CPAGs
INCOME-RELATED BENEFITS:
THE LEGISLATION

AUSTRALIA
The Law Book Company
Brisbane · Sydney · Melbourne · Perth

CANADA
Carswell
Ottawa · Toronto · Calgary · Montreal · Vancouver

Agents

Steimatzky's Agency Ltd., Tel Aviv;
N.M. Tripathi (Private) Ltd., Bombay;
Eastern Law House (Private) Ltd., Calcutta;
M.P.P. House, Bangalore;
Universal Book Traders, Delhi;
Aditya Books, Delhi;
MacMillan Shuppan KK, Tokyo;
Pakistan Law House, Karachi, Lahore

CPAGs
INCOME-RELATED BENEFITS:
THE LEGISLATION

1995 EDITION

Commentary By

JOHN MESHER, B.A., B.C.L., LL.M.
Barrister, Professor Associate of Law,
University of Sheffield

PENNY WOOD, LL.B., M.Sc.
Solicitor, Part-Time Chairman,
Social Security Appeal Tribunals

LONDON
SWEET & MAXWELL
1995

Published in 1995 by
Sweet & Maxwell Limited of
South Quay Plaza, 183 Marsh Wall,
London E14 9FT.
Computerset by Wyvern Typesetting, Bristol.
Printed in England
Clays Ltd., St. Ives plc.

No natural forests were destroyed to make this product.
Only farmed timber was used and re-planted.

A catalogue record for this book is
available from the British Library

British Cataloguing in Publication Data

ISBN 0 421 53990 9

©
SWEET & MAXWELL
1995

FOREWORD TO THE 1995 EDITION

This is the second edition of this established textbook under the editorship of Penny Wood. The transition from John Mesher to Penny has been seamless and the commentary retains the rigorously high standards which John set during the book's first decade. John still has a valuable input as consultant.

Any editor of *Mesher Wood* has to cope with the increasing complexity of this area of law. Many senior judges regard social security law as *the* most difficult they have to deal with. They appreciate how frustrating this is for claimants. This is what Lord Justice Glidewell said in the Court of Appeal in *Bate* last November:

'Even for this legislation, [the provisions in question] are particularly obscure in their meaning . . . it is deplorable that legislation which affects some of the most disadvantaged people in society should be couched in language which is so difficult for even a lawyer trained and practising in this field to understand.'

CPAG endorses those sentiments. We appreciate that means-testing inevitably involves a degree of complexity, not least because people's financial resources take a great many forms these days. As with tax law, every paragraph of every subsection of every section has budgetary implications for the Government and precision is therefore important.

However, there is no reason why the legislation has to be as impenetrable as it is. Much of the drafting leaves a great deal to be desired. Cross-references and exceptions abound. No self-respecting section or regulation is complete, so it would seem, without a double or even a triple negative. In one recent case brought by CPAG, a High Court judge even identified a quadruple negative! Clear and accessible the legislation is not.

The effect of all this is to make much of the legisation effectively a no-go area for all but the most resourceful claimants, the very people who need to know what it says. And, of course, the more complicated legislation is, the more uncertainties there are to be resolved by case law. Unfortunately, cases often throw up their own uncertainties. Commissioners sometimes disagree amongst themselves about the proper meaning of a provision; and gleaning the true *ratio* of a Commissioner or court decision is not always easy.

To the editor of *Mesher Wood* falls the unenviable task of making sense of this unseemly mess. It is to Penny Wood's great credit that her commentary succeeds in explaining and illuminating all the recent legislation and case law. She shows that accessibility and legal accuracy *can* be bedfellows. Tribunals, welfare rights workers and lawyers will all find the book invaluable, indeed indispensable.

Many of the cases Penny summarises show the capriciousness of the current system. CPAG believes that, essential as it is to help claimants understand the system, it is even more essential that the system should itself be made more equitable. If you would like more information about our campaigning work, or about our publications, please write to us at 1–5 Bath Street, London EC1V 9PY. Our publications include *CPAG's Housing Benefit and Council Tax Benefit Legislation* by Lorna Findlay, Richard Poynter and Martin Ward and, of course, the *National Welfare Benefits Handbook*. Both complement this book.

David Thomas
Legal Officer
Child Poverty Action Group

July 1995

PREFACE

One of the most controversial changes in the past year has been the introduction of an habitual residence test for income support. The test applies to all new claims from August 1, 1994 and has affected a far greater number of claimants than those who could be reasonably classified as "benefit tourists". Another development has been the child care costs disregard for family credit and disability working allowance (but not income support) effective from October 4, 1994. This welcome change recognises an important principle but is regretfully narrow in its scope. The major change from April 1995 has been the introduction of incapacity benefit and the new test of incapacity for work (see Bonner, *Non-Means Tested Benefits: the Legislation* (1995 ed.) for details). The new test has implications for income support and there are also associated changes in the income support rules, such as that affecting entitlement to the disability premium. New benefit reductions for some claimants who appeal against decisions on incapacity for work have also been introduced. Finally, there have been some significant Court decisions, most notably *Bate v. Chief Adjudication Officer and the Secretary of State for Social Security, The Times*, December 12, 1994 and *Chief Adjudication Officer v. Palfrey and Others, The Times*, February 17, 1995, together with the usual crop of Commissioners' decisions and amending regulations. All in all it has not been a quiet year.

The main objective of this book remains unaltered, to bring together the legislation, both Acts of Parliament and Regulations, governing cases which could come before a Social Security Appeal Tribunal in income support, family credit and social fund (maternity and funeral expenses and cold weather payments) appeals and on certain aspects of disability working allowance claims. In addition, Social Fund Directions given by the Secretary of State and Practice Directions to appeal tribunals issued by the President of the Independent Tribunal Service (ITS) are included. The book does not deal with all the income-related benefits contained in the Social Security Contributions and Benefits Act 1992. Housing benefit and council tax benefit are excluded. The legislation on these benefits, with a full commentary, can be found in Findlay and Ward, *CPAG's Housing Benefit and Council Tax Benefit: the Legislation.*

The book similarly continues to be structured in broadly the same way as earlier editions. It is divided into seven parts – I. Benefits Acts; II. Income Support; III. Family Credit; IV. Disability Working Allowance; V. The Social Fund; VI. Administration and Adjudication; and VII. ITS President's Practice Directions. Parts II to V contain no Acts of Parliament. The Social Security Contributions and Benefits Act 1992 in Part I deals with entitlements to all benefits. The sections of the Child Support Act 1991 dealing with reduced benefit directions (which can be applied to income support, family credit or disability working allowance) and deductions from income support as a contribution towards child maintenance are also included in Part I. Parts VI and VII contain the Social Security Administration Act 1992, the Social Security (Consequential Provisions) Act 1992 (which has provisions on the effects of the consolidation process in 1992), the regulations on claims, payments and adjudication and the Practice Directions issued by the President of the ITS.

The text of all the legislation is set out as amended and in force on April 18, 1995. All of the text has amendments and definitions noted. Under the "AMENDMENT" heading at the end of each section, Regulation or Schedule is a numbered note referring to any amending provision with the date on which the amendment came into force. Where a provision contains a reference to a statute as it existed before the 1992 consolidation a note in square brackets immediately follows it showing the location of the reference in the consolidating legislation. The Contributions and Benefits Act is abbreviated as "SSCBA" and the Administration Act as "SSAA". See section 2(4) of the Consequential Provisions act for the meaning of such references from July 1, 1992 (the date on which the consolidating legislation came into force) onwards. The old legislation of course remains relevant in relation to periods before July 1, 1992. After each section of the consolidating legislation is a "DERIVATION" heading showing which part of the old legislation has gone into the new provision. There are also Tables of Destinations near the front of the book showing in broad outline where provisions of the Social Security Act 1975 and the Social Security Act 1986 can be found in the consolidating legislation. It is hoped that this gives enough information for readers to continue to be able to work backwards and forwards between the old and the new legislation.

Apart from the normal updating, rewriting and correcting process and the incorporation of material contained in the 1994 Supplement, decisions of the courts and the Social Security Commissioners given up to about the end of April 1995 have been taken into account.

I am fortunate indeed to be able to call upon the accumulated wisdom of John Mesher in his consultative capacity and I am extremely grateful for his continuing and generous support. CPAG's support and co-operation, in particular through their legal officer, David Thomas, and Peter Ridpath in their publications department, has also continued unstintingly. In addition I want to thank Les Allamby, Martin Barnes, Simon Cox, Emma Knights, Beth Lakhani, Richard Poynter, Mary Shirley, Geoff Tait, Dave Wilcox, and those at Sweet and Maxwell who have been involved in the production of this book, for their assistance. My thanks also go to the DSS and ITS officials who have helped, beyond the normal limits of duty, in providing information which ensures as far as possible that the book is up to date. It should however of course be emphasised that all the comments in the book are made in a personal capacity and are in no way "official" or endorsed by the Independent Tribunal Service. Nor do the views expressed necessarily coincide with those of CPAG.

I warmly welcome comments from readers pointing out errors, ommissions or the need for clarification. These should be sent to me c/o Sweet and Maxwell, South Quay Plaza, 183 Marsh Wall, South Quay, London E14 9FT. I hope that this book will continue to be of practical assistance both to those who advise claimants and to those who adjudicate upon their claims and appeals.

PENNY WOOD

CONTENTS

PART I.
BENEFITS ACTS

PART II.
INCOME SUPPORT

S.I. No.

Contents

PART III.
FAMILY CREDIT

S.I. No.

PART IV.
DISABILITY WORKING ALLOWANCE

S.I. No.

PART V.
THE SOCIAL FUND

S.I. No.

PART VI.
ADJUDICATION AND ADMINISTRATION

Contents

PART VII.
ITS PRESIDENT'S PRACTICE DIRECTIONS

SOURCES OF INFORMATION

This book cannot provide a general introduction to the law and inevitably some familiarity with the system has been assumed. It may though help readers who are not already experts to have some information about the kinds of sources referred to in the notes and on sources of information about up-to-date developments.

Commissioners' decisions

There are many references to decisions of the Social Security Commissioners, who decide appeals from Social Security Appeal Tribunals. Their decisions are binding on tribunals and on the adjudication officers who make the initial decisions within the DSS. Each decision has a file number within the Commissioners' office (*e.g. CIS 1/1988:* "C" for Commissioner, "IS" for income support). Certain decisions which are circulated amongst other Commissioners to be considered for reporting are "starred". If the Chief Social Security Commissioner decides that a decision is to be reported, it is published by HMSO and receives a new reference (*e.g. R(IS) 1/90:* "R" for report). Copies of reported decisions can be bought from HMSO or inspected at local offices of the DSS. Copies will also be available at tribunal hearings.

It has been announced that from April 1, 1987, starred and other unreported decisions will be available for consultation at the Commissioners' offices in London and Edinburgh, and on subscription.

Although the Chief Commissioner has directed that so far as possible the authorities should refer to reported decisions only, the legal position is that all decisions of individual Commissioners have equal authority. A decision of a Tribunal of Commissioners binds individual Commissioners, unless there are compelling reasons for not following it. A tribunal or adjudication officer must follow a decision of a Tribunal of Commissioners in preference to a decision of an individual Commissioner. If decisions of individual Commissioners conflict, then prima facie a reported decision has more weight than an unreported one. This is because a decision will not be reported unless it commands the assent of a majority of Commissioners. However, a tribunal or adjudication officer is free to follow which-ever decision is considered correct and there is no obligation to prefer a later decision to an earlier one. See *R(I) 12/75* (an industrial injuries case) for the statement of these principles.

Commissioners' decisions, including unreported decisions and those awaiting publication, are noted and commented on in the *Journal of Social Security Law*, the *Journal of Social Welfare and Family Law* and in CPAG's *Welfare Rights Bulletin*. Summaries are sometimes published in the *Law Society Gazette*.

Decisions of the courts

Decisions of the courts bind the Social Security Commissioners and all below them in the system. However, it has been confirmed in *CSBO v. Leary*, appendix to *R(SB) 6/85*, that Divisional Court decisions on appeal from SBATs under the statutory right of appeal before 1980 do not bind the Commissioners. Divisional Court decisions on judicial review of the Commissioners do bind them (*Commock v. Chief Adjudication Officer*, appendix to *R(SB) 6/90*). Social security cases have not been well reported. Where possible references have been given to the ordinary series of law reports. Some older cases are only reported in an HMSO publication *Decisions of the courts relating to supplementary bene-fits and family income supplements legislation.* This is often called "the Little Yellow Book". Decisions are given a number, *e.g.* SB 24. Although the cover-age is full before 1980, more recent decisions are not included.

Once again court decisions will be noted and commented on in the *Journal of Social Security Law,* the *Journal of Social Welfare and Family Law* and CPAG's *Welfare Rights Bulletin.*

Official guidance

A ten volume Adjudication Officer's Guide, published by HMSO, contains guidance on entitlements across a wide range of benefits from the Chief Adju-dication Officer. Volume 3 covers income support and Volume 4 covers family credit and disability working allowance. The Income Support Guide (8 volumes) contains procedural instructions, and there are also other guides on specific sub-jects, for example, the Mortgage Interest Direct Guide. The Social Fund Guide contains guidance from the Secretary of State and the binding directions which are reproduced in this book.

Unofficial guidance

There is a large number of guides. CPAG's own *National Welfare Benefits Handbook,* published annually each spring, is unrivalled as a practical and com-prehensive introduction from the claimants' viewpoint.

TABLE OF DESTINATIONS

Social Security Act 1986

1986 Act	Contributions and Benefits Act 1992 Administration Act 1992
s.20	SSCBA, ss.123 124, 125, 129, 137
	SSAA, s.72
s.21	SSCBA, ss.124, 128, 129
s.22	SSCBA, ss.134, 135, 136
s.23	SSCBA, ss.126
s.23A	SSCBA, s.127
s.24	SSAA, s.106
s.24A	SSAA, s.107
s.24B	SSAA, s.108
s.26	SSAA, s.105
s.27	SSAA, s.74
s.27A	SSAA, s.126
s.32	SSCBA, ss.138, 140
	SSAA, s.64
s.33	SSCBA, ss.138, 139, 140
s.34	SSAA, s.66
s.35	SSAA, s.65
s.51	SSAA, s.5
s.51B	SSAA, s.7
s.53	SSAA, s.71
s.64A	SSAA, s.159
s.64B	SSAA, s.160
s.84(1)	SSCBA, s.137(1)
	SSAA, s.191

TABLE OF DESTINATIONS

Social Security Act 1975

1975 Act	Administration Act 1992
s.97	ss.38, 39, 41, 52
s.98	s.20
s.99	s.21
s.100	s.22
s.100A	s.30
s.100B	s.31
s.100C	s.32
s.100D	s.33
s.101	ss.23, 34
s.102	s.36
s.103	s.37
s.104	ss.25, 26, 27, 28, 29, 69
s.114	s.58
s.115	s.59
s.115A	s.53
s.115B	s.56
s.115C	s.54
s.116	s.57
s.117	s.60
s.119	s.61
s.160	s.124
s.165A	s.1
s.165B	s.2
s.165D	s.68
Sched. 10	Sched. 2
Sched. 13	Sched. 3

TABLE OF CASES

Table of Cases

Table of Cases

Table of Cases

Table of Cases

TABLE OF DECISIONS

Table of Decisions

PART I

BENEFITS ACTS

Social Security Contributions and Benefits Act 1992

(1992 c. 4)

3

PART VII

INCOME-RELATED BENEFITS

General

Income-related benefits

123.—(1) Prescribed schemes shall provide for the following benefits (in this Act referred to as "income-related benefits")—

   (a) income support;
   (b) family credit;
   (c) disability working allowance;
   (d) housing benefit; and
[¹(e) council tax benefit.]

(2) The Secretary of State shall make copies of schemes prescribed under subsection (1)(a), (b) or (c) above available for public inspection at local offices of the Department of Social Security at all reasonable hours without payment. [*Subss. (3) to (6) omitted as applying only to housing benefit and council tax benefit.*]

DERIVATION

Social Security Act 1986, s.20(1) and (2).

AMENDMENT

1. Local Government Finance Act 1992, Sched. 9, para. 1(1) (April 1, 1993).

Income support

Income support

124.—(1) A person in Great Britain is entitled to income support if—

   (a) he is of or over the age of 18 or, in prescribed circumstances and for a prescribed period, of or over the age of 16 or he is a person to whom section 125(1) below applies;
   (b) he has no income or his income does not exceed the applicable amount;
   (c) he is not engaged in remunerative work and, if he is a member of a married or unmarried couple, the other member is not so engaged; and
   (d) except in such circumstances as may be prescribed—
      (i) he is available for, and actively seeking, employment;
      (ii) he is not receiving relevant education.

(2) In subsection (1)(a) above "period" includes—

   (a) a period of a determinate length;
   (b) a period defined by reference to the happening of a future event; and

(c) a period of a determinate length but subject to earlier determination upon the happening of a future event.

(3) Circumstances may be prescribed in which a person must not only satisfy the condition specified in subsection (1)(d)(i) above but also be registered in the prescribed manner for employment.

(4) Subject to subsection (5) below, where a person is entitled to income support, then—

(a) if he has no income, the amount shall be the applicable amount; and

(b) if he has income, the amount shall be the difference between his income and the applicable amount.

(5) Where a person is entitled to income support for a period to which this subsection applies, the amount payable for that period shall be calculated in such manner as may be prescribed.

(6) Subsection (5) above applies—

(a) to a period of less than a week which is the whole period for which income support is payable; and

(b) to any other period of less than a week for which it is payable.

DERIVATION

Subs. (1): Social Security Act 1986, s.20(3).
Subs. (2): 1986 Act, s.20(4N).
Subs. (3): 1986 Act, s.20(4).
Subss. (4) to (6): 1986 Act, s.21(1) to (1B).

DEFINITIONS

"Great Britain"—see s.172(a).
"married couple"—see s.137(1).
"prescribed"—*ibid.*
"unmarried couple"—*ibid.*

GENERAL NOTE

Subsection (1)
Here the general conditions of entitlement to income support are set out. There is also a capital test under s.134(1). There is no contributions test or requirement of citizenship (but see para. 17 of Sched. 7 to the Income Support (General) Regulations on persons from abroad). However, although a person qualifies if he is in Great Britain, an habitual residence condition was introduced on August 1, 1994. See the additional definition of "person from abroad" in reg. 21(3) of the Income Support (General) Regulations, and the notes to that definition. Reg. 4 of those regulations allows an award to continue for a short period of temporary absence from Great Britain.

(a) Then the person must in general be at least 18. Until September 1988, the minimum age was 16. The government's view is that 16 and 17 year-olds no longer need the option of reliance on income support. They may remain in education (with parents entitled to child benefit), take employment or take up a place on the Youth Training Scheme (where a place is guaranteed for all 16 and 17 year-old school leavers).
There are exceptions to the general rule of exclusion. The prescribed circumstances are set out in reg. 13A of the Income Support (General) Regulations, which covers three different routes to entitlement and periods of entitlements. See the notes to reg. 13A, which in particular deal with the relationship with child benefit entitlement. If the claimant does not come into one of the prescribed circumstances, there may still be an escape under s.125, which depends entirely on decisions by the Secretary of State. Note that satisfying an exception only gets the claimant past subs. (1)(*a*). All the other conditions of entitlement must be met.

(b) The person's income (which includes the income of the claimant's family) must be less than the applicable amount (effectively the figure set for the family's requirements under s.135).

(c) The introduction of the condition in para. (*c*) marked an important change from the supplementary benefit rules. If either the claimant or his partner is in remunerative work (defined in regs. 5 and 6 of the Income Support Regulations) there is no entitlement to income support. For supplementary benefit, this condition was only applied to the claimant. The transitional

protection announced on April 28, 1988 (see p. 198 of the 1988 edition) has remained on an extra-statutory basis.
(d) The conditions in para. (d) are dealt with in regs. 7 to 13 of the Income Support (General) Regulations. For availability, see regs. 8 to 10 and 7(1). For the condition of actively seeking employment, see regs. 10A and 7(2). For relevant education, see regs. 12 and 13.

If there is entitlement under this subsection, the amount of income support is laid down in subss. (4) to (6).

Subsection (3)
See reg. 11 of the Income Support (General) Regulations.

Subsection (4)
This provision sets out the basic means test calculation for income support. Providing that the conditions of entitlement imposed by subs. (1) and the capital test under s.134(1) are satisfied, the claimant's income is set against his applicable amount, calculated according to regs. 17 to 22 of the Income Support (General) Regulations. The difference is the amount of benefit. The claimant's income includes that of the other members of his family (s.136(1)).

Subsections (5) and (6)
These provisions allow regulations to deal with entitlement for part-weeks. See regs. 73 to 77 of the Income Support (General) Regulations.

Severe hardship cases

125.—(1) If it appears to the Secretary of State—
(a) that a person of or over the age of 16 but under the age of 18 is not entitled to income support; and
(b) that severe hardship will result to that person unless income support is paid to him,
the Secretary of State may direct that this subsection shall apply to him.

(2) Any such direction may specify a period for which subsection (1) above is to apply to the person to whom the direction relates.

(3) The person to whom such a direction relates shall be treated in accordance with it, but if at any time it appears to the Secretary of State that there has been a change of circumstances as a result of which failure to receive income support need no longer result in severe hardship to him, he may revoke the direction.

(4) The Secretary of State may also revoke the direction if—
(a) he is satisfied that it was given in ignorance of some material fact or was based on a mistake as to some material fact; and
(b) he considers that but for his ignorance or mistake he would not have determined that failure to receive income support would result in severe hardship.

(5) In this section "period" includes—
(a) a period of a determinate length;
(b) a period defined by reference to the happening of a future event; and
(c) a period of a determinate length but subject to earlier determination upon the happening of a future event.

Derivation

Subss. (1) to (4): Social Security Act 1986, s.20(4A) to (4D).
Subs. (5): 1986 Act, s.20(4N).

General Note

Subsection (1)
A person may satisfy the condition of entitlement in s.124(1)(a) through the operation of this provision. Since it is a requirement of subs. (1) that the person under 18 is not entitled to income support, the person must fall outside the categories covered in reg. 13A of and Sched. 1A to the

Income Support (General) Regulations. The other main condition is that severe hardship will (not may) result if income support is not paid. The question of whether these two conditions are satisfied is for the Secretary of State, and even if they are, there is a discretion whether or not to allow benefit. There is no right of appeal to a social security appeal tribunal from the Secretary of State's decision. Although the test is very strict, early indications were that a high proportion of applications under the predecessor of subs. (1) were successful.

In November 1989, concern that claimants were incorrectly turned away before reaching this stage led to revised instructions being issued. All 16 and 17 year-old claimants should be interviewed, unless, for instance, they clearly do not qualify on capital or income grounds. The AO should then consider eligibility and automatically refer all claimants who fail at this stage to the Severe Hardship Cases Unit (which acts on behalf of the Secretary of State) for consideration. See 95 *Welfare Rights Bulletin 11* (April 1990). A direction under subs. (1) may be made for a definite period or until some future event (subss. (2) and (5)) and may be revoked if there is a change of circumstances under subs. (3). If a direction is made the AO must consider all the other conditions of entitlement.

Subsection (3)

Once a direction is made under subs. (1) the claimant satisfies s.124(1)(a), presumably until the age of 18 is reached. If the claimant ceases to satisfy the other conditions of entitlement, entitlement will cease. The Secretary of State has a general discretion to revoke a direction whenever there is a change of circumstances which means that severe hardship no longer need follow from non-payment of income support. This emphasises the strictness of the test under subs. (1). If severe hardship will not definitely follow from the non-payment of income support subs. (1) cannot operate. It appears that the revocation of the direction may be retrospective, from the date of the change of circumstances, and if there was a failure to disclose facts constituting the change the overpayment is recoverable under subs. (4) and s.72 of the Administration Act.

If a person ceases to satisfy subs. (1)(a) this does not seem to justify revocation.

Subsection (4)

There is a discretion to revoke a direction if it was originally given in ignorance of or under a mistake as to a material fact which would have altered the decision on the inevitability of severe hardship.

Trade disputes

126.—(1) This section applies to a person, other than a child or a person of a prescribed description—

    (a) who is disqualified under section 27 above for receiving unemployment benefit; or

    (b) who would be so disqualified if otherwise entitled to that benefit,

except during any period shown by the person to be a period of incapacity for work [² - -] or to be within the maternity period.

(2) In subsection (1) above "the maternity period" means the period commencing at the beginning of the 6th week before the expected week of confinement and ending at the end of the 7th week after the week in which confinement takes place.

(3) For the purposes of calculating income support—

    (a) so long as this section applies to a person who is not a member of a family, the applicable amount shall be disregarded;

    (b) so long as it applies to a person who is a member of a family but is not a member of a married or unmarried couple, the portion of the applicable amount which is included in respect of him shall be disregarded;

    (c) so long as it applies to one of the members of a married or unmarried couple—

        (i) if the applicable amount consists only of an amount in respect of them, it shall be reduced to one half; and

        (ii) if it includes other amounts, the portion of it which is included in respect of them shall be reduced to one-half and any further portion of it which is included in respect of the member of the couple to whom this section applies shall be disregarded;

(d) so long as it applies to both members of a married or unmarried couple—

    (i) if neither of them is responsible for a child or person of a prescribed description who is a member of the same household, the applicable amount shall be disregarded; and

    (ii) in any other case, the portion of the applicable amount which is included in respect of them and any further portion of it which is included in respect of either of them shall be disregarded.

(4) Where a reduction under subsection (3)(c) above would not produce a sum which is a multiple of 5p, the reduction shall be to the nearest lower sum which is such a multiple.

(5) Where this section applies to a person for any period, then, except so far as regulations provide otherwise—

(a) in calculating the entitlement to income support of that person or a member of his family the following shall be treated as his income and shall not be disregarded—

    (i) any payment which he or a member of his family receives or is entitled to obtain by reason of the person to whom this section applies being without employment for that period; and

    (ii) without prejudice to the generality of sub-paragraph (i) above, any amount which becomes or would on an application duly made become available to him in that period by way of repayment of income tax deducted from his emoluments in pursuance of section 203 of the Income and Corporation Taxes Act 1988; and

(b) any payment by way of income support for that period or any part of it which apart from this paragraph would be made to him, or to a person whose applicable amount is aggregated with his—

    (i) shall not be made if the weekly rate of payment is equal to or less than the relevant sum; or

    (ii) if it is more than the relevant sum, shall be at a weekly rate equal to the difference.

(6) In respect of any period less than a week, subsection (5) above shall have effect subject to such modifications as may be prescribed.

(7) Subject to subsection (8) below, the "relevant sum" for the purposes of subsection (5) above shall be [¹£25.00].

(8) If an order under section 150 of the Administration Act (annual up-rating) has the effect of increasing payments of income support, from the time when the order comes into force there shall be substituted, in subsection (5)(b) above, for the references to the sum for the time being mentioned in it references to a sum arrived at by—

(a) increasing that sum by the percentage by which the personal allowance under paragraph 1(1) of Part I of Schedule 2 to the Income Support (General) Regulations 1987 for a single person aged not less than 25 has been increased by the order; and]

(b) if the sum so increased is not a multiple of 50p, disregarding the remainder if it is 25p and, if it is not, rounding it up or down to the nearest 50p,

and the order shall state the substituted sum.

DERIVATION

Social Security Act 1986, s.23.

AMENDMENT

1. Social Security Benefits Up-rating Order 1995 (S.I. 1995 No. 559), art. 20 (April 10, 1995).
2. Social Security (Incapacity for Work) Act 1994, Sched. 1, para. 31 (April 13, 1995).

DEFINITIONS

"child"—see s.137(1).
"family"—*ibid.*
"married couple"—*ibid.*
"prescribed"—*ibid.*
"the Administration Act"—see s.174.
"unmarried couple"—see s.137(1).

GENERAL NOTE

The trade dispute rule, long an important part of the supplementary benefit scheme, was considerably simplified in the income support rules, although most of the stringency remains.

Subsection (1)

The rule applies to anyone other than a child or young person (Income Support (General) Regulations, reg. 14) who is disqualified for unemployment benefit, or would be disqualified, under s.27 of the Act. Thus the income support rule depends directly on the unemployment benefit rule, and the income support question need not be finally decided until the unemployment benefit question is resolved (Adjudication Regulations, reg. 64).

The rule does not apply when the person involved is incapable of work. There is no trade dispute disqualification for sickness or invalidity benefit. The rule also does not apply in the maternity period, defined in subs. (2).

If the rule applies there are consequences for the way in which applicable amounts are calculated. This is dealt with in subs. (3). There are also consequences for the way in which income is calculated. This is dealt with in subs. (5) and in a number of regulations. The most immediate effect is that the person is treated as in remunerative work for the seven days following the first day of the stoppage of work or the day on which the claimant withdrew his labour (Income Support Regulations, reg. 5(4)). The result is that neither the person nor his partner can be entitled to income support at all for those days (s.124(1)(c)).

Subsection (3)

This provision sets out the effect on the applicable amount if the claimant is not excluded by the conditions of entitlement.

(a) A single claimant with no child or young person in the household is to have no applicable amount, and so cannot be entitled to any benefit. There is the possibility of a crisis loan under the social fund for expenses which result from a disaster.

(b) For a single claimant with a child or young person in the household, the "portion of the applicable amount included in respect of" the claimant is disregarded. It is clear that the personal allowance for the claimant is taken out, and so is any premium based on the claimant's disability or age. Presumably the family premium and the lone parent premium are not included "in respect of" the claimant and so remain.

(c) For a couple where the trade dispute rule applies to only one of them, if they have no premiums on top of their personal allowance, that allowance is reduced by a half. This is a different rule from supplementary benefit, which would have left the other partner with the appropriate personal allowance for a single claimant. If there are any premiums, then the rule in para. (b) applies. It is easier to argue for the retention of the family premium here, since that would be paid to the remaining partner if the partner involved in the trade dispute disappeared. Obviously, the lone parent premium is not applicable because the couple remain a couple.

(d) For a couple where the trade dispute rule applies to both of them, the applicable amount is nil if there is no child or young person in the household. If there is a child or young person, then the family premium and any premium paid for that person's disability is allowed on top of the personal allowance for that person.

Subsection (5)

If the trade dispute rule applies, the normal rules about income are modified. Under para. (a) any payment which a member of the family receives or is entitled to obtain by reason of the person involved in the trade dispute being without employment must be taken into account. In *R(SB) 29/85* a loan from a local authority Social Work Department (the Scottish equivalent of a Social Services Department) to meet arrears of hire purchase repayments was held to be capable of being such a payment. The claimant had not been in arrears before the dispute and the loan was to be repaid on his return to work. But on the facts it was a payment of capital, not income. Now reg. 41(3) of the Income Support (General) Regulations secures that in trade dispute cases payments under ss.17 or 24 of the Children Act 1989 or ss.12, 24 or 26 of the Social Work (Scotland) Act 1968 (payments to families to prevent children being taken into care, etc.) are treated as income, not capital. Nor does the disregard of such income in para. 28 of Sched. 9 to the Income Support (General) Regulations apply in trade dispute cases. Other categories of income normally disregarded but counted here are income in kind (para. 21) and charitable or voluntary payments (para. 15). Holiday pay paid more than four weeks after the termination of employment (normally capital) is earnings (reg. 35(1)(d)).

The other main category under para. (a) is income tax refunds paid or due. The effect of reg. 48(2) is that in trade dispute cases refunds do not count as capital. The assumption is then that they count as income, but this does not seem to be provided for expressly.

Under para. (b) there is the final automatic deduction of the "relevant sum." This is the sum specified in subs. (6). as increased in future years under subs. (7). The sum was increased to £25.00 in April 1995. The relevant sum is often called "assumed strike pay," but is deducted regardless of whether the person involved is entitled to strike pay, a member of a union, or even on strike.

The "compensation" for this rule is that any payment from a trade union up to the amount of £25.00 is disregarded (Sched. 9, para. 34).

The cumulative result of these income rules, plus the reductions in applicable amounts, is that even married strikers will often receive very little benefit indeed. Their only resort is the social fund for crisis loans in disasters.

Effect of return to work

127. If a person returns to work with the same employer after a period during which section 126 above applies to him, and whether or not his return is before the end of any stoppage of work in relation to which he is or would be disqualified for receiving unemployment benefit—

    (a) that section shall cease to apply to him at the commencement of the day on which he returns to work; and

    (b) until the end of the period of 15 days beginning with that day section 124(1) above shall have effect in relation to him as if the following paragraph were substituted for paragraph (c)—

        "(c) in the case of a member of a married or unmarried couple, the other member is not engaged in remunerative work; and"; and

    (c) any sum paid by way of income support for that period of 15 days to him or, where he is a member of a married or unmarried couple, to the other member of that couple, shall be recoverable in the prescribed manner from the person to whom it was paid or from any prescribed person or, where the person to whom it was paid is a member of a married or unmarried couple, from the other member of the couple.

<small>DERIVATION</small>

Social Security Act 1986, s.23A.

<small>DEFINITIONS</small>

    "married couple"—see s.137(1).
    "prescribed"—*ibid.*
    "unmarried couple"—*ibid.*

<small>GENERAL NOTE</small>

This section allows income support to be paid for the first 15 days following a return to work from a trade dispute. Normally the work would exclude entitlement to benefit under s.124(1)(c) regardless of whether any wages were payable or not. The rules about the relevant sum and income tax refunds under s.126 do not apply, but the other adjustments to the income rules do apply. Applicable amounts are calculated in the ordinary way. Note that any advance of earnings or loan made by the employer counts as earnings (Income Support (General) Regulations, reg. 48(5) and

(6)). In addition, any payment of benefit under this section is recoverable under subs. (c) and Part VIII of the Payments Regulations.

Family credit

Family credit

128.—(1) Subject to regulations under section 5(1)(a) of the Administration Act, a person in Great Britain is entitled to family credit if, when the claim for it is made or is treated as made—
  (a) his income—
     (i) does not exceed the amount which is the applicable amount at such date as may be prescribed; or
     (ii) exceeds it, but only by such an amount that there is an amount remaining if the deduction for which subsection (2)(b) below provides is made;
  (b) he or, if he is a member of a married or unmarried couple, he or the other member of the couple, is engaged and normally engaged in remunerative work;
  (c) except in such circumstances as may be prescribed, neither he nor any member of his family is entitled to a disability working allowance; and
  (d) he or, if he is a member of a married or unmarried couple, he or the other member, is responsible for a member of the same household who is a child or a person of a prescribed description.
  (2) Where a person is entitled to family credit, then—
  (a) if his income does not exceed the amount which is the applicable amount at the date prescribed under subsection (1)(a)(i) above, the amount of the family credit shall be the amount which is the appropriate maximum family credit in his case; and
  (b) if his income exceeds the amount which is the applicable amount at that date, the amount of the family credit shall be what remains after the deduction from the appropriate maximum family credit of a prescribed percentage of the excess of his income over the applicable amount.
  (3) Family credit shall be payable for a period of 26 weeks or such other period as may be prescribed and, subject to regulations, an award of family credit and the rate at which it is payable shall not be affected by any change of circumstances during that period or by any order under section 150 of the Administration Act.
  (4) Regulations may provide that an award of family credit shall terminate—
  (a) if a person who was a member of the family at the date of the claim becomes a member of another family and some member of that family is entitled to family credit; or
  (b) if income support or a disability working allowance becomes payable in respect of a person who was a member of the family at the date of the claim for family credit.
  (5) Regulations shall prescribed the manner in which the appropriate maximum family credit is to be determined in any case.
  (6) The provisions of this Act relating to family credit apply in relation to persons employed by or under the Crown as they apply in relation to persons employed otherwise than by or under the Crown.

DERIVATION

Subs. (1): Social Security Act 1986, s.20(5) and (5A).
Subs. (2): 1986 Act, s.21(2) and (3).
Subs. (3): 1986 Act, s.20(6).
Subs. (4): 1986 Act, s.20(10).

Subs. (5): 1986 Act, s.21(6)(a).
Subs. (6): 1986 Act, s.79(3).

DEFINITIONS

"child"—see s.137(1).
"family"—*ibid.*
"Great Britain"—see s.172(1).
"married couple"—see s.137(1).
"prescribed"—*ibid.*
"the Administration Act"—see s.174.
"unmarried couple"—see s.137(1).

GENERAL NOTE

Subsection (1)

Here the general conditions of entitlement to family credit are set out, apart from the capital test under s.134(1). The condition must be met at the date of claim. Satisfaction at a later date will not do.

As for income support, the claimant must be in Great Britain, but here reg. 3 of the Family Credit (General) Regulations deems a person to be present or not present in certain circumstances. Family credit is a "family benefit" within Art. 4(1)(h) of EC Regulation 1408/71 and is not excluded from the scope of the Regulation as a form of social assistance under Art. 4(4) (*Hughes v. Chief Adjudication Officer* (ECJ, July 16, 1992)). Under Art. 73 the family of a person employed in a Member State is entitled to family benefits in that State although resident in another Member State. Thus, Mrs Hughes, who lived in the Republic of Ireland, could claim family credit in Northern Ireland because her husband worked there. With effect from June 1, 1992, the U.K. took advantage of an amendment to Art. 10 of Regulation 1408/71 to name family credit, (among other benefits) as a "special non-contributory benefit", to be confined exclusively to U.K. territory. However, the DSS now accepts that family credit is still payable to people in Mrs Hughes' position. This is because family credit falls within Art. 4(1) and so this overrides the fact that it has been named as a "special non-contributory benefit". Thus the residence rule for family credit still does not apply in these circumstances.

The most important condition is that the claimant or, if she has a partner, she or her partner is in remunerative work and normally engaged in remunerative work. See reg. 4 of the Family Credit Regulations. Although the minimum hours to qualify have been reduced from 24 to 16 for both income support and family credit in April 1992, the methods of calculating the hours differ. Also, a claimant may be excluded from income support by work, but fail to be entitled to family credit because the work is not normal. Another reason for the same result might be a failure to meet the condition in para. (d), that the claimant (or partner) is responsible for a child or "person of a prescribed description" in the household. A "person of a prescribed description" is a person aged 16 to 18 who is still in full time secondary-level education (Family Credit Regulations, reg. 6) (a "young person"). If an adult is treated as responsible for a child or young person under reg. 7, she is then treated as in the same household by reg. 8. Para. (c) spells out that if any member of the family is entitled to the new disability working allowance at the date of claim for family credit, then there can be no entitlement to family credit. Reg. 52 of the Family Credit Regulations lifts this condition where a claim for family credit is made within 42 days before the expiry of an award of disability working allowance for a period running on from the end of that award. See s.134(2) for the prevention of overlaps of entitlement.

If paras. (b) to (d) are met, then under para. (a) there is a test of the family's income against the applicable amount (see s.135 and Family Credit Regulations, reg. 47). It is crucial to the family credit scheme that the test is to be applied at the date of claim, although in principle evidence coming to light after that date may be relevant (*CFC 14/1991*). Satisfaction of the income test a few weeks later is not in itself any good. A fresh claim has to be made. If the income is less than the applicable amount, the maximum family credit is payable under subs. (2)(a). If the income exceeds the applicable amount, then the amount of benefit, if any, is calculated under subs. (2)(b).

Note that there is no age limit (upper or lower) for a claimant of family credit, although in practice the requirements of remunerative work for at least 16 hours a week and responsibility for a child or young person will exclude almost all under-16s.

A person under 16 cannot be one of a married or unmarried couple (*CFC 7/1992*).

Subsection (2)

Under para. (a) where the family's income does not exceed the applicable amount (Family Credit Regulations, reg. 47) the maximum family credit (reg. 46) is payable.

Under para. (b) where the family's income exceeds the applicable amount, then the maximum credit is reduced by 70 per cent. of the excess (reg. 48). Providing that what is left of the maximum credit is more than 49p. (Claims and Payments Regulations, reg. 27(2)), that amount is the benefit payable. If the maximum credit is eroded completely, there is no entitlement under subs. (1)(a) (ii).

Subsection (3)
The normal length of an award of family credit is to be 26 weeks. The 1987 Transitional Regulations allowed different periods to be fixed in the early months following the start of the scheme in April 1988. Once an award is made it will not be affected by a change in circumstances (although see subs. (4) and regs. 49, 51 and 51A of the Family Credit Regulations) or by the annual uprating of benefits under s.150 of the Administration Act during the currency of the award. An award may be reviewed if it was made in ignorance of or under a mistake as to a material fact (as in *R(FIS) 1/89*) or for error of law (Administration Act, s.25(1)(a) and (2), formerly s.104(1)(a) and (1A) of the Social Security Act 1975). There can be no review for an actual or anticipated change of circumstances (Administration Act, s.25(1)(b) and (bb), and formerly s.104(1)(b) and (bb) of the 1975 Act).

Subsection (4)
See reg. 50 of the Family Credit Regulations.

Subsection (5)
See reg. 46 of the Family Credit Regulations.

Disability working allowance

Disability working allowance

129.—(1) A person in Great Britain who has attained the age of 16 and [²qualifies under subsection (2) or (2A) below] is entitled to a disability working allowance if, when the claim for it is made or is treated as made—
  (a) he is engaged and normally engaged in remunerative work;
  (b) he has a physical or mental disability which puts him at a disadvantage in getting a job
  (c) his income—
      (i) does not exceed the amount which is the applicable amount at such date as may be prescribed; or
      (ii) exceeds it, but only by such an amount that there is an amount remaining if the deduction for which subsection (5)(b) below provides is made; and
  (d) except in such circumstances as may be prescribed, neither he nor, if he has a family, any member of it, is entitled to family credit.
  (2) Subject to subsection (4) below, a person qualifies under this subsection if—
  (a) for one or more of the 56 days immediately preceding the date when the claim for a disability working allowance is made or is treated as made there was payable to him one or more of the following—
      [³(i) the higher rate of short-term incapacity benefit or long-term incapacity benefit;]
      (ii) a severe disablement allowance;
      (iii) income support, housing benefit or [¹council tax benefit],
      or a corresponding benefit under any enactment having effect in Northern Ireland;
  (b) when the claim for a disability working allowance is made or is treated as made there was payable to him one or more of the following—
      (i) an attendance allowance;
      (ii) a disability living allowance;
      (iii) an increase of disablement pension under section 104 above;
      (iv) an analogous pension increase under a war pension scheme or an industrial injuries scheme,

or a corresponding benefit under any enactment having effect in Northern Ireland; or

(c) when the claim for a disability working allowance is made or is treated as made, he has an invalid carriage or other vehicle provided by the Secretary of State under section 5(2)(a) of the National Health Service Act 1977 and Schedule 2 to that Act or under section 46 of the National Health Service (Scotland) Act 1978 or provided under Article 30(1) of the Health and Personal Social Services (Northern Ireland) Order 1972.

[²(2A) A person qualifies under this subsection if—

(a) on one or more of the 56 days immediately preceding the date when the claim for a disability working allowance is made or is treated as made he was engaged in training for work and

(b) a relevant benefit was payable to him for one or more of the 56 days immediately preceding—

(i) the first day of training for work falling within the 56 days mentioned in paragraph (a) above or

(ii) an earlier day of training for work which formed part of the same period of training for work as that day.

(2B) For the purposes of subsection (2A) above—

(a) the following are relevant benefits—

(i) the higher rate of short-term incapacity benefit

(ii) long-term incapacity benefit

(iii) a severe disablement allowance,

or a corresponding benefit under any enactment having effect in Northern Ireland;

(b) "training for work" means training for work in pursuance of arrangements made under section 2(1) of the Employment and Training Act 1973 or section 2(3) of the Enterprise and New Towns (Scotland) Act 1990 or training of such other description as may be prescribed; and

(c) a period of training for work means a series of consecutive days of training for work, there being disregarded for this purpose such days as may be prescribed.]

(3) For the purposes of subsection (1) above a person has a disability which puts him at a disadvantage in getting a job only if he satisfies prescribed conditions or prescribed circumstances exist in relation to him.

(4) If the only benefit mentioned in paragraph (*a*) of subsection (2) above which is payable to a person as there mentioned is—

(a) a benefit mentioned in sub-paragraph (iii) of that paragraph; or

(b) a corresponding benefit under any enactment having effect in Northern Ireland,

he only qualifies under that subsection in prescribed circumstances.

(5) Where a person is entitled to a disability working allowance, then—

(a) if his income does not exceed the amount which is the applicable amount at the date prescribed under subsection (1)(c)(i) above, the amount of the disability working allowance shall be the amount which is the appropriate maximum disability working allowance in his case; and

(b) if his income exceeds that amount, the amount of the disability working allowance shall be what remains after the deduction from the appropriate maximum disability working allowance of a prescribed percentage of the excess of his income over that amount.

(6) A disability working allowance shall be payable for a period of 26 weeks or such other period as may be prescribed and, subject to regulations, an award of a disability working allowance and the rate at which it is payable shall not be affected by any change of circumstances during that period or by any order under section 150 of the Administration Act.

(7) Regulations may provide that an award of a disability working allowance to a person shall terminate if—

(a) a disability working allowance becomes payable in respect of some other person who was a member of his family at the date of his claim for a disability working allowance; or

(b) income support or family credit becomes payable in respect of a person who was a member of the family at that date.

(8) Regulations shall prescribe the manner in which the appropriate maximum disability working allowance is to be determined in any case.

(9) The provisions of this Act relating to disability working allowance apply in relation to persons employed by or under the Crown as they apply in relation to persons employed otherwise than by or under the Crown.

DERIVATION

Subs. (1): Social Security Act 1986, s.20(6A) and (6D).
Subss. (2) and (3): 1986 Act, s.20(6B) and (6C).
Subs. (4): 1986 Act, s.20(6E).
Subs. (5): 1986 Act, s.21(3A) and (3B).
Subs. (6): 1986 Act, s.20(6F).
Subs. (7): 1986 Act, s.27B(4).
Subs. (8): 1986 Act, s.21(6)(aa).
Subs. (9): 1986 Act, s.79(3).

AMENDMENTS

1. Local Government Finance Act 1992, Sched. 9, para. 2 (April 1, 1993).
2. Social Security (Incapacity for Work) Act 1994, s.10 (April 13, 1995).
3. Social Security (Incapacity for Work) Act 1994, Sched. 1, para. 32 (April 13, 1995)

DEFINITIONS

"family"—see s.137(1).
"Great Britain"—see s.172(1).
"industrial injuries scheme"—see s.137(1).
"prescribed"—*ibid*.
"the Administration Act"—see s.174.
"war pension scheme"—see s.137(1).

GENERAL NOTE

The disability working allowance was introduced by the Disability Living Allowance and Disability Working Allowance Act 1991 with effect from April 6, 1992. That Act amended the Social Security Act 1975 and the Social Security Act 1986. This section of the 1992 Act consolidates the amendments to ss.20 and 21 of the 1986 Act.

See the General Note at the beginning of the Disability Working Allowance (General) Regulations for the background and general structure of the benefit.

Subsection (1)

This provision sets out the general conditions of entitlement to disability working allowance, apart from the capital test under s.134(1). All of these conditions have to be satisfied at the date of claim. However, the adjudication rules for disability working allowance appear to make the choice of the exact date of claim slightly less crucial than in family credit. A claimant may within three months of an AO's decision denying entitlement apply for a review on any ground (Administration Act, s.30(1) and Adjudication Regulations, reg. 26A(1)). Any fresh claim made within this three-month period is treated as an application for review (Administration Act, s.30(13)). "Any ground" would seem to include a change of circumstances such that the conditions of s.129(1) are satisfied after the date of claim. Any award of benefit made on such a review can only take effect from the date of the application for review or fresh claim (Adjudication Regulations, reg. 70B(1)).

General conditions

The claimant must be present in Great Britain. See reg. 5 of the Disability Working Allowance (General) Regulations, which is very similar to reg. 3 of the Family Credit (General) Regulations. Disability working allowance has been named by the U.K. with effect from June 1, 1992, as a benefit which is for the purposes of EC Regulation 1408/71 exclusively confined to U.K. territory. See the notes to s. 128(1).

Secondly, the claimant must be at least 16. Presumably it was considered that since the test of responsibility for a child or young person is not part of the disability working allowance scheme, a different rule to that for family credit was necessary. Then the claimant must satisfy one of the four alternative qualifications in subss. (2) or (2A) and all four of the conditions in subs. (1)(a) to (d).

Remunerative work

On para. (a), see reg. 6 of the Disability Working Allowance Regulations. As for family credit and income support, work for less than 16 hours a week does not come within the definition of remunerative work. A claimant may fail to be entitled to disability working allowance because of not being "normally engaged" in remunerative work, but be excluded from income support by work of at least 16 hours in particular weeks. One effect of this test is that a claim made in advance of starting work will fail. Reg. 13B of the Claims and Payments Regulations only allows advance initial claims at the beginning of the scheme in March and April 1992. However, there is a political commitment to giving priority to claims from those who have just started work (Mr. N. Scott, Standing Committee E, col. 190, January 17, 1991), so that there is as little delay as possible in getting benefit to someone who cannot make a claim until work begins.

Physical or mental disability

On para. (b), what amounts to a physical or mental disability which puts the claimant at a disadvantage in getting a job is to be defined in regulations (subs. (3)). Reg. 3 of and Sched. 1 to the Disability Working Allowance Regulations prescribe a long list of alternative conditions. See the notes to Sched. 1 for the details. On an initial claim a claimant's declaration that he has such a disability is conclusive, unless either the claim or other evidence before the AO indicates that he does not (Administration Act, s.11(2) and Disability Working Allowance Regulations, reg. 4). On a repeat claim, one of the qualifying conditions must be met directly.

The question whether the claimant satisfies this condition is a "disability question." Any appeal from an AO's decision on a disability question is to a disability appeal tribunal (DAT) and not to a SSAT (Adjudication Regulations, reg. 26C). Indeed, if an appeal on disability working allowance raises a disability question along with other questions, the whole appeal goes to a DAT. If in the course of an appeal to a SSAT a disability question first arises, the SSAT cannot deal with it (Administration Act, s.36(2)). See the notes to that subsection for what follows in such circumstances.

Income

Under para. (c), the income of the claimant and any family is set against the applicable amount (prescribed in reg. 52 of the Disability Working Allowance Regulations). If income is less than the applicable amount, sub-para. (i) is met. If income exceeds the applicable amount, the same calculation is made under subs. (5)(b) as for family credit; 70 per cent. of the excess is deducted from the maximum disability working allowance. If some amount remains, sub-para. (ii) is met, but benefit of less than 50p is not payable (Claims and Payments Regulations, reg. 27(2)).

Non-entitlement to family credit

In general, under para. (d), if any member of a family is entitled to family credit no member of the family can be entitled to disability working allowance. Since the test under subs.(1) is applied at the date of claim, reg. 57 of the Disability Working Allowance Regulations lifts this condition when a claim for disability working allowance is made within 28 days before the expiry of a family credit award for a period running on from the end of that award.

Subsections (2), (2A) and (2B)

In addition to satisfying the conditions of subs. (1) the claimant must also at the date of claim fall into one of the four categories set out here. In all cases the equivalent Northern Ireland benefits count equally with the British benefits.

Under subs. (2)(a), either higher rate short-term incapacity benefit, long-term incapacity benefit (or invalidity benefit: reg. 18(1) of the Disability Working Allowance and Income Support (General) Amendment Regulations 1995, p.586), severe disablement allowance or income support, housing benefit or council tax benefit with the higher pensioner (on the ground of disability) or disability premium (subs. (4) and Disability Working Allowance Regulations, reg. 7) must have been payable for at least one day in the 56 days before the date of claim. All the conditions of entitlement and payability must be met. This condition operates normally on an initial claim. If it is satisfied on the initial claim then on any repeat claim (*i.e.* one made up to eight weeks after the expiry of the previous award) it is treated as still satisfied (Administration Act, s.11(3)).

Under subs. (2)(b), either attendance allowance, disability living allowance or constant attendance allowance under an industrial injuries scheme or a war pension scheme must be payable at the date of claim. The test is applied to initial and repeat claims. For claims made before April 6, 1992, mobility allowance is substituted for disability living allowance in s.20(6B)(b)(ii) of the Social Security Act 1986 (Disability Living Allowance and Disability Working Allowance Act 1991, s.6(5) and Social Security (Consequential Provisions) Act 1992, Sched. 4, para. 21).

Under subs. (2)(c), the claimant must have some kind of invalid carriage or vehicle provided under the legislation listed.

Under subss. (2A) and (2B), the claimant must have been undergoing training for work (see below) for at least one day in the eight weeks before the date of claim. In addition, he must have been getting higher rate short-term incapacity benefit, long-term incapacity benefit (or invalidity benefit: reg. 18(2) of the Disability Working Allowance and Income Support (General) Amendment Regulations 1995, p.586), or severe disablement allowance within the eight weeks before his first day of training for work started. This can be an earlier day which counts as part of the same period of training for work. "Training for work" means training arranged under s.2(1) of the Employment and Training Act 1973 or, in Scotland, s.2(3) of the Enterprise and New Towns (Scotland) Act 1990 (subs. (2B)(b)), or a course which a person attends for at least 16 hours a week and the main purpose of which is to teach occupational or vocational skills (reg. 7A of the Disability Working Allowance Regulations). Reg. 7B of the Disability Working Allowance Regulations lists the days that are disregarded under subs. (2B)(c).

Subsection (3)
See note to subs. (1)(b). The conditions and circumstances are prescribed in the Disability Working Allowance Regulations, reg. 3 and Sched. 1, subs. (4). See note to subs. (2)(a).

Subsection (5)
Under para. (a), where the family's income does not exceed the applicable amount (Disability Working Allowance Regulations, reg. 52) the maximum allowance (reg. 51) is payable.

Under para. (b), where the family's income exceeds the applicable amount, then the maximum allowance is reduced by 70 per cent. of the excess (reg. 53). Providing that what is left of the maximum allowance is more than 49p. (Claims and Payments Regulations, reg. 27(2)), that amount is the benefit payable. If the maximum allowance is eroded completely, there is no entitlement under subs. (1)(c)(ii).

Subsection (6)
The normal length of an award of disability working allowance is to be 26 weeks, the same as for family credit. Once an award is made, it and the rate of payment will not generally be affected by a change in circumstances (although see subs. (7), s.(30)(5)(b) of the Administration Act and regs. 54 to 56A of the Disability Working Allowance Regulations) or by the annual uprating of benefits under s. 150 of the Administration Act during the currency of the award. The process of appeal against an AO's decision has to start with an application within three months to review the decision "on any ground" (Administration Act, s.30(1)), but where an award has been made, this subsection seems to require that it is only the position as at the date of claim which can be considered. An application for an "ordinary" review can only be made later than three months after notice of the AO's decision (Administration Act, s.30(5) and Adjudication Regulations, reg. 26A(1)). Potential grounds of review include ignorance of or mistake as to a material fact (as in *R(FIS) 1/ 89* for family credit) and error of law (Administration Act, s.30(5)(a) and (c)). Advance awards under reg. 13B or 13C of the Claims and Payments Regulations can be reviewed if the conditions of entitlement are not satisfied at the start date of the award (s.30(5)(d)). Section 30(5)(b) allows regulations to prescribe situations in which there can be review for change of circumstances, which this subsection also allows. The only regulation made directly under this power is reg. 56 of the Disability Working Allowance Regulations. Reg. 54 (death of claimant) is made under s.5 of the Administration Act (formerly s.51 of the 1986 Act) and reg. 55 is made under subs. (7) of this section.

Subsection (7)
See reg. 55 of the Disability Working Allowance Regulations.

17

Subsection (8)
See reg. 51 of the Disability Working Allowance Regulations.

General

Exclusions from benefit

134.—(1) No person shall be entitled to an income-related benefit if his capital or a prescribed part of it exceeds the prescribed amount.

(2) Except in prescribed circumstances the entitlement of one member of a family to any one income-related benefit excludes entitlement to that benefit for any other member for the same period.

(3) [¹ . . .]

(4) Where the amount of any income-related benefit would be less than a prescribed amount, it shall not be payable except in prescribed circumstances.

DERIVATION

Subs. (1): Social Security Act 1986, s.22(6).
Subs. (2): 1986 Act, s.20(9).
Subs. (4): 1986 Act, s.21(7).

AMENDMENT

1. Local Government Finance Act 1992, Sched. 9, para. 7 (April 1, 1993).

DEFINITIONS

"family"—see s.137(1).
"prescribed"—*ibid.*

GENERAL NOTE

Subsection (1)
The capital limit for income support and family credit was raised to £8,000 from £6,000 in April 1990 (Income Support (General) Regulations, reg. 45 and Family Credit (General) Regulations, reg. 28). The limit for disability working allowance was set at £16,000, the same as for housing benefit, after a response from the Social Security Advisory Committee and pressure during the progress of the Disability Living Allowance and Disability Working Allowance Act 1991 through the House of Lords (Disability Working Allowance (General) Regulations, reg. 31). The basis for the difference is that the disabled may need to save up for expensive equipment or unexpected outlays.

Since the capital rule operates as an exclusion to benefit it is arguable that the burden of proof that a claimant's capital exceeds the limit is on the AO. The Tribunal of Commissioners in *CIS 417/ 1992* treat satisfaction of the capital rule as part of what the claimant has to prove in showing entitlement to income support. However, the contrary argument was not put to the Tribunal. But once it has been shown that the claimant possesses an item of capital, it is for him to prove that one of the disregards in Sched. 10 applies (*CIS 240/1992*). Similarly, if it has been established that the claimant is the legal owner of a property, the burden is on him to show that the beneficial ownership does not follow the legal ownership (*CIS 30/1993*).

Subsection (4)
See regs. 26(3) and 27(2) of the Claims and Payments Regulations.

The applicable amount

135.—(1) The applicable amount, in relation to any income-related benefit, shall be such amount or the aggregate of such amounts as may be prescribed in relation to that benefit.

(2) The power to prescribe applicable amounts conferred by subsection (1) above includes power to prescribe nil as an applicable amount.

[¹(3) In prescribing, for the purposes of income support, amounts under sub-section (1) above in respect of accommodation in any area for qualifying persons in cases where prescribed conditions are fulfilled, the Secretary of State shall take into account information provided by local authorities or other prescribed bodies or persons with respect to the amounts which they have agreed to pay for the provision of accommodation in relevant premises in that area.

(4) In subsection (3) above—

"accommodation" includes any board or care;

"local authority"—

    (a) in relation to areas in England and Wales, has the same meaning as it has in Part III of the National Assistance Act 1948; and

    (b) in relation to areas in Scotland, has the meaning given by section 1(2) of the Social Work (Scotland) Act 1968;

"qualifying person" means any person who falls within—

    (a) subsection (1) of section 26A of the National Assistance Act 1948 (which is inserted by the National Health Service and Community Care Act 1990 and relates to persons ordinarily resident in residential care or nursing homes immediately before the commencement of that section); or

    (b) subsection (1) of section 86A of the Social Work (Scotland) Act 1968 (the corresponding provision for Scotland),

or who would fall within either of those subsections apart from any regulations under subsection (3) of the section in question;

"relevant premises"—

    (a) in relation to areas in England and Wales, has the meaning given by section 26A(2) of the National Assistance Act 1948; and

    (b) in relation to areas in Scotland, has the meaning given section 86A(2) of the Social Work (Scotland) Act 1968.]

(5) In relation to income support, housing benefit and [²council tax benefit], the applicable amount for a severely disabled person shall include an amount in respect of his being a severely disabled person.

(6) Regulations may specify circumstances in which persons are to be treated as being or as not being severely disabled.

DERIVATION

Social Security Act 1986, s.22(1) to (4).

AMENDMENTS

1. To be omitted until s.9 of the Social Security Act 1990 is brought into force: Social Security (Consequential Provisions) Act 1992, s.6 and Sched. 4, Part I.

2. Local Government Finance Act 1992, Sched. 9, para. 8 (April 1, 1993).

DEFINITION

"prescribed"—see s.137(1).

GENERAL NOTE

Subsection (1)

See reg. 47 of the Family Credit (General) Regulations, regs. 17 to 22 of and Sched. 2 to the Income Support (General) Regulations and reg. 52 of the Disability Working Allowance (General) Regulations.

CIS 683/93 confirms that a claimant's applicable amount can only consist of elements specified in the relevant regulations. It cannot be increased by the amount of maintenance (or insurance premiums) the claimant is required to pay.

Subsection (2)

See reg. 21 of and Sched. 7 to the Income Support Regulations.

Subsections (3) and (4)

The predecessors of these subsections were inserted into s.22 of the 1986 Act by s.9 of the Social Security Act 1990 and are closely bound up with the Government's community care reforms. Those reforms under the National Health Service and Community Care Act 1990 were intended to come into force in April 1991, but after the passage of the Social Security Act 1990, it was announced that they would not come into effect until April 1993. These amendments have not yet come into force (see Social Security (Consequential Provisions) Act 1992, Sched. 4, paras. 1 and 4).

Subsections (5) and (6)

See para. 13 of Sched. 2 to the Income Support (General) Regulations. A provision requiring the payment of a community care addition to income support to very severely disabled people was put into the 1986 Act when it was going through the House of Lords. Although the Government did not wish to have this requirement in the legislation it did not seek to remove its spirit when the Bill returned to the House of Commons. But it put in its own amendments which have now become subss. (5) and (6).

In *CIS 372/1990* the Commissioner held that s.22(4) of the 1986 Act (the predecessor of subs. (6)) did not authorise the making of regulations prescribing conditions to be satisfied before a person counts as severely disabled other than conditions relating to the extent of that person's disablement. Otherwise, the mandatory provision of s.22(3) (the predecessor of subs. (5)) would be undermined. He therefore went on to hold that heads (ii) and (iii) of para. 13(2)a of Sched. 2, on the severe disability premium, were not validly part of the General Regulations. This was because they referred to the presence of a non-dependant in the claimant's household and to the receipt of invalid care allowance by another person, and not to the claimant's disability.

On appeal, the majority of the Court of Appeal took the opposite view, that s.22(4) gave the Secretary of State power to specify financial and domestic conditions as part of the circumstances in which a person was or was not to be treated as severely disabled (*Chief Adjudication Officer v. Foster* [1992] Q.B. 31, [1991] 3 All E.R. 846). Therefore the provisions were valid. Lord Donaldson M.R. dissented trenchantly, saying that if s.22(4) allowed regulations to specify conditions not relating to the severity of disability this would "emasculate the imperative contained in subsection (3) and indeed . . . render it otiose."

Now the House of Lords ([1993] A.C. 754, [1993] 1 All E.R. 705) has held the provisions to be valid. Lord Bridge agrees that subs. (3) (now subs. (5)) requires the applicable amount for a severely disabled person to include some amount in respect of being such a person. But subs. (4) (now subs. (6)) is a deeming provision which allows the Secretary of State to define who is to be treated as severely disabled. He may do this by reference to circumstances which either relate to the degree of disability or affect the extent of need for income support arising from the disability. If the only power intended to be given by subs. (4) were a power to define the degree of disability which qualifies as severe, the language used is totally inappropriate for that purpose (especially compared with the precise code for determining the degree of disability which qualifies someone for severe disablement allowance).

Lord Bridge would have reached this conclusion without looking at the Parliamentary history of the subsections in Hansard, but following *Pepper v. Hart* [1993] 1 All E.R. 42, [1992] 3 W.L.R. 1032 this can be consulted. The statements of Ministers in both Houses of Parliament on the government amendments made clear that it was intended to use the regulation-making power to prescribe that the severe disability premium should only be applicable where the person was receiving the higher rate of attendance allowance, was living in a household with no other adult able to care for him and had no-one eligible for invalid care allowance in respect of him. Therefore, the ambiguity in the regulation-making power should be resolved so as to authorise that use of the power.

The House of Lords' decision settles the scope of subss. (5) and (6). See the notes to para. 13 of Sched. 2 to the Income Support (General) Regulations for the conditions for the severe disability premium. On the powers of the Social Security Commissioners, SSATs and AOs to determine the validity or otherwise of regulations, see the notes to ss.21 and 23 of the Administration Act.

Income and capital

136.—(1) Where a person claiming an income-related benefit is a member of a family, the income and capital of any member of that family shall, except in prescribed circumstances, be treated as the income and capital of that person.

(2) Regulations may provide that capital not exceeding the amount prescribed under section 134(1) above but exceeding a prescribed lower amount shall be treated, to a prescribed extent, as if it were income of a prescribed amount.

(3) Income and capital shall be calculated or estimated in such manner as may be prescribed.

(4) A person's income in respect of a week shall be calculated in accordance with prescribed rules; and the rules may provide for the calculation to be made by reference to an average over a period (which need not include the week concerned).

(5) Circumstances may be prescribed in which—

(a) a person is treated as possessing capital or income which he does not possess;

(b) capital or income which a person does possess is to be disregarded;

(c) income is to be treated as capital;

(d) capital is to be treated as income.

DERIVATION

Subs. (1): Social Security Act 1986, s.22(5).
Subss. (2) to (5): 1986 Act, s.22(7) to (9).

DEFINITIONS

"family"—see s.137(1).
"prescribed"—*ibid.*

GENERAL NOTE

Subsection (1)
The general rule for income support, family credit and disability working allowance is that all of the family's (as defined in s.137(1)) income and capital should be aggregated together and treated as the claimant's. See reg. 23(1) of the Income Support (General) Regulations, reg. 10(1) of the Family Credit (General) Regulations and reg. 12(1) of the Disability Working Allowance (General) Regulations. The main exceptions are for children and young persons (see regs. 44 and 47 of the Income Support Regulations, regs. 27 and 30 of the Family Credit Regulations and regs. 30 and 33 of the Disability Working Allowance Regulations).

Subsection (2)
Reg. 53 of the Income Support Regulations and reg. 36 of the Family Credit Regulations provide for an income to be assumed to be produced from capital between £3,000 and £8,000. Because the capital limit for disability working allowance is £16,000, reg. 40 of the Disability Working Allowance Regulations provides for income to be assumed from capital between £3,000 and £16,000.

Subsections (3) to (5)
Large parts of the regulations deal with the matters covered by these subsections.

Interpretation of Part VII and supplementary provisions

137.—(1) In this Part of this Act, unless the context otherwise requires—

["billing authority" has the same meaning as in Part I of the Local Government Finance Act 1992;]

"child" means a person under the age of 16;

[¹ . . .]

"dwelling" means any residential accommodation, whether or not consisting of the whole or part of a building and whether or not comprising separate and self-contained premises;

"family" means—

(a) a married or unmarried couple;

(b) a married or unmarried couple and a member of the same household for whom one of them is or both are responsible and who is a child or a person of a prescribed description;

(c) except in prescribed circumstances, a person who is not a member of a married or unmarried couple and a member of the same household for whom that person is responsible and who is a child or a person of a prescribed description;

"industrial injuries scheme" means a scheme made under Schedule 8 to this Act or section 159 of the 1975 Act or under the Old Cases Act;

[¹"levying authority" has the same meaning as in Part II of the Local Government Finance Act 1992;]

"married couple" means a man and woman who are married to each other and are members of the same household;

[¹ . . .]

"prescribed" means specified in or determined in accordance with regulations;

"unmarried couple" means a man and woman who are not married to each other but are living together as husband and wife otherwise than in prescribed circumstances;

"war pension scheme" means a scheme under which war pensions (as defined in section 25 of the Social Security Act 1989) are provided;

"week", in relation to [¹council tax benefit], means a period of seven days beginning with a Monday.

(2) Regulations may make provision for the purposes of this Part of this Act—

(a) as to circumstances in which a person is to be treated as being or not being in Great Britain;

(b) continuing a person's entitlement to benefit during periods of temporary absence from Great Britain;

(c) as to what is or is not to be treated as remunerative work or as employment;

(d) as to circumstances in which a person is or is not to be treated as—
   (i) engaged or normally engaged in remunerative work;
   (ii) available for employment; or
   (iii) actively seeking employment;

(e) as to what is or is not to be treated as relevant education;

(f) as to circumstances in which a person is or is not to be treated as receiving relevant education;

(g) specifying the descriptions of pension increases under war pension schemes or industrial injuries schemes that are analogous to the benefits mentioned in section 129(2)(b)(i) to (iii) above;

(h) as to circumstances in which a person is or is not to be treated as occupying a dwelling as his home;

(i) for treating any person who is liable to make payments in respect of a dwelling as if he were not so liable;

(j) for treating any person who is not liable to make payments in respect of a dwelling as if he were so liable;

(k) for treating as included in a dwelling any land used for the purposes of the dwelling;

(l) as to circumstances in which persons are to be treated as being or not being members of the same household;

(m) as to circumstances in which one person is to be treated as responsible or not responsible for another.

DERIVATION

Subs. (1): Social Security Act, ss. 20(11) and 84(1).
Subs. (2): 1986 Act, s. 20(12).

AMENDMENT

1. Local Government Finance Act 1992, Sched. 9, para. 9 (April 1, 1993).

DEFINITIONS

"the 1975 Act"—see s. 174.
"the Old Cases Act"—*ibid.*

GENERAL NOTE

Subsection (1)

These definitions are important throughout the income-related benefit schemes.

"*child.*" Note the restricted definition which gives rise to the need to define "young persons" in regulations, to cater for the over-15s.

"*dwelling.*" See the notes to the definition of "dwelling occupied as the home" in reg. 2(1) of the Income Support (General) Regulations.

"*family.*" The definition effectively covers couples with or without children and single claimants with children. It may be that some contexts in the regulations require that single claimants without children are also included where a "family" is referred to.

Under para. (a), see the later definitions of married couple and unmarried couple.

Para. (b) covers couples and any child or young person (see reg. 14 of the Income Support Regulations, reg. 6 of the Family Credit (General) Regulations and reg. 8 of the Disability Working Allowance (General) Regulations) in the household for whom one of the couple is responsible. On the general test of membership of the household and children, see *England v. Secretary of State for Social Services* [1982] 3 F.L.R. 222, *R(FIS) 4/83* and *R(SB) 14/87*. See also notes under "married couple" and "unmarried couple". There are deeming rules in reg. 16 of the Income Support Regulations, regs. 8 and 9 of the Family Credit Regulations and regs. 9 and 10 of the Disability Working Allowance Regulations.

Para. (c) covers a single claimant who is responsible for a child in the same household.

"*married couple.*" The crucial question here is whether the couple are members of the same household. In *Santos v. Santos* [1972] 2 All E.R. 247 at 255 it was said that "household" refers to "people held together by a particular kind of tie". No doubt the approach taken in *R(SB) 13/82, R(SB) 4/83* and *CSB 463/1986* would apply here, subject to the deeming regulations mentioned above. The basic point of these and other decisions is that a house can contain a number of households. According to *R(SB) 4/83*, the concept of a household is a matter of commonsense and common experience. If a person in practice has exclusive occupation of separate accommodation from another person they do not live in the same household. In *CSB 463/1986* two claimants physically shared one room in a house as well as other facilities, but otherwise lived separately. They were in separate households. Thus a husband and wife can maintain separate households under the same roof. If the couple have decided to live apart in the same house, there can be separate households even if the husband is still maintaining the wife (*CIS 72/1994*). In *CIS 671/1992* the claimant and his wife shared a room in a home for the mentally ill. Both suffered from senile dementia and they did not understand that they were husband and wife. It is held that there must be some communality, something that can be identified as a domestic establishment. Mere presence in the same room did not turn them into a household. It is a question of fact in each case. In *CIS 81/1993* the same Commissioner similarly concludes that a husband and wife (who were not mentally incapacitated) were not members of the same household where they lived in separate rooms in a nursing home, were billed separately and had only limited contact with each other.

In *CIS 671/1992* the Commissioner also considers whether the claimant and his wife could be said to be members of some other household (the home as a whole). He refers to the decision of the House of Lords in *Simmons v. Pizzey* [1977] 2 All E.R. 432 (occupants of a woman's refuge not a single household), and concludes that all the residents of the home were not one household. A person under 16 cannot be a member of a married or unmarried couple (*CFC 7/1992*).

"*unmarried couple.*" The meaning and effect of this definition raises one of the most contentious issues in the whole of the law of social security—the cohabitation rule. The term "cohabitation" is now replaced by "living together as husband and wife," which is thought to be more neutral. The "rule" arises from the facts that the applicable amount for a couple is less than that for two single claimants and that a claimant is excluded from entitlement to income support if her partner is in remunerative work. The principle of aggregation between husband and wife is itself controversial, but while it remains, so it is argued, a couple living together as husband and wife must be treated in the same way. This is despite the fact that the legal position of such a couple in many other respects is different from that of a married couple.

While the law remains as it is, it is crucial to identify when a couple are living together as husband and wife. The first point to note is that the income support scheme recognises other ways of living together and has specific rules for determining the entitlement of claimants who live in someone else's household or have someone else living in their household. Webster J. put this very well in *Robson v. Secretary of State for Social Services* [1982] 3 F.L.R. 232, 236, when he said that "the legislation provides for three different situations: two persons who are living together being husband and wife is the first; two persons living together as husband and wife is the second; and two persons living together not as husband and wife is the third. It seems to me that where the facts show that there are two persons living together not being husband and wife, then both the second and third situations must be considered." Thus to show that a couple are living together is only the first step, not the final one, as so often happens in practice (see also, *e.g. Crake v SBC, Butterworth v. SBC* [1982] 1 All E.R. 498, 502, SB 38).

There have been a number of Commissioner's decisions on a similar rule in widow's benefit (the test is held to be the same in *R(SB) 17/81* and *R(G) 3/81* and the same principles will apply for the income-related benefits), but the position reached is fairly vague. Early attempts to obtain a judicial definition of "cohabitation" were unsuccessful ("for my part it is so well-known that nothing I could say about it could possibly assist in its interpretation hereafter," Lord Widgery C. J. in *R. v. S.W. London A.T., ex p. Barnett*, SB 4). The examination of three main matters is required in deciding if a woman is cohabiting with a man as his wife: "(1) their relationship in relation to sex: (2) their relationship in relation to money: (3) their general relationship. Although all three are as a rule relevant, no single one of them is necessarily conclusive" (*R(G) 3/71*). In *CIS 87/1993*, however, the Commissioner expresses the view that it is the parties' general relationship that is most important (see below).

In response to criticisms about the operation of the cohabitation rule the Supplementary Benefits Commission produced published guidelines. The last formulation in summary form was in the 1984 edition of the *Supplementary Benefits Handbook* (1984 ed.). A previous form of these guidelines had been approved as "an admirable signpost; the approach cannot be faulted" (Woolf J. in *Crake v SBC, Butterworth v. SBC, supra*) and were found to correspond to the *R(G) 3/71* test in *R(SB) 17/81*. The Handbook said (para. 2.13) that the main criteria are:

"1. Members of the same household
The couple must be living in the same household and neither partner will usually have any other home where they normally live. This implies that the couple live together, apart from absences necessary for employment, visits to relatives, etc.

2. Stability
Living together as husband and wife clearly implies more than an occasional or very brief association. When a couple first live together, it may be clear from the start that the relationship is similar to that of husband and wife (for example, if the woman has taken the man's name and borne his child), but in cases where at the outset the nature of the relationship is less clear it may be right not to regard the couple as living together as husband and wife until it is apparent that a stable relationship has been formed.

3. Financial support
In most husband and wife relationships one would expect to find financial support of one party by the other, or sharing of household expenses, but the absence of any such arrangement does not of itself prove that a couple are not living together.

4. Sexual relationship
Similarly, a sexual relationship is a normal part of a marriage and therefore of living together as husband and wife. But its absence at any particular time does not necessarily prove that a couple are not living as husband and wife.

5. Children
When a couple are caring for a child of their union, there is a strong presumption that they are living together as husband and wife.

6. Public acknowledgment
Whether the couple have represented themselves to other people as husband and wife is relevant. However, many couples living together do not wish to pretend that they are actually married. The fact that they retain their identity publicly as unmarried people does not mean that they cannot be regarded as living together as husband and wife."

The Handbook was wrong to claim that these guidelines had been approved by courts and a Commissioner, for there had been changes in form. The most important, in the paragraph on "sexual relationship," are devastatingly set out by the Commissioner in *R(SB) 35/85*. It was the 1979 version which was approved in *Crake* and *Butterworth* and in *R(SB) 17/81* and which referred to a sexual relationship as an important as well as a normal part of marriage and also noted that the presence of a sexual relationship did not necessarily prove that a couple were living as husband and wife. The 1982 edition added a new sentence "However, if a couple have never had such a relationship it is most unlikely that they should be regarded as living together as husband and wife." The 1983 edition "watered down" that sentence to suggesting that "it may be wrong" to regard the couple as living together as husband and wife in such circumstances. In the 1984 edition this final sentence disappeared altogether, along with the suggestion that the presence of a sexual relationship does not necessarily prove that a couple are living as husband and wife. In the meantime, the law has remained exactly the same. However, it is correct to stress that there is no single way by which the issue can be decided in every case. For the criteria tend not to help in making the basic distinction between couples living together as husband and wife and those living together in other ways. As *CIS 87/1993* emphasises, it is important to consider *why* the couple are living together.

The issues are now dealt with in Part 15 of the AOG, where the issues are discussed quite fully and with reference to a range of decisions. It is notable that in para. 15041 a sexual relationship is now described as an important as well as a normal part of marriage, and the presence of a sexual relationship is said not to be conclusive in itself of living together as husband and wife.

Household

Being members of the same household is obviously necessary. The approach to the meaning of "household" in the definition of "householder" for supplementary benefit purposes (see the notes on "married couple") may be relevant. In *R(SB) 30/83* the Commissioner holds that the issue is not decided on a week-by-week basis. So where the woman was absent during University terms living in a rented bedsitter, the couple were living together throughout. This principle was implicitly applied in *R(SB) 8/85*. The claimant lived with a Mr. G, whose employment brought him to the area and was said to go back to his wife at weekends. The Commissioner holds that a person can only be a member of one couple, and so of one household, at a time. This appears to leave open, to be determined according to the circumstances, whether Mr. G was living with the claimant for five days a week and with his wife for two days, or with only one of them. If a person maintains and from time to time lives in the same house as his lawful spouse there is an initial presumption that they form a married couple.

In *R(SB) 19/85* the claimant had been living together with (another) Mr. G as his wife in Manchester. She did not move with him to London because there was no place available for her in a London hospital for her to have dialysis on a kidney machine. Although *R(SB) 30/83* holds that the relationship can continue despite temporary absences, the Commissioner holds that the situation here was different. Effectively, the claimant and Mr. G had ceased to live together in the same accommodation. At the time, reg. 2(2) of the Supplementary Benefit (Aggregation) Regulations, deeming a couple still to be members of the same household through temporary absences, only applied to married couples, not as later also to unmarried couples. Now see reg. 16(1) of the Income Support Regulations.

Stability

The stability of a relationship is only of great weight if the relationship is one like husband and wife. There is no reason why a stable landlady-lodger relationship or flat-sharing relationship should not last for many years. However, it is sometimes suggested that an element of permanency in a relationship may differentiate it from, say, an employer-housekeeper relationship (*e.g. Campbell v. Secretary of State for Social Services* [1983] 4 F.L.R. 138, where the "housekeeper" had sold her furniture and intended to apply for a joint local authority tenancy with the man). This forward-looking approach does make sense.

Financial support

The approach to financial support seems to make almost any arrangement point the same way, except a very clearly fixed commercial rate. If the man pays a lot, he is supporting the woman. If he pays very little, this shows that the relationship is more than a commercial one. This makes it very difficult for parties who are friends, or where the man pays what he can afford, where the proper conclusion may merely be that the two people share a household.

Sexual relationship

There has been an attempt to decrease reliance on the existence of a sexual relationship, partly in response to criticism of "sex snoopers" and methods of investigation. Officers are now instructed not to initiate questions about sexual relationships and not to seek to inspect sleeping arrangements, but to note statements and evidence presented by the claimant. However, if a rule is to distinguish people living together as husband and wife from people living together in some other way it seems impossible not to give great significance to the nature of the sexual relationship. By playing down its importance, either as being present or absent, the Handbook inevitably shifted the test closer to one which simply tested whether the couple were living together in one household. The Commissioner in *CIS 87/1993* considers that where there has never been a sexual relationship, strong alternative grounds are needed to reach the conclusion that the relationship is akin to that of husband and wife. In his view, the instruction to DSS officers not to ask about the physical aspects of the relationship is inappropriate in an inquisitorial system, and if the information is not volunteered, such questions may have to be asked. But care will need to be taken to prevent any such investigation becoming over-intrusive.

In *CSB 150/1985* the Commissioner held that an unmarried couple who refrained on principle from any sexual relationship could not be described as living together as husband and wife. The claimant and his fiancee lived in the same house, but were Mormons. That religion forbids sexual relationships before marriage.

Children and public acknowledgment

The shared care of children, especially children of the couple, and public acknowledgment are obviously important factors. In *R(G) 1/79* the adoption of the same name on the electoral register was decisive. Other elements might be whether the couple visit relatives or friends, or go on holiday, together.

What these points come to is that the so-called "objective facts" of a relationship may be capable of being interpreted either way. This, then, leaves the authorities in a difficulty, although it is clear that the burden of proof, since the rule operates as a disqualification, is on the DSS. In two decisions the Divisional Court has stressed the importance of looking at the intention of the parties in explaining the "objective facts." In *Butterworth v. SBC, supra,* the claimant was disabled following a serious accident, and invited the man, whom she had known for five years, to move into her house, since she was then on her own. The man had his own bedroom, with a lock on the door. He did the cooking and household tasks, and they lived as one household. Woolf J. says:

"If the only reason that [the man] went to that house temporarily was to look after Mrs. Butterworth in her state of illness and, albeit, while doing so, acted in the same way as an attentive husband would behave towards his wife who suffered an illness, this does not amount to living together as husband and wife because it was not the intention of the parties that there should be such a relationship. Looked at without knowing the reason for the man going to live there, it would appear that they were living together as husband and wife, but when the reason was known that would explain those circumstances."

In *Robson's* case (above), the parties were both seriously disabled, needing wheelchairs and invalid cars. They had been friends for a long time before they were widowed. They moved together into a two-bedroom maisonette at their social worker's suggestion. They lived as one household. As so often the SBAT assumed that this was conclusive, and this was an error of law. In order to provide guidance to tribunals, Webster J. says that often it is only possible to decide into which category a relationship falls by considering the objective facts,

"because usually the intention of the parties is either unascertainable, or, if ascertainable, is not to be regarded as reliable. But if it is established to the satisfaction of the tribunal that the two persons concerned did not intend to live together as husband and wife and still do not intend to do so, in my judgment it would be a very strong case indeed sufficient to justify a decision that they are, or ought to be treated as if they are, husband and wife."

Although subsequent Divisional Court decisions (*e.g. Kaur v. Secretary of State for Social Services* [1982] 3 F.L.R. 237) have not referred to intention as a factor, it has not been rejected either. However, in *R(SB) 17/81* the Commissioner says that Webster J.'s words are of no real assistance to tribunals. For, he says, it is "the conduct of the person concerned to which regard has to be paid", *i.e.* "what he or she does or says at the relevant time." If *R(SB) 17/81* is taken as deciding that only the "objective facts" as identified by the Handbook criteria are relevant, and that the intention of the parties is not relevant, it need not be followed as being inconsistent with persuasive decisions of the Divisional Court. If *R(SB) 17/81* is taken as a reminder of the difficulties of establishing intention it is in line with those decisions, although evidence of intention should not be as limited as suggested. On the facts of *R(SB) 17/81* the couple shared a sexual relationship and one household, but said that there was nothing permanent about the relationship. The Commissioner points out that the fact that they did not intend to marry did not mean that they did not intend to live together as though they were married.

It is the second view of *R(SB) 17/81* which seems to have been applied in recent Commissioners' decisions, although AOs commonly rely on the first view in submissions to tribunals. *CSSB 145/*

1983 is a decision on facts reminiscent of *Robson's* case. Two disabled people living in a sheltered housing scheme moved into one flat to share living expenses and provide mutual support. At the beginning the Housing Association running the flats did not have the funds to divide the one bedroom. There was no sexual relationship. The SSAT had decided that the situation was no different from that of a married couple where one partner had a serious disability. The Commissioner holds this to be a wrong approach. A sharing of expenses and mutual support can arise between people of the same sex, or between brother and sister, and does not in itself amount to living together as husband and wife.

In *R(SB) 35/85* the claimant was a widow in her seventies. She had taken over the tenancy of her bungalow in 1976, on the death of her brother, with whom she had lived for some years. In 1974, Mr. W, who needed care and help, had moved into the household. By August 1984, he was a widower. The claimant did the cooking and there was a sharing of household expenses. The Commissioner holds that the SSAT, in finding the claimant and Mr W to be living together as husband and wife, had failed to see that the existence of a common household was only one ingredient in the decision. He adopts as helpful guidance the approach of Woolf J. in *Butterworth's* case that it is impossible to categorise all the kinds of explanation of why two people were sharing a household which would mean that the two were not living together as husband and wife.

In *CIS 87/1993* the claimant maintained that the only relationship between him and Mrs B, with whom he was living, was that of patient and carer. The Commissioner decides that the SSAT had failed to consider their general relationship and *why* they were living together. He expresses reservations about the "criteria" relied upon by AOs in cohabitation cases. He points out that Woolf J. in *Crake* and *Butterworth* considered it wrong to refer to them as "criteria" and preferred the description "admirable signposts". There was nothing in *R(SB) 17/81* to suggest that only these admirable signposts had to be considered. In the Commissioner's view, the admirable signposts failed to emphasise the significance of the parties' "general relationship". It was arguable that it was the parties' general relationship that was of paramount importance and that their sexual and their financial relationship were only relevant for the light they threw upon the general relationship.

Part VIII

The Social Fund

Payments out of the social fund

138.—(1) Payments may be made out of the social fund, in accordance with this Part of this Act—

(a) of prescribed amounts, whether in respect of prescribed items or otherwise, to meet, in prescribed circumstances, maternity expenses and funeral expenses; and

(b) to meet other needs in accordance with directions given or guidance issued by the Secretary of State.

(2) Payments may also be made out of fund, in accordance with this Part of this Act, of a prescribed amount or a number of prescribed amounts to prescribed descriptions of persons, in prescribed circumstances, to meet expenses for heating which appear to the Secretary of State to have been or to be likely to be incurred in cold weather.

(3) The power to make a payment out of the social fund such as is mentioned in subsection (1)(b) above may be exercised by making a payment to a third party with a view to the third party providing, or arranging for the provision of, goods or services for the applicant.

(4) In this section "prescribed" means specified in or determined in accordance with regulations.

DERIVATIONS

Subss. (1) and (2): Social Security Act 1986, s.32(2) and (2A).
Subs. (3): 1986 Act, s.33(1A).
Subs. (4): 1986 Act, s.84(1).

GENERAL NOTE

This book cannot contain any real discussion of the general social fund scheme. It is concerned with claims which can lead to an appeal to the SSAT. Since such appeals only lie from decisions of AOs, the decision of social fund officers (SFOs) cannot be appealed to the SSAT. A system of review is set out in s.66 of the Administration Act. If an applicant insists on appealing to a SSAT against a decision of a SFO, a SSAT chairman may dispose of the purported appeal as outside the SSAT's jurisdiction (Adjudication Regulations, reg. 3(6)). Only the payments for maternity and funeral expenses under subs. (1)(a) and for exceptionally cold weather under subs. (2) are dealt with by AOs and SSATs. Only the sections relating to these payments have substantial comments. But the primary legislation relating to the social fund is included, since it will be of use to many readers. In the later Social Fund section are the regulations on the review process and the general directions issued by the Secretary of State under s.140(2) to (4) (formerly ss.32(2)(b), 33(10) and (10A) of the Social Security Act 1986), which are binding on SFOs.

Subsection (1)(a)

This part of the social fund scheme was brought into operation in April 1987 to enable payments to be made for maternity and funeral expenses. These are made under the ordinary system of adjudication and under regulations required to be made by subs. (1)(a). They are not subject to any budget. See the Social Fund Maternity and Funeral Expenses (General) Regulations 1987. The death grant and the maternity grant, formerly payable under the Social Security Act 1975, were abolished (1986 Act, ss.38 and 41) and the provisions for maternity and funeral expenses under the supplementary benefit regulations were removed in April 1987 (General Regulations, regs. 13 to 15).

Subs. (1)(a) does little more than provide the framework for the detailed entitlement set out in the General Regulations. See s.78(4) of the Administration Act on the recovery of funeral payments from the estate of the deceased.

Subsection (1)(b)

This subsection gives the discretion ("may") to make payments to meet needs other than for maternity and funeral expenses. It also contains the general power for the Secretary of State to give directions and guidance, which are given particular statutory force under s.140(2) and (5) of this Act and s.66(7), (9) and (10) of the Administration Act. There are more specific powers in s.140(2) to (4) and s.66(8) and s.168(5) of the Administration Act. The Secretary of State's directions are set out in Part 4 of this book.

In *R. v. Social Fund Officer and Secretary of State for Social Security, ex parte Stitt* it was argued that the predecessor of subs. (1)(b) did not empower the Secretary of State to give directions which limited the categories of need which could be met from the social fund. The applicant and his wife already had three children when they had triplets. The applicant was then on an Employment Training course. He applied for a community care grant to assist with the care of the triplets. The application was rejected because direction 29 (by reference to direction 12(h)) excluded payments for domestic assistance. The Divisional Court (*The Times*, February 23, 1990, *The Independent*, February 23, 1990) held that the Secretary of State had power to give "such directions as can reasonably be regarded as being necessary for the proper 'control and management' of the Social Fund so as to enable that fund to meet the needs of applicants which cannot be met out of their own resources" (see s.167(2) of the Administration Act, formerly s.32(5) of the 1986 Act). This power covered directions defining needs. The Court of Appeal (*The Times*, July 4, 1990) agreed that the directions were validly made, but Butler-Sloss L.J. and Sir Patrick Connor found the power in ss.32(1)(b) and 33(10) of the 1986 Act (now this subsection and s.140(2)) rather than in s.32(5). All the judges expressed their surprise (at the least) at the scope of the unsupervised powers to give directions.

In *R. v. Secretary of State for Social Security, ex parte Healey* (and the associated actions in *Smith* and *Stitt II*), *The Independent*, April 18, 1991, *The Times*, April 22, 1991, the Divisional Court accepts that the Court of Appeal's decision means that the Secretary of State has power to define the categories of need to be met. The power is not limited to excluding needs which can be met by some body or person other than the social fund. The Secretary of State must not act irrationally in exercising the power, but this does not prevent him excluding needs which may not be met elsewhere. The Court of Appeal (*The Times*, December 31, 1991) confirms this decision and rejects the argument that a court may quash directions if it finds them merely unreasonable, rather than irrational.

Subsection (2)

Although the predecessor of this subsection was in force from April 1988, the regulations which it required were not in place until November 7, 1988 (Social Fund Cold Weather Payments (General)

Regulations 1988). The form of the scheme, as embodied in the 1988 Regulations, has been amended several times. The current form does not require a separate claim to be made for a severe weather payment. As for maternity and funeral expenses, the decisions are made by AOs, with appeals to the SSAT, and are not subject to any budget.

Awards by social fund officers

139.—(1) The questions whether a payment such as is mentioned in section 138(1)(b) is to be awarded and how much it is to be shall be determined by a social fund officer.

(2) A social fund officer may determine that an award shall be payable in specified instalments at specified times.

(3) A social fund officer may determine that an award is to be repayable.

(4) An award that is to be repayable shall be repayable upon such terms and conditions as before the award is paid the Secretary of State notifies to the person by or on behalf of whom the application for it was made.

(5) Payment of an award shall be made to the applicant unless the social fund officer determines otherwise.

DERIVATIONS

Subss. (1) to (4): Social Security Act 1986 Act, s.33(2) to (4A).
Subs. (5): 1986, s.33(11).

GENERAL NOTE

Subsection (1)
This provision secures that decisions on payments from the general social fund are made by social fund officers, so that there is no appeal to a SSAT.

Subsection (3)
This provision gives the power for payments to be made in the form of loans, although there is no power to charge interest. The Social Fund Directions specify what categories of need may be met by grants and which by loans. S.78 of the Administration Act is concerned with the mechanism of recovering loans. See the notes to s.78 and also the Social Fund (Recovery by Deductions from Benefits) Regulations 1988 in Part 4.

Principles of determination

140.—(1) In determining whether to make an award to the applicant or the amount or value to be awarded a social fund officer shall have regard, subject to subsection (2) below, to all the circumstances of the case and, in particular—
   (a) the nature, extent and urgency of the need;
   (b) the existence of resources from which the need may be met;
   (c) the possibility that some other person or body may wholly or partly meet it;
   (d) where the payment is repayable, the likelihood of repayment and the time within which repayment is likely;
   (e) any relevant allocation under section 168(1) to (4) of the Administration Act.

(2) A social fund officer shall determine any question in accordance with any general directions issued by the Secretary of State and in determining any question shall take account of any general guidance issued by him.

(3) Without prejudice to the generality of subsection (2) above, the Secretary of State may issue directions under that subsection for the purpose of securing that a social fund officer or group of social fund officers shall not in any specified period make awards of any specified description which in the aggregate exceed the amount, or a specified portion of the amount, allocated to that officer

or group of officers under section 168(1) to (4) for payments under awards of that description in that period.

(4) Without prejudice to the generality of subsection (2) above, the power to issue general directions conferred on the Secretary of State by that subsection includes power to direct—

(a) that in circumstances specified in the direction a social fund officer shall not determine an application and, without prejudice to the generality of this paragraph, that a social fund officer shall not determine an application which is made before the end of a specified period after the making of an application by the same person for a payment such as is mentioned in section 138(1)(b) above to meet the same need and without there having been any relevant change of circumstances since the previous application;

(b) that for a category of need specified in the direction a social fund officer shall not award less than an amount specified in the direction;

(c) that for a category of need specified in the direction a social fund officer shall not award more than an amount so specified;

(d) that payments to meet a category of need specified in the direction shall in all cases or in no case be made by instalments;

(e) that payments to meet a category of need specified in the direction shall in all cases or in no case be repayable; and

(f) that a payment such as is mentioned in section 138(1)(b) above shall only be awarded to a person if either—

(i) he is in receipt of a benefit which is specified in the direction and the circumstances are such as are so specified; or

(ii) in a case where the conditions specified in subparagraph (i) above are not satisfied, the circumstances are such as are specified in the direction;

and the power to issue general guidance conferred on him by that subsection includes power to give social fund officers guidance as to any matter to which directions under that subsection may relate.

(5) In determining a question a social fund officer shall take account (subject to any directions or guidance issued by the Secretary of State under this section) of any guidance issued by the social fund officer nominated for his area under section 64 of the Administration Act.

DERIVATIONS

Subss. (1) to (4): Social Security Act 1986, s.33(9) to (10A).
Subs. (5): 1986 Act, s.32(11).

GENERAL NOTE

Subsection (1)

The effect of subs. (1) is that the social fund officer (SFO) must have regard to the five statutory factors in every case, as well as all the circumstances of the particular case. However, subs. (1) is subject to subs. (2), which requires the SFO to follow directions given by the Secretary of State and to take account of guidance. Taking account seems to mean the same as having regard, so that Secretary of State's guidance can effectively be added to the list in subs. (1). The effect of subs. (5) is to add guidance given by area SFOs to the list, providing that that guidance is not contrary to Secretary of State's directions or guidance. But directions are overriding, provided that they are within the Secretary of State's statutory power, and so take precedence to the subs. (1) factors.

The requirement to have regard to the budget allocated to the local office (para. (e)) is of particular interest, since it is the budget which is responsible for many of the novel, if not unique, features of the Social Fund. In subs. (1) the state of the budget is just one factor to be taken into account and is given no overriding status. The Social Fund Directions did not originally deal with the budget. Paras. 2016 and 2054 of the Social Fund Manual (containing the guidance) said that a payment was not to be made if it would result in the local office budget being exceeded. In *R. v. Social*

Fund Inspector and Secretary of State for Social Security, ex parte Roberts, The Times, February 23, 1990, *The Independent* February 23, 1990, the Divisional Court struck down these, and some other, paragraphs as unlawful. They adopted the language of direction when there was no power to do so. Now see subs. (3).

Subsection (2)

A SFO must follow directions issued by the Secretary of State and must take account of guidance. The directions and guidance were originally published in the *Social Fund Manual*. They were then contained in Volumes 1 and 2 of the *Social Fund Officer's Guide*, produced by the Benefits Agency late in 1991, reissued as the *Social Fund Guide* in 1993. A new *Social Fund Guide* was issued on April 1, 1995, volume 1 containing guidance on the budget and community care grants, and volume 2 on loans, trade disputes and reviews. The Secretary of State's directions are in volume 2.

See the note to subs. (1) for the interaction of subss.(1) and (2). See subs. (5) for guidance by area SFOs.

Subsection (3)

The predecessor of subs. (3) (s.33(10ZA) of the 1986 Act) was introduced from July 13, 1990. Its intention was described by the Minister for Social Security as follows (H.C. Hansard, March 28, 1990, Vol. 170, col. 580).

"[It] is essential to the successful operation of the fund that its resources are managed so as not to exceed the amounts allocated for payments. Under the present legislation, it would be possible to issue directions on matters relating to the control of the budget. I have already mentioned the power that we are taking in respect of directions for the management and control of local budgets. The additional power that we are taking under the new clause will reinforce the effect of those directions by giving the Secretary of State explicit power to issue directions requiring social fund officers to keep within their allocations.

Such directions will, therefore, preclude a social fund officer, or a group of social fund officers, from making any award that would result in the sums allocated to that officer or group of officers being exceeded. This must be right if the scheme is to operate within the strict monetary limits, as Parliament originally intended, and as was recognised by the court."

It is clear that subs. (3) authorises such directions, which could anyway have been made under the general power of subs. (2). Directions were issued in September 1990 (see Part 4).

An extra £12.3 million was put into the 1990–91 budget to make up for the extra expenditure incurred as a result of the judgment in *Roberts* before the new directions were issued.

Subsection (4)

This provision lists some matters on which the Secretary of State may issue directions, without prejudicing the generality of subs. (2).

Subsection (5)

Under s.64(3) of the Administration Act the Secretary of State may nominate a SFO for an area who is to issue guidance to SFOs in the area about matters specified by the Secretary of State. Direction 41 requires the Area SFO to review and revise planned levels of expenditure and priorities each month.

PART XIII

GENERAL

Interpretation

Application of Act in relation to territorial waters

172. In this Act—
   (a) any reference to Great Britain includes a reference to the territorial waters of the United Kingdom adjacent to Great Britain;
   (b) any reference to the United Kingdom includes a reference to the territorial waters of the United Kingdom.

DERIVATION

Social Security Act 1986, s.84(4).

Age

173. For the purposes of this Act a person—
  (a) is over or under a particular age if he has or, as the case may be, has not attained that age; and
  (b) is between two particular ages if he has attained the first but not the second;

and in Scotland (as in England and Wales) the time at which a person attains a particular age expressed in years is the commencement of the relevant anniversary of the date of his birth.

DERIVATION

Social Security Act 1975, Sched. 20.

References to Acts

174. In this Act—
"the 1975 Act" means the Social Security Act 1975;
"the 1986 Act" means the Social Security Act 1986;
"the Administration Act" means the Social Security Administration Act 1992;
"the Consequential Provisions Act" means the Social Security (Consequential Provisions) Act 1992;
"the Northern Ireland Contributions and Benefits Act" means the Social Security Contributions and Benefits (Northern Ireland) Act 1992;
"the Old Cases Act" means the Industrial Injuries and Diseases (Old Cases) Act 1975; and
"the Pensions Act" means the Social Security Pensions Act 1975.

Subordinate legislation

Regulations, orders and schemes

175.—(1) Subject to section 145(5) above, regulations and orders under this Act shall be made by the Secretary of State.

(2) Powers under this Act to make regulations, orders or schemes shall be exercisable by statutory instrument.

(3) Except in the case of an order under section 145(3) above and in so far as this Act otherwise provides, any power under this Act to make regulations or an order may be exercised—
  (a) either in relation to all cases to which the power extends, or in relation to those cases subject to specified exceptions, or in relation to any specified cases or classes of case;
  (b) so as to make, as respects the cases in relation to which it is exercised—
    (i) the full provision to which the power extends or any less provision (whether by way of exception or otherwise),
    (ii) the same provision for all cases in relation to which the power is exercised, or different provision for different cases or different classes of case or different provision as respects the same case or class of case for different purposes of this Act;
    (iii) any such provision either unconditionally or subject to any specified condition;

and where such a power is expressed to be exercisable for alternative purposes it may be exercised in relation to the same case for any or all of those purposes; and powers to make regulations or an order for the purposes of any one provision of this Act are without prejudice to powers to make regulations or an order for the purposes of any other provision.

(4) Without prejudice to any specific provision in this Act, any power conferred by this Act to make regulations or an order (other than the power conferred in section 145(3) above) includes power to make thereby such incidental, supplementary, consequential or transitional provision as appears to the Secretary of State to be expedient for the purposes of the regulations or order.

(5) Without prejudice to any specific provisions in this Act, a power conferred by any provision of this Act except—

(a) sections 30, 47(6), [¹25B(2)(a)] and 145(3) above and paragraph 3(9) of Schedule 7 to this Act;

(b) section 122(1) above in relation to the definition of "payments by way of occupational or personal pension"; and

(c) Part XI,

to make regulations or an order includes power to provide for a person to exercise a discretion in dealing with any matter.

(6) *[Omitted as relating only to housing benefit and community charge benefit.]*

(7) Any power of the Secretary of State under any provision of this Act, except the provisions mentioned in subsection (5)(a) and (b) above and Part IX, to make any regulations or order, where the power is not expressed to be exercisable with the consent of the Treasury, shall if the Treasury so direct be exercisable only in conjunction with them.

(8) and (9) *[Omitted as relating only to ss.116 to 120.]*

(10) Any reference in this section or section 176 below to an order or regulations under this Act includes a reference to an order or regulations made under any provision of an enactment passed after this Act and directed to be construed as one with this Act; but this subsection applies only so far as a contrary intention is not expressed in the enactment so passed, and without prejudice to the generality of any such direction.

DERIVATION

Social Security Act 1986, ss. 83(1) and 84(1).

AMENDMENT

1. Social Security (Incapacity for Work) Act 1994, Sched. 1, para. 36 (April 13, 1995).

Parliamentary control

176.—(1) and (2) *[Omitted as not applying to income-related benefits.]*

(3) A statutory instrument—

(a) which contains (whether alone or with other provisions) any order, regulations or scheme made under this Act by the Secretary of State, other than an order under section 145(3) above; and

(b) which is not subject to any requirement that a draft of the instrument shall be laid before and approved by a resolution of each House of Parliament,

shall be subject to annulment in pursuance of a resolution of either House of Parliament.

DERIVATION

Social Security Act 1986, s.83(4).

Short title, commencement and extent

177.—(1) This Act may be cited as the Social Security Contributions and Benefits Act 1992.

(2) This Act is to be read, where appropriate, with the Administration Act and the Consequential Provisions Act.

(3) The enactments consolidated by this Act are repealed, in consequence of the consolidation, by the Consequential Provisions Act.

(4) Except as provided in Schedule 4 to the Consequential Provisions Act, this Act shall come into force on 1st July 1992.

(5) The following provisions extend to Northern Ireland—
>   section 16 and Schedule 2;
>   section 116(2); and
>   this section.

(6) Except as provided by this section, this Act does not extend to Northern Ireland.

DEFINITIONS

"the Administration Act"—see s.174.
"the Consequential Provisions Act"—*ibid*.

Child Support Act 1991

(1991 c. 48)

SECTIONS REPRODUCED

SCHEDULES REPRODUCED

GENERAL NOTE

This book does not deal directly with the system of child support maintenance, not least because appeals from decisions of child support officers (CSOs) go to child support appeal tribunals, rather than SSATs. For a full treatment, see Jacobs and Douglas, *Child Support Legislation*. The child support legislation provides for income-related benefits to be reduced where a parent on benefit fails to co-operate in the process of assessing maintenance from an absent parent. In addition, where an absent parent is on income support, a deduction can be made from his income support as a contribution towards child maintenance. Those parts of the legislation relevant to the reduction and the deduction are included.

Applications by those receiving benefit

6.—(1) Where income support, family credit or any other benefit of a prescribed kind is claimed by or in respect of, or paid to or in respect of, the parent of a qualifying child she shall, if—
>   (a) she is a person with care of the child; and
>   (b) she is required to do so by the Secretary of State,
authorise the Secretary of State to take action under the Act to recover child support maintenance from the absent parent.

(2) The Secretary of State shall not require a person ("the parent") to give him the authorisation mentioned in subsection (1) if he considers that there are reasonable grounds for believing that—
>   (a) if the parent were to be required to give that authorisation; or

(b) if she were to give it.

there would be a risk of her, or of any child living with her, suffering harm or undue distress as a result.

(3) Subsection (2) shall not apply if the parent requests the Secretary of State to disregard it.

(4) The authorisation mentioned in subsection (1) shall extend to all children of the absent parent in relation to whom the parent first mentioned in subsection (1) is a person with care.

(5) That authorisation shall be given, without unreasonable delay, by completing and returning to the Secretary of State an application—

(a) for the making of a maintenance assessment with respect to the qualifying child or qualifying children; and

(b) for the Secretary of State to take action under this Act to recover, on her behalf, the amount of child support maintenance so assessed.

(6) Such an application shall be made on a form ("a maintenance application form") provided by the Secretary of State.

(7) A maintenance application form shall indicate in general terms the effect of completing and returning it.

(8) Subsection (1) has effect regardless of whether any of the benefits mentioned there is payable with respect to any qualifying child.

(9) A person who is under a duty imposed by subsection (1) shall, so far as she reasonably can, comply with such regulations as may be made by the Secretary of State with a view to the Secretary of State or the child support officer being provided with the information which is required to enable—

(a) the absent parent to be traced;

(b) the amount of child support maintenance payable by the absent parent to be assessed; and

(c) that amount to be recovered from the absent parent.

(10) The obligation to provide information which is imposed by subsection (9)—

(a) shall not apply in such circumstances as may be prescribed; and

(b) may, in such circumstances as may be prescribed, be waived by the Secretary of State.

(11) A person with care who has authorised the Secretary of State under subsection (1) but who subsequently ceases to fall within that subsection may request the Secretary of State to cease acting under this section.

(12) It shall be the duty of the Secretary of State to comply with any request made under subsection (11) (but subject to any regulations made under subsection (13)).

(13) The Secretary of State may by regulations make such incidental or transitional provision as he thinks appropriate with respect to cases in which he is requested under subsection (11) to cease to act under this section.

(14) The fact that a maintenance assessment is in force with respect to a person with care shall not prevent the making of a new maintenance assessment with respect to her in response to an application under this section.

DEFINITIONS

"absent parent"
"child support maintenance"
"qualifying child"

GENERAL NOTE

Disability working allowance is prescribed as a benefit to which s. 6 applies along with income support and family credit (Child Support (Maintenance Assessment Procedure) Regulations 1992, reg. 34).

A parent who has claimed one of these benefits and who has care of a qualifying child has general obligations to authorise the Secretary of State to take action against the absent parent (subs. (1)) and to provide the necessary information. The Child Support (Information, Evidence and Disclosure) Regulations 1992 prescribe the information required. However, those obligations depend on the Secretary of State having under subs. (1)(b) required the parent to give authorisation. That requirement is not, under subs. (2), to be made if the Secretary of State considers that there are reasonable grounds for believing that there is a risk of harm or undue distress to her or any children living with her from compliance. There is no provision for appeal from the Secretary of State's decision to require the parent to authorise action, but no doubt there could be a challenge through judicial review.

If, once the obligations under subss. (1) and (9) have arisen, the Secretary of State considers that the parent has failed to comply he must serve a notice on the parent that he intends to refer the case to a CSO to take action under s. 46 and must then wait for six weeks before making the reference (Maintenance Assessment Procedure Regulations, reg. 35). The CSO may then consider making a reduced benefit direction. The parent has a right of appeal under s. 46(7) to a child support appeal tribunal against a CSO's decision to give a reduced benefit direction.

Special cases

Contribution to maintenance by deduction from benefit

43.—(1) This section applies where—
   (a) by virtue of paragraph 5(4) of Schedule 1, an absent parent is taken for the purposes of that Schedule to have no assessable income; and
   (b) such conditions as may be prescribed for the purposes of this section are satisfied.

(2) The power of the Secretary of State to make regulations under [¹section 5 of the Social Security Administration Act 1992 by virtue of subsection (1)(p),] (deductions from benefits) may be exercised in relation to cases to which this section applies with a view to securing that—
   (a) payments of prescribed amounts are made with respect to qualifying children in place of payments of child support maintenance; and
   (b) arrears of child support maintenance are recovered.

AMENDMENT

1. Social Security (Consequential Provisions) Act 1992, Sched. 2, para. 113 (July 1, 1992).

GENERAL NOTE

This section, Sched. 1, para. 5(4) and regs. 13 and 28 and Scheds. 4 and 5 of the Child Support (Maintenance Assessments and Special Cases) Regulations 1992 have been reproduced for the assistance of SSATs hearing appeals against the deduction of £2.35 from the income support of absent parents as a contribution towards the maintenance of their children. The conditions referred to in subs. (1)(b) are set out in reg. 28(1) of and Sched. 4 to the Maintenance Assessments and Special Cases Regulations. Any appeal concerning whether an absent parent is exempt from these deductions has to go to a child support appeal tribunal. The issues before a SSAT will be mainly whether there are other deductions that have a higher priority and whether there is sufficient income support in payment for the deduction to be made.

Miscellaneous and supplemental

Failure to comply with obligations imposed by section 6

46.—(1) This section applies where any person (''the parent'')—
   (a) fails to comply with a requirement imposed on her by the Secretary of State under section 6(1); or
   (b) fails to comply with any regulation made under section 6(9).

(2) A child support officer may serve written notice on the parent requiring her, before the end of the specified period, either to comply or to give him her reasons for failing to do so.

(3) When the specified period has expired, the child support officer shall consider whether, having regard to any reasons given by the parent, there are reasonable grounds for believing that, if she were to be required to comply, there would be a risk of her or of any children living with her suffering harm or undue distress as a result of complying.

(4) If the child support officer considers that there are such reasonable grounds, he shall—

(a) take no further action under this section in relation to the failure in question; and

(b) notify the parent, in writing, accordingly.

(5) If the child support officer considers that there are such reasonable grounds, he may give a reduced benefit direction with respect to the parent.

(6) Where the child support officer gives a reduced benefit direction he shall send a copy of it to the parent.

(7) Any person who is aggrieved by a decision of a child support officer to give a reduced benefit direction may appeal to a child support appeal tribunal against that decision.

(8) Sections 20(2) to (4) and 21 shall apply in relation to appeals under subsection (7) as they apply in relation to appeals under section 20.

(9) A reduced benefit direction shall take effect on such date as may be specified in the direction.

(10) Reasons given in response to a notice under subsection (2) may be given in writing or orally.

(11) In this section—

"comply" means to comply with the requirement or with the regulation in question; and "complied" and "complying" shall be construed accordingly;

"reduced benefit direction" means a direction, binding on the adjudication officer, that the amount payable by way of any relevant benefit to, or in respect of, the parent concerned be reduced by such amount, and for such period, as may be prescribed;

"relevant benefit" means income support, family credit or any other benefit of a kind prescribed for the purposes of section 6; and

"specified", in relation to any notice served under this section, means specified in the notice; and the period to be specified shall be determined in accordance with regulations made by the Secretary of State

GENERAL NOTE

For the CSO to act under s.46 the parent must have failed to comply with the obligations under s.6(1) or (9). The written notice under subs. (2) to comply or give reasons must give 14 days to do so (Maintenance Assessment Procedure Regulations, reg. 35(3)).

If the parent complies, s.46 ceases to apply. If she does not, the CSO must consider whether there are reasonable grounds for believing that there would be a risk of harm or undue distress to her or any children living with her from compliance. If not, he may give a reduced benefit direction (subs. (5)). Any appeal against that decision has to be to a child support appeal tribunal (subs. (7)). The direction is, under subs. (11), binding on the AO and requires the amount of income support, family credit or disability working allowance payable to or in respect of the parent to be reduced. See the Maintenance Assessment Procedure Regulations for the amount of the reduction, its length and the complicated provisions for its suspension, ending or extension. At April 1995 benefit rates the reduction will be £9.30 per week for the first 26 weeks and £4.65 for the next 52 weeks.

The intention seems to be that the giving of the direction will be a change of circumstances requiring a review by the AO of any existing award of benefit under s.25(1)(b) or 30(5)(b) of the Administration Act. See reg. 51A of the Family Credit (General) Regulations and reg. 56A of the Disability Working Allowance (General) Regulations for provisions allowing review of awards of family credit and disability working allowance when certain action is taken in relation to reduced benefit directions. Any appeal about such reviews or the resulting revised decisions must go to a SSAT, but the issues will be mainly arithmetical.

SCHEDULE 1

Section 11

MAINTENANCE ASSESSMENTS

PART I

CALCULATION OF CHILD SUPPORT MAINTENANCE

Assessable income

5.—(4) Where income support or any other benefit of a prescribed kind is paid to or in respect of a parent who is an absent parent or a person with care that parent shall, for the purposes of this Schedule, be taken to have no assessable income.

[The rest of the Schedule has not been reproduced.]

PART II

INCOME SUPPORT

Income Support (General) Regulations 1987

(S.I. 1987 No. 1967)

ARRANGEMENT OF REGULATIONS

PART I

GENERAL

PART II

CONDITIONS OF ENTITLEMENT

PART III

MEMBERSHIP OF A FAMILY

PART IV

APPLICABLE AMOUNTS

41

Income Support (General) Regulations 1987

PART I

GENERAL

Citation and commencement

1. These Regulations may be cited as the Income Support (General) Regulations 1987 and shall come into force on 11th April 1988.

Interpretation

2.—(1) In these Regulations, unless the context otherwise requires
"the Act" means the Social Security Act 1986;
"attendance allowance" means:—

> (a) an attendance allowance under section 35 of the Social Security Act [SSCBA, s.64];
> (b) an increase of disablement pension under section 61 or 63 of that Act [SSCBA, s.104 or 105];
> (c) a payment under regulations made in exercise of the power conferred by section 159(3)(b) of that Act;
> (d) an increase of an allowance which is payable in respect of constant attendance under section 5 of the Industrial Injuries and Diseases (Old Cases) Act 1975;
> (e) a payment by virtue of articles 14, 15, 16, 43 or 44 of the Personal Injuries (Civilians) Scheme 1983 or any analogous payment; or
> (f) any payment based on need for attendance which is paid as part of a war disablement pension;

"benefit week" has the meaning prescribed in paragraph 4 of Schedule 7 to the Social Security (Claims and Payments) Regulations 1987 [⁴and for the purposes of calculating any payment of income and of regulation 74(2)(a) "benefit week" shall also mean the period of 7 days ending on the day before the first day of the first benefit week following the date of claim or the last day on which income support is paid if it is in payment for less than a week;]
[⁶"board and lodging accommodation" means—

> (a) accommodation provided to a person or, if he is a member of a family, to him or any other member of his family, for a charge which is inclusive of the provision of that accommodation and at least some cooked or prepared meals which both are cooked or prepared (by a person other than the person to whom the accommodation is provided or a member of his family) and are consumed in that accommodation or associated premises; or
> (b) accommodation provided to a person in a hotel, guest house, lodging house or some similar establishment,

except accommodation provided by a close relative of his or of any other member of his family, or other than on a commercial basis;]

"claimant" means a person claiming income support;

"close relative" means a parent, parent-in-law, son, son-in-law, daughter, daughter-in-law, step-parent, step-son, step-daughter, brother, sister, or the spouse of any of the preceding persons or, if that person is one of an unmarried couple, the other member of that couple;

[[19]"community charge benefit" means community charge benefits under Part VII of the Contributions and Benefits Act as originally enacted;]

"concessionary payment" means a payment made under arrangements made by the Secretary of State with the consent of the Treasury which is charged either to the National Insurance Fund or to a Departmental Expenditure Vote to which payments of benefit under the Act, the Social Security Act or the Child Benefit Act 1975 are charged;

[[19]"the Contributions and Benefits Act" means the Social Security Contributions and Benefits Act 1992;]

"co-ownership scheme" means a scheme under which a dwelling is let by a housing association and the tenant, or his personal representative, will, under the terms of the tenancy agreement or of the agreement under which he became a member of the association, be entitled, on his ceasing to be a member and subject to any condition stated in either agreement, to a sum calculated by reference directly or indirectly to the value of the dwelling;

"couple" means a married or an unmarried couple;

"course of study" means any full-time course of study or sandwich course whether or not a grant is made for attending it;

"Crown tenant" means a person who occupies a dwelling under a tenancy or licence where the interest of the landlord belongs to Her Majesty in right of the Crown or to a government department or is held in trust for Her Majesty for the purposes of a government department, except (in the case of an interest belonging to Her Majesty in right of the Crown) where the interest is under the management of the Crown Estate Commissioners;

[[22]"date of claim" means the date on which the claimant makes, or is treated as making, a claim for income support for the purposes of regulation 6 of the Social Security (Claims and Payments) Regulations 1987;]

[[15]"disability living allowance" means a disability living allowance under section 37ZA of the Social Security Act [SSCBA, s.71];

"disability working allowance" means a disability working allowance under section 20 of the Act [SSCBA, s.129];]

"dwelling occupied as the home" means the dwelling together with any garage, garden and outbuildings, normally occupied by the claimant as his home including any premises not so occupied which it is impracticable or unreasonable to sell separately, in particular, in Scotland, any croft land on which the dwelling is situated;

"earnings" has the meaning prescribed in regulation 35 or, as the case may be, 37;

"employed earner" shall be construed in accordance with section 2(1)(a) of the Social Security Act [SSCBA, s.2(1)*a*];

[[4]"employment" except for the purposes of section 20(3)(d) of the Act [SSCBA, s.124(1)(d)], includes any trade, business, profession, office or vocation;]

"housing association" has the meaning assigned to it by section 1(1) of the Housing Associations Act 1985;

"housing benefit expenditure" means expenditure of a kind for which housing benefit may be granted;

"invalid carriage or other vehicle" means a vehicle propelled by petrol engine or by electric power supplied for use on the road and to be controlled by the occupant;

[14"last day of the course" has the meaning prescribed in regulation 61 for the purposes of the definition of "period of study";]

"liable relative" has the meaning prescribed in regulation 54;

"lone parent" means a person who has no partner and who is responsible for, and a member of the same household as, a child or young person;

"long tenancy" means a tenancy granted for a term of years certain exceeding twenty one years, whether or not the tenancy is, or may become, terminable before the end of that term by notice given by or to the tenant or by re-entry, forfeiture (or, in Scotland, irritancy) or otherwise and includes a lease for a term fixed by law under a grant with a covenant or obligation for perpetual renewal unless it is a lease by sub-demise from one which is not a long tenancy;

[6"lower rate" where it relates to rates of tax has the same meaning as in the Income and Corporation Taxes Act 1988 by virtue of section 832(1) of that Act;]

[22"maternity leave" means a period during which a woman is absent from work because she is pregnant or has given birth to a child, and at the end of which she has a right to return to work either under the terms of her contract of employment or under Part III of the Employment Protection (Consolidation) Act 1978;]

"mobility allowance" means an allowance under section 37A of the Social Security Act;

"mobility supplement" means any supplement under article 26A of the Naval, Military and Air Forces etc (Disablement and Death) Service Pensions Order 1983 including such a supplement by virtue of any other scheme or order or under Article 25A of the Personal Injuries (Civilians) Scheme 1983;

"net earnings" means such earnings as are calculated in accordance with regulation 36

"net profit" means such profit as is calculated in accordance with regulation 38;

"non-dependant" has the meaning prescribed in regulation 3;

"non-dependant deduction" means a deduction that is to be made under regulation 17(e) and paragraph 11 of Schedule 3;

"nursing home" has the meaning prescribed in regulation 19(3);

"occupational pension" means any pension or other periodical payment under an occupational pension scheme but does not include any discretionary payment out of a fund established for relieving hardship in particular cases;

"partner" means where a claimant—

(a) is a member of a married or an unmarried couple, the other member of that couple;

(b) is married polygamously to two or more members of his household, any such member;

"payment" includes a part of a payment;

[23"pay period" means the period in respect of which a claimant is, or expects to be, normally paid by his employer, being a week, a fortnight, four weeks, a month or other shorter or longer period as the case may be;]

[10"period of study" means the period beginning with the start of the course of study and ending with the last day of the course or such earlier date as the student abandons it or is dismissed from it; but any period of attendance by the student at his educational establishment in connection with the course which is outside the period of the course shall be treated as part of the period of study;]

[22"personal pension scheme" has the same meaning as in section 84(1) of the Act [PSA, s. 1] and, in the case of a self-employed earner, includes a scheme approved by the Inland Revenue under Chapter IV of Part XIV of the Income and Corporation Taxes Act 1988;]

"policy of life insurance" means any instrument by which the payment of money is assured on death (except death by accident only) or the happening of any contingency dependent on human life, or any instrument evidencing a contract which is subject to payment of premiums for a term dependent on human life;

[5"polygamous marriage" means any marriage during the subsistence of which a party to it is married to more than one person and the ceremony of marriage took place under the law of a country which permits polygamy;]

[18"preserved right" means a preserved right for the purposes of regulation 19;]

[16"qualifying person" means a person in respect of whom payment has been made from the Fund [21or the Eileen Trust];]

[3"registered person" means a person registered with a body mentioned in regulation 7D(1)(a)(i) to (iv) of the Child Benefit (General) Regulations 1976 for—

(a) work; or

(b) training under the youth training scheme;]

"relative" means close relative, grand-parent, grand-child, uncle, aunt, nephew or niece;

"relevant enactment" has the meaning prescribed in regulation 16(8)(a);

"remunerative work" has the meaning prescribed in regulation 5;

[4"residential accommodation" except in [8 regulation 19 and Schedule 3B] has the meaning prescribed in regulation 21(3);]

[18"residential allowance" means the weekly amount determined in accordance with paragraph 2A of Schedule 2;]

"residential care home" has the meaning prescribed in regulation 19(3);

"self-employed earner" shall be construed in accordance with section 2(1)(b) of the Social Security Act [SSCBA, s.2(1)(b)];

"single claimant" means a claimant who neither has a partner nor is a lone parent;

"Social Security Act" means the Social Security Act 1975;

"student" has the meaning prescribed in regulation 61;

"supplementary benefit" means a supplementary pension or allowance under section 1 or 4 of the Supplementary Benefits Act 1976;

"terminal date" in respect of a claimant means the terminal date in his case for the purpose of regulation 7 of the Child Benefit (General) Regulations 1976;

[21"the Eileen Trust" means the charitable trust of that name established on 29th March 1993 out of funds provided by the Secretary of State for the benefit of persons eligible for payment in accordance with its provisions;]

[16"the Fund" means moneys made available from time to time by the Secretary of State for the benefit of persons eligible for payment in accordance with the provisions of a scheme established by him on 24th April 1992 or, in Scotland, on 10th April 1992;]

[20"the Independent Living (Extension) Fund" means the Trust of that name established by a deed dated 25th February 1993 and made between the Secretary of State for Social Security of the one part and Robin Glover Wendt and John Fletcher Shepherd of the other part;]

[2"the Independent Living Fund" means the charitable trust established out of funds provided by the Secretary of State for the purpose of providing financial assistance to those persons incapacitated by or otherwise suffering from very severe disablement who are in need of such assistance to enable them to live independently;]

[20"the Independent Living (1993) Fund" means the Trust of that name established by a deed dated 25th February 1993 and made between the Secretary of State for Social Security of the one part and Robin Glover Wendt and John Shepherd of the other part;]

[20"the Independent Living Funds" means the Independent Living Fund, the Independent Living (Extension) Fund and the Independent Living (1993) Fund;]

[9"the Macfarlane (Special Payments) Trust" means the trust of that name, established on 29th January 1990 partly out of funds provided by the Secretary of State, for the benefit of certain persons suffering from haemophilia;]

[13"the Macfarlane (Special Payments) (No.2) Trust" means the trust of that name, established on 3rd May 1991 partly out of funds provided by the Secretary of State, for the benefit of certain persons suffering from haemophilia and other beneficiaries;]

[1"the Macfarlane Trust" means the charitable trust, established partly out of funds provided by the Secretary of State to the Haemophilia Society, for the relief of poverty or distress among those suffering from haemophilia;]

"training allowance" means an allowance (whether by way of periodical grants or otherwise) payable—.

    (a) out of public funds by a Government department or by or on behalf of the [12 Secretary of State for Employment] [11, Scottish Enterprise or Highlands and Islands Enterprise];

    (b) to a person for his maintenance or in respect of a member of his family; and

    (c) for the period, or part of the period, during which he is following a course of training or instruction provided by, or in pursuance of arrangements made with, that department or approved by that department in relation to him or so provided or approved by or on behalf of [12the Secretary of State for Employment] [11, Scottish Enterprise or Highlands and Islands Enterprise],

but it does not include an allowance paid by any Government department to or in respect of a person by reason of the fact that he is following a course of full-time education [7, other than under arrangements made under section 2 of the Employment and Training Act 1973,] or is training as a teacher;

[24"voluntary organisation" means a body, other than a public or local authority, the activities of which are carried on otherwise than for profit;]

[19"water charges" means—

    (a) as respects England and Wales, any water and sewerage charges under Chapter 1 of Part V of the Water Act 1991;

    (b) as respects Scotland, any water and sewerage charges under Schedule 11 to the Local Government Finance Act 1992;

in so far as such charges are in respect of the dwelling which a person occupies as his home.]

[23"year of assessment" has the meaning prescribed in section 832(1) of the Income and Corporation Taxes Act 1988;]

"young person" has the meaning prescribed in regulation 14,

[3"youth training scheme [12 or youth training]" means—

    (a) arrangements made under section 2 of the Employment and Training Act 1973 (functions of the Secretary of State); or

    (b) arrangements made by the Secretary of State for persons enlisted in Her Majesty's forces for any special term of service specified in regulations made under section 2 of the Armed Forces Act 1966 (power of Defence Council to make regulations as to engagement of persons in regular forces), for purposes which include the training of persons who, at the beginning of their training, are under the age of 18.]

(2) In these Regulations, unless the context otherwise requires, a reference—

(a) to a numbered Part is to the Part of these Regulations bearing that number;

(b) to a numbered regulation or Schedule is to the regulation in or Schedule to these Regulations bearing that number;

(c) in a regulation or Schedule to a numbered paragraph is to the paragraph in that regulation or Schedule bearing that number;

(d) in a paragraph to a lettered or numbered sub-paragraph is to the sub-paragraph in that paragraph bearing that letter or number.

(3) Unless the context requires otherwise, any reference to the claimant's family or, as the case may be, to being a member of his family, shall be construed for the purposes of these Regulations as if it included in relation to a polygamous marriage a reference to any partner and any child or young person who is treated as the responsibility of the claimant or his partner, where that child or young person is a member of the claimant's household.

AMENDMENTS

1 Income Support (General) Amendment Regulations 1988 (S.I. 1988 No. 663), reg. 2 (April 11, 1988).

2. Family Credit and Income Support (General) Amendment Regulations 1988 (S.I. 1988 No. 999), reg. 4 (June 9, 1988).

3. Income Support (General) Amendment No.3 Regulations 1988 (S.I. 1988 No. 1228), reg. 2 (August 29, 1988).

4. Income Support (General) Amendment No.4 Regulations 1988 (S.I. 1988 No. 1445), reg. 2 (September 12, 1988).

5. Income Support (General) Amendment No.5 Regulations 1988 (S.I. 1988 No. 2022), reg. 2(*b*) (December 12, 1988).

6. Income Support (General) Amendment No.5 Regulations 1988 (S.I. 1988 No. 2022), reg. 2(*a*) (April 10, 1989).

7. Income Support (General) Amendment No. 2 Regulations 1989 (S.I. 1989 No. 1323), reg. 2 (August 21, 1989).

8. Income Support (General) Amendment Regulations 1989 (S.I. 1989 No. 534), Sched. 1 para. 1, (October 9, 1989).

9. Income-related Benefits Schemes Amendment Regulations 1990 (S.I. 1990 No. 127), reg. 3 (January 31, 1990).

10. Social Security Benefits (Student Loans and Miscellaneous Amendments) Regulations 1990 (S.I. 1990 No. 1549), reg. 5(2) (September 1, 1990)

11. Enterprise (Scotland) Consequential Amendments Order 1991 (S.I. 1991 No. 387), art. 9 (April 1, 1991).

12. Income Support (General) Amendment Regulations 1991 (S.I. 1991 No. 236), reg. 2 (April 8, 1991).

13. Income-related Benefits Schemes and Social Security (Recoupment) Amendment Regulations 1991 (S.I. 1991 No. 1175), reg. 5 (May 11, 1991).

14. Income Support (General) Amendment No. 4 Regulations 1991 (S.I. 1991 No. 1559), reg. 2 (August 5, 1991).

15. Disability Living Allowance and Disability Working Allowance (Consequential Provisions) Regulations 1991 (S.I. 1991 No. 2742), reg. 11(2) (April 6, 1992).

16. Income-related Benefits Schemes and Social Security (Recoupment) Amendment Regulations 1992 (S.I. 1992 No. 1101), reg. 6(2) (May 7, 1992).

17. Income-related Benefits Schemes (Miscellaneous Amendments) (No.3) Regulations 1992 (S.I. 1992 No. 2155), reg. 12 (October 5, 1992).

18. Social Security Benefits (Amendments Consequential Upon the Introduction of Community Care) Regulations 1992 (S.I. 1992 No. 3147), reg. 2(1) (April 1, 1993).

19. Income-related Benefits Schemes (Miscellaneous Amendments) Regulations 1993 (S.I. 1993 No. 315), reg. 3 (April 12, 1993).

20. Social Security Benefits (Miscellaneous Amendments) (No. 2) Regulations 1993 (S.I. 1993 No. 963), reg. 2 (April 22, 1993).

21. Income-related Benefits Schemes and Social Security (Recoupment) Amendment Regulations 1993 (S.I. 1993 No. 1249), reg. 4 (May 14, 1993).

22. Income-related Benefits Schemes (Miscellaneous Amendments) (No. 4) Regulations 1993 (S.I. 1993 No. 2119), reg. 2 (October 4, 1993).
23. Income-related Benefits Schemes (Miscellaneous Amendments) (No. 5) Regulations 1994 (S.I. 1994 No. 2139), reg. 22 (October 3, 1994).
24. Income-related Benefits Schemes (Miscellaneous Amendments) Regulations 1995 (S.I. 1995 No. 516), reg. 17 (April 10, 1995).

DEFINITIONS

"dwelling"—see 1986 Act, s.84(1) (SSCBA, s.137(1)).
"family"—see 1986 Act, s.20(11) (SSCBA, s.137(1)).
"married couple"—*ibid.*
"occupational pension scheme"—see 1986 Act, s.84(1) (PSA, s. 1).
"unmarried couple"—see 1986 Act, s.20(11) (SSCBA, s.137(1)).

GENERAL NOTE

The significance of most of these definitions is mentioned in the notes to the regulations in which they occur. A few points are noted here.

"*Board and lodging accommodation.*" Now that since April 1989, there are no special calculations of benefit for claimants in board and lodging accommodation (as opposed to residential care or nursing homes), the definition is of less significance than in the past. Either the accommodation must be in some establishment like a hotel or lodging house or the charge must include the provision of some cooked or prepared meals in the accommodation or associated premises. The requirement in para. (a) that a charge is made for the accommodation has logically to be considered before the exclusion of non-commercial arrangements. In *CSB 1163/1988* the claimant moved with her two children into a house owned by the Jesus Fellowship Church (Baptist), where 17 other people also lived. Meals were provided. The terms of her occupation were that she should put all her income into a "common purse." A basic charge to cover food, accommodation and running costs was set, but any excess of the claimant's income was regarded as a donation to the Church. The Commissioner holds that the claimant was not a boarder because she did not pay a "charge." She was one of a joint community of persons, all sharing their income and outgoings. See also *R v. Sheffield Housing Benefits Review Board, ex parte Smith, Rugby Borough Council Housing Benefits Review Board, ex parte Harrison and Daventry District Council Housing Benefits Review Board, ex parte Bodden*, below. Some family arrangements may be of this kind. Similarly, if a person makes a contribution of whatever he can afford week by week to the household expenses, this is probably not a charge. On the other hand, a fixed, but low, amount may require the non-commercial basis exception to be examined. Recent cases on the meaning of "board" in the Rent Acts (*e.g. Otter v. Norman* [1988] 2 All E. R. 897, H.L) indicate that merely providing the ingredients will not amount to preparing a meal. This was specifically decided in the supplementary benefit context in *CSB 950/1987*. The argument that getting a packet of cornflakes out of a cupboard constituted preparation was rejected.

If this primary definition is met there is an exclusion either if the accommodation is provided by a close relative (see definition below) of the claimant or any member of his family (see s.137(1)) or if it is provided on other than a commercial basis. Provision by a limited company, of which a close relative of the resident is a director or a shareholder, is not provision by a close relative (*R(SB) 9/89*). In this case the company was formed well before the resident went into the home. It might be different if the company was a mere facade or had been formed for a fraudulent or improper purpose. In *R(IS) 2/91* the claimant became a resident in a nursing home of which his daughter was the sole proprietor. He was actually cared for by the staff employed by his daughter. Nonetheless, his accommodation and meals were "provided" by his daughter. "Provided" means "made available."

What is a commercial basis is unclear, although the Adjudication Officer's Guide suggests that the phrase should be interpreted broadly (para. 28044). If the charge and the arrangements are as one would expect in a commercial relationship it can clearly be argued that the basis is commercial. The AOG stresses that an intention to make a profit should not be required. If the intention is to cover the cost of food plus a reasonable amount for accommodation, this can be commercial. This approach is confirmed by *CSB 1163/1988* (above), where the SSAT had decided that "commercial basis" contained an element of profit. The Commissioner holds that this was an error of law and that the phrase means a basis that is intended to be more or less self-financing and not provided as part of a quasi "family" setting. On the facts, the lack of the intention to make a profit by the Church did not prevent the basis being commercial, but the "community" nature of the arrangement did. It was probable that if the claimant paid no income in for at least a short time, she would not have been asked to leave. In *R v. Sheffield Housing Benefits Review Board, ex parte Smith, Rugby Borough Council Housing Benefits Review Board, ex parte Harrison and Daventry District Council Housing Benefits Review Board, ex parte Bodden, The Times*, December 28, 1994, (housing benefit cases which also concerned the Jesus Fellowship Church) Blackburne J. reaches a similar conclusion. In deciding whether an arrangement was on a commercial basis, it was necessary to look at the arrangement as a whole. It was not correct only to consider the amount payable for the accommodation and to ignore the other terms of the agreement. As far as family arrangements are concerned, all the circumstances must be considered. If money has been spent adapting accommodation to a disabled person's needs, this may be relevant. It is not the case, as is often argued by AOs, that if a person enters into an arrangement with a friend or a non-close relative it is automatically non-commercial. In *CIS 195/1991* (confirmed in *CSIS 28/1992*, and *CSIS 40/1992*, to be reported as *R(IS) 17/94*) whether a family arrangement was on a commercial basis is held to be entirely a question of fact for the SSAT, which has to consider whether it is similar to that which might have been arranged with a paying lodger (see notes to reg. 3).

"close relative." The words "brother" and "sister" include half-brothers and half-sisters *(R(SB) 22/87)*. The same decision confirms that if a child is adopted it becomes the child of its adoptive parents and ceases to have any legal relationship with its natural parents or brothers or sisters. It is legal relationships which are referred to in the definition of "close relative."

"couple." "Married couple" and "unmarried couple" are defined in s.137(1) of the Contributions and Benefits Act (1986 Act, s.20(11)).

"date of claim." See the notes to reg. 6 of the Social Security (Claims and Payments) Regulations.

"dwelling occupied as the home." "Home" is no longer defined, but the present definition contains many similarities to that of "home" in the old Supplementary Benefit Requirements Regulations and Resources Regulations. Instead of referring to accommodation, it refers to a dwelling, but since the definition of "dwelling" in s.137(1) of the Contributions and Benefits Act (1986 Act, s.84(1)) refers to residential accommodation, there is probably not much difference. The s.137(1) definition does specify that a dwelling can be the whole or part of a building and need not comprise separate and self-contained premises. The dwelling must be normally occupied as the home by the claimant. There is no reference here to the claimant's family, but presumably if the claimant has a family within s.137(1) of the Contributions and Benefits Act (1986 Act, s.20(11)), the family's home will normally be his home, but see *CIS 81/1991* below.

It is probably the case that the reference to "the dwelling" means that only one dwelling at a time can meet the definition. However, it is not entirely clear that the normal rule that the singular includes the plural is excluded, and it is thought necessary to include several deeming rules on housing costs in para.4 of Sched. 3. *R(SB) 30/83* decided that two completely separate units could not constitute one home. *R(SB) 10/89* held that two units about 600 yards apart, neither of which on their own could accommodate the assessment unit were one home. The Commissioner relied on some Rent Act cases on when something is let as a separate dwelling (in particular, *Langford Property Co. Ltd. v. Goldrich* [1949] 1 K.B. 511). In *CIS 299/1992* it was held that a bungalow and an adjoining caravan constituted one dwelling. In *CIS 81/1991* the claimant lived in one house and members of his family slept in another. The second house did not come within the definition in reg. 2(1) as it was not occupied by the *claimant* as his home. The Commissioner distinguishes *R(SB) 10/89* on the grounds that it was decided in relation to the significantly different definition of "home" in the supplementary benefit regulations, which referred to ". . . the accommodation . . . normally occupied by the assessment unit . . .". He also holds that the reference in the definition of dwelling in s.137(1) (1986 Act, s.84(1)) to "separate and self-contained premises" does not mean that a dwelling can be spread over separate buildings. This decision may be correct where only members of the claimant's family live in the other property. However, where a claimant occupies two physically separate properties, both may still constitute the dwelling normally occupied by the claimant as his home depending on all the circumstances.

Para. 4 of Sched. 3 allows payments to be made for two homes in limited circumstances. It also appears that accommodation cannot be normally occupied until some person has actually moved in *(R(SB) 27/84, R(SB) 7/86)*, given the special rule created in para. 4(7) for periods before anyone moves in. In an unstarred decision, *CIS 4/1990*, the Commissioner doubts the existence of a rule that occupation requires residence. The same point was made in the supplementary benefit context in *CSB 524/1985* (not quoted by the Commissioner) and *CSSB 34/1987*. While it is right that the word used in the legislation is "occupy" and not "reside," it must also be noted that the definition requires not simply occupation, but occupation as the home. This point was the basis of *R(SB) 7/86*, also not mentioned in *CIS 4/1990*. It may be that the issue of what is sufficient to amount to occupation is one of fact in each set of circumstances.

The definition extends to any garden or outbuildings which are occupied as part of the home (like the toilet and coalstore in outbuildings in *R(SB) 13/84* or the "development land" in *R(SB)*

27/84 which might have been part of the garden). *CIS 427/1991* holds that the line between a garden and other land occupied with a dwelling is to be drawn according to the view of the ordinary man in the street.

If a building or a garden is occupied as part of the home it does not matter that they could be sold separately. This only comes into play when some buildings or land are not so occupied. Then those premises still count as part of the home if it is impracticable or unreasonable to sell them separately. A potential limit to this extension is exposed by *CSB 965/1986*, where the claimant was a tenant of a council house and owned a half-share in a small-holding two fields away. The small-holding was clearly not occupied as part of the home. The Commissioner holds that the extension could not apply since the home could not be sold and therefore the question of separate sale could not arise. This decision seems dubious, especially since the definition refers by way of example to croft land in Scotland, where the crofter is often only a tenant. But perhaps *CSB 965/1986* can be supported on the basis that if the small-holding was the only premises actually owned by the claimant it could not be unreasonable or impracticable to sell it separately. In *CIS 427/1991* the Commissioner holds that *R(SB) 13/84* was wrong in suggesting that property outside Scotland which is comparable to croft land is to be treated on the same principles. In considering reasonableness and practicability all the circumstances must be considered, including the use to which the premises are put, any profit made from them, etc. *(R(SB) 13/84* and *R(SB) 27/84).* In *CIS 427/1991* the state of health of the claimant's wife was a factor of which account could be taken in assessing whether it was unreasonable to sell land held with the home but not occupied as the home (she was a manic depressive who needed the adjoining fields for therapeutic walking). Medical evidence as to the therapeutic benefit would obviously be highly desirable in these circumstances.

CIS 616/1992 holds that the common parts of a block of flats (*e.g.* the entrance hall or staircases) do not come within the definition. It is not impracticable or unreasonable to sell such areas separately but quite simply impossible to do so.

"*employed earner.*" The meaning in s.2(1)(*a*) of the Contributions and Benefits Act (1975 Act, s.2(1)(*a*)) is "a person who is gainfully employed in Great Britain either under a contract of service, or in an office (including elective office) with emoluments chargeable to income tax under Schedule E."

"*occupational pension*". Section 1 of the Pension Schemes Act 1993 defines an "occupational pension scheme" as "any scheme or arrangement which is comprised in one or more instruments or agreements and which has, or is capable of having, effect in relation to one or more descriptions or categories of employments so as to provide benefits, in the form of pensions or otherwise, payable on termination of service, or on death or retirement, to or in respect of earners with qualifying service in an employment of any such description or category".

"*personal pension scheme*". The meaning in s.1 of the Pension Schemes Act 1993 (1986 Act, s.84(1)) is "any scheme or arrangement which is comprised in one or more instruments or agreements and which has, or is capable of having, effect so as to provide benefits, in the form of pensions or otherwise, payable on death or retirement to or in respect of employed earners who have made arrangements with the trustees or managers of the scheme for them to become members of it".

"*registered person.*" The bodies referred to in the Child Benefit Regulations are the Department of Employment, the Ministry of Defence and local education authorities within the meaning of s.114(1) of the Education Act 1944 (England and Wales) or of s.135(1) of the Education (Scotland) Act 1980 (Scotland).

"*self-employed earner.*" The meaning in s.2(1)(b) of the Contributions and Benefits Act (1975 Act, s.2(1)(b)) is "a person who is gainfully employed in Great Britain otherwise than in employed earner's employment (whether or not he is also employed in such employment)."

"*year of assessment.*" The meaning s.832(1) of the Income and Corporation Taxes Act 1988 is "with reference to any tax year, the year for which such tax was granted by any Act granting income tax." A tax year is the 12 months beginning with April 6 in any year.

Paragraph (3)
Note that special provision is only made for polygamous marriages. If the claimant is not married, the ordinary living together as husband and wife rules apply (Contributions and Benefits Act, s.137(1); 1986 Act, s.20(11)).

Definition of non-dependant

3.—(1) In these Regulations, "non-dependant" means any person, except someone [³ to whom paragraph (2), (2A) or (2B) applies], who normally resides with a claimant [⁴or with whom a claimant normally resides.]

[³(2) This paragraph applies to—

(a) any member of the claimant's family;

(b) a child or young person who is living with the claimant but who is not a member of his household by virtue of regulation 16 (circumstances in which a person is to be treated as being or not being a member of the household);

(c) a person who lives with the claimant in order to care for him or for the claimant's partner and who is engaged for that purpose by a charitable or [⁵voluntary organisation] which makes a charge to the claimant or the claimant's partner for the care provided by that person;

(d) the partner of a person to whom sub-paragraph (c) applies.

(2A) This paragraph applies to a person, other than a close relative of the claimant or the claimant's partner,—

(a) who is liable to make payments on a commercial basis to the claimant or the claimant's partner in respect of his occupation of the claimant's dwelling;

(b) to whom the claimant or the claimant's partner is liable to make payments on a commercial basis in respect of his occupation of that person's dwelling;

(c) who is a member of the household of a person to whom sub-paragraph (a) or (b) applies.

(2B) Subject to paragraph (2C), this paragraph applies to—

(a) person who jointly occupies the claimant's dwelling and who is either—
　(i) a co-owner of that dwelling with the claimant or the claimant's partner (whether or not there are other co-owners); or
　(ii) jointly liable with the claimant or the claimant's partner to make payments to a landlord in respect of his occupation of that dwelling;

(b) a partner of a person whom sub-paragraph (a) applies.

(2C) Where a person is a close relative of the claimant or the claimant's partner, paragraph (2B) shall apply to him only if the claimant's, or the claimant's partner's, co-ownership, or joint liability to make payments to a landlord in respect of his occupation, of the dwelling arose either before 11th April 1988, or, if later, on or before the date upon which the claimant or the claimant's partner first occupied the dwelling in question.]

(3) [². . .].

(4) For the purposes of this regulation a person resides with another only if they share any accommodation except a bathroom, a lavatory or a communal area [¹ but not if each person is separately liable to make payments in respect of his occupation of the dwelling to the landlord].

(5) In this regulation "communal area" means any area (other than rooms) of common access (including halls and passageways) and rooms of common use in sheltered accommodation.

AMENDMENTS

1. Income Support (General) Amendment Regulations 1989 (S.I. 1989 No. 534), reg. 2 (April 10, 1989).

2. Income Support (General) Amendment Regulations 1989 (S.I. 1989 No. 534), Sched. 1, para. 2 (October 9, 1989).

3. Income Support (General) Amendment No. 6 Regulations 1991 (S.I. 1991 No. 2334), reg. 2 (November 11, 1991).

4. Income-related Benefits Schemes (Miscellaneous Amendments) (No. 6) Regulations 1994 (S.I. 1994 No. 3061), reg. 2(2) (December 2, 1994).

5. Income-related Benefits Schemes (Miscellaneous Amendments) Regulations 1995 (S.I. 1995 No. 516), reg. 18 (April 10, 1995).

DEFINITIONS

"child"—see 1986 Act, s.20(11) (SSCBA, s.137(1)).
"claimant"—see reg. 2(1).

"dwelling"—see 1986 Act, s.84(1) (SSCBA, s.137(1)).
"family"—*ibid.*
"local authority"—see 1986 Act, s.84(1).
"partner"—see reg. 2(1).
"voluntary organisation"—*ibid.*
"young person"—*ibid.*, reg. 14.

GENERAL NOTE

Paragraph (1)

The definition of "non-dependant" is important for a number of purposes, particularly deductions from housing costs and qualification for the severe disability premium. Its use for different purposes causes difficulties. What might be a sensible test for determining when a contribution towards accommodation costs ought to be assumed from an independent person who shares the claimant's accommodation might be less sensible in determining a severely disabled person's financial needs.

A person who normally resides with the claimant, or, since December 2, 1994, with whom the claimant normally resides, unless within the important exceptions in paras. (2) to (2C), is a non-dependant. The December 1994 amendment to para. (1) was the government's immediate (within 48 hours) response to the decision in *Bate v. Chief Adjudication Officer and Secretary of State for Social Security* on November 30, 1994 (*The Times*, December 12, 1994). Ms Bate was a severely disabled person who lived in her parents' home. The Court of Appeal decided that because her parents were the "householders", in the sense that it was they who jointly occupied the home as tenants, they did not normally reside with *her*, but she normally resided with *them*. Thus they did not come within the definition of non-dependant at all. The Court recognised that this construction did not fit easily with the amendment to reg. 3(2)(d) on April 10, 1989 (now recast in para. (2A)), but did not consider that the meaning of the initial regulation could be determined by later amendments. The April 1989 amendment simply showed that the draftsman had assumed that "residing with the claimant" had the meaning which the Court had rejected.

The effect of the Court of Appeal's decision is that many claimants in Ms Bate's position should have been getting a severe disability premium since April 1988 if they otherwise satisfied the conditions of entitlement. However, review applications to obtain backdating of the premium are likely to be met by the application of the "anti-test case" rule in s.69 of the Administration Act. The *Bate* case was also concerned with the interpretation of this rule. For the Court of Appeal's judgment on this issue see the notes to s. 69. For suggestions as to how claimants affected by the *Bate* case may obtain arrears of the severe disability premium see Welfare Rights Bulletins 123 (the insert) and 124. See also the Court of Appeal's decision in *Chief Adjudication Officer v. Eggleton and Others* (March 17, 1995) in the notes to s.25 of the Administration Act. For an argument that the amendment does not affect claimants entitled to a severe disability premium before December 2, 1994 (even if that entitlement is established after December 2, 1994), but only applies to those first entitled after December 2, 1994, see CPAG's Welfare Rights Bulletin 124 (and see *CSIS 28/1992* and *CSIS 40/1992* below).

The Chief Adjudication Officer has been granted leave to appeal by the House of Lords, but the result of that appeal will not be known for some months.

The December 2, 1994 regulations (S.I. 1994 No. 3061) were introduced without first being referred to the Social Security Advisory Committee. Section 173(1)(a) of the Administration Act permits this if the Secretary of State considers it inexpedient to refer proposed regulations by reason of urgency. The failure to refer these proposed regulations is being challenged by Ms Bate (see Welfare Rights Bulletin 125). It is argued that the Court of Appeal decided that it was Parliament's intention that people in Ms Bate's position should be entitled to a severe disability premium (and therefore it intended that financial provision should be made for this) and so the Secretary of State cannot say that it was urgent that payment of the premium should stop. In addition, the Secretary of State should not be allowed to sidestep the consultation procedure, which Parliament clearly considered important, in this way. (See the comment of Hobhouse L.J. in *Chief Adjudication Officer v. Palfrey and Others* (Court of Appeal, February 8, 1995) that one reason at least for the consultation procedure is the "remarkable latitude" given to the maker of regulations in the Social Security Acts.) Leave to bring judicial review was refused by the High Court but the application is being renewed before the Court of Appeal. As Welfare Rights Bulletin 125 points out, tribunals may also be asked to consider the validity of the December 1994 regulations. See the notes to s. 23 of the Administration Act on the jurisdiction of the adjudicating authorities to determine the vires of regulations.

Paras. (4) and (5) provide a partial definition of "resides with." In its original form, para. (4) put forward only one necessary, but not on its own sufficient, condition about sharing accommodation. But the general test of para. (1) still had to be satisfied. The post-April 1989 form of para. (4) specifically excludes from the definition a situation where co-residents are separately liable to make payments to a landlord. Such a person is already paying for accommodation costs. "Landlord" does not require there to be a tenancy; licensees can come within the exclusion (*CSIS 43/1992*). Outside this exclusion the arrangement must still come within the general meaning of "residing with" and be the normal situation to come within the definition in para. (1). In *CSIS 100/1993* the claimant's daughter sometimes stayed in her mother's home and used that address for official correspondence. The Commissioner says that where correspondence is sent is a possible indicator that the daughter normally resided with the claimant, but equally, having regard to the other places the daughter stayed, it could be that she had no "fixed abode" (and thus did not normally reside with the claimant).

Paragraphs (2) to (2C)

These provisions except those who would otherwise count as non-dependants from coming within that category. The exceptions have been through a convoluted series of forms, whose meaning has been a matter of great controversy. The convolutions are traced in previous editions, and great care must be taken in identifying what form of the regulation is in effect at particular dates which may be relevant to outstanding claims and appeals. The House of Lords in *Foster v. Chief Adjudication Officer* [1993] A.C. 754; [1993] 1 All E.R. 705 holds that the amendment made on October 9, 1989 (to add the conditions now substantially contained in para. (2B)(a)(i) and (ii)) was not *ultra vires* on the ground of irrationality.

Note that regs. 4 to 6 of the Income Support (General) Amendment No. 6 Regulations 1991 provide transitional protection for claimants who were entitled to the severe disability premium before October 21, 1991, by virtue of the pre-November 1991 form of reg. 3 (see p.368).

In *CSIS 28/1992* and *CSIS 40/1992* (to be reported as *R(IS) 17/94*), a Tribunal of Commissioners states that SSATs, when considering, for example, a claimant's right to a severe disability premium, should deal with the position from the date of claim down to the date when the issues are finally decided (preferring the approach of *CIS 391/1992* and *CIS 417/1992* (Tribunal of Commissioners) to that of *CIS 649/1992*, where the Commissioner held that an adjudicating authority should only consider the position as at the date from which benefit is sought). *CIS 649/1992* is also inconsistent with, for example, *CIS 654/1991*, to be reported as *R(IS) 3/93*, (see the notes to reg. 25(2) of the Adjudication Regulations). In addition, *CSIS 28/1992* and *CSIS 40/1992* dealt with an argument that once a claimant had acquired a right to a severe disability premium, its removal by subsequent amendment of reg. 3(2) was prevented by s. 16(1)(c) of the Interpretation Act (protection of acquired rights). Section 16 applies unless the contrary intention appears. The Commissioners hold that the words "shall come into force in relation to a particular claimant" in reg. 1(1) of S.I. 1989 No. 534 (the regulations at issue) indicated that the regulations were intended to apply to existing claimants. A claim made after the regulations came into force would be subject to them without the need for these words. Thus they were clearly intended to provide for existing claimants. The December 1994 regulations (S.I. 1994 No. 3061), see above, do not contain this wording, which is the basis for the argument that they do not have retrospective effect (see Welfare Rights Bulletin 124).

Paragraph (2)

These four categories excluded from the definition of non-dependant have been in the regulation since 1988 and are relatively straightforward. They cover those who are not sufficiently independent of the claimant to be a non-dependant.

(a) A member of the family. This, by reference to s.137(1) of the Contributions and Benefits Act (1986 Act, s.20(11)), covers children and 16–18 year-olds treated as in full time secondary level education as well as partners, but only if members of the same household.

(b) Children who are not members of the family under the operation of the special rules in reg. 16.

(c) and (d) Certain carers provided at a charge by charities or voluntary bodies, plus the carer's partner.

Paragraph (2A)

This is a recasting in November 1991 of the previous para. (2)(d) to (db). The difference is that a close relative (defined in reg. 2(1)) of the claimant or his partner does not come within para. (2A). Thus, for instance, the parents of a severely disabled person may no longer come within para. (2A). If they are not to be non-dependants from November 1991, they must come within paras. (2B) and (2C). Outside the close relative exception, the effect of para. (2A) now is that where the relationship between the claimant (or the claimant's partner) and the other person (or a member of that person's household) is a commercial one, that person is not a non-dependant. No further contribution to accommodation costs is therefore appropriate.

There must be a legal liability (as distinct from a moral or ethical obligation (*CIS 754/1991*)) to make payments for accommodation, *i.e.* rent or a board and lodging charge, on a commercial basis. The first question is whether there is a liability to pay. It has been held on the pre-November 1991 version of para. (2A) that a severely disabled claimant, for example, living with his parents can be their licensee and therefore liable to pay for his accommodation in the sense that if no payment is made the licence could terminate (*CIS 195/1991, CIS 754/1991*). In deciding whether such a liability exists there would need to be findings as to the terms on which a claimant lives in his parent's home, the amount and regularity of the payments and the use made of the claimant's contributions. If the payments go towards rent or a mortgage that would be a stronger case than if they are used for the claimant's own personal needs (*CIS 754/1991*), but they need not be applied directly to accommodation costs. If the claimant's contributions go into a general fund used for household costs (including accommodation) that will suffice (*CSIS 28/1992* and *CSIS 40/1992*, to be reported as *R(IS)17/94*). It will then be necessary to conclude on the basis of the relevant findings whether there was an intention to create legal relations. Such an intention can be inferred from a course of conduct (see Scarman L.J. in *Horrocks v. Forray* [1976] 1 W.L.R. 230 at 239). *CIS 754/1991* holds that this might not be too difficult to infer where an adult member of the family is making regular payments in respect of his occupation. It may be easier to infer where the parents depend on the claimant's contributions because of their own financial circumstances. In his directions to the new SSAT in *CIS 754/1991* the Commissioner concludes:

"In essence there should be what I might call a broad approach to satisfaction of the condition keeping in mind that the AO has throughout accepted that in [*CIS 195/1991*] it was right to conclude that the claimant [had a liability to make payments in respect of his occupation]. I should have thought that the facts in many of the cases are likely to be essentially indistinguishable from those in [*CIS/195/1991*]."

The facts in *CIS/195/1991* were that the claimant's parents took £20 per week from his benefit. The rest of the money was used for his own needs. The SSAT found that the claimant lived in his parents' house as a licensee and paid them £20 in respect of his occupation of it.

But what of the situation where there can be no contractual liability because one of the parties lacks the capacity to make a contract? In *CIS 195/1991* the claimant was held to be capable of incurring a liability to make payment, despite his mental disability. Under English law the contract was voidable because of his mental disability, not void. However, in Scottish law an "incapax" is not capable of making any personal contract. *CSIS 28/1992* and *CSIS 40/1992* (to be reported as *R(IS) 17/94*) hold that in Scottish cases SSATs must first consider whether a claimant is so mentally incapacitated as to be incapax. But if this is the case, the doctrine of recompense may well apply to establish a liability on the incapax, so that the result is similar in practical terms to that in *CIS 195/1991* (see 1993 Supplement for fuller discussion of *CSIS 28/1992* and *CSIS 40/1992*). In *CIS 754/1991* the Commissioner expresses the *obiter* view that where a person has no contractual capacity at all, the doctrine of restitution does not seem available to assist claimants in England in the way that recompense can in Scotland. Thus in English cases for mentally disabled claimants it will generally be necessary for there to be a finding of sufficient contractual capacity. On the facts of both *CIS 195/1991* and *CIS 754/1991* the capacity required does not seem to be of a very high order. The claimant in *CIS 754/1991* was found to have sufficient contractual capacity despite having Downs syndrome and needing an appointee to act for her in social security matters.

Since October 1, 1990, the liability to pay has had to be on a commercial basis. The words "commercial basis" govern the nature of the liability, not just the quality of the payments made (*CSIS 28/1992* and *CSIS 40/1992*, to be reported as *R(IS)17/94*). For a discussion of "commercial basis" see *CSB 1163/1988* and the notes to the definition of "board and lodging accommodation" in reg. 2(1). In *CIS 195/1991* the Commissioner held that the question of whether an arrangement is on a commercial basis was entirely one of fact for the SSAT. What has to be considered is whether the arrangement is the sort that might have been entered into if the parents had taken in a lodger, instead of, in *CIS 195/1991*, their physically and mentally handicapped son. The Tribunal of Commissioners in *CSIS 28/1992* and *CSIS 40/1992* add to this that if members of SSATs bring local knowledge to bear on this question it must be exposed to the parties before the end of the hearing so that the parties can respond to it by comment or further evidence.

Although there might still be some scope for structuring an informal relationship to get within para. (2A), the requirement of a commercial basis (since October 1, 1990) and the exclusion of close relatives (from November 11, 1991) provide quite a stringent control. Note the transitional protection in regs. 4 to 6 of the Income Support (General) Amendment No. 6 Regulations 1991 (see page 368) for claimants entitled to the severe disability premium before October 21, 1991.

SSATs faced with sorting out severe disability premium entitlement, in particular for the periods October 9, 1989 to September 30, 1990 and October 1, 1990 to November 10, 1991, will need to pay particular regard to the Commissioners' decisions discussed above. They should deal with the position down to the date of the final decision (see above).

Paragraphs (2B) to (2C)

These provisions replace the previous para. (2)(c) on joint occupiers, and impose a considerably stricter test. The biggest change in November 1991 was to exclude joint occupiers who are close relatives (see reg. 2(1)) from the operation of para. (2B) except in restricted circumstances. This is done by para. (2C). If the close relative met the conditions of para. (2B) either before April 11, 1988, or as soon as the claimant or partner moved to the current home, then advantage can be taken of para. (2B). The aim is to exclude arrangements made within a family (in the non-income support sense) designed to take advantage of the definition of a non-dependant. The thinking is that if the arrangement was the basis on which the occupation of the home by the claimant started it is likely to be a genuine one. Existing claimants excluded by this rule may particularly benefit from the transitional protection mentioned above. *CIS 80/1994* rejects the argument that para. (2C) is invalid on the ground that it operates retrospectively. The Commissioner states that para. (2C) imposes a new condition of future eligibility (though with reference to past events). Thus it does not take away any vested right or create any new obligation in regard to events that have already past.

In *CIS 650/1993* the claimant had been a joint tenant of her home with her husband. When he died in 1990 she became the sole tenant. Later her sister came to live with her and they became joint tenants. The Commissioner rejects the claimant's contention that the previous joint liability of the claimant and her husband meant that para. (2C) was satisfied. In the context of reg. 3, para. (2C) only referred to the joint liability of the claimant and the person currently residing with her and not to any other joint liability.

The rest of para. (2B) is based on the provisions in force from October 1989. First, there must be joint occupation of the claimant's home. In *CIS 180/1989* the claimant was a single woman in receipt of attendance allowance, severe disablement allowance and income support. She lived with her parents, who owned the house. The Commissioner held that "jointly occupies" is not to be given a technical meaning, but its ordinary meaning. The phrase applies where "persons who normally reside together jointly occupy the premises in the sense of equality of access and use as distinct from a situation where restrictions are imposed in relation to those matters." It did not matter, under the legislation in force at the relevant time, that the claimant did not have any proprietary interest in the house. *CIS 180/1989* (approved by the Tribunal of Commissioners in *CSIS 28/1992* and *CSIS 40/1992*, to be reported as *R(IS)17/94*) has governed the position, particularly in severe disability premium cases, for the period before October 9, 1989, when amendments to impose the extra conditions now substantially contained in para. (2B)(a)(i) and (ii) were made. Indeed, it has been usual for AOs to concede that for the period before October 9, 1989, parents or other family members are not non-dependants.

It might be objected that the approach of *CIS 180/1989* expanded the exception on joint occupation so far that it excluded everyone who would be caught by the primary definition of a non-dependant. This is not so. People can reside together, but without the equality of access and use stressed by the Commissioner. The House of Lords in the *Foster* case, where it was conceded that the claimant's parents were joint occupiers up to October 9, 1989, expressed similar doubts that the exception, if widely construed, might eat up the rule, but did not reach any authoritative conclusion. In a decision on the equivalent housing benefit provision (*Fullwood v. Chesterfield Borough Council, The Times*, June 15, 1993) the Court of Appeal specifically rejects the basis of *CIS 180/1989*, holding that "jointly occupies" is a technical legal phrase, meaning "occupies by right jointly with one or more persons". Thus, joint occupation entails either a joint tenancy or joint liability to make payments under an agreement for occupation. This decision strictly only related to housing benefit, but the Court of Appeal in *Bate v. Chief Adjudication Officer and Secretary of State for Social Security* (see above) accepted that the phrase should be given the same meaning for the purposes of income support.

From October 9, 1989, it has been specifically provided that one of two extra conditions must be satisfied. One is that the claimant (or partner) is a co-owner of the home with the other person (or partner). This is unchanged since October 9, 1989. The other condition is that there is joint liability to make payments in respect of the occupation of the home to a landlord. This was changed in November 1991 from the October 9, 1989 form to specify that the payments must be to a landlord. The result is broadly to confirm the outcome of *CIS 299/1990* (discussed in the 1991 edition), and to remove the problem of interpretation addressed in that decision. These conditions narrowed the scope of para. (2B) considerably. Where there is separate, rather than joint, liability a person is deemed not to be residing with the claimant (para. (4)).

Paragraph (3)
The revocation removes the special rule for boarders and hostel-dwellers.

Paragraph (4)
The original form of para. (4) merely meant that if accommodation other than bathroom, lavatory or a communal area was not shared, one person was not "residing with" another. It did not mean that the person was "residing with" the other just because such accommodation was shared. The general test of para. (1) still has to be satisfied. See *CSIS 100/1993* above. Para. (4) now also

excludes from the definition of non-dependant a person who is separately liable to make payments to the landlord. See *CSIS 43/1992* above. Joint tenants and co-owners (other than close relatives of the claimant or partner) are excluded by para. (2B)(a).

[¹Permitted period

3A.—(1) For the purposes of regulation 17(6), paragraph 7(10) of Schedule 3, paragraph 7(6) of Schedule 3A, paragraph 6(3) of Schedule 3B and paragraphs 4 and 6 of Schedule 8 (applicable amounts, mortgage interest, protected sums and earnings to be disregarded), where a claimant has ceased to be entitled to income support—
   (a) because he or his partner becomes engaged in remunerative work the permitted period, subject to paragraph (2), shall be 12 weeks; or
   (b) for any other reason, the permitted period shall be eight weeks.
(2) Subject to paragraph (3), where the claimant or his partner has ceased to be engaged in the remunerative work referred to in paragraph (1)(a) the permitted period shall be eight weeks if—
   (a) the claimant's weekly applicable amounts is reduced under regulation 22 (reduction in applicable amounts in certain cases of actual or notional unemployment benefit disqualification) because of the cessation of that work; or
   (b) the claimant or his partner has ceased to be engaged in that work within six weeks of beginning it; or
   (c) at any time during the period of 26 weeks immediately preceding the beginning of that work, the person who has ceased to be engaged in it—
      (i) was engaged in remunerative work; or
      (ii) was in relevant education; or
      (iii) was a student.
(3) Paragraph (2)(b) or (c) shall not apply if, by virtue of section 20A(2) of the Social Security Act [SSCBA, s.29(2)] (exemption from disqualification for unemployment benefit) the person who has ceased to be engaged in remunerative work is exempted from disqualification for receiving unemployment benefit.]

AMENDMENT

1. Income Support (General) Amendment No. 3 Regulations 1989 (S.I. 1989 No. 1678), reg. 2 (October 9, 1989).

GENERAL NOTE

Reg. 3A provides a definition of the maximum permitted period of break in entitlement for the application of the variety of provisions set out in para. (1).

PART II

CONDITIONS OF ENTITLEMENT

Temporary absence from Great Britain

4.—(1) Where a claimant is entitled to income support for a period immediately preceding a period of temporary absence from Great Britain, his entitlement to income support [² shall continue only—
   (a) in the circumstances specified in paragraph (2), during the first 4 weeks of that period of temporary absence; and
   (b) in the circumstances specified in paragraph (3), during the first 8 weeks of that period.]

(2) The circumstances in which a claimant's entitlement to income support is to continue during the first four weeks of a temporary absence from Great Britain are that—

(a) the period of absence is unlikely to exceed 52 weeks; and

(b) while absent from Great Britain, the claimant continues to satisfy the other conditions of entitlement to income support; and

(c) any one of the following conditions apply—

    (i) the claimant is not required to be available for employment under regulation 8(1) and Schedule 1 other than paragraph 5, 10, 18 to 20 of that Schedule (persons not required to be available for employment); or

    (ii) he is not required to be available for employment under regulation 8(1) and paragraph 5 of Schedule 1 (incapacity for work) and his absence from Great Britain is for the sole purpose of receiving treatment from an appropriately qualified person for the incapacity by reason of which he is not required to be so available; or

    (iii) he is in Northern Ireland; or

    (iv) he is a member of a couple and he and his partner are both absent from Great Britain, and a premium referred to in paragraphs 9, 10, 11 or 13 of Schedule 2 (applicable amounts) is applicable in respect of his partner; [¹ or

[³(v) on the day on which the absence began he had satisfied the provisions of paragraph 5 of Schedule 1 (persons incapable of work) for a continuous period of not less than—

    (aa) 196 days in the case of a claimant who is terminally ill within the meaning of section 30B(4) of the Contributions and Benefits Act, or who is entitled to the highest rate of the care component of disability living allowance; or

    (bb) 364 days in any other case,

and for this purpose any two or more separate periods separated by a break of not more than 56 days shall be treated as one continuous period.]]

[²(3) The circumstances in which a claimant's entitlement to income support is to continue during the first 8 weeks of a temporary absence from Great Britain are that—

(a) the period of absence is unlikely to exceed 52 weeks; and

(b) the claimant continues to satisfy the other conditions of entitlement to income support; and

(c) the claimant is, or the claimant and any other member of his family are, accompanying a member of the claimant's family who is a child or young person solely in connection with arrangements made for the treatment of that child or young person for a disease or bodily or mental disablement; and

(d) those arrangements relate to treatment—

    (i) outside Great Britain;

    (ii) during the period whilst the claimant is, or the claimant and any member of his family are, temporarily absent from Great Britain; and

    (iii) by, or under the supervision of, a person appropriately qualified to carry out that treatment.

(4) In paragraphs (2) and (3) "appropriately qualified" means qualified to provide medical treatment, physiotherapy or a form of treatment which is similar to, or related to, either of those forms of treatment.]

AMENDMENTS

1. Income Support (General) Amendment Regulations 1988 (S.I. 1988 No. 663), reg. 3 (April 11, 1988).

2. Income Support (General) Amendment Regulations 1990 (S.I. 1990 No. 547), reg. 3 (April 9, 1990).

3. Disability Working Allowance and Income Support (General) Amendment Regulations 1995 (S.I. 1995 No. 482), reg. 5 (April 13, 1995).

DEFINITIONS

"claimant"—see reg. 2(1).
"couple"—*ibid.*
"disability living allowance"—*ibid.*
"partner"—*ibid.*

GENERAL NOTE

This provision takes over from reg. 3 of the old Conditions of Entitlement Regulations a limited right to benefit during the claimant's absence from Great Britain (normally excluded by s.124(1) of the Contributions and Benefits Act; 1986 Act, s.20(3)). Great Britain means England, Scotland and Wales. If it is the claimant's partner who is temporarily absent, see Sched. 7, para. 11.

Paragraph (1)
The absence must be temporary, on the meaning of which see *Chief Adjudication Officer v. Ahmed & Others, The Times,* April 6, 1994 (Court of Appeal). In *R. v. Social Security Commissioner, ex parte Akbar, The Times,* November 6, 1991, Hodgson J. had decided that temporary meant "not permanent". The Court of Appeal in *Ahmed* says that this is wrong, although the decision in *Akbar* itself was correct. However, the Court does agree with Hodgson J. that an absence can be temporary, even though the intended date for return remains uncertain. Thus *R(S) 1/85* should not be followed on this point. The Court of Appeal holds that the decision as to whether a person is temporarily absent is one of fact for the adjudicating authority concerned. Relevant factors include the claimant's intention (although this is not decisive) and the length of the absence. If a person initially has the intention of not returning or an intention to stay for some fixed period which goes beyond the temporary (*e.g.* a matter of years), the absence is not temporary from the outset. In practice, the 52–week period referred to in paras. (2)(a) and (3)(a) is likely to be the most important test.

The claimant must have been entitled to income support immediately before the temporary absence. Since the reference is to entitlement, it does not seem that income support must actually have been received. But a claim must have been made for that period before entitlement can arise (Administration Act, s.1).

If the conditions set out in para. (2) are met, entitlement at the rate which would have been payable if the claimant had remained in Great Britain, can continue for the first four weeks of the temporary absence. The 28 days begins on the first day after the day of leaving Great Britain (see para. 25070 of the *Adjudication Officers' Guide*).

If the conditions of para. (3) are met, entitlement can continue for the first eight weeks of absence, beginning on the first day after the day of departure (see para. 25070 of the *Adjudication Officers' Guide*).

If the claimant does not satisfy the conditions for continuing entitlement or the four or eight weeks are exhausted, any partner remaining in Great Britain may claim. If the absence is temporary, the couple ought on principle to remain members of the same household (although the effect of reg. 16(3)(d) is obscure).

Paragraph (2)
Sub-paras. (a) and (b) are self-explanatory. It is important that all the other conditions of entitlement must continue to be satisfied. The five conditions in sub-para. (c) are alternatives.

Head (i) covers claimants not required to be available for work, apart from by reason of incapacity for work (but see (ii) and (v)), secondary education, recent discharge from prison, trade disputes or being a person from abroad.

Some of the conditions which lead to the requirement of availability being lifted will obviously continue during absence abroad (*e.g.* pregnancy) but others may not (*e.g.* temporarily looking after children, if the children are left behind). Since the October 1993 change in the test of responsibility for a child, a lone parent who goes abroad temporarily without her children should continue to be exempt from the availability requirement under para. 1 of Sched. 1. This is because reg. 15(1) now makes receipt of child benefit the primary test of responsibility. Child benefit can continue to be paid while a claimant is temporarily absent from Great Britain for up to eight weeks. Only if no claim for child benefit has been made is the person with whom the child usually lives treated as responsible under reg. 15(2)(a). The matter has to be tested week by week (*CIS 49/1991*). See the 1993 edition for the potential problems for lone parents absent abroad prior to October 4, 1993.

Head (ii) covers incapacity for work, but only subject to these conditions (as applied to incapacity benefit by reg. 2(1) of the Social Security (Persons Aboard) Regulations 1975). See *R(S) 2/86* and *R(S) 1/90* for the conditions and head (v). Para. (4) defines when the person providing treatment is appropriately qualified.

Head (iii) is self explanatory.

Head (iv) refers to the pensioner and disability premiums, but only applies to couples who are both abroad. Para. 25055 of the *Adjudication Officers' Guide* says that for a premium to be "applicable" it must actually be in payment following a decision that it is payable. It is clearly arguable that "applicable" means "ought to be applied," so that entitlement will do.

Head (v) allows those incapable of work for at least 52 weeks, or 28 weeks if they are terminally ill (*i.e.* expected to die from a progressive disease within six months) or entitled to the highest rate care component of disability living allowance, to use the regulation free of the conditions of head (ii). Two or more periods of incapacity count as one continuous period unless there is a break of more than eight weeks. Before April 13, 1995 the minimum period was 28 weeks for all claimants, but it has been increased for most claimants in line with the changes following the introduction of incapacity benefit. For the details of incapacity benefit see *Bonner, Non-Means Tested Benefits: the Legislation*, (1995 ed.)

Paragraph (3)

The conditions in heads (a) and (b) are the same as in para. (2)(a) and (b). Then the effect of heads (c) and (d) is that where the claimant is accompanying a child or young person in their family abroad for that child or young person to receive treatment, entitlement can continue for eight weeks. The claimant's absence must be solely for that purpose. The treatment must be for a medical condition and be carried out by an appropriately qualified person within the meaning of para. (4). There seems to be no reason why a claimant accompanying a child should be more deserving than a claimant going abroad for treatment for himself.

Persons treated as engaged in remunerative work

5.—(1) Subject to the following provisions of this regulation, for the purposes of section 20(3)(c) of the Act [SSCBA, s.124(1)(*c*)] (conditions of entitlement to income support), remunerative work is work in which a person is engaged, or, where his hours of work fluctuate, he is engaged on average, for [⁶not less than 16 hours] a week being work for which payment is made or which is done in expectation of payment.

(2) [⁸Subject to paragraph (3B),] the number of hours for which a person is engaged in work shall be determined—

    (a) where no recognisable cycle has been established in respect of a person's work, by reference to the number of hours or, where those hours are likely to fluctuate, the average of the hours, which he is expected to work in a week;

    (b) where the number of hours for which he is engaged fluctuate, by reference to the average of hours worked over—

        (i) if there is a recognisable cycle of work, the period of one complete cycle (including, where the cycle involves periods in which the person does no work, those periods but disregarding any other absences);

        (ii) in any other case, the period of five weeks immediately before the date of claim or the date of review, or such other length of time as may, in the particular case, enable the person's average hours of work to be determined more accurately.

(3) A person shall be treated as engaged in remunerative work during any period for which he is absent from work referred to in paragraph (1) if the absence is either without good cause or by reason of a recognised, customary or other holiday.

[⁷(3A) A person shall not be treated as engaged in remunerative work on any day on which the person is on maternity leave or is absent from work because he is ill.]

[⁸(3B) Where for the purpose of paragraph (2)(b)(i), a person's recognisable cycle of work at a school, other educational establishment or other place of employment is one year and includes periods of school holidays or similar vacations during which he does not work, those periods and any other periods not forming part of such holidays or vacations during which he is not required to work shall be disregarded in establishing the average hours for which he is engaged in work.]

(4) A person who makes a claim and to whom or whose partner section 23 of the Act [SSCBA, s.126] (trade disputes) applies [¹or applied] shall, for the period of seven days following the date on which the stoppage of work due to a trade dispute at his or his partner's place of work commenced or, if there is no stoppage, the date on which he or his partner first withdrew his labour in furtherance of a trade dispute, be treated as engaged in remunerative work.

(5) A person who was, or was treated as being, engaged in remunerative work and in respect of that work earnings to which [⁴regulation 35(1)(b) to (d) and (i)] (earnings of employed earners) applies are [³paid] shall be treated as engaged in remunerative work for the period for which those earnings are taken into account in accordance with Part V.

[²(6) For the purposes of this regulation, in determining the number of hours in which a person is engaged or treated as engaged in remunerative work, no account shall be taken of any hours in which the person is engaged in an employment or a scheme to which paragraph (*a*) to [¹paragraph (k)] of regulation 6 (persons not treated as engaged in remunerative work) applies.]

[⁵(7) For the purposes of paragraphs (1) and (2), in determining the number of hours for which a person is engaged in work, that number shall include any time allowed to that person by his employer for a meal or for refreshment, but only where that person is, or expects to be, paid earnings in respect of that time.]

AMENDMENTS

1. Income Support (General) Amendment Regulations 1988 (S.I. 1988 No. 663), reg. 4 (April 11, 1988).
2. Income Support (General) Amendment No. 4 Regulations 1988 (S.I. 1988 No. 1445), reg. 3 (September 9, 1988).
3. Income Support (General) Amendment No. 5 Regulations 1988 (S.I. 1988 No. 2022), reg. 3 (December 12, 1988).
4. Income Support (General) Amendment No. 2 Regulations 1989 (S.I. 1989 No. 1323), reg. 3 (October 9, 1989).
5. Income Support (General) Amendment Regulations 1990 (S.I. 1990 No. 547), reg. 4 (April 9, 1990).
6. Income Support (General) Amendment No. 4 Regulations 1991 (S.I. 1991 No. 1559), reg. 3 (April 7, 1992).
7. Income-related Benefits Schemes (Miscellaneous Amendments) (No. 4) Regulations 1993 (S.I. 1993 No. 2119), reg. 3 (October 4, 1993).
8. Income-related Benefits Schemes (Miscellaneous Amendments) Regulations 1995 (S.I. 1995 No. 516), reg. 19 (April 10, 1995).

DEFINITIONS

"the Act"—see reg. 2(1).
"date of claim"—*ibid.*
"maternity leave"—*ibid.*
"partner"—*ibid.*

(S.I. 1987 No. 1967, reg. 5)

One of the most significant departures in income support, as compared to supplementary benefit, was the reduction of the limit for remunerative work to 24 hours per week and the application of the test to both the claimant and his partner. Then, from April 1992, the limit was reduced again to 16 hours, which excludes a significant number of part-time workers. Important transitional protection for existing claimants was provided in regs. 22 to 24 of the Income Support (General) Amendment No. 4 Regulations 1991 (see p.333). As part of the same package, the qualification for family credit (and disability working allowance) was reduced to 16 hours per week, but not everyone has children or is disabled.

Because income support is normally paid in arrears, the disentitlement applies immediately a person starts remunerative work, regardless of whether wages have been paid or when they will be paid. This situation is specifically mentioned in the Social Fund Guide (para. 5422) as one in which a crisis loan might be payable if no other resources are available. The details of the test are therefore important. Note the exceptions in reg. 6, brought in by para. (6).

Paragraph (1)

First note that the test is in terms of work, not employment. Therefore, the precise categorisation of the activities carried out may not be crucial. This is illustrated in two family credit decisions (remunerative work is a qualification for family credit). In *CFC 7/1989* the claimant's husband was working in connection with Moral Re-Armament, a Christian charity, for about 38 hours a week. He received payment by persuading individuals to covenant income to him. He was not employed by Moral Re-Armament or the covenantors, nor did he contract with them on a self-employed basis. But this did not matter, because what he did was undoubtedly work and he was paid for it. In *R(FC) 2/90* both the claimant and her husband were officers of the Salvation Army. It was accepted, following the decision of the Court of Appeal in *Rogers* v. *Booth* [1937] 2 All E.R. 751, that the relationship of officers to the Salvation Army is spiritual, not contractual. Nevertheless, the onerous duties of officers were "work."

Remunerative

Work is remunerative if payment is made for it, or it is done in the expectation of payment. There is a significant difference from the common law test (on which see *R(FIS) 1/83*), because the mere hope of or desire for payment is not the same as expectation. Thus in *CFC 3/1989*, the claimant's husband, who regarded himself as a self-employed writer, but who had not sold any manuscripts and did not anticipate any sales in the next six months, was not in remunerative work. The Commissioner puts forward a rule of thumb, not a binding principle, that for work to be done in the expectation of payment some payment must be expected within 26 weeks of the relevant date. This was based partly on the length of a family credit award, but there clearly should be one dividing line between the income support and family credit systems. In *R (IS) 1/93* the Commissioner holds that the guiding principle on when there is an expectation of payment should be common sense and an appreciation of the realities of the situation. The claimant, another writer, had sent several works to publishers, but had had negligible success in selling anything. She was working "on spec," with only the hope of payment, not an expectation. In *Kevin Smith v. Chief Adjudication Officer* (C.A., October 11, 1994) the claimant's partner, who was in receipt of an enterprise allowance, wished to establish herself as an agent for pop groups and spent a lot of time building up contacts in the pop music world. The Court of Appeal, having said that the question is really one of fact, distinguishes between work done to set up a business, which is not done in expectation of payment, and work carried out once the business is established, which it would be reasonable to infer was done in expectation of payment. On the facts of that case the claimant's partner was not engaged in remunerative work.

In *CIS 815/1992* the claimant's wife worked in a general shop owned by the two of them. For several months she had worked without pay and had no expectation of receiving any in the future because the business was making a loss. The Commissioner holds that the SSAT had been correct in concluding that on the facts she was not in remunerative work. This decision was upheld by the Court of Appeal in *Chief Adjudication Officer v. Ellis* (February 15, 1995). In *Ellis* the Court gives some general guidance on the questions to be considered when deciding whether a person is in remunerative work. In particular, the Court draws a distinction between a person providing a service (such as the claimant carrying on a translation agency in *Perrot v. SBC* [1980] 3 All E.R. 110 where the unprofitability of her business was irrelevant) and the position of a retail shop. The Court points out that the price paid for goods sold in a shop is not payment for the work of the salesman, but the price of the goods sold. Thus simply carrying on a retail business did not necessarily mean that a person was in remunerative work (so *CSIS 39/1994* should not be followed on this point).

But if the person was not expecting to make any money the question had to be asked why the shop was being kept open. In this case the answer was clear. The claimant's wife was carrying on the business in the hope of disposing of the goodwill. She was not in remunerative work.

In *CIS 181/1993* (to be reported as *R(IS) 5/95*), which concerned an employee, the Commissioner points out that expectation of payment means payment for current work. It may be that this is not the case for the self-employed, although the Court of Appeal in *Ellis* states that the question of whether work is done in expectation of payment is to be decided at the time the work is done, not at the end of the year or other accounting period.

The payment must be in return for the work *(R(FIS) 1/86)*, but need not derive from an employer. Thus the payments by covenantors in *CFC 7/1989* (see above) counted. So too did the payments from the Salvation Army in *R(FC) 2/90*, although they were not paid under contract and were aimed at providing for the officers' actual needs. There was a distinction from the maintenance grant paid to a student. Provision for actual needs went beyond mere maintenance. A grant is not in return for work *(R(FIS) 1/86)*, so that students and trainees *(R(FIS) 1/83)* will still not be said to be in remunerative work. The argument that enterprise allowance is paid in return for work was rejected by the Court of Appeal in *Kevin Smith v. Chief Adjudication Officer* (above). The Court holds that it is a payment to enable people to establish themselves in business, not for work. This conclusion was indicated both by the terms of the enterprise allowance scheme and reg. 37(1). If receipt of enterprise allowance by itself meant that a person had to be treated as engaged in remunerative work, the inclusion in reg. 37(1) of enterprise allowance as earnings was unnecessary since the calculation stage envisaged by reg. 37 would never be reached.

A payment in kind will count in the same way as a payment in cash. In *CFC 33/1993* the provision of rent-free accommodation and the payment of gas and electricity bills meant that the claimant's work was done for payment.

Hours of work

If the engagement is for a regular 16 hours or more, para. (1) seems to be satisfied directly. But para. (1) is silent on what is the appropriate period to look at when determining whether a person is engaged in work for 16 hours or more a week. This causes certain difficulties (see below). If the hours fluctuate, averaging must be carried out. Para. (2) says how.

It is hours during which the person is engaged in work and is paid (or at least expects payment) which are crucial. The calculation is usually relatively easy for employees. Thus in *CIS 3/1989* the claimant's paid one hour lunch break did not count towards the limit. He was not "engaged in" work for that hour. The precise result is reversed from April 1990, by para. (7), but the principle might apply in other situations. *R(FC) 1/92* suggests that where the nature of the job requires a person to work beyond the contractually specified hours, the longer hours count. But it is not clear just how this translates from the old family credit provision to income support. For the self-employed the test is not of hours costed and charged to a client, but of hours of activities which are essential to the undertaking *(R(FIS) 6/85)*. Thus time spent in preparation, research, doing estimates and accounts, travel for the purposes of the undertaking, keeping a shop open etc. must all count. But activities carried on merely in the hope, rather than expectation, of payment are not remunerative. The actual hours of work must be considered. In *CIS 815/1992*, although the shop in which the claimant's wife worked was open from 8.30am to 6.30pm Monday to Friday, she only spent three hours a day in it. The rest of the time she was in her home (which was in the same premises), ready to go into the shop if the shop bell rang. The Commissioner expresses the view (without finally deciding the point) that on the particular facts of that case (a small shop with little stock and fewer customers) the hours "on call" may not be hours of work. The decision in *CIS 815/1992* was upheld by the Court of Appeal in *Cheif Adjudication Officer v. Ellis* (see above), but the Court of Appeal does not deal with this particular point. In *CIS 665/1991* all the hours that a share fisherman was at sea (including those that he was not on watch or was sleeping) counted. The Commissioner referred to *Suffolk County Council v. Secretary of State for the Environment and another* [1984] I.C.R. 882 in which the House of Lords had distinguished between a regular fireman required to remain in the station while on duty and a retained fireman free to do as he pleases until called upon. The claimant could not do as he pleased during his rest period. He had to stay on the trawler and could be summoned to assist if, for example, there was a storm.

CIS 514/1990 holds that although recipients of enterprise allowance must undertake to work for at least 36 hours a week in their business, that does not mean that they must automatically be treated as doing so for benefit purposes (see *Kevin Smith v. Chief Adjudication Officer* above on whether enterprise allowance is paid in return for work). In *CIS 181/1993* (to be reported as *R(IS) 5/95*) where the claimant was both a director and an employee of a small limited company, the Commissioner states that it was necessary to consider in relation to each week whether he was working in his capacity as an employee or a director (although the functions of a director of a small private company were quite slight (*R(U)1/93*, para. 5)). The claimant had not been paid for some months due to the company's financial difficulties, but he had continued to work for 30 hours a week. If this work had been done as an employee it was only remunerative if any payment expected was in that capacity. The Commissioner points out that reg. 42(6) (notional earnings) would also need to be considered.

Para. (2) is exceptionally difficult to make sense of. Comprehensive restructuring of reg. 5, as has been carried out on the equivalent family credit provision, is required. The opening words of para. (2) suggest a mechanism for determining the hours worked in all cases, but sub-paras. (a) and (b) only apply in restricted circumstances. In particular, a person who works for a regular number of contracted hours seems to fall outside para. (2) and inside para. (1).

Sub-para. (a) can only apply where no recognisable cycle has been established. An obvious situation is where a person has just started work. But if a person works a contractually-set number of hours, with no overtime, is this a case where there is no "cycle" at all (so that sub-para. (*a*) applies) or is it an immediately recognisable cycle (so that para. (1) applies)? The Commissioner's definition in *CIS 493/1993* of a "cycle" as a "recurrent round" which contains within it a complete description of the work done, the end of one cycle being the beginning of another, is helpful but does not answer this kind of question. In *CIS 267/1993* the Commissioner emphasises that sub-para. (a) refers to where no recognised cycle has been *established*. Thus it applies not only when employment has just begun, but also when evidence of past hours of work does not reflect the current position (*e.g.* where there has been a change of hours), so that what has to be considered is what is likely to happen in the future (see below).

If sub-para. (a) does apply, the test is of the number of hours the person is expected to work, or be paid for a meal-break (para. (7)). Could this test go beyond contracted hours of work? If the hours are likely to fluctuate, an average is to be taken. There is no provision for the period over which the average is to be calculated, so that presumably whatever period is most appropriate to the circumstances must be chosen. (See *CIS 267/1993* below). It seems that only hours of actual work should count in the averaging (*R(FIS)2/82* and see *CIS 745/1993* below). On the effect of para. (3) see *R(IS) 15/94* below.

Sub-para. (b) can only apply if the hours worked do fluctuate. There is enormous difficulty in some cases in determining the period over which fluctuation should be tested. For example, school auxiliary workers may have contracts for absolutely regular hours during term-time, with no work required during school holidays. It is arguable that this is not an example of fluctuating hours, but of periods of work for non-fluctuating hours followed by periods of no work. The person would then be engaged in work for the regular number of hours in term-time and not so engaged outside term-time. But this is not the approach taken in *CIS 261/1990* or *CIS 745/1993*. In *CIS 261/1990* (unstarred), it was assumed that sub-para. (b) applies in such circumstances. However, the contrary argument was not put and the actual decision was on another ground. In *CIS 745/1993* the claimant worked 20 hours a week during term time (38 weeks) and was paid for an additional six weeks holiday. During the remaining eight weeks of the year she neither worked nor was paid. The Commissioner decides that over the academic year her hours fluctuated and so she came within sub-para. (b)(i). He follows *R(IS) 15/94* (and *CIS 261/1990*) in holding that in the case of a school ancillary worker the appropriate cycle is one year. But in *CIS 745/1993*, unlike *R(IS) 15/94*, the claimant's hours did not fluctuate during term time. The Commissioner in *CIS 745/1993* does not seem to have considered the possibility that sub-para. (b) might not apply at all in these circumstances. It should be noted that in both *CIS 261/1990* (where the claimant was paid a monthly salary throughout the year) and *CIS 745/1993*, the claimants' contracts of employment continued throughout the year; they did not have a separate one for each term. The argument against the application of sub-para. (b) will be much stronger if the person's contract terminates at the end of each period of work (and see *R(U) 2/87* referred to in the notes to para. (3)).

In *R(IS) 15/94* the claimant was a school receptionist whose contractual hours of work were 22 hours per week during term time only. However, her actual hours of work fluctuated each week (unlike the claimants' in *CIS 261/1990* and *CIS 745/1993*). She was not paid during the school holidays, although she did work on occasional days during the holidays when asked to do so. Her contract of employment was a continuing one. The Commissioner applies sub-para.(b)(i), holding that the recognisable cycle was a yearly one and that the school holidays were included in the cycle as "periods in which the person does no work". He disagrees with the Commissioner in *CIS 261/1990* that the school holidays were to be excluded as absences by reason of a recognised or customary holiday. He holds that para. (3), which treats a person as engaged in remunerative work during certain absences, including recognised or customary holidays, does not affect the question of averaging of hours. Para. (3) only applies once it has been ascertained that a claimant works 16 hours or more a week over the appropriate cycle. The claimant's averaged hours of work over the year were less than 24 a week (which was the limit for remunerative work at that time) and so she was not engaged in remunerative work. *R(IS) 15/94* is followed in *CIS 745/1993* (see above for the facts), although in *CIS 745/1993* the claimant's hours of work did not fluctuate during term time. It also holds that the notional hours attributable to the claimant's six weeks' paid holiday were not to be included in the total number of hours worked during the cycle. The Commissioner points out that para. (1) defines remunerative work as work "in (not *for*) which a person is engaged". This implied that the claimant actually had to be working. This interpretation was also supported by the meaning of para. (3) as explained in *R(IS) 15/94*, since the implication was that without para. (3) a person would be considered not in remunerative work during the period of holiday. Thus the claimant's total hours of work during the cycle were 760 (20 hours × 38 weeks), which when averaged over 52 weeks came to less than 16 a week. It will be noted, however, that the Commissioner did include the weeks of paid holiday within the cycle. In doing so he applied *R(IS) 15/94* where the Commissioner distinguishes between *ad hoc* holidays which would not be included in the cycle and holidays for which the contract made specific or advance provision, such as school holidays. These fell squarely within the phrase "periods in which the person does no work". But holidays (or absence due to sickness) during the period when the person is required to work will reduce the length of the cycle as these count as "other absences" (see the *Adjudication Officers' Guide* paras. 39424–5).

Although the interpretation adopted in *R(IS) 15/94* and *CIS 745/1993* could work to a claimant's advantage in establishing entitlement to income support, it was a disadvantage in family credit terms. The policy intention apparently was that benefit entitlement should be based on the average hours worked during term time and so para. (3B) has been introduced. This provides that if a person has an annual cycle of work which includes periods of no work, for example, school holidays, such periods are ignored in averaging hours of work. A similar rule has been introduced for family credit and disability working allowance (and housing and council tax benefit). The new rule will make it more difficult for workers like school ancillary workers to qualify for income support, and could operate harshly in some cases. For example, a school ancillary worker who is employed for 18 hours a week in term time under a continuing contract who has no dependent children will not be entitled to family credit, or income support (even during the holidays). If, however, her contract terminates at the end of each term, she should be able to claim income support during the school holidays. In these circumstances she is not engaged in work outside term time and so sub-para. (b) (and para. (3B)) does not apply at all, and the case has to be determined under the primary rule in para. (1). The same should apply to other employees who have periods of work interspersed with periods of no work (and no continuing contract of employment), for example, seasonal workers.

But in the case of such a worker who is self-employed (and so does not have a contract of employment) the position is less clear. Para. (1) does not state what is the appropriate period to look at when determining whether a person is engaged in remunerative work. Each case will therefore depend to some extent on its own facts. If, for example, a person carries on a business for six months of the year and does no work in connection with that business for the rest of the year, it must be arguable that the period to be looked at is the six months when his business is dormant and that during that time he is not engaged in work. Therefore the question of whether para. (2) applies simply does not arise. However, this is not the conclusion reached by the Commissioner in *CIS 493/93*. The claimant ran a guest house with a six-month season and did a minimal amount of work during the closed season. The claimant had argued that there were two cycles, or periods, one in which he worked more than 16 hours every week and the second during which he was not engaged in work at all. The Commissioner states that the first question was whether there was a recognisable cycle, and the second was whether the claimant's hours fluctuated within that cycle. The basis of this approach seems to have been that para. (2) is to be used to determine the number of hours for which a person is engaged in work. But para. (2) does not provide a rule for deciding the number of hours worked per week in all cases. It applies in the circumstances described in the opening words of sub-paras. (a) and (b) (*CIS 267/1993*). It is suggested that the first question is what is the appropriate period for deciding whether a claimant is engaged in remunerative work, which will depend on the facts of each case, before going on to consider whether the particular circumstances referred to in para. (2) apply. Para. (3B) would not seem to apply to the self-employed (see below).

Sub-para. (b)(ii) applies if the hours fluctuate but there is no recognisable cycle, in which case an average is taken, normally over the five weeks before the week of claim. An alternative period should only be used if it can be demonstrated that it will produce a more accurate average (*R(FIS) 1/81* and *R(FIS) 2/83*), and not, for example, because there is no evidence of the hours worked in one of those weeks (*CIS 665/1993*).

CIS 267/1993 concerns the application of reg. 5 in the case of a claimant who had been working a regular 37 hour week and went onto a period of short time, working one week on and one week off. There was the possibility that he could be called in on non-working weeks. The claimant therefore argued that his claim should be considered on a week by week basis under para. (2)(a). However, this was rejected by the Commissioner. He holds that the claim was to be treated as for an indefinite period under reg. 17(1) of the Claims and Payments Regulations (see the notes to reg. 17). He then considered whether para. (2) applied in this case. In his view, para. (2)(a) looked forward and was directed to the situation where there was no (or insufficient) evidence of recent working hours on which to decide the working hours for the week in question. Para. (2)(b) applied where there was such evidence, and that evidence showed a fluctuation of hours. The point at which the test shifted from a forward-looking one under sub-para. (a) to a backward-looking one under sub-para. (b) depended on the circumstances. A claimant's hours of work had to be considered week by week throughout the period in issue and were not fixed at the date of claim. The result was that sub-para. (a) applied at the beginning of the claim when it was expected that the claimant's hours would fluctuate; the appropriate period for averaging the hours at that time was two weeks. When there had been two two-week cycles of one week on and one week off sub-para. (b)(i) came into play. When later the recognisable cycle was broken because the claimant had less weeks off, sub-para. (b)(ii) applied. On any test the minimum hours that the claimant was working were more than 16 a week and so he was engaged in remunerative work throughout the period.

Paragraph (3)

A person is deemed to be in remunerative work, and so excluded from entitlement under s.124(1)(c) of the Contributions and Benefits Act (1986 Act, s.20(3)(c)), in these circumstances. Para. (3) does not come into play until it has been established under the terms of paras. (1) and (2) that the work from which the person is absent is normally carried on for at least 16 hours a week *(R(IS) 15/94)*. Absence for any kind of holiday, not just recognised or customary holidays (on which, see *R(SB) 7/84*) comes under para. (3). A distinction must be drawn between holidays and periods of non-working imposed by the employer. If a contract of employment comes to an end on the completion of a period of work the following period cannot be a holiday *(R(U) 2/87)* or a period of absence from work. (For the position of school ancillary and similar workers see above.) The category of absence without good cause is an open one. Absence due to incapacity to work through illness or disability will obviously be for a good cause. Such absence is now specifically covered by para. (3A).

Paragraph (3A)

This para. confirms that a person who is away sick or a woman on maternity leave is not treated as in remunerative work. The effect is that there is no automatic exclusion from entitlement under s.124(1)(c) of the Contributions and Benefits Act (1986 Act, s.20 (3) (c)) but any pay will be taken into account as income (regs. 35(2) and 40(4); note the disregards in paras. 1, 4 and 4A of Sched. 9). The definition of maternity leave in reg. 2(1) means that a woman counts as on maternity leave only if she has either a statutory or a contractual right to return to work. Prior to October 4, 1993, the same result could be achieved by treating such absences as for a good cause (see para. (3)). This will continue to be the case for absence due to paternity leave or other leave (*e.g.* compassionate leave).

Paragraph (3B)

See the notes on hours of work above. The wording of para. (3B) seems to indicate that it only applies to employees.

Paragraph 4

See the notes to s.126 of the Contributions and Benefits Act (1986 Act, s.23).

Paragraph 5

Where income payments in lieu of notice or remuneration are paid or (within four weeks of termination) holiday pay, the person is treated as in remunerative work for the period covered. See regs. 29 and 31.

Paragraph 7

Paid meal or refreshment breaks count in the calculation of the hours for which a person is engaged in work.

Persons not treated as engaged in remunerative work

6. A person shall not be treated as engaged in [² remunerative work in so far as—]

[³(a) he is mentally or physically disabled, and by reason of that disability—
  (i) his earnings are reduced to 75 per cent. or less of what a person without that disability and working the same number of hours would reasonably be expected to earn in that employment or in comparable employment in that area; or
  (ii) his number of hours of work are 75 per cent. or less of what a person without that disability would reasonably be expected to undertake in that employment or in comparable employment in that area.]
  (b) he is engaged in child minding in his home;
  (c) he is engaged by a charity or [⁷voluntary organisation [⁸- -],] or is a volunteer where the only payment received by him or due to be paid to him, is a payment which is to be disregarded under regulation 40(2) and paragraph 2 of Schedule 9 (sums to be disregarded in the calculation of income other than earnings);
  (d) he is engaged on a scheme for which a training allowance is being paid; [⁴ . . .]
  (e) subject to regulation 5(4) [² and (5)] (persons treated as engaged in remunerative work) he is a person to whom section 23 of the Act [SSCBA, s.126] (trade disputes) applies [¹ or in respect of whom section 20(3) of the Act [SSCBA, s.124(1)] (conditions of entitlement to income support) has effect as modified by section 23A(b) of the Act [SSCBA, s.127(b)] (effect of return to work)]; [⁴ . . .]
  (f) he is a person who is not required to be available for employment because regulation 8 and paragraph 4 of Schedule 1 (person caring for another) applies to him;
[⁶(g) he is in employment, and—
  (i) lives in, or is temporarily absent from, a residential care home, a nursing home or residential accommodation, and either
  (ii) his, or his partner's, applicable amount falls to be calculated in accordance with Part I of Schedule 4 (applicable amounts of persons in residential care and nursing homes) or, as the case may be, paragraphs 9, 10 to 10D, 13, 16 or 18 of Schedule 7 (applicable amounts in special cases), or
  (iii) he or his partner satisfies the conditions specified in paragraph 2A(2) of Part I of Schedule 2 (conditions for entitlement to a residential allowance);]
[⁴(h) he is engaged in any one of the employments mentioned in heads (a) to (d) of sub-paragraph (1) of paragraph 7 of Schedule 8 (which relates to persons serving as firemen, in coastal rescue activities etc); [⁵ . . .]
  (j) he is performing his duties as a councillor, and for this purpose ''councillor'' has the same meaning as in paragraph 2(6) of Schedule 8 to the Social Security Act 1989;][⁵ or
  (k) he is engaged in caring for a person who is accommodated with him by virtue of arrangements made under any of the provisions referred to in paragraph 26 [⁷or in accordance with paragraph 27] of Schedule 9 (sums to be disregarded in the calculation of income other than earnings) and is in receipt of any payment specified in [⁷those paragraphs].]

AMENDMENTS

1. Income Support (General) Amendment Regulations 1988 (S.I. 1988 No. 663), reg. 5 (April 11, 1988).
2. Income Support (General) Amendment No. 4 Regulations 1988 (S.I. 1988 No. 1445), reg. 4 (September 12, 1988).
3. Income Support (General) Amendment No. 4 Regulations 1991 (S.I. 1991 No. 1559), reg. 4 (October 7, 1991).

4. Income Support (General) Amendment Regulations 1992 (S.I. 1992 No. 468), reg. 2 (April 6, 1992).

5. Income-related Benefits Schemes (Miscellaneous Amendments) (No. 3) Regulations 1992 (S.I. 1992 No. 2155), reg. 13 (October 5, 1992).

6. Social Security Benefits (Miscellaneous Amendments) Regulations 1993 (S.I. 1993 No. 518), reg. 5 (April 1, 1993).

7. Income-related Benefits Schemes (Miscellaneous Amendments) (No. 5) Regulations 1994 (S.I. 1994 No. 2139), reg. 23 (October 3, 1994).

8. Income-related Benefits Schemes (Miscellaneous Amendments) Regulations 1995 (S.I. 1995 No. 516), reg. 20 (April 10, 1995).

DEFINITIONS

"the Act"—see reg. 2(1).
"remunerative work"—*ibid.*
"training allowance"—*ibid.*
"voluntary organisation"—*ibid.*

GENERAL NOTE

These categories must be deemed not to be in remunerative work for the time engaged in these activities, although the "not" could be better placed. The effect is that there is not an automatic exclusion from entitlement under s.124(1)(c) of the Contributions and Benefits Act (1986 Act, s.20(3)(c)). Any earnings from employment must still be taken into account as income. Most of the categories are self-explanatory.

The previous form of para. (a) made the test for the disabled a 75 per cent. reduction in earning capacity. The new form splits the test into two alternatives. The first, in sub-para. (i), compares the claimant's earnings with what a non-disabled person doing the same job for the same hours would earn. The second, in sub-para. (ii), compares the hours worked with what a non-disabled person would do in the same job. In either case, if the claimant falls below 75 per cent. of the comparison level he is deemed not to be engaged in remunerative work.

It is thought that most of those assisted by the old form of para. (a) will continue to be assisted by the new form, but there is a saving provision in regs. 22 to 24 of the Income Support (General) Amendment No. 4 Regulations 1991 (see p. 333) for those who lose out.

Under para. (c), para. 2 of Sched. 9 refers to payments solely of expenses to volunteers or people working for charitable or voluntary bodies. A volunteer is someone who without any legal obligation performs a service for another person without expectation of payment (*R(IS)12/92*).

Under para. (d), training allowances are most commonly paid on YTS schemes.

Under para. (e), reg. 5(4) deems those in trade disputes to be in remunerative work for the first seven days of stoppage and reg. 5(5) deems those who have received holiday pay or payments in lieu of notice or remuneration to be in remunerative work for the period covered.

Para. (g) deems residents in residential care and nursing homes (defined in reg. 19(3)) and residential accommodation (defined in reg. 21(3)) not to be engaged in remunerative work. The reference to Sched. 7 is to the paragraphs dealing with people who are in residential accommodation or who are temporarily in any of the three types of accommodation.

Under para. (j), the definition of "councillor" is—

"(a) in relation to England and Wales, a member of a London borough council, a county council, a district council, a parish or community council, the Common Council of the City of London or the Council of the Isles of Scilly; and

(b) in relation to Scotland, a member of a regional, islands or district council."

Under para. (k) foster-parents who receive statutory payments for fostering, or people receiving payments for providing temporary care in their home, are deemed not to be in remunerative work by reason of those payments.

Meaning of employment

7.—[¹(1)] For the purposes of section 20(3)(d) of the Act [SSCBA, s. 124(3)(d)] (conditions of entitlement to income support [¹in so far as it relates to the condition of availability for employment]) only work in employed earner's employment within the meaning of the Social Security Act [SSCBA]—

(a) which the claimant can reasonably be expected to do;

(b) or which payment is made or which is done in expectation of payment; and

(c) for which he would normally be engaged for not less than 24 hours a week or, if he is mentally or physically disabled, such lesser number of hours as, having regard to his disability, he is usually capable of working;

shall be treated as employment.

[¹(2) For the purposes of section 20(3)(d) of the Act [SSCBA, s.124(3)(d)] in so far as it relates to the condition of actively seeking employment, work which is treated as employment for the purposes of paragraph (1) and employment as a self-employed earner under any scheme for assisting claimants to become self-employed earners established under arrangements made pursuant to section 2 of the Employment and Training Act 1973 [²or section 2 of the Enterprise and New Towns (Scotland) Act 1990] shall be treated as employment.]

AMENDMENTS

1. Income Support (General) Amendment No. 2 Regulations 1989 (S.I. 1989 No. 1323), reg. 4 (October 9, 1989).

2. Enterprise (Scotland) Consequential Amendments Order 1991 (S.I. 1991 No. 387), art. 2 (April 1, 1991).

DEFINITIONS

"the Act"—see reg. 2(1).
"claimant"—*ibid.*
"Social Security Act"—*ibid.*

GENERAL NOTE

Paragraph (1)

This provision defines the kind of employment the claimant must be available for to satisfy s.124(1)(d) of the Contributions and Benefits Act (1986 Act, s.20(3)(d)). An amendment by reg. 5 of the Income Support (General) Amendment No. 4 Regulations 1991 (S.I. 1991 No. 1559) to alter the required number of hours from 24 to 16 was revoked before it came into force (Income Support (General) Amendment Regulations 1992 (S.I. 1992 No. 468), reg. 13).

Self-employment will not do. The definition of reg. 2(1) does not apply.

Paragraph (2)

The meaning of "employment" for the actively seeking employment test is slightly wider as it extends to self-employment covered by the enterprise allowance scheme for those who were previously unemployed.

Persons not required to be available for employment

8.—(1) A person, other than one to whom regulation 10(1)(h) applies (circumstances in which a person is to be treated as available for employment), to whom any paragraph of Schedule 1 (persons not required to be available for employment) applies in any week shall not be required to be available for employment in that week.

(2) A person, other than one to whom regulation 10(1)(h) applies, to whom none of the provisions of Schedule 1 [² . . .] applies, shall, where—

[³(a) an adjudication officer has determined for the purposes of section 171B of the Contributions and Benefits Act (the own occupation test) that that person is not incapable of work; and]

(b) that person's medical practitioner continues to supply evidence of his incapacity for work in accordance with regulation 2 of the Social Security (Medical Evidence) Regulations 1976 (evidence of incapacity for work); and

   (c) that person has made and is pursuing an appeal against the determination of an adjudication officer that he is not so incapable; and

   (d) that person, were he required to be available for employment, would not be treated as so available under regulation 9(1) (persons treated as available for employment),

not be required to be available for employment pending the determination of his appeal.

[³(2A) A person, other than one to whom paragraph (2) or regulation 10(1)(h) applies, to whom none of the provisions of Schedule 1 applies, shall, where—

   (a) an adjudication officer has determined for the purposes of section 171C of the Contributions and Benefits Act (the all work test) that that person is not incapable of work; and

   (b) that person has made and is pursuing an appeal against that determination; and

   (c) that person, were he required to be available for employment, would not be treated as so available under regulation 9(1) (persons treated as available for employment),

not be required to be available for employment pending the determination of his appeal.]

[¹(3) A person, other than one to whom [² [³paragraph (2) or (2A)] or] regulation 10(1)(h) applies, to whom none of the provisions of Schedule 1 applies, shall, for any period when—

   (a) he would, were he required to be available for employment, not be treated as so available under regulation 9(1); and

   (b) the adjudication officer is satisfied that, unless income support is paid, the claimant or a member of his family (if any) will suffer hardship,

not be required to be available for employment.]

AMENDMENTS

   1. Income Support (General) Amendment Regulations 1988 (S.I. 1988 No. 663), reg. 6 (April 11, 1988).

   2. Income Support (General) Amendment Regulations 1991 (S.I. 1991 No. 236), reg. 3 (April 8, 1991).

   3. Disability Working Allowance and Income Support (General) Amendment Regulations 1995 (S.I. 1995 No. 482), reg. 6 (April 13, 1995).

GENERAL NOTE

Paragraph (1)

   The main point here is to refer on to Sched. 1 for the categories of claimant who are not required to be available for employment (as defined in reg. 7). See the notes to Sched. 1. Reg. 10(1)(h) applies to most students throughout the entire length of their course (including vacations) and deems them to be unavailable. There are a few exceptions. Note that para. (3) effectively creates another last resort category to be added to the list in Sched. 1, and that paras. (2) and (2A) deal with a special category.

Paragraphs (2) and (2A)

   These provisions apply to people who have been receiving benefit on the ground of incapacity for work, but have been found fit for work and appeal against that decision. Para. (2A) and the new form of para. (2)(a) are necessary following the introduction of the new tests of incapacity for work from April 13, 1995. Para. (2) now applies where the person has been found capable of work on the basis of the "own occupation test", and para. (2A) where the person has failed to satisfy the "all work test". For the details of these tests and when they apply see *Bonner, Non-Means Tested Benefits: the Legislation,* (1995 ed.). Note reg. 19 of the Social Security (Incapacity for Work) (General) Regulations 1995 (S.I. 1995 No. 311) which provides that a decision that a person is capable, or incapable, of work in connection with a claim for one benefit is conclusive for the purposes of all other benefits.

The opening words of both paras. exclude most students and those who do not need these provisions because they qualify under Sched. 1 anyway. In addition, if the person would be treated as available for work, these provisions do not apply (para. (2)(d) and para. (2A)(c)).

For cases within para. (2), if the claimant's own doctor continues to certify that he is incapable of work while he is pursuing an appeal against the incapacity decision, he is not required to be available pending the determination of the appeal. This should mean the final determination of the appeal, *e.g.* if it is taken to the Social Security Commissioner. An amendment to the *Adjudication Officers' Guide* in May 1994 confirms this interpretation (para. 25499). If para. (2) applies, full benefit is payable.

If para. (2) does not apply, and the claimant is appealing about capacity for work on the basis of the all work test, there is no requirement under para. (2A) for him to continue to submit medical certificates from his own doctor. This is because these are no longer required once the all work test has been applied. Otherwise the conditions in sub-paras. (b) and (c) are the same as in para. (2)(c) and (d). But if para. (2A) applies, the claimant's income support is reduced by 20 per cent of the appropriate personal allowance for a single claimant of his age until the appeal is determined (reg. 22(1A), (5A) and (6)(d)). (If the appeal is successful, the reduction will be repaid.) See above for when an appeal is determined. In order to receive full income support, a claimant who is appealing against failure to satisfy the all work test will have to sign on as available for work (unless any of the other paras. of Sched. 1 apply). This could place the claimant in a dilemma if he is maintaining that he is unable to work. The best course may be for him to say that he has been found capable of work and that he will accept any suitable work having regard to his limitations. The Adjudication Officers' Guide states that the fact that a person has been available for employment should not prejudice the appeal about incapacity (para. 53585).

There is transitional protection for claimants to whom reg. 8(2) applied on April 12, 1995 and for those who appeal against an AO's decision on incapacity made on or before April 12, 1995. In these cases the old rules still apply (reg. 20(1) and (3) of the Disability Working Allowance and Income Support (General) Amendment Regulations 1995 (see p. 374)). In addition, full income support will be paid where a claimant appeals after failing his first all work test if he had been incapable of work for 28 weeks or in receipt of invalidity benefit or severe disablement allowance immediately before April 13, 1995 (reg. 19(5), see p. 375).

Note the possibility of invoking para. (3) if the conditions of paras. (2) or (2A) are not met.

Paragraph (3)

The list of categories in Sched. 1 of those not required to be available is a closed one. The old Supplementary Benefit (Conditions of Entitlement) Regulations contained an "analogous circumstances" provision. This is a limited replacement, in that it allows a claimant who is not actually available for work to receive a reduced amount of benefit. The test is of hardship (not exceptional or severe hardship) to any member of the family (as defined in s.137(1) of the Contributions and Benefits Act; 1986 Act, s.20(11)) or the claimant. Since the decision on whether hardship will (not might) result from the non-payment of income support is for the AO, a SSAT will be able to substitute its opinion on appeal. Students deemed to be unavailable and those who would be found to be available anyway are excluded.

If the claimant qualifies for income support under para. (3) the rate is reduced by 40 per cent. of the appropriate personal allowance under reg. 22, with the possibility of a 20 per cent. reduction in limited circumstances (reg. 22(5)).

Persons treated as available for employment

9.—(1) Except in a case to which regulation 10 (circumstances in which claimants are not to be treated as available for employment) applies, a claimant shall be treated as available for employment if, and only if—

    (a) he is available to be employed within the meaning of section 17(1)(a)(i) of the Social Security Act [SSCBA, s.57(1)(a)(i)] or Regulations made under it (requirement to be available to be employed for the purposes of unemployment benefit) in employment to which regulation 7 applies (meaning of employment); or

    (b) he is normally engaged for less than the number of hours prescribed in paragraph (c) of regulation 7 in respect of him in employment to which that regulation applies, and he is available, within the meaning of section 17(1)(a)(i) [SSCBA, s.57(1)(a)(i)] or Regulations made under it, for such further number of hours which would in aggregate with the number of hours for which he is normally engaged, be not less than the number of hours prescribed in paragraph (c) of regulation 7 for his case; or

(c) he satisfies the conditions in paragraph (2) and is attending—
  (i) a course of education at an establishment recognised by the Secretary of State as being, or as comparable to, a school or college; or
  (ii) a course of training or instruction analogous to a course for which a training allowance would be payable,
  and, in either case, he is prepared to terminate the course immediately if a suitable vacancy becomes available to him.

(2) The conditions referred to in paragraph (1) (c) are that either—

(a) the claimant was, for a continuous period of not less than three months falling immediately before the commencement date,—
  (i) in receipt of a qualifying benefit; or
  (ii) on a course of training or instruction organised by or on behalf of ['Scottish Enterprise, Highlands and Islands Enterprise or] the [²Secretary of State for Employment] as part of the Youth Training Scheme [²or Youth Training]; or

(b) during the period of six months falling immediately before the commencement date the claimant was—
  (i) for a period, or periods in aggregate, of not less than three months in receipt of a qualifying benefit or on a course of training or instruction organised by or on behalf of ['Scottish Enterprise, Highlands and Islands Enterprise or] the [²Secretary of State for Employment] as part of the Youth Training Scheme [²or Youth Training]; and
  (ii) after the period referred to in head (i) of this sub-paragraph or, in the case of periods in aggregate, after the first such period and throughout the remainder of the six months for which that head did not apply to him, engaged in appropriate work;

and that the period of three months referred to in sub-paragraph (*a*) or, as the case may be, the period of six months referred to in sub-paragraph (*b*) fell wholly after the terminal date.

(3) In this regulation—

"appropriate work" means remunerative work for the purpose of section 20(3)(c) of the Act [SSCBA, s. 124(1)(c) (conditions of entitlement to income support) or other work the emoluments from which are such as to disentitle the person engaged in it from a qualifying benefit;

"commencement date" means the date on which the claimant first attended the course of education or course of training or instruction;

"course" means a course in the pursuit of which the time spent receiving instruction or tuition, undertaking supervised study, examination or practical work or taking part in any exercise, experiment or project for which provision is made in the curriculum of the course does not, subject to paragraph (4), exceed 21 hours a week;

"qualifying benefit" means unemployment benefit or [³short-term incapacity benefit] or, in the case of a claimant who is required to be available for employment under section 20(3)(d) of the Act [SSCBA, s. 124(1)(d) (conditions of entitlement to income support) or who is not so required under paragraph 5 of Schedule 1 (persons not required to be available by reason of sickness or incapacity), income support.

(4) In calculating the time spent in pursuit of a course for the purpose of this regulation, no account shall be taken of time occupied by meal breaks or spent on unsupervised study, whether undertaken on or off the premises of the educational establishment or place of instruction or training.

Income Support (General) Regulations 1987

AMENDMENTS

1. Enterprise (Scotland) Consequential Amendments Order 1991 (S.I. 1991 No. 387), art. 9 (April 1, 1991).
2. Income Support (General) Amendment Regulations 1991 (S.I. 1991 No. 236), reg. 2 (April 8, 1991).
3. Disability Working Allowance and Income Support (General) Amendment Regulations 1995 (S.I. 1995 No. 482), reg. 7 (April 13, 1995).

DEFINITIONS

"claimant"—see reg. 2(1).
"Social Security Act"—*ibid.*
"training allowance"—*ibid.*
"Youth Training Scheme or Youth Training"—*ibid.*

GENERAL NOTE

Where a claimant is required to be available for employment (and is not deemed to be unavailable by reg. 10) reg. 9 provides an exhaustive test of availability. Any one of the three alternative conditions specified in para. (1) is both sufficient and necessary.

Paragraph (1)

The main test under sub-para. (a) is of availability for unemployment benefit purposes for the number of hours required by reg. 7 (normally 24). This question is listed in reg. 64(3)(c) of the Adjudication Regulations, so that if the income support AO considers that entitlement depends on that question and it cannot be determined immediately, he can proceed on the assumption that the decision of the unemployment benefit AO will be adverse to the claimant (reg. 64(1)). If the question is eventually decided in favour of the claimant, entitlement to income support will be adjusted (reg. 69(4)).

The basic principle of unemployment benefit law is that the person must be willing and able to accept at once any offer of suitable employment *(R(U) 1/53)*. Regulations allow availability on 24 hours notice in some circumstances (see Bonner *et al., Non-Means Tested Benefits: the Legislation* for the details). *CIS 142/1993* decides that the 24 hours should start to run when the claimant would receive notification of the job (in that case by a telephone call from his parents in the evening as he was doing voluntary work during the day). There is some authority that availability requires some active steps to draw attention to the person's availability *(R(U) 5/80)*, but this element is now covered by the test of actively seeking employment (see reg. 10A).

Sub-para. (b) applies to people with reduced working capacity. If they normally work for less than the hours they are capable of, they are treated as available if available for enough hours to make up the difference to 24.

Sub-para. (c) incorporates the 21 hour rule through the definition of "course" in para. (3). See the notes to reg. 7(2) of the Conditions of Entitlement Regulations in the 1987 edition for some of the history. Only the structure is sketched in here. Given the exclusion from benefit of 16 and 17 year-olds, the definition of "student" especially for those over 18 (reg. 61) and the expansion of Employment Training, the future role of the 21 hour rule is likely to be restricted. The rule also allows claimants to escape from the relevant education rule (see reg. 13(f)).

In order to benefit from this provision the claimant must be attending a course of education or training where the "contact hours" (carefully defined in para. (3)) are not more than 21 per week. The claimant must also be prepared to terminate the course immediately a suitable vacancy (for work) comes up. At this point there appears to be a wide-ranging opportunity for the unemployed to pursue part-time education while claiming benefit. The restriction comes in with the conditions of para. (2). Note also at this point that anyone who falls into the category of "student" cannot use the 21 hour rule because they are covered by reg. 10 and excluded by the opening words of para. (1).

Paragraph (2)

The main condition (sub-para. (a)) is that for the whole three months before the beginning of the course the claimant was either in receipt of a qualifying benefit or on a YTS course. Qualifying benefit means short-term incapacity benefit, unemployment benefit or income support while unemployed or sick. (Note the transitional provision for sickness benefit in reg. 19(1) of the Disability Working Allowance and Income Support (General) Amendment Regulations 1995, p. 374.) This is intended to introduce a requirement that the claimant should be primarily unemployed, and not simply wishing to continue to study on benefit. A person who leaves school in the summer will not be entitled to income support until the first Monday in September (see reg. 12) and thus will not have had three months on benefit in time to start a course before January.

"Commencement date" is defined in para. (3). If a claimant starts (say in September) a course whose contact hours are below 12, so as to be outside the definition of relevant education, and after three months on benefit increases the hours, it will often be very difficult to decide when the claimant first attended "the" course. The official view is that a mere change in hours does not mean that a new course starts, so that the three months benefit would have been at the wrong time, but that if the subjects taken change there will be a new course (*Adjudication Officers' Guide*, para. 25529). Receipt of benefit means entitlement to benefit, whether benefit is actually in payment or not (*R(SB) 12/87*).

Under sub-para. (b) a claimant can mix qualifying benefit, YTS and work over the six months, providing that the qualifying benefit and YTS add up to at least three months.

Paragraphs (3) and (4)
These definitions have already been discussed. Note that in computing the 21 hours for the purpose of the definition of "course" any number of courses can be put together, providing that they are properly educational and not recreational (*CSB 761/1986*). It does not matter that one course might be in the evening. In a decision relating to the definition of "student" in the supplementary benefit regulations (*CSB 1010/1989*) a Commissioner has said that "unsupervised study" should not be confused with study done not in the physical presence of the supervisor. Study can be supervised if set by the supervisor and done privately by the student in his own time. It is not clear that this approach fits the overall structure of paras.(3) and (4), particularly considering the level of course involved. In *R(F) 1/93* the Commissioner holds that, where schools are concerned, supervised study "would normally be understood to import the presence or close proximity of a teacher or tutor". The claimant's daughter did not receive such supervision and so was not in full–time education for the purposes of reg. 5 of the Child Benefit (General) Regulations 1976. The definition of "unsupervised study" would, therefore, seem to depend largely on the level of course involved.

Circumstances in which claimants are not to be treated as available for employment

10.—(1) A claimant shall not be treated as available for employment if he is a person to whom any one of the following sub-paragraphs applies—

(a) after a situation in any [³ . . .] employment has been properly notified to him as vacant or about to become vacant he has without good cause refused or failed to apply for that situation or refused to accept that situation when offered to him, and that situation is still vacant or open to application;

(b) he has neglected to avail himself of a reasonable opportunity of [³ . . .] employment and that opportunity is still available to him;

(c) he has failed to avail himself of a reasonable opportunity of short-term work which is available in the area in which he lives, and—

　(i) he is aged 18 or over but under 45;

　(ii) his partner, if any, is aged under 45;

　(iii) there is no child or young person who is a member of his family;

　(iv) his partner or, as the case may be, the claimant herself is not pregnant; and

　(v) neither he nor his partner, if any, is mentally or physically disabled;

(d) [³subject to paragraphs (4) to (6),] he has placed restrictions on the nature, hours, rate of remuneration or locality or other conditions of employment which he is prepared to accept and as a consequence of those restrictions he has no reasonable prospects of securing employment; but this sub-paragraph shall not apply where—

　(i) he is prevented from having reasonable prospects of securing employment consistent with those restrictions only as a result of adverse industrial conditions in the locality or localities concerned which may reasonably be regarded as temporary, and, having regard to all the circumstances, personal and other, the restrictions which he imposes are reasonable; or

[³(ii) the restrictions are nevertheless reasonable in view of his physical or mental condition; or

(iii) he has a usual occupation and those restrictions relate to it and are consistent with conditions which are usual in that occupation;]

(e) having failed to comply with a written notice given or sent to him by or on behalf of the Secretary of State or the [⁶Secretary of State for Employment] requesting him to report at a specified time, place and date to an officer of the Department of Social Security, the Department of Employment [⁶or a local education authority] for an interview in connection with his prospects of employment, he fails without good cause to comply with the requirements of a further notice given or sent to him within 14 days of the date specified in the first notice by or on behalf of the Secretary of State [². . .] and requesting him to report as aforesaid at a time, place and date specified in the further notice for the purpose of such an interview;

(f) he has been disallowed unemployment benefit on the ground that he failed to claim in the manner prescribed by regulation 4 of the Social Security (Claims and Payments) Regulations 1987 (making a claim for benefit) by virtue of the fact that the form approved by the Secretary of State for the purpose of claiming was not duly completed so far as it related to his availability for employment; or

(g) he is a share fisherman within the meaning of the Social Security (Mariners' Benefits) Regulations 1975 who is not entitled to unemployment benefit under the Social Security Act [SSCBA] because he has failed to satisfy the additional condition for receipt of that benefit in paragraph (5) or (8) of regulation 8 of those Regulations (that he performed no work as a sea-going or on-shore share fisherman and that he has not neglected to avail himself of a reasonable opportunity of employment as a fisherman);

[⁴(h) he is a student during the period of study, other than—

(i) one to whom paragraph 1, 2, [⁵7 to 7B], 11, 16 or 20 of Schedule 1 applies (persons not required to be available for employment) but in the case of paragraph 20 only where the student is a person to whom regulation 70(3)(a) applies (certain persons from abroad); or

(ii) one who has a partner who is also a student, if either he or his partner is treated as responsible for a child or young person, but this exception shall apply only for the period of the summer vacation appropriate to his course.]

(2) A determination that a claimant is not to be treated as available for employment—

(a) under paragraph (1)(a) shall apply for a period not exceeding—

(i) the period during which the situation in question remains vacant; or

(ii) [¹26] weeks,

whichever is the shorter;

(b) under paragraph (1)(b), shall apply for a period not exceeding—

(i) the period during which the opportunity is still available to him; or

(ii) [¹26] weeks,

whichever is the shorter;

(c) under paragraph (1)(c)—

(i) shall not apply until the claimant has been given 14 days' notice in writing and that period has expired, and then

(ii) shall apply for a period not exceeding the period during which the opportunity is still available to him or, if shorter, the period of [[1]26] weeks;

(d) under paragraph (1)(d), shall apply for so long as the claimant has no reasonable prospect of employment as a consequence of the restrictions referred to in that paragraph;

(e) under paragraph (1)(e), shall apply on the day specified in the further notice and any subsequent day falling before the day on which the claimant reports to an officer of the Department of Social Security, the Department of Employment [[6]or a local education authority] at the place specified in the notice and there attends an interview in connection with his prospects of employment or before the day on which the Secretary of State or, as the case may be, the [[6]Secretary of State for Employment] rescinds the further notice, whichever event first occurs;

(f) under paragraph (1)(f), shall apply for so long as the claimant fails to claim in the manner referred to in that paragraph;

(g) under paragraph (1)(g) or (h), shall apply for so long as that paragraph continues to apply to him.

(3) In this regulation—

(a) [[3] . . .];

(b) "properly notified" means notified by an officer acting on behalf of the Secretary of State, or by the [[6]Secretary of State for Employment], a local education authority or some other recognised agency, or by or on behalf of an employer.

[[3](4) A determination that paragraph (1)(d) does not apply by reason of the circumstances prescribed in head (iii) of that paragraph shall have effect for a period not exceeding 13 weeks beginning—

(a) in a case where the claimant is not entitled to unemployment benefit and has not been entitled to that benefit for any day since he was last in remunerative work, on the first day for which the claimant makes a claim for income support since the last day on which he was in remunerative work, or vocational training in his usual occupation, or incapable of work;

(b) in any other case, on the first day for which a claim for unemployment benefit is made since the claimant was last in remunerative work.

(5) In determining the length of the period for the purposes of paragraph (4) regard shall be had to—

(a) the claimant's usual occupation and any relevant skills and qualifications which he has acquired;

(b) the length of the periods during which he has undergone training relevant to his usual occupation;

(c) the length of the periods during which he has been employed in his usual occupation and the period since he was last so employed, and

(d) the availability and location of employment in his usual occupation.

(6) For the purposes of paragraph (1)(d), in deciding whether a claimant has no reasonable prospects of securing employment regard shall be had, in particular, to the length of the period during which he has been unemployed.]

AMENDMENTS

1. Income Support (General) Amendment Regulations 1988 (S.I. 1988 No. 663), reg. 7 (April 11, 1988).
2. Employment Act 1989, Sched. 5 paras. 1 and 4 (November 16, 1989).
3. Income Support (General) Amendment No. 2 Regulations 1989 (S.I. 1989 No. 1323), reg. 5 (October 9, 1989).
4. Social Security Benefits (Student Loans and Miscellaneous Amendments) Regulations 1990 (S.I. 1990 No. 1549), reg. 5(3) (September 1, 1990).

5. Income-Related Benefits Amendment Regulations 1990 (S.I. 1990 No. 1657), reg. 5(2) (September 1, 1990).

6. Income Support (General) Amendment Regulations 1991 (S.I. 1991 No. 236), reg. 2 (April 8, 1991).

DEFINITIONS

"claimant"—see reg. 2(1).
"child"—see, 986 Act, s.20(11) (SSCBA, s.137(1)).
"family"—*ibid.*
"partner"—see reg. 2(1).
"period of study"—*ibid.*
"student"—*ibid.*, reg. 61.
"young person"—*ibid.*, reg. 14.

GENERAL NOTE

Reg. 10 deems certain claimants not to be available for work, and thus not entitled to income support even though they might otherwise be treated as available under reg. 9. Apart from the case of students (para. (1)(h)), this provision constitutes the major control in the income support system over voluntary unemployment. See now also reg. 10A on actively seeking employment. A claimant denied entitlement in this way has access to the system of crisis loans under the social fund, because the applicant there does not have to be entitled to income support, but has to have insufficient resources for his needs.

Para. (1) defines the situations in which reg. 10 will apply.

Para. (2) says how long the disentitlement lasts.

Reg. 10 has been amended in consequence of the amendments to unemployment benefit law in and under the Social Security Act 1989. However, the new income support rules are at some points significantly different from the UB rules and the precise terms of the regulations must be examined carefully.

Paragraph (1)(a)

Here the word "suitable" has been removed from in front of "employment," as it has been from what was s.20(1)(b) of the 1975 Act (now SSCBA, s.28(1)(b)). The old partial definition of "suitable" in para.(3)(a) has been removed, as has the old form of s.20(4) of the 1975 Act (SSCBA, s.28(5)). But two additional conditions introduced into the UB disqualification provisions are absent from the income support rules.

The first is that s.20A(1)(now SSCBA, s.29(1)) provides that a claimant is not to be disqualified for UB by reason only of his refusal to seek or accept a situation vacant because of a trade dispute or (for the permitted period—up to 13 weeks: Social Security (Unemployment, Sickness and Invalidity Benefit) Regulations 1983, reg. 12F) a situation outside his usual occupation at his usual pay. The introduction of the permitted period is a significant restriction on the previous case law on suitability, but even this is not extended to income support claimants. The effect of para. (1)(a) is that if any vacancy is properly notified to the claimant he runs the risk of losing his entire entitlement to income support by not applying for or taking up that vacancy. It may be that the authorities who can "properly notify" vacancies (para. (3)(b)) will normally only notify claimants of vacancies which are appropriate under UB law, but this cannot be guaranteed. The main safeguard must be the concept of good cause.

The meaning of "good cause" is the second instance of a difference between UB and income support law. Section 20(4)(b) of the 1975 Act (now SSCBA, s.28(5)(b)) allows regulations to prescribe when a person is or is not to be treated as having good cause. The new reg. 12E of the 1983 Regulations does not give an exhaustive definition of good cause, but does provide that a person is to be treated as having good cause for refusing a vacancy notified by an agency or by or on behalf of an employer unless it is a job to which he is entitled to return or the vacancy was also notified by the Secretary of State. There is no such prescription for income support, where the ordinary meaning of good cause must be applied. In the past there has not been much need to separate good cause from suitability, and it seems that if a job would not be suitable in the particular circumstances of the claimant then he has good cause to refuse it (*cf. R(U) 20/60, R(U) 5/71* and *R(U) 2/77*). In *Crewe v. Social Security Commissioner* [1982] 2 All E. R. 745, 751 Slade L. J. suggested that good cause meant "reasonable cause" and involved a lower burden than showing "just cause," which required the balancing of individual interests against the interests of all the contributors to the National Insurance Fund. Personal and domestic circumstances, religious or moral beliefs, the location of employment and the level of remuneration will all be relevant. But the fact that income from work may be lower than income on benefit has in the past not been accepted as making a vacancy unsuitable *(R(U) 10/61* and *R(U) 15/62)*.

The question whether para. (1)(a) applies is one which the AO need not determine immediately (Adjudication Regulations, reg. 64(1), (3)(f), but in view of the difference from UB law it may often be the case that the income support AO ought to make a decision without waiting for an UB decision.

The disentitlement lasts for the shorter of the period for which the situation remains vacant or 26 weeks (para. (2)(a)).

Paragraph (1)(b)

Here also the word "suitable" has been removed. In the past the notions of "reasonable opportunity" and "neglect" have been considered to bring in all the factors which would be raised by a good cause exception. In the equivalent UB provision (1975 Act, s.20(1)(c); SSCBA, s.28(1)(c)), a good cause exception has been inserted by the 1989 Act, which will bring in reg. 12E of the 1983 Regulations for that purpose, but there is no such exception in para. (1)(b).

Although reg. 64 of the Adjudication Regulations (reg. 64(3)(c)) applies to this question, for the same reasons as in relation to para. (1)(a) it must be used with caution.

The disentitlement lasts for the shorter of the period the opportunity remains open or 26 weeks (para. (2)(b)).

Paragraph (1)(c)

This is the remnant of the notorious "four-week rule." See the notes to reg. 8(1)(e) of the Conditions of Entitlement Regulations in the 1987 edition for some history. The conditions for the application of the rule at heads (i) to (v) are largely self-explanatory.

"Mentally or physically disabled" has no special meaning. Note that the element of discretion retained in reg. 8(1)(e) of the old Conditions of Entitlement Regulations has disappeared. The actual test is a strange one. Only short-term work is relevant (young claimants at the seaside are perceived as a problem). "Failure to avail" means that the opportunity must have been available to the claimant *(R(SB) 10/83)* and probably that the job was suitable *(R(U) 5/71)*. What normality of residence is necessary to say that a claimant "lives" in an area? On area, see *R(SB) 8/84*. The disentitlement cannot apply until the claimant has been given 14 days' notice, which has expired. Then it lasts for the shorter of the period of availability of the opportunity or 26 weeks (para. (2)(c)).

Paragraph (1)(d)

The amendments to the rule on unreasonable restrictions are in line with the changes in UB law, in the new reg. 7B of the 1983 Regulations. The main alterations are to head (ii), which now extends to mental as well as physical conditions, and to head (iii), which replaces a test of general reasonableness with a test restricted to what is usual in the claimant's usual occupation. Paras. (4) and (5) restrict the length of time for which a claimant can escape under head (iii) to a maximum of 13 weeks. Para. (6) confirms that what are reasonable prospects of employment depends particularly on how long the claimant has been unemployed.

Reg. 64 of the Adjudication Regulations applies to the question whether para. (1)(d) applies, and here uniformity with the UB decision is possible. The disentitlement lasts for as long as the claimant has no reasonable prospect of employment as a result of the restrictions.

Paragraph (1)(e)

This is the sanction for not attending interviews (*e.g.* for Restart or by a Claimant Adviser) at the UBO, Benefits Agency, etc., about job prospects. Two notices must have been sent within 14 days of each other. There is an escape for good cause (*e.g.* illness, short notice, change of address, etc.). The disentitlement continues until the claimant attends for interview (para. (2)(e)). In *CIS 374/ 1993* the claimant tried to rearrange the first interview date as he had another appointment, but was told this was not possible. He did not attend that interview or the second one and his income support was stopped. The Commissioner decides that because para. (1)(e) refers to "failure to comply with a written notice", the terms of the notice had to be considered. The first notice envisaged the possibility of a rearranged interview. As the claimant had a good reason for not attending the first interview and had contacted the Department, he had complied with the notice. Thus the second notice was not valid and provided no ground for review of the claimant's income support.

Paragraph (1)(f)

This is the sanction for failing to answer the questions on the "initial test" of availability. It turns simply on whether unemployment benefit has been disallowed on this ground. Disentitlement lasts as long as the unemployment benefit claim remains defective (para. (2)(f)).

Paragraph (1)(g)

Reg. 64 of the Adjudication Regulations applies (reg. 64(3)(c)). The disentitlement lasts as long as the provision applies (para. (2)(g)).

Paragraph (1)(h)

In combination with the definition of "period of study" in reg. 2(1), reg. 10(1)(h) excludes students (defined in reg. 61) from entitlement to income support from the beginning of their course to the end and through all the vacations within the period of study. See the notes to reg. 61 for discussion of the definitions. This is part of the Government's policy to remove student support from the social security budget and to introduce student loans.

The exclusions in heads (i) and (ii) preserve the potential entitlement of various categories who might be vulnerable to hardship. Those covered by head (i) are lone parents, single people with a foster child, students who qualify for the disability or severe disability premium, disabled students with an existing entitlement on September 1, 1990, deaf students, recipients of a training allowance, refugees, and certain persons from abroad. Under head (ii) student couples with a child may claim, but only in the summer vacation. There was a late concession to exclude deaf students from the deeming of non-availability, but the Government was not prepared to accept the recommendation of the Social Security Advisory Committee that the Secretary of State should have a discretion to award income support to any student in the summer vacation in order to avoid hardship. Money has been provided to educational institutions for use in cases of hardship.

The disentitlement lasts as long as the provision applies (para. (2)(g)).

Paragraph (2)

Note the maximum disentitlement in many cases has been extended to 26 weeks in line with the maximum disqualification for unemployment benefit in s.28 of the Contributions and Benefits Act (1975 Act, s.20).

Paragraphs (4) to (6)

See notes to para. (1)(d).

[¹Actively seeking employment

10A.—(1) A claimant shall not be required to be a person who is actively seeking employment where, by virtue of regulation 8 (persons not required to be available for employment), he is not required to be available for employment.

[²(2) A claimant, other than a person to whom regulation 10(1)(h) applies, shall not be required to be a person who is actively seeking employment during any week in which—
   (a) the claimant—
      (i) is a single woman and is pregnant, and
      (ii) the adjudication officer is satisfied that, unless income support is paid, the claimant will suffer hardship; or
   (b) the claimant is a member of a married or unmarried couple where—
      (i) one member of that couple is pregnant, and
      (ii) the adjudication officer is satisfied that, unless income support is paid, that member will suffer hardship; or
   (c) the claimant is a member of a married or unmarried couple where—
      (i) he or his partner, or both of them, are responsible for a child or young person, and
      (ii) the adjudication officer is satisfied that, unless income support is paid, the child or young person will suffer hardship; or
   (d) the claimant's applicable amount includes a disability premium under Part III of Schedule 3 (premiums) and the adjudication officer is satisfied that, unless income support is paid, the person, whether the claimant or his partner, who satisfies the additional condition in paragraph 12 of that Schedule for the award of the premium will suffer hardship.]

(3) Subject to paragraph (4), a claimant shall be treated as actively seeking employment in any week if, and only if, he takes such steps in that week as he would be required to take under regulations made under sub-section (2)(aa)(i)

of section 17 of the Social Security Act [SSCBA, s.57(3)(b)(i)] in order to be recorded as actively seeking employed earner's employment in that week for the purposes of that section.

(4) A claimant shall be treated as actively seeking employment in respect of any week for which he is, or would have been had he made a claim for unemployment benefit, deemed to have been actively seeking employment under regulations made under section 17(1)(a)(i) of the Social Security Act [SSCBA, s.57(1)(a)(i)].

(5) For the purposes of this regulation, in relation to a claimant, "week" has the meaning prescribed in regulations made under section 17(2)(aa)(ii) of the Social Security Act [SSCBA, s.57(3)(b)(ii)] which—

(a) if he is entitled to unemployment benefit, applies in his case; and

(b) if he is not entitled to unemployment benefit, would have applied in his case if each of the days for which he claims income support would have fallen within a period of interruption of employment had he claimed unemployment benefit under the Act in respect of those days.]

AMENDMENTS

1. Income Support (General) Amendment) No. 2 Regulations 1989 (S.I. 1989 No. 1323), reg. 6 (October 9, 1989).
2. Income Support (General) Amendment (No. 3) Regulations 1992 (S.I. 1992 No. 2804), reg. 2 (December 3, 1992).

GENERAL NOTE

Reg. 10A deals with the application of the controversial actively seeking employment test introduced under s.20(3)(d)(i) of the 1986 Act, now s.124(1)(d)(i) of the Contributions and Benefits Act. "Employment" is defined in reg. 7(2). Reg. 64 of the Adjudication Regulations applies to the question of whether the test applies under paras. (3) and (4)(reg. 64(3)(g)).

In an administrative change connected with the December 1992 amendment to para. (2), the practice of issuing a warning letter to a claimant who appears not to have been seeking work actively in the preceding two weeks will be restricted to cases where the interviewing officer considers that the claimant has misunderstood earlier advice on the appropriate steps to take. In other cases, where the claimant does not satisfy the interviewing officer that he has taken sufficient steps in the preceding two weeks, the question of whether the test is met for those weeks will be submitted to the AO. In the meantime, a decision that income support is not payable will be given, under reg. 64 of the Adjudication Regulations, subject to the possibility of a hardship payment. If the AO's decision goes in favour of the claimant, the income support disallowance is reviewed (Adjudication Regulations, reg. 69(4)(b)). This change of practice may well produce many more disallowances and more appeals, because in the past the vast majority of claimants produced satisfactory evidence of job search after receiving a warning. From October 1989 to May 1990, 28,910 warning letters were issued, but only 5,161 cases of doubt were referred to the AO (Report of the Social Security Advisory Committee on the Income Support (General) Amendment (No. 3) Regulations 1992, Cm 2099, para. 14).

Paragraph (1)

The test does not apply to anyone who is not required to be available for employment under reg. 8. This covers all the categories set out in Sched. 1 (apart from students caught by reg. 10(1)(h)), including, for example, lone parents, some pregnant women, anyone in receipt of a training allowance and anyone aged at least 60. In addition, those assisted by reg. 8(2) (decision on capacity to work under appeal) or (3) (hardship) cannot have the test applied to them. The relationship with reg. 8(3) is quite complex. Reg. 8(3) can only apply where the person is not actually available for work. Then if hardship would result to the claimant or any member of the family, of whatever category, from non-payment of income support, the requirement of availability is lifted, although only a reduced rate of income support is payable. As a consequence reg. 10A cannot apply.

Paragraph (2)

The initial form of para. (2) lifted the test whenever the failure to pay income support would cause hardship to the claimant or a member of the family. The Government's view was that this

81

provision allowed some claimants to make only token efforts to satisfy the test and, by relying on hardship payments, to continue to receive benefit without any real intention of seeking work. As a result it put forward revised conditions for hardship payments. The Social Security Advisory Committee (see the Report cited above) recommended that the amendment should not be proceeded with while the administrative changes were monitored. The Government rejected this recommendation, but expanded the limited categories of those who can receive hardship payments from December 1992.

There is an initial problem that if the requirement of availability is lifted under reg. 8(3), the actively seeking work test cannot be applied at all. Thus if a claimant is not available for work at all, hardship payments are payable without limit. Para. (2) only bites on a claimant who was available for work (in the sense of being prepared to accept at once any offer of a suitable job), but did not take sufficient steps to seek work. It seems odd that in what seem to be the "worse" cases hardship payments are more freely available.

In order to qualify under para. (2) a claimant must come within one of the four categories set out. Sub-paras. (a) and (b) relate to pregnancy. A claimant who is incapable of work due to pregnancy or is in the 11 weeks before and eight weeks after the week of confinement is not required to be available for work (Sched. 1, para. 9). Sub-paras. (a) and (b) apply during pregnancy outside that period where there will be hardship if income support is not paid. Sub-para. (a) applies to a "single woman." The intention (supported by the SSAC Report) is that sub-paras. (a) and (b) between them should cover all cases of pregnancy, so that the words should be taken to mean "a female single claimant," rather than an unmarried woman. Otherwise married, but separated, women would be excluded. Under sub-para. (c), all couples who are responsible for children or young persons are excluded. Under para. 1 of Sched. 1 a single parent with responsibility for a child is not required to be available for work, but is required to be available once the last child turns into a young person. Such a person receives no protection under para. (2) when a couple does. Sub-para. (d), on the disability premium, is straightforward. The Government rejected arguments for the inclusion of other categories on the basis that in deciding under reg. 12B of the Social Security (Unemployment, Sickness and Invalidity Benefit) Regulations 1983 whether a claimant had taken reasonable steps to find work an AO has to take into account all the circumstances of the case. But that does not help the claimant while the AO is making up his mind.

As under reg. 8(3), there is a general test that hardship (not severe hardship) will (not might) result if income support is not paid. In both cases, income support is payable subject to the 40 per cent. reduction under reg. 22 (reg. 22(5)), with the possibility of a 20 per cent. reduction in limited circumstances.

Paragraph (3)

The general rule, if the test applies, is that the claimant satisfies it only if he takes the steps that he would have to take to satisfy the UB test. These steps are defined in reg. 12B of the Social Security (Unemployment, Sickness and Invalidity Benefit) Regulations 1983. The requirement is to take such of the steps which are reasonable in the claimant's case as offer him his best prospects of receiving offers of employment. Reg. 12B(4) of the 1983 Regulations lists some of the actions which can count as "steps" and reg. 12B(2) lists some of the factors to be taken into account in deciding whether a claimant has taken reasonable steps in any week. This is a very convoluted test, and income support AOs are unlikely to feel confident enough to make an immediate decision, even if the claimant has not claimed UB, but will defer the decision under reg. 64 of the Adjudication Regulations for a decision from the UB AO.

Note that a person who is assisted by para. (4) escapes the requirement under para. (3).

Paragraph (4)

A person who is or would be deemed to be actively seeking employment for UB purposes is also deemed to be doing so for income support purposes. The UB rules are contained in reg. 12D of the 1983 Regulations. These provide for deeming of seeking employment in the first week of claim, the last week of unemployment, up to two weeks a year of holiday away from home, some weeks associated with training courses or the enterprise allowance, and some cases involving lifeboatmen, firemen and emergency duties. Most of these categories can be quite easily applied in an income support case. The first week of claim refers to a claim for UB. Presumably, under para. (4) the week in which an income support claim was made can be substituted.

Paragraph (5)

"Week" is defined for these purposes in reg. 12C of the 1983 Regulations.

Registration for employment

11.—(1) Subject to [²paragraphs (2) and (2A)], a claimant who—

(a) is aged less than 18; and

(b) is required to be available for employment for the purposes of section 20(3)(d)(i) of the Act [SSCBA, s.124(1)(d)(i)] (conditions of entitlement to income support);

must also be registered for employment in accordance with paragraph (3).

(2) A claimant other than one to whom regulation 10(1)(h) (circumstances in which claimants are not to be treated as available for employment) applies and who would, but for this paragraph, be required to be registered for employment in accordance with paragraph (3), shall not be required so to register for employment if—

[²(a) an adjudication officer has determined for the purposes of section 171B of the Contributions and Benefits Act (the own occupation test) that that claimant is not incapable of work; and]

(b) the claimant's medical practitioner continues to supply evidence of his incapacity for work in accordance with regulation 2 of the Social Security (Medical Evidence) Regulations 1976 (evidence of incapacity); and

(c) the claimant has made and is pursuing an appeal against the determination of an adjudication officer that he is not so incapable.

[²(2A) A claimant, other than one to whom paragraph (2) or regulation 10(1)(h) applies, who would, but for this paragraph, be required to be registered for employment in accordance with paragraph (3), shall not be required so to register for employment if—

(a) an adjudication officer has determined for the purposes of section 171C of the Contributions and Benefits Act (the all work test) that that claimant is not incapable of work; and

(b) that claimant has made and is pursuing an appeal against that determination.]

(3) A claimant to whom paragraph (1) applies shall, except where the Secretary of State decides otherwise, be registered for employment by registering with the [¹ Secretary of State for Employment] or a local education authority.

AMENDMENTS

1. Income Support (General) Amendment Regulations 1991 (S.I. 1991 No. 236), reg. 2 (April 8, 1991).

2. Disability Working Allowance and Income Support (General) Amendment Regulations 1995 (S.I. 1995 No. 482), reg. 8 (April 13, 1995).

DEFINITIONS

"the Act"—see reg. 2(1).
"claimant"—*ibid.*

GENERAL NOTE

Registration for employment may be required in addition to availability (Contributions and Benefits Act, s.124(3); 1986 Act, s.20(4)). Reg. 11 prescribes it only for the under-18s who are required to be available for work. There are not many of these left.

Paragraphs (2) and (2A)
See the notes to reg. 8. There is similar transitional protection for claimants to whom reg. 11(2) applied on April 12, 1995 or who appeal against an AO's decision on incapacity made on or before April 12, 1995 (see reg. 20(2) and (3) of the Disability Working Allowance and Income Support (General) Amendment Regulations 1995, p. 374).

[¹Relevant Education

12.—(1) For the purposes of these Regulations a child or young person is to be treated as receiving relevant education if, and only if—

    (a) he is not receiving advanced education; but

    (b) he is receiving full-time education for the purposes of section 2 of the Child Benefit Act 1975 [SSCBA, s.142] (meaning of child) or, as the case may be, he is treated as a child for the purposes of that section.

(2) For the purposes of this regulation "receiving advanced education" means participating in any course (whether full-time or part-time)—

    (a) leading to a postgraduate degree or comparable qualification, a first degree or comparable qualification, a diploma of higher education, a higher national diploma, [²a higher national diploma or higher national certificate of either the Business & [³Technology] Education Council] or the Scottish Vocational Education Council or a teaching qualification; or

    (b) any other course which is a course of a standard above ordinary national diploma, [²a national diploma or national certificate of either the Business & [³Technology] Education Council or the Scottish Vocational Education Council], a general certificate of education (advanced level), a Scottish certificate of education [²(higher level)] or a Scottish certificate of sixth year studies.]

AMENDMENTS

1. Income Support (General) Amendment Regulations 1990 (S.I. 1990 No. 547), reg. 5 (April 9, 1990).

2. Income-related Benefits Schemes (Miscellaneous Amendments) (No. 3) Regulations 1992 (S.I. 1992 No. 2155), reg. 14 (October 5, 1992).

3. Income-related Benefits Schemes (Miscellaneous Amendments) (No. 4) Regulations 1993 (S.I. 1993 No. 2119), reg. 4 (October 4, 1993).

DEFINITIONS

    "child"—see 1986 Act, s.20(11) (SSCBA, s.137(1)).
    "young person"—see regs. 2(1) and 14.

GENERAL NOTE

    The general rule under s.124(1)(d)(ii) of the Contributions and Benefits Act (1986 Act. s.20(3)(d)(ii)) is that if a claimant is receiving relevant education he is not entitled to income support. Reg. 12 provides an exhaustive test of when a person is to be treated as receiving relevant education. The 1990 formulation is a tidying-up. Note that only a child or young person can qualify. There is a reference over to the child benefit legislation and the reg. 12 question is one which under reg. 64 of the Adjudication Regulations need not be determined immediately by the income support AO (reg. 64(3)(d)). The AO can proceed on the assumption that the child benefit decision will be adverse to the claimant in the income support sense, if it has not already been determined.

    See on the child benefit test, regs. 5, 6, 7, 7A, 7B, 7C and 7D of the Child Benefit (General) Regulations 1976 in Bonner *et al.*, *Non-Means Tested Benefits: the Legislation*. The effect used to be contained in reg. 10 of the old Supplementary Benefit (Conditions of Entitlement) Regulations (see 1987 edition of this book). Contact hours of at least 12 per week are required. Relevant education continues through temporary interruptions, like school holidays. When a person ceases actually to receive relevant education he is treated as doing so until the next terminal date: the first Monday in January, the first Monday after Easter Monday or the first Monday in September. From September 1988, there is the possibility of the person remaining a "child" for an extension period of 12 or 16 weeks beyond the terminal date, if registered for work or training (see also notes to reg. 13A).

    Note that reg. 13 allows certain claimants to recieve income support though in relevant education.

Circumstances in which persons in relevant education may be entitled to income support

    13.—(1) Notwithstanding that a person is to be treated as receiving relevant education under regulation 12 (relevant education) he shall, if paragraph (2) applies to him and he satisfies the other conditions of entitlement to income support, be entitled to income support.

(2) This paragraph applies to [³a person aged 16 or over but under 19 (hereinafter referred to as an eligible person)] who—

(a) is the parent of a child for whom he is treated as responsible under regulation 15 (circumstances in which a person is to be treated as responsible or not responsible for another) and who is treated as a member of his household under regulation 16 (circumstances in which a person is to be treated as being or not being a member of the household); or

(b) is severely mentally or physically handicapped and because of that he would be unlikely, even if he were available for employment, to obtain employment within the next 12 months; or

(c) has no parent nor any person acting in the place of his parents; or

[¹(d) of necessity has to live away from his [² parents and any] person acting in the place of his parents because—

   (i) he is estranged from his [² parents and that person]; or

   (ii) he is in physical or moral danger; or

   (iii) there is a serious risk to his physical or mental health;] or

[⁴(dd) has ceased to live in accommodation provided for him by a local authority under Part III of the Children Act 1989 (local authority support for children and families) and is of necessity living away from his parents and any person acting in place of his parents;]

(e) is living away from his parents and any person acting in the place of his parents in a case where his parents are or, as the case may be, that person is unable financially to support him and—

   (i) chronically sick or mentally or physically disabled; or

   (ii) detained in custody pending trial or sentence upon conviction or under a sentence imposed by a court; or

   (iii) prohibited from entering or re-entering Great Britain; or

(f) attending a course of education to which regulation 9 (person treated as available for employment) applies and satisfies the other conditions of that regulation; or

(g) has completed or terminated such a course and while attending that course satisfied the other conditions of that regulation; or

(h) he is a person to whom paragraph 16 of Schedule 1 (refugees not required to be available for employment) applies.

(3) In this regulation—

[⁵(a) any reference to a person acting in the place of an eligible person's parents includes—

   (i) for the purposes of paragraph (2)(c), (d) and (dd), a reference to a local authority or voluntary organisation where the eligible person is being looked after by them under a relevant enactment or where the eligible person is placed by the local authority or voluntary organisation with another person, that other person whether or not a payment is made to him;

   (ii) for the purposes of paragraph (2)(e), the person with whom the person is so placed;]

(b) "chronically sick or mentally disabled" means, in relation to a person to whom that expression refers, a person—

   (i) in respect of whom the condition specified in paragraph 12(1) of Schedule 2 (additional condition for the higher pensioner and disability premiums) is satisfied; or

   (ii) in respect of whom an amount under article 26 of the Naval, Military and Air Forces etc. (Disablement and Death) Services Pension Order 1983 (provision of expenses in respect of appropriate aids for disabled living) is payable in respect of the cost of providing a vehicle, or maintaining a vehicle to a disabled person; or

(iii) who is substantially and permanently disabled.

AMENDMENTS

1. Family Credit and Income Support (General) Amendment Regulations 1989 (S.I. 1989 No. 1034), reg. 4 (July 10, 1989).
2. Income Support (General) Amendment Regulations 1991 (S.I. 1991 No. 236), reg. 5 (April 8, 1991).
3. Income Support (General) Amendment No. 4 Regulations 1991 (S.I. 1991 No. 1559), reg. 6 (August 5, 1991).
4. Income Support (General) Amendment Regulations 1992 (S.I. 1992 No. 468), reg. 3 (April 6, 1992).
5. Income Support (General) Amendment Regulations 1992 (S.I. 1992 No. 468), Sched., para. 2 (April 6, 1992).

DEFINITIONS

"child"—see 1986 Act, s.20(11) (SSCBA, s.137(1)).
"local authority"—see 1986 Act, s.84(1).
"relevant enactment"—see reg. 2(1), reg. 16(8)(a).

GENERAL NOTE

In the circumstances set out in para. (2) a claimant, if he satisfies the other conditions of entitlement, is entitled to income support although in relevant education. The regulation can only benefit someone aged from 16 to 18 inclusive. If a claimant satisfies any of para. (2)(a) to (e), he is not required to be available for work (Sched. 1, para. 10) and is exempted from the minimum age limit of 18 (Sched. 1A, para. 1). If he satisfies para. (2)(f) he will be deemed to be available under the 21-hour rule in reg. 9. If a claimant clearly satisfies one of these tests it may not be necessary to explore the question of relevant education. Most of the tests are taken over from reg. 11 of the old Supplementary Benefit (Conditions of Entitlement) Regulations.

Paragraph (2)
Sub-para. (a). A person of at least 16 who is the parent of a child who is in the same household can claim although in relevant education.
Sub-para. (b). Severe mental or physical handicap has no special meaning. Qualification for one of the higher levels of the care component of disability living allowance would certainly do, although the *Adjudication Officers' Guide* requires medical evidence to be provided in support of the claim (paras. 25741 and 25743).
Sub-para. (c). A parent presumably means a natural parent or an adoptive parent. A person acting in place of parents may include some informal relationships (but see note to para. (3)(a)(i) below). If a person is claiming child benefit in respect of a pupil, this would be a strong factor. However, a sponsor under the Immigration Act 1971 is not a person acting in place of parents. A sponsor's duties are restricted to the maintenance and accommodation of the dependant without recourse to public funds and there is no responsibility for other aspects of the dependant's life (*R(IS) 9/94*).
Para. (3)(a)(i) specifically includes for this purpose local authorities and voluntary organisations who are looking after children (what used to be known as having them in care), and foster parents with whom the pupil has been placed by *the* local authority or voluntary organisation. Since head (i) refers to pupils placed by "the", not "a", local authority or voluntary organisation, it would seem that head (i) only applies where the pupil is being looked after by the local authority or voluntary organisation. If they are simply assisting them without looking after them under a relevant enactment, the person with whom the pupil has been placed does not seem to fall within head (i). *CIS 447/1994* confirms this.
Sub-para. (d). See sub-para. (c) above for the meaning of parent and of person acting in place of a parent. The 1991 amendment to the effect that the pupil must be living away from parents *and* substitutes (and see head (i) on estrangement) was described by the DSS as technical. However, this was a change of substance. The previous form referred to living away from or estrangement from parents *or* substitutes. When the Conditions of Entitlement Regulations were in this form, *CSB 677/1983* decided that the pupil qualified if estranged from his parents even though he was not estranged from a person acting in their place. Now the pupil has to be living away from or estranged from both. See sub-para. (dd) on pupils leaving care.

Head (i). Estrangement has "connotations of emotional disharmony" *(R(SB) 2/87)* and it seems that it could exist although financial support is being provided. It is hard to see how estrangement from a local authority can exist, but the regulation is clear. The 1989 form of sub-para. (d) is an attempt to provide a test of "genuine estrangement." It is in some respects stricter than the previous form because in addition to showing estrangement, the person in relevant education must also show that as a result, at least partly, of that he has of necessity to live away from his parents and any substitute. It is obviously a matter of judgment when estrangement is serious enough to necessitate that the young person leaves home. There is perhaps some widening in the addition of two extra categories which may lead to a need to leave home.

Head (ii). Under head (ii), the meaning of "physical or moral danger" is again a matter of judgment. It is not a term of art with an established meaning. Obvious points are that a person can be in danger from himself or from others and that a danger can exist before any harm has actually occurred (see *Kelly v. Monklands District Council* [1986] S. L. T. 169 on the phrase "at risk of sexual or financial exploitation" in the Code of Guidance on Homelessness). Nor is the danger specified to be immediate, but the test will no doubt be whether the danger is sufficient to necessitate living away from parents or their substitute. The danger does not have to emanate from the pupil's parents. In *R(IS) 9/94* the claimant's parents were in a refugee camp in Ethiopia, having fled there after civil war broke out in Somalia. It is held that he had to live away from his parents in view of the situation in Somalia, as otherwise he was in physical or moral danger; in addition, there was a serious risk to his physical or mental health under head (iii).

Head (iii). Under head (iii) there is an echo of the "serious risk to health" test of reg. 30 of the Supplementary Benefit (Single Payments) Regulations. There was there some dispute about how closely a SSAT had to define the seriousness of the risk (compare *R(SB) 5/81* and *CSB 11/81* with *R(SB) 3/82* and *R(SB) 8/82*). The nature of the risk must no doubt be identified (as the danger must be under head (ii)) and some reason given why it is serious enough to necessitate living away from parents or their substitute. See *R(IS) 9/94* in the notes to head (ii).

See the transitional protection in reg. 13 of the Family Credit and Income Support (General) Amendment Regulations 1989.

Sub-para. (dd). This provision protects the entitlement of pupils leaving local authority care who need to live away from their parents and any substitute without the necessity of proving estrangement or moral danger or one of the other conditions in sub-para. (d). See the note to sub-para. (c) for the meaning of parent and person acting in place of a parent.

Sub-para. (e). Here the pupil must be living away from both parents and persons acting in place of parents, and they must be unable to provide financial support. The reason for this inability must be one of those listed. See para. (3)(b) for the definition of chronically sick or mentally or physically disabled. See the note to sub-para. (c) for the meaning of parent and person acting in place of a parent.

Head (iii). In *R(IS) 9/94* the claimant's parents who were in a refugee camp in Ethiopia had no leave to enter the U.K. at the date of the AO's decision. Under s.3 of the Immigration Act 1971 (subject to certain exceptions) all persons who are not British citizens require leave to enter the U.K. The claimant's parents were thus prohibited from entering Great Britain.

Sub-para. (f). This condition refers over to the 21-hour rule in reg. 9. If the claimant gets through that rule, he is not excluded by the relevant education rule.

Sub-para. (g). This provision applies to those who have done a course which satisfied the 21-hour rule.

Sub-para. (h). This is a special case of refugees.

Paragraph (3)

The previous form of sub-para. (a) (see the Supplement to the 1991 edition) remains in force in Scotland. The new form was introduced on April 6, 1992, as a consequence of the Children Act 1989.

See the note to para. (2)(c).

[¹Persons under 18 years

13A.—(1) A person to whom this regulation applies and for the period specified in relation to him is a person within the prescribed circumstances and period mentioned in section 20(3)(a) of the Act [SSCBA, s.124(1)(a)] (conditions of entitlement for persons under 18).

(2) This regulation applies to a person of or over the age of 16—

(a) to whom any paragraph of Schedule 1A (circumstances in which a person aged 16 or 17 is eligible for income support) applies; and

(b) for the period for which that paragraph applies or, if the relevant date specified in paragraph (3) falls within that period, for so much thereof [³as falls on or before] that date

(3) In the case of a person—

(a) to whom any paragraph in Part I (persons eligible until 18) of Schedule 1A applies, the relevant date [³is the day before the date] on which he attains the age of 18;

(b) other than one to whom sub-paragraph (a) applies, to whom any paragraph in Part II (persons eligible until the relevant date) of that Schedule applies, the relevant date is the date determined in accordance with paragraph (7).

(4) This regulation also applies to a person of, or over, the age of 16, other than one to whom any paragraph in [³Part I of Schedule 1A] applies who is—

(a) incapable of work and training under the youth training scheme [²or youth training] by reason of some disease or bodily or mental disablement if, in the opinion of a medical practitioner, that incapacity is likely to end within a period of less than 12 months; or

(b) [³. . .]

(c) a registered person who has been discharged from any institution to which the Prison Act 1952 applied or from custody under the Criminal Procedure (Scotland) Act 1975 after the relevant date determined in accordance with paragraph (7) and who is within the circumstances specified in Part II of Schedule 1A.

[⁴(d) a registered person who has ceased to live in accommodation provided for him by a local authority under Part III of the Children Act 1989 (local authority support for children and families) and is of necessity living away from his parents and any person acting in place of his parents.]

[³(5) Paragraph (4)(a) shall have effect for a period—

(a) beginning on the date on which paragraph (4)(a) applies to that person which first falls after the relevant date determined in accordance with paragraph (7); and

(b) ending on the day before the date on which that person attains the age of 18 or the date on which paragraph (4)(a) ceases to apply to him, whichever first occurs.]

(6) Paragraph (4)(c) shall have effect for a period—

(a) beginning on [³the date] on which paragraph (4)(c) applies to that person which first falls [³. . .] after the relevant date determined in accordance with paragraph (7); and

[³(b) ending on the last day of the period of eight weeks beginning with the date specified in sub-paragraph (a) or on the day before the date on which that person attains the age of 18, whichever first occurs.]

[⁴(6A) Paragraph (4)(d) shall have effect for a period—

(a) beginning on the day on which that paragraph first applies to that person; and

(b) ending on the day before the day on which that person attains the age of 18 or the day at the end of a period of eight weeks immediately following the day on which paragraph (4)(d) first had effect in relation to him, whichever is the earlier.

(6B) The period mentioned in paragraph (6A) may include any week in which regulation 7 of the Child Benefit (General) Regulations 1976 (circumstances in which a person who has ceased to receive full-time education is to continue to be treated as a child) also applies to that person.]

(7) For the purposes of paragraphs (3)(*b*) and (4) to (6)—

(a) in the case of a person who ceases to be treated as a child by virtue of section 2(1)(a) of the Child Benefit Act 1975 [SSCBA, s.142(1)(*a*)] (meaning of child) or regulation 7 of the Child Benefit (General) Regulations 1976 (circumstances in which a person who has ceased to receive full-time education is to continue to be treated as a child)—

    (i) on or after the first Monday in September, but before the first Monday in January of the following year, the relevant date is the last day of the week which falls immediately before the week which includes the first Monday in January in that year;

    (ii) on or after the first Monday in January but before the Monday following Easter Monday in that year, the relevant date is the last day of the week which falls 12 weeks after the week which includes the first Monday in January in that year;

    (iii) at any other time of the year, the relevant date is the last day of the week which falls 12 weeks after the week which includes the Monday following Easter Monday in that year;

(b) in the case of a person who was not treated as a child by virtue of section 2(1)(a) of that Act [SSCBA, s.142(1)(a)] immediately before he was 16 and who has not been treated as a child by virtue of regulation 7 of those Regulations (interruption of full-time education), the relevant date is the date determined in accordance with sub-paragraph (a)(i), (ii) or (iii) as if he had ceased full-time education on the first date on which education ceased to be compulsory for a person of his age in England and Wales or, if he is resident in Scotland, in Scotland.]

[⁴(8) In this regulation, any reference to a person acting in place of a registered person's parents has the same meaning as it has in Schedule 1A by virtue of paragraph 10 of that Schedule.]

AMENDMENTS

    1. Income Support (General) Amendment No. 3 Regulations 1988 (S.I. 1988 No. 1228), reg. 4 (September 12, 1988).
    2. Income Support (General) Amendment Regulations 1991 (S.I. 1991 No. 236), reg. 2 (April 8, 1991).
    3. Income Support (General) Amendment Regulations 1991 (S.I. 1991 No. 236), reg. 6 (April 8, 1991).
    4. Income Support (General) Amendment Regulations 1992 (S.I. 1992 No. 468), reg. 3 (April 6, 1992).

DEFINITIONS

    "the Act"—see reg. 2(1).
    "period of study"—*ibid.*
    "registered person"—*ibid.*
    "student"—*ibid.*
    "youth training scheme and youth training"—*ibid.*

GENERAL NOTE

    Reg. 13A prescribes the circumstances in which 16 and 17 year-olds can be exempted from the ordinary lower age limit of 18 imposed by s.124(1)(a) of the Contributions and Benefits Act (1986 Act, s.20(3)(a)). Paras.(2) and (3) deal with those who meet the conditions of Parts I or II of Sched. 1A. Paras.(4) to (6) apply to a limited number of people who do not come under Part I of Sched. 1A. Note also that s.125(1) of the Contributions and Benefits Act (1986 Act, s.20(4A)) allows exemption from the 18 year-old limit outside the conditions of reg. 13A in cases of severe hardship.

Paragraphs (2) and (3)
    These provisions apply the conditions of Sched. 1A. Under para. (3)(a) someone who comes within Part I of Sched. 1A is exempt from the age test up to the 18th birthday. See the notes to Sched. 1A for the categories included. Note in particular, that a person who satisfies reg. 13(2)(e) on relevant education is not caught by the age limit. Under para. (3)(b) someone who comes within Part II of Sched. 1A is exempt until the relevant date defined in para. (7).

Paragraphs (4) to (6)

These provisions apply to people outside Part I of Sched. 1A. A person within the categories of Part II can also use these provisions. They allow exemption after the relevant date defined in para. (7) (*i.e.* broadly after the end of the child benefit extension period). Para. (4) defines the categories covered.

Sub-para. (a) A person whose incapacity for work or YTS training is unlikely to end within 12 months falls under para. 2 of Sched. 1A and is exempt until 18. Sub-para. (a) applies to more limited incapacities. Under para. (5)(a) the exemption lasts as long as the incapacity continues, up to the age of 18.

Sub-para. (b). This sub-paragraph has been omitted because most students are excluded from income support throughout their courses, including vacations.

Sub-para. (c). A person who is registered for work or YTS training who has been discharged from custody can continue to be exempted beyond the end of the extension period if one of the conditions in Part II of Sched. 1A continues to be satisfied. Under para. (6)(b) this exemption lasts for eight weeks or until the 18th birthday if earlier.

Sub-para. (d). A person who leaves local authority care and is registered as in sub-para. (c) is exempted if he has to live away from his parents and any substitute (on which see Sched. 1A, para. 10). Under paras. (6A) and (6B) the exemption lasts for eight weeks, or until the person reaches 18 if sooner. Any week in the child benefit extension period can count in the eight weeks, but only after the person registers for work or youth training.

Paragraph (7)

The definition of the "relevant date" in para. (7) is crucial for many purposes. It provides the end of exemption for those falling within Part II of Sched. 1A and the beginning of exemption under para. (4) above. It is in most cases the date at the end of the child benefit "extension period" during which a parent can continue to receive child benefit for a child (and income support for them as a dependant) after the "terminal date" (see notes to reg. 12). If the terminal date is the first Monday in September, the relevant date is immediately before the week containing the first Monday in January (*i.e.* 16 weeks later). If the terminal date is the first Monday in January or the Monday following Easter Monday the relevant date is 12 weeks later.

If a person was not treated as a child for child benefit purposes immediately before reaching 16 (as might be the case, for example, for some young people coming to this country from abroad) then the relevant date is to be fixed as if they had left school at the earliest legal date. This might mean that the relevant date has long passed before a claim is made.

PART III

MEMBERSHIP OF THE FAMILY

Persons of a prescribed description

14.—(1) Subject to paragraph (2), a person of a prescribed description for the purposes of section 20(11) of the Act [SSCBA, s.137(1)] as it applies to income support (definition of the family) and section 23(1) [¹and (3)] of the Act [SSCBA, s.126(1) and (3)] is a person aged 16 or over but under 19 who is treated as a child for the purposes of section 2 of the Child Benefit Act 1975 [SSCBA, s.142] (meaning of child), and in these Regulations such a person is referred to as a "young person".

(2) Paragraph (1) shall not apply to [²a person who is receiving advanced education within the meaning of regulation 12(2) (relevant education) or to] a person who is entitled to income support or would, but for section 20(9) of the Act [SSCBA, s.134(2)] (provision against dual entitlement of members of family), be so entitled.

AMENDMENTS

1. Income Support (General) Amendment No. 4 Regulations 1988 (S.I. 1988 No. 1445), reg. 5 (September 12, 1988).

2. Income Support (General) Amendment Regulation 1990 (S.I. 1990 No. 547), reg. 6 (April 9, 1990).

DEFINITION

"the Act"—see reg. 2(1).

GENERAL NOTE

For the circumstances in which a person of 16 to 18 is treated as a child for child benefit purposes, see reg. 12. If such a person is receiving advanced education or could be entitled to income support in their own right (see reg. 13), that person does not come within reg. 14.

Circumstances in which a person is to be treated as responsible or not responsible for another

15.—[¹(1) Subject to the following provisions of this regulation, a person is to be treated as responsible for a child or young person for whom he is receiving child benefit.

(1A) In a case where a child ("the first child") is in receipt of child benefit in respect of another child ("the second child"), the person treated as responsible for the first child in accordance with the provisions of this regulation shall also be treated as responsible for the second child.

(2) In the case of a child or young person in respect of whom no person is receiving child benefit, the person who shall be treated as responsible for that child or young person shall be—

(a) except where sub-paragraph (b) applies, the person with whom the child or young person usually lives; or

(b) where only one claim for child benefit has been made in respect of the child or young person, the person who made that claim.]

(3) Where regulation 16(6) (circumstances in which a person is to be treated as being or not being a member of the household) applies in respect of a child or young person, that child or young person shall be treated as the responsibility of the claimant for that part of the week for which he is under that regulation treated as being a member of the claimant's household.

(4) Except where paragraph (3) applies, for the purposes of these Regulations a child or young person shall be treated as the responsibility of only one person in any benefit week and any person other than the one treated as responsible for the child or young person under this regulation shall be treated as not so responsible.

AMENDMENT

1. Income-related Benefits Schemes (Miscellaneous Amendments) (No. 4) Regulations 1993 (S.I. 1993 No. 2119), reg. 5 (October 4, 1993).

DEFINITIONS

"benefit week"—see reg. 2(1).
"child"—see 1986 Act, s.20(11) (SSCBA, s.137(1)).
"claimant"—see reg. 2(1).
"young person"—*ibid.*, reg. 14.

GENERAL NOTE

Paragraph (1)
The definition of family in s.137(1) of the Contributions and Benefits Act (1986 Act, s.20(11)) refers to a person being responsible for a child or young person (on which see reg. 14). Reg. 15 now makes the test of responsibility receipt of child benefit. Up to October 4, 1993, the test was

"primary responsibility", and receipt of child benefit was only relevant in cases of doubt. See the notes to reg. 15 in the 1993 edition and *Whelan v. Chief Adjudication Officer, The Independent,* November 14, 1994. The Court of Appeal confirmed that the question of who had "primary responsibility" for a child had to be assessed on a week to week basis. On the facts, the claimant had primary responsibility for the children in the three weeks in the summer when they stayed with her.

The test for family credit and disability working allowance is still whether the child normally lives with the adult and receipt of child benefit only becomes relevant where this is unclear. The different rules may therefore make it possible in certain cases for one person to claim income support and another family credit or disability working allowance for the same child at the same time.

Paragraph (1A)

If a child (B) for whom a person (A) is responsible gets child benefit for another child (C), (A) is also treated as responsible for (C).

Paragraph (2)

If no one is receiving child benefit for the child, then if one claim only has been made, the person who made that claim is responsible. Otherwise the person responsible is the person with whom the child usually lives. (See the notes to reg. 7 of the Family Credit (General) Regulations on "living with".) Since para. (4) refers to consideration of responsibility on the basis of benefit weeks, the test of where a child usually lives should be applied week by week and not on some kind of overall assessment on a long-term basis (*CIS 49/1991*). In the vast majority of cases, however, the question of who is responsible for a child for the purposes of income support will now be determined by who is receiving child benefit. The rules for child benefit include methods of establishing priorities between claimants, and a child benefit claimant can agree that someone with lower priority should be paid it.

Paragraphs (3) and (4)

Para. (4) provides that only one person can be treated as responsible for a child in any one benefit week. There is no provision for dividing up income support where a child spends time in different households. The only exceptions are under para. (3), which allows a person to be treated as responsible for a child for the part of the week in which he is in the household, but only where the child is being looked after by a local authority or is in custody (reg. 16(6)). The result of the new test is that if someone else is in receipt of child benefit for a child in any one benefit week, an income support claimant cannot be treated as responsible for that child even if the child spends most of, or even all, his time with the claimant. This may provide for even greater administrative simplicity than the previous test of primary responsibility but at a cost of a lack of justice in certain situations. However, it may be possible, because of the different rules for family credit and disability working allowance, for one person to claim income support and another family credit or disability working allowance for the same child at the same time.

Circumstances in which a person is to be treated as being or not being a member of the household

16.—(1) Subject to paragraphs (2) and (5), the claimant and any partner and, where the claimant or his partner is treated as responsible under regulation 15 (circumstances in which a person is to be treated as responsible or not responsible for another) for a child or young person, that child or young person and any child of that child or young person shall be treated as members of the same household [¹notwithstanding that any of them] [⁷is temporarily living away from the other members of his family].

[⁷(2) Paragraph (1) shall not apply to a person who is living away from the other members of his family where—

(a) that person does not intend to resume living with the other members of his family; or

(b) his absence from the other members of his family is likely to exceed 52 weeks, unless there are exceptional circumstances (for example the person is in hospital or otherwise has no control over the length of his absence), and the absence is unlikely to be substantially more than 52 weeks.]

(3) Paragraph (1) shall not apply in respect of any member of a couple or of a polygamous marriage where—

   (a) one, both or all of them are patients detained in a hospital provided under section 4 of the National Health Service Act 1977 (special hospitals) or section 90(1) of the Mental Health (Scotland) Act 1984 (provision of hospitals for patients requiring special security); or

   (b) one, both or all of them are detained in custody pending trial or sentence upon conviction or whilst serving a sentence imposed by a court; or

   (c) [⁶. . .]

   (d) the claimant is abroad and does not satisfy the conditions of regulation 4 (temporary absence from Britain); or

   (e) one of them is permanently in residential accommodation or in a residential care or a residential nursing home.

(4) A child or young person shall not be treated as a member of the claimant's household where he is—

   [⁵(a) placed with the claimant or his partner by a local authority under section 23(2)(a) of the Children Act 1989 or by a voluntary organisation under section 59(1)(a) of that Act; or

   (b) placed with the claimant or his partner prior to adoption; or]

   (c) placed for adoption with the claimant or his partner pursuant to a decision under the Adoption Agencies Regulations 1983 or the Adoption Agencies (Scotland) Regulations 1984.

(5) Subject to paragraph (6), paragraph (1) shall not apply to a child or young person who is not living with the claimant [¹and who]—

   (a) [⁴in a case which does not fall within sub-paragraph (aa),] has been continuously absent from Great Britain for a period of more than four weeks commencing—

      (i) where he went abroad before the date of claim for income support, with that date;

      (ii) in any other case, [⁴on the day which immediately follows the day] on which he went abroad; or

   [⁴(aa) where regulation 4(3) or paragraph 11A or 12A of Schedule 7 (temporary absence abroad for the treatment of a child or young person) applies, has been continuously absent from Great Britain for a period of more than eight weeks, that period of eight weeks commencing—

      (i) where he went abroad before the date of the claim for income support, on the date of that claim;

      (ii) in any other case, on the day which immediately follows the day on which he went abroad; or]

   (b) has been an in-patient or in [¹accommodation provided under any of the provisions referred to in [²any of sub-paragraphs (a) to (d) [³(excluding heads (i) and (ii)] of sub-paragraph (d)) of the definition of residential accommodation] in regulation 21(3)] for a continuous period of more than 12 weeks commencing—

      (i) where he became an in-patient or, as the case may be, entered that accommodation, before the date of the claim for income support, with that date; or

      (ii) in any other case, with the date on which he became an in-patient or entered that accommodation,

   and, in either case, has not been in regular contact with either the claimant or any member of the claimant's household; or

   [⁵(c) is being looked after by a local authority under a relevant enactment; or

   (d) has been placed with a person other than the claimant prior to adoption; or]

(e) has been placed for adoption pursuant to a decision under the Adoption Agencies Regulations 1983 or the Adoption Agencies (Scotland) Regulations 1984; or

(f) is detained in custody pending trial or sentence upon conviction or under a sentence imposed by a court.

(6) A child or young person to whom any of the circumstances mentioned in sub-paragraphs (c) or (f) of paragraph (5) applies shall be treated as being a member of the claimant's household only for that part of any benefit week where that child or young person lives with the claimant.

(7) Where a child or young person for the purposes of attending the educational establishment at which he is receiving relevant education is living with the claimant or his partner and neither one is treated as responsible for that child or young person that child or young person shall be treated as being a member of the household of the person treated as responsible for him and shall not be treated as a member of the claimant's household.

(8) In this regulation—

[⁵(a) "relevant enactment" means the Army Act 1955, the Social Work (Scotland) Act 1968, the Matrimonial Causes Act 1973, the Adoption (Scotland) Act 1978, the Family Law Act 1986 and the Children Act 1989;]

(b) "voluntary organisation" has the meaning assigned to it in the [⁵Children Act 1989] or, in Scotland, the Social Work (Scotland) Act 1968.

AMENDMENTS

1. Income Support (General) Amendment Regulations 1988 (S.I. 1988 No. 663), reg. 8 (April 11, 1988).

2. Income Support (General) Amendment Regulations 1989 (S.I. 1989 No. 534), reg. 3 (April 10, 1989).

3. Income Support (General) Amendment Regulations 1989 (S.I. 1989 No. 534), Sched. 1, para. 3 (October 9, 1989).

4. Income Support (General) Amendment Regulations 1990 (S.I. 1990 No. 547), reg. 7 (April 9, 1990).

5. Income Support (General) Amendment Regulations 1992 (S.I. 1992 No. 468), Sched., para. 3 (April 6, 1992). *Note:* The previous form (see the 1991 edition) of sub-paras. (4)(a) and (b), (5)(c) and (d) and (8)(a) and (b) remains in force in Scotland. The new form was introduced on April 6, 1992, as a consequence of the Children Act 1989.

6. Social Security Benefits (Amendments Consequential Upon the Introduction of Community Care) Regulations 1992 (S.I. 1992 No. 3147), Sched. 1, para. 1 (April 1, 1993).

7. Income-related Benefits Schemes (Miscellaneous Amendments) (No. 4) Regulations 1993 (S.I. 1993 No. 2119), reg. 6 (October 4, 1993).

DEFINITIONS

"child"—see 1986 Act, s.20(11) (SSCBA, s.137(1)).
"claimant"—see reg. 2(1).
"couple"—*ibid.*
"date of claim"—*ibid.*
"dwelling occupied as the home"—*ibid.*
"local authority"—see 1986 Act, s.84(1).
"nursing home"—see reg. 2(1), reg. 19(3).
"partner"—see reg. 2(1).
"polygamous marriage"—*ibid.*
"residential accommodation"—*ibid.*, reg. 21(3).
"residential care home"—*ibid.*, reg. 19(3).
"young person"—*ibid.*, reg. 14.

GENERAL NOTE

Paragraph (1)

This provision does two things. The first is to provide that a claimant and partner are deemed to be members of the same household, notwithstanding that they are temporarily apart. Before October

4, 1993, the deeming applied notwithstanding one partner's absence from the dwelling occupied as the home (see below). Since a partner is one of a married or unmarried couple and it is an essential part of the definition of both kinds of couple that the parties should be members of the same household, para. (1) cannot subvert the general meaning of household referred to in the notes to s.137(1) of the Contributions and Benefits Act (see *CIS 671/1992*). Para. (1) must only mean that because one partner is temporarily living elsewhere this does not in itself mean that membership of the same household ceases. This means that the exceptions in para. (3) perhaps do not achieve much, but probably indicate that those circumstances do terminate membership of the household.

The other thing done by para. (1) is to deem that where an adult is responsible for a child or young person under reg. 15, the child or young person is to be treated as in the same household as the adult, notwithstanding that one of them is temporarily living elsewhere (again, before October 4, 1993, the test was absence from the home). This deeming is more significant. There are exceptions in paras. (4) and (5).

The test under para. (1) is now one of absence from other members of the family, rather than from the home. *CIS 209/1989* held that the old form of para. (1) only applied if there was a dwelling which could be regarded as the home of both partners. This is no longer required, but it is still necessary for the family to have previously lived as members of the same household. (See notes to s.137(1) of the Contributions and Benefits Act under *"married couple"* on the meaning of household.) The Commissioner in *CIS 508/1992* seems to have accepted that the home need not have been in this country; how this applies to the new test of absence from other members of the family is not entirely clear. Temporarily is not defined and each case will need to be decided on its particular facts (unless it falls within para. (2)). One of the main groups potentially affected by the changed test may be couples where the claimant has come to Britain in advance of the other partner. However, adjudicating authorities still need to investigate whether either of the conditions in para. (2) applies. On sub-para. (a), see *CIS 508/1992* and *CIS 484/1993* in the notes to para. 4 of Sched. 3.

Paragraph (2)

Para. (1) does not apply where the person living away does not intend to resume living together with the other members of the family or is likely to be away for more than 52 weeks (or longer in exceptional circumstances, provided it is not substantially longer). When either of these conditions applies membership of the same household immediately ceases.

Paragraph (3)

Para. (1) does not apply in these circumstances, as between partners and polygamous marriages. The intention seems to be that the members of the couple or marriage cease to be partners in these circumstances, but para. (3) does not exactly say so. Under sub-para. (b) a person required to live in a bail hostel is not "detained in custody" pending trial (*R(IS) 17/93*); see Sched. 7, para. 9 as to how his applicable amount is calculated if he is a member of a couple. However, once a person has been charged, he is detained in custody pending trial, even if subsequently no trial takes place (*CIS 255/1990*, to be reported as *R(IS) 1/94*). In *Chief Adjudication Officer v. Carr, The Times*, June 2, 1994, the Court of Appeal upheld the decision in *CIS 561/1992* that a person on home leave while serving a prison sentence was not "detained in custody" during the leave period. The definition of "prisoner" in reg. 21(3) has been amended with effect from April 10, 1995, so as to include periods of temporary release. But sub-para. (b) has not been similarly amended.

Paragraph (4)

Children or young persons are not to be members of the household of their foster-parents or the people they are placed with for adoption. They therefore cannot be a member of the family.

Paragraph (5)

Para. (1) does not apply to a child or young person who is not living with the claimant when one of heads (a) to (f) applies. Again, the intention seems to be that in these circumstances the child or young person is to be treated as not a member of the household, but para. (5) does not expressly say so. It may be that the general test of membership of the household is relevant.

See para. (8) for the meaning of "relevant enactment."

Paragraph (6)

This provision provides a limited exception to para. (5), allowing a claimant to receive benefit for children or young persons being looked after by a local authority or in custody for the days on which they are in the claimant's home.

Paragraph (7)

This is a special rule where children live away from home while at school.

PART IV

APPLICABLE AMOUNTS

Applicable amounts

17. Subject to regulations 18 to 22 and 70 (applicable amounts in other cases and reductions in applicable amounts and urgent cases), a claimant's weekly applicable amount shall be the aggregate of such of the following amounts as may apply in his case:
  (a) an amount in respect of himself or, if he is a member of a couple, an amount in respect of both of them, determined in accordance with paragraph 1(1), (2) or (3), as the case may be, of Schedule 2;
  (b) an amount determined in accordance with paragraph 2 of Schedule 2 in respect of any child or young person who is a member of his family, except a child or young person whose capital, if calculated in accordance with Part V in like manner as for the claimant, [⁷except as provided in regulation 44(1) (modifications in respect of children and young persons)], would exceed £3,000;
[⁶(bb) an amount in respect of himself, or where the claimant is a member of a family, an amount in respect of any member of the family aged 16 or over, determined in accordance with paragraph 2A of Schedule 2 (residential allowance);]
  (c) if he is a member of a family of which at least one member is a child or young person, an amount determined in accordance with Part II of Schedule 2 (family premium);
  (d) the amount of any premiums which may be applicable to him, determined in accordance with Parts III and IV of Schedule 2 (premiums);
  (e) any amounts determined in accordance with Schedule 3 (housing costs) which may be applicable to him in respect of mortgage interest payments or such other housing costs as are prescribed in that Schedule.
  [¹(f) any amounts determined in accordance with [²paragraphs (2) to (7)].
  [²(g) the amount of the protected sum which may be applicable to him determined in accordance with Schedule 3A [³or, as the case may be, 3B].]
  (2) Where—
  (a) a claimant has throughout the period beginning on 11th April 1988 and ending immediately before the coming into force of paragraphs 25 to 28 of Schedule 10 (capital to be disregarded) failed to satisfy the capital condition in section 22(6) of the Act (no entitlement to benefit if capital exceeds prescribed amount); and
  (b) as a consequence he is not entitled to any transitional addition, special transitional addition or personal expenses addition under Part II of the Transitional Regulations; and
  (c) had those paragraphs been in force on 11th April 1988 he would have satisfied that condition and been entitled to any such addition,
the amount applicable under this paragraph shall, subject to paragraph (3) be equal to the amount of any transitional addition, special transitional addition and personal expenses addition to which he would be entitled under Part II of the Transitional Regulations had he been entitled to any such addition in the week commencing 11th April 1988.
  (3) For the purposes of paragraph (2), in determining a claimant's total benefit income in his second benefit week for the purpose of calculating the amount of any transitional addition to which he would have been entitled, no account shall be taken of any payment referred to in paragraph (1)(j) of regulation 9 of the

Transitional Regulations (total benefit income) which is made in respect of that week to compensate for the loss of entitlement to income support.

(4) Subject to paragraph (6), where—
   (a) the claimant or any member of his family was temporarily absent from his home in the claimant's first or second benefit week (or both), because he was—
      (i) a patient; or
      (ii) outside Great Britain for the purpose of receiving treatment for any disease or bodily or mental disablement or for the purpose of accompanying a child or young person who is outside Great Britain for the purpose of receiving such treatment; or
      (iii) in a residential care or nursing home or in accommodation provided under any of the provisions referred to in any of subparagraphs (*a*) to (d) of the definition of residential accommodation in regulation 21(3) (special cases); or
      (iv) in the care of a local authority under a relevant enactment; or
      (v) staying with a person who was contributing to his maintenance; and
   (b) as a result—
      (i) in the claimant's first benefit week his requirements for the purpose of calculating his entitlement to supplementary benefit were increased or reduced or he was not entitled to that benefit; or
      (ii) in the claimant's second benefit week his applicable amount was increased or reduced or he was not entitled to income support; and
   (c) the period during which his requirements were, or his applicable amount was, increased or reduced, or he was not entitled to benefit, or any one or more of those circumstances existed, did not exceed eight weeks,
the amount applicable under this paragraph (4) shall be equal to the amount determined under paragraph (5).

(5) The amount for the purposes of paragraph (4) shall be an amount equal to the difference between—
   (a) the amount that his total benefit income in his first benefit week would have been had he been entitled in respect of that week to supplementary benefit calculated on the basis that he or any member of his family had not been absent from the home; and, if less,
   (b) the amount of his total benefit income in the first complete week after the period of temporary absence ends; but for the purpose of calculating his total benefit income in that week—
      (i) no account shall be taken of any payment referred to in paragraph (1)(j) of regulation 9 of the Transitional Regulations which is made in respect of that week to compensate for the loss (in whole or in part) of entitlement to income support; and
      (ii) if the period of temporary absence ends after the coming into force of paragraph (4), the amount of income support to be taken into account shall, notwithstanding regulation 9(6) of the Transitional Regulations, be calculated as if that paragraph were not in force.

(6) The amount under paragraph (4) shall cease to be applicable to a claimant if he ceases to be entitled to income support for a period exceeding [⁴the permitted period determined in accordance with regulation 3A (permitted period)].

[⁴(6A) For the purposes of paragraph (6), where a claimant has ceased to be entitled to income support because he or his partner is participating in arrangements for training made under section 2 of the Employment and Training Act 1973 [⁵or section 2 of the Enterprise and New Towns (Scotland) Act 1990] or attending a course at an employment rehabilitation centre established under that section [⁵of the 1993 Act], he shall be treated as if he had been entitled to income support for the period during which he or his partner is participating in such arrangements or attending such a course.]

(7) In this Regulation—

"first benefit week" and "second benefit week" have the meanings given to those expressions in regulations 2(1) of the Transitional Regulations and shall also include the week which would have been the claimant's "first benefit week" or, as the case may be, "second benefit week" had he been entitled to supplementary benefit or, as the case may be, income support in that week;

"total benefit income" has, subject to paragraphs (3) and (5)(b), the same meaning as in regulation 9 of the Transitional Regulations;

"Transitional Regulations" means the Income Support (Transitional Regulations 1987.]

AMENDMENTS

1. Income Support (General) Amendment No. 2 Regulations 1988 (S.I. 1988 No. 910), reg. 2 (May 30, 1988).

2. Income Support (General) Amendment No. 4 Regulations 1988 (S.I. 1988 No. 1445), Sched. 1, para. 11 (April 10, 1989).

3. Income Support (General) Amendment Regulations 1989 (S.I. 1989 No. 534), Sched. 1, para. 17 (October 9, 1989).

4. Income Support (General) Amendment No. 3 Regulations 1989 (S.I. 1989 No. 1678), reg. 4 (October 9, 1989).

5. Enterprise (Scotland) Consequential Amendments Order 1991 (S.I. 1991 No. 387), arts. 2 and 9 (April 1, 1991).

6. Social Security Benefits (Amendments Consequential Upon the Introduction of Community Care) Regulations 1992 (S.I. 1992 No. 3147), reg. 2(1) (April 1, 1993).

7. Income-related Benefits Schemes (Miscellaneous Amendments) (No. 4) Regulations 1993 (S.I. 1993 No. 2119), reg. 7 (October 4, 1993).

DEFINITIONS

"child"—see 1986 Act, s.20(11) (SSCBA, s.137(1)).
"claimant"—see reg. 2(1).
"couple"—*ibid.*
"family"—see 1986 Act, s.20(11) (SSCBA, s.137(1)).
"young person"—see reg. 2(1), reg. 14.

GENERAL NOTE

Reg. 17 sets out the categories which go towards the total applicable amount, which is then set against the claimant's income to determine entitlement.

The categories cover first a personal allowance for the claimant, as a single person or a member of a couple. The amount of the allowance is specified in Sched. 2. A personal allowance (again specified in Sched. 2) is also added for each child or young person who is a member of the family (defined in s.137 of the Contributions and Benefits Act; 1986 Act, s.20(11)). If the child's or young person's own capital exceeds £3,000, then no personal allowance is included for that child. In that case, any income of the child is not treated as the claimant's (reg. 44(5)). The capital of a child or young person is never treated as the claimant's (reg. 47). There is a specific residential allowance for new residents (from April 1993) in residential care and nursing homes. See para. 2A of Sched. 2. And see reg. 19 for the treatment of existing residents.

The second main category covers premiums. If a member of the claimant's family is a child or young person, the family premium is included (see Part II of Sched. 2). The other premiums are in Parts III and IV of Sched. 2.

The third category covers housing costs, set out in Sched. 3. Note reg. 64(1)(a) of the Adjudication Regulations.

The fourth category, in sub-paras. (f) and (g), covers transitional protection for a number of groups. Sub-para. (f) first deals with those assisted by paras. 25 to 28 of Sched. 10 on disregarded capital, which were inserted from May 30, 1988. The details are in paras. (2) and (3). Sub-para. (f) secondly deals with groups who lost out on the ordinary transitional protection because of temporary absence from home around April 11, 1988. Here the details are in paras. (4) to (6). Sub-para. (g) applies Scheds. 3A and 3B, giving transitional protection to certain claimants in board and lodging accommodation on the change in the income support system on April 10, 1989, and to hostel-dwellers and operators on the changes in October 1989. See the notes to Sched. 3A and 3B.

Paragraphs (2) and (3)

These provisions apply where a person was continuously excluded from entitlement to income support by the capital rule before the additional disregards were added with effect from May 30, 1988. If the person would have satisfied the capital rule on April 11, 1988, if those disregards had been in the regulations and would have been entitled to some transitional protection, then the amount of that protection is applicable from May 30, 1988. There is no statutory provision for filling the gap between April 11 and May 30, but extra-statutory payments were made. The effect of para. (3) is that in doing the calculations of total benefit income in the second benefit week around April 11, any extra-statutory payment is to be ignored.

Paragraphs (4) to (6A)

Where the calculation of total benefit income in either the first or second benefit week is affected by a person's temporary absence from home (for one of the reasons set out in para. (4)(a)), then the calculation can be done as if the person was still at home. The absence must not exceed eight (or sometimes 12) weeks (para. (4)(c)) and the addition applied will cease if there is a subsequent break in entitlement of more than eight (or sometimes 12) weeks (para. (6)).

There are special rules for particular categories in regs. 18 to 22, in particular for residents in residential care and nursing homes.

Polygamous marriages

18. [¹Subject to paragraph (2) and regulations] 19 to 22 and 70 (applicable amounts in other cases and reductions in applicable amounts and urgent cases), where a claimant is a member of a polygamous marriage his weekly applicable amount shall be the aggregate of such of the following amounts as may apply in his case:

   (a) the highest amount applicable to him and one of his partners determined in accordance with paragraph 1(3) of Schedule 2 as if he and that partner were a couple;

   (b) an amount equal to the differences between the amounts specified in [¹sub-paragraphs (3)(c)][⁴and (1)(e)] of paragraph 1 of Schedule 2 in respect of each of his other partners;

   (c) an amount determined in accordance with paragraph 2 of Schedule 2 (applicable amounts) in respect of any child or young person for whom he or a partner of his is responsible and who is a member of the same household except a child or young person whose capital, if calculated in accordance with Part V in like manner as for the claimant, [⁷except as provided in regulation 44(1) (modifications in respect of children and young persons)], would exceed £3,000;

   [⁶(cc) an amount, whether in respect of the claimant or any member of his household aged 16 or over, determined in accordance with paragraph 2A of Schedule 2 (residential allowance);]

   (d) if he or another partner of the polygamous marriage is responsible for a child or young person who is a member of the same household, the amount specified in Part II of Schedule 2 (family premiums);

   (e) the amount of any premiums which may be applicable to him determined in accordance with Parts III and IV of Schedule 2 (premiums);

   (f) any amounts determined in accordance with Schedule 3 (housing costs) which may be applicable to him in respect of mortgage interest payments or such other housing costs as are prescribed in that Schedule.

   [²(g) any amount determined in accordance with regulation 17(1)(f) (applicable amounts);]

   [³(h) the amount of the protected sum which may be applicable to him determined in accordance with Schedule 3A [⁵or, as the case may be, 3B].]

[¹(2) In the case of a partner who is aged less than 18, the amount which applies in respect of that partner shall be nil unless—
(a) that partner is treated as responsible for a child, or
(b) that partner is a person who—
  (i) had he not been a member of a polygamous marriage would have been eligible for income support by virtue of regulation 13A (circumstances in which a person aged 16 or 17 is eligible for income support); or
  (ii) is a person in respect of whom there is a direction under section 20(4A) of the Act [SSCBA, s.125] (income support to avoid severe hardship).]

AMENDMENTS

1. Income Support (General) Amendment No. 3 Regulations 1988 (S.I. 1988 No. 1228), reg. 5 (September 9, 1988).
2. Income Support (General) Amendment No. 4 Regulations 1988 (S.I. 1988 No. 1445), reg. 6 (September 9, 1988).
3. Income Support (General) Amendment No. 4 Regulations 1988 (S.I. 1988 No. 1445), Sched. 1, para. 12 (April 10, 1989).
4. Family Credit and Income Support (General) Amendment Regulations 1989 (S.I. 1989 No. 1034), reg. 5 (July 10, 1989).
5. Income Support (General) Amendment Regulations 1989 (S.I. 1989 No. 534), Sched. 1, para. 17 (October 9, 1989).
6. Social Security Benefits (Amendments Consequential Upon the Introduction of Community Care) Regulations 1992 (S.I. 1992 No. 3147), reg. 2(1) (April 1, 1993).
7. Income-related Benefits Schemes (Miscellaneous Amendments) (No. 4) Regulations 1993 (S.I. 1993 No. 2119) reg. 8 (October 4, 1993).

DEFINITIONS

"the Act"—see reg. 2(1).
"child"—see 1986 Act, s.20(11) (SSCBA, s.137(1)).
"claimant"—see reg. 2(1).
"couple"—*ibid.*
"partner"—*ibid.*
"polygamous marriage"—*ibid.*
"young person"—*ibid.*, reg. 14.

GENERAL NOTE

Reg. 18 contains special rules for polygamous marriages, but not for other kinds of relationships. There the ordinary living together as husband and wife rule in s.137(1) of the Contributions and Benefits Act (1986 Act, s.20(11)) applies.

Applicable amounts for persons in residential care and nursing homes

19.—[¹[⁶(1) Subject to regulation 22 (reduction of applicable amounts) where a claimant has a preserved right and either—
(a) lives in a residential care or nursing home; or
(b) is a member of a family and he and the members of his family live in such a home,]
his weekly applicable amount shall, except in a case to which regulation 21 (applicable amounts in special cases) or Part II of Schedule 4 (persons to whom regulation 19 does not apply) applies, be calculated in accordance with Part I of that Schedule.]

[⁵(1ZA) A person to whom paragraph (1) applies shall be treated as not being severely disabled.]

[⁶(1ZB) In this regulation a person has a preserved right, subject to paragraphs (1ZE) and (1ZF), where—

(a) on 31st March 1993, he was living in a residential care home or a nursing home, and—

    (i) was entitled to income support for the benefit week in which that day fell and his applicable amount was calculated in accordance with Part I of Schedule 4; or

    (ii) was not in that week entitled to income support because he was able to meet the cost of the accommodation from other sources available to him, but subsequently becomes entitled to income support; or

    [¹⁰(iii) was not in that week entitled to income support, but was residing with his partner as a member of a couple on the relevant date where the partner was a person to whom head (i) or (ii) applies; or]

(b) he would have been living in a residential care home or nursing home on 31st March 1993 but for an absence which, including that day, does not exceed—

    (i) except in a case to which head (ii) applies—

      (aa) where the person was before his absence a temporary resident in the home, 4 weeks, or

      (bb) where the person was before his absence a permanent resident in the home, 13 weeks; or

    (ii) where throughout the period of absence the person was a patient, 52 weeks,

and the provisions of sub-paragraph (a) would have applied to him but for that absence.

(1ZC) Subject to paragraphs (1ZD), (1ZE) and (1ZF), a person also has a preserved right where—

(a) on 31st March 1993 he was living in a residential care home or nursing home within the meaning of paragraph (3) as then in force, and was entitled to income support but his applicable amount was not calculated in accordance with Part I of Schedule 4 because he was a person to whom paragraph 14 of Schedule 4 applied (accommodation provided by a close relative); and

(b) after 31st March 1993, either—

    (i) he moved from the home in which he was residing on that date to another residential care home or nursing home, or

    (ii) the ownership of the home changed,

and in the home to which he moved, or as the case may be, following the change of ownership, the accommodation and meals (if any) are provided for him by a person other than a close relative of his [⁸or of any member] of his family, and are provided on a commercial basis.

(1ZD) Where a person has a preserved right under paragraph (1ZC), that right shall commence on the first full day of residence in the residential care home or nursing home to which he moved, or as the case may be, the day after the ownership of the [⁹home] changed.

(1ZE) [¹⁰In England and Wales,] a person does not have a preserved right by virtue of paragraph (1ZB) (a)(ii) or (1ZC) where the residential care home in which he was living provided both board and personal care for less than 4 persons.

[¹⁰(1ZEA) Where, in Scotland, a person would have had a preserved right by virtue of paragraph (1ZB)(a)(ii) or (1ZC) but for the provisions of paragraph (1ZE) as it originally had effect, that person shall be treated from the date this regulation has effect in respect of him as though the first two paragraphs referred to continued to have effect in his case.]

(1ZF) Paragraphs (1ZB) and (1ZC) shall cease to apply to a person who has a preserved right where he is absent from a residential care home or nursing home and that absence exceeds a period of—

   (a) except in a case to which sub-paragraph (b) applies—
      (i) 4 weeks, where the person was before his absence a temporary resident in the home; or
      (ii) 13 weeks, where the person was before his absence a permanent resident in the home; or
   (b) 52 weeks where throughout the period of absence the person was a patient.

(1ZG)—
   (a) A person who acquired a preserved right under paragraph (1ZB) or (1ZC) shall cease to have that right where either—
      (i) he moves from the home he resided in, or would but for an absence specified in paragraph (1ZB)(b) have resided in, on 31st March 1993 to another residential care home or nursing home, or
      (ii) the ownership of that home changes;
     and in the home to which he moves, or as the case may be, following the change of ownership, the accommodation and meals (if any) are provided for him by a close relative of his, [8or of any member] of his family, [8or are provided] otherwise than on a commercial basis;
   (b) a preserved right acquired under paragraph (1ZB) or (1ZC) which ceased to apply to a person in accordance with sub-paragraph (a) shall, notwithstanding that paragraph, revive and again apply in his case where—
      (i) he moves from the home mentioned in sub-paragraph (a)(i) to another residential care home or nursing home, or
      (ii) the ownership of that home changes, or in the case of a home mentioned in sub-paragraph (a)(ii), changes again,
     and in the home to which he moves, or as the case may be, following the change or further change of ownership, the accommodation and meals (if any) are provided for him otherwise than by a close relative of his, [8or of any member] of his family, and are provided on a commercial basis.

(1ZH) For the purposes of paragraphs (1ZB) and (1ZF) a person is a permanent resident in a residential care home or nursing home where the home is his principal place of abode, and a temporary resident where it is not.

(1ZJ) For the avoidance of doubt, the expression "residential care home" in paragraphs (1ZB) and (1ZE) has the meaning it bore on 31st March 1993.]

[8(1ZK) Where a person—
   (a) formerly had a preserved right by virtue of paragraph (1ZB); and
   (b) on 1st April 1993 was living in a home which was exempt from registration under Part I of the Registered Homes Act 1984 pursuant to section 1(4)(a) of that Act (exemption from registration in respect of certain homes) because one or more of the residents were treated as relatives pursuant to section 19(4) of that Act; and
   (c) is living in that home on 4th October 1993; and
   (d) between 1st April 1993 and 4th October 1993 he has not been absent from that home, or has been absent from it for a period not exceeding 13 weeks;
then subject to paragraph (1ZL) that person shall be treated for the purposes of this regulation as though he had a preserved right on and after 4th October 1993.

(1ZL) Paragraph (1ZK) shall cease to apply to a person who is treated as though he had a preserved right where he is absent from a residential care home or nursing home and that absence exceeds a period of—
   (a) except in a case to which sub-paragraph (b) applies, 13 weeks; or
   (b) 52 weeks where throughout the period of absence the person was a patient.]

[⁹(1ZM) Where a person is treated in accordance with paragraph (1ZK) as having a preserved right, paragraph (1ZG) shall apply to that person as if he had acquired a preserved right under paragraph (1ZB).]

[¹⁰(1ZN) Where a person—

(a) on 31st March 1993 was a member of a couple and his partner acquired a preserved right under paragraph (1ZB)(a)(i);

(b) before 3rd October 1994 ceased to be a member of a couple; and

(c) between 31st March 1993 and 3rd October 1994 has been living in a residential care home or a nursing home,

he shall be treated for the purposes of this regulation as having a preserved right from 3rd October 1994.

(1ZO) Subject to paragraph (1ZG), where a person would have been living in a residential care home or nursing home on 31st March 1993 but for an absence which, including that day, does not exceed—

(a) where the person was before his absence a temporary resident in the home, 4 weeks; or

(b) where the person was before his absence a permanent resident in the home, 13 weeks; or

(c) where throughout the period of absence the person was a patient, 52 weeks,

and the provisions of paragraph (1ZN) would have applied to him but for that absence, he shall be treated as having a preserved right from 3rd October 1994.

(1ZP) Where a person is treated as having a preserved right in accordance with paragraphs (1ZK), (1ZN) or (1ZO) above, paragraph (1ZG) shall apply to that person as if he had acquired a preserved right under paragraph (1ZB).

(1ZQ) Where a person to whom paragraph (IZO) refers is absent from a residential care home or nursing home in the period from 31st March 1993 to 3rd October 1994 for a period which exceeds a period to which paragraph (1ZO) refers and which is appropriate in his case, he shall cease to be treated as having a preserved right.]

[¹(1A) For the purposes of paragraph (1)(b) [⁴and Schedule 4] a claimant and the members of his family are to be taken as living in a residential care home or nursing home even during periods when one or more members of the family are temporarily absent from the home but only if the claimant or his partner is living in the home during any such period.]

(2) Where—

(a) a claimant immediately before 27th July 1987 was in receipt of supplementary benefit as a boarder in a residential care home which was not required to register under Part I of the Registered Homes Act 1984 because section 1(4) of that Act (registration) applied to it; and

(b) immediately before 11th April 1988 his appropriate amount fell to be determined, by virtue of regulation 3 of the Supplementary Benefit (Requirements and Resources) Amendment Regulations 1987 (transitional provisions), in accordance with paragraph 1 of Schedule 1A to the Supplementary Benefit Requirements Regulations 1983 (maximum amounts for residential care homes) or would have been so determined but for his temporary absence from the home,

his weekly applicable amount shall be calculated in accordance with Part I of Schedule 4 (applicable amounts of persons in residential care homes or nursing homes) as if the home was a residential care home within the meaning of this regulation if, and for so long as, the claimant remains resident in the same home apart from any temporary absence, and the home continues to provide accommodation with board and personal care for the claimant by reason of his old age, disablement, past or present dependence on alcohol or drugs or past or present mental disorder.

(3) In this regulation and Schedule 4—

"nursing home" means—

(a) premises which are a nursing home or mental nursing home within the meaning of the Registered Homes Act 1984 and which are either registered under Part II of that Act or exempt from registration under section 37 thereof (power to exempt Christian Science Homes); or

(b) any premises used or intended to be used for the reception of such persons or the provision of such nursing or services as is mentioned in any paragraph of subsection (1) of section 21 or section 22(1) of the Registered Homes Act 1984 (meaning of nursing home or mental nursing home) or, in Scotland, as are mentioned in section 10(2) of the Nursing Homes Registration (Scotland) Act 1938 (interpretation) and which are maintained or controlled by a body instituted by special Act of Parliament or incorporated by Royal Charter;

(c) in Scotland,
  (i) premises which are a nursing home within the meaning of section 10 of the Nursing Homes Registration (Scotland) Act 1938 which are either registered under that Act or exempt from registration under section 6 or 7 thereof (general power to exempt homes and power to exempt Christian Science Homes); or
  (ii) premises which are a private hospital within the meaning of section 12 of the Mental Health (Scotland) Act 1984 (private hospitals), and which are registered under that Act,;

"residential care home" means an establishment—

[¹(a) which is required to be registered under Part I of the Registered Homes Act 1984 and is so registered [⁷, or is deemed to be registered under section 2(3) of the Registered Homes (Amendment) Act 1991 (which refers to the registration of small homes where the application for registration has not been determined)]; or]

(b) [⁷ ...]

(c) run by the Abbeyfield Society including all bodies corporate or incorporate which are affiliated to that Society; or

(d) [²which provides residential accommodation with both board and personal care and is] managed or provided by a body incorporated by Royal Charter or constituted by Act of Parliament other than a local social services authority; or

(e) in Scotland, which is a home registered under section 61 of the Social Work (Scotland) Act 1968 or is an establishment provided by [⁷a housing association registered with Scottish Homes established by the Housing (Scotland) Act 1988] which provides care equivalent to that given in residential accommodation provided under Part IV of the Social Work (Scotland) Act [⁸1968; or]

[⁸(f) which is exempt from registration under Part I of the Registered Homes Act 1984 pursuant to section 1(4)(a) of that Act (exemption from registration in respect of certain homes) because one or more of the residents are treated as relatives pursuant to section 19(4) of that Act;]

[²and in paragraphs (b) and (d) of this definition "personal care" means personal care for persons in need of personal care by reason of [³old] age, disablement, past or present dependence on alcohol or drugs, or past or present mental disorder.]

"temporary absence" means—

(a) [¹in paragraph (2) or] in the case of a person who is over pensionable age, 52 weeks;

(b) in any other case, 13 weeks.

(4) In Schedule 4 the expressions "old age", "mental disorder", "mental handicap", "drug or alcohol dependence" and "disablement" have the same

meanings as those expressions have for the purposes of the Registered Homes Act 1984 and Regulations made thereunder.

[⁴(5) Notwithstanding the foregoing paragraphs of this regulation, where—
  (a) a person has been registered under the Registered Homes Act 1984 in respect of premises which have been carried on as a residential care home or, as the case may be, a nursing home, and that person has ceased to carry on such a home; and
  (b) an application for registration under that Act has been made by another person and that application has not been determined or abandoned,
the applicable amount of a person resident in those premises shall be determined under Schedule 4 as if the most recent registration under the Registered Homes Act 1984 in respect of those premises continued until the day on which the application is determined or abandoned.]

AMENDMENTS

1. Income Support (General) Amendment Regulations 1988 (S.I. 1988 No. 663), reg. 9 (April 11, 1988).
2. Income Support (General) Amendment No. 4 Regulations 1988 (S.I. 1988 No. 1445), reg. 7 (September 9, 1988).
3. Income Support (General) Amendment No. 5 Regulations 1988 (S.I. 1988 No. 2022), reg. 4 (December 12, 1988).
4. Income Support (General) Amendment No. 3 Regulations 1989 (S.I. 1989 No. 1678), reg. 5 (October 9, 1989).
5. Income Support (General) Amendment (No. 3) Regulations 1991 (S.I. 1991 No. 1033), reg. 2 (May 20, 1991).
6. Social Security Benefits (Amendments Consequential Upon the Introduction of Community Care) Regulations 1992 (S.I. 1992 No. 3147), reg. 3 (April 1, 1993).
7. Social Security Benefits (Amendments Consequential Upon the Introduction of Community Care) Regulations 1992 (S.I. 1992 No. 3147), Sched. 1, para. 2 (April 1, 1993).
8. Income-related Benefits Schemes (Miscellanous Amendments) (No. 4) Regulations 1993 (S.I. 1993 No. 2119), reg. 9 (October 4, 1993).
9. Income-related Benefits Schemes (Miscellanous Amendments) Regulations 1994 (S.I. 1994 No. 527), reg. 2 (April 11, 1994).
10. Income-related Benefits Schemes (Miscellaneous Amendments) (No. 5) Regulations 1994 (S.I. 1994 No. 2139), reg. 24 (October 3, 1994).

DEFINITIONS

"benefit week"—see reg. 2(1).
"claimant"—*ibid*.
"close relative"—*ibid*. "family"—see 1986 Act, s.20(11) (SSCBA, s.137(1)).
"partner"—see reg. 2(1).
"relative"—*ibid*.
"remunerative work"—*ibid*.
"supplementary benefit"—*ibid*.

GENERAL NOTE

A new system of income support for new residents of residential care and nursing homes was introduced from April 1, 1993. The system is described in the notes to para. 2A of Sched. 2. Essentially, new residents receive the ordinary income support entitlement plus a fixed residential allowance towards the cost of accommodation. It is then for the local authority to deal with the cost of the care provided in the home. But the existing system is maintained in force under reg. 19 and Sched. 4 for most of those who were resident in, or only temporarily absent from, homes on March 31, 1993.

Access to the existing system depends on the claimant having a "preserved right" (para.(1)). "Preserved right" is defined in paras. (1ZB) to (1ZQ).

Para. (1ZB) deals with most cases. Para. (1ZC) covers cases where the accommodation is provided by close relatives. The basic rule in para. (1ZB) applies to those resident in a residential care home (as defined on March 31, 1993: para. (1ZJ)) or nursing home on that date. Therefore, residential care homes with less than four residents are covered if they met the conditions in head (b) of the definition in reg. 19(3) as at March 31, 1993. However, in England and Wales (but now not Scotland) there is different treatment of those entitled to income support on March 31, 1993 (para. (1ZB)(a)(i)) and those who were not entitled to income support on that date because they were self-financing (para. (1ZB)(a)(ii)), or qualify for a preserved right under para. (1ZC). A person does not have a preserved right under paras. (1ZB)(a)(ii) or (1ZC) if resident in a residential care home with less than four residents (para. (1ZE)). The thinking is that it would be too difficult to check, possibly several years after April 1993, that such a home met the condition under the old reg. 19(3). Where a resident was entitled to income support on March 31, 1993, a check would necessarily have been made. In Scotland, homes with less than four residents were not exempt from the requirement to register before April 1993 and so this rationale does not apply. The effect of para. (1ZEA) is to extend preserved rights to claimants in Scotland who were self-financing residents on March 31, 1993, or who qualify for a preserved right under para. (1ZC), irrespective of the size of the home.

Under para. (1ZB)(a)(iii), from October 3, 1994, a claimant's partner also has a preserved right where the couple were resident in a residential care or nursing home on March 31, 1993, and the claimant fell within para. (1ZB)(a)(i) or (ii). This will protect the partner's position if, for example, the claimant dies. Para. (1ZN) provides that this applies to a partner of a resident entitled to income support on March 31, 1993 who ceased to be a member of a couple before October 3, 1994, and who has continued to live in a residential care or nursing home up to October 3, 1994; certain absences are ignored (paras. (1ZO) and (1ZQ)), and this preserved right can be lost (and revive) in accordance with para. (1ZG) (para. (1ZP)).

Due to the change in the definition of residential care home in para. (3) from April 1993, residents of small homes that remained exempt from registration (see below) could have a preserved right by virtue of para. (1ZB), but not be paid income support in accordance with Part I of Sched. 4 after April 1993. From October 4, 1993, the definition of residential care home has been expanded to include those small homes not required to register because one or more residents are treated as relatives for registration purposes (category (f): see below); residents of such homes have a preserved right from October 4, 1993 and will be entitled to income support under Part I of Sched. 4, if they satisfy the conditions of para. (1ZK). This preserved right can be lost (and revive) in accordance with para. (1ZG) (para. (1ZM)). A resident of such a home who was self-financing on March 31, 1993 would not have a preserved right because of para. (1ZE)).

If the person is temporarily absent from a home on March 31, 1933, there may still be a preserved right under the conditions of para. (1ZB)(b).

Under para. (1ZC) if a resident would have qualified for a preserved right under para. (1ZB) if the accommodation had not been provided by a close relative, there is a preserved right when that situation changes or there is a move to another home which qualifies.

Paras. (1ZF), (1ZG), (1ZL), (1ZM), (1ZP) and (1ZQ) define when a preserved right ceases to exist. Under paras. (1ZF), (1ZL) and (1ZQ) the preserved right is lost (and cannot revive) if one of the prescribed kinds of absence occurs. The absence has to be from any residential care or nursing home so that the preserved right can survive any number of moves. Each period of absence must be considered separately. There are no linking rules. Under paras. (1ZG), (1ZM) and (1ZP) the preserved right is lost temporarily if accommodation becomes provided by a close relative or on a non-commercial basis, but can revive.

If a claimant qualifies under para. (1), income support is calculated much as before the new system was introduced. The main rules are in Sched. 4

Part II of Sched. 4 lists people in homes who do not fall under reg. 19. They then have to be considered as ordinary claimants. There are also some special categories in reg. 21 and Sched. 7.

"Nursing home" and "residential care home" are defined in para. (3).

Nursing home In England and Wales, if the home is not run by a body set up by special Act of Parliament or Royal Charter (para. (b)), the home must not only come within the category of nursing home in the Registered Homes Act 1984, but actually be registered under that Act (para. (a)). Para. (c) applies the same rule through the Scottish legislation. See para. (5) for changes in the registered proprietor.

Residential care home The definition has been somewhat simplified from April 1993, since the Registered Homes (Amendment) Act 1991 requires the registration of homes with less than four residents (but see category (f) below). Now under para. (a) the basic test is registration by the local authority. The local authority will apply the criteria of board and personal care at that stage. A small home can be deemed to be registered while waiting for registration.

Categories (c) and (d) do not require registration. Under (c) all Abbeyfield Homes are included whether or not they provide board and personal care and whether or not they meet the conditions for registration (*R(SB) 11/91*). There is no special category for Abbeyfield Homes under the new system (Sched. 2, para. 2A).

In category (d), a decision is necessary on whether board and personal care is provided. By analogy with cases on the Rent Acts (see *Otter v. Norman* [1988] 2 All E. R. 897 for a discussion), "board" requires the provision of some prepared food or drink which goes beyond the trivial. It does not require any particular standard of substantiality, but a cup of cocoa, say, would not do on its own. "Personal care" is only defined to the extent of limiting the reasons why it has to be provided. The *Adjudication Officers' Guide* (AOG) (para. 28035) suggests that "Personal care" may be read as meaning:

> "all that the proprietors must do to preserve and promote the health, safety and emotional well being of the residents. It is broadly equivalent to the care which might be provided by a competent carer, and includes, help with washing, bathing, dressing, toiletry needs and administration of medicines. When a resident falls sick, it includes the kind of attention someone would receive from a carer under the guidance of a GP, nurse, or any other member of the primary health care service."

This is helpful, but should not be seen to imply that a particular level of personal care must be provided. If something beyond the trivial which counts as personal care is provided, then personal care is provided, even though much more care would be desirable.

Category (f) has been added from October 4, 1993 to include small homes not required to register because one or more residents are *treated* as relatives for the purposes of Part I of the Registered Homes Act 1984. Under s.1(4)(a), as amended by the Registered Homes (Amendment) Act 1991, and s.19(4) of the 1984 Act, homes with less than four residents are not required to register where the only residents are those who run the home, employees, their relatives or people who are treated as relatives because they have lived there for at least five years. Thus homes which are not required to register because the residents are genuine relatives are not covered by category (f). Residents of homes in category (f) will be entitled to income support under Part I of Sched. 4 from October 4, 1993 if they satisfy the conditions of para. (1ZK) (see above).

The consequence if a home fails to get into either of the definitions is that a resident does not qualify under para. (1) and may also not qualify for a residential allowance under para. 2A of Sched. 2, so being restricted to the ordinary allowances and premiums plus housing benefit.

There are other important definitions dealt with below under para. (4).

Once the category of home is settled, paras.(1) and (1A) deal with the residence of the claimant and his family (if any).

Para. (1ZA) secures that a person who qualifies under para. (1) does not qualify for the severe disability premium. The person's care needs are deemed to be taken care of by the residential care or nursing home.

Paragraph (2)

This provision continues the transitional protection formerly given by reg. 3 of the Supplementary Benefit (Requirements and Resources) Amendment Regulations 1987, dating from July 27, 1987. For receipt of supplementary benefit as a boarder, see *R(SB) 12/87* and *CSB 29/1986*.

Paragraph (4)

"Mental disorder" is defined in s.55 of the Registered Homes Act 1984 as "mental illness, arrested or incomplete development of mind, psychopathic disorder, and any other disorder or disability of mind." "Mental handicap" is defined in reg. 1(2) of the Residential Care Homes Regulations 1984 as "a state of arrested or incomplete development of mind which includes impairment of intelligence and social functioning." Thus, "mental disorder" can include "mental handicap." Senility is not a mental handicap, but it can amount to a mental disorder (*R(SB) 17/88*).

"Disablement" is defined in s.20(1) of the 1984 Act as meaning that the person concerned is "blind, deaf or dumb or substantially and permanently handicapped by illness, injury or congenital deformity or any other disability prescribed by the Secretary of State."

Paragraph (5)

This provision allows the definition to be met through gaps in registration when proprietors change.

Applicable amounts for persons in board and lodging accommodation and hostels

20.—[¹. . .]

1. Income Support (General) Amendment Regulations 1989 (S.I. 1989 No. 534), Sched. 1, para. 4 (October 9, 1989).

GENERAL NOTE

As from October 1989, most hostel-dwellers, unless their accommodation comes within the amended definition of residential accommodation in reg. 21(3), are entitled to the ordinary income support personal allowances and premiums and to housing benefit for their accommodation. See Sched. 3B for transitional protection from October 1989 and April 1990.

Boarders had already been transferred to a similar system from April 1989. Their transitional protection is under Sched. 3A.

Special cases

21.—(1) Subject to [⁴regulations 21A and 22] (reductions in applicable amounts) in the case of a person to whom any paragraph in column (1) of Schedule 7 applies (applicable amounts in special cases), the amount included in the claimant's weekly amount in respect of him shall be the amount prescribed in the corresponding paragraph in column (2) of that Schedule; but no amount shall be included in respect of a child or young person if the capital of that child or young person calculated in accordance with Part V in like manner as for the claimant, [¹³except as provided in regulation 44(1) (modifications in respect of children and young persons)], would exceed £3,000.

[⁶(1A) Except where the amount prescribed in Schedule 7 in respect of a person to whom paragraph (1) applies includes an amount applicable under regulation 17(1)(d) or 18(1)(e), a person to whom paragraph (1) applies shall be treated as not being severely disabled.]

(2) In Schedule 7, for the purposes of paragraph 1, 2, 3 or 18 (patients), where a person has been a patient for two or more distinct periods separated by one or more intervals each not exceeding 28 days, he shall be treated as having been a patient continuously for a period equal in duration to the total of those distinct periods.

(3) In Schedule 7—

"person from abroad" means a person, who—

    (a) has a limited leave as defined in section 33(1) of the Immigration Act 1971 (hereinafter referred to as "the 1971 Act") to enter or remain in the United Kingdom which was given in accordance with any provision of the immigration rules (as defined in that section) which refers to there being, or to there needing to be, no recourse to public funds or to there being no charge on public funds during that limited leave; but this sub-paragraph shall not apply to a person who is a national of a Member State, a state which is a signatory to the European Convention on Social and Medical Assistance (done in Paris on 11th December 1953), [⁵a state which is a signatory to the Council of Europe Social Charter (signed in Turin on 18th October 1961),] the Channel Islands or the Isle of Man[³, unless, in the case of a national of a state which is a signatory of that European Convention, he has made an application for the conditions of his leave to remain in the United Kingdom to be varied, and that application has not been determined or an appeal from that application is pending under Part II of the 1971 Act (appeals);] or

    (b) having a limited leave (as defined in section 33(1) of the 1971 Act) to enter or remain in the United Kingdom, has remained without further leave under that Act beyond the time limited by the leave; or

    (c) is the subject of a deportation order being an order under section

5(1) of the 1971 Act (deportation) requiring him to leave and prohibiting him from entering the United Kingdom; or

(d) is adjudged by the immigration authorities to be an illegal entrant (as defined in section 33(1) of the 1971 Act) who has not subsequently been given leave under that Act to enter or remain in the United Kingdom; or

(e) has been allowed temporary admission to the United Kingdom by virtue of paragraph 21 of Schedule 2 to the 1971 Act; or

(f) has been allowed temporary admission to the United Kingdom by the Secretary of State outside any provision of the 1971 Act; or

(g) has not had his immigration status determined by the Secretary of State; [¹¹or

(h) is a national of a member State and is required by the Secretary of State to leave the United Kingdom;]

[¹⁴"person from abroad" also means a claimant who is not habitually resident in the United Kingdom, the Republic of Ireland, the Channel Islands or the Isle of Man, but for this purpose, no claimant shall be treated as not habitually resident in the United Kingdom who is—

(a) a worker for the purposes of Council Regulation (EEC) No. 1612/68 or (EEC) No. 1251/70 or a person with a right to reside in the United Kingdom pursuant to Council Directive No. 68/360/EEC or No. 73/148/EEC; or

(b) a refugee within the definition in Article 1 of the Convention relating to the Status of Refugees done at Geneva on 28th July 1951, as extended by Article 1(2) of the Protocol relating to the Status of Refugees done at New York on 31st January 1967; or

(c) a person who has been granted exceptional leave to remain in the United Kingdom by the Secretary of State.]

"patient" means a person (other than a prisoner) who is regarded as receiving free in-patient treatment within the meaning of the Social Security (Hospital In-Patients) Regulations 1975;

[¹⁶"prisoner" means a person who—

(a) is detained in custody pending trial or sentence upon conviction or under a sentence imposed by a court; or

(b) is on temporary release in accordance with the provisions of the Prison Act 1952 or the Prisons (Scotland) Act 1989,

other than a person whose detention is under the provisions of the Mental Health Act 1983 or the Mental Health (Scotland) Act 1984;]

[⁹"residential accommodation" means, subject to the following provisions of this regulation, accommodation provided by a local authority in a home owned or managed by that or another local authority—

(a) under sections 21 to 24 [¹⁶. . .] of the National Assistance Act 1948 (provision of accommodation); or

(b) in Scotland, under section 13B or 59 of the Social Work (Scotland) Act 1968 (provision of residential and other establishments) [¹⁵. . .]; or

(c) under section 7 of the Mental Health (Scotland) Act 1984 (functions of local authorities),

where the accommodation is provided for a person whose stay in that accommodation has become other than temporary.]

[⁷(3A) Where on or after 12th August 1991 a person is in, or only temporarily absent from, residential accommodation within the meaning of paragraph (3) and that accommodation subsequently becomes a residential care home within the meaning of regulation 19 (applicable amounts for persons in residential care and nursing homes) that person shall continue to be treated as being in residential accommodation within the meaning of paragraph (3) if, and for so long as, he remains in the same accommodation and the local authority is under a duty to provide or make arrangements for providing accommodation for that person.]

[¹⁰(3B) In a case where on 31st March 1993 a person was in or was temporarily absent from accommodation provided under section 26 of the National Assistance Act 1948, the definition of "residential accommodation" in paragraph (3) shall have effect in relation to that case as if for the words "provided by a local authority in a home owned or managed by that or another authority" there were substituted the words "provided in accordance with arrangements made by a local authority", and for the words in sub-paragraph (a) "under sections 21 to 24 [¹⁶. . .]" there were substituted the words "under section 26".

(3C) In a case where on 31st March 1993 a person was in or was temporarily absent from accommodation provided by a local authority under section 21 of the National Assistance Act 1948, the definition of "residential accommodation" in paragraph (3) shall have effect in relation to that case as if, after the words "by that or another [¹²local] authority" there were inserted the words "or provided in accordance with arrangements made by a local authority".]

[¹⁵(3D) In Scotland, in a case where on the 31st March 1993 a person was in or was temporarily absent from accommodation provided under section 13B in a private or voluntary sector home, section 59(2)(c) of the Social Work (Scotland) Act 1968 or section 7 of the Mental Health (Scotland) Act 1984 in a voluntary or private sector home, the definition of "residential accommodation" in paragraph (3) shall have effect in that case as if—

(a) for the words "provided by a local authority in a home owned or managed by that or another local authority" there were substituted the words "provided in accordance with arrangements made by a local authority"; and

(b) for the words in sub-paragraph (b) "under section 13B or 59" there were substituted the words "under section 13B or 59(2)(c)";

and for the purpose of this paragraph the definition of "residential accommodation" above shall continue to have effect as though the words "other than in premises registered under section 61 of that Act (registration) and which are used for the rehabilitation of alcoholics or drug addicts." were retained at the end of sub-paragraph (b) of the definition.

(3E) In Scotland, in a case where on 31st March 1993 a person was in or was temporarily absent from accommodation the provision of which was secured by a local authority under section 13B in a home owned or managed by that or another local authority, section 59(2)(a) or (b) of the Social Work (Scotland) Act 1968, or section 7 of the Mental Health (Scotland) Act 1984 in a home owned or managed by that or another local authority, the definition of "residential accommodation" in paragraph (3) shall have effect in relation to that case as if, after the words "by that or another local authority" there were inserted the words "or provided in accordance with arrangements made by a local authority".]

(4) A person who would, but for this paragraph, be in residential accommodation within the meaning of paragraph (3) shall not be treated as being in residential accommodation if he is a person—

(a) who is under the age of 18 and in the care of a local authority under Part II or III of the Social Work (Scotland) Act 1968 (promotion of social welfare of children in need of care), or

(b) [¹⁶. . .]

(c) for whom board is not provided.]

[⁸(4A) [⁹In paragraph (4), sub-paragraph (c)] shall apply only to accommodation—

(a) where no cooked or prepared food is made available to the claimant in consequence solely of his paying the charge for the accommodation or any other charge which he is required to pay as a condition of occupying the accommodation, or both of those charges, or

(b) where such food is actually made available for his consumption on payment of a further charge or charges.]

[¹⁰(4B) In the case of a person who on 31st March 1993 was either in or only temporarily absent from, residential accommodation within the meaning of regulation 21(3) as then in force, paragraph (4) shall apply as if sub-paragraph (c) was omitted.]

(5) A claimant to whom paragraph 19 of Schedule 7 (disability premium) applies shall be entitled to income support for the period in respect of which that paragraph applies to him notwithstanding that his partner was also entitled to income support for that same period.

AMENDMENTS

1. Income Support (General) Amendment No. 4 Regulations 1988 (S.I. 1988 No. 1445), Sched. 1, para. 1 (April 10, 1989).
2. Income Support (General) Amendment Regulations 1989 (S.I. 1989 No. 534), Sched. 1, para. 5 (October 9, 1989).
3. Income Support (General) Amendment Regulations 1990 (S.I. 1990 No. 547), reg. 8 (April 9, 1990).
4. Income Support (General and Transitional) Amendment Regulations 1990 (S.I. 1990 No. 2324), reg. 2 (December 17, 1990).
5. Income Support (General) Amendment Regulations 1991 (S.I. 1991 No. 236), reg. 7 (April 8, 1991).
6. Income Support (General) Amendment (No. 3) Regulations 1991 (S.I. 1991 No. 1033), reg. 2 (May 20, 1991).
7. Income Support (General) Amendment (No. 5) Regulations 1991 (S.I. 1991 No. 1656), reg. 2 (August 12, 1991).
8. Income-related Benefits Schemes (Miscellaneous Amendments) (No. 3) Regulations 1992 (S.I. 1992 No. 2155), reg. 15 (October 5, 1992).
9. Social Security Benefits (Amendments Consequential Upon the Introduction of Community Care) Regulations 1992 (S.I. 1992 No. 3147), Sched. 1, para. 3 (April 1, 1993).
10. Social Security Benefits (Miscellaneous Amendments) Regulations 1993 (S.I. 1993 No. 518), reg. 5 (April 1, 1993).
11. Income-related Benefits Schemes (Miscellaneous Amendments) Regulations 1993 (S.I. 1993 No. 315), reg. 4 (April 12, 1993).
12. Income-related Benefits Schemes (Miscellaneous Amendments) (No. 4) Regulations 1993 (S.I. 1993 No. 2119), reg. 10 (October 4, 1993).
13. Income-related Benefits Schemes (Miscellaneous Amendments) Regulations 1994 (S.I. 1994 No. 527), reg. 3 (April 11, 1994).
14. Income-related Benefits Schemes (Miscellaneous Amendments) (No. 3) Regulations 1994 (S.I. 1994 No. 1807), reg. 4(1) (August 1, 1994).
15. Income-related Benefits Schemes (Miscellaneous Amendments) (No. 5) Regulations 1994 (S.I. 1994 No. 2139), reg. 25 (October 3, 1994).
16. Income-related Benefits Schemes (Miscellaneous Amendments) Regulations 1995 (S.I. 1995 No. 516), reg. 21 (April 10, 1995).

DEFINITIONS

"child"—see 1986 Act, s.20(11) (SSCBA, s.137(1)).
"claimant"—see reg. 2(1).
"local authority"—*ibid.*
"residential care home"—*ibid.*, reg. 19(3).
"young person"—*ibid.*, reg. 14.

GENERAL NOTE

Paragraph (1)
Applicable amounts in special cases are to be as prescribed in Sched. 7. It is confirmed that the rule in reg. 17(b), disallowing a personal allowance for a child or young person who has capital of more than £3,000, applies to Sched. 7.

Paragraph (1A)
This provision secures that, except where the particular paragraph of Sched. 7 expressly allows the payment of a premium, a person whose entitlement falls under Sched. 7 does not qualify for the severe disability premium.

Paragraph (2)
This provision supplies a linking rule for hospital patients (see para. (3)) who come out of hospital for short periods.

Paragraph (3)
This paragraph contains some important definitions for Sched. 7, which are also referred to in other parts of the Regulations.

"Person from abroad"
With the additional definition of "person from abroad" inserted into para. (3) from August 1, 1994, there are effectively eight categories:
(1) those present in the U.K. with limited leave subject to the condition that there is no recourse to public funds;
(2) overstayers;
(3) those subject to a deportation order;
(4) illegal entrants;
(5) those allowed temporary admission to the U.K.;
(6) those whose immigration status has not been determined; and
(7) EU nationals who are required to leave the U.K. (but see *CIS 472/1994* below).
(8) those who are not habitually resident in the U.K., Republic of Ireland, Channel Islands or the Isle of Man, subject to the exceptions in (a), (b) or (c) of that part of the definition.
See para. 17 of Sched. 7 for the special rules for persons from abroad.

(1) For this category (sub-para. (a)) to apply the person must need leave to enter or remain in the U.K. In *R(SB) 11/88* it was held that it was for a SSAT to decide for supplementary benefit purposes whether a person was a patrial and so did not need leave to enter the country. The claimant had mistakenly been granted limited leave in 1982, and the immigration authorities did not in fact lift immigration controls until 1985. Although a SSAT should approach the Home Office for information if an issue of patriality arises and the person does not have a certificate of entitlement, it was not bound to apply the decision of the immigration authorities from 1982. *R(SB) 2/85* and *R(SB) 25/85*, giving conclusive effect to the decisions of the immigration authorities on the terms of leave, are held to be confined to situations where it is clear that leave is required for entry. A proper statement of the terms of leave should be obtained from the Home Office (*CSB 137/1983*). These principles should also apply to income support.
Sub-para. (a) cannot apply to nationals of EU Member States or to nationals of so-called "convention countries," as well as the Channel Islands and the Isle of Man. The convention countries, apart from those which have joined the EU, are Iceland, Malta, Norway and Turkey. The 1991 amendment brings in signatories to the European Social Charter. This now only affects Cyprus, as Austria has joined the EU.
(2) Some people who do not fall into sub-para. (a) may be given limited leave to be present in the U.K. with no conditions about public funds and thus may fall into para. (b) if they remain beyond the time limited by their leave. This cannot apply to nationals of the Republic of Ireland, the Isle of Man or the Channel Islands, who have freedom of travel within the U.K. (Immigration Act 1971, s.1(3)).
In the past there was doubt as to whether EU nationals could have limited leave within this category and for that reason sub-para. (h) was added from April 1993. However, on July 20, 1994 s. 7(1) of the Immigration Act 1988 was brought into force, which expressly provides that a person exercising Community rights does not require leave to enter or remain in the U.K. The position of nationals of the European Economic Area (EEA) States (other than the U.K.) exercising Community rights of freedom of movement is now set out in the Immigration (European Economic Area) Order 1994 (S.I. 1994 No. 1895) (I(EEA) Order), also in force from July 20, 1994. The EEA comprises EU member states (Austria, Belgium, Denmark, Finland, France, Germany, Greece, Republic of Ireland, Italy, Luxembourg, the Netherlands, Portugal, Spain, Sweden and the U.K.) plus Norway and Iceland. Nationals of the EEA States have rights of free movement within the EEA from January 1, 1994 under the Agreement establishing the EEA. Broadly, those exercising Community rights include

workers, work seekers, self-employed people, providers or recipients of services within the meaning of article 60 of the EC Treaty, and others whose right of residence is subject to the condition that they are self-financing, including students and retired people. Under the I(EEA) Order EEA nationals who cease to be exercising Community rights are treated as if they required leave to enter or remain and can be removed from the U.K. They have a right of appeal under the Immigration Act 1971.

(3) A British citizen cannot be deported, nor can some citizens of the Commonwealth and the Republic of Ireland (Immigration Act 1971, s.7(1)).

(4) Under sub-para. (d) the judgment of the immigration authorities on the person's status as an illegal entrant has to be accepted by the AO and SSAT.

(5) Sub-paras. (e) and (f) cover all forms of temporary admission.

(6) Sub-para. (g) covers those whose immigration status has not been determined by the immigration authorities. This must be subject to the principles of *R(SB) 11/88*.

(7) This provision is likely to have less application now in view of the introduction of the habitual residence test (see below). And see *CIS 472/1994* below on the meaning of "required to leave", but note the power to remove EEA nationals in article 15 of the I(EEA) Order from July 20, 1994.

The question of an EU national's right to remain in the U.K. for an unlimited period for the purpose of seeking employment was considered by the ECJ in *R v. Immigration Appeal Tribunal ex parte Antonissen* [1991] ECR 1–745. The Court held that the six months allowed under para. 143 of the then current Statement of Changes in Immigration Rules (HC 169) during which a person should obtain work did not "appear in principle to be insufficient". However, the Court also said that if a person showed he had "genuine chances" of finding employment he could not be required to leave the host member state. Since August 1993, the Home Office has sent letters to those who have not found work after six months requiring them to leave. Similar letters are sent to those here in a non-economic capacity who have been claiming income support. These letters refer to the Secretary of State's view that the person is not lawfully resident under E.C. law and state that the person should make arrangements to leave the U.K. This "requirement" to leave is not enforced but results in the withdrawal of income support under sub-para. (h) (but now see *CIS 472/1994* below).

However, the power of the Secretary of State to so "require" an EU national to leave the U.K. was challenged in *R v. Secretary of State for Home Department ex parte Vitale and Do Amaral* (High Court, *The Times*, April 18, 1995). The main argument centred on whether the effect of Article 8a(1) of the EC Treaty, inserted by the Treaty of European Union from November 1, 1993, was to enable a national of a Member State to lawfully remain in the U.K., whether he was in work or seeking work or not. Article 8a(1) provides that every EU citizen has "the right to move and reside freely within the territory of the Member States, subject to the limitations and conditions laid down in this Treaty and by the measures adopted to give it effect". Judge J. held that Article 8a did not create an unqualified right of every EU citizen to reside in any Member State as and when they may wish. The limitations on the rights of free movement granted by Article 48 of the EC Treaty approved by the ECJ in *Antonissen* remained effective. Judge J. also rejected an argument that because the Home Office letters did not represent the exercise of any legal power they were "shams", designed to avoid the payment of income support. (The I(EEA) Order which authorises the removal of EEA nationals did not come into force until July 20, 1994.) He holds that when the letters were sent the applicants were no longer present in the U.K. exercising Community rights. The fact that the Secretary of State could not enforce the request to leave did not invalidate it. It would be up to the SSAT, to whom the applicants had appealed against the withdrawal of their income support, to decide whether on the facts they were lawfully present in the U.K. and thus whether sub-para. (h) applied. Another issue had been whether the applicants had adequate rights of appeal, as required by European law. Judge J. held that the present judicial review proceedings and the appeal to the SSAT indicated that there were sufficient remedies. However, he stated that the letters sent by the Home Office and the BA in these cases should be reworded to avoid the impression that there were no rights of appeal. It is understood that this decision is being appealed to the Court of Appeal.

As was accepted in *Vitale* and *Do Amaral*, it is possible to appeal to a SSAT against the application of sub-para. (h) on the grounds that the EU national is lawfully resident, *i.e.* that he does have "genuine chances" of finding work. But following the decision in *Vitale* and *Do Amaral*, *CIS 472/1994* considered the meaning of "required to leave" in sub-para. (h). The Commissioner points out that the test is not whether the person is not lawfully resident (or has been informed that in the Secretary of State's view he is not lawfully resident), but whether he has been required to leave the U.K. by the Secretary of State. The letter from the Home Office expresses the Secretary of State's view that the person is not lawfully resident in the U.K. and states that the person should arrange to leave. That form of words fell short of the necessary degree of compulsion or insistence for there to be a "requirement" to leave. They were words of "advice" that the person should make arrangements to leave, but no more. The Commissioner also decides that the judgment in *Vitale* and *Do Amaral* did not prevent him from reaching this conclusion. The main argument in those cases had been directed to the lawfulness of the Secretary of State's decisions about continued residence and it had been largely assumed that the wording of the Home Office letters triggered sub-para. (h). This assumption was not a necessary part of the decision and was not bindng on him. Thus the claimant was not a "person from abroad" and remained entitled to income support. The result of the decision in *CIS 472/1994* is to render sub-para. (h) of no effect in these circumstances.

Note that *CIS 472/1994* and *Vitale* and *Do Amaral* do not deal with removal under the I(EEA) Order, which would seem to fall within para. (7).

(8) This additional definition of "person from abroad" introduces an "habitual residence" test for income support from August 1, 1994. A similar rule has been introduced for housing benefit and council tax benefit. The validity of this new provision has already been the subject of challenge (see *Ex parte Sarwar, Getachew and Urbanek* below).

Background

Part of the Government's justification for this significant and controversial change in the conditions of entitlement for income support was its concern about the potential growth of "benefit tourism", particularly with the expansion of the EEA. No evidence, however, was produced to indicate that this is a widespread problem. Although the intended target of the new rule is EEA nationals, others, for example U.K. citizens, particularly those from ethnic minorities, with family ties in other countries who have spent time living and working in those countries, or U.K. nationals returning after working abroad for a prolonged period, may experience difficulties in satisfying the test. The Social Security Advisory Committee's recommendation (Cm. 2609) that an habitual residence condition should not be imposed without research being undertaken to quantify the perceived problem and the potential effects of the proposed test was not accepted. The Committee also made other recommendations were the proposals to be implemented, some of which are reflected in the regulation's final form.

The new test

All claimants, including U.K. nationals and nationals of other EEA States, are subject to the test, unless they fall within one of the exempted groups (see below). The test applies to all new and repeat claims for income support from August 1, 1994. Existing claimants are not affected (see reg. 4(2) of the Income-related Benefits Schemes (Miscellaneous Amendments) (No. 3) Regulations 1994 (p. 374)). The requirement only applies to the claimant, not a partner or dependant. Since this rule operates as an exclusion from benefit, it is arguable that the burden of proof should be on the AO. However the opposite view is taken in the DSS guidance (see para. 18 of Memo AOG 3/76).

The basic rule is that a claimant who is not habitually resident in any part of the Common Travel Area (CTA) of the U.K., the Republic of Ireland, the Channel Islands and the Isle of Man is defined as a "person from abroad" and will not be entitled to ordinary income support. (Note that a "person from abroad" who qualifies for income support under reg. 70(3) (urgent cases) will be entitled to this even if they do not satisfy the habitual residence test; thus a person who fails the test may be entitled under reg. 70(3) if they come within one of the other categories of "person from abroad" in para. (3). See the notes to reg. 70(3).) However, certain groups are treated as habitually resident (sub-paras. (a) to (c)) and these are considered first.

Who is exempt?

Sub-para. (a)

A person who is a "worker" for the purposes of E.C. Regulations 1612/68 or 1251/70, or who has a right of residence under E.C. Directives 68/360 or 731/48, is exempt. These Regulations and Directives apply to all EEA nationals (including U.K. nationals who are exercising Community rights: *R v. Immigration Appeal Tribunal and Surinder Singh, ex parte Secretary of State for the Home Department*, ECJ Case C-370/90, [1992] 3 All E.R. 798).

E.C. Regulations 1612/68 and 1251/70

Regulation 1612/68 provides for freedom of movement for workers and their families.

The main question is what is meant by "worker" in this context. "Worker" is not defined in Regulation 1612/68 (or in the E.C. Treaty). However, the word is to be interpreted broadly and as a matter of Community, not national, law (*Levin* [1982] E.C.R. 1035). A person's motives for working in another Member State are not relevant (*Bettray* [1989] E.C.R 1621). "Worker" includes those who work part-time or whose pay is below subsistence level, provided that they are pursuing an activity that is "genuine and effective" and not on such a small scale as to be "marginal and ancillary" (*Levin*, and *Kempf* [1986] E.C.R. 1741). If the work is very limited *and* only on an irregular or occasional basis, this may indicate that it is a marginal and ancillary activity (*Raulin* [1992] E.C.R. 1–1027). But if it can be described as an economic activity (*Levin*), as opposed to, for example, a hobby, this should count as work, even if it is for only a few hours a week.

If the person has genuinely worked, even for a very short period, they count as a worker. There seems to be no reason why this should not include work done during a previous stay in the U.K. (even if on this occasion the person has not yet obtained employment). If a worker becomes involuntarily unemployed or incapable of work, they remain a worker for the purposes of Regulation 1612/68. This was accepted by the ECJ in *Scrivner* [1984] E.C.R. 1027. Mr Scrivner had worked in Belgium but had given up his job for personal reasons and then registered as in search of work. The ECJ held that he was entitled to the Belgian "minimex" (a benefit which provided a "minimum means of subsistence"), as this was a social advantage within Article 7(2) of Regulation 1612/68 which could not be denied to migrant workers. However, this is not the view taken by the DSS who consider that a worker who is temporarily incapacitated or involuntarily unemployed has a right to reside under Article 7(1) of Directive 68/360, but does not retain worker status (see paras. 10 and 11 of Memo AOG Vol 3/76). Although both a "worker" and a person with a right to reside are exempt from the habitual residence test under sub-para. (a), a person's right to reside under Directive 68/360 may be time-limited (see below). Worker status is also retained by a person who has voluntarily given up work in order to take up vocational training which is linked to the previous job (*Lair* 1988] E.C.R. 3161). If the training has no link with the previous occupation, worker status is only retained in the case of a migrant worker who was involuntarily unemployed (*Raulin*).

But what about a person seeking work? By making the test whether a person is a worker for the purposes of Regulation 1612/68, it is apparently intended to exclude work seekers from sub-para. (a). See *Lebon* [1987] E.C.R. 2811 which holds that the right to equal treatment as regards social and tax advantages (which would include income support) in Article 7(2) of Regulation 1612/68 only applies to workers and not to those who move to seek employment. The ECJ states that people who move in order to seek employment only enjoy equal treatment as regards access to such employment in accordance with Article 48 of the Treaty and Articles 2 and 5 of Regulation 1612/68. But the question under sub-para. (a) is only whether a person is a worker for the purposes of 1612/68, not whether he can assert any right under it (or Article 48). It is certainly arguable, for example, that a person who has worked in an EEA state of which he is not a national and comes to the U.K. seeking work is a worker for the purposes of Regulation 1612/68 sub-para. (a) as does not say "worker in the U.K." (*c/f* "person with a right to reside in the United Kingdom"). If a person has actually worked in another EEA country it is difficult to see why he should not come within the category of "worker". To exclude such people from sub-para. (a) (quite apart from others who are genuinely seeking work), and, as a consequence, to deny them income support while they look for employment (unless they are habitually resident), does not fit easily with the concept of free movement of workers embodied in Article 48 of the EC Treaty.

Regulation 1251/70, *inter alia*, grants a right of residence after termination of employment to certain retired or incapacitated workers. For this to apply, a worker must have reached pension age when he stopped work, been employed in the host State for the last 12 months and lived there for more than three years, or ceased work due to a permanent incapacity and lived in the host State for more than two years (if the incapacity resulted from an accident at work or occupational disease entitling him to benefit there is no residence condition). If his spouse is a national there are no required periods of employment or residence.

E.C. Directives 68/360 and 73/148

People who have a right to reside under E.C. Directives 68/360 or 73/148 are also treated as habitually resident. (The I(EEA) Order implements, *inter alia*, Directives 68/360 and 73/148.) Directive 68/360 covers workers and members of their families who come within Regulations 1612/68 or 1251/70. Members of the worker's family who have a right to "install" themselves with the worker are his spouse, their children who are under the age of 21 or dependent, and their ascendant relatives who are dependent (Article 10(1) of Regulation 1612/68). In addition, Article 10(2) provides that Member States shall "facilitate the admission of" other members of a worker's family who are either dependent or who were living under his roof in the previous country. It is not clear whether the latter also have a right of residence for these purposes (see Wyatt and Dashwood, *European Community Law* (3rd ed.), pp. 246 and 282).

Directive 68/360 is concerned with the issue of residence permits, but the right to reside does not derive from the permit but from Community law itself (*Royer* [1976] E.C.R. 497, *Echternach* [1989] E.C.R. 723, *Raulin*). Thus workers who satisfy the conditions for obtaining (or retaining) a residence permit are covered, even if they have not applied for one. Residence permits are issued on the basis of confirmation from the employer of the worker's employment. They are for five years unless the employment is expected to last less than one year; where the expected period of the worker's employment is more than three months but less than a year a permit may be limited to this period. A worker whose employment is not expected to last more than three months has a right of residence without a residence permit for the expected duration of the employment. Seasonal workers, and frontier workers (*i.e.* those who return to another Member State at least once a week) also have a right of residence without a residence permit. A residence permit does not end if the worker becomes involuntarily unemployed or temporarily incapable of work. However, it may do so if the person leaves the U.K. for more than six months (unless this is for military service).

Directive 73/148, which is very similar to Directive 68/360, covers the self-employed and those who are providing or receiving services, and their families. It also applies to EEA nationals who are seeking self-employment, or to provide or receive services. As in the case of Directive 68/360, the permit does not create the right to reside which derives from the Treaty itself, but only confirms it. Residence permits for the self-employed are to be granted for at least five years; for providers or recipients of services they may be limited to the duration of the service. A permit is not to be withdrawn because the person is temporarily incapable of work. Services are those that are normally paid for, and include industrial, commercial, craft and professional activities (Article 60 of the Treaty). The ECJ has held that tourism, medical treatment and education are covered (*Luisi* [1984] E.C.R. 377). The Directive does not, for example, specify the level of service, or impose any qualifying period, in order for a right of residence to be granted. Thus its application could be quite wide.

Sub-paras. (b) and (c)

Refugees and people with exceptional leave to remain are treated as habitually resident.

Habitual residence
"Habitual residence" is not defined in the regulation and therefore the words must be given their natural and ordinary meaning (see *Shah v. Barnet London Borough Council* [1983] 2 A.C. 309, [1983] 1 All E.R. 226 below). Habitual residence is not the same as domicile (*R(U)8/88*). It is possible to be habitually resident in more than one country (although it is unusual); it is also possible to be habitually resident in none. A person does not have to be continually present in a country in order to be habitually resident. There is no time limit after which habitual residence is established, but the longer the length of stay the more likely the person is to be habitually resident. On the other hand, a person may be habitually resident very shortly (possibly from the first day) after arriving in a country depending on the circumstances. In practice, if a person states on their income support claim that they have not entered the U.K. within the last five years habitual residence will be assumed. The SSAC recommended that the trigger point for generating inquiries into habitual residence should be reduced to two years. The Government's reply was that they accepted this in principle and would decide on the time period to use in future after monitoring the operation of the test.

The concept of habitual residence occurs in European law, in particular in E.C. Regulation 1408/71 dealing with social security for migrant workers, and has been considered in several Commissioners' decisions on unemployment benefit (see *R(U)7/85, R(U)4/86, CU 285/1985* and in particular *R(U)8/88* which has appendices summarising these decisions together with references to the relevant European provisions and case law). The detailed guidance that has been issued to AOs on how to operate the test (since April 1995 in Memo AOG Vol 3/76, replacing Memo AOG 3/69; see also Income Support Circular ISG 15/94, revised November 1994) is largely based on this case law and thus focuses heavily on employment-related issues. This guidance sets out the following factors to be considered: the person's centre of interests (*i.e.* where are their links/ties, *e.g.* their family and their home/possessions}; employment record (the nature of any previous occupation; has the person got an offer of "genuine and effective" work in the U.K.?); length and continuity of residence elsewhere; why did the claimant come; and what are the claimant's intentions. The guidance states that AOs should consider all these factors, although not all will be relevant in each case. It emphasises that the list is neither exhaustive nor conclusive and that AOs "should reach a conclusion having regard to the overall circumstances of each case and taking into account existing case law". However, it is important to remember that the context of this case law is that of returning workers claiming to have retained their "habitual residence" while working elsewhere, in order to qualify for unemployment benefit. It is thus mainly concerned with looking at the past. Yet applying the test to income support will often require adjudicating authorities to look to the future and to reach judgments on the more subjective factors of the claimant's intentions and his reasons for coming to the CTA. An example of the problems of importing this test into income support is shown by *Di Paolo v. Office National de L'Emploi* [1977] E.C.R. 315 where the ECJ held that stable employment could outweigh other factors in determining habitual residence. However, in connection with claims for income support this factor will often be less relevant than others. The SSAC's report points out that the case law's emphasis on the length and stability of employment does not take account of the fact that part-time or temporary work, or short fixed-term contracts, may be the only available option for many people coming to the U.K. The DSS accepted that the changing nature of the labour market should be taken into consideration but this is not fully reflected in the guidance. Further, for people who are not required to be available for employment as a condition of receiving income support (*e.g.* lone parents), employment related factors may be of little assistance in determining whether thay are habitually residentl.

The concept of habitual residence also occurs in certain areas of U.K. law, *e.g.* tax, family and child support law. Here it has been equated to "ordinarily resident". See, for example *Kapur v. Kapur* [1984] F.L.R. 920, a case on the meaning of habitual residence in the Domicile and Matrimonial Proceedings Act 1973, which holds that there is no real distinction between "ordinary" and "habitual" residence. Bush J. in *Kapur* refers to the House of Lords' decision in *Shah* (which concerned the interpretation of "ordinarily resident" in the Education Act 1962) where ordinary residence was held to include habitual residence. Lord Scarman states that the words "ordinarily resident" were to be given their natural and ordinary meaning which was "habitually and normally resident, apart from temporary or occasional absences of long or short duration". Habitually meant that the residence had to be adopted voluntarily and for a settled purpose (see *IRC v. Lysaght* [1928] A.C. 234). In the light of the House of Lords' decision in *Shah* Bush J. declined to follow *Cruse v. Chittum* [1974] 2 All E.R. 940 which had held that habitual residence was something more than ordinary residence. In *Shah* Lord Scarman points out that a settled purpose could be for a limited period; there was no need to intend to stay indefinitely. Such a purpose could include education, employment, health, family or "merely love of the place". Thus in *CA 35/1992* a woman, who had gone to Malta for health reasons, intending to return within 18 months, was held to be ordinarily resident there. The fact that a person has a restricted right to stay in the U.K. does not prevent him from being habitually resident (*Shah* and *Kapur*). It is clear from these cases that habitual residence can be acquired very quickly. The proposition that it can be acquired in one day (*Macrae v. Macrae* [1949] 2 All E.R. 34) has been doubted, but certainly where there is a settled purpose a very short period may suffice, depending on the circumstances. The interpretation adopted in these cases would seem to be a more generous one, with the emphasis more on the person's intentions and purpose. In connection with claims for income support this may be more relevant than employment-centred factors.

The SSAC expressed regret that the chosen test was not ordinary residence as this was the test for family credit and disability working allowance and one with which U.K. adjudicators were more familiar. They understood that the DSS's view was that habitual residence implied "a stronger, more regular physical presence in the country and association with it" than did ordinarily resident. But they considered that the difference between the two was one of emphasis and they were unable to find any uniquely distinguishing factor.

Until an authoritative decision on the meaning of habitual residence in the context of income support emerges, the exact test to be applied remains unclear. As already stated, the DSS's guidance relies on the European case law, in particular the factors set out by the ECJ in *Di Paolo* (see above). But it is necessary to remember that the issue in *Di Paolo* was whether a person could claim unemployment benefit from the country to which he had returned on the basis of his habitual residence there. Thus it concerned the exception in Article 71(1)(b)(ii) of Regulation 1408/71 to the general rule that an unemployed person should receive unemployment benefit from the State where he was last employed. The ECJ emphasised the need for this exception to be strictly interpreted to prevent it nullifying the general rule. It is therefore arguable that this interpretation should be restricted to its particular context. On the other hand, the judgment of the House of Lords in *Shah* makes it clear that it is intended to be of more general application (see, for example, [1983] 1 All E.R. at p. 232, paras. e to f). Moreover, the purpose of the income support habitual residence rule is to provide an exception in the case of claimants who are not habitually resident to the general principle that a person in Great Britain is eligible for income support and so should be interpreted in that light.

Ultimately, the question of whether a person is habitually resident will have to be determined by looking at all the circumstances of each case. Clearly, as it is presently being interpreted, the test is highly complex, imprecise and subjective and requires adjudicating authorities to balance many competing factors. It leaves much room for argument and no doubt will often be the subject of appeal. The SSAC considered "that it will be extremely difficult to ensure that the test is applied fairly and consistently". Despite assurances that AOs would have comprehensive guidance on how to apply the test, the Committee remained of the view that it "would inevitably lead to cases of doubtful adjudication, refusal of benefit and consequent hardship". Early experience of the operation of the test seems to have borne this out. It has certainly had substantial impact, with 15,564 people being refused benefits because of it, 2,599 of them British citizens, in the first six months of its operation (*Hansard*, March 21, 1995, Col. 253).

If a person fails the habitual residence test this does not mean to say that he cannot satisfy it at a subsequent date, particularly if further information is produced or there is a change in circumstances, or simply due to passage of time.

Ex parte Sarwar, Getachew and Urbanek

Mr Sarwar was a U.K. national, Mr Getachew and Mr Urbanek and his mother were EEA nationals, who were refused income support on the ground that they were not habitually resident. In *R v. Secretary of State for Social Security ex parte Sarwar, Getachew and Urbanek* (High Court, April 11, 1995) they challenged that refusal, arguing that the regulation introducing the test was *ultra vires*; Mr Getachew and the Urbaneks also claimed that the test was unlawful under European law.

On the first point, it was contended that because s.124(1) of the Contributions and Benefits Act states that "a person in Great Britain is entitled to income support . . .", it was not within the Secretary of State's regulation-making powers to qualify this simple presence test by introducing the further requirement of habitual residence. The change was not limited to a class of claimants, but created a universal test of habitual residence (subject only to very limited exceptions) and thus was inconsistent with the primary legislation. It was significant that the regulation had not been made under s.137(2)(a) (circumstances in which a person is to be treated as being or not being in Great Britain), but under s.135(2) (power to prescribe nil applicable amount). If the new regulation had purported to treat anyone who was not habitually resident as not being in Great Britain, the fact that the test was being amended on a universal basis would have been more obvious. But prescribing a nil applicable amount for all claimants who are not habitually resident (subject to the limited exceptions) had the same effect. Indeed this was the intended effect (see the Secretary of State's statement in response to the SSAC's report on this proposed change: "These regulations will introduce a test of habitual residence into the Income Support, Housing Benefit and Council Tax Benefit schemes" (para. 2)).

However, the High Court rejected this argument and held that the provision was valid. The Court stated that Parliament had only intended that physical presence in Great Britain should be a necessary, but not a sufficient, condition for eligibility. If the test could have been introduced directly under s.137(2)(a), the Court saw no reason why this could not be done indirectly under s.135(1) and (2). This seems unsatisfactory and does not deal with the main argument. The Court's reasoning that s.137(2)(a) would be otiose if Parliament intended that every person physically present in Great Britain would be eligible for income support misses the point. It was not being argued that the Secretary of State did not have power to treat people as not being in Great Britain, but that he did not have power to introduce a universal test of habitual residence without amending the primary legislation.

The Court also held that the new test was not contrary to European law. Article 6 of the E.C. Treaty prohibits any discrimination on the grounds of nationality within the scope of the operation of the Treaty. Article 48 provides for freedom of movement for workers. Article 48(3) states that this includes the right to, *inter alia*, move freely within Member States to accept offers of employment actually made, stay in a Member State for the purpose of employment and remain there after the employment has ended (subject to the conditions set out in the implementing regulations). It was argued that the provision indirectly discriminates in favour of Irish nationals against other EEA nationals because Irish nationals are more likely to be habitually resident in Ireland and thus exempt from the test. The Court was prepared to accept that this could be discriminatory. But this did not assist the applicants because in *Lebon* the ECJ had decided that the right to equal treatment as regards social and tax advantages in Article 7(2) of Regulation 1612/68 only applied to workers, not work seekers. Although *Lebon* was decided under Regulation 1612/68, not the Treaty, this was immaterial as a Regulation could not detract from rights under the Treaty, although it might add to them. Since the applicants, as work seekers, had no right under Article 48 to income support, the issue as to whether the alleged discrimination was in favour of U.K. and Irish nationals, or just U.K. nationals, was irrelevant (see *Humbel* [1988] E.C.R. 5365). The rights of free movement and residence were not co-extensive with the right to maintenance (*Brown* [1988] E.C.R. 3205, *Raulin* [1992] E.C.R. 1027).

Article 8a (inserted by the Treaty of European Union) provides for the right to move and reside freely within the Member States, subject to the conditions in the Treaty and the implementing legislation. The question whether Article 8a confers additional rights (or is merely declaratory) and whether it is of direct effect had already been referred to the ECJ in *R v. Secretary of State for the Home Department ex parte Adams* [1995] All E.R. (EC) 177. But even if Article 8a did create a new right of residence, it was qualified by the last part of the provision, and so subject to the ECJ's decision in *Lebon*.

It is understood that an appeal has been made to the Court of Appeal, so that there will be a further opportunity for these important and fundamental issues to be fully aired.

Mr Getachew had also challenged decisions to refuse him an urgent cases payment under reg. 70(3) and an interim payment. See the notes to reg. 70(3) and to reg. 2(1) of the Payments Regulations.

"Patient"

Reg. 2(2) of the Hospital In-Patients Regulations requires that the person is or has been maintained free of charge while undergoing treatment in a NHS hospital or a similar institution. There have been amendments in November 1987 and November 1992 so that in all cases a person is to be regarded as maintained free of charge for a day unless the accommodation and services are provided under s.65 of the National Health Service Act 1987 (and the Scottish equivalent) or para. 14 of Sched. 2 to the National Health Service and Community Care Act 1990, which relate only to fee-paying patients in NHS and Trust hospitals. In *CS 249/1989* and *CIS 371/1990* (to be reported as *R(IS) 7/92*) the Commissioners regretfully apply the unambiguous effect of the 1987 amendment, which means that patients for whom considerable contributions to maintenance are made are still treated as patients, with the consequent reductions in income support specified in Sched. 7. *CIS 192/1991* holds that the deeming applies despite the person's absence from the hospital during each period of 24 hours.

In *White v. Chief Adjudication Officer, The Times*, August 2, 1993, the Health Authority had made an agreement with a nursing home under which the home agreed to reserve 18 places for people nominated by the Health Authority in return for a grant. The claimant who had been in hospital for some years was transferred to the nursing home under this arrangement. The Court of Appeal agreed with *CIS 371/1990* (to be reported as *R(IS) 7/92*) that the definition of "hospital" in s.128 of the National Health Service Act 1977 applied. In s.128 "hospital" includes "any institution for the reception and treatment of persons suffering from illness", and "illness" is defined to include mental disorder and "any injury or disability requiring medical or dental treatment or nursing". The claimant was mentally ill and required appropriate nursing. The nursing home had agreed to maintain appropriate staffing, including qualified mental nurses. Medication was dispensed (although not prescribed) by the nursing home. Thus the home was a hospital within the meaning of the Hospital In-Patient Regulations. It was not maintained under the National Health Service Act 1977, but the claimant was receiving treatment there pursuant to arrangements made by the Health Authority on behalf of the Secretary of State under the 1977 Act which was enough to bring the hospital within reg. 2(2)(b). The claimant was therefore not entitled to income support as his income exceeded his reduced applicable amount as a hospital in-patient.

Note: Reg. 2(2) of the Hospital In-Patient Regulations was amended on November 16, 1992. It is not clear whether such an arrangement will still fall within the terms of reg. 2(2) as amended.

"Prisoner"

A person is detained in custody pending trial once he has been charged. It does not matter that in fact no trial takes place because the proceedings are discontinued. For the period he was in custody he was a prisoner (*CIS 255/1990*, to be reported as R(IS) 1/94). However, a person required to live in a bail hostel is not detained in custody pending trial (*R(IS) 17/93*); see Sched. 7, para. 9 as to how his applicable amount is calculated if he is a member of a couple.

Sub-para. (b) of the definition has been added to reverse the effect of *Chief Adjudication Officer v. Carr, The Times*, June 2, 1994 (which was the appeal from *CIS 561/1992*). A majority of the Court of Appeal had upheld the Commissioner's decision that a person serving a prison sentence who was released for a period of home leave was not a prisoner during that leave period. A person on temporary release will now continue to count as a prisoner and will not be eligible for income support. A person on income support with whom the prisoner stays while released on temporary licence can apply for a community care grant for his living expenses (*Social Fund Guide*, para. 3621).

Only people detained in custody awaiting trial or sentence have a limited entitlement to income support (see Sched. 7, para. 8(b)).

"Residential accommodation"

This definition applies where the person's stay is more than temporary and controls the application of the so-called "Part III rate" under para. 13 of Sched. 7. Note that para. (4) excludes from the definition under-18s in care in Scotland (sub-para. (a)), and accommodation where board is not provided (sub-para. (c)). The effect of sub-para. (c) is that residents of some types of local authority hostels are not shifted onto ordinary income support and housing benefit with other hostel-dwellers. If board is available, residents remain entitled to the "Part III rate" under para. 13 of Sched. 7. See the notes to the definition of "residential care home" in reg. 19 for "board". Para. (4A) in effect provides that board is available where any cooked or prepared food is provided in return for an inclusive charge. The intention is that if residents buy their own food or meals when they want them they are not restricted to the Part III rate.

Paragraph (3A)

Local authorities have duties to provide accommodation under the statutes mentioned in the definition of residential accommodation in para.(3), either in their own homes or by meeting the costs of independent homes. Residents then make a contribution to the costs. By agreement between the Government and local authorities the minimum weekly charge has been set at 80 per cent. of the basic rate of retirement pension. The resident can qualify for the ordinary rates of income support.

The Government was concerned that some local authorities had transferred their own homes to independent bodies (or were planning to do so) and required residents who did not wish to move to sign undertakings to arrange their own accommodation. If this had the effect of absolving the local authority from their duty to provide accommodation, the costs would be transferred from the local authorities to the income support budget. There was concern that the long-term welfare of existing residents was at risk if the local authority's responsibility was removed. Thus para. (3A) provides that if residential accommodation becomes a residential care home after August 11, 1991, existing residents continue to be treated as if they were still in residential accommodation. There are two conditions to this. The first is that the person remains in the same accommodation. There may be scope for manipulation here. The second condition is that the local authority remains under a duty to provide or arrange for accommodation for the person. At the same time as reg. 21 was amended the Secretary of State issued Directions under the National Assistance Act 1948 and the National Health Service Act 1977 that in these circumstances of transfer the local authority remains under a duty. *CIS 298/1992* and *CIS 641/1992* decide that para. (3A) did effect a material change in the law and is not (as the AO had argued) merely declaratory. In both cases the claimants were resident in "Part III" homes for the elderly, the management of which was transferred by the local authority to a voluntary organisation before August 12, 1991. The residents were given the option of staying in the same home or moving to another home still run by the local authority. Both claimants stayed in their current home. The Commissioner holds that the evidence showed that the agreement between the local authority and the voluntary organisation in both cases did not come within s.26 of the National Assistance Act 1948. Thus the claimants were entitled to income support at the residential care home rate. The general approach of *CIS 298/1992* and *CIS 641/1992* is followed by the Commissioner in *CA 60/1993*, but he also points out that in deciding whether an arrangement is made under s.26 of the 1948 Act, s.26(5) is of central importance. If the residents are liable to make payments for their accommodation to the voluntary organisation a necessary characteristic of a s.26 arrangement is missing and the continued provision of accommodation is not pursuant to Part III of the 1948 Act. The Commissioner's decision in *CIS 298/1992* and *CIS 641/1992* was confirmed by the Court of Appeal in *Chief Adjudication Officer v. Harris* and *Chief Adjudication Officer v. Gibbon* (April 15, 1994). The CAO is appealing to the House of Lords.

Paragraphs (3B) to (3E)

The intention of these paragraphs is that where a local authority accepted responsibility for accommodating a person prior to April 1, 1993, they remain responsible for them.

[¹Reductions in applicable amounts in certain cases of failure to attend courses

21A.—(1) The weekly applicable amount of a claimant to whom paragraph (3) applies shall be reduced in each relevant week by a sum equal to the appropriate percentage of the relevant amount which applies in his case.

(2) A reduction under paragraph (1) shall, if it is not a multiple of 5p, be rounded to the nearest such multiple or, if it is a multiple of 2.5p but not of 5p, to the next lower multiple of 5p.

(3) Except where paragraph (4) applies, this paragraph applies to a claimant where—

(a) he has been notified of a relevant course;
(b) he has during the period of [²12 months] which ended on the day on which he was notified of that course been in receipt of benefit—
   (i) without any period of interruption;
   (ii) with a period of interruption which did not exceed 56 days; or
   (iii) with a number of periods of interruption, none of which exceeded 56 days;
(c) his entitlement to benefit during the whole of that period of [²12 months], or such part of it as the claimant in question was in receipt of benefit, was subject to the condition that he was available for employment;
(d) his entitlement to income support is not subject to a reduction in the relevant week under regulation 22 (reductions in applicable amounts in certain cases of actual or notional unemployment benefit disqualification); and
(e) he has failed to attend the whole or any part of that course.

(4) This paragraph shall apply where the claimant's failure to attend a relevant course is attributable to any of the following circumstances—

(a) the claimant in question was suffering from some disease or bodily or mental disablement on account of which—
   (i) he was not able to attend the relevant course in question; or
   (ii) his attendance at that course would have put at risk the health of other persons;
(b) the time it took, or would normally have taken, for the claimant to travel from his home to the course and back to his home by a route and means appropriate to his circumstances and to the course exceeded, or would normally have exceeded, one hour in either direction;
(c) the claimant was caring for a member of his household where—
   (i) that member was unable to care for himself;
   (ii) no other member of that household was available to care for him; and
   (iii) in the circumstances of the case it was not practical for the claimant to make other arrangements for the care of that member;
(d) the claimant was attending court [² . . .] as a party to any proceedings, or as a witness or as a juror;
(e) the claimant was arranging or attending the funeral of a partner or relative;
(f) the claimant was engaged in—
   (i) the manning or launching of a lifeboat; or
   (ii) the performance of duty as a part-time fireman in a fire brigade maintained in pursuance of the Fire Services Acts 1947 to 1959;
(g) the claimant was required to deal with some domestic emergency; or
(h) the claimant was providing assistance in response to an emergency.

(5) A claimant shall be treated as having provided assistance in response to an emergency for the purposes of paragraph (4)(h) [²only]—
[²(a) if he was a member of a group of persons organised wholly or partly for the purpose of providing such assistance and he was called upon to—
   (i) provide assistance to any person whose life might have been endangered or who might have been exposed to the risk of serious bodily injury or whose health might have been seriously impaired;
   (ii) protect property of substantial value from imminent risk of serious damage or destruction; or
   (iii) assist in measures being taken to prevent a serious threat to health; and]

(b) [²where the events which gave rise to an emergency included]—
    (i) a fire, flood or an explosion;
    (ii) a natural catastrophe;
    (iii) a railway or other accident;
    (iv) a cave or mountain accident; [²or]
    (v) a search for a person reported missing.

(6) For the purposes of this regulation—

"appropriate percentage" means 40 per cent. except that where the circumstances of a case fall within those set out in regulation 22(2) it means 20 per cent.;

"benefit" means income support or unemployment benefit or, if they are received in respect of the same benefit week, both of those benefits;

"notified" means notified in writing by the Secretary of State for Employment by a notice which specifies in relation to the relevant course which the claimant may attend—
    (i) the date of the course, or if the duration of the course is to exceed one day, the date of each day of the course;
    (ii) the time when the course is to begin, or if it is to begin at different times on different days, each of those times; and
    (iii) the place at which the course is to be held, or, if it is to be held at more than one place, each of those places;

"relevant amount" has the same meaning as in regulation 22(1);

"relevant course" means a course or programme provided by [²or on behalf of] the Secretary of State for Employment for the purpose of improving the prospects of unemployed persons entering or returning to employment other than any such course or programme which—
    (a) is provided for the purpose of training for employment or acquiring work experience; or
    (b) exceeds 5 weeks in duration;

"relevant week" means the benefit which includes the Friday which falls more than 6 but less than 14 days after the Saturday of the week in which the claimant in question failed to attend the whole or any part of a relevant course.]

AMENDMENTS

1. Income Support (General and Transitional) Amendment Regulations 1990 (S.I. 1990 No. 2324), reg. 3 (December 17, 1990).
2. Income-related Benefits Schemes (Miscellaneous Amendments) Regulations 1993 (S.I. 1993 No. 315), reg. 5 (March 29, 1993).

DEFINITIONS

"benefit week"—see reg. 2(1).
"claimant"—*ibid.*
"employment"—*ibid.*
"partner"—*ibid.*
"relative"—*ibid.*

GENERAL NOTE

The Social Security Advisory Committee, in their report on the regulations introducing reg. 21A (Cm. 1355), describe its purpose as to:

"provide for a reduction in the applicable amount of the income support of a person in certain circumstances where he or she has been notified of a Restart course but has failed to attend or to complete the course. The intention is that attendance at a relevant course would be mandatory for people unemployed for two years or more and who refused all offers of help at a Restart interview" (para. 3).

One-week Restart courses for the unemployed over 18 are normally voluntary. The proposal to make them mandatory is

"part of a package introduced in April 1990, to provide guidance and advice for long-term unemployed people. The Employment Service's Claimant Advisers had found that many people who had been unemployed for more than two years lacked the motivation and confidence to take advantage of the range of help on offer from the Employment Service ... [In] order to stimulate effective job search it was proposed to introduce a requirement to attend a Restart course as a condition of receiving full benefit" (paras. 6 and 7).

The courses were said to be:

"designed to help people who have particular difficulties in getting back to work and to restore their confidence and motivation. The course does not provide skills training or education but is essentially an enabling process. The intention is to help those individuals to reassess their strengths and skills, look at all the options, and to decide the way forward ... The courses are part of a six week period of intensive support from Employment Service staff" (paras. 8 and 9).

Selection for courses would be through the Restart interview programme. These normally take place at six month intervals. If a person has been continuously unemployed for at least two years and has refused or failed to take up all offers of help in finding a job, referral to a Restart course would be considered (para. 10).

The SSAC considered that what was envisaged was not really a "course," but was a programme of assessment. The majority did not object to making attendance at a one week course a condition of full benefit entitlement, but subject to safeguards which were not accepted by the Government.

In April 1993, the Government introduced a new one week assessment course for those who have been unemployed for a year, called Jobplan Workshop. People will be directed to the workshop if they refuse all other offers of help at an interview with a Claimant Adviser. The year's anniversary of becoming unemployed is thought to mark a significant watershed. The workshops will have two tutors instead of Restart's one and are to be aimed at encouraging people to be more positive about seeking work and to develop clear goals. Therefore, the terms of reg. 21A have been amended to enable the sanction for non-attendance to be applied to the new courses.

Paragraph (1)

Para. (1) applies the reduction in benefit for the specified period. The exact amount and length of the reduction is set by the definitions of "appropriate percentage" and "relevant week" in para. (6). Paras. (3) and (4) define which claimants can be made subject to reg. 21A. See the notes to those paragraphs.

Paragraph (3)

Para. (3) sets out five conditions which must be met before reg. 21A can be applied to a claimant. Para. (4) sets out exceptions.

(a) The claimant must have been notified of a relevant course. Under para. (6), "notified" means notified in writing of the precise dates, places and times of the course. "Relevant course" is quite restrictively defined in para. (6). It must be provided by or on behalf of the Secretary of State for Employment. By analogy with *R(IS) 2/91*, "provided" will mean "made available." The purpose of the course or programme must be to improve employment prospects and not to provide training or work experience. Although Restart and Jobplan workshop courses currently only last for one week, the para. (6) definition excludes courses of over five weeks. This leaves some scope for future changes in the nature of the courses. The purpose of the courses is reminiscent of what used to go on in Re-establishment Centres, where attendance for quite long periods could be a condition of entitlement to supplementary benefit.

(b) The basic rule is that the claimant must have been continuously in receipt of income support and/or unemployment benefit for the 12 months immediately before the date of notification under sub-para. (a). However, the effect of heads (ii) and (iii) is to allow any number of periods of interruption of receipt of benefit to count towards the limit provided that each interruption is shorter than 57 days. The 12-month period of benefit receipt could thus theoretically be far from continuous. Since the reference is to the exact period of 12 months and not to a period of at least 12 months, it appears to be necessary that the claimant was in receipt of benefit on the day exactly 12 months before the date of notification. Only periods of interruption within the 12-month period, *i.e.* preceded and followed by receipt of benefit within the 12-month period, can count.

(c) For the periods for which the claimant was in receipt of benefit, he must have been required to be available for employment. This is a general condition of entitlement to unemployment benefit. For income support, see reg. 8 and Sched. 1.

(d) If income support is already reduced on the grounds of voluntary unemployment under reg. 22 for the relevant week the reduction under reg. 21A is not to be applied on top.

(e) Reg. 21A is triggered by a failure to attend the course notified or any part of it. Failure to attend for a day or a part of a day counts, although absences of a few minutes could be ignored on the *de minimis* principle. Since sub-para. (e) does not simply say that the claimant does not attend, it may be arguable that the notion of "failure" imports a requirement of a breach of some obligation (see *R(SB) 21/82*) going beyond the limited categories of para. (4).

Note that some of the factors for selection of claimants for Restart and Jobplan workshop courses do not feature in the regulation. In particular, there is no legal requirement that the claimant must have refused all offers of help or that the course should be appropriate to his circumstances. The administrative instructions to Claimant Advisers will therefore be particularly important.

Paragraph (4)

Para. (4) lists circumstances relating to the failure to attend. The SSAC recommended that there should be a general good cause exception (Cm. 1355, para. 26). The Government rejected this recommendation, preferring a more clear-cut rule, but did expand the list of exemptions (Cm. 1355, Secretary of State's Statement, para. 6).

Most of the categories are self-explanatory and only a few comments are necessary.

(*a*) See s.57(1) of the Contributions and Benefits Act (Bonner *et al.*, *Non-Means Tested Benefits*).

(*b*) It appears that if either the normal or actual travel time by appropriate means in either direction was over an hour, the exemption applies.

(*c*) See notes to s.137(1) of the Contributions and Benefits Act (1986 Act, s.20(11)) and reg. 16 for membership of a household.

(*g*) Domestic emergency is not defined.

(*h*) The restrictive conditions of this exemption are set out in para. (5).

Paragraph (6)

The reduction applied for the relevant week is the same as that applied for voluntary unemployment under reg. 22, *i.e.* 40 per cent. or 20 per cent. of the claimant's personal applicable amount.

The definition of "relevant week" identifies the benefit week for which the reduction is to be applied. Whether the absence is from the whole course or only a small part, the sanction is the same, with no discretion to vary it. While the courses are limited to one week, it appears that there can only be one relevant week in relation to each course.

Reductions in applicable amounts in certain cases of actual or notional unemployment benefit disqualification

22.—(1) The weekly applicable amount of a claimant to whom paragraph (4) or (5) applies shall, subject to paragraph (2), be reduced by a sum equal to 40 per cent. of the following amount (hereinafter referred to as the "relevant amount")—

(a) in the case of a person to whom regulation 17 or 18 or paragraph 4 to 6, 9 to 12, 16, 17(c)(i) or (d)(i) of Schedule 7 applies—

(i) where he is a single claimant aged less than 18 or a member of a couple or a polygamous marriage where all the members, in either case, are less than 18, the amount specified in [²paragraph 1(1)(a), (b) or (c), as the case may be,] of Schedule 2 (applicable amounts);

(ii) where he is a single claimant aged not less than 18 but less than 25 [⁵or a member of a couple or polygamous marriage where one member is aged not less than 18 but less than 25 and the other member, or in the case of a polygamous marriage each other member, is a person under 18 who is not eligible for income support under regulation 13A (persons under 18 years), or is not the subject of a direction under section 20(4A) (severe hardship direction)], the amount specified in [²paragraph 1(1)(d)] of that Schedule;

(iii) where he is a single claimant aged not less than 25 or a member of a couple or a polygamous marriage [⁵(other than a member of a couple or polygamous marriage to whom head (ii) of this sub-paragraph applies)] at least one of whom is aged not less than 18, the amount specified in [²paragraph 1(1)(e)] of that Schedule;

(b) in the case of a person to whom [³regulation 19 (applicable amounts for persons in residential care or nursing homes) applies, the amount allowed for personal expenses for him specified in paragraph 13 of Schedule 4.]

[⁷(1A) The weekly applicable amount of a claimant to whom paragraph (5A) applies shall be reduced in accordance with paragraph (1) but for this purpose paragraph (1) shall be modified so that for the words "40 per cent" there are substituted the words "20 per cent".]

(2) Where—

(a) the claimant's capital calculated in accordance with Part V (including any capital treated as his) does not exceed £200; and

(b) he or any member of his family is either pregnant or seriously ill, his weekly applicable amount shall be reduced by a sum equal to 20 per cent. of the relevant amount in his case.

(3) A reduction under paragraph (1) or (2) shall, if it is not a multiple of 5p, be rounded to the nearest such multiple or, if it is a multiple of 2.5p but not of 5p, to the next lower multiple of 5p.

(4) This paragraph applies to a claimant—

(a) whose weekly applicable amount is calculated otherwise than in accordance with regulation 21 and paragraphs 1 to 3, 8(b), 13, 16 and 18 of Schedule 7; and

(b) whose right to income support is, under section 20(3)(d)(i) of the Act [SSCBA, s.124(1)(d)(i)] (conditions of entitlement to income support), subject to the condition of availability for employment; and

(c) who—

    (i) is disqualified for receiving unemployment benefit under section 20(1) of the Social Security Act [SSCBA, s.28(1)] (disqualifications etc); or

    (ii) has made a claim for unemployment benefit which has not been determined by an adjudication officer and in respect of which, in the opinion of an adjudication officer, a question as to disqualification under that section arises; or

    (iii) has not made a claim for unemployment benefit or has had such a claim disallowed other than by reason of section 20(1) [SSCBA, s.28(1)] and, in either case, would be so disqualified if he were to make such a claim or it had not been so disallowed.

(5) This paragraph applies to a claimant who is not required to be available for employment by virtue of regulation [⁶. . .][¹8(3)] (persons not required to be available for employment) [⁴or a claimant who is not required to be actively seeking employment by virtue of regulation 10A(2) (actively seeking employment)][⁶. . .].

[⁷(5A) This paragraph applies to a claimant who is not required to be available for employment by virtue of regulation 8(2A) (persons not required to be available for employment) or who is not required to register for employment by virtue of regulation 11(2A) (registration for employment).]

(6) This regulation shall apply—

(a) in a case to which head (i) of paragraph (4)(c) applies, for the period of the disqualification;

(b) in a case to which head (ii) of paragraph (4)(c) applies, for a period of [¹26] weeks except that where, on subsequent determination of the claim for unemployment benefit—

    (i) disqualification is not imposed, any reduction imposed under paragraph (1) or (2), as the case may be, shall be withdrawn,

    (ii) disqualification is imposed but for a period of less than [¹26] weeks, the period of such reduction shall be adjusted to correspond with the period of disqualification;

(c) in a case to which head (iii) of paragraph (4)(c) applies, for the period for which the claimant would be disqualified if he were to make a claim for unemployment benefit or if such a claim had not been disallowed for other reasons.

(d) in a case to which [⁷paragraph (5) or (5A)] applies, so long as that paragraph continues so to apply.

AMENDMENTS

1. Income Support (General) Amendment Regulations 1988 (S.I. 1988 No. 663), reg. 11 (April 11, 1988).
2. Family Credit and Income Support (General) Amendment Regulations 1989 (S.I. 1989 No. 1034), reg. 6 (July 10, 1989).
3. Income Support (General) Amendment Regulations 1989 (S.I. 1989 No. 534), Sched. 1, para. 6 (October 9, 1989).
4. Income Support (General) Amendment No. 2 Regulations 1989 (S.I. 1989 No. 1323), reg. 7 (October 9, 1989).
5. Income Support (General) Amendment Regulations 1990 (S.I. 1990 No. 547), reg. 9 (April 9, 1990).
6. Income Support (General) Amendment Regulations 1991 (S.I. 1991 No. 236), reg. 8 (April 8, 1991).
7. Disability Working Allowance and Income Support (General) Amendment Regulations 1995 (S.I. 1995 No. 482), reg. 9 (April 13, 1995).

DEFINITIONS

"claimant"—see reg. 2(1).
"couple"—*ibid.*
"family"—see 1986 Act, s.20(11) (SSCBA, s.137(1)).
"polygamous marriage"—see reg. 2(1)
"single claimant"—*ibid.*
"Social Security Act"—*ibid.*

GENERAL NOTE

This regulation reinforces the unemployment benefit disqualifications for misconduct, leaving voluntarily and refusing a job or training under s.28(1) of the Contributions and Benefits Act (1975 Act, s.20(1)) and the disentitlement for failing to be available for employment or to be actively seeking employment. It ensures that the disqualification has a financial bite by preventing the claimant's income from simply being made up by income support. With the extension of the maximum period of disqulification to 26 weeks, reg. 22 will have even greater visibility.

The basic rule is applied by para. (4). The person must be required to be available for work (sub-para. (b) and not be one of the specified cases in Sched. 7 (sub-para. (a): certain patients, prisoners, residents in residential accommodation etc.). Then under sub-para. (c) there are three alternatives. Head (i), an actual disqualification, is straightforward. The income support consequence follows the unemployment benefit decision, and can only be challenged (apart from questions as to the rate of the reduction under para. (2)) by appealing against the unemployment benefit decision. Under para. (6)(a), reg. 22 applies for as long as the disqualification. If, on appeal or review, the disqualification is lifted or its length is reduced, the decision under reg. 22 will be reviewed (Administration Act, s.25; 1975 Act, s.104). Head (ii) covers the case where an unemployment benefit claim has not been determined and a question arises as to disqualification. If the unemployment benefit AO suspends making a decision in order to investigate disqualification, it has to be accepted for income support purposes that a question arises *(R(SB) 18/81)*. Then reg. 22 applies for 26 weeks (regardless of the length of the suspension), subject to adjustment when the unemployment benefit decision is actually made (para. (6)(b)). Again, the only appeal against the substance of the decision can be against the unemployment benefit decision once it is made. Head (iii) covers other cases, where the question is whether the person would be disqualified if the issue arose. Then reg. 22 applies for the period for which the person would be disqualified (para. (6)(c)). This is a question to which the procedure of reg. 64 of the Adjudication Regulations applies (reg. 64(3)(b)), allowing the income support AO to assume an adverse decision if the question cannot be decided immediately. See Adjudication Regulations, reg. 69(4)(b).

In *CIS 640/1993* (to be reported as *R(IS)16/94*) the Commissioner points out that if the reduction in a claimant's income support starts from a later date than the unemployment benefit disqualification, it still ends when the disqualification period comes to an end. Para. (6)(a) refers to "the period of the disqualification", not "a period equal to the period of disqualification". The same point applies to the rest of para. (6).

If reg. 22 does apply, the reduction in benefit is 40 per cent. of the appropriate personal allowance under para. (1). Under para. (2), if the claimant's capital is no more than £200 and a member of the family is (not might be) pregnant or seriously ill (not defined) the reduction is by 20 per cent.

Para. (5) and para. (6)(d) apply the same reductions to claimants not required to be available for work or to seek work actively on grounds of hardship. The April 1991 amendments secured that a claimant who had been found capable of work. but was challenging that decision on appeal, and so was not required to be available for employment under reg. 8(2) or to register for employment under reg. 11(2), had no reduction made in his income support. But from April 13, 1995, this only applies if the claimant has been found capable of work on the basis of the "own occupation test". If that test does not apply and the claimant is appealing against a failure to satisfy the "all work test", his income support is reduced by 20 per cent of the appropriate personal allowance for a single claimant of his age (paras. (1A), (5A) and (6)(d)). See the notes to reg. 8 for the new provisions and for the transitional protection for some claimants.

PART V

INCOME AND CAPITAL

Chapter I

General

Calculation of income and capital of members of claimant's family and of a polygamous marriage

23.—(1) [¹Subject to paragraphs (2) and (4) and to regulation 44 (modifications in respect of children and young persons), the income and capital of a claimant's partner and] the income of a child or young person which by virtue of section 22(5) of the Act [SSCBA, s.136(1) is to be treated as income and capital of the claimant, shall be calculated in accordance with the following provisions of this Part in like manner as for the claimant; and any reference to the "claimant" shall, except where the context otherwise requires, be construed, for the purposes of this Part, as if it were a reference to his partner or that child or young person.

(2) Regulations 36(2) and 38(2), so far as they relate to paragraphs 1 to 10 of Schedule 8 (earnings to be disregarded) and regulation 41(1) (capital treated as income) shall not apply to a child or young person.

(3) [¹Subject to paragraph (5)] where a claimant or the partner of a claimant is married polygamously to two or more members of his household—

(a) the claimant shall be treated as possessing capital and income belonging to each such member and the income of any child or young person who is one of that member's family; and

(b) the income and capital of that member or, as the case may be, the income of that child or young person shall be calculated in accordance with the following provisions of this Part in like manner as for the claimant or, as the case may be, as for any child or young person who is a member of his family.

[¹(4) Where at least one member of a couple is aged less than 18 and the applicable amount of the couple falls to be determined under paragraph 1(3)(b), (e) or (f) of Schedule 2 (applicable amounts), the income of the claimant's partner shall not be treated as the income of the claimant to the extent that—

127

  (a) in the case of a couple where both members are aged less than 18, the amount specified in paragraph 1(3)(a) of that Schedule exceeds the amount specified in paragraph 1(3)(b) of that Schedule; and

  (b) in the case of a couple where only one member is aged less than 18, the amount specified in paragraph 1(3)(d) of that Schedule exceeds the amount which applies in that case which is specified in paragraph 1(3)(e) or (f) of that Schedule.

(5) Where a member of a polygamous marriage is a partner aged less than 18 and the amount which applies in respect of him under regulation 18(2) (polygamous marriages) is nil, the claimant shall not be treated as possessing the income of that partner to the extent that an amount in respect of him would have been included in the applicable amount if he had fallen within the circumstances set out in regulation 18(2)(a) or (b).]

AMENDMENT

1. Income Support (General) Amendment No. 3 Regulations 1988 (S.I. 1988 No. 1228), reg. 6 (September 12, 1988).

DEFINITIONS

  "child"—see 1986 Act, s.20(11) (SSCBA, s.137(1)).
  "claimant"—see reg. 2(1).
  "family"—see 1986 Act, s.20(11) (SSCBA, s.137(1)).
  "partner"—see reg. 2(1).
  "polygamous marriage"—*ibid.*
  "young person"—*ibid.*, reg. 14.

GENERAL NOTE

Resources are to be either capital or income. There is nothing in between. The distinction between capital and income is one which has given a good deal of trouble in the past, and in many other legal contexts. There is no attempt at any general definition in the Regulations, although see regs. 35, 41 and 48. The approach tends to be that around the borderlines a decision can go either way, and it is only if a decision is completely unreasonable that it embodies an error of law *(R. v. W. London SBAT, ex parte Taylor* [1975] 2 All E. R. 790). But ultimately the question is one of law (see *Lillystone v. SBC* [1982] 3 F.L.R. 52 (C.A.))

So far as general principle goes it has been said that the "essential feature of receipts by way of income is that they display an element of periodic recurrence. Income cannot include ad hoc receipts." (Bridge J. in *R. v. Supplementary Benefits Commission, ex parte Singer* [1973] 1 W. L. R. 713). This links the notion of recurrence (which may only be expected in the future) with the notion of a period to which the income is linked. Similar notions are applied by the Commissioner in *R(SB) 29/85* where the issue was the proper treatment of a £15 loan made to a striking miner by a local authority Social Work Department to meet arrears on hire purchase agreements. The Commissioner holds that this was a capital payment, since it was a "one-off" advance and there was no evidence that it was one of a series of payments. Earlier he had referred to income payments normally bearing a readily identifiable relationship with a period. However, periodic recurrence alone is not enough. The nature of the obligation (if any) under which a payment is made must be looked at. A capital payment may be made by instalments. Then in general each instalment is a capital payment, so that reg. 41 is necessary. The general rule is supported by the Court of Appeal in *Lillystone v. SBC* where the purchase price of a house was to be paid in monthly instalments over 10 years. It was agreed that each £70 instalment, when it was paid, was capital, not income.

In *R(SB) 2/83* the Tribunal of Commissioners says "In most cases capital resources arise out of income resources. They represent savings out of past earnings. However, before they undergo the metamorphosis from income to capital all relevant debts, including, in particular, tax liabilities, are first deducted." In *R(SB) 35/83* the Commissioner holds that accumulated earnings will not become capital until all relevant liabilities are deducted. Since the "relevant liabilities" seems to mean the deductions appropriate under the benefit legislation, presumably it is only the categories mentioned in reg. 36(3), if not already deducted, which can be considered, plus it seems, expenses necessarily incurred in obtaining the earnings (*R(FC) 1/90* and *R(IS) 16/93*—see the note to reg. 36(3)). *CIS 563/1991* decides that such expenses are not deductible in the case of income other than earnings (see the note to reg. 40(1)). There is no provision for deducting amounts which are to be used for ordinary current expenditure *(CIS 654/1991,* to be reported as *R(IS) 3/93). R(IS) 3/93* also confirms that a payment does not metamorphose into capital until the end of the period to which it is attributed as income.

This principle should apply to other forms of income as it does to earnings. Thus if, for instance, arrears of a social security benefit are paid, then any amount of those arrears left after the end of the period to which the benefit is properly attributed as income comes into the category of capital. *R(SB) 4/89,* holding arrears of special hardship allowance to be income, did not deal with this point.

Paragraph (1)

This provision contains the basic rule on the aggregation of resources. The income and capital of the claimant's partner is treated as the claimant's. Note that the definition of partner refers on to married and unmarried couples, defined in s.137(1) of the Contributions and Benefits Act (1986 Act, s.20(11)) (and see para. (3) for polygamous marriages). It is an essential part of the definition of both kinds of couple that the parties should be members of the same household, so that reg. 16 may also be relevant. There are special rules for couples where at least one member is under 18 and ineligible for benefit (paras.(4) and (5)).

Only the income of a child or young person in the claimant's household is aggregated with the claimant's (confirmed in reg. 47). If a child or young person has capital over £3,000 there is no personal allowance for that child (reg. 17(b)) and any income of the child is not aggregated (reg. 44(5)). The word "claimant" in the following regulations includes those whose income or capital is aggregated.

Paragraph (2)

Where a child or young person has earnings, the normal disregards in paras 1 to 10 of Sched. 8, which in particular include the £5 and £15 disregards, do not apply, but the rest do. The effect of para. 14 of Sched. 8 is that most earnings are disregarded. Reg. 41(1) on capital payable by instalments does not apply to children or young persons because there is special provision, referring to the £3,000 limit, in reg. 44(1).

Paragraph (4)

This paragraph applies where a couple receives less than the ordinary couple's rate of personal allowance because of the ineligibility of one partner under the 18 year-old limit (this is the effect of the reference to para. 1(3)(b), (e) and (f) of Sched. 2). The income of the ineligible partner is not treated as the claimant's except to the extent that it exceeds the difference between the reduced rate of personal allowance and the ordinary rate. The aggregation of capital is not affected.

Paragraph (5)

This makes similar provision for polygamous marriages.

Treatment of charitable or voluntary payments

24.—[¹. . .]

AMENDMENT

1. Income Support (General) Amendment No. 5 Regulations 1988 (S.I. 1988 No. 2022), reg.5 (December 12, 1988).

Liable relative payments

25. Regulations 29 to 44, 46 to 52 and Chapter VIII of this Part shall not apply to any payment which is to be calculated in accordance with Chapter VII thereof (liable relatives).

[¹Child support

25A. Regulations 29, 31, 32, 40 and 42 and Chapter VII of this Part shall not apply to any payment which is to be calculated in accordance with chapter VIIA of this Part (child support).]

AMENDMENT

1. Social Security (Miscellaneous Provisions) Amendment Regulations 1993 (S.I. 1993 No. 846), reg. 2 (April 19, 1993).

GENERAL NOTE

Reg. 25A takes payments of child support maintenance, paid under an assessment carried out in accordance with the Child Support Act 1991, out of the categories of income other than earnings and of liable relative payments. They may only be taken into account for income support purposes in accordance with regs. 60A to 60D.

Calculation of income and capital of students

26. The provisions of Chapters II to VI of this Part (income and capital) shall have effect in relation to students and their partners subject to the modifications set out in Chapter VIII thereof (students).

DEFINITIONS

"partner"—see reg. 2(1).
"student"—*ibid.*, reg. 61.

[¹Rounding of fractions

27. Where any calculation under this Part results in a fraction of a penny that fraction shall, if it would be to the claimant's advantage, be treated as a penny, otherwise it shall be disregarded.]

AMENDMENT

1. Income Support (General) Amendment Regulations 1988 (S.I. 1988 No. 663), reg. 13 (April 11, 1988).

Chapter II

Income

Calculation of income

28.—(1) For the purposes of section 20(3) of the Act [SSCBA, s.124(1)] (conditions of entitlement to income support), the income of a claimant shall be calculated on a weekly basis—

    (a) by determining in accordance with this Part, other than Chapter VI, the weekly amount of his income; and

    (b) by adding to that amount the weekly income calculated under regulation 53 (calculation of tariff income from capital).

[¹(2) For the purposes of paragraph (1) "income" includes capital treated as income under regulations 41 (capital treated as income) and income which a claimant is treated as possessing under regulation 42 (notional income).]

AMENDMENT

1. Income Support (General) Amendment No. 4 Regulations 1991 (S.I. 1991 No. 1559), reg. 7 (October 7, 1991).

DEFINITIONS

"the Act"—see reg. 2(1).
"claimant"—*ibid.*

Reg. 28 simply confirms that all resources which would come under the description of income, including resources specifically treated as earnings or income, are to be taken into account in the income calculation.

Calculation of earnings derived from employed earner's employment and income other than earnings

29.—(1) [¹. . .] Earnings derived from employment as an employed earner and income which does not consist of earnings shall be taken into account over a period determined in accordance with the following paragraphs and at a weekly amount determined in accordance with regulation 32 (calculation of weekly amount of income).

(2) Subject to [¹paragraphs (3) [²and (4A) to (4D)]], the period over which a payment is to be taken into account shall be—

(a) in a case where it is payable in respect of a period, a period equal to the length of that period;

(b) in any other case, a period equal to such number of weeks as is equal to the number obtained (and any fraction shall be treated as a corresponding fraction of a week) by dividing the net earnings, or in the case of income which does not consist of earnings, the amount of that income [³less any amount paid by way of tax on that income which is disregarded under paragraph 1 of Schedule 9 (income other than earnings to be disregarded)] by the amount of income support which would be payable had the payment not been made plus an amount equal to the total of the sums which would fall to be disregarded from that payment under Schedule 8 [³(earnings to be disregarded) or, as the case may be, any paragraph of Schedule 9 other than paragraph 1 of that Schedule,] as is appropriate in the claimant's case;

and that period shall begin on the date on which the payment is treated as paid under regulation 31 (date on which income is treated as paid).

(3) Where earnings not of the same kind are derived from the same source and the periods in respect of which those earnings would, but for this paragraph, fall to be taken into account—

(a) overlap, wholly or partly, those earnings shall be taken into account over a period equal to the aggregate length of those periods;

(b) and that period shall begin with the earliest date on which any part of those earnings would otherwise be treated as paid under regulation 31 (date on which income is treated as paid).

[²(4) In a case to which paragraph (3) applies, earnings under regulation 35 (earnings of employed earners) shall be taken into account in the following order of priority—

(a) earnings normally derived from the employment;

(b) any payment to which paragraph (1)(b) or (c) of that regulation applies;

(c) any payment to which paragraph (1)(i) of that regulation applies;

(d) any payment to which paragraph (1)(d) of that regulation applies.]

[¹(4A) Where earnings to which regulation 35(1)(b) to (d) (earnings of employed earners) applies are paid in respect of part of a day, those earnings shall be taken into account over a period equal to a day.]

[²(4B) Where earnings to which regulation 35(1)(i)(i) applies (earnings of employed earners) are paid in respect of or on the termination of any employment which is not part-time employment, the period over which they are to be taken into account shall be—

(a) a period equal to such number of weeks as is equal to the number (less any fraction of a whole number) obtained by dividing the net earnings by the maximum weekly amount which, on the date on which the payment of earnings is made, is specified in paragraph 8(1)(c) of Schedule 14 to the Employment Protection (Consolidation) Act 1978; or

(b) a period equal to the length of the specified period,

whichever is the shorter, and that period shall begin on the date on which the payment is treated as paid under regulation 31 (date on which income is treated as paid).

(4C) Any earnings to which regulation 35(1)(i)(ii) applies which are paid in respect of or on the termination of part-time employment, shall be taken into account over a period equal to one week.

(4D) In this regulation—

(a) "part-time employment" means employment in which a person is not to be treated as engaged in remunerative work under regulation 5 or 6 (persons treated, or not treated, as engaged in remunerative work);

(b) "specified period" means a period equal to—

(i) the period of notice which is applicable to a person, or would have been applicable if it had not been waived; less

(ii) any part of that period during which the person has continued to work in the employment in question or in respect of which he has received a payment to which regulation 35(1)(c) applies,

and for the purposes of this definition "period of notice" means the period of notice of termination of employment to which a person is entitled by statute or by contract, whichever is the longer, or, if he is not entitled to such notice, the period of notice which is customary in the employment in question.]

(5) For the purposes of this regulation the claimant's earnings and income which does not consist of earnings shall be calculated in accordance with Chapters III and V respectively of this Part.

AMENDMENTS

1 Income Support (General) Amendment No. 5 Regulations 1988 (S.I. 1988 No.2022), reg. 7 (December 12, 1988).

2 Income Support (General) Amendment No. 2 Regulations 1989 (S.I. 1989 No. 1323), reg. 9 (October 9, 1989).

3 Income Support (General) Amendment Regulations 1990 (S.I. 1990 No. 547), reg. 10 (April 9, 1990).

DEFINITIONS

"claimant"—see reg. 2(1), reg. 23(1).
"employed earner"—see reg. 2(1).

GENERAL NOTE

Paragraphs (1) and (2)

This regulation applies to the earnings of employees and income other than earnings. Thus it covers other social security benefits. Earnings from self-employment are dealt with in reg. 30. It defines the period over which income is to be taken into account and the date on which that period starts. The general rule is set out in para. (2). The first part (familiar from reg. 9(2)(a) of the old Resources Regulations) is that where a payment is in respect of a period it is to be taken into account for an equal period. A fortnight's unemployment benefit is to be taken into account for a fortnight (*R(SB) 17/82*), a month's salary for a month, an annual covenant for a year (*R(SB) 25/ 86*, but see Chapter VIII for students). There will be problems in determining the period in respect of which a payment is made in some cases. For instance, is holiday pay in terms of days, to be attributed to each of the seven days in a week (as done in *R(SB) 11/85* and *CSB 1004/1988*), or is it in terms of weeks, so that only five days' worth is attributed to each week? If a supply teacher works for a varying number of days in each month, being paid at the end of the month, is that payment in respect of the month or in respect of the number of days worked? Much will turn on the precise contractual situation and the terms used by the parties, as confirmed by *CIS 654/1991* (to be reported as *R(IS) 3/93*). Decisions on reg. 7(1)(g) of the Social Security (Unemployment, sickness and Invalidity Benefit) Regulations 1983 (like *R(U) 3/84*) may be helpful.

The question in relation to supply teachers was specifically considered in *CIS 242/1989*. The claimant had worked as a supply teacher for five days in the month of June. She was paid for work done in a month at the end of the following month. The Commissioner accepts that the claimant's contract with the local education authority was on a daily basis (see *R(U) 2/87*). But he rejected her argument that the period for which payment was made was five days. He holds that since she was employed on a daily basis, she was in fact paid for five different periods in June. Para. (2)(a) clearly only envisaged payment in respect of a single period, since neither para. (2) nor reg. 32(1) could operate satisfactorily if a single payment could be in respect of two or more periods. Thus the payment for the days worked in a particular month had to be attributed to the period of a month. *CIS 242/1989* is followed with some reluctance in *CIS 167/1992*. The result of this approach is that the period is determined by the employer's administrative arrangements for payment, rather than the terms of the employment. But it is surely arguable that the period in respect of which the payment was payable was one day. The terms of the claimant's employment were that she was paid £42.23 per session (*i.e.* day). The Commissioner's approach equates the period in respect of which a payment is *payable* with the period for which payment is *due to be made*, which is not necessarily the same. Moreover, the Commissioner does not seem to have taken account of the fact that "payment" can include part of a payment (see reg. 2(1)). Thus some of the operational difficulties referred to by the Commissioner could be overcome by dividing the claimant's monthly payment by the number of days worked in that month and attributing this on a daily basis. However, this does not deal with the point that all the payments would be due on one day. If the payments were due before the date of the claim, reg. 31(1)(a) would apply to attribute them all to that day; if they were paid during a claim see reg. 32(5) and reg. 31(1)(b). See also para. 13 of Sched. 8.

Note the special rules set out in paras. (4B) to (4D) for calculating the period over which compensation payments (see reg. 35(1)(i) and (3)) are to be taken into account.

If the payment is not in respect of a period then there is a mechanical rule in para. (2)(b) spreading it at the rate of income support which would otherwise be payable, taking account of any disregards.

Once the period is fixed, it begins on the date specified in reg. 31.

Paragraphs (3) and (4)

Para. (3) establishes an exception in the case of earnings only, to the rule about the date from which a payment is to be taken into account. It is to deal mainly with the situation on the termination of employment when a claimant may be entitled to regular earnings, week in hand payments, pay in lieu of notice or compensation for breach of contract and holiday pay. The effect is that each payment which is not disregarded (Sched. 8, paras. 1 to 3) is to be taken into account for the appropriate period, and the periods are to be put together consecutively. Then the aggregate period starts on the earliest date which would be fixed for any of the periods under reg. 31. Note that para. (3) only applies where the earnings are of different kinds, and derive from the same source. Thus it would not apply to payments from different employers.

Para. (4) deals with the order in which payments in lieu of notice, compensation payments and holiday pay are to be taken into account in conjunction with ordinary earnings.

Paragraph (4A)

Earnings paid in respect of a part of a day are taken into account for a day.

Paragraph (4B)

This provision defines the length of the period for which a payment of compensation on the termination of full-time employment is to be taken into account. The line between full-time and part-time is drawn by para. (4D)(a) and reg. 35(3)(c). What is a payment of compensation is defined in reg. 35(3)(*a*). There are two alternative periods, whichever is the shorter being applied. The first is obtained by dividing the amount of the payment by the maximum weekly sum specified at the relevant time for the purposes of calculating statutory redundancy payments and the basic award for unfair dismissal. From April 1, 1989, the sum was £172, from April 1, 1990, it was £184, from April 1, 1991, it was £198 and from April 1, 1992 (not increased in 1993, 1994 or 1995), it has been £205. This calculation will give an advantage to lower paid workers, for whom the period may be shorter than the number of weeks' wages represented by the payment. The second alternative is the "specified period," defined in para. (4D)(b) as the period of notice to which the person was legally entitled (or customarily entitled for civil servants with no contractual entitlement) less any period worked out or already covered by a payment in lieu of notice. This secures that if a person receives a payment which is larger than would be required to make up for the uncovered period of notice, he is not affected beyond the legal notice period.

Although the end of para. (4B) provides that the payment is to be treated as paid on the date fixed by reg. 31, this result may well be displaced by the operation of paras. (3) and (4).

Paragraph (4C)
Where a payment of compensation is made on the termination of part-time employment (para. (4D)(a) and reg. 35(3)(c)) it is to be taken into account for one week. See also reg. 32(7).

Calculation of earnings of self-employed earners

30.—(1) Except where paragraph (2) applies, where a claimant's income consists of earnings from employment as a self-employed earner the weekly amount of his earnings shall be determined by reference to his average weekly earnings from that employment—
    (a) over a period of [¹one year]; or
    (b) where the claimant has recently become engaged in that employment or there has been a change which is likely to affect the normal pattern of business, over such other period [¹. . .] as may, in any particular case, enable the weekly amount of his earnings to be determined more accurately.

(2) Where the claimant's earnings consist of royalties or sums paid periodically for or in respect of any copyright those earnings shall be taken into account over a period equal to such number of weeks as is equal to the number obtained (and any fraction shall be treated as a corresponding fraction of a week) by dividing the earnings by the amount of income support which would be payable had the payment not been made plus an amount equal to the total of the sums which would fall to be disregarded from the payment under Schedule 8 (earnings to be disregarded) as is appropriate in the claimant's case.

(3) For the purposes of this regulation the claimant's earnings shall be calculated in accordance with Chapter IV of this Part.

AMENDMENT

1. Income-related Benefits Schemes (Miscellaneous Amendments) (No. 4) Regulations 1993 (S.I. 1993 No. 2119), reg. 11 (October 4, 1993).

DEFINITIONS

    "claimant"—see reg. 2(1), reg. 23(1).
    "self-employed earner"—see reg. 2(1).

GENERAL NOTE

Reg. 30 applies to earnings from self-employment. The earnings (calculated under regs. 37 to 39) are generally to be averaged over a period of one year. Contrary to what was said in earlier editions, it does not seem necessary that the period immediately precedes the benefit week in question. Any one year period—normally the last year for which accounts are available—will do. The alternative period under para. (1)(b) can only be chosen if there has been a change likely to affect the normal pattern of business or if the self-employment has recently started. A more general exception is hidden in reg. 38(10), which allows the amount of any item of income or expenditure to be calculated over a different period if that will produce a more accurate figure.

Para. (2) supplies a special rule for payments of royalties or for copyright, which are to be spread in the same way as income of an employee not in respect of a period (reg. 29(2)(b)).

Note that the profit simply derived from a capital asset is not earnings, which must be derived from some employment or occupation. See *R(U) 3/77*.

Date on which income is treated as paid

31.—(1) Except where paragraph (2) applies, a payment of income to which regulation 29 (calculation of earnings derived from employed earner's employment and income other than earnings) applies shall be treated as paid—

    (a) in the case of a payment which is due to be paid before the first benefit week pursuant to the claim, on the date on which it is due to be paid;

    (b) in any other case, on the first day of the benefit week in which it is due to be paid or the first succeeding benefit week in which it is practicable to take it into account.

(2) Income support, unemployment benefit, [²maternity allowance,] [³short-term or long term incapacity benefit], or severe disablement allowance [³. . .],shall be treated as paid on the day of the benefit week in respect of which [¹it is payable].

AMENDMENTS

    1. Income Support (General) Amendment Regulations 1988 (S.I. 1988 No. 663), reg. 14 (April 11, 1988).
    2. Income Support (General) Amendment No. 4 Regulations 1988 (S.I. 1988 No. 1445), reg. 8 (September 12, 1988).
    3. Disability Working Allowance and Income Support (General) Amendment Regulations 1995 (S.I. 1995 No. 482), reg. 10 (April 13, 1995).

DEFINITIONS

    "benefit week"—see reg. 2(1).

GENERAL NOTE

Paragraph (1)
    This provision applies to determine when the period of attribution of earnings from employment and income other than the benefits specified in para. (2) (fixed in reg. 29) begins. The crucial date is that on which the payment is due to be paid. This date may well be different from the date of actual payment. Legal obligations must be considered, *e.g.* the terms of a contract of employment *(R(SB) 33/83)*. If a claimant's contract of employment is terminated without due notice any deferred holiday pay and wages withheld under week-in-hand arrangements are due immediately. So are any agreed payments in lieu of notice *(R(SB) 22/84* and *R(SB) 11/85)*. Note the operation of regs. 29(3) and (4) when different kinds of earnings are received for overlapping periods.
    In *CIS 590/1993* the claimant had been dismissed from her employment in April 1991 because she was pregnant. In June 1992 she was awarded compensation by an industrial tribunal under the Sex Discrimination Act 1975 which included one month's loss of earnings. The tribunal had deducted the income support paid to the claimant for the month after her dismissal. It is held that the loss of earnings element of the award was to be taken into account as earnings under reg. 35 (see the notes to reg. 35). For the purpose of reg. 31(1), the date on which it was due to be paid was the date when the lost earnings were due to be paid, not when the award was made. This was because the award was to be regarded as a payment in lieu of remuneration and the purpose of the sex discrimination legislation was to put the claimant in the position she would have been if the employer had not acted unlawfully. If the payment was treated as due at the date of the award this could produce unfairness. The result was that the earnings were to be attributed to a period of one month in April/May 1991 and she was to be treated as in remunerative work for that period. However, the income support that had been paid to the claimant for that period was not recoverable as there had been no failure to disclose or misrepresentation.
    If the payment is due before the first week pursuant to the claim (on which see Sched. 7 to the Claims and Payments Regulations), it is treated as paid on the date it is due. This date then starts the period under reg. 29. In other cases the payment is treated as paid on the first day of the benefit week in which it is due (or the next week if the main rule is impracticable).

Paragraph (2)
    It seems that the effect of para. (2) is that all these benefits are treated as paid on a daily basis. A proportion of the weekly rate is treated as paid for each day covered by the entitlement. This should avoid overlaps of the kind revealed in *R(SB) 15/82*. See regs. 75(b) and 32(4.

Calculation of weekly amount of income

    32.—(1) For the purposes of regulation 29 (calculation of earnings derived

from employed earner's employment and income other than earnings), subject to [³paragraphs (2) to (7)][¹. . .], where the period in respect of which a payment is made—
  (a) does not exceed a week, the weekly amount shall be the amount of that payment;
  (b) exceeds a week, the weekly amount shall be determined—
      (i) in a case where that period is a month, by multiplying the amount of the payment by 12 and dividing the product by 52;
      (ii) in a case where that period is three months, by multiplying the amount of the payment by 4 and dividing the product by 52;
      (iii) in a case where that period is a year by dividing the amount of the payment by 52;
      (iv) in any other case by multiplying the amount of the payment by 7 and dividing the product by the number equal to the number of days in the period in respect of which it is made.

(2) Where a payment for a period not exceeding a week is treated under regulation 31(1)(a) (date on which income is treated as paid) as paid before the first benefit week and a part is to be taken into account for some days only in that week (the relevant days), the amount to be taken into account for the relevant days shall be calculated by multiplying the amount of the payment by the number equal to the number of relevant days and dividing the product by the number of days in the period in respect of which it is made.

(3) Where a payment is in respect of a period equal to or in excess of a week and a part thereof is to be taken into account for some days only in a benefit week (the relevant days), the amount to be taken into account for the relevant days shall, except where paragraph (4) applies, be calculated by multiplying the amount of the payment by the number equal to the number of relevant days and dividing the product by the number of days in the period in respect of which it is made.

(4) In the case of a payment of—
  (a) unemployment benefit, [²maternity allowance], [⁴short-term or long-term incapacity benefit], or severe disablement allowance [⁴. . .], the amount to be taken into account for the relevant days shall be the amount of benefit [¹payable] in respect of those days;
  (b) income support, the amount to be taken into account for the relevant days shall be calculated by multiplying the weekly amount of the benefit by the number of relevant days and dividing the product by seven.

(5) Except in the case of a payment which it has not been practicable to treat under regulation 31(1)(b) as paid on the first day of the benefit week in which it is due to be paid, where a payment of income from a particular source is or has been paid regularly and that payment falls to be taken into account in the same benefit week as a payment of the same kind and from the same source, the amount of that income to be taken into account in any one benefit week shall not exceed the weekly amount determined under paragraph (1)(a) or (b), as the case may be, of the payment which under regulation 31(1)(b) (date on which income is treated as paid) is treated as paid first.

(6) Where the amount of the claimant's income fluctuates and has changed more than once, or a claimant's regular pattern of work is such that he does not work every week, the foregoing paragraphs may be modified so that the weekly amount of his income is determined by reference to his average weekly income—
  (a) if there is a recognisable cycle of work, over the period of one complete cycle (including, where the cycle involves periods in which the claimant does no work, those periods but disregarding any other absences);
  (b) in any other case, over a period of five weeks or such other period as

may, in the particular case, enable the claimant's average weekly income to be determined more accurately.

[³(7) Where any payment of earnings is taken into account under paragraph (4C) of regulation 29 (calculation of earnings derived from employed earner's employment and income other than earnings), over the period specified in that paragraph, the amount to be taken into account shall be equal to the amount of the payment.]

AMENDMENTS

1. Income Support (General) Amendment Regulations 1988 (S.I. 1988 No. 663), reg. 15 (April 11, 1988).
2. Income Support (General) Amendment Regulations 1988 (S.I. 1988 No. 1445), reg. 8 (September 12, 1988).
3. Income Support (General) Amendment No. 2 Regulations 1989 (S.I. 1989 No. 1323), reg. 10 (October 9, 1989).
4. Disability Working Allowance and Income Support (General) Amendment Regulations 1995 (S.I. 1995 No. 482), reg. 11 (April 13, 1995).

DEFINITIONS

"benefit week"—see reg. 2(1).
"claimant"—*ibid.*, reg. 23(1).

GENERAL NOTE

Paragraph (1)
This provision gives a straightforward method of converting payments to be taken into account for various periods to a weekly equivalent. Reg. 75 deals with the calculation for part-weeks of entitlement.

Paragraphs (2) to (4)
These provisions establish the rules where the period for which a payment is to be taken into account under regs. 29 and 31 does not coincide with a benefit week and some odd days ("the relevant days") come into a benefit week.

Paragraph (5)
There are two different rules, according to whether two payments from the same regular source fall into the same benefit week because of the rules of attribution or because of the operation of reg. 31(1)(b). The general rule is the first one, under which the maximum amount to be taken into account in the benefit week is the weekly amount of the payment due first. The *Adjudication Officers' Guide* (para. 29081) gives an example of how this could arise. A claimant has been receiving statutory sick pay from his employer every two weeks. He receives a payment for two weeks on July 15. This is attributed to the period July 15 to July 28 inclusive. The claimant is to return to work on August 1 and receives a final payment of two weeks' sick pay on July 22. Since this payment cannot be due later than it is paid, it is attributed to the period July 22 to August 4 inclusive. For the income support benefit week from July 22 to July 28 the amount of sick pay to be taken into account is limited to the weekly amount of the payment made on July 15. There is an exception to this rule in that if the first payment was due to be paid before the date of claim it is to be disregarded (Sched. 8, para. 13 and Sched. 9, para. 35). Then there will no longer be an overlap. The second rule applies where under reg. 31(1)(b) it has not been practicable to take a payment into account in the benefit week in which it was due to be paid. The payment then is taken into account in the first practicable benefit week. In this situation both payments can be taken into account in the same week, although each payment can have the appropriate disregard applied (Sched. 8, para. 10 and Sched. 9, para. 37). The disregards in para. 13 of Sched. 8 and para. 35 of Sched. 9 (see above) may also apply.

Paragraph (6)
This paragraph is oddly placed because it only allows the preceding paragraphs to be modified, not any of the other regulations on the calculation or attribution of income.

Paragraph (7)

Where a payment of compensation (reg. 35(3)(a) is made on the termination of part-time employment (reg. 29(4D)(e) and reg. 35(3)(c)) it is taken into account for a week (reg. 29(4C)). This provision confirms that the whole payment is taken into account for that week.

Weekly amount of charitable or voluntary payment

33.—(1) [¹. . .]

AMENDMENT

1. Income Support (General) Amendment No. 5 Regulations 1988 (S.I. 1988 No. 2022), reg. 8 (December 12, 1988).

Incomplete weeks of benefit

34. [¹. . .]

AMENDMENT

1. Income Support (General) Amendment Regulations 1988 (S.I. 1988 No. 663), reg. 16 (April 11. 1988).

Chapter III

Employed Earners

Earnings of employed earners

35.—(1) [²Subject to paragraphs (2) and (3),] "earnings" means in the case of employment as an employed earner, any remuneration or profit derived from that employment and includes—

(a) any bonus or commission;

(b) any payment in lieu of remuneration except any periodic sum paid to a claimant on account of the termination of his employment by reason of redundancy;

(c) any payment in lieu of notice [². . .];

(d) any holiday pay except any payable more than four weeks after the termination or interruption of employment but this exception shall not apply to a claimant to whom [¹section 23 of the Act [SSCBA, s.126] (trade disputes) applies or in respect of whom section 20(3) of the Act [SSCBA, s.124(1)] (conditions of entitlement to income support) has effect as modified by section 23A(*b*) of the Act [SSCBA, s.127(b)] (effect to return to work)];

(e) any payment by way of a retainer;

(f) any payment made by the claimant's employer in respect of expenses not wholly, exclusively and necessarily incurred in the performance of the duties of the employment, including any payment made by the claimant's employer in respect of—

   (i) travelling expenses incurred by the claimant between his home and place of employment;

   (ii) expenses incurred by the claimant under arrangements made for the care of a member of his family owing to the claimant's absence from home;

(g) any award of compensation made under section 68(2) or 71(2)(a) of the Employment Protection (Consolidation) Act 1978 (remedies for unfair dismissal and compensation);

(h) any such sum as is referred to in section 18(2) of the Social Security (Miscellaneous Provisions) Act 1977 (certain sums to be earnings for social security purposes).

[²(i) where—
   (i) a payment of compensation is made in respect of employment which is not part-time employment and that payment is not less than the maximum weekly amount, the amount of the compensation less the deductible remainder, where that is applicable;
   (ii) a payment of compensation is made in respect of employment which is part-time, the amount of the compensation.]

[²(1A) For the purposes of paragraph (1)(i)(i) the "deductible remainder"—
   (a) applies in cases where dividing the amount of compensation by the maximum weekly amount produces a whole number plus a fraction; and
   (b) is equal to the difference between—
       (i) the amount of the compensation; and
       (ii) the product of the maximum weekly amount multiplied by the whole number.]

(2) "Earnings" shall not include—
   (a) any payment in kind;
   (b) any remuneration paid by or on behalf of an employer to the claimant [⁴in respect of a period throughout which the claimant is on maternity leave or is absent from work because he is ill];
   (c) any payment in respect of expenses wholly, exclusively and necessarily incurred in the performance of the duties of the employment;
   (d) any occupational pension.

[²(3) In this regulation—
   (a) "compensation" means any payment made in respect of or on the termination of employment in a case where a person has not received or received only part of a payment in lieu of notice due or which would have been due to him had he not waived his right to receive it, other than—
       (i) any payment specified in paragraph (1)(a) to (h);
       (ii) any payment specified in paragraph (2)(a) to (d);
       (iii) any redundancy payment within the meaning of section 81(1) of the Employment Protection (Consolidation) Act 1978, and
       (iv) any refund of contributions to which that person was entitled under an occupational pension scheme within the meaning of section 66(1) of the Social Security Pensions Act 1975;
       [³(v) any compensation payable by virtue of section 173 or section 178(3) or (4) of the Education Reform Act 1988;]
   (b) "maximum weekly amount" means the maximum weekly amount which, on the date on which the payment of compensation is made, is specified in paragraph 8(1)(c) of Schedule 14 to the Employment Protection (Consolidation) Act 1978;
   (c) "part-time employment" means employment in which a person is not to be treated as engaged in remunerative work under regulation 5 or 6 (persons treated, or not treated, as engaged in remunerative work).]

AMENDMENTS

1. Income Support (General) Amendment Regulations 1988 (S.I. 1988 No. 663), reg. 17 (April 11, 1988).
2. Income Support (General) Amendment No. 2 Regulations 1989 (S.I. 1989 No. 1323), reg. 11 (October 9, 1989).
3. Education (Inner London Education Authority) (Transitional and Supplementary Provisions) (No. 2) Order 1990 (S.I. 1990 No. 774), art. 2 (April 1, 1990).

4. Income-related Benefits Schemes (Miscellaneous Amendments) (No. 4) Regulations 1993 (S.I. 1993 No. 2119), reg. 12 (October 4, 1993).

DEFINITIONS

"the Act"—see reg. 2(1).
"claimant"—*ibid.*, reg. 23(1).
"employed earner"—see reg. 2(1).
"family"—see 1986 Act, s.20(11) (SSCBA, s.137(1)).
"maternity leave"—see reg. 2(1).
"occupational pension"—see reg. 2(1).

GENERAL NOTE

Reg. 35 applies to earnings from employment as an employed earner. See the definition in reg. 2(1). The category of office-holder includes holders of elective office, such as local councillors. Some payments made to councillors (*e.g.* for travelling expenses and subsistence allowances: *CIS 89/1989*) will be excluded under para. (2)(*c*), but attendance allowances, which are not paid to meet specific expenses, count as earnings (*R(IS) 6/92*). *CIS 77/1993* decides that basic allowances are also earnings, but applies the disregard in para. (2)(c), reg.40(4) and Sched. 9, para. 3. The purpose of the basic allowance is to compensate the councillor for his time and to cover the expenses incurred in the execution of his duties. The expenses may, as in that case, absorb the total allowance. The Commissioner points out that since March 18, 1992, basic allowances have been disregarded for the purposes of reg. 7(1)(g)(i) of the Social Security (Unemployment, Sickness and Invalidity Benefit) Regulations 1983. The allowance will therefore be treated differently depending whether unemployment benefit or income support is claimed. See the notes to reg. 36(3).

Paragraph (1)
This paragraph first provides a general definition of earnings from employment as an employee—any remuneration or profit derived from that employment—and then deems certain payments to be earnings. Para. (2) provides a number of exceptions and Sched. 8 lists items which would otherwise count as earnings which are to be disregarded. In particular under paras. 1 to 3 final earnings due on the termination or interruption of employment are disregarded.

The general test covers straightforward wages or salary, but can extend to other remuneration derived from employment. According to *R(SB) 21/86*, these are wide words, which mean "having their origin in." Thus if it had been necessary to decide whether a compensatory award for unfair dismissal by an Industrial Tribunal was derived from employment, the Commissioner would have held that it did. *R(SB) 21/86* is followed in *CIS 590/1993*, which concerned the loss of earnings element in a compensation award for sex discrimination. Payments to a NCB employee in lieu of concessionary coal constituted remuneration derived from employment (*R(SB) 2/86*). Tips and gratuities would be an example of payments from third parties which are nonetheless derived from employment (see Williams, *Social Security Taxation*, paras. 4.21 to 4.22 for discussion of the income tax cases).

The particular categories in sub-paras. (a) to (i) are deemed to be earnings, whether they would in general count as earnings or not (*R(SB) 21/86*). Only a few categories require comment.

Sub-para. (b). A payment in lieu of remuneration will in its nature be an income payment. Capital payments (*e.g.* for the loss of the job itself) are excluded. *R(SB) 21/86* held that a compensatory award for unfair dismissal made by an Industrial Tribunal was a payment in lieu of remuneration, to be taken into account for the number of weeks specified in the award. Such an award is now expressly included in sub-para. (g), but if it can also fall into (b) it will lead to complete disentitlement to income support under reg. 5(5), regardless of the weekly amount of the award. In *CIS 590/1993* the claimant's award of compensation under the Sex Discrimination Act included amounts for injured feelings, the loss of a tax rebate and one month's loss of earnings. It was accepted that the first two items counted as capital. The Commissioner follows *R(SB) 21/86* and holds that the loss of earnings element fell to be treated as earnings under sub-para. (b). There was no reason for drawing a distinction between a compensatory award for unfair dismissal and that part of a sex discrimination award that was for loss of earnings. The fact that only the former was referred to in sub-para. (g) did not imply that the loss of earnings elements in sex (or race) discrimination awards (or indeed awards made by county courts for breach of employment contracts) were excluded from para. (1), since the categories listed in sub-paras. (a) to (i) were only included as examples. See the notes to reg. 31(1) as to when the earnings were treated as due to be paid.

Sub-para. (c). This sub-paragraph is now confined to payments in lieu of notice, whether full or partial. Presumably, it covers payments expressly in lieu of notice (see *CIS 400/1994*). "Global"

140

payments will fall under sub-para. (i). If earnings under this sub-paragraph are received, entitlement is excluded under reg. 5(5) for the period covered.

Sub-para. (d). Holiday pay which is payable (*i.e.* due to be paid, not received or paid: *R(SB) 15/82, R(SB) 33/83, R(SB) 11/85*) within four weeks of termination or interruption of employment counts as earnings. In cases of termination holiday pay will be due immediately, unless the contract of employment expressly provides otherwise. Therefore, whenever it is paid (and presumably it cannot count until it is actually paid) it will count as earnings to be taken into account for the benefit week in which it was due to be paid. Then s.74 of the Administration Act (1986 Act, s.27) might come into play. If employment is merely interrupted it is more likely that holiday pay will not be payable immediately. Earnings received under this sub-paragraph lead to disentitlement under reg. 5(5).

Holiday pay outside this sub-paragraph is capital (reg. 48(3)).

Sub-para. (e). CIS 743/1992 decides that a guarantee payment under s.12 of the Employment Protection (Consolidation) Act 1978 is a payment by way of a retainer.

Sub-para. (f). The conditions here are in line with those under which expenses are deductible from earnings for income tax purposes. Payment for all items beyond those solely necessary for the person to do the job are caught. The express mention of the expenses of travel to and from work and of looking after a family member merely spells this out. The reimbursement of a local councillor's home telephone expenses in *CIS 38/1989* is an example. On the evidence, the expenses were necessarily incurred, but not wholly or exclusively, in the performance of his duties as a councillor. On other evidence, such expenses could be apportioned between personal and employment purposes (*cf. R(FC) 1/91, CFC 26/1989* and *R(FIS) 13/91* on reg. 38(3)). There is helpful guidance in *R(FIS) 4/85.*

CIS 89/1989 holds that travel and subsistence allowances paid to a local councillor, which included travel from home to the place of employment, were for necessary etc. expenses, because a councillor's home is also a place of employment. *R(1S) 6/92* confirms this result, because under s.174(1) of the Local Government Act 1972 payments of travelling and subsistence allowances can only be made where the expenses have been necessarily incurred for the performance of any duty as a councillor. Therefore, such a payment must fall outside sub-para. (f) and within para. (2)(c). In *CIS 77/1993* it was accepted that a local councillor's expenses (*e.g.* the use of his home and telephone) could lead to the whole of his basic allowance being disregarded (see above). See the notes to reg. 36(3).

Sub-para. (g). If awards of compensation can only come under this sub-paragraph and not (b) they do not lead to complete disentitlement, but the amount must be considered.

Sub-para. (h). The sums referred to in s.18(2) of the 1977 Act are maternity pay under s.40 of the Employment Protection (Consolidation) Act 1978, arrears of pay under s.122(3)(a); arrears of pay under an order for reinstatement or re-engagement; a sum payable under an award for the continuation of a contract; and remuneration under a protective award.

Sub-para. (i). There was a significant change in 1989 in the treatment of lump sum payments made on the termination of employment, which is designed to simplify decision-making. It is along similar lines to the change in the UB rules, but introduces several differences. In *CIS 400/1994* the Commissioner draws attention to the different ways that termination payments at the end of a period of employment are treated by the income support and unemployment benefit legislation. In particular, the definition of ''compensation'' is not the same (*e.g.*, for unemployment benefit purposes ''compensation'' can include payments in lieu of notice; for income support it cannot).

There are separate provisions depending whether it is full-time or part-time employment which is terminated. The dividing line is defined in para. (6)(c) and reg. 29(4D)(a) by adopting the test of remunerative work in regs. 5 and 6.

Full-time employment. This new category of earnings is added to the list while sub-para. (c) is restricted to payments in lieu of notice and not payments of compensation for loss of employment. For full-timers sub-para. (i) applies to a payment of ''compensation'' which equals or exceeds the ''maximum weekly amount''.

''Compensation'' is defined in para. (3)(a). First, the person must not have received a payment in lieu of all the notice to which he was legally entitled. If this has happened, no other payment can be ''compensation'' within sub-para. (i) (confirmed in *CIS 400/1994*). Second, all the payments already counted as earnings by para. (1)(a) to (h) or excluded from that category by para. (2), statutory redundancy payments and refunds of pension contributions are excluded. Other payments made in respect of or on the termination of employment count as compensation. It does not particularly matter what the employer calls the payment, providing that it is connected to the termination (*cf. R(U) 4/92* and *R(U) 5/92*), so that merely calling the payment a capital payment (*e.g.* for loss of the job as a capital asset) does not take it outside sub-para. (i). The main categories will be payments from employers which are not precisely categorised (*e.g.* the ubiquitous ''*ex gratia*'' payment) and payments made in settlement of claims for unfair or wrongful dismissal (providing that a payment in lieu of full notice has not already been paid). But a payment solely in relation to racial discrimination during employment is not within the definition (*CU 88/1991*).

The "maximum weekly amount" is defined in para. (3)(b) and is the amount specified at the relevant time as the maximum to be used in calculating the basic award for unfair dismissal and redundancy payments. The figure in effect from April 1, 1989, was £172, from April 1,1990, was £184, from April 1, 1991, was £198 and from April 1, 1992 (not increased in 1993, 1994 or 1995) is £205.

If a payment is "compensation" then its amount has to be divided by the maximum weekly amount. If this division produces a whole number plus a fraction the portion of the amount of the compensation representing that fraction is ignored as earnings. It is the "deductible remainder" (para. (1B)). But it appears to be capital (reg. 48(11)). The payment less any deductible remainder is taken into account as income for the same number of weeks as the whole number (reg. 29(4B)(a)). However, the rigid application of this rule could result in the payment being taken into account for longer than the claimant's notice period. Therefore, under reg. 29(4B)(b) the payment is to be taken into account for a period equal to the person's notice entitlement (less any days of notice worked or covered by a payment in lieu of notice) if this is shorter. This is the "specified period" (reg. 29(4D)(b).

The date on which this period is to start is defined by reg. 31 (reg. 29(4B)). Often this will be the date of termination, but it may be later, *e.g.* where there is a settlement of an unfair dismissal claim. But see *CIS 590/1993* referred to above and in the notes to reg. 31(1). If there is an identifiable loss of earnings element in the settlement, such a payment may come within para (1)(a) to (h) (and thus fall outside the definition of "compensation") and be due to be paid on the date when the lost earnings, etc., were due to be paid. Note the effect of reg. 29(3) and (4).

Where the payment is small, less in total than the "maximum weekly amount," these provisions do not apply and the payment is treated as capital (reg. 48(11)).

Part-time employment. For part-time employment the whole payment of "compensation" is to be taken into account in one week (reg. 35(1)(i)(ii) and reg. 29(4C)), generally the week in which it is due to be paid (reg. 31).

Paragraph (2)

These amounts—payments in kind, contractual sick or maternity pay, reimbursement of necessary expenses and occupational pensions—are not earnings, but do count as other income (reg. 40(4)). However, income in kind is disregarded (Sched. 9, para. 21) and so are payments of necessary expenses (Sched. 9, para. 3). There is no provision for the disregard of ill-health payments or occupational pensions (confirmed in *CIS 6/1989*). If a person is remunerated by payments in kind, there is the possibility of notional earnings being attributed to the person under reg. 42(6).

See the notes to para. (1)(f) for what are necessary, etc., expenses.

In a decision on the equivalent provision in the Family Credit (General) Regulations (reg. 19(2)), the Commissioner suggested that its effect is that expenditure by the employee on necessary etc. expenses is to be deducted from the amount of his earnings (*CFC 2/1989*). This does not seem to be consistent with the pattern of reg. 35, which is otherwise concerned with payments to the employee, and is rejected in *R(FC) 1/90, R(IS) 16/93* and *CIS 77/1993*. See the notes to reg. 19(2) of the Family Credit Regulations for full discussion of the point. The payment can be by way of reimbursement to the employee for expenses initially met by him (*CIS 77/1993*). But the application of the principle of *Parsons v. Hogg* to the meaning of 'gross earnings' in reg. 36 will, it seems, permit the deduction from earnings of necessary, etc., expenses incurred by the employee. See the notes to reg. 36(3).

Calculation of net earnings of employed earners

36.—(1) For the purposes of regulation 29 (calculation of earnings of employed earners) the earnings of a claimant derived from employment as an employed earner to be taken into account shall, subject to paragraph (2), be his net earnings.

(2) There shall be disregarded from a claimant's net earnings, any sum specified in paragraphs 1 to 13 of Schedule 8.

(3) For the purposes of paragraph (1) net earnings shall be calculated by taking into account the gross earnings of the claimant from that employment less—

    (a) any amount deducted from those earnings by way of—

(i) income tax;
(ii) primary Class 1 contributions under the Social Security Act; and
(b) one-half of any sum paid by the claimant [¹in respect of a pay period]
by way of a contribution towards an occupational or personal pension
scheme.

AMENDMENT

1. Income-related Benefits Schemes (Miscellaneous Amendments) (No. 5) Regulations 1994 (S.I.
1994 No. 2139), reg. 26 (October 3, 1994).

DEFINITIONS

"claimant"—see reg. 2(1), reg. 23(1).
"employed earner"—see reg. 2(1).
"occupational pension scheme"—see 1986 Act, s.84(1). (PSA, s.1).
"pay period"–see reg. 2(1).
"personal pension scheme"—*ibid.*
"Social Security Act"—*ibid.*

GENERAL NOTE

Paragraph (1)
Earnings defined in reg. 35 are to be converted to net earnings before being taken into account.
This is to be done according to para. (3).

Paragraph (2)
After the conversion to net earnings has been carried out, the amounts specified in paras. 1 to 13
of Sched. 8 are to be disregarded. The disregards of paras. 1 to 10 do not apply to children or young
persons, but under reg. 44(6) paras. 14 and 15 do apply, which leads to the earnings of children or
young persons being disregarded in most cases.

Paragraph (3)
Only this limited list of deductions for payments made by the employee may be made from gross
earnings. Nothing is to be deducted for travel costs, child care expenses or meals at work. This
leads to a much simpler calculation than under supplementary benefit. The compensation is an
increase in the basic disregard from its previous £4 to £5. This will obviously affect different
claimants very differently. *R(FC) 1/90* holds that if the employee makes contributions to both an
occupational and a personal pension scheme, half of both contributions can be deducted.
There is, however, some doubt about the meaning of "gross earnings." In *R(FC) 1/90* the Commissioner refers to the principle adopted by the Court of Appeal in *Parsons v. Hogg* [1985] 2 All
E. R. 897, appendix to *R(FIS) 4/85*, and by the Commissioner in *R(FIS) 4/85*, that "earnings," even
associated with the word "gross," in the Family Income Supplements (General) Regulations 1980
meant not the remuneration actually received, but the receipts after payment of expenses wholly and
necessarily incurred in the course of winning those receipts. He applies this principle to the equivalent provision to reg. 36 in the Family Credit (General) Regulations (reg. 20) and holds that expenses
necessarily wholly and exclusively incurred by the employee in the performance of the duties of
employment are to be deducted from the gross receipts to produce a figure of gross earnings. The
same Commissioner applies the principle to income other than earnings in *CIS 25/1989*, but this has
not been followed in *CIS 563/1991* (see the note to reg. 40(1)). In *R(FC) 1/90*, the claimant's
expenditure on work equipment might be deducted, but not child-care expenses *(R(FIS) 2/88)*.
The wording of reg. 36 is not the same as was considered in *Parsons v. Hogg*, so that there was
some doubt about the application of the principle. In *R(IS) 6/92* the Commissioner held that an
attendance allowance paid to a local councillor had to be taken into account as earnings, subject
only to the £5 disregard, although the councillor incurred necessary, etc., expenses on such things
as stationery and telephone calls. However, the Commissioner referred only to reg. 35 and not to
reg. 36 or any of the decisions cited in the previous paragraph. In *CIS 77/1993*, which concerned a
local councillor's basic allowance, the same Commissioner considered that *Parsons v. Hogg* did not
apply, but decided that the allowance fell within reg. 35(2)(c). However, the application of *Parsons
v. Hogg* does produce a result where only resources actually available to the person are counted. It
is also the approach taken in paras. 29121 and 29165 of the *Adjudication Officers' Guide*; para.
29165 states that local councillors' necessary etc., expenses should be deducted in calculating their

earnings even where there is no reimbursement by the local authority. *R(IS) 16/93* has now expressly decided that the principle of *Parsons v. Hogg* applies to reg. 36.

In calculating the amount of necessary, etc., expenses to be deducted the principle established in *R(FC) 1/91*, *CFC 26/1989* and *R(IS) 13/91* should be applied. That is that if items have a dual private and work use, and that use can be apportioned on a time basis, the appropriate proportion should be deducted. See the note to reg. 38(3).

In *R(IS) 10/91*, a challenge to the inability to deduct child-care expenses from earnings as being discriminatory and therefore contrary to EC Directive 79/7 was rejected. On appeal, the Court of Appeal referred the question whether supplementary benefit and/or income support fall within art. 3 of the Directive to the European Court of Justice (*Cresswell v. Chief Adjudication Officer, Jackson v. Chief Adjudication Officer*, December 21, 1990).

A similar question in relation to housing benefit had been referred by the Divisional Court in *R. v. Secretary of State for Social Security, ex parte Smithson* (June 26, 1990). The Advocate General's opinion in *Smithson* (delivered on November 20, 1991) was that the provisions on higher pensioner premium were part of the statutory scheme protecting against the risks of invalidity and old age, so that they came within art. 3. The ECJ (February 4, 1992) disagreed, finding that the higher pensioner premium was an inseparable part of the whole scheme of housing benefit, which was intended to compensate for the fact that the beneficiary's income was insufficient to meet housing costs and not to provide protection against one of the risks specified in art. 3(1) (*e.g.* sickness, invalidity, old age). Although criteria concerning protection against old age and sickness were part of the criteria for determining the level against which the beneficiary's income was tested, that did not affect the purpose of the whole scheme.

Once that decision had been made, the ECJ's decision in *Cresswell and Jackson* (July 16, 1992) [1993] 3 All ER 265 followed fairly inevitably. Benefits such as supplementary benefit and income support could be granted in a variety of personal situations to persons whose means are insufficient to meet their needs as defined by statute. Therefore they did not come within article 3(1) of the Directive. In the particular cases the claimants' theoretical needs were set independently of any consideration of any of the risks specified in art. 3(1). Nor did the fact that the conditions of entitlement to a benefit affected a single parent's ability to take up access to vocational training or part-time employment bring that benefit within EC Directive 76/207 on equal treatment for men and women as regards access to employment, vocational training and promotion, and working conditions. Benefit schemes only come within Directive 76/207 if their subject matter is access to employment, etc., or working conditions.

These decisions seem to rule out challenges to the income support scheme under either Directive, as accepted in *CIS 8/1990* and *CIS 375/1990*.

However, the possibility of a challenge to the family credit scheme under Directive 76/207 remains. Family credit similarly did not, until October 4, 1994, permit the offsetting of any child care expenses against earnings. See regs. 13(1)(c) and 13A of the Family Credit Regulations and regs. 15(1)(c) and 15A of the Disability Working Allowance Regulations for the limited disregard of child care costs that has now been introduced for these benefits. In *CFC 19/1990 (Meyers)* the claimant is arguing that the previous family credit rule was discriminatory and in breach of Directive 76/207. It is contended that since the main purpose of family credit is to supplement the income of low-paid workers, family credit is directly concerned with access to employment and/or working conditions. An oral hearing before the ECJ on the question of whether family credit does come within the scope of Directive 76/207 took place on March 23, 1995. See the notes to reg. 13A of the Family Credit Regulations.

In addition, there may be a possibility of challenge under art. 7 of EC Regulation 1612/68 on social and tax advantages. In *O'Flynn v. Chief Adjudication Officer* (July 29, 1992) the Court of Appeal accepted that a social fund funeral payment is a social advantage within the Regulation. See the notes to reg. 7(1) of the Social Fund Maternity and Funeral Expenses Regulations.

Chapter IV

Self-Employed Earners

Earnings of self-employed earners

37.—(1) Subject to paragraph (2), "earnings", in the case of employment as a self-employed earner, means the gross receipts of the employment and shall include any allowance paid under section 2 of the Employment and Training

Act 1973 [¹or section 2 of the Enterprise and New Towns (Scotland) Act 1990] to the claimant for the purpose of assisting him in carrying on his business.

[²(2) "Earnings" shall not include—
(a) where a claimant is involved in providing board and lodging accommodation for which a charge is payable, any payment by way of such a charge;
[³(b) any payment to which paragraph 26 or 27 of Schedule 9 refers (payments in respect of a person accommodated with the claimant under an arrangement made by a local authority or voluntary organisation and payments made to the claimant by a health authority, local authority or voluntary organisation in respect of persons temporarily in the claimant's care).]]

AMENDMENTS

1. Enterprise (Scotland) Consequential Amendments Order 1991 (S.I. 1991 No. 387), art. 2 (April 1, 1991).
2. Income-related Benefits Schemes (Miscellaneous Amendments) (No. 3) Regulations 1992 (S.I. 1992 No. 2155), reg. 16 (October 5, 1992).
3. Income-related Benefits Schemes (Miscellaneous Amendments) (No. 5) Regulations 1994 (S.I. 1994 No. 2139), reg. 27 (October 3, 1994).

DEFINITIONS

"board and lodging accommodation"—see reg. 2(1).
"claimant"—see reg. 2(1), reg. 23(1).
"self-employed earner"—see reg. 2(1).
"voluntary organisation—*ibid.*

GENERAL NOTE

Paragraph (1)
The starting point for the self-employed is the figure of gross receipts, including enterprise allowance, to be reduced to net profits under reg. 38.

In *CFC 4/1991*, the claimant's husband had recently started a construction business. He received a loan of £5,500 from a relative and made part repayment of £4,000 not long afterwards. The AO and the SSAT treated the loan as part of the "gross receipts" of the self-employment. The repayment could not be deducted from the gross receipts because of reg. 22(5)(a) of the Family Credit (General) Regulations (the equivalent of reg. 38(5)(a) below). The result was that the net profit so calculated took the claimant above family credit level. The Commissioner found that the loan was a capital receipt, but concluded that the words of reg. 21(1) of the Family Credit Regulations (the equivalent of reg. 37(1)) were unambiguous and included capital receipts. On appeal under the name of *Kostanczwk*, an order of the Registrar of the Court of Appeal (dated August 21, 1992) allowed the appeal by consent and directed that capital receipts not generated by a claimant's business do not form part of the gross receipts of that employment for the purposes of reg. 21 of the Family Credit Regulations. As *CFC 3/1992* has now confirmed, since that direction was contained in an Order made by consent and without argument it was not binding on anyone other than the parties to the Order and the tribunal to whom the direction was made. But as the decision in *CFC 4/1991* had been set aside by the Court of Appeal, *CFC 24/1989* remained at that time the only authoritative Commissioner's decision on the point. In *CFC 24/1989* it was held that a grant of £900 from the Prince's Youth Business Trust to assist in the setting up of a business was not part of the gross receipts. The Commissioner focuses on the bizarre consequences if a capital receipt has to count as part of the gross receipts, when capital expenditure cannot be deducted from the gross receipts. The approach of *CFC 24/1989* was to be preferred as a matter of principle. In *CFC 23/1991* a legacy used to keep the claimant's business afloat was not a receipt of the business. The argument that since reg. 37 is placed within the income section of the regulations, gross receipts must mean "revenue receipts" and exclude loans or receipts from the sale of capital assets, etc., did seem to be a convincing one. This has now been confirmed by *CFC 3/1992*. In a comprehensive decision the Commissioner holds that neither a loan for business purposes nor the proceeds of sale of capital assets (in that case a car and a computer printer) form part of the gross receipts of the employment for the purposes of reg. 21 of the Family Credit Regulations (the equivalent of reg. 37).

Paragraph (2)
CIS 55/1989 decided that the predecessor of sub-para. (a), which referred to a claimant "employed" in providing board and lodging accommodation, applied whenever the claimant made

a charge for providing the accommodation. It was not necessary for the claimant to provide it by way of business. The substitution of the word "involved" reinforces this conclusion. The payments received count as income under reg. 40(4), but subject to disregards.

Sub-para. (b) applies to payments to foster-parents and to people for providing temporary care in their home. Those payments are disregarded as income other than earnings under paras. 26 and 27 of Sched. 9. Sub-para. (b) ensures that they are not treated as earnings. See also reg. 6(k).

Calculation of net profit of self-employed earners

38.—(1) For the purposes of regulation 30 (calculation of earnings of self-employed earners), the earnings of a claimant to be taken into account shall be—

(a) in the case of a self-employed earner who is engaged in employment on his own account, the net profit derived from that employment;

(b) in the case of a self-employed earner whose employment is carried on in partnership or is that of a share fisherman within the meaning of the Social Security (Mariners' Benefits) Regulations 1975, his share of the net profit derived from that employment less—

  (i) an amount in respect of income tax and of social security contributions payable under the Social Security Act [SSCBA] calculated in accordance with regulation 39 (deduction of tax and contributions for self-employed earners); and

  (ii) [¹one half of any premium paid [²in the period that is relevant under regulation 30] in respect of a retirement annuity contract or a personal pension scheme].

(2) There shall be disregarded from a claimant's net profit any sum, where applicable, specified in paragraphs 1 to 13 of Schedule 8.

(3) For the purposes of paragraph (1)(a) the net profit of the employment shall, except where paragraph (9) applies, be calculated by taking into account the earnings of the employment over the period determined under regulation 30 (calculation of earnings of self-employed earners) less—

(a) subject to paragraphs (5) to (7), any expenses wholly and exclusively defrayed in that period for the purposes of that employment;

(b) an amount in respect of—

  (i) income tax; and

  (ii) social security contributions payable under the Social Security Act [SSCBA],

  calculated in accordance with regulation 39 (deduction of tax and contributions for self-employed earners); and

(c) [¹one half of any premium paid[²in the period that is relevant under regulation 30] in respect of a retirement annuity contract or a personal pension scheme].

(4) For the purposes of paragraph (1)(b), the net profit of the employment shall be calculated by taking into account the earnings of the employment over the period determined under regulation 30 less, subject to paragraphs (5) to (7), any expenses wholly and exclusively defrayed in that period for the purposes of that employment.

(5) Subject to paragraph (6), no deduction shall be made under paragraph (3)(a) or (4) in respect of—

(a) any capital expenditure;

(b) the depreciation of any capital asset;

(c) any sum employed or intended to be employed in the setting up or expansion of the employment;

(d) any loss incurred before the beginning of the period determined under regulation 30 (calculation of earnings of self-employed earners);

   (e) the repayment of capital on any loan taken out for the purposes of the employment;

   (f) any expenses incurred in providing business entertainment.

  (6) A deduction shall be made under paragraph (3)(a) or (4) in respect of the repayment of capital on any loan used for—

   (a) the replacement in the course of business of equipment or machinery; and

   (b) the repair of an existing business asset except to the extent that any sum is payable under an insurance policy for its repair.

  (7) An adjudication officer shall refuse to make a deduction in respect of any expenses under paragraph (3)(a) or (4) where he is not satisfied that the expense has been defrayed or, having regard to the nature of the expense and its amount, that it has been reasonably incurred.

  (8) For the avoidance of doubt—

   (a) a deduction shall not be made under paragraph (3)(a) or (4) in respect of any sum unless it has been expended for the purposes of the business;

   (b) a deduction shall be made thereunder in respect of—

     (i) the excess of any VAT paid over VAT received in the period determined under regulation 30 (calculation of earnings of self-employed earners);

     (ii) any income expended in the repair of an existing asset except to the extent that any sum is payable under an insurance policy for its repair;

     (iii) any payment of interest on a loan taken out for the purposes of the employment.

  (9) Where a claimant is engaged in employment as a child minder the net profit of the employment shall be one-third of the earnings of that employment, less—

   (a) an amount in respect of—

     (i) income tax; and

     (ii) social security contributions payable under the Social Security Act [SSCBA],

    calculated in accordance with regulation 39 (deduction of tax and contributions for self-employed); and

   (b) [¹one half of any premium paid in respect of a retirement annuity contract or personal pension scheme].

  (10) Notwithstanding regulation 30 (calculation of earnings of self-employed earners) and the foregoing paragraphs, an adjudication officer may assess any item of a claimant's income or expenditure over a period other than that determined under regulation 30 as may, in the particular case, enable the weekly amount of that item of income or expenditure to be determined more accurately.

  (11) For the avoidance of doubt where a claimant is engaged in employment as a self-employed earner and he is also engaged in one or more other employments as a self-employed or employed earner any loss incurred in any one of his employments shall not be offset against his earnings in any other of his employments.

  [¹(12) In this regulation, "retirement annuity contract" means an annuity contract for the time being approved by the Board of Inland Revenue as having for its main object the provision of a life annuity in old age or the provision of an annuity for a partner or dependant and in respect of which relief from income tax may be given on any premium.]

AMENDMENT

  1. Income-related Benefits Schemes (Miscellaneous Amendments) (No. 4) Regulations 1993 (S.I. 1993 No. 2119), reg. 13 (October 4, 1993).

2. Income-related Benefits Schemes (Miscellaneous Amendments) (No. 5) Regulations 1994 (S.I. 1994 No. 2139), reg. 28 (October 3, 1994).

DEFINITIONS

"claimant"—see reg. 2(1), reg. 23(1).
"personal pension scheme"—see reg 2(1).
"self-employed earner"—see reg. 2(1).
"Social Security Act"—*ibid.*

GENERAL NOTE

The structure is as follows.
(1) General rule
(2) Disregards
(3) Net profit of sole traders
(4) Net profit of partners and share fishermen
(5) Deductions are not allowed
(6) Deductions allowed
(7) Tests for (3), (4) and (6)
(8) Tests for (3), (4) and (6)
(9) Child minders
(10) Period of calculation to be adjusted
(11) Two employments
(12) Definition

Paragraph (1)

This provision sets up two categories—
  (a) those in employment on their own account ("sole traders") and
  (b) partners and share fishermen.
For both, the earnings to be taken into account under reg. 30 are to be net profits. Under (b) the deductions for income tax, social security contributions and personal pension or retirement annuity (see para. (12)) premiums are put under para. (1). For (a), these appear in para. (3).

Paragraph (2)

See the notes to reg. 36(2).

Paragraph (3)

For sole traders apart from child minders (para. (9)) the starting point in calculating net profit under para. (1) is earnings, *i.e.* gross receipts (see notes to reg. 37(1) on the meaning of gross receipts). From that are deducted expenses. Any expenses wholly and exclusively defrayed may be deducted providing that they are reasonably incurred (para. (7)) and the rules of paras. (5) and (6) are applied. The expenses must have been actually defrayed, so that unpaid liabilities cannot be deducted (*CIS 212/1989*).

There has been considerable doubt about whether the cost of items which have a dual use, for business and private purposes, can be apportioned. *The Adjudication Officers' Guide* originally suggested that the cost of telephone calls, units of gas or electricity consumption and petrol could be apportioned (because consumption can be identified as for business or private purposes), but not, for instance, standing charges or road fund tax or insurance for a car. In a series of appeals heard together, the Commissioner convincingly demolished this approach (*R(FC) 1/91, CFC 26/1989* and *R(IS) 13/91*). He holds that where expenses can be apportioned on a time basis, this can identify the amount wholly and exclusively defrayed on business expenses. There remain some expenses, like the cost of lunches for clients, which are not capable of apportionment. The Commissioner also holds that the apportionment made by the Inspector of Taxes is cogent evidence of the amounts wholly and exclusively incurred for the purposes of the business, which should be accepted in the absence of evidence to the contrary. Para. 29463 of the *Adjudication Officers' Guide* has now been amended to reflect this decision.

The standard deductions for tax and social security contributions (see reg. 39) and personal pension or retirement annuity (see para. (12)) premiums are made.

Paragraph (4)

For partners and share fishermen the calculation is effectively the same apart from the standard deductions already in para. (1)(b).

Paragraph (5)
No deductions are allowed for these items, many of which will appear in profit and loss accounts. But see para. (6) for exceptions to (e).

Paragraph (6)
Deductions can be made for the repayment of capital on loans for these repairs or replacements. The interest on such a loan will be an allowable expense under the general test (and see para. (8)(b)(iii)).

Paragraph (7)
This provision confirms that an expense must have been actually paid out *(CIS 212/1988)*, and imposes a general test of reasonableness.

Paragraph (8)
The test of business purpose merely confirms the general requirement under paras. (3) and (4). It is useful to have the categories in (b) expressly confirmed.

Paragraph (9)
For child-minders the simple rule of taking profit as one third of gross receipts is used. The standard deductions are then made. Child-minders who work at home are treated as not in remunerative work (reg. 6(b)).

Paragraph (10)
This provision gives a very general power to average items over different periods from that set in reg. 30, where the basic rule is to take the previous one year.

Paragraph (11)
CFC 20/1991 (to be reported as *R(FC) 1/93*) applies the principle that a loss in one employment cannot be set off against a profit or earnings in another separate employment.

Paragraph (12)
The Commissioner in *CFC 5/1993* states that in his view this amendment (from October 4, 1993), combined with the amendments to paras. (1)(b)(ii), (3)(c) and (9)(b), is merely clarificatory, since a personal pension scheme capable of approval under s.633(1) of the Income and Corporation Taxes Act 1988 was an annuity contract within the meaning of the old form of para. (12).

Deduction of tax and contributions for self-employed earners

39.—(1) The amount to be deducted in respect of income tax under regulation 38(1)(b)(i), (3)(b)(i) or (9)(a)(i) (calculation of net profit of self-employed earners) shall be calculated on the basis of the amount of chargeable income and as if that income were assessable to income tax at [¹the lower rate or, as the case may be, the lower rate and the basic rate of tax] less only the personal relief to which the claimant is entitled under sections 8(1) and (2) and 14(1)(a) and (2) of the Income and Corporation Taxes Act 1970 (personal relief) as is appropriate to his circumstances; but, if the period determined under regulation 30 (calculation of earnings of self-employed earners) is less than a year, [¹the earnings to which the lower rate [³. . .] of tax is to be applied and] the amount of the personal relief deductible under this paragraph shall be calculated on a pro rata basis.

(2) The amount to be deducted in respect of social security contributions under regulation 38(1)(b)(i), (3)(b)(ii) or (9)(a)(ii) shall be the total of—

[²(a) the amount of Class 2 contributions payable under section 11(1) or, as the case may be, 11(3) of the Contributions and Benefits Act at the rate applicable at the date of claim except where the claimant's chargeable income is less than the amount specified in section 11(4) of that Act (small earnings exception) for the tax year in which the date of claim falls; but if the assessment period is less than a year, the amount specified for that tax year shall be reduced pro rata; and

(b) the amount of Class 4 contributions (if any) which would be payable under section 15 of that Act (Class 4 contributions recoverable under the Income Tax Acts) at the percentage rate applicable at the date of claim on so much of the chargeable income as exceeds the lower limit but does not exceed the upper limit of profits and gains applicable for the tax year in which the date of claim falls; but if the assessment period is less than a year, those limits shall be reduced pro rata.]

(3) In this regulation "chargeable income" means—

(a) except where sub-paragraph (b) applies, the earnings derived from the employment less any expenses deducted under paragraph (3)(a) or, as the case may be, (4) of regulation 38;

(b) in the case of employment as a child minder, one-third of the earnings of that employment.

AMENDMENTS

1. Income-related Benefits Schemes (Miscellaneous Amendments) (No. 3) Regulations 1992 (S.I. 1992 No. 2155), reg. 17 (October 5, 1992).

2. Income-related Benefits Schemes (Miscellaneous Amendments) (No. 4) Regulations 1993 (S.I. 1993 No. 2119), reg. 14 (October 4, 1993).

3. Income-related Benefits Schemes (Miscellaneous Amendments) (No. 5) Regulations 1994 (S.I. 1994 No. 2139), reg. 29 (October 3, 1994).

DEFINITIONS

"claimant"—see reg. 2(1), reg. 23(1).
"date of claim"—see reg. 2(1).
"lower rate"—see reg. 2(1).
"Social Security Act"—*ibid.*

GENERAL NOTE

Paragraph (1)

The deduction for income tax from the amount of earnings calculated under reg. 38 is to be made by applying the lower and basic rates of tax (*i.e.* currently 20 and 25 per cent. respectively) and the personal relief as a single or married person. This figure may well be higher than the actual tax payable. The references to the Income and Corporation Taxes Act 1970 need to be up-dated to the consolidating 1988 Act.

Paragraph (2)

Deductions are made for the Class 2 and Class 4 Social Security contributions payable on the amount calculated under reg. 38.

Chapter V

Other Income

Calculation of income other than earnings

40.—(1) For the purposes of regulation 29 (calculation of income other than earnings) the income of a claimant which does not consist of earnings to be taken into account shall, subject to paragraphs [²(2) to (3A)], be his gross income and any capital treated as income under regulations [¹...] 41 and 44 ([¹...] capital treated as income and modifications in respect of children and young persons).

(2) There shall be disregarded from the calculation of a claimant's gross income under paragraph (1), any sum, where applicable, specified in Schedule 9.

(3) Where the payment of any benefit under the benefit Acts is subject to any deduction by way of recovery the amount to be taken into account under paragraph (1) shall be the gross amount payable.

[²(3A) Where a loan is made to a person pursuant to arrangements made under section 1 of the Education (Student Loans) Act 1990 [³ or article 3 of the Education (Student Loans) (Northern Ireland) Order 1990] and that person ceases to be a student before the end of the academic year in respect of which the loan is payable or, as the case may be, before the end of his course, a sum equal to the weekly amount apportionable under paragraph (2) of regulation 66A shall be taken into account under paragraph (1) for each week, in the period over which the loan fell to be apportioned, following the date on which that person ceases to be a student; but in determining the weekly amount apportionable under paragraph (2) of regulation 66A so much of that paragraph as provides for a disregard shall not have effect.]

(4) For the avoidance of doubt there shall be included as income to be taken into account under paragraph (1) any payment to which regulation 35(2) or 37(2) (payments not earnings) applies.

AMENDMENTS

1. Income Support (General) Amendment No. 5 Regulations 1988 (S.I. 1988 No. 2022), reg. 9 (December 12, 1988).
2. Social Security Benefits (Student Loans and Miscellaneous Amendments) Regulations 1990 (S.I. 1990 No. 1549), reg. 5(4) (September 1, 1990).
3. Income Support (General) Amendment Regulations 1991 (S.I. 1991 No. 236), reg. 9 (March 13, 1991).

DEFINITIONS

"benefit Acts"—see 1986 Act, s.84(1).
"claimant"—see reg. 2(1), reg. 23(1).
"student"—see reg. 2(1), reg. 61.

GENERAL NOTE

Paragraph (1)
This paragraph mainly confirms that all forms of income other than earnings fall into this category, and provides that the gross amount is to be taken into account. *CIS 25/1989* holds that, applying the principle of *Parsons v. Hogg* [1985] 2 All E.R. 897, appendix to *R(FIS) 4/85*, expenditure necessary to produce the income is to be deducted to produce a figure of gross income. The claimant was entitled to £21.60 per month sickness benefit from the Ideal Benefit Society only while he continued to pay £60 annual payment to the Society. The monthly equivalent (£5) was to be deducted from the £21.60. However, in *CIS 563/1991* the Commissioner disagrees with *CIS 25/1989* and holds that gross income in para. (1) means without any deduction of the expenses incurred in gaining that income, except to the extent expressly allowed by Sched. 9. He considers that the various provisions in Sched. 9 relating to deduction of expenses incurred by the claimant would not be necessary if "gross income" meant income after deducting the expenses of obtaining it. In his view *CIS 25/1989*, in applying *Parsons v. Hogg* in this context, had not paid sufficient regard to the fact that that case was concerned with earnings of employed earners and involved different statutory provisions. The phrase "gross income" was an equivocal one, as indicated by the Court of Appeal's decision in *Parsons v. Hogg*, and the statutory context had to be considered. The principle of *Parsons v. Hogg* had been applied to earnings in *R(FC) 1/90* and *R(IS) 16/93*, (but (apparently not to attendance and basic allowances paid to councillors, which are counted as earnings, in *R(IS) 6/92* and *CIS 77/1993*). The Commissioner in *CIS 563/1991* considered that the statutory context of earnings of employed earners and income other than earnings was sufficiently different not to necessitate a uniform approach to the deduction of expenses, and so did not find it necessary to question the correctness of those decisions. The Commissioner acknowledges that the Tribunal of Commissioners in para. 37 of *CIS 85/1992* assumed that the rental income that was to be taken into account should be net of expenses. However, in his view, they were not expressing a firm conclusion on this question, but simply deciding that the same amount should be treated as capital under reg. 48(4) as would have been taken into account as income. (See the note to reg. 48(4) as to how income treated as capital is to be attributed.) The meaning of "gross income" was not dealt with by the Court of Appeal in *Chief Adjudication Officer v. Palfrey and Others, The Times*, February 17, 1995 (which is the appeal from *CIS 85/1992* and others). The approach adopted by the Commissioner in *CIS*

563/1991 is cogently argued and is to be preferred to that of *CIS 25/1989*. He adopts the same conclusion in *CIS 82/1993* which was heard at the same time. See the notes to reg. 36(3) on the application of *Parsons v. Hogg* to the meaning of "gross earnings".

Certain kinds of income are disregarded under Sched. 9 (para. (2)). There is now no special rule for charitable or voluntary payments. Note reg. 48 on income treated as capital.

The major form of such income for income support claimants will be from other social security benefits. All benefits of an income nature (presumably benefits like disablement gratuity and widow's payment continue to be treated as capital although there is now no classification in the regulations (*cf. R(SB) 4/89*)) count in full as income unless disregarded under Sched. 9. Benefits disregarded include housing benefit (para. 5), mobility allowance, the mobility component of disability living allowance or mobility supplement (paras. 6 and 8), attendance allowance or the care component of disability living allowance, except for residents of residential care and nursing homes (paras. 9 and 9A), social fund payments (para. 31) and council tax benefit (para. 52). Benefits which count as income are income whether they are paid on time or in the form of arrears (*R(SB) 4/89*). Then reg. 31 defines the date on which the income is treated as paid. The fact that there is a partial disregard of some kinds of benefit arrears as capital in para. 7 of Sched. 10 does not affect this conclusion. This is because the conclusion, and *R(SB) 4/89*, must be subject to the principle of *R(SB) 2/83* and *R(SB) 35/83* that at some point accumulated income turns into capital. The sensible approach would be that if any amount of income is still possessed after the end of the period to which it is properly attributed as income under regs. 29 and 31, then it becomes capital, subject to the deduction of relevant liabilities under *R(SB) 2/83* and *R(SB) 35/83*. See *CIS 654/1991*, to be reported as *R(IS)3/93*. Thus there is still something for para. 7 of Sched. 10 to bite on.

Paragraph (2)

This paragraph authorises the disregards in Sched. 9. See *CIS 563/1991* discussed in the note to para. 22 of Sched. 9 where more than one disregard applies. *CIS 683/1993* confirms that income can only be disregarded to the extent allowed for by Sched. 9. Therefore, no deduction could be made for the maintenance payments made by the claimant, whether under a court order or otherwise, or for his insurance premiums, in calculating his income.

Paragraph (3)

If deductions are made from social security benefits for recovery of overpayments or social fund loans the gross amount of benefit is used in the calculation of income support.

Paragraph (3A)

If a student ceases to be a student in the middle of a period for which a student loan is attributed under reg. 66A, the balance of the loan is treated as income under para. (3A).

Paragraph (4)

These amounts, which do not count as earnings, do count as other income. However, note the disregards in paras. 1, 3, 4, 4A, 18, 20 and 21 of Sched. 9.

Capital treated as income

41.—(1) Any capital payable by instalments which are outstanding on the first day in respect of which income support is payable or the date of the determination of the claim, whichever is earlier, or, in the case of a review, the date of any subsequent review shall, if the aggregate of the instalments outstanding and the amount of the claimant's capital otherwise calculated in accordance with Chapter VI of this Part exceeds [⁵£8,000], be treated as income.

(2) Any payment received under an annuity shall be treated as income.

(3) In the case of a person to whom section 23 of the Act [SSCBA, s.126] (trade disputes) applies [¹or in respect of whom section 20(3) of the Act [SSCBA, s.124(1)] (conditions of entitlement to income support) has effect as modified by section 23A(b) of the Act [SSCBA, s.127(b)] (effect of return to work)], any payment under [⁶section 17 or 24 of the Children Act 1989] [³or, as the case may be, section 12, 24 or 26 of the Social Work (Scotland) Act 1968 (local authorities' duty to promote welfare of children and powers to grant financial assistance to persons in, or formerly in, their care) shall be treated as income].

[²(4) In the case of a person to whom section 20(3) of the Act [SSCBA, s.124(1)] (conditions of entitlement to income support) has effect as modified by section 23A(b) of that Act [SSCBA, s.127(b)] (effect of return to work), any amount by way of repayment of income tax deducted from his emoluments in pursuance of section 203 of the Income and Corporation Taxes Act 1988, shall be treated as income.]

[⁴(5) Any earnings to the extent that they are not a payment of income shall be treated as income.]

AMENDMENTS

1. Income Support (General) Amendment Regulations 1988 (S.I. 1988 No. 663), reg. 18 (April 11, 1988).
2. Income Support (General) Amendment No. 4 Regulations 1988 (S.I. 1988 No. 1445), reg. 9 (September 12, 1988).
3. Family Credit and Income Support (General) Amendment Regulations 1989 (S.I. 1989 No. 104), reg. 7 (July 10, 1989).
4. Income Support (General) Amendment No. 2 Regulations 1989 (S.I. 1989 No. 1323), reg. 13 (October 9, 1989).
5. Income-related Benefits (Miscellaneous Amendments) Regulations 1990 (S.I. 1990 No. 671), reg. 5 (April 9, 1990).
6. Income Support (General) Amendment Regulations 1992 (S.I. 1992 No. 468), Sched., para. 4 (April 6, 1992).

DEFINITIONS

"the Act"—see reg. 2(1).
"claimant"—*ibid.*

GENERAL NOTE

Paragraph (1)
The value of the right to receive any outstanding instalments of capital payable by instalments is disregarded (Sched. 10, para. 16). See the notes to reg. 23 on the line between capital and income. Normally each instalment, when it is paid, would add to the claimant's capital (*Lillystone v. SBC* [1982] 3 F.L.R. 52). The literal effect of para. (1) is that if the amount of the instalments outstanding plus the claimant's (including partner's: reg. 23) other capital comes to more than £8,000, the whole amount outstanding is to be treated as income. What para. (1) does not say is what this means. A capital sum cannot simply be treated as income. The common sense rule would be that each instalment, when paid, was treated as a payment of income (as suggested in para. 30046 of the *Adjudication Officers' Guide*), but this is not expressed in para. (1).

Paragraph (2)
The value of the right to receive income under an annuity is disregarded as capital (Sched. 10, para. 11). The income under some "home income" schemes is disregarded under para. 17 of Sched. 9.

Paragraph (3)
R(SB) 29/85 decided that some payments under this legislation were capital. In trade dispute cases, all payments count as income.

Paragraph (4)
In trade dispute cases repayments of PAYE tax, normally capital, are to be treated as income.

Paragraph (5)
This seems merely to confirm that sums which are defined as earnings in reg. 35 which might under the general law be categorised as capital are income.

Notional income

42.—(1) A claimant shall be treated as possessing income of which he has deprived himself for the purpose of securing entitlement to income support or increasing the amount of that benefit.

(2) Except in the case of—

(a) a discretionary trust;

(b) a trust derived from a payment made in consequence of a personal injury;

(c) unemployment benefit under the Social Security Act [SSCBA] which may be payable to a claimant who is not required to be available for employment; or

(d) an increase of child benefit payable to a claimant under regulation 2(2) of the Child Benefit and Social Security (Fixing and Adjustment of Rates) Regulations 1976 (rates of child benefit),

[8(e) family credit;

(f) disability working allowance,]

income which would become available to the claimant upon application being made but which has not been acquired by him shall be treated as possessed by him but only from the date on which [1it could expected to be acquired were an application made.]

(3) Except in the case of a discretionary trust, or a trust derived from a payment made in consequence of a personal injury, any income which is due to be paid to the claimant but—

(a) has not been paid to him;

(b) is not a payment prescribed in regulation 9 or 10 of the Social Security (Payments on Account, Overpayment and Recovery) Regulations 1987 (duplication and prescribed payments or maintenance payments) and not made on or before the date prescribed in relation to it,

shall [10except for any amount to which paragraph (3A) or (3B) applies] be treated as possessed by the claimant.

[10(3A) This paragraph applies to an amount which is due to be paid to the claimant under an occupational pension scheme but which is not paid because the trustees or managers of the scheme have suspended or ceased payments [13. . .] due to an insufficiency of resources.

(3B) This paragraph applies to any amount by which a payment made to the claimant from an occupational pension scheme falls short of the payment to which he was due under the scheme where the shortfall arises because the trustees or managers of the scheme have insufficient resources available to meet in full the scheme's liabilities [13. . .].]

[2(4) Any payment of income made, other than a payment of income made under the Macfarlane Trust[5, the Macfarlane (Special Payments) Trust][6, the Macfarlane (Special Payments) (No. 2) Trust][9, the Fund][15, the Eileen Trust] or [14the Independent Living Funds], made—

(a) to a third party in respect of a single claimant or in respect of a member of the family (but not a member of the third party's family) shall be treated—

(i) in a case where the payment is derived from a payment of any benefit under the benefit Acts, a war disablement pension or war widow's pension, as possessed by that single claimant, if it is paid to him, or by that member, if it is paid to any member of that family;

(ii) in any other case, as possessed by that single claimant or by that member to the extent that it is used for the food, ordinary clothing or footwear, household fuel, rent or rates for which housing benefit is payable, [16or] [7. . .] any housing costs to the extent that they are met under regulations 17(1)(e) or 18(1)(f) (housing costs) [16. . .] [4. . .] [3. . .] [4. . .], of that single claimant or, as the case may be, of any member of that family[7, or is used for any [12council tax] or water charges for which that claimant or member is liable];

(b) to a single claimant or a member of the family in respect of a third party (but not in respect of another member of that family) shall be treated as possessed by that single claimant or, as the case may be, that member of the family to the extent that it is kept or used by him or used by or on behalf of any member of the family;

but, except where sub-paragraph (a)(i) applies and in the case of a person to whom section 23 of the Act [SSCBA, s.126] (trade disputes) applies, this paragraph shall not apply to any payment in kind.]

[¹⁶(4A) Where the claimant lives in a residential care home or a nursing home, or is temporarily absent from such a home, any payment made by a person other than the claimant or a member of his family in respect of some or all of the cost of maintaining the claimant or a member of his family in that home shall be treated as possessed by the claimant or by that member of his family.]

(5) Where a claimant's earnings are not ascertainable at the time of the determination of the claim or of any subsequent review the adjudication officer shall treat the claimant as possessing such earnings as is reasonable in the circumstances of the case having regard to the number of hours worked and the earnings paid for comparable employment in the area.

(6) Where—
(a) a claimant performs a service for another person; and
(b) that person makes no payment of earnings or pays less than that paid for a comparable employment in the area,

the adjudication officer shall treat the claimant as possessing such earnings (if any) as is reasonable for that employment unless the claimant satisfies him that the means of that person are insufficient for him to pay or to pay more for the service; but this paragraph shall not apply to a claimant who is engaged by a charitable or [¹⁹voluntary organisation] or is a volunteer if the adjudication officer is satisfied [¹⁹in any of those cases] that it is reasonable for him to provide his services free of charge.

(7) Where a claimant is treated as possessing any income under any of paragraphs (1) to (4) the foregoing provisions of this Part shall apply for the purposes of calculating the amount of that income as if a payment had actually been made and as if it were actual income which he does possess.

(8) Where a claimant is treated as possessing any earnings under paragraph (5) or (6) the foregoing provisions of this Part shall apply for the purposes of calculating the amount of those earnings as if a payment had actually been made and as if they were actual earnings which he does possess except that paragraph (3) of regulation 36 (calculation of net earnings of employed earners) shall not apply and his net earnings shall be calculated by taking into account the earnings which he is treated as possessing, less—
(a) an amount in respect of income tax equivalent to an amount calculated by applying to those earnings [¹¹the lower rate or, as the case may be, the lower rate and the basic rate of tax] in the year of assessment less only the personal relief to which the claimant is entitled under sections 8(1) and (2) and 14(1)(a) and (2) of the Income and Corporation Taxes Act 1970 (personal relief) as is appropriate to his circumstances; but, if the period over which those earnings are to be taken into account is less than a year, [¹¹the earnings to which the lower rate [¹⁸. . .] of tax is to be applied and] the amount of the personal relief deductible under this paragraph shall be calculated on a pro rata basis;
[¹⁶(b) where the weekly amount of those earnings equals or exceeds the lower earnings limit, an amount representing primary Class 1 contributions under the Contributions and Benefits Act, calculated by applying to those earnings the initial and main primary percentages in accordance with sections 8(1) (a) and (b) of that Act; and]

(c) one-half of any sum payable by the claimant [¹⁷in respect of a pay period] by way of a contribution towards an occupational or personal pension scheme.

[¹⁰(8A) In paragraphs (3A) and (3B) the expression "resources" has the same meaning as in the Social Security Pensions Act 1975 by virtue of section 66(1) of that Act.]

[²(9) In paragraph (4) the expression "ordinary clothing or footwear" means clothing or footwear for normal daily use, but does not include school uniforms, or clothing or footwear used solely for sporting activities.]

AMENDMENTS

1. Income Support (General) Amendment Regulations 1988 (S.I. 1988 No. 663), reg. 19 (April 11, 1988).
2. Income Support (General) Amendment (No. 4) Regulations 1988 (S.I. 1988 No. 1445), reg. 10 (September 12, 1988).
3. Income Support (General) Amendment (No. 4) Regulations 1988 (S.I. 1988 No. 1445), Sched. 1, para. 4 (April 10, 1989).
4. Income Support (General) Amendment Regulations 1989 (S.I. 1989 No. 534), Sched. 1, para. 7 (October 9, 1989).
5. Income-related Benefits Schemes Amendment Regulations 1990 (S.I. 1990 No. 127), reg. 3 (January 31, 1990).
6. Income-related Benefits Schemes and Social Security (Recoupment) Amendment Regulations 1991 (S.I. 1991 No.1175), reg. 5 (May 11, 1991).
7. Income Support (General) Amendment No. 4 Regulations 1991 (S.I. 1991 No. 1559), reg. 8 (October 7, 1991).
8. Income Support (General) Amendment Regulations 1992 (S.I. 1992 No. 468), reg. 4 (April 6, 1992).
9. Income-related Benefits Schemes and Social Security (Recoupment) Amendment Regulations 1992 (S.I. 1992 No. 1101), reg. 6 (May 7, 1992).
10. Income Support (General) Amendment (No. 2) Regulations 1992 (S.I. 1992 No. 1198), reg. 2 (May 22, 1992).
11. Income-related Benefits Schemes (Miscellaneous Amendments) (No. 3) Regulations 1992 (S.I. 1992 No. 2155), reg. 18 (October 5, 1992).
12. Income-related Benefits Schemes (Miscellaneous Amendments) Regulations 1993 (S.I. 1993 No. 315), Sched., para. 2 (April 1, 1993).
13. Income-related Benefits Schemes (Miscellaneous Amendments) Regulations 1993 (S.I. 1993 No. 315), reg. 6 (April 12, 1993).
14. Social Security Benefits (Miscellaneous Amendments) (No. 2) Regulations 1993 (S.I. 1993 No. 963), reg. 2(3) (April 22, 1993).
15. Income-related Benefits Schemes and Social Security (Recoupement) Amendment Regulations 1993 (S.I. 1993 No. 1249), reg. 4(3) (May 14, 1993).
16. Income-related Benefits Schemes (Miscellaneous Amendments) Regulations 1994 (S.I. 1994 No. 527), reg. 4 (April 11, 1994).
17. Income-related Benefits Schemes (Miscellaneous Amendments) (No. 5) Regulations 1994 (S.I. 1994 No. 2139), reg. 26 (October 3, 1994).
18. Income-related Benefits Schemes (Miscellaneous Amendments) (No. 5) Regulations 1994 (S.I. 1994 No. 2139), reg. 29 (October 3, 1994).
19. Income-related Benefits Schemes (Miscellaneous Amendments) Regulations 1995 (S.I. 1995 No. 516), reg. 22 (April 10, 1995).

DEFINITIONS

"the Act"—see reg. 2(1).
"benefit Acts"—see 1986 Act, s.84(1).
"claimant"—see reg. 2(1), reg. 23(1).
"earnings"—see reg. 2(1).
"family"—see 1986 Act, s.20(11) (SSCBA, s.137(1)).
"lower rate"—see reg. 2(1).
"occupational pension scheme"—see 1986 Act, s.84(1) (PSA, s.1).
"pay period"—see reg. 2(1).

"personal pension scheme"—*ibid.*
"primary Class 1 contribution"—*ibid.*
"single claimant"—see reg. 2(1).
"Social Security Act"—*ibid.*
"the Eileen Trust"—*ibid.*
"the Fund"—*ibid.*
"the Independent Living Funds"—*ibid.*
"the Macfarlane (Special Payments) Trust"—*ibid.*
"the Macfarlane (Special Payments) (No. 2) Trust"—*ibid.*
"the Macfarlane Trust"—*ibid.*
"voluntary organisation"—ibid.
"war widow's pension"—*ibid.*
"water charges"—see reg. 2(1).
"year of assessment"—*ibid.*

GENERAL NOTE

The structure is as follows.
(1) Deprivation of income
(2) Income available on application
(3) Income due
(3A) and (3B) Income from occupational pension schemes not paid
(4) Third parties
(5) Earnings not ascertainable
(6) Underpaid services
(7) Calculation
(8) Deductions
(8A) and (9) Definitions

Paragraph (1)
See notes to reg. 51(1). A social security benefit is "income" which a claimant may be treated as still possessing under para. (1) (*CIS 57/1992*).

Paragraph (2)
See notes to reg. 51(2). There are some extra excluded categories here. The fact that a number of social security benefits are excluded suggests that social security benefits generally are caught by the rule. It is not at all clear that such benefits "would become available upon application being made" if an award has not already been made. Stages of the gathering of evidence and a decision by the AO are necessary before a claimant becomes entitled to payment. The words "would become" may be broad enough to cover that process, but that could only be the case where entitlement is straightforward.

The exclusion of family credit from April 1992, is intended, in conjunction with regs. 22 to 24 of the Income Support (General) Amendment No. 4 Regulations 1991, to allow claimants a choice of which method of support they prefer on the change in the minimum working hours for family credit from 24 to 16. Income support may be claimed to top up family credit, but there is no penalty for not claiming family credit. There is similar protection on the introduction of disability working allowance.

Paragraph (3)
To start with the exclusion in sub-para. (b), the 1987 Payments Regulations have been revoked and replaced by the 1988 Regulations set out in this book. The reference to regs. 9 and 10 can be taken (under the Interpretation Act 1978) to be a reference to regs. 8 and 9 of the 1988 Regulations. This excludes almost all social security benefits from the operation of this paragraph (although abandoning entitlement might be a deprivation of income under para. (1)). The other exclusions are of income due, but not paid, under discretionary trusts and trusts of personal injury compensation, and entitlements under occupational pension schemes covered by paras. (3A) and (3B).

Outside these exclusions if income is due, *i.e.* legally due, it is to be treated as possessed by the claimant, and as income. The value of a debt would normally be a capital asset. Note that there is no discretion. An example would be of wages legally due but not paid, or payments on termination of employment due but not paid.

See reg. 70(2)(b) (urgent cases) for the possibility of payment when notional income is attributed under para. (3).

Paragraphs (3A) and (3B)

Where a payment due from an occupational pension scheme is either not made or is not made in full because of a deficiency in the scheme's resources (defined in para. (8A)) the amount not paid does not fall within para. (3). The original form of the provisions applied only where the scheme stopped making payments to members of the scheme. The amendment puts beyond doubt that if payments to relatives or dependants of members are stopped, para. (3) does not apply.

Paragraph (4)

See notes to reg. 51(3).

Paragraph (4A)

Any payment made by a third party towards the cost of a claimant and his family's residential care or nursing home fees counts as the claimant's income. However, under paras. 15, 15A, 30 and 30A of Sched. 9 certain "top-up" payments to people in residential care and nursing homes are disregarded.

Paragraph (5)

This is a very general discretion. The AO (or SSAT) must have regard to the number of hours worked and the going rate locally for comparable employment in deciding what is reasonable, but is not prevented from considering all relevant circumstances *(R(SB) 25/83, R(SB) 15/86, R(SB) 6/88)*.

Paragraph (6)

This provision has been tightened up in a number of respects in comparison with its supplementary benefit predecessor. If the two conditions in sub-paras. (a) and (b) are met there is no discretion whether or not to apply para. (6), unless the claimant comes within one of the specific exceptions. It appears that for sub-para. (a) any unpaid or underpaid service will do, subject to the exclusion of volunteers or workers for charities or voluntary organisations where it is reasonable for the person to make no charge. In *R(SB) 3/92* on the old law the Commissioner held that the rule applied where a mother provided services to her disabled adult son out of love and affection. On appeal in *Sharrock v. Chief Adjudication Officer* (March 26, 1991; appendix to *R(SB) 3/92)* the Court of Appeal agreed that such relationships came within the old provision, providing that the service provided was of a character for which an employer would be prepared to pay. In *CIS 93/1991* the Commissioner holds that the principle of *Sharrock* applies to reg. 42(6), which thus covers services provided within informal family relationships without any contract. Under supplementary benefit there was no proviso exempting volunteers etc. at the time. Now unpaid carers can be defined as volunteers *(CIS 93/1991)*, so that there is a discretion not to apply the rule (see below). In *CIS 422/1992* (which again concerned Mrs Sharrock), the Commissioner held that she was a volunteer and that it was reasonable for her to provide her services free. The evidence was that her son made a substantial contribution to the household expenses. If she were to charge for her services the whole basis of the arrangement between them would have to change, which could have a deleterious effect on their relationship. (However, the part of the son's contribution that was not in respect of *his* living and accommodation costs could not be disregarded under para. 18 of Sched. 9.) It is difficult to see in most cases it can be unreasonable for carers to look after a relative without payment. This is acknowledged by para. 29265 of the *Adjudication Officers' Guide*; para. 29266 lists factors to be considered in cases of doubt which are broadly in line with those suggested in *CIS 93/1991* (see below).

Under sub-para. (b) the "employer" must either make no payment or pay less than is paid for comparable employment in the area. Since the amount of notional earnings is set according to what is reasonable for that comparable employment, it seems that some comparable employment must exist in all cases.

Some of the points made in *R(SB) 13/86* on the old law will still apply to para. (6). It must be necessary to identify the employer for whom the services were provided. "Person" includes a company or other corporate employer (Interpretation Act 1978). Thus in *CIS 181/1993* where the claimant, who was an employee and director of a small company, was working unpaid because of the company's financial difficulties, it was necessary to consider whether para. (6) applied.

Particulars of the services provided and any payments made must be ascertained. Although payments of earnings in kind are disregarded in the calculation of income (reg. 35(2)(a) and Sched. 9, para. 21), presumably payments in kind should be considered in testing whether a claimant is paid at all or is paid less than the rate for comparable employment.

The claimant can then escape if he proves (on the balance of probabilities) that the person to whom he has provided the services has insufficient means to pay more. This could well cause difficulties for claimants reluctant to make embarrassing enquiries. But there is an interest in preventing employers from economising at the expense of the income support budget. The Court of Appeal in *Sharrock v. Chief Adjudication Officer* suggests that "means" refers simply to monetary resources and is a matter of broad judgment. No automatic test of ignoring certain benefits or regarding an income above income support level as available should be adopted. In *CIS 93/1991*, the claimant looked after his elderly and severely disabled father, but declined to give any information about the father's means. The Commissioner confirms that in such circumstances the basic rule of para. (6) must be applied, but subject to the proviso on volunteers.

The proviso allows volunteers or those engaged by charities or voluntary organisations not to have any notional earnings if it is reasonable for them to provide their services free of charge. Volunteer in this context means someone who without any legal obligation performs a service for another person without expectation of payment (*R(IS) 12/92*). Thus, it would seem that if any payment is made to the claimant, the proviso cannot apply. The Commissioner in *CIS 93/1991* holds that the means of the "employer" are a factor here, but other factors are relevant too. It may be more reasonable for close relatives to provide services free of charge than for others to do so. The basis on which the arrangement was made, the expectations of the family members concerned, the housing arrangements and the reason why the carer gave up any paid work might need to be considered. Anomalies like the loss of invalid care allowance if the carer accepted any payment should be considered. In *CIS 93/1991* the SSAT went wrong in not properly considering their discretion under the proviso and concentrating on the legitimate inference that the "employer" could afford to pay the going rate. It should be noted that the test is whether it is reasonable for the person to provide his services free of charge, rather than whether it is reasonable for payment not to be made for the service, although this is a factor (*CIS 147/1993*). If the claimant was receiving training while, or by doing, the work, this may be relevant (*R(IS) 12/92*).

In *CIS 93/1991* the Commissioner points out that the aim of the rule is clearly to prevent an employer who has the means to pay the going rate profiting at the expense of the public purse. If, therefore, a claimant volunteers to undertake painting work (as in *CIS 147/1993*), which otherwise would have remained undone, there is no element of financial profit to the employer in the claimant doing the work. If, however, the employer would have paid the claimant if he had not said he did not wish to be paid, it may be concluded that it was not reasonable for the claimant to offer his services free of charge.

Paragraphs (7) to (8)

If notional income counts it is to be calculated as though it was actual income. Notional deductions are to be made from earnings to get a net figure.

Paragraph (9)

Para. 29876 of the *Adjudication Officers' Guide* suggests that wellington boots are not for "normal daily use", nor are special shoes needed because of a disability (as these would not be for the normal daily use of children in general).

Notional earnings of seasonal workers

43. [¹. . .].

AMENDMENT

1. Income Support (General) Amendment No. 2 Regulations 1989 (S.I. 1989 No. 1323), reg. 14 (October 9, 1989).

GENERAL NOTE

The special rules for seasonal workers have been removed from the unemployment benefit scheme and consequently from income support also.

Modifications in respect of children and young persons

44.—(1) Any capital of a child or young person payable by instalments which are outstanding on the first day in respect of which income support is payable or at the date of the determination of the claim, whichever is earlier, or, in the case of a review, the date of any subsequent review shall, if the aggregate of the instalments outstanding and the amount of that child's or young person's other capital calculated in accordance with Chapter VI of this Part in like manner as for the claimant [². . .] would exceed £3000, be treated as income.

(2) In the case of a child or young person who is residing at an educational establishment at which he is receiving relevant education—

(a) any payment made to the educational establishment, in respect of that child's or young person's maintenance, by or on behalf of a person who is not a member of the family or by a member of the family out of funds contributed for that purpose by a person who is not a member of the family, shall be treated as income of that child or young person but it shall only be taken into account over periods during which that child or young person is present at that educational establishment; and

(b) if a payment has been so made, for any period in a benefit week in term-time during which that child or young person returns home, he shall be treated as possessing an amount of income in that week calculated by multiplying the amount of personal allowance and disabled child premium, if any, applicable in respect of that child or young person by the number equal to the number of days in that week in which he was present at his educational establishment and dividing the product by seven; but this sub-paragraph shall not apply where the educational establishment is provided under section 8 of the Education Act 1944 (duty of local authority to secure primary and secondary schools) by a local education authority or where the payment is made under section 49 or 50 of the Education (Scotland) Act 1980 (power of education authority to assist persons).

(3) Where a child or young person—

(a) is resident at an educational establishment and he is wholly or partly maintained at that establishment by a local education authority under section 8 of the Education Act 1944; or

(b) is maintained at an educational establishment under section 49 or 50 of the Education (Scotland) Act 1980,

he shall for each day he is present at that establishment be treated as possessing an amount of income equal to the sum obtained by dividing the amount of personal allowance and disabled child premium, if any, applicable in respect of him by seven.

(4) Where the income of a child or young person who is a member of the claimant's family calculated in accordance with [² Chapters I to V] of this Part exceeds the amount of the personal allowance and disabled child premium, if any, applicable in respect of that child or young person, the excess shall not be treated as income of the claimant.

(5) Where the capital of a child or young person if calculated in accordance with Chapter VI of this Part in like manner as for the claimant, [²except as provided in paragraph (1)], would exceed £3,000, any income of that child or young person shall not be treated as income of the claimant.

(6) In calculating the net earnings or net profit of a child or young person there shall be disregarded, (in addition to any sum which falls to be disregarded under paragraphs 11 to 13), any sum specified in paragraphs 14 and 15 of Schedule 8 (earnings to be disregarded).

(7) Any income of a child or young person which is to be disregarded under Schedule 9 (income other than earnings to be disregarded) shall be disregarded in such manner as to produce the result most favourable to the claimant.

(8) Where a child or young person is treated as possessing any income under paragraphs (2) and (3) the foregoing provisions of this Part shall apply for the purposes of calculating that income as if a payment had actually been made and as if it were actual income which he does possess.

[¹(9) For the purposes of this regulation, a child or young person shall not be treated as present at his educational establishment on any day if on that day he spends the night with the claimant or a member of his household.]

AMENDMENTS

1. Income Support (General) Amendment Regulations 1988 (S.I. 1988 No. 663), reg. 20 (April 11, 1988).
2. Income-related Benefits Schemes (Miscellaneous Amendments) (No. 4) Regulations 1993 (S.I. 1993 No. 2119), reg. 15 (October 4, 1993).

DEFINITIONS

"child"—see 1986 Act, s.20(11) (SSCBA, s.137(1)).
"claimant"—see reg. 2(1), reg. 23(1).
"family"—see 1986 Act, s.20(11) (SSCBA, s.137(1)).
"young person"—see reg. 2(1), reg. 14.

GENERAL NOTE

Paragraph (1)
See the notes to reg. 41(1) for the general test. If a child or young person has capital of more than £3,000, no personal allowance is included for him (reg. 17(b)) and his income is disregarded (para. (5)).

Paragraph (2)
If a child or young person is at a boarding school, payments made to the school for maintenance by, or from funds contributed to by, someone outside the family (as defined in s.137(1) of the Contributions and Benefits Act; 1986 Act, s.20(11)) are subject to these special rules. See para. (9).

Paragraph (3)
Children and young persons at maintained boarding schools are treated as possessing an income sufficient to wipe out their personal allowance and disabled child premium (if applicable). See para. (9).

Paragraph (4)
If a child's or young person's income exceeds his personal allowance, plus any disabled child premium, the excess is disregarded.

Paragraph (5)
If a child or young person has capital over £3,000, their income does not count as the claimant's. There is no personal allowance for the child or young person, but the rest of the family's benefit is not affected by that person's income.

Paragraph (6)
This paragraph brings in the disregard of the earnings of most children and young persons.

Paragraph (7)
The disregards in Sched.9 are to be applied in the most favourable way.

Paragraph (8)
Income under paras.(2) and (3) is to be calculated as if it was actual income.

Chapter VI

Capital

Capital limit

45. For the purposes of section 22(6) of the Act [SSCBA, s.134(1)] as it applies to income support (no entitlement to benefit if capital exceeds prescribed amount), the prescribed amount is [¹£8,000].

AMENDMENT

1. Income-Related Benefits (Miscellaneous Amendments) Regulations 1990 (S.I. 1990 No. 671), reg. 5 (April 9, 1990).

DEFINITION

"the Act"—see reg. 2(1).

GENERAL NOTE

Under s.134(1) of the Contributions and Benefits Act (1986 Act, s.22(6)) there is no entitlement to income support if the claimant's capital exceeds the prescribed amount. £8,000 is prescribed from April 9, 1990. The capital of a claimant's partner is aggregated with the claimant's (reg. 23(1)), but not that of children or young persons (reg. 47).

In *CIS 127/1993* the Commissioner raises the question of where the burden of proof lies when considering whether the capital rule is satisfied. The Tribunal of Commissioners in *CIS 417/1992* treat this as part of what the claimant has to prove in showing entitlement to income support. However, the argument that the capital rule operates as an exception to the conditions of basic entitlement does not appear to have been put. See sidenote to s.134 which is entitled "Exclusions from benefit". But once it has been shown that the claimant possesses an item of capital, it is for him to prove that one of the disregards in Sched. 10 applies (*CIS 240/1992*). Similarly, once it has been established that the claimant is the legal owner of a property, the burden is on her to show that she does not have any or all of the beneficial interest (*CIS 30/1993*).

Calculation of capital

46.—(1) For the purposes of Part II of the Act [SSCBA, Part VII] as it applies to income support, the capital of a claimant to be taken into account shall, subject to paragraph (2), be the whole of his capital calculated in accordance with this Part and any income treated as capital under [¹regulation 48 (income treated as capital)].

(2) There shall be disregarded from the calculation of a claimant's capital under paragraph (1) any capital, where applicable, specified in Schedule 10.

AMENDMENT

1. Income Support (General) Amendment No. 5 Regulations 1988 (S.I. 1988 No. 2022), reg. 10 (December 12, 1988).

DEFINITIONS

"the Act"—see reg. 2(1).
"claimant"—*ibid.*, reg. 23(1).

GENERAL NOTE

All the claimant's (and partner's) capital, both actual and notional, counts towards the £8,000 limit, subject to the disregards in Sched.10. There is a good deal of law on actual capital.

The first condition is of course that the capital resource is the claimant's or his partner's. This is not as simple as it sounds. In *CIS 634/1992* the claimant was made bankrupt on November 29, 1990. However, his trustee in bankruptcy was not appointed until April 1991. Between November 29 and December 28, 1990, when he claimed income support the claimant divested himself of most of his capital. Under the Insolvency Act 1986 (subject to certain exceptions) a bankrupt's property does not vest in his trustee in bankruptcy on the making of a bankruptcy order, but only when the trustee is appointed. The appointment does not have retrospective effect. It is held that since he had failed to give a satisfactory account of how he had disposed of his capital he was to be treated as still possessing it (*R(SB) 38/85* referred to in the notes to reg. 51(1)). Thus the claimant was not entitled to income support prior to the appointment of the trustee in bankruptcy because until then he possessed actual capital over the income support limit.

However, the mere fact that an asset or a bank or building society account is in the claimant's name alone does not mean that it belongs to the claimant. It is the "beneficial ownership" which matters. The claimant may hold the asset under a trust which means that he cannot simply treat the asset as his, but must treat it as if it belonged to the beneficiary or beneficiaries under the trust. It is they who are "beneficially entitled." A trustee may also be a beneficiary, in which case the rule of reg. 52 may come into play, or may have no beneficial interest at all.

An example of the first situation is *CIS 449/1990* (to be reported as *R(IS) 2/93*). The claimant had a building society account in her sole name, which she had had since before her marriage. Her husband deposited the bulk of the money in it, including his salary. On their separation, the AO and the SSAT treated the entire amount in the account as part of the claimant's capital. The Commissioner holds that she was not solely beneficially entitled to the money so that reg. 52 had to operate. There is helpful guidance on the limited circumstances in which the "presumption of advancement" (*i.e.* that when a husband puts an asset into his wife's name he intends to make an outright gift of it) will operate in modern circumstances. In *CIS 553/1991* where a house was in the husband's sole name it is held that its valuation should take into account the wife's statutory right of occupation under the Matrimonial Homes Act 1967. In most cases of spouses, in whoever's name the asset is, there will be some degree of joint ownership.

There have been several examples of the second situation, where the claimant has no beneficial interest at all. In *R(SB) 49/83* the claimant had bought a house, but said that this was on behalf of his son, who was paying off the loan. The Commissioner held that if this could be established, the claimant would hold the house on a resulting trust for his son. It would not then be part of his capital resources. See *CSB 200/1985* (applying *Cowcher v. Cowcher* [1972] 1 W. L. R. 425) for the position where another person provides part of the money. In *R(SB) 53/83* the claimant's son had paid him £2,850 to be used for a holiday in India. The claimant died without taking the holiday or declaring the existence of the money to the DHSS. The Commissioner, applying the principle of *Barclays Bank Ltd. v. Quistclose Investments Ltd.* [1970] A. C. 567, held that there was a trust to return the money to the son if the primary purpose of the loan was not carried out. Since the Commissioner held that there had been no overpayment while the claimant was alive, this must mean that the claimant held the money on trust to use it for the specified purpose or to return it. It was not part of the claimant's resources. This is an important decision, which overtakes some of the reasoning of *R(SB) 14/81* (see below). The actual decision in *R(SB) 53/83* was reversed (by consent) by the Court of Appeal, because the Commissioner had differed from the appeal tribunal on a point of pure fact. *R(SB) 1/85* holds that this does not affect its authority on the issue of principle. In *R(SB) 1/85*, the claimant's mother-in-law had some years previously provided the money for the purchase of the lease of a holiday chalet for the use of the claimant's mentally handicapped son, Keith. The lease was in the claimant's name and its current value was probably about £5,000. The AO's initial statement of the facts was that the mother-in-law had bought the chalet in the claimant's name. The Commissioner holds that this would give rise to a presumption of a resulting trust in her favour, so that the claimant would have no beneficial interest in the chalet—nothing he could sell. The presumption could be rebutted if in fact the mother-in-law had made an outright gift to the claimant, or to Keith. In the second case the claimant again would have no beneficial interest. In the first, he would be caught, for even if he had said that he intended to use the chalet purely for Keith, he had not made the necessary written declaration of trust (Law of Property Act 1925, s.53). Another possibility was that the mother-in-law had made a gift to the claimant subject to an express (but unwritten) trust in favour of Keith, when again the claimant clearly would not be the beneficial owner. This is a very instructive decision, which will give valuable guidance in sorting out many family-type arrangements. *CIS 30/1993* also sets out helpful guidance on the points to consider when deciding whether a resulting trust has been created. The claimant had purchased her flat with the proceeds of sale of her previous home. She had bought that home as a sitting tenant with the aid of a loan, the repayments on which had been made by her children. The Commissioner states that the children's contributions indicated a resulting trust in their favour in the beneficial interest in the house in proportion to their and the claimant's contributions to the purchase price. If the claimant had, as a sitting tenant, received a discount on the price, that would be treated as a contribution. The resulting trust would transfer to the flat on the sale of the house. However, the presumption of a resulting trust created by the children's contributions could be rebutted by proof of the purchasers' true intentions, *e.g.* that an outright gift was or different beneficial interests under the trust than those created by the presumption were intended.

The *Quistclose* principle was re-affirmed in *R(SB) 12/86*, where £2,000 was lent to the claimant on condition that she did not touch the capital amount, but only took the interest, and repaid the £2,000 on demand. The £2,000 was not part of her capital, never having been at her disposal. The

Commissioner in *CSB 975/1985* was prepared to apply the principle to a loan on mortgage from a Building Society for property renovation. But it would have to be found that the loan was made for no other purpose and was to be recoverable by the Building Society if for any reason the renovations could not be carried out. The dangers and difficulties of *Quistclose* are pointed out in *CSB 1137/1985*, particularly where family transactions are concerned. If a gift or loan is made with a particular motive, the whole sum becomes part of the recipient's resources. The intention to impose a trust must appear expressly (as in *R(SB) 12/86*) or by implication from the circumstances. Perhaps it is easier to prove (*e.g.* by contemporaneous documents) such an intention in business transactions. Often such evidence will be lacking in domestic situations, but the issue is one of proof, as is shown in *R(IS) 1/90*. There, the claimant established a Building Society account in his own name which was to be used solely to finance his son's medical education. He executed no documents about the account. It was argued that there was sufficient evidence of a declaration of trust over the account, but the Commissioner holds that the claimant had not unequivocally renounced his beneficial interest in the sum in the account. Although he had earmarked the money for the son's education, the situation was like an uncompleted gift and there was insufficient evidence of a declaration of trust. There is a thin line between an outright gift or loan, and one subject to an implied trust. In *CIS 69/1994* where the claimant had transferred her flat to her daughter partly on the condition that her daughter looked after her, it is held that the gift failed when this condition was not fulfilled and the daughter held the flat on trust for her mother.

The furthest extension so far of the *Quistclose* principle is in *CFC 21/1989*. The claimant's father paid her each month an amount to meet her mortgage obligation to a building society. The Commissioner accepts that the money was impressed with a trust that it should be used only for that purpose and did not form part of her capital. The extension is that the purpose was to meet expenditure on an item which could be covered by income support.

See also the doctrine of secret trusts, under which a person who receives property under an intestacy when the deceased refrained from making a will in reliance on that person's promise to carry out his expressed intentions, holds the property on trust to carry out those intentions (*CSB 989/1985*).

Another example of the legal owner having nothing to sell is *R(SB) 23/85*. The claimant's wife in a home-made and legally ineffective deed of gift purported to give an uninhabitable property to her son. He, as intended, carried out the works to make it habitable. The Commissioner holds that although a court will not normally ''complete'' such an ''uncompleted gift'' in favour of someone who has not given valuable consideration, one of the situations in which a transfer of the property will be ordered is where the intended recipient is induced to believe that he has or will have an interest in the property and acts on that belief to his detriment. Thus in the meantime the claimant's wife held the property merely as a ''bare trustee'' and could not lawfully transfer it to anyone but the son. There is discussion of what kind of action might give rise to the right to complete the gift in *R(SB) 7/87*. See also *CIS 807/1991* on proprietary estoppel.

There is also a remarkable range of interests in property which do have a present market value and so are actual capital resources. These are usually things in action (or choses in action), rights to sue for something. Debts, even where they are not due to be paid for some time, are things in action which can be sold. A good example is *R(SB) 31/83* where the claimant in selling a house allowed the purchaser a mortgage of £4,000, to be redeemed in six months. The debt conferred a right to sue and had to be valued at what could be obtained on the open market. Similarly, a life interest in a trust fund is a present asset which can be sold and has a market value (*R(SB) 2/84, R(SB) 43/84, R(SB) 15/86 and R(SB) 13/87*). The practical effect is reversed by para. 13 of Sched. 10.

A more direct way of holding capital is in a bank or building society account. In *CSB 296/1985* the claimant's solicitor received £12,000 damages on behalf of the claimant and placed the money on deposit, presumably in the solicitor's client account. The Commissioner held that the £12,000 was an actual resource of the claimant, on the basis that there was no difference in principle between monies being held by a solicitor on behalf of a client and monies held by a bank or building society on behalf of a customer. This decision was upheld by the Court of Appeal in *Thomas v. Chief Adjudication Officer* (reported as *R(SB) 17/87*). Russell L. J. says ''the possession of this money by the solicitors as the agent for the claimant was, in every sense of the term, possession by the claimant.'' This seems to involve valuing the amount of money directly, not as a technical chose in action. However, the importance of the legal relationship between a bank and a customer being one of debtor and creditor was revealed in *CSB 598/1987*. A large cheque was paid into the claimant's wife's bank account on October 9, 1987. The amount was credited to her account on that date, but the cheque was not cleared until October 15. The bank's paying-in slips reserved the bank's right to ''postpone payment of cheques drawn against uncleared effects which may have been credited to the account.'' The effect was that the bank did not accept the relationship of debtor and creditor on the mere paying in of a cheque. Thus the amount did not become part of the claimant's actual resources until October 15. A person who deliberately refrains from paying in a cheque may be fixed with notional capital under reg. 51.

The nature of interests in capital under trusts gives rise to several problems. The *Adjudication Officers' Guide* (paras. 30451 to 61) does not deal with all the issues. It is clear that a person may have an absolute vested interest under a trust, although payment is deferred, *e.g.* until the age of 21. This was the case in *R(SB) 26/86*, where the resource was held to be the person's share of the fund. However, an interest may be contingent on reaching a particular age. This appears to have been one of the assumptions on which the Court of Appeal decided the unsatisfactory case of *Peters v. Chief Adjudication Officer, R(SB) 3/89*. It was conceded that sums were held on trust to be paid over to each of three sisters on attaining the age of 18, with the power to advance up to 50 per cent. of the capital before then. In the end, the Court of Appeal accepted the valuation of half of the full value for each sister under 18. The precise finding may depend on the supplementary benefit rule on discretionary trusts, which has not been translated into the income support legislation. But some statements about the general market value of such interests are made. May L. J. says "in an appropriate market a discretionary entitlement of up to 50 per cent. now and at least 50 per cent. in, say, six months in a given case, or three to four years in another, could well be said to have a value greater than 50 per cent. of the capital value of the trust."

This clearly supports the view that a contingent interest has a market value and so is actual capital. Although often a potential benefit under a discretionary trust will have no market value, a discretion to advance capital before the contingency happens may affect the value of the contingent interest. In some circumstances also a purely discretionary trust may produce a capital asset, as where the claimant is the only real beneficiary under a "spendthrift" trust (*R(SB) 25/83*, especially para. 18). In the family law context, the courts are prepared to look at the realities of what a person is likely to receive under a discretionary trust in assessing financial resources under s.25 of the Matrimonial Causes Act 1973 (*Browne v. Browne* [1989] 1 F. L. R. 291 and *J. v. J. (C. intervening)* [1989] 1 F. L. R. 453). The income support law is not so flexible, but it is certain that all interests which can be sold or borrowed against should be considered.

R(SB) 18/83 stresses that there are more ways of realising assets than sale. In particular, assets can be charged to secure a loan which can be used to meet requirements. In that case the asset was a minority shareholding in a family company. The Commissioner says that only a person prepared to lend money without security would do so in such circumstances. The articles of association of the company provided that if a shareholder wanted to sell shares they were to be offered to the existing shareholders at the fair value fixed by the auditors. The Commissioner holds that the regulations do not require assets to be valued at a figure higher than anything the person would realise on them, *i.e.* the auditor's fair value. This is in line with the purpose of the capital cut-off that a claimant can draw on resources until they fall below the limit.

This approach to valuation can usefully deal with unrealisable assets. Sometimes their market value (see reg. 49) will be nil (*e.g.* a potential interest under a discretionary trust: *R(SB) 25/83*); sometimes it will be very heavily discounted. However, if the asset will be realisable after a time, it may have a current value. The claimant may be able to sell an option to purchase the asset in the future (see *R(IS) 8/92*) or borrow, using the asset as security. It should similarly be remembered that if, exceptionally, personal possessions are being taken into account (*e.g.* they have been bought to secure benefit), their value is not what was paid for them, but what could be obtained for them if sold as second-hand (*CIS 494/1990*). As the Tribunal of Commissioners in *R(SB) 45/83* point out, the market value (in this case of an interest in an entire trust fund) must reflect the outlay the purchaser would expect to incur in obtaining transfer of the assets and the profit he would expect as an inducement to purchase. If there might be some legal difficulty in obtaining the underlying asset (as there might have been in *R(SB) 21/83*) this must be taken into account. In *CIS 654/1993* the Commissioner accepts that the delay and inconvenience for a purchaser in obtaining good title (*e.g.* by means of a court order) where shares of £15,000 were held in the claimant's children's names reduced their value (although not sufficiently). See the Tribunal of Commissioners' decision in *CIS 391/1992* and *CIS 417/1992* discussed in the notes to reg.49 on the valuation of a deemed share under reg. 52 in jointly held capital.

The general rule is that the whole of a capital resource is to be taken into account. Liabilities are not to be deducted from the value (*R(SB) 2/83*). Otherwise, it is only if a debt is secured on the capital asset that it can be deducted, at the stage specifically required by reg. 49 or 50 (*R(IS) 21/93*). See the notes to reg. 49.

It is no part of the definition of capital that it should be immediately realisable. As suggested above, its market value may be affected by such factors, but it remains quite possible (especially in circumstances like those imposed by reg. 52 below) for a claimant to be fixed with a large amount of capital which is not available to him. If this takes the claimant over the £8,000 limit, a crisis loan may be appropriate while the claimant attempts to realise the asset or raise a commercial loan (*Social Fund Guide*, para. 5424).

Disregard of capital of child or young person

47. The capital of a child or young person who is a member of the claimant's family shall not be treated as capital of the claimant.

DEFINITIONS

"child"—see 1986 Act, s.20(11) (SSCBA, s.137(1)).
"claimant"—see reg. 2(1), reg. 23(1).
"family"—see 1986 Act, s.20(11) (SSCBA, s.137(1)).
"young person"—see reg. 2(1), reg. 14.

GENERAL NOTE

The capital of a child or young person is not aggregated with the claimant's. But if that person's capital is over £3,000 there is no personal allowance for that person (reg. 17(b)) and any income is not aggregated with the claimant's either (reg. 44(5)).

Income treated as capital

48.—(1) Any [². . .] bounty derived from employment to which paragraph 7 of Schedule 8 applies [²and paid at intervals of at least one year] shall be treated as capital.

(2) Except in the case of an amount to which section 23(5)(a)(ii) of the Act [SSCBA, s.126(5)(a)(ii)] (refund of tax in trade disputes cases) [²or regulation 41(4) (capital treated as income)] applies, any amount by way of a refund of income tax deducted from profits or emoluments chargeable to income tax under Schedule D or E shall be treated as capital.

(3) Any holiday pay which is not earnings under regulation 35(1)(d) (earnings of employed earners) shall be treated as capital.

(4) Except any income derived from capital disregarded under paragraph 1, 2, 4, 6, [³12 or 25 to 28] of Schedule 10, any income derived from capital shall be treated as capital but only from the date it is normally due to be credited to the claimant's account.

(5) Subject to paragraph (6), in the case of employment as an employed earner, any advance of earnings or any loan made by the claimant's employer shall be treated as capital.

[¹(6) Paragraph (5) shall not apply to a person to whom section 23 of the Act [SSCBA, s.126] (trade disputes) applies or in respect of whom section 20(3) of the Act [SSCBA, s.124(1)] (conditions of entitlement to income support) has effect as modified by section 23A(b) [SSCBA, s.127(b)] (effect of return to work).]

(7) Any payment under section 30 of the Prison Act 1952 (payments for discharged prisoners) or allowance under section 17 of the Prisons (Scotland) Act 1952 (allowances to prisoners on discharge) shall be treated as capital.

[⁷(8) Any payment made by a local authority which represents arrears of payments under paragraph 15 of Schedule 1 to the Children Act 1989 (power of local authority to make contributions to a person with whom a child lives as a result of a residence order) shall be treated as capital.]

[³(9) Any charitable or voluntary payment which is not made or not due to be made at regular intervals, other than one to which paragraph (10) applies, shall be treated as capital.

(10) This paragraph applies to a payment—
(a) which is made to a person to whom section 23 of the Act [SSCBA, s.126]

(trade disputes) applies or in respect of whom section 20(3) of the Act [SSCBA, s.124(1)] (conditions of entitlement to income support) has effect as modified by section 23A(b) of the Act [SSCBA, s.127(b)] (effect of return to work) or to a member of the family of such a person;
(b) to which regulation 44(2) (modification in respect of children and young persons) applies; or
(c) which is made under the Macfarlane Trust[⁵, or the Macfarlane (Special Payments) Trust][⁶, the Macfarlane (Special Payments) (No. 2) Trust] [⁸, the Fund][¹⁰, the Eileen Trust] or [⁹ the Independent Living Funds].]

[⁴(11) Any compensation within the meaning of regulation 35(3) (earnings of employed earners) which is made in respect of employment which is not part-time employment within the meaning of that regulation, to the extent that it is not earnings by virtue of regulation 35(1)(i)(i) shall be treated as capital.]

AMENDMENTS

1. Income Support (General) Amendment Regulations 1988 (S.I. 1988 No. 663), reg. 21 (April 11, 1988).
2. Income Support (General) Amendment No. 4 Regulations 1988 (S.I. 1988 No. 1445), reg. 11 (September 12, 1988).
3. Income Support (General) Amendment No. 5 Regulations 1988 (S.I. 1988 No. 2022), reg. 11 (December 12, 1988).
4. Income Support (General) Amendment No. 2 Regulations 1989 (S.I. 1989 No. 1323), reg. 15 (October 9, 1989).
5. Income-related Benefits Schemes Amendment Regulations 1990 (S.I. 1990 No. 127), reg. 33 (January 31, 1990).
6. Income-related Benefits Schemes and Social Security (Recoupment) Amendment Regulations 1991 (S.I. 1991 No. 1175), reg. 5 (May 11, 1991).
7. Income Support (General) Amendment Regulations 1992 (S.I. 1992 No. 468), Sched., para. 5 (April 6, 1992).
8. Income-related Benefits Schemes and Social Security (Recoupment) Amendment Regulations 1992 (S.I. 1992 No. 1101), reg. 6 (May 7, 1992).
9. Social Security Benefits (Miscellaneous Amendments) (No. 2) Regulations 1993 (S.I. 1993 No. 963), reg. 2(3) (April 22, 1993).
10. Income-related Benefits Schemes and Social Security (Recoupment) Amendment Regulations 1993 (S.I. 1993 No. 1249), reg. 4(3) (May 14, 1993).

DEFINITIONS

"the Act"—see reg. 2(1).
"child"—see 1986 Act, s.20(11) (SSCBA, s.137(1)).
"claimant"—*ibid.*, reg. 23(1).
"employed earner"—see reg. 2(1).
"family"—see 1986 Act, s.20(11) (SSCBA, s.137(1)).
"local authority"—see 1986 Act, s.84(1).
"the Eileen Trust"—see reg. 2(1).
"the Fund"—*ibid.*
"the Independent Living Funds"—*ibid.*
"the Macfarlane (Special Payments) Trust"—*ibid.*
"the Macfarlane (Special Payments) (No. 2) Trust"—*ibid.*
"the Macfarlane Trust"—*ibid.*

GENERAL NOTE

Most of these categories deemed to be capital are self-explanatory. They are then disregarded as income (Sched. 9, para. 32).

Paragraph (4)
The general rule is that the income from capital is not to be treated as income, but is added to the capital when it is credited. The excepted cases are premises and business assets plus trusts of personal injury compensation. The income must be derived from some capital asset of the claimant

(*CIS 25/1989*). A twelve month assured shorthold tenancy is not a capital asset and income from the subletting of rooms is not "derived from" the tenancy (*CIS 82/1993*). The income covered by this provision is disregarded as income (Sched. 9, para. 22), but remember that capital over £3,000 is deemed to produce a tariff income under reg. 53.

In *Chief Adjudication Officer v. Palfrey and Others, The Times*, February 17, 1995 (the appeal from *CIS 85/1992* and others), the Court of Appeal confirmed that property subject to a tenancy is disregarded as a reversionary interest under para. 5 of Sched. 10. *CIS 563/1991* and *CIS 615/1993* confirm that the disregard in para. 5 applies to leasehold as well as freehold property. Thus under para. (4), rent from a property let out to tenants counts as capital from the date it is due to be received. It is disregarded as income under Sched. 9, para. 22. In *CIS 563/1991* the Commissioner considers that the effect of para. (4) is to treat a payment of income as capital for the same length of time as it would have been taken into account as income. So, for example, a payment of a month's rent counts as capital for a month from the date that the claimant is due to receive it. After that, reg. 48(4) ceases to have effect. Money spent during that month cannot form part of the claimant's actual capital at the end of the month (subject to the possible effect of the notional capital rule in reg. 51(1)). Although saved-up income only metamorphoses into capital after deducting all relevant debts (see the notes to reg. 23), the Commissioner considers that where para. (4) has effected a statutory metamorphosis, any unspent money at the end of the period covered by para. (4) continues to count as capital; it does not change into income and then immediately back into capital. Thus any outstanding debts will only reduce the amount of the capital if they are secured on the capital itself (reg. 49(a)(ii)). *CIS 563/1991* also deals with the situation where the disregards in both paras. 5 and 26 (taking steps to dispose of premises) of Sched. 10 apply. If the para. 26 disregard applied, the rental income would count as income and would only be ignored to the extent allowed for by para. 22(2) of Sched. 9. The Commissioner concludes, however, that considering reg. 48(4) and para. 22 of Sched. 9 together, the primary rule was that income derived from capital was to be treated as capital. The disregard in para. 5 therefore took precedence, and the rental income counted as capital, even during periods when the property could also be disregarded under one or more of the provisions listed in para. 22 and reg. 48(4).

Paragraph (8)

The previous form of para. (8) (see the 1991 edition) remains in force in Scotland. The new form was introduced on April 6, 1992, as a consequence of the Children Act 1989.

Paragraphs (9) and (10)

Regs. 24 and 33 on charitable or voluntary payments have been revoked from December 1988. See the notes to para. 15 of Sched. 9 for the meaning of "charitable" and "voluntary." The general rule in para. (9) is that such payments not made or due to be made at regular intervals are to be treated as capital. This rule does not apply to the three kinds of payments set out in para. (10). However, there is nothing to say how such payments are to be treated. Presumably they must be treated as capital or income according to general legal principles (on which see the notes to reg. 23). Similarly, there is nothing expressly to say how payments which are made or due to be made regularly are to be treated, but no doubt they will usually have the character of income.

Paragraph (11)

The elements of compensation on the termination of full-time employment which do not count as earnings under reg. 35(1)(i) are payments of less than the "maximum weekly amount" and "deductible remainders" (see notes to reg. 35).

Calculation of capital in the United Kingdom

49. Capital which a claimant possesses in the United Kingdom shall be calculated—
  (a) except in a case to which sub-paragraph (b) applies, at its current market or surrender value, less —
    (i) where there would be expenses attributable to sale, 10 per cent.; and
    (ii) the amount of any incumbrance secured on it;
  (b) in the case of a National Savings Certificate—
    (i) if purchased from an issue the sale of which ceased before 1st July last preceding the first day on which income support is payable or the date of the determination of the claim, whichever is the earlier, or in the case of a review, the date of any subsequent review, at the

price which it would have realised on that 1st July had it been purchased on the last day of that issue;

(ii) in any other case, at its purchase price.

DEFINITION

"claimant"—see reg. 2(1), reg. 23(1).

GENERAL NOTE

The general rule is that the market value of the asset is to be taken. The surrender value will be taken if appropriate (although the surrender value of life insurance policies and of annuities is totally disregarded (Sched. 10, paras. 15 and 11)). The value at this stage does not take account of any incumbrances secured on the assets, since those come in under para. (a)(ii) *(R(IS) 21/93)*. In *R(SB) 57/83* and *R(SB) 6/84* the test taken is the price that would be commanded between a willing buyer and a willing seller at a particular date. In *R(SB) 6/84* it is stressed that in the case of a house it is vital to know the nature and extent of the interest being valued. Also, since what is required is a current market value, the Commissioner holds that an estate agent's figure for a quick sale was closer to the proper approach than the District Valuer's figure for a sale within three months. All the circumstances must be taken into account in making the valuation. In *CIS 553/1991* it is held that in valuing a former matrimonial home the wife's statutory right of occupation under the Matrimonial Homes Act 1967 has to be taken into account. See also the Tribunal of Commissioners' decisions in *CIS 391/1992* and *CIS 417/1992* below. Similarly, if personal possessions are being valued, it is what the possessions could be sold for which counts, not simply what was paid for them *(CIS 494/1990)*. Sometimes a detailed valuation is not necessary, such as where the value of an asset is on any basis clearly over the £8,000 limit *(CSIS 40/1989)*.

It is accepted that the test of the willing buyer and the willing seller is the starting point for the valuation of shares *(R(SB) 57/83, R(SB) 12/89* and *R(IS) 2/90)*. The latter case emphasises that in the income support context the value must be determined on the basis of a very quick sale, so that the hypothetical willing seller would be at a corresponding disadvantage. In the case of private companies there is often a provision in the articles of association that a shareholder wishing to sell must first offer the shares to other shareholders at a "fair value" fixed by the auditors (this was the case in *R(SB) 18/83* and *R(IS) 2/90)*. Then the value of the shares ought not to be higher than the fair value, but for income support purposes may well be less. The possible complications are set out in *CSB 488/1982* (quoted with approval in *R(SB) 12/89* and *R(IS) 2/90)*. In *R(IS) 8/92* it is suggested that the market value is what a purchaser would pay for the shares subject to the same restriction. Whether the shareholding gives a minority, equal or controlling interest is particularly significant. All the circumstances of the share structure of the company must be considered. For instance, in *R(SB) 12/89* shares could only be sold with the consent of the directors, which it was indicated would not be forthcoming. It seems to be agreed that valuation according to Inland Revenue methods is not appropriate *(R(SB) 18/83* and *R(IS) 2/90)*, although it is suggested in *R(SB) 12/89* that the Inland Revenue Shares Valuation Division might be able to assist SSATs. It is not known if this is so. What is absolutely clear is that the total value of the company's shareholding cannot simply be divided in proportion to the claimant's holding *(R(SB) 18/83)*. However, in the case of shares in companies quoted on the London Stock Exchange the Inland Revenue method of valuation should be used *(CIS 598/1992)*. This involves looking at all the transactions relating to the relevant share during the previous day, taking the lowest figure and adding to this a quarter of the difference between the lowest and the highest figure. The Commissioner considered that AOs could use the valuation quoted in newspapers (which is the mean between the best bid and best offer price at the close of business the previous day) to obtain approximate valuations. However, where a completely accurate valuation was essential, the Inland Revenue method would need to be adopted.

The proper approach to valuation can usefully deal with unrealisable assets. Sometimes their market value will be nil (*e.g.* a potential interest under a discretionary trust: *R(SB) 25/83)*; sometimes it will be very heavily discounted. However, if the asset will be realisable after a time, it may have a current value. The claimant may be able to sell an option to purchase the asset in the future (see *R(IS) 8/92)* or borrow, using the asset as security. It should similarly be remembered that if, exceptionally, personal possessions are being taken into account (*e.g.* they have been bought to secure benefit), their value is not what was paid for them, but what could be obtained for them if sold as second-hand. As the Tribunal of Commissioners in *R(SB) 45/83* point out, the market value (in this case of an interest in an entire trust fund) must reflect the outlay the purchaser would expect to incur in obtaining transfer of the assets and the profit he would expect as an inducement to purchase. If there might be some legal difficulty in obtaining the underlying asset (as there might have been in *R(SB) 21/83* and in *CIS 654/1993* where shares were held in the names of the claimant's children) this must be taken into account.

In *Chief Adjudication Officer v. Palfrey and Others, The Times*, February 17, 1995, the Court of Appeal confirmed the Tribunal of Commissioners' decisions in *CIS 391/1992* and *CIS 417/1992* that in a case to which reg. 52 (capital jointly held) applies, it is the deemed equal share that has to be valued, not the proportionate share of the overall value that has to be taken. The Tribunal of Commissioners gave detailed guidance as to the basis of a proper valuation in such cases. In both *CIS 391/1992* and *CIS 417/1992* ownership was shared with relatives who were unable or unwilling to sell the property or buy the claimant's interest. The Commissioners state that a valuer would have to express a view as to whether there is a market for shares in property of this kind, and, if so, take account of the likelihood that any application for sale of the house under s.30 of the Law of Property Act 1925 would be refused. The Commissioners recognised, as did the Court of Appeal, that the market value in such cases may well be nil. The Tribunal of Commissioners' approach to reg. 52 was followed in *CIS 127/1993* (*McNamara*, which was appealed to the Court of Appeal with *CIS 391/1992* and *CIS 417/1992*) and *CIS 413/1992*. *CIS 413/1992*, however, notes the differences that arise from the law of property in Scotland.

The general rule is that the whole of a capital resource is to be taken into account. Liabilities are not to be deducted from the value (*R(SB) 2/83*). Otherwise, it is only where a debt is secured on the capital asset that it is deducted under para. (a)(ii). The standard case would be a house that is mortgaged. The amount of capital outstanding would be deducted from the market value of the house. In *R(SB) 14/81* (see Sched. 10, para. 8) the claimant had been lent £5,000 for work on his bungalow, which was mortgaged to secure the debt. He had £3,430 left. Although he was obliged to make monthly repayments this liability could not be deducted from the £3,430, for the debt was not secured on the money. However, the principle of *R(SB) 53/83* (see the notes to reg. 46) would make the money not part of the claimant's resources. In *R(SB) 18/83* the Commissioner says that personal property such as shares (or money) can be charged by a contract for valuable consideration (*e.g.* a loan) without any writing or the handing over of any title documents. But this is not the case in Scots law (*R(SB) 5/88*). In *CIS 598/1992* the claimant's brokers had a lien on his shares for the cost of acquisition and their commission which fell to be offset against the value of the shares. *CIS 368/1993* concerned money held under a solicitor's undertaking. £40,000 of the proceeds of sale of the claimant's house was retained by his solicitors in pursuance of an undertaking to his bank given because of a previous charge on the property. The Commissioner decides that the undertaking was an incumbrance within para. (a)(ii). It was the equivalent of a pledge or lien and was secured on the proceeds of sale. Thus the £40,000 did not count as part of the claimant's resources. In *CIS 69/1994* the claimant transferred her flat to her daughter on the understanding that the daughter would care for her in the flat and pay off the mortgage. The daughter complied with the second condition, but evicted her mother from the flat. The Commissioner decides that the gift of the flat to the daughter had been subject to the condition that she looked after her mother. As that condition had not been fulfilled, the gift failed and the daughter held the property on trust for the claimant. In valuing the claimant's interest under para. (a), the mortgage was to be deducted because the daughter was to be treated as subrogated to the rights of the mortgagee. In addition, the costs of the litigation to recover the property from the daughter also fell to be deducted.

The first deduction to be made under para. (a) is a standard 10 per cent. if there would be any expenses attributable to sale, as there almost always will be. The second is the amount of any incumbrance secured on the asset. There is particularly full and helpful guidance on the nature of incumbrances on real property and the evidence which should be examined in *R(IS) 21/93*, and see above.

Calculation of capital outside the United Kingdom

50. Capital which a claimant possesses in a country outside the United Kingdom shall be calculated—
  (a) in a case in which there is no prohibition in that country against the transfer to the United Kingdom of an amount equal to its current market or surrender value in that country, at that value;
  (b) in a case where there is such a prohibition, at the price which it would realise if sold in the United Kingdom to a willing buyer,
less, where there would be expenses attributable to sale, 10 per cent. and the amount of any incumbrance secured on it.

"claimant"—see reg. 2(1), reg. 23(1).

GENERAL NOTE

There had been problems under supplementary benefit in valuing overseas assets. Now the standard rules about the deduction of 10 per cent. for sale expenses and the deduction of the amount of any incumbrance secured on the asset apply. But then there are two separate situations. Under para. (a), if there is no prohibition in the country where the asset is located against transferring to the U.K. an amount of money equal to the asset's value in that country, the market value there is the test. If there are merely restrictions or delays in transfer this does not seem to come within para. (a). If there is such a prohibition, under para. (b) the value is the market value in the U.K.

Notional capital

51.—(1) A claimant shall be treated as possessing capital of which he has deprived himself for the purpose of securing entitlement to income support or increasing the amount of that benefit [⁶ except—
    (a) where that capital is derived from a payment made in consequence of any personal injury and is placed on trust for the benefit of the claimant; or
    (b) to the extent that the capital which he is treated as possessing is reduced in accordance with regulation 51A (diminishing notional capital rule).]
    (2) Except in the case of—
    (a) a discretionary trust;
    (b) a trust derived from a payment made in consequence of a personal injury; or
    (c) any loan which would be obtainable if secured against capital disregarded under Schedule 10,
any capital which would become available to the claimant upon application being made but which has not been acquired by him shall be treated as possessed by him but only from the date on which [¹ it could be expected to be acquired were an application made.]
    [²(3) Any payment of capital, other than a payment of capital made under the Macfarlane Trust[⁵, or the Macfarlane (Special Payments) Trust][⁷, the Macfarlane (Special Payments) (No. 2) Trust][⁹, the Fund][¹², the Eileen Trust] or [¹¹the Independent Living Funds], made—
    (a) to a third party in respect of a single claimant or in respect of a member of the family (but not a member of the third party's family) shall be treated—
        (i) in a case where that payment is derived from a payment of any benefit under the benefit Acts, a war disablement pension or a war widow's pension as possessed by that single claimant, if it is paid to him, or by that member if it is paid to any member of the family;
        (ii) in any other case, as possessed by that single claimant or by that member to the extent that it is used for the food, ordinary clothing or footwear, household fuel, rent or rates for which housing benefit is payable, [⁸. . .] any housing costs to the extent that they are met under regulation 17(1)(e) and 18(1)(f) (housing costs) or accommodation charge to the extent that it is met under regulation 19 [⁴. . .] (persons in residential care or nursing homes [³. . .] [⁴. . .]), of that single claimant or, as the case may be, of any member of that family[⁸, or is used for any [¹⁰council tax] or water charges for which that claimant or member is liable];
    (b) to a single claimant or a member of the family in respect of a third party (but not in respect of another member of the family) shall be treated as

possessed by that single claimant or, as the case may be, that member of the family to the extent that it is kept or used by him or used by or on behalf of any member of the family.]

(4) Where a claimant stands in relation to a company in a position analogous to that of a sole owner or partner in the business of that company, he shall be treated as if he were such sole owner or partner and in such a case—

    (a) the value of his holding in that company shall, notwithstanding regulation 46 (calculation of capital), be disregarded; and

    (b) he shall, subject to paragraph (5), be treated as possessing an amount of capital equal to the value or, as the case may be, his share of the value of the capital of that company and the foregoing provisions of this Chapter shall apply for the purposes of calculating that amount as if it were actual capital which he does possess.

(5) For so long as the claimant undertakes activities in the course of the business of the company, the amount which he is treated as possessing under paragraph (4) shall be disregarded.

(6) Where a claimant is treated as possessing capital under any of paragraphs (1) to (4), the foregoing provisions of this Chapter shall apply for the purposes of calculating its amount as if it were actual capital which he does possess.

[[1](7) For the avoidance of doubt a claimant is to be treated as possessing capital under paragraph (1) only if the capital of which he has deprived himself is actual capital.]

[[2](8) In paragraph (3) the expression "ordinary clothing or footwear" means clothing or footwear for normal daily use, but does not include school uniforms, or clothing or footwear used solely for sporting activities].

AMENDMENTS

1. Income Support (General) Amendment Regulations 1988 (S.I. 1988 No. 663), reg. 22 (April 11, 1988).

2. Income Support (General) Amendment No. 4 Regulations 1988 (S.I. 1988 No. 1445), reg. 12 (September 12, 1988).

3. Income Support (General) Amendment No. 4 Regulations (S.I. 1988 No. 1445), Sched. 1, para. 4 (April 10, 1989).

4. Income Support (General) Amendment Regulations 1989 (S.I. 1989 No. 534), Sched. 1, para. 7 (October 9, 1989).

5. Income-related Benefits Schemes Amendment Regulations 1990 (S.I. 1990 No. 127), reg. 3 (January 31, 1990).

6. Income Support (General) Amendment No. 3 Regulations 1990 (S.I. 1990 No. 1776), reg. 5 (October 1, 1990).

7. Income-related Benefits Schemes and Social Security (Recoupment) Amendment Regulations 1991 (S.I. 1991 No. 1175), reg. 5 (May 11, 1991).

8. Income Support (General) Amendment No. 4 Regulations 1991 (S.I. 1991 No. 1559), reg. 8 (August 5, 1991).

9. Income-related Benefits Schemes and Social Security (Recoupment) Amendment Regulations 1992 (S.I. 1992 No. 1101), reg. 6 (May 7, 1992).

10. Income-related Benefits Schemes (Miscellaneous Amendments) Regulations 1993 (S.I. 1993 No. 315), Sched., para. 3 (April 1, 1993).

11. Social Security Benefits (Miscellaneous Amendments) (No. 2) Regulations 1993 (S.I. 1993 No. 963), reg. 2(3) (April 22, 1993).

12. Income-related Benefits Schemes and Social Security (Recoupment) Amendment Regulations 1993 (S.I. 1993 No. 1249), reg. 4(3) (May 14, 1993).

DEFINITIONS

"the benefit Acts"—see 1986 Act, s.84(1).
"claimant"—see reg. 2(1), reg. 23(1).
"family"—see 1986 Act, s.20(11) (SSCBA, s.137(1)).
"the Eileen Trust"—see reg. 2(1).

"the Fund"—*ibid.*
"the Independent Living Funds"—see reg. 2(1).
"the Macfarlane (Special Payments) Trust"—*ibid.*
"the Macfarlane (Special Payments) (No. 2) Trust"—*ibid.*
"the Macfarlane Trust"—*ibid.*
"war disablement pension"—see 1986 Act, s.84(1).
"war widow's pension"—*ibid.*
"water charges"—see reg. 2(1).

GENERAL NOTE

Paragraph (1)
In order for para. (1) to apply, only two elements must be proved by the AO—that the person has deprived himself of actual capital (see para. (7)) and that his purpose was to secure entitlement to or increase the amount of income support. It is clear that the principles applied to these questions for supplementary benefit purposes are to be applied to para. (1) *(CIS 24/1988, CIS 40/1989* and *R(IS) 1/91,* although the first decision is in error in failing to note the crucial difference identified in the next sentence). There is now no discretion (the regulation says "shall," not "may"). This was thought to give rise to the problems mentioned at the end of this note. (1). These problems led to the insertion of reg. 51(A), applying a diminishing capital rule. Capital subject to that rule is excluded from reg. 51(1) by sub-para. (b). *R(IS) 1/91* overturned the previous understanding of the effect of reg. 51(1) and is discussed at the end of this note and in the note to reg. 51A. Sub-para. (a) excludes the operation of reg. 51(1) where money derived from compensation for personal injury is placed on trust for the claimant.

Deprivation
Here the onus of proof is complicated by the relationship with the claimant's actual capital. Once it is shown that a person did possess, or received, an asset, the burden shifts to him to show that it has ceased to be a part of his actual capital, to be valued under reg. 49 *(R(SB) 38/85).* Therefore, para. (1) can only come into play after these two stages have been passed, with the second stage depending on the claimant. If he cannot satisfactorily account for the way in which an asset or a sum of money which he says he no longer has was disposed of, the proper conclusion is that it remains a part of his actual capital. In *CIS 634/1992* the claimant was made bankrupt on November 29, 1990. Between November 29 and December 28, 1990, when he claimed income support the claimant divested himself of most of his capital. His trustee in bankruptcy was not appointed until April 1991. Under the Insolvency Act 1986 (subject to certain exceptions) a bankrupt's property does not vest in his trustee on the making of a bankruptcy order but only when the trustee is appointed. However, s. 284 of the Insolvency Act 1986 makes any disposal of property or payment by a bankrupt between the presentation of a bankruptcy petition and the vesting of his estate in his trustee void (except with the consent or later ratification of the court). The claimant could not therefore in law deprive himself of any resources from November 29, onwards and reg. 51(1) could not apply. However, since he had failed to give a satisfactory account of how he had disposed of his capital, he was to be treated as still possessing it *(R(SB) 38/85).* Thus he was not entitled to income support prior to the appointment of the trustee in bankruptcy because until then he possessed actual capital over the income support limit.
"Deprive" is an ordinary English word and is not to be given any special legal definition *(R(SB) 38/85, R(SB) 40/85).* The result is that a person deprives himself of a resource if he ceases to possess it, regardless of the reason for doing so or the fact that he receives some other resource in return. This is the clear assumption in *R(SB) 38/85* and is expressly decided in *R(SB) 40/85.* That decision holds that the approach in the *S Manual* (para. 6042—set out on p. 177 of the second edition of this book), that a person had not deprived himself of a resource if he spent money or changed it into another form which is still available to him, was wrong. The effect is to put the main emphasis on the purpose of the deprivation. *CIS 494/1990* appears to adopt a different principle. The issue was the treatment of the use of capital to buy a vehicle, for the purpose of securing entitlement to benefit. The value of such a personal possession is not disregarded under para. 10 of Sched. 10. The Commissioner points out that the value of the vehicle will be considerably less than the purchase price, and appears to treat only this "depreciation" as notional capital under s.51(1). It seems that the Commissioner is not saying that the use of the capital to buy a personal possession is not a deprivation (which would be directly contrary to *R(SB) 40/85)* because he considers that the amount of notional capital will increase as the actual value of the possession decreases over time. But he suggests no reason why the full amount of the purchase price, rather than merely the depreciation, is not to be the amount of notional capital under reg. 51(1). These points were not necessary to the

decision in the case, but were part of the guidance to a new tribunal, and it is suggested that they should be regarded with caution. See also under *Diminishing capital*, below.

It is arguable that a person cannot deprive himself of something which he has never possessed, but it may be that a deliberate failure to acquire an asset is also a deprivation. In *CSB 598/1987* it is suggested that a deliberate failure to pay a cheque into a bank account could be a deprivation.

Purpose

Here the AO must show that the person's purpose is one of those mentioned in para. (1). There is unlikely to be direct evidence of purpose (although there might be contemporary letters or documents), so that primary facts must be found from which an inference as to purpose can be drawn (*CSB 200/1985, R(SB) 40/85*).

The view put forward in *CSB 28/81*, that the test is of the person's predominant purpose, is rejected in *R(SB) 38/85* and *R(SB) 40/85*. In *R(SB) 38/85* it was suggested that it was enough that a subsidiary purpose was to obtain supplementary benefit. In *R(SB) 40/85* the Commissioner says that this must be a "significant operative purpose." If the obtaining of benefit was a foreseeable consequence of the transaction then, in the absence of other evidence, it could be concluded that this was the person's purpose. This would exclude some cases caught by the width of the approach to deprivation, *e.g.* where a resource is converted into another form in which it is still taken into account. For then there would be no effect on eligibility for benefit. But beyond that situation there remain great difficulties. The Commissioners mention a number of relevant factors, *e.g.* whether the deprivation was a gift or in return for a service, the personal circumstances of the person (*e.g.* age, state of health, employment prospects, needs), whether a creditor was pressing for repayment of a loan. It must be an issue of fact when these other factors indicate that the reasonably foreseeable consequence of obtaining benefit was not a significant operative factor. The length of time since the disposal of the capital may be relevant (*CIS 264/1989*). Where the claimant had been warned about the consequences of a transaction by the local DSS office (*i.e.* that reg. 51(1) would be applied) and still went ahead, this showed that he could not have as any part of his purpose securing of entitlement, or continued entitlement, to income support (*CIS 621/1991*). In effect, the test seems to be whether the person would have carried out the transaction at the same time if there had been no effect on eligibility for benefit. The onus of proof on the AO may come into play in marginal cases.

A number of recent decisions have firmed up the principles to be applied. *CIS 124/1990* holds that it must be proved that the person actually knew of the capital limit rule, otherwise the necessary deliberate intention to obtain benefit could not have been present. It is not enough that the person ought to have known of the rule. The crunch comes, and the resolution with the approach in *R(SB) 40/85* (where it was suggested that the existence of some limit might be said to be common knowledge), in the assessment of the evidence about the person's knowledge. The Commissioner stresses that the person's whole background must be considered, including experience of the social security system and advice which is likely to have been received from the family and elsewhere. The burden of proof is on the AO, but in some circumstances a person's assertion that they did not know of the rule will not be credible. In *CIS 124/1990* itself the claimant was illiterate and spoke and understood only Gujerati. The Commissioner says that this should put her in no better or worse situation than a literate claimant whose mother tongue was English, but that the possibility of misunderstandings in interpretation should be considered. *CIS 124/1990* is followed in *R(SB) 12/91*, where the necessity of a positive finding of fact, based on sufficient evidence, that the person knew of the capital limit is stressed. Evidence that the person had been in receipt of supplementary benefit or income support for some years was not in itself enough. But information which the person has received, together with his educational standing and other factors, will be material in deciding whether actual knowledge exists or not. *CIS 30/1993* similarly holds that it is not possible to infer actual knowledge of the capital limits simply from the claimant signing a claim form which contained that information. The claimant was partially sighted and had not completed the claim form herself but merely signed it. It was necessary for the SSAT to indicate what evidence satisfied it that the claimant did know of the capital limits.

The Commissioner in *R(SB) 9/91* stresses that a positive intention to obtain benefit must be shown to be a significant operative purpose. It is not enough for the AO merely to prove that the obtaining of benefit was a natural consequence of the transaction in question. The claimant had transferred her former home to her two daughters. Evidence was given that her sole intention was to make a gift to her daughters, as she intended to leave the property to them in her will and it was no longer of any use to her (she being permanently in need of residential nursing care). The Commissioner notes that this did not explain why the transfer was made when it was, why the proceeds of sale of the property would not have been of use to the claimant and what she thought she would live on if she gave the property away. She had been in receipt of supplementary benefit for several years. On the evidence the obtaining of benefit was a significant operative purpose. In *CIS 242/1993*, another case where the claimant had gone into residential care, the Commissioner reaches the opposite conclusion on the facts. The claimant's son had cared for his mother for 15 years. When she went into a residential care home, she gave her share of the proceeds of sale of their jointly owned home to her son to be used towards the purchase of his flat. The Commissioner accepts that she had relinquished her share in gratitude to her son and not to secure income support. In *R(IS) 13/94* the claimant's capital was in excess of the statutory limit when he purchased his council house. The deposit used up enough of his capital to bring him below the limit. It was necessary to consider whether para. (1) applied to this use of the capital since the claimant was apparently dependent on income support to meet the mortgage interest.

In *CIS 109/1994* and *CIS 112/1994* the claimants had used their capital to purchase an annuity and a life insurance policy respectively. In *CIS 109/1994* the claimant was both physically and mentally frail and lived in a nursing home. The tribunal found that at the material time she had no knowledge of the income support capital and deprivation of capital rules, and entered into the transaction on her son's advice, who considered that this was the best use of her capital to enable her to stay in the nursing home. The Commissioner holds that the tribunal had not erred in concluding that she had not purchased the annuity in order to obtain income support. In *CIS 112/1994* the Commissioner decides that para. (1) did apply, but that para. 15 of Sched. 10 applied to disregard the life policy. The Commissioner also deals with "double counting" of notional and actual capital (see below).

If capital is used to repay debts which are immediately payable then this cannot be said to be for the purpose of obtaining benefit (*R(SB) 12/91*). In that particular case there were doubts whether the alleged debts, to members of the family, were legally enforceable debts and whether they were owed by the claimant personally.

CIS 40/1989 provides an interesting example on its facts of the securing or increase of benefit not being a significant operative purpose. The claimant had been on supplementary benefit and then income support since 1978. Her father died intestate. The estate consisted almost entirely of a house in which the claimant's sister had lived with the father. The claimant and her sister were the sole beneficiaries of the estate. Legal proceedings had to be taken to enforce a sale of the house. In March 1988 the claimant received £38,000 net of costs, which her solicitor divided equally between the claimant, her son, her daughter and her grand-daughter. After repaying a number of debts and buying a second-hand car, the amount possessed by the claimant quickly fell below £6,000. The AO and the SSAT found that she should be treated as still possessing the amounts given to her children and grandchild. The Commissioner, having heard the claimant give evidence and be cross-examined, accepted that her purpose was to carry out her father's wishes, which were that the house should be used to provide for his grandchildren and great-grandchildren. She had originally intended to take nothing, but had been encouraged by her children to take a quarter share. She knew of the capital limit, but did not know of the effect her actions would have on her benefit entitlement. On these particular facts, the Commissioner found that para. (1) did not apply.

There may be a problem in the transfer from the corresponding supplementary benefit regulation (Resources Regulations, reg. 4(1)). Reg. 51(1) only mentions income support. What if a person deprived himself of capital in December 1987, thinking only of supplementary benefit. On a claim for income support, can he be caught by reg. 51(1)? In *CIS 259/1990* (which was to be reported as *R(IS) 8/91*, but has been withdrawn from reporting) the Commissioner accepts that the purpose must be to secure or increase income support, but held that the claimant in March 1987, knew enough about the effect of depleting her resources on her means-tested benefit for her purpose to satisfy reg. 51(1). The Commissioner found that the claimant was aware that the existing means-tested benefit was to be replaced by another means-tested benefit (although the evidential basis for this finding does not appear). There was an appeal to the Court of Appeal, but the decision was set aside by consent. In *R(IS) 14/93* the Commissioner does not accept the reliance in *CIS 259/1990* on the enactment of the Social Security Act 1986 well before the income support scheme came into operation. He holds that a provision of a statute has no legal existence until it comes into force. Therefore, when in that case the claimant in November/December 1987, divested himself of capital he could not have done it with the intention of obtaining income support, because at that time it did not exist. Nor can the words "income support" be taken to refer to means-tested benefits which previously went under the name of supplementary benefit. This approach has the merit of not making the result depend on the vagaries of the particular claimant's advance knowledge of the nature of the income support reforms in April 1988.

Diminishing capital

There may also be problems from the removal of discretion in the shift to income support. Under the Supplementary Benefit (Resources) Regulations this was used in particular for two purposes.

One was to avoid double counting with the rule about personal possessions, now contained in para. 10 of Sched. 10. The value of personal possessions is not disregarded if they were acquired with the intention of reducing capital so as to gain entitlement to benefit. With no discretion at either end a claimant could have the market value of the possessions counted as part of his actual capital and the money he spent on them counted as notional capital under this paragraph. The Commissioner in *CIS 494/1990* avoids this problem by treating only the shortfall between the market value of the personal possessions from time to time and the purchase price (the "depreciation") as the notional capital to be imputed under reg. 51(1). However, he does not explain how reg. 51(1) should be interpreted so as not to make the whole purchase price the amount of the notional capital. It is also difficult to combine a rising level of notional capital over time, in line with the reduction in the market value of the personal possessions, with the diminishing notional capital rule under reg. 51A. Although *CIS 494/1990* satisfactorily avoids double counting, its suggestions cannot yet be confidently accepted.

In *CIS 112/1994* the Commissioner recognises the gross unfairness to a claimant if she were to be penalised twice because of the lack of discretion in para. (1). In the Commissioner's view this is not the intention of the regulation. But in that case double counting did not arise. The claimant had purchased a life insurance policy with a legacy. Although she was to be treated as still possessing the notional capital by virtue of para. (1), the actual capital (the life policy) could be disregarded under para. 15 of Sched. 10.

The second problem for which the use of discretion was useful was that it was unfair to fix a claimant with an amount of notional capital for eternity. If he had still had the capital and not been entitled to benefit, he would have had to use up the capital for living expenses. Thus the figure of notional capital could be reduced by the equivalent of the weekly benefit lost by the capital counting (*R(SB) 38/85, R(SB) 40/85*). There had seemed no possibility of such a process applying to reg. 51(1) until the decision of the Tribunal of Commissioners in *R(IS) 1/91*. The Tribunal concluded that the diminishing capital rule did apply. This is because para. (6) provides that regs. 45 to 50 apply to the calculation of notional capital as if it was actual capital. If a claimant has capital over the £8,000 limit, reasonable expenditure on living and other sensible expenses (not necessarily limited to income support rates) will reduce the amount of capital until it falls below the limit. He will then be entitled to income support. The same situation is held to apply where it is notional capital, rather than actual, which is held initially. The decision is wrong in principle, because if actual capital is held, the actual amount, reduced by any expenditure, must be considered week by week. This is not a consequence of any of regs. 45 to 50 and there is no analogy with the notional reduction of notional capital. Para. (6) is primarily concerned with the calculation of the market value of assets. Nonetheless, *R(IS) 1/91* must be followed in relation to weeks before October 1, 1990.

With effect from October 1, 1990, reg. 51A provides an express diminishing notional capital rule. *R(IS) 9/92* decides that while the principles of *R(IS) 1/91* apply up to that date, they do not apply thereafter. They are superseded by the rules laid down in reg. 51A.

Paragraph (2)

It is not at all clear what sort of capital would be caught by this rule. It must be available simply on application, with no other conditions, but not amount to actual capital (*cf. R(SB) 26/86* and *R(SB) 17/87*). Examples might be money held in court which would be released on application or arrears of employer's sick pay which needed to be applied for. Note the exclusions. Although discretionary trusts are specifically excluded, a potential beneficiary would not seem to be caught by para. (2) anyway. More than an application is needed for payment to be made: the discretion has to be exercised.

Paragraph (3)

Sub-para. (a) applies where payments are made to a third party in respect of the claimant or a member of the claimant's family. If the payment is derived from a benefit listed in head (i) it counts as the claimant's. In other cases it counts as the claimant's in so far as it is actually used for food, ordinary clothing or footwear, fuel or housing or accommodation costs.

"Ordinary clothing or footwear" is defined in para. (8). Para. 30356 of the *Adjudication Officers' Guide* suggests that wellington boots are not for "normal daily use", nor are special shoes needed because of a disability (as these would not be for the normal daily use of children in general).

If the payment is used for other items or costs it does not form part of the claimant's capital. Note that if the conditions are met, there is no discretion whether or not to apply para. (3). In this respect, as in others, *R(SB) 6/88* would be decided differently under income support.

The operation of sub-para. (b) is clear. In these circumstances the payment would not form part of the claimant's actual capital in view of the obligation to use it for a third party.

Paragraphs (4) and (5)

These two paragraphs establish an artificial method of dealing with one person companies or similar. The basic legal position is that if there is a company, the shareholders' assets are the value of the shares, not the value of the company's assets (*R(SB) 57/83*). But under para. (4), if the claimant is in a position analogous to a sole owner or partner in the business of the company (on which, see *R(IS) 8/92*), the value of his shareholding is disregarded, and he is treated as possessing a proportionate share of the capital of the company. The value is the net worth of the company's total assets taken together (*R(IS) 13/93*). The value of one particular asset within the total is not relevant in itself. However, as long as the claimant undertakes activities in the course of the business of the company, the amount produced by para. (4) is disregarded (para. (5)). Temporary interruptions in activity (*e.g.* holidays, short-term sickness) ought not to prevent para. (5) from applying. It is accepted in *R(IS) 13/93* that any activities which are more than *de minimis* satisfy para. (4).

Paragraph (6)

One of the effects of para. (6) is that the disregards in Sched. 10 can apply to notional capital. However, *CIS 30/1993* decides that the disregard in para. 26 of Sched. 10 (taking steps to dispose of premises) could not apply where the claimant had already disposed of the capital so as to trigger reg. 51(1). Reg. 51(6) did not provide any authority for altering the provisions of Sched. 10 which could only apply where their conditions were met. This is a different view from that taken in some other decisions. See the note to para. 26 of Sched. 10.

CIS 231/1991 confirms that it is not necessary for the disregard under Sched. 10 to have been applicable before the claimant deprived himself of the capital. The claimant had transferred his former home to his parents who were both over 60. When he claimed income support his parents were living in the home. The Commissioner holds that the former home fell to be disregarded under para. 4(a) of Sched. 10; the disregard in para. 4 applied to notional, as well as actual, capital.

Paragraph (7)

The capital of which a person has deprived himself must be actual capital. In *CIS 240/1992* and *CIS 30/1993* the Commissioner raises the question (without expressing a conclusion) as to whether para. (1) can apply when a claimant is deemed to possess an equal share in a capital asset under reg. 52. In *CIS 240/1992* the claimant had a quarter share in a property, but the effect of reg. 52 was to treat him as having a half share. The claimant's parents (his mother owned the other three-quarters of the property) then bought his share for £5,000, out of which he repaid them loans of £3,883. The Commissioner points out that as reg. 52 operated to treat the claimant as having a notional equal share in the property, his actual share should not also count, since otherwise there would be double counting. Therefore, when he sold his actual share to his parents, was there no disposal of *actual* capital at all, or no disposal to the extent that his notional share exceeded his actual share? Para. 30341 of the *Adjudication Officers' Guide* states that where under reg. 52 a claimant has been deemed to own more capital than he actually does, he is only to be treated under para. (1) as depriving himself of the capital he actually owns. But this does not entirely deal with the Commissioner's point. In fact, in *CIS 240/1992*, since the property was subject to a tenancy, even if under para. (1) the claimant was treated as still possessing his actual interest, the disregard in para. 5 of Sched. 10 would result in him having no capital. The new tribunal would also have to consider whether para. (1) applied when the claimant repaid the loans (see *R(SB) 12/91* above).

[¹**Diminishing notional capital rule**

51A.—(1) Where a claimant is treated as possessing capital under regulation 51(1) (notional capital), the amount which he is treated as possessing—
    (a) in the case of a week that is subsequent to—
        (i) the relevant week in respect of which the conditions set out in paragraph (2) are satisfied, or
        (ii) a week which follows that relevant week and which satisfies those conditions,
shall be reduced by an amount determined under paragraph (2);
    (b) in the case of a week in respect of which paragraph (1)(a) does not apply but where—
        (i) that week is a week subsequent to the relevant week, and
        (ii) that relevant week is a week in which the condition in paragraph (3) is satisfied,

shall be reduced by the amount determined under paragraph (3).

(2) This paragraph applies to a benefit week or part week where the claimant satisfies the conditions that—

(a) he is in receipt of income support; and

(b) but for regulation 51(1), he would have received an additional amount of income support in that benefit week or, as the case may be, that part week;

and in such a case, the amount of the reduction for the purposes of paragraph (1)(a) shall be equal to that additional amount.

(3) Subject to paragraph (4), for the purposes of paragraph (1)(b) the condition is that the claimant would have been entitled to income support in the relevant week, but for regulation 51(1), and in such a case the amount of the reduction shall be equal to the aggregate of—

(a) the amount of income support to which the claimant would have been entitled in the relevant week but for regulation 51(1); and for the purposes of this sub-paragraph if the relevant week is a part-week that amount shall be determined by dividing the amount of income support to which he would have been so entitled by the number equal to the number of days in the part-week and multiplying the quotient by 7;

(b) the amount of housing benefit (if any) equal to the difference between his maximum housing benefit and the amount (if any) of housing benefit which he is awarded in respect of the benefit week, within the meaning of regulation 2(1) of the Housing Benefit (General) Regulations 1987 (interpretation), which includes the last day of the relevant week;

(c) the amount of community charge benefit (if any) equal to the difference between his maximum community charge benefit and the amount (if any) of community charge benefit which he is awarded in respect of the benefit week, within the meaning of regulation 2(1) of the Community Charge Benefits (General) Regulations 1989 (interpretation) which includes the last day of the relevant week.

[²(d) the amount of council tax benefit (if any) equal to the difference between his maximum council tax benefit and the amount (if any) of council tax benefit which he is awarded in respect of the benefit week which includes the last day of the relevant week, and for this purpose "benefit week" has the same meaning as in regulation 2(1) of the Council Tax Benefit (General) Regulations 1992 (interpretation).]

(4) The amount determined under paragraph (3) shall be re-determined under that paragraph if the claimant makes a further claim for income support and the conditions in paragraph (5) are satisfied, and in such a case—

(a) sub-paragraphs (a), (b) and (c) of paragraph (3) shall apply as if for the words "relevant week" there were substituted the words "relevant subsequent week"; and

(b) subject to paragraph (6), the amount as re-determined shall have effect from the first week following the relevant subsequent week in question.

(5) The conditions are that—

(a) a further claim is made 26 or more weeks after—

(i) the date on which the claimant made a claim for income support in respect of which he was first treated as possessing the capital in question under regulation 51(1); or

(ii) in a case where there has been at least one re-determination in accordance with paragraph (4), the date on which he last made a claim for income support which resulted in the weekly amount being re-determined; or

(iii) the date on which he last ceased to be in receipt of income support; whichever last occurred; and

(b) the claimant would have been entitled to income support but for regulation 51(1).

(6) The amount as re-determined pursuant to paragraph (4) shall not have effect if it is less than the amount which applied in that case immediately before the re-determination and in such a case the higher amount shall continue to have effect.

(7) For the purpose of this regulation—

(a) "part-week" means a period to which sub-section (1A) of section 21 of the Act [SSCBA, s.124(5)] (amount etc. of income support) applies;

(b) "relevant week" means the benefit week or part-week in which the capital in question of which the claimant has deprived himself within the meaning of regulation 51(1)—

(i) was first taken into account for the purpose of determining his entitlement to income support; or

(ii) was taken into account on a subsequent occasion for the purpose of determining or re-determining his entitlement to income support on that subsequent occasion and that determination or re-determination resulted in his beginning to receive, or ceasing to receive, income support;

and where more than one benefit week or part-week is identified by reference to heads (i) and (ii) of this sub-paragraph the later or latest such benefit week or, as the case may be, the later or latest such part-week;

(c) "relevant subsequent week" means the benefit week or part-week which includes the day on which the further claim or, if more than one further claim has been made, the last such claim was made.]

AMENDMENTS

1. Income Support (General) Amendment No. 3 Regulations 1990 (S.I. 1990 No. 1776), reg. 6 (October 1, 1990).
2. Income-related Benefits Schemes (Miscellaneous Amendments) Regulations 1993 (S.I. 1993 No. 315), Sched., para. 4 (April 1, 1993).

GENERAL NOTE

See the note to reg. 51(1) for the general background. Reg. 51A provides for the reduction of the amount of notional capital fixed by reg. 51(1). If the amount of notional capital remaining is not sufficient to remove entitlement to income support altogether, it is to be treated as reducing each week by the amount by which income support would be increased if it did not exist at all (paras. (1)(a) and (2)). If the amount does remove entitlement it is to be treated as reducing each week by the amount of income support the person would receive if the notional capital had not been fixed plus the proportion of rent and council tax not met by housing benefit or council tax benefit (paras. (1)(b) and (3)). There are complicated provisions for redetermination and recalculation.

The inter-relationship of this regulation, which ties the reduction in notional capital very much to income support rates, and *R(IS) 1/91* is of considerable difficulty. The Tribunal of Commissioners' diminishing capital rule works on reasonable expenditure not necessarily limited to income support rates. Could a claimant take the benefit of this more generous rule, or had its implication from the regulations been destroyed by the introduction of this express provision? *R(IS) 9/92* holds that the second alternative is correct.

Capital jointly held

52. Except where a claimant possesses capital which is disregarded under regulation 51(4) (notional capital), where a claimant and one or more persons are beneficially entitled in possession to any capital asset they shall be treated as if each of them were entitled in possession to the whole beneficial interest therein in an equal share [¹and the foregoing provisions of this Chapter shall apply for the purposes of calculating the amount of capital which the claimant is treated as possessing as if it were actual capital which the claimant does possess.]

AMENDMENT

1. Income Support (General) Amendment No. 4 Regulations 1988 (S.I. 1988 No. 1445), reg. 13 (September 12, 1988).

DEFINITION

"claimant"—see reg. 2(1), reg. 23(1).

GENERAL NOTE

This regulation contains an extraordinary rule (a view endorsed in *CIS 408/1990*). In *CIS 807/ 1991* the rule is described as draconian. Shared interests in assets had caused difficult problems of valuation under supplementary benefit. The intention of reg. 52 was to provide a solution which is simple to apply, but the conceptual difficulties posed are formidable.

Except in the case of deemed ownership of a company's assets under reg. 51(4), if the claimant has any share of the beneficial interest (*i.e.* the right to dispose of something) in an asset he is treated as having an equal share in the interest, regardless of the legal and equitable position. Thus if a person has a 10 per cent. interest in a house, and another person has a 90 per cent. interest, each is treated as having a 50 per cent. interest. There are many situations in which such a division might occur. The same could apply to, say, joint bank accounts or Building Society accounts. The result can easily be, in conjunction with the rules on disregards in Sched. 10, that a claimant is fixed with capital assets which he is not legally entitled to at all, let alone able to realise immediately. Although crisis loans under the social fund may be available (Social Fund Guide, para. 5424), the guidance presently given is in terms of short-term support while assets are realised, which does not meet the case. Normally the claimant's "remedy" for the artificial effects of reg. 52 is to dispose of his share in the asset, when he will receive an amount appropriate to his actual legal share. But this will not always be possible.

However, the draconian effect of reg. 52 was mitigated by the Tribunal of Commissioners' decisions in *CIS 391/1992* and *CIS 417/1992* which have been upheld by the Court of Appeal in *Chief Adjudication Officer v. Palfrey and Others, The Times*, February 17, 1995. It is now clearly established that where reg. 52 applies, what has to be valued is the deemed equal share, rather than the whole asset that has to be valued and then divided by the number of shares (see also *CIS 24/ 1990* and *CIS 408/1990*). In *CIS 391/1992* the claimant and his daughter had bought as joint tenants the council house which he had previously rented. When the claimant went into a residential care home the AO decided that he was not entitled to income support on the grounds that his deemed half-share of the value of the house under reg. 52 exceeded the capital limit. In *CIS 417/1992* the claimant had purchased a house with her daughter and son-in-law. They had each contributed £25,000 to the purchase and the property was conveyed to them as beneficial tenants in common. When the claimant moved into a residential care home, she was refused income support on the basis of having capital in excess of the statutory limit. The Commissioners decided that the effect of reg. 52 was to deem the claimants to have an equal share in the property (which was what they actually had). It was the current market value of that deemed share that had to be taken, not a proportion of the market value of the whole asset. The Commissioners recognised that this may well produce a very low valuation, if not a nil one, where the ownership of the property is shared with a relative who is unable or unwilling to sell the property or buy the claimant's interest. See the 1993 Supplement for a summary of the Tribunal of Commissioners' decisions, which give detailed guidance on the application of reg. 52. The Court of Appeal, for differing reasons, agreed with the Tribunal of Commissioners' conclusion. Nourse L.J. and Hobhouse L.J. considered that the language of reg. 52 was directed to the creation of a deemed tenancy in common in equal shares and thus it was the claimant's deemed (or actual) share that had to be brought into account. Nourse L.J. points out that reg. 52 does not say "shall be treated as if each of them were entitled in possession to an equal share of the value of the whole beneficial interest therein". Sir Ralph Gibson did not consider that the provision was particularly directed at treating joint tenants as tenants in common or primarily concerned with dealing with real property. But in his view, clear language had to be used if the intention was to treat the claimant as possessing capital, or capital of a particular value, that he did not in fact possess. Since reg. 52 did not expressly provide that the division into equal shares had to follow the valuation, it should be construed in a way that accorded more with the true facts.

The Tribunal of Commissioners' decisions had been followed in *CIS 127/1993* (*McNamara,* which was appealed to the Court of Appeal with *CIS 391/1992* and *CIS 417/1992*) and *CIS 413/1992*. *CIS 413/1992,* however, notes the differences that arise from the law of property in Scotland. In *CIS 391/1992* and *CIS 417/1992* the Commissioners state that the SSAT should have exercised its inquisitorial jurisdiction to call for the documents under which the property was acquired in order to sort out the beneficial ownership. But in *CIS 127/1993* the Commissioner did not find this necessary, since it was not disputed that the house had been conveyed into the names of the claimant and her daughter, and the method of valuation was the same whether the claimant and her daughter actually had equal shares or were deemed to do so by reg. 52.

It was argued in *CIS 391/1992* and *CIS 417/1992* that reg. 52 was invalid on the ground of irrationality. The Commissioners held, given their ruling on valuation under reg. 52, that irrationality had not been made out and that reg. 52 was validly made. The Court of Appeal in *Palfrey* did not express a view as to whether reg. 52 was invalid, as this argument only became relevant if the CAO's construction of reg. 52 was correct.

The Tribunal of Commissioners in *CIS 417/1992* did not have to decide whether reg. 52 applied so as to deem actual unequal shares to be treated as equal shares. In *CIS 240/1992* the claimant had a one quarter share in a property which was held on a tenancy in common with his mother. The Commissioner decides that reg. 52 did apply to treat the claimant as having a half-share in the beneficial interest. However, in that case (unlike *CIS 391/1992* and *CIS 417/1992*) there was a possibility that the other co-owner would have been willing to purchase the claimant's notional share if it actually existed. It was possible, therefore, that she should form part of the market for the claimant's notional interest. But the price paid by the claimants' parents for his actual interest (he sold it to them some months later) was not decisive of the value of his deemed share (see *R(SB) 18/83*).

Note that reg. 52 only applies where the beneficial interest is shared. It does not apply merely because there is a separation between legal and beneficial interests, for instance where one person holds assets on trust for another. But if an interest in a trust fund is shared, then reg. 52 will apply. This was the case in *CIS 449/1990* (to be reported as *R(IS)2/93*), where a building society account in the claimant's sole name was in fact a joint asset of herself and her (separated) husband. She had to be treated as possessing half of the amount in the account, regardless of how it might be dealt with in matrimonial proceedings. But it is arguable that in the case of assets that are the subject of matrimonial dispute, reg. 52 should not apply and their value should be disregarded, until ownership is resolved.

Calculation of tariff income from capital

53.—(1) Where the claimant's capital calculated in accordance with this Part exceeds £3,000 it shall be treated as equivalent to a weekly income of £1 for each complete £250 in excess of £3,000 but not exceeding [²£8,000].

(2) Notwithstanding paragraph (1), where any part of the excess is not a complete £250 that part shall be treated as equivalent to a weekly income of £1.

(3) For the purposes of paragraph (1), capital includes any income treated as capital under regulations [¹ . . .] 48 and 60 ([¹ . . .] income treated as capital and liable relative payments treated as capital).

AMENDMENTS

1. Income Support (General) Amendment No. 5 Regulations 1988 (S.I. 1988 No. 2022), reg. 13 (December 12, 1988).

2. Income-Related Benefits (Miscellaneous Amendments) Regulations 1990 (S.I. 1990 No. 671), reg. 5 (April 9, 1990).

DEFINITION

"claimant"—see reg. 2(1), reg. 23(1).

GENERAL NOTE

The overall capital limit under reg. 45 was raised to £8,000 from £6,000 from April 1990. If the claimant and partner have capital over £3,000 but not over £8,000, it is treated as producing an income under this regulation. The actual income from most forms of capital is disregarded under para. 22 of Sched. 9.

The tariff income is £1 per week for each complete £250 between the two limits, and £1 per week for any odd amount left over. Thus if the claimant has exactly £6,000, that is treated as producing £12 per week. If he has £4,001, that is treated as producing £5 per week.

Chapter VII

Liable Relatives

Interpretation

54. In this Chapter, unless the context otherwise requires—
"claimant" includes a young claimant;
"liable relative" means—
   (a) a spouse or former spouse of a claimant or of a member of the claimant's family;
   (b) a parent of a child or young person who is a member of the claimant's family or of a young claimant;
   (c) a person who has not been adjudged to be the father of a child or young person who is a member of the claimant's family or of a young claimant where that person is contributing towards the maintenance of that child, young person or young claimant and by reason of that contribution he may reasonably be treated as the father of that child, young person or young claimant;
   (d) a person liable to maintain another person by virtue of section 26(3)(c) of the Act [SSAA, s.78(6)(c)] (liability to maintain) where the latter is the claimant or a member of the claimant's family,
and, in this definition, a reference to a child's, young person's or young claimant's parent includes any person in relation to whom the child, young person or young claimant was treated as a child or a member of the family;
"payment" means a periodical payment or any other payment made by or derived from a liable relative including, except in the case of a discretionary trust, any payment which would be so made or derived upon application being made by the claimant but which has not been acquired by him but only from the date on which [¹it could be expected to be acquired were an application made]; but it does not include any payment—
   (a) arising from a disposition of property made in contemplation of, or as a consequence of—
      (i) an agreement to separate; or
      (ii) any proceedings for judicial separation, divorce or nullity of marriage;
   (b) made after the death of the liable relative;
   (c) made by way of a gift but not in aggregate or otherwise exceeding £250 in the period of 52 weeks beginning with the date on which the payment, or if there is more than one such payment the first payment, is made; and, in the case of a claimant who continues to be in receipt of income support at the end of the period of 52 weeks, this provision shall continue to apply thereafter with the modification that any subsequent period of 52 weeks shall begin with the first day of the benefit week in which the first payment is made after the end of the previous period of 52 weeks;
   (d) to which regulation 44(2) applies (modifications in respect of children and young persons);

(e) made—
   (i) to a third party in respect of the claimant or a member of the claimant's family; or
   (ii) to the claimant or to a member of the claimant's family in respect of a third party,
   where having regard to the purpose of the payment, the terms under which it is made and its amount it is unreasonable to take it into account;
(f) in kind;
(g) to, or in respect of, a child or young person who is to be treated as not being a member of the claimant's household under regulation 16 (circumstances in which a person is to be treated as being or not being a member of the same household);
(h) which is not a periodical payment, to the extent that any amount of that payment—
   (i) has already been taken into account under this Part by virtue of a previous claim or determination; or
   (ii) has been recovered under section 27(1) of the Act [SSAA, s.74(1)] (prevention of duplication of payments) or is currently being recovered; or
   (iii) at the time the determination is made, has been used by the claimant except where he has deprived himself of that amount for the purpose of securing entitlement to income support or increasing the amount of that benefit;

"periodical payment" means—
   (a) A payment which is made or is due to be made at regular intervals in pursuance of a court order or agreement for maintenance;
   (b) in a case where the liable relative has established a pattern of making payments at regular intervals, any such payment;
   (c) any payment not exceeding the amount of income support payable had that payment not been made;
   (d) any payment representing a commutation of payments to which sub-paragraphs (a) or (b) of this definition applies whether made in arrears or in advance,
   but does not include a payment due to be made before the first benefit week pursuant to the claim which is not so made;

"young claimant" means a person aged 16 or over but under 19 who makes a claim for income support.

AMENDMENT

1. Income Support (General) Amendment Regulations 1988 (S.I. 1988 No. 663), reg. 23 (April 11, 1988).

DEFINITIONS

   "the Act"—see reg. 2(1).
   "benefit week"—*ibid.*
   "child"—see 1986 Act, s.20(11) (SSCBA, s.137(1)).
   "claimant"—see reg. 2(1), reg. 23(1).
   "family"—see 1986 Act, s.20(11) (SSCBA, s.137(1)).
   "young person"—see reg. 2(1), reg. 14.

GENERAL NOTE

   The rules for liable relative payments do not apply to payments of child support maintenance paid under an assessment carried out in accordance with the Child Support Act 1991 (reg. 25A). They are taken into account as income in accordance with regs. 60A to 60D.

"Liable relative."

Note that the definition for these purposes is not restricted to those who are obliged to maintain others under s.78(6) of the Administration Act (1986 Act, s.26(3)), but includes in particular, a former spouse and a person who may reasonably be treated as the father of a child (by reason of contributing to the maintenance of the child).

"Payment."

The general definition is very wide, including payments not yet acquired which would be made on application (*cf.* reg. 51(2)). The general category of "payment" is divided into "periodical payments" (further defined below) and "other payments." This division is important in the following regulations.

The list of exceptions is also very important—

(a) A payment arising from a disposition of property made in connection with an agreement to separate or matrimonial proceedings is not a liable relative payment (LRP). There had been great problems in construing the similar, but not identical, supplementary benefit provision, in particular in deciding when a payment "resulted from" a disposition of property. Although the words here are "arising from," the authoritative settlement of the supplementary benefit problem in *R(SB)1/89* should apply. The claimant received a payment of £2,500 from her ex-husband pursuant to a county court order. This was a consent order made on the basis that the claimant gave up any claims against her ex-husband's houses. The Tribunal of Commissioners holds that there must be a chain of causation, however short, between the disposition and the payment, and that the prior disposition does not have to be by way of sale. Where a payment is made in discharge of a claimant's proprietary interest (or a claim to such an interest) it results from a disposition of property. Where it is made in discharge of maintenance obligations the payment stands alone and does not result from a disposition. *R(SB) 1/89* approves the result of *CSB 1160/1986* where a husband and wife had a joint building society account. On their separation they agreed to split the account and as a result the husband paid £2,500 to the wife, who was receiving supplementary benefit. It was held that the building society account was "property" and that the agreement to split it was a "disposition." The payment then resulted from a disposition of property. It was not a LRP, and had to be dealt with under the ordinary rules on resources.

(b) Payments made after the liable relative's death are not LRPs.

(c) Gifts up to £250 in 52 weeks do not count as LRPs. In view of para. (f), para. (c) must apply to gifts of money or property.

(d) Reg. 44(2) applies to payments to residential schools for a child's or young person's maintenance.

(e) Payments from liable relatives to third parties in respect of the claimant or a member of the claimant's family do not count as LRPs if it would be unreasonable for them to do so. Here much of the guidance in *R(SB) 6/88* is still relevant. This indicates that while the factors mentioned must be considered, other relevant factors may also be considered. If the payment is not a LRP, see reg. 51(3).

Similar rules apply to payments to a member of the claimant's family for a third party (and see para. (9)).

(f) Payments in kind are not LRPs. This could be an important factor in benefit planning.

(g) Payments to or in respect of a child or young person who would otherwise be a member of the claimant's household, but is treated as not being in the household by reg. 16, do not count as LRPs. See reg. 51(3).

(h) Where an "other payment" is being considered, its amount is to be reduced if any of the three categories listed apply. Category (iii) is likely to be particularly important where there is a significant gap between the date of receipt of the payment in question and the date on which the claim for income support (or presumably a question arising on review) is determined. See the notes to reg. 51(1) for the difficulties of deciding when a claimant's purpose is to secure or increase entitlement to income support.

"Periodical payment."

This definition is also very wide, as the four categories are alternatives.

Sub-paras. (a) and (b) are relatively straightforward, covering the standard cases where payments are due to be made at regular intervals or a regular pattern has been established.

The effect of sub-para. (d) is that a payment of arrears of payments under (a) and (b), or a payment in advance, also counts as a periodical payment (subject to the final exception). If, however, a regular pattern of payments has ceased to exist and there is no court order or agreement to make regular payments, such a payment cannot be a commutation of payments under sub-paras. (a) or

(b) (*Bolstridge v. Chief Adjudication Officer, The Times*, May 5, 1993). It will be a matter of fact in each case by what date a regular pattern of payments ceases to exist. The facts in *Bolstridge* were that the claimant's ex-husband paid her maintenance of £40 per week on a voluntary basis up to July 31, 1986. He was then made redundant and ceased making payments. In September 1987 her ex-husband made her a payment of £10,500 "in lieu of future maintenance". In July 1988, she claimed income support. The Court of Appeal held that, in the absence of any subsisting contract or outstanding liability, it could not be said that by September 1987, there was an agreement for maintenace of any particular sum or any pattern of regular payment. Therefore, the £10,500 was not a periodical payment. It was an "other payment", to be taken into account under reg. 57. Any part of the total amount which fell outside the definition of "payment" (above) would not be taken into consideration at all. In particular, amounts which the claimant had already spent for "legitimate" purposes would be excluded under sub-para. (h)(iii) of the definition.

The intention of sub-para. (c) seems to be that relatively small payments (*i.e.* up to the amount of one week's income support) are to be treated as periodical payments.

The final exception is crucial to the working of the LRP system. If a payment was due to be made before the first benefit week, pursuant to the claim, but is paid in or after that benefit week, it is an "other payment," not a periodical payment. Thus the treatment of arrears will vary according to whether the claimant was or was not in receipt of benefit during the period to which the arrears relate (on which see *McCorquodale v. Chief Adjudication Officer (R(SB)1/88), The Times*, May 3, 1988).

Treatment of liable relative payments

55. Except where regulation 60(1) (liable relative payments to be treated as capital) applies a payment shall—
  (a) to the extent that it is not a payment of income, be treated as income;
  (b) be taken into account in accordance with the following provisions of this Chapter.

DEFINITION

"payment"—see reg. 54.

GENERAL NOTE

The general rule is that if a payment falls into the definition in reg. 54, it is to be taken into account as income. It is only in the limited circumstances described in reg. 60(1) that it can be treated as capital, and therefore be much less likely to affect benefit.

Period over which periodical payments are to be taken into account

56.—(1) The period over which a periodical payment is to be taken into account shall be—
  (a) in a case where the payment is made at regular intervals, a period equal to the length of that interval;
  (b) in a case where the payment is due to be made at regular intervals but is not so made, such number of weeks as is equal to the number (and any fraction shall be treated as a corresponding fraction of a week) obtained by dividing the amount of that payment by the weekly amount of that periodical payment as calculated in accordance with regulation 58(4) (calculation of the weekly amount of a liable relative payment);
  (c) in any other case, a period equal to a week.
  (2) The period under paragraph (1) shall begin on the date on which the payment is treated as paid under regulation 59 (date on which a liable relative payment is to be treated as paid).

DEFINITION

"periodical payment"—see reg. 54.

GENERAL NOTE

If a periodical payment is actually paid at regular intervals, it is to be taken into account for the length of the interval. If it is due to be paid regularly but is not, each payment is spread at the weekly rate of proper payment. In other cases (*e.g.* some payments within sub-para. (c) of the definition of periodical payment) the payment is taken into account for a week.

The application of reg. 56 to payments under sub-para. (d) of the definition of periodical payment is not straightforward. In *Bolstridge v. Chief Adjudication Officer, The Times*, May 5, 1993, it was accepted that reg. 56(1)(b) can be given a sensible meaning only if the word "payment" in that regulation sometimes applies to the commutated payment and sometimes to the payment that was due to be made at regular intervals.

Payments are taken into account from the date on which they are treated as paid under reg. 59.

Period over which payments other than periodical payments are to be taken into account

57.—(1) Subject to paragraph (2), the number of weeks over which any payment other than a periodical payment is to be taken into account shall be equal to the number (and any fraction shall be treated as a corresponding fraction of a week) obtained by dividing that payment by—

    (a) where the payment is in respect of the claimant or the claimant and any child or young person who is a member of the family, the aggregate of £2 and the amount of income support which would be payable if the payment had not been made;

[¹(b) where the payment is in respect of one, or more than one, child or young person who is a member of the family, the lesser of the amount (or the aggregate of the amounts) prescribed under Schedule 2, in respect of—

      (i) the personal allowance of the claimant and each such child or young person;

      (ii) any family and lone parent premium;

      (iii) any disabled child premium in respect of such a child; and

      (iv) any carer premium if, but only if, that premium is payable because the claimant is in receipt, or is treated as being in receipt, of invalid care allowance by reason of the fact that he is caring for such a child or young person who is severely disabled;

and the aggregate of £2 and the amount of income support which would be payable had the payment not been made.]

(2) Where a liable relative makes a periodical payment and any other payment concurrently and the weekly amount of that periodical payment, as calculated in accordance with regulation 58 (calculation of the weekly amount of a liable relative payment), is less than—

    (a) in a case where the periodical payment is in respect of the claimant or the claimant and any child or young person who is a member of the family, the aggregate of £2 and the amount of income support which would be payable had the payment not been made; or

    (b) in a case where the periodical payment is in respect of one or more than one child or young person who is a member of the family, the aggregate of the amount prescribed in Schedule 2 in respect of each such child or young person and any family and lone parent premium,

that other payment shall, subject to paragraph (3), be taken into account over a period of such number of weeks as is equal to the number obtained (and any fraction shall be treated as a corresponding fraction of a week) by dividing that payment by an amount equal to the extent of the difference between the amount referred to in sub-paragraph (a) or (b), as the case may be, and the weekly amount of the periodical payment.

(3) If—

    (a) the liable relative ceases to make periodical payments, the balance (if any) of the other payment shall be taken into account over the number of weeks equal to the number obtained (and any fraction shall be treated as a corresponding fraction of a week) by dividing that balance by the amount referred to in sub-paragraph (a) or (b) of paragraph (1), as the case may be;

(b) the amount of any subsequent periodical payment varies, the balance (if any) of the other payment shall be taken into account over a period of such number of weeks as is equal to the number obtained (and any fraction shall be treated as a corresponding fraction of a week) by dividing that balance by an amount equal to the extent of the difference between the amount referred to in sub-paragraph (a) or (b) of paragraph (2) and the weekly amount of the subsequent periodical payment.

(4) The period under paragraph (1) or (2) shall begin on the date on which the payment is treated as paid under regulation 59 (date on which a liable relative payment is treated as paid) and under paragraph (3) shall begin on the first day of the benefit week in which the cessation or variation of the periodical payment occurred.

AMENDMENT

1. Income Support (General) Amendment No. 3 Regulations 1990 (S.I. 1990 No. 1776), reg. 7 (October 15, 1990).

DEFINITIONS

"child"—see 1986 Act, s.20(11) (SSCBA, s.137(1)).
"claimant"—see reg. 2(1), reg. 23(1), reg. 54.
"family"—see 1986 Act, s.20(11) (SSCBA, s.137(1)).
"liable relative"—see reg. 54.
"payment"—*ibid.*
"periodical payment"—*ibid.*
"young person"—see reg. 2(1), reg. 14.

GENERAL NOTE

This regulation deals with payments other than periodical payments. The basic rule under para. (1) is to spread them at the rate of income support for the people the payment is for, plus £2 if one of them is the claimant. The new form of para. (1)(b) deems many more elements of the applicable amount to be treated as for a child. Paras. (2) and (3) modify this rule where the payment is in addition to periodical payments so as to spread the payments at the rate of the difference between the amount of the periodical payment and the amount identified in para. (1), as long as the periodical payments continue to be made.

See reg. 58(5) for the weekly amount to be taken into account.

Calculation of the weekly amount of a liable relative payment

58.—(1) Where a periodical payment is made or is due to be made at intervals of one week, the weekly amount shall be the amount of that payment.

(2) Where a periodical payment is made or is due to be made at intervals greater than one week and those intervals are monthly, the weekly amount shall be determined by multiplying the amount of the payment by 12 and dividing the product by 52.

(3) Where a periodical payment is made or is due to be made at intervals and those intervals are neither weekly nor monthly, the weekly amount shall be determined by dividing that payment by the number equal to the number of weeks (including any part of a week) in that interval.

(4) Where a payment is made and that payment represents a commutation of periodical payments whether in arrears or in advance, the weekly amount shall

be the weekly amount of the individual periodical payments so commutated, as calculated under paragraphs (1) to (3) as is appropriate.

(5) The weekly amount of a payment to which regulation 57 applies (period over which payments other than periodical payments are to be taken into account) shall be equal to the amount of the divisor used in calculating the period over which the payment or, as the case may be, the balance is to be taken into account.

DEFINITIONS

"payment"—see reg. 54.
"periodical payment"—*ibid.*

GENERAL NOTE

The weekly rate of periodical payments is normally calculated by dividing the payment into weekly bits depending on the intervals between payment dates (paras. (1) to (3)). For a commutation of periodical payments, whether in arrears or in advance (which itself comes within the definition of periodical payment), the weekly rate is the appropriate one for the recurring payments.

Date on which a liable relative payment is to be treated as paid

59.—(1) A periodical payment is to be treated as paid—
  (a) in the case of a payment which is due to be made before the first benefit week pursuant to the claim, on the day in the week in which it is to be paid which corresponds to the first day of the benefit week;
  (b) in any other case, on the first day of the benefit week in which it is due to be paid unless, having regard to the manner in which income support is due to be paid in the particular case, it would be more practicable to treat it as paid on the first day of a subsequent benefit week.

(2) Subject to paragraph (3), any other payment shall be treated as paid—
  (a) in the case of a payment which is made before the first benefit week pursuant to the claim, on the day in the week in which it is paid which corresponds to the first day of the benefit week;
  (b) in any other case, on the first day of the benefit week in which it is paid unless, having regard to the manner in which income support is due to be paid in the particular case, it would be more practicable to treat it as paid on the first day of a subsequent benefit week.

(3) Any other payment paid on a date which falls within the period in respect of which a previous payment is taken into account, not being a periodical payment, is to be treated as paid on the first day following the end of that period.

DEFINITIONS

"benefit week"—see reg. 2(1).
"payment"—see reg. 54.
"periodical payment"—*ibid.*

GENERAL NOTE

Paragraph (1)
This provision effectively applies the ordinary rule for income (see reg. 31) to periodical payments. Under sub-para. (a) for the payment still to be a periodical payment it must have been paid as well as been due before the first benefit week pursuant to the claim. Once the benefit week is determined under para. 4 of Sched. 7 to the Claims and Payments Regulations, prior weeks can be counted off and payments attributed to the first day of each week. Under sub-para. (b), for other periodical payments (which can include many payments of arrears) the crucial thing is the benefit week in which the payment is due, or, if it would be more practicable, a subsequent week. A payment of arrears within the definition of a periodical payment may well have been due in a large

number of past weeks, for which benefit has already been paid on the assumption that no LRP had been received. This would seem to trigger the application of s.74(1) of the Administration Act (1986 Act, s.27(1)). Para. 29932 of the *Adjudication Officers' Guide* suggests that in such circumstances it is more practicable to take the payment into account from the next benefit week in which the amount of benefit can be adjusted, although the *Guide* does not really face the problem of payments of arrears. If continuing periodical payments are being made, the spreading of a payment of arrears over future benefit weeks could lead to more than one periodical payment being taken into account in the same benefit week. Whether this leaves the claimant better off than if recovery under s.74(1) had been triggered depends on the levels of payment in relation to income support entitlement. It is not at all clear that this solution is "more practicable" than spreading the payment of arrears over the past period to which the arrears related. The latter solution, with the recovery of any overpayment under s.74(1), may be better.

Paragraph (2)

This provision applies to all "other payments", including payments of arrears identified in the final exception to the definition of "periodical payment". Here it is the date of actual payment, rather than the date on which payment is due, which is crucial. Sub-para. (a) applies to payments made before the first benefit week pursuant to the claim. Sub-para. (b) applies in all other cases, and allows attribution to a later benefit week than that of payment if that is more practicable.

The result for payments of arrears relating to a period before entitlement to benefit, is that the payment is treated as income to be spread at the rate identified in reg. 58 from the date of actual payment. This reverses the result of *McCorquodale v. Chief Adjudication Officer (R(SB)1/88), The Times,* May 3, 1988. If this results in one "other payment" being attributed to a benefit week to which another "other payment" has already been attributed, the attribution of the later payment is deferred until the first one runs out (para. (3)).

Liable relative payments to be treated as capital

60.—(1) Subject to paragraph (2), where a liable relative makes a periodical payment concurrently with any other payment, and the weekly amount of the periodical payment as calculated in accordance with regulation 58(1) to (4) (calculation of the weekly amount of a liable relative payment), is equal to or greater than the amount referred to in sub-paragraph (a) of regulation 57(2) (period over which payments other than periodical payments are to be taken into account) less the £2 referred to therein, or sub-paragraph (b) of that regulation, as the case may be, the other payment shall be treated as capital.

(2) If, in any case, the liable relative ceases to make periodical payments, the other payment to which paragraph (1) applies shall be taken into account under paragraph (1) of regulation 57 but, notwithstanding paragraph (4) thereof, the period over which the payment is to be taken into account shall begin on the first day of the benefit week following the last one in which a periodical payment was taken into account.

DEFINITIONS

    "benefit week"—see reg. 2(1).
    "liable relative"—see reg. 54.
    "payment"—*ibid.*
    "periodical payment"—*ibid.*

GENERAL NOTE

If a periodical payment at least equals the income support rate for the person(s) it is for, any other payment made at the same time is treated as capital. If the liable relative later stops making the periodical payments the other payment can be tapped as income under para. (2).

[¹*Chapter VIIA*

Child Support

Interpretation

60A. In this Chapter—

"child support maintenance" means such periodical payments as are referred to in section 3(6) of the Child Support Act 1991;

"maintenance assessment" has the same meaning as in the Child Support Act 1991 by virtue of section 54 of that Act.]

AMENDMENT

1. Social Security (Miscellaneous Provisions) Amendment Regulations 1993 (S.I. 1993 No. 846), reg. 3 (April 19, 1993).

GENERAL NOTE

Section 3(6) of the Child Support Act 1991 refers to "periodical payments which are required to be paid in accordance with a maintenance assessment." A "maintenance assessment" is defined in s.54 as "an assessment of maintenance made under [the Child Support Act 1991] and, except in prescribed circumstances, includes an interim maintenance assessment."

[¹Treatment of child support maintenance

60B. All payments of child support maintenance shall to the extent that they are not payments of income be treated as income and shall be taken into account on a weekly basis in accordance with the following provisions of this Chapter.]

AMENDMENT

1. Social Security (Miscellaneous Provisions) Amendment Regulations 1993 (S.I. 1993 No. 846), reg. 3 (April 19, 1993).

DEFINITIONS

"child support maintenance"—see reg. 60A.
"payment"—see reg. 2(1).

GENERAL NOTE

Since the definition of "child support maintenance" refers to payments which are required to be made periodically, it appears that payments in commutation of periodical payments, either in advance or in arrears, will be payments of child support maintenance, providing that there is a subsisting liability under a maintenance assessment (see *Bolstridge v. Chief Adjudication Officer, The Times*, May 5, 1993). They then have to be treated as payments of income. See reg. 60C(5) for commutation payments. Payments made at the periodical intervals required under the maintenance assessment would be income anyway, but are to be taken into account according to the rules set out in regs. 60C and 60D.

All income under Chapter VIIA is taken into account in full in assessing entitlement to income support. There are no disregards.

[¹Calculation of the weekly amount of payments of child support maintenance

60C.—(1) The weekly amount of child support maintenance shall be determined in accordance with the following provisions of this regulation.

(2) Where payments of child support maintenance are made weekly, the weekly amount shall be the amount of that payment.

(3) Where payments of child support maintenance are made monthly, the weekly amount shall be determined by multiplying the amount of the payment by 12 and dividing the product by 52.

(4) Where payments of child support are made at intervals and those intervals are not a week or a month, the weekly amount shall be determined by dividing that payment by the number equal to the number of weeks (including any part of a week) in that interval.

(5) Where a payment is made and that payment represents a commutation of child support maintenance the weekly amount shall be the weekly amount of the individual child support maintenance payments so commuted as calculated in accordance with paragraphs (2) to (4) as appropriate.

(6) Paragraph (2), (3) or, as the case may be, (4) shall apply to any payments made at the intervals specified in that paragraph whether or not—

(a) the amount paid is in accordance with the maintenance assessment, and

(b) the intervals at which the payments are made are in accordance with the intervals specified by the Secretary of State under regulation 4 of the Child Support (Collection and Enforcement) Regulations 1992].

AMENDMENT

1. Social Security (Miscellaneous Provisions) Amendment Regulations 1993 (S.I. 1993 No. 846), reg. 3 (April 19, 1993).

DEFINITIONS

"child support maintenance"—see reg. 60A.
"maintenance assessment"—*ibid.*
"payment"—see reg. 2(1).

GENERAL NOTE

The Secretary of State specifies the day and interval by reference to which payments of child support maintenance are to be paid by the liable person (Child Support (Collection and Enforcement) Regulations 1992, reg. 4). Paras. (2) to (4) work easily when payments of the full amount of the maintenance assessment are made at regular intervals. Then they supply simple arithmetical rules for working out the weekly amount and reg. 60D defines when each payment is to be treated as made. If the payments are not made at regular intervals, it is not clear whether para. (4) should apply, taking the interval since the last payment to define the weekly amount, or whether the payment should be treated as a commutation of past maintenance under para. (5). If regular payments are made of less than the maintenance assessment, the effect of para. (6) is that the actual amount paid should be treated as income, not the amount properly due. If later a payment of arrears is made in a lump sum, does para. (5) apply to that payment as a commutation of child support maintenance, or does the definition of child support maintenance mean that para. (5) only applies to payments which are multiples of the payments required to be made under the maintenance assessment? It would seem that the former is intended, because there can be recovery of overpaid income support under s.74(1) of the Administration Act when arrears of child support maintenance are paid only to take account of the period between the effective date of the maintenance assessment and the date when normal periodical payments start (Social Security (Payments on account, Overpayments and Recovery) Regulations 1988, reg. 7(1)(b): see below). In practice, where the parent with care is on income support, it is likely that payments of arrears by an absent parent for periods after normal periodical payments start will be made direct to the Child Support Agency who will retain an amount equal to the income support that would not have been paid if the child support maintenance had been paid on time. But if arrangements for payment direct to the Child Support Agency have not yet been made (*e.g.* where the absent parent has only just fallen into arrears), para. (5) may apply to any payments made in these circumstances.

Para. (5) deals with payments which are commutations of child support maintenance. Although nothing is said expressly, it would seem to cover commutations both in advance or in arrears. There is little problem over payments in advance.

[¹Date on which child support maintenance is to be treated as paid

60D. A payment of child support maintenance is to be treated as paid—

(a) in the case of a payment which is due to be paid before the first benefit week pursuant to the claim, on the day in the week in which it is due to be paid which corresponds to the first day of the benefit week;

(b) in any other case, on the first day of the benefit week in which it is paid or the first day of the first succeeding benefit week in which it is practicable to take it into account.]

AMENDMENT

1. Social Security (Miscellaneous Provisions) Amendment Regulations 1993 (S.I. 1993 No. 846), reg. 3 (April 19, 1993).

DEFINITIONS

"benefit week"—see reg. 2(1).
"child support maintenance"—see reg. 60A.

GENERAL NOTE

This is the same rule as in reg. 31(1).

Chapter VIII

Students

Interpretation

61. In this Chapter, unless the context otherwise requires—
"a course of advanced education" means—
  (a) a full-time course leading to a postgraduate degree or comparable qualification, a first degree or comparable qualification, a diploma of higher education, a higher national diploma, [⁵a higher national diploma or higher national certificate of either the Business & [⁶Technology] Education Council] or the Scottish Vocational Education Council or a teaching qualification; or
  (b) any other full-time course which is a course of a standard above ordinary national diploma, [⁵a national diploma or national certificate of either the Business and [⁶Technology] Education Council or the Scottish Vocational Education Council], a general certificate of education (advanced level) a Scottish certificate of education [⁵(higher level)] or a Scottish certificate of sixth year studies;
"contribution" means any contribution in respect of the income of any other person which a Minister of the Crown or an education authority takes into account in assessing the amount of the student's grant and by which that amount is, as a consequence, reduced;
"covenant income" means the income net of tax at the basic rate payable to a student under a Deed of Covenant by a person whose income is, or is likely to be, taken into account in assessing the student's grant or award;
"education authority" means a government department, a local education authority as defined in section 114(1) of the Education Act 1944 (interpretation), an education authority as defined in section 135(1) of the Education (Scotland) Act [¹1980] (interpretation), an education and library board established under Article 3 of the Education and Libraries (Northern Ireland) Order 1986, any body which is a research council for the purposes of the Science and Technology Act 1965 or any analogous government department, authority, board or body, of the Channel Islands, Isle of Man or any other country outside Great Britain;
"grant" means any kind of educational grant or award and includes any scholarship, studentship, exhibition, allowance or bursary [²but does not include a payment derived from funds made available by the Secretary of State for the purpose of assisting students in financial difficulties under

section 100 of the Education Act 1944, sections 131 and 132 of the Education Reform Act 1988 or section 73 of the Education (Scotland) Act 1980];

"grant income" means—

(a) any income by way of a grant;

(b) in the case of a student other than one to whom sub-paragraph (c) refers, any contribution which has been assessed whether or not it has been paid;

(c) in the case of a student to whom paragraph 1, 2 or 7 of Schedule 1 applies (lone parent or disabled student), any contribution which has been assessed and which has been paid;

and any such contribution which is paid by way of a covenant shall be treated as part of the student's grant income;

[³"last day of the course" means the date on which the last day of the final academic term falls in respect of the course in which the student is enrolled;]

"period of study" means—

(a) in the case of a course of study for one year or less, the period beginning with the start of the course [³and ending with the last day of the course];

(b) in the case of a course of study for more than one year, in the first or, as the case may be, any subsequent year of the course, [³other than the final year of the course,] the period beginning with the start of the course or, as the case may be, that year's start and ending with either—

(i) the day before the start of the next year of the course in a case where the student's grant is assessed at a rate appropriate to his studying throughout the year, or, if he does not have a grant, where it would have been assessed at such a rate had he had one; or

(ii) in any other case the day before the start of the normal summer vacation appropriate to his course;

[³(c) in the final year of a course of study of more than one year, the period beginning with that year's start and ending with the last day of the course;]

"periods of experience" has the meaning prescribed in paragraph 1(1) of Schedule 5 to the Education (Mandatory Awards) Regulations 1987;

"sandwich course" has the meaning prescribed in paragraph 1(1) of Schedule 5 to the Education (Mandatory Awards) Regulations 1987;

"standard maintenance grant" means—

(a) except where paragraph (b) applies, in the case of a student attending a course of study at the University of London or an establishment within the area comprising the City of London and the Metropolitan Police District, the amount specified for the time being in paragraph 2(2)(a) of Schedule 2 to the Education (Mandatory Awards) Regulations 1987 for such a student;

(b) in the case of a student residing at his parents' home the amount specified in paragraph 3(2) thereof;

(c) in any other case, the amount specified in paragraph 2(2) other than in sub-paragraph (a) or (b) thereof;

[⁴"student" means a person, other than a person in receipt of a training allowance,] aged less than 19 who is attending a full-time course of advanced education or, as the case may be, a person aged 19 or over but under pensionable age who is attending a full-time course of study at an educational establishment; and for the purposes of this definition—

(a) a person who has started on such a course shall be treated as attending it throughout any period of term or vacation within it, until [³the last day of the course] or such earlier date as he abandons it or is dismissed from it;

(b) a person on a sandwich course shall be treated as attending a full-time course of advanced education or, as the case may be, of study;

"year" in relation to a course, means the period of 12 months beginning on 1st January, 1st April or 1st September according to whether the academic year of the course in question begins in the spring, the summer or the autumn respectively.

AMENDMENTS

1. Income Support (General) Amendment No. 5 Regulations 1988 (S.I. 1988 No. 2022), reg. 14 (December 12, 1988).
2. Social Security Benefits (Student Loans and Miscellaneous Amendments) Regulations 1990 (S.I. 1990 No. 1549), reg. 5(5) (September 1, 1990).
3. Income Support (General) Amendment No. 4 Regulations 1991 (S.I. 1991 No. 1559), reg. 10 (August 5, 1991).
4. Income Support (General) Amendment Regulations 1992 (S.I. 1992 No. 468), reg. 5 (April 6, 1992).
5. Income-related Benefits Schemes (Miscellaneous Amendments) (No. 3) Regulations 1992 (S.I. 1992 No. 2155), reg. 19 (October 5, 1992).
6. Income-related Benefits Schemes (Miscellaneous Amendments) (No.4) Regulations 1993 (S.I. 1993 No. 2119), reg. 16 (October 4, 1993).

DEFINITION

"training allowance"—see reg. 2(1).

GENERAL NOTE

"Grant"
R(SB) 20/83 decided that "award" included a loan. However, in *CIS 758/1992* the Commissioner disagrees with *R(SB) 20/83*. In his view, "award", if given its everyday meaning, particularly in the context of academic grants and awards, implied an outright gift with no liability to repay. Thus the education loan received by the claimant's partner from the Norwegian Government did not fall within reg. 61, but was to be taken into account as income under reg. 40 (see *R(SB) 7/88*). Reg. 66A (concerning the student loan scheme) had been introduced simply for the removal of doubt and did not indicate that, without it, loans would not count as income.

"Grant income"
Note that in most cases a parental contribution is included whether paid or not.

"Student"
The definition of student here is important not just for Chapter VIII on the income of students, but also because it feeds back in through the additional definition of "period of study" in reg. 2(1) to remove most students' entitlement (see reg. 10(1)(h)).

Those in receipt of a training allowance are now excluded from the definition. This makes little practical difference for income support purposes, for such claimants are not deemed to be unavailable for work under reg. 10(1)(h). The amendment is to maintain the alignment with the housing benefit definition, where the change does make a difference.

There are two categories. A person under 19 is a student if attending a full-time course of advanced education. Advanced education is defined earlier in reg. 61.

A person of 19 or over (but under pensionable age) is a student if attending a full-time course of study at an educational establishment. It does not have to be any particular level. A person of 19 cannot be in relevant education, because that only applies to children or young persons (reg. 12). The reference is now to a course of study, rather than of education. This probably makes little difference, although it makes it harder to argue that students pursuing degrees purely by research, with no coursework, are not "attending" a course (see *(R(SB) 26/82)*, but pursuing or following it. The shifting of the words "full-time," as compared with the supplementary benefit definition, emphasises that it is the course which has to be full-time, not the attendance (see *(R(SB) 40/83, R(SB) 41/83, CSB 176/1987)*. Evidence from the educational establishment, an education authority or examining board, and the length of time the claimant is taking to complete the course will be relevant.

In *CIS 152/1994* the Commissioner recognises that recent developments in education have blurred the distinction between full-time and part-time courses, and that what is in essence the same course can often be accessed on either a full-time or a part-time basis. The claimant had begun a full-time course in 1992, studying 21 and three quarters hours a week. In 1993 he reduced the number of modules he was taking from seven to five, so that his hours of study became 15 a week. The Commissioner states that it is no longer sufficient just to look at the course. The overall circumstances (*e.g.* the hours of study, number of modules, length of time it would take to obtain the qualification on the basis of five as opposed to seven modules at a time, correspondence from the college, fees payable and any relevant information in the college prospectus) therefore had to be examined to ascertain whether the course the claimant was now attending was full or part-time.

R(SB) 25/87 decides that a pupil barrister is not a student because pupillage is not a course of education, but an assimilation of specific vocational skills by attending on the pupil master. Presumably, a pupil barrister would be said not to be attending a "course of study" (the phrase here) either. *CIS 50/1990* suggests that this approach is not lightly to be extended to other circumstances. The claimant was attending an intensive shorthand and typing course at a commercial Training Centre. There was little difficulty in deciding that this was a full-time course. The Commissioner holds that since there was active tuition, the claimant was engaged in study, regardless of the technical nature of the skills studied. The Centre was within the ordinary meaning of "educational establishment."

Note that the definition of student applies for the entire length of the course, as confirmed by the August 1991 amendments. This raises the question of what is meant by "course" (see *CIS 179/ 1994* below). The definition applies unless the student abandons the course or is dismissed from it. In *CIS 514/1992*, after the second year of her three year course the claimant was allowed to "intercalate" (that is, take a year off). The Commissioner decides that a course can be abandoned temporarily. It is irrelevant that the claimant has a right to resume her course at an agreed date. She has in the interim lost all the attributes of being a student (she was not allowed on the campus, had to give up her university accommodation, etc). In *CIS 413/1993* (heard at the same time) a student who was seeking a third intercalating year due to ill-health is held to have ceased to be a student from the date she last attended her course.

CIS 514/1992 and *CIS 413/1993* were appealed to the Court of Appeal. In *Chief Adjudication Officer and Secretary of State for Social Security v. Clarke and Faul, The Times,* February 22, 1995, the appeals were dismissed by a majority. All three judges considered that "abandon" in the context of the definition of "student" in reg. 61 meant "abandon permanently". However, the majority held that because the definition treats a student who has started a course as attending it "throughout any period of term or vacation within it" (until the course ends or he abandons, or is dismissed from, it), the claimants were not students during their intercalating years. There could be no period of term or vacation within a course when the student was not attending the course at all. The AO had submitted that these words simply emphasised that a student was deemed to be attending a course even when he was on vacation. Although this was a possible explanation, the claimants' construction accorded more with the purpose of the regulations. This was that a person should count as a student for income support purposes when he would be entitled to support under the students' grants and loans systems because he was attending a course. If he took time off from his course he was not eligible for such support. Thus during such time he should not be excluded from income support. Hoffmann L. J. concluded with a warning that the decision should not be taken as a licence for artificially creating gaps in courses in order to enable students to claim benefit. The AO was granted leave to appeal to the House of Lords, but the appeal is not being pursued. It may be noteworthy that the definition in para. (a) contains no reference to any temporary interruption of a student's attendance on a course (*cf.* for example, reg. 5(3) of the Social Security (Invalid Care Allowance) Regulations 1976).

The Court's reasoning will apply to others who are not attending a course, for example, those who have failed exams and who are only permitted to return if they successfully resit them a year later. It could perhaps also be argued that such a person had been "dismissed" from the course in the meantime, although the Court of Appeal in *Clarke* and *Faul* thought that dismissal from a course meant final dismissal. *CIS 368/1992* decided that a student who exercised the option of working in France for a year as part of her course remained a student throughout her four year course. Her course was continuing, even if in a different form. But following the Court of Appeal's judgment in *Clarke* and *Faul*, it is questionable whether during her year away from university the claimant in *CIS 368/1992* could have been said to be attending a "period of term or vacation" within her course.

In *CIS 179/1994* the claimant was training to be an architect. He had obtained his degree and had to find a year's placement with a firm before undertaking a further two years' study (to be followed by a further year's practical experience) in order to complete his professional training. The Commissioner holds that he was not a student during the year "out". In the Commissioner's view, a course was a "unified sequence of study, tuition and/or practical training ... intended to lead to one or more qualifications obtained on its completion". So if a profession required more than one qualification for which colleges did not provide a single sequence of tuition and/or experience, the person was not engaged on one continuous "course" throughout, but completed one "course" before moving onto another. After finishing his degree course the claimant was not within any period of term or vacation of that course. Thus para (a) of the definition of student did not apply to him. Para. (b) also did not apply as the claimant was not on a "sandwich course", since any periods of outside practical experience were not "associated with" his full-time study within the meaning of the Mandatory Awards Regulations.

Calculation of grant income

62.—(1) The amount of a student's grant income to be taken into account shall, subject to [⁴paragraphs (2) and (2A)], be the whole of his grant income.

(2) There shall be disregarded from the amount of a student's grant income any payment—

(a) intended to meet tuition fees or examination fees;

(b) intended to meet the cost of special equipment for a student on a course which began before 1st September 1986 in architecture, art and design, home economics, landscape architecture, medicine, music, ophthalmic optics, orthoptics, physical education, physiotherapy, radiography, occupational therapy, dental hygiene, dental therapy, remedial gymnastics, town and country planning and veterinary science or medicine;

(c) intended to meet additional expenditure incurred by a disabled student in respect of his attendance on a course;

(d) intended to meet additional expenditure connected with term time residential study away from the student's educational establishment;

(e) on account of the student maintaining a home at a place other than that at which he resides during his course but only to the extent that his rent or rates is not met by housing benefit;

(f) on account of any other person but only if that person is residing outside of the United Kingdom and there is no applicable amount in respect of him;

(g) intended to meet the cost of books and equipment (other than special equipment) or if not so intended an amount equal to [³£276] towards such costs;

(h) intended to meet travel expenses incurred as a result of his attendance on the course.

[²(2A) Where in pursuance of an award a student is in receipt of a grant in respect of maintenance under regulation 17(b) of the Education (Mandatory Awards) Regulations 1991, there shall be excluded from his grant income a sum equal to the amount from time to time specified in paragraph 7(4) of Schedule 2 to those Regulations, being the amount to be disregarded in respect of travel costs in the particular circumstances of his case.]

(3) A student's grant income [¹, except any amount intended for the maintenance of dependants under [²Part 3 of Schedule 2 to the Education (Mandatory Awards) Regulations 1991] or intended for an older student under Part 4 of that Schedule,] shall be apportioned—

(a) subject to paragraph (4), in a case where it is attributable to the period of study, equally between the weeks in that period;

(b) in any other case, equally between the weeks in the period in respect of which it is payable.

[¹(3A) Any amount intended for the maintenance of dependants or for an older student under the provisions referred to in paragraph (3) shall be apportioned equally over a period of 52 weeks or, if there are 53 benefit weeks (including part-weeks) in the year, 53.]

(4) In the case of a student on a sandwich course, any periods of experience within the period of study shall be excluded and the student's grant income shall be apportioned equally between the remaining weeks in that period.

AMENDMENTS

1. Income Support (General) Amendment Regulations 1988 (S.I. 1988 No. 663), reg. 24 (April 11, 1988).
2. Income Support (General) Amendment Regulations 1992 (S.I. 1992 No. 468), reg. 5 (April 6, 1992).
3. Income-related Benefits Schemes (Miscellaneous Amendments) (No. 2) Regulations 1994 (S.I. 1994 No. 1608), reg. 2 (September 1, 1994, or if the student's period of study begins between August 1 and 31, 1994, the first day of the period).
4. Income-related Benefits Schemes (Miscellaneous Amendments) (No. 3) Regulations 1992 (S.I. 1992 No. 2155), reg. 20 (October 5, 1992).

DEFINITIONS

"grant income"—see reg. 61.
"period of study"—*ibid.*
"periods of experience"—*ibid.*
"sandwich course"—*ibid.*
"student"—*ibid.*

GENERAL NOTE

A student's grant is first to be subject to the disregards listed in paras. (2) and (2A). In *CIS 91/ 1994* the claimant argued that the disregard for books in para. (2)(g) should be apportioned over 52 weeks. It would then reduce the dependants and mature student elements of her grant that were taken into account in calculating her income support during the summer vacation. But the Commissioner holds that the deduction in sub-para. (g) could only be applied to the basic maintenance grant, as this was clearly the part of the grant which contained provision for books.

Para. (2A) is necessary because the standard maintenance grant no longer contains a set amount intended for travel costs. This is confirmed by *CIS 497/1993* where the Commissioner decides that only the notional amount for travel expenses provided for in para. 7(4) of Sched. 2 to the Mandatory Awards Regulations (currently £149 for 1994/5) could be deducted from the claimant's partner's grant, not his actual, much higher, travel costs. Although para. 2(h) allowed the disregard of any sum "intended to meet travel expenses", the scheme of the Mandatory Awards Regulations made it clear that the basic grant was payable solely for maintenance. No amount was payable for travel expenses except in certain circumstances, which did not apply in this case. It was the intention of the grant-making authority, not of the student, that counted under sub-para. (h). *CIS 758/1992* similarly holds that in the case of the disregard for tuition fees under sub-para. (a), it is the intention of the provider of the payment that has to be considered. The fact that the claimant's partner spent all his grants from the Norwegian Government on tuition fees was irrelevant.

A grant is normally apportioned over the weeks of the period of study, *i.e.* from the beginning of the academic year to the day before the summer vacation (para. (3)). The elements of the grant for mature students or dependants are apportioned over 52 weeks (para. (3A)), but only while the person remains a student. *CIS 7/1988* holds that these elements of grant would ordinarily be attributable to the same period as the maintenance grant under the Education (Mandatory Awards) Regulations. *CIS 7/1988* is followed (with some reservation) in *CIS 179/1994*, where the Commissioner points out that under reg. 15(1) of the Mandatory Awards Regulations an award comes to an end on the expiry of the course. This supported the conclusion that in the final year the dependants and mature student elements were, like the ordinary maintenance grant, to be treated as payable for the period up to the day before the summer vacation. After that date the person was no longer a student and reg. 62 no longer applied.

In *CIS 33/1994* the claimant claimed income support for the summer vacation at the end of the first year of her course. Her grant included a dependants allowance and a single parent's allowance. The Commissioner decides that the single parent element had to be apportioned over 52 weeks. This was because the single parent's allowance was provided for in Sched. 4 to the Mandatory Awards Regulations. The effect of Sched. 4 was to increase in certain circumstances the amount awarded under Part III of Sched. 2 for the maintenance of dependants. Sched. 4 on its own awarded nothing. Thus the single parent's allowance was in fact merely an increase of the amount intended for the maintenance of dependants and so fell to be apportioned in accord with para. (3A). Even if this was not the case, the allowance had to be apportioned equally between the weeks in the period in respect of which it was payable (para. (3)(b)). That period was 52 weeks (see paras. 12(1) and 20 of Sched. 2 to the Mandatory Awards Regulations).

Subject to reg. 62, a student's grant will be taken into account as income under reg. 40. Thus any relevant disregards in Sched. 9 will apply (*CIS 758/1992*).

Calculation of covenant income where a contribution is assessed

63.—(1) Where a student is in receipt of income by way of a grant during a period of study and a contribution has been assessed, the amount of his covenant income to be taken into account for that period and any summer vacation immediately following shall be the whole amount of his covenant income less, subject to paragraph (3), the amount of the contribution.

(2) The weekly amount of the student's covenant income shall be determined—

  (a) by dividing the amount of income which falls to be taken into account under paragraph (1) by 52 or, if there are 53 benefit weeks (including part weeks) in the year, 53; and

  (b) by disregarding from the resulting amount, £5.

(3) For the purposes of paragraph (1), the contribution shall be treated as increased by the amount, if any, by which the amount excluded under [¹regulation 62(2)(h) (calculation of grant income) falls short of the amount for the time being specified in paragraph 7(4)(i) of Schedule 2 to the Education (Mandatory Awards) Regulations 1991 (travel expenditure).]

AMENDMENT

1. Income Support (General) Amendment Regulations 1992 (S.I. 1992 No. 468), reg. 5 (April 6, 1992).

DEFINITIONS

  "benefit week"—see reg. 2(1).
  "contribution"—see reg. 61.
  "covenant income"—*ibid.*
  "grant"—*ibid.*
  "period of study"—*ibid.*
  "standard maintenance grant"—*ibid.*
  "student"—*ibid.*

GENERAL NOTE

Although the number of covenants will drop away following the 1988 Budget, there may continue to be some existing covenants running, perhaps at inadequate levels.

If a student has a grant, with a parental contribution assessed, covenant income is only taken into account to the extent that it exceeds the assessed contribution (plus any addition under para. (3)). The definition of covenant income in reg. 61 confines it to the payment net of tax. Any excess is spread over the whole year, with a £5 per week disregard.

Covenant income where no grant income or no contribution is assessed

64.—(1) Where a student is not in receipt of income by way of a grant the amount of his covenant income shall be calculated as follows—

  (a) any sums intended for any expenditure specified in regulation 62(2)(a) to (f), (calculation of grant income) necessary as a result of his attendance on the course, shall be disregarded;

  (b) any covenant income, up to the amount of the standard maintenance grant, which is not so disregarded, shall be apportioned equally between the weeks of the period of study and there shall be disregarded from the covenant income to be so apportioned the amount which would have been disregarded under [¹regulation 62(2)(g) and (h) and (2A)] (calculation of grant income) had the student been in receipt of the standard maintenance grant;

(c) the balance, if any, shall be divided by 52 or, if there are 53 benefit weeks (including part weeks) in the year, 53 and treated as weekly income of which £5 shall be disregarded.

(2) Where a student is in receipt of income by way of a grant and no contribution has been assessed, the amount of his covenant income shall be calculated in accordance with sub-paragraphs (a) to (c) of paragraph (1), except that—

(a) the value of the standard maintenance grant shall be abated by the amount of his grant income less an amount equal to the amount of any sums disregarded under regulation 62(2)(a) to (f); and

(b) the amount to be disregarded under paragraph (1)(b) shall be abated by an amount equal to the amount of any sums disregarded under [¹regulation 62(2)(g) and (h) and (2A)].

AMENDMENT

1. Income Support (General) Amendment Regulations 1992 (S.I. 1992 No. 468), reg. 5 (April 6, 1992).

DEFINITIONS

"benefit week"—see reg. 2(1).
"contribution"—see reg. 61.
"covenant income"—*ibid.*
"grant"—*ibid.*
"grant income"—*ibid.*
"standard maintenance grant"—*ibid.*
"student"—*ibid.*

GENERAL NOTE

Paragraph (1)
If the student has no grant, first any sums earmarked for things listed in regs. 62(2)(a) to (f) are excluded. Then the amount of covenant income up to the rate of the standard maintenance grant (less the items specified above) is spread over the weeks of the period of study, disregarding items specified in regs. 62(2)(g) and (h) and (2A). Then any excess is spread over the whole year with a £5 p.w. disregard.

Paragraph (2)
If the student has a grant with no parental contribution, the effect is to spread the convenant income, after topping up any deficiency from the standard maintenance grant, over the whole year, as in para. (1).

Relationship with amounts to be disregarded under Schedule 9

65. No part of a student's convenant income or grant income shall be disregarded under paragraph 15 of Schedule 9 (charitable and voluntary payments) and any other income [¹to which sub-paragraph (1) of that paragraph applies shall be disregarded only to the extent that] the amount disregarded under regulation 63(2)(b) (calculation of convenant income where a contribution is assessed) or, as the case may be, 64(1)(c) (convenant income where no grant income or no contribution is assessed) is less than [¹£10].

AMENDMENT

1. Income Support (General) Amendment Regulations 1990 (S.I. 1990 No. 547), reg. 14 (April 9, 1990).

DEFINITIONS

"convenant income"—see reg. 61.
"grant income"—*ibid.*
"student"—*ibid.*

Other amounts to be disregarded

66.—(1) For the purposes of ascertaining income [¹other than grant income, covenant income and loans treated as income in accordance with regulation 66A], any amounts intended for any expenditure specified in regulation 62(2) (calculation of grant income) necessary as a result of his attendance on the course shall be disregarded but only if, and to the extent that, the necessary expenditure exceeds or is likely to exceed the amount of the sums disregarded under regulation 62(2) [¹and (2A)], 63(3) and 64(1)(a) or(b) (calculation of grant income and convenant income) on like expenditure.

(2) Where a claim is made in respect of any period in the normal summer vacation and any income is payable under a Deed of Convenant which commences or takes effect after the first day of that vacation, that income shall be disregarded.

AMENDMENT

1. Income-related Benefits Schemes (Miscellaneous Amendments) Regulations 1994 (S.I. 1994 No. 527), reg. 5 (April 11, 1994).

DEFINITIONS

"convenant income"—see reg. 61.
"grant income"—*ibid.*

GENERAL NOTE

Paragraph (2) will not be of any practical effect, because new covenants are unlikely to be made now that the tax advantages have been removed in the 1988 Budget.

[¹Treatment of student loans

66A.—(1) A loan which is made to a student pursuant to arrangements made under section 1 of the Education (Student Loans) Act 1990 [² or article 3 of the Education (Student Loans)(Northern Ireland) Order 1990] shall be treated as income.

(2) In calculating the weekly amount of the loan to be taken into account as income—

    (a) except where sub-paragraph (b) applies, the loan shall be apportioned equally between the weeks in the academic year in respect of which the loan is payable;

    (b) in the case of a loan which is payable in respect of the final academic year of the course or if the course is only of one academic year's duration, in respect of that year the loan shall be apportioned equally between the weeks in the period beginning with the start of the final academic year or, as the case may be, the single academic year and ending with [³the last day of the course,]

and from the weekly amount so apportioned there shall be disregarded £10.

(3) Any loan for which a student is eligible in respect of an academic year under the arrangements mentioned in paragraph (1) but which has not been acquired by him shall be treated as possessed by him and paragraphs (1) and

(2) shall apply accordingly; and for the purposes of this paragraph the loan for which a student is eligible is the maximum amount payable to him under those arrangements.]

AMENDMENTS

1. Social Security Benefits (Student Loans and Miscellaneous Amendments) Regulations 1990 (S.I. 1990 No. 1549), reg. 5(7) (September 1, 1990).
2. Income Support (General) Amendment Regulations 1991 (S.I. 1991 No. 236), reg. 9 (March 13, 1991).
3. Income Support (General) Amendment No. 4 Regulations 1991 (S.I. 1991 No. 1559), reg. 12 (August 5, 1991).

GENERAL NOTE

If a student is, exceptionally, entitled to income support the amount of the maximum student loan which he is eligible to apply for is treated as income, whether he actually receives a loan or not. The income is to be apportioned under para. (2) over the weeks covered by the loan, with a £10 disregard. See reg. 40(3A) for the position where a student ends the course prematurely.

See *CIS 758/1992* referred to in the note to "grant" in reg. 61.

Disregard of contribution

67. Where the claimant or his partner is a student and the income of one has been taken into account for the purpose of assessing a contribution to the student's grant, an amount equal to the contribution shall be disregarded for the purpose of calculating the income of the one liable to make that contribution.

DEFINITIONS

"claimant"—see reg. 2(1), reg. 23(1).
"contribution"—see reg. 61.
"grant"—*ibid.*
"partner"—see reg. 2(1).
"student"—see reg. 61.

Income treated as capital

68. Any amount by way of a refund of tax deducted from a student's income shall be treated as capital.

DEFINITION

"student"—see reg. 61.

Disregard of changes occurring during summer vacation

69. In calculating a student's income an adjudication officer shall disregard any change in the standard maintenance grant occurring in the recognised summer vacation appropriate to the student's course, if that vacation does not form part of his period of study, from the date on which the change occurred up to the end of that vacation.

DEFINITIONS

"period of study"—see reg. 61.
"standard maintenance grant"—*ibid.*
"student"—*ibid.*

PART VI

URGENT CASES

Urgent cases

70.—(1) In a case to which this regulation applies, a claimant's weekly applicable amount and his income and capital shall be calculated in accordance with the following provisions of this Part.

(2) Subject to paragraph (4), this regulation applies to—

  (a) a claimant to whom paragraph (3) (certain persons from abroad) applies;

  (b) a claimant who is treated as possessing income under regulation 42(3) (notional income);

  (c) [¹. . .].

(3) This paragraph applies to a person from abroad within the meaning of regulation 21(3) (special cases) who—

  (a) having, during any one period of limited leave of a kind referred to in sub-paragraph (a) of that definition (including any period as extended), supported himself without recourse to public funds other than any such recourse by reason of the previous application of this sub-paragraph, is temporarily without funds during that period of leave because remittances to him from abroad have been disrupted provided that there is a reasonable expectation that his supply of funds will be resumed;

[²(b) is an asylum seeker for the purposes of paragraph 3A;]

  (c) is awaiting the outcome of an appeal made under Part II of the 1971 Act (including any period for which the appeal is treated as pending under section 33(4) of that Act);

  (d) [². . .];

  (e) is a person to whom sub-paragraph (c) of that definition applies but whose removal from the United Kingdom has been deferred in writing by the Secretary of State;

  (f) is a person, other than someone to whom sub-paragraph (c) of that definition applies, who has been granted permission to remain in the United Kingdom pending the removal of a person to whom sub-paragraph (e) applies;

  (g) is a person who has no or no further right of appeal under the 1971 Act but has been allowed to remain in the United Kingdom while an application so to remain is, or representations on his behalf, are being considered by the Secretary of State;

  (h) is a person to whom sub-paragraph (d) of that definition applies and who has been allowed to remain in the United Kingdom with the consent in writing of the Secretary of State;

  (i) is a person to whom sub-paragraph (e), (f) or (g) of that definition applies and whose applicable amount, but for this sub-paragraph would if calculated in accordance with regulation 21 (special cases) be nil;

  (j) he is a person other than one to whom sub-paragraph (e) applies who is subject to a direction for his removal from the United Kingdom, but whose removal has been deferred in writing by the Secretary of State.

[²(3A) For the purposes of this paragraph, a person—

  (a) becomes an asylum seeker when he has submitted a claim for asylum to the Secretary of State that it would be contrary to the United Kingdom's obligations under the Convention for him to be removed from, or required to leave, the United Kingdom and that claim is recorded by the Secretary of State as having been made; and

(b) ceases to be an asylum seeker when his claim is recorded by the Secretary of State as having been finally determined or abandoned.

(3B) In paragraph (3A), "the Convention" means the Convention relating to the Status of Refugees done at Geneva on 28th July 1951 and the protocol to that Convention.]

(4) This regulation shall only apply to a person to whom paragraph (2)(b) [¹applies, where the income he is treated as possessing by virtue of regulation 42(3) (notional income)] is not readily available to him; and—

(a) the amount of income support which would be payable but for this Part is less than the amount of income support payable by virtue of the provisions of this Part; and

(b) the adjudication officer is satisfied that, unless the provisions of this Part are applied to the claimant, the claimant or his family will suffer hardship.

AMENDMENTS

1. Income Support (General) Amendment No. 2 Regulations 1989 (S.I. 1989 No. 1323), reg. 16 (October 9, 1989).

2. Income Support (General) Amendment No. 3 Regulations 1993 (S.I. 1993 No. 1679), reg. 2 (August 2, 1993).

DEFINITIONS

"the 1971 Act"—see reg. 21(3).
"claimant"—see reg. 2(1).
"family"—see 1986 Act, s. 20(11) (SSCBA, s.137(1)).
"partner"—see reg. 2(1).

GENERAL NOTE

Paragraphs (1) and (2)
The provision for urgent cases outside the normal scope of the income support rules is very limited. The two categories are certain persons from abroad (para. (3)) and claimants who are treated as possessing income which is due, but has not been paid. In the last case the notional income must not be readily available and the AO must be satisfied that the claimant or his family would suffer hardship if the normal income support entitlement was not brought up to the urgent cases rate (para. (4)). Applicable amounts are adjusted under reg. 71, and income and capital rules are in reg. 72.

Paragraph (3)
The first condition is that the person comes within the definition of "person from abroad" in reg. 21(3). Generally, under Sched. 7 such a person has an applicable amount of nil (para. 17). Then if the person falls into one of sub-paras. (a) to (j) there can be entitlement on the conditions of reg. 71. There is no requirement to be available for work (Sched. 1, para. 20).

The new form of para. (3), in force from August 2, 1993, deals with asylum seekers (defined in para. (3A)) and removes the entitlement to urgent cases payments of people who are applying for their leave to remain to be varied so as not to be subject to the public funds test. See reg. 2(4) of the Income Support (General) Amendment No. 3 Regulations 1993 for the continuing entitlement under the unamended reg. 70 of claimants entitled to benefit on August 2, 1993 (p.373).

The scope of para. (3) has not been extended following the insertion of an additional category of "person from abroad" in reg. 21(3) from August 1, 1994, which introduced an habitual residence test for income support. Thus claimants who are refused income support on the ground that they are not habitually resident will not be eligible for urgent cases payments unless they come within one of the other categories of "person from abroad" in reg. 21(3) who can qualify under para. (3).

An EEA national can bring himself within para. (3)(c) by applying for a residence permit under the Immigration (European Economic Area) Order 1994 (S.I. 1994 No. 1895) and then appealing any refusal (see Owen J.'s judgement on the Secretary of State's application to set aside leave to apply for judicial review in *R v. Secretary of State for the Home Department and Secretary of State for Social Security, ex parte Jager, Gallin and Urbanek*, High Court, December 15, 1994). Article 18 of the 1994 Order confirms that there is a right of appeal under s. 14 of the Immigration Act 1971. Counsel for the Secretary of State in *ex parte Jager, Gallin and Urbanek* also contended that sub-para. (g) could apply to an EEA national. But this argument failed in *R. v. Secretary of State for Social Security, ex parte Sarwar, Getachew and Urbanek* (High Court, April 11, 1995). Mr Getachew contended that as he had a right of residence under European law he could not acquire leave under the 1971 Act and so had no right of appeal under that Act. He had made representations regarding his residence status to the Home Office and therefore was entitled to an urgent cases payment under sub-para. (g). However, the Court disagreed. It held that to qualify under sub-para. (g) the claimant must require leave to remain, since otherwise he cannot be *allowed* to remain pending consideration of representations on his behalf. Mr Getachew did not require leave to remain as he had entered the U.K. as of right (see *Pieck* [1980] E.C.R. 2171).

But a U.K. national who fails the habitual residence test will not be able to bring himself within para. (3), and thus will be in a worse position than some non-U.K. nationals. It seems unlikely that this was Parliament's intention.

The only other possibility for those who are caught by the habitual residence rule is to apply for interim payments under reg. 2(1) of the Payments Regulations while their claim is determined, or their appeal heard. See the notes to reg. 2(1).

Applicable amounts in urgent cases

71.—(1) For the purposes of calculating any entitlement to income support under this Part—
- (a) except in a case to which [¹sub-paragraph (b), (c) or (d)] applies, a claimant's weekly applicable amount shall be the aggregate of—
  - (i) 90 per cent. of the amount applicable in respect of himself or, if he is a member of a couple or of a polygamous marriage, of the amount applicable in respect of both of them under paragraph 1(1), (2) or (3) of Schedule 2 or, as the case may be, the amount applicable in respect of them under regulation 18 (polygamous marriages); and where regulation 22 (reduction in applicable amounts in certain cases of actual or notional unemployment benefit disqualification) applies, the reference in this head to 90 per cent. of the amount applicable shall be construed as a reference to 90 per cent. of the relevant amount under that regulation reduced by the percentage specified in paragraph (1) or (2), as the case may be, of that regulation;
  - (ii) the amount applicable under paragraph 2 of Schedule 2 in respect of any child or young person who is a member of his family except a child or young person whose capital, if calculated in accordance with Part V in like manner as for the claimant, [¹⁰except as provided in regulation 44(1) (modifications in respect of children and young persons)], would exceed £3,000;
  - (iii) the amount, if applicable, specified in [⁵Part II or III of Schedule 2 (premiums)]; and
  - (iv) any amounts applicable under [²regulation 17(1)(e) or, as the case may be, 18(1)(f) (housing costs]; [⁴and
  - (v) the amount of the protected sum which may be applicable to him determined in accordance with Schedule 3A [⁷or, as the case may be, 3B];]
  [⁹(vi) the amount, if applicable, specified in paragraph 2A of Schedule 2;]
- (b) where the claimant is a resident in [³. . .] [⁶. . .] a residential care home or a nursing home [⁹and has a preserved right], his weekly applicable amount shall be the aggregate of—
  - (i) 90 per cent. of the amount of the allowance for personal expenses prescribed in paragraph 13(a) of Schedule 4 (applicable amounts of persons in residential care and nursing homes) [⁶. . .] or, if he is a member of a couple or of a polygamous marriage, of the amount applicable in respect of both or all of them; and where regulation 22 (reduction in applicable amounts in certain cases of actual or

notional unemployment benefit disqualification) applies, the reference in this head to 90 per cent. of the amount so reduced shall be construed as a reference to 90 per cent. of the relevant amount under that regulation reduced by the percentage specified in paragraph (1) or (2), as the case may be, of that regulation;

    (ii) the amount applicable under paragraph 13(b) to (e) of Schedule 4 [6. . .] in respect of any child or young person who is a member of his family except a child or young person whose capital, if calculated in accordance with Part V in like manner as for the claimant, [10except as provided in regulation 44(1) (modifications in respect of children and young persons)], would exceed £3,000;

    (iii) the amount in respect of the weekly charge for his accommodation calculated in accordance with regulation 19 and Schedule 4 [6. . .] except any amount in respect of a child or young person who is a member of the family and whose capital, if calculated in accordance with Part V in like manner as for the claimant, [10except as provided in regulation 44(1) (modifications in respect of children and young persons)], would exceed £3,000;

  (c) where the claimant is resident in residential accommodation, his weekly applicable amount shall be the aggregate of—

    (i) [898 per cent.] of the amount [9. . .] referred to in column (2) of paragraph 13(a) to (c) and (e) of Schedule 7 (applicable amounts in special cases) applicable to him;

    (ii) the amount applicable under column (2) of paragraph 13(d) of Schedule 7, in respect of any child or young person who is a member of his family except a child or young person whose capital, if calculated in accordance with Part V in like manner as for the claimant, [10except as provided in regulation 44(1) (modifications in respect of children and young persons)], would exceed £3,000;

    (iii) [8. . .]

[1(d) except where sub-paragraph (b) or (c) applies, in the case of a person to whom any paragraph, other than paragraph 17, in column (1) of Schedule 7 (special cases) applies, the amount shall be 90 per cent. of the amount applicable in column 2 of that Schedule in respect of the claimant and partner (if any), plus, if applicable—

    (i) any amount in respect of a child or young person who is a member of the family except a child or young person whose capital, if calculated in accordance with Part V in like manner as for the claimant, [10except as provided in regulation 44(1) (modifications in respect of children and young persons)], would exceed £3,000;

    (ii) any premium under [5Part II or III of Schedule 2]; and

  [2(iii) any amounts applicable under regulation 17(1)(e) or, as the case may be, 18(1)(f)]; [4and

    (iv) the amount of the protected sum which may be applicable to him determined in accordance with Schedule 3A [7or, as the case may be, 3B].]

(2) The period for which a claimant's weekly applicable amount is to be calculated in accordance with paragraph (1) where paragraph (3) of regulation 70 (urgent cases) applies shall be—

  (a) in a case to which sub-paragraph (a) of paragraph (3) of that regulation applies, any period, or the aggregate of any periods, not exceeding 42 days during any one period of leave to which that regulation applies;

  (b) in a case to which sub-paragraph (b) of paragraph (3) of that regulation applies—

    (i) the period ending not later than the date on which that determination is sent to the claimant; or

    (ii) if he has a right to appeal against the determination under Part II of the 1971 Act, the period ending not later than 28 days after the date on which that determination is sent to him;

(c) in a case to which sub-paragraph (c) of paragraph (3) of that regulation applies, the period ending not later than the end of the period for which that appeal is treated as pending under section 33(4) of the 1971 Act;

(d) in a case to which sub-paragraph (d) of paragraph (3) of that regulation applies, the period ending not later than—
    (i) where the application referred to in that regulation is successful, the date on which that determination is sent to the claimant; or
    (ii) where that application is refused, the date on which he is removed from the United Kingdom;

(e) in any case to which sub-paragraph (e), (f), (g), (h) or (j) of paragraph (3) of that regulation applies, the period ending not later than—
    (i) the date on which the claimant is removed from the United Kingdom; or
    (ii) where given leave (within the meaning of section 33 of the 1971 Act) to remain in the United Kingdom, or otherwise permitted in writing by the Secretary of State to remain in the United Kingdom, the date on which that leave was given;

(f) in a case to which sub-paragraph (i) of paragraph (3) of that regulation applies, the period ending not later than the date on which—
    (i) leave (within the meaning of section 33 of the 1971 Act) is granted; or
    (ii) he is removed from the United Kingdom; or
    (iii) his immigration status is determined by the Secretary of State,

[[1](3) Where the calculation of a claimant's applicable amount under this regulation results in a fraction of a penny that fraction shall be treated as a penny.]

AMENDMENTS

1. Income Support (General) Amendment Regulations 1988 (S.I. 1988 No. 663), reg. 25 (April 11, 1988).

2. Income Support (General) Amendment No. 4 Regulations 1988 (S.I. 1988 No. 1445), reg. 15 (September 12, 1988).

3. Income Support (General) Amendment No. 4 Regulations 1988 (S.I. 1988 No. 1445), Sched. 1, para. 5 (April 10, 1989).

4. Income Support (General) Amendment No. 4 Regulations 1988 (S.I. 1988 No. 1445), Sched. 1, para. 13 (April 10, 1989).

5. Family Credit and Income Support (General) Amendment Regulations 1989 (S.I. 1989 No. 1034), reg. 9 (July 10, 1989).

6. Income Support (General) Amendment Regulations 1989 (S.I. 1989 No. 534), Sched. 1, para. 8 (October 9, 1989).

7. Income Support (General) Amendment Regulations 1989 (S.I. 1989 No. 534), Sched. 1, para. 17 (October 9, 1989).

8. Social Security Benefits (Amendments Consequential Upon the Introduction of Community Care) Regulations 1992 (S.I. 1992 No. 3147), Sched. 1, para. 4 (April 1, 1993).

9. Income-related Benefits Schemes (Miscellaneous Amendments) (No. 4) Regulations 1993 (S.I. 1993 No. 2119), reg. 17 (October 4, 1993).

10. Income-related Benefits Schemes (Miscellaneous Amendments) Regulations 1994 (S.I. 1994 No. 527), reg. 6 (April 11, 1994).

DEFINITIONS

"the 1971 Act"—see reg. 21(3).
"child"—see 1986 Act, s.20(11) (SSCBA, s.137(1)).
"claimant"—see reg. 2(1).
"couple"—*ibid.*
"family"—see 1986 Act, s.20(11) (SSCBA, s.137(1)).

"nursing home"—see reg. 2(1), reg. 19(3).
"polygamous marriage"—see reg. 2(1).
"residential accommodation"—*ibid.*, reg. 21(3).
"residential care home"—*ibid.*, reg. 19(3).
"young person"—*ibid.*, reg. 14.

GENERAL NOTE

Paragraph (1)
The basic rule, with detailed variations, is that 90 per cent. of the applicable amount for the claimant and any partner is allowed, full personal allowance for children and young persons not excluded on capital grounds, (from July 1989) all premiums, and housing costs.

Paragraph (2)
Payments under reg. 70(2)(b) appear to last as long as the conditions for entitlement. But in the case of a person from abroad the length of payment is strictly limited.

Assessment of income and capital in urgent cases

72.—(1) The claimant's income shall be calculated in accordance with Part V subject to the following modifications—

[¹(a) any income, other than a payment of income [⁵or income in kind] made under the Macfarlane Trust [⁴or the Macfarlane (Special Payments) Trust][⁵, the Macfarlane (Special Payments) (No. 2) Trust][⁶, the Fund] [⁸, the Eileen Trust] or [⁷the Independent Living Funds] [²or income to which [⁵paragraph 5, 39(2), (3) or (4),] 40, [⁹ or 42] of Schedule 9 (disregard of income other than earnings) applies], possessed or treated as possessed by him shall be taken into account in full notwithstanding any provision in that Part disregarding the whole or any part of that income;]

(b) any income to which regulation 53 (calculation of tariff income from capital) applies shall be disregarded;

(c) income treated as capital by virtue of [² regulation 48(1), (2), (3) and (9)] (income treated as capital) shall be taken into account as income;

(d) in a case to which paragraph (2)(b) of regulation 70 (urgent cases) applies, any income to which regulation 42(3) (notional income) applies shall be disregarded;

(e) [³. . .].

(2) The claimant's capital calculated in accordance with Part V, but including any capital referred to in paragraphs 3 and, to the extent that such assets as are referred to in paragraph 6 consist of liquid assets, 6 [²and, except to the extent that the arrears referred to in paragraph 7 consist of arrears of housing benefit payable under Part II of the Act or Part II of the Social Security and Housing Benefits Act 1982 [SSCBA, Part VII], 7, 9(b), 19, 30 and 32 of Schedule 10] (capital to be disregarded) shall be taken into account in full and the amount of income support which would, but for this paragraph be payable under this regulation, shall be payable only to the extent that it exceeds the amount of that capital.

AMENDMENTS

1. Family Credit and Income Support (General) Amendment Regulations 1988 (S.I. 1988 No. 999), reg. 6 (June 9, 1988).

2. Income Support (General) Amendment No. 5 Regulations 1988 (S.I. 1988 No. 2022), reg. 15 (December 12, 1988).

3. Income Support (General) Amendment No. 2 Regulations 1989 (S.I. 1989 No. 1323), reg. 17 (October 9, 1989).

4. Income-related Benefits Schemes Amendment Regulations 1990 (S.I. 1990 No. 127, reg. 3 (January 31, 1990).

5. Income-related Benefits Schemes and Social Security (Recoupment) Amendment Regulations 1991 (S.I. 1991 No. 1175), reg. 5 (May 11, 1991).

6. Income-related Benefits Schemes and Social Security (Recoupment) Amendment Regulations 1992 (S.I. 1992 No. 1101), reg. 6 (May 7, 1992).

7. Social Security Benefits (Miscellaneous Amendments) (No. 2) Regulations 1993 (S.I 1993 No. 963), reg. 2(3) (April 22, 1993).

8. Income-related Benefits Schemes and Social Security (Recoupment) Amendment Regulations 1993 (S.I 1993 No. 1249), reg 4(3) (May 14, 1993).

9. Income-related Benefits Schemes (Miscellaneous Amendments) Regulations 1995 (S.I. 1995 No. 516), reg. 23 (April 10, 1995).

DEFINITIONS

"the Act"—see reg. 2(1).
"claimant"—*ibid.*
"the Eileen Trust"—*ibid.*
"the Fund"—*ibid.*
"the Independent Living Funds"—*ibid.*
"the Macfarlane (Special Payments) Trust"—*ibid.*
"the Macfarlane (Special Payments) (No. 2) Trust"—*ibid.*
"the Macfarlane Trust"—*ibid.*

GENERAL NOTE

Paragraph (1)
    This paragraph modifies the ordinary rules on income in urgent cases. All income is to be taken into account, free of any disregards, except for income from the Macfarlane Trusts (haemophiliacs), the Fund, the Eileen Trust or the Independent Living Funds, all forms of housing benefit and the notional income which causes the problem in cases under reg. 70(2)(b). The tariff income from capital under reg. 53 is disregarded, but that is of little consequence given para. (2). Under sub-para. (c) several items of income normally treated as capital retain their status as income.

Paragraph (2)
    The calculation of capital is much as normal. Categories normally disregarded which count for urgent cases purposes are the proceeds of sale of a former home, liquid assets of a business, arrears of certain benefits, certain sums deposited with Housing Associations, refunds of MIRAS tax, training bonuses under £200 and payments to compensate for loss of transitional protection. Once the capital has been calculated a payment for urgent cases is only to be made in so far as it exceeds the amount of capital. There is no £8,000, £3,000, £500 or £1 exemption.

[¹PART VII

CALCULATIONS OF INCOME SUPPORT FOR PART-WEEKS

Amount of income support payable

73.—(1) Subject to regulations 75 (modifications in income) and 76 (reduction in certain cases), where a claimant is entitled to income support for a period (referred to in this Part as a part-week) to which subsection (1A) of section 21 of the Act [SSCBA, s.124(5)] (amount etc. of income-related benefit) applies, the amount of income support payable shall, except where paragraph (2) applies, be calculated in accordance with the following formulae—

(a) if the claimant has no income, $\dfrac{N \times A}{7}$;

(b) if the claimant has income, $\dfrac{N \times (A - I)}{7} - B.$

(2) Subject to regulations 75 and 76, in the case of a claimant to whom regulation 19 [³. . .] (persons in residential care or nursing homes [³. . .]) applies, where the weekly charge for the accommodation is due to be paid during a part-week to which regulation 74(1)(*a*) or (*b*) applies, the amount of income support payable shall be calculated in accordance with the following formulae—

(a) if the claimant has no income, A;

(b) if the claimant has income, $(A - I) - B$.

(3) In this Regulation—

"A", subject to paragraph (4), means the claimant's weekly applicable amount in the relevant week;

"B" means the amount of any income support, unemployment benefit, [² maternity allowance,] [⁴short-term or long-term incapacity benefit], or severe disablement allowance payable in respect of any day in the part-week;

"I" means his weekly income in the relevant week less B;

"N" means the number of days in the part-week;

"relevant week" means the period of 7 days determined in accordance with regulation 74.

(4) In a case to which paragraph (2) applies, a claimant's weekly applicable amount shall be—

(a) where the weekly charge for the accommodation includes all meals, the aggregate of the following amounts—

(i) the weekly charge for the accommodation determined in accordance with paragraph 1(1)(a) of Schedule 4 [³. . .]; and

(ii) the amount calculated in accordance with the formula—

$$\frac{(N \times P)}{7} + \frac{(N \times H)}{7};$$

(b) where the weekly charge for the accommodation does not include all meals, the aggregate of the following amounts—

(i) the weekly charge for the accommodation determined in accordance with paragraph 1(1)(a) of Schedule 4 [³. . .] less M; and

(ii) The amount calculated in accordance with the formula—

$$\frac{(N \times M)}{7} + \frac{(N \times P)}{7} + \frac{(N \times H)}{7}.$$

(5) In paragraph (4)—

"H" means the weekly amount determined in accordance with paragraph 1(1)(c) of Schedule 4[³. . .];

"M" means the amount of the increase for meals calculated on a weekly basis in accordance with paragraph 2 of Schedule 4 [³. . .];

"P" means the weekly amount for personal expenses determined in accordance with paragraph 13 of Schedule 4 [³. . .].]

AMENDMENTS

1. Income Support (General) Amendment Regulations 1988 (S.I. 1988 No. 663), reg. 27 (April 11, 1988).

2. Income Support (General) Amendment No. 4 Regulations 1988 (S.I. 1988 No. 1445), reg. 17 (September 12, 1988).

3. Income Support (General) Amendment Regulations 1989 (S.I. 1988 No. 534), Sched. 1, para. 9 (October 9, 1989).

4. Disability Working Allowance and Income Support (General) Amendment Regulations 1995 (S.I. 1995 No. 482), reg. 12 (April 13, 1995).

DEFINITIONS

"the Act"—see reg. 2(1).
"claimant"—*ibid.*

Although the rules set out in regs. 73 to 77 do look very complex, they set out a relatively straightforward method of calculating benefit for part-weeks.

['Relevant week

74.—(1) Where the part-week—
   (a) is the whole period for which income support is payable or occurs at the beginning of the claim, the relevant week is the period of 7 days ending on the last day of that part-week; or
   (b) occurs at the end of the claim, the relevant week is the period of 7 days beginning on the first day of that part-week.

(2) Where during the currency of a claim the claimant makes a claim for a relevant social security benefit within the meaning of paragraph 4 of Schedule 7 to the Social Security (Claims and Payments) Regulations 1987 and as a result his benefit week changes, for the purpose of calculating the amount of income support payable—
   (a) for the part-week beginning on the day after his last complete benefit week before the date from which he makes a claim for the relevant social security benefit and ending immediately before that date, the relevant week is the period of 7 days beginning on the day after his last complete benefit week (the first relevant week);
   (b) for the part-week beginning on the date from which he makes a claim for the relevant social security benefit and ending immediately before the start of his next benefit week after the date of that claim, the relevant week is the period of 7 days ending immediately before the start of his next benefit week (the second relevant week).

(3) Where during the currency of a claim the claimant's benefit week changes at the direction of the Secretary of State under paragraph 3 of Schedule 7 to the Social Security (Claims and Payments) Regulations 1987, for the purpose of calculating the amount of income support payable for the part-week beginning on the day after his last complete benefit week before the change and ending immediately before the change, the relevant week is the period of 7 days beginning on the day after the last complete benefit week.]

1. Income Support (General) Amendment Regulations 1988 (S.I. 1988 No. 663), reg. 27 (April 11, 1988).

"benefit week"—see reg. 2(1).
"claimant"—*ibid.*

['Modifications in the calculation of income

75.—For the purposes of regulation 73 (amount of income support payable for part-weeks), a claimant's income and the income of any person which the claimant is treated as possessing under section 22(5) of the Act [SSCBA, s.136(1)] or regulation 23(3) shall be calculated in accordance with Part V and, where applicable, VI subject to the following modifications—
   (a) any income which is due to be paid in the relevant week shall be treated as paid on the first day of that week;
   (b) any income support, unemployment benefit, [²maternity allowance,] [³short-term or long-term incapacity benefit], or severe disablement

allowance [³. . .]payable in the relevant week but not in respect of any day in the part-week shall be disregarded;

(c) where the part-week occurs at the end of the claim, any income or any change in the amount of income of the same kind which is first payable within the relevant week but not on any day in the part-week shall be disregarded;

(d) where the part-week occurs immediately after a period in which a person was treated as engaged in remunerative work) under regulation 5(5) (persons treated as engaged in remunerative work) any earnings which are taken into account for the purposes of determining that period shall be disregarded;

(e) where regulation 74(2) (relevant week) applies, any payment of income which—
  (i) is the final payment in a series of payments of the same kind or, if there has been an interruption in such payments, the last one before the interruption;
  (ii) is payable in respect of a period not exceeding a week; and
  (iii) is due to be paid on a day which falls within both the first and second relevant weeks,

shall be taken into account in either the first relevant week or, if it is impracticable to take it into account in that week, in the second relevant week; but this paragraph shall not apply to a payment of income support, unemployment benefit, [²maternity allowance,] [³short-term or long-term incapacity benefit] or severe disablement allowance [³. . .];

(f) where regulation 74(2) applies, any payment of income which—
  (i) is the final payment in a series of payments of the same kind or, if there has been an interruption in such payments, the last one before the interruption;
  (ii) is payable in respect of a period exceeding a week but not exceeding 2 weeks; and
  (iii) is due to be paid on a day which falls within both the first and second relevant weeks,

shall be disregarded; but this sub-paragraph shall not apply to a payment of income support, unemployment benefit, [²maternity allowance,] [³short-term or long term incapacity benefit], or severe disablement allowance, [³. . .]

(g) where regulation 74(2) applies, if the weekly amount of any income which is due to be paid on a day which falls within both the first and second relevant weeks is more than the weekly amount of income of the same kind due to be paid in the last complete benefit week, the excess shall be disregarded;

(h) where only part of the weekly amount of income is taken into account in the relevant week, the balance shall be disregarded.]

AMENDMENTS

1. Income Support (General) Amendment Regulations 1988 (S.I. 1988 No. 663), reg. 27 (April 11, 1988).
2. Income Support (General) Amendment No. 4 Regulations 1988 (S.I. 1988 No. 1445), reg. 17 (September 12, 1988).
3. Disability Working Allowance and Income Support (General) Amendment Regulations 1995 (S.I. 1995 No. 482), reg. 13 (April 13, 1995).

DEFINITIONS

"claimant"—see reg. 2(1).
"Social Security Act"—*ibid.*

[¹Reduction in certain cases

76.—There shall be deducted from the amount of income support which would, but for this regulation, be payable for a part-week—

    (a) in the case of a claimant to whom regulation 22(1) or (2) (reductions in weekly applicable amounts in certain cases of unemployment benefit disqualification) applies, the proportion of the relevant amount specified therein appropriate to the number of days in the part-week;

    (b) where regulation 75(f) (modifications in the calculation of income) applies, one-half of the amount disregarded under regulation 75(f) less the weekly amount of any disregard under Schedule 8 or 9 appropriate to that payment.]

AMENDMENT

1. Income Support (General) Amendment Regulations 1988 (S.I. 1988 No. 663), reg. 27 (April 11, 1988).

DEFINITION

"claimant"—see reg. 2(1).

[¹Modification of section 23(5) of the Act [SSCBA, s.126(5)]

77.—Where income support is payable for a part-week, section 23(5) of the Act [SSCBA, s.126(5)] (trade disputes) shall have effect as if the following paragraph were substituted for paragraph (b)—

    "(b) any payment by way of income support for a part-week which apart from this paragraph would be made to him, or to a person whose applicable amount if aggregated with his—

        (i) shall not be made if the payment for the part-week is equal to or less than the proportion of the relevant sum appropriate to the number of days in the part-week; or

        (ii) if it is more than that proportion, shall be made at a rate equal to the difference."]

AMENDMENT

1. Income Support (General) Amendment Regulations 1988 (S.I. 1988 No. 663), reg. 27 (April 11, 1988).

DEFINITION

"the Act"—see reg. 2(1)

SCHEDULES

SCHEDULE 1   **Regulation 8**

PERSONS NOT REQUIRED TO BE AVAILABLE FOR EMPLOYMENT

Lone parents

1. A person who is a lone parent and responsible for a child who is a member of his household.

Single persons looking after foster children

2. A single claimant or a lone parent with whom a child [¹¹is placed] by a local authority or voluntary organisation within the meaning of the [¹¹Children Act 1989] or, in Scotland, the Social Work (Scotland) Act 1968.

Persons temporarily looking after children

3. A person who is—
(a) looking after a child because the parent of that child or the person who usually looks after him is ill or is temporarily absent from his home; or
(b) looking after a member of the family who is temporarily ill.

Persons caring for another person

[⁹**4.**—(1) A person (the carer)—
(a) who is regularly and substantially engaged in caring for another person if—
   (i) the person being cared for is in receipt of attendance allowance under section 35 of the Social Security Act [SSCBA, s.64] [¹⁰or the care component of disability living allowance at the highest or middle rate prescribed in accordance with section 37ZB(3) of the Social Security Act] [SSCBA, s.72(3)]; or
   (ii) the person being cared for has claimed attendance allowance under that section but only for the period up to the date of determination of the claim, or the period of 26 weeks from the date of that claim, whichever date is the earlier; or
   [¹⁰(iii) the person being cared for has claimed entitlement to a disability living allowance but only for the period up to the date of determination of that claim, or the period of 26 weeks from the date of that claim, whichever date is the earlier; or]
(b) who is engaged in caring for another person and who is in receipt of an invalid care allowance under section 37 of the Social Security Act [SSCBA, s.70].
(2) If paragraph (1) ceases to apply to the carer, he shall not be required to be available for employment for a period of eight weeks from the date upon which that paragraph ceased to apply to him.
4A. A person who, had he previously made a claim for income support, would not have been required to be available for employment by reason of sub-paragraph (1) of paragraph 4 for a period of 8 weeks from the date upon which that sub-paragraph would have ceased to apply to him.]

Persons incapable of work

[¹² **5.** A person who—
(a) is incapable of work in accordance with the provisions of Part XIIA of the Contributions and Benefits Act and the regulations made thereunder (incapacity for work); or
(b) is treated as capable of work by virtue of regulations made under section 171E(1) of that Act (disqualification etc); or
(c) is entitled to statutory sick pay.]

Disabled workers

[⁹**6.** A person to whom regulation 6(a) (persons not treated as engaged in remunerative work) applies.

Persons in employment living in residential care homes, nursing homes or residential accommodation

6A. A person to whom regulation 6(g) applies.]

Disabled students

[⁶[¹³ **7.** A person who is a student and—
- (a) whose applicable amount includes the disability premium or severe disability premium; or
- (b) who has satisfied the provisions of paragraph 5 for a continuous period of not less than 196 days, and for this purpose any two or more separate periods separated by a break of not more than 56 days shall be treated as one continuous period.]

7A .—(1) A person who is a student who—
- (a) immediately before 1st September 1990 was in receipt of income support by virtue of paragraph 7 as then in force; or
- (b) on or after that date makes a claim for income support and at a time during the period of 18 months immediately preceding the date of that claim was in receipt of support either by virtue of that paragraph or regulation 13(2)(b),

but this paragraph shall cease to apply where the person has ceased to be in receipt of income support for a continuous period of 18 months or more.]

[⁷**7B.**—(1) A person who is a student in respect of whom—
- (a) a supplementary requirement has been determined under paragraph 15 of Schedule 2 to the Education (Mandatory Awards) Regulations 1987 or the Education (Mandatory Awards) Regulations 1988, paragraph 12 of Schedule 2 to the Education (Mandatory Awards) Regulations 1989 or paragraph 12 of Schedule 2 to the Education (Mandatory Awards) Regulations 1990; or
- (b) an allowance or, as the case may be, bursary has been granted which includes a sum under paragraph (1)(d) of regulation 6 of the Students' Allowances (Scotland) Regulations 1987 or, as the case may be, the Education Authority Bursaries (Scotland) Regulations 1988 in respect of expenses incurred; or
- (c) a payment has been made under section 2 of the Education Act 1962; [⁸or
- (d) a supplementary requirement has been determined under paragraph 15 of Schedule 7 to the Students Awards Regulations (Northern Ireland) 1987, paragraph 15 of Schedule 7 to the Students Awards Regulations (Northern Ireland) 1988, paragraph 12 of Schedule 7 to the Students Awards Regulations (Northern Ireland) 1990 or paragraph 12 of Schedule 7 to the Students Awards (No.2) Regulations (Northern Ireland) 1990 or a payment has been made under article 50(3) of the Education and Libraries (Northern Ireland) Order 1986;]

on account of his disability by reason of deafness.

(2) A student to whom sub-paragraph (1) applies shall be treated as satisfying that sub-paragraph from the date on which he made a request for the supplementary requirement, allowance, bursary or payment, as the case may be, or 1st September 1990, whichever is later.]

Blind persons

8. A person who is a blind person registered in a register compiled by a local authority under section 29 of the National Assistance Act 1948 (welfare services) or, in Scotland, who has been certified as blind in a register maintained by or on behalf of a regional or islands council, but a person who has ceased to be so registered on regaining his eyesight shall nevertheless be treated as so registered for a period of 28 weeks following the date on which he ceased to be so registered.

Pregnancy

9. A woman who—

(a) is incapable of work by reason of pregnancy; or

(b) is or has been pregnant but only for the period commencing 11 weeks before her expected week of confinement and ending seven weeks after the date on which her pregnancy ends.

Persons in education

10. A person to whom any provision of regulation 13(2)(a) to (e) (persons receiving relevant education who are parents, persons severely handicapped, orphans and persons estranged from their parents or guardian) applies.

Training allowances

11. A person who is in receipt of a training allowance.

Open University students

12. A person who is following an Open University course and is attending, as a requirement of that course, a residential course.

Persons within 10 years of pensionable age

13. A person ['aged not less than 50 who]—

(a) has not been in remunerative work during the previous 10 years; and

(b) has no prospect of future employment in remunerative work; and

(c) during that period has not been required to be available for employment in accord-ance with section 20(3)(d)(i) of the Act [SSCBA, s.124(3)(d)(i)] (conditions of entitlement to income support), or would not have been so required had a claim to income support been made by or in respect of him.

Persons aged 60

14. A person aged not less than 60.

Allowances under the Job Release Act 1977

15. [3. . .]

Refugees

16. [6. . .] A person who is a refugee within the definition in Article 1 of the Convention relating to the Status of Refugees done at Geneva on 28th July 1951 as extended by Article 1(2) of the Protocol relating to the Status of Refugees done at New York on 31st January 1967 and who—

(a) is attending for more than 15 hours a week a course for the purpose of learning English so that he may obtain employment; and

(b) on the date on which that course commenced, had been in Great Britain for not more than 12 months.

but only for a period not exceeding nine months.

Persons required to attend court

17. A person who is required to attend court [9. . .] as a justice of the peace, a party to any proceedings, a witness or a juror.

Discharged prisoners

18. A person who has been discharged from detention in a prison, remand centre or youth custody institution but only for the period of seven days commencing with the date of his discharge.

Persons affected by a trade dispute

19. A person to whom section 23 of the Act [SSCBA, s.126] (trade disputes) applies or in respect of whom section 20(3) of the Act [SSCBA, s.124(1)] (conditions of entitlement to income support) has effect as modified by [¹section 23A(b) of the Act [SSCBA, s.127(b)] (effect of return to work).]

Persons from abroad

20. A person to whom regulation 70(3) (applicable amount of certain persons from abroad) applies.

Persons in custody

21. A person remanded in, or committed in, custody for trial or for sentencing.

[²Member of couple looking after children while other member temporarily abroad

22. A person who is a member of a couple and who is treated as responsible for a child who is a member of his household where the other member of that couple is temporarily [⁴not present in the United Kingdom].]

[⁵Persons taking a child or young person abroad for treatment

23. A person who is temporarily absent from Great Britain in the circumstances specified in regulation 4(3) (temporary absence abroad for the treatment of the child or young person).]

AMENDMENTS

1. Income Support (General) Amendment Regulation 1988 (S.I. 1988 No. 663), reg. 28 (April 11, 1988).
2. Income Support (General) Amendment No. 3 Regulations (S.I. 1988 No. 1228), reg. 7 (September 12, 1988).
3. Income Support (General) Amendment No. 4 Regulations 1988 (S.I. 1988 No. 1445), reg. 18 (April 10, 1989).
4. Income Support (General) Amendment No. 5 Regulations 1988 (S.I. 1988 No. 2022), reg. 16 (April 10, 1989).
5. Income Support (General) Amendment Regulations 1990 (S.I. 1990 No. 547), reg. 15 (April 9, 1990).
6. Social Security Benefits (Student Loans and Miscellaneous Amendments) Regulations 1990 (S.I. 1990 No. 1549), reg. 5(8) (September 1, 1990).
7. Income-related Benefits Amendment Regulations 1990 (S.I. 1990 No. 1657), reg. 5(3) (September 1, 1990).
8. Income Support (General) Amendment Regulations 1991 (S.I. 1991 No. 236), reg. 10 (March 13, 1991).
9. Income Support (General) Amendment No. 4 Regulations 1991 (S.I. 1991 No. 1559), reg. 13 (October 7, 1991).
10. Disability Living Allowance and Disability Working Allowance (Consequential Provisions) Regulations 1991 (S.I. 1991 No. 2742), reg. 11(3) (April 6, 1992).
11. Income Support (General) Amendment Regulations 1992 (S.I. 1992 No. 468), Sched., para. 6 (April 6, 1992).

12. Disability Working Allowance and Income Support (General) Amendment Regulations 1995 (S.I. 1995 No. 482), reg. 14 (April 13, 1995).

13. Disability Working Allowance and Income Support (General) Amendment Regulations 1995 (S.I. 1995 No. 482), reg. 15 (April 13, 1995).

DEFINITIONS

"the Act"—see reg. 2(1).
"child"—see 1986 Act, s.20(11) (SSCBA, s.137(1)).
"disability living allowance"—see reg. 2(1).
"lone parent"—*ibid.*
"single claimant"—*ibid.*
"Social Security Act"—*ibid.*
"student"—*ibid.*, reg. 61.
"training allowance"—see reg. 2(1).

GENERAL NOTE

Sched. 1 provides an exhaustive list of the circumstances in which a person is not required to be available for employment. There is no category of analogous circumstances as there was in reg. 6 of the Supplementary Benefit (Conditions of Entitlement) Regulations. But reg. 8(3) does allow a reduced rate of benefit to be paid to someone who is not available for work and does not fall into any of the categories specified in Sched. 1 to avoid hardship. *CIS 137/1992* holds that a SSAT should consider whether reg. 8(3) applies if Sched. 1 does not. If one of the categories applies for any part of a week, para. 25431 of the *Adjudication Officers' Guide* says that there is exemption for the whole week.

Paragraph 1
See reg. 16 for membership of the household. Once a child turns into a young person (reg. 14) or ceases to be a member of the family (Contributions and Benefits Act, s.137(1), 1986 Act, s.20(11)) a lone parent ceases to fall under para. 1.

Paragraph 2
Special provision is necessary for foster-children because they are not members of the foster-parent's household (reg. 16(4)).

Paragraphs 4 and 4A
There is no requirement that alternative arrangements cannot be made. Under para. 4(1)(a) the fact of being substantially and regularly engaged in providing care for someone in receipt of attendance allowance or one of the two higher care components of disability living allowance (or waiting for a decision on entitlement) is enough. For invalid care allowance purposes "substantial" is 35 hours a week. Under para. 4(1)(b) anyone in receipt of invalid care allowance does not have to be available for work.

The effect of para. 4(2) and 4A is that a carer does not have to be available for work in the eight weeks after ceasing to meet the conditions of para. 4(1).

Paragraph 5
The latest form of para. 5 is a consequence of the changes associated with the introduction of incapacity benefit (which replaces sickness and invalidity benefit from April 13, 1995) and the new tests for deciding incapacity for work. This book does not cover incapacity benefit or the new tests, but only deals with the consequences for income support (and disability working allowance) of their introduction. For the details see *Bonner, Non-Means-Tested Benefits: the Legislation*, 1995 edition. The framework for deciding whether a person is capable or incapable of work is now contained in Part XIIA of the Contributions and Benefits Act (s. 171A-G), inserted by s. 5 of the Social Security (Incapacity for Work) Act 1994, and s. 61A of the Administraton Act, inserted by s. 6(2) of the 1994 Act. As usual, the detail is in regulations. The rules for the new incapacity tests are in the Social Security (Incapacity for Work) (General) Regulations 1995 (S.I. 1995 No. 311). Note also regs. 19 to 21 which deal with adjudication. Reg. 19 provides that a decision on a person's capacity for work in connection with a claim for one benefit is conclusive for the purposes of all other benefits; reg. 20 that if a question of incapacity arises on a claim for any benefit, this is to be decided by an AO, even if other questions are decided by another authority (this will mean AOs and SSATs deciding incapacity questions that arise, for example, in connection with a disability premium on a

housing benefit claim); and reg. 21 that a SSAT must sit with a medical assessor in any case that involves consideration of whether the claimant satisfies the "all work test" (see the notes to s.61A(4) of the Administration Act).

First, a person who is incapable of work in accordance with the new rules is exempt from availability (sub-para. (a)). There are two tests for assessing whether a person is incapable of work. The following is only a brief summary; see *Bonner* for the details. For most people the "own occupation test" will apply for the first 28 weeks of incapacity; during this time the claimant must supply medical evidence to show that he is unable to work in his "own occupation". While this test applies a claimant is likely to satisfy sub-para. (a) if he sends in medical certificates, unless an AO decides that he is capable of work in his "own occupation". If the "own occupation test" does not apply (e.g. because the claimant has been unemployed for 13 or more weeks in the 21 weeks before the incapacity for work began), or after 28 weeks, the "all work test" applies. Claimants can be treated as incapable of work until they are assessed under this test, in which case they must submit, or continue to submit, medical evidence. Under the all work test a person's capacity for work is decided by measuring his ability to perform specified activities. If the person's disabilities result in him scoring the required number of points he will pass the all work test, and medical evidence will no longer be required. Non-medical considerations, such as age, education, previous work experience and other personal factors are no longer relevant, nor is the person's ability to undertake actual jobs. Some claimants are exempt from the test; a few are treated as incapable of work even if they fail the all work test. A person in hospital counts as incapable of work. If a person does any work (subject to certain exceptions) he is treated as capable of work on each day of that week (but only on the actual days worked if it is the first or last week of the claim), even if he has passed the all work test or is exempt; in addition, the rules on therapeutic work are more restrictive. There are also rules for treating a person as capable of work if he fails without good cause either to return the all work test questionnaire within the time limit, or to attend a medical examination of which at least seven days' written notice has been given.

Note that there is transitional protection for some existing claimants entitled to invalidity benefit, severe disablement allowance, or income support, housing benefit or council tax benefit with a disability premium, on April 12, 1995, provided they continue to submit medical evidence.

A claimant who is entitled to statutory sick pay is also exempt from availability (sub-para. (c)); so is a person who is treated as capable of work under reg. 18 of the Social Security (Incapacity for Work) (General) Regulations, made under s. 171E(1) of the Contributions and Benefits Act (sub-para. (b)). Reg. 18 provides that a person may be treated as capable of work for a period of up to six weeks if he has become incapable of work through his own misconduct (see *R(S) 2/53*), failed without good cause to have treatment (other than vaccination, inoculation or major surgery), or without good cause either behaved in a way that will retard his recovery or been absent from home without stating where he has gone.

See the notes to para. 5 in the 1994 edition for decisions on the previous forms of para. 5. *R(IS) 8/93*, followed in *CIS 714/1991*, decides that the 1989 form of para. 5 could be satisfied by the provision of retrospective medical statements. This should continue to be the case under this form. (See reg. 28 of the Social Security (Incapacity for Work) (General) Regulations 1995 under which the all work test can be treated as satisfied (subject to certain conditions, including the provision of medical evidence) until a person has been assessed under it.) For the form of para. 5 in force from March 31, 1994 to April 12, 1995 see the 1994 edition. Reg. 5 of the Social Security (Incapacity Benefit) (Transitional) Regulations 1995 (S.I. 1995 No. 310) allows for late claims for sickness or invalidity benefit to be made for a period before April 13, 1995.

See the notes to reg. 17(4) of the Claims and Payments Regulations for discussion of an AO's power to review an income support award when a claimant has been found no longer incapable of work.

If para. 5 does not apply, an adjudicating authority should go on to consider para. 6. However, even if para. 6 applies, para. 5 should always be considered as this may be the only route to enable the claimant to qualify for a disability premium under para. 12(1)(b) of Sched. 2, or a £15 earnings disregard under para. 4 of Sched. 8 (*CIS 137/1992*).

Paragraph 6

The text of para. 6, in both its pre and post-October 1991 form, applies to a "person", although the heading is "Disabled workers." The Commissioner in *CSIS 89/1990* convincingly shows that the heading is not relevant to the interpretation of the provision itself, being the equivalent of a marginal or side-note in a statute. Even if the heading were to be relevant, the words of para. 6 were plain, so that it applied to a person who was not a worker. The claimant in *CSIS 89/1990* had not been economically active for some years, but this did not prevent the application of para. 6.

The post-October 1991 form of para. 6, instead of setting out its conditions directly, refers on to reg. 6(a), which was also amended from October 1991. Before October 1991 the test under reg. 6(a) was a disabled person's reduced earning *capacity*. The post-October 1991 form of reg. 6(a), by comparing the claimant's earnings or hours of work with those of a non-disabled person, seems to require that the claimant is actually working. But what if the claimant's hours of work are nil? Reg. 6(a) itself would not be needed in such circumstances, but if a person satisfies its conditions (*i.e.*, he is not incapable of work but his earnings or hours of work are less because of his mental or physical disability) could he not come within para. 6? The new form of para. 6 still refers to a "person", not a "worker" and thus does not actually require that a person is economically active.

Paragraph 7

The definition of a disabled student was narrowed in September 1990, so that qualification for one of the disability premiums became the test, rather than reduction in earning capacity. The previous test was perhaps not very appropriate, but this test was strict. See para. 7A for transitional protection and para. 7B for deaf students.

But from April 13, 1995 the definition has been expanded to also include a student who has satisfied para. 5 for 28 weeks. Two or more periods, separated by not more than 8 weeks, count as continuous.

Paragraph 7A

This transitional provision protects disabled students in receipt of income support immediately before September 1, 1990, who no longer fell under para. 7. See *CIS 276/1989* on the old form of para. 7, holding that in asking whether the student was unlikely to obtain employment within a reasonable period of time, the period started with the date of claim, not with the end of the course.

Paragraph 7B

Students who are within the definition of "deaf" for one of the various grant purposes are not required to be available. They were unlikely to fall within the September 1990 form of para. 7.

Paragraph 8

Only those registered blind with the local authority can use this paragraph and the 28 weeks period of grace on regaining sight. But other categories may be available for the unregistered.

Paragraph 10

Although reg. 13 as a whole applies to persons in relevant education, none of the conditions in para. (2) refer to relevant education. However, para. (2) applies to "young persons," and for a 16 to 18-year old to be within that definition s/he must be treated as a child for child benefit purposes, *i.e.* be in relevant education.

Paragraph 13

The crucial age for both men and women is now 50, in place of the discriminatory use of 10 years before pensionable age in this context. This is a desirable move, although the European Court of Justice's decision in *Jackson and Cresswell v. Chief Adjudication Officer* [1993] 3 All E.R. 265 is that income support does not fall within the scope of EC Directive 79/7 on the progressive implementation of the principle of equal treatment for men and women in matters of social security. See the notes to reg. 36.

In *R(SB) 5/87* it was suggested that to have no prospect of future employment, a person has to have no realistic prospects of securing employment in his working life. It is not necessary to show that the person's prospects are nil, but the test is still strict and merely poor prospects will not do. The shift to the crucial age of 50 also means that the person must not have worked and must have been exempted from the requirement to be available since the age of 40.

Paragraph 18

A person has not been "discharged" while on a period of temporary release, since he is only "discharged" at the end of his sentence (*Chief Adjudication Officer v. Carr, The Times*, June 2, 1994).

Paragraph 21

A person required to live in a bail hostel is not "detained in custody" (*R(IS) 17/93*; note the effect of Sched. 7, para. 9, if a person in a bail hostel is a member of a couple). However, once a person has been charged, he is detained in custody pending trial, even if subsequently no trial takes place (*CIS 255/1990*, to be reported as (*R(IS) 1/94*). See the notes to "prisoner" in reg. 21(3). The definition of prisoner was amended from April 10, 1995 to reverse the effect of *Chief Adjudication Officer v. Carr* which held that a person serving a prison sentence was not "in custody" while on home leave.

Paragraph 22
   Someone in this situation could not come within para. 1 because they would not be a lone parent while the absence of the partner was only temporary, but clearly equally deserves exemption from availability.

Paragraph 23
   There is particularly generous treatment for people accompanying children abroad for medical treatment.

[¹SCHEDULE 1A   Regulation 13A

CIRCUMSTANCES IN WHICH A PERSON AGED 16 OR 17 IS ELIGIBLE FOR INCOME SUPPORT

PART I

Persons Eligible until 18

1. A person who is not required to be available for employment under any of the following paragraphs of Schedule 1 (persons not required to be available for employment)—

paragraph 1	(lone parents
paragraph 2	(single persons looking after foster children)
paragraph 3	(persons temporaily looking after another person)
paragraph 4	(persons caring for another person)
[¹paragraph 7	(disabled students)
paragraph 7A	
paragraph 7B]	
paragraph 8	(blind persons)
paragraph 9	(pregnancy)
paragraph 10	(persons in education)
paragraph 11	(training allowances)
paragraph 16	(refugees)
paragraph 20	(persons from abroad)
paragraph 22	(member of couple looking after children while other member temporarily abroad)
[³paragraph 23	(persons taking a child or young person abroad for treatment).]

2. A person who is incapable of work and training under the youth training scheme, by reason of some disease or bodily or mental disablement if, in the opinion of a medical practitioner, that incapacity is unlikely to end within 12 months because of the severity of that disease or disablement.

3. A person who is a member of a couple and is treated as responsible for a child who is a member of his household.

4. A person who is temporarily laid off employment and is available to be re-engaged in that employment.

PART II

Persons Eligible until the Relevant Date Determined under Regulation 13A(3)(b)

5. A registered person who is a member of a married couple where the other member of that couple is aged not less than 18 or is a registered person or a person to whom Part I of this Schedule applies.

6. A registered person who has no parent nor any person acting in the place of his parents.

7. A registered person who—

(a) is not living with his parents nor any person acting in the place of his parents; and

(b) [⁶was being looked after by a local authority pursuant to a relevant enactment who placed him with some person other than a close relative of his], or was in custody in any institution to which the Prison Act 1952 applied or under the Criminal Procedure (Scotland) Act 1975 immediately before he attained the age of 16.

8. A registered person who is in accommodation which is other than his parental home, [⁴and which is other than the home] of a person acting in the place of his parents, who entered that accommodation—

(a) as part of a programme of rehabilitation or resettlement, that programme being under the supervision of the probation service or a local authority; or

(b) in order to avoid physical or sexual abuse; or

(c) because of a mental or physical handicap or illness and needs such accommodation because of his handicap or illness.

9. A registered person who is living away from his parents and any person who is acting in the place of his parents in a case where his parents are or, as the case may be, that person is, unable financially to support him and his parents are, or that person is—

(a) chronically sick or mentally or physically disabled; or

(b) detained in custody pending trial or sentence upon conviction or under a sentence imposed by a court; or

(c) prohibited from entering or re-entering Great Britain.

[²**9A.** A registered person who of necessity has to live away from his parents [⁴and any person] acting in the place of his parents because—

(a) he is estranged from [⁴his parents and that person]; or

(b) he is in physical or moral danger; or

(c) there is a serious risk to his physical or mental health.]

10. In this Schedule—

[⁶(a) any reference to a person acting in place of a registered person's parents includes a reference—

(i) except in a case to which head (ii) applies, to any person with parental responsibility for the child, and for this purpose "parental responsibility" bears the meaning it has in the Children Act 1989 by virtue of section 3 of that Act; or

(ii) where the person is being looked after by a local authority or voluntary organisation who place him with a family, a relative of his, or some other suitable person, the person with whom the person is placed, whether or not any payment is made to him in connection with the placement; and]

(b) "chronically sick or mentally or physically disabled" has the same meaning as in regulation 13(3)(b) (circumstances in which persons in relevant education are to be entitled to income support.]

AMENDMENTS

1. Income Support (General) Amendment No. 3 Regulations 1988 (S.I. 1988 No. 1228). reg. 8 (September 12, 1988).

2. Family Credit and Income Support (General) Amendment Regulations 1989 (S.I. 1989 No. 1034), reg. 10 (July 10, 1989).

3. Income Support (General) Amendment Regulations 1990 (S.I. 1990 No. 547), reg. 16 (April 9. 1990).

4. Income Support (General) Amendment Regulations 1991 (S.I. 1991 No. 236), reg. 11 (April 8, 1991).

5. Income Support (General) Amendment No. 4 Regulations 1991 (S.I. 1991 No. 1559), reg. 14 (August 5, 1991).

6. Income Support (General) Amendment Regulations 1992 (S.I. 1992 No. 468), Sched., para. 7 (April 6, 1992) (amendments in respect of England and Wales only, not Scotland. For the previous form see the 1991 edition).

DEFINITIONS

"close relative"—see reg. 2(1).
"couple"—*ibid.*
"employment"—*ibid.*
"local authority"—see 1986 Act, s.84(1).
"married couple"—see 1986 Act, s.20(11) (SSCBA, s.137(1)).
"registered person"—see reg. 2(1).
"youth training scheme"—*ibid.*

GENERAL NOTE

Sched. 1A defines the categories of 16 and 17 year-olds who may still be eligible for income support. As the result of reg. 13A(3)(a), anyone who falls into Part I of the Schedule is eligible until the age of 18. Under reg. 13A(2)(b) and (3)(b) anyone who falls under Part II is eligible until the relevant date defined by reg. 13A(7), *i.e.* effectively the end of the child benefit extension period. Part II applies to registered persons, *i.e.* those registered either for work or the youth training scheme with the Department of Employment, the Ministry of Defence or a local education authority (see reg. 2(1)). There is no such restriction in Part I.

Paragraph 1
Most of the categories of those not required to be available for employment which are appropriate to 16 or 17 year-olds apply here. The major exception is para. 5 of Sched. 1 (incapacity for work), but this is dealt with in para. 2 of Sched. 1A and reg. 13A(4)(a). Note the inclusion of para. 10 of Sched. 1, which refers on to reg. 13(2)(a) to (e).

Paragraph 2
The concepts of incapacity for work and disease or bodily or mental disablement are familiar from benefits for people incapable of work. But it remains to be worked out what amounts to incapacity for training. Medical evidence will obviously be necessary to prove incapacity, but it is only conclusive on the likely length of the incapacity. Note that if the incapacity is likely to end within 12 months reg. 13A(4)(a) can apply.

Paragraphs 3 and 4
These are straightforward.

Paragraph 5
This is the first provision in Part II. If the couple are responsible for a child, then para. 3 in Part I will apply. Para. 5 applies to registered persons who are part of a married couple (living together as husband and wife will not do) provided that the partner is either over 17 or registered or within Part I.

Paragraph 6
See para. 10 for definitions, and notes to reg. 13(2)(c). Someone still in education who meets these conditions will qualify under para. 1.

Paragraph 7
See para. 10 for definitions, and reg. 2(1) for "close relative." The condition is similar to that in reg. 13(2)(d) except that instead of estrangement from parents etc. is substituted the test of having been in care or custody. The limited protection for this group has produced particular criticism, but now see reg. 13(4)(d).

Paragraph 8
These groups are expected to be particularly vulnerable.

Paragraph 9
See notes to reg. 13(2)(e).

Paragraph 9A
See notes to reg. 13(2)(d).

SCHEDULE 2   **Regulations 17 [³(1)] and 18**

APPLICABLE AMOUNTS

[²⁵PART I

Personal Allowances

1. The weekly amounts specified in column (2) below in respect of each person or couple specified in column (1) shall be the weekly amounts specified for the purposes of regulations 17(1) and 18(1) (applicable amounts and polygamous marriages).

Column (1)	Column (2)
Person or Couple	*Amount*
(1) Single claimant aged—	
(a) except where head (b) or (c) of this sub-paragraph applies, less than 18;	(1)(a) £28.00;
(b) less than 18 who falls within any of the circumstances specified in Part II of Schedule 1A or who, had he been a registered person, would fall within any of those circumstances, and who—	(b) £36.80;
(i) is eligible for income support under regulation 13A; or	
(ii) is the subject of a direction under section 125(1) of the Contributions and Benefits Act;	
(c) less than 18 who satisfies the condition in paragraph 11(a);	(c) £36.80;
(d) not less than 18 but less than 25;	(d) £36.80;
(e) not less than 25.	(e) £46.50
(2) Lone parent aged—	(2)
(a) except where head (b) or (c) of this sub-paragraph applies, less than 18;	(a) £28.00;
(b) less than 18 who falls within any of the circumstances specified in Part II of Schedule 1A or who, had he been a registered person, would fall within any of those circumstances, and who—	(b) £36.80;
(i) is eligible for income support under regulation 13A; or	
(ii) is the subject of a direction under section 125(1) of the Contributions and Benefits Act;	
(c) less than 18 who satisfies the condition in paragraph 11(a);	(c) £36.80;
(d) not less than 18.	(d) £46.50.
(3) Couple—	(3)
(a) Where both members are aged less than 18 and—	(*a*) £55.55;
(i) at least one of them is treated as responsible for a child; or	
(ii) had they not been members of a couple, each would be eligible for income support under regulation 13A (circumstances in which a person aged 16 or 17 is eligible for income support); or	

Column (1)	Column (2)
Person or Couple	*Amount*

(iii) they are married and each member is either a registered person or a person to whom Part I of Schedule 1A applies; or
  (iv) there is a direction under section 125(1) of the Contributions and Benefits Act (income supportr to avoid severe hardship) in respect of each member; or
  (v) there is a direction under section 125(1) of the 1992 Act in respect of one of them and the other is eligible for income support under regulation 13A;	

(aa) where both members are aged less than 18 and sub-paragraph (3)(a) does not apply but one member of the couple falls within any of the circumstances specified in Part II of Schedule 1A or who, had he been a registered person, would fall within any of those circumstances and that member—
  (i) is eligible for income support under regulation 13A; or
  (ii) is the subject of a direction under section 125(1) of the Contributions and Benefits Act;
	(aa) £36.80

(b) where both members are aged less than 18 and sub-paragraph (3)(a) or (aa) above does not apply but one member of the couple—
  (i) is eligible for income support under regulation 13A; or
  (ii) is the subject of a direction under section 125(1);
	(b) £28.00;

(c) where both members are; aged not less than 18;	(c) £73.00.

(d) where one member is aged not less than 18 and the other member is a person under 18 who—
  (i) is eligible for income support under regulation 13A; or
  (ii) is the subject of a direction under section 125(1);
	(d) £73.00.

(e) where one member is aged not less than 18 but less than 25 and the other member is a person under 18 who—
  (i) is not eligible for income support under regulation 13A; or
  (ii) is not the subject of a direction under section 125(1);
	(e) £36.80

(f) where one member is aged not less than 25 and the other member is a person under 18 who—
  (i) is not eligible for income support under regulation 13A; and
  (ii) is not the subject of a direction under section 125(1).
	(f) £46.50.

2. The weekly amounts specified in column (2) below in respect of each person specified in column (1) shall be the weekly amounts specified for the purposes of regulations 17(1)(b) and 18(1)(c).

Column (1)	Column (2)
Child or Young Person	*Amount*
Person aged— (a) less than 11; (b) not less than 11 but less than 16; (c) not less than 16 but less than 18; (d) not less than 18.	(a) £15.95; (b) £23.40; (c) £28.00; (d) £36.80.

[¹⁷**2A.**—(1) The weekly amount for the purposes of regulation 17(1)(bb) and 18(1)(cc) (residential allowance) in respect of a person who satisfies the conditions specified in sub-paragraph (2) shall be—

 (a) except in a case to which head (b) applies, £51.00; and

(b) where the home in which the person resides is situated within the area described in Schedule 3C (the Greater London area), £57.00.]

(2) Subject to sub-paragraphs [^{20}(3), (4) and (4A)], the conditions are—

(a) the person resides in a residential care home or a nursing home [^{20}or is regarded pursuant to sub-paragraph (4A) as residing in such a home];

[^{18}(aa) the person both requires personal care and is provided with it in the home and for this purpose "personal care" means care which includes assistance with bodily functions where such assistance is required;]

(b) he does not have a preserved right;

(c) he is aged 16 or over;

(d) both the person's accommodation and such meals (if any) as are provided for him are provided on a commercial basis; and

(e) no part of the weekly charge for accommodation is met by housing benefit.

(3) For the purposes of sub-paragraph (2), but subject to sub-paragraph (4), a person resides in a residential care home where the home in which he resides—

(a) is registered under Part I of the Registered Homes Act 1984 or is deemed to be so registered by virtue of section 2(3) of the Registered Homes (Amendment) Act 1991 (registration of small homes where application for registration not determined);

(b) is managed or provided by a body incorporated by Royal Charter or constituted by Act of Parliament (other than a social services authority) and provides both board and personal care for the claimant; or

(c) is in Scotland and is registered under section 61 of the Social Work (Scotland) Act 1968 or is an establishment provided by a housing association registered with Scottish Homes established by the Housing (Scotland) Act 1988 which provides care equivalent to that given in residential accommodation provided under Part IV of the Social Work (Scotland) Act 1968;

and a person resides in a nursing home where the home in which he resides is such a home for the purposes of regulation 19.

(4) A person shall not be regarded as residing in a nursing home for the purposes of sub-paragraph (2) where the home in which he resides is a hospice, and for this purpose "hospice" means a nursing home which—

(a) if situate in England and Wales, is registered under Part II of the Registered Homes Act 1984, or

(b) if situate in Scotland, is exempted from the operation of the Nursing Homes Registration (Scotland) Act 1938 by virtue of section 6 of that Act,

[^{21}and whose primary function is to provide palliative care for persons resident there who are suffering from a progressive disease in its final stages].

[^{20}(4A) For the purposes of sub-paragraph (2)(a), where a person's principal place of residence is a residential care home or nursing home, and he is temporarily absent from that home, he shall be regarded as continuing to reside in that home—

(a) where he is absent because he is a patient, for the first six weeks of any such period of absence, and for this purpose—

  (i) "patient" has the meaning it has in Schedule 7 by virtue of regulation 21(3), and

  (ii) periods of absence separated by not more than 28 days shall be treated as a single period of absence equal in duration to all those periods; and

(b) for the first three weeks of any other period of absence.]

(5) Where—

(a) a person has been registered under the Registered Homes Act 1984 in respect of premises which have been carried on as a residential care home or, as the case may be, a nursing home, and that person has ceased to carry on such a home; and

(b) an application for registration under that Act has been made by another person and that application has not been determined or abandoned,

then any question arising for determination under this paragraph shall be determined as if the most recent registration in respect of those premises continued until the day on which the application is determined or abandoned.]

PART II

Regulations 17[³(1)](c)
[³and 18(1)](d)

Family Premium

3. The weekly amount for the purposes of regulations 17[³(1)](c) [³and 18(1)](d) in respect of a family of which at least one member is a child or young person shall be [²⁶£10.25].

PART III

Regulations 17[³(1)](d)
[³and 18(1)](e)

Premiums

4. Except as provided in paragraph 5, the weekly premiums specified in Part IV of this Schedule shall, for the purposes of regulations 17[³(1)](d)[³ and 18(1)](e), be applicable to a claimant who satisfies the condition specified in paragraphs [¹⁰8 to 14ZA] in respect of that premium.

5. Subject to paragraph 6, where a claimant satisfies the conditions in respect of more than one premium in this Part of this Schedule, only one premium shall be applicable to him and, if they are different amounts, the higher or highest amount shall apply.

6.—(1) The severe disability premium to which paragraph 13 applies may be applicable in addition to [⁷any other premium which may apply under this Schedule.]

(2) [¹⁰The disabled child premium and carer premium to which paragraphs 14 and 14ZA respectively apply] may be applicable in addition to any other premium which may apply under this Schedule.

7.—[¹⁰(1) Subject to sub-paragraph (2)] for the purposes of this Part of this Schedule, once a premium is applicable to a claimant under this Part, a person shall be treated as being in receipt of any benefit—

(a) in the case of a benefit to which the Social Security (Overlapping Benefits) Regulations 1979 applies, for any period during which, apart from the provisions of those Regulations, he would be in receipt of that benefit; and

(b) for any period spent by a claimant in undertaking a course of training or instruction provided or approved by the [¹²Secretary of State for Employment] under section 2 of the Employment and Training Act 1973 [¹¹, or by Scottish Enterprise or Highlands and Islands Enterprise under section 2 of the Enterprise and New Towns (Scotland) Act 1990,] [⁷or for any period during which he is in receipt of a training allowance].

[¹⁰(2) For the purposes of the carer premium under paragraph 14ZA, a person shall be treated as being in receipt of invalid care allowance by virtue of sub-paragraph (1)(a) only if and for so long as the person in respect of whose care the allowance has been claimed remains in receipt of attendance allowance[¹⁵, or the care component of disability living allowance at the highest or middle rate prescribed in accordance with section 37ZB(3) of the Social Security Act [SSCBA, s.72(3)]].]

Lone Parent Premium

8. The condition is that the claimant is a member of a family but has no partner.

[Pensioner premium for persons under 75

9. The condition is that the claimant—

(a) is a single claimant or lone parent aged not less than 60 but less than 75; or

226

(b) has a partner and is, or his partner is, aged not less than 60 but less than 75.

Pensioner premium for persons 75 and over

9A. The condition is that the claimant—
(a) is a single claimant or lone parent aged not less than 75 but less than 80; or
(b) has a partner and is, or his partner is, aged not less than 75 but less than 80.]

Higher Pensioner Premium

10.—(1) Where the claimant is a single claimant or a lone parent, the condition is that—
(a) he is aged not less than 80; or
(b) he is aged less than 80 but not less than 60, and
    (i) the additional condition specified in paragraph 12(1)(a) [¹or (c)] is satisfied; or
    (ii) he was entitled to income support and the disability premium was applicable to him in respect of a benefit week within eight weeks of his 60th birthday and he has, subject to sub-paragraph (3), remained continuously entitled to income support since attaining that age.
(2) Where the claimant has a partner, the condition is that—
(a) he or his partner is aged not less than 80; or
(b) he or his partner is aged less than 80 but not less than 60 and either—
    (i) the additional condition specified in paragraph 12(1)(a) [¹or (c)] is satisfied [¹⁶. . .]; or
    (ii) he was entitled to income support and the disability premium was applicable to him in respect of a benefit week within eight weeks of his 60th birthday and he has, subject to sub-paragraph (3), remained continuously entitled to income support since attaining that age.
(3) For the purposes of this paragraph and paragraph 12—
(a) once the higher pensioner premium is applicable to a claimant, if he then ceases, for a period of eight weeks or less, to be entitled to income support, he shall, on becoming re-entitled to income support, thereafter be treated as having been continuously entitled thereto;
(b) in so far as sub-paragraphs (1)(b)(ii) and (2)(b)(ii) are concerned, if a claimant ceases to be entitled to income support for a period not exceeding eight weeks which includes his 60th birthday, he shall, on becoming re-entitled to income support, thereafter be treated as having been continuously entitled thereto.

Disability Premium

11. The condition is that—
(a) where the claimant is a single claimant or a lone parent, he is aged less than 60 and the additional condition specified in paragraph 12 is satisfied; or
(b) where the claimant has a partner, either—
    (i) the claimant is aged less than 60 and the additional condition specified in paragraph [¹12(1)(a), (b) or (c)] is satisfied by him; or
    (ii) his partner is aged less than 60 and the additional condition specified in paragraph 12(1)(a) [¹or (c)] is satisfied by his partner.

Additional condition for the Higher Pensioner and Disability Premiums

12.—(1) Subject to sub-paragraph (2) and paragraph 7 the additional condition referred to in paragraphs 10 and 11 is that either—

(a) the claimant or, as the case may be, his partner—
    (i) is in receipt of one or more of the following benefits: attendance allowance, [15disability living allowance, disability working allowance], mobility supplement, [28long-term incapacity benefit] under [22Part II of the Contributions and Benefits Act or severe disablement allowance under Part III of that Act] [1but, in the case of [28 long-term incapacity benefit] or severe disablement allowance only where it is paid in respect of him]; or
    (ii) is provided by the Secretary of State with an invalid carriage or other vehicle under section 5(2) of the National Health Service Act 1977 (other services) or, in Scotland, under section 46 of the National Health Service (Scotland) Act 1978 (provision of vehicles) or receives payments by way of grant from the Secretary of State under paragraph 2 of Schedule 2 to that 1977 Act (additional provisions as to vehicles) or, in Scotland, under that section 46; or
    (iii) is registered as blind in a register compiled by a local authority under section 29 of the National Assistance Act 1948 (welfare services) or, in Scotland, has been certified as blind and in consequence he is registered as blind in a register maintained by or on behalf of a regional or islands council; or
[29(b) the claimant—
    (i) is entitled to statutory sick pay or is incapable of work in accordance with the provisions of Part XIIA of the Contributions and Benefits Act and the regulations made thereunder (incapacity for work), and
    (ii) has been so entitled or so incapable for a continuous period of not less than—
        (aa) 196 days in the case of a claimant who is terminally ill within the meaning of section 30B(4) of the Contributions and Benefits Act; or
        (bb) 364 days in any other case;
        and for these purposes any two or more periods of entitlement or incapacity separated by a break of not more than 56 days shall be treated as one continuous period; or]
(c) the claimant or, as the case may be, his partner was in receipt of either—
    [15(i) [28long-term incapacity benefit] under [22Part II of the Contributions and Benefits Act] when entitlement to that benefit ceased on account of the payment of a retirement pension under [22that Act] and the claimant has since remained continuously entitled to income support and, if the [28long-term incapacity benefit] was payable to his partner, the partner is still alive; or]
    (ii) except where paragraph 1(a), (b), (c)(ii) or (d)(ii) of Schedule 7 (patients) applies, attendance allowance [14or disability living allowance but payment of benefit has been suspended in accordance with regulations made under [24section 113(2) of the Contributions and Benefits Act 1992 or otherwise abated as a consequence of the claimant or his partner becoming a patient within the meaning of regulation 21(3) (special cases)],]
    and, in either case, the higher pensioner premium or disability premium has been applicable to the claimant or his partner.

(2) For the purposes of sub-paragraph (1)(a)(iii), a person who has ceased to be registered as blind on regaining his eyesight shall nevertheless be treated as blind and as satisfying the additional condition set out in that sub-paragraph for a period of 28 weeks following the date on which he ceased to be so registered.

(3) [29. . .]

(4) For the purpose of sub-paragraph (1)(c), once the higher pensioner premium is applicable to the claimant by virtue of his satisfying the condition specified in that provision, if he then ceases, for a period of eight weeks or less, to be entitled to income support, he shall on again becoming so entitled to income support, immediately thereafter be treated as satisfying the condition in sub-paragraph (1)(c).

[⁴(5) For the purposes of sub-paragraph (1)(b), once the disability premium is applicable to a claimant by virtue of his satisfying the additional condition specified in that provision, he shall continue to be treated as satisfying that condition for any period spent by him in undertaking a course of training provided under section 2 of the Employment and Training Act 1973 [⁷or for any period during which he is in receipt of a training allowance].]

[²⁸(6) For the purposes of sub-paragraph (1)(a)(i) and (c)(i), a reference to a person in receipt of long-term incapacity benefit includes a person in receipt of short-term incapacity benefit at a rate equal to the long-term rate by virtue of section 30B(4)(a) of the Contributions and Benefits Act (short-term incapacity benefit for a person who is terminally ill), or who would be or would have been in receipt of short-term incapacity benefit at such a rate but for the fact that the rate of short-term incapacity benefit already payable to him is or was equal to or greater than the long-term rate.]

Severe Disability Premium

13.—(1) The condition is that the claimant is a severely disabled person.

(2) For the purposes of sub-paragraph (1), a claimant shall be treated as being a severely disabled person if, and only if—

(a) in the case of a single claimant[¹⁹, a lone parent or a claimant who is treated as having no partner in consequence of sub-paragraph (2A)]—
  (i) he is in receipt of attendance allowance [¹⁵or the care component of disability living allowance at the highest or middle rate prescribed in accordance with section 37ZB(3) of the Social Security Act [SSCBA, s.72(3)]], and
  (ii) subject to sub-paragraph (3), he has no non-dependants aged 18 or over [²³normally residing with him or with whom he is normally residing,] and
  (iii) [⁷ . . .] an invalid care allowance under section 37 of the Social Security Act [SSCBA, s.70] [⁷is not in payment to anyone] in respect of caring for him;
(b) if he has a partner—
  (i) he is in receipt of attendance allowance [¹⁵, or the care component of disability living allowance at the highest or middle rate prescribed in accordance with section 37ZB(3) of the Social Security Act [SSCBA, s.72(3)]]; and
  (ii) his partner is also in receipt of such an allowance or, if he is a member of a polygamous marriage, all the partners of that marriage are in receipt thereof; and
  (iii) subject to sub-paragraph (3), he has no non-dependants aged 18 or over [²³normally residing with him or with whom he is normally residing,]
  and either [⁷an invalid care allowance is in payment to someone] in respect of caring for only one of the couple or, in the case of a polygamous marriage, for one or more but not all the partners of the marriage, or, as the case may be, [⁷such an allowance is not in payment to anyone] in respect of caring for either member of the couple or any partner of the polygamous marriage.

[¹⁹(2A) Where a claimant has a partner who does not satisfy the condition in sub-paragraph (2)(b)(ii), and that partner is blind or is treated as blind within the meaning of paragraph 12(1)(a)(iii) and (2), that partner shall be treated for the purposes of sub-paragraph (2) as if he were not a partner of the claimant.]

(3) For the purposes of sub-paragraph (2)(a)(ii) and (2)(b)(iii) no account shall be taken of—

(a) a person receiving attendance allowance [¹⁵, or the care component of disability living allowance at the highest or middle rate prescribed in accordance with section 37ZB(3) of the Social Security Act [SSCBA, s.72(3)]]; or
(b) [²¹ . . .]
(c) subject to sub-paragraph (4), a person who joins the claimant's household for the

first time in order to care for the claimant or his partner and immediately before
so joining the claimant or his partner was treated as a severely disabled person;
[[19] or

(d) a person who is blind or is treated as blind within the meaning of paragraph
12(1)(a)(iii) and (2).]

[[1](3A)For the purposes of sub-paragraph (2)(b) a person shall be treated as being in
receipt of—

(a) attendance allowance[[15], or the care component of disability living allowance at
the highest or middle rate prescribed in accordance with section 37ZB(3) of the
Social Security Act [SSCBA, s.72(3)]] if he would, but for his being a patient for
a period exceeding 28 days, be so in receipt;

(b) invalid care allowance if he would, but for the person for whom he was caring
being a patient in hospital for a period exceeding 28 days, be so in receipt.]

[[22](3ZA) For the purposes of sub-paragraph (2)(a)(iii) and (2)(b), no account shall be
taken of an award of invalid care allowance to the extent that payment of such an award
is back-dated for a period before the date on which the award is made.]

(4) Sub-paragraph (3)(c) shall apply only for the first 12 weeks following the date on
which the person to whom that provision applies first joins the claimant's household.

Disabled Child Premium

14. The condition is that a child or young person for whom the claimant or a partner
of his is responsible and who is a member of the claimant's household—

(a) has no capital or capital which, if calculated in accordance with Part V in like
manner as for the claimant, [[21]except as provided in regulation 44(1)
(modifications in respect of children and young persons)], would not exceed
£3,000; and

(b) is in receipt of [[15]disability living allowance] or is no longer in receipt of that
allowance because he is a patient provided that the child or young person continues to be a member of the family; or

(c) is blind or treated as blind within the meaning of paragraph 12(1)(a)(iii) and
(2).

[[10]Carer premium

14ZA.—(1) [[13]Subject to sub-paragraphs (3) and (4),] the condition is that the claimant
or his partner is, or both of them are, in receipt of invalid care allowance under section
37 of the Social Security Act [SSCBA, s.70].

(2) If a claimant or his partner, or both of them, would be in receipt of invalid care
allowance but for the provisions of the Social Security (Overlapping Benefits) Regulations 1979, where—

(a) the claim for that allowance was made on or after 1st October 1990, and

(b) the person or persons in respect of whose care the allowance has been claimed
remains or remain in receipt of attendance allowance[[15], or the care component of
disability living allowance at the highest or middle rate prescribed in accordance
section 37ZB(3) of the Social Security Act [SSCBA, s.72(3)]]]

he or his partner, or both of them, as the case may be, shall be treated for the purposes
of sub-paragraph (1) as being in receipt of invalid care allowance.]

[[14](3) Where a carer premium is awarded but the person in respect of whom it has
been awarded either ceases to be in receipt of, or ceases to be treated as in receipt of,
invalid care allowance, the condition for the award of the premium shall be treated as
satisfied for a period of eight weeks from the date on which that person ceased to be in
receipt of, or ceased to be treated as in receipt of, invalid care allowance.

(4) Where a person who has been receiving, or who has been treated as receiving
invalid care allowance ceases to be in receipt of, or ceases to be treated as in receipt, of

that allowance and makes a claim for income support, the condition for the award of the carer premium shall be treated as satisfied for a period of eight weeks from the date that the person was last in receipt of, or was last treated as being in receipt of, invalid care allowance.]

[³ Persons in receipt of concessionary payments

14A. For the purpose of determining whether a premium is applicable to a person [¹²under paragraphs 12 to 14A], any concessionary payment made to compensate that person for the non-payment of any benefit mentioned in those paragraphs shall be treated as if it were a payment of that benefit.]

[⁸Person in receipt of benefit

14B. For the purposes of this Part of this Schedule, a person shall be regarded as being in receipt of any benefit if, and only if, it is paid in respect of him and shall be so regarded only for any period in respect of which that benefit is paid.]

[²⁷PART IV

Weekly Amounts of Premiums Specified in Part III

Column (1)	Column (2)
Premium	*Amount*
15.—(1) Lone parent premium	(1) £5.20.
(2) Pensioner premium for persons aged under 75—	(2)
(a) where the claimant satisfies the condition in paragraph 9(a);	(a) £18.60;
(b) where the claimant satisfies the condition in paragraph 9(b).	(b) £28.05.
(2A) Pensioner premium for persons aged 75 and over—	(2A)
(a) where the claimant satisfies the condition in paragraph 9A(a);	(a) £20.70;
(b) where the claimant satisfies the condition in paragraph 9A(b).	(b) £30.95.
(3) Higher Pensioner Premium—	(3)
(a) where the claimant satisfies the condition in paragraph 10(1)(a) or (b);	(a) £25.15;
(b) where the claimant satisfies the condition in paragraph 10(2)(a) or (b).	(b) £35.95.
(4) Disability Premium—	(4)
(a) where the claimant satisfies the condition in paragraph 11(a);	(a) £19.80;
(b) where the claimant satisfies the condition in paragraph 11(b).	(b) £28.30.
(5) Severe Disability Premium—	(5)
(a) where the claimant satisfies the condition in paragraph 13(2)(a);	(a) £35.05;
(b) where the claimant satisfies the condition in paragraph 13(2)(b).	(b)
(i) if there is someone in receipt of an invalid care allowance or if he or any partner satisfies that condition only by virtue of paragraph 13(3A);	(i) £35.05;
(ii) if on-one is in receipt of such an allowance.	(ii) £70.10.

Column (1)	Column (2)
Premium	*Amount*
(6) Disability Child Premium—	(6) £19.80 in respect of each child or young person in respect of whom the conditions specified in paragraph 14 are satisfied.
(7) Carer Premium—	(7) £12.60 in respect of each person who satisfied the condition specified in paragraph 14ZA.]

PART V

Rounding of Fractions

16. Where income support is awarded for a period which is not a complete benefit week and the applicable amount in respect of that period results in an amount which includes a fraction of a penny that fraction shall be treated as a penny.

AMENDMENTS

1. Income Support (General) Amendment Regulations 1988 (S.I. 1988 No. 663), reg. 29 (April 11, 1988).
2. Income Support (General) Amendment No. 3 Regulations 1988 (S.I. 1988 No. 1228). reg. 9 (September 12, 1988).
3. Income Support (General) Amendment No. 4 Regulations 1988 (S.I. 1988 No. 1445), reg. 19 (September 12, 1988).
4. Income Support (General) Amendment No. 5 Regulations 1988 (S.I. 1988 No. 2022), reg. 17(*b*) (December 12, 1988).
5. Income Support (General) Amendment No. 5 Regulations 1988 (S.I. 1988 No. 2022), reg. 17(*a*) (April 10, 1989).
6. Income Support (General) Amendment Regulations 1989 (S.I. 1989 No. 534), reg. 5 (October 9, 1989).
7. Income Support (General) Amendment No. 3 Regulations 1989 (S.I. 1989 No. 1678), reg. 6 (October 9, 1989).
8. Income Support (General) Amendment Regulations 1990 (S.I. 1990 No. 547), reg. 17 (April 9, 1990).
9. Income Support (General) Amendment No. 2 Regulations 1990 (S.I. 1990 No. 1168). reg. 2 (July 2, 1990).
10. Income Support (General) Amendment No. 3 Regulations 1990 (S.I. 1990 No. 1776), reg. 8 (October 1, 1990).
11. Enterprise (Scotland) Consequential Amendments Order 1991 (S.I. 1991 No. 3870, art. 9 (April, 19910.
12. Income Support (General) Amendment Regulations 1991 (S.I. 1991 No. 236), reg. 2 (April 8, 1991).
13. Income Support (General) Amendment No. 4 Regulations 1991 (S.I. 1991 No. 236). reg. 15 (August 5, 1991).
14. Income Support (General) Amendment No. 4) Regulations 1991 (S.I. 1991 No. 1559), reg. 15 (October 7, 1991).
15. Disability Living Allowance and Disability Working Allowance (Consequential Provisions) Regulations 1991 (S.I. 1991 No. 2742), reg. 11(4) (April 6, 1992).

16. Income Support (General) Amendment Regulations 1992 (S.I. 1992 No. 468), reg. 6 (April 6, 1992).

17. Social Security Benefits (Amendments Consequential Upon the Introduction of Community Care) Regulations 1992 (S.I. 1992 No. 3147), reg. 2 (April 1, 1993).

18. Social Security Benefits (Miscellaneous Amendments) Regulations 1993 (S.I. 1993 No. 518), reg. 5 (April 1, 1993).

19. Income-related Benefits Schemes (Miscellaneous Amendments) (No. 2) Regulations 1993 (S.I. 1993 No. 1150), reg. 3 (May 25, 1993).

20. Income Support (General) Amendment (No. 2) Regulations 1993 (S.I. 1993 No. 1219), reg. 2 (May 31, 1993).

21. Income-related Benefits Schemes (Miscellaneous Amendments) (No. 4) Regulations 1993 (S.I. 1993 No. 2119), reg. 18 (October 4, 1993).

22. Income-related Benefits Schemes (Miscellaneous Amendments) (No. 5) Regulations 1994 (S.I. 1994 No. 2139), reg. 30 (October 3, 1994).

23. Income-related Benefits Schemes (Miscellaneous Amendments) (No. 6) Regulations 1994 (S.I. 1994 No. 3061), reg. 2(3) (December 2, 1994).

24. Income-related Benefits Schemes (Miscellaneous Amendments) Regulations 1995 (S.I. 1995 No. 516), reg. 24 (April 10, 1995).

25. Social Security Benefits Uprating Order 1995 (S.I. 1995 No. 559), art. 18(3) and Sched. 4 (April 10, 1995).

26. Social Security Benefits Uprating Order 1995 (S.I. 1995 No. 559), art. 18(4) (April 10, 1995).

27. Social Security Benefits Uprating Order 1995 (S.I. 1995 No. 559), art. 18(5) and Sched. 5 (April 10, 1995).

28. Disability Working Allowance and Income Support (General) Amendment Regulations 1995 (S.I. 1995 No. 482), reg. 16 (April 13, 1995).

29. Disability Working Allowance and Income Support (General) Amendment Regulations 1995 (S.I. 1995 No. 482), reg. 17 (April 13, 1995).

DEFINITIONS

"attendance allowance"—see reg. 2(1).
"benefit week"—*ibid.*
"child"—see 1986 Act, s. 20(11) (SSCBA, s.137(1)).
"claimant"—see reg. 2(1).
"couple"—*ibid.*
"disability living allowance"—*ibid.*
"disability working allowance"—*ibid.*
"family"—see 1986 Act. s.20(11) (SSCBA, s.137(1)).
"invalid carriage or other vehicle"—see reg. 2(1).
"lone parent"—*ibid.*
"mobility supplement"—*ibid.*
"non-dependent"—see reg. 3.
"nursing home"—see regs. 2(1) and 19(3).
"partner"—see reg. 2(1).
"polygamous marriage"—*ibid.*
"preserved right"—see reg. 2(1) and 19.
"residential care home"—see regs. 2(1) and 19(3).
"single claimant"—*ibid.*
"Social Security Act"—*ibid.*
"young person"—*ibid.*, reg. 14.

GENERAL NOTE

The details of the personal allowances and premiums are at the heart of the income support system. Their adequacy or otherwise is crucial to the success of the scheme. The personal allowances can be looked at as a simplified version of the supplementary benefit scale rates (specific differences are noted below), but the premiums were a new departure in April 1988. Instead of an attempt, through supplementary benefit additional requirements, to tailor the level of benefit to the individual needs and circumstances of the claimant and his family, higher amounts of benefit are now targeted on fairly broad categories of claimant. In such a structure benefit may be adequate for those with routine and predictable needs (although of course there is always room for argument about the adequacy of particular rates), but it is almost impossible to make it adequate for those with unusually high needs. The Transitional Regulations protected transferring claimants to some extent, but had the effect, particularly for those with large transitional additions, of preventing any real increase in benefit for, in some cases, several years. An improvement of the structure for pensioners was introduced in October 1989 and for those caring for the disabled in October 1990.

Paragraphs 1 and 2

Much of this is taken over from the supplementary benefit system, particularly the children's rates. Note that there is no long-term rate and no special rate for pensioners. All additions to weekly benefit are through the premiums. For couples the significant age-break comes when one of them reaches 18. The removal of general entitlement for 16 and 17 year-olds has led to the immense complexity of para. 1(3). Where both partners are aged less than 18, the lower couple's rate is only applied if either a child is a member of the family or if both partners are eligible for benefit. If only one of them is eligible for income support under reg. 13A or s.125 of the Contributions and Benefits Act (1986 Act, s.20(4A)), then the personal allowance is the same as for a single person under 18 under para. 1(1). Where one partner is 18 or over and the other is under 18, the higher couple's rate is only paid if the partner under 18 is eligible for income support under reg. 13A or s.125. If that partner is not eligible, the personal allowance is the same as for a single claimant, with another age-break at 25.

Single claimants under 18 qualify for the 18–24 year-old rate if they meet the conditions of para. 1(1)(b).

The crucial age for lone parents is also currently 18. Lone parents of 16 and 17 are always eligible under reg. 13A. But for single claimants there is another very significant break at the age of 25. This is connected to the absence of any distinction in the personal allowances between householders and non-householders. Instead, the assumptions are made that most single people of 25 and over are responsible for their own households and that most single people under 25 are not responsible for independent households, typically living with parents. Thus a higher rate is paid to those of 25. Both these assumptions are correct, looking at the entire age-groups involved, but clearly have no direct applicability to the needs and circumstances of individuals. Young single claimants were one of the losing groups in the 1988 reforms.

See para. 2A for the treatment of residents in residential care and nursing homes and Sched. 7 for special cases, such as hospital patients. From April 1989 there are no special rules for people in board and lodging accommodation and from October 1989 no special rules for residents in most hostels.

Paragraph 2A

A new structure of benefit for residents in residential care and nursing homes was introduced in April 1993. Anyone with a "preserved right" is excluded from the new system (sub-para. (2)(b)). People who were resident in a home on March 31, 1993 (apart from residents, not entitled to income support, in residential care homes in England and Wales with less than four residents) have preserved rights, which means that they can continue to receive income support under the old system of reg. 19(3) and Sched. 4. See reg. 19 (1ZB) to (1ZQ) for details.

If a person is not excluded by the "preserved right" provisions, the new system was described as follows by the DSS to the Social Security Advisory Committee (Appendix 2 to Cm. 2215, para. 6).

"Under the new Community Care arrangements from April 1993 people entering residential care and nursing homes at public expense will be able to claim Income Support on a similar basis to those living in their own home. Additionally, they will be able to receive a Residential Allowance, as part of their Income Support entitlement, as a contribution towards their 'accommodation costs'. They will have their care needs assessed by the local authority who will meet any extra cost involved. In deciding the ability of an individual to contribute towards their fees in the care home, the local authority will carry out a financial assessment. This will largely follow the rules which currently apply to Income Support under regulations being prepared by the Department of Health.

Resources will be transferred to the local authorities to enable them to meet their new responsibilities. The White Paper commitment is that the Government will transfer to local authorities what it would otherwise have spent on DSS benefits, taking into account expenditure on existing cases and the continuing eligibility for benefit of new residents."

The residential allowance is set at £51 (£57 for London) for each adult resident. Outside the conditions of para. 2A there may be entitlement to ordinary income support and housing benefit, or to the "Part III" rate for "residential accommodation." There are detailed conditions in sub-para. (2)

(a) The person must be a resident in a residential care or nursing home. Through reg. 2(1), the definitions in reg. 19(3) are incorporated, subject to some special rules in para. 2A. Thus, for residential care homes, the home must be in one of the three categories specified in sub-para

(3). There is no separate category for Abbeyfield Homes, so that they only qualify if registered under the 1984 Act. Under the Registered Homes (Amendment) Act 1991 residential care homes with less than four residents have to be registered. The local authority has to apply the standards of board and personal care.

From May 31, 1993, the period for which claimants who are absent from their residential care or nursing home can continue to receive a residential allowance has been extended. The previous limit was six days. Now it will continue for six weeks where the claimant is in hospital and three weeks in any other case. Periods in hospital separated by not more than 28 days count as one period. There is a transitional provision applying to claimants who had been temporarily absent from a home for more than six days on May 31, 1993: see Income Support (General) Amendment (No. 2) Regulations 1993 (S.I. 1993 No. 1219) p. 373.

(aa) This condition ensures that the person concerned requires personal care and is not simply a resident in a home which provides such care to others.

(b) The person must not have a preserved right (reg. 19).

(c) Under-16s are not entitled to residential allowances.

(d) On a "commercial basis": see the notes to reg. 2(1) on "board and lodging accommodation."

(e) It is a condition that housing benefit is not received for the accommodation. Generally there can be no entitlement to housing benefit if there is potential entitlement to a residential allowance. But for Royal Charter/Act of Parliament homes, where there is a care test under sub-para. (3)(b), housing benefit can be claimed as an alternative without the need to meet the care test.

Paragraph 3

The family premium is treated differently from the other premiums. It is awarded whenever there is a child or young person in the claimant's family. Thus it goes to lone parents and couples with children or young persons. It is of the same amount whether there is one child or 10 in the family. It does not matter that no personal allowance is included for the child, *e.g.* because he has capital over £3,000.

Paragraphs 4 to 7

These provisions establish the general framework for the other premiums, in paras. 8 to 14. Para. 4 provides that in each case the premium is applicable to the claimant, although often the condition relates to some other member of his family. The general rule is that only one of these premiums is applicable. If the claimant satisfies the conditions for more than one, the highest is applicable (para. 5). But a number of exceptions appear in para. 6. The severe disability premium (SDP) is allowed in addition to any other premium, as is the disabled child premium (DCP) and the carer premium (CP), rather like the family premium (FP).

Many of the conditions for premiums are based on the receipt of other social security benefits. Para. 7(1) deals with two situations where, once a premium has been allowed, the person concerned ceases actually to receive the other benefit. It allows entitlement to the premium to continue if the person has only ceased to receive the relevant benefit because of another, overlapping, benefit or is on a government training course or in receipt of a training allowance (the main example being YT). See para. 14B on the meaning of receipt of benefit.

Under para. 7(2), the above rules do not allow the CP to continue unless the person cared for continues to receive attendance allowance or one of the two higher rates of the care component of disability living allowance.

Paragraph 8

The qualification is to meet the definition of lone parent. The premium is £5.20 (para. 15(1)).

Paragraphs 9 and 9A

These provisions, together with the increases in the higher pensioner premium under para. 15(3), implemented the Government's commitment to give increased help to needy pensioners in October 1989. The ordinary pensioner premium under para. 9 is now limited to people aged 60 to 74. Para. 9A provides a separate premium for those aged 75 to 79, with a current differential over the ordinary pensioner premium of £2.10 for a single person and £2.90 for a couple (para. 15(2A)). The effect of reg. 14(1D) of the Transitional Regulations is that these increases do not affect any transitional addition in payment.

Paragraph 10

The first qualification for the HPP is that the claimant or any partner is aged 80 or over. If this is not satisfied there are another two alternatives, providing that at least one of the claimants or any partner is aged at least 60. The first was originally that the person of 60-plus satisfies the disability test in para. 12(1)(a) or (c). From April 1992 the test may be satisfied by a partner who is under 60. The second is that the person was entitled to income support with the disability premium in the eight weeks before his 60th birthday and has been continuously entitled to income support since that birthday. Although there are linking rules in sub-para. (3), this test is most arbitrary. All sorts of things might cause a person not to be entitled to income support just before a 60th birthday (obtaining capital from the proceeds of an endowment or retirement annuity policy, for instance), which have nothing to do with future disability needs. In addition, *CIS 458/1992* decides that a premium is not applicable unless it actually forms part of the claimant's applicable amount.

Sub-para. (3)(a) allows breaks of eight weeks once the HPP has been allowed. Sub-para. (3)(b) allows a break of eight weeks if it straddles the 60th birthday.

The premium is £25.15 if the claimant does not have a partner, £35.95 for a couple (para. 15(3)). It thus takes precedence over the pensioner premium.

Paragraph 11

The qualification for the DP can be for the claimant personally to satisfy one of the conditions in para. 12. If it is the claimant's partner who might qualify, then only para. 12(1)(a) or (c), not (b), will do. In either case, the person qualifying must be under 60. The premium is £19.80 if the claimant does not have a partner, £28.30 for a couple (para. 15(4)).

Paragraph 12

Sub-para. (1) prescribes three alternative disablement conditions for HPP and DP. Heads (a) and (c) can be satisfied by either the claimant or his partner; head (b) can only be satisfied by the claimant. As far as possible the conditions are made to depend on decisions already taken by other authorities, so that decision-making here should be routine.

Head (a) applies to receipt of the benefits listed in head (i), provision of or grant towards an invalid carriage, or being registered blind. From April 1990, para. 14B defines receipt of benefit in terms of payment, reversing the effect of *R(SB) 12/87*. Long-term incapacity benefit requires 52 weeks of incapacity for work, and has a contribution test. (Previously invalidity pension required only 28 weeks of incapacity.) Note sub-para. (6), the effect of which is to treat a person who is terminally ill as in receipt of long-term incapacity benefit after 28 weeks. Severe disablement allowance is non-contributory, but has an additional (and tough) test of disablement. The extension to all levels of the new disability living allowance brought in some previously excluded claimants. See sub-para. (2) for blindness, and notes to para. 8 of Sched. 1.

The upper age limits for claims for long-term incapacity benefit (and previously invalidity benefit) and, until October 28, 1994, initial claims for severe disablement allowance, which are a consequence of the UK's different pensionable ages for men and women, discriminate against women. These limits can in turn affect entitlement to HPP. As a result of the ECJ's decision in *Jackson and Cresswell v. Chief Adjudication Officer* [1993] 3 All E.R. 265, also reported as Appendix 2 to *R(IS)10/91*, (see notes to reg. 36), it is not possible to directly challenge the rules for the income support premium as being contrary to EC Directive 79/7 on equal treatment for men and women in matters of social security. However, the ECJ decided in *Secretary of State for Social Security v. Thomas* [1993] 4 All E.R. 556 that it was contrary to Directive 79/7 to deny severe disablement allowance to a woman aged 60 and over when a man could establish entitlement up to the age of 65. It was not disputed that severe disablement allowance came within art.3 of the Directive (protection against the risk of sickness, invalidity, old age, etc), but the U.K. Government argued that the different treatment was permitted by art. 7(1)(a) of the Directive (possible consequences for other benefits of different retirement ages). However, the ECJ held that this was not covered by the derogation in art. 7(1)(*a*) and was therefore unlawful. Thus both men and women could make an initial claim for severe disablement allowance up to the age of 65 simply by satisfying the normal conditions. As a result of the ECJ's decision, the rules were eventually changed from October 28, 1994: see Social Security (Severe Disablement Allowance and Invalid Care Allowance) Amendment Regulations 1994 (S.I. 1994 No. 2556). Women who became 65 before October 28, 1994 can receive severe disablement allowance after 65 if they would have been entitled to it immediately before their sixty-fifth birthday but for the previously discriminatory rule.

CS 27/1991 (Graham) decides that the different treatment of men and women in relation to invalidity benefit is also in breach of Directive 79/7. The DSS has appealed against this decision and the Court of Appeal referred the case to the ECJ in January 1994. The main question in *Graham* is whether since invalidity benefit is a contributory benefit, the different treatment is necessary to "avoid disrupting the complex financial equilibrium" and "ensure the consistency" of the U.K.'s social security system, and so is within the scope of the derogation in art. 7(1) (a). (See the ECJ's judgment in the *Thomas* case and in *R.v. Secretary of State for Social Security, ex parte Equal*

Opportunities Commission [1992] 3 All E.R. 577.) The hearing before the ECJ took place on April 6, 1995. At the time of writing the decision is not known. The result of the Commissioner's decision in *Graham* is that the discriminatory rules in relation to invalidity benefit should not have been applied. In practice the Secretary of State is suspending payment of awards to other claimants until the ECJ's decision is known (see regs. 37 and 37A of the Claims and Payments Regulations and the notes to these regs; in cases of particular hardship the Secretary of State *may* be persuaded to exercise his discretion not to suspend). One of the complications in these cases is that women may have claimed retirement pension and then wish to "deretire" to take advantage of *Graham*. *CS/51/ 1992* decides that it was not possible for a claimant who had deretired to resume entitlement to invalidity benefit without first going through a further period of 28 weeks' entitlement to sickness benefit. To deretire a woman must be under 65, whereas the age limit for a man is 70 (s. 54(1) of the Contributions and Benefits Act; reg. 2(1) of the Social Security (Widow's Benefit and Retirement Pensions) Regulations 1979 (S.I. 1979 No. 642)). *CP/1/1994* holds, based on the decision of the ECJ in *R v. Secretary of State for Social Security, ex parte Smithson*, ECJ Case 243/90, that this rule is not contrary to Directive 79/7. But it is suggested that the Commissioner's interpretation of the ECJ's decision is not correct. *Smithson* was a housing benefit case. Mrs Smithson was 67 and wished to deretire in order to be able to claim sickness, and then invalidy benefit, so that she could qualify for a higher pensioner premium. The ECJ held that housing benefit was not covered by Directive 79/7. It was argued before the Commissioner that the Court's judgment did not dispose of the separate question whether it was a breach of the Directive to prevent a woman exercising an option to claim a benefit (such as sickness benefit) that *was* covered by the Directive, albeit that the motive was thus to qualify for a premium in a benefit not within the scope of the Directive. The Commissioner decided that he was bound by *Smithson*. But it does not seem to have been sufficiently appreciated by the Commissioner (or indeed the ECJ) that this separate issue had been raised by the second question referred to the ECJ in *Smithson*. It appears to have been for this reason that the ECJ did not answer that question. A decision dealing directly with this issue as a separate question would be helpful, but for the amount *CP/1/1994* will apply.

The position under the new incapacity benefit regime is that long-term incapacity benefit is not payable at all after pensionable age (whereas, provided retirement pension had not been claimed, invalidity benefit was payable for a further five years at the rate at which retirement pension would have been paid). The discrimination against women therefore remains. See *CPAG's Rights Guide to Non-Means Tested Benefits* for more details on the implications of the *Graham* case, and in particular the position of women reaching 60 after April 12, 1995.

The new form of head (b) is a consequence of the changes associated with the introduction of incapacity benefit (which replaced sickness benefit and invalidity benefit from April 13, 1995). It is no longer linked to para. 5 of Sched. 1 (see the 1994 edition for notes on the previous form of head (b)), although it employs the same criteria as heads (a) and (c) of para. 5. See the notes to para. 5 of Sched. 1. The test must now be satisfied for a continuous period of at least 52 weeks before a disability or higher pensioner premium can be awarded under head (b), unless the claimant is terminally ill when the period is 28 weeks. Two or more periods separated by not more than eight weeks count as one continuous period. A person is defined as terminally ill if he is expected to die from a progressive disease within six months. If the person has been incapable of work (or entitled to statutory sick pay) for 28 weeks by the time an AO decides he is terminally ill, head (b) will immediately apply. Before April 13, 1995 the qualifying period under head (b) was 28 weeks. There is some transitional protection, see below. In the case of a couple, head (b) can only be satisfied by the claimant.

A person is entitled to statutory sick pay from the first day of incapacity (even though it is not paid for the first three "waiting days"). Otherwise it is only days on which it is accepted that the claimant is incapable of work in accordance with the new rules for determining incapacity for work (see the notes to para. 5 of Sched. 1) that count. A claimant does not have to be in receipt of income support during the qualifying period, so if a person has been incapable of work for 52 weeks before claiming income support head (b) will immediately apply. Any days when the claimant is treated as capable of work under the new incapacity rules (see the notes to para. 5 of Sched. 1) will not count, but note the linking rule. A person may be treated as capable of work for a maximum of 6 weeks under reg. 18 of the Social Security (Incapacity for Work) (General) Regulations; or indefinitely in other cases. Thus the effect of a decision to treat a claimant as capable of work may (depending on the circumstances) only result in that period not counting towards establishing entitlement to a disability or higher pensioner premium, rather than necessitate a return to square one. If the claimant has already been awarded a premium it will not be payable while he is treated as capable of work. But if this is for eight weeks or less it will apply again immediately after the break.

If a claimant makes a late claim for a benefit on the grounds of incapacity for work, the days on which it is accepted that he was incapable of work should count under head (b). It does not matter that there is no entitlement to the benefit, for example, because the claimant cannot show "good cause" for the late claim. See *R(IS) 8/93* (but note the amendments to reg. 2(1) of the Social Security (Medical Evidence) Regulations 1976 (S.I. 1976 No. 615) from April 13, 1995).

There is transitional protection for claimants entitled to a disability premium on April 12, 1995 under head (b) as then in force. The premium will continue to be paid as long as they remain incapable of work (in accordance with the new rules, including the transitional protection). Note the linking rule. In addition, any period immediately before April 13, 1995 during which a claimant satisfied para. 5 of Sched. 1 as then in force (see the 1994 edition) counts towards the qualifying period under head (b). See reg. 19(2) to (4) of the Disability Working Allowance and Income Support (General) Amendment Regulations 1995 (p. 374).

Head (c) applies where receipt of some benefits specified in (a) only ceased because of age limits or going into hospital. Note sub-para. (6) in relation to incapacity benefit, the effect of which is to treat a person who is terminally ill as in receipt of long-term incapacity benefit after 28 weeks. There is transitional protection for claimants entitled to a higher pensioner premium under the old form of head (c)(i) at any time in the eight weeks before April 12, 1995 (*i.e.* those who transferred to retirement pension from invalidity benefit): see reg. 20(4) of the Disability Working Allowance and Income Support (General) Amendment Regulations 1995 (p. 374).

CIS 587/1990 exposes a gap in the legislation which has not yet been closed. The claimant transferred from invalidity benefit to retirement pension in 1982. He could not qualify under head (c) because he had not been continuously entitled to income support since the transfer. If he had delayed the transfer until after April 10, 1988, he would have qualified. The extent of his need at the relevant date (April 1990) was identical under either alternative. See sub-para. (4) for linking rules. Another gap is highlighted by *CIS 458/1992* which holds that the condition that a premium has been applicable requires that it should have been part of the claimant's applicable amount. So where a claimant had been in a residential care home he could not use head (c), because Sched. 4 has no provision for premiums.

Paragraph 13

The presence of this category is required by s.22(3) of the 1986 Act, now s.135(5) of the Contributions and Benefits Act. The concern which prompted the inclusion of that subsection was that a severely disabled claimant on supplementary benefit might be getting high additional requirements for a range of extra needs (*e.g.* heating, laundry, diet, wear and tear on clothes, etc.), which the ordinary disability premium would go nowhere near matching. However, the conditions for the SDP are so tight that very few will qualify. The Independent Living Fund was set up to provide further cash help to the very severely disabled, but its budget was usually fully spent part way through its financial year. The Fund was suspended in 1992. From April 1, 1993, it has been replaced by two new funds, the Independent Living (Extension) Fund which took over payments to existing beneficiaries and the Independent Living (1993) Fund for new applications.

First note that the SDP can only apply to the claimant, not to his partner. But since a couple has a free choice as to which of them should be the claimant (Claims and Payments Regulations, reg. 4) this should not be a problem.

If the claimant has no partner, he first must be in receipt of attendance allowance or one of the two higher rates of the care component of disability living allowance, *i.e.* he must require attention or supervision (sub-para. (2)(a)(i)). Then there must be no non-dependants of 18 or over residing with him (sub-para. (2)(a)(ii)). The addition of the words "with whom he is normally residing" from December 2, 1994 is to reverse the effect of the Court of Appeal's decision in *Bate v. Chief Adjudication Officer and Secretary of State for Social Security* on November 30, 1994 (*The Times*, December 12, 1994). See the notes to reg. 3 for the implications of this decision. The effect of sub-para. (3) is that adults in receipt of attendance allowance or one of the two higher rates of care component of disability living allowance or who are registered as blind or treated as blind or carers for the first 12 weeks of residence do not count for this purpose. "Non-dependant" is defined in reg. 3. See the notes to that regulation for the intricacies of the definition. Care must be taken to apply the particular form of reg. 3 in force at the relevant time. The current version makes it very difficult for the parents with whom an adult claimant is living not to be regarded as non-dependants (but see the notes to reg. 3 for a possible argument that the December 2, 1994 amendment does not affect claimants entitled to a severe disability premium before December 2, 1994). Finally, no-one must be receiving invalid care allowance for caring for the claimant (sub-para. (2)(a)(iii)). *R(IS) 14/94* held that where arrears of ICA were awarded, it had been "in payment" for the period covered by the arrears. "In payment" in sub-para. (2)(a)(iii) did not mean timeously in payment. Thus an SDP that had been paid for the same period could be recovered under s. 74(4) of the Administration Act (s. 27(4) of the 1986 Act). This was despite the fact that the recipient of the SDP and the recipient of the ICA were different people whose requirements and resources were not aggregated for the purposes of income support. See the notes to s. 74 for a full discussion of *R(IS) 14/94*. The claimant was granted leave to appeal to the Court of Appeal, but the appeal was not proceeded with as the DSS issued internal guidance stating that such overpayments were not to be recovered. Now sub-para. (3ZA) provides that where an award of ICA is made which includes arrears, entitlement to the severe disability premium only ceases from the date the award of ICA is actually made. This should avoid any question of an overpayment of an SDP by reason of a backdated award of invalid care allowance.

If the claimant has a partner, the assumption is that the partner can care for the claimant. So there is an additional qualification that the partner is also in receipt of a qualifying allowance (sub-para. (2)(b)(ii)) or, if not, is registered as blind or treated as blind (sub-para. (2A)). There must be no eligible non-dependants in residence (see above), and at least one of the couple must not have a carer receiving invalid care allowance.

In *CIS 372/1990* and a number of associated appeals, the Commissioner held that sub-para. (2)(a)(ii) and (iii) were not validly made, since s.22(4) of the Social Security Act 1986 (now s.135(6) of the Contributions and Benefits Act) only gave power to prescribe conditions relating to a claimant's disability. Section 22(3) (SSCBA, s.135(5)) requires a severely disabled person's applicable amount to include a special premium. Heads (ii) and (iii) are concerned with the presence of others in the household and the benefit entitlement of other people, which are not connected to the claimant's disability. This cogently argued decision was reversed by the Court of Appeal in *Chief Adjudication Officer v. Foster* [1992] Q.B. 31, [1991] 3 All E.R. 846, which held by a majority that the provisions were valid. The House of Lords has confirmed this part of the Court of Appeal's decision (*Foster v. Chief Adjudication Officer* [1993] A.C. 754, [1993] 1 All E.R. 705). Therefore, the full conditions of para. 13 must be applied at all points of its history. See the notes to s.135 of the Contributions and Benefits Act for more details, and the notes to s.23 of the Administration Act for the power of the Social Security Commissioners and others to determine whether regulations have been validly made.

The premium is high, since it is in addition to DP or HPP (para. 6(1)). For a claimant without a partner it is £35.05. For a couple (where both partners have to qualify) it is £35.05 for each of them who does not have a carer with invalid care allowance (para. 15(5)).

It was argued in *R(IS) 10/94* that for periods before April 1990, (when para. 14B was introduced) where a lone parent received attendance allowance in respect of a child under 16, para. 13(2)(a)(i) was satisfied. Reg. 6(4) of the Social Security (Attendance Allowance) (No. 2) Regulations 1975 made the parent entitled to the attendance allowance in these circumstances. But if the parent, and not the child, were treated as in receipt of attendance allowance, that would mean that a child could never have satisfied the conditions of para. 14(b) on the DCP. *R(IS) 10/94* decides that in the context of para. 14(b) a child is in receipt of attendance allowance when the child satisfies the prescribed conditions and the meaning must be the same in para. 13(2)(a)(i). The introduction of para. 14B in April 1990, providing that a person is to be regarded as in receipt of any benefit only where it is paid in respect of that person was to clarify the law, not to change it. *R(IS) 10/94* has been appealed to the Court of Appeal.

Note that from November 14, 1994, entitlement to a severe disability premium has been added to the list of questions that the AO need not determine immediately (Adjudication Regulations, reg. 64(1)(b) and (3)(h)).

Paragraph 14

Since the DP applies to the claimant or partner only, and the SDP to the claimant only, separate provision has to be made for children. The child must either be receiving disability living allowance (or only not be, because of being a patient) or be registered blind or treated as blind. See para. 14B for receipt of benefit and *R(IS) 10/94* in the notes to para. 13. Any level of either the care or the mobility component will do. The child is excluded if his capital exceeds £3,000. The premium has from April 1990 been increased to the same rate as that of the adult DP, *i.e.* £19.80 (para. 15(6)), and is paid in addition to any other premium. The range of need within this category will also be vast. A disabled child would have qualified a claimant for very large supplementary benefit additional requirements. The limit of £19.80 on top of what would be paid for the presence of any child is now somewhat more realistic for severe disabilities.

Paragraph 14ZA

The carer premium is part of the Government's shift of resources amongst the disabled. It goes to a person who is receiving invalid care allowance, or is treated as receiving it (sub-para. (2)). The amount is £12.60 for each person who qualifies. The CP may encourage the claiming of ICA, against which must be balanced the possible loss of SDP for the disabled person being cared for. See *R(IS) 14/94* above and para. 13(3ZA). Under sub-paras. (3) and (4) entitlement to the premium continues for eight weeks after ceasing to receive ICA.

Paragraph 14A

In paras.12 to 14ZA receipt of a concessionary (*i.e* extra-statutory) payment to compensate for non-payment of a benefit is to be equated with actual payment of that benefit.

Paragraph 14B

This important definition of receipt of benefit in terms of payment, not entitlement, reverses the effect of *R(SB) 12/87*. It makes for a further simplification of decision-making. It also ended the argument that it was the parent of a child under 16 who qualified for attendance allowance who received the benefit. See the note to para. 13.

SCHEDULE 3   **Regulations 17(1)(*e*)**
and 18(1)(*f*)

HOUSING COSTS

Eligible Housing Costs

1. Subject to the following provisions of this Schedule, the amounts which may be applicable to a person in respect of mortgage interest payments or other prescribed housing costs under [²regulation 17(1)(e) or 18(1)(f)] (applicable amounts) are—
- (a) mortgage interest payments;
- [³(aa) interest payments under a hire purchase agreement to buy the dwelling occupied as a home;]
- (b) interest on loans for repairs and improvements to the dwelling occupied as the home[¹⁶, including interest on a loan for any service charge imposed to meet the cost of such repairs and improvements;]
- [¹(c) payments by way of rent or ground rent relating to a long tenancy and, in Scotland, payments by way of feu duty,]
- (d) payments under a co-ownership scheme;
- (e) payments under or relating to a tenancy or licence of a Crown tenant;
- (f) service charges;
- (g) where the dwelling occupied as the home is a tent, payments in respect of the tent and the site on which it stands;
- (h) [¹⁶...]
- [²²(i) payments by way of rentcharge within the meaning of section 1 of the Rent Charges Act 1977.]

Basic condition of entitlement to housing costs

2. Subject to the following provisions of this Schedule, the housing costs referred to in paragraph 1 shall be met where the claimant, or if he is one of a family, he or any member of his family is treated as responsible for the expenditure to which that cost relates in respect of the dwelling occupied as the home which he or any member of his family is treated as occupying.

Circumstances in which a person is to be treated as responsible for housing costs

3.—(1) A person is to be treated as responsible for the expenditure which relates to housing costs where—
- (a) he or his partner is liable to meet those costs other than to a member of the same household;
- (b) because the person liable to meet those costs is not doing so, he has to meet those costs in order to continue to live in the dwelling occupied as the home and either he was formerly the partner of the person liable, or he is some other person whom it is reasonable to treat as liable to meet the cost;
- (c) he in practice shares those costs with other members of his household, other than

close relatives of his or his partner, at least one of whom either is responsible under the preceding provisions of this paragraph or has an equivalent responsibility for housing benefit expenditure and for which it is reasonable in the circumstances to treat him as sharing responsibility.

(2) Where any one or more, but not all, members of the claimant's family are affected by a trade dispute, the housing costs shall be treated as those of those members of the family not so affected.

Circumstances in which a person is or is not to be treated as occupying a dwelling as his home

4.—(1) Subject to the following provisions of this paragraph, a person shall be treated as occupying as his home the dwelling normally occupied as his home by himself or, if he is a member of a family, by himself and his family and he shall not be treated as occupying any other dwelling as his home.

(2) In determining whether a dwelling is the dwelling normally occupied as the claimant's home for the purposes of sub-paragraph (1) regard shall be had to any other dwelling occupied by the claimant or by him and his family whether or not that dwelling is in Great Britain.

(3) Subject to sub-paragraph (4) where a single claimant or a lone parent is a student or is on a training course and is liable to make payments (including payments of mortgage interest or, in Scotland, payments under heritable securities or, in either case, analogous payments) in respect of either (but not both) the dwelling which he occupies for the purpose of attending his course of study or his training course or, as the case may be, the dwelling which he occupies when not attending his course, he shall be treated as occupying as his home the dwelling in respect of which he is liable to make payments.

(4) A full-time student shall not be treated as occupying a dwelling as his home for any week of absence from it, other than an absence occasioned by the need to enter hospital for treatment, outside the period of study, if the main purpose of his occupation during the period of study would be to facilitate attendance on his course.

(5) Where a claimant has been required to move into temporary accommodation by reason of essential repairs being carried out to the dwelling normally occupied as his home and he is liable to make payments (including payments of mortgage interest or, in Scotland, payments under heritable securities or, in either case analogous payments) in respect of either (but not both) the dwelling normally occupied or the temporary accommodation, he shall be treated as occupying as his home the dwelling in respect of which he is liable to make payments.

(6) Where a person is liable to make payments in respect of two (but not more than two) dwellings, he shall be treated as occupying both dwellings as his home only—

(a) where he has left and remains absent from the former dwelling occupied as the home through fear of violence in that dwelling or by a former member of his family and it is reasonable that housing costs should be met in respect of both his former dwelling and his present dwelling occupied as the home; or

(b) in the case of a couple or a member of a polygamous marriage where a partner is a student or is on a training course and it is unavoidable that he or they should occupy two separate dwellings and reasonable that housing costs should be met in respect of both dwellings;

(c) in the case where a person has moved into a new dwelling occupied as the home, except where sub-paragraph (5) applies, for a period not exceeding four benefit weeks if his liability to make payments in respect of two dwellings is unavoidable.

(7) Where—

(a) a person has moved into a dwelling and was liable to make payments in respect of that dwelling before moving in; and

(b) had claimed income support before moving in and either that claim has not yet been determined or it has been determined but an amount has not been included under this Schedule and if the claim has been refused a further claim has been made within four weeks of the date on which the claimant moved into the new dwelling occupied as the home; and

(c) the delay in moving into the dwelling in respect of which there was liability to make payments before moving in was reasonable and—

    (i) that delay was necessary in order to adapt the dwelling to meet the disablement needs of the claimant or any member of his family; or

    (ii) the move was delayed pending the outcome of an application under Part III of the Act [SSCBA, Part VIII] for a social fund payment to meet a need arising out of the move or in connection with setting up home in the dwelling and either a member of the claimant's family is aged five or under or the claimant's applicable amount includes a premium under [⁵paragraph 9, 9A,] 10, 11, 13 or 14 of Schedule 2; or

    (iii) the person became liable to make payments in respect of the dwelling while he was a patient or in residential accommodation,

he shall be treated as occupying the dwelling as his home for any period not exceeding four weeks immediately prior to the date on which he moved into the dwelling and in respect of which he was liable to make payments.

[²⁹(7A) This paragraph shall apply to a person who enters residential accommodation—

(a) for the purpose of ascertaining whether the accommodation suits his needs, and

(b) with the intention of returning to the dwelling which is normally occupied by him as his home should, in the event, the residential accommodation prove not to suit his needs, and

(c) while the part of the dwelling which is normally occupied by him as his home is not let, or as the case may be, sublet.

(7B) A person to whom paragraph (7A) applies shall be treated as if he is occupying the dwelling he normally occupies as his home for a period not exceeding, subject to an overall limit of 52 weeks on the absence from that home, 13 weeks beginning from the first day he enters a residential accommodation.]

(8) [²⁹ Subject to sub-paragraph (8B),] a person shall be treated as occupying a dwelling as his home for [²⁹ a period not exceeding 13 weeks beginning from the first day of that absence from the home] while he is temporarily absent therefrom only if—

(a) he intends to return to occupy the dwelling as his home; and

(b) the part of the dwelling normally occupied by him has not been let or, as the case may be, sub-let; and

(c) the period of absence is unlikely to exceed [²⁹ 13 weeks.]

[²⁹(8A) This sub-paragraph shall apply to a person who is temporarily absent from the dwelling he normally occupies as his home ("absence"), if—

(a) he intends to return to occupy the dwelling as his home; and

(b) while the part of the dwelling which is normally occupied by him has not been let, or as the case may be, sublet; and

(c) he is—

    (i) detained in custody on remand pending trial or, as a condition of bail, required to reside in a hostel approved under section 27(1) of the Probation Services Act 1993, or, as the case may be, detained pending sentence upon conviction, or

    (ii) resident in a hospital or similar institution as a patient, or

    (iii) undergoing, or as the case may be, his partner or his dependent child is undergoing, in the United Kingdom or elsewhere, medical treatment, or medically approved convalescence, in accommodation other than residential accommodation, or

    (iv) following, in the United Kingdom or elsewhere, a training course, or

    (v) undertaking medically approved care of a person residing in the United Kingdom or elsewhere, or

    (vi) undertaking the care of a child whose parent or guardian is temporarily absent from the dwelling normally occupied by that parent or guardian for the purpose of receiving medically approved care or medical treatment, or

(vii) a person who is, in the United Kingdom or elsewhere, receiving medically approved care provided in accommodation other than residential accommodation, or

(viii) a student to whom sub-paragraph (3) or (6)(b) does not apply, or

(ix) a person who is receiving care provided in residential accommodation other than a person to whom sub-paragraph (7A) applies, or

(x) a person who has left the dwelling he occupies as his home through fear of violence, in that dwelling, or by a person who was formerly a member of the family of the person first mentioned, and to whom sub-paragraph (6)(a) does not apply; and

(d) the period of his absence is unlikely to exceed 52 weeks or, in exceptional circumstances is unlikely substantially to exceed that period.

(8B) A person to whom sub-paragraph (8A) applies shall be treated as occupying the dwelling as his home during a period not exceeding 52 weeks of his absence beginning from the first day of that absence.]

(9) In this paragraph—

[²⁹(za) "medically approved" means certified by a medical practitioner;]

(a) "patient" means a person who is undergoing medical or other treatment as an in-patient in any hospital or similar institution;

(b) "residential accommodation" means accommodation

(i) provided under sections 21 to 24 and 26 of the National Assistance Act 1948 (provision of accommodation); or

(ii) [²⁷. . .]

(iii) provided under [²⁷sections 13B and] 59 of the Social Work (Scotland) Act 1968 (provision of residential and other establishments) where board is available to the claimant; or

(iv) which is a residential care home within the meaning of that expression in regulation 19(3) (persons in residential care or nursing homes) other than sub-paragraph (b) of that definition; or

(v) which is a nursing home;

[²⁹(c) "training course" means a course of training or instruction provided wholly or partly by or on behalf of or in pursuance of arrangements made with, or approved by or on behalf of, Scottish Enterprise, Highlands and Islands Enterprise, a government department or the Secretary of State.]

Circumstances in which no amount of housing costs may be met

5. No amount may be met under the provisions of this Schedule—

(a) in respect of housing benefit expenditure; or

(b) where the claimant is in accommodation unless [²²which is a residential care home or a nursing home for the purposes of regulation 19 (applicable amounts for persons in residential care and nursing homes)], unless his absence from the dwelling occupied as his home in such accommodation is only temporary within the meaning of paragraph 4(8).

[²⁶Other Housing Costs which are not met

5A.—(1) Subject to the following provisions of this paragraph, the housing costs referred to in paragraph 1(a), (aa) and (b) shall not be met during the relevant period where those costs were incurred—

(a) after 2nd May 1994; and

(b) during that same relevant period.

(2) The "relevant period" is any period during which the person who incurred the cost is either—

(a) entitled to income support; or

(b) living as a member of a family one of whom is entitled to income support, together with any linked period that is to say a period falling between two such periods of entitlement to income support separated by not more than 26 weeks; and for the purposes of this paragraph two or more periods of entitlement and any intervening linked periods form a single relevant period.

(3) Where in the relevant period, before the housing costs referred to in sub-paragraph (1) were incurred (''the new liability''), housing costs of a kind referred to in paragraph 1(a), (aa) or (b) were applicable in the case of the claimant or a member of his family (''the former liability'') then, in sub-paragraph (1), the housing costs which are not to be met are such costs, except those costs mentioned in sub-paragraphs (4) and (5)—

    (a) except in a case to which head (b) applies, as are equal to an amount (if any) by which the new liability exceeds the former liability; and

    (b) where—

        (i) the former liability has remained and the new liability was incurred in addition to the former liability, and

        (ii) paragraph 4(6) (payments in respect of two dwellings) does not apply in respect of the former liability and the new liability,

as are equal to the amount of the new liability.

(4) The housing costs mentioned in this sub-paragraph are any housing costs in excess of the former liability which are attributable solely to movements in interest rates, and not to an increase in the amount borrowed.

(5) The housing costs mentioned in this sub-paragraph are those met under paragraph 8 (interest on loans for repairs and improvements to the dwelling occupied as the home), but as if for head (*k*) in sub-paragraph (3) of that paragraph, there was substituted the following head—

    ''(k) provision of separate sleeping accommodation for children of different sexes aged 10 or over who are part of the same family as the claimant.''.

(6) Notwithstanding sub-paragraph (1), the housing costs shall be met in accordance with the provisions of this Schedule in the case of a claimant who satisfies the conditions specified in sub-paragraph (7), (8), (9) or (10) below, but—

    (a) subject to any additional limitations imposed by the sub-paragraph; and

    (b) where the claimant satisfies the conditions in more than one of those sub-paragraphs, only one sub-paragraph shall apply in his case and the one that applies shall be the one most favourable to him.

(7) The conditions specified in this sub-paragraph are that—

    (a) during the relevant period the claimant or a member of his family acquires an interest (''the relevant interest'') in a dwelling which he then occupies as his home; and

    (b) in the week preceding the week in which the relevant interest was acquired, housing benefit was payable to the claimant or a member of his family;

so however that the amount to be met in accordance with this Schedule shall initially not exceed the aggregate of—

        (i) the housing benefit payable for that week; and

        (ii) any amount included in the applicable amount of the claimant or a member of his family in accordance with regulation 17(1)(e) or 18(1)(f) in that week;

and shall be increased subsequently only to the extent that it is necessary to take account of any increase, arising after the date of the acquisition, in expenditure on housing costs.

(8) [[27]Subject to sub-paragraph (8A),] the conditions specified in this sub-paragraph are that the loan was taken out, or an existing loan increased, either—

    (a) to make adaptations to an existing property to meet the special needs of a disabled person; or

    (b) to acquire alternative accommodation more suited to the special needs of a disabled person than the accommodation which was occupied before the acquisition by the claimaint;

and in this sub-paragraph a disabled person is a person in respect of whom a disability premium, disabled child premium, higher pensioner premium or pensioner premium for persons aged 75 or over is included in his applicable amount or would be so included but for his failure to satisfy other conditions of entitlement to income support.

[²⁷(8A) For the purposes of sub-paragraph (8), a person shall not cease to be a disabled person on account of his being disqualified for receiving benefit or treated as capable of work by virtue of the operation of section 171E of the Contributions and Benefits Act (incapacity for work, disqualification etc.).]

(9) The conditions specified in this sub-paragraph are that—
(a) the loan commitment increased in consequence of the disposal of the dwelling occupied as the home and the acquisition of an alternative such dwelling; and
(b) the change of dwelling was made solely by reason of the need to provide separate sleeping accommodation for children of different sexes aged 10 or over who are part of the same family as the claimant.

(10) The conditions specified in this sub-paragraph are that—
(a) during the relevant period the claimant or a member of his family acquires an interest ("the relevant interest") in a dwelling which he then occupies as his home; and
(b) in the week preceding the week in which the relevant interest was acquired, the applicable amount of the claimant or a member of his family included an amount determined by reference to paragraph 1(c) to (i) [²⁷ and did not include an amount determined by reference to paragraph 1(a), 1(aa) or 1(b);]

so however that the amount to be met in accordance with this Schedule shall initially not exceed the amount so determined, and shall be increased subsequently only to the extent that it is necessary to take account of any increase, arising after the date of the acquisition, in expenditure on housing costs.

(11) Sub-paragraph (1) shall not apply in relation to—
(a) any accumulated arrears of interest whenever accumulated; and
(b) any interest on a loan for service charges imposed to meet the cost of repairs and improvements to the dwelling occupied as the home.

(12) The following provisions of this Schedule shall have effect subject to the provisions of this paragraph.]

Apportionment of housing costs

6.—[⁸(1) [¹²Where the dwelling occupied as the home is a composite hereditary and—]
(a) before 1st April 1990 for the purposes of section 48(5) of the General Rate Act 1967 (reduction of rates on dwellings), it appeared to a rating authority or it was determined in pursuance of sub-section (6) of that section 48 that the hereditament including the dwelling occupied as the home was a mixed hereditament and that only a proportion of the rateable value of the hereditament was attributable to use for the purpose of a private dwelling; or
(b) in Scotland, before 1st April 1989 an assessor acting pursuant to section 45(1) of the Water (Scotland) Act 1980 (provision as to valuation roll) has apportioned the net annual value of the premises including the dwelling occupied as the home between the part occupied as a dwelling and the remainder,

the amounts applicable under this Schedule shall be such proportion of the amounts applicable in respect of the hereditament or premises as a whole as is equal to the proportion of the rateable value of the hereditament attributable to the part of the hereditament used for the purposes of a private tenancy or, in Scotland, the proportion of the net annual value of the premises apportioned to the part occupied as a dwelling house.]

[¹²(1A) Subject to sub-paragraph (1) and the following provisions of this paragraph, where the dwelling occupied as the home is a composite hereditament, the amount applicable under this Schedule shall be the relevant fraction of the amount which would otherwise be applicable under this Schedule in respect of the dwelling occupied as the home.

(1B) For the purposes of sub-paragraph (1A), the relevant fraction shall be obtained in accordance with the formula—

$$\frac{A}{A + B}$$

Where—

"A" is the current market value of the claimant's interest in that part of the composite hereditament which is domestic property within the meaning of section 66 of the Act of 1988;

"B" is the current market value of the claimant's interest in that part of the composite hereditament which is not domestic property within that section.

(1C) In this paragraph—

"composite hereditament" means—

    (a) as respects England and Wales, any hereditament which is shown as a composite hereditament in a local non-domestic rating list;

    (b) as respects Scotland, any lands and heritages entered in the valuation roll which are part residential subjects within the meaning of section 26(1) of the Act of 1987;

"local non-domestic rating list" means a list compiled and maintained under section 41(1) of the Act of 1988;

"the Act of 1987" means the Abolition of Domestic Rates Etc. (Scotland) Act 1987;

"the Act of 1988" means the Local Government Finance Act 1988.]

(2) Where responsibility for expenditure which relates to housing costs met under this Schedule is shared, the amounts applicable shall be calculated by reference to the appropriate proportion of that expenditure for which the claimant is responsible.

Interest on loans to acquire an interest in the dwelling occupied as the home

7.—(1) Subject to [⁷the following sub-paragraphs of this paragraph], the following amounts shall be met under this paragraph—

    (a) if the claimant or, if he is a member of a couple, or if a member of a polygamous marriage, he or any partner of his is aged 60 or over, 100 per cent. of the eligible interest in his case;

    (b) [¹except where sub-paragraph (1) (a) applies,] if the claimant or, if he is a member of a couple, or if a member of a polygamous marriage, he and any partner of his are aged under 60—

        (i) where the claimant has been in receipt of income support in respect of a continuous period of not less than 16 weeks, 100 per cent. of the eligible interest in his case;

        (ii) in any other case, 50 per cent. of the eligible interest in that case.

(2) Where in a case to which sub-paragraph (1)(b)(ii) applies—

    (a) either—

        (i) the claim for income support is refused; or

        (ii) an award of income support is terminated on appeal or review,

solely because the claimant's income exceeds his applicable amount by virtue of the fact that only 50 per cent. of the eligible interest in this case is to be met under sub-paragraph (1)(b)(ii); and

    (b) the claimant or any partner of his makes a further claim no later than 20 weeks after—

        (i) where the original claim for income support was refused, the date of that claim; or

        (ii) where an award of income support was terminated on appeal or review the date of the claim in respect of which that award was made,

the amount to be met under this paragraph commencing on a date not before the expiry of 16 weeks from the date specified in (i) or (ii) above, as the case may be, shall be 100 per cent. of the eligible interest in that case and until that date shall be the amount specified in sub-paragraph (1)(b)(ii).

(3) Subject to [²⁰sub-paragraphs (3A) to (6B) and paragraphs 7A and 7B], in this paragraph "eligible interest" means the amount of interest on a loan, whether or not secured by way of a mortgage or, in Scotland, under a heritable security, taken out to defray money applied for the purpose of—

(a) acquiring an interest in the dwelling occupied as the home; or

(b) paying off another loan but only to the extent that interest on that other loan would have been eligible interest had the loan not been paid off.

[³(3A) For the purpose of this paragraph any reference to a loan includes a reference to payments specified in paragraph 1(aa).]

[¹⁰(4) Subject to sub-paragraph (3A), the following provisions of this paragraph, and paragraph 6, the weekly amount of eligible interest shall be the amount calculated by the formula—

$$\frac{A \times B}{52}$$

where—

A = the gross annual interest calculated by the formula $C \times D$;

B = the difference between 100 per cent. and [²⁴the applicable percentage of income tax within the meaning of section 369(1A) of the Income and Corporation Taxes Act 1988] for the year of assessment in which the payment of interest becomes due;

C = the amount of the loan which from time to time is outstanding and in respect of which eligible interest is payable; and

D = the rate of interest chargeable on that loan or any part thereof expressed as a percentage.

(4A) Where section 369 of the Income and Corporation Taxes Act 1988 (mortgage interest payable under deduction of tax) does not apply to the interest on a loan or to part of a loan, sub-paragraph (4) shall apply in respect of that loan or part as if it contained no reference to factor B.

(4B) Where the eligible interest is charged at more than one rate, the amount of that interest shall be calculated by making a separate calculation under sub-paragraph (4) in respect of each of those rates of interest and aggregating the results.

(4C) Where evidence supplied by the lender shows that the eligible interest charged is different from that calculated under sub-paragraph (4), the weekly amount of eligible interest shall be calculated by reference to the interest charged.]

(5) Where a loan is applied only in part for the purpose specified in [³sub-paragraphs (3) and (3A)], only such proportion of the interest thereon as is equal to the proportion of the loan applied for that purpose shall qualify as eligible interest.

(6) Where, under the terms of a loan taken out for a purpose specified in [³sub-paragraphs (3) and (3A)], interest is payable on accumulated arrears of interest (whether or not those arrears have been consolidated with the outstanding capital), the amount of such interest shall be met under this paragraph as if it were eligible interest but only in so far as it represents interest on arrears incurred during any period—

(a) when sub-paragraph (1)(b)(ii) applied in that case; or

(b) when the claimant was not entitled to income support which fell within the period of 20 weeks specified in sub-paragraph (2)(b), [¹⁰or

(c) where, under the terms or conditions on which a loan has been made, for an initial period of at least 2 years the whole or part of the interest on that loan is not, or has not been, payable;

and, where either head (a) or (b) applies only to the extent that the arrears do not exceed 50 per cent. of the eligible interest that otherwise would have been payable during the period in question and where head (c) applies only to the extent that interest is deferred and accrues further interest under the terms or conditions on which the loan is made.]

[¹⁰(6A) For the purposes of sub-paragraph (6), in determining whether interest is, or is not, payable regard shall not be had to any obligation to pay interest which, under the terms or conditions on which a loan has been granted, is deferred for an initial period of at least 2 years.]

[²⁰(6B) Where for the time being a loan exceeds, or in a case where more than one loan is to be taken into account, the aggregate of those loans exceeds the appropriate amount specified below for the purposes of this sub-paragraph, then the amount of the loan, or as the case may be, the aggregate amount of those loans, shall for the purposes of paragraph 7 be the appropriate amount and only the interest attributable to that amount shall qualify as eligible interest.

(6C) Subject to the following provisions of this paragraph the appropriate amount specified for the purposes of sub-paragraph (6B) is—

(a) before 11th April 1994 £150,000;

(b) after 10th April 1994 £125,000.

[²⁷(c) after 9th April 1995 £100,000.]

(6D) Where a person is treated under paragraph 4(6) (payments in respect of two dwellings) as occupying two dwellings as his home, and has loans of a kind specified in sub-paragraphs (3) and (3A) or met under sub-paragraph (7) in respect of both those dwellings, then the restrictions imposed by sub-paragraph (6B) shall be applied separately to the loans for each dwelling, and the eligible interest for the purposes of this paragraph shall be the aggregate of the eligible interest for the loans on both dwellings.

(6E) In a case where paragraph 6 (apportionment of housing costs) applies, the appropriate amount for the purposes of sub-paragraph (6B) shall be the lower of—

(a) a sum determined by applying the formula—

$P \times Q$, where—

P = the relevant fraction for the purposes of paragraph 6, and

Q = the amount or, as the case may be, the aggregate amount for the time being of any loan or loans of a kind specified in sub-paragraphs (3) and (3A) or met under sub-paragraph (7); or

(b) the sum for the time being specified in sub-paragraph (6C).

(6F) In a case where sub-paragraph (5) (loans which qualify in part only) applies, the appropriate amount for the purposes of sub-paragraph (6B) shall be the lower of—

(a) a sum representing for the time being the part of the loan applied for the purposes specified in sub-paragraphs (3) and (3A); or

(b) the sum for the time being specified in sub-paragraph (6C).]

(7) Where a person who was formerly one of a couple or a polygamous marriage—

(a) has taken out, either solely or jointly with his former partner, a loan secured on the dwelling occupied as the home for a purpose other than one specified in [³sub-paragraphs (3) and (3A)]; and

[²⁵(b) has left that dwelling and either cannot or will not pay the interest on the loan, or has died,]

and, if that person's former partner has to pay the interest on the loan in order to continue to live in the dwelling occupied as the home, there shall be met in respect of the former partner under this paragraph the amount of interest on the loan calculated as if it were a loan taken out for a purpose specified in [³sub-paragraphs (3) and (3A)].

(8) [²⁵. . .]

(9) [³⁰Subject to sub-paragraphs (10) to (12)] for the purpose of sub-paragraph (1)—

(a) a person shall be treated as being in receipt of income support during the following periods—

(i) any period in respect of which it was subsequently held, on appeal or review, that he was so entitled; and

(ii) any period of eight weeks or less in respect of which he was not in receipt of income support and which fell immediately between periods in respect of which he was in receipt thereof or to which (i) above applies;

(b) a person shall be treated as not being in receipt of income support during any period other than a period to which (a)(ii) above applies in respect of which it is subsequently held on appeal or review that he was not so entitled;

(c) where the claimant—
  (i) was a member of a couple or a polygamous marriage; and
  (ii) his partner was, in respect of a past period, in receipt of income support for himself and the claimant; and
  (iii) the claimant is no longer a member of that couple or polygamous marriage; and
  (iv) the claimant made his claim for income support within eight weeks of ceasing to be a member of that couple or polygamous marriage,

  he shall be treated as having been in receipt of income support for the same period as his former partner had been or had been treated, for the purposes of sub-paragraph (1), as having been;

(d) where the claimant's partner's applicable amount was determined in accordance with paragraph 1(1) (single claimants) or paragraph 1(2) (lone parent) of Schedule 2 (applicable amounts) in respect of a past period, provided that the claim was made within eight weeks of the claimant and his partner becoming one of a couple or polygamous marriage, the claimant shall be treated as having been in receipt of income support for the same period as his partner had been or been treated, for the purposes of sub-paragraph (1), as having been;

(e) where the claimant is a member of a couple or a polygamous marriage and his partner was, in respect of a past period in receipt of income support for himself and the claimant, and the claimant has become in receipt as a result of an election by the members of the couple or polygamous marriage, he shall be treated as having been in receipt of income support for the same period as his partner had been or had been treated, for the purposes of sub-paragraph (1), as having been;

[²(f) where—
  (i) the claimant was a member of a family of a person (not being a former partner) entitled to income support and at least one other member of that family was a child or young person; and
  (ii) the claimant becomes a member of another family which includes that child or young person; and
  (iii) the claimant made his claim for income support within 8 weeks of the date on which the person entitled to income support mentioned in (i) above ceased to be so entitled,

  the claimant shall be treated as being in receipt of income support for the same period as that person had been or had been treated, for the purposes of sub-paragraph (1), as having been.]

[⁷(10) Where—
  (a) a claimant has ceased to be in receipt of income support because he or his partner becomes engaged in remunerative work; and
  (b) immediately before ceasing to be so in receipt amount under sub-paragraph (1)(b)(i) was applicable to him

sub-paragraph (9)(a)(ii) shall apply to him as if for the words "any periods of eight weeks or less" there were substituted the words "any period not exceeding the permitted period determined in accordance with regulation 3A (permitted period)".

(11) For the purposes of sub-paragraph (1)(b)(i), where—
  (a) a claimant has ceased to be entitled to income support because he or his partner is participating in arrangements for training made under section 2 of the Employment and Training Act 1973 or attending a course at an employment rehabilitation centre established under that section; and
  (b) immediately before so ceasing an amount under that sub-paragraph was applicable to him,

he shall be treated as if he had been in receipt of income support for the period during which he or his partner was participating in such arrangements or attending such a course.]

[³⁰(12) Where a claimant, with the care of a child, has ceased to be in receipt of income support in consequence of the payment of child support maintenance under the Child Support Act 1991 and immediately before ceasing to be so in receipt an amount under sub-paragraph (1)(b)(i) was applicable to him. then—

(a) if the child support maintenance assessment concerned is terminated or replaced on review by a lower assessment in consequence of the coming into force on or after 18th April 1995 of regulations made under the Child Support Act 1991; or

(b) where the child support maintenance assessment concerned is an interim maintenance assessment and, in circumstances other than those referred to in sub-paragraph (a), it is terminated or replaced after termination by another interim maintenance assessment or by a maintenance assessment made in accordance with Part I of Schedule 1 to the Child Support Act 1991, in either case of a lower amount than the assessment concerned,

sub-paragraph (9)(a)(ii) shall apply to him as if for the words "any period of eight weeks or less" there were substituted the words "any period of 26 weeks or less".]

[²⁰Apportionment of qualifying loans

7A.—(1) For the purposes of determining whether the appropriate amount for the time being specified for the purposes of paragraph 7(6B) has been exceeded, any loan taken out for a purpose specified in paragraph 8(1) shall, subject to paragraph 7B, be aggregated with any loan taken out for a purpose specified in paragraph 7(3) or (3A) or met under paragraph 7(7).

(2) Where in any case the amount for the time being specified for the purpose of paragraph 7(6B) is exceeded and there are 2 or more loans to be taken into account under either paragraph 7 or paragraph 8 or under the two paragraphs, then the amount of eligible interest in respect of each of those loans to the extent that the loans remain outstanding shall be determined as if each loan had been reduced to a sum equal to the qualifying portion of that loan.

(3) For the purposes of sub-paragraph (2), the qualifying portion of a loan shall be determined by applying the formula—

$$R \times \frac{S}{T}$$

where—

R = the amount for the time being specified for the purposes of paragraph 7(6B);

S = the amount of the outstanding loan to be taken into account; and

T = the aggregate of all outstanding loans to be taken into account under paragraphs 7 and 8.

(4) For the purposes of this paragraph a loan is to be taken into account only to the extent that eligible interest is payable on it.]

[²⁰Disabled Persons

7B.—(1) Any loan taken out to adapt a dwelling for the special needs of a disabled person shall be disregarded in determining whether the appropriate amount for the time being specified for the purposes of paragraph 7(6B) is exceeded and an amount in respect of interest payable on such a loan shall be met in accordance with paragraph 8.

(2) For the purposes of sub-paragraph (1) a disabled person is a person—

(a) in respect of whom a disability premium, a disabled child premium, a pensioner premium for persons 75 or over or a higher pensioner premium is included in his applicable amount or the applicable amount of a person living with him; or

(b) who is a non-dependant but who, had he in fact been entitled to income support, would have had included in his applicable amount a disability premium, a disabled child premium, a pensioner premium for persons aged 75 or over or a higher pensioner premium.

[^{27}(3) For the purposes of sub-paragraph (1) a person shall not cease to be a disabled person on account of his being disqualified for receiving benefit or treated as capable of work by virtue of the operation of section 171E of the Contributions and Benefits Act (incapacity for work, disqualification etc.).]]

Interest on loans for repairs and improvements to the dwelling occupied as the home

[^{25}8.—(1) Subject to paragraph 7A, there shall be met under this paragraph interest payable on any loan which is taken out, with or without security, for the purpose of—
  (a) repairs and improvements to which paragraph 1(b) refers; or]
  (b) paying off another loan but only to the extent that interest on that other loan would have been met under this paragraph had the loan not been paid off,
and which is used for that purpose or is to be so used within six months of the date of receipt or such further period as is reasonable, and the amount to be met under this paragraph shall be calculated as if the loan were a loan to which paragraph 7 applied.
  (2) [^{9}. . .]
  (3) In this paragraph "repairs and improvements" means major repairs necessary to maintain the fabric of the dwelling occupied as the home [^{23}or where the dwelling forms part of a building any part of the building containing that dwelling] and any of the following measures undertaken with a view to improving its fitness for occupation—
  (a) installation of a fixed bath, shower, wash basin, sink or lavatory, and necessary associated plumbing;
  (b) damp proofing measures;
  (c) provision or improvement of ventilation and natural lighting
  (d) provision of electric lighting and sockets;
  (e) provision or improvement of drainage facilities;
  (f) improvement in the structural condition of the dwelling occupied as the home [^{23}or where the dwelling forms part of a building any part of the building containing that dwelling];
  (g) improvements to the facilities for storing, preparing and cooking food;
  (h) provision of heating, including central heating;
  (i) provision of storage facilities for fuel and refuse;
  (j) improvements to the insulation of the dwelling occupied as the home [^{23}or where the dwelling forms part of a building any part of the building containing that dwelling];
  (k) other improvements which are reasonable in the circumstances.
  (4) [^{9}. . .]

Other housing costs

9.—(1) Subject to sub-paragraph (5), there shall be met under this paragraph the amounts, calculated on a weekly basis, in respect of the housing costs specified in paragraph 1 [^{22}(c) to (i)] subject to the deductions specified in sub-paragraph (2).
  (2) Subject to sub-paragraph (3), the deductions to be made from the weekly amounts to be met under this paragraph are—
  (a) where the costs are inclusive of any of the items mentioned in paragraph 5(2) to Schedule 1 of the Housing Benefit (General) Regulations 1987 (payment in respect of fuel charges), the deductions prescribed in that paragraph unless the claimant provides evidence on which the actual or approximate amount of the service charge for fuel may be estimated, in which case the estimated amount;
  (b) where the costs are inclusive of ineligible service charges within the meaning of paragraph 1 to Schedule 1 of the Housing Benefit (General) Regulations 1987 (ineligible service charges) the amounts attributable to those ineligible service charges or where that amount is not separated from or separately identified within the housing costs to be met under this paragraph, such part of the payments made

251

in respect of those housing costs which are fairly attributable to the provision of those ineligible services having regard to the costs of comparable services;

[²³(c) any amount for repairs and improvements, and for this purpose the expression "repairs and improvements" has the same meaning it has in paragraph 8(3).]

(3) Where arrangements are made for the housing costs mentioned in paragraph 1[²²(c) to (i)] payable for a year, to be paid for 53 weeks, or irregularly, or so that no such costs are payable for or collected in certain periods, or so that the costs for different periods in the year are of different amounts, the weekly amount shall be the amount payable for the year divided by 52.

(4) Where as compensation for work carried out by way of reasonable repairs or redecoration which are not normally the responsibility of the claimant or other member of his family, payment of the costs mentioned in paragraph 1 [²² (c) to (i)] are waived, they shall, for a period not exceeding eight weeks, be treated as payable.

[⁸(5) Where in England and Wales an amount calculated on a weekly basis in respect of housing costs specified in paragraph 1(e) (Crown tenants) includes water charges, that amount shall be reduced—

> (a) where the amount payable in respect of water charges is known, by that amount;
>
> (b) in any other case, by the amount which would be the likely weekly charge had the property not been occupied by a Crown tenant.]

Restriction on meeting housing costs under this Schedule

10.—(1) Subject to sub-paragraph (2), where—

(a) the dwelling occupied as the home is occupied with security of tenure, that is to say—

> (i) under a protected or statutory tenancy for the purposes of the Rent Act 1977 or the Rent (Scotland) Act 1984, excluding any case in which the tenant has been given a notice to which any Case in Part II of Schedule 15 to the Act of 1977 or, as the case may be, Part II of Schedule 3 to the Act of 1984 (cases in which Court must order possession where dwelling-house subject to regulated tenancy) applies;
>
> (ii) under a secure tenancy for the purposes of Chapter II of Part I of the Housing Act 1980 or Part II of the Tenants' Rights Etc (Scotland) Act 1980 (security of tenure of public sector tenants);
>
> (iii) where the tenant is a protected occupier or statutory tenant for the purposes of the Rent (Agriculture) Act 1976; [⁹ . . .]
>
> (iv) under a crofting tenancy for the purposes of the Crofters (Scotland) Acts 1955 and 1961;
>
> [⁹(v) under an assured tenancy for the purposes of section 1 of the Housing Act 1988 or section 12 of the Housing (Scotland) Act 1988;·or
>
> (vi) under an assured agricultural occupancy for the purposes of section 24 of the Housing Act 1988;]

(b) the claimant or, if he is a member of a family, any member of the family acquires some other interest in the dwelling occupied as the home; and

(c) in consequence of the acquisition the aggregate of any amounts which would, but for this paragraph, be applicable under paragraphs 7, 8 and 9 exceed the amount of the eligible rent for the purposes of regulation 10 of the Housing Benefit (General) Regulations 1987 (rent) immediately before the acquisition,

the aggregate amount so applicable shall initially be restricted to the amount of the eligible rent immediately before the acquisition and shall be increased subsequently only to the extent that this is necessary to take account of any increase, after the date of the acquisition, in expenditure on any housing costs.

(2) Sub-paragraph (1)—

(a) shall not apply where the claimant or the member of the family became liable to complete the acquisition at a time when income support was not payable in respect of him;

(b) shall cease to apply if its application becomes inappropriate by reason of any major change in the circumstances of the family affecting their ability to meet expenditure on housing costs;

(c) shall cease to apply where income support ceases to be payable in respect of the claimant or his family except that it shall reapply wherever income support again becomes payable within a period of eight weeks or less.

(3) Where the amounts to be met under paragraphs 7 to 9 and, subject to any deduction applicable under paragraph 11 are excessive, they shall be subject to restriction in accordance with sub-paragraphs (4) [¹⁰to (6A)].

(4) [¹⁰ . . .]The amounts to be met shall be regarded as excessive [¹⁰where—]

(a) the dwelling occupied as the home, excluding any part which is let [⁴ . . .], is larger than is required by the claimant and his family and any child or young person to whom regulation 16(4) applies (foster children) and any other non-dependants having regard, in particular, to suitable alternative accommodation occupied by a household of the same size; or

(b) the immediate area in which the dwelling occupied as the home is located is more expensive than other areas in which suitable alternative accommodation exists; or

(c) the outgoings of the dwelling occupied as the home in respect of which the amounts to be met under paragraphs 7 to 10 are higher than the outgoings of suitable alternative accommodation in the area,

[¹⁰but for the purposes of this sub-paragraph no regard shall be had to the capital value of the dwelling occupied as the home.]

(5) Where, having regard to the relevant factors, it is not reasonable to expect the claimant and his family to seek alternative cheaper accommodation no restrictions shall be made [⁷under sub-paragraph (3)].

(6) Where sub-paragraph (5) does not apply and the claimant (or other member of the family) was able to meet the financial commitments for the dwelling occupied as the home when these were entered into, no restriction shall be made under this paragraph during the first six months of any period of entitlement to income support nor during the next six months if and so long as the claimant uses his best endeavours to obtain cheaper accommodation [¹²or, as the case may be, no restriction shall be made under this paragraph on review during the six months from the date of the review nor during the next six months if and so long as the claimant so uses his best endeavours.]

[²¹(6ZA) For the purposes of calculating any period of 6 months referred to in sub-paragraph (6), and for those purposes only, a person shall be treated as entitled to income support for any period of 8 weeks or less in respect of which he was not in receipt of income support and which fell immediately between periods in respect of which he was in receipt thereof.

(6ZB) Any period in respect of which—

(a) income support was paid to a person, and

(b) it was subsequently determined on appeal or review that he was not entitled to income support for that period,

shall be treated for the purposes of sub-paragraph (6ZA) as a period in respect of which he was not in receipt of income support.

(6ZC) Heads (c) to (f) of sub-paragraph (9) of paragraph 7 shall apply to sub-paragraph (6ZA) as they apply to sub-paragraph (1) of paragraph 7 but with the modification that the words "Subject to sub-paragraphs (10) and (11)" were omitted and references to "the claimant" were references to the person mentioned in sub-paragraph (6ZA).]

[¹⁰(6A) Where sub-paragraph (4) applies the amounts to be met shall be restricted and the excess over the amounts which the claimant would need to obtain suitable alternative accommodation shall not be allowed.]

(7) [⁷In sub-paragraph (5)] "the relevant factors" are—

(a) the availability of suitable accommodation and the level of housing costs in the area; and

(b) the circumstances of the family including in particular the age and state of health of its members, the employment prospects of the claimant and, where a change in accommodation is likely to result in a change of school, the effect on the education of any child or young person who is a member of his family, or any child or young person who is not treated as part of his family by virtue of regulation 16(4) (foster children).

Non-dependant deductions

11.—[⁹(1) Subject to the following provisions of this paragraph, the following deductions from the amount to be met under the preceding paragraphs of this Schedule in respect of housing costs shall be made in respect of a non-dependant—

    (a) in respect of a non-dependant aged 18 or over who is in remunerative work, [²⁸£30.00];

    (b) in respect of a non-dependant aged 18 or over to whom head (*a*) does not apply, [²⁸£5.00].]

[¹⁰(2) In the case of a non-dependant aged 18 or more to whom sub-paragraph (1)(*a*) applies because he is in remunerative work, where the claimant satisfies the adjudication officer that the non-dependant's gross weekly income [¹⁴is—

    (i) less than [²⁸£74.00], the deduction to be made under this paragraph shall be the deduction specified in sub-paragraph (1)(*b*);

    (ii) not less than [²⁸£74.00] but less than [²⁸£111.00], the deduction to be made under this paragraph shall be [²⁸£10.00];

    (iii) not less than [²⁸£111.00] but less than [²⁸£145.00], the deduction to be made under this paragraph shall be [²⁸£14.00]].]

(3) Only one deduction shall be made under this paragraph in respect of a couple or, as the case may be, the members of a polygamous marriage, and [¹⁷where, but for this sub-paragraph, the amount that would fall to be deducted in respect of one member of a couple or polygamous marriage is higher than the amount (if any) that would fall to be deducted in respect of the other, or any other, member, the higher amount shall be deducted.]

(4) In applying the provisions of sub-paragraph (2) in the case of a couple or, as the case may be, a polygamous marriage, regard shall be had, for the purpose of sub-paragraph (2) to the couple's or, as the case may be, all the members of the polygamous marriage's, joint weekly income.

(5) Where a person is a non-dependant in respect of more than one joint occupier of a dwelling (except where the joint occupiers are a couple or members of a polygamous marriage), the deduction in respect of that non-dependant shall be apportioned between the joint occupiers (the amount so apportioned being rounded to the nearest penny) having regard to the number of joint occupiers and the proportion of the housing costs in respect of the dwelling occupied as the home payable by each of them.

(6) No deduction shall be made in respect of any non-dependants occupying the dwelling occupied as the home of the claimant, if the claimant or any partner of his is—

    (a) blind or treated as blind by virtue of paragraph 12 of Schedule 2 (additional condition for the higher pensioner and disability premiums); or

[¹⁴(b) receiving in respect of himself either—

        (i) attendance allowance; or

        (ii) the care component of the disability living allowance.]

(7) No deduction shall be made in respect of a non-dependant—

    (a) if, although he resides with the claimant, it appears to the adjudication officer that the dwelling occupied as his home is normally elsewhere; or

    (b) if he is in receipt of a training allowance paid in connection with a Youth Training Scheme established under section 2 of the Employment and Training Act 1973 [¹¹or section 2 of the Enterprise and New Towns (Scotland) Act 1990] [¹¹ . . .]; or

    (c) if he is a full-time student during a period of study [¹⁰or, if he is not in remunerative work, during a recognised summer vacation appropriate to his course;] or

(d) if he is aged under 25 and in receipt of income support [[9] . . .]; or

(e) in respect of whom a deduction in the calculation of a rent rebate or allowance falls to be made under regulation 63 of the Housing Benefit (General) Regulations 1987 [[13](non-dependant deductions); or]

[[13](f) to whom, but for paragraph (2C) of regulation 3 (definition of non-dependant), paragraph (2B) of [[13]that regulation would apply; or]]

[[13](g) if he is not residing with the claimant because he has been a patient for a period in excess of six weeks, or a prisoner, and for these purposes—

    (i) "patient" and "prisoner" respectively have the meanings given in regulation 21(3) (special cases), and

    (ii) the period of six weeks shall be calculated by reference to paragraph (2) of that regulation as if that paragraph applied in his case.

[(8) In the case of a non-dependant to whom sub-paragraph (2) applies because he is in remunerative work, there shall be disregarded from his gross income—

[[15](a) any attendance allowance or disability living allowance received by him;

(b) any payment made under the Macfarlane Trust, the Macfarlane (Special Payments) Trust, the Macfarlane (Special Payments) (No. 2) Trust, the Fund[[19], the Eileen Trust] or [[18]the Independent Living Funds] which had his income fallen to be calculated under regulation 40 (calculation of income other than earnings) would have been disregarded under paragraph 21 of Schedule 9 (income in kind); and

(c) any payment which had his income fallen to be calculated under regulation 40 would have been disregarded under paragraph 39 of Schedule 9 (payments under certain trusts and certain other payments).]]

Rounding of fractions

12. Where any calculation made under this Schedule results in a fraction of a penny, that fraction shall be treated as a penny.

Amendments

1. Income Support (General) Amendment Regulations 1988 (S.I. 1988 No. 663), reg. 30 (April 11, 1988).

2. Income Support (General) Amendment No. 4 Regulations 1988 (S.I. 1988 No. 1445), reg. 20 (September 12, 1988).

3. Income Support (General) Amendment No. 5 Regulations 1988 (S.I. 1988 No. 2022), reg. 18 (December 12, 1988).

4. Income Support (General) Amendment No. 4 Regulations 1988 (S.I. 1988 No. 1445), Sched. 1, para. 6 (April 10, 1989).

5. Income Support (General) Amendment Regulations 1989 (S.I. 1989 No. 534), reg. 6 (April 10, 1989).

6. Income Support (General) Amendment Regulations 1989 (S.I. 1989 No. 534), Sched. 1, para. 10 (October 9, 1989).

7. Income Support (General) Amendment No. 3 Regulations 1989 (S.I. 1989 No. 1678), reg. 7 (October 9, 1989).

8. Income Support (General) Amendment Regulations 1990 (S.I. 1990 No. 547), reg. 18 April 1, 1990).

9. Income Support (General) Amendment Regulations 1990 (S.I. 1990 No. 547), reg. 18 (April 9, 1990).

10. Income Support (General) Amendment No. 3 Regulations 1990 (S.I. 1990 No. 1776), reg. 9 (October 1, 1990).

11. Enterprise (Scotland) Consequential Amendments Order 1991 (S.I. 1991 No. 387), art. 9 (April).

12. Income Support (General) Amendment Regulations 1991 (S.I. 1991 No. 236), reg. 12 (April 8, 1991).

13. Income Support (General) Amendment No. 6 Regulations 1991 (S.I. 1991 No. 2334), reg. 3 (November 11, 1991).

14. Income-related Benefits Schemes (Miscellaneous Amendments) Regulations 1992 (S.I. 1992 No. 50), reg. 3 (April 6, 1992).

15. Income-related Benefits Schemes (Miscellaneous Amendments) (No. 3) Regulations 1992 (S.I. 1992 No. 2155), reg. 21 (October 5, 1992).

16. Income Support (General) Amendment Regulations 1993 (S.I. 1993 No. 30), reg. 2 (February 2, 1993).

17. Income-related Benefits Schemes (Miscellaneous Amendments) Regulations 1993 (S.I. 1993 No. 315), reg. 7 (April 12, 1993).

18. Social Security Benefits (Miscellaneous Amendments) (No. 2) Regulations 1993 (S.I. 1993 No. 963), reg. 2(3) (April 22, 1993).

19. Income-related Benefits Schemes and Social Security (Recoupment) Amendment Regulations 1993 (S.I. 1993 No. 1249), reg. 4(3) (May 14, 1993).

20. Income Support (General) Amendment No. 3 Regulations 1993 (S.I. 1993 No. 1679), reg. 3 (August 2, 1993).

21. Income Support (General) Amendment No. 3 Regulations 1993 (S.I. 1993 No. 1679), reg. 5 (August 2, 1993).

22. Income-related Benefits Schemes (Miscellaneous Amendments) (No. 4) Regulations 1993 (S.I. 1993 No. 2119), reg. 19 (October 4, 1993).

23. Income Support (General) Amendment (No. 4) Regulations 1993 (S.I. 1993 No. 3121), reg. 2 (January 10, 1994).

24. Income-related Benefits Schemes (Miscellaneous Amendments) Regulations 1994 (S.I. 1994 No. 527), reg. 8(1) and (2) (March 31, 1994).

25. Income-related Benefits Schemes (Miscellaneous Amendments) Regulations 1994 (S.I. 1994 No. 527), reg. 8(3) and (4) (April 11, 1994).

26. Income Support (General) Amendment Regulations 1994 (S.I. 1994 No. 1004), reg. 2 (May 2, 1994).

27. Income-related Benefits Schemes (Miscellaneous Amendments) Regulations 1995 (S.I. 1995 No. 516), reg. 25 (April 10, 1995).

28. Social Security Benefits Up-rating Order 1995 (S.I. 1995 No. 559), art. 18 (April 10, 1995).

29. Housing Benefit, Council Tax Benefit and Income Support (Amendments) Regulations 1995 (S.I. 1995 No. 625), reg. 5 (April 10, 1995).

30. Child Support and Income Support (Amendment) Regulations 1995 (S.I. 1995 No. 1045), reg. 62 (April 18, 1995).

DEFINITIONS

"the Act"—see reg. 2(1).
"attendance allowance"—*ibid.*
"benefit week"—*ibid.*
"claimant"—*ibid.*
"close relative"—*ibid.*
"couple"—*ibid.*
"course of study"—*ibid.*
"dwelling occupied as the home"—*ibid.*
"family"—see 1986 Act, s.20(11) (SSCBA, s.137(1)).
"housing benefit expenditure"—see reg. 2(1).
"lone parent"—*ibid.*
"non-dependant"—see reg. 3.
"nursing home"—see reg. 2(1), reg. 19(3).
"partner"—see reg. 2(1).
"period of study"—*ibid.*
"polygamous marriage"—*ibid.*
"single claimant"—*ibid.*
"social fund payment"—see 1986 Act, s.84(1).
"Social Security Act"—see reg. 2(1).
"student"—*ibid.*, reg. 61.
"the Eileen Trust"—see reg. 2(1).
"the Fund"—*ibid.*
"the Independent Living Funds"—*ibid.*
"the Macfarlane (Special Payments) Trust"—*ibid.*
"the Macfarlane (Special Payments) (No.2) Trust"—*ibid.*
"the Macfarlane Trust"—*ibid.*
"training allowance"—*ibid.*

"water charges"—*ibid.*
"year of assessment"—*ibid.*

GENERAL NOTE

Much of this Schedule takes over what was in the old Requirements Regulations for supplementary benefit purposes, but there are crucial differences. Some more detail is given in the notes in the 1987 edition of this book to Part IV of the Requirements Regulations.

Since August 1993 there have been increasing restrictions on the amount of housing costs met by income support. The upper limit for loans, first introduced on August 2, 1993, has been reduced twice and is now (from April 10, 1995) £100,000 (see para. (7)(6B) to (6F). Since May 2, 1994, interest on loans taken out or increased while a person is entitled to income support (or caught by the 26 weeks linking rule), which increases their housing costs, is not met, subject to certain exceptions (see para. 5A). These restrictions are in addition to those in para. 10 (tenants buying their homes and too large or expensive accommodation). All these limits should be borne in mind when considering the other paragraphs of this Schedule.

From October 2, 1995, the government intends to introduce major changes to the rules for payment of housing costs by income support. The existing Sched. 3 will be replaced, and there will also be amendments to paras. 29 and 30 of Sched. 9 to the Income Support Regulations and Scheds. 9 and 9A of the Social Security (Claims and Payments) Regulations. The main proposals are that for people under 60, housing costs on new loans (*i.e.* taken out after October 1, 1995) will only be payable after 39 weeks in receipt of income support (if a claim for unemployment benefit, statutory sick pay or incapacity benefit has been made, this will count as being in receipt of income support in certain circumstances, as will receiving payments under a mortgage protection policy), and no housing costs will be paid on existing loans (*i.e.* taken out before October 2, 1995) for the first eight weeks and only 50 per cent for the following 19 weeks; mortgage interest payments will be calculated using a standard rate of interest and all payments will be made directly to lenders who participate in the mortgage interest direct scheme; interest on loans for repairs and improvements will only be met if they are necessary to "maintain fitness for occupation", or to provide separate sleeping accommodation for children of different sexes aged 10 or over, or to adapt a home for the needs of a disabled person; the standard linking period will be 12 weeks; interest payments on loans for non-approved purposes for separated partners will cease and interest on accumulated arrears of interest will not be covered in any circumstances. There will be some transitional protection for existing claimants. See the 1995 Supplement for details of the new regulations.

Paragraph 1—Eligible Housing Costs
Housing costs are limited to the categories mentioned here. Note that rent, board and lodging and hostel charges are not mentioned, nor is council tax (as its predecessors, the community charge (poll tax) and rates were not). To be doubly sure, housing benefit expenditure is excluded by para. 5. Although only a maximum of 80 per cent. of general rates could be met by housing benefit from April 4, 1988, there was no specific provision for the 20 per cent. of rates which claimants had to pay. This was to be paid out of the personal allowances, which contained an element said to represent a national average for 20 per cent. of rates paid by claimants. The same applied to the community charge, but for council tax there is a 100 per cent. rebate for those on income support, or at an equivalent level of income.

Note that water rates are not included. They are to be paid out of the personal allowances. The supplementary benefit allowance for maintenance and insurance for owner-occupiers has gone, and is intended to be subsumed into the rates of personal allowance. See the notes on para. 1(h) for the consequences of this policy.

Note also reg. 64(1)(a) of the Adjudication Regulations which specifically provides that where a claimant's housing costs cannot be immediately determined, an AO can decide the claim on the basis of those costs that can be immediately determined.

CIS 636/1992 (confirmed by the Court of Appeal in *Brain v. Chief Adjudication Officer*, December 2, 1993) holds that an amount for housing costs is limited to what the claimant is actually required to pay. Under the terms of her mortgage the claimant was not liable to pay any capital or interest so long as the amount outstanding (including accrued interest) did not exceed 75 per cent. of the value of the mortgaged property. She was not entitled to an amount for mortgage interest while she was not liable to pay it. See also *CIS 743/1993* in the note to para. 3(a).

The conditions for meeting costs in sub-paras. (c) to (g) and (i) are contained in para. 9. The conditions for meeting costs in sub-paras. (a) and (aa) are contained in para. 7. The conditions for meeting the costs in sub-para. (b) are contained in para. 8. The addition in sub-para. (b) of the interest on loans for service charges to pay for repairs and improvements is the compensation for the abolition in February 1993, of the category of "analogous payments." *R(IS) 3/94* confirms that para. 1(a) to (h) (now (a) to (i)) sets out heads of entitlement only, which are expanded and explained in subsequent paragraphs. Both paras. 1 and 2 are subject to the following paragraphs of the Schedule. So the effect of para. 1(a) is restricted by para. 7, and the effect of para. 1(b) by para. 8.

Para. 1(h) was an interesting survival from the supplementary benefit scheme, but since the range of payments to which an analogy could be made was curtailed, its operation was also cut back. It was not clear what sorts of liabilities might fall within sub-para. (h), although *R(SB) 3/87* and *CSB 864/1986* decided on a similar supplementary benefit provision that other forms of credit arrangement might be analogous to loans. "Analogous" means similar in attributes relevant to the question in issue *(R(SB) 5/87)*. Although category (h) mentioned an analogy "to those [payments] mentioned in this paragraph," the approach of *R(SB) 3/87* to similar words was that an analogy to any one payment would suffice. Then *CSIS 4/1990* held that an analogy could be found to a common thread running through para. 1(a) to (g). The decision identified common threads as the relationship to the dwelling occupied as the home and payments required to others for what the others are doing to facilitate the claimant's occupation of the dwelling or the sufficiency of the building for such occupancy. The Commissioner went on to decide that premiums for buildings insurance paid by an owner-occupier, and required by the terms of his mortgage, were analogous to the payments mentioned in sub-paras. (a) to (g) taken as a whole. The decision did not deal with *R(SB) 3/87*, and an appeal to the Court of Session was made, but the Government decided to amend Sched. 3 immediately to remove what it saw as double provision. The Court of Session allowed the appeal (*Secretary of State for Social Security v. McSherry*, March 17, 1994). It held that the omission of insurance payments from para. 1 (in contrast to the express provision of a sum for routine maintenance and insurance under the supplementary benefit scheme) was deliberate, and that, properly construed, para. 1(h) only allowed for items analogous to the specific items in sub-paras. (a) to (g).

The result is the complete removal of sub-para. (h). It was thought that the provision had been used to pay the interest on loans to meet service charges for repairs and improvements to the home, so the specific addition was made to sub-para. (b). The intention is that any other existing payments under sub-para. (h) would be continued on an extra-statutory basis and that other specific provisions would be added to Sched. 3 if deserving cases emerge. This does not seem to be a satisfactory way of proceeding. It was for this reason that sub-para. (i) was added in October 1993 since payments of this kind had previously been met under sub-para. (h).

For the period up to February 3, 1993, the analogy provision applies (as construed by the Court of Session in the *McSherry* case). In *R(IS) 3/91* and *R(IS) 4/91* a Tribunal of Commissioners suggests, without finally deciding, that there may be no other charges which can be analogous to service charges (category (f)) under category (h). Either something is a service charge (for which see notes to para. 9) or it is something different. This view is approved by the Court of Session in *McSherry*.

Paragraph 2—Basic Condition of Entitlement to Housing Costs

To be entitled to a sum for housing costs the claimant or another member of the family must be treated as responsible for that expenditure on the home. See *CIS 636/1992* and *R(IS) 3/94* referred to in notes to para. 1. Para. 3 deals with responsibility. Whether a person is occupying a dwelling as his home is essentially a question of fact (*CIS 480/1992*).

Paragraph 3—Responsibility for Housing Costs

Three situations are specified, to satisfy para. 2.

(a) Any form of legal liability will do, except to a member of the same household. See *R(SB) 13/82, R(SB) 4/83, CSB 145/1984* and *CSB 463/1986*, and the notes to s.137(1) of the Contributions and Benefits Act (1986 s.20(11)).

Where a separated spouse or cohabitee has a joint mortgage with the former partner who has left the home, normally the liability for the mortgage will be a joint and several one (although each case will depend on the exact terms of the mortgage deed or loan agreement). This means that each party will be legally liable for the whole payment. Even if each party is liable separately for a defined share of the payment, then the claimant will in most circumstances of separation be treated as responsible for the other party's share under sub-para. (b), if the other party is not paying this. But if the claimant is only paying half the mortgage interest (even though she is jointly and severally liable), because payments for the other half are being made by someone else, the amount of her housing costs will be restricted to what she actually pays (*CIS 743/1993*, and see *CIS 636/1992* in the note to para. 1). See para. 6(2).

(b) The standard situation here is the deserted wife whose husband is solely liable for mortgage repayments, but is not making them. There is discretion to extend this to other situations, if reasonable. An example is *R(IS) 12/94*. The claimant lived with her daughter and grandson.

Her daughter had a mortgage on their home. Following the death of her daughter the claimant applied for income support. The Commissioner holds that "the person" liable can include an incorporeal person such as the estate of a deceased person. The daughter's estate was liable to pay the mortgage but was not doing so. It was reasonable to treat the claimant as liable for the mortgage interest under sub-para. (1)(b).

In *CIS 14/1993* the claimant lived with her daughter in a home in their joint names. The daughter took out a hire purchase agreement for a central heating boiler and a cooker. The claimant reimbursed her daughter for half of the hire purchase payments. The claimant argued that she could bring herself within sub-para. (1)(b) because there was a possibility that if the payments were not made, British Gas would apply for a charging order on the home under the Charging Orders Act 1979. The Commissioner holds that for sub-para. (1)(b) to apply, there had to be an immediate threat to the continued occupation of the home, not a theoretical possibility of this in the future. On its particular facts this decision would seem to be correct (the daughter was in fact making the payments). But it is suggested that importing a requirement of an immediate threat to possession into sub-para. (1)(b) is not justified by the wording of the provision and so this decision should be restricted to its particular circumstances.

(c) Only sharing with another member of the same household will do, but see the definition of close relative. This enables sharers, who may be liable to pay a share of rent to one person, who pays to the landlord or lender, to get their proportionate share of housing costs.

Paragraph 4—Occupying a Dwelling as the Home

Generally a claimant can only have one home—the one normally occupied (sub-paras. (1) and (2)), although in some circumstances two separate units of accommodation may constitute one dwelling (see notes to reg. 2(1)). *R(SB) 7/86* holds that premises cannot be "normally occupied as the home" if the claimant has never actually resided in them. Doubts expressed about this rule in *CSB 524/1985* and *CIS 4/1990* may lead to the issue being one of fact in each case.

Sub-paras. (3) and (4) give special rules for choosing the home of students with a term-time and a vacation base.

In some circumstances payments will be made for two homes. The limit in para. 7(6C) will be applied separately to each home (para. 7(6D)).

Sub-para. (5) covers moving into temporary accommodation while repairs are done. Sub-para. (6) allows payments in three cases where there is an overlap of liability. *R(SB) 7/86* decides that there must be a liability at both the "outgoing" end and the "ingoing" end. It was suggested that a legal liability at the outgoing end might not be necessary, but *CSSB 564/1987* decides that the liability in respect of the old home had to constitute a responsibility for housing expenditure within reg. 14 of the Requirements Regulations. It was argued there that the claimant was liable to make payments to her father as a licensee, but she could not be responsible under reg. 14 because the payment was to another member of the same household (differing from *CSB 865/1986*).

It is not clear how these principles might apply to income support. Para. 3 deals with responsibility (including in sub-para. (a) an exclusion of liability to a member of the same household), but only for housing costs. Items which count as housing costs are restricted under para. 1 and do not include ordinary rent or payments as a licensee to occupy a dwelling. A straightforward application of *CSSB 564/1987* would conclude that there could be no overlap of liability if there was only an obligation to make these kinds of payments at the ingoing end. However, it is necessary to look at the problem to which sub-para. (6) is directed. This is that the "new home" would not ordinarily count as "the dwelling occupied as the home" when the claimant had not moved in, or the family more regularly lived elsewhere (reg. 2(1), sub-para. (1), *R(SB) 7/86*). Sub-para. (6) is to enable the "new home" to be treated as occupied as the home. In the circumstances it does not seem to matter that the liability in respect of the "old home" was not one included as a housing cost, provided that there was a true liability. But the reference in sub-para. (6)(a) and (b) to meeting two lots of housing costs raises doubts. See sub-para. (7).

Of the three cases covered, one is fear of violence in the former home or by a former member of the family. This can continue as long as reasonable. The fear of violence leading to the claimant leaving the former home has to be directed against the claimant, not caused by him (*CIS 339/1993*). The second is where one of a couple is a student or on a training course and the double expenditure is unavoidable. This can also continue as long as reasonable. The third is an unavoidable overlap of liability on moving home. What is unavoidable is a matter of fact. This can last for a maximum of four weeks.

Sub-para. (7) is an important provision allowing a person in certain circumstances to be treated as occupying a dwelling as his home for up to four weeks before moving in. This has consequences for entitlement to housing benefit and may fill in some of the gaps in sub-para. (6). The decision can only be made once the claimant has moved in. Then the claimant can be treated as occupying the dwelling for up to four weeks before the date of the move. The delay in moving while there was a liability to make payments must have been reasonable and fall into one of the three categories set out in sub-para. (7)(c). The categories cover: (i) delay necessary for adaptations for disablement needs; (ii) delay while a social fund application is determined and a member of the family is aged under six, over 59 or is disabled; and (iii) the move is from being a patient or in residential accommodation (see sub-para. (9)).

See para. 6(6) of Sched.7 to the Claims and Payments Regulations.

The new sub-paras. (7A), (7B), (8A) and (8B), together with the amended sub-para. (8), deal with temporary absences from home. See also the definitions in sub-para. (9). Similar changes have been made to housing benefit and council tax benefit. The Government considered that the previous temporary absence rules were too generous in some cases, but no estimate of the numbers affected or the savings that would result (except in the case of housing benefit for convicted prisoners) was produced. The Social Security Advisory Committee (Cm. 2783) recommended that the changes should not proceed, as there was no evidence of any widespread abuse and the changes could have far-ranging consequences for various groups, some of them unintended. This recommendation was rejected. SSAC also made recommendations about the details of the proposed changes, if they were to be implemented. A limited number of these have been incorporated into the final form of the new provisions.

The primary rule is in sub-para. (8). Sub-paras. (8A) and (8B) deal with absences in special cases and there is a separate provision for absences due to trial periods in residential accommodation (sub-paras. (7A) and (7B)).

Under sub-para. (8) a person is to be treated as occupying the home during a temporary absence of up to 13 weeks from the first day of that absence. All three of heads (a) to (c) have to be safisfied (see the Northern Ireland decision *R 1/91 (IS)* and *R(IS) 17/93*). *CIS 508/1992* and *CIS 484/1993* decide that the intention to return in head (a) must be an unqualified one. It is not enough for the intention to be contingent on the outcome of an event (such as a partner's admission into the U.K.: *CIS 508/1992*, or the obtaining of employment: *CIS 484/1993*). The same should apply to sub-para. (8A) (see below). Note that there is now no discretion in head (c), as there was under the previous rule. If the absence is likely to exceed 13 weeks, the person is not treated as occupying the home.

Sub-para. (8A) and (8B) deal with absences for particular reasons. Sub-para. (8A)(c) lists those people who can be treated as occupying the home during temporary absences of up to 52 weeks. They are: people remanded in custody pending trial or sentence, and those required to live in a bail hostel; patients; people (or whose partner, or dependant child is) undergoing medical treatment or medically approved convalescence in the U.K. or abroad (but not in residential accommodation); people providing or receiving (but not in residential accommodation) medically approved care in the U.K. or abroad; people caring for a child whose parent or guardian is temporarily away from home in order to receive medical treatment or medically approved care; people in residential accommodation, other than on a trial basis; people on a training course (defined in sub-para. (9)(c)) in the U.K. or abroad; people in fear of violence who are not covered by sub-para. (6)(a); eligible students not covered by sub-paras. (3) or (6)(b). Several of the categories refer to "medically approved" care (or convalescence: head (iii)), which is defined in sub-para. (9)(za). According to DSS guidance, some kind of corroboration from a doctor (or nurse) will do, not necessarily in the form of a medical certificate. There does not seem to be any restriction on who can provide the care.

A person in one of the categories in head (c) must also satisfy the conditions in heads (a), (b) and (d). Heads (a) and (b) are the same as heads (a) and (c) in sub-para. (8), except that the use of the word "while" in head (b) confirms that if there has been a letting, the person can satisfy sub-para. (8A) when it terminates. On head (a), see *CIS 508/1992* and *CIS 484/1993* above. Under head (d) (as was the case under the pre-April 1995 rule), sub-para (8B) can apply where the absence is unlikely substantially to exceed 52 weeks and there are exceptional circumstances. Presumably a stay in hospital or other circumstances over which the person has no control (which were previously given as examples under the old rule) should qualify.

Sub-paras. (7A) and (7B) apply where a person has gone into residential accommodation (defined in sub-para. (9)(b)) for a trial period with the intention of returning to his own home if the accommodation proves unsuitable. If the person has entered the home for the purpose of, for example, respite care, or convalescence, the 52 weeks rule, not this one, should apply (see sub-para. (8A)(ix)). There will obviously be some grey areas here; as was pointed out to SSAC in the course of their consultation on these regulations, the answer to the question as to the reason for entry into a residential home may well vary depending on who is asked. Note that, in this case, unlike absences covered by sub-paras. (8) and (8A), the person does not have to intend to return home within a specified period. He will be treated as occupying his home during the first 13 weeks of the absence, starting with the day he first goes into "a residential accommodation", (*not* the date his absence from home begins) even if it is likely at the outset that he will be away for longer. A new 13 week period will start to run every time a person enters a residential home, so a person will be able to try out different homes. The 13 weeks is subject to a maximum of 52 weeks for that period of absence. So, for example, if the person has been in hospital for 40 weeks before going into a residential home for a trial period, he will only be treated as occupying his own home for a further 12 weeks.

If the reason for the absence changes, the rule governing absence for the latest reason will apply. The intention is that the absence will count from the first day the person left his own home, not the date the reason changed, except where the special rule for trial periods in residential accommodation applies.

There are no linking rules for any of these provisions. This means that provided the person returns to his own home for a period, he can be treated as occupying his own home for repeated 13 or 52 week absences. As the regulations do not specify any length of time for which the person must return to his own home, presumably a very short period (24 hours?) will suffice. SSAC recommended that guidance should be provided on how long a person's return home should last before he requalifies for a further period of temporary absence. But any such guidance cannot of course override the terms of the regulations.

The people affected by these changes will usually be single people. In the case of couples, where only one member is temporarily absent, housing costs should continue to be paid.

Sub-paras. (7A) to (8B) apply to absences starting on or after April 10, 1995. Claimants whose absence began before April 10, 1995, remain subject to the previous temporary absence rule (52 weeks irrespective of the reason for the absence: see the 1994 edition) while that absence continues. See the Housing Benefit, Council Tax Benefit and Income Support (Amendments) Regulations 1995 (S.I. 1995 no. 625), reg. 7 (p. 376).

Paragraph 5—Exclusions

Housing benefit expenditure is excluded. If a person is in a residential care or nursing home no housing costs can usually be paid. But if the person is temporarily absent from his home, see para. 4(7A) to (8B) as to when housing costs for that dwelling can continue to be met although the person is in the residential care home, etc.

Paragraph 5A—Other Housing Costs which are not met

Para. 5A came into force on May 2, 1994. Its aim is to restrict the payment of interest on loans for house purchase or (some) repairs and improvements taken out or increased while income support is being claimed (or a person is caught by the linking rule). It stemmed from the Government's concern about possible "upmarketing" at the expense of the benefit system. However, no figures were produced as to the numbers of people said to have been exploiting income support by taking on bigger mortgages while on benefit. There may be many reasons why a claimant needs to take out or increase a loan while in receipt of income support which have nothing to do with "upmarketing" (*e.g.* if urgent repairs are required to the home, to accommodate a growing family or an elderly or disabled relative, to move to an area where there are better job prospects, to buy out a former partner after a relationship breakdown, etc). Some of these concerns, but by no means all, were taken into account in the final form of the provision. Furthermore, as the Social Security Advisory Committee pointed out (Cm 2537), "not only has it been Government policy to encourage home ownership, but . . . the rented sector is unable to meet the demands placed on it".

Where para. 5A applies the effect is that the specified housing costs which would otherwise be included in the claimant's applicable amount are not met, or are met only subject to extra conditions.

Sub-para. (1). This provision contains the basic rule. It makes clear that the restriction does not apply to the housing costs specified in paras. 1(c) to (i). It only applies to mortgage and loan interest payments mentioned in paras. 1(a), (aa) and (b). That means that para. 5A applies to interest on loans for major repairs or improvements to the claimant's home, but many such loans are taken out of the scope of sub-para. (3) by sub-para (5). Interest on loans for service charges for repairs and improvements is also exempt (sub-para. (11)(b)).

The wording of sub-para. (1) gives rise to uncertainty. The underlying intention is that where a claimant (or a member of the claimant's family) takes out, or increases, a loan for house purchase or (some) repairs or improvements after May 2, 1994 while entitled to income support, or caught by the linking rule in sub-para. (2), the restriction will apply. However, sub-para. (1) does not use terms like "taking out a loan" or "incurring a liability", but applies where housing costs of a specified category were incurred after May 2, 1994, and during the relevant period. Housing costs are the weekly amounts included in a claimant's applicable amount, and relate to a liability to pay existing in each week of entitlement. In the abstract, one would say that a housing cost is incurred week by week. Sub-para. (1) does not say that it applies when a particular housing cost is *first* incurred. Its express words therefore seem to catch loans taken out before May 2, 1994, or outside

261

the relevant period where liability to pay interest on that loan subsists during the relevant period. That conclusion would have a draconian effect and would make nonsense of sub-para. (3). It could no doubt be avoided by a purposive interpretation of para. 5A as a whole, but it is unfortunate that such an uncertainty lies at the heart of this provision.

Assuming that sub-para. (1) bites when a housing cost of a specified category is first incurred during the relevant period, then its effect is that the interest is not met, or, if the claimant is already entitled to have loan interest met as a housing cost, the increase only is excluded (sub-para. (3)). So if the claimant moves, or remortgages his home, interest on the new loan will be met if there is no increase, or will be met up to the previous level. The restriction only applies to loans taken out (by the claimant or a member of the family) during the claimant's current entitlement to income support or a period of non-entitlement included in the "relevant period" by the operation of sub-para. (2). If entitlement to income support ceases for more than 26 weeks, the claimant will be paid the full amount of his loan interest if he makes a further claim (subject to the 16 weeks rule (para. 7(1)) and the ceiling on loans (para. 7(6C))). In addition, loans taken out *before* a claimant or his partner claimed income support are not caught (subject to the 26 week linking rule).

There are exceptions in sub-paras. (4) to (11). Note that sub-paras. (4) and (5) only remove the effect of sub-para. (3), not sub-para. (1).

Sub-para. (2). Periods of entitlement to income support separated by 26 weeks or less are treated as continuous for the purposes of sub-para. (1). So a loan taken out or increased during a period of 26 weeks or less that falls between two periods of entitlement to income support would be subject to the restriction. The 26 weeks is much more stringent than the normal eight week linking rule. There is also no provision along the lines of para. 10(2)(*b*) for the restriction to cease to apply if there is a major change of circumstances.

Sub-para. (3). Sub-para. (3) is not straightforward. For example, it seems to use "liability" to refer to both the interest payable on the loan and the loan itself which adds to the confusion. The intention is that if interest on a loan for house purchase or repairs or improvements was already being met (note the linking rule in sub-para. (2)), the interest payments are restricted to the amount previously payable.

The effect of sub-paras. (2) and (3) is that if a couple who are in receipt of income support separate, the restriction will also apply to the partner who was not the claimant if s/he claims income support within 26 weeks. Sub-para. (3) refers to specified housing costs that were applicable to the claimant *or* a member of his family. The DSS's intention is that each former partner will be entitled to loan interest up to the previous amount (*i.e.* each would receive interest on a £30,000 loan if that was the amount of the loan they had as a couple). But an increase above that amount (*e.g.* to buy out the other partner's share) will not be met if it is incurred during the relevant period. If the couple were not in receipt of income support, the restriction will not apply if the loan, or increased loan, to buy out the other partner's share is taken out before a claim for income support is made (subject to the 26 week linking rule).

So if the interest payable is not increased, or even decreases (*e.g.*, because of a move to a cheaper house), sub-para. (3) does not apply. However, if there is a gap between leaving one mortgaged home and moving into another, and the claimant (or a member of the family) receives housing benefit during this period, sub-para. (7) would seem to restrict interest payments to the amount of housing benefit payable in the intervening period, even if the second home is cheaper than the first. The restriction does not operate if the new or increased loan is taken out in circumstances to which para. 4(6) applies.

Sub-para. (4). The restriction under sub-para. (3) does not apply to increases in housing costs that are due to increased mortgage interest rates.

Sub-para. (5). This exempts interest on loans for repairs or improvements met under para. 8. However, because it is expressed as an exception to sub-para. (3), it may be that the exemption under this sub-paragraph only applies where the claimant is already entitled to some loan interest (unless the loan falls within sub-paras. (6) to (11)). Note the restricted form of para. 8(3)(k) for the purposes of the exemption.

Sub-para. (7). A person receiving housing benefit who buys a home will be paid housing costs but only up to the level of the housing benefit payable in the week before the purchase, together with any amount for housing costs that he was being paid that week. Because sub-para (7)(a) refers to a person buying a home which he *then* occupies, it seems that this restriction will apply where a different home is purchased, and para. 10(1) and (2) where a tenant buys his own home. This is the view taken in the Adjudication Officers' Guide (see para. 27759). The restriction under para. 10(1) is to the amount of the eligible rent for housing benefit purposes, whereas sub-para. (7) refers to the housing benefit that was payable. Deductions that are made from the eligible rent in order to calculate the housing benefit that is payable (such as non-dependant deductions) could make a difference here. There can be an increase in the restricted level equivalent to any subsequent increase in housing costs, *e.g.* an increase in mortgage interest rates. There is no provision for subsequent reductions (see *R(IS) 8/94* referred to in the notes to para. 10(1)).

Sub-para. (8). If the loan is taken out, or increased, to adapt a home, or to acquire another home, to meet the needs of a disabled person, this is exempt from restriction under sub-para. (1). This should cover people wanting to move into sheltered accommodation. A person counts as disabled if he qualifies for the disability, disabled child, higher pensioner or enhanced pensioner premium, or would do so if entitled to income support (including periods when he is disqualified from receiving benefit or treated as capable of work under the new incapacity rules, see notes to para. 5 of Sched. 1). This definition is quite restrictive and may exclude some people who need care even though they do not qualify for these premiums. The disabled person does not have to be a member of the claimant's family, or to have previously lived with the claimant. "Adaptations" should include the building of an extension, for example. See notes to para. 8 on the meaning of reasonable improvements to the home to improve its fitness for occupation.

Sub-para. (9). Increased loans taken out because of a need to move to provide separate sleeping accommodation for male and female children aged 10 or over who are members of the claimant's family are exempt.

Sub-para. (10). Claimants who were only receiving housing costs specified in para. 1(c) to (i) before they purchased their home will have their loan interest met up to the level of their previous housing costs. The rule is similar to that for claimants previously in receipt of housing benefit in sub-para. (7). The restricted level can be increased for subsequent increases in mortgage interest rates (see notes to sub-para. (7)).

Sub-para. (11)(a). This covers, for example, arrears of interest accrued during the 16 week rule. It is also intended to cover deferred interest mortgages.

Sub-para. (11)(b). The restriction does not apply to interest on loans for service charges for repairs and improvements.

Paragraph 6—Apportionment of Housing Costs

Sub-para. (1). This allows the expenditure on premises used for mixed purposes (*e.g.* business and domestic) to be apportioned and the part attributable to a private dwelling met (subject to the limit in para. 7(6E)). Where the "composite hereditament" existed before the community charge came into force the apportionment follows the rateable value of each part of the premises (sub-para. (1)). Where the composite hereditament comes into existence after the advent of the community charge, the apportionment is to follow the current market value of each part (sub-paras. (1A) to (1C)).

Sub-para. (2). In *CIS 743/1993* the Commissioner holds that "responsible" at the end of sub-para. (2) did not mean legally responsible (as it did elsewhere in the Schedule), but referred to the proportion of the shared responsibility that a claimant was actually paying. The claimant was jointly and severally liable with her ex-husband under the terms of the mortgage, but only paid half the mortgage interest. She was only entitled to housing costs for the amount she actually paid.

Where para. 6 applies, the effect of para. 7(6E) is that the ceiling on loans is applied to the eligible part of the loan.

Paragraph 7—Interest on Loans for Purchase of Home

The structure is as follows.

(1) General rule.
(2) 16 week rule.
(3) Eligible interest.
(3A) Hire purchase.
(4) Amount of eligible interest.
(4A) Non-MIRAS loans.
(4B) Mixed rates of interest.
(4C) Actual interest charged.
(5) Mixed purpose loans.
(6) Interest on arrears.
(6A) Initial interest deferred for more than two years.
(6B) to (6F) Limit on loans.
(7) Former partners and ineligible loans.
(8) (. . .)
(9)–(12) Deeming.

Note the exclusion of housing costs incurred while in receipt of income support by para. 5A as well as the limits imposed under sub-paras. (6B) to (6F) and para. 10.

Sub-para. (1). What is eligible interest is dealt with in sub-para. (3). Sub-para. (1) is concerned with what proportion of that interest is to be allowed as a housing cost. Under head (a), if the claimant or partner is aged at least 60, 100 per cent. of eligible interest is met. In other cases, under head (b), 100 per cent. of the eligible interest is met once the claimant has been in receipt of income support for a continuous period of 16 weeks (see sub-paras. (9) to (12) for the meaning of "receipt" and for continuity). Otherwise, only 50 per cent. of the eligible interest is met. Note the avoidance of a "mortgage trap" under sub-para. (2). *R(IS) 2/94* rejects the argument that receipt of income support on any claim for a continuous period of 16 weeks is sufficient. The 16 week period recommences each time a fresh claim for income support is made (subject to the linking rules in sub-paras. (9) to (12)).

This system was taken over from supplementary benefit. See p. 174 of the 1987 edition for the circumstances of its introduction.

Interest is only met when the claimant is actually required to pay it (*CIS 636/1992 (Brain)* and *CIS 743/1993* referred to in the notes to para. 1).

Only interest is covered, not the capital element in loan repayments. There are a number of ways round this deficiency. First, the lender may be prepared to accept repayments of interest only. Second, if the claimant sub-lets part of the home, the first £4 of any payments (£9.20, if heating is included) is disregarded (Sched. 9, para. 19). Contributions to living or accommodation expenses by someone who normally resides with the claimant are disregarded entirely (Sched. 9, para. 18) (but see para. 11 of this Schedule). Payments from others to meet capital repayments are disregarded (Sched. 9, para. 30). Payments from liable relatives would not be disregarded, but if made direct to the lender might be excluded from the liable relative provisions (reg. 54). Payments from mortgage protection policies are disregarded to the extent that they cover, among other things, capital repayments (Sched. 9, para. 29). Finally, the operation of sub-para. (8) may in the past have occasionally allowed some capital repayments to be met.

There is no provision to cover the cost of premiums on insurance policies connected with the loan.

Sub-para. (2). This provision is necessary to avoid the creation of a "mortgage trap." If the result of initially limiting a claimant to 50 per cent. of the eligible interest was that he did not qualify for income support, he could never clock up the necessary 16 weeks' entitlement to qualify for 100 per cent. under the ordinary operation of sub-para. (1). In these circumstances, set out in head (a), providing that another claim is made within 20 weeks of the crucial date, 100 per cent. of the eligible interest is met after 16 weeks have expired from the crucial date. If an initial claim is turned down because the 50 per cent. restriction takes the claimant's applicable amount below his income, the crucial date is the date of claim. If benefit is removed on review for the same reason, the crucial date is the date of claim for the award subject to review, not the date of review.

Sub-para. (3). This provision deals with the purposes of a loan (or hire-purchase agreement: sub-para. (3A)) in determining what is eligible interest. It is subject to sub-para. (4) on amounts, sub-para. (5) on mixed purposes, sub-para. (6) on interest on arrears, and sub-para. (6B) and paras. 7A and 7B on limits on loans. There may also be restrictions under paras. 5A or 10 or deductions under para. 11.

The eligible interest is the whole amount of interest on the appropriate amount (sub-para. (6C)) of a loan for a qualifying purpose. Para. 3 deals with when a claimant is treated as responsible for a housing cost, so that it can be included in the applicable amount. See the notes to para. 3 for the problems of joint loans after partners separate but note sub-para. (7).

The loan (or any increase in the loan, *CIS 141/1993*) must either be for the purpose of acquiring an interest in the home, or paying off another loan which was for an approved purpose. In the second situation interest is only allowed to the extent that interest on the old loan would have qualified. *CIS 119/1994* decides that sub-para. (3)(b) can apply even though the replaced loan was interest free. The Commissioner points out that the interest on the replacement loan is not restricted (in percentage terms) to the interest that was payable on the replaced loan. He considered it significant that the word "the" had been omitted between "that" and "interest" and accepted that the provision was to be read as if the word "any" appeared there instead. Thus interest on the mortgage, which the claimant had taken out to repay loans from friends used towards the purchase of his home, was covered by head (b).

"Interest" includes a "further interest". In *R(IS) 7/93*, the claimant had been living in leasehold property for some time and receiving housing costs for the interest on the loan to acquire that interest. He received a further advance to enable him to buy the freehold reversion. It is held that the loan to acquire a further interest was for a qualifying purpose, and it did not matter that he already had one interest. "An interest" in the home should include both legal and equitable interests. In *CIS 465/1994* the Commissioner holds that "acquiring an interest" covers the situation where the owner does not have a present right of possession and takes out a mortgage to buy out sitting tenants so that she can move into the property. The tenants were statutory tenants under the Rent Act 1977. The Commissioner states that the primary purpose of Sched. 3 was to help with the costs of acquiring or keeping a roof over one's head. Interest in sub-para. (3)(a) was not restricted to "an interest in land" in the Law of Property Act sense, although it did contemplate "an interest of a proprietary nature or some closely analogous right of tenure or occupancy similar to that of a true tenant". Moreover, acquiring an interest could include purchasing an interest only for the purpose of extinguishing it (see *CIS 63/1993* in the notes to para. 3 of Sched. 10 which regards a similar transaction as a saie from the tenant's point of view). The Commissioner distinguished *CIS 454/ 1993* (see below) on the ground partly that the right of occupation at issue in that case was not a right of exclusive occupation.

Sub-paras. (3)(a) and (b) are not mutually exclusive, so eligible interest can be allowed under both heads.

In *R(IS) 6/94* the claimant and his wife had bought their home in joint names with the help of a mortgage. They were equitable joint tenants. The claimant was made bankrupt and a trustee in bankruptcy appointed. The trustee in bankruptcy sold the claimant's former interest in the home to the claimant's wife. She obtained a mortgage to pay for this and to discharge the original mortgage (among other things). When the claim for income support was made, interest was only allowed on an amount equal to the original loan under sub-para. (b). The Commissioner points out that on the appointment of the trustee in bankruptcy the claimant's estate vested in him and the equitable joint tenancy was severed (*In re Dennis (a Bankrupt)* [1992] 3 W.L.R. 204). It was replaced by an equitable tenancy in common, under which the trustee and the claimant's wife held equal shares. Therefore, when buying the claimant's former interest in the home, his wife was acquiring a further interest in it and the interest on the part of the mortgage advanced for that purpose was payable under sub-para. (a).

When a claimant buys a former partner's interest in the home this will constitute acquiring a further interest in a home (but note para. 5A). However, if they still count as a couple, the acquisition by one of them of the other's interest in the home, does not come within sub-para. (3)(a). They are one entity for the purposes of income support, and any transaction between them, when together they previously owned the entire interest, does not give rise to eligible interest (*CIS 526/1993*, to be reported as *R(IS) 1/95*). *CIS 454/1993* (to be reported as *R(IS) 4/95*) decides that a Class F land charge (registered by a spouse to protect his or her rights under the Matrimonial Homes Act 1983) is not "an interest in the dwelling occupied as the home", but a mere right of occupation (see *Wroth v. Tyler* [1974] Ch. 30).

R(IS) 11/94 holds that "dwelling occupied as the home" in sub-para. (3)(a) includes any dwelling intended to be occupied as the home, since most properties are acquired before they become a home. If a person acquires a site and then builds a home on it, all the costs connected with the acquisition of the site and the subsequent building work constitute "money applied for the purpose of acquiring an interest" in the home. Such building costs include the value of the claimant's own labour (put in this case at £9,000) and all bank charges (including overdraft interest) necessary to enable the home to be built. However, any interest accruing after the claimant moves into the home is not eligible interest. In addition, any new liabilities that the claimant incurred after going into occupation had to be brought within para. 8. In *CIS 679/1992* a loan taken out to purchase a strip of land to extend the claimant's garden was for the purpose of acquiring an interest in what was, at the date of the claim, the dwelling occupied as the home.

CIS 297/1994 holds that the intention to make the property the home has to be formed at the date of acquisition and implemented as soon as practicable. But it would seem at least arguable that the wording of para. 7(3)(a) does not actually require this, and that if the dwelling is now occupied as the home, even if this was not the case, or the intention, at the time the interest was acquired, sub-para. (3)(a) can apply.

In *R(IS) 18/93* the land certificate of the claimant's home had been deposited with a Bank as security for a company loan. When the Bank threatened to call in the loan when the company was in trouble, the claimant obtained a mortgage to discharge the debt to the Bank. This loan was not for a qualifying purpose. The deposit of the land certificate may have been evidence of the creation of an incumbrance on the claimant's title to the home, but the Bank did not acquire an interest in the home. Therefore the mortgage loan was not to acquire the Bank's interest. *CIS 336/1993* reaches a similar conclusion. It made no difference that the bank's charge had been created by way of a legal mortgage rather than deposit of the land certificate. By effecting the charge the claimant had not parted with an interest in his home. When he obtained release of the charge he did not acquire any interest.

CIS 563/1991 considered when money is being *applied* for an approved purpose. Clearly this is the case if it is spent directly on the purchase price and the legal and other expenses of the purchase. The Commissioner considers that it could also include money used for the purchase of goods or some other interest in property that then formed part of the consideration for the transfer of the interest in the home.

The possibility that loans for purposes not squarely within sub-para. (3) could be housing costs on the basis of analogy *(cf. CSB 847/1985)* is no longer open after the revocation of para. 1(h).

Sub-para. (3A). Loans include hire purchase agreements.

Sub-paras. (4) to (4C). Once the proper proportion of any loan is fixed under sub-para. (5), the amount of interest eligible in an ordinary case is the interest actually payable under the MIRAS (mortgage interest relief at source) scheme (but see sub-paras. (6B) and (6C) and para. 7A). If the loan is outside MIRAS, then the amount of interest payable is taken.

Sub-para. (5). The proportion of a loan for an eligible purpose under sub-para. (3) defines the proportion of the total interest which is eligible (subject to the limit in sub-para. (6F)).

Sub-para. (6). Interest on arrears accrued during a period subject to the 50 per cent. restriction is allowed, but not beyond the "missing" 50 per cent. Sub-para. (c) relates to "low-start" mortgages. Interest on arrears incurred in other circumstances is not allowed. This would be a "discouragement to thrift" *(CSB 467/1983).*

The rule can cause problems because of the terms of some mortgages. In *CIS 141/1993* the claimant's mortgage gave him the option when he was notified of a change in interest rates of continuing payments at the existing rate. The claimant had exercised this option on the occasion of most interest rate increases with the result that the capital sum owing had risen from its original £7,900 to £11,000. His housing costs were limited to the interest due on £7,900. It is held that sub-para. (6) was of no assistance to him as under the terms of his mortgage the whole of the interest was payable for an initial, albeit short, period. In *CIS 146/1993* the claimant's mortgage repayments were adjusted annually. Any arrears due to changes in interest rates during the year were capitalised, divided into 12 and added to the monthly instalments for the following year. The Commissioner holds that the claimant's mortgage payments consisted of (i) interest on the original loan; (ii) repayment of the capitalised interest and (iii) interest on the unpaid capitalised interest. The capitalised interest was not arrears but part of the interest payable in the following year. Thus it qualified as eligible interest. But the interest on the capitalised interest was to be treated as arrears and so was not payable.

Sub-para. (6A). Interest which is deferred for more than two years from the beginning of a loan counts as interest that is not payable for the purposes of sub-para. (6). It cannot be treated as eligible interest during the period of deferment *(CIS 141/1993).*

Sub-paras. (6B) to (6F). These provisions were introduced in August 1993, as a response to the meeting of the interest on some very large mortgages under the general rules on housing costs. Sub-paras. (6B) and (6C) provide that there is an absolute limit on the size of loans taken out to acquire an interest in the home or to pay for major repairs or improvements to the home which can be taken into account in calculating eligible interest. The limit was £150,000 from August 2, 1993, until April 10, 1994, £125,000 from April 11, 1994, to April 9, 1995, and is £100,000 from April 10, 1995, onwards. All qualifying loans (except any loan taken out to adapt a home for a disabled person (para. 7B)) are aggregated and the total amount outstanding is subject to the ceiling (para. 7A(1)). Para. 7A(3) provides that the restriction is to be applied proportionately to each loan where the total outstanding exceeds the ceiling. If a claimant qualifies for loan interest for two homes the limit is applied separately to the loans for each home (sub-para. (6D)). If only a proportion of the loan is for a qualifying purpose, or the property is used for mixed purposes (*e.g.* business and domestic), the limit is applied to the proportion of the loan covered by income support (sub-paras. (6E) and (6F)).

The rules apply to loans taken out before August 2, 1993, but there is transitional protection for existing claimants in reg. 4 of the Income Support (General) Amendment No. 3 Regulations 1993 (see p. 373). The effect of reg. 4 is that there is no limit on the existing loans of claimants entitled to income support on August 2, 1993 (or who are treated as entitled by virtue of reg. 4(2) and the linking rules in sub-para. (9)(c) to (f), see below), while their entitlement continues. For claimants who do not qualify for this protection but who are entitled (or treated as entitled under reg. 4(2)) to income support on April 11, 1994, the ceiling on their existing loans is £150,000 while they remain entitled to income support. Similar transitional protection is provided in reg. 28 of the Income-related Benefits Schemes (Miscellaneous Amendments) Regulations 1995 (see p. 376) in connection with the reduction of the limit to £100,000 from April 10, 1995. But the new limits do apply to any loan taken out or increased after August 2, 1993, April 11, 1994, or April 9, 1995, respectively.

The limit applies from the beginning of a claim, so that the 50% rule is applied to the restricted amount of a loan. The ceiling on loans is in addition to the existing rules on "excessive" housing costs (see para. 10). The disregard in Sched. 9, para. 29 of payments from mortgage protection policies has been extended to include interest payments on the amount of a loan that is above the limit.

The DSS estimated that less than 1 per cent of mortgage holders, and less than 2,000 new claimants, would be affected by the £150,000 limit, but it was accepted that the effect would be mainly in London and the South East. The Social Security Advisory Committee (Cm 2272) recommended that the changes should be deferred until the Government had been assured that mortgage protection insurance would be available to existing borrowers. The recommendation was rejected. The Government's view is that decisions on very large mortgages are not influenced by the availability or otherwise of income support.

Sub-para. (7). A separated spouse or cohabitee may have the interest on a loan whose purpose is not approved under sub-para. (3) met if that is necessary for the person to stay in the home. It is necessary that the former partner (although not the claimant) was a party to the loan and has left the home, but cannot or will not pay the interest on the loan. *CIS 450/1993* decides that it does not matter that the loan was taken out after the former partner left the home. For approved purpose loans, see para. 3(1)(b).

CIS 89/1992 held that the claimant could not benefit from sub-para. (7) after her husband died. The Commissioner differed from *CIS 177/1991* in holding that the words "has left" are restricted to a living person leaving the home. Sub-para. (7) has now been amended to include a former partner who has died.

Sub-para. (8). This has been revoked. Sub-para. (8) used to provide that if interest rates fell or some capital was paid off, but the claimant had no option but to continue repayments at the same level, then the amount allowed as a housing cost was not to be recalculated until there was a review for some other change of circumstance under s.25(1)(b) of the Administration Act (1975 Act, s.104(1)(b)). This amendment may affect in particular those claimants whose mortgage repayments are reviewed annually. But it is arguable that if the amount of interest actually charged by the lender does not alter until the annual review date, the effect of sub-para. (4C) is that there should be no alteration of eligible interest until that date. *CSB 717/1985* held that if the claimant had the choice of reducing the amount of the repayments, then the amount he was liable to pay had altered.

Sub-paras. (9), (10), (11) and (12). These are important linking rules for the 16-week rule.

Paragraph 7A–Apportionment of Loans
See notes to sub-paras. (6B) to (6F).

Paragraph 7B–Loans for adaptations for disabled people
If a loan was to "adapt a dwelling" for the special needs of a disabled person, that loan is ignored in calculating whether the limit on loans in sub-para. (6C) is exceeded. A person counts as disabled if he qualifies for the disability, disabled child, higher pensioner or enhanced pensioner premium, or would do if entitled to income support (sub-para. (2)) (including periods when he is disqualified from receiving benefit or treated as capable of work under the new incapacity rules, see notes to para. 5 of Sched. 1). This definition is quite restrictive and may exclude some people who need care even though they do not qualify for any of these premiums. The disabled person does not have to be a member of the claimant's family. "Adapt a dwelling" is not defined, but this should include the building of an extension, for example. See notes to para. 8 on the meaning of reasonable improvements to the home to improve its fitness for occupation.

Paragraph 8–Interest on Loans for Repairs or Improvements
Sub-para. (1). Interest on a loan for the purpose of repairs or improvements to the home, or for service charges to pay for repairs or improvements, or on a loan to pay off such loans, is allowed. In *CIS 616/1992* it was held that repairs to the common parts of a block of flats were not repairs to the dwelling occupied as the claimant's home (*i.e.* her own flat). Such areas did not come within the last part of the definition of "dwelling occupied as the home" in reg. 2(1) (see notes to reg. 2(1)). So sub-para. (3) has now been amended to include repairs and improvements to any part of the building containing the claimant's home. *CIS 659/1994* holds that the loan has to be for repairs or improvements to the home that is currently occupied. Thus the claimant was not entitled to interest on a bank loan for central heating after he moved from that home. "Repairs and improvements" are defined in sub-para. (3). The loan has to be used for the repairs, etc., within six months or some further reasonable period. The capital amount of the loan is disregarded under para. 8(b) of Sched. 10.

The calculation of the interest as if para. 7 applies means that there is a restriction to 50 per cent. of the interest for the first 16 weeks on benefit for most claimants, and that the overall limit on loans applies (but note the exception in para. 7B). See also the restrictions on the payment of housing costs incurred while in receipt of income support in para. 5A, (note the effect of sub-paras. (5) and (11)(b) in particular), as well as the general limits in para. 10. From April 1990 the level of a claimant's capital does not affect this allowance.

Sub-para. (3). There must either be a major repair to maintain the fabric of the home, or the building containing the claimant's home, or one of the measures listed in heads (a) to (k) undertaken with a view to improving its fitness for occupation.

The line between major and minor repairs must be an issue of fact (*cf. CSB 265/1987* on chimney-sweeping). External redecoration might in some circumstances be a major repair to maintain the fabric of the home or possibly an improvement *(CSB 420/1985)*.

On improvements, several decisions have considered the meaning of head (k). *CIS 278/1992* holds that in deciding whether an improvement was reasonable in the circumstances, the home's fitness for occupation had to be tested against the size of the claimant's family and its particular needs. *CIS 689/1991*, heard at the same time, decides that this could include the needs of, for example, an elderly parent. In *CIS 278/1992* the claimant lived in a two-bedroomed house with his wife and three children, one of whom was mentally handicapped. He borrowed £26,000 to build an extension including an extra bedroom for his mentally handicapped son. The Commissioner holds that the claimant was not excluded from para. 8 because the home was perfectly fit for occupation by an "ordinary" family. Head (k) was not limited to measures analogous to those listed in heads (a) to (j). All the relevant circumstances had to be considered, including whether it was reasonable for the claimant to spend money on his existing home rather than moving. In *CIS 689/1991*, the loan was partly to convert a garage into a bedsit for the claimant's mother of 84. The fact that she was not a member of the claimant's family for income support purposes, but was a non-dependant, did not prevent the use of para. 8. It was one of the circumstances to be considered under head (k). *CIS 749/1991* concerned a loan for a loft conversion to create a study-bedroom for the claimant's teenage son. The Commissioner agrees with *CIS 278/1992* that head (k) is not restricted to items analogous to those in heads (a) to (j), and that the question of whether the work improved the home's fitness for occupation was subjective, but considers that the reasonableness test in head (k) was objective. In *CIS 453/1993* (to be reported as *R(IS) 3/95*) the loan was for an extension to house a new kitchen and a shower room with a toilet. The Commissioner disagrees with *CIS 749/1991* that the test in head (k) is objective. Whether a particular improvement was reasonable is not to be viewed solely from a subjective or objective standpoint, but overall in the broadest possible fashion. The Commissioner gives as an example of a reasonable improvement, an extension that is built because the claimant has a large young family, and is likely to live there for many years. But if the children are on the point of leaving home it might not be reasonable. The question of whether the improvement increased the value of the property could also be relevant. In *CIS 129/1993* the construction of an access road (mainly over a neighbour's land) to enable renovation work to be carried out to the claimant's home came within sub-para. (k). So did a loan for the clearance of a strip of land that the claimant had purchased and incorporated into his garden. The land was rat-infested and had been used as a tip (*CIS 679/1992*).

A different test for deciding the question of reasonableness is put forward in *CIS 643/1993*. The Commissioner holds first that the words "with a view to improving [the home's] fitness for occupation" should be interpreted very broadly. If the claimant considered that the work would improve the property this should be accepted, save in the most exceptional cases. Thus, all the work in this case (which included a six room extension, a double garage and driveway (see the definition of "dwelling occupied as the home" in reg. 2(1) which includes a garage), a porch and a sink and fitted units in the main bedroom could be said to improve the home's fitness for occupation. The crunch came in applying the test of reasonableness in head (k). In the Commissioner's view, the question was whether it was reasonable that income support should meet the interest on the loan for the improvement. The answer to this depended on the claimant's position when the work was undertaken. If the claimant could reasonably have expected to meet the financial commitment involved without recourse to income support when the work was done, it should be regarded as a reasonable improvement. If not, the question was whether the advantage to the claimant justified the cost to the taxpayer.

Paragraph 9—Other Housing Costs

This provision covers the miscellaneous items listed in para. 1(c) to (i).

Of these items, the category of "service charges" (para. 1(f)) is probably of most interest. This phrase is given no special definition. *CSB 157/1989* suggested that it means charges in respect of a service rendered to a tenant by the landlord. The Tribunal of Commissioners in *R(IS) 3/91* and *R(IS) 4/91* decides that the category can extend to owner-occupiers as well. The essence is the determination and arranging of what would otherwise be left for the occupier to do for himself, on the basis of an arrangement which the terms of occupation of the property make binding on all those with the same interest in the property. However, things within the housing benefit definition of ineligible service charges are excluded (para. 9(2)(b)). This list covers charges in respect of day-to-day living expenses, a number of personal services and other services "not connected with the provision of adequate accommodation." Under sub-para. (2)(c) charges for the cost of repairs and improvements, as defined in para. 8(3), are also deducted. Thus service charges to cover, for example, minor repairs are not excluded. For interest on loans for service charges for repairs and improvements, see para. 8.

In *R(IS) 3/91* a tenant's share of the cost of roof repairs was a service charge. The obligation was imposed on the claimant by the conditions of her occupation and the service was connected with the provision of adequate accommodation, so that the exclusion in sub-para. (2)(b) did not bite. But the exclusion in sub-para. (2)(c) would now apply. In *R(IS) 4/91* the claimant, an owner-occupier, had to pay £93 a year to have his cess-pit emptied. The appeal had to be returned to the SSAT for further findings of fact, but it was suggested that if the service was carried out by an outside contractor engaged by the claimant, the cost would not be a service charge.

In *R(IS) 4/92* it was held that sums required to be paid by a tenant under the terms of the lease to reimburse the landlord for the cost of property insurance were a service charge within the principles set out in *R(IS) 3/91* and *R(IS) 4/91*. The Commissioner also found that the landlord's obligation to use any money paid out under the insurance policy as a result of fire on reinstatement of the property meant that the charge was connected with the provision of adequate accommodation. The Commissioner in *CSIS 4/1990* doubted that building insurance was so connected (referring to the earlier decision in *CIS 17/1988* where there was a suggestion to the contrary). The Court of Session in the *McSherry* case (which is the appeal in *CSIS 4/1990*) does not deal with this point. However, in *R(IS) 19/93* the Commissioner agrees with *R(IS) 4/92* and dissents from the suggestion in *CIS 17/1988*. The weight of authority would therefore seem to favour the interpretation taken in *R(IS) 4/92* in relation to payments by tenants to reimburse landlords for the cost of building insurance. Note the effect of para. 5(a) discussed below.

In *Dunne v. Department of Health and Social Security* (September 10, 1993), the Court of Appeal in Northern Ireland decided that the building insurance premium paid by the claimant as an owner occupier was not a service charge. Although the claimant was obliged to take out such insurance under the terms of both his building lease and his mortgage, it did not fulfill the test laid down in *R(IS) 3/91* and *R(IS) 4/91*. Such a premium was to be distinguished from payment required to be made to the landlord for building insurance by occupiers of a block of flats which clearly was a service charge. In *Secretary of State for Social Security v. McSherry* (March 17, 1994) the property insurance premium at issue was mandatory under the terms of the claimant's mortgage. The Court of Session agrees with the decision in *Dunne*, holding that the omission of insurance premiums from para. 1 (in contrast to the express provision for routine maintenance and insurance in the supplementary benefit scheme) was deliberate. (*R(SB) 1/90* holds that although decisions of the Court of Appeal of Northern Ireland are not binding on Commissioners in Great Britain, identically worded provisions operating in both Northern Ireland and Great Britain are to be interpreted uniformly. Decisions of the Court of Session are binding.)

R(IS) 19/93 had come to a similar conclusion. The Commissioner states that the claimant's obligation to pay the insurance premium to his building society was not an obligation arising from his interest or estate in the property, but from his mortgage. It was a consequence of the claimant's financial arrangements, not his ownership of the property itself, and thus was not a service charge. In essence, the payment was no different from a house insurance premium paid under an ordinary contract between an owner/occupier and his insurance company (which had been held in *CIS 17/1988* not to constitute a service charge).

The result is that whether the obligation to pay insurance charges or to reimburse a landlord for the payment of insurance premiums constitutes a service charge depends upon it coming within the principles set out in *R(IS) 3/91* and *R(IS) 4/91*. It seems clear that payments required to be made to the landlord from occupiers of a block of flats to cover insurance for the building are a service charge, whereas a building insurance premium payable under the terms of a claimant's mortgage is not. An insurance charge of the kind concerned in *R(IS) 4/92* also constitutes a service charge. On the other hand, an obligation on the claimant to effect insurance under the terms of a lease would not qualify.

Since housing benefit expenditure is excluded generally under para. 5(a), this means that no service charge, payment of which by a tenant is a condition for the occupation of the home (and therefore within the definition of rent), can count under Sched. 3. In *R(IS) 4/92* the Commissioner made his award subject to enquiries whether the reimbursement of the landlord's insurance premiums would be included in the claimant's rent for housing benefit purposes. If a charge includes fuel charges, deductions are to be made. The standard amounts to be deducted under sub-para. (2)(a) are (from April 1995): heating (apart from hot water), £9.20; hot water, £1.10; lighting, 75p; cooking, £1.10. The standard amounts can be altered on evidence of the actual or estimated charge.

Paragraph 10—Restrictions on Meeting Housing Costs

This covers two specific forms of restriction on the amount of housing costs to be met.

Sub-paras. (1) and (2) cover cases where tenants buy their homes. Sub-paras. (3) to (7) cover accommodation which is too large or expensive. These restrictions are in addition to the ceiling on loans (paras. 7(6B) and (6C) and 7A), and the restriction on loans taken out, or increased, while the claimant is entitled to income support (para. 5A).

Sub-para. (1). If the claimant's home is occupied under a tenancy with security of tenure or (from April 1990) under an assured tenancy and the claimant or a member of the family acquires an interest in the home any housing costs are initially (*R(IS) 8/94*) restricted to the amount of eligible rent (for housing benefit purposes) payable immediately before the acquisition. (Sub-para. 5A(7) applies (from May 2, 1994) a similar (although not identical) restriction to anyone receiving housing benefit who moves into owner-occupation.) It is a condition of the application of sub-para. (1) that at the date of liability to complete the acquisition income support was payable in respect of the new owner.

In *R(IS) 13/94* the claimant used his capital in excess of the statutory limit as the deposit for the purchase of his council house. As his income support award could not start until after he had divested himself of this capital (*i.e.* the day after he completed the purchase), the limitation on eligible interest in sub-para. 2(a) did not apply. In some cases (*e.g.* where a claimant's entitlement to income support is very small) it may be worth withdrawing a claim for a period and then reclaiming free of this provision. The existence of sub-para. (1) (and now para. 5A) is perhaps ironic given the Government's encouragement of council tenants to buy their homes and of owner-occupation in general. There can be an increase in the restricted level equivalent to any subsequent increase in housing costs, *e.g.* an increase in mortgage interest rates. But there is no provision for subsequent reductions. So if interest rates later fall, a claimant can continue to enjoy the partial relief from restriction due to the previous increase in mortgage interest rates (*R(IS) 8/94*). The restriction can cease to apply under sub-para. (2)(b) or (c). If the eligible interest falls below the restricted level the allowable housing costs are the lower figure (*R(IS) 8/94*).

Sub-para. (2). Head (a) is dealt with above. Under head (b) the restriction ceases to apply if there is a major change in the family's circumstances affecting their ability to meet the housing costs. What is major is a matter of opinion. It might cover the loss of a partner's earnings, the loss of some benefit which is normally disregarded or a significant depletion of capital. If the claimant believes that the mortgage payments will be met by someone else, but this does not materialise, this could be a major change of circumstances (*CIS 404/1992*).

In *CIS 546/1993* the major change was the claimant's son leaving the home which they were jointly purchasing. The Commissioner decides that "family" was to be defined as in s. 137(1) SSCBA and so head (b) did not assist the claimant. The effect of this is that single people without children cannot benefit from head (b). There seems to be no clear policy reason for this unfairness to single claimants. The Commissioner in *CIS 546/1993* notes that the claimant was now being allowed her son's share of the mortgage interest (under para. 3(1)(b)) but that seems to be beside the point. What about a single claimant who, for example, suffers a reduction in his benefit income? In the case of a couple (with or without children) this could be treated as a major change in circumstances. It is difficult to see why there should be different treatment for a single claimant in this situation. The predecessor of sub-para. (2)(b) was reg. 20(2) of the Supplementary Benefit (Requirements) Regulations which referred to "any major change in the circumstances of the assessment unit". Although the concept of assessment unit under the supplementary benefit scheme was roughly equivalent to that of "family" under income support, crucially an assessment unit could consist of a single claimant (reg. 2(1) of the Requirements Regulations). Thus reg. 20(2) did apply to single claimants. The definition of "family" in s. 137(1) does not apply if the context otherwise requires. This would seem to be a case where "family" should include a single claimant without children. (See *CIS 104/1991* referred to in the note to sub-para. (4) where the Commissioner did read in the words "if any" after "the claimant and his family").

Under head (c) a break in entitlement to income support of more than eight weeks removes the restriction.

Sub-para. (3). This indicates that any deduction for the presence of a non-dependant under para. 11 should be made first. Then if the level of housing costs is excessive there is to be a reduction here.

Sub-para. (4). There are three sets of circumstance in which a restriction can be applied under sub-para. (3). The first is that the home is unnecessarily large for the claimant's family, including any foster children and non-dependants living in the household. An absolutely literal reading of the provision would lead to the result that it does not apply to a single claimant, who does not have a family. *CIS 104/1991* decides that the words must be read as "the claimant and his family (if any)." Any part of the home which is let is ignored in assessing the size of the accommodation against the needs of its occupants. At base is an issue of opinion about what is unnecessarily large. Some common situations caught by this provision (*e.g.* a married couple whose children have left home, or a deserted spouse) may escape under sub-para. (5) or (6).

The second set of circumstances, under head (b), is that the immediate area of the home is more expensive than other areas in which suitable alternative accommodation is available. It is not at all clear how restricted the immediate area might be, but it will probably be more limited than the area under (c). *CSB 1016/1982* suggests that the delimitation of an area is likely to be within the knowledge of SSATs. It must be possible also to identify another cheaper area (using the *CSB 1016/1982* definition) in which suitable alternative accommodation exists. The condition of suitability will limit the distance within which other areas can be sought *(R(IS) 12/91)*.

Finally, under head (c), there is a restriction if the outgoings of the home are higher than for suitable alternative accommodation in the area (not the immediate area). In *CSB 1016/1982* (in relation to an earlier formulation of this rule) "area" was said to connote "something more confined, restricted and more compact than a locality or district. It might consist of dwelling houses or flats contiguous to a road or a number of roads, refer to a neighbourhood or even to a large block of flats. It is not capable of precise definition." This approach was commended for the purposes of sub-para. (4) in *CIS 34/1989* and *R(IS) 12/91*.

If sub-para. (4) applies, sub-para. (6A) provides that the excess expenditure over that for a home of suitable size or expense will not be met. Sub-paras. (5) and (6) contain exceptions to the operation of sub-para. (4).

R(IS) 9/91 decides that sub-para. (4) operates in the same way as *R(SB) 6/89* decided that the old reg. 21 of the Requirements Regulations did. The excess is not the difference between the actual expenditure and the maximum that would be allowed for a family of similar size in a home of the necessary size or in an acceptably cheaper area. The excess is the difference between the actual expenditure and the housing costs which would be incurred by the claimant in the alternative accommodation. On the facts of *R(IS) 9/91*, the net proceeds of sale of the existing home would have completely covered the cost of acquiring alternative accommodation, so that there would be no income support housing costs. Thus the entire actual expenditure was "excess."

Sub-para. (5). If it is not reasonable to expect the claimant to seek alternative cheaper accommodation, no restriction is to be made at all. It must already have been determined under sub-para. (4) that cheaper alternative accommodation which is suitable exists. All the relevant factors set out in sub-para. (7) must be considered.

Under head (a) the availability of suitable accommodation must be judged objectively *(R(SB) 7/89* and *R(IS) 10/93)*. The particular circumstances of the claimant and his family are taken into account under head (b). The reference in head (a) to area is particularly obscure. Does it mean the area in which the home is situated or can it include another area in which suitable accommodation is available? In *CSB 1016/1982* it is suggested that it only governs the level of housing costs, not the availability of suitable accommodation, but it seems to be assumed in *R(SB) 7/89* that it governs both matters.

Sub-para. (7)(b) brings in all the relevant circumstances, not just those mentioned *(R(SB) 6/89, R(SB) 7/89* and *R(IS) 10/93)*. One relevant factor mentioned in *CSB 1016/1982* was that the home had only just come into the claimant's occupation in matrimonial proceedings. In *CSB 617/1988* the claimant was assured by the manager of the local DSS office before she moved from a house with a mortgage of £25,000 to a house with a mortgage of £69,890 that the full interest on the new mortgage would be met by supplementary benefit. Although such an assurance could not bind the AO by creating an estoppel *(R(SB) 14/88)* it was one of the circumstances to be considered. (*CSB 617/1988* is reported as *R(SB) 14/89*, but it is the unreported version that should be referred to, as the reported decision omits the last three paragraphs which are the relevant ones here.)

Financial hardship is also a relevant factor. In *R(SB) 6/89* the invidious financial position the claimant would be put in if she were forced to sell the home in which she had lived for many years before its renovation was complete was relevant. As was the claimant's inability to find a buyer because of the stagnant housing market (*CIS 347/1992*). In that case the claimant had been advised of a price range for selling his home and would suffer financial hardship if forced to sell below that price. In *CIS 434/1992* the not uncommon problem of a negative equity was relevant. A further factor mentioned in *R(SB) 7/89* was that if the claimant sold his home, his lenders would not be prepared to lend to him again, but if the proceeds of sale were not put to purchasing another house, the capital would disentitle him from benefit. Thus rented accommodation may not be a straightforward alternative. *R(IS) 10/93* holds that the inability of the claimant to obtain suitable accommodation is a relevant factor. As in that case, that inability may stem from the fact that the claimant is unable to sell his existing home, despite making all reasonable efforts to do so.

Sub-para. (6). If the restriction is not removed completely under sub-para. (5) there can be a limited exemption here. If the claimant (or a member of the family) was able to meet the financial commitments for the home when they were first entered into, there is to be no restriction under para. 10(3) (but the ceiling in para. 7(6C) may apply) for the first six months on income support or from the date on which the housing costs are determined on review to be excessive. This should include a person who was a member of the family when the mortgage was taken on (*e.g.* where a couple have separated). The exemption can be extended for up to another six months so long as the claimant uses his best endeavours to obtain cheaper accommodation. What are the best endeavours is an issue of fact. *R(SB) 7/89* holds that a claimant can only be penalised for failing to use his best endeavours if he has been given some advance notice of the necessity to do so. In *R(IS) 13/92* the claimant's housing costs were restricted by the AO from the beginning of the claim to £146.85 a week, the amount appropriate to interest on a capital sum of £110,000. At the time the capital and accrued unpaid interest amounted to £696,063.44. The Commissioner agreed that a restriction under sub-paras. (4) and (5) was indicated, but on the evidence the claimant was able to meet the financial commitments for the dwelling at the time the mortgage was obtained. Therefore the absence of restriction for the first six months under sub-para. (6) was mandatory. The Commissioner did however consider that the initial improper restriction by the AO operated as a notice of the intention to restrict housing costs after the six months under *R(SB) 7/89*. The Court of Appeal in *Secretary of State for Social Security v. Julien, The Times*, April 21, 1992, has confirmed the Commissioner's decision, saying that the issue is ability to meet the financial commitments, not prudence.

In *CIS 104/1991* the Commissioner takes the approach of *R(SB) 7/89* a little further. He holds that if the claimant could afford the housing commitments when he took them on there cannot be a restriction until there has been an explicit notice in an AO's decision that there may be a restriction in six months' time. The para. 10(6) meter has to be started explicitly and it has to run for six months. In *CIS 104/1991* only two months notice was given. The claimant had to be allowed another four months and then the question of using the best endeavours to obtain cheaper accommodation had to be explored.

Sub-paras. (6ZA) to (6ZC). A person can now (since August 2, 1993) only requalify for the deferment of a restriction under para. 10(6) if there is a break in entitlement to income support of more than eight weeks. Previously any break in entitlement, however short, sufficed. Note that the linking rules in para. 7(9)(c) to (f) apply.

Sub-para. (7). See notes to sub-para. (5).

Paragraph 11—Non-Dependant Deductions

Non-dependant is defined in reg. 3. The standard deductions depend on whether the non-dependant is in work or not, and the level of earnings (sub-paras. (1) and (2)). A wider range of deductions was introduced in April 1992, so as to be more discriminating among differing levels of earnings. The same deduction is made for a couple as for a single person. Note that no deduction is made from the benefit of a claimant who (or whose partner) is blind or who is in receipt of attendance allowance or the care component of disability living allowance for himself (sub-para. (6)). Note also the list in sub-para. (7) of non-dependants for whom no deduction is made. Those covered include those getting a YT allowance (head (b)), students (head (c)), under-25s on income support (head (d)), those for whom a deduction has already been made from rent allowance or rebate (head (e)), people who would not count as non-dependants under reg. 3(2B) but for reg. 3(2C) (*e.g.*, co-owners or their partners who are close relatives, even if the co-ownership arose after 11.4.88) (head (f)) and patients and prisoners absent from home for more than six weeks (head (g)).

[¹SCHEDULE 3A   **Regulations 17(1)(*g*),
                                  18(1)(*h*) and 71(1)(*a*)(v)
                                  and (*d*)(iv)**

PROTECTED SUM

Interpretation

1.—(1) In this Schedule—
[³"eligible housing benefit" means
    (a) for the period of 7 consecutive days beginning on 3rd April 1989, the amount of housing benefit to which the claimant or his partner was entitled in that period which relates to the board and lodging accommodation normally occupied as the home by him or, if he has a partner, by him and his partner;
    (b) for the period of 7 consecutive days beginning on 10th April 1989 or, in a case to which paragraph 7(7)(b) applies, for the period of 7 consecutive days referred to in that paragraph, the amount of the claimant's or his partner's maximum housing benefit determined in accordance with regulation 61 of

the Housing Benefit (General) Regulations 1987 (maximum housing benefit) which relates to that accommodation;]

"first week" means the benefit week beginning on a day during the period of 7 days commencing on 3rd April 1989;

"income support" includes any sum payable under Part II of the Income Support (Transitional) Regulations 1987;

"protected sum" means the amount applicable under this Schedule [³to a claimant who in the first week is living in board and lodging accommodation or who or whose partner is temporarily absent in that week from that accommodation];

[³"protected total" means—

(a) the total of the claimant's applicable amount under regulation 20 (applicable amounts for persons in board and lodging accommodation) in the first week or, in a case to which paragraph 7(7) applies, if the protected person or any partner of his is temporarily absent from his accommodation in that week, the amount which would have fallen to be calculated under that regulation for that week as if there had been no temporary absence; and

(b) the amount of any eligible housing benefit for the period of 7 consecutive days beginning 3rd April 1989;]

"relevant provisions" means—

(a) regulation 17(1)(a) to (f) (applicable amounts);

(b) regulation 18(1)(a) to (g) (polygamous marriages);

(c) regulation 71(1)(a)(i) to (iv) (urgent cases);

(d) regulation 71(1)(d)(i) to (iii);

(e) in relation to a case to which paragraph 17(b)(ii) or (c)(i) of Schedule 7 (persons from abroad) applies, the regulations specified in that paragraph but as if the reference to regulation 17(1)(g) in that paragraph were omitted; or

(f) in relation to a case to which paragraph 17(d)(i) of that Schedule applies, the regulations specified in that paragraph but as if the reference to regulation 18 were a reference to regulation 18(1)(a) to (g) only;

"second week" means the benefit week beginning on a day during the period of 7 days commencing on 10th April 1989.

[³"third week" means the benefit week beginning on a day during the period of 7 days commencing on 17th April 1989.]

(2) For the purposes of this Schedule—

(a) in determining a claimant's applicable amount in his first week, second week or any subsequent benefit week no account shall be taken of any reduction under regulation 22 (reduction in certain cases of unemployment benefit disqualification);

(b) [²except in so far as it relates to any temporary absence to which paragraph 7(7) refers,] where a change of circumstances takes effect in the claimant's second week which, had it taken effect in the first week, would have resulted in a lesser applicable amount in respect of that week, his applicable amount in the first week shall be determined as if the change of circumstances had taken effect in that week.

Protected sum

2. [³Subject to sub-paragraph (2) and the following paragraphs] of this Schedule, where the protected total of a claimant is more than—

(a) his applicable amount in the second week determined in accordance with the relevant provisions; and

(b) any eligible housing benefit for the period [³of 7 consecutive days] beginning 10th April 1989,

the protected sum applicable to the claimant shall be an amount equal to the difference.

[³(2) Where—

(a) in the second week a claimant's income calculated in accordance with Part V or, as the case may be, VI exceeds the aggregate of his applicable amount determined in accordance with the relevant provisions and X; and

(b) the amount of income support to which he is entitled in the first week is more than the amount of housing benefit to which he would, but for this sub-paragraph, have been entitled in the period of 7 consecutive days beginning on 10th April 1989.

the protected sum applicable to the claimant shall, subject to sub-paragraph (3), be an amount equal to $X + Y + 10$ pence.

(3) Where a claimant or his partner is, or both are, entitled in the first, second and third weeks to a relevant social security benefit or to more than one such benefit and consequent upon the Social Security Benefits Up-rating Order 1989 the claimant or his partner is, or both are, entitled to an increase in any one or more of those benefits in the third week, the protected sum under sub-paragraph (2) shall be increased by an amount equal to the difference between—

(a) the amount of benefit or aggregate amount of those benefits to which the claimant or his partner is, or both are, entitled in the third week; and, if less,

(b) the amount of benefit or aggregate amount of those benefits to which the claimant or his partner is, or both are, entitled in the second week.

(4) In this paragraph—

"X" means the sum which, but for sub-paragraph (2), would be the protected sum applicable under sub-paragraph (1);

"Y" means the amount of the excess to which sub-paragraph (2)(a) refers;

"relevant social security benefit" means—

(a) child benefit;

(b) any benefit under the Social Security Act [SSCBA];

(c) war disablement pension;

(d) war widow's pension;

(e) any payment under a scheme made under the Industrial Injuries and Diseases (Old Cases) Act 1975;

(f) any concessionary payment.]

Persons not entitled to a protected sum

3. A protected sum shall not be applicable to a claimant where in the first week—

(a) he is aged under 25 and, if he is a member of a couple, his partner is also aged under 25; and

(b) he is required to be available for employment for the purposes of section 20(3)(d)(i) of the Act [SSCBA, s.124(1)(d)(i)]; and

(c) he was not in receipt of supplementary benefit as a boarder on November 24, 1985; and

(d) none of the conditions in paragraph 16(4) of Schedule 5 (applicable amounts of persons in board and lodging accommodation or hostels) applies to him.

[²(2) A protected sum shall not be applicable to a claimant [³unless he, or any partner of his, is entitled to housing benefit for the period of 7 consecutive days beginning 10th April 1989 or, where paragraph 7(7)(b) applies, for the period of 7 consecutive days referred to in that paragraph in respect of] the board and lodging accommodation normally occupied as the home by him, or if he has a partner, by him and his partner.

(3) Subject to paragraph 7, a protected sum shall not be applicable to a claimant where he changes or vacates his accommodation during the period of 7 consecutive days beginning 10th April 1989.]

Period of application

4. Subject to paragraph 7, the protected sum shall not be applicable to a claimant for more than—

(a) in the case of a claimant who is a member of a family and that family includes a child or young person and during the first week that family was in accommodation not provided or secured by a local authority under section 63 or 65(2) or (3)(a) of the Housing (Scotland) Act 1987, a period of 52 weeks beginning with the second week;

(b) in any other case, a period of 13 weeks beginning with the second week.

Reduction of protected sum

5.—(1) Subject to [⁸sub-paragraphs (2) to (6)], the protected sum shall be reduced by the amount of any increase, in a benefit week subsequent to the second week, in the claimant's applicable amount determined in accordance with the relevant provisions.

(2) Where regulation 22 (reduction in certain cases of unemployment benefit disqualification) [⁶or regulation 21A (reductions in certain cases of failure to attend courses)] ceases to apply to a claimant and as a result his applicable amount increases no account shall be taken of that increase.

[³(3) Where by virtue of the coming into force of regulation 5 of the Income Support (General) Amendment Regulations 1989 the claimant's applicable amount increases in his benefit week beginning on a day during the period of 7 days commencing on 9th October 1989, no account shall be taken of that increase.]

[⁵(4) Where a claimant's applicable amount increases because a child or young person mentioned in paragraph (5)(c) of regulation 16 (circumstances in which a person is treated or not treated as a member of the household) is treated as a member of the claimant's household under paragraph (6) of that regulation, the claimant's protected sum shall not be reduced by the amount of that increase unless the child or young person has been treated as a member of the household for a continuous period which exceeds 8 weeks.]

[⁷(5) Where by virtue of the coming into force of regulation 15(a), (b) or (c) of the Income Support (General) Amendment No. 4 Regulations 1991 a claimant's applicable amount increases in his benefit week beginning on a day during the period of 7 days commencing on 1st October 1991, no account shall be taken of that increase.]

[⁸(6) Where by virtue of the coming into force of regulation 3(1) and (2) of the Income-Related Benefits Amendment Regulations 1992 a claimant's applicable amount increases in his benefit week beginning on a day during the period of 7 days commencing on 5th October 1992, no account shall be taken of that increase.]

Termination of protected sum

6. Subject to paragraph 7, the protected sum shall cease to be applicable if—
(a) that amount is reduced to nil under paragraph 5; or
(b) the claimant changes or [²vacates] his accommodation; or
(c) the claimant ceases to be entitled to income support.

Protected persons

7.—(1) Subject to sub-paragraph (2), for the purposes of this paragraph a protected person is a claimant, where—
(a) in respect of the first week he is entitled to an increase under paragraph 7 of Schedule 5 (applicable amounts of persons in board and lodging accommodation or hostels) because either he or, if he is one of a couple or a member of a polygamous marriage, he or his partner satisfies any of the conditions in paragraph 8 of that Schedule; or
(b) in the first week the claimant or, if he has a partner, either he or his partner—
  (i) is in need of personal care by reason of [²old age,] mental or physical disablement, mental illness, or dependence on alcohol or drugs; and
  (ii) is receiving both board and personal care in accommodation other than a

residential care home or nursing home or residential accommodation within the meaning of regulation 21(3) (special cases) [³ . . .]; and

(iii) is in accommodation which he entered under arrangements for his personal care made by a statutory authority or a voluntary or charitable body and those arrangements are being supervised on a continuing basis by that authority or body; or

(c) he or, if he has a partner, either he or his partner but for his temporary absence from his accommodation for a period not exceeding 13 weeks, which includes the first week, would have satisfied (a) or (b) above.

(2) A claimant is not a protected person if he or, if he has a partner, he or his partner, in the first week, is temporarily living in board and lodging accommodation and that accommodation is not the accommodation normally occupied as the home.

(3) Paragraph 4 shall not apply to a protected person.

(4) Paragraph 6(b) shall not apply to a protected person if:

(a) he moves to accommodation where he satisfies conditions (i) to (iii) of sub-paragraph (1)(b); or

(b) he becomes a patient within the meaning of regulation 21(3); or

(c) on his ceasing to be a patient within the meaning of regulation 21(3), either he returns to the accommodation which he occupied immediately before he became a patient, or he moves to other accommodation where he satisfies conditions [²(i) to (iii)] of sub-paragraph (1)(b); or

(d) in a case to which sub-paragraph (6) applies, on his becoming re-entitled to income support, he is either in the accommodation which he occupied immediately before he ceased to be entitled to income support, or in accommodation where he satisfies conditions (i) to (iii) of sub-paragraph (1)(b).

[³(5) Except where sub-paragraph (7) applies, where a protected sum was applicable to a protected person immediately before he or any partner of his became a patient within the meaning of regulation 21(3) for a period of 14 weeks or less, he shall, subject to sub-paragraph (4)(c), on his or, as the case may be, his partner's easing to be a patient, be entitled to a protected sum equal to—

(a) the amount by which his protected total exceeds his applicable amount determined in accordance with the relevant provisions in the first benefit week in which his applicable amount ceases to be determined under paragraph 1 of Schedule 7 and either—

(i) any eligible housing benefit for the period of 7 consecutive days beginning on 10th April 1989; or, if greater,

(ii) in a case where sub-paragraph (7)(b) applied, any eligible housing benefit for the period of 7 consecutive days referred to in that sub-paragraph; or

(b) the amount of the protected sum to which he was entitled in the immediately preceding benefit week,

whichever is the lower.

(6) Paragraph 6(c) shall not apply to a protected person who has ceased to be entitled to income support for [⁴a period not exceeding the permitted period determined in accordance with regulation 3A (permitted period)]—

(a) if immediately before he ceased to be so entitled a protected sum was applicable to him; and

(b) except where sub-paragraph (7) applies, if during that period the protected person becomes re-entitled, or would by virtue of this sub-paragraph be re-entitled, to income support he shall, subject to sub-paragraph (4)(d), be entitled to a protected sum equal to—

(i) the amount by which his protected total exceeds his applicable amount determined in accordance with the relevant provisions in the first complete benefit week in which he becomes so re-entitled and either any eligible housing benefit for the period of 7 consecutive days beginning 10th April 1989 or, if greater, in a case to which sub-paragraph (7)(*b*) applied, any eligible housing benefit for the period of 7 consecutive days referred to in that sub-paragraph; or

(ii) the amount of the protected sum to which he was previously entitled,

whichever is the lower.

(7) Where a protected person or any partner of his is temporarily absent from his accommodation for a period not exceeding 13 weeks which includes the first or second week (or both)—

(a) in a case where a protected sum was applicable to the protected person immediately before his or, as the case may be, his partner's return to that accommodation and the full charge was made for the accommodation during the temporary absence, on the protected person's or, as the case may be, his partner's return to that accommodation, the protected person shall be entitled to a protected sum equal to—

    (i) the amount by which his protected total exceeds his applicable amount determined in accordance with the relevant provisions in the first complete benefit week after his or, as the case may be, his partner's return to that accommodation and any eligible housing benefit for the period of 7 consecutive days beginning 10th April 1989; or

    (ii) the amount of the protected sum which was applicable to him in the immediately preceding benefit week,

whichever is the lower;

(b) in a case where—

    (i) a protected sum has not at any time been applicable to the protected person; or

    (ii) immediately before the protected person's or, as the case may be, his partner's return to that accommodation a protected sum was applicable but a reduced charge was made for the accommodation during the temporary absence.

the protected person on his or, as the case may be, his partner's return to that accommodation shall, subject to sub-paragraph (8), be entitled to a protected sum equal to the amount by which his protected total exceeds his applicable amount determined in accordance with the relevant provisions in the first complete benefit week after his or, as the case may be, his partner's return to that accommodation and the amount of eligible housing benefit for the period of 7 consecutive days beginning on the date determined in accordance with regulation 65 or, as the case may be, 68(2) of the Housing Benefit (General) Regulations 1987 (date on which entitlement is to commence or change of circumstances is to take effect) following that person's return to that accommodation.

(8) Where, in a case to which sub-paragraph (7)(b)(i) applies—

(a) in the first complete benefit week after the protected person's or, as the case may be, his partner's return to his accommodation the protected person's income calculated in accordance with Part V or, as the case may be, VI exceeds the aggregate of his applicable amount determined in accordance with the relevant provisions and X; and

(b) the amount of income support to which he was entitled in the first week is more than the amount of housing benefit to which he would, but for this sub-paragraph, have been entitled in the period of 7 consecutive days beginning on the date determined in accordance with regulation 65 or, as the case may be, 68(2) of the Housing Benefit (General) Regulations 1987 following the case may be, his partner's return to that accommodation.

the protected sum applicable shall, subject to sub-paragraph (9), be an amount equal to X + Y + 10 pence.

(9) Where the protected person or, as the case may be, his partner returns to the accommodation in the second week and he or his partner is, or both are, entitled in the first, second and third weeks to a relevant social security benefit or to more than one such benefit and consequent upon the Social Security Benefits Up-rating Order 1989 he

or his partner is, or both are, entitled to an increase in any one or more of those benefits in the third week, the protected sum under sub-paragraph (8) shall be increased by an amount equal to the difference between—

    (a) the amount of benefit or aggregate amount of those benefits to which the protected person or his partner is, or both are, entitled in the third week; and, if less,

    (b) the amount of benefit or aggregate amount of those benefits to which the protected person or his partner is, or both are, entitled in the second week.

    (10) In sub-paragraph (8)—

    "X" means the sum which, but for sub-paragraph (8), would be the protected sum applicable in a case to which sub-paragraph (7)(b)(i) applies;

    "Y" means the amount of the excess to which sub-paragraph (8)(*a*) refers;

    "relevant social security benefit" has the same meaning as in paragraph 3(4).]]

AMENDMENTS

    1. Income Support (General) Amendment No. 4 Regulations 1988 (S.I. 1988 No. 1445), Sched. 2 (April 10, 1989).

    2. Income Support (General) Amendment No. 5 Regulations 1988 (S.I. 1988 No. 2022), reg. 19 (April 10, 1989).

    3. Income Support (General) Amendment Regulations 1989 (S.I. 1989 No. 534), reg. 7 and Sched. 1 (April 10, 1989).

    4. Income Support (General) Amendment No. 3 Regulations 1989 (S.I. 1989 No. 1678), reg. 8 (October 9, 1989).

    5. Income Support (General) Amendment Regulations 1990 (S.I. 1990 No. 547), reg. 19 (April 9, 1990).

    6. Income Support (General and Transitional) Amendment Regulations 1990 (S.I. 1990 No. 2324), reg. 4 (December 17, 1990).

    7. Income Support (General) Amendment No. 4 Regulations 1991 (S.I. 1991 No. 1559), reg. 17 (October 1, 1991).

    8. Income-related Benefits Amendment Regulations 1992 (S.I. 1992 No. 1326), reg. 3(3) (October 5, 1992).

DEFINITIONS

    "the Act"—see reg. 2(1).
    "benefit week"—*ibid.*
    "board and lodging accommodation"—*ibid.*
    "child"—see 1986 Act, s.20(11) (SSCBA, s.137(1)).
    "claimant"—see reg. 2(1).
    "couple"—*ibid.*
    "employment"—*ibid.*
    "family"—see 1986 Act, s.20(11) (SSCBA, s.137(1)).
    "local authority"—see 1986 Act, s.84(1).
    "partner"—see reg. 2(1).
    "polygamous marriage"—*ibid.*
    "young person"—*ibid.*, reg. 14.

GENERAL NOTE

    Sched. 3A is made necessary by the removal from the Regulations of the special treatment of those in board and lodging accommodation. Before April 1989, such claimants received their board and lodging charge (subject to a maximum amount, and a maximum length of time for some under-25s) plus a personal allowance, but were not eligible for housing benefit. From April 1989, they receive ordinary personal allowances and premiums, but are eligible for housing benefit. Sched.3A provides transitional protection if there is a loss of income for existing claimants, in the form of a "protected sum" to make up the difference.

    R(IS) 2/92 holds that to be a protected person within para. 7(1)(a) a person must actually have been entitled to an increase of the maximum amount for boarders under para. 7 of Sched. 5 immediately before the benefit week beginning in the week from April 3, 1989.

[¹SCHEDULE 3B **Regulations 17(1)(*g*),
18(1)(*h*) and 71(1)(*a*)(v)
and (*d*)(iv)**

PROTECTED SUM

Interpretation

1.—(1) In this Schedule—
"eligible housing benefit" means—
   (a) for the period of 7 consecutive days beginning on 2nd October 1989, the amount of housing benefit to which the claimant or his partner was entitled in that period which relates to the hostel normally occupied as the home by him or, if he has a partner, by him and his partner;
   (b) for the period of 7 consecutive days beginning on 9th October 1989 or, in a case to which paragraph 6(4) (*b*) applies, for the period of 7 consecutive days referred to in that paragraph, the amount of the claimant's or his partner's maximum housing benefit determined in accordance with regulation 61 of the Housing Benefit (General) Regulations 1987 (maximum housing benefit) which relates to that accommodation.
"first week" means the benefit week beginning on a day in the period of 7 days commencing on 2nd October 1989;
"hostel" means any establishment which immediately before the commencement of this Schedule was a hostel within the meaning of regulation 20(2) (applicable amounts for persons in hostels);
"Income support" includes any sum payable under Part II of the Income Support (Transitional) Regulations 1987;
"March benefit week" means the benefit week beginning on a day during the period of 7 consecutive days beginning 20th March 1989;
"protected sum" means the amount applicable under this Schedule to a claimant who in the first week is living in a hostel or who or whose partner is temporarily absent in that week from that accommodation;
"protected total" means—
   (a) the total of the claimant's applicable amount under regulation 20 in the first week or, [² ...] if the claimant or any partner of his is temporarily absent from his accommodation [²for a period not exceeding 14 weeks which includes that week], the amount which would have fallen to be calculated under that regulation for that week as if there had been no temporary absence; and
   (b) the amount of any eligible housing benefit for the period of 7 consecutive days beginning 2nd October 1989;
"relevant benefit week" means the benefit week beginning on a day during that period of 7 consecutive days commencing on 9th April 1990;
"relevant provisions" means—
   (a) regulation 17(1)(a) to (f) (applicable amounts);
   (b) regulation 18(1)(a) to (g) (polygamous marriages);
   (c) regulation 71(1)(a)(i) to (iv) (urgent cases);
   (d) regulation 71(1)(d)(i) to (iii);
  [²(dd) paragraph 13 of Schedule 7 (persons in residential accommodation);]
   (e) in relation to a case to which paragraph 17(b)(ii) or (c)(i) of Schedule 7 (persons from abroad) applies, the regulations specified in that paragraph but as if the reference to regulation 17(1)(g) in that paragraph were omitted; or
   (f) in relation to a case to which paragraph 17(d)(i) of that Schedule applies, the regulations specified in that paragraph but as if the reference to regulation 18 were a reference to regulation 18(1)(a) to (g) only;

"second week" means the benefit week beginning on a day during the period of 7 consecutive days commencing on 9th October 1989.

(2) For the purposes of this Schedule—

(a) in determining a claimant's applicable amount in his first week, second week or any subsequent benefit week no account shall be taken of any reduction under regulation 22 (reduction in certain cases of unemployment benefit disqualification);

(b) except in so far as it relates to any temporary absence to which paragraph 6(4) refers, where a change of circumstances takes effect in the claimant's second week which, if it had taken effect in the first week, would have resulted in a lesser applicable amount in respect of that week, his applicable amount in the first week shall be determined as if the change of circumstances had taken effect in that week.

Protected sum

2.—(1) Subject to the following provisions of this paragraph and the following paragraphs of this Schedule, where the protected total of a claimant is more than—

(a) his applicable amount in the second week determined in accordance with the relevant provisions less the amount of any increase consequent on the coming into force of regulation 5 of the Income Support (General) Amendment Regulations 1989; and

(b) any eligible housing benefit for the period of 7 consecutive days beginning 9th October 1989,

the protected sum applicable to the claimant shall be an amount equal to the difference.

(2) Where—

(a) in the second week a claimant's income calculated in accordance with Part V or, as the case may be, VI exceeds the aggregate of his applicable amount determined in accordance with the relevant provisions and X; and

(b) the amount of income support to which he is entitled in the first week is more than the amount of housing benefit to which he would, but for this sub-paragraph, have been entitled in the period of 7 consecutive days beginning on 9th October 1989,

the protected sum applicable to the claimant shall be an amount equal to $X + Y + 10$ pence.

(3) In sub-paragraph (2)—

"X" means the sum which, but for sub-paragraph (2), would be the protected sum applicable under sub-paragraph (1);

"Y" means the amount of the excess to which sub-paragraph (2)(a) refers.

(4) For the period beginning with the claimant's relevant benefit week the protected sum applicable to the claimant shall, subject to sub-paragraph (6), and the following paragraphs of this Schedule, be—

(a) the total of—

(i) the amount of the allowance for personal expenses for the claimant or, if he is a member of a family, for him and for each member of his family in the first week determined, or which, but for any temporary absence, would have been determined, in accordance with paragraph 11 of Schedule 5 as then in force;

(ii) [³subject to sub-paragraph (7)] the amount of any increase for meals in the first week determined, or which, but for any temporary absence, would have been determined, in accordance with paragraph 2 of that Schedule; and

(iii) the amount or, if he is a member of a family, the aggregate of the amounts determined in accordance with sub-paragraph (5),

less the aggregate of his applicable amount in the second week determined, or which, but for any temporary absence, would have been determined, in accordance with the relevant provisions and, where applicable, the amount of any reduction in the protected sum made by virtue of paragraph 4 in a benefit week occurring before the relevant benefit week; or

(b) the amount of the protected sum which was applicable to him in the immediately preceding benefit week,

whichever is the lower.

(5) For the purposes of sub-paragraph (4)(a), where in the first week the accommodation charge makes or, but for any temporary absence, would have made, provision or no provision for meals, as respects each person an amount shall be determined as follows—

(a) in a case where the provision is for at least three meals a day—
    (i) for the claimant, £17.20;
    (ii) for a member of his family aged 16 or over, £12.50;
    (iii) for a member of the family aged less than 16, £6.25;

(b) except where head (c) applies, in a case where the provision is for less than three meals a day—
    (i) for the claimant, £13.85;
    (ii) for a member of his family aged 16 or over, £8.30;
    (iii) for a member of his family aged less than 16, £4.15;

(c) in a case where the provision is for breakfast only—
    (i) for the claimant, £7.05;
    (ii) for a member of his family, £1.50;

(d) in a case where there is no provision for meals, for the claimant or, if he is a member of a family, for the claimant and for the members of his family for whom there is no such provision, £5.55;

(6) Where in the relevant benefit week the claimant is in, or only temporarily absent from, residential accommodation, the protected sum applicable to the claimant for the period beginning with that week shall[², subject to the following paragraphs of this Schedule,] be—

(a) equal to the difference between—
    (i) the amount of the allowance for personal expenses for the claimant or, if he is a member of a family, for him and for each member of his family in the first week determined, or which, but for any temporary absence, would have been determined, in accordance with paragraph 11 of Schedule 5 as then in force; and
    (ii) the amount of the allowance for personal expenses for the claimant or, if he is a member of a family, for him and for each member of his family in the second week determined, or which, but for any temporary absence would have been determined, under paragraph 13 of Schedule 7 (persons in residential accommodation),

less, where applicable, the amount of any reduction in the protected sum made by virtue of paragraph 4 in a benefit week occurring before the relevant benefit week; or

(b) the amount of the protected sum which was applicable to him in the immediately preceding benefit week,

whichever is the lower.

[³(7) In the case of a member of a family who in the first week is a child aged less than 11, the amount of any increase for meals under sub-paragraph (4)(a)(ii) shall be either—

(a) the amount of any such increase in the first week determined, or which, but for any temporary absence, would have been determined, in accordance with paragraph 2 of Schedule 5 as then in force; or

(b) £17.65,

whichever is the lower.]

Persons not entitled to a protected sum

3.—(1) Subject to paragraph 6, a protected sum shall not be applicable to a claimant where he changes or vacates his hostel during the period of 7 consecutive days beginning 9th October 1989.

(2) Except where regulation 8(2)(b) of the Housing Benefit (General) Regulations 1987 (eligible housing costs) applies, a protected sum shall not be applicable to a claimant unless he, or any partner of his, is entitled to housing benefit for the period of 7 consecutive days beginning 9th October 1989 or, where paragraph 6(4)(b) applies, for the period of 7 consecutive days referred to in that paragraph, in respect of the hostel normally occupied as the home by him, or if he has a partner, by him and his partner.

(3) A protected sum shall not be applicable to a claimant where—

(a) he has been or would, but for any temporary absence, have been in the same accommodation in both the March benefit week and the second week, and—

    (i) his applicable amount in both those weeks fell or would have fallen, but for any temporary absence, to be determined under paragraph 13(1) of Schedule 7; or

    (ii) his applicable amount in the second week fell or would have fallen, but for any temporary absence, to be determined under that paragraph and would also have fallen to be so determined in the March benefit week had his stay in that accommodation been other than temporary; or

(b) his applicable amount in the second week fell or would have fallen, but for any temporary absence, to be determined under that paragraph and would also have fallen to be so determined in the March benefit week had he been in the same accommodation in that week and had his stay in that accommodation been other than temporary[²; or

(c) his applicable amount in the first week fell or would have fallen, but for any temporary absence, to be determined under regulation 20 but would not have fallen to be so determined in the March benefit week had he been in the same accommodation in that week and had his stay in that accommodation been other than temporary.

(4) For the purposes of sub-paragraph (3), where—

(a) a claimant's applicable amount in respect of the March benefit week has been determined under paragraph 13(1) of Schedule 7 and it is subsequently determined on review that it fell to be determined under regulation 20, he shall, notwithstanding that review, be treated as if his applicable amount fell to be determined under that paragraph;

(b) a claimant has been temporarily absent from his accommodation in the March benefit week and immediately before the period of temporary absence his applicable amount was determined under paragraph 13(1) of Schedule 7, he shall be treated as if his applicable amount would have fallen to be determined under that paragraph during the period of temporary absence notwithstanding that it is subsequently determined on review that immediately before the period of temporary absence it fell to be determined under regulation 20;

(c) a claimant has entered his accommodation after the March benefit week, he shall be treated as if his applicable amount, had he been in that accommodation in the March benefit week, would not have fallen to be determined under regulation 20 in that week if the applicable amounts of other claimants in that accommodation in that week were determined otherwise than under that regulation notwithstanding that it is subsequently determined on review that they fell to be determined under regulation 20.]

Reduction of protected sum

4.—(1) Subject to [⁶sub-paragraphs (2) to (5)], the protected sum shall be reduced by the amount of any increase, in a benefit week subsequent to the second week, in the claimant's applicable amount determined in accordance with the relevant provisions.

(2) Where regulation 22 (reduction in certain cases of unemployment benefit disqualification) [⁴or regulation 21A (reductions in certain cases of failure to attend courses)] ceases to apply to a claimant and as a result his applicable amount increases no account shall be taken of that increase.

[³(3) Where a claimant's applicable amount increases because a child or young person mentioned in paragraph (5)(c) of regulation 16 (circumstances in which a person is treated or not treated as a member of the household) is treated as a member of the claimant's household under paragraph (6) of that regulation, the claimant's protected sum shall not be reduced by the amount of that increase unless the child or young person has been treated as a member of the household for a continuous period which exceeds 8 weeks.]

[⁵(4) Where by virtue of the coming into force of regulation 15(a), (b) or (c) of the Income Support (General) Amendment No. 4 Regulations 1991 a claimant's applicable amount increases in his benefit week beginning on a day during the period of 7 days commencing on 1st October 1991, no account shall be taken of that increase.]

[⁶(5) Where by virtue of the coming into force of regulation 3(1) and (2) of the Income-Related Benefits Amendment Regulations 1992 a claimant's applicable amount increases in his benefit week beginning on a day during the period of 7 days commencing on 5th October 1992, no account shall be taken of that increase.]

Termination of protected sum

5. Subject to paragraph 6, the protected sum shall cease to be applicable if—
(a) that amount is reduced to nil under paragraph 4; or
(b) the claimant changes or vacates his hostel; or
(c) the claimant ceases to be entitled to income support.

Modifications in cases of temporary absence and loss of entitlement to income support

6.—(1) Paragraph 5(b) shall not apply to a claimant if—
(a) he becomes a patient within the meaning of regulation 21(3) (special cases); or
(b) on ceasing to be a patient within the meaning of regulation 21(3), he returns to the hostel which he occupied immediately before he became a patient; or
(c) in a case to which sub-paragraph (3) applies, on his becoming re-entitled to income support, he is in the accommodation which he occupied immediately before he ceased to be entitled to income support.

(2) Except where sub-paragraph (4) applies, where a protected sum was applicable to the claimant immediately before he or any partner of his became a patient within the meaning of regulation 21(3) for a period of 14 weeks or less, he shall, subject to sub-paragraph (1)(b), on his or, as the case may be, his partner ceasing to be a patient be entitled to a protected sum equal to—
(*a*) the amount by which his protected total exceeds his applicable amount determined in accordance with the relevant provisions in the first benefit week in which his applicable amount ceases to be determined under paragraph 1 of Schedule 7 and either—
(i) any eligible housing benefit for the period of 7 consecutive days beginning on 9th October 1989; or, if greater,
(ii) in a case where sub-paragraph (4)(b) applied, any eligible housing benefit for the period of 7 consecutive days referred to in that sub-paragraph; or
[³(aa) where the first benefit week in which his applicable amount ceases to be determined under paragraph 1 of Schedule 7 is the relevant benefit week, the amount determined under paragraph 2(4) or, as the case may be, paragraph 2(6), less any reduction under paragraph 4(1) other than a reduction which arises by virtue of his ceasing to be a patient within the meaning of regulation 21(3); or]
(b) the amount of the protested sum to which he was entitled in the immediately preceding benefit week
whichever is the lower.

(3) Paragraph 5(*c*) shall not apply to a claimant who has ceased to be entitled to income support for [²a period not exceeding the permitted period determined in accordance with regulation 3A (permitted period)]—

(a) if immediately before he ceased to be so entitled a protected sum was applicable to him; and

(b) except where sub-paragraph (4) applies, if during that period he becomes re-entitled, or would by virtue of this sub-paragraph be re-entitled, to income support he shall, subject to sub-paragraph (1)(c), be entitled to a protected sum equal to—

    (i) the amount by which his protected total exceeds his applicable amount determined in accordance with the relevant provisions in the first benefit week in which he becomes so re-entitled and either any eligible housing benefit for the period of 7 consecutive days beginning 9th October 1989 or, if greater, in a case to which sub-paragraph (4)(b) applied, any eligible housing benefit for the period of 7 consecutive days referred to in that sub-paragraph; or

    [³(ii) where the first benefit week in which he becomes so re-entitled is the relevant benefit week, the amount determined under paragraph 2(4) or, as the case may be, paragraph 2(6), less any reduction under paragraph 4(1) in that benefit week; or

    (iii) where the first benefit week in which he becomes so re-entitled is a week subsequent to the relevant benefit week, the amount which would have been determined under paragraph 2(4) or, as the case may be, paragraph 2(6) had he been entitled in the relevant benefit week, less any reduction under paragraph 4(1) in the benefit week in which he becomes re-entitled; or

    (iv) the amount of the protested sum to which he was previously entitled,]
whichever is the lower.

(4) Where a claimant or any partner of his temporarily absent from his accommodation for a period not exceeding 14 weeks which includes the first or second week (or both)—

(a) in a case where a protected sum was applicable to the claimant immediately before his or, as the case may be, his partner's return to that accommodation and the full charge was made for that accommodation during the temporary absence, on the claimant's or, as the case may be, his partner's return to that accommodation, the claimant shall be entitled to a protected sum equal to—

    (i) the amount by which his protected total exceeds his applicable amount determined in accordance with the relevant provisions in the first complete benefit week after his, or as the case may be, his partner's return to that accommodation and any eligible housing benefit for the period of 7 consecutive days beginning 9th October 1989; or

    (ii) the amount of the protected sum which was applicable to him in the immediately preceding benefit week,
whichever is the lower.

(b) in a case where—

    (i) a protected sum has not at any time been applicable to the claimant; or

    (ii) immediately before the claimant's or, as the case may be, his partner's return to that accommodation a protected sum was applicable to the claimant but a reduced charge was made for the accommodation during the temporary absence,

the claimant on his or, as the case may be, his partner's, return to that accommodation shall, subject to sub-paragraph (5), be entitled to a protected sum equal to the amount by which his protected total exceeds his applicable amount determined in accordance with the relevant provisions in the first complete benefit week after his or, as the case may be, his partner's return to that accommodation and the amount of eligible housing benefit for the period of 7 consecutive days beginning on the date determined in accordance with regulation 65 or, as the case may be, 68(2) of the Housing Benefit (General) Regulations 1987 (date on which entitlement is to commence or change of circumstances is to take effect) following that person's return to that accommodation.

(5) Where, in a case to which sub-paragraph (4)(b)(i) applies—

(a) in the first complete benefit week after the claimant's or, as the case may be, his partner's return to his accommodation the claimant's income calculated in accordance with Part V or, as the case may be, VI exceeds the aggregate of his applicable amount determined in accordance with the relevant provisions and X; and

(b) the amount of income support to which he was entitled in the first week is more than the amount of housing benefit to which he would, but for this sub-paragraph, have been entitled in the period of 7 consecutive days beginning on the date determined in accordance with regulation 65 or, as the case may be, 68(2) of the Housing Benefit (General) Regulations 1987 following his or, as the case may be, his partner's return to that accommodation,

the protected sum applicable to the claimant shall be an amount equal to $X + Y + 10$ pence.

(6) In sub-paragraph (5)—

"X" means the sum which, but for sub-paragraph (5), would be the protected sum applicable in a case to which sub-paragraph (4)(b)(i) applies;

"Y" means the amount of the excess to which sub-paragraph (5) (a) refers.

(7) The foregoing provisions of this paragraph shall not apply to a claimant if he or, if he has a partner, he or his partner, in the first week is temporarily living in a hostel and that accommodation is not the accommodation normally occupied as the home.]

AMENDMENTS

1. Income Support (General) Amendment Regulations 1989 (S.I. 1989 No. 534), Sched. 1, para. 18 and Sched. 2 (October 9, 1989).
2. Income Support (General) Amendment No. 3 Regulations 1989 (S.I. 1989 No. 1678), reg. 9 (October 9, 1989).
3. Income Support (General) Amendment Regulations 1990 (S.I. 1990 No. 547), reg. 20 (April 9, 1990).
4. Income Support (General and Transitional) Amendment Regulations 1990 (S.I. 1990 No. 2324), reg. 5 (December 17, 1990).
5. Income Support (General) Amendment No. 4 Regulations 1991 (S.I. 1991 No. 1559), reg. 17 (October 1, 1991).
6. Income-related Benefits Amendment Regulations 1992 (S.I. 1992 No. 1326), reg. 3(4) (October 5, 1992).

GENERAL NOTE

These complex provisions provide transitional protection for those hostel-dwellers who are moved on to housing benefit in October 1989. A full description cannot be given here, but there is a helpful summary on pp.4 and 5 of *Welfare Rights Bulletin* 91 (August 1989).

The main provision is in para. 2. Sub-paras. (1) to (3) deal with the position from October 9, 1989. For claimants who are residents in or only temporarily absent from a hostel in the week before that date, their protected sum is normally the difference between their applicable amount in that week and their applicable amount plus housing benefit in the following week (para. 2(1)). If the claimant's income is too high for entitlement to income support on the ordinary rules there is a special calculation in para. 2(2). Note that the transitional protection ceases if the claimant changes or vacates his hostel or ceases to be entitled to income support (para. 5) subject to the exceptions in para. 6.

Para. 2(4) to (6) deals with protection from April 9, 1990. See *CIS 168/1990* and *CIS 340/1990* on the definition of "hostel" and *CIS 142/1991*.

[¹SCHEDULE 3C   **Regulation 2A(1)(*b*)**

THE GREATER LONDON AREA

The area described in this Schedule comprises—

(*a*) the Boroughs of

Barking	Hillingdon
Barnet	Hounslow
Bexley	Islington
Brent	Kensington and Chelsea
Bromley	Kingston-Upon-Thames
Camden	Lambeth
City of Westminster	Lewisham
Croydon	Merton
Ealing	Newham
Enfield	Redbridge
Greenwich	Richmond-Upon-Thames
Hackney	Southwark
Haringey	Sutton
Hammersmith & Fulham	Tower Hamlets
Harrow	Waltham Forest
Havering	Wandsworth

(b) the City of London;
(c) in the County of Essex that part of the district of Epping Forest which comprises the parishes of Chigwell and Waltham Holy Cross;
(d) in the County of Hertfordshire, that part of the Borough of Broxbourne which lies south of Cheshunt Park, including Slipe Lane, and that part of the district of Hertsmere which comprises the former parishes of Elstree, Ridge, Shenley and South Mimms;
(e) in the County of Surrey, the Borough of Spelthorne and that part of the Borough of Elmbridge which was formerly administered by the Old Esher District Council.]

AMENDMENT

1. Social Security Benefits (Amendments Consequential Upon the Introduction of Community Care) Regulations 1992 (S.I. 1992 No. 3147), reg. 2(3) and Sched. 2 (April 1, 1993).

SCHEDULE 4   **Regulation 19**

PART I

Applicable Amounts of Persons in Residential Care and Nursing Homes

1. Subject to sub-paragraph (2), the weekly applicable amount of a claimant to whom regulation 19 applies shall be the aggregate of—
(a) subject to paragraph 3, the weekly charge for the accommodation, including all meals and services, provided for him or, if he is a member of a family, for him and his family increased, where appropriate, in accordance with paragraph 2 but, except in a case to which paragraph 12 applies, subject to the maximum determined in accordance with paragraph 5; and
(b) a weekly amount for personal expenses for him and, if he is a member of a family, for each member of his family determined in accordance with paragraph 13; and
(c) where he is only temporarily in such accommodation any amount applicable under [²regulation 17(1)(e) or 18(1)(f)] (housing costs) in respect of the dwelling normally occupied as the home; [²and
(d) any amount in accordance with regulation 17(1)(f) or 18(1)(g) (applicable amounts).]

(2) No amount shall be included in respect of any child or young person who is a member of the claimant's family if the capital of that child or young person calculated

in accordance with Part V in like manner as for the claimant, except where otherwise provided, would exceed £3,000.

2.—(1) Where, in addition to the weekly charge for accommodation, a separate charge is made for the provision of heating, attention in connection with bodily functions, supervision, extra baths, laundry or a special diet needed for a medical reason, the weekly charge for the purpose of paragraph 1(1)(a) shall be increased by the amount of that charge.

(2) Where the weekly charge for accommodation does not include the provision of all meals, it shall, for the purpose of paragraph 1(1)(a), be increased in respect of the claimant or, if he is a member of a family, in respect of each member of his family by the following amount:

    (a) if the meals can be purchased within the residential care or nursing home, the amount equal to the actual cost of the meals, calculated on a weekly basis; or

    (b) if the meals cannot be so purchased, the amount calculated on a weekly basis—

        (i) for breakfast, at a daily rate of £1.10;

        (ii) for a midday meal, at a daily rate of £1.55; and

        (iii) for an evening meal, at a daily rate of £1.55;

except that, if some or all of the meals are normally provided free of charge or at a reduced rate, the amount shall be reduced to take account of the lower charge or reduction.

3. Where any part of the weekly charge for the accommodation is met by housing benefit, an amount equal to the part so met shall be deducted from the amount calculated in accordance with paragraph 1(1)(a).

4. [¹. . .]

5.—(1) Subject to paragraph 12 the maximum referred to in paragraph 1(1)(a) shall be—

    (a) in the case of a single claimant, the appropriate amount in respect of that claimant specified in or determined in accordance with paragraphs 6 to 11;

    [⁵(b) in the case of a claimant who is a member of a family the aggregate of the following amounts—

        (i) in respect of the claimant, the appropriate amount in respect of him specified in or determined in accordance with paragraph 6 to 11;

        (ii) in respect of each member of his family who lives in the home aged under 11, $1\frac{1}{2}$ times the amount specified in paragraph 2(a) of Schedule 2;

        (iii) in respect of each member of his family aged not less than 11 who lives in the home, an amount which would be the appropriate amount specified in or determined in accordance with paragraph 6 to 11 if the other member were the claimant.]

(2) The maximum amount in respect of a member of the family aged under 11 calculated in the manner referred to in sub-paragraph (1)(b)(i) shall be rounded to the nearest multiple of 5p by treating an odd amount of 2.5p or more as 5p and by disregarding an odd amount of less than 2.5p.

Residential care homes

[¹⁰**6.**—(1) Subject to sub-paragraph (2) and paragraphs 8 to 11, where the accommodation provided for the claimant is a residential care home for persons in need of personal care by virtue of—

    (a) old age, the appropriate amount shall be £197.00 per week;

    (b) past or present mental disorder but excluding mental handicap, the appropriate amount shall be £207.00 per week;

    (c) past or present drug or alcohol dependence, the appropriate amount shall be £207.00 per week;

    (d) mental handicap, the appropriate amount shall be £237.00 per week;

    (e) physical disablement, the appropriate amount shall be—

        (i) in the case of a person to whom paragraph 8 applies, £267.00 per week, or

    (ii) in any other case £197.00 per week; or
  (f) any condition not falling within sub-paragraphs (*a*) to (*e*) above, the appropriate amount shall be £197.00 per week.]
  (2) Where the claimant is over pensionable age and—
[³(a) he is registered as blind in a register compiled by a local authority under section 29 of the National Assistance Act (welfare services) or, in Scotland has been certified as blind and in consequence he is registered as blind in a register maintained by or on behalf of a regional or islands council; or]
[⁸(b) he—
    (i) is entitled to attendance allowance at the higher rate in accordance with section 65(3) of the Contributions and Benefits Act, or the care component of disability living allowance at the highest rate prescribed in accordance with section 72(3) of the Contributions and Benefits Act, or
    (ii) has made a claim for attendance allowance or disability living allowance and, in respect of that claim, a decision has been made that he satisfies the disability conditions, but he has not yet completed the qualifying period for that benefit; or]
  (c) he is in receipt of any payment based on need for attendance which is payable—
    (i) under section 61 of the Social Security Act [SSCBA, s.104], or
    (ii) by virtue of article 14 of the Naval, Military and Air Forces etc (Disablement and Death) Service Pensions Order 1983 or article 14 of the Personal Injuries (Civilians) Scheme 1983,
the appropriate amount shall, except where sub-pargraph (1)(d) or (e)(i) applies, be [⁹£227.00] per week.
  [⁸(3) In this paragraph—
  (a) "the disability conditions" means—
    (i) in the case of attendance allowance, the conditions in section 64(2) and (3) of the Contributions and Benefits Act; and
    (ii) in the case of disability living allowance, the conditions in section 72(1)(b) and (c) of the Contributions and Benefits Act;
  (b) "the qualifying period" means—
    (i) in the case of attendance allowance, the period specified in section 65(1)(b) of the Contributions and Benefits Act; and
    (ii) in the case of disability living allowance, the period specified in section 72(2)(a) of the Contributions and Benefits Act.]

Nursing homes

[¹⁰7. Subject to paragraphs 8 to 11, where the accommodation provided for the claimant is a nursing home for persons in need of personal care by virtue of—
  (a) past or present mental disorder but excluding mental handicap, the appropriate amount shall be £296.00 per week;
  (b) mental handicap, the appropriate amount shall be £301.00 per week;
  (c) past or present drug or alcohol dependence, the appropriate amount shall be £296.00 per week;
  (d) physical disablement, the appropriate amount shall be—
    (i) in the case of a person to whom paragraph 8 applies, £331.00 per week, or
    (ii) in any other case, £295.00 per week;
  (e) terminal illness, the appropriate amount shall be £295.00 per week; or
  (f) any condition not falling within sub-paragraphs (a) to (e), the appropriate amount shall be £295.00 per week.]
  8. For the purposes of paragraphs 6(e) and 7(d) this paragraph applies to a person under pensionable age or a person over pensionable age who, before attaining pensionable age, had become physically disabled.
  9. The appropriate amount applicable to a claimant in a residential care home or nursing home shall, subject to paragraph 10, be determined—

(a) where the home is a residential care home registered under Part I of the Registered Homes Act 1984, by reference to the particulars recorded in the register kept by the relevant registration authority for the purposes of that Act; or

(b) where the home is a residential care home not so registered or a nursing home, by reference to the type of care which, taking into account the facilities and accommodation provided, the home is providing to the claimant.

10.—(1) Where more than one amount would otherwise be applicable, in accordance with paragraph 9, to a claimant in a residential care home or a nursing home, the appropriate amount in any case shall be determined in accordance with the following sub-paragraphs.

(2) Where the home is a residential care home registered under Part I of the Registered Homes Act 1984 and where the personal care that the claimant is receiving corresponds to the care received by a category of residents for whom the register indicates that the home provides accommodation, the appropriate amount shall be the amount, in paragraph 6 or 8, as the case may be, as is consistent with that personal care.

(3) Where the home is a residential care home which is so registered but where the personal care that the claimant is receiving does not correspond to the care received by a category of residents for whom the register indicates that the home provides accommodation, the appropriate amount shall be the lesser or least amount, in paragraphs 6 or 8, as the case may be, as is consistent with those categories.

(4) In any case not falling within sub-paragraph (2) or (3), the appropriate amount shall be whichever amount of the amounts applicable in accordance with paragraph 6 or 7 or 9 is, having regard to the types of personal care that the home provides, most consistent with the personal care being received by the claimant in that accommodation.

11.—[¹⁰(1) Where the accommodation provided for the claimant is a residential care home or a nursing home which is, in either case, situated in the Greater London area and the actual charge for that accommodation exceeds the appropriate amount in his case by virtue of the preceding paragraphs of this Schedule, that amount shall be increased by any excess up to—

(a) in the case of a residential care home, £34.00;

(b) in the case of a nursing home, £39.00.]

(2) In sub-paragraph (1), "the Greater London area" means all those areas specified [⁸in Schedule 3C.]

Circumstances in which the maximum is not to apply

12.—(1) Where a claimant who satisfies the conditions in sub-paragraph (2) has been able to meet the charges referred to in paragraphs 1 or 2 without recourse to income support or supplementary benefit, the maximum determined in accordance with paragraph 5 shall not apply for the period of 13 weeks or, if alternative accommodation is found earlier, such lesser period following the date of claim except to the extent that the claimant is able to meet out of income disregarded for the purposes of Part V the balance of the actual charge over the maximum.

(2) The conditions for the purposes of sub-paragraph (1) are that—

(a) the claimant has lived in the same accommodation for more than 12 months; and

(b) he was able to afford the charges in respect of that accommodation when he took up residence; and

(c) having regard to the availability of suitable alternative accommodation and to the circumstances mentioned in paragraph 10(7)(b) of Schedule 3 (housing costs), it is reasonable that the maximum should not apply in order to allow him time to find alternative accommodation; and

(d) he is not a person who is being accommodated—

(i) by a housing authority under Part III of the Housing Act 1985 (housing the homeless), or

(ii) by a local authority under [⁷ section 20 of the Children Act 1989 (provision of accommodation for children: general)] or, in Scotland, section 12 of the Social Work (Scotland) Act 1968 (general welfare); and

(e) he is seeking alternative accommodation and intends to leave his present accommodation once alternative accommodation is found.

(3) Where—

(a) the claimant was a resident in a residential care home or nursing home immediately before 29 April 1985 and has continued after that date to be resident in the same accommodation, apart from any period of temporary absence; and

(b) immediately before that date, the actual charge for the claimant's accommodation was being met either wholly or partly out of the claimant's resources, or, wholly or partly out of other resources which can no longer be made available for this purpose; and

(c) since that date the local authority have not at any time accepted responsibility for the making of arrangements for the provision of such accommodation for the claimant; and

(d) the Secretary of State, in his discretion, has determined that this sub-paragraph shall have effect in the particular case of the claimant in order to avoid exceptional hardship,

the maximum amount shall be the rate specified in sub-paragraph (4) if that rate exceeds the maximum which, but for this sub-paragraph, would be determined under paragraph 5.

(4) For the purposes of sub-paragraph (3) the rate is either—

(a) the actual weekly charge for the accommodation immediately before 29 April 1985 plus £10; or

(b) the aggregate of the following amounts—
   (i) the amount estimated under regulation 9(6) of the Supplementary Benefit (Requirements) Regulations 1983 as then in force as the reasonable weekly charge for the area immediately before that date;
   (ii) £26.15; and
   (iii) if the claimant was entitled at that date to attendance allowance under section 35 of the Social Security Act at the higher rate £28.60 or, as the case may be, at the lower rate, £19.10,

whichever is the lower amount.

Personal allowances

[¹⁰13. The allowance for personal expenses for the claimant and each member of his family referred to paragraph 1(1)(b) shall be—

(a) for the claimant £13.35; and if he has a partner, for his partner, £13.35;

(b) for a young person aged 18, £13.35;

(c) for a young person aged under 18 but over 16, £9.25;

(d) for a child aged under 16 but over 11, £8.00;

(e) for a child aged under 11, £5.50.]

PART II

Persons to Whom Regulation 19 Does Not Apply

[¹14. A claimant or, if he is a member of a family, the claimant and the members of his family where the accommodation and meals (if any) of the claimant or, as the case may be, the claimant and the members of his family are provided in whole or in part by a close relative of his or of any member of his family, or other than on a commercial basis.]

15. A person who is on holiday and during a period which has not continued for more than 13 weeks is absent from his home or from a hospital or similar institution in which he is normally a patient.

16. A person who has entered a residential care or nursing home for the purpose of receiving an amount of income support to which he would not otherwise be entitled.

17. A person aged 16 or over but under 19 [⁷who is being looked after by a local authority] under a relevant enactment except someone who is personally liable to pay the cost of his accommodation and maintenance direct to someone other than a local authority.

[⁶**18.** A person who is living in a residential care home within the meaning of paragraph (d) of the definition of "residential care home" in regulation 19(3) and who is not in receipt of personal care by reason of old age, disablement, past or present dependence on alcohol or drugs or past or present mental disorder.]

AMENDMENTS

1. Income Support (General) Amendment Regulations 1988 (S.I. 1988 No. 663), reg. 31 (April 11, 1988).
2. Income Support (General) Amendment No. 4 Regulations 1988 (S.I. 1988 No. 1445), reg. 21 (September 12, 1988).
3. Income Support (General) Amendment No. 5 Regulations 1988 (S.I. 1988 No. 2022), reg. 20 (December 12, 1988).
4. Income Support (General) Amendment Regulations 1989 (S.I. 1989 No. 534), reg. 8 (April 10, 1989).
5. Income Support (General) Amendment No. 3 Regulations 1989 (S.I. 1989 No. 1678), reg. 10 (October 9, 1989).
6. Income Support (General) Amendment No. 4 Regulations 1991 (S.I. 1991 No. 1559), reg. 18 (October 7, 1991).
7. Income Support (General) Amendment Regulations 1992 (S.I. 1992 No. 468), Sched., para. 8 (April 6, 1992) (amendment to para. 17 in respect of England and Wales only, not Scotland. For the previous form of para. 17 see the 1991 edition.)
8. Income-related Benefits Schemes (Miscellaneous Amendments) (No. 4) Regulations 1993 (S.I. 1993 No. 2119), reg. 20 (October 4, 1993).
9. Social Security Benefits Up-rating Order 1995 (S.I. 1995 No. 559) art. 18(8) (April 10, 1995).
10. Social Security Benefits Up-rating Order 1995 (S.I. 1995 No. 559) Art. 18, and Sched. 6 (April 10, 1995).

DEFINITIONS

"attendance allowance"—see reg. 2(1).
"benefit week"—*ibid.*
"child"—see 1986 Act, s.20(11) (SSCBA, s.137(1)).
"claimant"—see reg. 2(1).
"date of claim"—*ibid.*
"disability living allowance"—*ibid.*
"disablement"—see reg. 19(4).
"drug or alcohol dependence"—*ibid.*
"family"—see 1986 Act, s.20(11) (SSCBA, s.137(1)).
"local authority"—see 1986 Act, s.84(1).
"mental disorder"—see reg. 19(4).
"mental handicap"—*ibid.*
"nursing home"—see reg. 2(1), reg. 19(3).
"old age"—see reg. 19(4).
"partner"—see reg. 2(1).
"relevant enactment"—*ibid.*, reg. 16(8)(a).
"residential care home"—see reg. 2(1), reg. 19(3).
"single claimant"—see reg. 2(1).
"supplementary benefit"—*ibid.*
"temporary absence"—see reg. 19(3).
"young person"—see reg. 2(1), reg. 14.

GENERAL NOTE

The history of the supplementary benefit provisions on residential care and nursing homes has been of continuing complexity and difficulty, with terrible technical problems. Sched. 4 is still complicated, but at least the rules can be made sense of. The Government's programme for community care had significant implications for income support (for the original proposals see Chap. 9 of the White Paper *Caring for People: Community Care in the Next Decade and Beyond*). Sched. 4 now only applies to claimants who have a "preserved right" under reg. 19 to receive income support under the pre-April 1993 arrangements. New residents, excluded from Sched. 4, may only resort to ordinary income support plus the residential allowance under para. 2A of Sched. 2.

"Residential care home" and "nursing home" are defined in reg. 19(3). See the notes to that regulation.

Paragraph 1

There are four elements in the applicable amount of a resident in a residential care or nursing home with a preserved right: (a) the weekly charge for accommodation, board, services, and any separate charge for items mentioned in para. 2(1), plus an amount for any extra meals under para. 2(2), all subject to the maximum set in para. 5; (b) the personal allowance under para. 13; (c) any housing costs for the claimant's old home if he is only temporarily in the residential care or nursing home; and (d) any transitional protection under reg. 17(2) to (7).

Paragraph 2

For a separate charge to be met under sub-para. (1) it must be made by the home in which the claimant is resident. Only charges for services provided by the home, not third parties count (*CSB 754/1988*, confirmed in *Pearce v. Chief Adjudication Officer, The Times*, May 10, 1990).

Under sub-para. (2) the amounts for meals have not changed for several years.

Paragraph 3

If any part of the charge is met by housing benefit, it is deducted from the charge to be met under para. 1(1)(a).

Paragraph 5

The maximum to be met under para. 1(1)(a) is set by paras. 6 to 11 for adults and children over also living in the home. For children under 11, it is one and a half times the ordinary personal allowance for a child under 11.

Paragraph 6

On the various categories, see the definitions in the notes to reg. 19(4). The Residential Care Homes Regulations 1984 require the register kept by the local authority of homes which are registered to record the number of residents in defined categories which coincide with those specified in para. 6(1)(a) to (e). Note the effect of para. 8 on para. 6(1)(e), and of para. (2) on the disabled over pensionable age. Attendance allowance and the care component of disability living allowance is not disregarded for residents in residential care or nursing homes (Sched. 9, para. 9). The maximum can be increased under para. 11 for homes in Greater London.

Paragraph 7

See the notes to reg. 19(4) for definitions, and note to para. 6 above. Nursing homes are not registered for particular categories.

Paragraph 8

In *R(SB) 16/88* the Tribunal of Commissioners raises the possibility that the differential age for men and women, created by the use of "pensionable age" might infringe EC Directive 79/7 on equal treatment, but see the note to para. 13 of Sched. 1.

Paragraph 9

For residential care homes which are registered, under sub-para. (a) the appropriate maximum is to be determined by reference to the register under the 1984 Act. This is effectively the result reached on the supplementary benefit provisions by the Tribunal of Commissioners in *R(SB) 15/88*, *R(SB) 16/88* and *R(SB) 17/88*. Thus, if a home is registered for only one category, that is the maximum to be applied, regardless of the care actually received by the resident. If more than one category is on the register, para. 10 applies.

For nursing homes and for unregistered residential care homes (*e.g.* before April 1993 those with less than four residents which have not registered voluntarily), the test is the type of care being provided to the claimant. This should normally produce an appropriate category (contrary to the view of the Commissioner in *CSIS 2/1991*), but para. 10 still makes reference to this class of homes. The emphasis on the care provided to the claimant is different from the rules produced on the supplementary benefit provision by the Tribunal of Commissioners in *R(SB) 12/88, R(SB) 13/88* and *R(SB) 14/88.* In *CIS 263/1991* the claimant suffered from osteoporosis and osteoarthritis. She was not terminally ill but received similar care to those who were. The Commissioner holds that the appropriate category is para. 7(e) because this was most consistent with the personal care she actually received. The SSAT had erred in concluding that because she was not terminally ill she could not receive this rate.

Paragraph 10
This provision only applies where the rules of para. 9 produce alternative amounts. This should only be a real possibility in the case of registered residential care homes. Here the rules are set out in sub-paras. (2) and (3). If the care which the claimant is receiving corresponds to a category for which the home is registered, that category supplies the maximum. If the care received by the claimant does not correspond to such a category, the maximum is to be the lowest of the amounts specified for the categories for which the home is registered. Note that a home can only be registered for categories corresponding to para. 6(1)(a) to (e). It cannot be registered for "any condition not falling within sub-paragraphs (a) to (e)" (sub-para. (f)).

In any other case, which should not exist, the test is what is most consistent with the personal care being received by the claimant.

Paragraph 11
This provision allows the extension of the maximum by £34.00 (residential care homes) or £39.00 (nursing homes) in the Greater London area.

Paragraphs 12(1) and (2)
There is a period of grace in these circumstances in which a charge over the maximum will be met. In *CIS 515/1990,* the Commissioner held that although there was then no definition of date of claim in the Income Support Regulations, the definition of "claim for benefit" in reg. 2(1) of the Claims and Payments Regulations could be incorporated. This included at the time an application for the review of an award or decision in order to obtain any increase of benefit. Therefore, although the claimant first claimed and was awarded income support in February 1989, the 13 week period under sub-para. (1) could run from December 1989, when an application to increase the amount of income support to cover the full fees was made. This decision must be wrong in importing a definition used for very different Regulations and ignoring the natural meaning of the words "date of claim." However, there does not appear to be any other Commissioner's decision to the contrary. With effect from March 9, 1992, the definition of "claim for benefit" in the Claims and Payments Regulations has been narrowed, so as not to cover reviews aimed at increasing the amount of a benefit. "Date of claim" is now (from October 4, 1993) defined in reg. 2(1), which cross-refers to the Claims and Payments Regulations.

CIS 515/1990 also decides that the condition in sub-para. (1) of having been able to meet the home's charges without recourse to income support does not have to be met immediately before the date of claim. Sub-para. (c) was also held to be satisfied, because alternative accommodation was being sought. But since the evidence was that no suitable alternative accommodation was available, there must be doubt that it was reasonable to allow time to find alternative accommodation.

Paragraphs 12(3) and (4)
This provision contains a transitional rule protecting those who were resident in residential care or nursing homes immediately before April 29, 1985, although not necessarily claimants. The rule can only apply if, in addition to meeting the conditions in sub-para. (3)(a) to (c), the Secretary of State has exercised his discretion in favour of the claimant to avoid exceptional hardship. The rule produces a choice of protected amounts, which will replace the maximum calculated under para. 5 if either is higher than that amount. The first is the actual charge immediately before April 29, 1985, plus £10. The second is the total of the three amounts listed in head (b). For the estimation of the reasonable weekly charge under the Requirements Regulations as in force immediately before April 29, 1985, see *R(SB) 12/88* which indicates that many of the estimates made by AOs could have been too low. The maximum should be fixed at the highest amount being charged for full board and lodging by establishments in the area providing a suitable standard for the needs of occupants, having disregarded charges which are way above those of the majority.

Part II.
Paras. 14 to 18 prescribe the categories of resident who are not allowed to receive benefit under the special rules of reg. 19.

Paragraph 14

See the notes to the definitions of "board and lodging accommodation" and "close relative" in reg. 2(1).

Paragraph 18

This provision is only concerned with residential care homes run by statutory bodies or bodies incorporated by Royal Charter. The form of para. (d) of the definition in reg. 19 includes such homes if they provide personal care to at least one resident. The effect then seemed to be to give all residents, whether receiving personal care or not, access to the special level of benefit. Para. 18 removes that possibility and limits access to those receiving personal care for the specified reasons.

It is not clear that the unintended effect removed by para. 18 is limited to homes within para. (d) of the definition.

SCHEDULE 7   **Regulation 21**

APPLICABLE AMOUNTS IN SPECIAL CASES

Column (1)	Column (2)
[20**Patients** **1.** Subject to paragraphs 2, 2A, 3 and 18, a person who has been a patient for a period of more than six weeks and who is—	**1.**
(a) a single claimant;	(a) £14.70 plus any amount applicable under regulation 17(1)(e), (f) or (g);
(b) a lone parent;	(b) £14.70 plus any amounts applicable to him under regulation 17(1)(b), (c), (e), (f) or (g) or under regulation 17(1)(d) because of paragraph 8 or 14 of Schedule 2 (applicable amounts);
(c) a member of a couple— (i) where only one of the couple is a patient or, where both members of the couple are patients but only one has been a patient for that period; (ii) where both members of the couple have been a patient for that period;	(c) (i) the amount applicable in respect of both of them under regulation 17(1) reduced by £11.75. (ii) £29.40 plus any amounts which may be applicable under regulation 17(1)(b), (c), (e), (f), or (g) or under regulation 17(1)(d) because of paragraph 14 of Schedule 2;
(d) a member of a polygamous marriage— (i) where at least one member of the polygamous marriage is not a patient or has not been a patient for more than that period; (ii) where all the members of the polygamous marriage have been patients for more than that period.	(d) (i) the applicable amount under regulation 18 (polygamous marriages) shall be reduced by £11.75 in respect of each such member who is a patient; (ii) the applicable amount shall be £14.70 in respect of each member plus any amounts applicable under regulation 18(1)(c), (d), (f), (g) or (h) or (e) because of his satisfying the condition specified in paragraph 14 of Schedule 2.
2. A single claimant who has been a patient for a continuous period of more than 52 weeks, where— (a) the following conditions are satisfied— (i) a person has been appointed to act for him under regulation 33 of the Social Security (Claims and Payments) Regulations 1987 (persons unable to act); and (ii) his income support is payable to an	**2.** (a) Such amount (if any) not exceeding £11.75 as is reasonable having regard to the views of the hospital staff and the patient's relatives if available as to the amount necessary for this personal use;

Column (1)	Column (2)
administrative officer of the hospital or other institution either as or at the request of the person so appointed; and	
(iii) a registered medical practitioner treating him certifies that all or part of his income support cannot be used by him or on his behalf; or	
(b) those conditions are not satisfied.	(b) £11.75.
2A. A single claimant who is detained under the provisions of the Mental Health Act 1983 or the Mental Health Act (Scotland) Act 1984 and who immediately before his detention under either of those Acts was a prisoner.	**2A.** £11.75.
3. Subject to paragraph 18—	**3.**
(a) a claimant who is not a patient and who is a member of a family of which another member is a child or young person who has been a patient for a period of more than 12 weeks; or	(a) The amount applicable to him under regulation 17(1) or 18 except that the amount applicable under regulation 17(1)(b) or 18(1)(c) in respect of the child or young person referred to in Column (1) of this paragraph shall be £11.75 instead of an amount determined in accordance with paragraph 2 of Schedule 2; or
(b) where the person is a member of a family and paragraph 1 applies to him and another member of the family who is a child or young person has been a patient for a period of more than 12 weeks.	(b) the amount applicable to him under paragraph 1 except that the amount applicable under regulation 17(1) (b) or 18(1)c) in respect of the child or young person referred to in Column (1) of this paragraph shall be £11.75 instead of an amount deter mined in accordance with paragraph 2 of Schedule 2.]
4. [⁶. . .].	
5. [⁶. . .].	
Claimants without accommodation	
6. A claimant who is without accommodation.	**6.** The amount applicable to him under regulation 17[³(1)](a) only.
Members of religious orders	
7. A claimant who is a member of and fully maintained by religious order.	**7.** Nil.
Prisoners	
8. A person—	**8.**
(a) except where sub-paragraph (b) applies, who is a prisoner;	(a) Nil;
(b) who is detained in custody pending trial or sentence following conviction by a court.	(b) only such amount, if any, as may be applicable under regulation 17[³(1)](e).
Specified cases of temporarily separated couples	
9. A claimant who is a member of a couple and who is temporarily separated from his partner [¹⁰where—	**9.** Either—
(a) one member of the couple is—	(a) the amount applicable to him as a member of a couple under regulation 17; or

Column (1)	Column (2)

(i) not a patient but is resident in a nursing home, or
(ii) resident in a residential care home, or
(iii) resident in premises used for the rehabilitation of alcoholics or drug addicts, or
(iv) resident in accommodation provided under section 3 of and Part II of the Schedule to, the Polish Resettlement Act 1947 (provision of accommodation in camps), or
(v) participating in arrangements for training made under section 2 of the Employment and Training Act 1973 [¹² or section 2 of the Enterprise and New Towns (Scotland) Act 1990] or attending a course at an employment rehabilitation centre established under that section [¹² of the 1973 Act], where the course requires him to live away from the dwelling occupied as the home, or
(vi) in a probation or bail hostel approved for the purpose by the Secretary of State; and
(b) the other member of the couple is—
  (i) living in the dwelling occupied as the home, or
  (ii) a patient, or
  (iii) in residential accommodation, or
  (iv) resident in a residential care home or nursing home;]
	(b) the aggregate of his applicable amount and that of his partner assessed under the provisions of these Regulations as if each of them were a single claimant, or a lone parent, whichever is the greater.

Polygamous marriages where one or more partners are temporarily separated

10. A claimant who is a member of a polygamous marriage and who is temporarily separated from a partner of his, where one of them is living in the home while the other member is—

(a) not a patient but is resident in a nursing home; or

(b) resident in a residential care home; or
(c) [¹. . .]
(d) resident in premises used for the rehabilitation of alcoholics or drug addicts; or
(e) attending a course of training or instruction provided or approved by the [¹²Secretary of State for Employment] where the course requires him to live away from home; or
(f)in a probation or bail hostel approved for the purpose by the Secretary of State.

10. Either—
(a) the amount applicable to the members of the polygamous marriage under regulation 18; or
(b) the aggregate of the amount applicable for the members of the polygamous marriage who remain in the home under regulation 18 and the amount applicable in respect of those members not in the home calculated as if each of them were a single claimant, or a lone parent, whichever is the greater.

Column (1)	Column (2)
[²⁰**Single claimants temporarily in local authority accommodation** **10A.** A single claimant who is temporarily in accommodation referred to in any of sub-paragraphs (a) to (d) (excluding heads (i) and (ii) of sub-paragraph (d)) of the definition of residential accommodation in regulation 21(3) (special cases).	**10A.** £58.85 of which £13.35 is for personal expenses plus any amounts applicable under regulation 17(1)(e), (f) or (g).

Couples and members of polygamous marriages where one member is or all are temporarily in local authority accommodation
   10B.—(1) A claimant who is a member of a couple and temporarily separated from his partner where one of them is living in the home while the other is in accommodation referred to in any of sub-paragraphs (a) to (d) (excluding heads (i) and (ii) of sub-paragraph (d) of the definition of residential accommodation in regulation 21(3) (special cases).
   (2) A claimant who is a member of a polygamous marriage and who is temporarily separated from a partner of his where one is, or some are, living in the home while one is, or some are, in accommodation referred to in sub-paragraph (1).
   (3) A claimant who is a member of a couple or a member of a polygamous marriage where both members of that couple or all the members of that marriage are in accommodation referred to in sub-paragraph (1).
	10B.—(1) The aggregate of the amount applicable for the member who remains in the home calculated as if he were a single claimant under regulation 17(1), 19 or 21 and in respect of the other member £58.85 of which £13.35 is for personal expenses.
	
	   (2) The aggregate of the amount applicable, for the members of the polygamous marriage who remain in the home, under regulation 18 and in respect of each member not in the home £58.85 of which £13.35 is for personal expenses.
	   (3) For each member of that couple or marriage £58.85 of which £13.35 is for personal expenses plus, if appropriate, the amount applicable under regulation 17(1)(e), (f) or (g) or 18(1)(f) or (h).

Lone parents who are in residential accommodation temporarily **10C.** A claimant who is a lone parent who has entered residential accommodation temporarily.	**10C.** £58.85 of which £13.35 is for personal expenses, plus— (a) in respect of each child or young person who is a member of his family, the amount in respect of him prescribed in paragraph 2(a), (b), (c) or (d) of Schedule 2 or under this Schedule as appropriate; and (b) any amount which would be applicable to the claimant if he were not temporarily living away from the dwelling occupied as his home, under regulation 17(1)(c), (e), (f) or (g), or (d) in so far as that amount relates to the lone parent premium under paragraph 8 of Schedule 2.]
10D. [¹⁵. . .]	
Couples where one member is abroad. **11.** [¹¹Subject to paragraph 11A] a claimant who is a member of a couple and whose partner is temporarily not present in [³United Kingdom].	**11.** For the first four weeks of that absence, the amount applicable to them as a couple under regulation 17, or [⁹19 or 21] as the case

Column (1)	Column (2)
	may be and thereafter the amount applicable to the claimant in Great Britain under regulation 17 or [⁹19 or 21] as the case may be as if the claimant were a single claimant or, as the case may be, a lone parent.

[¹¹**Couple or member of couple taking child or young person abroad for treatment**
11A. [¹⁵—(1)] A claimant who is a member of a couple where either—
(a) he or his partner is, or,
(b) both he and his partner are
absent from the United Kingdom [¹⁴in the circumstances specified in paragraph (2).
(2) For the purposes of sub-paragraph (1), the specified circumstances are—
  (a) in respect of a claimant, those in regulation 4(3)(a) to (d);
  (b) in respect of a claimant's partner as if regulation 4(3)(a) to (d) applies to that partner.]
	11A. For the first eight weeks of that absence, the amount applicable to the claimant under regulation 17(1), 19 or 21, as the case may be, and, thereafter, if the claimant is in Great Britain the amount applicable to him under regulation 17(1), 19 or 21, as the case may be, as if the claimant were a single claimant, or, as the case may be, a lone parent.

Polygamous marriages where any member is abroad **12.** Subject to paragraph 12A, a claimant who is a member of a polygamous marriage where— (a) he or one of his partners is, or (b) he and one or more of his partners are, or (c) two or more of his partners are, temporarily absent from the United Kingdom.	**12.** For the first four weeks of that absence, the amount applicable to the claimant under regulations 17 to 21, as the case may be, and thereafter, if the claimant is in Great Britain the amount applicable to him under regulations 18 to 21, as the case may be, as if any member of the polygamous marriage not in the United Kingdom were not a member of the marriage.

Polygamous marriage: taking child or young person abroad for treatment
12A. [¹⁵—(1)] A claimant who is a member of a polygamous marriage where—
(a) he or one of his partners is,
(b) he and one or more of his partners are, or
(c) two or more of his partners are,
absent from the United Kingdom [¹⁴in the circumstances specified in paragraph (2).
(2) For the purposes of sub-paragraph (1), the specified circumstances are—
  (a) in respect of a claimant, those in regulation 4(3)(a) to (d);
  (b) in respect of a claimant's partner or partners, as the case may be, as if regulation 4(3)(a) to (d) applied to that partner or those partners.]
	12A. For the first 8 weeks of that absence the amount applicable to the claimant under regulations 18 to 21, as the case may be, as if any member of the polygamous marriage not in the United Kingdom were not a member of the marriage.]

[²⁰**Persons in residential accommodation.**
13.—(1) Subject to sub-paragraph (2), a person in or only temporarily absent from residential accommodation who is—
  (a) a single claimant;
	13.—(1) Any amount applicable under regulation 17(1)(f) or (g) or 18(1)(g) or (h), plus—
	  (a) £58.85 of which £13.35 is for personal expenses;

Column (1)	Column (2)
(b) a lone parent;	(b) the amount specified in sub-paragraph (a) of this column;
(c) one of a couple;	(c) twice the amount specified in sub-paragraph (a) of this column;
(d) a child or young person;	(d) the appropriate amount in respect of him prescribed in paragraph 2 of Schedule 2 (applicable amounts);
(e) a member of a polygamous marriage.	(e) the amount specified in sub-paragraph (a) of this column multiplied by the number of members of the polygamous marriage in or only temporarily absent from that accommodation.
(2) A single claimant who has become a patient and whose residential accommodation was provided by and managed by a local authority.	(2) Any amount applicable under regulation 17(1)(f) or (g), plus £13.35.

Polish Resettlement

13A. [¹⁹(1)] A claimant for whom accommodation is provided under section 3 of, and Part II of the Schedule to, the Polish Resettlement Act 1947 (provision of accommodation in camps) [¹⁹where the claimant both requires personal care and is provided with it in the accommodation and—

(a) is resident in that accommodation on 31st March 1995 or is temporarily absent on that date; or

(b) is first provided with such accommodation and care on or after 1st April 1995; or

(c) is re-admitted to such accommodation on or after 1st April 1995 where his absence has been other than temporary.

(2) In this paragraph "personal care" means care which includes assistance with bodily functions where such assistance is required.

(3) An absence is temporary for the purposes of sub-paragraph (1) where the absent resident with the agreement of the manager of the accommodation intends to return to the accommodation in due course.]

13A. —(1) The aggregate of—

(a) the weekly charge for the accommodation provided for him, or if he is a member of a family, for him and his family subject to the maximum determined in accordance with sub-paragraph (2); and

(b) a weekly amount for personal expenses for him or, if he is a member of a family, for him and for each member of his family determined in accordance with sub-paragraph (3) [¹⁹or, in the case of a claimant to whom sub-paragraph (1)(b) or (c) of Column (1) applies, determined in accordance with sub-paragraph (3A) below.]

(2) The maximum referred to in sub-paragraph (1)(a) shall be—

(a) in the case of a single claimant, £331.00.

(b) in the case of a claimant who is a member of a family the aggregate of the following amounts—

(i) in respect of the claimant, £331.00.

(ii) in respect of each member of his family who lives in the accommodation aged under 11, $1\frac{1}{2}$ times the amount specified in paragraph 2(a) of Schedule 2;

(iii) in respect of each member of his family aged not less than 11 who lives in the accommodation, £331.00; and

(iv) where the claimant is a lone parent, in respect of each member of the family who does not live in the accommodation, the amount which would be applicable in respect of that member under Schedule 2.

(3) [¹⁹Except where the claimant is a

Column (1)	Column (2)
	person to whom sub-paragraph (1)(b) or (c) of Column (1) refers,] the amount for personal expenses referred to in sub-paragraph (1)(b) shall be— (a) for the claimant, £17.35; (b) for his partner, £17.35; (c) for a young person aged 18, £15.55; (d) for a young person aged under 18 but over 16, £9.25; (e) for a child aged under 16 but over 11, £8.00; (f)for a child under 11, £5.50. [19(3A) In the case of a claimant to whom sub-paragraph (1)(b) or (c) of Column (1) applies, the amount for personal expenses referred to in sub-paragraph (1)(b) above, shall be the aggregate of the amounts which are relevant to him and which are referred to in Schedule 4 paragraph 13.] (4) The maximum amount in respect of a member of a family aged under 11 calculated in the manner referred to in [19sub-paragraph (2)(b)(ii)] shall be rounded to the nearest multiple of 5p by treating an odd amount of 2.5p or more as 5p and by disregarding an odd amount of less than 2.5p.]
[18Polish resettlement: Persons temporarily absent from accommodation **13B.** Where a claimant or his partner is temporarily absent from accommodation to which paragraph 13A applies for which the claimant is liable to pay a retaining fee, and but for that absence from that accommodation his applicable amount would be calculated in accordance with that paragraph and the absent person— (a) is a patient; or (b) is a person to whom sub-paragraph (a) does not apply. **Polish resettlement** **14.** [9. . .] **Resettlement units** **15.** [9. . .]	**13B.** The amount otherwise applicable to him under these Regulations may be increased to take account of the retaining fee— (a) in a case to which sub-paragraph (a) of Column 1 applies— (i) where the person has been a patient for a period of 6 weeks or less, by an amount not exceeding the maximum amount referred to in paragraph 13A(2)(a); (ii) where the person has been a patient for a period of more than 6 weeks, by an amount not exceeding 80 per cent. of the normal weekly charge for that accommodation, but any such increase shall not be for a continuous period of more than 52 weeks; (b) in a case of a person to whom sub-paragraph (b) of Column 1 applies, by an amount not exceeding 80 per cent. of the normal weekly charge for that accommodation, but any such increase shall not be for a continuous period of more than 4 weeks.]

Column (1)	Column (2)
Persons temporarily absent from a hostel, residential care or nursing home **16.** [¹⁷Where a person is temporarily absent from accommodation for which he is liable to pay a retaining fee, and but for his temporary absence from that accommodation his applicable amount would be calculated in accordance with regulation 19 (applicable amounts for persons in residential care and nursing homes), and]—	**16.** The amount otherwise applicable to him under these Regulations may be increased to take account of the retaining fee by an amount not exceeding 80 per cent. of the applicable amount referred to in paragraph 1(1)(a) of Schedule 4 (applicable amounts of persons in residential care or nursing homes) and—
(a) he is a person in accommodation referred to in [⁸any of sub-paragraphs (a) to (d) ([⁹excluding heads (i) and (ii)] of sub-paragraph (d) of the definition of residential accommodation] [¹in regulation 21(3)] (special cases) and paragraph 13 does not apply to him by reason only that his stay in that accommodation has not become other than temporary; or	(a) in a case to which sub-paragraph (a) to (b) of column 1 applies any such increase shall not be for a continuous period of more than 52 weeks;
(b) he is a person to whom paragraph 1 to 3 [³ or 18(b)(i), (b)(ii) case two, or (b)(iv) cases one and three (patients)] applies; or	(b) in a case of a person to whom only sub-paragraph (c) of column 1 applies, any such increase shall not be for a continuous period of more than four weeks.
(c) he is absent for a period of at least one week from that accommodation being accommmodation either in a residential care home or nursing home and he is not required to be available for employment.	
17. Except in relation to a person from abroad to whom regulation 70(3) applies (urgent cases)—	**17.**
(a) a person from abroad who is a single claimant;	(a) Nil;
(b) a lone parent—	(b)
(i) where he is a person from abroad;	(i) nil;
(ii) [¹⁴. . .];	(ii) [¹⁴. . .];
(c) a member of a couple	(c)
(i) where the claimant is not a person from abroad but his partner is such a person, whether or not regulation 70 applies to that partner;	(i) the amount applicable in respect of him only under regulation 17[³(1)](a) plus in respect of any child or young person who is a member of his family and who is not a person from abroad, any amounts which may be applicable to him under regulation 17[³(1)](b), (c) or (d) plus the amount applicable to him under [⁷regulation 17(1)(e), (f) and (g)] [³or as the case may be,] [⁹regulation 19 or 21];
(ii) where the claimant is a person from abroad but his partner is not such a person;	(ii) nil;
(iii) where the claimant and his partner are both persons from abroad;	(iii) nil;

301

Column (1)	Column (2)
(*d*) where regulation 18 (polygamous marriages) applies and— (i) the claimant is not a person from abroad but one or more but not all of his partners are persons from abroad;	(d) (i) the amounts determined in accordance with that regulation or [⁹regulation 19 or 21] in respect of the claimant and any partners of his and any child or young person for whom he or any partner is treated as responsible, who are not persons from abroad;
(ii) the claimant is a person from abroad, whether or not one or more of his partners are persons from abroad;	(ii) nil;
(iii) the claimant and all his partners are persons from abroad;	(iii) nil;
(e) where any amount is applicable to the claimant under regulation 17(d) because of Part III of Schedule 2 because he or his partner satisfies the conditions prescribed therein and he or his partner as the person so satisfying the condition is a person from abroad.	(e) no amount shall be applicable under regulation 17(d) because of Part III of Schedule 2.

[²⁰**Persons in residential care or nursing homes who become patients**

18. A claimant to whom regulation 19 (persons in residential care or nursing homes) applies immediately before he or a member or his family became a patient where—

18.

(a) he or any member of his family has been a patient for a period of six weeks or less and the claimant—

(a)

(i) continues to be liable to meet the weekly charge for the accommodation without reduction in respect of himself or that member of his family who is a patient;	(i) the amount which would be applicable under regulation 19 as if the claimant or the member of the family who is a patient were resident in the accommodation to which regulation 19 applies;
(ii) continues to be liable to meet the weekly charge for the accommodation but at a reduced rate;	(ii) the amount which would be applicable under regulation 19 having taken into account the reduced charge, as if the claimant or the member of the family who is a patient were resident in the accommodation to which regulation 19 applies;
(iii) is a single claimant and is likely to return to the accommodation, but has ceased to be liable to meet the weekly charge for that accommodation; or	(iii) the amount applicable to him (if any) under paragraph 2(2) of Schedule 4 (meal allowances) plus the amount in respect of him as an allowance for personal expenses under paragraph 13 of Schedule 4 as if he were residing in the accommodation to which regulation 19 applies plus any amount applicable under regulation 17(1)(f);
(iv) is a single claimant who ceases to be liable to meet the weekly charge for the accommodation, and who	(iv) the amount which would be applicable to him under regulation 17(1);

Column (1)	Column (2)
is unlikely to return to the accommodation;	
(b) he or his partner has been a patient for a period of more than six weeks and the patient is—	(b)
(i) a single claimant;	(i) £14.70, plus any amount applicable under regulation 17(1)(f), plus either the amount prescribed in paragraph 16 in respect of any retaining fee he is liable to pay for the accommodation or the amount applicable by virtue of regulation 17(1)(e), but not both;
(ii) a lone parent;.	(ii) where one or more children or young persons remain in the accommodation, the amount applicable to the family as if regulation 19, having taken into account any reduction in charge, continued to apply to all the members of the family except that where the lone parent is the patient no amount shall be applicable in respect of him under paragraph 2(2) of Schedule 4 (meals allowances) and for the amount in respect of the allowance for personal expenses prescribed by paragraph 13 of Schedule 4, there shall be substituted the amount £14.70;
	—where all the children or young persons are absent from the accommodation, £14.70 plus any amounts applicable to him under regulation 17(1)(b), (c), (d) or (f) plus, if appropriate, either the amount applicable under Column (2) of paragraph 16(a) or the amount applicable by virtue of regulation 17(1)(e) (housing costs) but not both;
	—where one or more children or young persons are also patients and have been so for more than 12 weeks, in respect of those children and young persons remaining in the accommodation and the lone parent patient the amount specified in case one of Column (2) of sub-paragraph (b)(ii) save that the child or young person who has been a patient for more than 12 weeks shall be disregarded as a member of the family in assessing the amount applicable under regulation 19, and in respect of each such child or young person there shall be added the amount of £14.70;
(iii) one of a couple or polygamous marriage and one of that couple or marriage is not a patient or has	(iii) where the members of the family not patients remain in the accommodation, the amount applicable to

Column (1)	Column (2)
been a patient or has been a patient for six weeks or less;	the family as if regulaton 19 having taken into account any reduction in charge, continued to apply to all the members of the family except that in respect of the member of the couple or polygamous marriage who has been a patient for more than six weeks no amount shall be applicable in respect of him under paragraph 2(2) of Schedule 4 and for the amount in respect of the allowance for personal expenses prescribed by paragraph 13 of Schedule 4 there shall be substituted the amount of £14.70; —where one or more children or young persons are also patients and have been so for more than 12 weeks, in respect of those children and young persons and the member of the couple or polygamous marriage remaining in the accommodation the amount specified in case one of column (2) of sub-paragraph (*b*)(iii) save that the child or young person who has been a patient for more than 12 weeks shall be disregarded as a member or the family in assessing the amount applicable under regulation 19 and in respect of each such child or young person there shall be added the amount of £11.75;
(iv) one of a couple or polygamous marriage where all the members of that couple or marriage are patients and have been so for more than six weeks;	(iv) where there is no child or young person in the family £14.70 in respect of each member of the couple or polygamous marriage plus any amount applicable under regulation 17(1)(*f*) or 18(1)(*g*), plus either the amount prescribed in paragraph 16 in respect of any retaining fee for the accommodation he is liable to pay or the amount applicable by virtue of regulation 17(1)(*e*) or 18(1)(*f*), but not both; —where there is a child or young person remaining in the accommodation, the amount which would be applicable in respect of the family as if regulation 19 having taken into account any reduction in charge continued to apply to all the members of the family except that in respect of each member of the couple of polygamous marriage no amount shall be applicable in respect of him under paragraph 2(2) of Schedule 4, and for the amount in respect of the allowance

Column (1)	Column (2)
	for personal expenses prescribed by paragraph 13 of Schedule 4 in respect of each member there shall be substituted the amount of £14.70; —where there is a child or young person in the family but no child or young person remains in the accommodation, the amount applicable under paragraph 1(*c*) or 1(*d*) as is appropriate plus either the amount applicable under Column (2) of paragraph 16(*a*) or the amount applicable by virtue of regulation 17(1)(*e*) or 18(1)(*f*) but not both; —where one or more children or young persons are also patients and have been so for more than 12 weeks, in respect of those children and young persons remaining in the accommodation and the members of the couple or polygamous marriage, the amount specified in case two of Column (2) of sub-paragraph (*b*)(iv) save that the child or young person who has been a patient for more than 12 weeks shall be disregarded as a member of the family in assessing the amount applicable under regulation 19, and in respect of each such child or young person there shall be added the amount of £11.75.
(*c*) a child or young person who has been a patient for a period of more than 12 weeks.	(*c*) the amount applicable under regulation 19 as if that child or young person was not a member of the family plus an amount of £11.75 in respect of that child or young person.]

Claimants entitled to the disability premium for a past period

19. A claimant—

(*a*) whose time for claiming income support has been extended under regulation 19(2) of the Social Security (Claims and Payments) Regulations 1987 (time for claiming benefit); and

(*b*) whose partner was entitled to income support in respect of the period beginning with the day on which the claimant's claim is treated as made under [¹⁹regulation 6(3) of those Regulations] and [¹⁹ending with the day before the day] on which the claim is actually made; and

(*c*) who satisfied the condition in paragraph 11(*b*) of Schedule 2 and the additional condition referred to in that

19. The amount only of the disability premium applicable by virtue of paragraph 11(*b*) of Schedule 2 as specified in paragraph 15(4)(*b*) of that Schedule.

Column (1)	Column (2)
paragraph and specified in paragraph 12(1)(*b*) of that Schedule in respect of that period. **Rounding of fractions** **20.** Where any calculation under this Schedule or as a result of income support being awarded for a period less than one complete benefit week results in a fraction of a penny that fraction shall be treated as a penny.	

1. Income Support (General) Amendment Regulations 1988 (S.I. 1988 No. 663), reg. 33 (April 11, 1988).
2. Employment Act 1988, s.24(3) (May 26, 1988).
3. Income Support (General) Amendment No. 4 Regulations 1988 (S.I. 1988 No. 1445), reg. 23 (September 12, 1988).
4. Income Support (General) Amendment No. 5 Regulations 1988 (S.I. 1988 No. 2022), reg. 21 (December 12, 1988).
5. Income Support (General) Amendment No. 4 Regulations 1988 (S.I. 1988 No. 1445), Sched. 1, para. 1 (April 10, 1989).
6. Income Support (General) Amendment No. 4 Regulations 1988 (S.I. 1988 No. 1445), Sched. 1, para. 10 (April 10, 1989).
7. Income Support (General) Amendment No. 4 Regulations 1988 (S.I. 1988 No. 1445), Sched. 1, para. 15 (April 10, 1989).
8. Income Support (General) Amendment Regulations 1989 (S.I. 1989 No. 534), reg. 9 (April 10, 1989).
9. Income Support (General) Amendment Regulations 1989 (S.I. 1989 No. 534), Sched. 1, para. 13 (October 9, 1989).
10. Income Support (General) Amendment No. 3 Regulations 1989 (S.I. 1989 No. 1678), reg. 11 (October 9, 1989).
11. Income Support (General) Amendment Regulations 1990 (S.I. No. 547), reg. 21 (April 9, 1990).
12. Enterprise (Scotland) Consequential Amendments order 1991 (S.I. 1991 No. 387), art. 2 (April 1, 1991.
13. Income Support (General) Amendment Regulations 1991 (S.I. 1991 No. 236), reg. 2(1) (April 8, 1991).
14. Income Support (General) Amendment Regulations 1991 (S.I. 1991 No. 236), reg. 13 (April 8, 1991).
15. Income Support (General) Amendment No. 4 Regulations 1991 (S.I. 1991 No. 1559), reg. 19 (October 7, 1991).
16. Social Security Benefits (Amendments Consequential Upon the Introduction of Community Care) Regulations 1992 (S.I. 1992 No. 3147), Sched. 1, para. 6 (April 1, 1993).
17. Income-related Benefits Schemes (Miscellaneous Amendments) (No. 4) Regulations 1993 (S.I. 1993 No. 2119), reg. 21 (October 4, 1993).
18. Income-related Benefits Schemes (Miscellaneous Amendments) (No. 5) Regulations 1994 (S.I. 1994 No. 2139), reg. 31 (October 3, 1994).
19. Income-related Benefits Schemes (Miscellaneous Amendments) Regulations 1995 (S.I. 1995 No. 516), reg. 26 (April 10, 1995).
20. Social Security Benefits Up-rating Order 1995 (S.I. 1995 No. 559), art. 18(10) and Sched. 7 (April 10, 1995).

"child"—see 1986 Act, s.20(11) (SSCBA, s.137(1)).
"claimant"—see reg. 2(1).
"couple"—*ibid*.
"family"—see 1986 Act, s.20(11) (SSCBA, s.137(1)).
"lone parent"—see reg. 2(1).
"nursing home"—see reg. 2(1), reg. 19(3).
"partner"—see reg. 2(1).
"patient"—see reg. 21(3).
"person from abroad"—*ibid*.
"polygamous marriage"—see reg. 2(1).
"prisoner"—see reg. 21(3).
"relative"—see reg. 2(1).
"residential accommodation"—see reg. 21(3).
"residential care home"—see reg. 2(1), reg. 19(3).
"single claimant"—see reg. 2(1).
"young person"—*ibid*., reg. 14.

See the notes to reg. 21.

SCHEDULE 8   **Regulations 36(2), 38(2)
and 44(6)**

SUMS TO BE DISREGARDED IN THE CALCULATION OF EARNINGS

1. In the case of a claimant who has been engaged in remunerative work as an employed earner [¹or, had the employment been in Great Britain would have been so engaged]—

(a) any earnings paid or due to be paid [²in respect of that employment which has terminated]—
   (i) by way of retirement but only if on retirement he is entitled to a retirement pension under the Social Security Act [SSCBA], or would be so entitled if he satisfied the contribution conditions;
   (ii) otherwise than by retirement except earnings to which regulation 35(1)(b) to (e) and [⁵(g) to (i)] applies (earnings of employed earners);

[¹⁰(b) where—
   (i) the employment has not been terminated, but
   (ii) the claimant is not engaged in remunerative work,
   any earnings in respect of that employment except earnings to which regulation 35(1)(d) and (e) applies; but this sub-paragraph shall not apply where the claimant has been suspended from his employment.]

[¹⁰**2.**—In the case of a claimant who, before the date of claim—
   (a) has been engaged in part-time employment as an employed earner or, where the employment has been outside Great Britain, would have been so engaged had the employment been in Great Britain, and
   (b) has ceased to be engaged in that employment, whether or not that employment has been terminated,
any earnings in respect of that employment except any payment to which regulation 35(1)(e) applies; but this paragraph shall not apply where the claimant has been suspended from his employment.]

3. In the case of a claimant who has been engaged in remunerative work or part-time employment as a self-employed earner [¹or, had the employment been in Great Britain, would have been so engaged] and who has ceased to be so employed, from the date of the cessation of his employment any earnings derived from that employment except earnings to which regulation 30(2) (royalties etc.) applies.

[⁴**4.**—(1) In a case to which this paragraph applies, £15; but notwithstanding regulation 23 (calculation of income and capital of members of claimant's family and of a polygamous marriage), if this paragraph applies to a claimant it shall not apply to his partner except where, and to the extent that, the earnings of the claimant which are to be disregarded under this paragraph are less than £15.

(2) This paragraph applies where the claimant's applicable amount includes, or but for his being an in-patient or in accommodation in a residential care home or nursing home or in residential accommodation would include, an amount by way of a disability premium under Schedule 2 (applicable amounts).

(3) This paragraph applies where—
   (a) the claimant is a member of a couple, and—
      (i) his applicable amount would include an amount by way of the disability premium under Schedule 2 but for the higher pensioner premium under that Schedule being applicable; or

      (ii) had he not been an in-patient or in accommodation in a residential care home or nursing home or in residential accommodation his applicable amount would include the higher pensioner premium under that Schedule and had that been the case he would also satisfy the condition in (i) above; and

  (b) he or his partner is under the age of 60 and at least one is engaged in part-time employment.

(4) This paragraph applies where—

  (a) the claimant's applicable amount includes, or but for his being an in-patient or in accommodation in a residential care home or nursing home or in residential accommodation would include, an amount by way of the higher pensioner premium under Schedule 2; and

  (b) the claimant or, if he is a member of a couple, either he or his partner has attained the age of 60; and

  (c) immediately before attaining that age he or, as the case may be, he or his partner was engaged in part-time employment and the claimant was entitled by virtue of sub-paragraph (2) or (3) to a disregard of £15; and

  (d) he or, as the case may be, he or his partner has continued in part-time employment.

(5) This paragraph applies where—

  (a) the claimant is a member of a couple and—

      (i) his applicable amount would include an amount by way of the disability premium under Schedule 2 but for the pensioner premium for persons aged 75 and over under that Schedule being applicable; or

      (ii) had he not been an in-patient or in accommodation in a residential care home or nursing home or in residential accommodation his applicable amount would include the pensioner premium for persons aged 75 and over under that Schedule and had that been the case he would also satisfy the condition in (i) above; and

  (b) he or his partner has attained the age of 75 but is under the age of 80 and the other is under the age of 60 and at least one member of the couple is engaged in part-time employment.

(6) This paragraph applies where—

  (a) the claimant is a member of a couple and he or his partner has attained the age of 75 but is under the age of 80 and the other has attained the age of 60; and

  (b) immediately before the younger member attained that age either member was engaged in part-time employment and the claimant was entitled by virtue of sub-paragraph (5) to a disregard of £15; and

  (c) either he or his partner has continued in part-time employment.

[⁶(7) For the purposes of this paragraph—

  (a) except where head (b) or (c) applies, no account shall be taken of any period not exceeding eight consecutive weeks occurring—

      (i) on or after the date on which the claimant or, if he is a member of a couple, he or his partner attained the age of 60 during which either was or both were not engaged in part-time employment or the claimant was not entitled to income support; or

      (ii) immediately after the date on which the claimant or his partner ceased to participate in arrangements for training made under section 2 of the Employment and Training Act 1973 [⁷or section 2 of the Enterprise and New Towns (Scotland) Act 1990] or to attend a course at an employment rehabilitation centre established under that section [⁷of the 1973 Act];

  (b) in a case where the claimant has ceased to be entitled to income support because he, or if he is a member of a couple, he or his partner becomes engaged in remunerative work, no account shall be taken of any period, during which he was not entitled to income support, not exceeding the permitted period determined in accordance with regulation 3A (permitted period) occurring on or after the date on which the claimant or, as the case may be, his partner attained the age of 60;

(c) no account shall be taken of any period occurring on or after the date on which the claimant or, if he is a member of a couple, he or his partner attained the age of 60 during which the claimant was not entitled to income support because he or his partner was participating in arrangements for training made under section 2 of the Employment and Training Act 1973 [⁷or section 2 of the Enterprise and New Towns (Scotland) Act 1990] or attending a course at an employment rehabilitation centre established under that section [⁷of the 1973 Act].]]

5. If an amount by way of a lone parent premium under Schedule 2 (applicable amounts) is, or but for the pensioner premium being applicable to him or for his accommodation in a residential care home nursing home [⁴. . .] [³. . .] or in residential accommodation would be, included in the calculation of the claimant's applicable amount, £15.

6.—(1) In a case where paragraph 4 does not apply, if the claimant is one of a couple and both members of that couple are under age 60 and one of the couple has for a continuous period of two years been in receipt of income support in respect of a couple (whether or not the same couple) and during that period—

    (a) neither member has been engaged in remunerative work; or

    (b) neither member has been [⁶in relevant education or a student];

for a period exceeding eight consecutive weeks, £15; but, notwithstanding regulation 23 (calculation of income and capital of members of claimant's family and of a polygamous marriage), if this paragraph applies to one of the couple it shall not apply to the other except where, and to the extent that, the earnings of the one which are to be disregarded under this paragraph are less than £15;

[⁶(2) For the purposes of this paragraph in determining whether one of a couple has been in receipt of income support for a continuous period of two years—

    (a) no account shall be taken of any period not exceeding eight weeks during which the claimant was not a member of a couple;

    (b) subject to sub-paragraphs (2A) and (2C), no account shall be taken of any period not exceeding eight weeks during which the claimant was not in receipt of income support;

    (c) consecutive periods during which either member was in receipt of income support in respect of a couple shall be treated as periods during which one of that couple had been so in receipt.

    (2A) Where—

    (a) a claimant has ceased to be in receipt of income support because he or the other member of the couple becomes engaged in remunerative work; and

    (b) immediately before ceasing to be so in receipt this paragraph applied to him,

sub-paragraph (2)(b) shall apply to him as if for the words "not exceeding eight weeks" there were substituted the words "not exceeding the permitted period determined in accordance with regulation 3A (permitted period)".

    (2B) In a case where sub-paragraph (2A) applies, sub-paragraph (1) shall apply as if for the words "a period exceeding eight consecutive weeks" there were substituted the words "a period exceeding the permitted period determined in accordance with regulation (3A)".

    (2C) For the purposes of this paragraph, where—

    (a) a claimant has ceased to be in receipt of income support because he or the other member of the couple is participating in arrangements for training made under section 2 of the Employment and Training Act 1973 [⁷or section 2 of the Enterprise and New Towns (Scotland) Act 1990] or attending a course at an employment rehabilitation centre established under that section [⁷of the 1973 Act]; and

    (b) immediately before ceasing to be so in receipt this paragraph applied to him,

he shall be treated as if he had been in receipt of income support in respect of a couple for the period during which he or his partner is participating in such arrangements or attending such a course and no account shall be taken of any period during that time in which the other member is engaged in remunerative work, in relevant education or a student.]

(3) For the purposes of this paragraph—

(a) any period beginning before the commencement of these regulations during supplementary benefit in respect of a couple, and immediately preceding the receipt of income support, is to be taken into account as if it were a period of income support except where during that period either the claimant or the other member was engaged in remunerative work or receiving relevant education within the meaning of section 6 of the Supplementary Benefits Act 1976;

(b) any period during which the claimant or the other member of the couple is in receipt of income support under the Social Security (Northern Ireland) Order 1986 or was in receipt of supplementary benefit under the Supplementary Benefit (Northern Ireland) Order 1977 and immediately preceding the receipt of income support is to be taken into account as if it were a period of income support;

and in determining whether any such period is continuous [⁶sub-paragraphs (2) to (2C)] hereof shall apply by analogy.

[⁹6A.—(1) In a case to which none of paragraphs 4 to 6 applies to the claimant, and subject to sub-paragraph (2), where the claimant's applicable amount includes an amount by way of the carer premium under Schedule 2 (applicable amounts), £15 of the earnings of the person who is, or at any time in the preceding eight weeks was, in receipt of invalid care allowance or treated in accordance with paragraph 14ZA(2) of that Schedule as being in receipt of invalid care allowance.

(2) Where the carer premium is awarded in respect of the claimant and of any partner of his, their earnings shall for the purposes of this paragraph be aggregated, but the amount to be disregarded in accordance with paragraph (1) shall not exceed £15 of the aggregated amount.

6B. Where the carer premium is awarded in respect of a claimant who is a member of a couple and whose earnings are less than £15, but is not awarded in respect of the other member of the couple, and that other member is engaged in an employment—

(a) specified in paragraph 7(1), so much of the other member's earnings as would not when aggregated with the amount disregarded under paragraph 6A exceed £15;

(b) other than one specified in paragraph 7(1), so much of the other member's earnings from such other employment up to £5 as would not when aggregated with the amount disregarded under paragraph 6A exceed £15.]

7.—(1) In a case to which none of paragraphs [⁹4 to 6B] applies to the claimant, £15 of earnings derived from one or more employments as—

(a) a part-time fireman in a fire brigade maintained in pursuance of the Fire Services Acts 1947 to 1959;

(b) an auxiliary coastguard in respect of coast rescue activities;

(c) a person engaged part time in the manning or launching of a lifeboat;

(d) a member of any territorial or reserve force prescribed in Part I of Schedule 3 to the Social Security (Contributions) Regulations 1979;

but, notwithstanding regulation 23 (calculation of income and capital of members of claimant's family and of a polygamous marriage), if this paragraph applies to a claimant it shall not apply to his partner except to the extent specified in sub-paragraph (2).

(2) If the claimant's partner is engaged in employment—

(a) specified in sub-paragraph (1) so much of his earnings as would not in aggregate with the amount of the claimant's earnings disregarded under this paragraph exceed £15;

(b) other than one specified in sub-paragraph (1) so much of his earnings from that employment up to £5 as would not in aggregate with the claimant's earnings disregarded under this paragraph exceed £15.

8. Where the claimant is engaged in one or more employments specified in paragraph 7(1) but his earnings derived from such employments are less than £15 in any week and he is also engaged in any other part-time employment so much of his earnings from that other employment up to £5 as would not in aggregate with the amount of his earnings disregarded under paragraph 7 exceed £15.

9. In a case to which none of paragraphs 4 to 8 applies to the claimant, £5.

10. Notwithstanding [⁹paragraphs 6 to 7] or 9, where two or more payments of the same kind and from the same source are to be taken into account in the same benefit week, there shall be disregarded from each payment the sum specified in that paragraph; but this paragraph shall only apply in the case of a payment which it has not been practicable to treat under regulation 31(1)(b) (date on which income treated as paid) as paid on the first day of the benefit week in which it is due to be paid.

11. Any earnings derived from employment which are payable in a country outside the United Kingdom for such period during which there is a prohibition against the transfer to the United Kingdom of those earnings.

12. Where a payment of earnings is made in a currency other than sterling, any banking charge or commission payable in converting that payment into sterling.

13. Any earnings which are due to be paid before the date of claim and which would otherwise fall to be taken into account in the same benefit week as a payment of the same kind and from the same source.

14. Any earnings of a child or young person except earnings to which paragraph 15 applies.

15. [⁸In the case of earnings of a child or young person who although not receiving full-time education for the purposes of section 2 of the Child Benefit Act 1975 [SSCBA, s.142] (meaning of "child") is nonetheless treated for the purposes of these Regulations as receiving relevant education and] who is engaged in remunerative work, if—

(a) an amount by way of a disabled child premium under Schedule 2 (applicable amounts) is, or but for his accommodation in a [⁴residential care home or nursing home] would be, included in the calculation of his applicable amount and his earning capacity is not, by reason of his disability, less than 75 per cent of that which he would, but for that disability normally be expected to earn, £15;

(b) in any other case, £5.

16. In this Schedule "part-time employment" means employment in which the person is not to be treated as engaged in remunerative work under regulation 5 or 6 (persons treated, or not treated, as engaged in remunerative work).

AMENDMENTS

1. Income Support (General) Amendment Regulations 1988 (S.I. 1988 No. 663). reg. 34 (April 11, 1988).

2. Income Support (General) Amendment No. 4 Regulations 1988 (S.I. 1988 No. 1445), reg. 24 (September 12, 1988).

3. Income Support (General) Amendment No. 4 Regulations 1988 (S.I. 1988 No. 1445), Sched. 1, para. 8 (April 10, 1989).

4. Income Support (General) Amendment Regulations 1989 (S.I. 1989 No. 534), reg. 10 and Sched. 1 (October 9, 1989).

5. Income Support (General) Amendment No. 2 Regulations 1989 (S.I. 1989 No. 1323), reg. 18 (October 9, 1989).

6. Income Support (General) Amendment No. 3 Regulations 1989 (S.I. 1989 No. 1678), reg. 12 (October 9, 1989).

7. Enterprise (Scotland) Consequential Amendments Order 1991 (S.I. 1991 No. 387), arts. 2 and 9 (April 1, 1991).

8. Income Support (General) Amendment Regulations 1992 (S.I.1992 No. 468), reg. 7 (April 6, 1992).

9. Income-related Benefits Schemes (Miscellaneous Amendments) Regulations 1993 (S.I. 1993 No. 315), reg. 8 (April 12, 1993).

10. Income-related Benefits Schemes (Miscellaneous Amendments) (No. 4) Regulations 1993 (S.I. 1993 No. 2119), reg. 22 (October 4, 1993).

DEFINITIONS

"benefit week"—see reg. 2(1).
"child"—see 1986 Act, s.20(11) (SSCBA, s.137(1)).
"claimant"—see reg. 2(1).
"couple"—*ibid.*

"date of claim"—*ibid.*
"employed earner"—*ibid.*
"family"—see 1986 Act, s.20(11) (SSCBA, s.137(1)).
"nursing home"—see reg. 2(1), reg. 19(3).
"partner"—see reg. 2(1).
"polygamous marriage"—*ibid.*
"remunerative work"—*ibid.*
"residential accommodation"—see reg. 2(1), reg. 21(3).
"residential care home"—see reg. 2(1), reg. 19(3).
"Social Security Act"—see reg. 2(1).
"supplementary benefit"—*ibid.*
"young person" *ibid.*, reg. 14.

GENERAL NOTE

Paras. 1 to 13 apply to adults. Paras. 14 and 15 apply to children and young persons only. Paras. 1 to 10 do not apply to children or young persons (reg. 23(2)).

Paragraph 1
This disregard is crucial to entitlement following the termination of full time (*i.e.* 16 hours or more per week) employment. The effect, under sub-para. (a)(ii), is that final payments of wages and salary are disregarded. This means that entitlement can begin immediately, unless a payment in lieu of wages or notice or holiday pay is due or a compensation payment is made. If any of these payments are made, reg. 5(5) treats the claimant as in full-time work for the number of weeks covered by the payments (regs. 29(3) and (4)). Once that period has ended, any money remaining counts as capital (*CIS 104/1989* and *CIS 654/1991*, to be reported as *R(IS) 3/93*). The disregard is more extensive if the employment has not terminated but the claimant is working less than 16 hours a week (or none at all). The old form of para. 1(b) applied the disregard if the employment had been "interrupted". In *CIS 301/1989* it was held that a shift from full-time to part-time employment with the same employer was an interruption of "the" employment. If the evidence had supported the replacement of one contract with another this would have been a termination. The new wording should cover this type of situation with less linguistic contortion. The disregard in sub-para. (b) does not apply if the claimant has been suspended. Payments by way of a retainer (reg. 35(1)(e)) are not disregarded under sub-para. (a)(ii) or (b). *CIS 743/1992* decides that a guarantee payment under s. 12 of the Employment Protection (Consolidation) Act 1978 counts as a retainer.
If the claimant retires at pensionable age no earnings due on termination are taken into account.

Paragraph 2
There is a more extensive disregard where the claimant's part-time (*i.e.* less than 16 hours per week: para. 16) work has stopped before the claim (provided he has not been suspended). On payments within reg. 35(1)(e) see *CIS 743/1992* in the note to para. 1. It is not necessary for the employment to have ended. If the part-time work ends while the claimant is claiming income support, payments are taken into account as earnings in the usual way.

Paragraph 3
When a self-employed person leaves that employment, only royalties or payments for copyright count.

Paragraph 4
This provision allows a disregard of £15 between the claimant and any partner, if the claimant meets the basic conditions for a disability premium or if the conditions for the enhanced or higher pensioner premium are met, with the restrictive extra conditions of sub-paras. (3)(b) and (5)(b).

Paragraph 5
If the claimant is a lone parent the first £15 of net earnings are disregarded.

Paragraph 6
If both members of a couple are under 60 and one of them has been in receipt of income support or supplementary benefit for a couple for a continuous period of two years the disregard between the couple is £15. It is a condition that neither partner has been in remunerative work (as defined in reg. 5) or full-time education for more than eight weeks in the two-year period.

This is designed as an incentive for the long-term unemployed. It is one of the few examples under income support of length of time on benefit affecting entitlement.

Paragraphs 6A and 6B

Where the carer premium is payable, the first £15 of the earnings of the carer are disregarded. If the carer does not use up the disregard, what is spare may be applied to a (non-carer) partner's earnings under para. 6B. Only £5 may be disregarded in this way, except for the employments mentioned in para. 7(1).

Paragraph 7

Earnings from these activities attract a £15 disregard, but a couple cannot have a total disregard of more than £15.

Paragraph 9

The basic disregard of net earnings from part-time work is £5. Para. 29226 of the *Adjudication Officers' Guide* says that if both members of a couple are in part-time work they should each be allowed a £5 disregard.

Paragraph 10

See notes to reg. 32(5).

Paragraph 13

Where earnings are due before the date of claim, overlaps with payments of the same kind are avoided. See notes to reg. 32(5).

Paragraphs 14 and 15

The general rule is that the earnings of children and young persons are disregarded, but where such a person has left school and is treated as in relevant education until the next terminal date, earnings from "remunerative work" do count, subject to a £5 disregard (£15 for the disabled). See the transitional protection for Easter school leavers who were working for more than 16 hours a week, but less than 24, immediately before April 6, 1992 in reg. 10 of the Income Support (General) Amendment Regulations 1992 (see p.371). Remunerative work for the purposes of excluding payment of child benefit in these circumstances remains 24 hours a week (regs. 1(2) and 7(3) of the Child Benefit (General) Regulations).

SCHEDULE 9   **Regulation 40(2)**

Sums to be Disregarded in the Calculation of Income other than Earnings

1. Any amount paid by way of tax on income which is taken into account under regulation 40 (calculation of income other than earnings).

2. Any payment in respect of any expenses incurred by a claimant who is—

(a) engaged by a charitable or [32voluntary organisation]; or

(b) a volunteer,

if he otherwise derives no remuneration or profit from the employment and is not to be treated as possessing any earnings under regulation 42(6) (notional income).

3. In the case of employment as an employed earner, any payment in respect of expenses wholly, exclusively and necessarily incurred in the performance of the duties of the employment.

4. In the case of a payment of statutory sick pay under Part I of the Social Security and Housing Benefits Act 1982 or statutory maternity pay under Part V of the Act or any remuneration paid by or on behalf of an employer to the claimant who for the time being is unable to work due to illness or maternity—

(a) any amount deducted by way of primary Class 1 contributions under the Social Security Act [SSCBA];

(b) one-half of any sum paid by the claimant by way of a contribution towards an occupational or personal pension scheme.

[1**4A.** In the case of the payment of statutory sick pay under Part II of the Social Security (Northern Ireland) Order 1982 or statutory maternity pay under Part VI of the Social Security (Northern Ireland) Order 1986—

314

(a) any amount deducted by way of primary Class 1 contributions under the Social Security (Northern Ireland) Act 1975;

(b) one-half of any sum paid by way of a contribution towards an occupational or personal pension scheme.]

5. Any housing benefit.

6. Any mobility allowance [¹⁸or the mobility component of disability living allowance].

7. Any concessionary payment made to compensate for the non-payment of—

(a) any payment specified in [¹⁸paragraph 6, 9 or 9A];

(b) income support.

8. Any mobility supplement or any payment intended to compensate for the non-payment of such a supplement.

[²⁵**9.** Any attendance allowance or the care component of disability living allowance, but, where the claimant's applicable amount falls to be calculated in accordance with Part I of Schedule 4 only to the extent that it exceeds the amount for the time being specified as the higher rate of attendance allowance for the purposes of section 64(3) of the Social Security Contributions and Benefits Act 1992 or, as the case may, be the highest rate of the care component of disability living allowance for the purposes of section 72(4)(a) of that Act.]

[²⁹**9A.** . . .]

10. Any payment to the claimant as holder of the Victoria Cross or George Cross or any analogous payment.

11. Any sum in respect of a course of study attended by a child or young person payable by virtue of regulations made under section 81 of the Education Act 1944 (assistance by means of scholarships and otherwise), or by virtue of section 2(1) of the Education Act 1962 (awards for courses of further education) or section 49 of the Education (Scotland) Act 1980 (power to assist persons to take advantage of educational facilities).

12. In the case of a claimant to whom regulation 9(1) (persons treated as available for employment) applies, any sums intended for any expenditure specified in paragraph (2) of regulation 62 (calculation of grant income) necessary as a result of his attendance on his course.

[¹**13.** In the case of a claimant participating in arrangements for training made under section 2 of the Employment and Training Act 1973 [¹³or section 2 of the Enterprise and New Towns (Scotland) Act 1990] or attending a course at an employment rehabilitation centre established under that section [¹³of the 1973 Act]—

(a) any travelling expenses reimbursed to the claimant;

(b) any living away from home allowance under section 2(2)(d) [¹³of the 1973 Act or section 2(4)(c) of the 1990 Act] but only to the extent that his rent or rates payable in respect of accommodation not normally occupied by him as his home are not met by housing benefit;

(c) any training premium,

but this paragraph, except in so far as it relates to a payment under sub-paragraph (a), (b) or (c), does not apply to any part of any allowance under section 2(2)(d) [¹³of the 1973 Act or section 2(4)(c) of the 1990 Act].]

14. Any Job Start Allowance payable pursuant to arrangements made under section 2(1) of the Employment and Training Act 1973.

[¹⁰**15.**—[²⁹(1) Subject to sub-paragraph (3) and paragraphs 36, 37 and 39, £10 of any charitable payment or of any voluntary payment made or due to be made at regular intervals, except any payment to which sub-paragraph (2) or paragraph 15A applies.]

(2) Subject to [²⁹sub-paragraphs (3) and (6)] and paragraph 39, any charitable payment of voluntary payment made or due to be made at regular intervals which is intended and used for an item other than food, ordinary clothing or footwear, household fuel, rent or rates for which housing benefit is payable, [¹⁶. . .] any housing costs to the extent that they are met under regulation 17(1) (e) or 18(1)(f) (housing costs) or any accommodation charges to the extent that they are met under regulation 19 (persons in residential care or nursing homes)[³⁰. . .], of a single claimant or, as the case may be, of the claimant or

any other member of his family[16], or is used for any [23council tax] or water charges for which that claimant or member is liable].

(3) Sub-paragraphs (1) and (2) shall not apply—

(a) to a payment which is made by a person for the maintenance of any member of his family or of his former partner or of his children;

(b) in the case of a person to whom section 23 of the Act [SSCBA, s.126] (trade disputes) applies or in respect of whom section 20(3) of the Act [SSCBA, s.124(1)] (conditions of entitlement to income support) has effect as modified by section 23A(b) of the Act [SSCBA, s.127(b)] (effect of return to work).

(4) For the purposes of sub-paragraph (1) where a number of charitable or voluntary payments fall to be taken into account in any one week they shall be treated as though they were one such payment.

(5) For the purposes of sub-paragraph (2) the expression "ordinary clothing or footwear" means clothing or footwear for normal daily use, but does not include school uniforms, or clothing or footwear used solely for sporting activities.]

[29(6) Sub-paragraph (2) shall apply to a claimant in a residential care home or nursing home only if his applicable amount falls to be calculated in accordance with regulation 19.]

[2515A.—(1) Subject to the following provisions of this paragraph, in the case of a claimant placed in a residential care home or nursing home by a local authority under section 26 of the National Assistance Act 1948, [32sections 13A, 13B and 59(2)(c) of the Social Work (Scotland) Act 1968 or section 7 of the Mental Health (Scotland) Act 1984] any charitable payment or voluntary payment made or due to be made at regular intervals.

(2) This paragraph shall apply only where—

(a) the claimant was placed in the residential care or nursing home by the local authority because the home was the preferred choice of the claimant, and

(b) the cost of the accommodation was in excess of what the authority would normally expect to pay having regard to the needs of the claimant assessed in accordance with section 47 of the National Health Service and Community Care Act 1990.

(3) This paragraph shall not apply in the case of a person whose applicable amount falls to be calculated under regulation 19 (persons in residential care or nursing homes with preserved rights).

(4) The amount to be disregarded under sub-paragraph (1) shall not exceed the difference between the actual cost of the accommodation provided by the local authority and the cost the authority would normally incur for a person with the particular needs of the claimant.]

16. Subject to paragraphs 36 and 37, [10£10] of any of the following, namely—

(a) a war disablement pension or war widow's pension or a payment made to compensate for the non-payment of such a pension[29, except in so far as such a pension or payment falls to be disregarded under paragraphs 8 or 9];

[16(b) a pension paid by the government of a country outside Great Britain and which is either—

(i) analogous to a war disablement pension; or

(ii) analogous to a war widow's pension;]

(c) a pension paid under any special provision made by the law of the Federal Republic of Germany or any part of it or of the Republic of Austria, to victims of National Socialist persecution.

17. Where a person receives income under an annuity purchased with a loan which satisfies the following conditions—

(a) that the loan was made as part of a scheme under which not less than 90 per cent. of the proceeds of the loan were applied to the purchase by the person to whom it was made of an annuity ending with his life or with the life of the survivor of two or more persons (in this paragraph referred to as "the annuitants") who include the person to whom the loan was made;

   (b) that the interest on the loan is payable by the person to whom it was made or by one of the annuitants;

   (c) that at the time the loan was made the person to whom it was made or each of the annuitants had attained the age of 65;

   (d) that the loan was secured on a dwelling in Great Britain and the person to whom the loan was made or one of the annuitants owns an estate or interest in that dwelling; and

   (e) that the person to whom the loan was made or one of the annuitants occupies the accommodation on which it was secured as his home at the time the interest is paid,

the amount, calculated on a weekly basis equal to—

     [³¹(i) where, or insofar as, section 369 of the Income and Corporation Taxes Act 1988 (mortgage interest payable under deduction of tax) applies to the payments of interest on the loan, the interest which is payable after deduction of a sum equal to income tax on such payments at the applicable percentage of income tax within the meaning of section 369(1A) of that Act;]

     (ii) in any other case the interest which is payable on the loan without deduction of such a sum.

[³²**18.** Any payment made to the claimant by a person who normally resides with the claimant, which is a contribution towards that person's living and accommodation costs, except where that person is residing with the claimant in circumstances to which paragraph 19 or 20 refers.]

[³⁰**19.** Where the claimant occupies a dwelling as his home and the dwelling is also occupied by [³²another person], and there is a contractual liability to make payments to the claimant in respect of the occupation of the dwelling by that person or a member of his family—

   (a) £4 of the aggregate of any payments made in respect of any one week in respect of the occupation of the dwelling by that person or a member of his family, or by that person and a member of his family; and

   (b) a further [³³£9.20], where the aggregate of any such payments is inclusive of an amount for heating.]

[³⁰**20.** Where the claimant occupies a dwelling as his home and he provides in that dwelling board and lodging accommodation, an amount, in respect of each person for whom such accommodation is provided for the whole or any part of a week, equal to—

   (a) where the aggregate of any payments made in respect of any one week in respect of such accommodation provided to such person does not exceed £20.00, 100 % of such payments; or

   (b) where the aggregate of any such payments exceeds £20.00, £20.00 and 50 % of the excess over £20.00.]

[¹**21.**—(1) Subject to sub-paragraph (2), except where regulation 42(4)(a)(i) (notional income) applies or in the case of a person to whom section 23 of the Act [SSCBA, s.126] (trade disputes) applies and for so long as it applies, any income in kind;

(2) The exception under sub-paragraph (1) shall not apply where the income in kind is received from the Macfarlane Trust[⁸, the Macfarlane (Special Payments) Trust] [¹⁵, the Macfarlane (Special Payments) (No. 2) Trust][²¹, the Fund][²⁷, the Eileen Trust] [² or [²⁶the Independent Living Funds]].]

22.—(1) Any income derived from capital to which the claimant is or is treated under regulation 52 (capital jointly held) as beneficially entitled but, subject to sub-paragraph (2), not income derived from capital disregarded under paragraph 1, 2, 4, 6 [³12 or 25 to 28] of Schedule 10.

(2) Income derived from capital disregarded under paragraph 2 [³4 or 25 to 28] of Schedule 10 but [²⁴only to the extent of—

   (a) any mortgage repayments made in respect of the dwelling or premises in the period during which that income accrued; or

(b) any council tax or water charges which the claimant is liable to pay in respect of the dwelling or premises and which are paid in the period during which that income accrued.

(3) The definition of "water charges" in regulation 2(1) shall apply to subparagraph (2) with the omission of the words "in so far as such charges are in respect of the dwelling which a person occupies as his home".]

23. Any income which is payable in a country outside the United Kingdom for such period during which there is a prohibition against the transfer to the United Kingdom of that income.

24. Where a payment of income is made in a currency other than sterling, any banking charge or commission payable in converting that payment into sterling.

25.—(1) Any payment made to the claimant in respect of a child or young person who is a member of his family—

[20(a) in accordance with regulations made pursuant to section 57A of the Adoption Act 1976 or with a scheme approved by the Secretary of State under section 51 of the Adoption (Scotland) Act 1978 (schemes for payment of allowances to adopters);

(b) which is a payment made by a local authority in pursuance of section 15(1) of, and paragraph 15 of Schedule 1 to, the Children Act 1989 (local authority contribution to a child's maintenance where the child is living with a person as a result of a residence order);]

to the extent specifed in sub-paragraph (2).

(2) In the case of a child or young person—

(a) to whom regulation 44(5) (capital in excess of £3,000) applies, the whole payment;

(b) to whom that regulation does not apply, so much of the weekly amount of the payment as exceeds the applicable amount in respect of that child or young person and where applicable to him any amount by way of a disabled child premium.

26. Any payment made by a local authority to the claimant with whom a person is [20accommodated by virtue of arrangements made under section 23(2)(a) of the Children Act 1989 (provision of accommodation and maintenance for a child whom they are looking after)] or, as the case may be, [3section 21] of the Social Work (Scotland) Act 1968 or by a voluntary organisation under [20section 59(1)(a) of the 1989 Act (provision of accommodation by voluntary organisations)] or by a care authority under regulation 9 of the Boarding Out and Fostering of Children (Scotland) Regulations 1985 (provision of accommodation and maintenance for children in care).

27. Any payment made by a health authority, local authority or voluntary organisation to the claimant in respect of a person who is not normally a member of the claimant's household but is temporarily in his care.

28. Except in the case of a person to whom section 23 of the Act [SSCBA, s.126] (trade disputes) applies [1or in respect of whom section 20(3) of the Act [SSCBA, s.124(1)] (conditions of entitlement to income support) has effect as modified by section 23A(b) of the Act [SSCBA, s.127(b)] (effect of return to work)], [6any payment made by a local authority [20in accordance with section 17 or 24 of the Children Act 1989] or, as the case may be, section 12, 24 or 26 of the Social Work (Scotland) Act 1968 (local authorities' duty to promote welfare of children and powers to grant financial assistance to persons in, or formerly in, their care).]

29.—(1) [29Subject to sub-paragraph (3),] any payment received under an insurance policy, taken out to insure against the risk of being unable to maintain repayments on a loan to which paragraph 7 or 8 of Schedule 3 applies (interest on loans to acquire an interest in the dwelling, or for repairs and improvements to the dwelling, occupied as the home) and used to meet such repayments, to the extent that it does not exceed—

(a) subject to sub-paragraph (2), the amount, calculated on a weekly basis, of any interest which is excluded [28under paragraphs 7, 8 and 10 of Schedule 3];

(b) the amount of the payment, calculated on a weekly basis, due on the loan attributable to the repayment of capital; and

(c) the amount, calculated on a weekly basis, of the premium due on that policy.

[²⁸(2) The amount to which sub-paragraph (1)(a) refers shall be taken into account in calculating the amount to be excluded under this paragraph only for such period during which either—

(a) there is applicable to the claimant 50 per cent. of his eligible interest under paragraph 7 of Schedule 3; or

(b) the amount of the loan to be taken into account is restricted by virtue of paragraph 7(6B) or 10 of Schedule 3.]

[²⁹(3) This paragraph shall not apply to any payment which is treated as possessed by the claimant by virtue of regulation 42(4)(a)(ii) (notional income).]

30. Except where [¹paragraph 29] applies, any payment made to the claimant which is intended and used as a contribution towards—

(a) the amount of eligible interest which is not met under paragraph 7 or 8 of Schedule 3 (interest on loans to acquire an interest in the dwelling, or for repairs and improvements to the dwelling, occupied as the home);

(b) the capital repayments—

    (i) where the loan is one specified in paragraph 7(3)(a) or 8(1)(a) of Schedule 3; or

    (ii) where the loan is one specified in paragraph 7(3)(b) or 8(1)(b) of Schedule 3 only to the extent that the capital outstanding on that loan represents the capital balance outstanding on the previous loan at the time when the loan was taken out;

(c) any payment or charge specified in paragraph 1 of Schedule 3 to the extent that that payment or charge has not been met;

(d) his rent in respect of the dwelling occupied by him as his home but only to the extent that it is not met by housing benefit; or his accommodation charge but only to the extent that the [⁷actual charge increased, where appropriate, in accordance with paragraph 2 of Schedule 4 exceeds the amount determined in accordance with regulation 19 (residential care and nursing homes) [²²or the amount payable by a local authority in accordance with Part III of the National Assistance Act 1948].]

[²⁹**30A.**—(1) Subject to sub-paragraphs (2) and (3), in the case of a claimant in a residential care home or nursing home, any payment, whether or not the payment is charitable or voluntary but not a payment to which paragraph 15A applies, made to the claimant which is intended to be used and is used to meet the cost of maintaining the claimant in that home.

(2) This paragraph shall not apply to a claimant for whom accommodation in a residential care home or nursing home is provided by a local authority under section 26 of the National Assistance Act 1948, or whose applicable amount falls to be calculated in accordance with regulation 19.

(3) The amount to be disregarded under this paragraph shall not exceed the difference between—

(a) the claimant's applicable amount less any of the amounts referred to in paragraph 13 of Schedule 4 (personal allowances) which would be applicable to the claimant if his applicable amount fell to be calculated in accordance with that Schedule, and

(b) the weekly charge for the accommodation.]

[¹⁹**31.** Any social fund payment made pursuant to Part III of the Act [SSCBA, Part VIII].]

32. Any payment of income which under regulation 48 (income treated as capital) is to be treated as capital.

33. Any payment under paragraph 2 of Schedule 6 to the Act [SSCBA, s. 148] (pensioners' Christmas bonus).

34. In the case of a person to whom section 23 of the Act [SSCBA, s.126] (trade disputes) applies and for so long as it applies, any payment up to the amount of the relevant sum within the meaning of sub-section (6) of that section made by a trade union; but, notwithstanding regulation 23 (calculation of income and capital of members of claimant's family and of a polygamous marriage) if this paragraph applies to a claimant it shall not apply to his partner except where, and to the extent that, the amount to be disregarded under this paragraph is less than the relevant sum.

35. Any payment which is due to be paid before the date of claim which would otherwise fall to be taken into account in the same benefit week as a payment of the same kind and from the same source.

36. The total of a claimant's income or, if he is a member of a family, the family's income and the income of any person which he is treated as possessing under regulation 23(3) (calculation of income and capital of members of claimant's family and of a polygamous marriage) to be disregarded under regulation 63(2)(b) and 64(1)(c) (calculation of covenant income where a contribution assessed)[¹¹, regulation 66A(2) (treatment of student loans)] and [¹⁰paragraphs 15(1)] and 16 shall in no case exceed [¹⁰£10] per week.

37. Notwithstanding paragraph 36 where two or more payments of the same kind and from the same source are to be taken into account in the same benefit week, there shall be disregarded from each payment the sum which would otherwise fall to be disregarded under this Schedule; but this paragraph shall only apply in the case of a payment which it has not been practicable to treat under regulation 31(1)(b) (date on which income treated as paid) as paid on the first day of the benefit week in which it is due to be paid.

[¹**38.** Any resettlement benefit which is paid to the claimant by virtue of regulation 3 of the Social Security (Hospital In-Patients) Amendment (No. 2) Regulations 1987.

[¹⁵**39.**—(1) Any payment made under the Macfarlane Trust, the Macfarlane (Special Payments) Trust, the Macfarlane (Special Payments) (No. 2) Trust ("the Trusts"), [²¹the Fund][²⁷, the Eileen Trust] or [²⁶the Independent Living Funds].

(2) Any payment by or on behalf of a person who is suffering or who suffered from haemophilia [²¹or who is or was a qualifying person], which derives from a payment made under any of the Trusts to which sub-paragraph (1) refers and which is made to or for the benefit of—

(a) that person's partner or former partner from whom he is not, or where that person has died was not, estranged or divorced;

(b) any child who is a member of that person's family or who was such a member and who is a member of the claimant's family; or

(c) any young person who is a member of that person's family or who was such a member and who is a member of the claimant's family.

(3) Any payment by or on behalf of the partner or former partner of a person who is suffering or who suffered from haemophilia [²¹or who is or was a qualifying person] provided that the partner or former partner and that person are not, or if either of them has died were not, estranged or divorced, which derives from a payment made under any of the Trusts to which sub-paragraph (1) refers and which is made to or for the benefit of—

(a) the person who is suffering from haemophilia [²¹or who is a qualifying person];

(b) any child who is a member of that person's family or who was such a member and who is a member of the claimant's family; or

(c) any young person who is a member of that person's family or who was such a member and who is a member of the claimant's family.

(4) Any payment by a person who is suffering from haemophilia [²¹or who is a qualifying person], which derives from a payment under any of the Trusts to which sub-paragraph (1) refers, where—

(a) that person has no partner or former partner from whom he is not estranged or divorced, nor any child or young person who is or had been a member of that person's family; and

(b) the payment is made either—

(i) to that person's parent or step-parent, or

(ii) where that person at the date of the payment is a child, a young person or a student who has not completed his full-time education and has no parent or step-parent, to his guardian,

but only for a period from the date of the payment until the end of two years from that person's death.

(5) Any payment out of the estate of a person who suffered from haemophilia [²¹or who was a qualifying person], which derives from a payment under any of the Trusts to which sub-paragraph (1) refers, where—

(a) that person at the date of his death (the relevant date) had no partner or former partner from whom he was not estranged or divorced, nor any child or young person who was or had been a member of his family; and

(b) the payment is made either—

    (i) to that person's parent or step-parent, or

    (ii) where that person at the relevant date was a child, a young person or a student who had not completed his full-time education and had no parent or step-parent, to his guardian,

but only for a period of two years from the relevant date.

(6) In the case of a person to whom or for whose benefit a payment referred to in this paragraph is made, any income which derives from any payment of income or capital made under or deriving from any of the Trusts.]

[²¹(7) For the purposes of sub-paragraphs (2) to (6), any reference to the Trusts shall be construed as including a reference to the Fund [²⁷and the Eileen Trust].]]

[³**40.** Any payment made by the Secretary of State to compensate for the loss (in whole or in part) of entitlement to housing benefit.]

[⁴**41.** Any payment made by the Secretary of State to compensate a person who was entitled to supplementary benefit in respect of a period ending immediately before 11th April 1988 but who did not become entitled to income support in respect of a period beginning with that day.

42. Any payment made by the Secretary of State to compensate for the loss of housing benefit supplement under regulation 19 of the Supplementary Benefit (Requirements) Regulations 1983.

43. Any payment made to a juror or a witness in respect of attendance at a court other than compensation for loss of earnings or for the loss of a benefit payable under the benefit Acts.

44. [²³ . . .].]

[⁹**45.** Any community charge benefit.

46. Any payment in consequence of a reduction of a personal community charge pursuant to regulations under section 13A of the Local Government Finance Act 1988 or section 9A of the Abolition of Domestic Rates Etc (Scotland) Act 1987 (reduction of liability for personal community charges) [²³or reduction of council tax under section 13 or, as the case may be, section 80 of the Local Government Finance Act 1992 (reduction of liability for council tax).]

47. Any special war widows payment made under—

(a) the Naval and Marine Pay and Pensions (Special War Widows Payment) Order 1990 made under section 3 of the Naval and Marine Pay and Pensions Act 1865;

(b) the Royal Warrant dated 19th February 1990 amending the Schedule to the Army Pensions Warrant 1977;

(c) the Queen's Order dated 26th February 1990 made under section 2 of the Air Force (Constitution) Act 1917;

(d) the Home Guard War Widows Special Payments Regulations 1990 made under section 151 of the Reserve Forces Act 1980;

(e) the Orders dated 19th February 1990 amending Orders made on 12th December 1980 concerning the Ulster Defence Regiment made in each case under section 140 of the Reserve Forces Act 1980;

and any analogous payment made by the Secretary of State for Defence to any person who is not a person entitled under the provisions mentioned in subparagraphs (a) to (e) of this paragraph.]

[¹²**48.**—(1)Any payment or repayment made—

(a) as respects England and Wales, under regulation 3, 5 or 8 of the National Health Service (Travelling Expenses and Remission of Charges) Regulations 1988 (travelling expenses and health service supplies);

(b) as respects Scotland, under regulation 3, 5 or 8 of the National Health Service (Travelling Expenses and Remission of Charges) (Scotland) Regulations 1988 (travelling expenses and health service supplies).

(2) Any payment or repayment made by the Secretary of State for Health, the Secretary of State for Scotland or the Secretary of State for Wales which is analogous to a payment or repayment mentioned in sub-paragraph (1).

49. Any payment made under regulation 9 to 11 or 13 of the Welfare Food Regulations 1988 (payments made in place of milk tokens or the supply of vitamins).

50. Any payment made either by the Secretary of State for the Home Department or by the Secretary of State for Scotland under a scheme established to assist relatives and other persons to visit persons in custody.]

[[19]**51.** Any payment (other than a training allowance) made, whether by the Secretary of State or by any other person, under the Disabled Persons (Employment) Act 1944 or in accordance with arrangements made under section 2 of the Employment and Training Act 1973 to assist disabled persons to obtain or retain employment despite their disability.]

[[23]**52.** Any council tax benefit.]

[[30]**53.** Where the claimant is in receipt of any benefit under Parts II, III or V of the Contributions and Benefits Act, any increase in the rate of that benefit arising under Part IV (increases for dependants) or section 106(a) (unemployability supplement) of that Act where the dependant in respect of whom the increase is paid is not a member of the claimant's family.]

[[31]**54.** Any supplementary pension under article 29(1A) of the Naval, Military and Air Forces etc. (Disablement and Death) Service Pensions Order 1983 (pensions to widows).

55. In the case of a pension awarded at the supplementary rate under article 27(3) of the Personal Injuries (Civilians) Scheme 1983 (pensions to widows), the sum specified in paragraph 1(c) of Schedule 4 to that Scheme.

56.—(1) Any payment which is—

(a) made under any of the Dispensing Instruments to a widow of a person—
    (i) whose death was attributable to service in a capacity analogous to service as a member of the armed forces of the Crown; and
    (ii) whose service in such capacity terminated before 31st March 1973; and

(b) equal to the amount specified in article 29(1A) of the Naval, Military and Air Forces etc. (Disablement and Death) Service Pensions Order 1983 (pensions to widows).

(2) In this paragraph "the Dispensing Instruments" means the Order in Council of 19th December 1881, the Royal Warrant of 27th October 1884 and the Order by His Majesty of 14th January 1922 (exceptional grants of pay, non-effective pay and allowances).]

AMENDMENTS

1. Income Support (General) Amendment Regulations 1988 (S.I. 1988 No. 663), reg. 35 (April 11, 1988).

2. Family Credit and Income Support (General) Amendment Regulations 1988 (S.I. 1988 No. 999), reg. 5 (June 9, 1988).

3. Income Support (General) Amendment No. 4 Regulations 1988 (S.I. 1988 No. 1445), reg. 25 (September 12, 1988).

4. Income Support (General) Amendment No. 5 Regulations 1988 (S.I. 1988 No. 2022), reg. 22 (December 12, 1988).

5. Income Support (General) Amendment No. 4 Regulations 1988 (S.I. 1988 No. 1445), Sched. 1, para. 9 (April 10, 1989).

6. Family Credit and Income Support (General) Amendment Regulations 1989 (S.I. 1989 No. 1034), reg. 12 (July 10, 1989).

7. Income Support (General) Amendment Regulations 1989 (S.I. 1989 No. 534), Sched. 1, para. 15 (October 9, 1989).

8. Income-related Benefits Schemes Amendment Regulations 1990 (S.I. 1990 No. 127), reg. 3 (January 31, 1990).

9. Income Support (General) Amendment Regulations 1990 (S.I. 1990 No. 547), reg. 22(e) (April 1, 1990).

10. Income Support (General) Amendment Regulations 1990 (S.I. 1990 No. 547), reg. 22 (April 1, 1990).

11. Income-related Benefits Amendment Regulations 1990 (S.I. 1990 No. 1657), reg. 5(4) (September 1, 1990).

12. Income Support (General) Amendment No. 3 Regulations 1990 (S.I. 1990 No. 1776), reg. 10 (October 1, 1990).

13. Enterprise (Scotland) Consequential Amendments Order 1991 (S.I. 1991 No. 387), arts. 2 and 9 (April 1, 1991).

14. Income Support (General) Amendment Regulations 1991 (S.I. 1991 No. 236), reg. 14 (April 8, 1991).

15. Income-related Benefits Schemes and Social Security (Recoupment) Amendment Regulations 1991 (S.I. 1991 No. 1175), reg. 5 (May 11, 1991).

16. Income Support (General) Amendment No. 4 Regulations 1991 (S.I. 1991 No. 1559), reg. 20 (October 7, 1991).

17. Social Security Benefits Up-rating (No. 2) Order 1991 (S.I. 1991 No. 2910), art. 13(13) (April 6, 1992).

18. Disability Living Allowance and Disability Working Allowance (Consequential Provisions) Regulations 1991 (S.I. 1991 No. 2742), reg. 11(6) (April 6, 1992).

19. Income Support (General) Amendment Regulations 1992 (S.I. 1992 No. 468), reg. 8 (April 6, 1992).

20. Income Support (General) Amendment Regulations 1992 (S.I. 1992 No. 468), Sched., para. 9 (April 6, 1992).

21. Income-related Benefits Schemes and Social Security (Recoupment) Amendment Regulations 1992 (S.I. 1992 No. 1101), reg. 6 (May 7, 1992).

22. Social Security Benefits (Amendments Consequential Upon the Introduction of Community Care) Regulations 1992 (S.I. 1992 No. 3147), Sched. 1, para. 7 (April 1, 1993).

23. Income-related Benefits Schemes (Miscellaneous Amendments) Regulations 1993 (S.I. 1993 No. 315), Sched., para. 5 (April 1, 1993).

24. Income-related Benefits Schemes (Miscellaneous Amendments) Regulations 1993 (S.I. 1993 No. 315), reg. 9 (council tax and council tax benefit: April 1, 1993; otherwise April 12, 1993).

25. Social Security Benefits (Miscellaneous Amendments) Regulations 1993 (S.I. 1993 No. 518), reg. 5 (April 1, 1993).

26. Social Security Benefits (Miscellaneous Amendments) (No. 2) Regulations 1993 (S.I. 1993 No. 963), reg. 2(3) (April 22, 1993).

27. Income-related Benefits Schemes and Social Security (Recoupment) Amendment Regulations 1993 (S.I. 1993 No. 1249), reg. 4(4) (May 14, 1993).

28. Income Support (General) Amendment No. 3 Regulations 1993 (S.I. 1993 No. 1679), reg. 6 (August 2, 1993).

29. Income-related Benefits Schemes (Miscellaneous Amendments) (No. 4) Regulations 1993 (S.I. 1993 No. 2119), reg. 23 (October 4, 1993).

30. Income-related Benefits Schemes (Miscellaneous Amendments) Regulations 1994 (S.I. 1994 No. 527), reg. 9 (April 11, 1994).

31. Income-related Benefits Schemes (Miscellaneous Amendments) (No. 5) Regulations 1994 (S.I. 1994 No. 2139), reg. 32 (October 3, 1994).

32. Income-related Benefits Schemes (Miscellaneous Amendments) Regulations 1995 (S.I. 1995 No. 516), reg. 27 (April 10, 1995).

33. Social Security Benefits Uprating Order 1995 (S.I. 1995 No. 559), art. 18(13) (April 10, 1995).

DEFINITIONS

"the Act"—see reg. 2(1).
"attendance allowance"—*ibid.*
"benefit week"—*ibid.*
"child"—see 1986 Act, s.20(11) (SSCBA, s.137(1)).
"claimant"—see reg. 2(1).
"course of study"—*ibid.*
"disability living allowance"—*ibid.*
"dwelling occupied as the home"—*ibid.*
"employed earner"—*ibid.*

"family"—see 1986 Act, s.20(11) (SSCBA, s.137(1)).
"local authority"—see 1986 Act, s.84(1).
"mobility allowance"—see reg. 2(1).
"mobility supplement"—*ibid.*
"nursing home"—*ibid.*, reg. 19(3).
"occupational pension scheme"—see 1986 Act, s.84(1).
"personal pension scheme"—*ibid.*
"primary Class 1 contribution"—*ibid.*
"qualifying person"—*ibid.*
"residential care home"—see reg. 2(1), reg. 19(3).
"Social fund payment"—see 1986 Act, s.84(1).
"Social Security Act"—see reg. 2(1).
"the Eileen Trust"—*ibid.*
"the Fund"—*ibid.*
"the Independent Living Funds"—*ibid.*
"the Macfarlane (Special Payments) Trust"—*ibid.*
"the Macfarlane (Special Payments) (No.2) Trust"—*ibid.*
"the Macfarlane Trust"—*ibid.*
"training allowance"—*ibid.*
"voluntary organisation"—*ibid.*
"young person"—*ibid.*, reg. 14.

GENERAL NOTE

Paragraph 1
There is no provision in Chapter V itself for deducting tax. So if taxable payments are treated as income under reg. 40 a disregard is needed.

Paragraph 2
A payment purely of expenses to a volunteer or someone working for a charity or a voluntary organisation is disregarded unless the person is caught by reg. 42(6) on underpaid services. A volunteer is someone who without any legal obligation performs a service for another person without expectation of payment (*R(IS) 12/92*).

Paragraph 3
Such payments are not earnings (reg. 35(2)), but are income (reg. 40(4)). See the notes to reg. 35(1)(f) for "wholly, exclusively and necessarily." *CFC 2/1989* might suggest that payments made by the employee for necessary, etc., expenses out of such income are to be deducted from that income. But that is not consistent with the scheme of the legislation and is rejected in *R(FC) 1/90*, *R(IS) 16/93* and *CIS 77/1993*. See the notes to reg. 35(2), and to reg. 19(2) of the Family Credit Regulations. However, note the effect of the application of the principle in *Parsons v. Hogg* to the meaning of "gross earnings" (see the notes to reg. 36(3)).

Paragraphs 4 and 4A
The standard deductions are to be made from contractual or statutory sick or maternity pay, which are not earnings (reg. 35(2)), but are income (reg. 40(4)).

Paragraph 5
See also paras. 40, 42, 44, 45, 46 and 52.

Paragraph 6
Mobility allowance or the mobility component of disability living allowance is disregarded. See also paras. 7 and 8.

Paragraph 9
The general rule is that attendance allowance and the care component of disability living allowance is disregarded.
Before April 1993 attendance allowance was not disregarded as income for residents in residential care or nursing homes, on the basis that the claimant's attendance needs would be met in the home. Until April 1991 this applied to all such residents, even though their benefit was not calculated under the special provisions in Sched. 4. From April 1991 if the claimant was in one of the excluded categories in Part II of Sched. 4 (and so restricted to the ordinary benefit calculation, rather than

having the home's fees met by the higher level of income support), the attendance allowance was disregarded. It would be needed in those circumstances.

With the introduction of the care in the community reforms in April 1993, the system has changed. Attendance allowance and the care component of disability living allowance will normally cease to be payable after a claimant has been a resident in a residential care or nursing home for four weeks. (See *CPAG's Rights Guide to Non-Means-Tested Benefits* as to when people in residential care and nursing homes may continue to receive attendance allowance or the care component of disability living allowance without restriction.) For that four weeks, there is a disregard under para. 9 for new residents after April 1, 1993, who will not fall under Sched. 4 at all, but will be entitled to the residential allowance under para. 2A of Sched. 2. Only existing residents who have preserved rights will continue to be eligible for the higher rate of income support under Sched. 4. For such residents attendance allowance and the care component of disability living allowance will only be disregarded under para. 9 in so far as it exceeds the ordinary maximum amount. It is possible for an attendance allowance to do this because of the width of the definition in reg. 2(1).

Paragraph 11

Educational maintenance allowances are disregarded in full, instead of in part, as under supplementary benefit.

Paragraph 13

These elements of training allowances are disregarded.

Paragraph 15

If charitable or voluntary payments are intended and used for items other than those listed in sub-para. (2) they are disregarded (sub-para. (2)). For claimants in residential care and nursing homes this disregard only applies if they have a preserved right (sub-para. (6)). Note the exceptions in sub-para. (3) and para. 39. Otherwise the normal disregard of regular charitable or voluntary payments is £10 (sub-para. (1)). The provision assumes that such payments amount to income. For irregular payments, see reg. 48(9).

There is no special definition of "charitable" or "voluntary." The words must be applied to whoever makes the payment. In *R. v. Doncaster Borough Council, ex parte Boulton, The Times*,December 31, 1992, on the equivalent provision in housing benefit, Laws J. holds that the word "charitable" appearing in a statute providing for the distribution and calculation of legal rights must refer only to payments under a charitable trust, rather than referring to acts done for some generous motive. He finds the legislative purpose to be to allow charities to make payments to claimants knowing that they will not simply reduce the amount of benefit. That decision must be highly persuasive, but does not pre-empt the income support position.

Laws J. also takes a different view to that expressed in the 1992 edition on the meaning of "voluntary." He holds that it does not refer to a payment which is not compulsory or not legally enforceable, but to a payment for which the person making the payment gets nothing in return. It does not matter that in voluntarily undertaking the payment the person comes under an obligation. The legislative purpose would then be consistent with that for charitable payments. He then had to apply this principle to payments by the National Coal Board in lieu of concessionary coal to a miner's widow. The concessionary coal scheme and the conditions for the payment of cash in lieu, including to widows, is contained in a collective agreement which is incorporated into miners' contracts of employment. Laws J. holds that neither he nor the Housing Benefit Review Board had sufficient evidence of the particular contractual arrangements to be able to conclude that under the principle of *Beswick v. Beswick* [1968] A.C. 58 the widow could as administratrix of her husband's estate obtain specific performance of the contract to make payments to his widow. However, he was satisfied that the NCB did receive something in return for payments made under the collective agreement, in the promotion of the efficient running of the coal industry. An element of this purpose was seeing that employees, ex-employees and their spouses were properly looked after. Therefore, he finds that the payments were not voluntary and the disregard did not apply. On this point also, the *Boulton* case cannot be conclusive for income support purposes, but is cogently argued and persuasive. It has been applied to para. 15 in *R(IS) 4/94*. In *CIS 702/1991* an annuity had been purchased for the claimant under the terms of her friend's will. It was argued that the payments under the annuity were "voluntary" as in essence there was a gift of them from the friend under the will. It is held that the disregard in para. 15 did not apply since the payments under the annuity were contractual in nature. That was consistent with the decision of Laws J. in the *Boulton* case. See also *CIS 492/1992*.

If regular payments are not charitable or voluntary they count as ordinary income with no disregard.

Paragraph 15A

Where a claimant is newly placed after April 1, 1993, by a local authority in a residential care or nursing home whose fee is more expensive than would normally be met, charitable or voluntary payments may be disregarded in so far as they make up the difference. This is only so if the reason for the placement is the choice of the claimant.

Paragraph 16

The £10 disregard under sub-para. (a) only applies if the payment is not fully disregarded under paras. 8 or 9.

Paragraph 17

If a person takes out one of these schemes for converting the capital value of the home into income, then so much of the annuity as goes to the mortgage interest is disregarded. The conditions are complicated. Only schemes entered by those aged at least 65 count.

Paragraph 18

The inter-relationship of this and the following two paragraphs is now much clearer. The new form of this paragraph, together with the amendment to para. 19, has been introduced from April 10, 1995, following the decision in *CIS 82/1993*. The Commissioner held that on the previous wording the dividing line between paras. 18 and 19 was not whether a payment for accommodation was made under a contractual obligation, but whether or not the payment was made by a person who normally resided with the claimant. Para. 19 only applied where the person did not normally reside with the claimant. (See the 1994 Supplement for a summary of the Commissioner's reasoning.) "Normally resides" in para. 18 had no special meaning (*cf.* reg. 3) and could include someone who was liable to make payments to the claimant for his occupation of the claimant's home. On the facts, the two "lodgers" who shared the claimant's flat, and each paid him £70 per week, did reside with him. The result was that para. 18, not para. 19, applied. "Payment" could include part of a payment (see reg. 2(1)), so the proportion of each payment that went to meeting the "lodger's" living and accommodation costs could be disregarded under para. 18 (*CIS 422/1992* followed). The evidence was that the benefit of the outgoings on the flat was shared more or less equally between the three occupants, so the Commissioner divided the rent, water rates and fuel costs by three and added to this the cost of the services provided by the claimant (*e.g.* laundry, routine repairs and replacements). This led to a much larger proportion of each payment (£47) being disregarded, than would have been the case if para. 19 applied.

The new form of para. 18, and the amendment to para. 19, have dealt with most of the difficulties exposed in *CIS 82/1993* regarding the inter-relationship of these two paragraphs. Paras. 18, 19 and 20 can now all apply where the person is residing with the claimant, so the problem identified in previous editions of this book (see the note to para. 19 of the 1994 edition) no longer exists. If para. 18 applies, payments by someone who normally resides with the claimant towards his own living and accommodation costs continue to be wholly disregarded. The new wording confirms, as decided in *CIS 422/1992* and *CIS 82/1993*, that it is only payments towards the "lodger's" living expenses that are disregarded (see above). However, para. 18 does not apply in the circumstances covered by paras. 19 and 20, so that those provisions must be looked at first. The intention is that payments from sub-tenants and licensees should fall within para. 19, not para. 18 (see below).

If the person making the payment is a non-dependant (see reg. 3), note that standard deductions are made from housing costs for the presence of a non-dependant in the household. (see para. 11 of Sched. 3).

Paragraph 19

Whenever the person occupying the claimant's home has a contractual liability to make payments this paragraph will now apply. This is certainly wide enough to cover income from sub-tenants and licensees. The disregard is small. People referred to in paras. 18 and 20 are no longer excluded, but para. 18 does not apply if the circumstances come within para. 19 (see above). Although payments from a person could fall within both para. 19 and para. 20, it does not matter that there is no provision for choosing between them, for a claimant can simply take advantage of the more generous disregard in para. 20 when the conditions of that paragraph are met (*CIS 82/1993*).

In *CIS 82/1993* the Commissioner raised the possibility of whether the disregard in para. 30(d) (contribution intended and used towards rent) might apply to payments by a sub-tenant or licensee of a tenant. He accepted the AO's submission that in view of the specific provisions in paras. 18., 19 and 20, para. 30(d) did not cover such payments, but did consider that legislative clarification of the relationship between para. 30 and paras. 18, 19 and 20 would be useful. It is not clear on the wording of para. 30(d) why payments from a sub-tenant or licensee should be excluded, provided that they are intended and used as a contribution towards rent not met by housing benefit. Payments may be disregarded under more than one paragraph of Sched. 9, provided this is not specifically proscribed. Para. 30(d) does not refer to payments under paras. 18, 19 or 20; the only payments that are specifically excluded from para. 30 are those covered by para. 29. Moreover, there is nothing in Sched. 9 (or reg. 40(2)) for establishing any order of priority if different paragraphs of Sched. 9 are applicable.

In April 1994 the wording of para. 19 was tightened up so that only one disregard per week applies to payments for each licence or subtenancy. On the pre-April 1994 form a separate disregard could have applied to each payment regardless of the period covered by it (*e.g.* daily).

Paragraph 20

This disregard (and not para. 18) applies when a person provides board and lodging accommodation home. The post-April 1994 form makes it clear that only one disregard is allowed per week per boarder (see the notes to para. 19).

Paragraph 21

Income in kind is normally disregarded. Earnings in kind are not earnings (reg. 35(2)), but are income. There is considerable scope for benefit planning here.

Paragraph 22

The general rule is that the actual income derived from capital is disregarded as income. It can go to increase the amount of capital under reg. 48(4). But income in the categories specified—premises, business assets and trusts of personal injury compensation—is not disregarded. Where this income is from premises whose capital value is disregarded, any mortgage repayments, water charges and council tax can be set off against it. Mortgage repayments in sub-para. (2)(a) include capital and interest, buildings insurance, and if an endowment policy is a condition of the mortgage, premiums on that policy (*CFC 13/1993*).

In *Chief Adjudication Officer v. Palfrey and Others, The Times*, February 17, 1995 (the appeal from *CIS 85/1992* and others), the Court of Appeal confirmed that property subject to a tenancy is disregarded as a reversionary interest under para. 5 of Sched. 10. Thus rent from a property let out to tenants is disregarded as income and counts as capital under reg. 48(4). *CIS 563/1991* confirms that the disregard in para. 5 applies to leasehold as well as freehold property, and explains how income treated as capital under reg. 48(4) is to be attributed. *CIS 563/1991* also decides that where the property could be disregarded under both para. 5 of Sched. 10 and one of the excepted provisions in reg. 48(4) and para. 22, the general rule to treat the rental income as capital applied (see the note to reg. 48(4)).

Paragraph 25

Payments to adopters are taken into account up to the level of the personal allowance applicable for the adopted child plus any disabled child premium. Anything above that level is disregarded.

The previous form of para. 25(1)(b) (see the 1991 edition) remains in force in Scotland. The new form was introduced on April 6, 1992, as a consequence of the Children Act 1989.

Paragraph 26

Payments to foster-parents are disregarded completely. Foster-children are not members of the family (reg. 16(4)).

The amendments to para. 26 introduced on April 6, 1992, as a consequence of the Children Act 1989, do not apply in Scotland.

Paragraph 28

Reg. 41(3) deems all such payments in trade dispute cases to be income and not capital. Then this disregard does not apply in trade dispute cases. Outside that special situation payments under the legislation (broadly to prevent children going into care) can be capital or income (*R(SB) 29/85*). Income is disregarded here and capital under para. 17 of Sched. 10.

Paragraph 29

The proceeds of mortgage protection policies can be used to cover capital repayments, the maintenance of the premium on the policy, the missing 50 per cent of the interest repayments for the first 16 weeks on income support, and the excluded interest under para. 10 of Sched. 3 (tenants buying own homes, too large or expensive homes) or where loans exceed the limit in para. 7(6B) of Sched. 3. The excess counts as income. This provision has not been amended to take account of the new para. 5A of Sched. 3. Sub-para. (3) seems merely declaratory as the disregard only applies to payments for housing costs that are not met by income support.

Paragraph 30
Payments other than under para. 29, earmarked for these elements of housing expenditure, are disregarded. Note that payments from liable relatives are dealt with in reg. 54.
See the note to para. 19 as to whether para. 30 can apply to payments from sub-tenants and licensees.

Paragraph 30A
Where a claimant in a residential care or nursing home does not have a preserved right under reg. 19, and whose accommodation has not been arranged by a local authority, payments towards the cost of the home's fees are disregarded. The amount ignored is the difference between the claimant's applicable amount less personal expenses and the weekly charge for the accommodation.

Paragraph 34
This is the compensation for the automatic counting of the "relevant sum" as part of the family's income under s.126(5)(b) of the Contributions and Benefits Act (1986 Act, s.23(5)(b)). From April 1995 the relevant sum is £25.00.

Paragraph 35
See notes to reg. 32(5).

Paragraph 37
See notes to reg. 32(5).

Paragraph 39
The disregard now extends to payments to haemophiliacs from the three trusts, and to non-haemophiliacs from the Fund and the Eileen Trust, and to distributions of income payments to the close family, or to a slightly wider class for the two years following such a person's death. Any payments from the Independent Living Funds are ignored.

Paragraph 47
These are the special payments to compensate pre-1973 war widows who had not benefited from amendments to the Armed Forces Pension Scheme. There was a commitment that the payments would not affect means-tested benefits. See paras. 54–56.

Paragraph 51
These are payments from certain Department of Employment special schemes for disabled people, such as the "business on own account" scheme, the "personal reader service" and the "fares to work" scheme.

Paragraph 53
Increases for dependants who are not residing with the claimant paid with certain benefits (*e.g.* retirement pension, invalidity benefit) are disregarded. Such increases are only paid if the claimant is contributing at least that amount to the maintenance of the dependant.

Paragraphs 54–56
See para. 47. These new disregards arise from the transfer of responsibility for the payment of most pre-1973 war widows' pensions from the Ministry of Defence to the DSS from October 1994 and give details of the additional powers under which these payments will be made.

SCHEDULE 10   **Regulation 46(2)**

CAPITAL TO BE DISREGARDED

1. The dwelling occupied as the home but, notwithstanding regulation 23 (calculation of income and capital of members of claimant's family and of a polygamous marriage), only one dwelling shall be disregarded under this paragraph.

2. Any premises acquired for occupation by the claimant which he intends to occupy [⁴as his home] within 26 weeks of the date of acquisition or such longer period as is reasonable in the circumstances to enable the claimant to obtain possession and commence occupation of the premises.

3. Any sum directly attributable to the proceeds of sale of any premises formerly occupied by the claimant as his home which is to be used for the purchase of other premises intended for such occupation within 26 weeks of the date of sale or such longer period as is reasonable in the circumstances to enable the claimant to complete the purchase.

4. Any premises occupied in whole or in part by—

(a) a partner or relative of [¹²a single claimant or any member of] the family [⁴as his home] where that person is aged 60 or over or is incapacitated;

(b) the former partner of a claimant [² . . .] as his home; but this provision shall not apply where the former partner is a person from whom the claimant is estranged or divorced.

5. Any reversionary interest.

6.—[¹²(1)] The assets of any business owned in whole or in part by the claimant and for the purposes of which he is engaged as a self-employed earner or, if he has ceased to be so engaged, for such period as may be reasonable in the circumstances to allow for disposal of any such asset.

[¹²(2) The assets of any business owned in whole or in part by the claimant where—

(a) he is not engaged as a self-employed earner in that business by reason of some disease or bodily or mental disablement; but

(b) he intends to become engaged (or, as the case may be, re-engaged) as a self-employed earner in that business as soon as he recovers or is able to become engaged, or re-engaged, in that business;

for a period of 26 weeks from the date on which the claim for income support is made, or is treated as made, or, if it is unreasonable to expect him to become engaged or re-engaged in that business within that period for such longer period as is reasonable in the circumstances to enable him to become so engaged or re-engaged.]

7. Any arrears of, or any concessionary payment made to compensate for arrears due to the non-payment of,—

(a) any payment specified in paragraph 6, [¹⁶8, 9 or 9A] of Schedule 9 (other income to be disregarded);

(b) an income-related benefit or supplementary benefit, family income supplement under the Family Income Supplements Act 1970 or housing benefit under Part II of the Social Security and Housing Benefits Act 1982;

but only for a period of 52 weeks from the date of the receipt of the arrears or of the concessionary payment.

8. Any sum—

(a) paid to the claimant in consequence of damage to, or loss of the home or any personal possession and intended for its repair or replacement; or

(b) acquired by the claimant (whether as a loan or otherwise) on the express condition that it is to be used for effecting essential repairs or improvements to the home,

and which is to be used for the intended purpose, for a period of 26 weeks from the date on which it was so paid or acquired or such longer period as is reasonable in the circumstances to enable the claimant to effect the repairs, replacement or improvements.

9. Any sum—

(a) deposited with a housing association as defined in section 189(1) of the Housing Act 1985 or section 338(1) of the Housing (Scotland) Act 1987 as a condition of occupying the home;

(b) which was so deposited and which is to be used for the purchase of another home, for the period of 26 weeks of such longer period as is reasonable in the circumstances to complete the purchase.

10. Any personal possessions except those which had or have been acquired by the claimant with the intention of reducing his capital in order to secure entitlement to supplementary benefit or income support or to increase the amount of that benefit.

11. The value of the right to receive any income under an annuity and the surrender value (if any) of such an annuity.

[¹²**12.** Where the funds of a trust are derived from a payment made in consequence of any personal injury to the claimant, the value of the trust fund and the value of the right to receive any payment under that trust.]

13. The value of the right to receive any income under a life interest or from a liferent.

14. The value of the right to receive any income which is disregarded under paragraph 11 of Schedule 8 or paragraph 23 of Schedule 9 (earnings or other income to be disregarded).

15. The surrender value of any policy of life insurance.

16. Where any payment of capital falls to be made by instalments, the value of the right to receive any outstanding instalments.

17. Except in the case of a person to whom section 23 of the Act [SSCBA, s.126] (trade disputes) applies [¹or in respect of whom section 20(3) of the Act [SSCBA, s.124(1)] (conditions of entitlement to income support) has effect as modified by section 23A(b) of the Act [SSCBA, s.127(b)] (effect of return to work)], [⁶any payment made by a local authority [¹⁸in accordance with section 17 or 24 of the Children Act 1989] or, as the case may be, section 12, 24 or 26 of the Social Work (Scotland) Act 1968 (local authorities' duty to promote welfare of children and powers to grant financial assistance to persons in, or formerly in, their care).]

[¹⁷**18.** Any social fund payment made pursuant to Part III of the Act [SSCBA, Part VIII].]

19. Any refund of tax which fell to be deducted under section 26 of the Finance Act 1982 (deductions of tax from certain loan interest) on a payment of relevant loan interest for the purpose of acquiring an interest in the home or carrying out repairs or improvements in the home.

20. Any capital which under [¹¹regulation 41, 44(1) or 66A (capital treated as income, modifications in respect of children and young persons or treatment of student loans)] is to be treated as income.

21. Where a payment of capital is made in a currency other than sterling, any banking charge or commission payable in converting that payment into sterling.

[¹**22.**—[¹⁴(1) Any payment made under the Macfarlane Trust, the Macfarlane (Special Payments) Trust, the Macfarlane (Special Payments) (No. 2) Trust ("the Trusts"), [¹⁹the Fund][²³, the Eileen Trust] or [²¹the Independent Living Funds].

(2) Any payment by or on behalf of a person who is suffering or who suffered from haemophilia [¹⁹or who is or was a qualifying person], which derives from a payment made under any of the Trusts to which sub-paragraph (1) refers and which is made to or for the benefit of—

(a) that person's partner or former partner from whom he is not, or where that person has died was not, estranged or divorced;

(b) any child who is a member of that person's family or who was such a member and who is a member of the claimant's family; or

(c) any young person who is a member of that person's family or who was such a member and who is a member of the claimant's family.

(3) Any payment by or on behalf of the partner or former partner of a person who is suffering or who suffered from haemophilia [¹⁹or who is or was a qualifying person] provided that the partner or former partner and that person are not, or if either of them has died were not, estranged or divorced, which derives from a payment made under any of the Trusts to which sub-paragraph (1) refers and which is made to or for the benefit of—

(a) the person who is suffering from haemophilia [¹⁹or who is a qualifying person];

(b) any child who is a member of that person's family or who was such a member and who is a member of the claimant's family; or

(c) any young person who is a member of that person's family or who was such a member and who is a member of the claimant's family.

(4) Any payment by a person who is suffering from haemophilia [¹⁹or who is a qualifying person], which derives from a payment under any of the Trusts to which sub-paragraph (1) refers, where—

(a) that person has no partner or former partner from whom he is not estranged or divorced, nor any child or young person who is or had been a member of that person's family; and

(b) the payment is made either—
   (i) to that person's parent or step-parent, or
   (ii) where that person at the relevant date was a child, a young person or a student who had not completed his full-time education and had no parent or step-parent, to his guardian,

but only for a period of two years from the date of the payment until the end of two years from that person's death.

(5) Any payment out of the estate of a person who suffered from haemophilia [¹⁹or who was a qualifying person], which derives from a payment under any of the Trusts to which sub-paragraph (1) refers, where—

(a) that person at the date of his death (the relevant date) had no partner or former partner from whom he was not estranged or divorced, nor any child or young person who was or had been a member of his family; and

(b) the payment is made either—
   (i) to that person's parent or step-parent, or
   (ii) where that person at the relevant date was a child, a young person or a student who had not completed his full-time education and had no parent or step-parent, to his guardian,

but only for a period of two years from the relevant date.

(6) In the case of a person to whom or for whose benefit a payment referred to in this paragraph is made, any capital resource which derives from any payment of income or capital made under or deriving from any of the Trusts.]

[¹⁹(7) For the purposes of sub-paragraphs (2) to (6), any reference to the Trusts shall be construed as including a reference to the Fund [²³and the Eileen Trust].]

23. The value of the right to receive an occupational [¹⁵or personal] pension.

24. The value of the right to receive any rent.]

[²**25.** Where a claimant has ceased to occupy what was formerly the dwelling occupied as the home following his estrangement or divorce from his former partner, that dwelling for a period of 26 weeks from the date on which he ceased to occupy that dwelling.

26. Any premises where the claimant is taking reasonable steps to dispose of those premises, for a period of 26 weeks from the date on which he first took such steps, or such longer period as is reasonable in the circumstances to enable him to dispose of those premises.

[⁵**27.** Any premises which the claimant intends to occupy as his home, and in respect of which he is taking steps to obtain possession and has sought legal advice or has commenced legal proceedings, with a view to obtaining possession, for a period of 26 weeks from the date on which he first sought such advice or first commenced such proceedings whichever is earlier, or such longer period as is reasonable in the circumstances to enable him to obtain possession and commence occupation of those premises.]

28. Any premises which the claimant intends to occupy as his home to which essential repairs or alterations are required in order to render them fit for such occupation, for a period of 26 weeks from the date on which the claimant first takes steps to effect those repairs or alterations, or such longer period as is reasonable in the circumstances to enable those repairs or alterations to be carried out and the claimant to commence occupation of the premises.]

[⁴**29.** Any payment in kind made by a charity [⁸or under the Macfarlane (Special Payments) Trust][¹⁹, the Macfarlane (Special Payments) (No. 2) Trust][²², the Fund or the Independent Living (1993) Fund].

30. [[24]£200 of any payment, or, if the payment is less than £200, the whole of any payment] made under section 2 of the Employment and Training Act 1973 (functions of the Secretary of State) [[13]or section 2 of the Enterprise and New Towns (Scotland) Act 1990] as a training bonus to a person participating in arrangements for training made under that section [[13]of the 1973 Act].

31. Any payment made by the Secretary of State to compensate for the loss (in whole or in part) of entitlement of housing benefit.]

[[5]**32.** Any payment made by the Secretary of State to compensate a person who was entitled to supplementary benefit in respect of a period ending immediately before 11th April 1988 but who did not become entitled to income support in respect of a period beginning with that day.

33. Any payment made by the Secretary of State to compensate for the loss of housing benefit supplement under regulation 19 of the Supplementary Benefit (Requirements) Regulations 1983.

34. Any payment made to a juror or a witness in respect of attendance at a court other than compensation for loss of earnings or for the loss of a benefit payable under the benefit Acts.

35. [[20]. . .].]

[[9]**36.** Any payment in consequence of a reduction of a personal community charge pursuant to regulations under section 13A of the Local Government Finance Act 1988 or section 9A of the Abolition of Domestic Rates Etc (Scotland) Act 1987 (reduction of liability for personal community charge) [[20]or reduction of council tax under section 13 or, as the case may be, section 80 of the Local Government Finance Act 1992 (reduction of liability for council tax)] but only for a period of 52 weeks from the date of the receipt of the payment.]

[[10]**37.** Any grant made to the claimant in accordance with a scheme made under section 129 of the Housing Act 1988 or section 66 of the Housing (Scotland) Act 1988 (schemes for payments to assist local housing authority and local authority tenants to obtain other accommodation) which is to be used—

   (a) to purchase premises intended for occupation as his home; or
   (b) to carry out repairs or alterations which are required to render premises fit for occupation as his home

for a period of 26 weeks from the date on which he received such a grant or such longer period as is reasonable in the circumstances to enable the purchase, repairs or alterations to be completed and the claimant to commence occupation of those premises as his home.]

[[12]**38.**— (1) Any payment or repayment made—

   (a) as respects England and Wales, under regulation 3, 5 or 8 of the National Health Service (Travelling Expenses and Remission of Charges) Regulations 1988 (travelling expenses and health service supplies);
   (b) as respects Scotland, under regulation 3, 5 or 8 of the National Health Service (Travelling Expenses and Remission of Charges) (Scotland) Regulations 1988 (travelling expenses and health service supplies);

but only for a period of 52 weeks from the date of receipt of the payment or repayment.

(2) Any payment or repayment made by the Secretary of State for Health, the Secretary of State for Scotland or the Secretary of State for Wales which is analogous to a payment or repayment mentioned in sub-paragraph (1); but only for a period of 52 weeks from the date of receipt of the payment or repayment.

39. Any payment made under regulation 9 to 11 or 13 of the Welfare Food Regulations 1988 (payments made in place of milk tokens or the supply of vitamins), but only for a period of 52 weeks from the date of receipt of the payment.

40. Any payment made either by the Secretary of State for the Home Department or by the Secretary of State for Scotland under a scheme established to assist relatives and other persons to visit persons in custody, but only for a period of 52 weeks from the date of receipt of the payment.

41. Any arrears of special war widows payment which is disregarded under paragraph 47 of Schedule 9 (sums to be disregarded in the calculation of income other than earnings) [²⁵ or of any amount which is disregarded under paragraph 54, 55 or 56 of that Schedule], but only for a period of 52 weeks from the date of receipt of the arrears.]

[¹⁷**42.** Any payment (other than a training allowance, or a training bonus under section 2 of the Employment and Training Act 1973) made, whether by the Secretary of State or by any other person, under the Disabled Persons (Employment) Act 1944 or in accordance with arrangements made under section 2 of the Employment and Training Act 1973 to assist disabled persons to obtain or retain employment despite their disability.

43. Any payment made by a local authority under section 3 of the Disabled Persons (Employment) Act 1958 to homeworkers under the Blind Homeworkers' Scheme.]

[²⁵**44.** Any sum of capital administered on behalf of a person under the age of 18 by the High Court under the provisions of Order 80 of the Rules of the Supreme Court, the County Court under Order 10 of the County Court Rules 1981, or the Court of Protection, where such sum derives from—

(a) an award of damages for a personal injury to that person; or

(b) compensation for the death of one or both parents.]

45. Any sum of capital administered on behalf of a person under the age of 18 in accordance with an order made under Rule 43.15 of the Act of Sederunt (Rules of the Court of Session 1994) 1994 or under Rule 131 of the Act of Sederunt (Rules of the Court, consolidation and amendment) 1965, or under Rule 36.14 of the Ordinary Cause Rules 1993 or under Rule 128 of the Ordinary Cause Rules, where such sum derives from—

(a) an award of damages for a personal injury to that person; or

(b) compensation for the death of one or both parents.]

AMENDMENTS

1. Income Support (General) Amendment Regulations 1988 (S.I. 1988 No. 663), reg. 36 (April 11, 1988).
2. Income Support (General) Amendment No. 2 Regulations 1988 (S.I. 1988 No. 910), reg. 3 (May 30, 1988).
3. Family Credit and Income Support (General) Amendment Regulations 1988 (S.I. 1988 No. 999), reg. 5 (June 9, 1988).
4. Income Support (General) Amendment No. 4 Regulations 1988 (S.I. 1988 No. 1445), reg. 26 (September 12, 1988).
5. Income Support (General) Amendment No. 5 Regulations 1988 (S.I. 1988 No. 2022), reg. 23 (December 12, 1988).
6. Family Credit and Income Support (General) Amendment Regulations 1989 (S.I. 1989 No. 1034), reg. 12 (July 10, 1989).
7. Income Support (General) Amendment Regulations 1989 (S.I. 1989 No. 534), Sched. 1, para. 18 (October 9, 1989).
8. Income-related Benefits Schemes Amendment Regulations 1990 (S.I. 1990 No. 127), reg. 3 (January 31, 1990).
9. Income Support (General) Amendment Regulations 1990 (S.I. 1990 No. 547), reg. 23(a) (April 1, 1990).
10. Income Support (General) Amendment Regulations 1990 (S.I. 1990 No. 547), reg. 23(b) (April 9, 1990).
11. Social Security Benefits (Student Loans and Miscellaneous Amendments) Regulations 1990 (S.I. 1990 No. 1549), reg. 5(9) (September 1, 1990).
12. Income Support (General) Amendment No. 3 Regulations 1990 (S.I. 1990 No. 1776), reg. 11 (October 1, 1990).
13. Enterprise (Scotland) Consequential Amendments Order 1991 (S.I. 1991 No. 387), arts, 2 and 9 (April 1, 1991).
14. Income-related Benefits Schemes and Social Security (Recoupment) Amendment Regulations 1991 (S.I. 1991 No. 1175), reg. 5 (May 11, 1991).
15. Income Support (General) Amendment No. 4 Regulations 1991 (S.I. 1991 No. 1559), reg. 21 (October 7, 1991).
16. Disability Living Allowance and Disability Working Allowance (Consequential Provisions) Regulations 1991 (S.I. 1991 No. 2742), reg. 11(7) (April 6, 1992).
17. Income Support (General) Amendment Regulations 1992 (S.I. 1992 No. 468), reg. 9 (April 6, 1992).

18. Income Support (General) Amendment Regulations 1992 (S.I. 1992 No. 468), Sched., para. 10 (April 6, 1992).

19. Income-related Benefits Schemes and Social Security (Recoupment) Amendment Regulations 1992 (S.I. 1992 No. 1101), reg. 6(8) (May 7, 1992).

20. Income-related Benefits Schemes (Miscellaneous Amendments) Regulations 1993 (S.I. 1993 No. 315), Sched., para. 6 (April 1, 1993).

21. Social Security Benefits (Miscellaneous Amendments) (No. 2) Regulations 1993 (S.I. 1993 No. 963), reg. 2(3) (April 22, 1993).

22. Social Security Benefits (Miscellaneous Amendments) (No. 2) Regulations 1993 (S.I. 1993 No. 963), reg. 2(5) (April 22, 1993).

23. Income-related Benefits Schemes and Social Security (Recoupment) Amendment Regulations 1993 (S.I. 1993 No. 1249), reg. 4(5) (May 14, 1993).

24. Income-related Benefits Schemes (Miscellaneous Amendments) (No. 4) Regulations 1993 (S.I. 1993 No. 2119), reg. 24 (October 4, 1993).

25. Income-related Benefits Schemes (Miscellaneous Amendments) (No. 5) Regulations 1994 (S.I. 1994 No. 2139), reg. 33 (October 3, 1994).

DEFINITIONS

"the Act"—see reg. 2(1).
"child"—see 1986 Act, s.20(11) (SSCBA, s.137(1)).
"claimant"—see reg. 2(1).
"dwelling occupied as the home"—*ibid.*
"family"—see 1986 Act, s.20(11) (SSCBA, s.137(1)).
"income-related benefit"—see 1986 Act, s.84(1).
"occupational pension"—see reg. 2(1).
"partner"—*ibid.*
"payment"—*ibid.*
"policy of life insurance"—*ibid.*
"qualifying person"—*ibid.*
"relative"—*ibid.*
"self-employed earner"—*ibid.*
"supplementary benefit"—*ibid.*
"the Eileen Trust"—*ibid.*
"the Fund"—*ibid.*
"the Independent Living Funds"—*ibid.*
"the Macfarlane (Special Payments) Trust"—*ibid.*
"the Macfarlane (Special Payments) (No. 2) Trust"—*ibid.*
"the Macfarlane Trust"—*ibid.*
"training allowance"—*ibid.*
"young person"—*ibid.*, reg. 14.

GENERAL NOTE

Capital may be disregarded under more than one paragraph of Sched. 10 at the same time, or in succession. There is no provision in reg. 46(2) or Sched. 10 for establishing any order of priority if different paragraphs of Sched. 10 are applicable, so the claimant will be entitled to the benefit of the most favourable disregard (this is also the case for Sched. 9). The disregards in Sched. 10 apply to notional capital (*CIS 25/1990, CIS 81/1991, CIS 562/1992* and *CIS 30/1993*), provided that their conditions are met (*CIS 30/1993*). See the note to para. 26.

Paragraph 1

The value of the home is disregarded. Para. 4 of Sched. 3 contains rules about when a person is or is not to be treated as occupying a dwelling as his home. The fact that Sched. 10 did not originally contain paras. 25 to 28 gave rise to a number of problems (for which see p.178 of the 1988 edition). The introduction of, in particular, a disregard of the value of premises which are for sale will solve, or at least postpone, many of the problems. See reg. 17(f) and (2) to (7) for transitional protection for those excluded from income support from April 11, 1988 to May 29, 1988, and Sched. 9, para. 41 and Sched. 10, para. 32.

On the meaning of "dwelling occupied as the home", see notes to reg. 2(1). Para. 1 can apply to notional capital (*CIS 81/1991* (although it was not necessary to the decision) and *CIS 30/1993*).

Paragraph 2

The value must be disregarded for the first 26 weeks after the acquisition. Thereafter all the circumstances must be looked at in deciding what is reasonable. There must be some realistic prospect of occupation starting. Previous editions suggested that the requirement that the premises have been "acquired for occupation by the claimant" would exclude some forms of acquisition (*e.g.* inheritance). But according to para. 30245 of the *Adjudication Officers' Guide*, this disregard applies where premises intended for occupation have been "purchased, inherited or acquired by some other means".

The income from premises whose value is disregarded under this provision counts as income (Sched. 9, para. 22), but mortgage repayments, water charges and council tax can be set off against it.

Paragraph 3

The sum must be directly attributable to the proceeds of sale of a home, and must be intended for the purchase of another home (not repairs or refurbishment: *R(SB) 14/85*; *CIS 368/1993*). *CIS 63/1993* decides that para. 3 is not restricted to circumstances where a claimant is free to sell to a third party but can apply where a statutory tenancy of a home has been surrendered to the landlord. The claimant had sold his home, albeit technically by a surrender rather than a sale, and it was irrelevant to whom he had sold it.

In *CIS 222/92* the claimant intended to use her share of the proceeds of sale of her deceased mother's house to purchase her own council house. The claimant had lived in her mother's house for a short time some 10 years before. The Commissioner rejects the argument that the claimant was entitled to the benefit of the disregard in para. 3 because she formerly occupied her mother's home as her home. He finds that the conditions for a purposive construction of para. 3 were satisfied (see Lord Diplock at p. 105 in *Jones v. Wrotham Park Settled Estates Ltd.* [1980] AC 74), and holds that para. 3 only applied where the claimant had owned the property when she had lived there.

CIS 685/1992 decides that it is not necessary, in order for there to be an extension of the primary 26 week period, that an intention to occupy specific premises should have been formed before the end of that period. If the proceeds of sale have not been used at the end of the 26 weeks there is a general discretion for the AO (or SSAT) to allow a longer period for the finding of another home and the completion of its purchase. However, a mere hope that the proceeds may be used at some future date for another home is not sufficient. The Commissioner declines to follow the more restricted view of para. 3 adopted in *CIS 321/1990* which decided that if sufficient negotiations were not in being at the end of the 26 week period there could be no extension.

Paragraph 4

"Relative" is defined in reg. 2(1). "Incapacitated" is not. Para. 30237 of the Adjudication Officers' Guide suggests that receipt of sickness benefit, invalidity benefit (now incapacity benefit), statutory sick pay (as well as more rigorous benefits like severe disablement allowance and attendance allowance) or an equivalent degree of incapacity will do. Occupation by a former partner does not count if there has been estrangement or divorce, but see para. 25. Under supplementary benefit, occupation was held to connote occupation as a residence, not merely as a holiday home *(R(SB) 1/ 85)*. Under sub-para. (b) it does not now matter that the claimant also occupies the home.

In *CIS 231/1991* the claimant had transferred his former home to his parents who were both over 60. When he claimed income support they were living in the home. The Commissioner decides that para. 4(a) applied to the former home; the disregard applied to notional, as well as actual, capital.

Paragraph 5

A reversionary interest is an interest in property which will not vest in possession until some event happens. It does not include a life assurance policy (*CSB 624/1981*).

In *Chief Adjudication Officer v. Palfrey and others, The Times,* February 17, 1995, the Court of Appeal upheld the Tribunal of Commissioners' decision in *CIS 85/1992* that property subject to a tenancy is a reversionary interest and so is to be disregarded under para. 5. The Commissioners had held that *R(SB) 3/86* was not to be followed, preferring the decision of a Tribunal of Commissioners in Northern Ireland in *C71/91(IS)*. In *CIS 85/1992* the rented property was freehold, but *CIS 563/ 1991* and *CIS 615/1993* confirm that the disregard in para. 5 applies to leasehold as well as freehold property. The value of the right to receive rent is also disregarded (para. 24), and rent, as and when it is received, counts as capital, not income (Sched. 9, para. 22), under reg. 48(4).

Paragraph 6

The business assets of a self-employed person are primarily disregarded under sub-para. (1) if he is engaged in the business. Para. 30271 of the *Adjudication Officers' Guide* states that a person should be treated as engaged in a business for as long as he performs some work in it, even for as little as half an hour a week. Business assets have to be distinguished from personal assets by asking if they are "part of the fund employed and risked in the business" *(R(SB) 4/85)*. The income tax and accounting position are factors to be taken into account, but are not conclusive (*CFC 10/1989*).

CFC 15/1990 holds that the ownership by an individual of a tenanted house is not a business. But an interest in a property that has been let to tenants is disregarded as a reversionary interest (see the notes to para. 5). If the claimant ceases to be engaged in the business, the value of the assets is disregarded for a period which is reasonable to allow them to be disposed of. Where the self-employed person is temporarily not engaged in the business because of illness, there is a disregard under sub-para. (2).

Income from capital disregarded under para. 6 is not disregarded (Sched. 9, para. 22).

Paragraph 7

Arrears of benefit which would be income when paid on the proper date retain their character as income (*R(SB) 4/89*). However, if any money is left after the end of the period to which the benefit is attributed as income then this will be capital (see notes to reg. 40(1)). Para. 7 applies, under sub-para. (a), to mobility allowance or supplement, attendance allowance and any care or mobility component of disability living allowance and, under sub-para. (b), to income support, family credit, housing benefit, council tax benefit, supplementary benefit and FIS. For these benefits there is a disregard for 52 weeks from the date of receipt. See also paras. 38 to 41.

Paragraph 8

This meets the problems in *R(SB) 14/81* and para. 8(2) of *R(SB) 14/85*. Such sums may not be part of the claimant's capital anyway (see *CSB 975/1985* and the notes to reg. 46).

CIS 63/1993 decides that sub-para. (a) only applies where the claimant has suffered damage to, or the loss of, his property against his will, not where he has deliberately brought this about. Thus it did not cover payment received for the surrender of a statutory tenancy of the claimant's home. *CIS 368/1993* rejects the argument that money (in that case proceeds of sale of a previous home) earmarked for the renovation of the claimant's home came within sub-para. (b). The Commissioner decides that the money had not been "acquired on the express condition" that it was to be used for the renovation, but as a consequence of the sale.

Paragraph 9

Sub-para (b) gets round the problem in *R(SB) 4/87*.

Paragraph 10

The supplementary benefit exceptions to the general disregard of the value of personal possessions have been considerably narrowed. Now it is only possessions bought with the intention of reducing capital so as to gain supplementary benefit or income support which count. See the notes to reg. 51(1) for "purpose" and for possible problems of double counting with para. 10. If the value of personal possessions does count, it is their current market value which must be included (reg. 49). See *CIS 494/1990* and CIS *112/1994*.

Presumably anything which is not real property is a personal possession. providing that it is an object and not a right to sue for something, like a debt. But hard lines might have to be drawn between coins and bank-notes (obviously capital) and investments like paintings, stamps, furniture (apparently disregarded). What about gold bars?

Paragraph 12

The unlimited disregard of the value of trusts deriving from payments in compensation for personal injury, previously restricted to children and young persons, has been extended to all claimants. This seems particularly generous compared to the treatment of other forms of capital. If there is no trust the amount of compensation counts as capital, even though it is in a solicitor's hands (*Thomas v. Chief Adjudication Officer (R(SB) 17/87)*). If the claimant then transfers the compensation to trustees, the exception in reg. 51(1)(a) operates so that he will not be treated as having deprived himself of the capital placed on trust. Although putting money into a trust would normally count as deprivation, to do so in the case of trusts of personal injury compensation would defeat the purpose of para. 12. It is not necessary for the trust to be set up before the compensation is received as suggested in the 1993 edition. See para. 30309 of the *Adjudication Officers' Guide*.

Paragraph 13

This reverses the result of *R(SB) 43/84*.

Paragraph 14

The provisions mentioned deal with situations where foreign income or earnings cannot be transmitted to the United Kingdom.

Paragraph 15
The surrender value of all life insurance policies is disregarded. In supplementary benefit there was a limit of £1,500.

Paragraph 16
See reg. 41(1).

Paragraph 17
Although in ordinary cases the nature of such payments as capital or income depends on general principles of law *(R(SB) 29/85)*, in trade dispute cases reg. 41(3) secures that they are all treated as income.

Paragraph 20
This is to avoid double counting.

Paragraph 22
These funds are intended to provide extra cash help to haemophiliacs and non-haemophiliacs who have contracted HIV through blood or tissue transfusions, their families and the severely disabled. All are government-funded. The disregard extends to distributions of capital to the close family of haemophiliacs and non-haemophiliacs, or to a slightly wider class for the two years after the haemophiliac's or non-haemophiliac's death.

Paragraph 23
Accrued rights to receive an occupational or personal pension in the future are often amongst a person's most valuable assets, but they are not capable of being bought or sold, and so have no market value anyway.

Paragraph 24
See the notes to para. 5. This paragraph expressly excludes the capital value of the element of possession involved in a tenanted property.

Paragraph 25
This paragraph applies where a claimant has ceased to be part of a couple because of estrangement or divorce and has left what was formerly the home. In these circumstances the claimant may well have an actual or deemed (see reg. 52) interest in the dwelling, but no longer be able to get within para. 1. Divorce is an easily proved event, but estrangement is a less hard edged concept. It has "connotations of emotional disharmony" *(R(SB) 2/87)*, but no doubt is to be given its ordinary, everyday meaning. Since the two people concerned must no longer be partners, there must be more than a temporary absence (and see reg. 16).
The disregard is limited to 26 weeks from the date on which the claimant left the dwelling, with no extension. In this time arrangements must be made.

Paragraph 26
This provision restores some of the effect of the similar supplementary benefit disregard. It applies if reasonable steps are being taken to dispose of premises. What are reasonable steps must be a question of fact. The disregard starts when the claimant first takes such steps, which may well be before a property is put on the open market. The initial disregard is for 26 weeks, but can be extended where reasonable to enable the disposal to be carried out. This amendment will ease some of the problems noted on p.178 of the 1988 edition, but not all of them.
In *CIS 562/1992* it is held that the 26 weeks does not run from the beginning of each fresh claim for income support, but from the day on which the claimant first took steps to dispose of the property. On its particular facts (it was several years since the property was first put on the market and the claimant had transferred ownership of it to his son for some time but then taken it back) this decision seems right. However, if a property is up for sale, then is genuinely taken off the market and put up for sale again later, it must be arguable that the time under para. 26 runs from the second occasion of taking steps to dispose of the property.
CIS 30/1993 decides that this disregard cannot apply to notional capital if the claimant has already disposed of the same capital so as to trigger reg. 51(1). This is because para. 26 is only applicable where the *claimant* is taking steps to dispose of premises. The Commissioner in *CIS 30/1993* acknowledges that this view is different from that taken in some other decisions, but having reviewed these *(R(SB) 9/91, CIS 25/1990, CIS 81/1991* and *CIS 562/1992)* concludes that the only one in which this question had been central to the appeal was *CIS 25/1990* and in that case the point had

not been argued in any detail. He was therefore not bound by it. (*R1/92 (IS)*, a decision of the Chief Commissioner in Northern Ireland, had come to the same conclusion as he had done.) It had been argued on behalf of the claimant that if the property was put up for sale by the actual possessor of it, para. 26 should apply. The AO had submitted, first, that the wording of para. 26 made it clear that the disregard only applied if the claimant was taking steps to dispose of the premises; second, that the purpose of the disregard in para. 26 was to allow the claimant a reasonable time to liquidate assets to provide money to live on. There could be no guarantee that the third party would allow the proceeds of sale to be used to support the claimant and thus there was no reason to delay counting the notional capital. The Commissioner holds that the words of para. 26 were plain and unambiguous and could not apply because the claimant could not be taking steps to dispose of what she had already disposed of. This seems unfair in that a claimant deemed to have notional capital may suffer an additional penalty through not being able to benefit from the disregard in para.26. But contrary to what was suggested in the 1994 edition, the Commissioner's conclusion would seem to be correct.

Paragraph 27

In these circumstances the claimant will have an interest in the premises, but it would be unfair to count the value of the interest. The initial disregard is for 26 weeks, with an extension as reasonable.

In *CIS 240/1992* the legal advice given to the claimant was that he could not obtain possession of the premises until the end of the current tenancy. The Commissioner states that for para. 27 to apply the claimant must be taking steps to obtain possession and rejects a submission that a failure to take steps that were bound to be unsuccessful did not preclude the application of para 27. But in seeking legal advice was not the claimant taking such steps? Para. 27 does not require the claimant to have commenced legal proceedings for the disregard to apply; it is sufficient if he has sought legal advice with a view to obtaining possession. Provided that a claimant is willing to commence proceedings immediately the tenancy ends (which did not appear to be the case in *CIS 240/1992*) it is difficult to see what other steps he could take in such circumstances.

Paragraph 28

Since the value of the home is disregarded, this is a limited extension. Then the disregard is for 26 weeks, with an extension as reasonable.

Paragraph 29

Payments of earnings or other income in kind are disregarded (see regs. 35(2) and 40(4) and Sched. 9, para. 21). Most payments of capital in kind would be personal possessions (see para. 10).

Paragraph 42

These are capital payments from special Department of Employment schemes to assist disabled people, such as the "business on own account" scheme and the "personal reader service."

Paragraph 43

Start-up capital payments under the Blind Homeworkers' Scheme are disregarded, but payments of income are taken into account.

Paragraphs 44–45

Damages for personal injury or compensation for the death of a parent held in court for a person under 18 under these provisions are disregarded as capital. See para. 12 for the disregard of compensation payments for personal injury placed on trust.

Income Support (Liable Relatives) Regulations 1990

(S.I. 1990 No. 1777)

Made by the Secretary of State under s.166(1) to (3A) of the Social Security Act 1975 and ss. 24A(1), 24B(5) and 84(1) of the Social Security Act 1986

Citation, commencement and interpretation

1.—(1) These Regulations may be cited as the Income Support (Liable Relatives) Regulations 1990 and shall come into force on 15th October 1990.

(2) In these Regulations—
"the Act" means the Social Security Act 1986; and
"the Income Support Regulations" means the Income Support (General) Regulations 1987.

Prescribed amounts for the purposes of section 24A of the Act [SSAA, s.107]

2.—(1) For the purposes of section 24A of the Act [SSAA, s.107] (recovery of expenditure on income support: additional amounts and transfer of orders) the amount which may be included in the sum which the court may order the other parent to pay under section 24(4) of the Act [SSAA, s.106(2)] shall be the whole of the following amounts which are payable to or for the claimant—

(a) any personal allowance under paragraph 2 of Part I of Schedule 2 to the Income Support Regulations for each of the children whom the other parent is liable to maintain;

(b) any family premium under paragraph 3 of Part II of that Schedule;

(c) any lone parent premium under paragraph 8 of Part III of that Schedule;

(d) any disabled child premium under paragraph 14 of Part III of that Schedule in respect of a child whom the other parent is liable to maintain; and

(e) any carer premium under paragraph 14ZA of Part III of that Schedule if, but only if, that premium is payable because the claimant is in receipt, or is treated as being in receipt, of invalid care allowance by reason of the fact that he is caring for a severely disabled child or young person whom the other parent is liable to maintain.

(2) If the court is satisfied that in addition to the amounts specified in paragraph (1) above the liable parent has the means to pay, the sum which the court may order him to pay under section 24 of the Act [SSAA, s. 106] may also include all or some of the amount of any personal allowance payable to or for the claimant under paragraph 1 of Part I of Schedule 2 to the Income Support Regulations.

Notice to the Secretary of State of applications to alter etc. maintenance orders

3.—(1) For the purposes of section 24B(5) of the Act [SSAA, s.108(5)] (prescribed person in prescribed circumstances to notify the Secretary of State of application to alter etc. a maintenance order) the prescribed person is, and in paragraph (2) below that expression means,—

(a) in England and Wales—

(i) in relation to the High Court, where the case is proceeding in the deputy principal registry the senior registrar of that registry, and where the case is proceeding in a district registry the district registrar;

(ii) in relation to a county court, the proper officer of that court within the meaning of Order 1, Rule 3 of the County Court Rules 1981; and

(iii) in relation to a magistrates' court, the clerk to the justices of that court; and

(b) in Scotland—

(i) in relation to the Court of Session, the deputy principal clerk of session; and

(ii) in relation to a sheriff court, the sheriff clerk.

(2) For the purposes of that subsection the prescribed circumstances are that before the final determination of the application the Secretary of State has made

a written request to the prescribed person that he be notified of any such application, and has not made a written withdrawal of that request.

GENERAL NOTE

See the notes to ss.107 and 108 of the Administration Act.

The Income Support (Transitional) Regulations 1987

(S.I. 1987 No. 1969)

Made by the Secretary of State under ss.84(1) and 89(1) of the Social Security Act 1986

ARRANGEMENT OF REGULATIONS

PART I

TRANSITIONAL ARRANGEMENTS

PART II

TRANSITIONAL PROTECTION

Citation and commencement

1. These Regulations may be cited as the Income Support (Transitional) Regulations 1987 and shall come into force on 23rd November 1987.

Interpretation

2.—(1) In these Regulations, unless the context otherwise requires—
"the Act" means the Social Security Act 1986;
"adjudicating authority" means any person or body with responsibility under the Social Security Acts 1975 to 1986, and regulations made thereunder, for the determination of claims for any benefit under those Acts and questions arising in connection with a claim for, or award of, or disqualification for receiving such benefit;

"benefit week"—
  (a) in relation to supplementary benefit, has the meaning given to it in regulation 7 of the Supplementary Benefit (Determination of Questions) Regulations 1980;
  (b) in relation to income support, has the meaning given to it by paragraph 4 of Schedule 7 to the Social Security (Claims and Payments) Regulations 1987;
"domestic assistance addition" means an additional requirement under paragraph 15 of Schedule 4 to the Requirements Regulations;
"first benefit week" means the benefit week beginning on a day during the period of 7 days commencing on 4th April 1988;
"former beneficiary" means a person who, for a period immediately preceding 11th April 1988, is entitled to supplementary benefit;
"former housing benefit supplement recipient" means a person in respect of whom an amount is applicable under regulation 19 of the Requirements Regulations for a period immediately preceding 4th April 1988;
"General Regulations" means the Income Support (General) Regulations 1987;
"income support" means income support under Part II of the Act [SSCBA, Part VII];
"Requirements Regulations" means the Supplementary Benefit (Requirements) Regulations 1983;
"second benefit week" means the benefit week beginning on a day during the period of 7 days commencing on 11th April 1988;
"Social Security Act" means the Social Security Act 1975;
"patient" has the same meaning as in regulation 21(3) of the General Regulations;
"personal expenses addition" means an amount of income support payable in accordance with regulation 13 in addition to any income support to which a person may be entitled under Part II of the Act [SSCBA, Part VII];
"special transitional addition" means an amount of income support payable in accordance with regulation 15 in addition to any income support to which a person may be entitled under Part II of the Act [SSCBA, Part VII];
"supplementary benefit" means a supplementary pension or allowance under the Supplementary Benefits Act 1976;
"transitional addition" means an amount of income support payable in accordance with regulations 10 to 13 in addition to any income support to which a person may be entitled under Part II of the Act [SSCBA, Part VII];
"unemployed person" means a person who is or is required to be available for employment;
and other expressions have the same meaning as in the General Regulations.

(2) Unless the context otherwise requires, any reference in these Regulations to a numbered regulation or Part is a reference to the regulation or Part bearing that number in these Regulations, and any reference in a regulation to a numbered paragraph is a reference to the paragraph bearing that number in that regulation.

[¹Permitted period

2A.—(1) For the purposes of regulations 14 and 15 (reduction and termination of transitional addition and special transitional addition) where a claimant has ceased to be entitled to income support—

    (a) because he or his partner becomes engaged in remunerative work the permitted period, subject to paragraph (2), shall be 12 weeks; or

    (b) for any other reason, the permitted period shall be eight weeks.

    (2) Subject to paragraph (3), where the claimant or his partner has ceased to be engaged in remunerative work referred to in paragraph (1)(a) the permitted period shall be eight weeks if—

    (a) the claimant's weekly applicable amount is reduced under regulation 22 of the General Regulations (reduction in applicable amounts in certain cases of actual or notional unemployment benefit disqualification) because of the cessation of that work; or

    (b) the claimant or his partner has ceased to be engaged in that work within 6 weeks of beginning it; or

    (c) at any time during the period of 26 weeks immediately preceding the beginning of that work, the person who has ceased to be engaged in it—
        (i) was engaged in remunerative work; or
        (ii) was in relevant education; or
        (iii) was a student.

    (3) Paragraph (2)(b) or (c) shall not apply if, by virtue of section 20A(2) of the Social Security Act [SSCBA, s.29(2)] (exemption from disqualification for unemployment benefit), the person who has ceased to be engaged in remunerative work is exempted from disqualification for receiving unemployment benefit.]

AMENDMENT

1. Income Support (Transitional) Amendment Regulations 1989 (S.I. 1989 No. 1626), reg. 2 (October 9, 1989).

Part I

Transitional Arrangements

Claims for income support made before 11th April 1988

    3.—(1) A claim for income support may be made on or after 14th March 1988 and before 11th April 1988, and a claim for supplementary benefit made during that period may be treated in addition as a claim for income support.

    (2) Paragraph (1) and regulation 4 (deeming of claims for income support by former beneficiaries) shall not apply in the case of a person affected by a trade dispute (that is to say a person in respect of whom the applicable amount or a proportion of the applicable amount falls to be disregarded by virtue of section 23 of the Act [SSCBA, s.126]).

    (3) Subject to the provisions of this regulation, any claim for income support made or treated as made in accordance with paragraph (1) may be determined before 11th April 1988 in accordance with the Act and Regulations made under that Act as if those provisions were in force.

    (4) Any claim made or treated as made in accordance with paragraph (1) shall be treated as made for a period commencing on 11th April 1988.

    (5) A decision which is given awarding income support on such a claim as is referred to in paragraph (1)—

    (a) may award the benefit from 11th April 1988 if it appears probable that the conditions for entitlement to income support for the person who made that claim will be satisfied;

    (b) shall be subject to the conditions for entitlement being so satisfied on the date from which the benefit is awarded;

(c) may be reviewed if any question arises as to the satisfaction of those conditions.

"applicable amount"—see 1986 Act, s.84(1).
"the Act"—see reg. 2(1).
"income support"—*ibid.*
"supplementary benefit"—*ibid.*

Deeming of claims for income support by former beneficiaries

4.—(1) Notwithstanding the provisions of section 165A of the Social Security Act [SSAA, s.1], but subject to regulation 3(2) (persons affected by a trade dispute), in the case of a former beneficiary or a former housing benefit supplement recipient it shall not be a condition of entitlement to income support for a period commencing in the week beginning 11th April 1988 that he makes a claim for such benefit and the provisions of the Act and Regulations made thereunder shall apply, subject to the following provisions of this Part, as if a claim for that benefit had been duly made by the former beneficiary or the former housing benefit supplement recipient in respect of a period commencing on the first day of his second benefit week.

(2) Where by virtue of paragraph (1) a person's entitlement to income support falls to be determined as if a claim for it had been duly made, the claimant's entitlement in respect of a period commencing in the week beginning 11th April 1988 may nevertheless be determined at an earlier date if the claimant is entitled to supplementary benefit at the date of the determination; and any such claim shall be determined in accordance with the Act and Regulations made under that Act as if those provisions were in force.

(3) A decision which is given awarding income support on a determination made under this regulation—

(a) may award the benefit from the first day of his second benefit week if it appears probable that the conditions for entitlement to income support will be satisfied;

(b) shall be subject to the conditions for entitlement being so satisfied on the date from which the benefit is awarded;

(c) may be reviewed if any question arises as to the satisfaction of those conditions.

"the Act"—see reg. 2(1).
"former beneficiary"—*ibid.*
"former housing benefit recipient"—*ibid.*
"income support"—*ibid.*
"second benefit week"—*ibid.*
"Social Security Act"—*ibid.*
"supplementary benefit"—*ibid.*

[¹Payments on account of income support

4A.—(1) Where, by virtue of regulation 4 (deeming of claims by former beneficiaries), a person's entitlement to income support, for a period commencing in the week beginning 11th April 1988, falls to be determined as if a claim for it had been duly made and no determination has been made by that date, the Secretary of State may make a payment on account of income support and the amount of such payment shall be offset by the adjudicating authority in reduction of any income support, any transitional payment of income support under regulation 7 (transitional payments for former beneficiaries) and any addition under Part II, subsequently awarded.

(2) Where a payment on account has been made under paragraph (1) and the adjudicating authority determines that there is no entitlement to income support, or that the entitlement is less than the amount of the payment on account, that authority shall determine the amount of the overpayment.

(3) The amount of any overpayment determined under paragraph (2) shall be recoverable by the Secretary of State by the same procedures and subject to the same conditions as if it were recoverable under section 53(1) of the Act [SSAA, s.71] (over-payments).

(4) A payment on account under this regulation may be made by means of an instrument of payment or such other means as appears to the Secretary of State to be appropriate in the circumstances of any particular case and, notwithstanding the repeal of any enactment, may be made by an instrument of payment or book of serial orders issued for the purpose of paying supplementary benefit.]

AMENDMENT

1. Income Support (Transitional) Amendment Regulations 1988 (S.I. 1988 No. 521), reg. 2 (April 11, 1988).

DEFINITIONS

"the Act"—see reg. 2(1).
"adjudicating authority"—*ibid.*
"former beneficiary"—*ibid.*
"income support"—*ibid.*
"supplementary benefit"—*ibid.*

Questions deemed to have been determined and treatment of income

5.—(1) Where, for a period commencing on or after 11th April 1988, it appears that the entitlement of a former beneficiary to income support, or the amount of such benefit to which he is entitled, depends upon the determination of any question by an adjudicating authority and such a question has been so determined in respect of that former beneficiary's entitlement to supplementary benefit immediately before 11th April 1988, that question shall be deemed to have been so determined for the purposes of the said entitlement to income support.

(2) For the purposes of determining a claimant's entitlement to income support for a period commencing on or after 11th April 1988, any earnings paid before that date on the termination or interruption of—

(a) the claimant's employment shall be taken into account in accordance with Part V of the General Regulations (income and capital) as if that Part were in force at the date of the termination or interruption of the employment and, except in the case of a claimant who was not treated as engaged in remunerative full-time work within the meaning of regulation 9(1)(a) of the Supplementary Benefit (Conditions of Entitlement) Regulations 1981 (circumstances in which persons are to be treated as engaged in remunerative full-time work), the claimant shall be treated as being engaged in remunerative work for that part of the period (if any), falling on or after 11th April 1988, for which those earnings are to be taken into account;

(b) the employment of the partner of a former beneficiary, except where the partner was engaged in that employment for less than 30 hours per week, shall notwithstanding the revocation of the Supplementary Benefit (Resources) Regulations 1981, be taken into account in accordance with those Regulations as if they were still in force.

(3) Except in the case of earnings to which paragraph (2) applies or would, but for the exception specified in sub-paragraph (b) thereof, apply, where in the case of a former beneficiary to whom regulation 4 applies a payment of income would, but for this paragraph, fall to be treated as paid under regulation 31(1)(a) of the General Regulations (date on which income treated as paid) before the first day of the benefit week in which he is first entitled to income support, that payment shall be treated as paid on that day and any part of the payment which has been taken into account in determining the former beneficiary's entitlement to supplementary benefit shall, notwithstanding Part V of the General Regulations, be disregarded in determining his entitlement to income support.

(4) Where an adjudicating authority has determined that payment of an amount of supplementary benefit awarded to a former beneficiary for a period immediately preceding 11th April 1988 should be paid to another person or body, such determination shall be deemed to have been made for the purposes of income support to which the former beneficiary is entitled on or after 11th April 1988.

(5) For the purposes of the application of paragraph 14 of Schedule 4 to the General Regulations (applicable amounts of persons in residential care and nursing homes), or paragraph 12 of Schedule 5 to those Regulations (applicable amounts of persons in board and lodging accommodation), to a former beneficiary in respect of whom income support becomes payable for a period immediately following a period in respect of which supplementary benefit was payable, the expression "close relative" shall, for so long as he continues to be entitled without interruption to income support, be given the meaning assigned to it immediately before 11th April 1988 by regulation 2 of the Requirements Regulations (interpretation).

[[1](6) For the purposes of determining a claimant's entitlement to income support for a period commencing on or after 11th April 1988, regulation 43 of the General Regulations (notional earnings of seasonal workers) shall apply for the purposes of determining a person's earnings in the period of his off-season or last period of normal employment beginning before that date as if that regulation and Parts IV and V of the General Regulations (applicable amounts and income and capital) were in force throughout that period.]

AMENDMENT

1. Income Support (Transitional) Amendment Regulations 1988 (S.I. 1988 No. 521), reg. 3 (April 11, 1988).

DEFINITIONS

"adjudicating authority"—see reg. 2(1).
"benefit week"—*ibid.*
"earnings"—see General Regulations, reg. 2(1).
"former beneficiary"—see reg. 2(1).
"General Regulations"—*ibid.*
"income support"—*ibid.*
"partner"—see General Regulations, reg. 2(1).
"payment"—*ibid.*
"supplementary benefit"—see reg. 2(1).

GENERAL NOTE

CSIS 89/1990 holds that para. (1) only applies where entitlement to or the amount of income support depends on the determination of a question and the same question has already been determined for supplementary benefit. So a decision for supplementary benefit purposes to lift the requirement to be available for employment was not carried over into income support, because neither entitlement to income support nor its amount depends on that question.

Appointments for former beneficiaries unable to act

6. Where the Secretary of State has made an appointment under regulation 26 of the Supplementary Benefit (Claims and Payments) Regulations 1981 of a person to exercise any right to which a former beneficiary may be entitled under the Supplementary Benefits Act 1976 and to receive and deal on his behalf with any sums payable to that former beneficiary under or by virtue of that Act, and such appointment has not, before 11th April 1988, been revoked by the Secretary of State or terminated by the resignation of the person appointed, that appointment shall be deemed, for the purposes of income support for that former beneficiary, to be an appointment made under regulation 33 of the Social Security (Claims and Payments) Regulations 1987 (persons unable to act).

DEFINITIONS

"former beneficiary"—see reg. 2(1).
"income support"—*ibid.*

Transitional payments for former beneficiaries

7.—(1) Where a former beneficiary is entitled to income support on the first day of his second benefit week—
   (a) he shall, notwithstanding the repeal or revocation of any enactment, be entitled to and be paid supplementary benefit for the period commencing on 11th April 1988 and ending with the day 6 days after the first day of his first benefit week except where that benefit week commences on 4th April 1988;
   (b) if the former beneficiary is a person to whom income support is payable in arrears, he shall also be entitled to a transitional payment of income support in respect of a period of, or two consecutive periods of, 7 days determined in accordance with paragraph (2).
   (2) For the purposes of paragraph (1)(b)—
   (a) in the case of a former beneficiary who is an unemployed person whose supplementary benefit had been paid by means of a book of serial orders or who is not an unemployed person, the transitional payment shall be in respect of the period of 7 days commencing with the day following the last day in respect of which supplementary benefit is payable in his case;
   (b) in any other case, the transitional payment shall be in respect of two consecutive periods of 7 days commencing with the day following the last day in respect of which supplementary benefit is payable in his case.
   (3) The amount of the transitional payment in respect of any such period shall be equal to the amount of income support payable in arrears for the benefit week or, in the case of a claimant whose entitlement to income support is for a period of less than a benefit week the amount which would have been payable had he been entitled to income support for the benefit week, commencing in the same calendar week as the period of seven days in respect of which the transitional payment is made.
   (4) The transitional payment shall be made in advance and, in a case to which paragraph (2)(b) applies, the transitional payment may be made in two instalments if it appears to the Secretary of State to be appropriate in the circumstances of the particular case.
   (5) In calculating the income of a former beneficiary for the purpose of determining his entitlement to income support in respect of any day for which that benefit becomes payable to him in arrears there shall be disregarded any supplementary benefit or any transitional payment payable to him under this regulation.

(6) Where a former beneficiary is not entitled to income support on the first day of his second benefit week he shall, notwithstanding the repeal or revocation of any enactment, be entitled to and be paid supplementary benefit for the period commencing on 11th April 1988 and ending with the day 6 days after the first day of his first benefit week except where that benefit week commences on 4th April 1988.

DEFINITIONS

"benefit week"—see reg. 2(1).
"first benefit week"—*ibid.*
"former beneficiary"—*ibid.*
"income support"—*ibid.*
"second benefit week"—*ibid.*
"supplementary benefit"—*ibid.*
"unemployed person"—*ibid.*

[¹Transitional payments for persons claiming supplementary benefit

7A.—(1) Except where regulation 7 applies (transitional payments for former beneficiaries), where a person makes a claim for supplementary benefit in the week commencing 4th April 1988 and, but for regulation 7(1)(a) of the Supplementary Benefit (Determination of Questions) Regulations 1980 (date of commencement of entitlement), he would have been entitled to supplementary benefit for a week beginning with the day on which the claim is made, he shall, if—
  (a) he is entitled to income support on the first day of his second benefit week; and
  (b) he is a person to whom income support is payable in arrears,
be entitled to a transitional payment of income support in respect of a period of, or two consecutive periods of, 7 days determined in accordance with paragraph (2).
  (2) For the purposes of paragraph (1)—
  (a) in the case of an unemployed person, the transitional payment shall be in respect of two consecutive periods of 7 days commencing with the first day of his second benefit week;
  (b) in any other case, the transitional payment shall be in respect of the period of 7 days commencing with the first day of his second benefit week.
  (3) Subject to paragraph (4), the amount of the transitional payment in respect of any such period shall be equal to the amount of income support payable in arrears for the benefit week or, in the case of a claimant whose entitlement to income support is for a period of less than a benefit week, the amount which would have been payable had he been entitled to income support for the benefit week, commencing in the same calendar week as the period of seven days in respect of which the transitional payment is made.
  (4) Where a person is entitled to income support for a period falling before the first day of his second benefit week, the amount of the transitional payment shall be reduced by the amount of income support payable for that period.
  (5) The transitional payment shall be made in advance and, in a case to which paragraph (2)(a) applies, the transitional payment may be made in two instalments if it appears to the Secretary of State to be appropriate in the circumstances of the particular case.
  (6) In calculating the income of a person entitled to a transitional payment under this regulation for the purpose of determining his entitlement to income support in respect of any day for which income support becomes payable to him in arrears there shall be disregarded any transitional payment payable to him under this regulation.

347

(7) Where a person is entitled to a transitional payment under this regulation or, but for his being a person to whom income support is payable in advance, would have been so entitled, Part II shall apply to him—

(a) as if he were a former beneficiary who had been entitled to supplementary benefit in the first benefit week; and

(b) as if that benefit week began on the day on which the claim for supplementary benefit was made.

(8) Where paragraph (7) applies, the amount of supplementary benefit to which that person is, for the purposes of Part II, to be treated as entitled shall be equal to the amount which would have been payable in the first benefit week had he been entitled to supplementary benefit for that week.]

AMENDMENT

1. Income Support (Transitional) Amendment Regulations 1988 (S.I. 1988 No. 521), reg. 4 (April 11, 1988).

DEFINITIONS

"benefit week"—see reg. 2(1).
"former beneficiary"—*ibid.*
"income support"—*ibid.*
"second benefit week"—*ibid.*
"supplementary benefit"—*ibid.*
"unemployed person"—*ibid.*

Treatment for income support purposes of periods relating to supplementary benefit

8.—(1) For the purpose of determining under regulation 4(1) of the General Regulations (temporary absence from Great Britain) whether a claimant is entitled to income support during a period of absence, that provision shall be construed as though there were inserted immediately after the words "entitled to income support" the words "or supplementary benefit".

(2) For the purpose of determining under regulation 21(4)(b)(ii) of the General Regulations (special cases) whether a local authority has accepted, in relation to a former beneficiary responsibility therein referred to for a period of not less than 2 years immediately before that person attained pensionable age, that provision shall be construed as though there were inserted immediately after the words "under and by virtue of that regulation" the words "or under or by virtue of the Supplementary Benefits Act 1976".

(3) Where, in relation to supplementary benefit for a former beneficiary in respect of a period immediately before 11th April 1988, his normal requirements fell to be reduced by virtue of regulation 8 of the Requirements Regulations 1983 (actual or notional unemployment benefit disqualification), regulation 22 of the General Regulations (reduction of applicable amount in cases of voluntary unemployment) shall apply to the calculation of that former beneficiary's applicable amount on 11th April 1988 with the modification that the relevant period specified in paragraph (6) of that regulation shall be reduced by the number of whole benefit weeks corresponding to the number of such weeks immediately preceding that date during which his normal requirements had been so reduced.

(4) For the purpose of determining whether, in any case, the additional condition for higher pensioner premium or disability premium, specified in paragraph 12(1)(b) of Schedule 2 to the General Regulations (applicable amounts), is satisfied for any period before 24th October 1988, that provision shall be construed as though there were inserted therein, immediately after the reference to the Social Security Act, a reference to the Supplementary Benefits Act 1976.

(5) For the purposes of paragraph 7 of Schedule 3 to the General Regulations (housing costs), any reference to income support shall be construed as if it included a reference to supplementary benefit and in sub-paragraph (2)(a) of that paragraph references to a claimant's income and applicable amount shall be construed as if they included references to his resources and requirements determined for the purposes of entitlement to supplementary benefit.

(6) Where, in relation to supplementary benefit for a former beneficiary in respect of a period immediately before 11th April 1988, his housing requirements fell to be restricted by virtue of regulation 20 or 21 of the Requirements Regulations (special cases and restrictions where amounts are excessive)—

(a) paragraph 10 of Schedule 3 to the General Regulations (housing costs) shall apply to the calculation of that former beneficiary's applicable amount in his second benefit week with the modification that the references in paragraph 10(2)(a) and (6) of that Schedule to income support shall be construed as if they included a reference to supplementary benefit; and

(b) in computing the 8 week period referred to in paragraph 10(2)(c) of that Schedule any week falling before 11th April 1988 which is within that 8 week period and during which supplementary benefit was payable shall be treated as a week in which income support was payable.

<small>DEFINITIONS</small>

"applicable amount"—see 1986 Act, s.84(1).
"benefit week"—see reg. 2(1).
"former beneficiary"—*ibid.*
"General Regulations"—*ibid.*
"income support"—*ibid.*
"local authority"—see 1986 Act, s.84(1).
"Requirements Regulations"—see reg. 2(1).
"Social Security Act"—*ibid.*
"supplementary benefit"—*ibid.*

PART II

TRANSITIONAL PROTECTION

Total benefit income

9.—(1) In this Part a person's total benefit income in his first benefit week means, subject to paragraphs (2) to (5) and (7), and regulation 13(1) (special provisions for persons in residential care and nursing homes), the aggregate of the amount of any of the following benefits or payments to which he or his partner was, or both were, entitled in respect of that week—

(a) supplementary benefit;
(b) family income supplement;
(c) child benefit;
(d) any benefit under the Social Security Act;
(e) war disablement pension;
(f) war widow's pension;
(g) any payment made under a scheme made under the Industrial Injuries and Diseases (Old Cases) Act 1975;
(h) statutory maternity pay under Part V of the Act;
(i) statutory sick pay under Part I of the Social Security and Housing Benefits Act 1982;

(j) any payment made otherwise than in accordance with any of the Acts under which the benefits or payments specified in sub-paragraphs (a) to (g) are made under arrangements made by the Secretary of State with the consent of the Treasury which is charged to the National Insurance Fund or to a Departmental Expenditure Vote to which payments of any benefit or payment specified in those sub-paragraphs are charged.

(2) Where a change of circumstances takes effect in a person's second benefit week which, had it taken effect in his first benefit week, would have resulted in a lesser amount of supplementary benefit being payable in respect of that week, the amount of supplementary benefit taken into account for the purpose of calculating his total benefit income in his first benefit week shall be the amount (if any) that would have been payable had the change of circumstances taken effect in that week ['but this paragraph shall not apply where the change of circumstances is the admission to hospital of the person in his second benefit week.]

(3) If a former beneficiary's requirements for the purpose of calculating his entitlement to supplementary benefit in his first benefit week include an amount in respect of housing requirements under Part IV of the Requirements Regulations to which he is entitled by virtue of regulation 14(4) of those Regulations (housing requirements) and, in a case to which sub-paragraph (a) of that provision applies, if in that week he has been absent from his home for 52 weeks or more, the amount of supplementary benefit taken into account for the purpose of calculating his total benefit income in that benefit week shall be reduced by the amount of those housing requirements.

(4) If, in respect of his first benefit week, a former beneficiary who is entitled to supplementary benefit in respect of that benefit week is also entitled to housing benefit in the form of a rate rebate, his total benefit income in that benefit week shall be increased by—

(a) if he is a single claimant aged under 25, £1.00;

(b) in any other case, £1.30.

(5) Where a claimant, other than one whose requirements were modified under regulation 10(2) or (3) of the Requirements Regulations (modifications of normal requirements in special cases), is—

(a) a member of a couple and either he or his partner has been in hospital immediately before 11th April 1988 for at least 6, but not more than 9, weeks; or

(b) a lone parent who immediately before that date has been in hospital for at least 6 weeks,

the amount of supplementary benefit to be taken into account for the purpose of calculating his total benefit income in his first benefit week shall be the amount (if any) that would have been payable had his requirements fallen to be determined in accordance with paragraph 2 of Schedule 3 to the Requirements Regulations (modifications in the case of patients).

(6) In this Part a person's total benefit income in relation to his second and any subsequent benefit week means, subject to paragraph (7) and regulations 11 and 13(1) (persons in residential care and nursing homes), the aggregate of the following amounts—

(a) the amount of any income support, family credit and child benefit to which he or his partner is, or both are, entitled in respect of that week;

(b) where he or his partner is, or both are, entitled in respect of that week to any benefit or payment specified in paragraph (1)(d) to (i), the amount of the weekly rate of that benefit to which he is normally entitled as increased, if appropriate, by the order made by the Secretary of State under section 63 of the Act with effect from 11th April 1988;

(c) any payment referred to in paragraph (1)(j) which he or his partner receives, or both receive, in respect of that week.

350

(7) The amount of any of the benefits specified in sub-paragraphs (a) to (c) of this paragraph shall, to the extent that it is disregarded for the purpose of calculating a person's resources under the Supplementary Benefit (Resources) Regulations 1981 or a person's income under the General Regulations, be disregarded for the purpose of calculating a person's total benefit income in his first, second or any subsequent benefit week—

(a) mobility allowance;

(b) mobility supplement; and

(c) attendance allowance.

(8) In this Part references to a person's income in a benefit week subsequent to his first benefit week are references to his income, and the income of any member of his family which would be treated as his under section 22(5) of the Act, calculated under Part V of the General Regulations (income and capital).

[[1](9) For the purposes of paragraph (1)(a) or (6)(a), where a claimant is a person to whom regulation 8 of the Requirements Regulations or regulation 22 of the General Regulations (reductions in certain cases of unemployment disqualification) applies, the amount of supplementary benefit or income support to be taken into account shall be the amount to which the claimant would have been entitled but for that regulation.]

AMENDMENT

1. Income Support (Transitional) Amendment Regulations 1988 (S.I. 1988 No. 521), reg. 5 (April 11, 1988).

DEFINITIONS

"the Act"—see reg. 2(1).
"benefit week"—*ibid.*
"claimant"—see General Regulations, reg. 2(1).
"couple"—*ibid.*
"family"—see 1986 Act, s.20(11) (SSCBA, s.137(1)).
"first benefit week"—see reg. 2(1).
"former beneficiary"—*ibid.*
"General Regulations"—*ibid.*
"lone parent"—see General Regulations, reg. 2(1).
"mobility allowance"—*ibid.*
"mobility supplement"—*ibid.*
"partner"—*ibid.*
"Requirements Regulations"—see reg. 2(1).
"second benefit week"—*ibid.*
"single claimant"—see General Regulations, reg. 2(1).
"Social Security Act"—see reg. 2(1).
"supplementary benefit"—*ibid.*
"war disablement pension"—see 1986 Act, s.84(1).
"war widow's pension"—*ibid.*

GENERAL NOTE

Reg. 9 does not create any right to payment of benefit in the week beginning April 4, 1988 (*CIS 6/1988*).

Transitional addition

10.—(1) Except in a case to which regulation 11 or 12 applies (special provisions for patients and persons in board and lodging accommodation and hostels) and subject to the following provisions of this Part, where—

(a) a former beneficiary was entitled to supplementary benefit in respect of his first benefit week; and

(b) either—
   (i) he is awarded income support in respect of his second benefit week; or
   (ii) he is not entitled to income support in respect of that week only because his applicable amount calculated in accordance with the General Regulations does not exceed his income; and
(c) his total benefit income in his second benefit week is less than his total benefit income in his first benefit week,

he shall be entitled to a transitional addition.

(2) Subject to regulation 12(2), 13(5) or 14 (special provision for persons in residential care or nursing homes and reduction and termination of transitional addition), and except in a case to which paragraph (3) applies, the amount of the transitional addition to which a former beneficiary is entitled under paragraph (1) shall be the difference between his total benefit income in his first and second benefit weeks.

(3) Subject to regulation 14 the amount of the transitional addition applicable to a former beneficiary who in respect of his first benefit week was entitled to a domestic assistance addition of £10 or more shall be the amount (if any) obtained by subtracting from his total benefit income in his first benefit week the amount of his domestic assistance addition, the sum determined under paragraph (4) and, where applicable, (5).

(4) The sum for the purposes of paragraph (3) shall be—
   (a) in a case where in his second benefit week a severe disability premium is applicable to the former beneficiary for the purpose of calculating his applicable amount under Part IV of the General Regulations (applicable amounts), his total benefit income in his second benefit week less the amount of that premium;
   (b) in any other case, his total benefit income in his second benefit week.

(5) If the amount of the former beneficiary's domestic assistance addition is less than the amount of his severe disability premium, the sum for the purposes of paragraph (3) shall be the amount of the difference between the addition and the premium.

DEFINITIONS

   "applicable amount"—see General Regulations, reg. 2(1).
   "domestic assistance addition"—see reg. 2(1).
   "first benefit week"—*ibid.*
   "former beneficiary"—*ibid.*
   "General Regulations"—*ibid.*
   "income support"—*ibid.*
   "second benefit week"—*ibid.*
   "supplementary benefit"—*ibid.*

GENERAL NOTE

   CIS 193/1989 holds that reg. 10 cannot be impugned as discriminatory under the Sex Discrimination Act 1975 because it was made under powers provided in the Social Security Act 1986, which therefore to that extent impliedly repealed the Sex Discrimination Act 1975. The discrimination complained of arises because the protection under reg. 10 is given to a former beneficiary, *i.e.* a claimant. The claimant of supplementary benefit within a couple would usually have been the man. If the woman has to claim income support in her own right, because, for example, the man dies or they separate, she is not entitled to the transitional protection.

Special provisions for patients

11.—(1) Where, immediately before 11th April 1988—
   (a) a claimant was a member of a married or unmarried couple for the pur-

poses of paragraph 3(1) of Schedule 1 to the Supplementary Benefits Act 1976 or a spouse of a polygamous marriage; and

(b) he or any partner was entitled to supplementary benefit; and

(c) he was not himself a patient but any partner of his had been a patient for a period of 52 weeks or more,

he shall, subject to regulations 12 to 14 and 16 (special cases and reduction and termination of, and persons not entitled to, transitional additions), be entitled to a transitional addition calculated in accordance with paragraph (2).

(2) Subject to regulation 14, the amount of the transitional addition to which a claimant is entitled under paragraph (1) shall be the amount (if any) obtained by subtracting from his total benefit income in his first benefit week the amount of his total benefit income in the second benefit week ['and the amount of his partner's total benefit income in his partner's second benefit week].

(3) In this regulation, references to a claimant's partner are references to the person who, immediately before 11th April 1988 was the other member of a married or unmarried couple for the purposes of paragraph 3(1) of Schedule 1 to the Supplementary Benefits Act 1976 or was a spouse to whom the former beneficiary was polygamously married.

AMENDMENT

1. Income Support (Transitional) Amendment Regulations 1988 (S.I. 1988 No. 521), reg. 6 (April 11, 1988).

DEFINITIONS

"claimant"—see General Regulations, reg. 2(1).
"first benefit week"—see reg. 2(1).
"former beneficiary"—*ibid.*
"patient"—*ibid.*, General Regulations, reg. 21(3).
"polygamous marriage"—see General Regulations, reg. 2(1).
"second benefit week"—see reg. 2(1).
"supplementary benefit"—*ibid.*

Special provisions for persons in board and lodging accommodation and hostels

12.—(1) Where a claimant is temporarily absent for ['a period of less than 13 weeks which includes his first and second benefit week (or both)] from his board and lodging accommodation or his hostel and, in the case of board and lodging accommodation was immediately before his absence entitled to an increase under regulation 9(7) of the Requirements Regulations (modifications of requirements of boarders), he shall, notwithstanding regulation 14 (reduction and termination of transitional addition), on his return to that accommodation be entitled to a transitional addition of an amount equal to the difference between—

(a) the amount that his total benefit income in his first benefit week would have been had he been entitled in respect of that week to supplementary benefit on the basis that he was in that board and lodging accommodation or hostel; and, if less,

(b) the amount of his total benefit income in the first complete benefit week in respect of which his applicable amount for the purpose of calculating his entitlement to income support is to be calculated under Schedule 5 to the General Regulations (applicable amounts for persons in board and lodging accommodation and hostels).

(2) If a claimant becomes entitled to a transitional addition under paragraph (1) he shall cease to be entitled to any transitional addition to which he would, but for this provision, be entitled under regulation 10 (transitional addition) while not in board and lodging accommodation or a hostel.

353

(3) Where a claimant who is in board and lodging accommodation or a hostel and who is entitled to a transitional addition under paragraph (1) or regulation 10 (transitional addition) temporarily leaves his board and lodging accommodation or a hostel for a period of 8 weeks or less or, if he becomes a patient, for a period of 14 weeks or less and, in the case of board and lodging accommodation he is entitled to an increase under paragraph 7 of Schedule 5 to the General Regulations, any increase in his applicable amount for the purpose of calculating his entitlement to income support on his return to that accommodation shall be disregarded for the purpose of regulation 14(1) (reduction in transitional addition).

(4) Regulation 14(3) [¹and (4)] (re-entitlement to a transitional addition after periods of 8 weeks or less) shall apply to a claimant who is in board and lodging accommodation and entitled to an increase under paragraph 7 of Schedule 5 to the General Regulations, or in a hostel and who, in either case was immediately before the period of 8 weeks, entitled to a transitional addition under paragraph (1) or regulation 10 notwithstanding that the amount of the transitional addition to which he is entitled is less than £10.

AMENDMENT

1. Income Support (Transitional) Amendment Regulations 1988 (S.I. 1988 No. 521), reg. 7, (April 11, 1988).

DEFINITIONS

"applicable amount"—see 1986 Act, s.84(1).
"benefit week"—see General Regulations, reg. 2(1).
"claimant"—*ibid.*
"first benefit week"—see reg. 2(1).
"General Regulations"—*ibid.*
"income support"—*ibid.*
"patient"—*ibid.*, General Regulations, reg. 21(3).
"Requirements Regulations"—see reg. 2(1).
"second benefit week"—*ibid.*
"supplementary benefit"—*ibid.*

Special provisions for persons in residential care and nursing homes

13.—(1) For the purpose of calculating the total benefit income of a claimant who is in a residential care or nursing home, where in his first benefit week an allowance for personal expenses is applicable under regulation 9(17)(e) of the Requirements Regulations (personal expenses for boarders)—

(a) in that benefit week, the amount of that allowance shall be deducted from the amount of supplementary benefit to which he is entitled in respect of that week; and

(b) in his second benefit week, the amount in respect of personal expenses applicable in his case under paragraph 13 of Schedule 4 to the General Regulations (applicable amounts of persons in residential care or nursing homes) shall be deducted from the amount of income support to which he is entitled in respect of that week.

(2) Subject to paragraph (3) and to regulation 16 (persons not entitled to personal expenses addition), a former beneficiary to whom paragraph (1) applies shall be entitled, in addition to any transitional addition to which he may be entitled under paragraph (5) or regulation 10 (transitional addition), to a personal expenses addition of an amount equal to the difference between the amount of the allowance for personal expenses under regulation 9(17)(e) of the Requirements Regulations referred to in paragraph (1) and, if less, the amount of the allowance for personal expenses referred to in paragraph (1)(b).

(3) The amount of the personal expenses addition under paragraph (2) [¹(6) or (8)] shall be reduced by the amount of any increase in the amount in respect of personal expenses referred to in paragraph (1)(b).

(4) Subject to paragraphs (5) and (8), a claimant who ceases to reside or, if he is a member of a family, who and whose family cease to reside, in a residential care or nursing home [¹. . .], shall cease to be entitled to any transitional addition and personal expenses addition under this Part [¹except where he ceases or, as the case may be, he and his family cease, to reside in the home in the circumstances specified in paragraph 16 or 18 of column (1) of Schedule 7 to the General Regulations (applicable amounts in special cases) and he intends or, as the case may be, they intend to return to the home].

(5) Notwithstanding regulation 14 (reduction and termination of transitional and personal expenses addition), where a claimant is temporarily absent from his residential care or nursing home for a period which includes his [¹first and second benefit week (or both)], he shall be entitled on his return to a residential care or nursing home to a transitional addition of an amount equal to the difference between—

  (a) the amount that his total benefit income in his first benefit week would have been had he been entitled in respect of that week to supplementary benefit calculated on the basis that he was a boarder in that residential care or nursing home for that week; and, if less,

  (b) the amount of his total benefit income in the first complete week in respect of which his applicable amount for the purpose of calculating his entitlement to income support is to be calculated in accordance with Schedule 4 to the General Regulations (applicable amounts for claimants in residential care and nursing homes).

(6) A claimant to whom paragraph (5) applies and to whom in respect of his first benefit week an allowance for personal expenses would have been applicable under regulation 9(17)(e) of the Requirements Regulations shall also be entitled to a personal expenses addition of an amount equal to the difference between the amount that his personal expenses allowance would have been in respect of his first benefit week and, if less, the amount in respect of personal expenses applicable under paragraph 13 of Schedule 4 to the General Regulations.

(7) If a claimant becomes entitled to a transitional addition under paragraph (5) he shall cease to be entitled to any transitional addition to which he would, but for this provision, be entitled under regulation 10 (transitional addition) while not in a residential care or nursing home.

(8) Notwithstanding regulation 14 (reduction and termination of transitional and personal expenses addition), where a claimant is temporarily absent from his residential care or nursing home for a period after his second benefit week (whether or not he thereby ceases to be entitled to income support), he shall be entitled on his return to a residential care or nursing home to—

  [¹(a) a transitional addition equal to the amount to which he was entitled immediately before his period of temporary absence less, if his applicable amount would have increased had he not been absent, the amount of the increase; and for the purposes of this sub-paragraph, any increase in the amount of personal expenses where a personal expenses addition is in payment shall be disregarded:

  (b) a personal expenses addition equal to the amount to which he was entitled immediately before his period of temporary absence less, if the amount of personal expenses applicable in his case under paragraph 13 of Schedule 4 to the General Regulations would have increased had he not been absent, the amount of that increase.]

(9) For the purposes of paragraphs (5), (8) and (10) a claimant is temporarily absent only if the period of his temporary absence does not exceed—

(a) in the case of a person who is of pensionable age, 52 weeks; or

(b) in any other case, 13 weeks.

(10) Where a claimant—

(a) was in receipt of supplementary benefit as a boarder in a residential care or nursing home within the meaning of regulation 9 of the Requirements Regulations (boarders) and immediately before 11th April 1988 his requirements fell to be determined in accordance with paragraph (17)(a) to (e) or (i) to (k) of that regulation (protected amounts); or

(b) would have satisfied the conditions in sub-paragraph (*a*) above but for his being temporarily absent from such a home,

and he ceases to be entitled to income support and a transitional addition or personal expenses addition or both, he shall notwithstanding regulation 14, if he becomes re-entitled to income support, become re-entitled to such an addition of the same amount as he would have been entitled to had he not ceased to be entitled to income support, provided that he has continued since that date to be resident in a residential care or nursing home.

(11) Where—

(a) the claimant's partner has died; and

(b) immediately before his death the partner was entitled to a transitional addition or personal expenses addition or both under this Part; and

(c) after the partner's death the claimant has continued to be a resident in the same accommodation as he and his partner occupied immediately before the partner's death,

the claimant shall be entitled to a transitional addition or personal expenses addition or both equal to one-half of the amount to which his partner was entitled immediately before his death.

AMENDMENT

1. Income Support (Transitional) Amendment Regulations 1988 (S.I. 1988 No. 521), reg. 8 (April 11, 1988).

DEFINITIONS

"benefit week"—see reg. 2(1).
"claimant"—see General Regulations, reg. 2(1).
"first benefit week"—see reg. 2(1).
"former beneficiary"—*ibid.*
"General Regulations"—*ibid.*
"income support"—*ibid.*
"nursing home"—see General Regulations, reg. 2(1), reg. 19(3).
"partner"—see General Regulations, reg. 2(1).
"personal expenses addition"—see reg. 2(1).
"Requirements Regulations'—*ibid.*
"residential care home"—see General Regulations, reg. 2(1), reg. 19(3).
"second benefit week"—see reg. 2(1).
"supplementary benefit"—*ibid.*
"transitional addition"—*ibid.*

Reduction and termination of transitional and personal expenses addition

14.—(1) The amount of a claimant's transitional addition shall be reduced—

(a) if, in respect of any benefit week subsequent to his second benefit week, he is entitled to income support as well as a transitional addition and his applicable amount under Part IV [³or VI] of the General Regulations increases, by the amount of that increase [¹but this subparagraph shall not apply to an increase to which regulation 13(3) applies (increase in personal expenses)];

(b) if, in respect of any benefit week subsequent to his second benefit week, he is entitled only to a transitional addition [¹or, as the case may be, to a transitional addition and a special transitional addition], by the amount of any increase in his income.

(c) if, in respect of any benefit week subsequent to his second benefit week, he is entitled only to a transitional addition and personal expenses addition under regulation 13(2) (special provisions for persons in residential care or nursing homes), by the amount of any increase in his income;

(d) if, in respect of any benefit week subsequent to his second benefit week he becomes entitled to income support as a result of an increase in his applicable amount under Part IV [³or VI] of the General Regulations and immediately before that increase he was entitled only to a transitional addition, by the amount of that increase less the amount by which his income exceeded his applicable amount prior to that increase;

(e) if, in respect of any benefit week subsequent to his second benefit week he ceases to be entitled to income support because his income exceeds his applicable amount, by the amount by which his income exceeds the applicable amount.

[¹(1A) Notwithstanding paragraph (1)(a) or (d) where [⁵regulation 21A or 22] of the General Regulations (reductions in applicable amounts) ceases to apply to the claimant and as a result his applicable amount increases, his transitional addition shall not be reduced by the amount of that increase.

(1B) Notwithstanding paragraph (1)(a) or (d) where a person has entered accommodation referred to in any of sub-paragraphs (a) to (d) of the definition of residential accommodation in regulation 21(3) of the General Regulations (special cases), or a residential care home or nursing home, for a period of 8 weeks or less and as a result his applicable amount increases, his transitional addition shall not be reduced by the amount of that increase.]

[²(1C) Notwithstanding paragraph (1)(b), (c) or (e) the amount of a claimant's transitional addition shall not be reduced if, and to the extent that, the increase in his income or, as the case may be, the reason his income exceeds his applicable amount, is attributable to the receipt of a training allowance.]

[⁷(1CA) Notwithstanding paragraph (1)(b), (c) or (e) the amount of a claimant's transitional addition shall not be reduced if, and to the extent that, the increase in his income or, as the case may be, the reason his income exceeds his applicable amount is attributable to the amendment made by regulation 2 of the Child Benefit and Social Security (Fixing and Adjustment of Rates) Amendment No.2 Regulations 1991.]

[⁷(1D) Notwithstanding paragraph (1)(a) or (d), the amount of a claimant's transitional addition shall not be reduced if, and to the extent that, the increase in his applicable amount is attributable to the amendments made by regulation 5(a) and (c) of the Income Support (General) Amendment Regulations 1989 and that increase in his applicable amount takes effect in his benefit week beginning on a day during the period of 7 days commencing on 9th October 1989.]

[⁷(1DA) Notwithstanding paragraph (1)(a) or (d), the amount of a claimant's transitional addition shall not be reduced if, and to the extent that, the increase in his applicable amount is attributable to the amendments made by regulation 15(a), (b) or (c) of the Income Support (General) Amendment No.4 Regulations 1991 and that increase in his applicable amount takes effect in his benefit week beginning on a day during the period of 7 days commencing on 1st October 1991.]

[⁷(1DZA) Notwithstanding paragraph (1)(a) or (d), the amount of a claimant's transitional addition shall not be reduced if, and to the extent that, the increase in his applicable amount is attributable to the amendments made by regulation 3(1) and (2) of the Income-Related Benefits Amendment Regulations 1992 and that increase in his applicable amount takes effect in his benefit week beginning on a day during the period of 7 days commencing on 5th October 1992.]

[³(1E) Notwithstanding paragraph (1)(a) or (d), where a claimant's applicable amount increases by virtue of his or his partner's participation or ceasing to participate in arrangements for training under section 2 of the Employment and Training Act 1973 [⁶or section 2 of the Enterprise and New Towns (Scotland) Act 1990] or his or his partner's attendance or ceasing to attend at a course at an employment rehabilitation centre established under that section [⁶of the 1993 Act], his transitional addition shall not be reduced by the amount of that increase.

(1F) Notwithstanding paragraph (1)(a) or (d), where—

(a) a claimant has ceased to be entitled to a transitional addition because he or his partner becomes engaged in remunerative work and immediately before he so ceased a higher pensioner premium or a disability premium was applicable to him under paragraph 10 or, as the case may be, 11 of Schedule 2 to the General Regulations (applicable amounts); and

(b) he becomes re-entitled to that addition by virtue of paragraph (3A) or (4A) or regulation 15(4) (special transitional addition),

his transitional addition shall not be reduced if the higher pensioner premium or the disability premium again becomes applicable to him to the extent that any increase in his applicable amount is attributable to that premium.]

[⁴(1G) Notwithstanding paragraph (1)(a) or (d), where a claimant's applicable amount increases because a child or young person mentioned in paragraph (5)(c) of regulation 16 of the General Regulations (circumstances in which a person is treated or not treated as a member of the household) is treated as a member of the claimant's household under paragraph (6) of that regulation, the claimant's transitional addition shall not be reduced by the amount of that increase unless the child or young person has been treated as a member of the household for a continuous period which exceeds eight weeks.]

(2) A claimant shall cease to be entitled to a transitional addition if—

(a) in the case of a claimant who is entitled to income support as well as a transitional addition—

(i) subject to regulation 15(4) (special transitional addition), he ceases to be entitled to income support for a reason other than that his applicable amount under Part IV of the General Regulations (applicable amounts) does not exceed his income; or

(ii) the amount of his transitional addition is reduced to nil by virtue of paragraph (1); or

(b) in the case of a claimant to whom paragraph (1)(b), (c) or (e) applies—

(i) subject to regulation 15(4), he would no longer, if he claimed, be entitled to income support for a reason other than that his applicable amount under Part IV of the General Regulations does not exceed his income; or

(ii) the amount of his transitional addition is reduced to nil by virtue of paragraph (1).

(3) [³Except where paragraph (3A) applies,] a claimant who either—

(a) has ceased to be entitled to income support but remained entitled to a transitional addition; or

(b) has ceased to be entitled to income support and a transitional addition,

and immediately before he so ceased was entitled to a transitional addition of £10 or more shall, [¹if he becomes re-entitled to income support not more than 8 weeks after the day on which he has ceased to be so entitled, in the benefit week in which he becomes re-entitled, be re-entitled to a transitional addition of an amount equal to the amount of the transitional addition to which he was previously entitled subject to any reduction in that amount which would have occurred under paragraph (1)(a) had he remained entitled to income support.]

[³(3A) A claimant who has ceased to be entitled to income support and a transitional addition because he or his partner has become engaged in remunerative work shall, if during the permitted period determined in accordance with regulation 2A (permitted period) beginning with the day after the day on which he ceased to be so entitled he or his partner has ceased to be engaged in that work, be re-entitled to a transitional addition of an amount equal to the amount of transitional addition to which he was previously entitled subject to any reduction in that amount which would have occurred under paragraph (1)(a) had he remained entitled to income support.]

(4) [³Except where paragraph (4A) applies,] a claimant who, was entitled only to a transitional addition of £10 or more and who has ceased to be entitled to such an addition—

(a) for a reason other than that his income exceeds his applicable amount; or

(b) because his income exceeds his applicable amount and the amount of his transitional addition,

shall, [¹if not more than 8 weeks after the day on which he ceased to be so entitled neither the reason in sub-paragraph (a) nor (b) applies to him, be re-entitled to a transitional addition of an amount equal to the amount by which his total benefit income in his first benefit week exceeds his total benefit income in the benefit week in which neither sub-paragraph applies to him, or the amount to which he was previously entitled, whichever is the lower.]

[³(4A) A claimant who was entitled only to a transitional addition and who has ceased to be entitled to such an addition because he or his partner became engaged in remunerative work shall, if during the permitted period determined in accordance with regulation 2A beginning with the day after the day on which he has ceased to be so entitled he or his partner ceased to be engaged in that work, be re-entitled to a transitional addition of an amount equal to the amount by which his total benefit income in his first benefit week exceeds his total benefit income in the benefit week in which he becomes re-entitled, or the amount to which he was previously entitled, whichever is the lower.]

(5) The amount of a claimant's personal expenses addition shall be reduced if, in any benefit week, he is entitled only to a personal expenses addition, by the amount of any increase in his income [²but not if, and to the extent that, the increase is attributable to the receipt of a training allowance.]

(6) A claimant shall cease to be entitled to a personal expenses addition if—

(a) in the case of a claimant who is entitled to income support as well as a personal expenses addition—

   (i) he ceases to be entitled to income support for a reason other than that his applicable amount under Part IV of the General Regulations (applicable amounts) does not exceed his income; or

   (ii) the amount of his personal expenses addition is reduced to nil by virtue of paragraph (5) or regulation 13(3).

(b) in the case of a claimant who is entitled only to a personal expenses addition—

   (i) he would no longer, if he claimed, be entitled to income support for a reason other than that his applicable amount under Part IV of the General Regulations does not exceed his income; or

   (ii) the amount of his personal expenses addition is reduced to nil by virtue of paragraph (5) or regulation 13(3).

AMENDMENTS

1. Income Support (Transitional) Amendment Regulations 1988 (S.I. 1988 No. 521), reg. 9 (April 11, 1988).
2. Income Support (Transitional) Amendment No. 2 Regulations 1988 (S.I. 1988 No. 670). reg. 2 (April 11, 1988).

3. Income Support (Transitional) Amendment Regulations 1989 (S.I. 1989 No. 1626), reg. 3 (October 9, 1989).

4. Income Support (Transitional) Amendment No. 2 Regulations 1989 (S.I. 1989 No. 2340), reg. 2 (December 14, 1989).

5. Income Support (General and Transitional) Amendment Regulations 1990 (S.I. 1990 No. 2324), reg. 6 (December 17, 1990).

6. Enterprise (Scotland) Consequential Amendments Order 1991 (S.I. 1991 No. 387) arts. 2 and 10 (April 1, 1991).

7. Income Support (Transitional) Amendment Regulations 1991 (S.I. 1991 No. 1600), reg. 2 (October 1, 1991).

8. Income-related Benefits Amendment Regulations 1992 (S.I. 1992 No. 1326), reg. 3(4) (October 5, 1992).

DEFINITIONS

"applicable amount"—see 1986 Act, s.84(1).
"benefit week"—see reg. 2(1).
"claimant"—see General Regulations, reg. 2(1).
"first benefit week"—see reg. 2(1).
"General Regulations"—*ibid.*
"income support"—*ibid.*
"personal expenses addition"—*ibid.*
"second benefit week"—*ibid.*
"transitional addition"—*ibid.*

GENERAL NOTE

Paragraph (1)

Two Commissioner's decisions have held that sub-para. (a) only applies to increases in the applicable amount in relation to its amount in the "second benefit week," *i.e.* the first week of the income support scheme in April 1988. In *CSIS 30/1989* the claimant's wife went into hospital for more than six weeks, so that the claimant's applicable amount was reduced under para. 1 of Sched. 7 to the Income Support (General) Regulations. When she came out of hospital, his applicable amount was increased to its previous level. The AO treated this as an increase under para. (1) and reduced the claimant's transitional addition by the same amount. The Commissioner held that there was not an increase under para. (1) because there was no increase against the base of the second benefit week. In *R(IS) 6/93* one of the claimant's children was taken into care and his applicable amount was accordingly reduced. The child later came back to live with the claimant and the applicable amount was restored. The AO reduced his transitional addition to nil. The Commissioner applied the principle of *CSIS 30/1989* to produce the same result. At the relevant time para. (1G) was not in force and so could not affect the interpretation of para. (1). But the Commissioner considered that it might not affect the principle anyway. An appeal to the Court of Appeal in *R(IS) 6/93* upholds the Commissioner's decision (*Chief Adjudication Officer v. Dommett*, March 12, 1992, appendix to *R(IS) 6/93*). But the Court of Appeal stresses the temporary nature of the change which produced the effect on the applicable amount.

Paragraph (2)

CIS 255/1990 (to be reported as *R(IS) 1/94*) holds that where a person is detained in custody pending trial and his applicable amount is reduced to nil under para. 8(b) of Sched. 7, he ceases to be entitled to a transitional addition by virtue of sub-para. (a)(i). However, this does not seem correct. Sub-para. (a)(i) applies where a claimant ceases to be entitled to income support for a reason other than that his applicable amount does not exceed his income. But in *CIS 255/1990* the claimant ceased to be entitled because his applicable amount, reduced to nil, no longer exceeded his income, also apparently nil. Reg. 16(3) removes a prisoner's entitlement to a transitional addition, but arguably that only applies during the period in custody and does not cause the entitlement to cease. In *CIS 255/1990* the claimant's transitional addition was less than £10 and so he could not have relied on para. (3) for its restoration on his release in any event. In *CIS 223/1993*, which concerned another prisoner, the Commissioner takes the view that what led to his ceasing to be entitled to income support *was* the fact that his applicable amount had become nil and thus could not exceed his income.

Paragraph (3)

CIS 223/1993 (to be reported as *R(IS) 2/95*) decides that where a person's applicable amount has been reduced to nil under para. 8 of Sched. 7 because he is a prisoner, this means that he has ceased to be entitled to income support. This is not a case where payment is denied of an underlying entitlement but under Sched. 7, para. 8, there is no entitlement at all. However, the claimant was not entitled to restoration of his transitional addition when he was released as he did not meet the other conditions of para. (3).

Special transitional addition

15.—(1) Subject to regulation 16 (persons not entitled to transitional additions), where the amount of a claimant's domestic assistance addition in respect of his first benefit week is £10 or more and is greater than the amount (if any) of the severe disability premium for the purpose of calculating his applicable amount under Part IV of the General Regulations (applicable amounts) [¹in his second benefit week], he shall be entitled to a special transitional addition of an amount equal to the difference between his domestic assistance addition and the severe disability premium [¹(if any)].

(2) Where a claimant is not entitled to income support or a transitional addition, the amount of a special transitional addition under paragraph (1) to which he is entitled shall be reduced by the amount of any increase in his income [²but not if, and to the extent that, the increase is attributable to the receipt of a training allowance] [⁴or to the receipt of an increase in the weekly rate of child benefit which is attributable to the amendments made by regulation 2 of the Child Benefit and Social Security (Fixing and Adjustment of Rates) Amendment No. 2 Regulations 1991.]

(3) Subject to paragraph (4) a claimant shall cease to be entitled to a special transitional addition under paragraph (1) if—

(a) he ceases to be entitled to income support for a reason other than that his applicable amount under Part IV of the General Regulations (applicable amounts) does not exceed his income; or

(b) his applicable amount for the purposes of calculating his entitlement to income support falls to be determined under Schedule 4 to, or paragraphs 1 to 4, 13 and 18 of Schedule 7 to, the General Regulations (applicable amounts for persons in residential care and nursing homes or residential accommodation or hospital patients); [¹or

(c) in the case of a claimant who is entitled to income support as well as a transitional addition he ceases to be entitled to income support and a transitional addition for a reason other than that his applicable amount under Part IV of the General Regulations does not exceed his income; or

(d) in the case of a claimant who is entitled to a transitional addition and a special transitional addition he would not, if he claimed, be entitled to income support for a reason other than that his applicable amount under Part IV of the General Regulations does not exceed his income; or

(e) he would, but for this sub-paragraph, be entitled only to a special transitional addition and he would not, if he claimed, be entitled to income support for a reason other than that his applicable amount does not exceed his income; or

(f) the amount of his special transitional addition is reduced to nil by virtue of paragraph (2).]

(4) Where a claimant ceases to be entitled to a special transitional addition—

[¹(a) by virtue of paragraph (3)(a), (c), (d) or (e) he shall be re-entitled to such an addition of the same amount as previously if, [³during the permitted period determined in accordance with regulation 2A (permitted period) beginning with the day after] the day on which he ceased to be so entitled, he becomes re-entitled to income support or a transitional addition;]

(b) by virtue of paragraph (3)(b) he shall be re-entitled to such an addition of the same amount as previously if, [³during the permitted period determined in accordance with regulation 2A (permitted period) beginning with the day after] [¹the day on which his applicable amount fell to be determined under the provisions of the General Regulations referred to in paragraph (3)(b), those provisions ceased to apply to him.]

[¹(c) by virtue of paragraph (3) (f) he shall be re-entitled to such an addition of the same amount as previously if [³during the permitted period determined in accordance with regulation 2A (permitted period) beginning with the day after] the day on which he ceased to be so entitled the reason for the cessation ceased to apply to him.]

AMENDMENTS

1. Income Support (Transitional) Amendment Regulations 1988 (S.I. 1988 No. 521), reg. 10 (April 11, 1988).
2. Income Support (Transitional) Amendment No. 2 Regulations 1988 (S.I. 1988 No. 670), reg. 2(3) (April 11, 1988).
3. Income Support (Transitional) Amendment Regulations 1989 (S.I. 1989 No. 1626), reg. 4 (October 9, 1989).
4. Income Support (Transitional) Amendment Regulations 1991 (S.I. 1991 No. 1600), reg. 3 (October 1, 1991).

DEFINITIONS

"applicable amount"—see 1986 Act, s.84(1).
"claimant"—see General Regulations, reg. 2(1).
"domestic assistance addition"—see reg. 2(1).
"General Regulations"—*ibid.*
"income support"—*ibid.*
"transitional addition"—*ibid.*

GENERAL NOTE

The amounts of special transitional additions have been up-rated annually, most recently by 1.8 per cent. from April 10, 1995 under art. 19 of the Social Security Benefits Up-rating Order 1995 (S.I. 1995 No. 559).

Paragraph (3)
CIS 223/1993 (to be reported as *R(IS) 2/95*) decides that where a person's applicable amount is reduced to nil under para. 8 of Sched. 7, he has ceased to be entitled to income support. Since the reason for this was that his applicable amount (nil) no longer exceeded his income (also nil), the claimant could not bring himself within sub-para. (c). He therefore could not rely on para. (4)(a) (even if he met its other conditions) for the restoration of his special transitional addition on his release.

Persons not entitled to transitional additions

16.—(1) A person without accommodation shall not be entitled to a transitional addition, personal expenses addition or a special transitional addition.

(2) A person who is in board and lodging accommodation or a hostel shall not be entitled to a special transitional addition.

[¹(3) A prisoner within the meaning of regulation 21(3) of the General Regulations (special cases) shall not be entitled to a transitional addition, personal expenses addition or special transitional addition.]

AMENDMENT

1. Income Support (Transitional) Amendment Regulations 1988 (S.I. 1988 No. 521), reg. 11 (April 11, 1988).

DEFINITIONS

"General Regulations"—see reg. 2(1).

"personal expenses addition"—*ibid.*
"special transitional addition"—*ibid.*
"transitional addition"—*ibid.*

GENERAL NOTE

Paragraph (3)
See *CIS 255/1990* (to be reported as *R(IS) 1/94*) and *CIS 223/1993* (to be reported as *R(IS) 2/95*) in the notes to regs. 14 and 15.

Income Support (Transitional) Regulations 1988

(S.I. 1988 No. 1229)

Made by the Secretary of the State under s. 18(4) of the Social Security Act 1988

GENERAL NOTE

These regulations protect couples where one partner is less than 18 who were entitled to benefit on September 11, 1988. Reg. 4 allows advance decisions reviewing entitlement from September 12, 1988.

Citation, commencement and interpretation

1.—(1) These Regulations may be cited as the Income Support (Transitional) Regulations 1988 and shall come into force as follows—
  (a) regulations 1 and 4, on 5th August 1988;
  (b) regulations 2 and 3, on 12th September 1988.
  (2) In these Regulations "the General Regulations" means the Income Support (General) Regulations 1987 and unless the context otherwise requires the expressions used in these regulations shall have the same meaning as in the General Regulations.

Couples

2.—(1) This regulation applies where, on 11th September 1988—
  (a) the claimant is a member of a couple and has continued after that date to be a member of the same couple; and
  (b) the claimant is entitled to income support; and
  (c) the claimant is aged not less than 18; and
  (d) the other member of that couple is aged less than 18 and had ceased full-time education on or before 11th April 1988.
  (2) This regulation shall cease to apply where the member of the couple to whom paragraph (1)(d) above refers attains the age of 18.
  (3) Where this regulation applies—
  (a) the claimant's applicable amount for the purpose of determining his entitlement to income support shall be determined as if paragraph 1(3)(c) of Schedule 2 to the General Regulations (applicable amounts) applied and paragraph 1(3)(a), (b), (d), (e) and (f) of that Schedule shall not apply; and
  (b) regulation 23(4) of the General Regulations (calculation of income and capital) and paragraph 1(3) of Schedule 5 to the General Regulations (applicable amounts of persons in board and lodging accommodation or hostels) shall not apply.

Polygamous marriages

3.—(1) This regulation applies where, on 11th September 1988—

(a) the claimant is a member of a polygamous marriage and has continued after that date to be a member of that polygamous marriage; and

(b) the claimant is entitled to income support; and

(c) the claimant is aged not less than 18; and

(d) at least one other member of that marriage is aged less than 18 and had ceased full-time education on or before 11th April 1988

(2) This regulation shall cease to apply where the member of the polygamous marriage to whom paragraph (1)(d) above refers has, or if there is more than one such member, those members have, attained the age of 18.

(3) Where this regulation applies the claimant's applicable amount for the purpose of determining his entitlement to income support shall be determined as if regulations 18(2) and 23(5) of the General Regulations (polygamous marriages) did not apply.

Review of awards of income support

4.—(1) This regulation shall apply to a person who will be aged less than 18 on 12th September 1988.

(2) Any decision awarding income support to a person to whom this regulation applies may be reviewed under section 104 of the Social Security Act before 12th September 1988 as if—

(a) regulations 2 and 3 of these Regulations; and

(b) any amendments to the Act and any Regulations made under the Act to come into force not later than 12th September 1988,

were already in force.

(3) Any decision given on review in accordance with paragraph (2) shall have effect as from 12th September 1988.

Family Credit and Income Support (General) Amendment Regulations 1989

(S.I. 1989 No. 1034)

Made by the Secretary of State under ss.20(3)(a) and (d), 22(1), (8) and (9) and 84(1) of the Social Security Act 1986 and s.166(1) to (3A) of the Social Security Act 1975

[In force July 10, 1989]

Transitional provision

13. Where, immediately before the coming into force of regulation 4 of these Regulations, a person was entitled to income support by virtue of paragraph (2)(d) of regulation 13 of the Income Support Regulations, notwithstanding that he was to be treated as receiving relevant education under regulation 12 of those Regulations, that paragraph shall continue to apply to him as if the substitution made by regulation 4 of these Regulations had not been made for so long as he continues to satisfy the other conditions of entitlement to income support.

GENERAL NOTE

This regulation came into force on July 10, 1989, the same date as did the amendment to reg. 13 of the Income Support (General) Regulations. Anyone entitled under the old form of reg. 13(2)(d) on July 9, 1989, continues to have their entitlement determined under that provision. If there is any break in the claimant's satisfaction of the other conditions of entitlement to income support this transitional protection is lost. There can be a break in actual receipt of benefit providing that the conditions of entitlement are still met. But these conditions will include not only those set out in s.124(1) of the Contributions and Benefits Act (1986 Act, s.20(3)), but also the requirement to make a claim imposed by s.1 of the Administration Act (1975 Act, s.165A).

Social Security Benefits (Student Loans and Miscellaneous Amendments) Regulations 1990

(S.I. 1990 No. 1549)

Made by the Secretary of State under ss.20(3)(d), (8) and (12)(d), (g) to (i), 22(8) and (9), 29(3), 31C(3) and 84(1) of the Social Security Act 1986 and ss.17(2)(a), 20(3) and 166(1) to (3A) of the Social Security Act 1975

[In force September 1, 1990]

Transitional provision

7.—(1) Where, immediately before 1st September 1990, a student was entitled to housing benefit, income support or unemployment benefit, as the case may be, the Housing Benefit Regulations, the Income Support Regulations or the Unemployment Benefit Regulations, as the case may be, shall continue to apply to him as if the amendments made by regulation 4(2) to (6) and (9) to (11), 5(2) to (5) and (7) to (9) or 6 of these Regulations had not been made but only for the period ending immediately before the date on which he is due to start or is due to resume his course of study.

(2) In paragraph (1) the expression ''student'' has the same meaning as in the Housing Benefit Regulations, Income Support Regulations or Unemployment Benefit Regulations, as the case may be, as in force immediately before 1st September 1990.

GENERAL NOTE

The Housing Benefit Regulations are the Housing Benefit (General) Regulations 1987, the Income Support Regulations are the Income Support (General) Regulations 1987 and the Unemployment Benefit Regulations are the Social Security (Unemployment, Sickness and Invalidity Benefit) Regulations 1983.

Income Support (General) Amendment No. 4 Regulations 1991

(S.I. 1991 No. 1559)

Made by the Secretary of State under ss.20(3)(a) and (d)(i), (12)(c) and (d)(i), 22(1), (8), (9)(a) and (b) and 84(1) of the Social Security Act 1986 and s.166(1) to (3A) of the Social Security Act 1975

[In force, in relation to the amendments to reg. 6(a) of and to para. 6 of Sched. 1 to the General Regulations, on October 7, 1991, and in relation to the amendment to reg. 5(1) of the General Regulations, on April 7, 1992]

Saving provision

22.—(1) Where this regulation applies to a person, regulation 5 of, or, as the case may be, regulation 6(a) of, and paragraph 6 of Schedule 1 to, the General Regulations shall continue to apply to him until the occurrence of one of the events specified in regulation 23 of these Regulations as if the amendments made by regulation 3 or, as the case may be, regulations 4(a) and 13(b) of these Regulations, had not been made.

(2) This regulation applies to a person—

(a) who satisfied the relevant qualifying conditions in the week immediately preceding the date on which regulation 3 or, as the case may be, regulations 4(a) and 13(b) of these Regulations came into force; and

(b) who in that week was, or whose partner was, entitled to income support.

(3) This regulation applies to a person—

(a) who satisfied the relevant qualifying condition in at least one of the eight weeks immediately preceding the date on which regulation 3 or, as the case may be, regulations 4(a) and 13(b) of these Regulations came into force, but who did not satisfy that condition in the week immediately preceding that date; and

(b) who in the week in which he satisfied that condition was, or whose partner was, entitled to income support; and

(c) who in a week commencing not more than eight weeks after the date on which he last satisfied the relevant qualifying condition, again satisfies that condition and in that week he, or his partner, is entitled to income support.

(4) This regulation applies to a person—

(a) who, or whose partner, ceased to be entitled to income support because he, or his partner, became engaged in remunerative work for a period not exceeding the permitted period determined in accordance with regulation 24 of these Regulations and that period had commenced but had not ended before the coming into force of regulation 3 or regulations 4(a) and 13(b) of these Regulations, as the case may be; and

(b) who satisfied the relevant qualifying condition in the week immediately before that period commenced; and

(c) who in the week which commences immediately after the date on which that period ends, again satisfies the relevant qualifying condition and in that week he, or his partner, is entitled to income support.

(5) This regulation applies to a person—

(a) who, or whose partner, was entitled to income support immediately before he or his partner participated in arrangements for training made under section 2 of the Employment and Training Act 1973 or section 2 of the Enterprise and New Towns (Scotland) Act 1990 or attended a course at an employment rehabilitation centre established under section 2 of the Employment and Training Act 1973 and that training or course had commenced but had not ended before the coming into force of regulation 3 or regulations 4(a) and 13(b) of these Regulations, as the case may be; and

(b) who satisfied the relevant qualifying condition in the week immediately before the commencement of the period during which he or his partner participated in that training or attended that course; and

(c) who in a week commencing not more than eight weeks after the date on which that period ends, again satisfies the relevant qualifying condition and in that week he, or his partner, is entitled to income support.

(6) For the purpose of determining whether—

(a) regulation 5 of the General Regulations continues to apply to a person as if the amendment made thereto by regulation 3 of these Regulations had not been made, the relevant qualifying condition is that he is engaged in work, or where the hours of work fluctuate, engaged on average, for at least 16 hours but less than 24 hours a week; or

(b) regulation 6(a) of, and paragraph 6 of Schedule 1 to, the General Regulations continue to apply to a person as if the amendments made thereto by regulations 4(a) and 13(b) of these Regulations had not been made, the relevant qualifying condition is that he is engaged in work, he is mentally or physically disabled and his earning capacity is, by reason of that disability, reduced to 75 per cent. or less of what he would, but for that disability, be reasonably expected to earn.

(7) In this regulation and in regulations 23 and 24 of these Regulations except where the context otherwise requires, the terms used have the same meanings as in the General Regulations.

Circumstances in which regulation 22 ceases to apply

23.—(1) Subject to paragraph (2) of this regulation, regulation 22 of these Regulations shall cease to apply to a person if—

  (a) he ceases to satisfy the relevant qualifying condition; or

  (b) he, or his partner, ceases to be entitled to income support,

for a period in excess of eight consecutive weeks.

(2) For the purposes of paragraph (1) of this regulation—

  (a) except where sub-paragraph (b) of this paragraph applies, in a case where the person, or his partner, ceases to be entitled to income support because he, or his partner, becomes engaged in remunerative work, no account shall be taken of any period during which he, or his partner, was not entitled to income support, not exceeding the permitted period determined in accordance with regulation 24 of these Regulations;

  (b) no account shall be taken of—

    (i) any period during which the person, or his partner, was participating in arrangements for training made under section 2 of the Employment and Training Act 1973 or section 2 of the Enterprise and New Towns (Scotland) Act 1990 or attending a course at an employment rehabilitation centre established under section 2 of the Employment and Training Act 1973; and

    (ii) a further period not exceeding eight consecutive weeks commencing immediately after the end of the period referred to in head (i) of this sub-paragraph.

Permitted period

24.—(1) For the purposes of regulations 22 and 23 of these Regulations, where a person has ceased to be entitled to income support—

  (a) because he, or his partner, becomes engaged in remunerative work the permitted period, subject to paragraph (2) of this regulation, shall be twelve weeks; or

  (b) for any other reason, the permitted period shall be eight weeks.

(2) Subject to paragraph (3) of this regulation, where that person, or his partner, has ceased to be engaged in the remunerative work referred to in paragraph (1)(a) of this regulation the permitted period shall be eight weeks if—

  (a) that person's weekly applicable amount is reduced under regulation 22 of the General Regulations (reductions in applicable amounts in certain cases of actual or notional unemployment benefit disqualification) because of the cessation of that work; or

  (b) that person, or his partner, has ceased to be engaged in that work within 6 weeks of beginning it; or

  (c) at any time during the period of 26 weeks immediately preceding the beginning of that work, the person who has ceased to be so engaged—

    (i) was engaged in remunerative work; or

    (ii) was in relevant education; or

    (iii) was a student.

(3) Paragraph (2)(b) or (c) of this regulation shall not apply if, by virtue of section 20A(2) of the Social Security Act 1975 (exemptions from disqualification for unemployment benefit), the person who has ceased to be engaged in

remunerative work is exempted from disqualification for receiving unemployment benefit.

Income Support (General) Amendment No. 6 Regulations 1991

(S.I. 1991 No. 2334)

Made by the Secretary of State under ss.22(1) and 84(1) of the Social Security Act 1986 and s.166(1) to (3A) of the Social Security Act 1975

[In force November 11, 1991]

Saving Provision in relation to Severe Disability Premium

4.—(1)The provisions of this regulation are subject to regulation 5.

(2) Where paragraph (3), (4), (5) or (6) applies to a claimant, sub-paragraph (2)(a)(ii), or, as the case may be, sub-paragraph (2)(b)(iii) of paragraph 13 of Schedule 2 to the General Regulations shall have effect as if the relevant amendment had not been made.

(3) This paragraph applies to a claimant who satisfied both the qualifying conditions in the week immediately preceding 21st October 1991.

(4) This paragraph applies to a claimant—

(a) who satisfied both the qualifying conditions in at least one of the eight weeks immediately preceding 21st October 1991, but did not satisfy either or both of those conditions in the week immediately preceding that date; and

(b) who in a week commencing not more than eight weeks after the date on which he last satisfied both the qualifying conditions, would again have satisfied both those conditions if the relevant amendment had not been made.

(5) This paragraph applies to a claimant—

(a) who ceased to be entitled to income support because he became engaged in remunerative work for a period not exceeding the permitted period determined in accordance with regulation 6 and that period had commenced but had not ended before 21st October 1991; and

(b) who satisfied both the qualifying conditions in the week ending on the day before the first day of that period commenced; and

(c) who in the week which commences on the day immediately following the day on which that period ends, would again have satisfied both the qualifying conditions if the relevent amendment had not been made.

(6) This paragraph applies to a claimant—

(a) who satisfied both the qualifying conditions immediately before he—

    (i) participated in arrangements for training made under section 2 of the Employment and Training Act 1973 or section 2 of the Enterprise and New Towns (Scotland) Act 1990; or

    (ii) attended a course at an employment rehabilitation centre established under section 2 of the Employment and Training Act 1973,

and he had begun the training or joined the course before 21st October 1991 and was still continuing with the training or course at that date; and

(b) who in the week which commences on the day immediately following the last day he attended the training or course, would again have satisfied both the qualifying conditions if the relevant amendment had not been made.

(7) The "qualifying conditions" means the two qualifying conditions set out in paragraph (8)(a) and (b) below.

(8) For the purposes of paragraph (7)—

(a) the first qualifying condition is that the claimant—

    (i) has made a claim for income support which has not been determined, but had it been determined and an award made, his applicable amount would have included severe disability premium; or

    (ii) has a current award of income support and the applicable amount appropriate to that award includes severe disability premium; or

    (iii) has a current award of income support and has before 21st October 1991 made an application in writing in accordance with section 104(2) of the Social Security Act requesting a review of that award, where the ground, or one of the grounds for review, is that—

        (aa) he has become a co-owner with a close relative of the dwelling which he and that close relative jointly occupy as their home; or

        (bb) he has become jointly liable with a close relative to make payments to a landlord in respect of the dwelling which he and that close relative jointly occupy as their home,

whether or not there are other co-owners or other persons jointly liable to make such payments and, if revised, the applicable amount appropriate to the award includes severe disability premium in respect of a period prior to that date;

(b) the second qualifying condition is that the person is—

    (i) a co-owner, with a close relative, of the dwelling he and that close relative jointly occupy as their home, whether or not there are other co-owners; or

    (ii) jointly liable, with a close relative, to make payments to a landlord in respect of the dwelling he and that close relative jointly occupy as their home, whether or not there are other persons jointly liable to make such payments.

[¹(9) For the purposes of paragraph (8)(b) and regulation 5(2)(b), where a person has satisfied the second qualifying condition, but his circumstances change so that he no longer satisfies it, he shall nonetheless be treated as satisfying it for so long as he is a person to whom paragraph (10) applies.

(10) This paragraph applies to a person—

(a) who was, together with a close relative of his, either a co-owner of, or jointly liable to make payments to a landlord in respect of, the dwelling which he and that close relative jointly occupied as their home; and

(b) who has since become, with that close relative or any other close relative, either—

    (i) jointly liable to make payments to a landlord in respect of that dwelling or any other dwelling; or

    (ii) a co-owner of that dwelling or any other dwelling,

which he and the close relative jointly occupy as their home (whether or not there are other co-owners, or other persons jointly liable to make such payments).]

AMENDMENT

1. Income-related Benefits Schemes (Miscellaneous Provisions) Amendment Regulations 1991 (S.I. 1991 No. 2695), reg. 5 (December 27, 1991).

DEFINITIONS

"claimant"—see General Regulations, reg. 2(1).
"close relative"—*ibid.*
"dwelling occupies as the home"—*ibid.*
"partner"—*ibid.*
"permitted period"—see reg. 6.

"relevant amendment"—see General Note.
"remunerative work"—see General Regulations, reg. 2(1).
"Social Security Act"—*ibid.*

GENERAL NOTE

The 'relevant amendment' is the amendment to the definition of non-dependant in reg. 3 of the Income Support (General) Regulations with effect from November 11, 1991, by reg. 2 of these Regulations (reg. 1(3)). These Regulations were made on October 21, 1991, which is why that is the date used in reg. 4 to fix the transitional protection. Reg. 4 allows existing claimants to continue to receive the benefit of the severe disability premium where they previously met the new conditions for joint occupiers of the home, except that the joint occupation was with a close relative.

Reg. 5 defines when the protection of reg. 4 ceases to apply.

Circumstances in which regulation 4 ceases to apply

5.—(1) Regulation 4 shall cease to apply to a claimant, or his partner, on the relevant day and shall not apply on any day thereafter.

(2) The relevant day is the first day after a period of eight consecutive weeks throughout which—

(a) subject to paragraph (3), he is not entiled to income support; or

(b) he is unable to satisfy, or be treated as satisfying, the second qualifying condition.

(3) For the purpose of calculating a period in excess of eight weeks in paragraph (2)(a) above the following periods shall be disregarded—

(a) where the claimant, or his partner, becomes engaged in remunerative work, any period during which he, or his partner, was not entitled to income support, not exceeding the permitted period determined in accordance with regulation 6;

(b) any period during which the claimant, or his partner, was participating in arrangements for training made under section 2 of the Employment and Training Act 1973 or section 2 of the Enterprise and New Towns (Scotland) Act 1990 or attending a course at an employment rehabilitation centre established under section 2 of the Employment and Training Act 1973.

DEFINITIONS

"claimant"—see General Regulations, reg. 2(1).
"partner"—*ibid.*
"permitted period"—see reg. 6.
"qualifying condition"—see reg. 4(7).

Definition of 'permitted period' for the purposes of regulations 4 and 5

6.—(1) For the purposes of regulations 4(5) and 5(3)(a), where a claimant has ceased to be entitled to income support because he or his partner became engaged in remunerative work, subject to paragraph (2), the permitted period shall be a period of 12 consecutive weeks.

(2) Subject to paragraph (3), where that claimant, or his partner, has ceased to be engaged in the remunerative work referred to in paragraph (1) above the permitted period shall be eight weeks where—

(a) the claimant's weekly applicable amount is reduced under regulation 22 of the General Regulations (reductions in applicable amounts in certain cases of actual or notional unemployment benefit disqualification) because of the cessation of that work; or

(b) the claimant, or his partner, has ceased to be engaged in that work within 6 weeks of the day he started it; or

(c) at any time during the period of 26 weeks immediately preceding the day he started that work, the claimant, or his partner, who has ceased to be so engaged—
   (i) was engaged in remunerative work; or
   (ii) was in relevant education; or
   (iii) was a student.

(3) Paragraph (2)(b) or (c) shall not apply if, by virtue of section 20A(2) of the Social Security Act 1975 [SSCBA, s.29(2)] (exemptions from disqualification for unemployment benefit), the claimant who has ceased to be engaged in remunerative work is exempted from disqualification for receiving unemployment benefit.

DEFINITIONS

"claimant"—see General Regulations, reg. 2(1).
"partner"—*ibid.*
"relevant education"—see General Regulations, reg. 12.
"remunerative work"—see General Regulations, reg. 2(1).
"student"—*ibid.*

Income Support (General) Amendment Regulations 1992

(S.I. 1992 No. 468)

Made by the Secretary of State under ss.20(3)(a) and (d) and (12)(c), (d)(i), (f) and (k), 22(1), (8) and (9) and 84(1) of the Social Security Act 1986, s.166(1) to (3A) of the Social Security Act 1975 and s.5(1) of the Disability Living Allowance and Disability Working Allowance Act 1991

[In force April 6, 1992]

Saving provision for children and young persons working 16 or more, but less than 24, hours a week

10.—(1) Paragraph (2) below shall apply subject to paragraph (3) below where in the benefit week which in relation to a particular claimant commences on or after 7th April but before 14th April 1992, a child or young person in respect of whom a sum is brought into account in determining the claimant's applicable amount would but for this regulation—
   (a) be engaged in remunerative work by reason of the fact that the work in which he is engaged, or where his hours of work fluctuate, in which he is engaged on average, amounts to 16 or more but less than 24 hours a week, being work for which payment is made or which is done in expectation of payment; and
   (b) have earnings from that work which fall to be disregarded in accordance with regulation 44(6) of and paragraph 15 of Schedule 8 to the General Regulations.

(2) Where this paragraph applies, regulation 5(1) of the General Regulations (persons treated as engaged in remunerative work) shall have effect in relation to the child or young person mentioned in paragraph (1) above as if for the reference to 16 hours there was substitued a reference to 24 hours; so however that this paragraph shall not apply in relation to him on any day on which he is neither a child nor a young person.

(3) Paragraph (2) above shall not apply where, in relation to the particular claimant, the benefit week mentioned in paragraph (1) above is his first benefit week pursuant to the claim.

(4) In this regulation, the expression 'young person' has the same meaning as it has in the General Regulations (by virtue of regulation 14).

DEFINITIONS

"child"—see 1986 Act, s.20(11) (SSCBA, s.137(1)).
"the General Regulations"—the Income Support (General) Regulations 1987 (reg. 1(4)).

GENERAL NOTE

Normally any earnings of a child or young person who is a member of the claimant's family are completely disregarded (General Regulations, Sched. 8, para. 14). But under para. 15 of Sched. 8, as amended from April 1992, if the child or young person has ceased actually to be in relevant education and is treated as continuing in relevant education up to the next "terminal date," earnings from employment for more hours than the limit for part-time work are not completely disregarded. Before April 1992 the limit was 24 hours. On April 7, 1992, it changed to 16 hours. This provision protects the position of a claimant with a child or young person in this position who was working for less than 24 hours a week, but more than 16 hours a week, immediately before the change. The protection is short-lived, as the status of child or young person will expire when the terminal date is reached.

Introduction of disability living allowance

11.—(1) Any payment of disability living allowance made pursuant to the Social Security Act 1975 [SSCBA] which, in accordance with regulation 31 of the General Regulations is treated as paid on a day before this regulation comes into force, shall be treated for the purposes of Parts V and VI of those Regulations (which contain provisions for the calculation of income and capital)—
- (a) as a payment of mobility allowance, to the extent that it consists of mobility component; and
- (b) as a payment of attendance allowance, to the extent that it consists of care component.

(2) Where—
- (a) on or after the date this regulation comes into force a payment falls to be made and that payment includes an amount in respect both of disability living allowance and of attendance allowance, mobility allowance or both ('the former benefits'); and
- (b) payment of disability living allowance and the former benefits would but for this regulation be regarded, pursuant to regulation 29(2) of the General Regulations as being made for concurrent periods commencing on the same day,

then that regulation shall have effect as if the payment falling to be made consisted solely of disability living allowance.

(3) In this regulation—
- (a) attendance allowance means an attendance allowance under section 35 of the Social Security Act 1975 [SSCBA, s.64];
- (b) mobility allowance means an allowance under section 37A of that Act;
- (c) disability living allowance means an allowance under section 37ZA of that Act [SSCBA, s.71]; and
- (d) any reference to the day the regulation comes into force is a reference to the day determined, in the particular case, in accordance with regulation 1(2) above.

DEFINITION

"the General Regulations"—the Income Support (General) Regulations 1987 (reg. 1(4)).

Income Support (General) Amendment (No. 2) Regulations 1993

(S.I. 1993 No. 1219)

Made by the Secretary of State under ss.135(1), 137(1) and 175(1) to (5) of the Social Security Contributions and Benefits Act 1992

[In force May 31, 1993]

Transitional provisions

3. Where—
(a) on 31st May 1993 a person is temporarily absent from a home, and his absence forms part of a period which on that day exceeded 6 days, and
(b) before that day paragraph 2A of Schedule 2 to the principal Regulations as in force on 30th May 1993 applied to him,
he shall be treated for the purposes of paragraph 2A of Schedule 2 to the principal Regulations, as amended by regulation 2 above, as if his first day of absence was 31st May 1993.

GENERAL NOTE

See the notes to para. 2A of Sched. 2 to the Income Support (General) Regulations. Para. 2A of Sched. 2 was amended by reg. 2 of these Regulations on May 31, 1993.

Income Support (General) Amendment No. 3 Regulations 1993

(S.I. 1993 No. 1679)

Made by the Secretary of State under ss.135(1), 136(5)(b), 137(1) and 175(1) to (4) of the Social Security Contributions and Benefits Act 1992

[In force August 2, 1993]

Reg. 2

(4) In the case of a claimant who was entitled to income support by virtue of regulation 70 of the Income Support Regulations for the benefit week which includes 2nd August 1993, then in respect of each day after that date on which the claimant's entitlement to income support continues, regulation 70 shall continue to apply in his case as if the preceding provisions of this regulation had not been made.

GENERAL NOTE

See the notes to reg. 70(3). Reg. 70(3) was amended by reg. 2(1) to (3) of these Regulations on August 2, 1993.

Saving

4.—(1) In the case of a claimant who was entitled to income support for the benefit week which included 2nd August 1993 then, but subject to paragraph (3), in respect of each day after that date on which the claimant's entitlement to income support continues, Schedule 3 to the Income Support Regulations shall continue to apply in his case as if regulation 3 of these Regulations had not been made.

(2) Heads (c) to (f) of sub-paragraph (9) of paragraph 7 of Schedule 3 to the Income Support Regulations shall apply to paragraph (1) above as they apply to sub-paragraph (1) of paragraph 7, but with the modification that for the words "in receipt of income support", wherever they occur, there were substituted the words "entitled to income support" and that the words "Subject to sub-paragraphs (10) and (11)" were omitted.

(3) In its application to any loan taken out or increased after 2nd August 1993 Schedule 3 to the Income Support Regulations shall have effect as amended by regulation 3 of these Regulations.

(4) Paragraphs (1) and (3) above shall apply as from 11th April 1994 as if for the references to "2nd August 1993" wherever they occur there were substituted references to "11th April 1994".

GENERAL NOTE

See the notes to para. 7(6B) to (6F) of Sched. 3 to the Income Support (General) Regulations. Para. 7 of Sched. 3 was amended by reg. 3 of these regulations on August 2, 1993.

Income-related Benefits Schemes (Miscellaneous Amendments) (No. 3) Regulations 1994

(S.I. 1994 No. 1807)

Made by the Secretary of State under ss.131(3)(b), 135(1), 137(1) and (2)(i) and 175(1), (3) and (4) of the Social Security Contributions and Benefits Act 1992

[In force August 1, 1994]

Reg. 4

(2) The provisions of this regulation shall only apply in the case of a claimant who was entitled to income support on 31st July 1994 where a claim for income support is made or treated as made by or in respect of him after that date, and where those provisions do apply they shall apply from the first day of the period in respect of which that claim is made.

GENERAL NOTE

See the note to the amendment to reg. 21(3) of the Income Support Regulations inserted by reg. 4(1) of these regulations.

Where there is a change of circumstances a claimant may be required to fill in a new claim form for administrative purposes, but this is not necessarily a new or repeat claim. If a person is protected by this provision and there is a review of his claim (*e.g.* because of a change of circumstances) he should continue to have the benefit of that protection.

Disability Working Allowance and Income Support (General) Amendment Regulations 1995

(S.I. 1995 No. 482)

Made by the Secretary of State under ss.124(1)(d)(i) and (3), 129(2B)(b) and (c) and (8), 135(1), 137(1) and 175(1), (3) and (4) of the Social Security Contributions and Benefits Act 1992 and s.12(1) of the Social Security (Incapacity for Work) Act 1994

[In force April 13, 1995]

Transitional provisions with respect to the Income Support Regulations

19.—(1) Sickness benefit shall be a qualifying benefit for the purposes of regulation 9(2)(a)(i) of the Income Support Regulations, and for this purpose "sickness benefit" means sickness benefit under section 31 of the Social Security Contributions and Benefits Act 1992 as in force on 12th April 1995.

(2) Where the disability premium was applicable to a claimant on 12th April 1995 by virtue of paragraph 12(1)(b) of Schedule 2 to the Income Support Regulations as in force on that date, the disability premium shall continue to be applicable to that claimant for so long as paragraph 12(1)(b)(i) of that Schedule applies to him.

(3) Paragraph (2) shall not apply to a claimant to whom paragraph 12(1)(b)(i) of Schedule 2 to the Income Support Regulations has ceased to apply for a period of more than 56 continuous days.

(4) Where on 12th April 1995 paragraph 5 of Schedule 1 to the Income Support Regulations (persons incapable of work) as in force on that date applied to a claimant, but the disability premium was not applicable to him, that claimant shall be treated for the purposes of paragraph 12(1) of Schedule 2 to the Income Support Regulations as if, throughout the period that paragraph 5 of Schedule 1 had applied to him, paragraph 12(1)(b)(i) of Schedule 2 applied to him.

(5) Where an adjudication officer on or after 13th April 1995, determines that a claimant fails to satisfy the incapacity for work test, in accordance with regulations made under section 171C of the Contributions and Benefits Act (the all work test), on its first application to the claimant concerned, and the claimant, immediately prior to that date, was either—

(a) incapable of work and had been so for a continuous period of 28 weeks in circumstances to which paragraph 5 of Schedule 1 of the Income Support Regulations refers (persons incapable of work not required to be available for employment); or

(b) in receipt of invalidity benefit or severe disablement allowance,

then, in a case in which either regulations 8(2A) or 11(2A) of the Income Support Regulations applies (persons not required to be available for employment and registration for employment), notwithstanding regulation 22(1A) and (5A) of the Income Support Regulations (reductions in applicable amounts), the amount of any income support to which the claimant is entitled shall be calculated in accordance with regulation 17 of those Regulations.

Savings with respect to the Income Support Regulations

20.—(1) Where a person was not required to be available for employment on 12th April 1995 by virtue of regulation 8(2) of the Income Support Regulations as in force on that date, that regulation shall continue to apply in that person's case as if regulation 6 of these Regulations had not been made.

(2) Where a claimant was not required to register for employment on 12th April 1995 by virtue of regulation 11(2) of the Income Support Regulations as in force on that date, that regulation shall continue to apply in that claimant's case as if regulation 8 of these Regulations had not been made.

(3) Where a claimant appeals against a decision of an adjudication officer that he is not incapable of work, and that decision was made on or before 12th April 1995, regulations 8 and 11 of the Income Support Regulations shall apply in that claimant's case as if these Regulations had not been made.

(4) Where the higher pensioner premium was applicable to a claimant on, or at any time during the 8 weeks immediately preceding, 12th April 1995 by virtue of paragraph 12(1)(c)(i) of Schedule 2 to the Income Support Regulations

as in force on that date, paragraph 12 of that Schedule shall continue to apply in that claimant's case as if regulation 16 of these Regulations had not been made.

GENERAL NOTE

These transitional and saving provisions relate to some of the amendments made to the Income Support Regulations as a consequence of the introduction of incapacity benefit and the new tests for deciding incapacity for work from April 13, 1995. See the notes to those regulations.

Income-related Benefits Schemes (Miscellaneous Amendments) Regulations 1995

(S.I. 1995 No. 516)

Made by the Secretary of State under ss.123(1)(a) to (c), 128(5), 129(4) and (8), 135(1), 136(3), (5)(a) and (b), 137(1), (2)(c) and (d)(i) and 175(1), (3) and (4) of the Social Security Contributions and Benefits Act 1992

[In force April 10, 1995]

Saving

28.—(1) In the case of a claimant who was entitled to income support for the benefit week which included 9th April 1995 then, but subject to paragraph (3), in respect of each day after that date on which the claimant's entitlement to income support continues, Schedule 3 to the Income Support Regulations shall continue to have effect as though regulation 25(c) of these Regulations had not been made.

(2) Heads (c) to (f) of sub-paragraph (9) of paragraph 7 of Schedule 3 to the Income Support Regulations shall apply to paragraph (1) above as they apply to sub-paragraph (1) of paragraph 7, but with the modification that for the words "in receipt of income support", wherever they appear, there were substituted the words "entitled to income support" and that the words "Subject to sub-paragraphs (10) and (11)" were omitted.

(3) In its application to any loan taken out or increased after 9th April 1995, Schedule 3 to the Income Support Regulations shall have effect as amended by regulation 25(c) of these Regulations.

DEFINITION

"claimant"—see General Regulations, reg. 2(1).

GENERAL NOTE

See the notes to para. 7(6B) to (6F) of Sched. 3 to the Income Support (General) Regulations. Para. 7(6C) of Sched. 3 was amended by reg. 25(c) of these Regulations on April 10, 1995.

Housing Benefit, Council Tax Benefit and Income Support (Amendments) Regulations 1995

(S.I. 1995 No. 625)

Made by the Secretary of State under ss.123(1)(d) and (e), 131(11), 135(1), 137(1) and (2)(h) and (i) and 175(1) and (3) to (6) of the Social Security Contributions and Benefits Act 1992 and ss.5(1)(k) and 6(1)(l) of the Social Security Administration Act 1992

[In force April 1, 1995]

Saving

7. In the case of a claimant who is absent from the dwelling he normally occupies as his home before the coming into force of these Regulations, regulation 5 of the Housing Benefit Regulations and paragraph 4 of Schedule 3 to the Income Support Regulations shall have effect, while that absence continues, as if regulation 2 or 5, as the case may be, of these Regulations had not been made.

DEFINITION

"claimant"—see General Regulations, reg. 2(1).

GENERAL NOTE

See the notes to para. 4 of Sched. 3 to the Income Support (General) Regulations. Para. 4 of Sched. 3 was amended by reg. 5 of these Regulations on April 10, 1995.

Community Charges (Deductions from Income Support) (No. 2) Regulations 1990

(S.I. 1990 No. 545)

Made by the Secretary of State under ss.22(3) and 146(6) and Sched. 4 para. 6 of the Local Government Finance Act 1988

GENERAL NOTE

The first version of these Regulations (S.I. 1990 No. 107) was defective and has been replaced.
The Community Charges (Deductions from Income Support) (Scotland) Regulations 1989 (S.I. 1989 No. 507) made provision for Scotland from April 10, 1989. They have been amended by S.I. 1990 No. 113 to bring them into line with these Regulations, but are not reproduced.

Citation, commencement and interpretation

1.—(1) These Regulations may be cited as the Community Charges (Deductions from Income Support) (No. 2) Regulations 1990 and shall come into force on 1st April 1990.

(2) In these Regulations, unless the context otherwise requires—
"the 1975 Act" means the Social Security Act 1975;
"the 1986 Act" means the Social Security Act 1986;
"adjudication officer" means an officer appointed in accordance with section 97(1) of the 1975 Act [SSAA, s.38];
"appropriate social security office" means an office of the Department of Social Security which is normally open to the public for the receipt of claims for income support and includes an office of the Department of Employment which is normally open to the public for the receipt of claims for unemployment benefit;
"Commissioner" means the Chief or any other Social Security Commissioner appointed in accordance with section 97(3) of the 1975 Act or section 13(5) of the Social Security Act 1980 [SSAA, s.52], and includes a Tribunal of 3 Commissioners constituted in accordance with section 116 of the 1975 Act [SSAA, s.57];
"couple" means a married or unmarried couple;
"debtor" means a person against whom a liability order has been obtained;
"5 per cent. of the personal allowance for a single claimant aged not less than 25" and

"5 per cent. of the personal allowance for a couple where both members are
aged not less than 18" means, in each case, where the percentage is not
a multiple of 5 pence, the sum obtained by rounding that 5 per cent. to
the next higher such multiple;

"income support" means income support within the meaning of the 1986
Act;

"liability order" means an order under regulation 29 of the Community
Charges (Administration and Enforcement) Regulations 1989;

"married couple" has the meaning ascribed to it in section 20(11) of the
1986 Act [SSCBA, s.137(1)];

"payments to third parties" means direct payments to third parties in accordance with Schedule 9 to the Social Security (Claims and Payments)
Regulations 1987;

"polygamous marriage" means a marriage to which section 22B of the Social
Security Act 1986 [SSCBA, s.133] refers;

"single debtor" means a debtor who is not a member of a couple;

"tribunal", except in relation to a Tribunal of 3 Commissioners, means a
social security appeal tribunal constituted in accordance with section
97(2) to (2E) of the 1975 Act [SSAA, s.41]; and

"unmarried couple" has the meaning ascribed to it in section 20(11) of the
1986 Act [SSCBA, s.137(1)].

(3) Unless the context otherwise requires, any reference in these Regulations
to a numbered regulation or Schedule is a reference to the regulation and Schedule bearing that number in the Regulations and any reference in a regulation or
Schedule to a numbered paragraph is a reference to the paragraph of that regulation or Schedule having that number.

Deductions from income support

2.—(1) Where a debtor is entitled to income support, an authority may apply
to the Secretary of State by sending an application in respect of the debtor or,
where a liability order is made against a couple in respect of both of the couple,
to an appropriate social security office asking the Secretary of State to deduct
sums from any amount payable to the debtor, or as the case may be either of
the couple by way of income support.

(2) An application from an authority shall be in writing and shall contain the
following particulars—

(a) the name and address of the debtor or where the liability order is made
against a couple, the names and address of both of them;

(b) the name and place of the court which made the liability order;

(c) the date when the liability order was made;

(d) the total amount of the arrears specified in the liability order;

(e) the total amount which the authority wishes to have deducted from
income support.

(3) Where it appears to the Secretary of State that an application from an
authority gives insufficient particulars to enable the debtor to be identified he
may require the authority to furnish such further particulars as may reasonably
be required.

(4) Subject to paragraph (5), where the Secretary of State receives an application from an authority, he shall refer it to an adjudication officer who shall
determine the following questions—

(a) whether there is sufficient entitlement to income support to enable the
Secretary of State to make any deduction—

(i) where a liability order is made against a single debtor, or a debtor
who is a member of a couple, or a member of a polygamous marriage, at a rate of 5 per cent. of the personal allowance set out in

Schedule 2 to the Income Support (General) Regulations 1987, [²paragraph 1(1)(e)] (single claimant aged not less than 25); or

   (ii) where a liability order is made against a couple and income support is payable in respect of both of them, at a rate of 5 per cent. of the personal allowance set out in Schedule 2 to the Income Support (General) Regulations 1987, paragraph 1(3)(c) (couple where both members are aged not less than 18),

and, if the amount payable by way of income support to the debtor were to be 10 pence or more after any such deduction, the adjudication officer shall determine that there is sufficient entitlement;

  (b) the priority of any sum to be deducted as against any payments to third parties where there is insufficient entitlement to income support to meet both the deduction in respect of arrears of community charges and those payments to third parties, and the following priorities shall apply—

    [¹(zi) any liability mentioned in regulation 34A of the Social Security (Claims and Payments) Regulation 1987 (mortgage interest);]

    (i) any liability mentioned in paragraph 3 of Schedule 9 (housing costs) to the Social Security (Claims and Payments) Regulations 1987;

    (ii) any liability mentioned in paragraph 5 of Schedule 9 (service charges for fuel, and rent not falling within paragraph 2(1)(a)) to those Regulations;

    (iii) any liability mentioned in paragraph 6 of Schedule 9 (fuel costs) to those Regulations;

    (iv) any liability mentioned in paragraph 7 of Schedule 9 (water charges) to those Regulations;

    (v) any liability for arrears in respect of community charges,

and the adjudication officer shall determine these questions so far as is practical within 14 days of receipt of the reference.

(5) Where at the time the Secretary of State is making deductions in respect of an application from an authority he receives one or more further applications [²or one or more applications under regulation 2 of the Council Tax (Deductions from Income Support) Regulations 1993] from an authority in respect of the person from whom the deductions are being made, he shall refer those further applications to the adjudication officer in accordance with the following order of priority, namely, the one bearing the earliest date shall be referred first and each subsequent application shall be referred, one at a time and in date order, only after deductions under any earlier application have ceased.

(6) Subject to any right of appeal or review under these Regulations, the decision of the adjudication officer shall be final.

AMENDMENTS

1. Social Security (Claims and Payments) Amendment Regulation 1992 (S.I. 1992 No. 1026), reg. 7 (May 25, 1992).
2. Social Security (Claims and Payments) Amendment (No. 3) Regulations 1993 (S.I. 1993 No. 2113), reg. 5 (September 27, 1993).

DEFINITIONS

"adjudication officer"—see reg. 1(2).
"authority"—see Local Government Finance Act 1988, s.144.
"appropriate social security officer"—see reg. 1(2).
"couple"—*ibid.*
"debtor"—*ibid.*
"5 per cent. of the personal allowance for a single claimant aged not less than 25"—*ibid.*
"5 per cent. of the personal allowance for a couple where both members are aged not less than 18"—*ibid.*
"income support"—*ibid.*

"liability order"—*ibid.*
"payments to third parties"—*ibid.*
"polygamous marriage"—*ibid.*

GENERAL NOTE

R(IS) 3/92 holds that if the Secretary of State accepts the validity of an application under para. (2), the AO or SSAT must also accept it.

Notification of decision

3. The Secretary of State shall notify the debtor in writing of the adjudication officer's decision as soon as is practicable after he receives that decision and at the same time he shall notify the debtor of his right of appeal.

DEFINITIONS

"adjudication officer"—see reg. 1(2).
"debtor"—*ibid.*

Circumstances, time of making and termination of deductions

4.—(1) The Secretary of State shall make deductions from income support only—
   (a) where the debtor is entitled to income support throughout any benefit week and the amount to which he is entitled is sufficient to enable him to make the deductions; and
   (b) in respect of one application at a time.
   (2) The Secretary of State shall make deductions from income support at a time which corresponds to the payment of income support to the debtor and he shall cease making deductions when—
   (a) a payment to a third party has priority;
   (b) there is insufficient entitlement to income support to enable him to make the deduction;
   (c) entitlement to income support ceases;
   (d) an authority withdraws its application for deductions to be made; or
   (e) the debt in respect of which he was making the deductions is discharged.
   (3) Payments shall be made to the authority at such intervals as the Secretary of State may decide.

DEFINITIONS

"adjudication officer"—see reg. 1(2).
"authority"—see Local Government Finance Act 1988, s.144.
"debtor"—see reg. 1(2).
"income support"—*ibid.*

Appeal

5.—(1) Where the adjudication officer has decided a question under regulation 2(4), the debtor may appeal to a tribunal.
   (2) Subject to paragraph (5), an appeal lies to a Commissioner from any decision of a tribunal on the grounds that the decision of that tribunal was erroneous in point of law and the persons who may appeal are the debtor and the adjudication officer.
   (3) If it appears to the Chief Commissioner or, in the case of his inability to act, to such other of the Commissioners as he may have nominated to act for that purpose, that an appeal falling to be heard by one of the Commissioners

involves a question of law of special difficulty, he may direct that the appeal be dealt with, not by that Commissioner alone but by a Tribunal consisting of any 3 of the Commissioners and if the decision is not unanimous, the decision of the majority shall be the decision of the Tribunal.

(4) Subject to paragraph (5), an appeal on a question of law lies to the Court of Appeal from any decision of a Commissioner on a question of law and the persons who may appeal are—

(a) the debtor;

(b) the adjudication officer; and

(c) the Secretary of State.

(5) No appeal lies—

(a) to the Commissioner from a decision of a tribunal without the leave of the chairman of the tribunal which gave the decision or, if he refuses leave, without the leave of the Commissioner, or

(b) to the Court of Appeal from a decision of a Commissioner, without the leave of the Commissioner who decided the case, or if he refuses, without the leave of the Court of Appeal.

(6) Where in any case it is impracticable, or it would be likely to cause undue delay for an application for leave to appeal against a decision of a tribunal to be determined by the person who was the chairman of that tribunal, that application shall be determined by any other person qualified under section 97(2D) of the 1975 Act [SSAA, s.41(4)] to act as a chairman of tribunals.

(7) In a case where the Chief Commissioner considers that it is impracticable, or would be likely to cause undue delay, for an application for leave to appeal to the Court of Appeal to be determined by the Commissioner who decided the case, that application shall be determined—

(a) where the decision was a decision of an individual Commissioner, by the Chief Commissioner or a Commissioner selected by the Chief Commissioner, and

(b) where the decision was a decision of a Tribunal of Commissioners, by a differently constituted Tribunal of Commissioners selected by the Chief Commissioner.

(8) If the office of Chief Commissioner is vacant, or if the Chief Commissioner is unable to act, paragraph (7) shall have effect as if the expression "the Chief Commissioner" referred to such other of the Commissioners as may have been nominated to act for the purpose either by the Chief Commissioner or, if he has not made such nomination, by the Lord Chancellor.

DEFINITIONS

"adjudication officer"—see reg. 1(2).
"Commissioner"—*ibid.*
"debtor"—*ibid.*
"tribunal"—*ibid.*

Review

6.—(1) Any decision under these Regulations of an adjudication officer, a tribunal or a Commissioner may be reviewed at any time by an adjudication officer if—

(a) the officer is satisfied that the decision was given in ignorance of, or was based on a mistake as to, some material fact; or

(b) there has been a relevant change of circumstances since the decision was given.

(2) Any decision of an adjudication officer may be reviewed by an adjudication officer on the grounds that the decision was erroneous in point of law.

(3) A question may be raised with a view to review under this regulation by means of an application in writing to an adjudication officer, stating the grounds of the application.

(4) On receipt of any such application, the adjudication officer shall take it into consideration and, so far as is practicable, dispose of it within 14 days of its receipt.

(5) A decision given by way of revision or a refusal to review under this regulation shall be subject to appeal in the same manner as an original decision and regulation 5(1) and Schedule 2 shall apply with the necessary modification in relation to a decision given on review as they apply to the original decision on a question.

DEFINITIONS

"adjudication officer"—see reg. 1(2).
"Commissioner"—*ibid.*
"tribunal"—*ibid.*

Correction of accidental errors

7.—(1) Subject to regulation 9, accidental errors in any decision or record of a decision made under regulations 2(4), 5 and 6 and Schedule 2 may at any time be corrected by the person or tribunal by whom the decision was made or a person or tribunal of like status.

(2) A correction made to, or to the record of, a decision shall be deemed to be part of the decision or, of that record, and written notice of it shall be given as soon as practicable to every party to the proceedings.

DEFINITIONS

"tribunal"—see reg. 1(2).

Setting aside decisions on certain grounds

8.—(1) Subject to regulation 9, on an application made by a party to the proceedings, a decision, made under regulations 2(4), 5, 6 and Schedule 2 by an adjudication officer, a tribunal or a Commissioner ("the adjudicating authority"), together with any determination given on an application for leave to appeal to a Commissioner or the Court of Appeal against such a decision may be set aside by the adjudicating authority which gave the decision or an authority of like status, in a case where it appears just to set that decision aside on the grounds that—

(a) a document relating to the proceedings in which the decision was given was not sent to, or was not received at an appropriate time by a party or their representative or was not received at the appropriate time by the person or tribunal who gave the decision;

(b) in the case of an appeal to a tribunal or an oral hearing before a Commissioner a party to the proceedings in which the decision was given or the party's representative was not present at the hearing relating to the proceedings; or

(c) the interests of justice so require.

(2) An application under this regulation shall be made in accordance with regulation 10 and Schedule 1.

(3) Where an application to set aside is made under paragraph (1) every party to the proceedings shall be sent a copy of the application and shall be afforded a reasonable opportunity of making representations on it before the application is determined.

(4) Notice in writing of a determination on an application to set aside a decision shall be given to every party to the proceedings as soon as may be practicable and the notice shall contain a statement giving the reasons for the determination.

(5) For the purpose of determining under these Regulations an application to set aside a decision, there shall be disregarded, but subject to any contrary intention, any provision in any enactment or instrument to the effect that any notice or other document required or authorised to be given or sent to any person shall be deemed to have been given or sent if it was sent to that person's last known notified address.

DEFINITIONS

"adjudication officer"—see reg. 1(2).
"Commissioner"—*ibid.*
"tribunal"—*ibid.*

Provisions common to regulations 7 and 8

9.—(1) In calculating any time specified in Schedule 1 there shall be disregarded any day falling before the day on which notice was given of a correction of a decision or the record thereof pursuant to regulation 7 or on which notice is given that a determination of a decision shall not be set aside following an application under regulation 8, as the case may be.

(2) There shall be no appeal against a correction made under regulation 7 or a refusal to make such a correction or against a determination under regulation 8.

(3) Nothing in regulation 7 or 8 shall be construed as derogating from any inherent or other power to correct errors or set aside decisions which is exercisable apart from these Regulations.

Manner of making applications or appeals and time limits

10.—(1) Any application or appeal set out in Column (1) of Schedule 1 shall be made or given by sending or delivering it to the appropriate office within the specified time.

(2) In this regulation—
   (a) "appropriate office" means the office specified in Column (2) of Schedule 1 opposite the description of the relevant application or appeal listed in Column (1); and
   (b) "specified time" means the time specified in Column (3) of that Schedule opposite the description of the relevant application or appeal so listed.

(3) The time specified by this regulation and Schedule 1 for the making of any application or appeal (except an application to the chairman of a tribunal for leave to appeal to a Commissioner) may be extended for special reasons, even though the time so specified may already have expired, and any application for an extension of time under this paragraph shall be made to and determined by the person to whom the application or appeal is sought to be made or, in the case of a tribunal, its chairman.

(4) An application under paragraph (3) for an extension of time (except where it is made to a Commissioner) which has been refused may not be renewed.

(5) Any application or appeal set out in Column (1) of Schedule 1 shall be in writing and shall contain—
   (a) the name and address of the appellant or applicant;
   (b) the particulars of the grounds on which the appeal or application is to be made or given; and

(c) his address for service of documents if it is different from that in sub-paragraph (a);

and in the case of an appeal to the Commissioner, but subject to paragraph 21(2) of Schedule 2, the notice of appeal shall have annexed to it a copy of the determination granting leave to appeal and a copy of the decision against which leave to appeal has been granted.

(6) Where it appears to an adjudication officer, or chairman of a tribunal, or Commissioner that an application or appeal which is made to him, or the tribunal, gives insufficient particulars to enable the question at issue to be determined, he may require, and in the case of a Commissioner, direct that the person making the application or appeal shall furnish such further particulars as may reasonably be required.

(7) The conduct and procedure in relation to any application or appeal shall be in accordance with Schedule 2.

DEFINITIONS

"adjudication officer"—see reg. 1(2).
"Commissioner"—*ibid.*
"tribunal"—*ibid.*

Manner and time for the service of notices etc.

11.—(1) Any notice or other document required or authorised to be given or sent to any person under these Regulations shall be deemed to have been given or sent if it was sent by post properly addressed and pre-paid to that party at his ordinary or last notified address.

(2) Any notice or other document required or authorised to be given to an appropriate social security office or office of the clerk to a tribunal shall be treated as having been so given or sent on the day that it is received in the appropriate social security office or office of the clerk to the tribunal.

(3) Any notice or document required to be given, sent or submitted to, or served on, a Commissioner—

(a) shall be given, sent or submitted to an office of the Social Security Commissioners;

(b) shall be deemed to have been given, sent or submitted if it was sent by post properly addressed and pre-paid to an office of the Social Security Commissioners.

DEFINITIONS

"appropriate social security office"—see reg. 1(2).
"Commissioner"—*ibid.*
"tribunal"—*ibid.*

Revocation

12. The Community Charges (Deductions from Income Support) Regulations 1990 are hereby revoked.

SCHEDULE 1   **Regulation 10(1)**

TIME LIMITS FOR MAKING APPLICATIONS OR APPEALS

Column (1)	Column (2)	Column (3)
Application or Appeal	*Appropriate Office*	*Specified time*
1. Appeal to a tribunal from an adjudication officer's decision (regulation 5).	An appropriate social security office.	3 months beginning with the date when notice in writing of the decision was given to the appellant.
2. Application to the Chairman for leave to appeal to a Commissioner from the decision of a tribunal (paragraph 16, Schedule 2).	The office of the Clerk to the tribunal.	3 months beginning with the date when a copy of the record of the decision was given to the applicant.
3. Application to— (*a*) an adjudication officer; (*b*) a tribunal; or (*c*) a Commissioner, to set aside decision (regulation 8).	(*a*) An appropriate social security office; (*b*) The office of the clerk to the tribunal; (*c*) An office of the Social Security Commissioners;	(*a*) and (*b*) 3 months beginning with the date when notice in writing of the decision was given to the applicant. (*c*) 30 days from the date on which notice in writing of the decision was given to the applicant by an officer of the Social Security Commissioners.
4. Application for leave to appeal to the Commissioner where the chairman has refused leave (paragraph 17, Schedule 2).	An office of the Social Security Commissioners.	42 days beginning with the date when notice in writing of the decision by the chairman to refuse leave was given to the applicant.
5. Appeal to the Commissioner (regulation 5).	An office of the Social Security Commissioners.	42 days beginning with the date when notice in writing of the decision was given to the applicant.
6. Leave to appeal to the Court of Appeal (regulation 5(5) and Schedule 2).	An office of the Social Security Commissioners.	3 months beginning with the date when notice in writing of the decision was given to the applicant.

DEFINITIONS

"adjudication officer"—see reg. 1(2).
"appropriate social security office"—*ibid.*
"Commissioner"—*ibid.*
"tribunal"—*ibid.*

SCHEDULE 2 **Regulation 10(7)**

CONDUCT AND PROCEDURE IN RELATION TO APPEALS AND APPLICATIONS

Common provisions in connection with appeals and applications

1.—(1) Subject to the provisions of these Regulations—

(a) the procedure in connection with the consideration of any appeal, or any application in relation to questions to which these Regulations relate, shall be such as the adjudication officer, chairman of the tribunal or the Commissioner may determine;

(b) any person who by virtue of these Regulations has the right to be heard at a hearing may be accompanied and represented by another person whether having professional qualifications or not, and for the purposes of any proceedings at any hearing any such representative shall have all the rights and powers to which the person whom he represents is entitled under these Regulations.

(2) Nothing in these Regulations shall prevent a member of the Council on Tribunals in his capacity as such from being present at any oral hearing before a tribunal or a Commissioner, notwithstanding that the hearing is not in public.

2. Reasonable notice (being not less than 10 days beginning on the day on which notice is given and ending on the day before the hearing of the appeal) of the time and place of any oral hearing before the tribunal or the Commissioner shall be given to every party to the proceedings, and if such notice had not been given to a person to whom it should have been given under the provisions of this paragraph the hearing may only proceed with the consent of that person.

3. At any oral hearing any party shall be entitled to be present and be heard.

Postponements and adjournments

4.—(1) Where a person to whom notice of an oral hearing has been given wishes to apply for that hearing to be postponed he shall do so in writing to the chairman of the tribunal or the Commissioner stating his reasons for the application and the chairman or the Commissioner may grant or refuse the application as he sees fit.

(2) An oral hearing may be adjourned at any time on the application of any party to the proceedings or on the motion of the tribunal or the Commissioner.

Striking out of proceedings for want of prosecution

5.—(1) The chairman of a tribunal or the Commissioner may, subject to sub-paragraph (2), on the application of any party to the proceedings or of his own motion, strike out any appeal or application for want of prosecution.

(2) Before making an order under sub-paragraph (1) the chairman of a tribunal or the Commissioner, as the case may be, shall send notice to the person against whom it is proposed that any order should be made giving him a reasonable opportunity to show cause why such an order should not be made.

(3) The chairman of a tribunal or the Commissioner, as the case may be, may, on application by the party concerned, give leave to reinstate any application or appeal which has been struck out in accordance with sub-paragraph (1).

Application and Appeals to the Tribunal

Procedure in connection with determinations

6. For the purpose of arriving at its decision a tribunal shall, and for the purpose of discussing any question of procedure may, notwithstanding anything in these Regulations, order all persons not being members of the tribunal other than its clerk to withdraw from the sitting of the tribunal except that—

(a) a member of the Council on Tribunals, the President of Social Security Appeal Tribunals and any full-time chairman; and

(b) with the leave of the chairman of the tribunal, if no person having the right to be heard objects, any person mentioned in paragraph 13(1)(b) and (d) (except a person undergoing training as an adjudicating officer).

may remain present at any such sitting.

Oral hearings

7. A tribunal shall hold an oral hearing of every appeal made to them.

8. If a party to the proceedings to whom notice has been given under paragraph 2 should fail to appear at the hearing, the tribunal may, having regard to all the circumstances, including any explanation offered for the absence, proceed with the case notwithstanding his absence or give such directions with a view to the determination of the case as they think fit.

9. Any oral hearing before a tribunal shall be in public except that the hearing shall be in private where the debtor requests a private hearing, or where the chairman is satisfied in the particular circumstances of the case that intimate personal or financial circumstances may have to be disclosed, or that considerations of public security are involved.

10. Any case may with the consent of the debtor or his representative, but not otherwise, be proceeded with in the absence of any one member other than the chairman.

11. Where an oral hearing is adjourned and at the hearing after the adjournment the tribunal is differently constituted otherwise than through the operation of paragraph 10, the proceedings at that hearing shall be by way of a complete rehearing of the case.

12.—(1) The decision of the majority of the tribunal shall be the decision of the tribunal but, where the tribunal consists of an even number, the chairman shall have a second or casting vote.

(2) The chairman of a tribunal shall—

(a) record in writing all its decisions; and

(b) include in the record of every decision a statement of the reasons for such decision and of their findings on questions of fact material thereto; and

(c) if a decision is not unanimous, record a statement that one of the members dissented and the reasons given by him for so dissenting.

(3) As soon as may be practicable after a case has been decided by a tribunal, a copy of the record of the decision made in accordance with this paragraph shall be sent to every party to the proceedings who shall also be informed of the conditions governing appeals to a Commissioner.

13.—(1) The following persons shall be entitled to be present at an oral hearing (whether or not it is in private) but shall take no part in the proceedings—

(a) the President of Social Security Appeal Tribunals;

(b) any person undergoing training as a chairman or other member of a tribunal, or as a clerk to a tribunal, or as an adjudication officer;

(c) any person acting on behalf of the President of the Social Security Appeal Tribunals, the Chief Adjudication Officer appointed under section 97(1B) of the 1975 Act, or the Secretary of State, in the training or supervision of clerks to tribunals or adjudication officers or officers of the Secretary of State or in the monitoring of standards of adjudication by adjudication officers;

(d) any regional or full-time chairman of appeal tribunals appointed under paragraph 1A of Schedule 10 to the 1975 Act; and

(e) with the leave of the chairman of the tribunal and with the consent of every party to the proceedings actually present, any other person.

(2) Nothing in sub-paragraph (1) affects the rights of any person mentioned in heads (a) and (b) at any oral hearing where he is sitting as a member of the tribunal or acting

as its clerk, and nothing in this paragraph prevents the presence at an oral hearing of any witness.

14. Any person entitled to be heard at an oral hearing may address the tribunal, may give evidence, may call witnesses and may put questions directly to any other person called as a witness.

Withdrawal of Appeals

15. Any appeal to the tribunal under these Regulations may be withdrawn by the person who made the appeal—
   (a) before the hearing begins by giving written notice of intention to withdraw to the tribunal and with the consent in writing of the adjudication officer who made the decision; or
   (b) after the hearing has begun with the leave of the chairman of the tribunal at any time before the determination is made.

Application to a Chairman for leave to appeal from a tribunal to a Commissioner

16.—(1) Subject to the following provisions of this paragraph, an application to the chairman of a tribunal for leave to appeal to a Commissioner from a decision of the tribunal shall be made—
   (a) orally at the hearing after the decision is announced by the tribunal; or
   (b) as provided by regulation 10 and Schedule 1.
(2) Where an application in writing for leave to appeal is made by an adjudication officer, the clerk to the tribunal shall, as soon as may be practicable, send a copy of the application to every other party to the proceedings.
(3) The decision of the chairman on an application for leave to appeal made under sub-paragraph (1)(a) shall be recorded in the record of the proceedings of the tribunal, and an application under sub-paragraph (1)(b) shall be recorded in writing and a copy shall be sent to each party to the proceedings.
(4) A person who has made an application to the chairman of a tribunal for leave to appeal to a Commissioner may withdraw his application at any time before it is determined by giving written notice of intention to the chairman.

[Paras. 17 to 36 on appeals to the Commissioner and the Court of Appeal omitted.]

DEFINITIONS

   "adjudication officer"—see reg. 1(2).
   "Commissioner"—*ibid.*
   "debtor"—*ibid.*
   "tribunal"—*ibid.*

Fines (Deductions from Income Support) Regulations 1992

(S.I. 1992 No. 2182)

Made by the Secretary of State under ss. 24 and 30 of the Criminal Justice Act 1991.

Citation, commencement and interpretation

1.—(1) These Regulations may be cited as the Fines (Deductions from Income Support) Regulations 1992 and shall come into force on 1st October 1992.
(2) In these Regulations, unless the context otherwise requires—
   "the 1971 Act" means the Vehicles (Excise) Act 1971;
   "the 1973 Act" means the Powers of the Criminal Courts Act 1973;

"the 1992 Act" means the Social Security Administration Act 1992;

"adjudication officer" means an officer appointed in accordance with section 38(1) of the 1992 Act;

"application" means an application made under regulation 2 in the form and containing the information specified in regulation 3(1);

"appropriate appeal court" means, except in regulation 9(9), the appropriate court as determined in accordance with regulation 9(9) and 9(10);

"benefit week" has the meaning prescribed in regulation 2(1) of the Income Support Regulations;

"the Claims and Payments Regulations" means the Social Security (Claims and Payments) Regulations 1987;

"Commissioner" means the Chief or any other Social Security Commissioner appointed in accordance with section 52(1) or (2) of the 1992 Act and includes a Tribunal of Commissioners constituted in accordance with section 57(1) of that Act;

"court" means in England and Wales a magistrates' court and in Scotland a court;

"5 per cent. of the personal allowance for a single claimant aged not less than 25" means, where the percentage is not a multiple of 5 pence, the sum obtained by rounding that 5 per cent. to the next higher such multiple;

"Income Support Regulations" means the Income Support (General) Regulations 1987;

"payments to third parties" means direct payments to third parties in accordance with Schedules 9 and 9A to the Claims and Payments Regulations, regulation 2(4) of the Community Charges (Deductions from Income Support) (No. 2) Regulations 1990 and regulation 2(4) of the Community Charges (Deductions from Income Support) (Scotland) Regulations 1989 [¹and regulation 2 of the Council Tax (Deductions from Income Support) Regulations 1993];

"personal allowance for a single claimant aged not less than 25" means the amount specified in paragraph 1(1)(e) of column 2 of Schedule 2 to the Income Support Regulations;

"social security office" means an office of the department of Social Security which is open to the public for the receipt of claims for income support and includes an office of the Department of Employment which is open to the public for the receipt of claims for unemployment benefit;

"tribunal" means a social security appeal tribunal constituted in accordance with section 41 of the 1992 Act; and

(3) Unless the context otherwise requires, any reference in these Regulations to a numbered regulation, Part or Schedule bearing that number in these Regulations and any reference in a regulation or Schedule to a numbered paragraph is a reference to the paragraph of that regulation or Schedule having that number.

AMENDMENT

1. Deductions from Income Support (Miscellaneous Amendment) Regulations 1993 (S.I. 1993 No. 495), reg. 3 (April 1, 1993).

Application for deductions from income support

2.—(1) Where a fine has been imposed on an offender by a court or a sum is required to be paid by a compensation order which has been made against an offender by a court and (in either case) the offender is entitled to income support, the court may, subject to paragraph (2), apply to the Secretary of State asking him to deduct sums from any amounts payable to the offender by way of income support, in order to secure the payment of any sum which is or forms part of the fine or compensation.

(2) Before making an application the court shall make an enquiry as to the offender's means.

<small>DEFINITION</small>

"court"—see reg. 1(2).

Contents of application

3.—(1) An application shall be made in the form set out in Schedule 3, or a form to like effect, and shall contain the following information—
- (a) the name and address of the offender, and, if it is known, his date of birth;
- (b) the date when the fine was imposed or the compensation order made;
- (c) the name and address of the court imposing the fine or making the compensation order;
- (d) the amount of the fine or the amount payable by the compensation order as the case may be;
- (e) the date on which the application is made;
- (f) the date on which the court enquired into the offender's means;
- (g) whether the offender has defaulted in paying the fine, compensation order or any instalment of either.

(2) A court making an application shall serve it on the Secretary of State by sending or delivering it to a social security office.

(3) Where it appears to the Secretary of State that an application from a court gives insufficient information to enable the offender to be identified, he may require the court to furnish such further information as he may reasonably require for that purpose.

<small>DEFINITIONS</small>

"application"—see reg. 1(2).
"court"—*ibid.*
"social security office"—*ibid.*

[¹Reference to adjudication officer

4.—(1) Where the Secretary of State receives an application from a court in respect of an offender, he shall, subject to regulation 7(5), refer it forthwith to an adjudication officer who shall determine whether there is sufficient entitlement to income support to enable the Secretary of State to make any deduction.

(2) The adjudication officer shall determine there is sufficient entitlement to income support to enable the Secretary of State to make a deduction—
- (a) if the amount payable by way of income support after any deduction to be made under regulation 6 is 10 pence or more; and
- (b) if the aggregate amount payable under one or more of the following provisions, namely paragraphs 3(2)(a), 5(6), 6(2)(a), 7(3)(a) and 7(5)(a) of Schedule 9 to the Claims and Payments Regulations, paragraph 3(5) of Schedule 9A to the Claims and Payments Regulations and regulation 2 of the Council Tax (Deductions from Income Support) Regulations 1993, together with the amount to be deducted under regulation 6 does not exceed an amount equal to 3 times 5 per cent of the personal allowance for a single claimant aged not less than 25 years.

(3) The adjudication officer shall determine whether there is sufficient entitlement to income support to enable a deduction to be made, so far as is practicable, within 14 days of receipt of the reference from the Secretary of State.]

AMENDMENT

1. Deductions from Income Support (Miscellaneous Amendment) Regulations 1993 (S.I. 1993 No. 495), reg. 3 (April 1, 1993).

DEFINITIONS

"adjudication officer"—see reg. 1(2).
"application"—*ibid.*
"the Claims and Payments Regulations"—*ibid.*
"court"—*ibid.*
"5 per cent. of the personal allowance for a single claimant aged not less than 25"—*ibid.*
"payments to third parties"—*ibid.*

Notification of decision

5. The Secretary of State shall notify the offender and the court in writing of the adjudication officer's decision so far as is practicable within 14 days from the date on which he receives that decision and at the same time he shall notify the offender of his right of appeal.

DEFINITIONS

"adjudication officer"—see reg. 1(2).
"court"—*ibid.*

Deductions from offender's income support

6. Where the adjudication officer has determined that there is sufficient entitlement to income support the Secretary of State may deduct a sum equal to 5 per cent. of the personal allowance for a single claimant aged not less than 25 and pay that sum to the court towards satisfaction of the fine or the sum required to be paid by compensation order.

DEFINITIONS

"adjudication officer"—see reg. 1(2).
"court"—*ibid.*
"5 per cent. of the personal allowance for a single claimant aged not less than 25"—*ibid.*

Circumstances, time of making and termination of deductions

7.—(1) The Secretary of State may make deductions from income support under regulation 6 only if—
  (a) the offender is entitled to income support throughout any benefit week; and
  (b) no deductions are being made in respect of the offender under any other application.
(2) The Secretary of State shall not make a deduction unless—
  (a) the offender at the date of application by the court is aged not less than 18;
  (b) the offender is entitled to income support; and
  (c) the offender has defaulted in paying the fine, compensation order or any instalment of either.
(3) The Secretary of State shall make deductions from income support by reference to the times at which payment of income support is made to the offender.
(4) The Secretary of State shall cease making deductions from income support if—

(a) there is no longer sufficient entitlement to income support to enable him to make the deduction;

(b) entitlement to income support ceases;

(c) a court withdraws its application for deductions to be made; or

(d) the liability to make payment of the fine or under the compensation order as the case may be has ceased.

(5) Where at any time during which the Secretary of State is making deductions in respect of an application he receives one or more further applications in respect of the offender from whom the deductions are being made, he shall refer those further applications to the adjudication officer in accordance with the following order of priority, namely, the one bearing the earliest date shall be referred first and each subsequent application shall be referred, one at a time and in date order, only after deductions under any earlier application have ceased.

(6) Payments of sums deducted from income support by the Secretary of State under these Regulations shall be made to the court at intervals of 13 weeks.

(7) Where the whole of the amount to which the application relates has been paid, the court shall so far as is practicable give notice of that fact within 21 days to the Secretary of State.

(8) The Secretary of State shall notify the offender in writing of the total of the sums deducted by him under any application—

(a) on receipt of a written request for such information from the offender; or

(b) on the termination of deductions made under any such application.

DEFINITIONS

"adjudication officer"—see reg. 1(2).
"authority"—*ibid.*
"benefit week"—*ibid.*
"court"—*ibid.*

Withdrawal of application

8. A court may withdraw an application at any time by giving notice in writing to the social security office to which the application was sent or delivered.

DEFINITIONS

"application"—see reg. 1(2).
"court"—*ibid.*
"social security office"—*ibid.*

Appeal

9.—(1) Where the adjudication officer has determined a question under regulation 4, the offender may appeal to a tribunal.

(2) Subject to paragraph (5), an appeal lies to a Commissioner from any decision of a tribunal on the grounds that the decision of that tribunal was erroneous in point of law and the persons who may appeal are the offender and the adjudication officer.

(3) If it appears to the Chief Commissioner or, in the case of his inability to act, to such other of the Commissioners, as he may have nominated to act for that purpose, that an appeal falling to be heard by one of the Commissioners involves a question of law of special difficulty, he may direct that the appeal be dealt with, not by that Commissioner alone but by a Tribunal consisting of any three of the Commissioners and if the decision is not unanimous, the decision of the majority shall be the decision of the Tribunal.

(4) Subject to paragraph (5), an appeal on a question of law lies to the appropriate appeal court from any decision of a Commissioner and the persons who may appeal are—

(a) the offender;

(b) the adjudication officer; and

(c) the Secretary of State.

(5) No appeal lies—

(a) to the Commissioner from a decision of a tribunal without the leave of the chairman of the tribunal which gave the decision or, if he refuses leave, without the leave of the Commissioner, or

(b) to the appropriate appeal court from a decision of a Commissioner, without the leave of the Commissioner who decided the case, or if he refuses, without the leave of the appropriate appeal court.

(6) Where in any case it is impracticable, or it would be likely to cause undue delay, for an application for leave to appeal against a decision of a tribunal to be determined by the person who was the chairman of that tribunal, that application shall be determined by any other person qualified under section 41(4) of the 1992 Act to act as a chairman of tribunals.

(7) In a case where the Chief Commissioner considers that it is impracticable, or would be likely to cause undue delay, for an application for leave to appeal to the appropriate appeal court to be determined by the Commissioner who decided the case, that application shall be determined—

(a) where the decision was a decision of an individual Commissioner, by the Chief Commissioner or a Commissioner selected by the Chief Commissioner, and

(b) where the decision was a decision of a Tribunal of Commissioners, by a differently constituted Tribunal of Commissioners selected by the Chief Commissioner.

(8) If the office of Chief Commissioner is vacant, or if the Chief Commissioner is unable to act, paragraph (7) shall have effect as if the expression "the Chief Commissioner" referred to such other of the Commissioners as may have been nominated to act for the purpose either by the Chief Commissioner or, if he has not made such nomination, by the Lord Chancellor.

(9) On an application to a Commissioner for leave under this regulation it shall be the duty of the Commissioner to specify as the appropriate court—

(a) the Court of Appeal if it appears to him that the relevant place is in England and Wales; and

(b) the Court of Session if it appears to him that the relevant place is in Scotland;

except that if it appears to him, having regard to the circumstances of the case and in particular to the convenience of the persons who may be parties to the proposed appeal, that he should specify a different court mentioned in paragraphs (a) and (b) above as the appropriate court, it shall be his duty to specify that court as the appropriate court.

(10) In paragraph (9)—

"the relevant place", in relation to an application for leave to appeal from a decision of a Commissioner, means the premises where the tribunal whose decision was the subject of the Commissioner's decision usually exercises its functions

DEFINITIONS

"the 1992 Act"—see reg. 1(2).
"adjudication officer"—*ibid.*
"appropriate appeal court"—*ibid.*
"Commissioner"—*ibid.*
"tribunal"—*ibid.*

Review

10.—(1) Any decision under these Regulations of an adjudication officer, a tribunal or a Commissioner may be reviewed at any time by an adjudication officer, if—

    (a) the officer is satisfied that the decision was given in ignorance of, or was based on a mistake as to, some material fact; or

    (b) there has been a relevant change of circumstances since the decision was given.

(2) Any decision of an adjudication officer may be reviewed by an adjudication officer on the grounds that the decision was erroneous in point of law.

(3) A question may be raised with a view to review under this regulation by means of an application in writing to an adjudication officer, stating the grounds of the application.

(4) On receipt of any such application, the adjudication officer shall take it into consideration and, so far as is practicable, dispose of it within 14 days of its receipt.

(5) A decision given by way of revision or a refusal to review under this regulation shall be subject to appeal in the same manner as an original decision and regulation 9(1) and Schedule 2 shall apply with the necessary modification in relation to a decision given on review as they apply to the original decision on a question.

DEFINITIONS

    "adjudication officer"—see reg. 1(2).
    "Commissioner"—*ibid.*
    "tribunal"—*ibid.*

Correction of accidental errors

11.—(1) Subject to regulation 13, accidental errors in any decision or record of a decision made under regulations 4, 9 and 10 and Schedule 2 may at any time be corrected by the person or tribunal by whom the decision was made or a person or tribunal of like status.

(2) A correction made to, or to the record of, a decision shall be deemed to be part of the decision, or of that record, and written notice of it shall be given as soon as practicable to every party to the proceedings.

DEFINITION

    "tribunal"—see reg. 1(2).

Setting aside decisions on certain grounds

12.—(1) Subject to regulation 13, on an application made by a party to the proceedings, a decision, made under regulation 4, 9, 10 and Schedule 2 by an adjudication officer, a tribunal or a Commissioner ("the adjudicating authority"), together with any determination given on an application for leave to appeal to a Commissioner or the Court of Appeal against such a decision may be set aside by the adjudicating authority which gave the decision or an authority of like status, in a case where it appears just to set that decision aside on the grounds that—

    (a) a document relating to the proceedings in which the decision was given was not sent to, or was not received at an appropriate time [¹by a party to the proceedings or the party's representative] or was not received at the appropriate time by the person or tribunal who gave the decision;

(b) in the case of an appeal to a tribunal or an oral hearing before a Commissioner a party to the proceedings in which the decision was given or the party's representative was not present at the hearing relating to the proceedings; or

(c) the interests of justice so require.

(2) An application under this regulation shall be made in accordance with regulation 14 and Schedule 1.

(3) Where an application to set aside is made under paragraph (1) every party to the proceedings shall be sent a copy of the application and shall be afforded a reasonable opportunity of making representations on it before the application is determined.

(4) Notice in writing of a determination on an application to set aside a decision shall be given to every party to the proceedings as soon as may be practicable and the notice shall contain a statement giving the reasons for the determination.

(5) For the purpose of determining under these Regulations an application to set aside a decision, there shall be disregarded, but subject to any contrary intention, any provision in any enactment or instrument to the effect that any notice or other document required or authorised to be given or sent to any person shall be deemed to have been given or sent if it was sent to that person's last known notified address.

AMENDMENT

1. Deductions from Income Support (Miscellaneous Amendment) Regulations 1993 (S.I. 1993 No. 495), reg. 3 (April 1, 1993).

DEFINITIONS

"adjudication officer"—see reg. 1(2).
"Commissioner"—*ibid.*
"tribunal"—*ibid.*

Provisions common to regulations 11 and 12

13.—(1) In calculating any time specified in Schedule 1 there shall be disregarded any day falling before the day on which notice was given of a correction of a decision or the record there of pursuant to regulation 11 or on which notice is given that a determination of a decision shall not be set aside following an application under regulation 12, as the case may be.

(2) There shall be no appeal against a correction made under regulation 11 or a refusal to make such a correction or against a determination under regulation 12.

(3) Nothing in regulation 11 or 12 shall be construed as derogating from any inherent or other power to correct errors or set aside decisions which is exercisable apart from these Regulations.

Manner of making applications or appeals and time limits

14.—(1) Any application or appeal set out in Column (1) of Schedule 1 shall be made or given by sending or delivering it to the appropriate office within the specified time.

(2) In this regulation—
(a) "appropriate office" means the office specified in Column (2) of Schedule 1 opposite the description of the relevant application or appeal listed in Column (1); and
(b) "specified time" means the time specified in Column (3) of that Sched-

ule opposite the description of the relevant application or appeal so listed.

(3) The time specified by this regulation and Schedule 1 for the making of any application or appeal (except an application to the chairman of a tribunal for leave to appeal to a Commissioner) may be extended for special reasons, even though the time so specified may already have expired, and any application for an extension of time under this paragraph shall be made to and determined by the person to whom the application or appeal is sought to be made or, in the case of a tribunal, its chairman.

(4) An application under paragraph (3) for an extension of time (except where it is made to a Commissioner) which has been refused may not be renewed.

(5) Any application or appeal set out in Column (1) of Schedule 1 shall be in writing and shall contain—

(a) the name and address of the appellant or applicant;

(b) the particulars of the grounds on which the appeal or application is to be made or given; and

(c) his address for service of documents if it is different from that in sub-paragraph (a);

and in the case of an appeal to the Commissioner, but subject to paragraph 21(2) of Schedule 2, the notice of appeal shall have annexed to it a copy of the determination granting leave to appeal and a copy of the decision against which leave to appeal has been granted.

(6) Where it appears to an adjudication officer, chairman of a tribunal or Commissioner that an application or appeal which is made to him, or to the tribunal, gives insufficient particulars to enable the question at issue to be determined, he may require, and in the case of a Commissioner, direct that the person making the application or appeal shall furnish such further particulars as may reasonably be required.

(7) The conduct and procedure in relation to any application or appeal shall be in accordance with Schedule 2.

DEFINITIONS

"adjudication officer"—see reg. 1(2).
"Commissioner"—*ibid.*
"tribunal"—*ibid.*

Manner and time for the service of notices etc.

15.—(1) Any notice or other document required or authorised to be given or sent to any person under these Regulations shall be deemed to have been given or sent if it was sent by post properly addressed and pre-paid to [¹that person] at his ordinary or last notified address.

(2) Any notice or other document required or authorised to be given to an appropriate social security office or office of the clerk to a tribunal shall be treated as having been so given or sent on the day that it is received in the appropriate social security office or office of the clerk to the tribunal.

(3) Any notice or document required to be given, sent or submitted to, or served on, a Commissioner—

(a) shall be given, sent or submitted to an office of the Social Security Commissioners;

(b) shall be deemed to have been given, sent or submitted if it was sent by post properly addressed and pre-paid to an office of the Social Security Commissioners.

AMENDMENT

1. Deductions from Income Support (Miscellaneous Amendment) Regulations 1993 (S.I. 1993 No. 495), reg. 3 (April 1, 1993).

DEFINITIONS

"Commissioner"—see reg. 1(2).
"social security office"—*ibid.*
"tribunal"—*ibid.*

[Scheds. 1 to 3 are omitted. Scheds. 1 and 2 are substantially the same as Scheds. 1 and 2 to the Community Charges (Deductions from Income Support) (No. 2) Regulations 1990. Sched. 3 sets out the form to be used under reg. 3(1)]

Council Tax (Deductions from Income Support) Regulations 1993

(S.I. 1993 No. 494)

Made by the Secretary of State under ss.14(3), 97(5), 113 and 116(1) of and Scheds. 4, paras. 1 and 6, and 8, para. 6, to the Local Government Finance Act 1992

Citation, commencement and interpretation

1.—(1) These Regulations may be cited as the Council Tax (Deductions from Income Support) Regulations 1993 and shall come into force on 1st April 1993.
(2) In these Regulations, unless the context otherwise requires—
"the Administration Act" means the Social Security Administration Act 1992;
"adjudication officer" means an officer appointed in accordance with section 38(1) of the Administration Act;
"application" means an application made under regulation 2 or regulation 3 containing the information specified in regulation 4;
"appropriate appeal court" means the appropriate court as determined in accordance with regulation 10(9) and 10(10);
"authority" means—
    (a) in relation to England and Wales, a billing authority, and
    (b) in relation to Scotland, a levying authority;
"benefit week" has the meaning prescribed in regulation 2(1) of the Income Support (General) Regulations 1987;
"Claims and Payments Regulations" means the Social Security (Claims and Payments) Regulations 1987;
"Commissioner" means the Chief or any other Social Security Commissioner appointed in accordance with section 52(1) or (2) of the Administration Act, and includes a Tribunal of Commissioners constituted in accordance with section 57(1) of that Act;
"debtor"—
    (a) in relation to England and Wales, has the same meaning as in paragraph 6 of Schedule 4 to the Local Government Finance Act, and
    (b) in relation to Scotland, has the same meaning as in paragraph 6 of Schedule 8 to that Act;
"5 per cent. of the personal allowance for a single claimant aged not less than 25" means, where the percentage is not a multiple of 5 pence, the sum obtained by rounding that 5 per cent. to the next higher such multiple;

"income support" means income support within the meaning of the Social Security Contributions and Benefits Act 1992;

"the Local Government Finance Act" means the Local Government Finance Act 1992;

"personal allowance for a single claimant aged not less than 25" means the amount specified in paragraph 1(1)(e) of column 2 of Schedule 2 to the Income Support (General) Regulations 1987;

"social security office" means an office of the Department of Social Security which is open to the public for the receipt of claims for income support and includes an office of the Department of Employment which is open to the public for the receipt of claims for unemployment benefit;

"tribunal", except in relation to a Tribunal of three Commissioners, means a social security appeal tribunal constituted in accordance with section 41 of the Administration Act.

(3) Unless the context otherwise requires, any reference in these Regulations to a numbered regulation or Schedule is a reference to the regulation or Schedule bearing that number in these Regulations and any reference in a regulation or Schedule to a numbered paragraph is a reference to the paragraph of that regulation or Schedule having that number.

Application for deductions from income support: England and Wales

2. Where a liability order has been made against a debtor by a magistrates' court and the debtor is entitled to income support the billing authority concerned may apply to the Secretary of State asking him to deduct sums from any amounts payable to the debtor by way of income support in order to secure the payment of any outstanding sum which is or forms part of the amount in respect of which the liability order was made.

DEFINITIONS

"debtor"—see reg. 1(2).
"income support"—*ibid.*

Application for deductions from income support: Scotland

3.—(1) Where a levying authority has obtained a summary warrant or a decree against a debtor in respect of arrears of sums payable under paragraph 1(1) of Schedule 8 to the [¹Local Government Finance Act] and the debtor is entitled to income support, the levying authority may, without prejudice to its right to pursue any other means of recovering such arrears, apply to the Secretary of State asking him to deduct sums from any amounts payable to the debtor by way of income support in order to secure the payment of any outstanding sum which is or forms part of the amount in respect of which the summary warrant or decree was granted.

AMENDMENT

1. Social Security (Claims and Payments) Amendment (No. 3) Regulations 1993 (S.I. 1993 No. 2113), reg. 6 (September 27, 1993).

DEFINITIONS

"debtor"—see reg. 1(2).
"income support"—*ibid.*
"Local Government Finance Act"—*ibid.*

Contents of application

4.—(1) An application shall contain the following particulars—

(a) the name and address of the debtor;

(b) the name and address of the authority making the application;

(c) the name and place of the court which made the liability order or granted the summary warrant, or decree as the case may be;

(d) the date on which the liability order was made or the summary warrant or decree granted as the case may be;

(e) the amount specified in the liability order, summary warrant or decree as the case may be;

(f) the total sum which the authority wishes to have deducted from income support.

(2) An authority making application shall serve it on the Secretary of State by sending or delivering it to a social security office.

(3) Where it appears to the Secretary of State that an application from an authority gives insufficient particulars to enable the debtor to be identified he may require the authority to furnish such further particulars as may reasonably be required for that purpose.

Reference to adjudication officer

5.—(1) Where the Secretary of State receives an application from an authority, he shall, subject to regulation 8(4), refer it forthwith to an adjudication officer who shall determine whether there is sufficient entitlement to income support to enable the Secretary of State to make any deduction.

(2) The adjudication officer shall determine there is sufficient entitlement to income support to enable the Secretary of State to make a deduction—

(a) if the amount payable by way of income support after any deduction to be made under regulation 7 is 10 pence or more;

(b) if the aggregate amount payable under one or more of the following provisions, namely paragraphs 3(2)(a), 5(6), 6(2)(a), 7(3)(a), 7(5)(a) of Schedule 9 and paragraph 3(5) of Schedule 9A to the Claims and Payments Regulations, together with the amount to be deducted under regulation 7, does not exceed an amount equal to 3 times 5 per cent. of the personal allowance for a single claimant aged not less than 25 years.

(3) The adjudication officer shall determine whether there is sufficient entitlement to income support to enable a deduction to be made, so far as is practicable, within 14 days of receipt of the reference from the Secretary of State.

Notification of decision

6. The Secretary of State shall notify the debtor and the authority in writing of the adjudication officer's decision so far as is practicable within 14 days from the date on which he receives that decision and at the same time he shall notify the debtor of his right of appeal.

> "adjudication officer"—see reg. 1(2).
> "authority"—*ibid.*
> "debtor"—*ibid.*

Deductions from debtor's income support

7. Where the adjudication officer has determined that there is sufficient entitlement to income support the Secretary of State may deduct a sum equal to 5 per cent. of the personal allowance for a single claimant aged not less than 25 and pay that sum to the authority towards satisfaction of any outstanding sum which is or forms part of the amount in respect of which the liability order was made or the summary warrant or the decree was granted.

DEFINITIONS

> "adjudication officer"—see reg. 1(2).
> "authority"—*ibid.*
> "debtor"—*ibid.*
> "5 per cent. of the personal allowance for a single claimant aged not less than 25"—*ibid.*
> "income support"—*ibid.*

Circumstances, time of making and termination of deductions

8.—(1) The Secretary of State may make deductions from income support under regulation 7 only if—
   (a) the debtor is entitled to income support throughout any benefit week;
   (b) no deductions are being made in respect of the debtor under any other application; and
   (c) no payments are being made under regulation 2 of the Community Charge (Deductions from Income Support) (Scotland) Regulations 1989 or regulation 2 of the Community Charge (Deductions from Income Support) (No. 2) Regulations 1990.
   (2) The Secretary of State shall make deductions from income support by reference to the times at which payment of income support is made to the debtor.
   (3) The Secretary of State shall cease making deductions from income support if—
   (a) there is no longer sufficient entitlement to income support to enable him to make the deduction;
   (b) an authority withdraws its application for deductions to be made; or
   (c) the debt in respect of which he was making deductions is discharged.
   (4) Where at any time during which the Secretary of State is making deductions in respect of an application he receives one or more further applications in respect of the debtor from whom the deductions are being made, he shall refer those further applications to the adjudication officer in accordance with the following order of priority, namely, the one bearing the earliest date shall be referred first and each subsequent application shall be referred, one at a time and in date order, only after deductions under any earlier application have ceased.
   (5) Payments of sums deducted from income support by the Secretary of State under these Regulations shall be made to the authority concerned, as far as is practicable, at intervals not exceeding 13 weeks.

(6) Where the whole of the amount to which the application relates has been paid, the authority concerned shall, so far as is practicable, give notice of that fact within 21 days to the Secretary of State.

(7) The Secretary of State shall notify the debtor in writing of the total of the sums deducted by him under any application—

(a) on receipt of a written request for such information from the debtor; or

(b) on the termination of deductions made under any such application.

DEFINITIONS

"adjudication officer"—see reg. 1(2).
"authority"—*ibid.*
"benefit week"—*ibid.*
"debtor"—*ibid.*
"income support"—*ibid.*

[Regs. 9 to 16 and Scheds. 1 and 2 are omitted as being substantially the same as regs. 8 to 15 of and Scheds. 1 and 2 to the Fines (Deductions from Income Support) Regulations 1992, with the substitution of "debtor" and "authority" for "offender" and "court".]

Child Support (Maintenance Assessment Procedure) Regulations 1992

(S.I. 1992 No. 1813)

Made by the Secretary of the State under various provisions of the Child Support Act 1991

REGULATIONS REPRODUCED

PART I

GENERAL

1. Citation, commencement and interpretation

PART IX

REDUCED BENEFIT DIRECTIONS

GENERAL NOTE

Only the regulations necessary to understand how a reduced benefit direction operates are reproduced. There are no notes or definitions after each individual regulation. Most relevant definitions are in reg. 1, although there also needs to be some reference to the Child Support Act 1991.

Once a reduced benefit direction is given by a CSO it is binding on the AO (Child Support Act 1991, s. 46(11)). The AO must then apply the reduction in making any initial decision on a claim for income support, family credit or disability working allowance and review any existing award on a relevant change of circumstances. See reg. 51A of the Family Credit (General) Regulations and reg. 56A of the Disability Working Allowance (General) Regulations for the authority to review those benefits. For income support, the power in s. 25(1)(*b*) of the Administration Act appears to be sufficient.

Reg. 36 specifies that the reduction is to be of a fixed amount for a fixed period. There is no discretion to alter either element whatever the circumstances. Under para. (2) for the first 26 weeks of the direction, the reduction is by 20 per cent. of the income support personal allowance for a single claimant aged not less than 25. From April 1995, the amount is £9.30. For the following 52 weeks the reduction is 10 per cent., *i.e.* £4.65. These amounts are subject to reg. 37, under which a reduction will be adjusted so as not to reduce the amount of income-related benefit below a minimum amount. The minimum is 10p for income support and 50p for family credit and disability working allowance. A direction is suspended where income support is payable under the special rules applying to hospital patients or persons in residential accommodation or residential care or nursing homes.

If the parent complies with her obligations under s. 6 of the Child Support Act 1991 (presumably to be determined by a CSO) the direction ceases to be in force (reg. 41). If she gives additional reasons for not complying, a CSO may review and lift the requirement to comply, in which case the direction ceases to be in force (reg. 42). If all of the relevant benefits cease to be payable the direction is suspended (reg. 38). The balance of the reduction period is applied if benefit becomes payable again within 52 weeks. The same applies if the sole qualifying child ceases to be a child or to be qualifying (reg. 48).

The general rule is that once a direction has been in operation for the full period, another direction cannot be given in relation to the children covered by the direction (reg. 36(9)). But if an additional qualifying child appears a further direction may be given (reg. 47).

PART I

GENERAL

Citation, commencement and interpretation

1.—(1) These Regulations may be cited as the Child Support (Maintenance Assessment Procedure) Regulations 1992 and shall come into force on 5th April 1993.

(2) In these Regulations, unless the context otherwise requires—

"the Act" means the Child Support Act 1991;

"applicable amount" is to be construed in accordance with Part IV of the Income Support Regulations;

"applicable amounts Schedule" means Schedule 2 to the Income Support Regulations;

"award period" means a period in respect of which an award of family credit or disability working allowance is made;

"balance of the reduction period" means, in relation to a direction that is or has been in force, the portion of the period specified in a direction in respect of which no reduction of relevant benefit has been made;

"benefit week", in relation to income support, has the same meaning as in the Income Support Regulations, and, in relation to family credit and disability working allowance, is to be construed in accordance with the Social Security (Claims and Payments) Regulations 1987;

"direction" means reduced benefit direction;

"disability working allowance" has the same meaning as in the Social Security Contributions and Benefits Act 1992;

[*definitions omitted as not relating to reduced benefit directions*]

"Income Support Regulations" means the Income Support (General) Regulations 1987;

[*definitions omitted as not relating to reduced benefit directions*]

"obligation imposed by section 6 of the Act" is to be construed in accordance with section 46(1) of the Act;

"parent with care" means a person who, in respect or the same child or children, is both a parent and a person with care;

"the parent concerned" means the parent with respect to whom a direction is given;

[*definition omitted as not relating to reduced benefit directions*]

"relevant benefit" means income support, family credit or disability working allowance;

[*definition omitted as not relating to reduced benefit directions*]

(3) In these Regulations, references to a direction as being "in operation", "suspended", or "in force" shall be construed as follows—

a direction is "in operation" if, by virtue of that direction, relevant benefit is currently being reduced;

a direction is "suspended" if either—

   (a) after that direction has been given, relevant benefit ceases to be payable, or becomes payable at one of the rates indicated in regulation 40(3); or

   (b) at the time that the direction is given, relevant benefit is payable at one of the rates indicated in regulation 40(3),

and these Regulations provide for relevant benefit payable from a later date to be reduced by virtue of the same direction;

a direction is "in force" if it is either in operation or is suspended,

and cognate terms shall be construed accordingly.

(4) The provisions of Schedule 1 shall have effect to supplement the meaning of "child" in section 55 of the Act.

[*Paras. (5) to (9) not reproduced*]

PART IX

REDUCED BENEFIT DIRECTIONS

Prescription of disability working allowance for the purposes of section 6 of the Act

34. Disability working allowance shall be a benefit of a prescribed kind for the purposes of section 6 of the Act.

Periods for compliance with obligations imposed by section 6 of the Act

35.—(1) Where the Secretary of State considers that a parent has failed to comply with an obligation imposed by section 6 of the Act he shall serve written notice on that parent that, unless she complies with that obligation, he intends to refer the case to a child support officer to take action under section 46 of the Act if the child support officer considers such action to be appropriate.

(2) The Secretary of State shall not refer a case to a child support officer prior to the expiry of a period of 6 weeks from the date he serves notice under paragraph (1) on the parent in question, and the notice shall contain a statement to that effect.

(3) Where the Secretary of State refers a case to a child support officer and the child support officer serves written notice on a parent under section 46(2) of the Act, the period to be specifies in that notice shall be 14 days.

Amount of and period of reduction of relevant benefit under a reduced benefit direction

36.—(1) The reduction in the amount payable by way of a relevant benefit to, or in respect of, the parent concerned and the period of such reduction by virtue of a direction shall be determined in accordance with paragraphs (2) to (9).

(2) Subject to paragraph (6) and regulations 37, 38(7) and 40, there shall be a reduction for a period of 26 weeks from the day specified in the direction under the provisions of section 46(9) of the Act in respect of each such week equal to

$$0.2 \times B$$

where B is an amount equal to the weekly amount, in relation to the week in question, specified in column (2) of paragraph 1(1)(e) of the applicable amounts Schedule.

(3) Subject to paragraph (6) and regulations 37, 38(7) and 40, at the end of the period specified in paragraph (2) there shall be a reduction from the day immediately succeeding the last day of that period for a period of 52 weeks of an amount in respect of each such week equal to

$$0.1 \times B$$

where B has the same meaning as in paragraph (2).

(4) [¹Subject to paragraphs (5), (5A) and (5B)], a direction shall come into operation on the first day of the second benefit week following the review, carried out by the adjudication officer in consequence of the direction, of the relevant benefit that is payable.

(5) Where the relevant benefit is income support and the provisions of regulation 26(2) of the Social Security (Claims and Payments) Regulations 1987 (deferment of payment of different amount of income support) apply, a direction shall come into operation on such later date as may be determined by the Secretary of State in accordance with those provisions.

[¹(5A) Where the relevant benefit is family credit or disability working allowance and, at the time a direction is given, a lump sum payment has already been made under the provisions of regulation 27(1A) of the Social Security (Claims and Payments) Regulations 1987 (payment of family credit or disability working allowance by lump sum) the direction shall, subject to paragraph (5B), come into operation on the first day of any benefit week which immediately follows the period in respect of which the lump sum payment was made, or the first day of any benefit week which immediately follows 18th April 1995 if later.

(5B) Where the period in respect of which the lump sum payment was made is not immediately followed by a benefit week, but family credit or disability working allowance again becomes payable, or income support becomes payable, during a period of 52 weeks from the date the direction was given, the direction shall come into operation on the first day of the second benefit week which immediately follows the expiry of a period of 14 days from service of the notice specified in paragraph (5C).

(5C) Where paragraph (5B) applies, the parent to or in respect of whom family credit or disability working allowance has again become payable, or income support has become payable, shall be notified in writing by a child support officer that the amount of family credit, disability working allowance or income support paid to or in respect of her will be reduced in accordance with the provisions of paragraph (5B) if she continues to fail to comply with the obligations imposed by section 6 of the Act.

(5D) Where—
(a) family credit or disability working allowance has been paid by lump sum under the provisions of regulation 27(1A) of the Social Security (Claims and Payments) Regulations 1987 (whether or not a benefit week immediately follows the period in respect of which the lump sum payment was made); and
(b) where income support becomes payable to or in respect of a parent to or in respect of whom family credit or disability working allowance was payable at the time the direction referred to in paragraph (5A) was made, income support shall become a relevant benefit for the purposes of that direction and the amount payable by way of income support shall be reduced in accordance with that direction.

(5E) In circumstances to which paragraph (5A) or (5B) applies, where no relevant benefit has become payable during a period of 52 weeks from the date on which a direction was given, it shall lapse.]

(6) Where the benefit payable is income support and there is a change in the benefit week whilst a direction is in operation, the periods of the reductions specified in paragraphs (2) and (3) shall be—
(a) where the reduction is that specified in paragraph (2), a period greater than 25 weeks but less than 26 weeks;
(b) where the reduction is that specified in paragraph (3), a period greater than 51 weeks but less than 52 weeks,
and ending on the last day of the last benefit week falling entirely within the period of 26 weeks specified in paragraph (2), or the period of 52 weeks specified in paragraph (3), as the case may be.

(7) Where the weekly amount specified in column (2) of paragraph 1(1)(e) of the applicable amounts Schedule changes on a day when a direction is in operation, the amount of the reduction of the relevant benefit shall be changed—
(a) where the benefit is income support, the first day of the first benefit week to commence for the parent concerned on or after the day that weekly amount changes;
(b) where the benefit is family credit or disability working allowance, from the first day of the next award period of that benefit for the parent concerned commencing on or after the day that weekly amount changes.

(8) Only one direction in relation to a parent shall be in force at any one time.

(9) Where a direction has been in operation for the aggregate of the periods specified in paragraphs (2) and (3) ("the full period"), no further direction shall be given with respect to the same parent on account of that parent's failure to comply with the obligations imposed by section 6 of the Act in relation to any child in relation to whom the direction that has been in operation for the full period was given.

AMENDMENT

1. Child Support and Income Support (Amendment) Regulations 1995 (S.I. 1995 No. 1045), reg. 38 (April 18, 1995).

Modification of reduction under a reduced benefit direction to preserve minimum entitlement to relevant benefit

37. Where in respect of any benefit week the amount of the relevant benefit that would be payable after it has been reduced following a direction would, but for this regulation, be nil or less than the minimum amount of that benefit that is payable as determined—

(a) in the case of income support, by regulation 26(4) of the Social Security (Claims and Payments) Regulations 1987;

(b) in the case of family credit and disability working allowance, by regulation 27(2) of those Regulations,

the amount of that reduction shall be decreased to such extent as to raise the amount of that benefit to the minimum amount that is payable.

Suspension of a reduced benefit direction when relevant benefit ceases to be payable

38.—(1) Where relevant benefit ceases to be payable to, or in respect of, the parent concerned at a time when a direction is in operation, that direction shall, subject to paragraph (2), be suspended for a period of 52 weeks from the date the relevant benefit has ceased to be payable.

(2) Where a direction has been suspended for a period of 52 weeks and no relevant benefit is payable at the end of the period, it shall cease to be in force.

(3) Where a direction is suspended and relevant benefit again becomes payable to or in respect of the parent concerned, the amount payable by way of that benefit shall, subject to regulation 40, 41 and 42, be reduced in accordance with that direction for the balance of the reduction period.

(4) The amount or, as the case may be, amounts of the reduction to be made during the balance of the reduction period shall be determined in accordance with regulation 36(2) and (3).

(5) No reduction in the amount of benefit under paragraph (3) shall be made before the expiry of a period of 14 days from service of the notice specified in paragraph (6), and the provisions of regulation 36(4) shall apply as to the date when the direction again comes into operation.

(6) Where relevant benefit again becomes payable to or in respect of a parent with respect to whom a direction is suspended she shall be notified in writing by a child support officer that the amount of relevant benefit paid to or in respect of her will again be reduced, in accordance with the provisions of paragraph (3), if she continues to fail to comply with the obligations imposed by section 6 of the Act.

(7) Where a direction has ceased to be in force by virtue of the provisions of paragraph (2), a further direction in respect of the same parent given on account of that parent's failure to comply with the obligations imposed by section 6 of the Act in relation to one or more of the same qualifying children shall, unless it also ceases to be in force by virtue of the provisions of paragraph (2), be in operation for the balance of the reduction period relating to the direction that has ceased to be in force, and the provisions of paragraph (4) shall apply to it.

Reduced benefit direction where family credit or disability working allowance is payable and income support becomes payable

39.—(1) Where a direction is in operation in respect of a parent to whom or in respect of whom family credit or disability working allowance is payable, and income support becomes payable to or in respect of that parent, income support shall become a relevant benefit for the purposes of that direction, and the amount payable by way of income support shall be reduced in accordance with that direction for the balance of the reduction period.

(2) The amount or, as the case may be, the amounts of the reduction to be made during the balance of the reduction period shall be determined in accordance with regulation 36(2) and (3).

Suspension of a reduced benefit direction when a modified applicable amount is payable

40.—(1) Where a direction is given or is in operation at a time when income support is payable to or in respect of the parent concerned but her applicable amount falls to be calculated under the provisions mentioned in paragraph (3), that direction shall be suspended for so long as the applicable amount falls to be calculated under the provisions mentioned in that paragraph, or 52 weeks, whichever period is the shorter.

[²(1A) Where a direction is given or is in operation at a time when income support is payable to or in respect of the parent concerned, but her applicable amount includes a residential allowance under regulation 17 of, and paragraph 2A of Schedule 2 to, the Income Support Regulations (applicable amounts for those in residential care or nursing homes), that direction shall be suspended for as long as her applicable amount includes a residential allowance under regulation 17 and paragraph 2A of Schedule 2, or 52 weeks, whichever period is the shorter.]

(2) Where a case falls within paragraph (1) [² or (1A)] and a direction has been suspended for a period of 52 weeks, it shall cease to be in force.

(3) The provisions of paragraph (1) shall apply where the applicable amount in relation to the parent concerned falls to be calculated under—

(a) regulation 19 of and Schedule 4 to the Income Support Regulations (applicable amounts for persons resident in residential care and nursing homes);

(b) regulation 21 of and paragraphs 1 to 3 of Schedule 7 to the Income Support Regulations (patients);

(c) regulation 21 of and paragraphs 10B, 10C [¹ ...] and 13 of Schedule 7 to the Income Support Regulations (persons in residential accommodation).

AMENDMENT

1. Child Support (Miscellaneous Amendments) Regulations 1993 (S.I. 1993 No. 913), reg. 13 (April 5, 1993).
2. Child Support and Income Support (Amendment) Regulations 1995 (S.I. 1995 No. 1045), reg. 39 (April 18, 1995).

Termination of a reduced benefit direction following compliance with obligations imposed by section 6 of the Act

41.—(1) Where a parent with care with respect to whom a direction is in force complies with the obligations imposed by section 6 of the Act, that direction shall cease to be in force on the date determined in accordance with paragraph (2) or (3), as the case may be.

(2) Where the direction is in operation, it shall cease to be in force on the last day of the benefit week during the course of which the parent concerned complied with the obligations imposed by section 6 of the Act.

(3) Where the direction is suspended, it shall cease to be in force on the date on which the parent concerned complied with the obligations imposed by section 6 of the Act.

Review of a reduced benefit direction

42.—(1) Where a parent with care with respect to whom a direction is in force [¹or some other person] gives the Secretary of State reasons—

(a) additional to any reasons given by [¹the parent with care] in response to the notice served on her under section 46(2) of the Act for having failed to comply with the obligations imposed by section 6 of the Act; or

(b) as to why [¹the parent with care] should no longer be required to comply with the obligations imposed by section 6 of the Act,
the Secretary of State shall refer the matter to a child officer who shall conduct a review of the direction (''a review'') to determine whether the direction is to continue or is to cease to be in force.

(2) Where a parent with care with respect to whom a direction is in force [¹or some other person] gives a child support officer reasons of the kind mentioned in paragraph (1), a child support officer shall conduct a review to determine whether the direction is to continue or is to cease to be in force.

[¹(2A) Where a direction is in force and the Secretary of State becomes aware that a question arises as to whether the welfare of a child is likely to be affected by the direction continuing in force, he shall refer the matter to a child support office who shall conduct a review to determine whether the direction is to continue or is to cease to be in force.

(2B) Where a direction is in force and a child support officer becomes aware that a question arises as to whether the welfare of a child is likely to be affected by the direction continuing to be in force a child support officer shall conduct a review to determine whether the direction is to continue or is to cease to be in force.]

(3) A review shall not be carried out by the child support officer who gave the direction with respect to the parent concerned.

(4) Where the child support officer who is conducting a review considers that the parent concerned is no longer to be required to comply with the obligations imposed by section 6 of the Act, the direction shall cease to be in force on the date determined in accordance with paragraph (5) or (6), as the case may be.

(5) Where the direction is in operation, it shall cease to be in force on the last day of the benefit week during the course of which [¹the reasons specified in paragraph (1) were given] [² or the Secretary of State or a child support officer becomes aware of a question of a kind mentioned in paragraph (2A) or (2B)].

(6) Where the direction is suspended, it shall cease to be in force on the date on which [¹the reasons specified in paragraph (1) were given].

(7) [¹ ...]

(8) A child support officer shall on completing a review immediately notify the parent concerned of his decision, so far as that is reasonably practicable, and shall give the reasons for his decision in writing.

[¹(9) A parent with care who is aggrieved by a decision of a child support officer following a review may appeal to a child support appeal tribunal against that decision.

(10) Sections 20(2) to (4) and 21 of the Act shall apply in relation to appeals under paragraph (9) as they apply in relation to appeals under section 20 of the Act.

(11) A notification under paragraph (8) shall include information as to the provision of paragraph (9) and (10).]

AMENDMENT

1. Child Support (Miscellaneous Amendments) Regulations 1993 (S.I. 1993 No. 913), reg. 14 (April 5, 1993).
2. Child Support and Income Support (Amendment) Regulations 1995 (S.I. 1995 No. 1045), reg. 40 (April 18, 1995).

Termination of a reduced benefit direction where a maintenance assessment is made following an application by a child under section 7 of the Act

43. Where a qualifying child of a parent with respect to whom a direction is in force applies for a maintenance assessment to be made with respect to him under section 7 of the Act, and an assessment is made in response to that application in respect of all of the qualifying children in relation to whom the parent concerned failed to comply with the obligations imposed by section 6 of the Act, that direction shall cease to be in force from the date determined in accordance with regulation 45.

Termination of a reduced benefit direction where a maintenance assessment is made following an application by an absent parent under section 4 of the Act

44. Where—
(a) an absent parent applies for a maintenance assessment to be made under section 4 of the Act with respect to all of his qualifying children in relation to whom the other parent of those children is a person with care;
(b) a direction is in force with respect to that other parent following her failure to comply with the obligations imposed by section 6 of the Act in relation to those qualifying children; and
(c) an assessment is made in response to that application by the absent parent for a maintenance assessment,
that direction shall cease to be in force on the date determined in accordance with regulation 45.

Date from which a reduced benefit direction ceases to be in force following a termination under regulation 43 or 44

45.—(1) The date a direction ceases to be in force under the provisions of regulation 43 or 44 shall be determined in accordance with paragraphs (2) and (3).

(2) Where the direction is in operation, it shall cease to be in force on the last day of the benefit week during the course of which the Secretary of State is supplied with the information that enables a child support officer to make the assessment.

(3) Where the direction is suspended, it shall cease to be in force on the date on which the Secretary of State is supplied with the information that enables a child support officer to make the assessment.

Cancellation of a reduced benefit direction in cases of error

46. Where a child support officer is satisfied that a direction was given as a result of an error on the part of the Secretary of State or a child support officer, or though not given as a result of such an error has not subsequently ceased to be in force as a result of such an error, the child support officer shall cancel the direction and it shall be treated as not having been given, or as having ceased to be in force on the date it would have ceased to be in force if that error had not been made, as the case may be.

Reduced benefit directions where there is an additional qualifying child

47.—(1) Where a direction is in operation or would be in operation but for the provisions of regulation 40 and a child support officer gives a further direction with respect to the same parent on account of that parent failing to comply with the obligations imposed by section 6 of the Act in relation to an additional qualifying child of whom she is a person with care, the earlier direction shall cease to be in force on the last day of the benefit week preceding the benefit week on the first day of which, in accordance with the provisions of regulation

36(4), the further direction comes into operation, or would come into operation but for the provisions of regulation 40.

(2) Where a further direction comes into operation in a case falling within paragraph (1), the provisions of regulation 36 shall apply to it.

(3) Where a direction has ceased to be in force by virtue of regulation 38(2) and a child support officer gives a direction with respect to the same parent on account of that parent failing to comply with the obligations imposed by section 6 of the Act in relation to an additional qualifying child, no further direction shall be given with respect to that parent on account of her failure to comply with the obligations imposed by section 6 of the Act in relation to one or more children in relation to whom the direction that has ceased to be in force by virtue of regulation 38(2) was given.

(4) Where a case falls within paragraph (1) or (3) and the further direction, but for the provisions of this paragraph would cease to be in force by virtue of the provisions of regulation 41 or 42, but the earlier direction would not have ceased to be in force by virtue of the provisions of those regulations, the later direction shall continue in force for a period ("the extended period") calculated in accordance with the provisions of paragraph (5) and the reduction of relevant benefit shall be determined in accordance with paragraphs (6) and (7).

(5) The extended period for the purposes of paragraph (4) shall be

(78—F—S) weeks

where—

F is the number of weeks for which the earlier direction was in operation; and

S is the number of weeks for which the later direction has been in operation.

(6) Where the extended period calculated in accordance with paragraph (5) is greater than 52 weeks, there shall be a reduction of relevant benefit in respect of the number of weeks in excess of 52 determined in accordance with regulation 36(2), and a reduction of relevant benefit in respect of the remaining 52 weeks determined in accordance with regulation 36(3).

(7) Where the extended period calculated in accordance with paragraph (5) is equal to 52 weeks, there shall be a reduction of relevant benefit in respect of that period determined in accordance with regulation 36(3).

(8) In this regulation "an additional qualifying child" means a qualifying child of whom the parent concerned is a person with care and who was either not such a qualifying child at the time the earlier direction was given or had not been born at the time the earlier direction was given.

Suspension and termination of a reduced benefit direction where the sole qualifying child ceases to be a child or where the parent concerned ceases to be a person with care

48.—(1) Where, whilst a direction is in operation—
  (a) there is, in relation to that direction, only one qualifying child, and that child ceases to be a child within the meaning of the Act; or
  (b) the parent concerned ceases to be a person with care,
the direction shall be suspended from the last day of the benefit week during the course of which the child ceases to be a child within the meaning of the Act, or the parent concerned ceases to be a person with care, as the case may be.

(2) Where, under the provisions of paragraph (1), a direction has been suspended for a period of 52 weeks and no relevant benefit is payable at that time, it shall cease to be in force.

(3) If during the period specified in paragraph (1) the former child again becomes a child within the meaning of the Act or the parent concerned again becomes a person with care and relevant benefit is payable to or in respect of

that parent, a reduction in the amount of that benefit shall be made in accordance with the provisions of paragraphs (3) to (7) of regulation 38.

Notice of termination of a reduced benefit direction

49.—(1) Where a direction ceases to be in force under the provisions of regulations 41 to 44 or 46 to 48, or is suspended under the provisions of regulation 48, a child support officer shall serve notice of such termination or suspension, as the case may be, on the adjudication officer and shall specify the date on which the direction ceases to be in force or is suspended, as the case may be.

(2) Any notice served under paragraph (1) shall set out the reasons why the direction has ceased to be in force or has been suspended.

(3) The parent concerned shall be served with a copy of any notice served under paragraph (1).

Rounding provisions

50. Where any calculation made under this Part of these Regulations results in a fraction of a penny, that fraction shall be treated as a penny if it exceeds one half, and shall otherwise be disregarded.

Child Support (Maintenance Assessments and Special Cases) Regulations 1992

(S.I. 1992 No. 1815)

Made by the Secretary of State under various provisions of the Child Support Act 1991

REGULATIONS REPRODUCED

PART II

Calculation or estimation of child support maintenance
13. The minimum amount

PART III

Special cases
28. Amount payable where absent parent is in receipt of income support or other prescribed benefit.

GENERAL NOTE

See the note to s. 43 of the Child Support Act 1991.

PART II

The minimum amount

13.—(1) Subject to regulation 26, for the purposes of paragraph 7(1) of Schedule 1 to the Act the minimum amount shall be for 5 per centum of the amount specified in paragraph 1(1)(e) of the relevant Schedule (income support personal allowance for single claimant aged not less than 25).

(2) Where an amount calculated under paragraph (1) results in a sum other than a multiple of 5 pence, it shall be treated as the sum which is the next higher multiple of 5 pence.

PART III

Amount payable where absent parent is in receipt of income support or other prescribed benefit

28.—(1) Where the condition specified in section 43(1)(a) of the Act is satisfied in relation to an absent parent (assessable income to be nil where income support or other prescribed benefit is paid), the prescribed conditions for the purposes of section 43(1)(b) of the Act are that—

(a) the absent parent is aged 18 or over;

(b) he does not satisfy the conditions in paragraph 3 of the relevant Schedule (income support family premium) [¹and does not have day to day care of any child (whether or not a relevant child)]; and

(c) [¹his income does not include] one or more of the payments or awards specified in Schedule 4 (other than by reason of a provision preventing receipt of overlapping benefits or by reason of a failure to satisfy the relevant contribution conditions).

(2) For the purposes of section 43(2)(a) of the Act, the prescribed amount shall be equal to the minimum amount prescribed in regulation 13(1) for the purposes of paragraph 7(1) of Schedule 1 to the Act.

[¹[²(3) Subject to paragraph (4), where—

(a) an absent parent is liable under section 43 of the Act and this regulation to make payments in place of payments of child support maintenance with respect to two or more qualifying children in relation to whom there is more than one parent with care; or

(b) that absent parent and his partner (within the meaning of regulation 2(1) of the Social Security (Claims and Payments) Regulations 1987) are both liable to make such payments,

the prescribed amount mentioned in paragraph (2) shall be apportioned between the persons with care in the same ratio as the maintenance requirements of the qualifying child or children in relation to each of those persons with care bear to each other.]

(4) If, in making the apportionment required by paragraph (3), the effect of the application of regulation 2(2) would be such that the aggregate amount payable would be different from the amount prescribed in paragraph (2) the Secretary of State shall adjust the apportionment so as to eliminate that difference; and that adjustment shall be varied from time to time so as to secure that, taking one week with another and so far as is practicable, each person with care receives the amount which she would have received if no adjustment had been made under this paragraph.

(5) The provisions of Schedule 5 shall have effect in relation to cases to which section 43 of the Act and this regulation apply.]

AMENDMENTS

1. Child Support (Miscellaneous Amendments) Regulations 1993 (S.I. 1993 No. 913), reg. 26 (April 5, 1993).
2. Child Support (Maintenance Assessment and Special Cases) Amendment Regulations 1993 (S.I. 1993 No. 925), reg. 2(2) (April 26, 1993).

SCHEDULE 4   Regulation 26(1)(b)(i)

CASES WHERE CHILD SUPPORT MAINTENANCE IS NOT TO BE PAYABLE

The payments and awards specified for the purposes of regulation 26(1)(b)(i) are—

(a) the following payments under the Contribution and Benefits Act—

[²(i) incapacity benefit under section 30A;
  (ii) long-term incapacity benefit for widows under section 40;
 (iii) long-term incapacity benefit for widowers under section 41;]
 (iv) maternity allowance under section 35;
  (v) [² . . .];
 (vi) attendance allowance under section 64;
 (vii) severe disablement allowance under section 68;
(viii) invalid care allowance under section 70;
 (ix) disability living allowance under section 71;
  (x) disablement benefit under section 103;
 (xi) disability working allowance under section 129;
 (xii) statutory sick pay within the meaning of section 151;
(xiii) statutory maternity pay within the meaning of section 164;
(b) awards in respect of disablement made under (or under provisions analogous to)—
  (i) the War Pensions (Coastguards) Scheme 1944 (S.I. 1944 No. 500);
  (ii) the War Pensions (Naval Auxiliary Personnel) Scheme 1964 (S.I. 1964 No. 1985);
 (iii) the Pensions (Polish Forces) Scheme 1964 (S.I. 1964 No. 2007);
 (iv) the War Pensions (Mercantile Marine) Scheme 1964 (S.I. 1964 No. 2058);
  (v) the Royal Warrant of 21st December 1964 (service in the Home Guard before 1945) (Cmnd. 2563);
 (vi) the Order by Her Majesty of 22nd December 1964 concerning pensions and other grants in respect of disablement or death due to service in the Home Guard after 27th April 1952 (Cmnd. 2564);
 (vii) the Order by Her Majesty (Ulster Defence Regiment) of 4th January 1971 (Cmnd. 4567);
(viii) the Personal Injuries (Civilians) Scheme 1983 (S.I. 1983 No. 686);
 (ix) the Naval, Military and Air Forces Etc. (Disablement and Death) Service Pensions Order 1983 (S.I. 1983 No. 883); and
(c) payments from [¹the Independent Living (1993) Fund or the Independent Living (Extension) Fund].

AMENDMENTS

1. Child Support (Miscellaneous Amendments) Regulations 1993 (S.I. 1993 No. 913), reg. 34 (April 5, 1993).
2. Child Support and Income Support (Amendment) Regulations 1995 (S.I. 1995 No. 1045), reg. 58 (April 13, 1995).

[¹SCHEDULE 5   Regulation 28(5)

PROVISIONS APPLYING TO CASES TO WHICH SECTION 43 OF THE ACT AND REGULATION 28 APPLY

1. In this Schedule—
[²(a)] "relevant decision" means a decision of a child support officer given under section 43 of the Act (contribution to maintenance by deduction from benefit) and regulation 28[²; and
  (b) "relevant person" has the same meaning as in regulation 1(2) of the Maintenance Assessment Procedure Regulations.]
[³**2.** A relevant decision may be reviewed by a child support officer, either on application by a relevant person or of his own motion—
  (a) if it appears to him that the absent parent has at some time after that decision was given satisfied the conditions prescribed by regulation 28(1) or, as the case may be, no longer satisfies those conditions; or

(b) if it appears to him that the relevant decision was wrong in law or was made in ignorance of, or based on a mistake as to, a material fact.]

3. A relevant decision [³ made on or before 18th April 1994] shall be reviewed by a child support officer[³ after] it has been in force for 52 weeks.

[³**3A.** A relevant decision made after 18th April 1994 shall be reviewed by a child support officer after it has been in force for 104 weeks.]

4.—(1) Before conducting a review under paragraph 6 the child support officer shall—

(a) give 14 days' notice of the proposed review to the relevant persons [² . . .]; and

(b) invite representations, either in person or in writing, from the relevant persons on any matter relating to the review and set out the provisions of sub-paragraphs (2) to (4) in relation to such representations.

(2) Subject to sub-paragraph (3), where the child support officer conducting the review does not, within 14 days of the date on which notice of the review was given, receive a request from a relevant person to make representations in person, or receives such a request and arranges for an appointment for such representations to be made but that appointment is not kept, he may complete the review in the absence of such representations from that person.

(3) Where the child support of officer conducting the review is satisfied that there was good reason for failure to keep an appointment, he shall provide for a further opportunity for the making of representations by the relevant person concerned before he completes the review.

(4) Where the child support officer conducting the review does not receive written representations from a relevant person within 14 days of the date on which notice of the review was given, he may complete the review in the absence of written representations from that person.

5. After completing a review under paragraph 2, 3 or 6, the child support officer shall notify all relevant persons of the result of the review and—

(a) in the case of a review under paragraph 2 or 3, of the right to apply for a further review under paragraph (6); and

(b) in the case of a review under [²paragraph 6], of the right of appeal under section 20 of the Act as applied by paragraph 8.

6. Where a child support officer has made a decision under regulation 28 or paragraph 2 or 3, any relevant person may apply to the Secretary of State for a review of that decision and, subject to the modifications set out in paragraph 7, the provisions of section 18(5) to (7) of the Act shall apply to such a review.

7. The modifications to the provisions of section 18(5) to (7) of the Act referred to in paragraph 6 are—

(a) any reference in those provisions to a maintenance assessment shall be read as a reference to a relevant decision; and

(b) subsection 6 shall apply as if the reference to the cancellation of an assessment was omitted.

[²**7A.** If, on a review under paragraph 2, 3, or 6, the relevant decision is revised (''the revised decision'') the revised decision shall have effect—

(a) if the revised decision is that no payments such as are mentioned in section 43 of the Act are to be made, from the date on which the event giving rise to the review occurred: or

(b) if the revised decision is that such payments are to be made, from the date on which the revised decision is given.]

8. The provisions of section 20 of the Act (appeals) shall apply in relation to a review or a refusal to review under paragraph 6.

9. The provisions of paragraphs (1) and (2) of regulation 5 of the Child Support (Collection and Enforcement) Regulations 1992 shall apply to the transmission of payments in place of child support maintenance under section 43 of the Act and regulation 28 as they apply to the transmission of payments of child support maintenance.]

AMENDMENTS

1. Child Support (Miscellaneous Amendments) Regulations 1993 (S.I. 1993 No. 913), reg. 26(3) and Sched. (April 5, 1993).

2. Child Support (Maintenance Assessment and Special Cases) Amendment Regulations 1993 (S.I. 1993 No. 925), reg. 2(3) (April 26, 1993).

3. Child Support and Income Support (Amendment) Regulations 1995 (S.I. 1995 No. 1045), reg. 59 (April 18, 1995).

PART III

FAMILY CREDIT

The Family Credit (General) Regulations 1987

(S.I. 1987 No. 1973)

Made by the Secretary of State under ss.20(1), (5)(c), (6), (10), (11) and (12), 21(3) and (6)(a), 22(1) and (5) to (9), 51(1)(h) and 84(1) of the Social Security Act 1986 and ss.104(5) and 166(1) to (3A) of the Social Security Act 1975.

ARRANGEMENT OF REGULATIONS

PART I

GENERAL

PART II

PRESENCE IN GREAT BRITAIN AND REMUNERATIVE WORK

PART III

MEMBERSHIP OF A FAMILY

PART IV

INCOME AND CAPITAL

Chapter I

General

Chapter II

Normal Weekly Income

45. Disregard of changes occurring during summer vacation

PART V

CALCULATION OF ENTITLEMENT

46. Determination of appropriate maximum family credit
47. Applicable amount of family credit
48. Entitlement to family credit where income exceeds the applicable amount

PART VI

CHANGES OF CIRCUMSTANCES

49. Death of claimant
50. Prevention of duplication of awards of family credit and income support
51. Overlapping awards of family credit
51A. Reduced benefit direction

PART VII

ENTITLEMENT TO FAMILY CREDIT AND DISABILITY WORKING ALLOWANCE

52. Prescribed circumstances for entitlement to family credit

SCHEDULES

1. Sums to be disregarded in the calculation of earnings
2. Sums to be disregarded in the calculation of income other than earnings
3. Capital to be disregarded
4. Determination of maximum family credit: adult, child and young person credits

GENERAL NOTE

The family credit scheme was described as "the jewel in the crown" of the April 1988 social security reforms. Some £200 million p.a. over and above what was spent on family income supplement (FIS) was allowed in the family credit estimates. In October 1994, 577,660 families were on family credit receiving an average of £49.54 p.w.

Although there are superficial similarities between FIS and family credit, the differences are important. First, the calculations are made on net income, rather than gross. This eases the worst of the poverty trap problems. Second, the maximum family credit is paid at all levels of income up to the applicable amount (reg. 47). Third, if income is above that level the maximum family credit is reduced by 70p for every £1 of excess, rather than by 50p. Fourth, the income support £8000/£3000 capital rule is applied (regs. 28 and 36). Fifth, the definition of full-time work was changed to 24 hours per week (reg. 4), rather than 30 for most claimants.

One of the most important subsequent changes was a further reduction in the qualifying hours to 16 per week in April 1992. At the same time, there was a slight easing in the way in which the test is applied. The combination brought more claimants within family credit rather than income support.

In April 1992 a disregard of the first £15 of maintenance was introduced and there were further changes in April 1993 to accommodate the child support system.

Since October 4, 1994, certain family credit claimants have been able to offset child care costs of up to £40 per week against their earnings. This also applies to disability working allowance (and housing and council tax benefit), but not income support. Although this is an important change in principle the scope of the disregard is limited (see the notes to regs. 13 and 13A).

As part of its emphasis on increasing in-work benefits (at the expense of out-of-work benefits), the Government has announced that from July 1995 the maximum credit for family credit will be increased by £10 for those who work 30 hours or more a week. The same will apply to disability working allowance. There will also be provision to ensure that this gain is not lost by decreased housing benefit/council tax benefit. Other changes are also planned, *e.g.*, from April 1996 most new family credit claims will be paid within five days, and people who have been out of work for six months or more will be allowed to keep their existing rate of housing benefit and council tax benefit for four weeks after taking up a job.

PART I

GENERAL

Citation and commencement

1. These Regulations may be cited as the Family Credit (General) Regulations 1987, and shall come into force on 11th April 1988.

Interpretation

2.—(1) In these Regulations, unless the context otherwise requires—

"the Act" means the Social Security Act 1986;

[6"assessment period" means, in the case of an employed earner, a period determined in accordance with [13regulation 14 or, as the case may be, 14A] and, in the case of a self-employed earner, a period determined in accordance with regulation 15;]

"claim" means a claim for family credit;

"claimant" means a person claiming family credit;

"close relative" means a parent, parent-in-law, son, son-in-law, daughter, daughter-in-law, step-parent, step-son, step-daughter, brother, sister, or the spouse of any of the preceding persons or, if that person is one of an unmarried couple, the other member of that couple;

[9"community charge benefit" means community charge benefits under Part VII of the Contributions and Benefits Act 1992 as originally enacted;]

"concessionary payment" means a payment made under arrangements made by the Secretary of State with the consent of the Treasury which is charged either to the National Insurance Fund or to a Departmental Expenditure Vote to which payments of benefit under the Act, the Social Security Act or the Child Benefit Act 1975 [SSCBA] are charged;

[9"the Contributions and Benefits Act" means the Social Security Contributions and Benefits Act 1992;]

[14"Crown property" means property held by Her Majesty in right of the Crown or by a government department or which is held in trust for Her Majesty for the purposes of a government department, except (in the case of an interest held by Her Majesty in right of the Crown) where the interest is under the management of the Crown Estate Commissioners;]

"date of claim" means the date on which the claimant makes, or is treated as making, a claim for family credit;

[13"director" means a director of a company, and for this purpose "company" means a company within the meaning of section 735(1) of the Companies Act 1985 or a body corporate to which, by virtue of section 718 of that Act, any provision of that Act applies;]

[5"disability living allowance" means a disability living allowance under section 372A of the Social Security Act [SSCBA, s.71];

"disability working allowance" means a disability working allowance under section 20 of the Act [SSCBA, s.129];]

"earnings" has the meaning prescribed in regulation 19 or, as the case may be, 21;

"employed earner" shall be construed in accordance with section 2(1)(*a*) of the Social Security Act [SSCBA, s.2(1)(*a*)];

[14"lone parent" means a person who has no partner and who is responsible for, and a member of the same household as, a child or young person;]

[8"lower rate" where it relates to rates of tax has the same meaning as in the Income and Corporation Taxes Act 1988 by virtue of section 832(1) of that Act;]

[12"maternity leave" means a period during which a woman is absent from work because she is pregnant or has given birth to a child, and at the end of which she has a right to return to work either under the terms of her contract of employment or under Part III of the Employment Protection (Consolidation) Act 1978;]

[5"mobility allowance" means an allowance under section 37A of the Social Security Act;

"mobility supplement" means any supplement under article 26A of the Naval, Military and Air Forces etc. (Disablement and Death) Service Pensions Order 1983 including such a supplement by virtue of any other scheme or order or under Article 25A of the Personal Injuries (Civilians) Scheme 1983;

"net earnings" means such earnings as are calculated in accordance with regulation 20;

"net profit" means such profit as is calculated in accordance with regulation 22;

"occupational pension" means any pension or other periodical payment under an occupational pension scheme but does not include any discretionary payment out of a fund established for relieving hardship in particular cases;

"partner" means, where a claimant—
  (a) is a member of a married or unmarried couple, the other member of that couple,
  (b) is married polygamously to two or more members of the same household, any such member;

[6"pay period" has the meaning given in regulation 14(7)(b);]

"payment" includes a part of a payment;

[12"personal pension scheme" has the same meaning as in section 84(1) of the Act and, in the case of a self-employed earner, includes a scheme approved by the Inland Revenue under Chapter IV of Part XIV of the Income and Corporation Taxes Act 1988;]

"policy of life insurance" means any instrument by which the payment of money is assured on death (except death by accident only) or the happening of any contingency dependent on human life, or any instrument evidencing a contract which is subject to payment of premiums for a term dependent on human life;

[7"qualifying person" means a person in respect of whom payment has been made from the Fund [11 or the Eileen Trust];]

"self-employed earner" shall be construed in accordance with section 2(1)(b) of the Social Security Act [SSCBA, s.2(1)(b)];

"Social Security Act" means the Social Security Act 1975;

"student" has the meaning prescribed in regulation 37;

[11"the Eileen Trust" means the charitable trust of that name established on 29th March 1993 out of funds provided by the Secretary of State for the benefit of persons eligible for payment in accordance with its provisions;]

[7"the Fund" means moneys made available from time to time by the Secretary of State for the benefit of persons eligible for payment in accordance with the provisions of a scheme established by him on 24th April 1992 or, in Scotland, on 10th April 1992;]

[10"the Independent Living (Extension) Fund" means the Trust of that name established by a deed dated 25th February 1993 and made between the Secretary of State for Social Security of the one part and Robin Glover Wendt and John Fletcher Shepherd of the other part;]

[²"the Independent Living Fund" means the charitable trust established out of funds provided by the Secretary of State for the purpose of providing financial assistance to those persons incapacitated by or otherwise suffering from very severe disablement who are in need of such assistance to enable them to live independently;]

[¹⁰"the Independent Living (1993) Fund" means the Trust of that name established by a deed dated 25th February 1993 and made between the Secretary of State for Social Security of the one part and Robin Glover Wendt and John Fletcher Shepherd of the other part;]

[¹⁰"the Independent Living Funds" means the Independent Living Fund, the Independent Living (Extension) Fund and the Independent Living (1993) Fund;]

[³"the Macfarlane (Special Payments) Trust" means the trust of that name, established on 29th January 1990 partly out of funds provided by the Secretary of State, for the benefit of certain persons suffering from haemophilia;]

[⁴"the Macfarlane (Special Payments) (No. 2) Trust" means the trust of that name, established on 3rd May 1991 partly out of funds provided by the Secretary of State, for the benefit of certain persons suffering from haemophilia and other beneficiaries;]

[¹"the Macfarlane Trust" means the charitable trust, established partly out of funds provided by the Secretary of State to the Haemophilia Society, for the relief of poverty or distress among those suffering from haemophilia;]

[⁶"training allowance" means an allowance (whether by way of periodical grants or otherwise) payable—

(a) out of public funds by a Government department or by or on behalf of the Secretary of State, Scottish Enterprise or Highlands and Islands Enterprise;

(b) to a person for his maintenance or in respect of a member of his family; and

(c) for the period, or part of the period, during which he is following a course of training or instruction provided by, or in pursuance of arrangements made with, that department or approved by that department in relation to him or so provided or approved by or on behalf of the Secretary of State, Scottish Enterprise or Highlands and Islands Enterprise,

but it does not include an allowance paid by any Government department to or in respect of a person by reason of the fact that he is following a course of full-time education, other than arrangements made under section 2 of the Employment and Training Act 1973, or is training as a teacher;]

[¹⁵"voluntary organisation" means a body, other than a public or local authority, the activities of which are carried on otherwise than for profit;]

[⁹"water charges" means—

(a) as respects England and Wales, any water and sewerage charges under Chapter I of Part V of the Water Industry Act 1991;

(b) as respects Scotland, any water and sewerage charges under Schedule 11 to the Local Government Finance Act 1992;]

"week" means a period of seven days beginning with midnight between Saturday and Sunday;

"week of claim" means the week which includes the date of claim;

"year of assessment" has the same meaning prescribed in section 526(5) of the Income and Corporation Taxes Act 1970;

"young person" has the meaning prescribed in regulation 6.

(2) Unless the context otherwise requires, any reference in these Regulations to a numbered regulation, Part or Schedule is a reference to the regulation, Part or Schedule bearing that number in these Regulations and any reference in a regulation or Schedule to a numbered paragraph is a reference to the paragraph in that regulation or Schedule bearing that number.

AMENDMENTS

1. Family Credit (General) Amendment Regulations 1988 (S.I. 1988 No. 660), reg. 2 (April 11, 1988).
2. Family Credit and Income Support (General) Amendment Regulations 1988 (S.I. 1988 No. 999), reg. 2 (June 9, 1988).
3. Income-related Benefits Schemes Amendment Regulations 1990 (S.I. 1990 No. 127), reg. 2 (January 31, 1990).
4. Income-related Benefits Schemes and Social Security (Recoupment) Amendment Regulations 1991 (S.I. 1991 No. 1175), reg. 5 (May 11, 1991).
5. Disability Living Allowance and Disability Working Allowance (Consequential Provisions) Regulations 1991 (S.I. 1991 No. 2742), reg. 13(2) (April 6, 1992).
6. Family Credit (General) Amendment Regulations 1992 (S.I. 1992 No. 573), reg. 2 (April 7, 1992).
7. Income-related Benefits Schemes and Social Security (Recoupment) Amendment Regulations 1992 (S.I. 1992 No. 1101), reg. 6 (May 7, 1992).
8. Income-related Benefits Schemes (Miscellaneous Amendments) (No. 3) Regulations 1992 (S.I. 1992 No. 2155), reg. 4 (October 5, 1992).
9. Income-related Benefits Schemes (Miscellaneous Amendments) Regulations 1993 (S.I. 1993 No. 315), reg. 10 (April 13, 1993).
10. Social Security Benefits (Miscellaneous Amendments) (No. 2) Regulations 1993 (S.I. 1993 No. 963), reg. 3(2) (April 22, 1993).
11. Income-related Benefits Schemes and Social Security (Recoupment Amendment Regulations 1993 (S.I. 1993 No. 1249), reg. 2(2) (May 14, 1993).
12. Income-related Benefits Schemes (Miscellaneous Amendments) (No. 4) Regulations 1993 (S.I. 1993 No. 2119), reg. 25 (October 5, 1993).
13. Income-related Benefits Schemes (Miscellaneous Amendments) Regulations 1994 (S.I. 1994 No. 527), reg. 10 (April 12, 1994).
14. Income-related Benefits Schemes (Miscellaneous Amendments) (No. 4) Regulations 1994 (S.I. 1994 No. 1924), reg. 4(2) (October 4, 1994).
15. Income-related Benefits Schemes (Miscellaneous Amendments) Regulations 1995 (S.I. 1995 No. 516), reg. 10 (April 11, 1995).

DEFINITION

"occupational pension scheme"—see 1986 Act, s.84(1) (PSA, s.1).

GENERAL NOTE

"*date of claim.*" See the Claims and Payments Regulations, reg. 6.
"*employed earner.*" The meaning in s.2(1)(a) of the Contributions and Benefits Act (1975 Act, s.2(1)(a)) is "a person who is gainfully employed in Great Britain either under a contract of service, or in an office (including elective office) with emoluments chargeable to income tax under Schedule E."
"*partner.*" See the notes to s.137(1) of the Contributions and Benefits Act for "married couple" and "unmarried couple."
"*self-employed earner.*" The meaning in s.2(1)(b) of the Contributions and Benefits Act (1975 Act, s.2(1)(b)) is "a person who is gainfully employed in Great Britain otherwise than in employed earner's employment (whether or not he is also employed in such employment)."
"*year of assessment.*" The meaning in s.526(5) of the Income and Corporation Taxes Act 1970 (s.832(1) of the consolidating 1988 Act) is "with reference to any tax year, the year for which such tax was granted by any Act granting income tax." A tax year is the 12 months beginning with April 6 in any year.

PART II

PRESENCE IN GREAT BRITAIN AND REMUNERATIVE WORK

Circumstances in which a person is treated as being or as not being in Great Britain

3.—(1) A person shall be treated as being in Great Britain if, on the date of claim—

(a) he is present and ordinarily resident in Great Britain; and

(b) his partner, if any, is ordinarily resident in the United Kingdom; and

(c) his earnings or the earnings of his partner, if any, derive at least in part from remunerative work in the United Kingdom; and

(d) his earnings do not wholly derive from remunerative work outside the United Kingdom nor do the earnings of his partner, if any.

(2) A person shall be treated as not being in Great Britain during any period for which he, or his partner, is entitled to be paid family credit ['or disability working allowance] under the law of Northern Ireland.

AMENDMENT

1. Disability Living Allowance and Disability Working Allowance (Consequential Provisions) Regulations 1991 (S.I. 1991 No. 2742), reg. 13(3) (April 6, 1992).

DEFINITIONS

"date of claim"—see reg. 2(1).
"disability working allowance"—*ibid.*
"earnings"—*ibid.*
"partner"—*ibid.*

GENERAL NOTE

The requirement for the claimant to be in Great Britain at the date of claim appears in s.128(1) of the Contributions and Benefits Act (1986 Act, s.20(5)). See the notes to s. 128(1) for the compatibility of the rule with EC Regulation 1408/71. By s.137(2) (1986 Act, s.20(12)(a)) regulations may provide for circumstances in which a person is to be treated as being or not being in Great Britain.

Paragraph (1)
The form of this provision is peculiar. It sets out a composite sufficient condition for treating a person as being in Great Britain. But because the opening phrase is "if," not "if and only if " (or even "only if "), it appears to remain open to a person to show actual presence in Great Britain on a straightforward factual basis. It would then only be the limited category defined in para. (2) which is deemed not to be present. However, in *R(FC) 2/93* the Commissioner has specifically rejected this view, because it would involve giving no meaning to para. (1)(a). He holds that para. (1) prescribes exhaustively the circumstances in which a person is to be treated as present in Great Britain, so that if the circumstances fall outside para. (1) the person is to be treated as not present. Then para. (2) applies to people who would otherwise come within para. (1). Although the drafting is unsatisfactory, *R(FC) 2/93* must be followed by SSATs.

Sub-paras. (a) and (b). The phrase "ordinarily resident" was considered in R(M) 1/85, where the Commissioner adopted the approach of Lord Scarman in *R. v. Barnet London Borough Council, ex parte Shah* [1983] 2 A. C. 309, that the words must be given their natural and ordinary meaning unless there is something in the statute to indicate otherwise. The ordinary meaning is that the person must be habitually and normally resident apart from temporary or occasional absences. The word "habitually" imports that the residence has been adopted voluntarily and for settled purposes as part of the regular order of his life for the time being, although not necessarily with the intention of remaining indefinitely or for more than a limited period. This may be slightly wider than the approach adopted in *R(P) 1/78* and *R(F) 1/62* (see CA 35/1992). Residence which is unlawful cannot be ordinary residence. See also the notes to the additional definition of "person from abroad" introduced into reg. 21(3) of the Income Support Regulations from August 1, 1994 on the meaning of ''habitual residence''.

The presence of the claimant is a matter of fact. The claimant's partner need not be present in Great Britain, but for para. (1) to apply must be ordinarily resident in the United Kingdom (on which see above). Note that if a claimant's spouse is not a member of the same household as the claimant the spouse does not come within the definition of ''partner'' in reg. 2(1) (*CFC 11/1992*).

Sub-paras. (c) and (d). Remunerative work is defined in reg. 4. Either the claimant or the partner must work for at least 16 hours a week in the United Kingdom (which includes Northern Ireland as well as Great Britain (Interpretation Act 1978, Sched.1)). But if either the claimant or partner derives all their income from remunerative work outside the United Kingdom, then under sub-para. (d) the deeming provision cannot operate.

Paragraph (2)
If either the claimant or the partner is entitled to family credit or disability working allowance in Northern Ireland, the claimant is to be treated as not present in Great Britain.

[¹Remunerative work

4.—(1) For the purposes of Part II of the Act [SSCBA, Part VII] as it applies to family credit, and subject to paragraph (3), a person shall be treated as engaged in remunerative work where—
  (a) the work he undertakes is for not less than 16 hours per week;
  (b) the work is done for payment or in expectation of payment; and
  (c) he is employed at the date of claim and satisfies the requirements of paragraph (5).
  (2) A person who does not satisfy all the requirements of sub-paragraphs (a) to (c) of paragraph (1) shall not be treated as engaged in remunerative work.
  [³(3) A person who otherwise satisfies all the requirements of paragraph (1) shall not be treated as engaged in remunerative work insofar as—
  (a) he is engaged by a charitable or voluntary organisation or is a volunteer, where the only payment received by him or due to be paid to him is a payment which is to be disregarded under regulation 24(2) and paragraph 2 of Schedule 2 (sums to be disregarded in the calculation of income other than earnings);
  (b) he is engaged in caring for a person in respect of whom he receives payments to which paragraph 24 of Schedule 2 refers; or
  (c) he is engaged on a scheme for which a training allowance is being paid.]
  (4) [⁴Subject to paragraph (4A),] in determining for the purposes of sub-paragraph (a) of paragraph (1) whether the work a person undertakes is for not less than 16 hours per week—
  (a) there shall be included in the calculation any time allowed for meals or refreshment but only where the person is, or expects to be, paid earnings in respect of that time; and
  (b) if he is a person to whom regulation 14(5) (normal weekly earnings of employed earners) applies, the hours worked shall be calculated by reference to the average number of hours which his employer expects him to work in a week; or
  (c) where paragraph (b) does not apply and—
    (i) a recognised cycle of working has been established at the date of claim, the hours worked shall be calculated by reference to the average number of hours worked in a week over the period of one complete cycle (including where the cycle involves periods in which the person does not normally work, those periods, but disregarding any other absences); or
    (ii) no recognised cycle of working has been established at the date of claim, the hours worked shall be calculated by reference to—
      (aa) the average number of hours worked over the five weeks imme-

diately preceding the week of claim, or such other longer time preceding that week as may, in the particular case, enable the person's weekly average hours of work to be determined more accurately; or

(bb) where he is a self-employed earner and he has worked for less than 5 weeks at the date of claim, the average number of hours he expects to work in a week.

[⁴(4A) Where for the purpose of paragraph (4)(c)(i), a person's recognised cycle of work at a school, other educational establishment or other place of employment is one year and includes periods of school holidays or similar vacations during which he does not work, those periods and any other periods not forming part of such holidays or vacations during which he is not required to work shall be disregarded in establishing the average hours for which he is engaged in work.]

(5) Subject to paragraph (6), the requirements of this paragraph are that the person—

(a) worked not less than 16 hours in either—
    (i) the week of claim; or
    (ii) either of the two weeks immediately preceding the week of claim; or

(b) is expected by his employer to work or, where he is a self-employed earner he expects to work, not less than 16 hours in the week next following the week of claim; or

(c) cannot satisfy the requirements of either sub-paragraph (a) or (b) above and at the date of claim he is absent from work by reason of a recognised, customary or other holiday but he is expected by his employer to work, or where he is a self-employed earner he expects to work, not less than 16 hours in the week following his return to work from that holiday,

and for the purposes of calculating the number of hours worked, sub-paragraph (a) of paragraph (4) shall apply to this paragraph as it applies to sub-paragraph (a) of paragraph (1).

[²(6) For the purposes of paragraph (5)—

(a) work which a person does only qualifies if—
    (i) it is the work he normally does, and
    (ii) it is likely to last for a period of 5 weeks or more beginning with the week of claim; and

(b) a person shall be treated as not on a recognised, customary or other holiday on any day on which the person is on maternity leave or is absent from work because he is ill.]

(7) Where a person is treated as engaged in remunerative work in accordance with the above paragraphs, he shall also be treated as normally engaged in remunerative work.]

[³(8)[⁴. . . .]]

AMENDMENTS

1. Family Credit (General) Amendment Regulations 1992 (S.I. 1992 No. 573), reg. 3 (April 7, 1992).

2. Income-related Benefits Schemes (Miscellaneous Amendments) (No. 4) Regulations 1993 (S.I. 1993 No. 2119), reg. 26 (October 5, 1993).

3. Income-related Benefits Schemes (Miscellaneous Amendments) (No. 5) Regulations 1994 (S.I. 1994 No. 2139), reg. 11 (October 4, 1994).

4. Income-related Benefits Schemes (Miscellaneous Amendments) Regulations 1995 (S.I. 1995 No. 516), reg. 11 (April 11, 1995).

DEFINITIONS

"the Act"—see reg. 2(1).

"claim"—*ibid.*
"date of claim"—*ibid.*
"maternity leave"—*ibid.*
"training allowance"—*ibid.*
"voluntary organisation"—*ibid.*
"week"—*ibid.*
"week of claim"—*ibid.*

GENERAL NOTE

Under s.128(1)(b) of the Contributions and Benefits Act (1986 Act, s.20(5)(b)) it is a condition of entitlement that at the date of claim either the claimant or her partner (if any) is engaged and normally engaged in remunerative work. Reg. 4 now provides an exhaustive test of whether this condition is satisfied. In April 1992 the test was somewhat simplified and definitely clarified in its compression into one regulation. It was previously very confusingly split between regs. 4 and 5. The family credit regulation is now very close to that adopted for disability working allowance. In the past there has been an attempt (not by any means successful) to maintain a uniform test for income support and family credit, so that if a claimant or a partner did not qualify as in remunerative work for family credit purposes, he should not be excluded from income support as being in remunerative work. However, the income support provisions have not been reformed as the family credit provisions have been and there seems now to be even more scope for different decisions between the two benefits.

Para. (1) breaks down the question of remunerative work into three conditions, all of which must be satisfied. If any one of them is not met, then the person is deemed not to be in remunerative work (para. (2)). The three conditions are that

(a) the work is for at least 16 hours per week;
(b) the work is remunerative; and
(c) there has been or will be 16 hours work in a specified week.

Even if all three conditions are met, a volunteer or a person working for a charity or voluntary organisation who receives only expenses is excluded under para. (3)(a). (A volunteer is someone who without any legal obligation performs a service for another person without expectation of payment (*R(IS) 12/92*)). So also from October 4, 1994, is a person being paid by a health or local authority or voluntary organisation for providing temporary care in their home (para. (3)(b)), and a person in receipt of a training allowance (para. (3)(c)). *CDWA 1/1992* had held that a trainee on a YTS scheme was in remunerative work for the purposes of disability working allowance and the same principle would have applied to family credit. However, sub-para. (c) now specifically excludes this possibility.

The following notes deal with each of the three conditions in turn, rather than proceed paragraph by paragraph.

Work for at least 16 hours per week

First, note that the test is not in terms of employment, but in terms of work, which is a broader concept. See, in particular, *R(FC) 2/90* and *CFC 7/1989*, discussed in the notes to reg. 5 of the Income Support (General) Regulations. *R(FIS) 1/86* suggests that a student is engaged in "work," but will normally be knocked out by the fact that the work is not remunerative. Note the exclusions in para. (3).

Para. 39381 of the *Adjudication Officers' Guide* states that the total hours can be made up from more than one job.

Second, note that the concept of "activities in the course of work" has disappeared from the regulations. The terms are simply "work" or "working." There will be difficult questions deciding what sort of activities count as work. The only help in the regulation itself is that meal or refreshment breaks count only if they are paid (para. (4)(a)). Presumably, "working" means actually being at work, as undertaking activities in the course of work did (*R(FIS) 2/81, R(FIS) 2/82* and *R(FIS) 1/85*). It is clear that the focus is on the hours actually worked, rather than the hours specified in any contract. The approach of *R(FC) 1/92*, that in each case it must be asked what time is necessarily spent carrying out activities in the course of the work, may be helpful. It was suggested there that in some jobs (*e.g.* teaching or in the health service) it may not be practicable to work to precise time limits. In *R(FC) 1/92*, the claimant worked as an ambulance transport clerk and gave evidence that she regularly had to stay on after hours because of delays. In other cases, it may be shown that preparation outside contractual hours is necessary. For the self-employed, the test will be the hours of activity essential to the undertaking (see *R(FIS) 6/85*). However, in some cases the activity need not be very active, *e.g.* keeping a shop or workshop open to the public. See the notes to reg. 5 of the Income Support (General) Regulations.

Para. (4) defines how hours of work are to be calculated for the 16 hour test under para. (1)(*a*). The effect is that in most cases it is the period before the date of claim which has to be looked at. The first exception is under sub-para. (b). Where a person has only recently started or resumed work as an employed earner, within the limits supplied by reg. 14(5), the number of hours which the employer expects the person to work are taken. See sub-para. (c)(ii)(bb) below for a similar effect for the self-employed.

Outside sub-para. (b), the calculation is to be made under sub-para. (c), which now clearly covers all cases. If a recognised cycle of working has been established as at the date of claim, then an average must be taken over one complete cycle (head (i)). Whether a cycle has been established and its length is a matter of judgment for the AO or the SSAT. It is not clear that the word "recognised" adds anything to the provision, even if it means something different from "recognisable," the word in the old regulation. Does a "cycle" imply some fluctuation in hours or of periods of work and no work? It is arguable that it does, so that someone who works absolutely regular hours would not come within head (i). However, this is not the view taken by the *Adjudication Officers' Guide* (see para. 39412). Periods of no work which are built into the cycle are included in the averaging (although now see para. (4A)), but not other absences. *R(IS) 15/94* held that in the case of a school receptionist the school holidays were periods of no work. Her contract of employment continued during the holidays but she was not paid, except for the occasional day's work that she was asked to do. The Commissioner disagreed with *CIS 261/1990* (unstarred) which suggested that school holidays counted as other absences to be excluded in the averaging (see the note to reg. 5(1) of the Income Support Regulations). He held that the claimant's recognisable cycle was a yearly one. *CIS 745/1993* further held that where a school ancillary worker was paid for 44 weeks each year but only required to work during term time (38 weeks), it was the total number of hours she actually worked (20 hours × 38 weeks) that had to be averaged over the one year cycle. The approach of *R(IS) 15/94* and *CIS 745/1993* produced a lower weekly figure which could assist a claimant in qualifying for income support, but caused difficulty for certain family credit claimants. The policy intention apparently was that benefit entitlement should be based on the average hours worked during term time and so para. (4A) has been introduced. This provides that if a person has an annual cycle of work which includes periods of no work, for example, school holidays, such periods are ignored in averaging hours of work. A similar rule has been introduced for income support and disability working allowance (and housing benefit and council tax benefit). The new rule will benefit those claiming family credit and disability working allowance but will work to the disadvantage of income support claimants. It should be noted that para. (4B) only applies where the recognised cycle is a year. This may not always be the case, for example, if a person has a separate contract of employment for each period of work. See the notes to reg. 5 of the Income Support (General) Regulations.

If no recognised cycle has been established, the calculation in most cases is under head (ii)(aa). The basic rule is to take an average over the five weeks before the week of claim. If it will enable the person's average weekly hours of work to be determined more accurately, a longer period before the week of claim may be used. But it must positively be shown that the result is more accurate than that produced by the normal rule *(R(FIS) 1/81* and *R(FIS) 2/83)*. It is not enough that the AO does not like the result of applying the normal rule.

Head (ii)(bb) deals with a self-employed person who has worked for less than five weeks at the date of claim, and so has not had time to establish a cycle of working. If the hours worked have been uniform, this is not a cycle. If they fluctuate, there has not been time to see if there is a pattern. The test is then the average number of hours the person expects to work. This must turn mainly on what the person declares his expectations to be. There is no requirement for the expectations to be reasonable, but there will be a point at which something is so unrealistic that an adjudicating authority can conclude that it cannot truly be part of a person's expectations.

Remunerative work

The condition laid down in para. (1)(b) is not elaborated any further in the regulation. See above and the notes to reg. 5 of the Income Support Regulations.

16 hours work in specified weeks

The condition in para. (1)(c) is in fact quite complex. The first part is that the person must be employed at the date of claim. This appears to mean that there must be an employment situation in existence. It does not require the person actually to be working. The second part is to satisfy the requirements of para. (5). Here, the major test is of 16 hours work in a specified week, but para. (6)(a) applies extra tests of normality.

The weeks in which the 16 hour test can be satisfied are the week of claim (sub-para. (a)(i)), either of the two weeks before the week of claim (sub-para. (a)(ii)), the week following the week of claim, on the basis of what is expected (sub-para. (b)) or the week following an absence on holiday, again on the basis of what is expected (sub-para. (c)). Sub-paras. (b) and (c) were new in April 1992, and remove the difficulties exposed in decisions such as *CFC 1/1989* and *R(FC) 2/91*, where the claimant happened to have holiday absences in the then crucial weeks although it was absolutely clear that she normally worked the required number of hours. There could also be problems where someone started work and immediately claimed family credit. The new flexibility is wholly welcome. But note that sub-para. (c) only applies where the claimant's absence from work at the date of claim is by reason of a recognised, customary or other holiday. In *CFC 15/1992* the Commissioner holds that "or other holiday" can mean a day that is a non-working day by agreement between employers and workers and that this could include maternity leave. Para. (6)(b) now specifically provides that in the case of absence through sickness or maternity leave a person is not treated as on holiday. A claimant in this situation will have to claim income support for the period not worked. The definition of maternity leave in reg. 2(1) means that a woman counts as on maternity leave only if she has either a statutory or a contractual right to return to work.

Work cannot count towards the 16 hours in one of the specified weeks if it is not the work which the person normally does and it is not likely to last for five weeks or more from (and including) the week of claim. There was a test of normality for family income supplement. "Normal" was said to have its ordinary everyday meaning (*R(FIS) 2/83*). In *R(FIS) 6/83* the claimant was working full-time as a temporary porter at the date of claim. This was in the summer following the end of a three-year degree course. He had the offer of a place on a further degree course starting the next term, but had not decided whether or not to take it up. The Commissioner holds that on the appropriate time-scale, the claimant was not normally engaged in full-time work. Since the award of benefit was for 52 weeks, something like the situation at the date of claim needed to be expected to prevail for 52 weeks. In *R(FIS) 1/84* the claimant was on a four year "sandwich" degree course, as part of which he had a job from May to September 1982. The Commissioner holds that the SSAT was entitled to take account of the fact that the claimant was primarily a student and of the length of an award in excluding the claimant. Although the same general principle will apply to family credit, the fact that the normal length of an award is 26 weeks (Contributions and Benefits Act, s.128(3); 1986 Act, s.20(6)) changes the context. But the fact that a person is primarily a student, or that a job is known to be coming to an end in the near future, will still be relevant.

The requirement that the work is likely to continue for at least five weeks from the week of claim then seems merely to provide a short cut in some cases. If the work is likely to end within five weeks it will not be normal, but it is easier to strike it out under para. (6)(a)(ii). However, work which is likely to last for more than five weeks is not necessarily normal. Para. (6)(a)(ii) does not impose a limit on the operation of para. (5)(c) because the counting is from the week of claim, not from the week of expected return from holiday.

It is the rule about normality which is the major cause of claimants being excluded from both income support and family credit. If the claimant or any partner works for at least 16 hours in any week, there cannot be entitlement to income support in that week (Contributions and Benefits Act, s.124(1)(c); 1986 Act, s.20(3)(c)). But if the work is not normal there will not be entitlement to family credit either.

Engagement in remunerative work and normal engagement

5. [¹ . . .]

AMENDMENT

1. Family Credit (General) Amendment Regulations 1992 (S.I. 1992 No. 573), reg. 3 (April 7, 1992).

PART III

MEMBERSHIP OF A FAMILY

Persons of a prescribed description

6.—(1) Subject to paragraph (2), a person of a prescribed description for the purposes of section 20(5)(c) [SSCBA, s.128(1)(d)] (entitlement) and section

20(11) of the Act [SSCBA, s.137(1)] (definition of the family) as it applies to family credit is a person aged 16 or over but under 19 who is receiving full-time education within section 2(1)(b) of the Child Benefit Act 1975 [SSCBA, s.142(1)(b)] (meaning of child), and in these Regulations such a person is referred to as "a young person."

[¹(2) Paragraph (1) shall not apply to a person—

(a) who is entitled to income support or would, but for section 20(9) of the Act [SSCBA, s.134(2)] (provision against dual entitlement of members of family), be so entitled;

(b) who is receiving advanced education within the meaning of regulation 1(2) of the Child Benefit (General) Regulations 1976; or

(c) who has ceased to receive full-time education but is to continue to be treated as a child by virtue of regulation 7 of the Child Benefit (General) Regulations 1976.]

AMENDMENT

1. Family Credit (General) Amendment Regulations 1992 (S.I. 1992 No. 574), reg. 4 (April 10, 1992).

DEFINITION

"the Act"—see reg. 2(1).

GENERAL NOTE

Para. (1) is very similar to, although not identical with, reg. 14(1) of the Income Support (General) Regulations. Reg. 14 refers to a person who is treated as a child for the purposes of s.142 of the Contributions and Benefits Act (Child Benefit Act 1975, s.2). Reg. 6 refers to a person who is receiving full-time education within s.142(1)(b) (Child Benefit Act 1975 s.2(1)(b)). *CFC 21/1990* shows that this difference is significant where a person has just left school. In the period up to the next "terminal date" the person is treated under reg. 7 of the Child Benefit (General) Regulations as a child. This brings the person within reg. 14 of the Income Support Regulations, but not within reg. 6(1), because the person is not treated as still in full-time education. See the notes to reg. 14 of the Income Support Regulations for further details. In both cases, the person is called a "young person."

The operation of para. (2) is to much the same effect as reg. 14(2) of the Income Support Regulations. Sub-para. (c), excluding school-leavers until the terminal date, seems unnecessary, for such people are not receiving full-time education within s.142(1)(b) of the Contributions and Benefits Act (Child Benefit Act 1975, s.2(1)(b)). And see *CFC 21/1990*. But it marks a difference from the income support rule. Such school-leavers count as young persons under reg. 14, as do people until the end of the child benefit extension period. Neither category is a young person for family credit purposes.

Circumstances in which a person is to be treated as responsible or not responsible for another

7.—(1) Subject to the following provisions of this regulation, a person shall be treated as responsible for a child or young person who is normally living with him.

(2) Where a child or young person spends equal amounts of time in different households, or where there is a question as to which household he is living in, the child or young person shall be treated for the purposes of paragraph (1) as normally living with—

(a) the person who is receiving child benefit in respect of him; or

(b) if there is no such person—

(i) where only one claim for child benefit has been made in respect of him, the person who made that claim, or

(ii) in any other case the person who has the primary responsibility for him.

(3) For the purposes of these Regulations a child or young person shall be treated as the responsibility of only one person during the period of an award and any person other than the one treated as responsible for the child or young person under the foregoing paragraphs shall be treated as not so responsible.

DEFINITIONS

"child"—see 1986 Act, s.20(11) (SSCBA. s.137(1)).
"young person"—see reg. 2(1), reg. 6.

GENERAL NOTE

Under s.128(1)(d) of the Contributions and Benefits Act (1986 Act, s.20(5)(c)) it is a condition that one of the adults in the family is responsible for a child or young person who is a member of the same household. Reg. 8 deals with membership of the household. Reg. 7 deals with responsibility. The effect of para. (3) is that paras. (1) and (2) provide an exhaustive test of responsibility.

Para. (1) starts by making the test whether the child or young person is normally living with the adult. This exact test is a new one, although the phrase "living with" is used in the child benefit legislation (see, in particular *R(F) 2/79* and *R(F) 2/81*). In the great majority of cases there will be no difficulty at all, but if there is doubt about the household the child is in, then para. (2) comes into play. The sloppy use of language here is very unfortunate (*e.g.* the reference to living in a household, when the question is of normally living with a particular person), but the most helpful interpretation is that para. (2) applies in all cases of doubt about para. (1). It is also possible that a child may be normally living with two people living separately, when para. (2) is also needed. There is then a series of tests. The first is receipt of child benefit, whose rules include methods of establishing priorities between claimants. If no-one is receiving child benefit then if only one person has claimed child benefit, that person has priority. If there have been no claims or more than one, the final test is who has "primary responsibility." Until October 4, 1993, this concept also appeared in reg. 15 of the Income Support (General) Regulations. "Responsibility" has no special meaning in the legislation and so must be determined according to the ordinary everyday meaning of the word.

It would seem that under reg. 7 responsibility or the normality of living may be judged on an overall basis over a period. This is different from the income support provision, where the test of responsibility has to be applied week by week (*CIS 49/1991* and *Whelan v. Chief Adjudication Officer* (C.A., October 21, 1994, unreported)).

Para. (3) secures that a child or young person, once attached to an adult, is only to be treated as the responsibility of that person for the duration of a family credit award. Also if a person meets the tests of paras. (1) and (3), no-one else can allege that they are responsible for the child for the purposes of family credit. But see the notes to reg. 15(4) of the Income Support Regulations where another person is claiming income support.

Membership of the same household

8.—(1) Except in a case to which paragraph (2) applies, where a claimant or any partner is treated as responsible for a child or young person by virtue of regulation 7 (circumstances where a person is treated as responsible or not responsible for another), that child or young person and any child of that child or young person shall be treated as a member of the claimant's household.

(2) A child or young person shall not be treated as a member of the claimant's household in any case where the child or young person—

(a) is a patient or in residential accommodation on account of physical or mental handicap or physical or mental illness and has been so accommodated for the 12 weeks immediately before the date of claim and is no longer in regular contact with the claimant or any member of the claimant's household; or

[¹(b) has been placed with the claimant or his partner prior to adoption; or

(c) has been placed with the claimant or his partner by a local authority under section 23(2)(a) of the Children Act 1989 or by a voluntary organisation under section 59(1)(a) of that Act; or]

(d) has been placed for adoption with the claimant or his partner pursuant to a decision under the Adoption Agencies Regulations 1983 or the Adoption Agencies (Scotland) Regulations 1984; or

(e) is detained in custody under a sentence imposed by a court.

(3) In this regulation—

(a) "patient" means a person (other than a person who is serving a sentence imposed by a court in a prison or youth custody institution) who is regarded as receiving free in-patient treatment within the meaning of the Social Security (Hospital In-Patients) Regulations 1975.

(b) [¹. . .];

(c) "residential accommodation" means accommodation for a person whose stay in the accommodation has become other than temporary which is provided under—

    (i) sections 21 to 24 and 26 of the National Assistance Act 1948; or

    (ii) section 21(1) of, and paragraph 1 or 2 of Schedule 8 to, the National Health Service Act 1977 (prevention, care and after-care) or, in Scotland, for the purposes of section 27 of the National Health Services (Scotland) Act 1947 (prevention of illness and after-care) or under section 59 of the Social Work (Scotland) Act 1968 (provision of residential and other establishments) or under section 7 of the Mental Health (Scotland) Act 1984 (functions of local authorities).

AMENDMENT

1. Family Credit (General) Amendment Regulations 1992 (S.I. 1992 No. 573), Sched., para. 2 (April 7, 1992).

DEFINITIONS

"child"—see 1986 Act, s.20(11) (SSCBA, s.137(1)).
"claimant"—see reg. 2(1).
"date of claim"—*ibid.*
"partner"—*ibid.*
"voluntary organisation"—*ibid.*
"young person"—*ibid.*, reg. 6.

GENERAL NOTE

Paragraph (1)
The general rule is that if an adult is treated as responsible for a child or young person under reg. 7 the child or young person is to be treated as a member of the adult's household.

Paragraph (2)
This provision supplies exceptions to the general rule. It is necessary because there are circumstances in which entitlement to child benefit can continue, sometimes for a specified number of weeks, despite the absence of the child.
The previous form (see the 1991 edition) of sub-paras. (b) and (c) remains in force in Scotland. The new form was introduced on April 7, 1992, as a consequence of the Children Act 1989.

Paragraph (3)
This supplies the necessary definitions. See the notes to reg. 21(3) of the Income Support (General) Regulations for "patient."
The definition of "relevant enactment" previously contained in sub-para. (b) remains in force in Scotland (see the 1991 edition). It was no longer necessary for England and Wales because of the new form of para. (2)(c), introduced as a consequence of the Children Act 1989.

Circumstances in which a person is to be treated as being no longer a member of the same household

9.—[²(1) Subject to the following provisions of this regulation, where the claimant and any partner of his are living apart from each other they shall be treated as members of the same household unless they do not intend to resume living together.]

(2) Where one of the members of a married or unmarried couple is a hospital [¹patient] or [¹detained in custody] he shall not be treated, on this account, as ceasing to be a member of the same household as his partner—

(a) unless he has been [¹a patient] in a hospital for 52 weeks or more; or

(b) unless he is a patient detained in a hospital provided under section 4 of the National Health Service Act 1977 (special hospitals) or section 90(1) of the Mental Health (Scotland) Act 1984 (provision of hospitals for patients requiring special security); or

(c) unless he is [¹detained in custody whilst] serving a sentence of 52 weeks or more imposed by a court,

but shall be treated as not being a member of the same household as his partner wherever the conditions in sub-paragraphs (a), (b) or (c) are fulfilled.

[¹(3) In this regulation "patient" has the same meaning as in regulation 8(3)(a) (membership of the same household).]

AMENDMENTS

1. Family Credit (General) Amendment Regulations 1988 (S.I. 1988 No. 660), reg. 3 (April 11, 1988).
2. Income-related Benefits Schemes (Miscellaneous Amendments) (No. 4) Regulations 1993 (S.I. 1993 No. 2119), reg. 27 (October 5, 1993).

DEFINITIONS

"partner"—see reg. 2(1).
"married couple"—see 1986 Act, s.20(11) (SSCBA, s.137(1)).
"unmarried couple"—*ibid.*

GENERAL NOTE

A single parent or a couple can be entitled to family credit, and the basic calculation of benefit is the same.

The old form of reg. 9 (up to October 5, 1993) only dealt with some specific cases in which a couple no longer counted as members of the same household. Para. (1) now contains a more general rule that a claimant and her partner are deemed to be members of the same household, notwithstanding that they are living apart unless they do not intend to resume living together. (On intention see *CIS 508/1992* and *CIS 484/1993* in the notes to para. 4 of Sched. 3 to the Income Support Regulations.) There are exceptions in para. (2). This brings the family credit provision more in line with the test in reg. 16(1) and (2) of the Income Support Regulations but there are differences. For family credit purposes, unless the couple do not intend to resume living together, the deeming applies whether or not the absence is temporary, or likely to last more than 52 weeks (unless para. (2) applies). However, for the reasons given in the notes to reg. 16(1), para. (1) cannot subvert the general meaning of household (see the notes to s. 137(1) of the Contributions and Benefits Act and *CIS 671/1992*). Para. (1) must only mean that because a couple are living apart this does not in itself mean that membership of the same household ceases.

In addition, for para. (1) to operate, it is necessary for there to be a finding that the couple previously lived as members of the same household. The Commissioner in *CIS 508/1992* seems to have accepted that the home in which the couple previously lived need not have been in this country. But how this applies to the current test of living apart from the other partner is not entirely clear.

Membership of the same household is crucial in deciding whether a particular adult's income or capital is to be treated as the claimant's. It is also relevant to the question whether a claimant satisfies the residence test in reg. 3. So, for example, in the case of a couple where one partner has come to this country ahead of the other, para. (1) may mean that the claimant is not entitled to family credit if her partner is not ordinarily resident in the U.K.; or has earnings all of which derive from work outside the U.K. See the notes to reg. 3 on the meaning of "ordinarily resident".

Paragraph (2)

A partner ceases to be a member of the household if he has been a hospital in-patient (see reg. 8(3)(a)) for at least 52 weeks, is detained in a special hospital, or is serving a prison or youth custody sentence of at least 52 weeks. Until in-patients have clocked up 52 weeks, they are still to be treated as members of the household, as are prisoners with sentences under 52 weeks.

PART IV

INCOME AND CAPITAL

Chapter I

General

Calculation of income and capital of members of claimant's family and of a polygamous marriage

10.—(1) The income and capital of a claimant's partner and, subject to regulation 27 (modifications in respect of children and young persons), the income of a child or young person, which by virtue of section 22(5) of the Act [SSCBA, s.136(1)] is to be treated as income and capital of the claimant, shall be calculated or estimated in accordance with the following provisions of this Part in like manner as for the claimant; and any reference to the "claimant" shall, except where the context otherwise requires, be construed, for the purposes of this Part, as if it were a reference to his partner or that child or young person.

(2) Where a claimant or the partner of a claimant is married polygamously to two or more members of the same household—

(a) the claimant shall be treated as possessing capital and income belonging to each such member and the income of any child or young person who is one of that member's family; and

(b) the income and capital of that member or, as the case may be, the income of that child or young person shall be calculated in accordance with the following provisions of this Part in like manner as for the claimant or, as the case may be, as for any child or young person who is a member of his family.

DEFINITIONS

   "the Act"—see reg. 2(1).
   "child"—see 1986 Act, s.20(11) (SSCBA, s.137(1)).
   "claimant"—see reg. 2(1).
   "family"—see 1986 Act, s.20(11) (SSCBA, s.137(1)).
   "partner"—see reg. 2(1).
   "young person"—*ibid.*, reg. 6.

GENERAL NOTE

   The income and capital of married and unmarried couples (see Contributions and Benefits Act, s.137(1); 1986 Act, s.20(11)) are to be put together and treated as the claimant's (normally the woman: Claims and Payments Regulations, reg. 4(2)). Although s.136(1) (1986 Act, s.22(5)) and this regulation require the income and capital of a child or young person also to be treated as the claimant's, reg. 27, in conjunction with reg. 46(4) and (5), contains special rules for this situation, and under para. 2 of Sched. 1 the earnings of a child or young person are to be disregarded completely.
   Note that para. (2) only applies to polygamous marriages, not to polygamous relationships generally.

Calculation of income and capital of students

11. The provisions of Chapters II to VI of this Part (income and capital) shall have effect in relation to students and their partners subject to the modifications set out in Chapter VII thereof (students).

DEFINITIONS

"partner"—see reg. 2(1).
"student"—*ibid.*

[¹Rounding of fractions

12. Where any calculation under this Part results in a fraction of a penny that fraction shall, if it would be to the claimants' advantage, be treated as a penny, otherwise it shall be disregarded.]

AMENDMENT

1. Family Credit (General) Amendment Regulations 1988 (S.I. 1988 No. 660), reg. 4 (April 11, 1988).

Chapter II

Normal Weekly Income

Calculation of income on a weekly basis

13.—(1) For the purposes of section 20(5) of the Act [SSCBA, s.128(1)] (conditions of entitlement to family credit), the income of a claimant shall be calculated on a weekly basis—
(a) by ascertaining in accordance with this Chapter and Chapter V of this Part (other income) the amount of his normal weekly income; [². . .]
(b) by adding to that amount the weekly income calculated under regulation 36 (calculation of tariff income from capital); [²and]
[²(c) by then deducting any relevant child care charges to which regulation 13A (treatment of child care charges) applies from any earnings which form part of the normal weekly income, up to a maximum deduction in respect of the claimant's family of £40 per week.]
[¹(2) For the purposes of paragraph (1) "income" includes capital treated as income under regulation 25 (capital treated as income) and income which a claimant is treated as possessing under regulation 26 (notional income).]

AMENDMENT

1. Family Credit (General) Amendment Regulations 1991 (S.I. 1991 No. 1520), reg. 3 (October 8, 1991).
2. Income-related Benefits Schemes (Miscellaneous Amendments) (No. 4) Regulations 1994 (S.I. 1994 No. 1924), reg. 4(3) (October 4, 1994).

DEFINITIONS

"the Act"—see reg. 2(1).
"claimant"—*ibid.*, reg. 10(1).
"earnings"—see reg. 2(1).
"family"—see 1986 Act, s.20(11) (SSCBA, s. 137(1)).
"relevant child care charges"—see reg. 13A.

GENERAL NOTE

A claimant's income means hers and her partner's plus any income of a child or young person which counts (regs. 10(1) and 27). The categories are earnings of employed earners, earnings of directors, self-employed earnings, other income (including that mentioned in para. (2)) and the tariff income from capital (reg. 36). Regs. 14, 14A, 15 and 16 respectively start the chain of regulations for calculating each of the first four categories of income.

Para. (1)(c) and reg. 13A provide for the child care disregard that was introduced for family credit from October 4, 1994. The disregard is limited in scope as only certain claimants and types of child care are covered and the ceiling for the charges that can be deducted is very low. The limit is the same regardless of the number of children in the family and care for children aged 11 and over is not included. The disregard also applies to disability working allowance (and housing and council tax benefit), but not income support. Before income support was introduced in April 1988, the full cost of child care (and other work-related expenses such as fares) could be offset against earnings when calculating entitlement to supplementary benefit.

Sub-para. (c) contains the basic rule and most of the detail is in reg. 13A. "Relevant child care charges" (defined in reg. 13A(2)) up to a maximum of £40 a week for the family (not per child) can be offset against earnings. Because of the taper in the family credit calculation, the maximum increase in family credit that will be payable is £28. Since the recommended rates for full-time child care with a registered childminder range from £60 to £90 per week per child, this new allowance will thus be no more than a contribution towards child care costs in many cases.

[¹Treatment of child care charges

13A.—(1) This regulation applies where a claimant is incurring relevant child care charges and—
>   (a) is a lone parent and is engaged in remunerative work;
>   (b) is a member of a couple both of whom are engaged in remunerative work; or
>   (c) is a member of a couple where one member is engaged in remunerative work and the other member is incapacitated.

(2) In this regulation—
>   "local authority" means, in relation to England and Wales, the council of a county or district, a metropolitan district, a London Borough, the Common Council of the City of London or the Council of the Isles of Scilly or, in relation to Scotland, a regional, islands or district council;
>   "relevant child care charges" means the charges paid by the claimant for care provided for any child of the claimant's family who is under the age of 11 years, other than charges paid in respect of the child's compulsory education, [² or charges paid by a claimant to a partner or by a partner to a claimant in respect of any child for whom either or any of them is responsible in accordance with regulation 7 (circumstances in which a person is to be treated as responsible or not responsible for another),] where the care is provided—
>>   (a) by persons registered under section 71 of the Children Act 1989 (registration of child minders and persons providing day care for young children);
>>   (b) for children aged 8 and over but under 11, out of school hours, by a school on school premises or by a local authority; or
>>   (c) by a child care scheme operating on Crown property where registration under section 71 of the Children Act 1989 is not required, [² or
>>   (d) in schools or establishments which are exempted from registration under section 71 of the Children Act 1989 by virtue of section 71(16) of and paragraph 3 or 4 of Schedule 9 to that Act,]
>   and shall be calculated on a weekly basis in accordance with paragraphs (3) to (6);
>   "school term-time" means the school term-time applicable to the child for whom care is provided.

[²(2A) The age of a child referred to in paragraph (2), shall be determined by reference to the age of the child at the date on which the period under section 128(3) of the Contributions and Benefits Act (period of award) begins.]

(3) Subject to paragraphs (4) to (6), relevant child care charges shall be calculated in accordance with the formula—

$$\frac{X + Y}{52}$$

where—

   X is the average weekly charge paid for child care in the most recent 4 complete weeks which fall in school term-time in respect of the child or children concerned, multiplied by 39; and

   Y is the average weekly charge paid for child care in the most recent 2 complete weeks which fall out of school term-time in respect of that child or those children, multiplied by 13.

(4) Subject to paragraph (5), where child care charges are being incurred in respect of a child who does not yet attend school, the relevant child care charges shall mean the average weekly charge paid for care provided in respect of that child in the most recent 4 complete weeks.

(5) Where in any case the charges in respect of child care are paid monthly, the average weekly charge for the purposes of paragraph (3) shall be established—

   (a) where the charges are for a fixed monthly amount, by multiplying that amount by 12 and dividing the product by 52;

   (b) where the charges are for variable monthly amounts, by aggregating the charges for the previous 12 months and dividing the total by 52.

(6) In a case where there is no information or insufficient information for establishing the average weekly charge paid for child care in accordance with paragraphs (3) to (5). the average weekly charge for care shall be estimated in accordance with information provided by the child minder or person providing the care or, if such information is not available, in accordance with information provided by the claimant.

(7) For the purposes of paragraph (1)(c) the other member of a couple is incapacitated where—

   (a) either council tax benefit or housing benefit is payable under Part VII of the Contributions and Benefits Act to the other member or his partner and the applicable amount of the person entitled to the benefit includes—

      (i) a disability premium; or

      (ii) a higher pensioner premium by virtue of the satisfaction of—

         (aa) in the case of council tax benefit, paragraph 11(2)(b) of Schedule 1 to the Council Tax Benefit (General) Regulations 1992;

         (bb) in the case of housing benefit, paragraph 10(2)(b) of Schedule 2 to the Housing Benefit (General) Regulations 1987,

on account of the other member's incapacity; [²or either regulation 13A(1)(c) of the Council Tax Benefit (General) Regulations 1992 (treatment of child care charges) or, as the case may be, regulation 21A(1)(c) of the Housing Benefit (General) Regulations 1987 (treatment of child care charges) applies in that person's case;]

   (b) there is payable in respect of him one or more of the following pensions or allowances—

      (i) invalidity pension under section 33, 40 or 41 of the Contributions and Benefits Act;

      (ii) attendance allowance under section 64 of that Act;

      (iii) severe disablement allowance under section 68 of that Act;

      (iv) disability living allowance under section 71 of that Act;

      (v) increase of disablement pension under section 104 of that Act;

      (vi) a pension increase under a war pension scheme or an industrial injuries scheme which is analogous to an allowance or increase of disablement pension under head (ii), (iv) or (v) above;

(c) a pension or allowance to which head (ii), (iv), (v) or (vi) of sub-paragraph (b) above refers, was payable on account of his incapacity but has ceased to be payable in consequence of his becoming a patient within the meaning of regulation 8(3)(a) (membership of the same household);

(d) sub-paragraph (b) or (c) would apply to him if the legislative provisions referred to in those sub-paragraphs were provisions under any corresponding enactment having effect in Northern Ireland; or

(e) he has an invalid carriage or other vehicle provided to him by the Secretary of State under section 5(2)(a) of and Schedule 2 to the National Health Service Act 1977 or under section 46 of the National Health Service (Scotland) Act 1978 or provided by the Department of Health and Social Services for Northern Ireland under Article 30(1) of the Health and Personal Social Services (Northern Ireland) Order 1972.]

AMENDMENTS

1. Income-related Benefits Schemes (Miscellaneous Amendments) (No. 4) Regulations 1994 (S.I. 1994 No. 1924), reg. 4(4) (October 4, 1994).
2. Income-related Benefits Schemes (Miscellaneous Amendments) Regulations 1995 (S.I. 1995 No. 516), reg. 12 (April 11, 1995).

DEFINITIONS

"claimant"—see reg. 2(1), reg. 10(1).
"Contributions and Benefits Act"—see reg. 2(1).
"Crown property"—*ibid.*
"lone parent"—*ibid.*
"partner"—*ibid.*

GENERAL NOTE

To qualify for the disregard in reg. 13(1)(c) the claimant must be a lone parent or a member of a couple where both partners are working full-time (16 hours or more a week), or where one is working full-time and the other is incapacitated (para. (1)). A person counts as incapacitated if (i) they are in receipt of any of the following (or its Northern Ireland equivalent): (a) short-term (higher rate) or long-term incapacity benefit (under s. 13(2)(b) of the Social Security (Incapacity for Work) Act 1994 any reference in primary or secondary legislation to invalidity benefit or invalidity pension is treated as a reference to higher rate short-term incapacity benefit or long-term incapacity benefit from April 13, 1995) or severe disablement allowance, or (b) attendance allowance, disability living allowance or constant attendance allowance (or an equivalent to any of the last three under a war pension or industrial injuries scheme), or they would be but for the fact that they are in hospital; or (ii) they have an invalid carriage or similar vehicle; or, (iii) housing benefit or council tax benefit is payable which includes on account of that person's incapacity a disability premium, a higher pensioner premium or a child care costs disregard (para. (7)).

Para. (2) specifies the types of child care costs that are eligible. The disregard only applies to charges (but not charges made by one member of a couple to the other) paid for care of children under 11 at the date the family credit award begins. The care has to be provided by a registered childminder or nursery/playscheme (sub-para. (a)), or in schools (charges for compulsory education are excluded) or other establishments (*e.g.* hospitals or children's homes) exempt from registration under the Children Act 1989 (sub-para. (d)), or, for children between the ages of 8 and 11 out of school hours, by a school on school premises or by a local authority (sub-para. (b)). In addition, child care schemes run on Crown property also qualify (sub-para. (c)).

Paras. (3) to (6) provide the method for calculating the weekly amount of deductible child care costs. The formula in para. (3) applies where the child attends school and is intended to take account of the fact that child care costs are likely to vary considerably between term-time (defined in para. (2)) and holiday periods. For pre-school children the average weekly charge for the most recent four full weeks is taken (para. (4)). But in any case where the charges are paid monthly, para. (5) applies. If there is no, or insufficient, information to calculate the child care costs under these rules (such as when child care has only recently been arranged), an estimate will be made based on information from the person providing care or, if that is not available, the claimant (para. (6)).

Until October 4, 1994 family credit did not permit the offsetting of child care expenses against earnings. In *CFC 19/1990 (Meyers)* the claimant is arguing that this indirectly discriminated against women in breach of EC Directive 76/207, which prohibits discrimination on the grounds of sex as regards access to employment, vocational training and promotion, and working conditions. It is contended that the inability to deduct child care costs created a barrier to equal access to employment, which particularly affected lone parents, nine out of 10 of whom are women. The question as to whether family credit comes within the scope of Directive 76/207 was referred to the ECJ by the Commissioner. The argument is that since the main purpose of family credit is to supplement the income of low-paid workers, family credit is directly concerned with access to employment and/or working conditions. The oral hearing before the ECJ took place on March 23, 1995 and the result should be known in about three months. If the ECJ does hold that family credit comes within Directive 76/207, the case will then return to the Commissioner for him to decide the discrimination question. If the claimant is ultimately successful, the principle will also apply to the new rules because of the limited nature of the current disregard.

[¹Normal weekly earnings of employed earners

14.—(1) Where a claimant's income consists of earnings from employment as an employed earner, [²except where those earnings arise from employment as a director,] his normal weekly earnings shall, subject to paragraphs (3) to (6), be determined by reference to [²his earnings from that employment received in] the assessment period relevant to his case.

(2) A claimant's assessment period, subject to [³paragraphs (2A) to (6)], shall be, in respect of a claimant whose pay period is—

[³(a) a week—
- (i) except where head (ii) applies, a period of 6 consecutive weeks immediately preceding the week of claim; or
- (ii) where the adjudication officer has insufficient information for the claimant's normal weekly earnings to be determined in accordance with head (i), a period of 6 consecutive weeks ending with the week before the week immediately preceding the week of claim;
- (aa) a fortnight, a period of three consecutive fortnights in the 7 weeks immediately preceding the week of claim;]
- (b) four weeks or a month, a period of 12 consecutive weeks or, as the case may be, 3 consecutive months, immediately preceding the week of claim;
- (c) any period of less than one month (a shorter period), other than one to which sub-paragraph (a) or (b) refers, 6 consecutive shorter periods immediately preceding the week of claim;
- (d) any period of more than one month (a longer period), a period of one year ending immediately before the week of claim.

[³(2A) Where an adjudication officer considers, on the basis of available evidence, that the claimant has elected to work fewer hours than he would otherwise have worked in the whole or part of the assessment period referred to in paragraph (2) with the result that, but for this paragraph, he would secure entitlement or increased entitlement to family credit, the adjudication officer may determine the claimant's normal weekly earnings by reference to his earnings during the period equal to, and ending immediately before, the period determined in accordance with paragraph (2), unless the claimant satisfies him that the reason for reducing his hours of work was otherwise than to secure such an entitlement or increased entitlement.]

(3) Where during a claimant's assessment period his earnings are reduced because of his involvement in a trade dispute at his place of employment, that assessment period shall be varied in that—
- (a) any pay period during which his earnings are so reduced shall be omitted from it; and
- (b) subject to sub-paragraph (c), his assessment period shall commence one pay period earlier (the extra period) for each period so omitted;

(c) where any extra period under sub-paragraph (*b*) is one in which his earnings are reduced because of his involvement in a trade dispute at his place of employment, that extra period shall also be omitted from his assessment period and his assesssment period shall commence one pay period earlier, for each extra period so omitted,

but so that his assessment period remains a period equal in length to the assessment period which would otherwise apply in his case under paragraph (2) but as if the words "consecutive" and "immediately" were omitted from that paragraph on each occasion where they appear.

(4) Where a claimant's earnings, whether during his assessment period or not, include a bonus or commission which is paid within 52 weeks preceding the week of claim and that bonus or commission is paid separately from his other earnings or is paid in respect of a period longer than the pay period relating to the other earnings with which it is paid, his normal weekly earnings shall be treated as including an amount in respect of that bonus or commission calculated in accordance with regulation 20A (calculation of bonus or commission).

(5) Where at the date if claim—
  (a) the claimant—
      (i) has been in his employment, or
      (ii) after a continuous period of interruption exceeding four weeks, has resumed his employment, or
      (iii) has changed the number of hours for which he is contracted to work; and
  (b) the period of his employment or the period since he resumed his employment or the period since the change in the number of hours took place, as the case may be, is less than the assessment period in paragraph (2) appropriate in his case,

his normal weekly earnings shall be determined in accordance with paragraph (6).

(6) In a case to which this paragraph applies, the Secretary of State shall require the claimant's employer to furnish him with an estimate of the claimant's likely earnings for the pay period for which he is or will normally be paid and the claimant's normal weekly earnings shall be determined by reference to that estimate.

(7) For the purposes of this regulation—
  (a) the claimant's earnings shall be calculated in accordance with Chapter III of this Part;
  (b) "pay period" means the period in respect of which a claimant is, or expects to be [³normally] paid by his employer, being a week, a fortnight, four weeks, a month or other shorter or longer period, as the case may be.]

AMENDMENTS

1. Family Credit (General) Amendment Regulations 1992 (S.I. 1992 No. 573), reg. 4 (April 7, 1992).

2. Income-related Benefits Schemes (Miscellaneous Amendments) Regulations 1944 (S.I. 1994 No. 527), reg. 11 (April 12, 1994).

3. Income-related Benefits Schemes (Miscellaneous Amendments) (No. 5) Regulations 1994 (S.I. 1994 No. 2139), reg. 12 (October 4, 1994).

DEFINITIONS

"claim"—see reg. 2(1).
"claimant"—*ibid*, reg.10(1).
"director"—see reg. 2(1).
"earnings"—see reg. 2(1), reg. 19.
"employed earner"—see reg. 2(1).
"trade dispute"—see 1986 Act, s.84(1).

"week"—see reg. 2(1).
"week of claim"—*ibid.*

GENERAL NOTE

Paras. (1) and (2) supply the general rule for defining the period over which earnings from employment are averaged. There are separate rules for earnings of directors in reg. 14A.

Para. (3) deals with trade disputes. Para. (4) deals with payments of bonus or commission. Paras. (5) and (6) deal with employees who have just started or resumed employment. The calculation of "earnings" is dealt with in regs. 19 and 20. Although "the claimant" is referred to throughout, this word includes any member of the family whose earnings are taken into account (reg. 10(1)).

Paragraphs (1) and (2)

These provisions, in conjunction with the new (from April 1992) reg. 20(5), produce a much simplified method of calculating the earnings of employees. This should enable decisions to be taken more quickly and reliably, but at the cost of a certain amount of rough justice.

The normal assessment period, over which the earnings of an employee received in that time are taken, is set in para. (2) according to the length of the person's pay period. The pay period is the period in respect of which the person is, or expects to be, normally paid by the employer (para. (7)(b)). In the standard cases of payment by the week or month, the assessment period is the six consecutive weeks (sub-para. (a)(ii)) or the three consecutive months (sub-para. (b)) before the week of claim. The assessment period is fixed and there is no longer any discretion to use a shorter or longer period. The new form of sub-para. (a) from October 1994 removes, in the case of a weekly paid person, the previous very limited flexibility whereby six consecutive weeks out of the seven before the week of the claim were taken. Now the six weeks which end one week before the week of claim can only be used where all the earnings information is not available (sub-para. (a)(ii)). The rule for those who are fortnightly paid is now in sub-para. (aa). Before April 1992, there was a power to exclude weeks from the assessment period under reg. 17 where earnings in a week were irregular or unusual. This power has been removed and reg. 17 now only applies to the self-employed. Instead there is a relatively mechanical formula under reg. 20(5) under which abnormal weeks are to be excluded.

Paragraph (2A)

If an AO thinks that a claimant has chosen to work less hours in her normal assessment period, he can take the preceding assessment period, unless the claimant proves (on the balance of probabilities) that securing entitlement to, or increasing the amount of, family credit was not the reason for the reduction in hours. The rule is discretionary and will require the AO to form a judgment on a number of questions. According to the DSS, this provision is designed to deal with a small number of cases of blatant manipulation of the benefit rules; it is not proposed that AOs should normally seek this information.

Paragraph (3)

If the person's earnings are reduced because of his involvement in a trade dispute at his place of employment, then the assessment period is shifted backwards so that it contains no pay periods affected by such a reduction, while remaining the same length. There is no definition of "trade dispute" specifically for the purposes of family credit, although no doubt the meaning in s.27(3)(b) of the Contributions and Benefits Act (1975 Act, s.19(2)(b)) would be adopted. There is no requirement that there should be a stoppage of work, so that a reduction in wages due to a work-to-rule or overtime ban will be covered. But there may in some cases be difficult questions about what amounts to involvement in a trade dispute.

Paragraph (4)

Where a bonus or commission is paid separately from normal remuneration or for a longer pay period a special rule applies. The amount calculated in reg. 20A is included in the claimant's normal weekly earnings and the actual payment is excluded (reg. 20(3)(c)).

Paragraphs (5) and (6).

These provisions apply where a person has recently started work or resumed work after a gap of at least four weeks or changed his contractual hours. Then if the period from that event to the date of claim is less than the appropriate assessment period in para. (2), the special rule in para. (6) applies. There is no discretion to apply this rule or not. If the time condition is met, para. (6) must be applied. This requires the employer to estimate the person's likely earnings, which must then be taken as the normal earnings.

[¹Normal weekly earnings of directors

14A.—(1) Subject to paragraph (2) and regulation 17 (periods to be disregarded), where a claimant's income includes earnings from employment as a director, his normal weekly earnings from that employment shall be determined by reference to his earnings from that employment received in the year immediately preceding the week of claim.

(2) Where at the date of claim the claimant has been in employment as a director for less than a year, his normal weekly earnings from that employment shall be determined by reference to any earnings received in the period that he has been in that employment and by reference to an estimate of the earnings likely to be received in the remainder of the first year of the employment.]

AMENDMENT

1. Income-related Benefits Schemes (Miscellaneous Amendments) Regulations 1994 (S.I. 1994 No. 527), reg. 12 (April 12, 1994).

DEFINITIONS

"claimant"—see reg. 2(1), reg. 10(1).
"date of claim"—see reg. 2(1).
"director"—*ibid.*
"earnings"—*ibid.* reg. 19.
"week of claim"—see reg. 2(1).

GENERAL NOTE

This new regulation contains separate rules for the assessment period over which earnings as a director are to be taken. This is one year before the week of claim (para. (1)). Weeks in which no work is done and no pay is received are disregarded (reg. 17(b)). If the claimant has been employed as a director for less than a year at the date of claim the earnings received so far from the employment are taken together with an estimate of the likely earnings over the remainder of the 52 weeks (para. (2)). This brings directors more in line with the self-employed.

Normal weekly earnings of self-employed earners

15.—(1) Subject to regulation 17 (periods to be disregarded), where a claimant's income consists of earnings from employment as a self-employed earner, his normal weekly earnings shall be determined, subject to paragraph (2), by reference to his weekly earnings from that employment—

[²(a) except where a sub-paragraph (aa) or (b) applies, over a period of 6 consecutive complete months up to and including the second last complete month immediately preceding the date of claim; or

(aa) except where sub-paragraph (b) applies, where the claimant provides in respect of the employment a statement of his earnings and expenses for the six consecutive complete months up to and including the las complete month immediately preceding the date of claim, over that period of six months; or]

[¹(b) where the claimant provides in respect of the employment a profit and loss account and, where appropriate, a trading account or a balance sheet or both, and the profit and loss account is in respect of a period of at least six months but not exceeding 15 months and that period terminates within the 12 months preceding the date of claim, over that period; or]

(c) over such other period of weeks [³or months] preceding the week in which [¹ the date of claims falls] as may, in any particular case, enable his normal weekly earnings to be determined more accurately.

[¹(1A) In paragraph (1)(b)
(a) "balance sheet" means a statement of the financial position of the employment disclosing its assets, liabilities and capital at the end of the period in question;
(b) "profit and loss account" means a financial statement showing the net profit or loss of the employment for the period in question; and
(c) "trading account" means a financial statement showing the revenue from sales, the cost of those sales and the gross profit arising during the period in question.]

[²(2) Subject to regulation 17, in a case where the claimant has been in employment as a self-employed earner for less than 7 complete months, his normal weekly earnings shall be determined over a period of 6 consecutive complete months commencing with the first complete month after the claimant began that employment, and that determination shall be based on either—
(a) where the claimant provides in relation to that employment a statement of his earnings and expenses for the complete months up to and including the last complete month immediately preceding the date of claim, the earnings he received in those months, or
(b) where no such statement is provided, any earnings he received in the period up to and including the second last complete month immediately preceding the date of claim,
together with an estimate of the earnings likely to be received in the balance of the 6 month period.].

(3) For the purposes of this regulation, the claimant's earnings shall be calculated in accordance with Chapter IV of this Part.

[²(4) In this regulation a "complete month" begins on the first day of the month and ends on the last day of the month.]

AMENDMENTS

1. Family Credit (General) Amendment No. 4 Regulations 1988 (S.I. 1988 No. 1970), reg. 3 (December 5, 1988).
2. Income-related Benefits Schemes (Miscellaneous Amendments) Regulations 1994 (S.I. 1994 No. 527), reg. 13 (April 12, 1994).
3. Income-related Benefits Schemes (Miscellaneous Amendments) (No. 5) Regulations 1994 (S.I. 1994 No. 2139), reg. 13 (October 4, 1994).

DEFINITIONS

"claim"—see reg. 2(1).
"claimant"—*ibid.*, reg. 6.
"date of claim"—see reg. 2(1).
"earnings"—see reg. 2(1), reg. 21.
"self-employed earnings"—see reg. 2(1).
"week"—*ibid.*

GENERAL NOTE

Paragraph (1)
The new form of this provision applies where the person has been in self-employment for at least seven calendar (see para. (4)) months (see para. (2)). The basic rule is now contained in sub-para. (b). If the claimant provides accounts for a period between six and 15 months ending in the year before the date of claim these are taken. If these are not produced but the claimant provides a statement of earnings and expenses for the six calendar months before the date of claim this is taken (sub-para. (aa)). If this is not provided the claimant's earnings over the six calendar months which end one calendar month before the date of claim are taken (sub-para. (a)). Alternatively, sub-para. (c) allows another past period to be chosen, if it produces a more accurate determination of normal earnings.

In *CFC 5/1993* the claimant's husband ran a shoe shop. Her claim for family credit made in June 1991, was originally assessed on the basis of the pre-April 1994 form of para. (a) and refused as the earnings figure was too high. By the SSAT hearing accounts for the years to August 1990, and August 1991, were available. The SSAT decided that family credit was not payable even on the lower earnings figure provided by the accounts. The Commissioner holds that sub-para. (c) provides an alternative to either sub-para (a) or (b) (now (a), (aa) or (b)). To apply sub-para. (c) an adjudicating authority must be satisfied that there is an alternative period the use of which will (not might) enable normal weekly earnings at the date of claim to be determined more accurately. The alternative period does not have to be a 26 week period. Evidence in the accounts for the year to August 1991, as to the pattern of the claimant's husband's expenditure on stock did suggest that an alternative period under sub-para. (c) should be used. Although the period covered by the accounts for the year to August 1991, could not be used under sub-para. (b) because it ended after the date of claim, evidence contained in those accounts could be considered in deciding whether an alternative period should be adopted under sub-para. (c).

See also *CFC 19/1993*, *CFC 10/1993* and *CFC 41/1993* on the valuation of opening and closing stock where earnings are assessed under sub-para. (b) in the notes to reg. 22(3A).

Note also the effect of reg. 17, under which weeks in which no activities are carried out are excluded from the period by reference to which earnings are calculated.

Paragraph (1A)
Simply provides definitions for para. (1)(b).

Paragraph (2)
If the person has been in self-employment for less than seven calendar months the assessment period is six calendar months starting from the beginning of the first complete month of the person's self-employment. Either the claimant can produce a statement of earnings and expenses for the calendar months before the date of claim, or earnings actually received up to the beginning of the last calendar month before the date of claim are taken. To this is added an estimate of the likely earnings over the remainder of the six month period. Until October 1992 reference to other evidence which would enable normal weekly earnings to be estimated more accurately was allowed. The Commissioner in *CFC 14/1991* held that that allowed a SSAT on an appeal to take into account the claimant's actual earnings since the date of claim. The removal of the power to consider such evidence from the old form of para. (2) was intended to reverse the effect of *CFC 14/1991*. It now appears that a SSAT must consider what could have been estimated as future earnings on the information which was available at the date of claim, even if that estimate turns out to have been mistaken. But the SSAT must consider what would be a realistic and proper estimate on that information. It is not obliged to accept the claimant's, or anyone else's, estimate.

The useful FIS power to make an award for less than the usual period in cases of doubt has gone (see *R(FIS) 1/82* for an example).

Reg. 17 may operate to exclude certain weeks from the assessment period.

Normal weekly income other than earnings

16.—(1) Subject to [²paragraphs (2) and (2A)], [³where a claimant's normal weekly income does not consist of earnings, or includes income that does not consist of earnings, that income] shall be determined by reference to his weekly income over a period of 26 weeks immediately preceding [¹the week in which the date of claim falls] or over such period immediately preceding [¹that week] as may, in any particular case, enable his weekly income to be determined more accurately.

(2) Where a claimant's income consists of any payments made by a person, whether under a court order or not, for the maintenance of any member of [²the claimant's family], and those payments are made or due to be made at regular intervals, his normal weekly income shall[², except where paragraph (2A) applies,] be determined—

(a) if before the date of claim those payments are made at regular intervals [³and of regular amounts], by reference to the normal weekly amount;

(b) if they are not so made, by reference to the average of such payments received in the 13 weeks immediately preceding the week in which [¹the date of claim falls].

[²(2A) Where a claimant's income consists of child support maintenance, his normal weekly income in respect of that maintenance shall be determined—

(a) if before the date of claim those maintenance payments are made at regular intervals [³and of regular amounts], by reference to the normal weekly amount;

(b) if they are not so made, [³except in a case to which sub-paragraph (*c*) applies,] by reference to the average of such payments received in the 13 weeks immediately preceding the week in which the date of claim falls,

[³(c) where the maintenance assessment has been notified to the claimant under regulation 10 of the Child Support (Maintenance Assessment Procedure) Regulations 1992 during the 13 weeks immediately preceding the week of claim, by reference to the average of such payments, calculated on a weekly basis, received in the interim period,]

and if the resulting sum exceeds the amount of child maintenance due under the maintenance assessment, the normal weekly income shall be the amount due under the maintenance assessment.]

(3) For the purposes of this regulation, income other than earnings shall be calculated in accordance with Chapter V of this Part.

[²(4) In this regulation—

(a) "child support maintenance" means such periodical payments as are referred to in section 3(6) of the Child Support Act 1991;

(b) "maintenance assessment" has the same meaning as in the Child Support Act 1991 by virtue of section 54 of that Act.]

[³(c) "the interim period" means the week in which the date of notification of the maintenance assessment falls and the subsequent period up to and including the week immediately preceding the week of claim.]

AMENDMENTS

1. Family Credit (General) Amendment No. 4 Regulations 1988 (S.I. 1988 No. 1970), reg. 4 (December 5, 1988).
2. Income-related Benefits Schemes (Miscellaneous Amendments) Regulations 1993 (S.I. 1993 No. 315), reg. 11 (April 13, 1993).
3. Income-related Benefits Schemes (Miscellaneous Amendments) (No. 4) Regulations 1993 (S.I. 1993 No. 2119), reg. 28 (October 5, 1993).

DEFINITIONS

"claim"—see reg. 2(1).
"claimant"—*ibid.*, reg. 10(1).
"date of claim"—see reg. 2(1).
"earnings"—*ibid.*, reg. 19.
"family"—see 1986 Act, s.20(11) (SSCBA, s.137(1)).
"payment"—see reg. 2(1).
"week"—*ibid.*

GENERAL NOTE

Note that reg. 16 is not subject to reg. 17.

Paragraph (1)
This provision deals with income which is not earnings and is not maintenance (see para. (2)). See Chapter V for what falls into this category. The general rule is to take the 26 weeks before the week in which the date of claim falls. Another period may be taken, if it produces a more accurate determination.

Paragraph (2)
This provision applies a special rule to payments of maintenance, apart from payments assessed under the Child Support Act 1991 (for which, see para. (2A)). "Maintenance" is not defined, and it seems that it is not restricted to payments from liable relatives as defined in s.78(6) of the Administration Act (1986 Act, s.26).

The first £15 per week of any maintenance payments made by a former partner of the claimant or her current partner or by an absent parent of a child or young person is disregarded (Sched. 2, para. 47, in effect from April 7, 1992).

If payments of maintenance are made to the claimant or another member of her family (reg. 10(1)) of regular amounts and at regular intervals, then the normal weekly amount (calculated under reg. 18) is taken. Otherwise the receipts in the 13 weeks before the week of claim are averaged. It is the date of receipt by the claimant that counts, not the court or the DSS where maintenance is paid to them. They were not acting as the claimant's agent in these circumstances (*CFC 48/1993*).

Any payments not either made or due to be made at regular intervals count as capital (reg. 31(6)).

Paragraph (2A)

"Child support maintenance" is defined in para. (4) to cover payments required by an assessment under the Child Support Act 1991. The weekly amount is to be calculated as under para. (2), except that if the claimant has only been notified of the maintenance assessment in the 13 weeks before the week of the family credit claim, just the payments received from the week of the notification are averaged. But the amount due under the assessment supplies a maximum. If an absent parent pays more than required by the assessment (for instance, if a payment includes arrears) the excess does not affect the claimant's family credit entitlement.

The first £15 of whatever amount is calculated is disregarded under para. 47 of Sched. 2.

Periods to be disregarded

[¹17. For the purposes of ascertaining a claimant's normal weekly earnings there shall be disregarded—

    (a) where the claimant is a self-employed earner, any week or period of weeks in his assessment period during which no activities have been carried out for the purposes of the business;

    (b) where the claimant is a director, any week or period of weeks in his assessment period during which he has done no work and in respect of which he has received no earnings; and

his normal weekly earnings shall be determined by reference to his earnings in the remainder of that period (the reduced period) and in these Regulations any reference to an assessment period shall in its application to such a case be construed as a reference to that reduced period.]

AMENDMENT

1. Income-related Benefits Schemes (Miscellaneous Amendments) Regulations 1994 (S.I. 1994 No. 527), reg. 14 (April 12, 1994).

DEFINITIONS

    "assessment period"—see reg. 2(1), reg. 15.
    "claimant"—*ibid.*, reg. 10(1).
    "director"—see reg. 2(1).
    "earnings"—*ibid.*
    "self-employed earner"—*ibid.*
    "week"—*ibid.*

GENERAL NOTE

Reg. 17 modifies the period used for calculation of earnings from self-employment under reg. 15 and as a director under reg. 14A. With the amendment of regs. 14 and 20 from April 1992 no extra provision is needed for employed earners.

Para. (a). This requires weeks in which the person did not carry out any activities for the purpose of the self-employment to be disregarded. The concept of activities in the course of work is no longer part of reg. 4, which since April 1992 simply refers to hours of work. No doubt the approach put forward in *R(FIS) 6/85* would be applicable. It was held there that activities were not limited to those which could be charged to a particular client, but extended to activities, like preparation and planning, which were essential to the self-employment. Only weeks (*i.e.* Sunday to Saturday) in which no activities at all are carried out can be excluded under reg. 17. The obvious examples are periods of holiday or incapacity.

Para. (b). Weeks in which the person has not worked as a director and for which he has not been paid are disregarded.

Calculation of weekly amount of income

18. For the purposes of regulations [¹14 and 16] (normal weekly income), where the period in respect of which a payment is made—
- (a) does not exceed a week, the weekly amount shall be the amount of that payment;
- (b) exceeds a week, the weekly amount shall be determined—
  - (i) in a case where that period is a month, by multiplying the amount of the payment by 12 and dividing the product by 52;
  - (ii) in a case where that period is 3 months, by multiplying the amount of the payment by 4 and dividing the product by 52;
  - (iii) in a case where that period is a year, by dividing the amount of the payment by 52;
  - (iv) in any other case, by multiplying the amount of the payment by 7 and dividing the product by the number equal to the number of days in the period in respect of which it is made.

[²(2) For the purposes of regulation 15 (normal weekly earnings of self-employed earners) the weekly amount of earnings of a claimant shall be determined—
[³(a) except where sub-paragraph (b) applies, by multiplying by 7 his earnings—
  - (i) received in the assessment period, or
  - (ii) estimated for the assessment period, or
  - (iii) both received in and estimated for that period,
as the case may be, and dividing the product by the number equal to the number of days in that period;]
- (b) in a case where regulation 15(1)(b) applies, by multiplying his earnings relevant to the assessment period (whether or not received in that period) by 7 and dividing the product by the number equal to the number of days in that period.]

[³(3) For the purposes of regulation 14A (normal weekly earnings of directors) the weekly amount of earnings of a claimant shall be determined by dividing his earnings—
  - (i) received in the assessment period, or
  - (ii) estimated for the assessment period, or
  - (iii) both received in and estimated for that period,
as the case may be, by the number equal to the number of weeks in that period.]

AMENDMENTS

1. Family Credit (General) Amendment No. 3 Regulations 1988 (S.I. 1988 No. 1438), reg. 4 (September 12, 1988).
2. Family Credit (General) Amendment No. 4 Regulations 1988 (S.I. 1988 No. 1970), reg. 5 (December 5, 1988).
3. Income-related Benefits Schemes (Miscellaneous Amendments) Regulations 1994 (S.I. 1994 No. 527), reg. 15 (April 12, 1994).

DEFINITIONS

"assessment period"—see reg. 2(1).
"claimant"—*ibid.*
"director"—*ibid.*

"payment"—*ibid.*
"week"—*ibid.*

GENERAL NOTE

See notes to reg. 32(1) of the Income Support (General) Regulations, except for paras. (2) and (3).

Chapter III

Employed Earners

Earnings of employed earners

19.—(1) Subject to paragraph (2), "earnings" means in the case of employment as an employed earner, any remuneration or profit derived from that employment and includes—

(a) any bonus or commission;

(b) any holiday pay except any payable more than 4 weeks after termination of the employment;

(c) any payment by way of a retainer;

(d) any payment made by the claimant's employer in respect of any expenses not wholly, exclusively and necessarily incurred in the performance of the duties of the employment, including any payment made by the claimant's employer in respect of—

    (i) travelling expenses incurred by the claimant between his home and place of employment;

    (ii) expenses incurred by the claimant under arrangements made for the care of a member of his family owing to the claimant's absence from home;

(e) any award of compensation made under section 68(2) or 71(2)(*a*) of the Employment Protection (Consolidation) Act 1978 (remedies and compensation for unfair dismissal);

(f) any such sum as is referred to in section 18(2) of the Social Security (Miscellaneous Provisions) Act 1977 (certain sums to be earnings for social security purposes);

[¹(g) any statutory sick pay under Part I of the Social Security and Housing Benefits Act 1982 [SSCBA, Part XI];

(h) any statutory sick pay under Part II of the Social Security (Northern Ireland) Order 1982.]

(2) Earnings shall not include—

(a) subject to paragraph (3), any payment in kind;

(b) any payment in respect of expenses wholly, exclusively and necessarily incurred in the performance of the duties of the employment;

(c) any occupational pension;

[²(d) any statutory maternity pay or a corresponding benefit under any enactment having effect in Northern Ireland.]

(3) Where living accommodation is provided for a claimant by reason of his employment, the claimant shall be treated as being in receipt of weekly earnings of an amount equal to—

(a) where no charge is made in respect of the provision of that accommodation, £12;

(b) where a charge is made and that weekly charge is less than £12, the amount of the difference,

except that where the claimant satisfies the adjudication officer that the weekly value to him of the provision of that accommodation is an amount less than the amount in sub-paragraph (a) or (b), as the case may be, he shall be treated as being in receipt of that lesser value.

1. Family Credit (General) Amendment Regulations 1992 (S.I. 1992 No. 573), reg. 6 (April 7, 1992).
2. Income-related Benefits Schemes (Miscellaneous Amendments) Regulations 1993 (S.I. 1993 No. 315), reg. 12 (April 13, 1993).

DEFINITIONS

"the Act"—see reg. 2(1).
"claimant"—*ibid.*, reg. 10(1).
"employed earner"—see reg. 2(1).
"family"—see 1986 Act, s.20(11) (SSCBA, s.137(1)).
"occupational pension"—see reg. 2(1).
"payment"—*ibid.*
"week"—*ibid.*

GENERAL NOTE

Paragraph (1)
See the notes to reg. 35(1) of the Income Support (General) Regulations for most categories of earnings. The differences are noted here. Categories in those Regulations which do not appear here are payments in lieu of remuneration and in lieu of notice. Presumably they are excluded as not relating to actual work, but will, as payments of income, fall into reg. 24. Holiday pay is counted subject to slightly different conditions. Sub-paras. (g) and (h) specifically including statutory sick pay (but not, from April 1992, statutory maternity pay) do not appear in the Income Support Regulations. Statutory maternity pay is from April 1993 expressly excluded from the category of earnings by para. (2)(d). Sched. 2, paras. 27 and 31 provide that statutory maternity pay and maternity allowance are disregarded as income.
Note the disregarded categories set out in Sched. 1 (reg. 20(2)), and that notional earnings under reg. 26 may be included.

Paragraph (2)
Payments in kind (see notes to reg. 35(2) of the Income Support (General) Regulations) are excluded from earnings, except where living accommodation is provided under para. (3). See the notes to reg. 35 for necessary expenses and occupational pensions.
In some earlier editions it has been asserted rather loosely that the rule on expenses effectively legislates the decision in *Parsons v. Hogg* [1985] 2 All E.R. 897 (*R(FIS) 4/85*). It is certainly the case that the part of the Commissioner's decision in *R(FIS) 4/85* which was not challenged in the Court of Appeal is confirmed by para. (1)(d) and (2)(b), *i.e.* payments from the employer which are simply reimbursement of necessary, etc. expenses do not count as earnings, but reimbursement of expenses outside that category (including for child care) does count. However, the major issue in the Court of Appeal in *Parsons v. Hogg* was whether expenses necessarily incurred by the employee were to be deducted in calculating the claimant's gross earnings. It was held that sums which the claimant necessarily had to spend to secure those earnings should be deducted for FIS purposes. Child care expenses did not fall into that category (*R(FIS) 2/88*). See the notes to reg. 20 on the application of the principle of *Parsons v. Hogg* to the meaning of "gross earnings" in reg. 20(3). See also regs. 13(1)(c) and 13A for the limited disregard for child care expenses introduced from October 4, 1994. In *CFC 19/1990 (Meyers)* the claimant is arguing that the previous inability to offset child care costs against earnings indirectly discriminated against women contrary to EC Directive 76/207 (see the notes to reg. 13A).
The intention seems to be that reg. 19 should apply to payments from the employer, while reg. 20(3) deals with which expenditure by the employee can be deducted. However, the decision in *CFC 2/1989* raised the possibility that such payments by the employee should be excluded from the calculation of gross earnings under reg. 19(2)(b). The Commissioner in fact held that the payments in question (for child care expenses) did not fall into the necessary, etc., category (following *R(FIS) 2/88*). But if they had done so it was apparently not disputed that the exclusion under reg. 19(2)(b) would follow. That provision does not say "payments by the employer," so that it can be argued that it also covers payments by the employee. But in the context of reg. 19 as a whole this seems unlikely. Para. (1) is expressly subject to para. (2) and lists a variety of payments made by the employer to the employee. Para. (2)(a) and (c) clearly refer to forms of payment made by the employer. The context suggests that para. (2)(b) refers only to payments by the employer in respect

of necessary etc. expenses rather than the ordinary remuneration for work done, and not to expenditure by the employee. The Commissioner's decision in *R(FC) 1/90* rejects the view expressed in *CFC 2/1989* and is to be preferred. See also *R(IS) 16/93* and *CIS 77/1993*. However, the effect of this construction is mitigated by the application of the principle of *Parsons v. Hogg* to the meaning of "gross earnings" in reg. 20(3) (see the notes to reg. 20).

The categories excluded as earnings under para. (2) are income under reg. 24 (reg. 24(5)), but note the disregards in paras. 20, 27, 31 and 32 of Sched. 2.

Paragraph (3)

In *R(FC) 2/90* both the claimant and her husband worked for the Salvation Army and were provided with free accommodation. Only one sum of £12 was to be assumed as part of their earnings, even if they had two separate employments. They only had one house provided. In *R(FC) 1/94* the claimant's husband was a vicar who until April 1990, was provided with accommodation free of rent and rates. After that date they became liable to pay the community charge, which, they argued, should be deducted from the £12 as the value of the free accommodation had decreased. It is held that para. (3) imposes a mandatory sum to be assumed as income where free accommodation is provided (subject to the proviso). The proviso did not permit the deduction of community charge liability.

Calculation of net earnings of employed earners

20.—[¹(1) For the purposes of regulation 14 (normal weekly earnings of employed earners) the earnings of a claimant to be taken into account shall be his average weekly net earnings derived from, or likely to be derived from, his employment as an employed earner either during the assessment period relevant to his case or, where an estimate of earnings has been made in his case, as estimated, and those weekly net earnings shall be determined in accordance with the following paragraphs.]

(2) There shall be disregarded from a claimant's net earnings, any sum, where applicable, specified in Schedule 1.

(3) [¹A claimant's net earnings shall, except where paragraph (4) applies, be calculated by taking into account his gross earnings from that employment] over the assessment period, less—

    (a) any amount deducted from those earnings by way of—
        (i) income tax;
        (ii) primary Class 1 contributions under the Social Security Act [SSCBA]; and
    (b) one-half of any sum paid by the claimant [⁵in respect of a pay period] by way of a contribution towards an occupational or personal pension scheme; [¹and
    (c) the net amount of bonus or commission (if any) which is paid separately from his other earnings or is paid in respect of a period longer than the pay period relating to the other earnings with which it is paid and that net amount shall be the gross amount of that bonus or commission after deducting from it sums calculated in accordance with paragraphs (a) to (c) of regulation 20A (calculation of bonus or commission).]

(4) Where the earnings of a claimant are [¹estimated under paragraph (6)] of regulation 14 (normal weekly earnings of employed earners), his net earnings shall be calculated by taking into account those earnings over [²the period in respect of which the estimate is made], less—

    (a) an amount in respect of income tax equivalent to an amount calculated by applying to those earnings [²the lower rate or, as the case may be, the lower rate and the basic rate of tax] in the year of assessment in which the claim was made less only the personal relief to which the claimant is entitled under sections 8(1) and (2) and 14(1)(a) and (2) of the Income and Corporation Taxes Act 1970 (personal relief) as is appropriate to his circumstances; but, if the assessment period is less than a year, [²the earnings to which the lower rate [⁴ . . .] of tax is to be applied and] the amount of the personal relief deductible under this sub-paragraph shall be calculated on a pro rata basis;

[³(b) where the weekly amount of those earnings equals or exceeds the lower earnings limit, an amount representing primary Class 1 contributions under the Contributions and Benefits Act, calculated by applying to those earnings the initial and main primary percentages applicable at the date of claim in accordance with section 8(1)(a) and (b) of that Act; and]

[⁵(c) one half of any sum which would be payable by the claimant by way of a contribution towards an occupational or personal pension scheme, if the earnings so estimated were actual earnings.]

[¹(5) When a claimant's net earnings have been calculated in accordance with paragraph (3), his average net earnings have in respect of his pay period shall be calculated as follows—

(a) the net earnings in each of the pay periods in his assessment period shall be aggregated, that total shall then be divided by the number of pay periods in his assessment period and the resulting amount shall be the average net earnings for his pay period;

(b) where in respect of any pay period, a claimant's net earnings are twenty per cent. or more higher, or twenty per cent. or more lower, than his average net earnings, those net earnings and that pay period shall be omitted, his assessment period shall be reduced accordingly and his average net earnings shall, subject to sub-paragraph (c), be re-calculated in accordance with sub-paragraph (a);

(c) where the operation of sub-paragraph (b) results in no pay period remaining in a claimant's assessment period there shall be omitted from the assessment period any pay period in which no earnings are received or in which the net earnings received are for a period longer than his normal pay period and his average net earnings shall be re-calculated in accordance with sub-paragraph (a);

(d) where the operation of sub-paragraph (c) results in no pay periods remaining, paragraph (6) of regulation 14 (normal weekly earnings of employed earners) and paragraph (4) of this regulation shall apply in his case.

(6) Where a claimant's average net earnings for his pay period have been calculated in accordance with paragraph (5) and his pay period is—

(a) a week, a fortnight or four weeks, his average net earnings for his pay period shall be divided by the number of weeks in that period;

(b) a month, his average net earnings shall be multiplied by 12, the resulting product divided by 52;

(c) any shorter or longer period than those referred to in sub-paragraphs (a) and (b), his average net earnings for his pay period shall be multiplied by seven and the product divided by the number equal to the number of days in his pay period,

and the resulting amount shall be his average weekly net earnings.]

AMENDMENTS

1. Family Credit (General) Amendment Regulations 1992 (S.I. 1992 No. 573), reg. 7 (April 7, 1992).

2. Income-related Benefits Schemes (Miscellaneous Amendments) (No. 3) Regulations 1992 (S.I. 1992 No. 2155), reg. 6 (October 5, 1992).

3. Income-related Benefits Schemes (Miscellaneous Amendments) Regulations 1994 (S.I. 1994 No. 527), reg. 16 (April 12, 1994).

4. Income-related Benefits Schemes (Miscellaneous Amendments) (No. 5) Regulations 1994 (S.I. 1994 No. 2139), reg. 14 (October 4, 1994).

5. Income-related Benefits Schemes (Miscellaneous Amendments) (No. 5) Regulations 1994 (S.I. 1994 No. 2139), reg. 15 (October 4, 1994).

"assessment period"—see reg. 2(1), reg. 14.
"claimant"—see reg. 2(1), reg. 10(1).
"earnings"—see reg. 2(1).
"employed earner"—*ibid.*
"lower rate"—*ibid.*
"occupational pension scheme"—see 1986 Act, s.84(1) (PSA, s.1).
"pay period"—see reg. 2(1), reg. 14(7)(b).
"personal pension scheme"—see 1986 Act, s.84(1) (PSA, s.1).
"primary Class 1 contribution"—*ibid.*
"Social Security Act"—see reg. 2(1).
"year of assessment"—*ibid.*

GENERAL NOTE

One of the main differences between family credit and FIS is that for family credit net, rather than gross, earnings are used for calculating benefit. Para. (1) expresses this rule, and requires that what is to be taken into account are average weekly net earnings. Para. (2) incorporates a limited number of disregards, set out in Sched. 1. Payments which are disregarded under this provision cannot be counted as income other than earnings under reg. 24. This is because the payments do not cease to be "earnings" and reg. 24 only applies to income which does not consist of earnings.

Para. (3) sets out how net earnings are to be calculated from gross earnings. The basic process is as in reg. 36(3) of the Income Support (General) Regulations. See the notes to that provision, where there is discussion of the decision in *R(FC) 1/90*, which applies the principle of *Parsons v. Hogg* (see notes to reg. 19(2)) to the meaning of "gross earnings" in para. (3). *R(IS) 16/93* has now expressly decided that the principle of *Parsons v. Hogg* applies to reg. 36 of the Income Support Regulations. The result is that expenditure by the employee which had to be incurred in order to secure the earnings should first be deducted, before the deductions expressly listed in para. (3) are made. Para. (4) is necessary to estimate the deductions in a case where future earnings are estimated under reg. 14(6).

Paragraphs (5) and (6)

Para. (5) takes the process on from the identification of net earnings for each pay period under para. (3). The first step under sub-para. (a) is to put together all the net earnings in the pay periods in the assessment period and produce the average net earnings for those pay periods. Then under sub-para. (b) the net earnings for each pay period must be inspected. If the figure for any pay period is 20 per cent. or more higher or lower than the average net earnings, that pay period is excluded and a new figure of average net earnings is calculated using the net earnings from the remaining pay periods. If the result of sub-para. (b) would be that no pay period at all would remain, then sub-para. (c) applies instead. Only pay periods in which no earnings are received or in which the earnings received are for a longer period than the pay period are excluded before the new average is calculated. If the result of sub-para. (c) would be that no pay periods at all would remain, sub-para. (d) applies and an estimate by the employer under reg. 14(6) must be accepted.

This mechanical process removes all issues of judgment. It should allow for quick and accurate calculations, although the result may be rather crude in some cases.

Finally, para. (6) converts the average net earnings for the pay period into the average weekly net earnings.

[¹Calculation of net earnings of directors

20ZA.—(1) For the purposes of regulation 14A (normal weekly earnings of directors) the earnings of a claimant to be taken into account shall be his net earnings derived from, or likely to be derived from, his employment as a director during the assessment period relevant to his case, and those net earnings shall be determined in accordance with the following paragraphs.

(2) There shall be disregarded from a claimant's net earnings any sum, where applicable, specified in Schedule 1.

(3) A claimant's net earnings shall, except where paragraph (4) applies, be calculated by taking into account his gross earnings from that employment, less—

(a) any amount deducted from those earnings by way of—

(i) income tax;

(ii) primary Class 1 contributions under the Contributions and Benefits Act; and

(b) one-half of any sum paid by the claimant [²in respect of a pay period] by way of a contribution towards an occupational or personal pension scheme.

(4) Where some or all of the claimant's earnings are estimated under regulation 14A(2), those net earnings shall be calculated by taking into account the estimated gross earnings, less—

(a) an amount representing income tax, calculated by applying to those earnings the lower rate or, as the case may be, the lower rate and the basic rate of income tax in the year of assessment in which the claim was made, taking into account the personal relief to which the claimant would be entitled under sections 257(1), 257A(1) and 259 of the Income and Corporation Taxes Act 1988 (personal relief); except that if the period in respect of which the estimate is made is less than a year, [²the earnings to which the lower rate of tax is to be applied] and the amount of the personal relief allowable under this sub-paragraph shall be reduced pro-rata;

(b) where the weekly amount of those earnings equals or exceeds the lower earnings limit, an amount representing primary Class 1 contributions under the Contributions and Benefits Act, calculated by applying to those earnings the initial and main primary percentages applicable at the date of claim in accordance with section 8(1)(a) and (b) of that Act; and

(c) one-half of any sum which would be payable by the claimant by way of a contribution towards an occupational or personal pension scheme[², if the earnings so estimated were actual earnings].]

AMENDMENT

1. Income-related Benefits Schemes (Micellanous Amendments) Regulations 1994 (S.I. 1994 No. 527), reg. 17 (April 12, 1994).

2. Income-related Benefits Schemes (Miscellaneous Amendments) (No. 5) Regulations 1994 (S.I. 1994 No. 2139), reg. 16 (October 4, 1994).

DEFINITIONS

"assessment period"—see reg. 2(1), reg. 14A.
"claimant"—see reg. 2(1), reg. 10(1).
"director"—see reg. 2(1)
"earnings"—*ibid.*
"lower rate"—*ibid.*
"occupational pension scheme"—see 1986 Act, s.84(1) (PSA, s.1).
"pay period"—see reg.2(1), reg. 14(7)(b).
"personal pension scheme"—see 1986 Act, s.84(1) (PSA, s.1).
"year of assessment"—see reg. 2(1).

GENERAL NOTE

The earnings to be taken into account under reg. 14A are the earnings derived from employment as a director less income tax, social security contributions, half of any contribution to an occupational or personal pension and any applicable disregards in Sched. 1. If any of the earnings are estimated, the tax, social security contributions and pension contributions will be assessed notionally.

[¹Calculation of bonus or commission

20A. Where a claimant's earnings include a bonus or commission to which [²paragraph (4)] of regulation 14 (normal weekly earnings of employed earners) applies that part of his earnings shall be calculated by aggregating any payments of bonus or commission and [³deducting from it—]

    (a) an amount in respect of income tax equivalent to an amount calculated by applying to that part of the earnings the basic rate of tax in the year of assessment in which the claim is made; and

[⁴(b) an amount representing primary Class 1 contributions under the Contributions and Benefits Act, calculated by applying to that part of the earnings the main primary percentage applicable at the date of claim; and]

    (c) one-half of any sum payable by the claimant in respect of that part of the earnings by way of a contribution towards an occupational pension [³scheme;

and dividing the resulting sum by 52.]]

AMENDMENTS

1. Family Credit (General) Amendment Regulations 1990 (S.I. 1990, No. 574), reg. 8 (April 10, 1990).

2. Family Credit (General) Amendment Regulations 1992 (S.I. 1992 No. 573), reg. 8 (April 7, 1992).

3. Income-related Benefits Schemes (Miscellaneous Amendments) (No. 3) Regulations 1992 (S.I. 1992 No. 2155), reg. 7 (October 5, 1992).

4. Income-related Benefits Schemes (Miscellaneous Amendments) Regulations 1994 (S.I. 1994 No. 527), reg. 18 (April 12, 1994).

DEFINITIONS

"claimant"—see reg. 2(1).
"occupational pension scheme"—see 1986 Act, s.84(1) (PSA, s.1).
"Social Security Act"—see reg. 2(1).
"year of assessment"—*ibid.*

GENERAL NOTE

The effect of reg. 14(4) is that any bonus or commission separate from ordinary earnings which is paid in the 52 weeks before the week of claim is to be brought into the calculation of earnings. Under reg. 20A the aggregate of such payments is divided by 52 to reach a weekly figure. The standard deductions are to be made under paras. (a) to (c) before doing the division. But there seems to be no scope for a *Parsons v. Hogg* deduction (see notes to reg. 20) and paras. (a) and (c) are defective in not referring to the lower rate of income tax (applicable from April 1992) or to contributions to personal pension schemes.

See reg. 20(3)(c) for the exclusion of the actual payment of such bonus or commission from the calculations.

Chapter IV

Self-employed earners

Earnings of self-employed earners

21.—(1) Subject to [³ paragraphs (2) and (3)], "earnings", in the case of employment as a self-employed earner, means the gross receipts of the employment and shall include any allowance paid under section 2 of the Employment and Training Act 1973 [²or section 2 of the Enterprise and New Towns (Scotland) Act 1990] to the claimant for the purpose of assisting him in carrying on his business unless at the date of claim the allowance has been terminated.

(2) Where a claimant is employed in providing board and lodging accommodation for which a charge is payable, any income consisting of payments of such a charge shall only be taken into account under this Chapter as earnings if it forms a major part of the total of the claimant's weekly income less any sums

disregarded under Schedule 2 [¹other than under paragraph 40 of that Schedule.]

[³(3) "Earnings" shall not include any payments to which paragraph 24 of Schedule 2 refers (sums to be disregarded in the calculation of income other than earnings).]

AMENDMENTS

1. Family Credit (General) Amendment Regulations 1990 (S.I. 1990 No. 574), reg. 9 (April 10, 1990).
2. Enterprise (Scotland) Consequential Amendments order 1991 (S.I. 1991 No. 387), art. 2 (April 1, 1991).
3. Income-related Benefits Schemes (Miscellaneous Amendments) (No. 5) Regulations 1994 (S.I. 1994 No. 2139), reg. 17 (October 4, 1994).

DEFINITIONS

"claimant"—see reg. 2(1), reg. 10(1).
"date of claim"—see reg. 2(1).
"payment"—*ibid.*
"self-employed earner"—*ibid.*

GENERAL NOTE

Paragraph (1)
The starting point in the calculations for the self-employed is the amount of the gross receipts, although reg. 22 immediately shifts to net profits. The receipts are to include any enterprise allowance paid to the person unless the allowance has been terminated at the date of claim. This appears to mean that even though enterprise allowance has been paid in most of the 26 weeks period under reg. 15(1), it should not count in the calculation if it has ended by the date of claim (which is not necessarily the same as the date on which the claim is received). The timing of a claim may thus be crucial.
See the notes to reg. 37(1) of the Income Support (General) Regulations for discussion of the general meaning of "gross receipts" and in particular the vexed question of capital receipts, now comprehensively resolved by *CFC 3/1992*.

Paragraph (2)
The income from taking boarders does not count as earnings from self-employment unless it forms "a major part" of the family's income which is not disregarded under Sched. 2 (apart from the provision on income from boarders). "A major part" presumably means more than 50 per cent. A person is "employed" in providing board and lodging providing that he is occupied in doing so. It does not have to be by way of business (*CIS 55/1989*). For "charge," see the notes to the definition of "board and lodging accommodation" in reg. 2(1) of the Income Support (General) Regulations.
If the income does not count under para. (2), see reg. 24.

Paragraph (3)
This applies to payments to people for providing temporary care in their home. These payments are disregarded as income other than earnings under para. 24 of Sched. 2. Para. (3) ensures that they are not treated as earnings.

Calculation of net profit of self-employed earners

22.—(1) For the purposes of regulation 15 (normal weekly earnings of self-employed earners), the earnings of a claimant to be taken into account shall be—

    (a) in the case of a self-employed earner who is engaged in employment on his own account, the net profit derived from that employment;

    (b) in the case of a self-employed earner whose employment is carried on in partnership or is that of a share fisherman within the meaning of the Social Security (Mariners' Benefits) Regulations 1975, his share of the net profit derived from that employment less—

        (i) an amount in respect of income tax and social security contributions payable under the Social Security Act [SSCBA] calculated in accordance with regulation 23 (deduction of tax and contributions for self-employed earners); and

        (ii) [³one half of the amount in respect of any qualifying premium calculated in accordance with paragraph (13)].

(2) There shall be disregarded from a claimant's net profit any sum, where applicable, specified in Schedule 1.

(3) For the purposes of paragraph (1)(a) the net profit of the employment shall, except where paragraph [¹(3A),] (9) or (10) applies, be calculated by taking into account the earnings of the employment [¹received in the assessment period], less—

(a) subject to paragraphs (5) to (7), any expenses wholly and exclusively defrayed in that period for the purposes of that employment;

(b) an amount in respect of—

        (i) income tax; and

        (ii) social security contributions payable under the Social Security Act [SSCBA], calculated in accordance with regulation 23 (deduction of tax and contributions for self-employed earners); and

(c) [³one half of the amount in respect of any qualifying premium calculated in accordance with paragraph (13)].

[³(3A) For the purposes of paragraph (1)(a), in a case where the assessment period is determined under regulation 15(1)(b), the net profit of the employment shall, except where paragraph (9) applies, be calculated by taking into account the earnings of the employment relevant to that period (whether or not received in that period), less—

(a) subject to paragraphs (5) to (7), any expenses relevant to that period (whether or not defrayed in that period) and which were wholly and exclusively incurred for the purposes of that employment;

(b) an amount in respect of—

        (i) income tax; and

        (ii) social security contributions payable under the Social Security Act [SSCBA], calculated in accordance with regulation 23; and

(c) [³one half of the amount in respect of any qualifying premium calculated in accordance with paragraph (13)].]

(4) For the purposes of paragraph (1)(b) the net profit of the employment shall, except where paragraph [¹(4A), (9) or] (10) applies, be calculated by taking into account the earnings of the employment [¹received in the assessment period] less, subject to paragraphs (5) to (7), any expenses wholly and exclusively defrayed in that period for the purposes of that employment.

[¹(4A) For the purposes of paragraph (1)(b), in a case where the assessment period is determined under regulation 15(1)(b) the net profit of the employment shall, except where paragraph (9) applies, be calculated by taking into account the earnings of the employment relevant to that period (whether or not received in that period) less, subject to paragraphs (5) to (7), any expenses relevant to that period (whether or not defrayed in that period) and which were wholly and exclusively incurred for the purposes of that employment.]

(5) Subject to paragraph (6), no deduction shall be made under [¹paragraphs (3)(a), (3A)(a), (4) or (4A), as the case may be,] in respect of—

(a) any capital expenditure;

(b) the depreciation of any capital asset;

(c) any sum employed, or intended to be employed, in the setting up or expansion of the employment;

(d) any loss incurred before the beginning of the assessment period;

(e) the repayment of capital on any loan taken out for the purposes of the employment;

(f) any expenses incurred in providing business entertainment.

(6) A deduction shall be made under ['paragraphs (3)(a), (3A)(a), (4) or (4A), as the case may be,] in respect of the repayment of capital on any loan used for—

(a) the replacement in the course of business of equipment or machinery; and

(b) the repair of an existing business asset except to the extent that any sum is payable under an insurance policy for its repair.

(7) An adjudication officer shall refuse to make a deduction in respect of any expenses under ['paragraphs (3)(a), (3A)(a), (4) or (4A), as the case may be,] where he is not satisfied that the expense has been defrayed or given the nature and the amount of the expense that it has been reasonably incurred.

(8) For the avoidance of doubt—

(a) a deduction shall not be made under ['paragraphs (3)(a), (3A)(a), (4) or (4A), as the case may be,] in respect of any sum unless it has been expended for the purposes of the business;

(b) a deduction shall be made thereunder in respect of—

(i) the excess of any VAT paid over VAT received in the assessment period;

(ii) any income expended in the repair of an existing business asset except to the extent that any sum is payable under an insurance policy for its repair;

(iii) any payment of interest on a loan taken out for the purposes of the employment.

(9) Where a claimant is engaged in employment as a child minder the net profit of the employment to be taken into account shall be one-third of the earnings of that employment, less—

(a) an amount in respect of—

(i) income tax; and

(ii) social security contributions payable under the Social Security Act [SSCBA],

calculated in accordance with regulation 23 (deduction of tax and contributions for self-employed earners); and

(b) [³one half of the amount in respect of any qualifying premium calculated in accordance with paragraph (13)].

[¹(10) Where regulation 15(2) (normal weekly earnings of self-employed earners) applies—

(a) for the purposes of paragraph (1)(a), the net profit derived from the employment shall be calculated by taking into account the claimant's estimated and, where appropriate, actual earnings from the employment less the amount of the deductions likely to be made and, where appropriate, made under sub-paragraphs (a) to (c) of paragraph (3); or

(b) for the purposes of paragraph (1)(b), his share of the net profit of the employment shall be calculated by taking into account the claimant's estimated and, where appropriate, his share of the actual earnings from the employment less the amount of his share of the expenses likely to be deducted and, where appropriate, deducted under paragraph (4); or

(c) in the case of employment as a child-minder, the net profit of the employment shall be calculated by taking into account one-third of the claimant's estimated earnings and, where appropriate, actual earnings from the employment less the amount of the deductions likely to be made and, where appropriate made under sub-paragraphs (a) and (b) of paragraph (9).]

(11) For the avoidance of doubt where a claimant is engaged in employment as a self-employed earner and he is also engaged in one or more other employments as a self-employed or employed earner any loss incurred in any one of

his employments shall not be offset against his earnings in any other of his employments.

[²(12) [³In this regulation—

(a) "qualifying premium" means any premium which at the date of claim is payable periodically in respect of a retirement annuity contract or a personal pension scheme;

(b)] "retirement annuity contract" means an annuity contract for the time being approved by the Board of Inland Revenue as having for its main object the provision of a life annuity in old age or the provision of an annuity for a partner or dependant and in respect of which relief from income tax may be given on any premium.]

[³(13) The amount in respect of any qualifying premium shall be calculated by multiplying the daily amount of the qualifying premium by the number equal to the number of days in the assessment period; and for the purposes of this regulation the daily amount of the qualifying premium shall be determined—

(a) where the qualifying premium is payable monthly, by multiplying the amount of the qualifying premium by 12 and dividing the product by 365;

(b) in any other case, by dividing the amount of the qualifying premium by the number equal to the number of days in the period to which the qualifying premium relates.]

AMENDMENTS

1. Family Credit (General) Amendment No. 4 Regulations 1988 (S.I. 1988 No. 1970), reg. 6 (December 5, 1988).
2. Income-related Benefits Schemes (Miscellaneous Amendments) (No.4) Regulations 1993 (S.I. 1993 No. 2119), reg. 59 (October 3, 1993).
3. Income-related Benefits Schemes (Miscellaneous Amendments) Regulations 1994 (S.I. 1994 No. 527) reg. 19 (April 12, 1994).

DEFINITIONS

"assessment period"—see reg. 2(1), reg. 15.
"claimant"—see reg. 2(1), reg. 10(1).
"earnings"—see reg. 2(1).
"employed earner"—*ibid.*
"self-employed earner"—*ibid.*
"Social Security Act"—*ibid.*

GENERAL NOTE

See the notes to reg. 38(1) to (9) and (11) to (12) of the Income Support (General) Regulations for the substance of this provision. Para. (10) here deals with estimated earnings. The main differences otherwise are in the cross-references and the provision in paras. (3A) and (4A) for the assessment period identified in reg. 15(1)(b).

Paragraphs (3A) and (4A).
CFC 19/1993 decides that in calculating the net profit of a business under para. (3A) it is necessary to take account of the opening and closing stock. The claimant had produced a profit and loss account and the claim was assessed on the basis of reg. 15(1)(b). It was argued on behalf of the AO that "expenses" in para. (3A) was confined to purchases during the year. The Commissioner rejects that approach. In order to produce sales stock had to be consumed. Stock constituted an expense deductible under para. (3A). Such stock comprised both the opening stock and purchases during the year less the closing stock. In taking this view the Commissioner differs from that taken in *C2/89* (a decision of the Chief Commissioner of Northern Ireland) which has been followed by some Commissioners in England (see *CFC 22/1989* and *CFC 19/1992*). The Commissioner in *CFC 10/1993* declines to follow *CFC 19/1993*. In his view regs. 21(1) and 22(7) make clear that only earnings actually received and expenses actually defrayed may be taken into account. The Commissioner observes that for tax purposes there are clearly strong arguments for taking a long-term view

and making the notional adjustments to income and expenditure involved in taking into account stock valuation. But in his view it is consistent with the purposes of a social security scheme that only money actually received or actually expended should be taken into account. The Commissioner also points out that variations in stock valuation will not always operate in a claimant's favour. The issue was also considered in *CFC 41/1993*. The Commissioner follows *CFC 19/1993*, pointing to the use of the phrase "whether or nor received in that period" in reg. 22(3A) in relation to earnings and a similar wording as regards expenses. Thus there was nothing in the family credit scheme to indicate that normal accountancy procedures should not be applied. The definition of "trading account" in reg. 15(1A)(c) which referred to "the cost of *those* sales" also supported this conclusion. Reg. 22(3A) was to be contrasted with the position where accounts were not supplied when a strictly cash basis was applied by reg. 22(3). While this conflict of view between the Commissioners continues, SSATs faced with an appeal on this issue will have to decide which approach they prefer, but the current weight of authority seems to be in favour of taking account of opening and closing stock.

Paragraphs (12) and (13)
   The Commissioner in *CFC 5/1993* considered that the amendments to reg. 22(12) introduced in October 1993 (which have been further expanded in April 1994), were merely clarificatory. In his view a personal pension scheme capable of approval under s.633(1) of the Income and Corporation Taxes Act 1988 was an annuity contract within the meaning of reg. 22(12) before its amendment in October 1993.

Deduction of tax and contributions for self-employed earners

   23.—(1) The amount to be deducted in respect of income tax under regulation 22(1)(b)(i), (3)(b)(i)[², (3A)(b)(i)] or (9)(a)(i) (calculation of net profit of self-employed earners) shall be calculated on the basis of the amount of chargeable income, and as if that income were assessable to income tax at [³the lower rate or, as the case may be, the lower rate and the basic rate of tax] in the year of assessment in which the claim was made, less only the personal relief to which the claimant is entitled under sections 8(1) and (2) and 14(1)(a) and (2) of the Income and Corporation Taxes Act 1970 (personal relief) as is appropriate to his circumstances; but, if the assessment period is less than a year [³the earnings to which the lower rate [⁴ . . .] of tax is to be applied and] the amount of the personal relief deductible under this paragraph shall be calculated on a pro rata basis.
   (2) The amount to be deducted in respect of social security contributions under regulation 22(1)(b)(i), (3)(b)(ii)[², (3A)(b)(ii)] or (9)(a)(ii) shall be the total of—
   [¹(a) the amount of Class 2 contributions payable under section 7(1) or, as the case may be, (4) of the Social Security Act [SSCBA, s.11(1) or (3)] at the rate applicable at the date of claim except where the claimant's chargeable income is less than the amount specified in section 7(5) of that Act [SSCBA, s.11(4)] (small earnings exception) for the tax year in which the date of claim falls; but if the assessment period is less than a year, the amount specified for that tax year shall be calculated on a pro rata basis; and
   (b) the amount of Class 4 contributions (if any) which would be payable under section 9(2) of that Act [SSCBA, s. 15(3)] (Class 4 contributions) at the percentage rate applicable at the date of claim on so much of the chargeable income as exceeds the lower limit but does not exceed the upper limit of profits and gains applicable for the tax year in which the date of claim falls; if the assessment period is less than a year, those limits shall be calculated on a pro rata basis.]
   [²(3) In this regulation "chargeable income" means—
   (a) except where sub-paragraph (b) or (c) applies, the earnings derived from the employment, less any expenses deducted under paragraph (3)(a), (3A)(a), (4) or (4A), as the case may be, of regulation 22;

(b) except where sub-paragraph (c)(iii) applies, in the case of employment as a child minder one-third of the earnings of that employment; or

(c) where regulation 15(2) applies (normal weekly earnings of self-employed earners)

   (i) in the case of a self-employed earner who is engaged in employment on his own account, the claimant's estimated and, where appropriate, actual earnings from the employment less the amount of the deductions likely to be made and, where appropriate, made under sub-paragraph (a) of paragraph (3) of regulation 22;

   (ii) in the case of a self-employed earner whose employment is carried on in partnership or is that of a share fisherman within the meaning of the Social Security (Mariners' Benefits) Regulations 1975, the claimant's estimated and, where appropriate, his share of the actual earnings from the employment less the amount of his share of the expenses likely to be deducted and, where appropriate, deducted under paragraph (4) of regulation 22;

   (iii) in the case of employment as a child minder, one-third of the claimant's estimated and, where appropriate, actual earnings from that employment.]

AMENDMENTS

1. Family Credit (General) Amendment Regulations 1988 (S.I. 1988 No. 660), reg. 7 (April 11, 1988).

2. Family Credit (General) Amendment No. 4 Regulations 1988 (S.I. 1988 No. 1970), reg. 7 (December 5, 1988).

3. Income-related Benefits Schemes (Miscellaneous Amendments) (No.3) Regulations 1992 (S.I. 1992 No. 2155), reg. 8 (October 5, 1992).

4. Income-related Benefits Schemes (Miscellaneous Amendments) (No. 5) Regulations 1994 (S.I. 1994 No. 2139), reg. 14 (October 4, 1994).

DEFINITIONS

"assessment period"—see reg. 2(1), reg. 15.
"claim"—see reg. 2(1).
"claimant"—*ibid.*, reg. 10(1).
"earnings"—see reg. 2(1).
"self-employed earner"—*ibid.*
"Social Security Act"—*ibid.*
"year of assessment"—*ibid.*

GENERAL NOTE

Paragraph (1)
Since the actual income tax to be paid by the self-employed may take some time to calculate (and is normally not payable until the tax year after that in which the profits are made) this provision supplies a simple rule to be applied immediately. The basic rate of income tax for the tax year in which the claim is made is applied, less the personal relief for a year or part of a year.

Paragraph (2)
The appropriate amounts of Class 2 (flat-rate) and Class 4 (profit-related) social security contributions for the period over which earnings are averaged are to be deducted.

Paragraph (3)
This paragraph defines the earnings on which the deductions for tax and social security contributions are to be calculated.

Chapter V

Other Income

Calculation of income other than earnings

24.—(1) For the purposes of regulation 16 (normal weekly income other than earnings), the income of a claimant which does not consist of earnings to be taken into account shall, subject to paragraphs [²(2) to (4A)], be his gross income and any capital treated as income under [⁴regulations 25 and 27 (capital treated as income and modifications in respect of children and young persons).]

(2) There shall be disregarded from the calculation of a claimant's gross income under paragraph (1), any sum, where applicable, specified in Schedule 2.

(3) [¹. . .]

(4) Where the payment of any benefit under the benefit Acts is subject to any deduction by way of recovery the amount to be taken into account under paragraph (1) shall be the gross amount payable.

[²(4A) Where a loan is made to a person pursuant to arrangements made under section 1 of the Education (Student Loans) Act 1990 [³or Article 3 of the Education (Student Loans) (Northern Ireland) Order 1990] and that person ceases to be a student before the end of the academic year in respect of which the loan is payable or, as the case may be, before the end of his course, a sum equal to the weekly amount apportionable under paragraph (2) of regulation 42A shall be taken into account under paragraph (1) for each week, in the period over which the loan fell to be apportioned, following the date on which that person ceases to be a student; but in determining the weekly amount apportionable under paragraph (2) of regulation 42A so much of that paragraph as provides for a disregard shall not have effect.]

(5) For the avoidance of doubt there shall be included as income to be taken into account under paragraph (1) any payment to which regulation 19(2) applies (payments not earnings).

AMENDMENTS

1. Family Credit (General) Amendment Regulations 1990 (S.I. 1990 No. 574), reg. 10 (April 10, 1990).

2. Social Security Benefits (Student Loans and Miscellaneous Amendments) Regulations 1990 (S.I. 1990 No. 1549), reg. 3(2) (September 1, 1990).

3. Family Credit (General) Amendment Regulations 1991 (S.I. 1991 No. 1520), reg. 4 (August 6, 1991).

4. Income-related Benefits Schemes (Miscellaneous Amendments) (No. 4) Regulations 1993 (S.I. 1993 No. 2119), reg. 30 (October 5, 1993).

DEFINITIONS

"the benefit Acts"—see 1986 Act, s.84(1).
"claimant"—see reg. 2(1), reg. 10(1).
"earnings"—see reg. 2(1).

GENERAL NOTE

Paragraph (1)

Income which is not earnings comes into this category. It specifically includes capital treated as income under reg. 25 and reg. 27 (capital payable by instalments), and must also include the tariff income from capital between £3,000 and £8,000 under reg. 36. Perhaps the main category covered will be social security benefits which are not disregarded under Sched. 2 (in particular, child benefit is disregarded). The intention seems to be that income from boarders which does not count as earnings from self-employment under reg. 21(2) should count here, but after the revocation of para. (3) it is not clear that this works. It is not income other than earnings. The income to be taken into account is the gross amount, *i.e.* without any deductions. See the notes to reg. 40(1) of the Income Support Regulations.

Note the disregard of the first £15 of maintenance payments under reg. 16(2) and (2A) (Sched. 2, para. 47).

Paragraph (2)

There is a long list of disregards in Sched. 2.

Paragraph (4)

If a social security benefit is to be taken into account any deduction by way of recovery (*e.g.* of an overpayment or of a social fund loan) is ignored. The gross amount is taken.

Paragraph (5)

Payments which are excluded from the category of earnings by reg. 19(2) count as income, but see the disregard of payments in kind (para. 20), statutory maternity pay (para. 27) and payments for necessary, etc., expenses (para. 32) in Sched. 2. Earnings which are disregarded under Sched. 1 do not count as income because they remain "earnings" and reg. 24 only applies to income which does not consist of earnings.

Capital treated as income

25.—(1) Any capital payable by instalments which are outstanding at the date of the claim shall, if the aggregate of the instalments outstanding and the amount of the claimant's capital otherwise calculated in accordance with Chapter VI of this Part exceeds [¹£8,000], be treated as income.

(2) Any payment received under an annuity shall be treated as income.

AMENDMENT

1. Income-related Benefits (Miscellaneous Amendments) Regulations 1990 (S.I. 1990 No. 671), reg. 3 (April 9, 1990).

DEFINITIONS

"claimant"—see reg. 2(1), reg. 10(1).
"date of claim"—see reg. 2(1).

GENERAL NOTE

Paragraph (1)

The value of the right to receive any outstanding instalments of capital to be paid by instalments is disregarded under para. 17 of Sched. 3 as a capital asset. Generally, each instalment, when it is paid, is added to the person's capital. However, if the person's existing capital plus the amount of any outstanding instalments comes to more than £8,000, this provision applies. The sensible result would then be that each instalment received when para. (1) applied would be treated as income. However, this is not what para. (1) says. It appears to require all of the capital payable by instalments to be treated as income, but there is no clue how this might be done. Perhaps the sensible result is the only possible outcome. See reg. 27(1) for payments to a child or young person.

See *Lillystone v. SBC* [1982] 3 F.L.R. 52 for an example of a capital sum payable by instalments.

Paragraph (2)

The value of the right to receive income under an annuity is disregarded as a capital asset under para. 12 of Sched. 3.

Notional income

26.—(1) A claimant shall be treated as possessing income of which he has deprived himself for the purpose of securing entitlement to family credit or increasing the amount of that benefit.

(2) Except in the case of a discretionary trust or a trust derived from a payment made in consequence of a personal injury, any income which would become available to the claimant upon application being made, but which has not been acquired by him, shall be treated as possessed by the claimant.

(3) Any payment of income[¹, other than a payment of income made under the Macfarlane Trust[⁵, the Macfarlane (Special Payments) Trust][⁶, the Macfarlane (Special Payments) (No. 2) Trust][⁸, the Fund][¹², the Eileen Trust] [²or [¹¹the Independent Living Funds]],] made—

[³(a) to a third party in respect of a member of [⁴the family] (but not a member of the third party's family) shall be treated as possessed by that member of the family to the extent that it is used for his food, ordinary clothing or footwear, household fuel [⁷. . .] or housing costs [⁷or is used for any personal community [¹⁰charge,] collective community charge contribution [¹⁰or council tax] for which that member is liable]; and in this sub-paragraph the expression "ordinary clothing or foot-wear" means clothing or footwear for normal daily use, but does not include school uniforms, or clothing or footwear used solely for sporting activities;]

    (b) to a member of the family in respect of a third party (but not in respect of another member of that family) shall be treated as possessed by that member to the extent that it is kept him or used by or on behalf of any member of the family.

(4) Where—

    (a) a claimant performs a service for another person; and

    (b) that person makes no payment of earnings or pays less than that paid for a comparable employment in the area; and

    (c) the adjudication officer is satisfied that the means of that person are sufficient for him to pay or to pay more for the service,

the adjudication officer shall treat the claimant as possessing such earnings (if any) as is reasonable for that employment; but this paragraph shall not apply to a claimant who is engaged by a charitable or [¹⁵voluntary organisation] or is a volunteer if the adjudication officer is satisfied [¹⁵in any of those cases] that it is reasonable for him to provide his services free of charge.

(5) Where a claimant is treated as possessing any income under any of paragraphs (1) to (3), the foregoing provisions of this Part shall apply for the purposes of calculating the amount of that income as if a payment had actually been made and as if it were actual income which he does possess.

(6) Where a claimant is treated as possessing any earnings under paragraph (4), the foregoing provisions of this Part shall apply for the purposes of calculating the amount of those earnings as if a payment had actually been made and as if they were actual earnings which he does possess, except that paragraph (3) of regulation 20 (calculation of net earnings of employed earners) shall not apply and his net earnings shall be calculated by taking into account those earnings which he is treated as possessing, less—

    (a) an amount in respect of income tax equivalent to an amount calculated by applying to those earnings [⁹the lower rate or, as the case may be, the lower rate and the basic rate of tax] in the year of assessment in which the claim was made less only the personal relief to which the claimant is entitled under sections 8(1) and (2) and 14(1)(a) and (2) of the Income and Corporation Taxes Act 1970 (personal relief) as is appropriate to his circumstances; but, if the assessment period is less than a year, [⁹the earnings to which the lower rate [¹⁴. . .] of tax is to be applied and] the amount of the personal relief deductible under this sub-paragraph shall be calculated on a pro rata basis;

[¹³(b) where the weekly amount of those earnings equals or exceeds the lower earnings limit, an amount representing primary Class 1 contributions under the Contributions and Benefits Act, calculated by applying to those earnings the initial and main primary percentages applicable at the date of claim in accordance with section 8(1)(a) and (b) of that Act; and]

    (c) one-half of any sum payable by the claimant by way of a contribution towards an occupational or personal pension scheme.

AMENDMENTS

1. Family Credit (General) Amendment Regulations 1988 (S.I. 1988 No. 660), reg. 8 (April 11, 1988).

2. Family Credit and Income Support (General) Amendment Regulations 1988 (S.I. 1988 No. 999), reg. 3 (June 9, 1988).

3. Family Credit (General) Amendment No. 3 Regulations 1988 (S.I. 1988 No. 1438), reg. 5 (September 12, 1988).

4. Family Credit (General) Amendment No. 4 Regulations 1988 (S.I. 1988 No. 1970), reg. 8 (December 5, 1988).

5. Income-related Benefits Schemes Amendment Regulations 1990 (S.I. 1990 No. 127), reg. 2 (January 31, 1990).

6. Income-related Benefits Schemes and Social Security (Recoupment) Amendment Regulations 1991 (S.I. 1991 No. 1175), reg. 3 (May 11, 1991).

7. Family Credit (General) Amendment Regulations 1991 (S.I. 1991 No. 1520), reg. 5 (October 8, 1991).

8. Income-related Benefits Schemes and Social Security (Recoupment) Amendment Regulations 1992 (S.I. 1992 No. 1101), reg. 4(3) (May 7, 1992).

9. Income-related Benefits Schemes (Miscellaneous Amendments) (No. 3) Regulations 1992 (S.I. 1992 No. 2155), reg. 9 (October 5, 1992).

10. Income-related Benefits Schemes (Miscellaneous Amendments) Regulations 1993 (S.I. 1993 No. 315), Sched., para. 7 (April 1, 1993).

11. Social Security Benefits (Miscellaneous Amendments) (No. 2) Regulations 1993 (S.I. 1993 No. 963), reg. 3(3) (April 22, 1993).

12. Income-related Benefits Schemes and Social Security (Recoupment) Amendment Regulations 1993 (S.I. 1993 No. 1249), reg. 2(3) (May 14, 1993).

13. Income-related Benefits Schemes (Miscellaneous Amendments) Regulations 1994 (S.I. 1994 No. 527), reg. 20 (April 12, 1994).

14. Income-related Benefits Schemes (Miscellaneous Amendments) (No. 5) Regulations 1994 (S.I. 1994 No. 2139), reg. 14 (October 4, 1994).

15. Income-related Benefits Schemes (Miscellaneous Amendments) Regulations 1995 (S.I. 1995 No. 516), reg. 13 (April 11, 1995).

DEFINITIONS

"assessment period"—see reg. 2(1).
"claimant"—*ibid.*, reg. 10(1).
"earnings"—see reg. 2(1).
"family"—see 1986 Act, s.20(11) (SSCBA, s.137(1)).
"occupational pension scheme"—see 1986 Act, s.84(1) (PSA, s.1).
"payment"—see reg. 2(1).
"personal pension scheme"—see 1986 Act, s.84(1) (PSA, s.1).
"primary Class 1 contribution"—*ibid.*
"the Eileen Trust"—see reg. 2(1).
"the Fund"—*ibid.*
"the Independent Living Funds"—*ibid.*
"the Macfarlane (Special Payments) Trust"—*ibid.*
"the Macfarlane (Special Payments) (No. 2) Trust"—*ibid.*
"the Macfarlane Trust"—*ibid.*
"voluntary organisation"—*ibid.*
"year of assessment"—*ibid.*

GENERAL NOTE

Paragraph (1)
See the notes to reg. 42(1) of the Income Support (General) Regulations. However, this provision only applies if the purpose is to gain entitlement to family credit. The approach of *R(IS) 14/93* suggests that if the purpose is to gain entitlement to income support or supplementary benefit or family income supplement, this provision cannot apply.

Paragraph (2)
See the notes to reg. 42(2) of the Income Support (General) Regulations for when income would become available upon application. Here the only exceptions are discretionary trusts and trusts of payments of compensation for personal injury.

Paragraph (3)
See the notes to reg. 42(4) of the Income Support (General) Regulations for the general tests. There are slight differences only.

Paragraph (4)

See the notes to reg. 42(6) of the Income Support (General) Regulations. Sub-para. (c) of this paragraph is not separated out in reg. 42(6), with the effect that the burden of proof is different. In reg. 42(6), if the other conditions are met, the provision applies unless the claimant satisfies the AO that the person's means are insufficient to pay the going rate. Here, the AO must be satisfied that the person's means are sufficient before para. (4) can apply.

Paragraphs (5) and (6)

Notional income and earnings are to be treated as actual income and earnings, including the appropriate deductions to reach a figure of net earnings.

Modifications in respect of children and young persons

27.—(1) Any capital of a child or young person payable by instalments which are outstanding at the date of claim shall, if the aggregate of the instalments outstanding and the amount of that child's or young person's other capital calculated in accordance with Chapter VI of this Part in like manner as for the claimant, [².. .], would exceed £3,000, be treated as income.

(2) Where the income of a child or young person, other than income consisting of payments of maintenance whether under a court order or not, calculated in accordance with [²Chapters I to V] of this Part exceeds the sum specified as a credit for that child or young person in Schedule 4 and regulation 46(5) (sum for child or young person who has income in excess to be nil) applies, that income shall not be treated as income of the claimant.

(3) Where the capital of a child or young person, if calculated in accordance with Chapter VI of this Part in like manner as for the claimant, [²except as provided in paragraph (1)], would exceed £3,000, any income of that child or young person[¹, other than income consisting of any payment of maintenance whether under a court order or not] shall not be treated as income of the claimant.

(4) Any income of a child or young person which is to be disregarded under Schedule 2 shall be disregarded in such manner as to produce the result most favourable to the claimant.

AMENDMENTS

1. Income-related Benefits Schemes (Miscellaneous Amendments) Regulations 1993 (S.I. 1993 No. 315), reg. 13 (April 13, 1993).
2. Income-related Benefits Schemes (Miscellaneous Amendments) (No. 4) Regulations 1993 (S.I. 1993 No. 2119), reg. 31 (October 5, 1993).

DEFINITIONS

"child"—see 1986 Act, s.20(11) (SSCBA, s.137(1)).
"claimant"—see reg. 2(1), reg. 10(1).
"date of claim"—see reg. 2(1).
"payment"—*ibid.*
"young person"—*ibid.*, reg. 6.

GENERAL NOTE

There are important modifications where children or young persons in the family have capital or income. Note that the earnings of a child or young person are disregarded under para. 2 of Sched. 1.

Paragraph (1)

See reg. 25(1) for the general treatment of capital payable by instalments. If the payment is to a child or young person, the rule comes in at £3,000.

Paragraph (2)

If the income of a child or young person exceeds the amount of the credit for a person of that age specified in Sched. 4, then under reg. 46(5) the credit for that person is nil. As compensation, the child's or young person's income is not treated as the claimant's. It is as if the child or young person had been taken out of the family. See also the effect of para. (3).

Paragraph (3)

If the capital of a child or young person exceeds £3,000, then under reg. 46(4) the credit for that person is nil. Any capital of a child or young person is not in any circumstances treated as the claimant's (reg. 30). This paragraph means that any income of the child or young person, other than maintenance, is ignored when reg. 46(4) applies.

Paragraph (4)

Self-explanatory.

Chapter VI

Capital

Capital limit

28. For the purposes of section 22(6) of the Act [SSCBA, s.134(1)] as it applies to family credit (no entitlement to benefit if capital exceeds prescribed amount), the prescribed amount is [¹£8,000].

AMENDMENT

1. Income-related Benefits (Miscellaneous Amendments) Regulations 1990 (S.I. 1990 No. 671), reg. 3 (April 9, 1990).

DEFINITION

"the Act"—see reg. 2(1).

GENERAL NOTE

There was no capital limit for FIS. The introduction of a limit for family credit in s.22(6) of the 1986 Act (now s.134(1) of the Contributions and Benefits Act) was an important reform. Reg. 28 adopts the same limit as for income support, raised from £6,000 to £8,000 in April 1990. The limit applies to all the capital of the family which is treated as the claimant's under reg. 10(1). Capital belonging to children and young persons is disregarded under reg. 30, but see the effect on the entitlement through reg. 46(4).

See reg. 29 for the calculation of capital.

Calculation of capital

29.—(1) For the purposes of Part II of the Act [SSCBA, Part VII] as it applies to family credit, the capital of a claimant to be taken into account shall, subject to paragraph (2), be the whole of his capital calculated in accordance with this Part and any income treated as capital under regulation 31 (income treated as capital).

(2) There shall be disregarded from the calculation of a claimant's capital under paragraph (1) any capital, where applicable, specified in Schedule 3.

DEFINITIONS

"the Act"—see reg. 2(1).
"claimant"—*ibid.*, reg. 10(1).

GENERAL NOTE

The main point here, apart from confirming the effect of reg. 31, is to provide for the capital specified in Sched. 3 to be disregarded.

Disregard of capital of child or young person

30. The capital of a child or young person who is a member of the claimant's family shall not be treated as capital of the claimant.

DEFINITIONS

"child"—see 1986 Act, s.20(11) (SSCBA, s.137(1)).
"claimant"—see reg. 2(1), reg. 10(1).
"family"—see 1986 Act, s.20(11) (SSCBA, s.137(1)).
"young person"—see reg. 2(1), reg. 6.

GENERAL NOTE

Where the claimant's family includes a child or young person, any capital belonging to the child or young person is not treated as the claimant's, and so does not count towards the £8,000 limit. If an individual child or young person has capital of more than £3,000, no credit is allowed for that person (reg. 46(4)).

Income treated as capital

31.—(1) Any amount by way of a refund of income tax deducted from profits or emoluments chargeable to income tax under Schedule D or E shall be treated as capital.

(2) Any holiday pay which is not earnings under regulation 19(1)(*b*) (earnings of employed earners) shall be treated as capital.

[²(3) Any charitable or voluntary payment which is not made or is not due to be made at regular intervals, other than a payment which is made under the Macfarlane Trust, the Macfarlane (Special Payments) Trust, the Macfarlane (Special Payments) (No. 2) Trust[³, the Fund][⁵, the Eileen Trust] or [⁴the Independent Living Funds] shall be treated as capital.]

(4) Except any income derived from capital disregarded under paragraph 1, 2, 4, 6[¹, 13 or 26 to 30] of Schedule 3, any income derived from capital shall be treated as capital but only from the date it is normally due to be credited to the claimant's account.

(5) In the case of employment as an employed earner, any advance of earnings or any loan made by the claimant's employer shall be treated as capital.

(6) Any maintenance payment other than one to which regulation 16(2) [⁶or (2A)](normal weekly income other than earnings) applies shall be treated as capital.

AMENDMENTS

1. Family Credit (General) Amendment No. 4 Regulations 1988 (S.I. 1988 No. 1970), reg. 9 (December 5, 1988).
2. Income-related Benefits Schemes and Social Security (Recoupment) Amendment Regulations 1991 (S.I. 1991 No. 1175), reg. 3 (May 11, 1991).
3. Income-related Benefits Schemes and Social Security (Recoupment) Amendment Regulations 1992 (S.I. 1992 No. 1101). reg. 6 (May 7, 1992).
4. Social Security Benefits (Miscellaneous Amendments) (No. 2) Regulations 1993 (S.I. 1993 No. 963), reg. 3(3) (April 22, 1993).
5. Income-related Benefits Schemes and Social Security (Recoupment) Amendment Regulations 1993 (S.I. 1993 No. 1249), reg. 2(3) (May 14, 1993).
6. Income-related Benefits Schemes (Miscellaneous Amendments) (No. 5) Regulations 1994 (S.I. 1994 No. 2139), reg. 18 (October 4, 1994).

DEFINITIONS

"claimant"—see reg. 2(1), reg. 10(1).

"earnings"—see reg. 2(1).
"employed earner"—*ibid.*
"the Eileen Trust"—*ibid.*
"the Fund"—*ibid.*
"the Independent Living Funds"—*ibid.*
"the Macfarlane (Special Payments) Trust"—*ibid.*
"the Macfarlane (Special Payments) (No. 2) Trust"—*ibid.*
"the Macfarlane Trust"—*ibid.*

GENERAL NOTE

If income is treated as capital under this regulation, it is to be disregarded as income (Sched. 2, para. 26).

Paragraph (1)
Refunds of income tax under Schedule E (PAYE) or Schedule D are capital.

Paragraph (2)
Holiday pay payable more than four weeks after the termination of employment is capital.

Paragraph (3)
Charitable or voluntary payments which are due to be made at regular intervals will be income (subject to the disregard in para. 13 of Sched. 2). See the notes to para. 15 of Sched. 9 to the Income Support (General) Regulations. If the payment is not made, or not due to be made, at regular intervals it is capital. There is an exception for payments from the government-funded trusts for haemophiliacs, non–haemophiliacs and the severely disabled.

Paragraph (4)
The general rule is that the income derived from capital is treated as capital from the date on which it increases the existing balance. The exceptions are premises the capital value of which is disregarded, plus business assets and trust funds derived from compensation for personal injury.

Paragraph (5)
Any advance of earnings or loan made by an employer to an employee is capital.

Paragraph (6)
Reg. 16(2) deals with maintenance payments (rather vaguely defined) which are made or due to be made at regular intervals. If the payments are neither made nor due to be made at regular intervals, they count as capital when they arrive. There is obvious scope for benefit planning here (compared to the rigidity of the income support rules).
Para. (6) has now (from October 1994) been amended to take account of child support maintenance under the Child Support Act 1991, which falls under reg. 16(2A) and not reg. 16(2).

Calculation of capital in the United Kingdom

32. Capital which a claimant possesses in the United Kingdom shall be calculated—
  (a) except in a case to which sub-paragraph (b) applies, at its current market or surrender value less—
     (i) where there would be expenses attributable to sale, 10 per cent.; and
     (ii) the amount of any incumbrance secured on it;
  (b) in the case of a National Savings Certificate—
     (i) if purchased from an issue the sale of which ceased before 1st July last preceding the date of claim, at the price which it would have realised on that 1st July had it been purchased on the last day of that issue;
     (ii) in any other case, at its purchase price.

DEFINITION

"claimant"—see reg. 2(1), reg. 10(1).

See the notes to reg. 49 of the Income Support (General) Regulations.

Calculation of capital outside the United Kingdom

33. Capital which a claimant possesses in a country outside the United Kingdom shall be calculated—
- (a) in a case where there is no prohibition in that country against the transfer to the United Kingdom of an amount equal to its current market or surrender value in that country, at that value;
- (b) in a case where there is such a prohibition, at the price which it would realise if sold in the United Kingdom to a willing buyer,

less, where there would be expenses attributable to sale, 10 per cent. and the amount of any incumbrance secured on it.

DEFINITION

"claimant"—see reg. 2(1), reg. 10(1).

GENERAL NOTE

See the notes to reg. 50 of the Income Support (General) Regulations.

Notional capital

34.—(1) A claimant shall be treated as possessing capital of which he has deprived himself for the purpose of securing entitlement to family credit or increasing the amount of that benefit [6except—
- (a) where that capital is derived from a payment made in consequence of any personal injury and is placed on trust for the benefit of the claimant; or
- (b) to the extent that the capital which he is treated as possessing is reduced in accordance with regulation 34A (diminishing notional capital rule).]

(2) Except in the case of a—
- (a) a discretionary trust;
- (b) a trust derived from a payment made in consequence of a personal injury; or
- (c) any loan which would be obtainable only if secured against capital disregarded under Schedule 3,

any capital which would become available to the claimant upon application being made but which has not been acquired by him shall be treated as possessed by him.

(3) Any payment of capital[1, other than a payment of capital made under the Macfarlane Trust[5, the Macfarlane (Special Payments) Trust][7, the Macfarlane (Special Payments) (No. 2) Trust][9, the Fund][12, the Eileen Trust] [2or [11the Independent Living Funds]],] made—
- [3(a) to a third party in respect of a member of [4the family] (but not a member of the third party's family) shall be treated as possessed by that member of the family to the extent that it is used for his food, ordinary clothing or footwear, household fuel [8. . .] or housing costs [8or is used for any personal community [10charge,] collective community charge contribution [10or council tax] for which that member is liable]; and in this subparagraph the expression "ordinary clothing or footwear" means clothing or footwear for normal daily use, but does not include school uniforms, or clothing or footwear used solely for sporting activities;]
- (b) to a member of the family in respect of a third party (but not in respect of another member of the family) shall be treated as possessed by that

member to the extent that it is kept by him or used on behalf of any member of the family.

(4) Where a claimant stands in relation to a company in a position analogous to that of a sole owner or partner in the business of that company, he shall be treated as if he were such sole owner or partner and in such a case—

(a) the value of his holding in that company shall, notwithstanding regulation 29 (calculation of capital) be disregarded; and

(b) he shall, subject to paragraph (5), be treated as possessing an amount of capital equal to the value or, as the case may be, his share of the value of the capital of that company and the foregoing provisions of this Chapter shall apply for the purposes of calculating that amount as if it were actual capital which he does possess.

(5) For so long as the claimant undertakes activities in the course of the business of the company, the amount which he is treated as possessing under paragraph (4) shall be disregarded.

(6) Where a claimant is treated as possessing capital under any of paragraphs (1) to (4) the foregoing provisions of this Chapter shall apply for the purposes of calculating its amount as if it were actual capital which he does possess.

[[1](7) For the avoidance of doubt a claimant is to be treated as possessing capital under paragraph (1) only if the capital of which he has deprived himself is actual capital.]

AMENDMENTS

1. Family Credit (General) Amendment Regulations 1988 (S.I. 1988 No. 660), reg. 9 (April 11, 1988).

2. Family Credit and Income Support (General) Amendment Regulations 1988 (S.I. 1988 No. 999), reg. 3 (June 9, 1988).

3. Family Credit (General) Amendment No. 3 Regulations 1988 (S.I. 1988 No. 1438), reg. 5 (September 12, 1988).

4. Family Credit (General) Amendment No. 4 Regulations 1988 (S.I. 1988 No. 1970), reg. 10 (December 5, 1988).

5. Income-related Benefits Schemes Amendment Regulations 1990 (S.I. 1990 No. 127), reg. 2 (January 31, 1990).

6. Family Credit (General) Amendment No. 2 Regulations 1990 (S.I. 1990 No. 1774), reg. 3 (October 2, 1990).

7. Income-related Benefits Schemes and Social Security (Recoupment) Amendment Regulations 1991 (S.I. 1991 No. 1175), reg. 3 (May 11, 1991).

8. Family Credit (General) Amendment Regulations 1991 (S.I. 1991 No. 1520), reg. 5 (October 8, 1991).

9. Income-related Benefits Schemes and Social Security (Recoupment) Amendment Regulations 1992 (S.I. 1992 No. 1101), reg. 6 (May 7, 1992).

10. Income-related Benefits Schemes (Miscellaneous Amendments) Regulations 1993 (S.I. 1993 No. 315), Sched., para. 8 (April 1, 1993).

11. Social Security Benefits (Miscellaneous Amendments) (No. 2) Regulations 1993 (S.I. 1993 No. 963), reg. 3(3) (April 22, 1993).

12. Income-related Benefits Schemes and Social Security (Recoupment) Amendment Regulations 1993 (S.I. 1993 No. 1249), reg. 2(3) (May 14, 1993).

DEFINITIONS

"claimant"—see reg. 2(1), reg. 10(1).
"family"—see 1986 Act, s.20(11) (SSCBA, s.137(1)).
"the Eileen Trust"—see reg. 2(1).
"the Fund"—*ibid.*
"the Independent Living Funds"—*ibid.*
"the Macfarlane (Special Payments) Trust"—*ibid.*
"the Macfarlane (Special Payments) (No. 2) Trust"—*ibid.*
"the Macfarlane Trust"—*ibid.*

Paragraph (1)

See the notes to reg. 51(1) of the Income Support (General) Regulations. Note, however, that this paragraph only applies where the purpose is to gain entitlement to family credit. The approach of *R(IS) 14/93* suggests that if the purpose is to gain entitlement to income support or housing benefit or supplementary benefit or family income supplement, the family credit rule cannot apply. The effect of para. (7) is to confirm that para. (1) only operates if the person has deprived himself of actual capital.

Paragraph (2)

See the notes to reg. 51(2) of the Income Support (General) Regulations. There are slight differences in wording.

Paragraph (3)

See the notes to reg. 51(3) of the Income Support (General) Regulations and the differences in sub-para. (a).

Paragraphs (4) to (6)

See the notes to reg. 51(4) to (6) of the Income Support (General) Regulations.

[¹Diminishing notional capital rule

34A.—(1) Where a claimant is treated as possessing capital under regulation 34(1) (notional capital), the amount which he is treated as possessing—
  (a) in the case of a benefit week which is subsequent to—
    (i) the relevant week in respect of which the conditions set out in paragraph (2) are satisfied, or
    (ii) a week which follows that relevant week and which satisfies those conditions,
  shall be reduced by an amount determined under paragraph (3);
  (b) in the case of a benefit week in respect of which paragraph (1)(a) does not apply but where—
    (i) that week is a week subsequent to the relevant week, and
    (ii) that relevant week is a week in which the condition in paragraph (4) is satisfied,
  shall be reduced by the amount determined under paragraph (4).

(2) This paragraph applies to a benefit week where the claimant satisfies the conditions that—
  (a) he is entitled to family credit; and
  (b) but for regulation 34(1), he would have been entitled to an additional amount of family credit in that benefit week.

(3) In a case to which paragraph (2) applies, the amount of the reduction for the purposes of paragraph (1)(a) shall be equal to the aggregate of—
  (a) the additional amount of family credit to which the claimant would have been entitled; and
  [²(b) if the claimant would, but for regulation 43(1) of the Housing Benefit (General) Regulations 1987 (notional capital), have been entitled to housing benefit or to an additional amount of housing benefit in respect of the benefit week in which the date of the last claim for family credit falls, the amount (if any) which is equal to—
    (i) in a case where no housing benefit is payable, the amount to which he would have been entitled, or
    (ii) in any other case, the amount equal to the additional amount of housing benefit to which he would have been entitled; and
  (c) if the claimant would, but for regulation 33(1) of the Community Charge Benefits (General) Regulations 1989 (notional capital) have been entitled to community charge benefit or to an additional amount of community

charge benefit in respect of the benefit week in which the date of the last claim for family credit falls, the amount (if any) which is equal to—
    (i) in a case where no community charge benefit is payable, the amount to which he would have been entitled, or
    (ii) in any other case, the amount equal to the additional amount of community charge benefit to which he would have been entitled[³; and
 (d) if the claimant would, but for regulation 34(1) of the Council Tax Benefit (General) Regulations 1992 (notional capital), have been entitled to council tax benefit or to an additional amount of council tax benefit in respect of the benefit week in which the date of the last claim for family credit falls, the amount (if any) which is equal to—
    (i) in a case where no council tax benefit is payable, the amount to which he would have been entitled, or
    (ii) in any other case, the amount equal to the additional amount of council tax to which he would have been entitled.]]

(4) Subject to paragraph (5), for the purposes of paragraph (1)(b) the condition is that the claimant would have been entitled to family credit in the relevant week, but for regulation 34(1) and in such a case the amount shall be equal to the aggregate of—
 (a) the amount of family credit to which the claimant would have been entitled in the relevant week but for regulation 34(1);
[²(b) if the claimant would, but for regulation 43(1) of the Housing Benefit (General) Regulations 1987 have been entitled to housing benefit or to an additional amount of housing benefit in respect of the benefit week in which the first day of the relevant week falls, the amount (if any) which is equal to—
    (i) in a case where no housing benefit is payable, the amount to which he would have been entitled, or
    (ii) in any other case, the amount equal to the additional amount of housing benefit to which he would have been entitled; and
 (c) if the claimant would, but for regulation 33(1) of the Community Charge Benefits (General) Regulations 1989 have been entitled to community charge benefit or to an additional amount of community charge benefit in respect of the benefit week in which the first day of the relevant week falls, the amount (if any) which is equal to—
    (i) in a case where no community charge benefit is payable, the amount to which he would have been entitled, or
    (ii) in any other case, the amount equal to the additional amount of community charge benefit to which he would have been entitled[³; and
 (d) if the claimant would, but for regulation 34(1) of the Council Tax Benefit (General) Regulations 1992 (notional capital), have been entitled to council tax benefit or to an additional amount of council tax benefit in respect of the benefit week in which the first day of the relevant week falls, the amount (if any) which is equal to—
    (i) in a case where no council tax benefit is payable, the amount to which he would have been entitled, or
    (ii) in any other case, the amount equal to the additional amount of council tax to which he would have been entitled.]]

(5) The amount determined under paragraph (4) shall be re-determined under that paragraph if the claimant makes a further claim for family credit and the conditions in paragraph (6) are satisfied, and in such a case—
 (a) sub-paragraphs (a), (b) and (c) of paragraph (4) shall apply as if for the words "relevant week" there were substituted the words "relevant subsequent week"; and
 (b) subject to paragraph (7), the amount as re-determined shall have effect from the first week following the relevant subsequent week in question.

(6) The conditions are that—
(a) a further claim is made 22 or more weeks after—
    (i) the first day of the relevant week;
    (ii) in a case where there has been at least one re-determination in accordance with paragraph (5), the first day of the relevant subsequent week which last occurred;
    whichever last occurred; and
(b) the claimant would have been entitled to family credit but for regulation 34(1).

(7) The amount as re-determined pursuant to paragraph (5) shall not have effect if it is less than the amount which applied in that case immediately before the re-determination and in such a case the higher amount shall continue to have effect.

(8) For the purpose of this regulation—
(a) "benefit week" has the meaning prescribed in regulations 16 (date of entitlement under an award) and 27 (family credit) of the Social Security (Claims and Payments) Regulations 1987 except where it appears in paragraphs [³(3)(b), (c) and (d) and (4)(b), (c) and (d)] where it has the meaning prescribed in regulation 2(1) of the Housing Benefit (General) Regulations [³1987 (interpretation),] regulation 2(1) of the Community Charge Benefits (General) Regulations 1989 (interpretation) [³or regulation 2(1) of the Council Tax Benefit (General) Regulations 1992 (interpretation)] as the case may be;
(b) "relevant week" means the benefit week in which the capital in question of which the claimant has deprived himself within the meaning of regulation 34(1)—
    (i) was for the first time taken into account for the purpose of determining his entitlement to family credit; or
    (ii) was taken into account on a subsequent occasion for that purpose other than in respect of either a benefit week to which paragraph (2) applies or a further claim to which paragraph (5) applies;
    and, where more than one benefit week is identified by reference to heads (i) and (ii) of this sub-paragraph, the later or latest such benefit week;
(c) "relevant subsequent week" means the benefit week in which any award of family credit in respect of the further claim referred to in paragraph (6)(a) would, but for regulation 34(1), have commenced, but it shall not be earlier than the twenty-seventh week after the week in which the existing amount took effect.]

AMENDMENTS

1. Family Credit (General) Amendment No. 2 Regulations 1990 (S.I. 1990 No. 1774), reg. 3 (October 2, 1990).
2. Family Credit (General) Amendment Regulations 1991 (S.I. 1991 No. 1520), reg. 6 (October 8, 1991).
3. Income-related Benefits Schemes (Miscellaneous Amendments) Regulations 1993 (S.I. 1993 No. 315), Sched., para. 9 (April 1, 1993).

DEFINITION

"claimant"—see regs. 2(1), 10(1).

GENERAL NOTE

See reg. 51A of the Income Support (General) Regulations.

Capital jointly held

35. Except where a claimant possesses capital which is disregarded under regulation 34(4) (notional capital), where a claimant and one or more persons are beneficially entitled in possession to any capital asset they shall be treated as if each of them were entitled in possession to the whole beneficial interest therein in an equal share [¹and the foregoing provisions of this Chapter shall apply for the purpose of calculating the amount of capital which the claimant is treated as possessing as if it were actual capital which the claimant does possess.]

AMENDMENT

1. Family Credit (General) Amendment No. 3 Regulations 1988 (S.I. 1988 No. 1438), reg. 6 (September 12, 1988).

DEFINITION

"claimant"—see reg. 2(1), reg. 10(1).

GENERAL NOTE

See the notes to reg. 52 of the Income Support (General) Regulations.

Calculation of tariff income from capital

36.—(1) Where the claimant's capital calculated in accordance with this Chapter exceeds £3,000, it shall be treated as equivalent to a weekly income of £1 for each complete £250 in excess of £3,000 but not exceeding [¹£8,000].

(2) Notwithstanding paragraph (1), where any part of the excess is not a complete £250 that part shall be treated as equivalent to a weekly income of £1.

(3) For the purposes of paragraph (1), capital includes any income treated as capital under regulation 31 (income treated as capital).

AMENDMENT

1. Income-related Benefits (Miscellaneous Amendments) Regulations 1990 (S.I. 1990 No. 671), reg. 3 (April 9, 1990).

DEFINITION

"claimant"—see reg. 2(1), reg. 10(1).

GENERAL NOTE

The treatment of capital between £3,000 and £8,000 is the same as for income support. Each complete £250 between those levels is treated as producing a weekly income of £1. If the capital does not divide exactly into £250 chunks anything left over is treated as producing £1 a week. Thus if the claimant capital is exactly £8,000 the tariff income is £20 a week. If the claimant's capital is £4,001, the tariff income is £5 a week.

Para. (3) merely confirms the effect of reg. 31. Notional capital must also count although not expressly mentioned.

Note reg. 30 on the capital of children and young persons.

Chapter VII

Students

Interpretation

37. In this Chapter, unless the context otherwise requires—
"a course of advanced education" means—

(a) a full-time course leading to a postgraduate degree or comparable qualification, a first degree or comparable qualification, a diploma of higher education, a higher national diploma, [⁴a higher national diploma or higher national certificate of either the Business & [⁵Technology] Education Council] or the Scottish Vocational Education Council or a teaching qualification; or

(b) any other full-time course which is a course of a standard above ordinary national diploma, [⁴a national diploma or national certificate of either the Business & [⁵Technology] Education Council or the Scottish Vocational Education Council], a general certificate of education (advanced level), a Scottish certificate of education [⁴(higher level)] or a Scottish certificate of sixth year studies;

"contribution" means any contribution in respect of the income of any other person which a Minister of the Crown or an education authority takes into account in assessing the amount of the student's grant and by which that amount is, as a consequence, reduced;

"course of study" means any full-time course of study or sandwich course whether or not a grant is made for attending it;

"covenant income" means the gross income payable to a student under a Deed of Covenant by a person whose income is, or is likely to be, taken into account in assessing the student's grant or award;

"education authority" means a government department, a local education authority as defined in section 114(1) of the Education Act 1944 (interpretation), an education authority as defined in section 135(1) of the Education (Scotland) Act 1980 (interpretation), an education and library board established under Article 3 of the Education and Libraries (Northern Ireland) Order 1986, any body which is a research council for the purposes of the Science and Technology Act 1965 or any analogous government department, authority, board or body, of the Channel Islands, Isle of Man or any other country outside Great Britain;

"grant" means any kind of educational grant or award and includes any scholarship, studentship, exhibition, allowance or bursary [¹but does not include a payment derived from funds made available by the Secretary of State for the purpose of assisting students in financial difficulties under section 100 of the Education Act 1944, sections 131 and 132 of the Education Reform Act 1988 or section 73 of the Education (Scotland) Act 1980];

"grant income" means—

(a) any income by way of a grant;

(b) any contribution which has been assessed whether or not it has been paid,

and any such contribution which is paid by way of a covenant shall be treated as part of the student's grant income;

[²"last day of the course" means the date on which the last day of the final academic term falls in respect of the course in which the student is enrolled;]

"period of study" means—

(a) in the case of a course of study for one year or less, the period beginning with the start of the course to the end,

(b) in the case of a course of study for more than one year, in the first or, as the case may be, any subsequent year of the course, the period beginning with the start of the course or, as the case may be, that year's start and ending with either—

(i) the day before the start of the next year of the course in a case where the student's grant is assessed at a rate appropriate to his studying throughout the year, or, if he does not have a grant, where it would have been assessed at such a rate had he had one; or

(ii) in any other case the day before the start of the normal summer vacation appropriate to his course;

[²(c) in the final year of a course of study of more than one year, the period beginning with that year's start and ending with the last day of the course;]

"periods of experience" has the meaning prescribed in paragraph 1(1) of Schedule 5 to the Education (Mandatory Awards) Regulations 1987;

"sandwich course" has the meaning prescribed in paragraph 1(1) of Schedule 5 to the Education (Mandatory Awards) Regulations 1987;

"standard maintenance grant" means—

(a) except where paragraph (b) applies, in the case of a student attending a course of study at the University of London or an establishment within the area comprising the City of London and the Metropolitan Police District, the amount specified for the time being in paragraph 2(2)(a) of Schedule 2 to the Education (Mandatory Awards) Regulations 1987 for such a student; and

(b) in the case of a student residing at his parents' home, the amount specified in paragraph 3(2) thereof;

(c) in any other case; the amount specified in paragraph 2(2) other than in sub-paragraph (a) or (b) thereof.

[³"student" means a person, other than a person in receipt of a training allowance, who is aged less than 19 and attending a full-time course of advanced education or, as the case may be, who is aged 19 or over and attending a full-time course of study] at an educational establishment; and for the purposes of this definition—

(a) a person who has started on such a course shall be treated as attending it throughout any period of term or vacation within it until [²the last day of the course] or such earlier date as he abandons it or is dismissed from it;

(b) a person on a sandwich course shall be treated as attending a full-time course of advanced education or, as the case may be, of study;

"year" in relation to a course, means the period of 12 months beginning on 1st January, 1st April or 1st September according to whether the academic year of the course in question begins in the spring, the summer or the autumn respectively.

AMENDMENTS

1. Social Security Benefits (Student Loans and Miscellaneous Amendments) Regulations 1990 (S.I. 1990 No. 1549), reg. 2(3) (September 1, 1990).

2. Family Credit (General) Amendment Regulations 1991 (S.I. 1991 No. 1520), reg. 7 (August 6, 1991).

3. Family Credit (General) Amendment Regulations 1992 (S.I. 1992 No. 573), reg. 9 (April 7, 1992).

4. Income-related Benefits Schemes (Miscellaneous Amendments) (No. 3) Regulations 1992 (S.I. 1992 No. 2155), reg. 10 (October 5, 1992).

5. Income-related Benefits Schemes (Miscellaneous Amendments) (No. 4) Regulations 1993 (S.I. 1993 No. 2119), reg. 32 (October 5, 1993).

GENERAL NOTE

See the notes to reg. 61 of the Income Support (General) Regulations. There are a few differences. There is a definition of "course of study" here, which is in reg. 2(1) of the Income Support Regulations. The definition of "covenant income" here means the gross income payable to a student rather than the income net of tax, as for income support. A significant difference. The definition of "grant income" here does not have any special provision for single parents or disabled students. The definition of "student" here can extend to a person over pensionable age!

Calculation of grant income

38.—(1) The amount of a student's grant income to be taken into account shall, subject to [²paragraphs (2) and (2A)], be the whole of his grant income.

(2) There shall be disregarded from a student's grant income any payment—

(a) intended to meet tuition fees or examination fees;

(b) intended to meet the cost of special equipment for a student on a course which began before 1st September 1986 in architecture, art and design, home economics, landscape architecture, medicine, music, ophthalmic optics, orthoptics, physical education, physiotherapy, radiography, occupational therapy, dental hygiene, dental therapy, remedial gymnastics, town and country planning and veterinary science or medicine;

(c) intended to meet additional expenditure incurred by a disabled student in respect of his attendance on a course;

(d) intended to meet additional expenditure connected with term time residential study away from the student's educational establishment;

(e) on account of the student maintaining a home at a place other than that at which he resides during his course;

(f) intended to meet the cost of books and equipment (other than special equipment) or, if not so intended, an amount equal to [³£276] towards such costs;

(g) intended to meet travel expenses incurred as a result of his attendance on the course.

[²(2A) Where in pursuance of an award a student is in receipt of a grant in respect of maintenance under regulation 17(b) of the Education (Mandatory Awards) Regulations 1991, there shall be excluded from his grant income a sum equal to the amount specified in paragraph 7(4) of Schedule 2 to those Regulations, being the amount to be disregarded in respect of travel costs in the particular circumstances of his case.]

(3) A student's grant income[¹, except any amount intended for the maintenance of dependants under [²Part 3 of Schedule 2 to the Education (Mandatory Awards) Regulations 1991] or intended for an older student under Part 4 of that Schedule,] shall be apportioned—

(a) subject to paragraph (4), in a case where it is attributable to the period of study, equally between the weeks in that period;

(b) in any other case, equally between the weeks in the period in respect of which it is payable.

[¹(3A) Any amount intended for the maintenance of dependants or for an older student under the provisions referred to in paragraph (3) shall be apportioned equally over a period of 52 weeks commencing with the week in which the period of study begins.]

(4) In the case of a student on a sandwich course, any periods of experience within the period of study shall be excluded and the student's grant income shall be apportioned equally between the remaining weeks in that period.

AMENDMENTS

1. Family Credit (General) Amendment Regulations 1988 (S.I. 1988 No. 660), reg. 10 (April 11, 1988).

2. Family Credit (General) Amendment Regulations 1992 (S.I. 1992 No. 573), reg. 10 (April 7, 1992).

3. Income-related Benefits Schemes (Miscellaneous Amendments) (No. 2) Regulations 1994 (S.I. 1994 No. 1608), reg. 2 (September 6, 1994 or, where a student's period of study begins between August 1 and 31 1994, the first Tuesday of the period).

DEFINITIONS

"grant income"—see reg. 37.

"payment"—see reg. 2(1).
"period of study"—see reg. 37.
"periods of experience"—*ibid.*
"sandwich course"—*ibid.*
"student"—*ibid.*
"week"—see reg. 2(1).

GENERAL NOTE

See the notes to reg. 62 of the Income Support (General) Regulations. There is one less disregard in para. (2) here (payments for dependants outside the United Kingdom).

Para. (2)(e) is more comprehensive than the income support counterpart, having no reference to housing benefit.

Calculation of covenant income where a contribution is assessed

39.—(1) Where a student is in receipt of income by way of a grant during a period of study and a contribution has been assessed, the amount of his covenant income to be taken into account shall be the whole amount of his covenant income less, subject to paragraph (3), the amount of the contribution.

(2) The weekly amount of the student's covenant income shall be determined—

(a) by dividing the amount of income which fails to be taken into account under paragraph (1) by 52; and

(b) by disregarding from the resulting amount, £5.

(3) For the purposes of paragraph (1), the contribution shall be treated as increased by the amount, if any, by which the amount excluded under [¹regulation 38(2)(*g*) (calculation of grant income) falls short of the amount specified in paragraph 7(4)(*i*) of Schedule 2 to the Education (Mandatory Awards) Regulations 1991 (travel expenditure).]

AMENDMENT

1. Family Credit (General) Amendment Regulations 1992 (S.I. 1992 No. 573), reg. 11 (April 7, 1992).

DEFINITIONS

"contribution"—see reg. 37.
"covenant income"—*ibid.*
"grant"—*ibid.*
"student"—*ibid.*

GENERAL NOTE

See the notes to reg. 63 of the Income Support (General) Regulations. The differences are that this provision makes no reference to the period over which the covenant income is to be taken into account and that the annual amount is simply divided by 52 to reach the weekly figure.

Covenant income where no grant income or no contribution is assessed

40.—(1) Where a student is not in receipt of income by way of a grant the amount of his covenant income shall be calculated as follows—

(a) any sums intended for any expenditure specified in regulation 38(2)(a) to (*e*) (calculation of grant income), necessary as a result of his attendance on the course, shall be disregarded;

(b) any covenant income, up to the amount of the standard maintenance grant, which is not so disregarded, shall be apportioned equally between the weeks of the period of study and there shall be disregarded from the covenant income to be so apportioned the amount which would have been disregarded under [¹regulation 38(2)(f) and (g) and (2A)] had the student been in receipt of the standard maintenance grant; and

(c) the balance, if any, shall be divided by 52 and treated as weekly income of which £5 shall be disregarded.

(2) Where a student is in receipt of income by way of a grant and no contribution has been assessed, the amount of his covenant income shall be calculated in accordance with sub-paragraphs (a) to (c) of paragraph (1), except that—

(a) the value of the standard maintenance grant shall be abated by the amount of his grant income less an amount equal to the amount of any sums disregarded under regulation 38(2)(a) to (e); and

(b) the amount to be disregarded under paragraph (1)(b) shall be abated by an amount equal to the amount of any sums disregarded under [¹regulation 38(2)(f) and (g) and (2A)].

AMENDMENT

1. Family Credit (General) Amendment Regulations 1992 (S.I. 1992 No. 573), reg. 12 (April 7, 1992).

DEFINITIONS

"covenant income"—see reg. 37.
"grant"—*ibid.*
"grant income"—*ibid.*
"period of study"—*ibid.*
"standard maintenance grant"—*ibid.*
"student"—*ibid.*
"week"—see reg. 2(1).

GENERAL NOTE

See the notes to reg. 64 of the Income Support (General) Regulations. There is a difference in that the annual amount is simply divided by 52 to reach the weekly figure.

Relationship with amounts to be disregarded under Schedule 2

41. No part of a student's covenant income or grant income shall be disregarded under paragraph 13 of Schedule 2 and any [¹other income to which sub-paragraph (1) of that paragraph applies shall be disregarded thereunder only to the extent that] the amount disregarded under regulation 39(2)(b) (calculation of covenant income where a contribution is assessed) or, as the case may be, 40(1)(c) (covenant income where no grant income or no contribution is assessed) is less than [¹£10].

AMENDMENT

1. Family Credit (General) Amendment Regulations 1990 (S.I. 1990 No. 574), reg. 13 (April 10, 1990).

DEFINITIONS

"covenant income"—see reg. 37.
"grant income"—*ibid.*
"student"—*ibid.*

GENERAL NOTE

See the notes to reg. 65 of the Income Support (General) Regulations. Para. 13 of Sched. 2 deals with charitable or voluntary payments.

Other amounts to be disregarded

42. For the purposes of ascertaining income [¹other than grant income, covenant income and loans treated as income in accordance with regulation 42A], any amounts intended for any expenditure specified in regulation 38(2) (calculation of grant income) necessary as a result of his attendance on the course shall be disregarded but only if, and to the extent that, the necessary expenditure exceeds or is likely to exceed the amount of the sums disregarded under regulation 38(2) [¹and (2A)], 39(3) and 40(1)(a) or (b) (calculation of grant income and covenant income) on like expenditure.

AMENDMENT

1. Income-related Benefits Schemes (Miscellaneous Amendments) Regulations 1994 (S.I. 1994 No. 527), reg. 21 (April 12, 1994).

DEFINITIONS

"covenant income"—see reg. 37.
"grant income"—*ibid.*

GENERAL NOTE

See the notes to reg. 66(1) of the Income Support (General) Regulations.

[¹Treatment of student loans

42A.—(1) A loan which is made to a student pursuant to arrangements made under section 1 of the Education (Student Loans) Act 1990 [²or Article 3 of the Education (Student Loans) (Northern Ireland) Order 1990] shall be treated as income.

(2) In calculating the weekly amount of the loan to be taken into account as income—

   (a) except where sub-paragraph (b) applies, the loan shall be apportioned equally between the weeks in the academic year in respect of which the loan is payable;

   (b) in the case of a loan which is payable in respect of the final academic year of the course or if the course is only of one academic year's duration, in respect of that year the loan shall be apportioned equally between the weeks in the period beginning with the start of the final academic year or, as the case may be, the single academic year and ending with [²the last day of the course],

and from the weekly amount so apportioned there shall be disregarded £10.

(3) Any loan for which a student is eligible in respect of an academic year under the arrangements mentioned in paragraph (1) but which has not been acquired by him shall be treated as possessed by him and paragraphs (1) and (2) shall apply accordingly; and for the purposes of this paragraph the loan for which a student is eligible is the maximum amount payable to him under those arrangements.]

AMENDMENTS

1. Social Security Benefits (Student Loans and Miscellaneous Amendments) Regulations 1990 (S.I. 1990 No. 1549), reg. 3(5) (September 1, 1990).
2. Family Credit (General) Amendment Regulations 1991 (S.I. 1991 No. 1520), reg. 9 (August 6, 1991).

GENERAL NOTE

See reg. 66A of the Income Support (General) Regulations.

Disregard of contribution

43. Where the claimant or his partner is a student and the income of one has been taken into account for the purpose of assessing a contribution to the student's grant, an amount equal to the amount of the contribution shall be disregarded for the purpose of calculating the income of the one liable to make that contribution.

DEFINITIONS

"claimant"—see reg. 2(1), reg. 10(1).
"contribution"—see reg. 37.
"grant"—*ibid.*
"partner"—see reg. 2(1).
"student"—see reg. 37.

GENERAL NOTE

See the notes to reg. 67 of the Income Support (General) Regulations. There is a trivial difference in drafting.

Disregard of tax refund

44. Any amount by way of a refund of tax deducted from a student's covenant income shall be disregarded in calculating the student's income or capital.

DEFINITIONS

"covenant income"—see reg. 37.
"student"—*ibid.*

GENERAL NOTE

Because for family credit purposes "covenant income" covers the gross amount payable under the covenant (reg. 37) it is necessary to disregard any refund to the student of tax deducted by the payer.

Disregard of changes occurring during summer vacation

45. In calculating a student's income there shall be disregarded any change in the standard maintenance grant occurring in the recognised summer vacation appropriate to the student's course, if that vacation does not form part of his period of study, from the date on which the change occurred to the end of that vacation.

DEFINITIONS

"period of study"—see reg. 37.
"standard maintenance grant"—*ibid.*
"student"—*ibid.*

GENERAL NOTE

See the notes to reg. 69 of the Income Support (General) Regulations. The differences in drafting do not seem to affect the substance.

PART V

CONDITIONS OF ENTITLEMENT

Determination of maximum family credit

46.—(1) Subject to [¹paragraphs (2) to (7)] of this regulation, the appropriate maximum family credit shall be the aggregate of the following credits—

(a) in respect of a claimant or, if he is a member of a married or unmarried couple, in respect of the couple, the credit specified in column (2) of Schedule 4 against paragraph 1 (adult);

(b) in respect of any child or young person for whom the claimant or his partner is treated as responsible by virtue of regulation 7 (circumstances in which a person is treated as responsible, or not responsible, for another), the credit specified in column (2) of Schedule 4 against whichever description in either paragraph 2 or 3 of column (1) fits the child or young person concerned.

(2) Where a claimant or, as the case may be, the partner of a claimant is married polygamously to two or more members of the same household, the maximum amount shall include, in respect of every such member but the first, an additional credit which equals—

(a) in the case of a person aged less than 18 years, the credit specified in column (2) of Schedule 4 against paragraph 3(*a*) in column (1); or

(b) in any other case, the credit specified in column (2) of Schedule 4 against paragraph 3(*b*) in column (1).

(3) For the purposes of paragraph (2), a person shall not be treated as a member of the same household as someone to whom he is married polygamously if he would not be so treated in the case of a monogamous marriage.

(4) Where the capital of a child or young person, if calculated in accordance with Part IV (income and capital) in like manner as for the claimant, [²except as provided in regulation 27(1) (modifications in respect of children and young persons)], would exceed £3,000, the credit in respect of that child or young person shall be nil.

(5) Where the income of a child or young person, other than income consisting of payments of maintenance whether under a court order or not, calculated in accordance with Part IV, exceeds the amount specified for that child or young person in Schedule 4, the credit in respect of that child or young person shall be nil.

(6) Where a child or young person is, for the purposes of regulation 8(2)(*a*) (membership of the same household), a patient or in residential accommodation on account of physical or mental handicap or physical or mental illness and has been so accommodated for the 52 weeks immediately before the date of claim, the credit in respect of that child or young person shall be nil.

[¹(7) For the purposes of this regulation the amount of any credit and the age of any child or young person shall be determined by reference to the credit specified in Schedule 4 and the age of the child or young person at the date on which the period under [³section 128(3) of the Contributions and Benefits Act] (period of award) begins.]

AMENDMENTS

1. Family Credit (General) Amendment Regulations 1988 (S.I. 1988 No. 660), reg. 11 (April 11, 1988).

2. Income-related Benefits Schemes (Miscellaneous Amendments) (No. 4) Regulations 1993 (S.I. 1993 No. 2119), reg. 33 (October 5, 1993).

3. Income-related Benefits Schemes (Miscellaneous Amendments) Regulations 1995 (S.I. 1995 No. 516), reg. 14 (April 11, 1995).

DEFINITIONS

"child"—see 1986 Act, s.20(11) (SSCBA, s.137(1)).
"claimant"—see reg. 2(1).
"partner"—*ibid.*
"young person"—*ibid.*, reg. 6.

The determination of the maximum family credit is the essential starting point in the calculation of benefit. If the family's income is not more than the applicable amount specified in reg. 47, the maximum family credit is payable (Contributions and Benefits Act, s.128(2)(a); 1986 Act, s.21(2)). If the income is above that amount, the maximum family credit is to be reduced at the rate specified in reg. 48 (Contributions and Benefits Act, s.128(2)(b); 1986 Act, s.21(3)).

Paragraph (1)
The maximum family credit is made up of an adult credit (the same for a single person or a couple) plus the appropriate amount for children and young persons for whom an adult is responsible. See paras. (4) to (6) below for details. The amounts are specified in Sched. 4. The effect of para. (7) is that the amount of the credit is set according to the ages of children and the amounts specified as at the beginning of the award. See reg. 16(1A) and (1B) of the Claims and Payments Regulations.

Paragraph (2)
In the case of polygamous marriages (but not other polygamous relationships) extra members of the family beyond the first two qualify for extra credits.

Paragraph (4)
If the capital belonging to a child or young person exceeds £3,000, no credit is allowed for that person. The capital of a child or young person is not treated as the claimant's (reg. 30), so that it does not count against the usual £8,000 or £3,000 limits. Nor does that person's income count (reg. 27(3)).

Paragraph (5)
If a child's or young person's income (apart from maintenance payments) exceeds the credit for that person, no credit is allowed. That person's income is then not treated as the claimant's for calculating the entitlement of the family in general (reg. 27(2)). Maintenance payments, even if paid directly to the child, are treated as income of the claimant.

Paragraph (6)
This provision is necessary because of the odd definition of the children for whom a credit is allowed in para. (1). In order to qualify for family credit an adult must have at least one child or young person who is a member of the same household (Contributions and Benefits Act, s.128(1)(d); 1986 Act, s.20(5)). But, providing that this qualification is met, para. (1) appears to allow a credit for any child or young person for whom the adult is responsible, even though that person is not a member of the household. The test of responsibility under reg. 7 is whether the child "normally lives" with the adult, referring to who gets child benefit in cases of doubt. Thus, para. (6) specifically excludes children in these circumstances, where, if there is still contact by parents, the child would be normally living with the parent, and part of the household.

Paragraph (7)
See para. (1).

[²Applicable amount of family credit

47. The applicable amount] for the purposes of section 20(5)(a) of the Act [SSCBA, s.128(1)(a)] (conditions of entitlement to family credit) shall be [³£73.00] per week.

[¹(2) For the purposes of section 20(5A) of the Act [SSCBA, s.128(2)] (date on which applicable amount is to be determined) the prescribed date is the date on which the period under section 20(6) of the Act [SSCBA, s.128(3)] (period of the award) begins.]

1. Family Credit (General) Amendment Regulations 1988 (S.I. 1988 No. 660), reg. 12 (April 11, 1988).
2. Income-related Benefits Schemes (Miscellaneous Amendments) (No. 3) Regulations 1992 (S.I. 1992 No. 2155), reg. 11 (October 5, 1992).

3. Social Security Benefits Up-rating Order 1995 (S.I. 1995 No. 559), art. 16(c) (April 11, 1995).

DEFINITION

"the Act"—see reg. 2(1).

GENERAL NOTE

See the note to reg. 46 for the calculation of benefit (and s.128(2) of the Contributions and Benefits Act; 1986 Act, s.21(2) and (3)). The applicable amount prescribed at the beginning of the period of award controls the calculation.

Entitlement to family credit where income exceeds the applicable amount

48. The prescribed percentage for the purpose of section 21(3) of the Act [SSCBA, s.128(2)(b)] (percentage of excess of income over applicable amount which is deducted from maximum family credit) shall be 70 per cent.

DEFINITION

"the Act"—see reg. 2(1).

GENERAL NOTE

Where the income exceeds the applicable amount the maximum family credit is reduced by 70 per cent. of the excess. The taper of 70 per cent. is higher than that of 50 per cent. for FIS, but since the calculation is now based on net earnings, cumulative effective tax rates of more than 100 per cent. will be avoided.

PART VI

CHANGES OF CIRCUMSTANCES

Death of claimant

49.—(1) Except as provided in paragraph (2), an award of family credit shall cease to have effect upon the death of the claimant.

(2) Where a claimant dies and is survived by a partner who was the claimant's partner at the date of claim, an award of family credit made in the claimant's favour shall have effect for its unexpired period as if originally made in favour of the partner.

DEFINITIONS

"claimant"—see reg. 2(1).
"partner"—*ibid.*

GENERAL NOTE

Death of a single claimant terminates an award, but if one partner dies, an award of family credit continues to be paid to the surviving partner.

Prevention of duplication of awards of family credit and income support

50. Where provision is made for the same child or young person in awards for overlapping periods, the first being an award of family credit and the second an award of [¹family credit, income support or disability working allowance], and at the start of the period of overlap that child or young person is no longer a member of the household of the claimant under the first award, the first award shall terminate with effect from the start of the period of overlap.

AMENDMENT

1. Disability Living Allowance and Disability Working Allowance (Consequential Provisions) Regulations 1991 (S.I. 1991 No. 2742), reg. 13(4) (April 6, 1992).

DEFINITIONS

"child"—see 1986 Act, s.20(11) (SSCBA, s.137(1)).
"claimant"—see reg. 2(1).
"disability working allowance"—*ibid.*
"young person"—*ibid.*, reg. 6.

[¹Overlapping awards

51.—(1) An award of family credit (the new award) which is made in consequence of a claim in respect of a period beginning before the commencement of an existing award of family credit (the existing award) and which overlaps with the period of the existing award, shall be treated as a relevant change of circumstances affecting the existing award and the existing award shall be reviewed and shall terminate with effect from the date on which the decision of the adjudication officer making the new award is notified to the claimant.

(2) An award of disability working allowance which is made in consequence of a claim in respect of a period beginning before the commencement of an existing award of family credit (the existing award) and which overlaps with the period of the existing award, shall be treated as a change of circumstances affecting the existing award and the existing award shall be reviewed and shall terminate with effect from the date on which the decision of the adjudication officer awarding disability working allowance is notified to the claimant.]

AMENDMENT

1. Income-related Benefits Schemes (Miscellaneous Amendments) (No. 5) Regulations 1994 (S.I. 1994 No. 2139), reg. 19 (October 4, 1994).

DEFINITIONS

"claimant"—see reg. 2(1).
"disability working allowance"—*ibid.*

GENERAL NOTE

The previous form of reg. 51 applied only where an overlapping award of family credit was made on review or appeal. The new form covers any award of family credit or disability working allowance made for an earlier and overlapping period (*e.g.* where the claimant has made a late claim for the earlier period). It also makes it clear that the original award will end on the date that the claimant is notified of the new award.

[¹Reduced benefit direction

51A.—(1) The following occurrences shall be changes of circumstances which affect an award of family credit and the rate at which it is payable—
  (a) a reduced benefit direction given by a child support officer under section 46(5) of the Child Support Act 1991;

(b) the cessation or cancellation of a reduced benefit direction under Part IX of the maintenance regulations;

(c) the suspension of a reduced benefit direction under regulation 48(1) of the maintenance regulations;

(d) the removal of a suspension imposed under paragraph (1) of regulation 48 of the maintenance regulations in accordance with paragraph (3) of that regulation.

(2) In this regulation—

(a) "child support officer" means a person appointed in accordance with section 13 of the Child Support Act 1991;

(b) "the maintenance regulations" means the Child Support (Maintenance Assessment Procedure) Regulations 1992.]

AMENDMENT

1. Income-related Benefits Schemes (Miscellaneous Amendments) Regulations 1993 (S.I. 1993 No. 315), reg. 14 (April 13, 1993).

GENERAL NOTE

Where a parent with care of a child who claims family credit (as well as income support or disability working allowance) fails to authorise the Secretary of State to take action against the absent parent under the Child Support Act 1991 (s.6(1)) or to give the information required to trace the absent parent (s.6(9)) the child support officer may make a reduced benefit direction against the parent with care under s.46(5) of the 1991 Act. The amount of the reduction is specified in reg. 36 of the Child Support (Maintenance Assessment Procedure) Regulations 1992, and is at the higher rate for 26 weeks followed by the lower rate for 52 weeks. The direction can be given effect to at the beginning of a family credit award. Reg. 51A allows the amount of an existing award to be altered when a direction becomes effective or when some change affecting the reduction happens.

[¹PART VII

ENTITLEMENT TO FAMILY CREDIT AND DISABILITY WORKING ALLOWANCE

Prescribed circumstances for entitlement to family credit

52. For the purposes of section 20(5)(bb) of the Act [SSCBA, s.128(1)(c)] (prescribed circumstances) where a claimant or a member of his family is entitled to disability working allowance, he is entitled to family credit, if—

(a) at the date of the claim for family credit the award of disability working allowance for him or a member of his family will expire within 42 days; and

(b) the claimant is or would otherwise be entitled to family credit by virtue of these Regulations; and

(c) the claim for family credit is made in respect of a period which commences immediately after the expiry of the award of disability working allowance.]

AMENDMENT

1. Disability Working Allowance (General) Regulations 1991 (S.I. 1991 No. 2887), reg. 58 (April 7, 1992).

DEFINITIONS

"the Act"—see reg. 2(1).

"claimant"—*ibid.*
"date of claim"—*ibid.*
"disability working allowance"—*ibid.*
"family"—see 1986 Act, s.20(11) (SSCBA, s.137(1)).

GENERAL NOTE

The general rule, under s.128(1) of the Contributions and Benefits Act (1986 Act, s.20(5)), is that the conditions of entitlement to family credit, including not being entitled to disability working allowance, must be satisfied at the date of claim. This provision allows a claim for family credit in advance of the expiry of an award of disability working allowance to succeed from the end of that award.

SCHEDULES

SCHEDULE 1   **Regulations 20(2) and 22(2)**

SUMS TO BE DISREGARDED IN THE CALCULATION OF EARNINGS

1. Any earnings derived from employment which are payable in a country outside the United Kingdom where there is a prohibition against the transfer to the United Kingdom of those earnings.
2. Any earnings of a child or young person.
3. Where a payment of earnings is made in a currency other than sterling, any banking charge or commission payable in converting that payment to sterling.

DEFINITIONS

"child"—see 1986 Act, s.20(11) (SSCBA, s.137(1)).
"earnings"—see reg. 2(1).
"young person"—*ibid.*, reg. 6.

GENERAL NOTE

The most important of these disregards is that in para. 2. Earnings of children and young persons are disregarded in all circumstances.

SCHEDULE 2   **Regulation 24(2)**

SUMS TO BE DISREGARDED IN THE CALCULATION OF INCOME OTHER THAN EARNINGS

1. Any amount paid by way of tax on income which is taken into account under regulation 24 (calculation of income other than earnings).
2. Any payment in respect of any expenses incurred by a claimant who is—
(a) engaged by a charitable or [25voluntary organisation]; or
(b) a volunteer,
if he otherwise derives no remuneration or profit from the employment and is not to be treated as possessing any earnings under regulation 26(4) (notional income).
3. Any housing benefit or income support.
4. Any mobility allowance[12, disability living allowance or disability working allowance.]
5. Any concessionary payment made to compensate for the non-payment of—

489

    (a) any payment specified paragraph 4 or 7;

    (b) income support.

    6. Any mobility supplement or any payment intended to compensate for the non-payment of such a supplement.

    7. Any payment which is—

    (a) an attendance allowance under section 35 of the Social Security Act [SSCBA, s.64];

    (b) an increase of disablement pension under sections 61 or 63 of that Act [SSCBA, s.104 or 105];

    (c) a payment made under regulations made in exercise of the power conferred by section 159(3)(b) of that Act [SSCBA, Sched. 8, para. 7(2)(b)];

    (d) an increase of allowance payable in respect of constant attendance under section 5 of the Industrial Injuries and Diseases (Old Cases) Act 1975;

    (e) payable by virtue of articles 14, 15, 16, 43 or 44 of the Personal Injuries (Civilians) Scheme 1983 or any analogous payment; or

    (f) a payment based on need for attendance which is paid as part of a war disablement pension.

    8. Any payment to the claimant as holder of the Victoria Cross or of the George Cross or any analogous payment.

    9. Any sum in respect of a course of study attended by a child or young person payable by virtue of regulations made under section 81 of the Education Act 1944 (assistance by means of scholarship or otherwise), or by virtue of section 2(1) of the Education Act 1962 (awards for courses of further education) or section 49 of the Education (Scotland) Act 1980 (power to assist persons to take advantage of educational facilities).

    10. In the case of a student, any sums intended for any expenditure specified in paragraph (2) of regulation 38 (calculation of grant income) necessary as a result of his attendance on his course.

    [¹**11.** In the case of a claimant participating in arrangements for training made under section 2 of the Employment and Training Act 1973 [⁹or section 2 of the Enterprise and New Towns (Scotland) Act 1990] or attending a course at an employment rehabilitation centre established under that section [⁹of the 1973 Act]—

    (a) any travelling expenses reimbursed to the claimant; and

    (b) any living away from home allowance under section 2(2)(d) [⁹of the 1973 Act or section 2(4)(c) of the 1990 Act];

    (c) any training premium,

but this paragraph, except insofar as it relates to a payment under sub-paragraph (a), (b) or (c), does not apply to any part of any allowance under section 2(2)(d) [⁹of the 1973 Act or section 2(4)(c) of the 1990 Act].]

    12. Any Job Start Allowance payable pursuant to arrangements made under section 2(1) of the Employment and Training Act 1973.

    [⁶**13.**—(1) Except where sub-paragraph (2) applies and subject to sub-paragraph (3) and paragraphs 29 and 34, £10 of any charitable payment or of any voluntary payment made or due to be made at regular intervals.

    (2) Subject to sub-paragraph (3) and paragraph 34, any charitable payment or voluntary payment made or due to be made at regular intervals which is intended and used for an item other than food, ordinary clothing or footwear, household fuel, community charge, [¹¹or housing costs of any member of the family or is used for any personal community [¹⁸charge,] collective community charge contribution [¹⁸or council tax] for which any member of the family is liable].

    [¹³(3) Sub-paragraphs (1) and (2) shall not apply to a payment which is made or due to be made by—

    (a) a former partner of the claimant, or a former partner of any member of the claimant's family; or

    (b) the parent of a child or young person where that child or young person is a member of the claimant's family.]

(4) For the purposes of sub-paragraph (1) where a number of charitable or voluntary payments fall to be taken into account they shall be treated as though they were one such payment.

(5) For the purposes of sub-paragraph (2) the expression "ordinary clothing or footwear" means clothing or footwear for normal daily use, but does not include school uniforms, or clothing or footwear used solely for sporting activities.]

14. Subject to paragraph 29, [⁶£10] of any of the following, namely—

(a) war disablement pension or war widow's pension or a payment made to compensate for the non-payment of such a pension [²² except in so far as such a pension or payment falls to be disregarded under paragraphs 6 or 7];

[¹¹(b) a pension paid by the government of a country outside Great Britain which is either—

(i) analogous to a war disablement pension; or

(ii) analogous to a war widow's pension;]

(c) a pension paid under any special provision made by the law of the Federal Republic of Germany or any part of it, or of the Republic of Austria, to victims of National Socialist persecution.

15. Any child benefit under Part I of the Child Benefit Act 1975 [SSCBA, Part IX].

16.—(1) Any income derived from capital to which the claimant is, or is treated under regulation 35 (capital jointly held) as, beneficially entitled but, but subject to sub-paragraph (2), not income derived from capital disregarded under paragraph 1, 2, 4, [²13or 26 to 30] of Schedule 3.

(2) Income derived from capital disregarded under paragraph 2[², 4 or 26 to 30] of Schedule 3 but [¹⁹only to the extent of—

(a) any mortgage repayments made in respect of the dwelling or premises in the period during which that income accrued; or

(b) any council tax or water charges which the claimant is liable to pay in respect of the dwelling or premises and which are paid in the period during which that income accrued.]

17. Where a person receives income under an annuity purchased with a loan which satisfies the following conditions—

(a) that the loan was made as part of a scheme under which not less than 90 per cent. of the proceeds of the loan were applied to the purchase by the person to whom it was made of an annuity ending with his life or with the life of the survivor of two or more persons (in this paragraph referred to as "the annuitants") who include the person to whom the loan was made;

(b) that the interest on the loan is payable by the person to whom it was made or by one of the annuitants;

(c) that at the time the loan was made the person to whom it was made or each of the annuitants had attained the age of 65;

(d) that the loan was secured on a dwelling in Great Britain and the person to whom the loan was made or one of the annuitants owns an estate or interest in that dwelling; and

(e) that the person to whom the loan was made or one of the annuitants occupies the dwelling on which it was secured as his home at the time the interest is paid,

the amount, calculated on a weekly basis equal to—

[²⁴(i) where, or insofar as, section 369 of the Income and Corporation Taxes Act 1988 (mortgage interest payable under deduction of tax) applies to the payments of interest on the loan, the interest which is payable after deduction of a sum equal to income tax on such payments at the applicable percentage of income tax within the meaning of section 369(1A) of that Act;]

(ii) in any other case the interest which is payable on the loan without deduction of such a sum.

[²⁵**18.** Any payment made to the claimant by a person who normally resides with the claimant, which is a contribution towards that person's living and accommodation costs, except where that person is residing with the claimant in circumstances to which paragraph 19 or 40 or regulation 21(2) (earnings of self-employed earners) refers.]

[²³19. Where the claimant occupies a dwelling as his home and the dwelling is also occupied by [²⁵another person], and there is a contractual liability to make payments to the claimant in respect of the occupation of the dwelling by that person or a member of his family—

    (a) £4 of the aggregate of any payments made in respect of any one week in respect of the occupation of the dwelling by that person or a member of his family, or by that person and a member of his family; and

    (b) a further [²⁶£9.20], where the aggregate of any such payments is inclusive of an amount for heating.]

    20. Any income in kind.

    21. Any income which is payable in a country outside the United Kingdom where there is a prohibition against the transfer to the United Kingdom of that income.

    22.—(1) Any payment made to the claimant in respect of a child or young person who is a member of his family—

[¹⁶(a) in accordance with regulations made pursuant to section 57A of the Adoption Act 1976 (permitted allowances) or with a scheme approved by the Secretary of State under section 51 of the Adoption (Scotland) Act 1978 (schemes for payments of allowances to adopters);

    (b) which is a payment made by a local authority in pursuance of section 15(1) of, and paragraph 15 of Schedule 1 to, the Children Act 1989 (local authority contribution to a child's maintenance where the child is living with a person as a result of a residence order),]

to the extent specified in sub-paragraph (2).

    (2) In the case of a child or young person—

    (a) to whom regulation 27(2) applies (capital in excess of £3,000), the whole amount;

    (b) to whom that regulation does not apply, so much of the weekly amount of the payment as exceeds the credit in respect of that child or young person under Schedule 4.

[¹⁶23. Any payment made by a local authority to the claimant with whom a person is accommodated by virtue of arrangements made under section 23(2)(a) of the Children Act 1989 or, as the case may be, section 21 of the Social Work (Scotland) Act 1968 or by a voluntary organisation under section 59(1)(a) of the 1989 Act or by a care authority under regulation 9 of the Boarding Out and Fostering of Children (Scotland) Regulations 1985 (provision of accommodation and maintenance for children by local authorities and voluntary organisations).]

    24. Any payment made by a health authority, local authority or voluntary organisation to the claimant in respect of a person who is not normally a member of the claimant's household but is temporarily in his care.

[¹⁶25. Any payment made by a local authority in accordance with section 17 or 24 of the Children Act 1989 or, as the case may be, section 12, 24 or 26 of the Social Work (Scotland) Act 1968 (provision of services for children and their families and advice and assistance to certain children).]

    26. Any payment of income which under regulation 31 (income treated as capital) is to be treated as capital.

[¹⁵27. Any maternity allowance under section 22 of the Social Security Act [SSCBA, s.35] or statutory maternity pay under Part V of the Act [SSCBA, Part XII].]

    28. Any payment under paragraph 2 of Schedule 6 to the Act [SSCBA, s.148] (pensioners Christmas bonus).

    29. The total of a claimant's income or, if he is a member of a family, the family's income and the income of any person which he is treated as possessing under regulation 10(2) (calculation of income and capital of members of claimant's family and of a polygamous marriage) to be disregarded under regulation 39(2)(b) (calculation of covenant income where a contribution assessed)[⁷, regulation 42A(2) (treatment of student loans)] and paragraphs [⁶13(1)] and 14, shall in no case exceed [⁶£10] per week.

30. Where a payment of income is made in a currency other than sterling, any banking charge or commission payable in converting that payment into sterling.

[^{15}**31.** Any maternity allowance under section 22 of the Social Security (Northern Ireland) Act 1975 or statutory maternity pay under Part VI of the Social Security (Northern Ireland) Order 1986.]

[^{1}**32.** Any payment in respect of expenses to which regulation 19(2) (earnings of employed earners) applies.

33. Any resettlement benefit which is paid to the claimant by virtue of regulation 3 to the Social Security (Hospital In-Patients) Amendment (No. 2) Regulations 1987 (transitional provisions)].

[^{9}**34.**—(1) Any payment made under the Macfarlane Trust, the Macfarlane (Special Payments) Trust, the Macfarlane (Special Payments) (No. 2) Trust (''the Trusts''), [^{16}the Fund][^{21}, the Eileen Trust] or [^{20}the Independent Living Funds].

(2) Any payment by or on behalf of a person who is suffering or who suffered from haemophilia [^{17}or who is or was a qualifying person], which derives from a payment made under any of the Trusts to which sub-paragraph (1) refers and which is made to or for the benefit of—

(a) that person's partner or former partner from whom he is not, or where that person has died was not, estranged or divorced;

(b) any child who is a member of that person's family or who was such a member and who is a member of the claimant's family; or

(c) any young person who is a member of that person's family or who was such a member and who is a member of the claimant's family.

(3) Any payment by or on behalf of the partner or former partner of a person who is suffering or who suffered from haemophilia [^{17}or who is or was a qualifying person] provided that the partner or former partner and that person are not, or if either of them has died were not, estranged or divorced, which derives from a payment made under any of the Trusts to which sub-paragraph (1) refers and which is made to or for the benefit of—

(a) the person who is suffering from haemophilia [^{17}or who is a qualifying person];

(b) any child who is a member of that person's family or who was such a member and who is a member of the claimant's family; or

(c) any young person who is a member of that person's family or who was such a member and who is a member of the claimant's family.

(4) Any payment by a person who is suffering from haemophilia [^{17}or who is a qualifying person], which derives from a payment under any of the Trusts to which sub-paragraph (1) refers, where—

(a) that person has no partner or former partner from whom he is not estranged or divorced, nor any child or young person who is or had been a member of that person's family; and

(b) the payment is made either—

   (i) to that person's parent or step-parent, or

   (ii) where that person at the date of the payment is a child, a young person or a student who has not completed his full-time education and has no parent or step-parent, to his guardian,

but only for a period from the date of the payment until the end of two years from that person's death.

(5) Any payment out of the estate of a person who suffered from haemophilia [^{17}or who was a qualifying person], which derives from a payment under any of the Trusts to which sub-paragraph (1) refers, where—

(a) that person at the date of his death (the relevant date) had no partner or former partner from whom he was not estranged or divorced, nor any child or young person who was or had been a member of his family; and

(b) the payment is made either—

   (i) to that person's parent or step-parent, or

   (ii) where that person at the relevant date was a child, a young person or a student who had not completed his full-time education and had no parent or step-parent, to his guardian,

but only for a period of two years from the relevant date.

(6) In the case of a person to whom or for whose benefit a payment referred to in this paragraph is made, any income which derives from any payment of income or capital made under or deriving from any of the Trusts.]

[[17](7) For the purposes of sub-paragraphs (2) to (6), any reference to the Trusts shall be construed as including a reference to the Fund [[21]and the Eileen Trust].]

[[2]35. Any payment made by the Secretary of State to compensate for the loss (in whole or in part) of entitlement to housing benefit.]

[[3]36. Any payment made by the Secretary of State to compensate a person who was entitled to supplementary benefit in respect of a period ending immediately before 11th April 1988 but who did not become entitled to income support in respect of a period beginning with that day.

37. Any payment made by the Secretary of State to compensate for the loss of housing benefit supplement under regulation 19 of the Supplementary Benefit (Requirements) Regulations 1983.

38. Any payment made to a juror or witness in respect of attendance at court other than compensation for loss of earnings or for the loss of a benefit payable under the benefit Acts.

39. [[18]. . .].]

[[23]40. Where the claimant occupies a dwelling as his home and he provides in that dwelling board and lodging accommodation, an amount, in respect of each person for whom such accommodation is provided for the whole or any part of a week, equal to—

(a) where the aggregate of any payments made in respect of any one week in respect of such accommodation provided to such person does not exceed £20.00, 100 per cent of such payments; or

(b) where the aggregate of any such payments exceeds £20.00, £20.00 and 50 per cent of the excess over £20.00.]

[[5]41. Any community charge benefit.

42. Any payment in consequence of a reduction of a personal community charge pursuant to regulations under section 13A of the Local Government Finance Act 1988 or section 9A of the Abolition of Domestic Rates Etc (Scotland) Act 1987 (reduction of liability for personal community charge) [[18]; or reduction of council tax under section 13 or, as the case may be, section 80 of the Local Government Finance Act 1992 (reduction of liability for council tax).]

43. Any special war widows payment made under—

(a) the Naval and Marine Pay and Pensions (Special War Widows Payment) Order 1990 made under section 3 of the Naval and Marine Pay and Pensions Act 1865;

(b) the Royal Warrant dated 19th February 1990 amending the Schedule to the Army Pensions Warrant 1977;

(c) the Queen's Order dated 26th February 1990 made under section 2 of the Air Force (Constitution) Act 1917;

(d) the Home Guard War Widows Special Payments Regulations 1990 made under section 151 of the Reserve Forces Act 1980;

(e) the Orders dated 19th February 1990 amending Orders made on 12th December 1980 concerning the Ulster Defence Regiment made in each case under section 140 of the Reserve Forces Act 1980;

and any analogous payment by the Secretary of State for Defence to any person who is not a person entitled under the provisions mentioned in sub-paragraphs (*a*) to (*e*) of this paragraph.]

[[8]44.—(1) Any payment or repayment made—

(a) as respects England and Wales, under regulation 3, 5 or 8 of the National Health Service (Travelling Expenses and Remission of Charges) Regulations 1988 (travelling expenses and health service supplies);

(b) as respects Scotland, under regulation 3, 5 or 8 of the National Health Service

(Travelling Expenses and Remission of Charges) (Scotland) Regulations 1988 (travelling expenses and health service supplies).

(2) Any payment or repayment made by the Secretary of State for Health, the Secretary of State for Scotland or the Secretary of State for Wales which is analogous to a payment or repayment mentioned in sub-paragraph (1).

45. Any payment made under regulation 9 to 11 or 13 of the Welfare Food Regulations 1988 (payments made in place of milk tokens or the supply of vitamins).

46. Any payment made either by the Secretary of State for the Home Department or by the Secretary of State for Scotland under a scheme established to assist relatives and other persons to visit persons in custody.]

[[13]**47.**—(1) £15 of any payment of maintenance, whether under a court order or not which is made or due to be made by—

(a) the claimant's former partner, or the claimant's partner's former partner; or

(b) the parent of a child or young person where that child or young person is a member of the claimant's family except where that parent is the claimant or the claimant's partner.

(2) For the purposes of sub-paragraph (1), where more than one maintenance payment falls to be taken into account in any week, all such payments shall be aggregated and treated as if they were a single payment.]

[[15]**48.** Any payment (other than a training allowance) made, whether by the Secretary of State or any other person, under the Disabled Persons (Employment) Act 1944 or in accordance with arrangements made under section 2 of the Employment and Training Act 1973 to assist disabled persons to obtain or retain employment despite their disability.]

[[19]**49.** Any council tax benefit.

50. Any guardian's allowance.]

[[23]**51.** Where the claimant is in receipt of any benefit under Parts II, III or V of the Contributions and Benefits Act, any increase in the rate of that benefit arising under Part IV (increases for dependants) or section 106(a) (unemployability supplement) of that Act where the dependant in respect of whom the increase is paid is not a member of the claimant's family.]

[[24]**52.** Any supplementary pension under article 29(1A) of the Naval, Military and Air Forces etc. (Disablement and Death) Service Pensions Order 1983 (pensions to widows).

53. In the case of a pension awarded at the supplementary rate under article 27(3) of the Personal Injuries (Civilians) Scheme 1983 (pensions to widows), the sum specified in paragraph (1)(c) of Schedule 4 to that Scheme.

54.—(1) Any payment which is—

(a) made under any of the Dispensing Instruments to a widow of a person—

(i) whose death was attributable to service in a capacity analogous to service as a member of the armed forces of the Crown; and

(ii) whose service in such capacity terminated before 31st March 1973; and

(b) equal to the amount specified in article 29(1A) of the Naval, Military and Air Forces etc. (Disablement and Death) Service Pensions Order 1983 (pensions to widows).

(2) In this paragraph "the Dispensing Instruments" means the Order in Council of 19th December 1881, the Royal Warrant of 27th October 1884 and the Order by His Majesty of 14th January 1922 (exceptional grants of pay, non-effective pay and allowances).]

[[25]**55.** Any payment made by the Secretary of State to compensate for a reduction in a maintenance assessment made under the Child Support Act 1991.]

AMENDMENTS

1. Family Credit (General) Amendment Regulations 1988 (S.I. 1988 No. 660), reg. 13 (April 11, 1988).

2. Family Credit (General) Amendment No. 3 Regulations 1988 (S.I. 1988 No. 1438), reg. 8 (September 12, 1988).

3. Family Credit (General) Amendment No. 4 Regulations 1988 (S.I. 1988 No. 1970), reg. 11 (December 5, 1988).

4. Family Credit and Income Support (General) Amendment Regulations 1989 (S.I. 1989 No. 1034), reg. 3 (July 10, 1989).

5. Family Credit (General) Amendment Regulations 1990 (S.I. 1990 No. 574), reg. 14(f) (April 3, 1990).

6. Family Credit (General) Amendment Regulations 1990 (S.I. 1990 No. 574), reg. 14(a) to (e) (April 10, 1990).

7. Income-related Benefits Amendment Regulations 1990 (S.I. 1990 No. 1657), reg. 3(2) (September 1, 1990).

8. Family Credit (General) Amendment No. 2 Regulations 1990 (S.I. 1990 No. 1774), reg. 4 (October 2, 1990).

9. Enterprise (Scotland) Consequential Amendments order 1991 (S.I. 1991 No. 387), arts. 2 and 12 (April, 1991).

10. Income-related Benefits Schemes and Social Security (Recoupment) Amendment Regulations 1991 (S.I. 1991 No. 1175), reg. 3 (May 11, 1991).

11. Family Credit (General) Amendment Regulations 1991 (S.I. 1991 No. 1520), reg. 10 (October 8, 1991).

12. Disability Living Allowance and Disability Working Allowance (Consequential Provisions) Regulations 1991 (S.I. 1991 No. 2742), reg. 13(5) (April 6, 1992).

13. Income-related Benefits Schemes (Miscellaneous Provisions) Amendment Regulations 1991 (S.I. 1991 No. 2695), reg. 3 (April 7, 1992).

14. Social Security Benefits Up-rating (No. 2) Order 1991 (S.I. 1991 No. 2910), art. 12 (April 7, 1992).

15. Family Credit (General) Amendment Regulations 1992 (S.I. 1992 No. 573), reg. 13 (April 7, 1992).

16. Family Credit (General) Amendment Regulations 1992 (S.I. 1992 No. 573), Sched., para. 3 (April 7, 1992).

17. Income-related Benefits Schemes and Social Security (Recoupment) Amendment Regulations 1992 (S.I. 1992 No. 1101), reg. 4(6) (May 7, 1992).

18. Income-related Benefits Schemes (Miscellaneous Amendments) Regulations 1993 (S.I. 1993 No. 315), Sched., para. 10 (April 1, 1993).

19. Income-related Benefits Schemes (Miscellaneous Amendments) Regulations 1993 (S.I. 1993 No. 315), reg. 15 (April 13, 1993).

20. Social Security Benefits (Miscellaneous Amendments) (No. 2) Regulations 1993 (S.I. 1993 No. 963), reg. 3(3) (April 22, 1993).

21. Income-related Benefits Schemes and Social Security (Recoupment) Amendment Regulations 1993 (S.I. 1993 No. 1249), reg. 2(4) (May 14, 1993).

22. Income-related Benefits Schemes (Miscellaneous Amendments) (No. 4) Regulations 1993 (S.I. 1993 No. 2119), reg. 34 (October 5, 1993).

23. Income-related Benefits Schemes (Miscellaneous Amendments) Regulations 1994 (S.I. 1994 No. 527), reg. 22 (April 12, 1994).

24. Income-related Benefits Schemes (Miscellaneous Amendments) (No. 5) Regulations 1994 (S.I. 1994 No. 2139), reg. 20 (October 4, 1994).

25. Income-related Benefits Schemes (Miscellaneous Amendments) Regulations 1995 (S.I. 1995 No. 516), reg. 15 (April 11, 1995).

26. Social Security Benefits Up-rating Order 1995 (S.I. 1995 No. 559), art. 16(d) (April 11, 1995).

DEFINITIONS

"the Act"—see reg. 2(1).
"child"—see 1986 Act, s.20(11) (SSCBA, s.137(1)).
"claimant"—see reg. 2(1).
"disability living allowance"—*ibid.*
"disability working allowance"—*ibid.*
"dwelling"—see 1986 Act, s.84(1) (SSCBA, s.137(1)).
"family"—see 1986 Act, s.20(11) (SSCBA, s.137(1)).
"local authority"—see 1986 Act, s.84(1).
"mobility allowance"—see reg. 2(1).
"mobility supplement"—*ibid.*
"payment"—*ibid.*
"student"—*ibid.* reg. 37.

"the Eileen Trust"—see reg. 2(1).
"the Fund"—*ibid.*
"the Independent Living Funds"—*ibid.*
"the Macfarlane (Special Payments) Trust"—*ibid.*
"the Macfarlane (Special Payments) (No. 2) Trust"—*ibid.*
"the Macfarlane Trust"—*ibid.*
"voluntary organisation"—*ibid.*
"year of assessment"—see reg. 2(1).
"young person"—*ibid.*, reg. 6.

GENERAL NOTE

Many of these disregarded categories of income coincide with those listed in Sched. 9 to the Income Support (General) Regulations (Sched. 9 (IS)), apart from necessary differences in cross-references.

Paragraphs 1 and 2
See paras. 1 and 2 of Sched. 9 (IS).

Paragraph 3
Any payments of income support or housing benefit are ignored.

Paragraphs 4 to 6
See paras. 6 to 8 of Sched. 9 (IS).

Paragraph 7
Attendance allowance and analogous payments are disregarded.

Paragraphs 8 to 12
See paras. 10 to 14 of Sched. 9 (IS).

Paragraph 13
The substance is the same as para. 15 of Sched. 9 (IS). Para. 29 limits the total disregard under paras. 13(1) and 14 and reg. 39(2)(b). Para. 34 covers payments from certain trusts.

Paragraph 14
See para. 16 of Sched. 9 (IS). The £10 disregard under sub-para. (a) only applies if the payment is not fully disregarded under paras. 6 or 7.

Paragraph 15
Child benefit (including one parent benefit) is disregarded in the calculation of family credit. This is an important difference from income support.

Paragraph 16
The general rule is that income from capital is disregarded as income. It can then add to the total of capital under reg. 31(4). The exceptions cover the income from certain categories of disregarded capital, mainly premises whose value is ignored. Under sub-para. (2) income from premises whose capital value is disregarded is itself disregarded in so far as it is put towards mortgage repayments, council tax or water charges for those premises. See the notes to para. 22 of Sched. 9(IS).

Paragraphs 17 to 19
See paras. 17 to 19 of Sched. 9 (IS).

Paragraph 20
All forms of income in kind are disregarded. The general rule is the same for earnings from employment (reg. 19(2)(a)) but these are then treated as income under reg. 24(5) before being disregarded under this provision.

Paragraph 21
See para. 23 of Sched. 9 (IS).

Paragraphs 22 to 25

See paras. 25 to 28 of Sched. 9 (IS). Note that there is no special rule for trade disputes in para. 25 as there is in the equivalent income support provision.

Paragraph 26

This provision confirms that income treated as capital under reg. 31 cannot also count as income.

Paragraph 27

Statutory maternity pay and the maternity allowance is disregarded as income other than earnings. Statutory sick pay is no longer (from April 1992) disregarded under this provision, and is treated as earnings from employment under reg. 19(1)(g). Statutory maternity pay is now (April 1993) expressly deemed not to be earnings (reg. 19(2)(d).

Paragraph 28

See para. 33 of Sched. 9 (IS).

Paragraph 29

This provision limits the total disregard under paras. 13(1) and 14 and reg. 39(2)(b) to £10 per week.

Paragraph 30

See para. 24 of Sched. 9 (IS).

Paragraph 31

This applies the same rule as in para. 27 to payments under the Northern Ireland legislation.

Paragraph 32

A payment of necessary expenses by an employer to an employee is disregarded as income. It is excluded from earnings by reg. 19(2).

Paragraphs 33 and 34

See paras. 38 and 39 of Sched. 9 (IS).

Paragraphs 35 to 38

See paras. 40 to 43 of Sched. 9 (IS).

Paragraph 40

See para. 20 of Sched. 9 (IS).

Paragraphs 41 to 46

See paras. 45 to 50 of Sched. 9 (IS).

Paragraph 47

The important disregard of the first £15 of any maintenance payments was a forerunner of the more radical reforms to the system of child support brought into operation in April 1993. "Maintenance" is not defined, but the payment must come from one of the people identified in sub-paras. (a) and (b). It will include payments due under an assessment of child support maintenance.

Maintenance payments count as income other than earnings, to be calculated under reg. 16(2) or (2A).

Paragraphs 48 and 49

See paras. 51 and 52 of Sched. 9 (IS). Any payment of council tax benefit is disregarded.

Paragraph 50

Payments of guardian's allowance are disregarded.

Paragraph 51

See para. 53 of Sched. 9 (IS).

Paragraphs 52–54
See para. 43 and the notes to paras. 54 to 56 of Sched. 9 (IS).

SCHEDULE 3   **Regulation 29(2)**

CAPITAL TO BE DISREGARDED

1. The dwelling, together with any garage, garden and outbuildings, normally occupied by the claimant as his home including any premises not so occupied which it is impracticable or unreasonable to sell separately, in particular, in Scotland, any croft land on which the dwelling is situated; but, notwithstanding regulation 10 (calculation of income and capital of members of claimant's family and of a polygamous marriage), only one dwelling shall be disregarded under this paragraph.

2. Any premises acquired for occupation by the claimant which he intends to occupy [³as his home] within 26 weeks of the date of acquisition or such longer period as is reasonable in the circumstances to enable the claimant to obtain possession and commence occupation of the premises.

3. Any sum directly attributable to the proceeds of sale of any premises formerly occupied by the claimant as his home which is to be used for the purchase of other premises intended for such occupation within 26 weeks of the date of sale or such longer period as is reasonable in the circumstances to enable the claimant to complete the purchase.

4. Any premises occupied in whole or in part by a partner or relative (that is to say any close relative, grandparent, grandchild, uncle, aunt, nephew or niece) of any member of the family, [³as his home] where that person is aged 60 or over or has been incapacitated for a continuous period of at least 13 weeks immediately preceding the date of the claim.

5. Any reversionary interest.

6.—[¹⁰(1)] The assets of any business owned in whole or in part by the claimant and for the purposes of which he is engaged as a self-employed earner or, if he has ceased to be so engaged, for such period as may be reasonable in the circumstances to allow for disposal of any such asset.

[¹⁰(2) The assets of any business owned in whole or in part by the claimant where—
- (a) he has ceased to be engaged as a self-employed earner in that business by reason of some disease or bodily or mental disablement; and
- (b) he intends to become re-engaged as a self-employed earner in that business as soon as he recovers or is able to be re-engaged in that business;

for a period of 26 weeks from the date on which the claimant last ceased to be engaged in that business, or, if it is unreasonable to expect him to become re-engaged in that business within that period, for such longer period as is reasonable in the circumstances to enable him to become so re-engaged.]

7. Any sum attributable to the proceeds of sale of any asset of such a business which is re-invested or to be re-invested in the business within 13 weeks of the date of sale or such longer period as may be reasonable to allow for the re-investment.

8. Any arrears of, or any concessionary payment made to compensate for arrears due to non-payment of—
- (a) any payment specified in paragraphs 4, 6, or 7 of Schedule 2;
- (b) an income-related benefit or supplementary benefit under the Supplementary Benefits Act 1976, family income supplement under the Family Income Supplements Act 1970 or housing benefit under Part II of the Social Security and Housing Benefits Act 1982,

but only for a period of 52 weeks from the date of the receipt of the arrears or of the concessionary payment.

9. Any sum—
- (a) paid to the claimant in consequence of damage to, or loss of, the home or any personal possession and intended for its repair or replacement; or

499

  (b) acquired by the claimant (whether as a loan or otherwise) on the express condition that it is to be used for effecting essential repairs or improvements to the home,

which is to be used for the intended purpose, for a period of 26 weeks from the date on which it was so paid or acquired or such longer period as is reasonable in the circumstances to enable the claimant to effect the repairs, replacement or improvements.

  10. Any sum—

  (a) deposited with a housing association as defined in section 1(1) of the Housing Associations Act 1985 or section 338(1) of the Housing (Scotland) Act 1987 as a condition of occupying the home;

  (b) which was so deposited and which is to be used for the purchase of another home, for the period of 26 weeks or such longer period as may be reasonable in the circumstances to complete the purchase.

  11. Any personal possessions except those which have been acquired by the claimant with the intention of reducing his capital in order to secure entitlement to family credit or to increase the amount of that benefit.

  12. The value of the right to receive any income under an annuity or the surrender value (if any) of such an annuity.

  [¹⁰**13.** Where the funds of a trust are derived from a payment made in consequence of any personal injury to the claimant, the value of the trust fund and the value of the right to receive any payment under that trust.]

  14. The value of the right to receive any income under a life interest or from a liferent.

  15. The value of the right to receive any income which is disregarded under paragraph 1 of Schedule 1 or 21 of Schedule 2.

  16. The surrender value of any policy of life insurance.

  17. Where any payment of capital falls to be made by instalments, the value of the right to receive any outstanding instalments.

  [¹⁵**18.** Any payment made by a local authority in accordance with section 17 or 24 of the Children Act 1989 or, as the case may be, section 12, 24 or 26 of the Social Work (Scotland) Act 1968 (provision of services for children and their families and advice and assistance to certain children).]

  [¹⁴**19.** Any social fund payment made pursuant to Part III of the Act [SSCBA, Part VIII].]

  20. Any refund of tax which falls to be deducted under section 26 of the Finance Act 1982 (deductions of tax from certain loan interest) on a payment of relevant loan interest for the purpose of acquiring an interest in the home or carrying out repairs or improvements to the home.

  [²¹**21.**—Any capital which by virtue of regulations 25 (capital treated as income), 27(1) (modifications in respect of children and young persons) or 42A (treatment of student loans) is to be treated as income.]

  22. Where a payment of capital is made in a currency other than sterling, any banking charge or commission payable in converting that payment to sterling.

  [¹²**23.**—(1) Any payment made under the Macfarlane Trust, the Macfarlane (Special Payments) Trust, the Macfarlane (Special Payments) (No. 2) Trust ("the Trusts"), [¹⁶the Fund] [²⁰, the Eileen Trust] or [¹⁸the Independent Living Funds].

  (2) Any payment by or on behalf of a person who is suffering or who suffered from haemophilia [⁶or who is or was a qualifying person], which derives from a payment made under any of the Trusts to which sub-paragraph (1) refers and which is made to or for the benefit of—

  (a) that person's partner or former partner from whom he is not, or where that person has died was not, estranged or divorced;

  (b) any child who is a member of that person's family or who was such a member and who is a member of the claimant's family; or

  (c) any young person who is a member of that person's family or who was such a member and who is a member of the claimant's family.

(3) Any payment by or on behalf of the partner or former partner of a person who is suffering or who suffered from haemophilia [[16]or who is or was a qualifying person] provided that the partner or former partner and that person are not, or if either of them has died were not, estranged or divorced, which derives from a payment made under any of the Trusts to which sub-paragraph (1) refers and which is made to or for the benefit of—

(a) the person who is suffering from haemophilia [[16]or who is a qualifying person];

(b) any child who is a member of that person's family or who was such a member and who is a member of the claimant's family; or

(c) any young person who is a member of that person's family or who was such a member and who is a member of the claimant's family.

(4) Any payment by a person who is suffering from haemophilia [[16]or who is a qualifying person], which derives from a payment under any of the Trusts to which sub-paragraph (1) refers, where—

(a) that person has no partner or former partner from whom he is not estranged or divorced, nor any child or young person who is or had been a member of that person's family; and

(b) the payment is made either—

(i) to that person's parent or step-parent, or

(ii) where that person at the date of the payment is a child, a young person or a student who has not completed his full-time education and has no parent or step-parent, to his guardian,

but only for a period from the date of the payment until of end of two years from that person's death.

(5) Any payment out of the estate of a person who suffered from haemophilia [[16]or who was a qualifying person], which derives from a payment under any of the Trusts to which sub-paragraph (1) refers, where—

(a) that person at the date of his death (the relevant date) had no partner or former partner from whom he was not estranged or divorced, nor any child or young person who was or had been a member of his family; and

(b) the payment is made either—

(i) to that person's parent or step-parent, or

(ii) where that person at the relevant date was a child, a young person or a student who had not completed his full-time education and had no parent or step-parent, to his guardian.

but only for a period of two years from the relevant date.

(6) In the case of a person to whom or for whose benefit a payment referred to in this paragraph is made, any capital resource which derives from any payment of income or capital made under or deriving from any of the Trusts.]

[[16](7) For the purposes of sub-paragraphs (2) to (6), any reference to the Trusts shall be construed as including a reference to the Fund [[20]and the Eileen Trust].]

[[1]24. The value of the right to receive an occupational [[13]or personal] pension.

25. The value of the right to receive any rent.]

[[2]26.—(1) Where a claimant has ceased to occupy what was formerly the dwelling occupied as the home following his estrangement or divorce from his former partner, that dwelling for a period of 26 weeks from the date on which he ceased to occupy that dwelling.

(2) In this paragraph "dwelling" includes any garage, garden and out-buildings which were formerly occupied by the claimant as his home and any premises not so occupied which it is impracticable or unreasonable to sell separately, in particular, in Scotland, any croft land on which the dwelling is situated.

27. Any premises where the claimant is taking reasonable steps to dispose of those premises, for a period of 26 weeks from the date on which he first took such steps, or such longer period as is reasonable in the circumstances to enable him to dispose of those premises.]

[⁴28. Any premises which the claimant intends to occupy as his home, and in respect of which he is taking steps to obtain possession and has sought legal advice, or has commenced legal proceedings, with a view to obtaining possession, for a period of 26 weeks from the date on which he first sought such advice or first commenced such proceedings whichever is the earlier, or such longer period as is reasonable in the circumstances to enable him to obtain possession and commence occupation of those premises.]

[²29. Any premises which the claimant intends to occupy as his home to which essential repairs or alterations are required in order to render them fit for such occupation, for a period of 26 weeks from the date on which the claimant first takes steps to effect those repairs or alterations, or such longer period as is reasonable in the circumstances to enable those repairs or alterations to be carried out and the claimant to commence occupation of the premises.

30. Any premises occupied in whole or in part by the former partner of a claimant as his home; but this provision shall not apply where the former partner is a person from whom the claimant is estranged or divorced.]

[³31. Any payment in kind made by a charity [⁶or under the Macfarlane (Special Payments) Trust][¹⁶or, the Macfarlane (Special Payments) (No. 2) Trust [¹⁹, the Fund or the Independent Living (1993) Fund]].

32. [²¹£200 of any payment, or, if the payment is less than £200, the whole of any payment] made under section 2 of the Employment and Training Act 1973 (functions of the Secretary of State) [¹¹or under section 2 of the Enterprise and New Towns (Scotland) Act 1990] as a training bonus to a person participating in arrangements for training made under [¹¹either of those sections] [⁴but only for a period of 52 weeks from the date of the receipt of that payment.]

33. Any payment made by the Secretary of State to compensate for the loss (in the whole or in part) of entitlement to housing benefit.]

[⁴34. Any payment made by the Secretary of State to compensate a person who was entitled to supplementary benefit in respect of a period ending immediately before 11th April 1988 but who did not become entitled to income support in respect of a period beginning with that day.

35. Any payment made by the Secretary of State to compensate for the loss of housing benefit supplement under regulation 19 of the Supplementary Benefit (Requirements) Regulations 1983.

36. Any payment made to a juror or witness in respect of attendance at court other than compensation for loss of earnings or for the loss of a benefit payable under the benefit Acts.

37. [¹⁷ . .].]

[⁷38. Any payment in consequence of a reduction of a personal community charge pursuant to regulations under section 13A of the Local Government Finance Act 1988 or section 9A of the Abolition of Domestic Rates Etc (Scotland) Act 1987 (reduction of liability for personal community charge) [¹⁷or reduction of council tax under section 13 or, as the case may be, section 80 of the local Government Finance Act 1992 (reduction of liability for council tax),] but only for a period of 52 weeks from the date of receipt of the payment.]

[⁸39. Any grant made to the claimant in accordance with a scheme made under section 129 of the Housing Act 1988 or section 66 of the Housing (Scotland) Act 1988 (schemes for payments to assist local housing authority and local authority tenants to obtain other accommodation) which is to be used—
  (a) to purchase premises intended for occupation as his home; or
  (b) to carry out repairs or alterations which are required to render premises fit for occupation as his home.
for a period of 26 weeks from the date on which he received such a grant or such longer period as is reasonable in the circumstances to enable the purchase, repairs or alterations to be completed and the claimant to commence occupation of those premises as his home.]

[¹⁰·**40.**—(1) Any payment or repayment made—

(a) as respects England and Wales, under regulation 3, 5 or 8 of the National Health Service (Travelling Expenses and Remission of Charges) Regulations 1988 (travelling expenses and health service supplies);

(b) as respects Scotland, under regulation 3, 5 or 8 of the National Health Service (Travelling Expenses and Remission of Charges) (Scotland) Regulations 1988 (travelling expenses and health service supplies);

but only for a period of 52 weeks from the date of receipt of the payment or repayment.

(2) Any payment or repayment made by the Secretary of State for Health, the Secretary of State for Scotland or the Secretary of State for Wales which is analogous to a payment or repayment mentioned in sub-paragraph (1); but only for a period of 52 weeks from the date of receipt of the payment or repayment.

41. Any payment made under regulation 9 to 11 or 13 of the Welfare Food Regulations 1988 (payments made in place of milk tokens or the supply of vitamins), but only for a period of 52 weeks from the date of receipt of the payment.

42. Any payment made either by the Secretary of State for the Home Department by the Secretary of State for Scotland under a scheme established to assist relatives and other persons to visit persons in custody, but only for a period of 52 weeks from the date of receipt of the payment.

43. Any arrears of special war widows payment which is disregarded under paragraph 43 of Schedule 2 (sums to be disregarded in the calculation of income other than earnings) [²²or of any amount which is disregarded under paragraph 52, 53 or 54 of that Schedule], but only for a period of 52 weeks from the date of receipt of the arrears.]

[¹⁴**44.** Any payment (other than a training allowance or training bonus under section 2 of the Employment and Training Act 1973) made, whether by the Secretary of State or any other person, under the Disabled Persons (Employment) Act 1944 or in accordance with arrangements made under section 2 of the Employment and Training Act 1973 to assist disabled persons to obtain or retain employment despite their disability.

45. Any payment made by a local authority under section 3 of the Disabled Persons (Employment) Act 1958 to homeworkers assisted under the Blind Homeworkers' Scheme.]

[²²**46.** Any sum of capital administered on behalf of a person under the age of 18 by the High Court under the provisions of Order 80 of the Rules of the Supreme Court, the County Court under Order 10 of the County Court Rules 1981, or the Court of Protection, where such sum derives from—

(a) an award of damages for a personal injury to that person; or

(b) compensation for the death of one or both parents.

47. Any sum of capital administered on behalf of a person under the age of 18 in accordance with an order made under Rule 43.15 of the Act of Sederunt (Rules of the Court of Session 1994) 1994 or under Rule 131 of the Act of Sederunt (Rules of the Court, consolidation and amendment) 1965, or under Rule 36.14 of the Ordinary Cause Rules 1993, or under Rule 128 of the Ordinary Cause Rules, where such sum derives from—

(a) an award of damages for a personal injury to that person; or

(b) compensation for the death of one or both parents.]

[²³**48.** Any payment made by the Secretary of State to compensate for a reduction in a maintenance assessment made under the Child Support Act 1991, but only for a period of 52 weeks from the date of receipt of that payment.]

AMENDMENTS

1. Family Credit (General) Amendment Regulations 1988 (S.I. 1988 No. 660), reg. 14 (April 11, 1988).

2. Family Credit (General) Amendment No. 2 Regulations 1988 (S.I. 1988 No. 908), reg. 2 (May 30, 1988).

3. Family Credit (General) Amendment No. 3 Regulations 1988 (S.I. 1988 No. 1438), reg. 9 (September 12, 1988).

4. Family Credit (General) Amendment No. 4 Regulations 1988 (S.I. 1988 No. 1970), reg. 12 (December 5, 1988).

5. Family Credit and Income Support (General) Amendment Regulations 1989 (S.I. 1989 No. 1034), reg. 3 (July 10, 1989).

6. Income-related Benefits Schemes Amendment Regulations 1990 (S.I. 1990 No. 127), reg. 2 (January 31, 1990).

7. Family Credit (General) Amendment Regulations 1990 (S.I. 1990 No. 574), reg. 15(a) (April 3, 1990).

8. Family Credit (General) Amendment Regulations 1990 (S.I. 1990 No. 574), reg. 15(b) (April 10, 1990).

9. Social Security Benefits (Student Loans and Miscellaneous Amendments) Regulations 1990 (S.I. 1990 No. 1549), reg. 3(6) (September 1, 1990).

10. Family Credit (General) Amendment No. 2 Regulations 1990 (S.I. 1990 No. 1774), reg. 5 (October 2, 1990).

11. Enterprise (Scotland) Consequential Amendments Order (S.I. 1991 No. 387), arts. 2 and 12 (April 1, 1991).

12. Income-related Benefits Schemes and Social Security (Recoupment) Amendment Regulations 1991 (S.I. 1991 No. 1175), reg. 3 (May 11, 1991).

13. Family Credit (General) Amendment Regulations 1991 (S.I. 1991 No. 1520), reg. 11 (October 8, 1991).

14. Family Credit (General) Amendment Regulations 1992 (S.I. 1992 No. 573), reg. 14 (April 7, 1992).

15. Family Credit (General) Amendment Regulations 1992 (S.I. 1992 No. 573), Sched. para. 4 (April 7, 1992).

16. Income-related Benefits Schemes and Social Security (Recoupment) Amendment Regulations 1992 (S.I. 1992 No. 1101), reg. 4(7) (May 7, 1992).

17. Income-related Benefits Schemes (Miscellaneous Amendments) Regulations 1993 (S.I. 1993 No. 315), Sched., para. 11 (April 1, 1993).

18. Social Security Benefits (Miscellaneous Amendments) (No. 2) Regulations 1993 (S.I. 1993 No. 963), reg. 3(3) (April 22, 1993).

19. Social Security Benefits (Miscellaneous Amendments) (No. 2) Regulations 1993 (S.I. 1993 No. 963), reg. 3(5) (April 22, 1993).

20. Income-related Benefits Schemes and Social Security (Recoupment) Amendment Regulations 1993 (S.I. 1993 No. 1249), reg. 2(5) (May 14, 1993).

21. Income-related Benefits Schemes (Miscellaneous Amendments) (No. 4) Regulations 1993 (S.I. 1993 No. 2119), reg. 35 (October 5, 1993).

22. Income-related Benefits Schemes (Miscellaneous Amendments) (No. 5) Regulations 1994 (S.I. 1994 No. 2139), reg. 21 (October 4, 1994).

23. Income-related Benefits Schemes (Miscellaneous Amendments) Regulations 1995 (S.I. 1995 No. 516), reg. 16 (April 11, 1995).

DEFINITIONS

"claimant"—see reg. 2(1), reg. 10(1).
"close relative"—see reg. 2(1).
"date of claim"—*ibid.*
"dwelling"—see 1986 Act, s.84(1) (SSCBA, s.137(1)).
"family"—see 1986 Act, s.20(11) (SSCBA, s.137(1)).
"income-related benefit"—see 1986 Act, s.84(1).
"occupational pension"—*ibid.*
"partner"—see reg. 2(1).
"policy of life insurance"—*ibid.*
"the Eileen Trust"—*ibid.*
"the Fund"—*ibid.*
"the Independent Living Funds"—*ibid.*
"the Independent Living (1993) Fund"—*ibid.*
"Macfarlane (Special Payments) Trust"—*ibid.*
"Macfarlane (Special Payments) (No. 2) Trust"—*ibid.*
"the Macfarlane Trust"—*ibid.*

GENERAL NOTE

Many of these categories of disregarded capital are the same in substance (there are occasional differences in cross references) as in Sched. 10 of the Income Support (General) Regulations (Sched. 10 (IS)). More substantial differences are noted.

Paragraphs 1 to 3
    See paras. 1 to 3 of Sched. 10 (IS).

Paragraph 4
    This is almost identical to para. 4 of Sched. 10 (IS), with the spelling out of the meaning of "relative," defined in reg. 2(1) of the Income Support (General) Regulations. But there is no requirement in Sched. 10 (IS) that the person has been incapacitated for at least 13 weeks.

Paragraphs 5 to 6
    See paras. 5 and 6 of Sched. 10 (IS).

Paragraph 7
    The proceeds of sale of a business asset, which are to be re-invested in the business, are disregarded. This provision has no equivalent in Sched. 10 (IS).

Paragraphs 8 to 10
    See paras. 7 to 9 of Sched. 10 (IS).

Paragraph 11
    The basic rule here is the same as that in para. 10 of Sched. 10 (IS), but in order for the value of personal possessions to count the intention in buying them must have been to reduce capital to gain entitlement to family credit. If the intention was to gain entitlement to income support or supplementary benefit, or even family income supplement, para. 11 will not apply.

Paragraph 13
    See para. 12 of Sched. 10 (IS).

Paragraphs 14 to 25
    See paras. 13 to 24 of Sched. 10 (IS).

Paragraphs 26 to 29
    See paras. 25 to 28 of Sched. 10 (IS).

Paragraph 30
    See para. 4(b) of Sched. 10 (IS).

Paragraphs 31 to 36
    See paras. 29 to 34 of Sched. 10 (IS).

Paragraphs 38 to 39
    See paras. 36 and 37 of Sched. 10 (IS).

Paragraphs 40 to 43
    See paras. 38 to 41 of Sched. 10 (IS).

Paragraphs 44 to 45
    See paras. 42 and 43 of Sched. 10 (IS).

Paragraphs 46 to 47
    See paras. 44 and 45 of Sched. 10 (IS).

[¹SCHEDULE 4   **Regulation 46**

DETERMINATION OF MAXIMUM FAMILY CREDIT: ADULT, CHILD AND YOUNG
PERSON CREDITS

Column (1)	Column (2)
Adult, child, young person	*Amount of Credit*
1. Adult	[²£45.10];
2. Child— (a) aged less than 11 years; (b) aged not less than 11 but less than 16 years;	(a) [²£11.40]; (b) [²£18.90];
3. Young person— (a) aged not less than 16 but less than 18 years; (b) aged not less than 18 years but less than 19 years.	(a) [²£23.45]; (b) [²£32.80].

AMENDMENTS

1. Social Security Benefits Up-rating Order 1990 (S.I. 1990 No. 320), art. 13 and Sched. 2 (April 10, 1990).
2. Social Security Benefits Up-rating Order 1995 (S.I. 1995 No. 559), art. 16(e) and Sched. 2 (April 11, 1995).

DEFINITIONS

"child"—see 1986 Act, s.20(11) (SSCBA, s.137(1)).
"young person"—see reg. 2(1), reg. 6

The Family Credit (Transitional) Regulations 1987

(S.I. 1987 No. 1974)

Made by the Secretary of State under ss.84(1) and 89(1) of the Social Security Act 1986.

ARRANGEMENT OF REGULATIONS

1.   Citation and commencement
2.   Interpretation
3.   Claims for family credit treated as made on 11th April 1988
4.   Claims for family credit treated as including renewal claims for family income supplement
5.   Claims for family income supplement to be determined first
6.   Determination of circumstances where family credit replaces, or arises out of a claim for, family income supplement
7.   Determination of circumstances where family credit is claimed before 11th April 1988
8.   Entitlement to family credit following entitlement to family income supplement
9.   Initial periods of family credit

Citation and commencement

1. These Regulations may be cited as the Family Credit (Transitional) Regulations 1987 and shall come into force on 1st January 1988.

Interpretation

2.—(1) In these Regulations, unless the context otherwise requires—

"the Act" means the Social Security Act 1986;

"appropriate office" means an office of the Department of Health and Social Security;

"child" has the same meaning as in Part II of the Act [SSCBA, Part VII];

"family" has the same meaning as in Part II of the Act [SSCBA, Part VII];

"family income supplement" means benefit under the Family Income Supplements Act 1970;

"married or unmarried couple" has the same meaning as in Part II of the Act [SSCBA, Part VII];

"renewal claim" means a claim for family income supplement which is so described in regulation 3(2) of the Family Income Supplements (General) Regulations 1980;

"young person" means a person aged 16 or over but under 19 who is receiving full-time education within section 2(1)(b) of the Child Benefit Act 1975 [SSCBA, s.142(1)(b)].

(2) Unless the context otherwise requires, any reference in these Regulations to a numbered regulation is a reference to the regulation bearing that number in these Regulations, and any reference in a regulation to a numbered paragraph is a reference to the paragraph bearing that number in that regulation.

Claims for family credit treated as made on 11th April 1988

3.—(1) A written claim for family credit which is delivered or sent to an appropriate office on or after 1st March 1988 and received on or before 11th April 1988 shall be treated as made on 11th April 1988.

(2) Where family income supplement is payable to a person under an award for a period which includes 5th April 1988 and does not exceed 51 weeks it shall not be a condition of entitlement to family credit for a period beginning 11th April 1988 that the person makes a claim for such benefit and a claim, in such a case, for family credit shall be treated as made on 11th April 1988.

(3) Where a claim for family income supplement is made on or after 1st March 1988 but on or before 5th April 1988, but no award of that benefit is made, that claim shall, if the Secretary of State in his discretion so determines, be treated as including a claim for family credit made on 11th April 1988.

(4) Where, after 5th April 1988, a claim is made for family income supplement which is neither a renewal claim nor a claim in respect of a period before 11th April 1988 it shall be treated as a claim for family credit which shall be treated as made on 11th April 1988 if received at an appropriate office on or before that date but otherwise on the date on which it is received at such an office.

(5) In a case to which paragraph (2), (3) or (4) applies, where the claim for family income supplement was made by a married or unmarried couple, the claim for family credit shall be treated as made by the woman except that the claim shall be treated as made by the man if the Secretary of, State is satisfied, in that case, as that it would be reasonable so to treat it.

(6) A claim which is treated as made on 11th April 1988 by virtue of the provisions of this regulation may nevertheless be determined at any earlier date on which the conditions for treating it as made on 11th April 1988 are satisfied; and any such claim shall be determined in accordance with the Act and Regulations made under that Act as if those provisions were in force.

DEFINITIONS

"appropriate office"—see reg. 2(1).
"family income supplement"—*ibid.*
"married couple"—*ibid.*, 1986 Act, s.20(11) (SSCBA, s.137(1)).
"renewal claim"—see reg. 2(1), General Regulations, reg. 3(2).

"unmarried couple"—see reg. 2(1), 1986 Act, s.20(11) (SSCBA, s.137(1)).

GENERAL NOTE

Paragraph (1)
Claims for family credit could be made from March 1, 1988. If received before April 12, 1988, they were treated as made on April 11, 1988. See para. (6) and regs. 4 and 7.

Paragraph (2)
Any awards of FIS starting after March 24, 1987, were adjusted so as to expire before April 11, 1988, instead of running for the usual 52 weeks. Where such an award includes April 5, 1988, and has not been for a full 52 weeks, it is assumed that a family credit award on such a claim will be for the balance of 52 weeks from the beginning of the last FIS award (reg. 9(1)). See reg. 6.

Paragraph (3)
An unsuccessful FIS claim made after February 29, 1988, may be treated as a family credit claim made on April 11, 1988, at the discretion of the Secretary of State. See reg. 6.

Paragraph (4)
A fresh claim for FIS made after April 5, 1988, is to be treated as a family credit claim.

Paragraph (5)
A family credit claim usually has to be made by the woman (Claims and Payments Regulations, reg. 4(2)). Para. (5) allows this condition to be treated as met where a FIS claim is treated as a family credit claim.

Paragraph (6)
This provision allows decisions to be made in advance of April 11, 1988. This was necessary to secure continuity of payments, the printing of order books, etc.

Claims for family credit treated as including renewal claims for family income supplement

4. Where a claim for family credit is treated as made on 11th April 1988 by virtue of regulation 3(1) (claim received before 11th April 1988) and a renewal claim could properly have been made on the date when the claim for family credit was received at an appropriate office, such a renewal claim shall be treated as so made.

DEFINITIONS

"appropriate office"—see reg. 2(1).
"renewal claim"—*ibid.*, General Regulations, reg. 3(2).

Claims for family income supplement to be determined first

5. Where, before 11th April 1988, a person makes a claim for family credit and also claims family income supplement in respect of a period before 11th April 1988, the determination of the claim for family credit shall be postponed or, if it has already been determined, shall be of no effect until, and may be reviewed when, the claim for family income supplement has been determined.

DEFINITION

"family income supplement"—see reg. 2(1).

Determination of circumstances where family credit replaces, or arises out of a claim for, family income supplement

6.—(1) Subject to paragraphs (2) and (3), in a case to which regulation 3(2) or (3) applies (family credit treated as claimed on 11th April 1988 where family income supplement awarded or claimed) the provisions of [¹section 20(5)] of the Act [SSCBA, s.128(1)] (conditions of entitlement to family credit) shall be modified to the extent that entitlement to family credit shall be determined upon the assumption that the circumstances of the family (but not the ages of its members except where a young person attains the age of 19 on or before 11th April 1988) are the same on 11th April 1988 as they were at the date of the claim for family income supplement.

(2) In a case to which regulation 3(2) or (3) applies, the weekly earnings of the claimant and, if he is a member of a married or unmarried couple, those of the other member shall be calculated by deducting from the weekly earnings as calculated for the purpose of assessing entitlement to family income supplement—

(a) an amount in respect of income tax equivalent to an amount calculated by applying the basic rate of tax for the tax year 1987/88 to those earnings, less only the personal relief, appropriate to a week, to which the claimant is entitled under sections 8(1) and (2) and 14(1)(a) and (2) of the Income and Corporation Taxes Act 1970 (personal and additional relief); and

(b) an amount in respect of primary Class I contributions under the Social Security Act 1975 [SSCBA, Part I] equivalent to an amount calculated by applying the appropriate percentage rate specified in section 4(6B) of that Act [SSCBA, s.8(2)] in respect of the tax year 1987/88 to those earnings.

(3) In a case to which regulation 3(2) or (3) applies the weekly income of a claimant and, if he is a member of a married or unmarried couple, that of the other member of the couple, other than earnings to which paragraph (2) applies, shall be calculated by deducting from the gross weekly income as calculated for the purpose of assessing entitlement to family income supplement the sums, where applicable, specified in Schedule 2 to the Family Credit (General) Regulations 1987 (income other than earnings to be disregarded).

AMENDMENT

1. Family Credit (Transitional) Amendment Regulation 1988 (S.I. 1988 No. 239), reg. 2 (February 20, 1988).

DEFINITIONS

"the Act"—see reg. 2(1).
"family"—*ibid.*, 1986 Act, s.20(11) (SSCBA, s.137(1)).
"family income supplement"—see reg. 2(1).
"married couple"—*ibid.*, 1986 Act, s.20(11) (SSCBA, s.137(1)).
"primary Class 1 contributions"—see 1986 Act, s.84(1).
"unmarried couple"—see reg. 2(1), 1986 Act, s.20(11) (SSCBA, s.137(1)).
"young person"—see reg. 2(1).

GENERAL NOTE

Paragraph (1)
Where reg. 3(2) or (3) applies, the family credit claim is to be determined as if the number and ages of the children on April 11, 1988, are the same as they were at the date of the FIS claim. The one exception is where a young person has reached 19, and so ceases to qualify for a credit. The family's income at the date of this FIS claim is also taken. In the case of a reg. 3(2) claim the family credit award will only be for the balance of 52 weeks from the date of the FIS award (reg. 9(1)).

Paragraph (2)
In a case falling under para. (1), the gross earnings for FIS are converted to net earnings.

Paragraph (3)

The disregarded categories of income in Sched. 2 to the Family Credit (General) Regulations apply to cases falling under para. (1).

Determination of circumstances where family credit is claimed before 11th April 1988

7. In a case to which regulation 3(1) applies (claim received before 11th April 1988), ['sections 20(5) and 22(6)] of the Act [SSCBA, ss.128(1) and 134(1)] (conditions of entitlement to family credit) shall be modified to the extent that the circumstances of the family (but not the ages of its members) shall be determined as at the date when the claim is received at an appropriate office.

AMENDMENT

1. Family Credit (Transitional) Amendment Regulations 1988 (S.I. 1988 No. 239), reg. 2 (February 20, 1988).

DEFINITIONS

"the Act"—see reg. 2(1).
"the family"—*ibid.*, 1986 Act, s.20(11) (SSCBA, s.137(1)).

GENERAL NOTE

Where an advance claim for family credit was made before April 11, 1988, it was to be determined on the circumstances as at the date on which the claim was actually received, but of course according to family credit rules (since the claim was treated as made on April 11, 1988).

Entitlement to family credit following entitlement to family income supplement

8.—(1) Where a claim for family credit is treated as made on 11th April 1988, by virtue of regulation 3(2) (pre-existing entitlement to family income supplement) and all the conditions of entitlement to family credit as modified by regulation 6 (determination of circumstances where family credit replaces family income supplement), are satisfied, including the capital conditions in section 22(6) of the Act [SSCBA, s.134(1)] and the income conditions in section 20(5)(a) of the Act [SSCBA, s.128(1)(a)], family credit shall be awarded at the rate at which family income supplement was payable on 5th April 1988, together with an additional £2.55 per week for each child or young person included in the family for which family income supplement was payable on 5th April 1988, except where such a rate would be lower than the rate at which family credit would otherwise be payable.

(2) Where a claim for family credit is treated as made on 11th April 88, by virtue of regulation 3(2), and, apart from the income conditions in section 20(5)(a) of the Act [SSCBA, s.128(1)(b)], all the conditions of entitlement to family credit as modified by regulation 6, including the capital conditions in section 22(6) of the Act [SSCBA, s.134(1)], are satisfied, family credit shall be awarded at the rate at which family income supplement was payable on 5th April 1988, together with an additional £2.55 per week for each child or young person included in the family for which family income supplement was payable on 5th April 1988.

(3) In the case of an award of family credit on a claim treated as made on 11th April 1988 by virtue of regulation 3(1) or (2), in respect of a person for whom family income supplement was payable on 5th April 1988, the first day of the award (namely 11th April 1988) shall be treated as a week for the purpose of calculating—

(a) the amount payable; and
(b) the number of weeks for which family credit should be payable under section 20(6) of the Act [SSCBA, s.128(3)] (period for which family credit payable), as modified by regulation 3 (initial periods of family credit).

DEFINITIONS

"the Act"—see reg. 2(1).
"child"—*ibid.*, 1986 Act, s.20(11) (SSCBA, s.137(1)).
"family"—*ibid.*
"family income supplement"—see reg. 2(1).
"young person"—*ibid.*

GENERAL NOTE

Reg. 8 contains the transitional protection for families entitled to FIS immediately before the start of family credit.

Paragraph (1)
This provision applies where the claimant met the £6,000 capital rule and also qualifies for family credit on income grounds, and any other conditions. If the amount of FIS payable on April 5, 1988, plus £2.55 for each child or young person in the family (to take account of the loss of entitlement to free school meals and milk), exceeded the amount of family credit calculated in the ordinary way, family credit was to be paid at the higher rate. This protection only applied to the initial claim treated as made on April 11, 1988, by virtue of reg. 3(2) and thus expired when that award (limited by reg. 9(1)) expired.

Paragraph (2)
This provision applied when the conditions of para. (1) were met except that on the income tests there was no entitlement on family credit. Family credit was paid at the FIS rate for April 5 1988, plus £2.55 for each child or young person.

Initial periods of family credit

9.—(1) In the case of an award of family credit on a claim treated as made on 11th April 1988 by virtue of regulation 3(2) (pre-existing entitlement to family income supplement), section 20(6) of the Act [SSCBA, s.128(3)] shall be modified by substituting for the words "for a period of 26 weeks or such other period as may be prescribed, beginning with the week in which the claim is made or is treated as made" the words "for a period beginning with the week in which a claim for it is made or is treated as made and ending 52 weeks after the start of the most recent award of family income supplement, or on such earlier date as the Secretary of State shall in any case decide, and".

(2) In the case of an award of family credit on any claim made or treated as made before 5th October 1988, except an award to which paragraph (1) applies, section 20(6) of the Act [SSCBA, s.128(3)] shall be modified by substituting for the words "for a period of 26 weeks or such other period as may be prescribed" the words "for such period of at least 14 weeks but not more than 39 weeks, as the Secretary of State shall in any case decide".

DEFINITIONS

"the Act"—see reg. 2(1).
"family income supplement"—ibid.

GENERAL NOTE

Paragraph (1)
On a claim under reg. 3(2) an award of family credit was to be for the balance of 52 weeks from the beginning of the last FIS award. Subsequent awards will be for 26 weeks, unless para. (2) applies.

Paragraph (2)

In the case of any family credit claim before October 5, 1988, the Secretary of State has power to depart from the normal 26 week award, within limits of 14 and 39 weeks. This will enable the expiry of awards to be staggered, so that there is not a disproportionate burden of administrative work at one point in the year. This provision is not limited to claimants moving from FIS to family credit (*CFC 13/1989*).

Family Credit (General) Amendment Regulations 1992

(S.I. 1992 No. 573)

[In force, April 7, 1992]

Extension of award period

15.—(1) In the case of an award of family credit on any claim to which paragraph (4) of regulation 13 of the Social Security (Claims and Payments) Regulations 1987 applies (advance claims and awards), for the purposes of section 20(6) of the Social Security Act 1986 [SSCBA, s. 128(3)] the prescribed period shall be determined in accordance with paragraph (2) of this regulation.

(2) For the purposes of determining the prescribed period the Secretary of State shall assign a number to the claim in question (the claim number), and where that claim number—

   (a) is exactly divisible by 13, the prescribed period shall be 27 weeks;
   (b) is not exactly divisible by 13, the remainder shall be multiplied by 13 and the prescribed period shall be the number of weeks equal to the sum of the resulting product plus 27.]

GENERAL NOTE

Reg. 13(4) of the Claims and Payments Regulations allows for advance claims for family credit immediately before the change in the minimum qualifying hours from 24 to 16 on April 7, 1992, by claimants who did not previously meet that qualification. This provision secures that all the awards made on such claims do not run out on the same date and thus impose an impracticable administrative burden. Awards are intended to be for a randomly chosen period between 27 and 39 weeks, but para. (2)(b) appears to allow a period of up to 183 weeks!

PART IV

DISABILITY WORKING ALLOWANCE

The Disability Working Allowance (General) Regulations 1991

(S.I. 1991 No. 2887)

Made by the Secretary of State under ss.20(1), (5)(bb), (6A)(d), (6C) to (6F), (11) and (12), 21(3B) and (6)(aa), 22(1) and (5) to (9), 27B(2) and (4) and 84(1) of the Social Security Act 1986 and s.166(1) to (3A) of the Social Security Act 1975.

Part VI

Calculation of Entitlement

Part VII

Changes of Circumstances

Part VIII

Entitlement to Family Credit and Disability Working Allowance

Schedules

General Note

For many years one of the biggest gaps in the British social security system has been that there was no provision for partial capacity for work. A person was either incapable of any work he could reasonably be expected to do, and so entitled to incapacity benefits, or he was not incapable. There was no special recognition of a lesser reduction in working and earning ability. This was one of the weaknesses identified in the Social Security Advisory Committee's special report, *Benefits for Disabled People: a Strategy for Change* (1988). The Government's White Paper, *The Way Ahead: Benefits for Disabled People* (1990, Cm 917) proposed a new benefit along the lines of family credit, but restricted to disabled people and not limited to people with children. Disability working allowance is the result.

Even with the shift in the minimum hours to 16 a week for the income-related benefits generally, disabled people who can only do a little work will still be excluded. The need to satisfy the criterion of entitlement to some other incapacity or disability benefit under s.129(2) of the Contributions and Benefits Act (1986 Act, s.20(6B)), will also exclude some claimants who are partially capable of work. The initial estimates were that about 50,000 claimants would benefit from disability working allowance, so that it is designed to be a limited scheme.

If a person has the choice of claiming family credit or disability working allowance, they will generally be better off on disability working allowance, because the applicable amounts incorporate the equivalent of the income support disability premium. In addition, a disabled child's allowance

517

has been introduced for disability working allowance (but not for family credit) from April 11, 1995. However, in the past disability working allowance did not operate as a passport to schemes like those for exemption from prescription charges and dental and optician's charges. It has been announced that this is to be remedied from April 1995, but only for recipients of disability working allowance who have capital of £8,000 or less.

Since October 4, 1994, certain disability working allowance claimants have been able to offset child care costs of up to £40 per week against their earnings. This also applies to family credit (and housing and council tax benefit) but not income support. Although this is an important change in principle, the scope of the disregard is limited (see regs. 15 and 15A and the notes to regs. 13 and 13A of the Family Credit Regulations).

Most of the issues which might come to SSATs will be familiar from the family credit scheme. But it is worth noting that the capital limit is £16,000.

PART I

GENERAL

Citation and commencement

1. These Regulations may be cited as the Disability Working Allowance (General) Regulations 1991, and shall come into force on 7th April 1992.

Interpretation

2.—(1) In these Regulations, unless the context otherwise requires—
"the Act" means the Social Security Act 1986;
"assessment period" means such period as is prescribed in regulations 16 to 19 over which income falls to be calculated;
"attendance allowance" means—
(a) an attendance allowance under section 35 of the Social Security Act [SSCBA, s.64];
(b) an increase of disablement pension under section 61 or 63 of that Act [SSCBA, ss.104 or 105];
(c) a payment under regulations made in exercise of the power conferred by section 159(3)(b) of that Act [SSCBA, Sched. 8, para. 7(2)(b)];
(d) an increase of an allowance which is payable in respect of constant attendance under section 5 of the Industrial Injuries and Diseases (Old Cases) Act 1975;
(e) a payment by virtue of article 14, 15, 16, 43 or 44 of the Personal Injuries (Civilians) Scheme 1983 or any analogous payment; or
(f) any payment based on need for attendance which is paid as part of a war disablement pension;
"claim" means a claim for disability working allowance;
"claimant" means a person claiming disability working allowance;
"close relative" means a parent, parent-in-law, son, son-in-law, daughter, daughter-in-law, step-parent, step-son, step-daughter, brother, sister, or the spouse of any of the preceding persons or, if that person is one of an unmarried couple, the other member of that couple;
[3"community charge benefit" means community charge benefits under Part VII of the Contributions and Benefits Act as originally enacted;]
"concessionary payment" means a payment made under arrangements made by the Secretary of State with the consent of the Treasury which is charged either to the National Insurance Fund or to a Departmental

Expenditure Vote to which payments of benefit under the Act, the Social Security Act or the Child Benefit Act 1975 are charged;

[3"the Contributions and Benefits Act" means the Social Security Contributions and Benefits Act 1992;]

[7"Crown property" means property held by Her Majesty in right of the Crown or by a government department or which is held in trust for Her Majesty for the purposes of a government department, except (in the case of an interest held by Her Majesty in right of the Crown) where the interest is under the management of the Crown Estate Commissioners;]

"date of claim" means the date on which the claimant makes, or is treated as making, a claim for disability working allowance;

"earnings" has the meaning prescribed in regulation 21 or, as the case may be, 24;

"employed earner" shall be construed in accordance with section 2(1)(a) of the Social Security Act [SSCBA, s.2(1)(a)];

"lone parent" means a person who has no partner and who is responsible for, and a member of the same household as, a child or young person;

[2"lower rate" where it relates to rates of tax has the same meaning as in the Income and Corporation Taxes Act 1988 by virtue of section 832(1) of that Act;]

[6"maternity leave" means a period during which a woman is absent from work because she is pregnant or has given birth to a child, and at the end of which she has a right to return to work either under the terms of her contract of employment or under Part III of the Employment Protection (Consolidation) Act 1978;]

"mobility allowance" means an allowance under section 37A of the Social Security Act;

"mobility supplement" means any supplement under article 26A of the Naval, Military and Air Forces etc. (Disablement and Death) Service Pensions Order 1983 including such a supplement by virtue of any other scheme or order or under Article 25A of the Personal Injuries (Civilians) Scheme 1983;

"net earnings" means such earnings as are calculated in accordance with regulation 22;

"net profit" means such profit as is calculated in accordance with regulation 25;

"occupational pension" means any pension or other periodical payment under an occupational pension scheme but does not include any discretionary payment out of a fund established for relieving hardship in particular cases;

"partner" means, where a claimant—

    (a) is a member of a married or unmarried couple, the other member of that couple,

    (b) is married polygamously to two or more members of the same household, any such member;

"payment" includes a part of a payment,

[6"personal pension scheme" has the same meaning as in section 84(1) of the Act [PSA, s.1] and, in the case of a self-employed earner, includes a scheme approved by the Inland Revenue under Chapter IV of Part XIV of the Income and Corporation Taxes Act 1988;]

"policy of life insurance" means any instrument by which the payment of money is assured on death (except death by accident only) or the happening of any contingency dependent on human life, or any instrument evidencing a contract which is subject to payment of premiums for a term dependent on human life;

[1"qualifying person" means a person in respect of whom payment has been made from the Fund [5or the Eileen Trust];]

"self-employed earner" shall be construed in accordance with section 2(1)(b) of the Social Security Act [SSCBA, s.2(1)(b)];

"single claimant" means a claimant who has neither a partner nor is a lone parent;

"Social Security Act" means the Social Security Act 1975;

"student" has the meaning prescribed in regulation 41;

[⁵"the Eileen Trust" means the charitable trust of that name established on 29th March 1993 out of funds provided by the Secretary of State for the benefit of persons eligible for payment in accordance with its provisions;]

[¹"the Fund" means moneys made available from time to time by the Secretary of State for the benefit of persons eligible for payment in accordance with the provisions of a scheme established by him on 24th April 1992 or, in Scotland, on 10th April 1992;]

[⁴"the Independent Living (Extension) Fund" means the Trust of that name established by a deed dated 25th February 1993 and made between the Secretary of State for Social Security of the one part and Robin Glover Wendt and John Fletcher Shepherd of the other part;]

"the Independent Living Fund" means the charitable trust established out of funds provided by the Secretary of State for the purpose of providing financial assistance to those persons incapacitated by or otherwise suffering from very severe disablement who are in need such assistance to enable them to live independently;

[⁴"the Independent Living (1993) Fund" means the Trust of that name established by a deed dated 25th February 1993 and made between the Secretary of State for Social Security of the one part and Robin Glover Wendt and John Fletcher Shepherd of the other part;]

[⁴"the Independent Living Funds" means the Independent Living Fund, the Independent Living (Extension) Fund and the Independent Living (1993) Fund;]

"the Macfarlane (Special Payments) Trust" means the trust of that name, established on 29th January 1990 partly out of funds provided by the Secretary of State, for the benefit of certain persons suffering from haemophilia;

"the Macfarlane (Special Payments) (No. 2) Trust" means the trust of that name, established on 3rd May 1991 partly out of funds provided by the Secretary of State, for the benefit of certain persons suffering from haemophilia and other beneficiaries;

"the Macfarlane Trust" means the charitable trust, established partly out of funds provided by the Secretary of State to the Haemophilia Society, for the relief of poverty or distress among those suffering from haemophilia;

[²"training allowance" means an allowance (whether by way of periodical grants or otherwise) payable—

(a) out of public funds by a Government department or by or on behalf of the Secretary of State, Scottish Enterprise or Highlands and Islands Enterprise;

(b) to a person for his maintenance or in respect of a member of his family; and

(c) for the period, or part of the period, during which he is following a course of training or instruction provided by, or in pursuance of arrangements made with, that department or approved by that department in relation to him or so provided or approved by or on behalf of the Secretary of State, Scottish Enterprise or Highlands and Islands Enterprise, but it does not include an allowance paid by any Government department to or in respect of a person by reason of the fact that he is following a course of full-time education, other than an allowance paid pursuant to arrangements made under section

2 of the Employment and Training Act 1973, or is training as a teacher;]

[8"voluntary organisation" means a body, other than a public or local authority, the activities of which are carried on otherwise than for profit;]

[3"water charges" means—

    (a) as respects England and Wales, any water and sewerage charges under chapter I of Part V of the Water Industry Act 1991;

    (b) as respects Scotland, any water and sewerage charges under Schedule 11 to the Local Government Finance Act 1992;]

"week" means a period of seven days beginning with Sunday;

"week of claim" means the week which includes the date of claim;

"year of assessment" has the same meaning prescribed in section 832(1) of the Income and Corporation Taxes Act 1988;

"young person" has the meaning prescribed in regulation 8.

(2) Unless the context otherwise requires, any reference in these Regulations to a numbered regulation, Part or Schedule is a reference to the regulation, Part or Schedule bearing that number in these Regulations and any reference in a regulation or Schedule to a numbered paragraph is a reference to the paragraph in that regulation or Schedule bearing that number.

AMENDMENTS

1. Income-related Benefits Schemes and Social Security (Recoupment) Amendment Regulations 1992 (S.I. 1992 No. 1101), reg. 6(2) (May 7, 1992).

2. Income-related Benefits Schemes (Miscellaneous Amendments) (No. 3) Regulations 1992 (S.I. 1992 No. 2155), reg. 2 (October 5, 1992).

3. Income-related Benefits Schemes (Miscellaneous Amendments) Regulations 1993 (S.I. 1993 No. 315), reg. 16 (April 13, 1993).

4. Social Security Benefits (Miscellaneous Amendments) (No.2) Regulations 1993 (S.I. 1993 No. 963), reg 6(2) (April 22, 1993).

5. Income-related Benefits Schemes and Social Security (Recoupment) Amendment Regulations 1993 (S.I. 1993 No. 1249), reg 5(2) (May 14, 1993).

6. Income-related Benefits Schemes (Miscellaneous Amendments) (No.4) Regulations 1993 (S.I. 1993 No. 2119), reg. 36 (October 5, 1993).

7. Income-related Benefits Schemes (Miscellaneous Amendments) (No. 4) Regulations 1994 (S.I. 1994 No. 1924), reg. 3(2) (October 4, 1994).

8. Income-related Benefits Schemes (Miscellaneous Amendments) Regulations 1995 (S.I. 1995 No. 516), reg. 2 (April 11, 1995).

DEFINITIONS

"married couple"—see 1986 Act, s.84(1) (SSCBA, s.137(1)).
"occupational pension scheme"—see 1986 Act, s.84(1) (PSA, s.1).
"unmarried couple"—see 1986 Act, s.84(1) (SSCBA, s.137(1)).

GENERAL NOTE

"*the Act.*" The amendments inserted into the Social Security Act 1986 on entitlement to disability working allowance with effect from April 7, 1992, by the Disability Living Allowance and Disability Working Allowance Act 1991 are (from July 1, 1992) consolidated into s.129 of the Contributions and Benefits Act and the Administration Act. This is the form which appears in this book. See the Preface for how cross-referencing is done.

"*date of claim.*" See the Claims and Payments Regulations, reg. 6.

"*employed earner.*" The meaning in s.2(1)(a) of the Social Security Act 1975 (SSCBA, s.2(1)(a)) is "a person who is gainfully employed in Great Britain either under a contract of service, or in an office (including elective office) with emoluments chargeable to income tax under Schedule E."

"*lone parent.*" See regs. 9 to 11 for responsibility and membership of the household.

"*occupational pension.*" An "occupational pension scheme" is defined in s.84(1) of the 1986 Act as having the same meaning as in s.66(1) of the Social Security Pensions Act 1975. This definition is not carried over into the Contributions and Benefits Act, but is now in s.1 of the Pension Schemes Act 1993.

"*partner*" See the notes to s.137(1) of the Contributions and Benefits Act for "married couple" and "unmarried couple."

"*self-employed earner*." The meaning in s.2(1)(b) of the Social Security Act 1975 (SSCBA, s.2(1)(b)) is "a person who is gainfully employed in Great Britain otherwise than in employed earner's employment (whether or not he is also employed in such employment)."

"*year of assessment*." The meaning in s.832(1) of the Income and Corporation Taxes Act 1988 is "with reference to any tax year, the year for which such tax was granted by any Act granting income tax." A tax year is the 12 months beginning with April 6 in any year.

PART II

DISABILITY TEST

Person at a disadvantage in getting a job

3.—(1) A person has a disability which puts him at a disadvantage in getting a job where—
   (a) in respect of an initial claim one or more of the paragraphs in Parts I, II or III of Schedule 1 apply to him;
   (b) In respect of a repeat claim one or more of the paragraphs in Part I or II of Schedule 1 apply to him.

(2) In this regulation and in regulation 4, the expressions "initial claim" and "repeat claim" the same meanings as in section 27B of the Act [SSAA, s.11].

GENERAL NOTE

See s.129(1)(b) and (3) of the Contributions and Benefits Act (1986 Act, s.20(6A)(b) and (6C)). A person is only to be treated as having a disability which puts him at a disadvantage in getting a job in the circumstances specified in Sched. 1. Different conditions apply to initial claims and to repeat claims. On an initial claim, the claimant's declaration that he has such a disability is conclusive (Administration Act, s.11(2); 1986 Act, s.27B(2)) subject to the exceptions in reg. 4.

The question of whether a person satisfies this condition is a "disability question" which on appeal can never be determined by a SSAT, but has to go to a DAT (Adjudication Regulations, reg. 26C).

Declaration by claimant

4. On an initial claim, a declaration by the claimant that he has a physical or mental disability which puts him at a disadvantage in getting a job is not conclusive that for the purposes of section 20(6A)(b) of the Act [SSCBA, s.129(1)(b)] he has a disability, where—
   (a) the claim itself contains contrary indications, or
   (b) the adjudication officer has before him other evidence which contradicts that declaration.

DEFINITIONS

"the Act"—see reg. 2(1).
"claim"—*ibid.*
"claimant"—*ibid.*

GENERAL NOTE

See Administration Act, s.11(2) (1986 Act, s.27B(2)). The "claim" here presumably means the information and evidence, including the self-assessments, entered on the claim form by or on behalf of the claimant. It is a matter of judgment how strong a contrary indication is required before the claimant's declaration is not treated as conclusive.

PART III

Circumstances in which a person is treated as being or as not being in Great Britain

5.—(1) A person shall be treated as being in Great Britain if, on the date of claim—
- (a) he is present and ordinarily resident in Great Britain; and
- (b) his partner, if any, is ordinarily resident in the United Kingdom; and
- (c) his earnings or the earnings of his partner, if any, derive at least in part from remunerative work in the United Kingdom; and
- (d) his earnings do not wholly derive from remunerative work outside the United Kingdom nor do the earnings of his partner, if any.

(2) A person shall be treated as not being in Great Britain during any period for which he, or his partner, is entitled to be paid disability working allowance or family credit under the law of Northern Ireland.

DEFINITIONS

    "claim"—see reg. 2(1).
    "date of claim"—*ibid.*
    "partner"—*ibid.*

GENERAL NOTE

    The requirement for the claimant to be in Great Britain at the date of claim appears in s.129(1) of the Contributions and Benefits Act (1986 Act, s.20(6A)). By s.137(2)(a) (1986 Act, s.20(12)(a)) regulations may provide for circumstances in which a person is to be treated as being or not being in Great Britain. See the notes to reg. 3 of the Family Credit (General) Regulations.

Remunerative work

6.—(1) [¹For the purposes of Part VII of the Social Security Contributions and Benefits Act 1992 as it applies to disability working allowance and subject to paragraph (3), a person shall be treated as engaged in remunerative work] where—
- (a) the work he undertakes is for not less than 16 hours per week;
- (b) the work is done for payment or in expectation of payment; and
- (c) he is employed at the date of claim and satisfies the requirements of paragraph (5).

(2) A person who does not satisfy all the requirements of sub-paragraphs (a) to (c) of paragraph (1) shall not be treated as engaged [¹. . .] in remunerative work.

[³(3) A person who otherwise satisfies all the requirements of paragraph (1) shall not be treated as engaged in remunerative work insofar as—
- (a) he is engaged by a charitable or voluntary organisation or is a volunteer, where the only payment received by him or due to be paid to him is a payment which is to be disregarded under regulation 27(2) and paragraph 2 of Schedule 3 (sums to be disregarded in the calculation of income other than earnings);
- (b) he is engaged in caring for a person in respect of whom he receives payments to which paragraph 24 of Schedule 3 refers; or
- (c) he is engaged on a scheme for which a training allowance is being paid.]

(4) [⁴Subject to paragraph (4A),] in determining for the purposes of sub-paragraph (a) of paragraph (1) whether a person has undertaken work of not less than 16 hours per week—

  (a) there shall be included in the calculation any time allowed—
    (i) for meals or refreshment; or
    (ii) for visits to a hospital, clinic or other establishment for the purpose only of treating or monitoring the person's disability,

  but only where the person is, or expects to be, paid earnings in respect of that time; and

  (b) where at the date of claim the claimant has within the previous 5 weeks—
    (i) started a new job;
    (ii) resumed work after a break of at least 13 weeks; or
    (iii) changed his hours,

  the hours worked shall be calculated by reference to the number of hours, or where these are expected to fluctuate, the average number of hours, which he is expected to work in a week; or

  (c) where none of heads (i) to (iii) of [¹this paragraph] apply, and
    (i) a recognised cycle of working has been established at the date of claim, the hours worked shall be calculated by reference to the average number of hours worked in a week over the period of one complete cycle (including where the cycle involves periods in which the person does not work, those periods, but disregarding any other absences); or
    (ii) no recognised cycle of working has been established at that date, the hours worked shall be calculated by reference to the average number of hours worked over the 5 weeks immediately preceding the week in which the claim is made, or such other length of time preceding that week as may, in the particular case, enable the person's weekly average hours of work to be determined more accurately.

[⁴(4A) Where for the purpose of paragraph (4)(c)(i), a person's recognised cycle of work at a school, other educational establishment or other place of employment is one year and includes periods of school holidays or similar vacations during which he does not work, those periods and any other periods not forming part of such holidays or vacations during which he is not required to work shall be disregarded in establishing the average hours for which he is engaged in work.]

(5) Subject to paragraph (6), the requirements of this paragraph are that the person—

  (a) worked not less than 16 hours in either—
    (i) the week of claim; or
    (ii) either of the two weeks immediately preceding the week of claim; or
  (b) is expected by his employer to work [¹or, where he is a self-employed earner he expects to work,] not less than 16 hours in the week next following the week of claim; or
  (c) cannot satisfy the requirements of sub-paragraph (a) or (b) above at the date of claim because he is or will be absent from work by reason of a recognised, customary or other holiday but he is expected by his employer to work [¹or, where he is a self-employed earner he expects to work,] not less than 16 hours in the week following his return to work, and for the purposes of calculating the number of hours worked, sub-paragraph (a) of paragraph (4) shall apply to this paragraph as it applies to sub-paragraph (a) of paragraph (1).

[²(6) For the purposes of paragraph (5)—
  (a) work which a person does only qualifies if—
    (i) it is the work which he normally does, and

    (ii) it is likely to last for a period of 5 weeks or more beginning with the week in which the claim is made; and

  (b) a person shall be treated as not on a recognised, customary or other holiday on any day on which the person is on maternity leave or is absent from work because he is ill.]

[[1](7) Where a person is treated as engaged in remunerative work in accordance with the above paragraphs, he shall also be treated as normally engaged in remunerative work.]

[[3](8) [[4]...]]

AMENDMENTS

  1. Income-related Benefits Schemes (Miscellaneous Amendments) (No. 3) Regulations 1992 (S.I. 1992 No. 2155), Sched., para. 2 (October 5, 1992).

  2. Income-related Benefits Schemes (Miscellaneous Amendments) (No. 4) Regulations 1993 (S.I. 1993 No. 2119), reg. 37 (October 5, 1993).

  3. Income-related Benefits Schemes (Miscellaneous Amendments) (No. 5) Regulations 1994 (S.I. 1994 No. 2139), reg. 2 (October 4, 1994).

  4. Income-related Benefits Schemes (Miscellaneous Amendments) Regulations 1995 (S.I. 1995 No. 516), reg. 3 (April 11, 1995).

DEFINITIONS

  "the Act"—see reg. 2(1).
  "claim" —*ibid.*
  "claimant"—*ibid.*
  "maternity leave"—*ibid.*
  "self-employed earner"—*ibid.*
  "voluntary organisation"—*ibid.*
  "week"—*ibid.*
  "week of claim"—*ibid.*

GENERAL NOTE

  See the notes to reg. 4 of the Family Credit (General) Regulations. The October 1992 amendments bring the form of reg. 6 into line with that of reg. 4.

  Para. (3)(c) was introduced to reverse the effect of *CDWA 1/1992* which had decided that a claimant who was a trainee on a YTS scheme was in remunerative work. At that time there was no provision in the Disability Working Allowance Regulations (or the Family Credit Regulations) corresponding to reg. 6(d) of the Income Support Regulations. For family credit, now see reg. 4(3)(c) of the Family Credit Regulations.

Income-related benefits

  7. For the purposes of subsection (6E) of section 20 of the Act [SSCBA, s.129(4)] the prescribed circumstances are that the person's weekly applicable amount included a higher pensioner or disability premium in respect of him, determined—

  (a) [[1]in the case of] income support, in accordance with paragraphs 10(1)(b) [[3], 10(2)(b)] or 11, and 12 of Part III of Schedule 2 to the Income Support (General) Regulations 1987 (applicable amounts);

  (b) in the case of housing benefit, in accordance with paragraphs 10(1)(b) [[3], 10(2)(b)] or 11, and 12 of Part III of Schedule 2 to the Housing Benefit (General) Regulations 1987 (applicable amounts);

  (c) in the case of community charge benefit, in accordance with paragraphs 11 or 12, and 13 of Part III of Schedule 1 to the Community Charge Benefits (General) Regulations 1989 (applicable amounts); [[2]...]

  [[2](ca) in the case of council tax benefit, in accordance with paragraphs [[3]11(1)(b), 11(2)(b)] or 12, and 13 of Part III of Schedule 1 to the Council Tax Benefit (General) Regulations 1992; or]

(d) in accordance with any provision equivalent to one of those specified in [¹paragraphs [²(a) to (ca)]] above and having effect in Northern Ireland.

AMENDMENTS

1. Income-related Benefits Schemes (Miscellaneous Amendments) (No. 3) Regulations 1992 (S.I. 1992 No. 2155), Sched., para. 3 (October 5, 1992).
2. Income-related Benefits Schemes (Miscellaneous Amendments) Regulations 1993 (S.I. 1993 No. 315), Sched., para. 12 (April 1, 1993).
3. Income-related Benefits Schemes (Miscellaneous Amendments) Regulations 1995 (S.I. 1995 No. 516), reg. 4 (April 11, 1995).

DEFINITION

"the Act"—see reg. 2(1).

GENERAL NOTE

See the notes to s. 129 of the Contributions and Benefits Act.

[¹Definition of "training for work"

7A. For the purposes of section 129(2A) of the Contributions and Benefits Act (which provides that a period of training for work may count towards the period of qualification for disability working allowance) "training for work" also includes any training received on a course which a person attends for 16 hours or more a week, the primary purpose of which is the teaching of occupational or vocational skills.]

AMENDMENT

1. Disability Working Allowance and Income Support (General) Amendment Regulations 1995 (S.I. 1995 No. 482), reg. 2 (April 13, 1995).

GENERAL NOTE

See the notes to s. 129(2A) of the Contributions and Benefits Act.

[¹Days to be disregarded

7B.—(1) For the purposes of section 129(2B)(c) of the Contributions and Benefits Act (days to be disregarded in determining a period of training for work) there shall be disregarded any day on which the claimant was—
   (a) on holiday;
   (b) attending court as a justice of the peace, a party to any proceedings, a witness or a juror;
   (c) suffering from some disease or bodily or mental disablement as a result of which he was unable to attend training for work, or his attendance would have put at risk the health of other persons;
   (d) unable to participate in training for work because—
      (i) he was looking after a child because the person who usually looked after that child was unable to do so;
      (ii) he was looking after a member of his family who was ill;
      (iii) he was required to deal with some domestic emergency; or
      (iv) he was arranging or attending the funeral of his partner or a relative; or

(e) authorised by the training provider to be absent from training for work.

(2) For the purposes of paragraph (1)(d)(iv), "relative" means close relative, grandparent, grandchild, uncle, aunt, nephew or niece.]

AMENDMENT

1. Disability Working Allowance and Income Support (General) Amendment Regulations 1995 (S.I. 1995 No. 482), reg. 2 (April 13, 1995).

DEFINITION

"child"—see SSCBA, s. 137(1).
"claimant"—see reg. 2(1).
"close relative"—*ibid.*
"partner"—*ibid.*

GENERAL NOTE

See the notes to s. 129(2B) of the Contributions and Benefits Act.

PART IV

MEMBERSHIP OF A FAMILY

Persons of a prescribed description

8.—(1) Subject to paragraph (2), a person of a prescribed description for the purposes of section 20(11) of the Act [SSCBA, s.137(1)] (meaning of the family) as it applies to disability working allowance is a person aged 16 or over but under 19 who is receiving full-time education within section 2(1)(b) of the Child Benefit Act 1975 (meaning of child), and in these Regulations such a person is referred to as "a young person".

(2) Paragraph (1) shall not apply to a person—

(a) who is entitled to income support or would, but for section 20(9) of the Act [SSCBA, s.134(2)] (provision against dual entitlement of members of family), be so entitled;

(b) who is receiving advanced education within the meaning of regulation 1(2) of the Child Benefit (General) Regulations 1976; or

(c) who has ceased to receive full-time education but is to continue to be treated as a child by virtue of regulation 7 of the Child Benefit (General) Regulations 1976.

DEFINITION

"the Act"—see reg. 2(1).

GENERAL NOTE

See the notes to reg. 6 of the Family Credit (General) Regulations.

Circumstances in which a person is to be treated as responsible or not responsible for another

9.—(1) Subject to the following provisions of this regulation, a person shall be treated as responsible for a child or young person who is normally living with him.

(2) Where a child or young person spends equal amounts of time in different households, or where there is a question as to which household he is living in, the child or young person shall be treated for the purposes of paragraph (1) as normally living with—

    (a) the person who is receiving child benefit in respect of him; or

    (b) if there is no such person—

        (i) where only one claim for child benefit has been made in respect of him, the person who made that claim, or

        (ii) in any other case the person who has the primary responsibility for him.

(3) For the purposes of these Regulations a child or young person shall be treated as the responsibility of only one person during the period of an award and any person other than the one treated as responsible for the child or young person under the foregoing paragraphs shall be treated as not so responsible.

DEFINITIONS

    "child"—see 1986 Act, s.20(11) (SSCBA, s.137(1)).
    "young person"—see reg. 2(1), reg. 8.

GENERAL NOTE

    See the notes to reg. 7 of the Family Credit (General) Regulations.

Membership of the same household

    10.—(1) Except in a case to which paragraph (2) applies, where a claimant or any partner is treated as responsible for a child or young person by virtue of regulation 9 (circumstances where a person is treated as responsible or not responsible for another), that child or young person and any child of that child or young person shall be treated as a member of the claimant's household.

    (2) A child or young person shall not be treated as a member of the claimant's household in any case where the child or young person—

    (a) is a patient or in residential accommodation on account of physical or mental handicap or physical or mental illness and has been so accommodated for the 12 weeks immediately before the date of claim and is no longer in regular contact with the claimant or any member of the claimant's household; or

    (b) is in a foster placement, or in Scotland boarded out, with the claimant or his partner prior to adoption; or

    (c) is in a foster placement, or in Scotland boarded out, with the claimant or his partner under a relevant enactment; or

    (d) has been placed for adoption with the claimant or his partner pursuant to a decision under the Adoption Agencies Regulations 1983 or the Adoption Agencies (Scotland) Regulations 1984; or

    (e) is detained in custody under a sentence imposed by a court.

    (3) In this regulation—

    (a) "patient" means a person (other than a person who is serving a sentence imposed by a court in a prison or youth custody institution) who is regarded as receiving free in-patient treatment within the meaning of the Social Security (Hospital In-Patients) Regulations 1975;

    (b) "relevant enactment" means the Army Act 1955, the Air Force Act 1955, the Naval Discipline Act 1957, the Adoption Act 1958, the Matrimonial Proceedings (Children) Act 1958, the Social Work (Scotland) Act 1968, the Family Law Reform Act 1969, the Children and Young Persons Act 1969, the Matrimonial Causes Act 1973, the Guardianship Act 1973, the Children Act 1975, the Adoption Act 1976, the Domestic Proceedings and Magistrates' Courts Act 1978, the Adoption (Scotland) Act 1978, the Child Care Act 1980 and the Children Act 1989;

(c) "residential accommodation" means accommodation for a person whose stay in the accommodation has become other than temporary which is provided under—

    (i) sections 21 to 24 and 26 of the National Assistance Act 1948 (provision of accommodation); or

    (ii) section 21(1) of, and paragraph 1 or 2 of Schedule 8 to, the National Health Service Act 1977 (prevention, care and after-care) or, in Scotland, for the purposes of section 27 of the National Health Services (Scotland) Act 1947 (prevention of illness and after-care) or under section 59 of the Social Work (Scotland) Act 1968 (provision of residential and other establishments) or under section 7 of the Mental Health (Scotland) Act 1984 (functions of local authorities).

"child"—see 1986 Act, s.20(11) (SSCBA, s.137(1)).
"claimant"—see reg. 2(1).
"date of claim"—*ibid.*
"partner"—*ibid.*
"young person"—*ibid.*, reg. 8.

GENERAL NOTE

See the notes to reg. 8 of the Family Credit (General) Regulations. Reg. 10 has not been up-dated to take account of the implementation of the Children Act 1989.

Circumstances in which a person is to be treated as being no longer a member of the same household

11.—[[1](1) Subject to the following provisions of this regulation, where the claimant and any partner of his are living apart from each other they shall be treated as members of the same household unless they do not intend to resume living together.]

(2) Where one of the members of a married or unmarried couple is a hospital patient or detained in custody he shall not be treated, on this account, as ceasing to be a member of the same household as his partner—

(a) unless he has been a patient in a hospital for 52 weeks or more; or

(b) unless he is a patient detained in a hospital provided under section 4 of the National Health Service Act 1977 (special hospitals) or section 90(1) of the Mental Health (Scotland) Act 1984 (provision of hospitals for patients requiring special security); or

(c) unless he is detained in custody whilst serving a sentence of 52 weeks or more imposed by a court,

but shall be treated as not being a member of the same household as his partner wherever the conditions in sub-paragraphs (a), (b) or (c) are fulfilled.

(3) In this regulation "patient" has the same meaning as in regulation 10(3)(a) (membership of the same household).

AMENDMENT

1. Income-related Benefits Schemes (Miscellanous Amendments) (No. 4) Regulations 1993 (S.I. 1993 No. 2119), reg. 38 (October 5, 1993).

DEFINITIONS

"partner"—see reg. 2(1).

"married couple"—see 1986 Act, s.20(11) (SSCBA, s.137(1)).
"unmarried couple"—*ibid.*

GENERAL NOTE

See the notes to reg. 9 of the Family Credit (General) Regulations.

PART V

INCOME AND CAPITAL

Chapter I

General

Calculation of income and capital of members of claimant's family and of a polygamous marriage

12.—(1) The income and capital of a claimant's partner and, subject to regulation 30 (modifications in respect of children and young persons), the income of a child or young person, which by virtue of section 22(5) of the Act [SSCBA, s.136(1)] is to be treated as income and capital of the claimant, shall be calculated or estimated in accordance with the following provisions of this Part in like manner as for the claimant; and any reference to the "claimant" shall, except where the context otherwise requires, be construed, for the purposes of this Part, as if it were a reference to his partner or that child or young person.

(2) Where a claimant or the partner of a claimant is married polygamously to two or more members of the same household—

(a) the claimant shall be treated as possessing capital and income belonging to each such member and the income of any child or young person who is one of that member's family; and

(b) the income and capital of that member or, as the case may be, the income of that child or young person shall be calculated in accordance with the following provisions of this Part in like manner as for the claimant or, as the case may be, as for any child or young person who is a member of his family.

DEFINITIONS

"the Act"—see reg. 2(1).
"child"—see 1986 Act, s.20(11) (SSCBA, s.137(1)).
"claimant"—see reg. 2(1).
"family"—see 1986 Act, s.20(11) (SSCBA, s.137(1)).
"partner"—see reg. 2(1).
"young person"—*ibid.*, reg. 8.

GENERAL NOTE

See the notes to reg. 10 of the Family Credit (General) Regulations.

Calculation of income and capital of students

13. The provisions of Chapters II to VI of this Part (income and capital) shall have effect in relation to students and their partners subject to the modifications set out in Chapter VII thereof (students).

DEFINITIONS

"partner"—see reg. 2(1).
"student"—*ibid.*, reg. 41.

Rounding of fractions

14. Where any calculation under this Part results in a fraction of a penny that fraction shall, if it would be to the claimant's advantage, be treated as a penny, otherwise it shall be disregarded.

Chapter II

Normal Weekly Income

Calculation of income on a weekly basis

15.—(1) For the purposes of section 20(6A) of the Act [SSCBA, s.129(1)] (conditions of entitlement to disability working allowance), the income of a claimant shall be calculated on a weekly basis—
  (a) by ascertaining in accordance with this Chapter and Chapter V of this Part (other income) the amount of his normal weekly income; [¹. . .]
  (b) by adding to that amount the weekly income calculated under regulation 40 (calculation of tariff income from capital) [and
[¹(c) by then deducting any relevant child care charges to which regulation 15A (treatment of child care charges) applies from any earnings which form part of the normal weekly income, up to a maximum deduction in respect of the claimant's family of £40 per week.]
  (2) For the purposes of paragraph (1) "income" includes capital treated as income under regulation 28 (capital treated as income) and income which a claimant is treated as possessing under regulation 29 (notional income).

AMENDMENT

1. Income-related Benefits Schemes (Miscellaneous Amendments) (No. 4) Regulations 1994 (S.I. 1994 No. 1924), reg. 3(3) (October 4, 1994).

DEFINITIONS

"the Act"—see reg. 2(1).
"claimant"—*ibid.*, reg. 12(1).
"earnings"—see reg. 2(1).
"family"—see 1986 Act, s.20(11) (SSCBA, s.137(1)).
"relevant child care charges"—see reg. 15A.

GENERAL NOTE

See the notes to reg. 13 of the Family Credit (General) Regulations.

[¹Treatment of child care charges

15A.—(1) This regulation applies where a claimant is incurring relevant child care charges and—
  (a) is a lone parent and is engaged in remunerative work;
  (b) is a member of a couple both of whom are engaged in remunerative work; or
  (c) is a member of a couple where one member is engaged in remunerative work and the other member is incapacitated.

(2) In this regulation—

"local authority" means, in relation to England and Wales, the council of a county or district, a metropolitan district, a London Borough, the Common Council of the City of London or the Council of the Isles of Scilly or, in relation to Scotland, a regional, islands or district council;

"relevant child care charges" means the charges paid by the claimant for care provided for any child of the claimant's family who is under the age of 11 years, other than charges paid in respect of the child's compulsory education, [²or charges paid by a claimant to a partner or by a partner to a claimant in respect of any child for whom either or any of them is responsible in accordance with regulation 9 (circumstances in which a person is to be treated as responsible or not responsible for another),] where the care is provided—

(a) by persons registered under section 71 of the Children Act 1989 (registration of child minders and persons providing day care for young children);

(b) for children aged 8 and over but under 11, out of school hours, by a school on school premises or by a local authority; or

(c) by a child care scheme operating on Crown property where registration under section 71 of the Children Act 1989 is not required, [²or

(d) in schools or establishments which are exempted from registration under section 71 of the Children Act 1989 by virtue of section 71(16) of and paragraph 3 or 4 of Schedule 9 to that Act,]

and shall be calculated on a weekly basis in accordance with paragraphs (3) to (6);

"school term-time" means the school term-time applicable to the child for whom care is provided.

[²(2A) The age of a child referred to in paragraph (2) shall be determined by reference to the age of the child at the date on which the period under section 129(6) of the Contributions and Benefits Act (period of award) begins.]

(3) Subject to paragraphs (4) to (6), relevant child care charges shall be calculated in accordance with the formula—

$$\frac{X + Y}{52}$$

where—

X is the average weekly charge paid for child care in the most recent 4 complete weeks which fall in school term-time in respect of the child or children concerned, multiplied by 39; and

Y is the average weekly charge paid for child care in the most recent 2 complete weeks which fall out of school term-time in respect of that child or those children, multiplied by 13.

(4) Subject to paragraph (5), where child care charges are being incurred in respect of a child who does not yet attend school, the relevant child care charges shall mean the average weekly charge paid for care provided in respect of that child in the most recent 4 complete weeks.

(5) Where in any case the charges in respect of child care are paid monthly, the average weekly charge for the purposes of paragraph (3) shall be established—

(a) where the charges are for a fixed monthly amount, by multiplying that amount by 12 and dividing the product by 52;

(b) where the charges are for variable monthly amounts, by aggregating the charges for the previous 12 months and dividing the total by 52.

(6) In a case where there is no information or insufficient information for establishing the average weekly charge paid for child care in accordance with

paragraphs (3) to (5), the average weekly charge for care shall be estimated in accordance with information provided by the child minder or person providing the care or, if such information is not available, in accordance with information provided by the claimant.

(7) For the purposes of paragraph (1)(c) the other member of a couple is incapacitated where—

(a) either council tax benefit or housing benefit is payable under Part VII of the Contributions and Benefits Act to the other member or his partner and the applicable amount of the person entitled to the benefit includes—

   (i) a disability premium; or

   (ii) a higher pensioner premium by virtue of the satisfaction of—

     (aa) in the case of council tax benefit, paragraph 11(2)(b) of Schedule 1 to the Council Tax Benefit (General) Regulations 1992;

     (bb) in the case of housing benefit, paragraph 10(2)(b) of Schedule 2 to the Housing Benefit (General) Regulations 1987,

on account of the other member's incapacity; [²or either regulation 13A(1)(c) of the Council Tax Benefit (General) Regulations 1992 (treatment of child care charges) or, as the case may be, regulation 21A(1)(c) of the Housing Benefit (General) Regulations 1987 (treatment of child care charges) applies in that person's case;]

(b) there is payable in respect of him one or more of the following pensions or allowances—

   (i) invalidity pension under section 33, 40 or 41 of the Contributions and Benefits Act 1992;

   (ii) attendance allowance under section 64 of that Act;

   (iii) severe disablement allowance under section 68 of that Act;

   (iv) disability living allowance under section 71 of that Act;

   (v) increase of disablement pension under section 104 of that Act;

   (vi) a pension increase under a war pension scheme or an industrial injuries scheme which is analogous to an allowance or increase of disablement pension under head (ii), (iv) or (v) above;

(c) a pension or allowance to which head (ii), (iv), (v) or (vi) of sub-paragraph (b) above refers was payable on account of his incapacity but has ceased to be payable in consequence of his becoming a patient within the meaning of regulation 10(3)(a) (membership of the same household);

(d) sub-paragraph (b) or (c) above would apply to him if the legislative provisions referred to in those sub-paragraphs were provisions under any corresponding enactment having effect in Northern Ireland; or

(e) he has an invalid carriage or other vehicle provided to him by the Secretary of State under section 5(2)(a) of and Schedule 2 to the National Health Service Act 1977 or under section 46 of the National Health Service (Scotland) Act 1978 or provided by the Department of Health and Social Services for Northern Ireland under Article 30(1) of the Health and Personal Social Services (Northern Ireland) Order 1972.]

AMENDMENTS

1. Income-related Benefits Schemes (Miscellaneous Amendments) (No. 4) Regulations 1994 (S.I. 1994 No. 1924), reg. 3(4) (October 4, 1994).
2. Income-related Benefits Schemes (Miscellaneous Amendments) Regulations 1995 (S.I. 1995 No. 516), reg. 5 (April 11, 1995).

DEFINITIONS

"claimant"—see reg. 2(1).
"Contributions and Benefits Act"—*ibid.*
"Crown property"—*ibid.*

"lone parent"—*ibid.*
"partner"—*ibid.*

<small>GENERAL NOTE</small>

See the notes to reg. 13A of the Family Credit (General) Regulations.

Normal weekly earnings of employed earners

16.—(1) Subject to regulation 19, where the claimant's income consists of earnings from employment as an employed earner, his normal weekly earnings shall be determined by reference to his earnings from that employment in accordance with the following provisions of this regulation.

(2) Subject to paragraph (7), where the claimant is paid weekly, his normal weekly earnings shall be determined by reference to his earnings over 5 consecutive weeks in the 6 weeks immediately preceding the week in which the date of claims falls.

(3) Subject to paragraph (7), where at the date of claim there is a trade dispute or period of short-time working at the claimant's place of employment, then his normal weekly earnings shall be determined by reference to his earnings over the 5 weeks immediately preceding the start of that dispute or period of short-time working.

(4) Subject to paragraph (7), where the claimant is paid monthly, his normal weekly earnings shall be determined by reference to his earnings—
- (a) over a period of 2 months immediately preceding the week in which the date of claim falls; or
- (b) where, at the date of claim, there is a trade dispute or a period of short-time working at his place of employment, over a period of 2 months immediately preceding the date of the start of that dispute or period of short-time working.

(5) Subject to paragraph (7), whether or not paragraph (2), (3) or (4) applies, where a claimant's earnings fluctuate or are not likely to represent his weekly earnings, his normal weekly earnings shall be determined by reference to his weekly earnings over such other period preceding the week in which the date of claim falls as may, in any particular case, enable his normal weekly earnings to be determined more accurately.

(6) Where a claimant's earnings include a bonus or commission which is paid within 52 weeks preceding the week in which the date of claim falls, and the bonus or commission is paid separately or relates to a period longer than a period relating to the other earnings with which it is paid, his normal weekly earnings shall be treated as including an amount calculated in accordance with regulation 23 (calculation of bonus or commission).

(7) Where at the date of claim—
- (a) the claimant—
  - (i) has been in his employment; or
  - (ii) after a continuous period of interruption exceeding 13 weeks, has resumed his employment; or
  - (iii) has changed the number of hours for which he is contracted to work; and
- (b) the period of his employment or the period since he resumed his employment or the period since the change in the number of hours took place, as the case may be, is less than 9 weeks,

his normal weekly earnings shall be determined in accordance with paragraph (8).

(8) In a case to which this paragraph applies, the Secretary of State shall require the claimant's employer to furnish an estimate of the claimant's average likely earnings for the period for which he will normally be paid and the claim-

ant's normal weekly earnings shall be determined by reference to that estimate.

(9) For the purposes of this regulation—

(a) the claimant's earnings shall be calculated in accordance with Chapter III of this Part;

(b) "a period of short-time working" means a continuous period not exceeding 13 weeks during which the claimant is not required by his employer to be available to work the full number of hours normal in his case under the terms of his employment.

DEFINITIONS

"claim"—see reg. 2(1).
"claimant"—*ibid.*, reg. 12(1).
"earnings"—see reg. 2(1), reg. 21.
"employed earner" see reg. 2(1).
"trade dispute"—see 1986 Act, s.84(1).
"week"—see reg. 2(1).

GENERAL NOTE

Although the test of hours of remunerative work under reg. 6 is the same as the April 1992 family credit test, the method of calculation of earnings for employees is not in line with the April 1992 form of reg. 14 of the Family Credit (General) Regulations. Instead, a slightly refined version of the pre-April 1992 family credit test is used (for which, see p. 307 of the 1991 edition).

Paras. (2) to (4) supply the general rules for defining the period over which the earnings of weekly paid and monthly paid employees are to be calculated. There appears to be no provision for those paid regularly at different intervals. Para. (5) provides a general power to use a different period to produce a more accurate figure. Para. (6) deals with bonuses and commission. Paras. (7) and (8) contain special rules where the person has recently started work or changed contractual hours. Reg. 19 allows certain weeks within the period fixed under reg. 16 to be discarded from the calculation.

Regs. 21 to 23 define what count as earnings.

Paragraphs (2) and (3)

Normally, for weekly paid employees, earnings are to be calculated over five consecutive weeks (*i.e.* Sunday to Saturday) in the six weeks immediately before the week of claim. The effect is that either the first or the last of the six weeks can be discarded, presumably whichever is more favourable to the claimant. A different period can be taken under the conditions of para. (5) and weeks within the period discarded under reg. 19.

If, at the date of claim, there is a trade dispute or a period of short-time working (defined in para. (9)) at the person's place of employment, the six weeks immediately before the beginning of that interruption must be taken (para. (3)). It is not necessary that there should be a stoppage of work, merely a trade dispute (presumably as defined in s.27 of the Contributions and Benefits Act). Thus a work-to-rule or overtime ban at the person's own place of employment (also defined in s.27) will affect the choice of period. Para. (3) is only triggered by the circumstances at the date of claim. If earnings in the weeks which would otherwise form the period of assessment are affected by a dispute or period of short-time working which has finished by the date of claim, then para. (5) or (7) or reg. 19 might need consideration.

Paragraph (4)

The period of assessment for the monthly paid is set in the same way as under paras. (2) and (3), except that the standard period is the two months immediately preceding the week of claim.

Paragraph (5)

Where a person's earnings fluctuate or are not likely to represent his weekly earnings a different period from that produced by paras. (2) to (4) may be taken. Para. (5) may cover employees paid otherwise than by the week or month, but not, it seems, if there is absolutely regular payment. The equivalent family credit provision had caused considerable difficulties and its simplification in April 1992 was overdue. Those difficulties remain for disability working allowance.

The two conditions are alternative. On fluctuation, the immediate problem is over what period fluctuation is to be considered. Arguably, if there is no fluctuation within the period fixed by paras. (2) to (4) there is no warrant for choosing another period. On the second condition, there seems to be a circular process required. In order to determine that earnings in the period fixed by paras. (2) to (4) are not likely to represent the person's weekly earnings, a standard of normality or usualness has to be set up, but no basis is provided for that standard. Only when the condition is satisfied can the authorities look at a different period for a more accurate figure. However, despite the logical difficulties, a similar process was approved for family income supplement purposes by the Court of Appeal in *Lowe v. Adjudication Officer* [1985] 2 All E.R. 903 (*R(FIS) 2/85*) and the Commissioner in *R(FIS) 1/87*. In *Lowe* the claimant was on strike. In *R(FIS) 1/87* the claimant was on maternity leave. It was found that during the periods affected by these events, the claimant, if asked what her/his normal earnings were, would have replied that normally they were X, but at present they were less because of the strike/maternity leave. Perhaps this is the only sort of test which can be used, which will now have to be applied in a context of a 26 week award, rather than the 52 weeks of family income supplement. There is a very large element of judgment involved.

Once one of the conditions is satisfied, another period should be chosen only if it will enable normal weekly earnings to be more accurately determined. Thus there is a burden on the AO to show that some other period will produce a more accurate figure than the basic five weeks or two months (see *R(FIS) 1/81* and *R(FIS) 2/83*).

Paragraph (6)

There is a special rule for payments of bonus or commission paid separately from other earnings or in relation to different periods. See regs. 19(a)(ii) and 23.

Paragraphs (7) and (8)

There is a special rule where a person has been in his employment for less than nine weeks. Then the earnings figure is to be based on estimates from the employer of average likely earnings. The same rule applies to resumption of employment after an interruption of more than 13 weeks or to a change in contractual hours. What counts as an interruption is far from clear. It clearly does not require the contract of employment to be terminated. Could it cover any period of non-working, such as absences for sickness, pregnancy, personal reasons, strikes, holidays, etc.?

Normal weekly earnings of self-employed earners

17.—(1) Subject to regulation 19 (periods to be disregarded), where a claimant's income consists of earnings from employment as a self-employed earner, his normal weekly earnings shall be determined, subject to paragraph (2), by reference to his weekly earnings from that employment—
- (a) except where sub-paragraph (b) applies, over a period of 26 weeks immediately preceding the week in which the date of claim falls; or
- (b) where the claimant provides in respect of the employment a profit and loss account and, where appropriate, a trading account or a balance sheet or both, and the profit and loss account is in respect of a period of at least 6 months but not exceeding 15 months and that period terminates within the 12 months preceding the date of claim, over that period; or
- (c) over such other period of weeks ['or months] preceding the week in which the date of claims falls as may, in any particular case, enable his normal weekly earnings to be determined more accurately.

(2) In paragraph (1)(b)—
- (a) "balance sheet" means a statement of the financial position of the employment disclosing its assets, liabilities and capital at the end of the period in question;
- (b) "profit and loss account" means a financial statement showing the net profit or loss of the employment for the period in question; and
- (c) "trading account" means a financial statement showing the revenue from sales, the cost of those sales and the gross profit arising during the period in question.

(3) Subject to regulation 19, where the claimant has been in employment as a self-employed earner for less than the period specified in paragraph (1)(*a*) his normal weekly earnings shall be determined by reference to an estimate of his likely weekly earnings over the 26 weeks next following the date of claim.

(4) For the purposes of this regulation, the claimant's earnings shall be calculated in accordance with Chapter IV of this Part.

AMENDMENT

1. Income-related Benefits Schemes (Miscellaneous Amendments) (No. 5) Regulations 1994 (S.I. 1994 No. 2139), reg. 3 (October 4, 1994.)

DEFINITIONS

"claim"—see reg. 2(1).
"claimant"—*ibid.*, reg. 8.
"earnings"—see reg. 2(1), reg. 24.
"self-employed earner"—see reg. 2(1).
"week"—*ibid.*

GENERAL NOTE

See the notes to reg. 15 of the Family Credit (General) Regulations, although para. (3) is a simplification of reg. 15(2).

Normal weekly income other than earnings

18.—(1) Subject to [¹paragraphs (2) and (2A)], [²where a claimant's normal weekly income does not consist of earnings, or includes income that does not consist of earnings, that income] shall be determined by reference to his weekly income over a period of 26 weeks immediately preceding the week in which the date of claim falls or over such period immediately preceding that week as may, in any particular case, enable his normal weekly income to be determined more accurately.

(2) Where a claimant's income consists of any payments made by a person, whether under a court order or not, for the maintenance of any member of [¹the claimant's family], and those payments are made or due to be made at regular intervals, his normal weekly income shall [¹, except where paragraph (2A) applies,] be determined—

(a) if before the date of claim those payments are made at regular intervals [²and of regular amounts], by reference to the normal weekly amount;

(b) if they are not so made, by reference to the average of such payments received in the 13 weeks immediately preceding the week in which the date of claim falls.

[¹(2A) Where a claimant's income consists of child support maintenance, his normal weekly income in respect of that maintenance shall be determined—

(a) if before the date of claim those maintenance payments are made at regular intervals [²and of regular amounts], by reference to the normal weekly amount;

(b) if they are not so made, [²except in a case to which sub-paragraph (c) applies], by reference to the average of such payments received in the 13 weeks immediately preceding the week in which the date of claim falls,

[²(c) where the maintenance assessment has been notified to the claimant under regulation 10 of the Child Support (Maintenance Assessment Procedure) Regulations 1992 during the 13 weeks immediately preceding the week of claim, by reference to the average of such payments, calculated on a weekly basis, received in the interim period,]

and if the resulting sum exceeds the amount of child support maintenance due under the maintenance assessment, the normal weekly income shall be the amount due under the maintenance assessment.]

(3) For the purposes of this regulation, income other than earnings shall be calculated in accordance with Chapter V of this Part.

[¹(4) In this regulation—

    (a) "child support maintenance" means such periodical payments as are referred to in section 3(6) of the Child Support Act 1991;

    (b) "maintenance assessment" has the same meaning as in the Child Support Act 1991 by virtue of section 54 of that Act];

    [²(c) "the interim period" means the week in which the date of notification of the maintenance assessment falls and the subsequent period up to and including the week immediately preceding the week of claim.]

AMENDMENTS

1. Income-related Benefits Schemes (Miscellaneous Amendments) Regulations 1993 (S.I. 1993 No. 315), reg. 17 (April 13, 1993).

2. Income-related Benefits Schemes (Miscellaneous Amendments) (No. 4) Regulations 1993 (S.I. 1993 No. 2119), reg. 39 (October 5, 1993).

DEFINITIONS

"claim"—see reg. 2(1).
"claimant"—*ibid.*, reg. 12(1).
"date of claim"—see reg. 2(1).
"earnings"—*ibid.*, regs. 21 and 24.
"family"—see 1986 Act, s.20(11) (SSCBA, s.137(1)).
"payment"—see reg. 2(1).
"week"—*ibid.*

GENERAL NOTE

See the notes to reg. 16 of the Family Credit (General) Regulations.

Periods to be disregarded

19. For the purposes of ascertaining a claimant's normal weekly earnings there shall be disregarded—

    (a) for the purposes of regulation 16(1) (normal weekly earnings of employed earners), in the case of an employed earner—

        (i) any period in the assessment period where the earnings of the claimant are irregular or unusual;

        (ii) any period in the assessment period in which a bonus or commission to which regulation 16(6) applies is paid where that bonus or commission is in respect of a period longer than the period relating to the other earnings with which it is paid.

    (b) in the case of a self-employed earner, any week or period of weeks in the assessment period during which no activities have been carried out for the purposes of the business,

and his normal weekly earnings shall be determined by reference to his weekly earnings in the remainder of that period and in such a case any reference in these Regulations to a claimant's assessment period shall be construed as a reference to the latter period.

DEFINITIONS

"assessment period"—see reg. 2(1).
"claimant"—*ibid.*, reg. 12(1).
"earnings"—see reg. 2(1).
"employed earner"—*ibid.*
"self-employed earner"—*ibid.*
"week"—*ibid.*

GENERAL NOTE

Para. (a). Para. (*a*) allows modification of the period of assessment established for an employee by reg. 16. It requires particular weeks to be discarded from that period. Sub-para. (i) applies to weeks in which earnings are "irregular or unusual." This is a very vague test. The meaning of "irregular" is particularly obscure when other provisions deal with fluctuating earnings. It is an issue of judgment when earnings are far enough away from the norm to be "unusual." There appears to be no necessity for any identifiable special factor to have caused the unusualness, but no doubt weeks in which, say, large tax refunds or accrued holiday pay are paid, or large deductions are made would be excluded. For family credit from April 1992, the regulations require any week in which the earnings deviate from the average by at least 20 per cent to be discarded (Family Credit (General) Regulations, reg. 20).

Sub-para. (ii) covers bonus and commission payments under reg. 16(6).

Para. (b). See reg. 17 of the Family Credit Regulations.

Calculation of weekly amount of income

20. For the purposes of regulations 16 and 18 (normal weekly income), where the period in respect of which a payment is made—
   (a) does not exceed a week, the weekly amount shall be the amount of that payment;
   (b) exceeds a week, the weekly amount shall be determined—
      (i) in a case where that period is a month, by multiplying the amount of the payment by 12 and dividing the product by 52;
      (ii) in a case where that period is 3 months, by multiplying the amount of the payment by 4 and dividing the product by 52;
      (iii) in a case where that period is a year, by dividing the amount of the payment by 52;
      (iv) in any other case, by multiplying the amount of the payment by 7 and dividing the product by the number equal to the number of days in the period in respect of which it is made.

(2) For the purposes of regulation 17 (normal weekly earnings of self-employed earners) the weekly amount of earnings of a claimant shall be determined—
   (a) except where sub-paragraph (b) applies, by dividing his earnings received in the assessment period or, as the case may be, estimated for that period by the number equal to the number of weeks in that period;
   (b) in a case where regulation 17(1)(b) applies, by multiplying his earnings relevant to the assessment period (whether or not received in that period) by 7 and dividing the product by the number equal to the number of days in that period.

DEFINITIONS

"assessment period"—see reg. 2(1).
"claimant"—*ibid.*
"payment"—*ibid.*
"week"—*ibid.*

GENERAL NOTE

See notes to reg. 32(1) of the Income Support (General) Regulations, except for para. (2).

Chapter III

Employed Earners

Earnings of employed earners

21.—(1) Subject to paragraph (2), "earnings" means in the case of employment as an employed earner, any remuneration or profit derived from that employment and includes—

(a) any bonus or commission;

(b) any holiday pay except any payable more than 4 weeks after termination of the employment;

(c) any payment by way of a retainer;

(d) any payment made by the claimant's employer in respect of any expenses not wholly, exclusively and necessarily incurred in the performance of the duties of the employment, including any payment made by the claimant's employer in respect of—

(i) travelling expenses incurred by the claimant between his home and place of employment;

(ii) expenses incurred by the claimant under arrangements made for the care of a member of his family owing to the claimant's absence from home;

(e) any award of compensation made under section 68(2) or 71(2)(a) of the Employment Protection (Consolidation) Act 1978 (remedies and compensation for unfair dismissal);

(f) any such sum as is referred to in section 18(2) of the Social Security (Miscellaneous Provisions) Act 1977 (certain sums to be earnings for social security purposes);

(g) any statutory sick pay under Part I of the Social Security and Housing Benefits Act 1982 [SSCBA, Part XI];

(h) any statutory sick pay under Part II of the Social Security (Northern Ireland) Order 1982;

(i) any payment made by the claimant's employer in respect of any Community Charge ['or council tax] to which the claimant is subject.

(2) Earnings shall not include—

(a) subject to paragraph (3), any payment in kind;

(b) any payment in respect of expenses wholly, exclusively and necessarily incurred in the performance of the duties of the employment;

(c) any occupational pension;

[²(d) any statutory maternity pay or a corresponding benefit under any enactment having effect in Northern Ireland.]

(3) Where living accommodation is provided for a claimant by reason of his employment, the claimant shall be treated as being in receipt of weekly earnings of an amount equal to—

(a) where no charge is made in respect of the provision of that accommodation, £12;

(b) where a charge is made and that weekly charge is less than £12, the amount of the difference,

except that where the claimant satisfies the adjudication officer that the weekly value to him of the provision of that accommodation is an amount less than the amount in sub-paragraph (a) or (b), as the case may be, he shall be treated as being in receipt of that lesser value.

AMENDMENTS

1. Income-related Benefits Schemes (Miscellaneous Amendments) Regulations 1993 (S.I. 1993 No. 315), Sched., para. 13 (April 1, 1993).

2. Income-related Benefits Schemes (Miscellaneous Amendments) Regulations 1993 (S.I. 1993 No. 315), reg. 18 (April 13, 1993).

DEFINITIONS

"the Act"—see reg. 2(1).

"claimant"—*ibid.*, reg. 12(1).

"employed earner"—see reg. 2(1).
"family"—see 1986 Act, s.20(11) (SSCBA, s.137(1)).
"occupational pension"—see reg. 2(1).
"payment"—*ibid.*
"week"—*ibid.*

GENERAL NOTE

See the notes to reg. 19 of the Family Credit (General) Regulations.

Calculation of net earnings of employed earners

22.—(1) For the purposes of regulation 16 (normal weekly earnings of employed earners), the earnings of a claimant derived or likely to be derived from employment as an employed earner to be taken into account shall, subject to paragraph (2), be his net earnings.

(2) There shall be disregarded from a claimant's net earnings, any sum, where applicable, specified in Schedule 2.

(3) For the purposes of paragraph (1), net earnings shall, except where paragraph (4) applies, be calculated by taking into account the gross earnings of the claimant from that employment over the assessment period, less—

(a) any amount deducted from those earnings by way of—
  (i) income tax;
  (ii) primary Class 1 contributions under the Social Security Act [SSCBA]; and
(b) one-half of any sum paid by the claimant [⁴in respect of a pay period] by way of a contribution towards an occupational or personal pension scheme.

(4) Where the earnings of a claimant are estimated under paragraph (8) of regulation 16 (normal weekly earnings of employed earners), his net earnings shall be calculated by taking into account those earnings over the assessment period, less—

(a) an amount in respect of income tax equivalent to an amount calculated by applying to those earnings [¹the lower rate of tax or, as the case may be, the lower rate and the basic rate of tax] in the year of assessment in which the claim was made less only the personal relief to which the claimant is entitled under sections 257(1), (6) and (7) and 259 of the Income and Corporation Taxes Act 1988 (personal relief) as is appropriate to his circumstances; but, if the assessment period is less than a year, [¹the earnings to which the lower rate [³. . .] of tax is to be applied and] the amount of the personal relief deductible under this sub-paragraph shall be calculated on a pro rata basis;
[²(b) where the weekly amount of those earnings equals or exceeds the lower earnings limit, an amount representing primary Class 1 contributions under the Contributions and Benefits Act, calculated by applying to those earnings the initial and main primary percentages applicable at the date of claim in accordance with section 8(1)(a) and (b) of that Act; and]
[⁴(c) one half of any sum which would be payable by the claimant by way of a contribution towards an occupational or personal pension scheme, if the earnings so estimated were actual earnings.]

AMENDMENTS

1. Income-related Benefits Schemes (Miscellaneous Amendments) (No. 3) Regulations 1992 (S.I. 1992 No. 2155), Sched., para. 4 (October 5, 1992).
2. Income-related Benefits Schemes (Miscellaneous Amendments) Regulations 1994 (S.I. 1994 No. 527), reg. 23 (April 12, 1994).

3. Income-related Benefits Schemes (Miscellaneous Amendments) (No. 5) Regulations 1994 (S.I. 1994 No. 2139), reg. 4 (October 4, 1994).

4. Income-related Benefits Schemes (Miscellaneous Amendments) (No. 5) Regulations 1994 (S.I. 1994 No. 2139), reg. 5 (October 4, 1994).

DEFINITIONS

"assessment period"—see reg. 2(1).
"claimant"—*ibid.*, reg. 12(1).
"date of claim"—see reg. 2(1).
"earnings"—*ibid.*
"employed earner"—*ibid.*
"lower rate"—*ibid.*
"occupational pension scheme"—see 1986 Act, s.84(1) (PSA, s.1).
"personal pension scheme"—*ibid.*
"primary Class 1 contribution"—*ibid.*
"Social Security Act"—see reg. 2(1).
"year of assessment"—*ibid.*

GENERAL NOTE

See the notes to reg. 20 of the Family Credit (General) Regulations.

Calculation of bonus or commission

23. Where a claimant's earnings include a bonus or commission to which paragraph (6) of regulation 16 (normal weekly earnings of employed earners) applies that part of his earnings shall be calculated by aggregating any payments of bonus or commission and [¹deducting from it—]
  (a) an amount in respect of income tax equivalent to an amount calculated by applying to that part of the earnings the basic rate of tax in the year of assessment in which the claim is made; and
  [²(b) an amount representing primary Class 1 contributions under the Contributions and Benefits Act, calculated by applying to that part of the earnings the main primary percentage applicable at the date of claim; and]
  (c) one-half of any sum payable by the claimant in respect of that part of the earnings by way of a contribution towards an occupational or personal pension [¹scheme;
and dividing the resulting sum by 52.]

AMENDMENTS

1. Income-related Benefits Schemes (Miscellaneous Amendments) (No. 3) Regulations 1992 (S.I. 1992 No. 2155), Sched., para. 5 (October 5, 1992).

2. Income-related Benefits Schemes (Miscellaneous Amendments) Regulations 1994 (S.I. 1994 No. 527), reg. 24 (April 12, 1994).

DEFINITIONS

"claimant"—see reg. 2(1).
"date of claim"—*ibid.*
"occupational pension scheme"—see 1986 Act, s.84(1) (PSA, s.1).
"personal pension scheme"—*ibid.*
"Social Security Act"—see reg. 2(1).
"year of assessment"—*ibid.*

GENERAL NOTE

See the notes to reg. 20A of the Family Credit (General) Regulations. Reg. 23(*c*) applies to contributions to personal pension schemes as well as to occupational pension schemes.

Chapter IV

Self-Employed Earners

Earnings of self-employed earners

24.—(1) Subject to [¹paragraphs (2) and (3)], "earnings", in the case of employment as a self-employed earner, means the gross receipts of the employment and shall include any allowance paid under section 2 of the Employment and Training Act 1973 or section 2 of the Enterprise and New Towns (Scotland) Act 1990 to the claimant for the purpose of assisting him in carrying on his business unless at the date of claim the allowance has been terminated.

(2) Where a claimant is employed in providing board and lodging accommodation for which a charge is payable, any income consisting of payments of such a charge shall only be taken into account under this Chapter as earnings if it forms a major part of the total of the claimant's weekly income less any sums disregarded under Schedule 3 other than under paragraph 38 of that Schedule.

[¹(3) "Earnings" shall not include any payments to which paragraph 24 of Schedule 3 refers (sums to be disregarded in the calculation of income other than earnings).]

AMENDMENT

1. Income-related Benefits Schemes (Miscellaneous Amendments) (No. 5) Regulations 1994 (S.I. 1994 No. 2139), reg. 6 (October 4, 1994).

DEFINITIONS

"claimant"—see reg. 2(1), reg. 12(1).
"date of claim"—see reg. 2(1).
"payment"—*ibid.*
"self-employed earner"—*ibid.*

GENERAL NOTE

See the notes to reg. 21 of the Family Credit (General) Regulations.

Calculation of net profit of self-employed earners

25.—(1) For the purposes of regulation 17 (normal weekly earnings of self-employed earners), the earnings of a claimant to be taken into account shall be—

    (a) in the case of a self-employed earner who is engaged in employment on his own account, the net profit derived from that employment;

    (b) in the case of a self-employed earner whose employment is carried on in partnership or is that of a share fisherman within the meaning of the Social Security (Mariners' Benefits) Regulations 1975, his share of the net profit derived from that employment less—

        (i) an amount in respect of income tax and social security contributions payable under the Social Security Act [SSCBA] calculated in accordance with [¹regulation 26] (deduction of tax and contributions for self-employed earners); and

        (ii) [³one half of the amount in respect of any qualifying premium calculated in accordance with paragraph (15)].

(2) There shall be disregarded from a claimant's net profit any sum, where applicable, specified in Schedule 2.

(3) For the purposes of paragraph (1)(a) the net profit of the employment shall, except where paragraph (4), (11) or (12) applies, be calculated by taking into account the earnings of the employment received in the assessment period, less—

(a) subject to paragraphs (7) to (9), any expenses wholly and exclusively defrayed in that period for the purposes of that employment;

(b) an amount in respect of—
 (i) income tax; and
 (ii) social security contributions payable under the Social Security Act [SSCBA], calculated in accordance with regulation 26 (deduction of tax and contributions for self-employed earners); and

(c) [³one half of the amount in respect of any qualifying premium calculated in accordance with paragraph (15)].

(4) For the purposes of paragraph (1)(a), in a case where the assessment period is determined under regulation 17(1)(b), the net profit of the employment shall, except where paragraph (11) applies, be calculated by taking into account the earnings of the employment relevant to that period (whether or not received in that period), less—

(a) [¹subject to paragraphs (7) to (10)], any expenses relevant to that period (whether or not defrayed in that period) and which were wholly and exclusively incurred for the purposes of that employment;

(b) an amount in respect of—
 (i) income tax; and
 (ii) social security contributions payable under the Social Security Act [SSCBA], calculated in accordance with regulation 26; and

(c) [³one half of the amount in respect of any qualifying premium calculated in accordance with paragraph (15)].

(5) For the purposes of [¹paragraph] (1)(b) the net profit of the employment shall, except where [¹paragraph] (6), (11) or (12) applies, be calculated by taking into account the earnings of the employment received in the assessment period less, subject to paragraphs (7) to (9), any expenses wholly and exclusively defrayed in that period for the purposes of that employment.

(6) For the purposes of paragraph (1)(b), in a case where the assessment period is determined [¹under regulation 17(1)(b) (normal weekly earnings of self-employed earners)], the net profit of the employment shall, except where paragraph (11) applies, be calculated by taking into account the earnings of the employment relevant to that period (whether or not received in that period) less, subject to paragraphs (7) to (9), any expenses relevant to that period (whether or not defrayed in that period) and which were wholly and exclusively incurred for the purposes of that employment.

(7) Subject to paragraph (8), no deduction shall be made under paragraphs (3)(a), (4)(a), (5) or (6), as the case may be, in respect of—

(a) any capital expenditure;

(b) the depreciation of any capital asset;

(c) any sum employed, or intended to be employed, in the setting up or expansion of the employment;

(d) any loss incurred before the beginning of the assessment period;

(e) the repayment of capital on any loan taken out for the purposes of the employment;

(f) any expenses incurred in providing business entertainment.

(8) A deduction shall be made under paragraphs (3)(a), (4)(a), (5) or (6), as the case may be, in respect of the repayment of capital on any loan used for—

(a) the replacement in the course of business of equipment or machinery; and

(b) the repair of an existing business asset except to the extent that any sum is payable under an insurance policy for its repair.

(9) An adjudication officer shall refuse to make a deduction in respect of any expenses under paragraphs (3)(a), (4)(a), (5) or (6), as the case may be, where he is not satisfied that the expense has been defrayed or given the nature and the amount of the expense that it has been reasonably incurred.

(10) For the avoidance of doubt—

(a) a deduction shall not be made under paragraphs (3)(a), (4)(b), (5) or (6), as the case may be, in respect of any sum unless it has been expended for the purposes of the business;

(b) a deduction shall be made thereunder in respect of—

(i) the excess of any VAT paid over VAT received in the assessment period;

(ii) any income expended in the repair of an existing business asset except to the extent that any sum is payable under an insurance policy for its repair;

(iii) any payment of interest on a loan taken out for the purposes of the employment.

(11) Where a claimant is engaged in employment as a child-minder the net profit of the employment to be taken into account shall be one-third of the earnings of that employment, less—

(a) an amount in respect of—

(i) income tax; and

(ii) social security contributions payable under the Social Security Act [SSCBA], calculated in accordance with regulation 26 (deduction of tax and contributions for self-employed earners); and

(b) [³one half of the amount in respect of any qualifying premium calculated in accordance with paragraph (15)].

(12) Where regulation 17(3) (normal weekly earnings of self-employed earners) applies—

(a) for the purposes of paragraph (1)(a), the net profit derived from the employment shall be calculated by taking into account the claimant's estimated and, where appropriate, actual earnings from the employment less the amount of the deductions likely to be made and, where appropriate, made under sub-paragraphs (a) to (c) of paragraph (3); or

(b) for the purposes of paragraph (1)(b), his share of the net profit of the employment shall be calculated by taking into account the claimant's estimated and, where appropriate, his share of the actual earnings from the employment less the amount of his share of the expenses likely to be deducted and, where appropriate, deducted under paragraph (5); or

(c) in the case of employment as a child-minder, the net profit of the employment shall be calculated by taking into account one-third of the claimant's estimated earnings and, where appropriate, actual earnings from the employment less the amount of the deductions likely to be made and, where appropriate, made under sub-paragraphs (a) and (b) of paragraph (11).

(13) For the avoidance of doubt where a claimant is engaged in employment as a self-employed earner and he is also engaged in one or more other employments as a self-employed or employed earner any loss incurred in any one of his employments shall not be offset against his earnings in any other of his employments.

[²(14) [³In this regulation—

(a) "qualifying premium" means any premium which at the date of claim is payable periodically in respect of a retirement annuity contract or a personal pension scheme;

(b)] "retirement annuity contract" means an annuity contract for the time being approved by the Board of Inland Revenue as having for its main object the provision of a life annuity in old age or the provision of an annuity for a partner or dependant and in respect of which relief from income tax may be given on any premium.]

[³(15) The amount in respect of any qualifying premium shall be calculated by multiplying the daily amount of the qualifying premium by the number equal to the number of days in the assessment period; and for the purposes of this regulation the daily amount of the qualifying premium shall be determined—

    (a) where the qualifying premium is payable monthly, by multiplying the amount of the qualifying premium by 12 and dividing the product by 365;

    (b) in any other case, by dividing the amount of the qualifying premium by the number equal to the number of days in the period to which the qualifying premium relates.]

AMENDMENTS

1. Income-related Benefits Schemes (Miscellaneous Amendments) (No. 3) Regulations 1992 (S.I. 1992 No. 2155), Sched., para. 6 (October 5, 1992).
2. Income-related Benefits Schemes (Miscellaneous Amendments) (No. 4) Regulations 1993 (S.I. 1993 No. 2119), reg. 40 (October 5, 1993).
3. Income-related Benefits Schemes (Miscellaneous Amendments) Regulations 1994 (S.I. 1994 No. 527), reg. 25 (April 12, 1994).

DEFINITIONS

"assessment period"—see reg. 2(1).
"claimant"—*ibid.*, reg. 12(1).
"earnings"—see reg. 2(1).
"employed earner"—*ibid.*
"self-employed earner"—*ibid.*
"Social Security Act"—*ibid.*

GENERAL NOTE

See the notes to reg. 22 of the Family Credit (General) Regulations.

Deduction of tax and contributions for self-employed earners

26.—(1)The amount to be deducted in respect of income tax under regulation 25(1)(b)(i), (3)(b)(i), (4)(b)(i) or (11)(a)(i) (calculation of net profit of self-employed earners) shall be calculated on the basis of the amount of chargeable income, and as if that income were assessable to income tax at [¹the lower rate or, as the case may be the basic rate of tax] in the year of assessment in which the claim was made, less only the personal relief to which the claimant is entitled under [¹sections 257(1), (6) and (7) and 259] of the Income and Corporation Taxes Act 1988 (personal relief) as is appropriate to his circumstances; but, if the assessment period is less than a year [¹the earnings to which the lower rate [². . .] of tax is to be applied and] the amount of the personal relief deductible under this paragraph shall be calculated on a pro rata basis.

(2) The amount to be deducted in respect of social security contributions under regulation 25(1)(b)(i), (3)(b)(ii) (4)(b)(ii) or (11)(a)(ii) shall be the total of—

    (a) the amount of Class 2 contributions payable under section 7(1) or, as the case may be, (4) of the Social Security Act [SSCBA, s.11(1) and (3)] at the rate applicable at the date of claim except where the claimant's chargeable income is less than the amount specified in section 7(5) of that Act [SSCBA, s.11(4)] (small earnings exception) for the tax year in which the date of claim falls; but if the assessment period is less than a year, the amount specified for that tax year shall be calculated on a pro rata basis; and

(b) the amount of Class 4 contributions (if any) which would be payable under section 9(2) of that Act [SSCBA, s.15(1)] (Class 4 contributions) at the percentage rate applicable at the date of claim on so much of the chargeable income as exceeds the lower limit but does not exceed the upper limit of profits and gains applicable for the tax year in which the date of claim falls; but, if the assessment period is less than a year, those limits shall be calculated on a pro rata basis.]

(3) In this regulation "chargeable income" means—

(a) except where sub-paragraph (b) or (c) applies, the earnings derived from the employment, less any expenses deducted under paragraph (3)(a), (4)(a), (5) or (6), as the case may be, of regulation 25;

(b) except where sub-paragraph (c)(iii) applies, in the case of employment as a child minder one-third of the earnings of that employment; or

(c) where regulation 17(3) applies (normal weekly earnings of self-employed earners)—

   (i) in the case of a self-employed earner who is engaged in employment on his own account, the claimant's estimated and, where appropriate, actual earnings from the employment less the amount of the deductions likely to be made and, where appropriate, made under sub-paragraph (a) of paragraph (3) of regulation 25;

   (ii) in the case of a self-employed earner whose employment is carried on in partnership or is that of a share fisherman within the meaning of the Social Security (Mariners' Benefits) Regulations 1975, the claimant's estimated and, where appropriate, his share of the actual earnings from the employment less the amount of his share of the expenses likely to be deducted and, where appropriate, deducted ['under paragraph (5)] of regulation 25;

   (iii) in the case of employment as a child minder, one-third of the claimant's estimated and, where appropriate, actual earnings from that employment.

AMENDMENT

1. Income-related Benefits Schemes (Miscellaneous Amendments) (No. 3) Regulations 1992 (S.I. 1992 No. 2155), Sched., para. 7 (October 5, 1992).

2. Income-related Benefits Schemes (Miscellaneous Amendments) (No. 5) Regulations 1994 (S.I. 1994 No. 2139), reg. 4 (October 4, 1994).

DEFINITIONS

"assessment period"—see reg. 2(1).
"claim"—*ibid.*
"claimant"—*ibid.*, reg. 12(1).
"date of claim"—see reg. 2(1).
"lower rate"—*ibid.*
"earnings"—*ibid.*
"self-employed earner"—*ibid.*
"Social Security Act"—*ibid.*
"year of assessment"—*ibid.*

GENERAL NOTE

See the notes to reg. 23 of the Family Credit (General) Regulations.

Chapter V

Other Income

Calculation of income other than earnings

27.—(1) For the purposes of regulation 18 (normal weekly income other than earnings), the income of a claimant which does not consist of earnings to be taken into account shall, subject to paragraphs to (2) to (5), be his gross income and any capital treated as income under [¹ regulations 28 and 30 (capital treated as income and modifications in respect of children and young persons).]

(2) There shall be disregarded from the calculation of a claimant's gross income under paragraph (1), any sum, where applicable, specified in Schedule 3.

(3) Where the payment of any benefit under the benefit Acts is subject to any deduction by way of recovery the amount to be taken into account under paragraph (1) shall be the gross amount payable.

(4) Any payment to which regulation 21(2) applies (payments not earnings) shall be taken into account as income for the purpose of paragraph (1).

(5) Where a loan is made to a person pursuant to arrangements made under section 1 of the Education (Student Loans) Act 1990 or Article 3 of the Education (Student Loans) (Northern Ireland) Order 1990 and that person ceases to be a student before the end of the academic year in respect of which the loan is payable or, as the case may be, before the end of his course, a sum equal to the weekly amount apportionable under paragraph (2) of regulation 47 shall be taken into account under paragraph (1) for each week, in the period over which the loan fell to be apportioned, following the date on which that person ceases to be a student; but in determining the weekly amount apportionable under paragraph (2) of regulation 47 so much of that paragraph as provides for a disregard shall not have effect.

AMENDMENT

1. Income-related Benefits Schemes (Miscellaneous Amendments) (No. 4) Regulations 1993 (S.I. 1993 No. 2119), reg. 41 (October 5, 1993).

DEFINITIONS

"the benefit Acts"—see 1986 Act, s.84(1).
"claimant—see reg. 2(1), reg. 12(1).
"earnings"—see reg. 2(1).

GENERAL NOTE

See the notes to reg. 24 of the Family Credit (General) Regulations.

Capital treated as income

28.—(1) Any capital payable by instalments which are outstanding at the date of the claim shall, if the aggregate of the instalments outstanding and the amount of the claimant's capital otherwise calculated in accordance with Chapter VI of this Part exceeds £16,000, be treated as income.

(2) Any payment received under an annuity shall be treated as income.

DEFINITIONS

"claimant"—see reg. 2(1), reg. 12(1).
"date of claim"—see reg. 2(1).

GENERAL NOTE

See the notes to reg. 25 of the Family Credit (General) Regulations, with the substitution of £16,000 for £8,000 as the capital limit.

Notional income

29.—(1) A claimant shall be treated as possessing income of which he has deprived himself for the purpose of securing entitlement to disability working allowance or increasing the amount of that benefit.

(2) Except in the case of a discretionary trust or a trust derived from a payment made in consequence of a personal injury, any income which would become available to the claimant upon application being made, but which has not been acquired by him, shall be treated as possessed by the claimant.

(3) Any payment of income, other than a payment of income made under the Macfarlane Trust, the Macfarlane (Special Payments) Trust, the Macfarlane (Special Payments) (No. 2) Trust[1, the Fund][5, the Eileen Trust] or [4the Independent Living Funds], made—

(a) to a third party in respect of a single claimant or member of the family (but not a member of the third party's family) shall be treated as possessed by [1that single claimant or] that member of the family to the extent that it is used for his food, ordinary clothing or footwear, household fuel, or housing costs or is used for any personal community [3charge,] collective community charge contribution [3or council tax] for which that member is liable; and in this subparagraph the expression "ordinary clothing or footwear" means clothing or footwear for normal daily use, but does not include school uniforms, or clothing or footwear used solely for sporting activities;

[2(b) to a single claimant or a member of the family in respect of a single claimant or a third party (but not in respect of another member of the family) shall be treated as possessed by that single claimant or, as the case may be, that member of the family to the extent that it is kept or used by him or used by or on behalf of any member of the family.]

(4) Where—

(a) a claimant performs a service for another person; and

(b) that person makes no payment of earnings or pays less than that paid for a comparable employment in the area;

the adjudication officer shall treat the claimant as possessing such earnings (if any) as is reasonable for that employment unless the claimant satisfies him that the means of that person are insufficient for him to pay or to pay more for the service, but this paragraph shall not apply to a claimant who is engaged by a charitable or [8voluntary organisation] or is a volunteer if the adjudication officer is satisfied [8in any of those cases] that it is reasonable for him to provide his services free of charge.

(5) Where a claimant is treated as possessing any income under any of paragraphs (1) to (3), the foregoing provisions of this Part shall apply for the purposes of calculating the amount of that income as if a payment had actually been made and as if it were actual income which he does possess.

(6) Where a claimant is treated as possessing any earnings under paragraph (4), the foregoing provisions of this Part shall apply for the purposes of calculating the amount of those earnings as if a payment had actually been made and as if they were actual earnings which he does possess, except that paragraph (3) of regulation 22 (calculation of net earnings of employed earners) shall not apply and his net earnings shall be calculated by taking into account those earnings which he is treated as possessing, less—

(a) an amount in respect of income tax equivalent to an amount calculated by applying to those earnings [2the lower rate or, as the case may be, the lower rate and the basic rate of tax] in the year of assessment in which the claim was made less only the personal relief to which the claimant is entitled under sections 257(1), (6) and (7) and 259 of the Income and Corporation Taxes Act 1988 (personal relief) as is appropriate to his circumstances; but, if the assessment period is less than a year, [2the earnings to which the lower rate [7. . .] of tax is to be applied and] the amount of the personal relief deductible under this sub-paragraph shall be calculated on a pro rata basis;

[⁶(b) where the weekly amount of those earnings equals or exceeds the lower earnings limit, an amount representing primary Class 1 contributions under the Contributions and Benefits Act, calculated by applying to those earnings the initial and main primary percentages applicable at the date of claim in accordance with section 8(1)(a) and (b) of that Act; and]

(c) one-half of any sum payable by the claimant by way of a contribution towards an occupational or personal pension scheme.

AMENDMENTS

1. Income-related Benefits Schemes and Social Security (Recoupment) Amendment Regulations 1992 (S.I. 1992 No. 1101), reg. 3(3) (May 7, 1992).
2. Income-related Benefits Schemes (Miscellaneous Amendments) (No. 3) Regulations 1992 (S.I. 1992 No. 2155), Sched., para. 8 (October 5, 1992).
3. Income-related Benefits Schemes (Miscellaneous Amendments) Regulations 1993 (S.I. 1993 No. 315), Sched., para. 14 (April, 1993).
4. Social Security Benefits (Miscellaneous Amendments) (No. 2) Regulations 1993 (S.I. 1993 No. 963), reg. 6(3) (April 22, 1993).
5. Income-related Benefits Schemes and Social Security (Recoupment) Amendment Regulations 1993 (S.I. 1993 No. 1249), reg. 5(3) (May 14, 1993).
6. Income-related Benefits Schemes (Miscellaneous Amendments) Regulations 1994 (S.I. 1994 No. 527), reg. 26 (April 12, 1994).
7. Income-related Benefits Schemes (Miscellaneous Amendments) (No. 5) Regulations 1994 (S.I. 1994 No. 2139), reg. 4 (October 4, 1994).
8. Income-related Benefits Schemes (Miscellaneous Amendments) Regulations 1995 (S.I. 1995 No. 516), reg. 6 (April 11, 1995).

DEFINITIONS

"assessment period"—see reg. 2(1).
"claimant"—*ibid*, reg. 12(1).
"earnings"—see reg. 2(1).
"family"—see 1986 Act, s.20(11) (SSCBA, s.137(1)).
"lower rate"—see reg. 2(1).
"occupational pension scheme"—see 1986 Act, s.84(1) (PSA, s.1).
"payment"—see reg. 2(1).
"personal pension scheme"—see 1986 Act, s.84(1) (PSA, s.1).
"primary Class 1 contribution"—*ibid*.
"single claimant"—see reg. 2(1).
"Social Security Act"—*ibid*.
"the Eileen Trust"—*ibid*.
"the Fund"—*ibid*.
"the Independent Living Funds"—*ibid*.
"the Macfarlane (Special Payments) Trust"—*ibid*.
"the Macfarlane (Special Payments)(No. 2) Trust"—*ibid*.
"the Macfarlane Trust"—*ibid*.
"voluntary organisation"—*ibid*.
"year of assessment"—*ibid*.

GENERAL NOTE

See, in general, the notes to reg. 26 of the Family Credit (General) Regulations.

Paragraph (1)

It is only income which the claimant deprives himself of for the purpose of entitlement to disability working allowance which he is to be treated as possessing under this provision. If the purpose is solely to secure entitlement to some other benefit, para. (1) cannot apply. See the notes to reg. 51(1) of the Income Support (General) Regulations (at the end of the section on *Purpose*) for discussion of the problem of deprivations occurring before a benefit comes into effect.

Paragraph (4)

This provision adopts the formula, with its different balance of burdens of proof, of reg. 42(6) of the Income Support (General) Regulations, rather than reg. 26(4) of the Family Credit Regulations.

Modifications in respect of children and young persons

30.—(1) Any capital of a child or young person payable by instalments which are outstanding at the date of claim shall, if the aggregate of the instalments outstanding and the amount of that child's or young person's other capital calculated in accordance with Chapter VI of this Part in like manner as for the claimant, [².. .], would exceed £3,000, be treated as income.

(2) Where the income of a child or young person, other than income consisting of payments of maintenance whether under a court order or not, calculated in accordance with [²Chapters I to V] of this Part exceeds the sum specified as an allowance for that child or young person in Schedule 5 and regulation 51(5) (sum for child or young person who has income in excess to be nil) applies, that income shall not be treated as income of the claimant.

(3) Where the capital of a child or young person, if calculated in accordance with Chapter VI of this Part in like manner as for the claimant, [²except as provided in paragraph 1], would exceed £3,000, any income of that child or young person[¹, other than income consisting of any payment of maintenance whether under a court order or not,] shall not be treated as income of the claimant.

(4) Any income of a child or young person which is to be disregarded under Schedule 3 shall be disregarded in such manner as to produce the result most favourable to the claimant.

AMENDMENTS

1. Income-related Benefits Schemes (Miscellaneous Amendments) Regulations 1993 (S.I. 1993 No. 315), reg. 19 (April 13, 1993).
2. Income-related Benefits Schemes (Miscellaneous Amendments) (No. 4) Regulations 1993 (S.I. 1993 No. 2119), reg. 42 (October 5, 1993).

DEFINITIONS

"child"—see 1986 Act, s.20(11) (SSCBA, s.137(1)).
"claimant"—see reg. 2(1), reg. 12(1).
"date of claim"—see reg. 2(1).
"payment"—*ibid.*
"young person"—*ibid.*, reg. 8.

GENERAL NOTE

See the notes to reg. 27 of the Family Credit (General) Regulations.

Chapter VI

Capital

Capital limit

31. For the purposes of section 22(6) of the Act [SSCBA, s.134(1)] as it applies to disability working allowance (no entitlement to benefit if capital exceeds prescribed amount), the prescribed amount is £16,000.

DEFINITION

"the Act"—see reg. 2(1).

See the notes to reg. 28 of the Family Credit (General) Regulations. One of the most significant differences in the structure of assessment adopted for disability working allowance, as compared to family credit, is that the Government was persuaded to make the capital limit £16,000, rather than £8,000. The thinking of the SSAC, one of the main proponents of the change, was that the disabled have different needs to the non-disabled population and may have to pay out sums for special equipment, adaptations or services. Therefore, they may need a larger reserve of capital.

Calculation of capital

32.—(1) For the purposes of Part II of the Act [SSCBA, Part VI] as it applies to disability working allowance, the capital of a claimant to be taken into account shall, subject to paragraph (2), be the whole of his capital calculated in accordance with this Part and any income treated as capital [¹under regulation 34] (income treated as capital).

(2) There shall be disregarded from the calculation of a claimant's capital under paragraph (1) any capital, where applicable, specified in Schedule 4.

AMENDMENT

1. Income-related Benefits Schemes (Miscellaneous Amendments) (No. 3) Regulations 1992 (S.I. 1992 No. 2155), Sched., para. 9 (October 5, 1992).

DEFINITIONS

"the Act"—see reg. 2(1).
"claimant"—*ibid.*, reg. 12(1).

GENERAL NOTE

See the notes to reg. 29 of the Family Credit (General) Regulations.

Disregard of capital of child or young person

33. The capital of a child or young person who is a member of the claimant's family shall not be treated as capital of the claimant.

DEFINITIONS

"child"—see 1986 Act, s.20(11) (SSCBA, s.137(1)).
"claimant"—see reg. 2(1), reg. 12(1).
"family"—see 1986 Act, s.20(11) (SSCBA, s.137(1)).
"young person"—see reg. 2(1), reg. 8.

GENERAL NOTE

See the notes to reg. 30 of the Family Credit (General) Regulations.

Income treated as capital

34.—(1) Any amount by way of a refund of income tax deducted from profits or emoluments chargeable to income tax under Schedule D or E shall be treated as capital.

(2) Any holiday pay which is not earnings under regulation 21(1)(b) earnings of employed earners) shall be treated as capital.

(3) Any charitable or voluntary payment which is not made or is not due to be made at regular intervals, other than a payment which is made under the Macfarlane Trust, the Macfarlane (Special Payments) Trust, the Macfarlane

(Special Payments) (No. 2) Trust[¹, the Fund] [³, the Eileen Trust] or [²the Independent Living Funds] shall be treated as capital.

(4) Except any income derived from capital disregarded under paragraph 1, 2, 4, 6, 13 or 26 to 30 of Schedule 4, any income derived from capital shall be treated as capital but only from the date it is normally due to be credited to the claimant's account.

(5) In the case of employment as an employed earner, any advance of earnings or any loan made by the claimant's employer shall be treated as capital.

(6) Any maintenance payment other than one to which regulation 18(2) [⁴or (2A)] (normal weekly income other than earnings) applies shall be treated as capital.

AMENDMENTS

1. Income-related Benefits Schemes and Social Security (Recoupment) Amendment Regulations 1992 (S.I. 1992 No. 1101), reg. 3(4) (May 7, 1992).
2. Social Security Benefits (Miscellaneous Amendments) (No. 2) Regulations 1993 (S.I. 1993 No. 963), reg. 6(3) (April 22, 1993).
3. Income-related Benefits Schemes and Social Security (Recoupment) Amendment Regulations 1993 (S.I. 1993 No. 1249), reg. 5(3) (May 14, 1993).
4. Income-related Benefits Schemes (Miscellaneous Amendments) (No. 5) Regulations 1994 (S.I. 1994 No. 2139), reg. 7 (October 4, 1994).

DEFINITIONS

"claimant"—see reg. 2(1), reg. 12(1).
"earnings"—see reg. 2(1).
"employed earner"—*ibid.*
"payment"—*ibid.*
"the Eileen Trust"—*ibid.*
"the Fund"—*ibid.*
"the Independent Living Funds"—*ibid.*
"the Macfarlane (Special Payments) Trust"—*ibid.*
"the Macfarlane (Special Payments) (No. 2) Trust"—*ibid.*
"the Macfarlane Trust"—*ibid.*

GENERAL NOTE

See the notes to reg. 31 of the Family Credit (General) Regulations.

Calculation of capital in the United Kingdom

35. Capital which a claimant possesses in the United Kingdom shall be calculated—
  (a) except in a case to which [¹paragraph] (b) applies, at its current market or surrender value less—
    (i) where there would be expenses attributable to sale, 10 per cent.; and
    (ii) the amount of any incumbrance secured on it;
  (b) in the case of a National Savings Certificate—
    (i) if purchased from an issue the sale of which ceased before 1st July last preceding the date of claim, at the price which it would have realised on that 1st July had it been purchased on the last day of that issue;
    (ii) in any other case, at its purchase price.

AMENDMENT

1. Income-related Benefits Schemes (Miscellaneous Amendments) (No. 3) Regulations 1992 (S.I. 1992 No. 2155), Sched., para.10 (October 5, 1992).

DEFINITIONS

"claimant"—see reg. 2(1), reg. 12(1).
"date of claim"—see reg. 2(1).

GENERAL NOTE

See the notes to reg. 49 of the Income Support (General) Regulations.

Calculation of capital outside the United Kingdom

36. Capital which a claimant possesses in a country outside the United Kingdom shall be calculated—
- (a) in a case where there is no prohibition in that country against the transfer to the United Kingdom of an amount equal to its current market or surrender value in that country, at that value;
- (b) in a case where there is such a prohibition, at the price which it would realise if sold in the United Kingdom to a willing buyer,

less, where there would be expenses attributable to sale, 10 per cent. and the amount of any incumbrance secured on it.

DEFINITION

"claimant"—see reg. 2(1), reg. 12(1).

GENERAL NOTE

See the notes to reg. 50 of the Income Support (General) Regulations.

Notional capital

37.—(1) [2. . .] A claimant shall be treated as possessing capital of which he has deprived himself for the purpose of securing entitlement to disability working allowance or increasing the amount of that benefit except—
- (a) where that capital is derived from a payment made in consequence of any personal injury and is placed on trust for the benefit of the claimant; or
- (b) to the extent that the capital which he is treated as possessing is reduced in accordance with regulation 38 (diminishing notional capital rule).

(2) Except in the case of—
- (a) a discretionary trust;
- (b) a trust derived from a payment made in consequence of a personal injury; or
- (c) any loan which would be obtainable only if secured against capital disregarded under Schedule 4,

any capital which would become available to the claimant upon application being made but which has not been acquired by him shall be treated as possessed by him.

(3) Any payment of capital, other than a payment of capital made under the Macfarlane Trust, the Macfarlane (Special Payments) Trust, the Macfarlane (Special Payments) (No. 2) Trust[1, the Fund][5, the Eileen Trust] or [4the Independent Living Funds], made—
- (a) to a third party in respect of a single claimant or a member of the family (but not a member of the third party's family) shall be treated as possessed by that single claimant or member of the family to the extent that it is used for his food, ordinary clothing or footwear, household fuel, or housing costs or is used for any personal community [3charge,] collective community charge contribution [3or council tax] for which that member is liable; and in this sub-paragraph the expression "ordinary clothing or

554

footwear" means clothing or footwear for normal daily use, but does not include school uniforms, or clothing or footwear used solely for sporting activities;

(b) to a single claimant or a member of the family in respect of a third party (but not in respect of another member of the family) shall be treated as possessed by that single claimant or member to the extent that it is kept by him or used on behalf of any member of the family.

(4) Where a claimant stands in relation to a company in a position analogous to that of a sole owner or partner in the business of that company, he shall be treated as if he were such sole owner or partner and in such a case—

(a) the value of his holding in that company shall, notwithstanding regulation 32 (calculation of capital), be disregarded; and

(b) he shall, subject to paragraph (5), be treated as possessing an amount of capital equal to the value or, as the case may be, his share of the value of the capital of that company and the foregoing provisions of this Chapter shall apply for the purposes of calculating that amount as if it were actual capital which he does possess.

(5) For so long as the claimant undertakes activities in the course of the business of the company, the amount which he is treated as possessing under paragraph (4) shall be disregarded.

(6) Where a claimant is treated as possessing capital under any of paragraphs (1) to (4) the foregoing provisions of this Chapter shall apply for the purposes of calculating its amount as if it were actual capital which he does possess.

(7) For the avoidance of doubt a claimant is to be treated as possessing capital under paragraph (1) only if the capital of which he has deprived himself is actual capital and not capital which he is treated as possessing under regulation 39.

AMENDMENTS

1. Income-related Benefits Schemes and Social Security (Recoupment) Amendment Regulations 1992 (S.I. 1992 No. 1101), reg. 6 (May 7, 1992).

2. Income-related Benefits Schemes (Miscellaneous Amendments) (No. 3) Regulations 1992 (S.I. 1992 No. 2155), Sched., para. 11 (October 5, 1992).

3. Income-related Benefits Schemes (Miscellaneous Amendments) Regulations 1993 (S.I. 1993 No. 315), Sched., para. 15 (April 1, 1993).

4. Social Security Benefits (Miscellaneous Amendments) (No. 2) Regulations 1993 (S.I. 1993 No. 963), reg. 6(3) (April 22, 1993).

5. Income-related Benefits Schemes and Social Secuirty (Recoupment) Amendment Regulations 1993 (S.I. 1993 No. 1249), reg. 5(3) (May 14, 1993).

DEFINITIONS

"claimant"—see reg. 2(1), reg. 12(1).
"family"—see 1986 Act, s.20(11) (SSCBA, s.137(1)).
"single claimant"—see reg. 2(1).
"the Eileen Trust"—*ibid.*
"the Fund"—*ibid.*
"the Independent Living Funds"—see reg. 2(1).
"the Macfarlane (Special Payments) Trust"—*ibid.*
"the Macfarlane (Special Payments) (No. 2) Trust"—*ibid.*
"the Macfarlane Trust"—*ibid.*

GENERAL NOTE

Paragraph (1)
See the notes to reg. 51(1) of the Income Support (General) Regulations. Note, however, that this paragraph only applies where the purpose is to gain entitlement to or to increase the amount of disability working allowance. If the purpose is solely to gain entitlement to some other benefit

the disability working allowance rule is not triggered. The effect of para. (7) is to confirm that para. (1) only operates if the person has deprived himself of actual capital. It further confirms that a deemed share in jointly held capital (reg. 39) does not count as actual capital for this purpose.

Paragraph (2)

See the notes to reg. 51(2) of the Income Support (General) Regulations. There are slight differences in wording.

Paragraph (3)

See the notes to reg. 51(3) of the Income Support (General) Regulations and the differences in sub-para. (a).

Paragraph (4)

See the notes to reg. 51(4) to (6) of the Income Support (General) Regulations.

Diminishing notional capital rule

38.—(1) Where a claimant is treated as possessing capital under regulation 37(1) (notional capital), the amount which he is treated as possessing—
  (a) in the case of a benefit week which is subsequent to—
    (i) the relevant week in respect of which the conditions set out in paragraph (2) are satisfied; or
    (ii) a week which follows that relevant week and which satisfies those conditions, shall be reduced by an amount determined under paragraph (3);
  (b) in the case of a benefit week in respect of which paragraph (1)(*a*) does not apply but where—
    (i) that week is a week subsequent to the relevant week; and
    (ii) that relevant week is a week in which the condition in paragraph (4) is satisfied, shall be reduced by the amount determined under paragraph (4).
  (2) This paragraph applies to a benefit week where the claimant satisfies the conditions that—
  (a) he is entitled to disability working allowance; and
  (b) but for regulation 37, he would have been entitled to an additional amount of disability working allowance in that benefit week.
  (3) In a case to which paragraph (2) applies, the amount of the reduction for the purposes of paragraph (1)(a) shall be equal to the aggregate of—
  (a) the additional amount of disability working allowance to which the claimant would have been entitled; and
  (b) if the claimant would, but for regulation 43(1) of the Housing Benefit (General) Regulations 1987 (notional capital), have been entitled to housing benefit or to an additional amount of housing benefit in respect of the benefit week in which the date of the last claim for disability working allowance falls, the amount (if any) which is equal to—
    (i) in a case where no housing benefit is payable, the amount to which he would have been entitled, or
    (ii) in any other case, the amount equal to the additional amount of housing benefit to which he would have been entitled; and
  (c) if the claimant would, but for regulation 33(1) of the Community Charge Benefits (General) Regulations 1989 (notional capital) have been entitled to community charge benefit or to an additional amount of community charge benefit in respect of the benefit week in which the date of the last claim for disability working allowance falls, the amount (if any) which is equal to—
    (i) in a case where no community charge benefit is payable, the amount to which he would have been entitled, or

    (ii) in any other case, the amount equal to the additional amount of community charge benefit to which he would have been [¹entitled; and

(d) if the claimant would, but for regulation 34(1) of the Council Tax Benefit (General) Regulations 1992 (notional capital), have been entitled to council tax benefit or to an additional amount of council tax benefit in respect of the benefit week in which the date of the last claim for disability working allowance falls, the amount (if any) which is equal to—

    (i) in a case where no council tax benefit is payable, the amount to which he would have been entitled, or

    (ii) in any other case, the amount equal to the additional amount of council tax benefit to which he would have been entitled.]

(4) Subject to paragraph (5), for the purposes of paragraph (1)(b) the condition is that the claimant would have been entitled to disability working allowance in the relevant week, but for regulation 37(1) and in such a case the amount shall be equal to the aggregate of—

(a) the amount of disability working allowance to which the claimant would have been entitled in the relevant week but for regulation 37(1);

(b) if the claimant would, but for regulation 43(1) of the Housing Benefit (General) Regulations 1987 (notional capital), have been entitled to housing benefit or to an additional amount of housing benefit in respect of the benefit week in which the first day of the relevant week falls, the amount (if any) which is equal to—

    (i) in a case where no housing benefit is payable, the amount to which he would have been entitled, or

    (ii) in any other case, the amount equal to the additional amount of housing benefit to which he would have been entitled; and

(c) if the claimant would, but for regulation 33(1) of the Community Charge Benefits (General) Regulations 1989 (notional capital) have been entitled to community charge benefit or to an additional amount of community charge benefit in respect of the benefit week in which the first day of the relevant week falls, the amount (if any) which is equal to—

    (i) in a case where no community charge benefit is payable, the amount to which he would have been entitled, or

    (ii) in any other case, the amount equal to the additional amount of community charge benefit to which he would have been [¹entitled; and

(d) if the claimant would, but for regulation 34(1) of the Council Tax Benefit (General) Regulations 1992 (notional capital), have been entitled to council tax benefit or to an additional amount of council tax benefit in respect of the benefit week in which the first day of the relevant week falls, the amount (if any) which is equal to—

    (i) in a case where no council tax benefit is payable, the amount to which he would have been entitled, or

    (ii) in any other case, the amount equal to the additional amount of council tax benefit to which he would have been entitled.]

(5) The amount determined under paragraph (4) shall be re-determined under that paragraph if the claimant makes a further claim for disability working allowance and the conditions in paragraph (6) are satisfied, and in such a case—

(a) sub-paragraphs (a), (b) and (c) of paragraph (4) shall apply as if for the words "relevant week" there were substituted the words "relevant subsequent week",

(b) subject to paragraph (7), the amount as re-determined shall have effect from the first week following the relevant subsequent week in question.

(6) The conditions are that—

(a) a further claim is made 20 or more weeks after—

    (i) the first day of the relevant week;

    (ii) in a case where there has been at least one re-determination in accordance with paragraph (5), the first day of the relevant subsequent week which last occurred;

    whichever last occurred; and

(b) the claimant would have been entitled to disability working allowance but for regulation 37(1).

(7) The amount as re-determined pursuant to paragraph (5) shall not have effect if it is less than the amount which applied in that case immediately before the re-determination and in such a case the higher amount shall continue to have effect.

(8) For the purpose of this regulation—

(a) "benefit week" has the meaning prescribed in regulations 16 (date of entitlement under an award) and 27 (family credit and disability working allowance) of the Social Security (Claims and Payments) Regulations 1987 except where it appears in paragraphs [[1](3)(b), (c) and (d) and (4)(b), (c) and (d)] where it has the meaning prescribed in regulation 2(1) of the Housing Benefit (General) Regulations [[1]1987 (interpretation),] regulation 2(1) of the Community Charge Benefits (General) Regulations 1989 (interpretation) [[1]or regulation 2(1) of the Council Tax Benefit (General) Regulations 1992 (interpretation)] as the case may be;

(b) "relevant week" means the benefit week in which the capital in question of which the claimant has deprived himself within the meaning of regulation 37(1)—

    (i) was for the first time taken into account for the purpose of determining his entitlement to disability working allowance; or

    (ii) was taken into account on a subsequent occasion for that purpose other than in respect of either a benefit week to which paragraph (2) applies or a further claim to which paragraph (5) applies;

    and, where more than one benefit week is identified by reference to heads (i) and (ii) of this sub-paragraph, the later or latest such benefit week;

(c) "relevant subsequent week" means the benefit week in which any award of disability working allowance in respect of the further claim referred to in paragraph (6)(a) would, but for regulation 37(1), have commenced, but it shall not be earlier than the twenty-seventh week after the week in which the existing amount took effect.

AMENDMENT

1. Income-related Benefits Schemes (Miscellaneous Amendments) Regulations 1993 (S.I. 1993 No. 315), Sched., para. 16 (April 1, 1993).

DEFINITION

    "claimant"—see regs. 2(1), 12(1).

GENERAL NOTE

    See reg. 51A of the Income Support (General) Regulations.

Capital jointly held

39. Except where a claimant possesses capital which is disregarded under regulation 37(4) (notional capital), where a claimant and one or more persons are beneficially entitled in possession to any capital asset they shall be treated as if each of them were entitled in possession to the whole beneficial interest therein in an equal share and the foregoing provisions of this Chapter shall apply for the purpose of calculating the amount of capital which the claimant is treated as possessing as if it were actual capital which the claimant does possess.

DEFINITION

"claimant"—see reg. 2(1), reg. 12(1).

GENERAL NOTE

See the notes to reg. 52 of the Income Support (General) Regulations.

Calculation of tariff income from capital

40.—(1) Where the claimant's capital calculated in accordance with this Chapter exceeds £3,000, it shall be treated as equivalent to a weekly income of £1 for each complete £250 in excess of £3,000 but not exceeding £16,000.

(2) Notwithstanding paragraph (1), where any part of the excess is not a complete £250 that part shall be treated as equivalent to a weekly income of £1.

(3) For the purposes of paragraph (1), capital includes any income treated as capital under regulation 34 (income treated as capital).

DEFINITION

"claimant"—see reg. 2(1), reg. 12(1).

GENERAL NOTE

The treatment of capital over £3,000 is the same as for family credit and income support, except that the tariff income is derived from capital up to £16,000. Each complete £250 between those levels is treated as producing a weekly income of £1. If the capital does not divide exactly into £250 chunks anything left over is treated as producing £1 a week. Thus if the claimant's capital is exactly £16,000 the tariff income is £40 a week. If the claimant's capital is £4,001, the tariff income is £5 a week.

Para. (3) merely confirms the effect of reg. 34. Notional capital must also count although not expressly mentioned.

Note reg. 33 on the capital of children and young persons.

Chapter VII

Students

Interpretation

41. In this Chapter, unless the context otherwise requires—
"a course of advanced education" means—
  (a) a full-time course leading to a postgraduate degree or comparable qualification, a first degree or comparable qualification, a diploma of higher education, a higher national diploma, ['a higher national diploma or higher national certificate of either the Business & [²Technology] Education Council] or the Scottish Vocational Education Council or a teaching qualification; or
  (b) any other full-time course which is a course of a standard above ordinary national diploma, ['a national diploma or national certificate of either the Business & [²Technology] Education Council or the Scottish Vocational Education Council], a general certificate of education (advanced level), a Scottish certificate of education ['(higher level)] or a Scottish certificate of sixth year studies;

"contribution" means any contribution in respect of the income of any other person which a Minister of the Crown or an education authority takes into account in assessing the amount of the student's grant and by which that amount is, as a consequence, reduced;

"course of study" means any full-time course of study or sandwich course whether or not a grant is made for attending it;

"covenant income" means the gross income payable to a student under a Deed of Covenant by a person whose income is, or is likely to be, taken into account in assessing the student's grant or award;

"education authority" means a government department, a local education authority as defined in section 114(1) of the Education Act 1944 (interpretation), an education authority as defined in section 135(1) of the Education (Scotland) Act 1980 (interpretation), an education and library board established under Article 3 of the Education and Libraries (Northern Ireland) Order 1986, any body which is a research council for the purposes of the Science and Technology Act 1965 or any analogous government department, authority, board or body, of the Channel Islands, Isle of Man or any other country outside Great Britain;

"grant" means any kind of educational grant or award and includes any scholarship, studentship, exhibition, allowance or bursary but does not include a payment derived from funds made available by the Secretary of State for the purpose of assisting students in financial difficulties under section 100 of the Education Act 1944, sections 131 and 132 of the Education Reform Act 1988 or section 73 of the Education (Scotland) Act 1980;

"grant income" means—

(a) any income by way of a grant;

(b) any contribution which has been assessed whether or not it has been paid,

and any such contribution which is paid by way of a covenant shall be treated as part of the student's grant income;

"last day of the course" means the date on which the last day of the final academic term falls in respect of the course in which the student is enrolled;

"period of study" means—

(a) in the case of a course of study for one year or less, the period beginning with the start of the course and ending with the last day of the course;

(b) in the case of a course of study for more than one year, in the first or, as the case may be, any subsequent year of the course, the period beginning with the start of the course or, as the case may be, that year's start and ending with either—

(i) the day before the start of the next year of the course in a case where the student's grant is assessed at a rate appropriate to his studying throughout the year, or, if he does not have a grant, where it would have been assessed at such a rate had he had one; or

(ii) in any other case the day before the start of normal summer vacation appropriate to his course;

(c) in the final year of a course of study of more than one year, the period beginning with that year's start and ending with the last day of the course;

"periods of experience" has the meaning prescribed in paragraph 1(1) of Schedule 5 to the Education (Mandatory Awards) Regulations 1991;

"sandwich course" has the meaning prescribed in paragraph 1(1) of Schedule 5 to the Education (Mandatory Awards) Regulations 1991;

"standard maintenance grant" means—

(a) except where paragraph (b) applies, in the case of a student attending a course of study at the University of London or an establishment within the area comprising the City of London and the Metropolitan Police District, the amount specified for the time being in paragraph 2(2)(a) of Schedule 2 to the Education (Mandatory Awards) Regulations 1991 for such a student; and

(b) in the case of a student residing at his parent's home, the amount specified in paragraph 3(2) thereof; and

(c) in any other case, the amount specified in paragraph 2(2) other than in sub-paragraph (a) or (b) thereof;

[¹"student" means a person,other than a person in receipt of a training allowance, who is aged less than 19 and attending a full-time course of advanced education or, as the case may be, who is aged 19 or over and attending a full-time course of study] at an educational establishment; and for the purposes of this definition—

(a) a person who has started on such a course shall be treated as attending it throughout any period of term or vacation within it until the last day of the course or such earlier date as he abandons it or is dismissed from it;

(b) a person on a sandwich course shall be treated as attending a full-time course of advanced education or, as the case may be, of study;

"year" in relation to a course, means the period of 12 months beginning on 1st January, 1st April or 1st September according to whether the academic year of the course in question begins in the spring, the summer or the autumn respectively.

AMENDMENTS

1. Income-related Benefits Schemes (Miscellaneous Amendments) (No. 3) Regulations 1992 (S.I. 1992 No. 2155), Sched., para.12 (October 5, 1992).

2. Income-related Benefits Schemes (Miscellaneous Amendments) (No. 4) Regulations 1993 (S.I. 1993 No. 2119), reg. 43 (October 5, 1993).

DEFINITION

"training allowance"—see reg. 2(1).

GENERAL NOTE

See the notes to reg. 37 of the Family Credit (General) Regulations.

Calculation of grant income

42.—(1) The amount of a student's grant income to be taken into account shall, subject to [²paragraphs (2) and (2A)], be the whole of his grant income.

(2) There shall be disregarded from a student's grant income any payment—

(a) intended to meet tuition fees or examination fees;

(b) intended to meet additional expenditure incurred by a disabled student in respect of his attendance on a course;

(c) intended to meet additional expenditure connected with term time residential study away from the student's educational establishment;

(d) on account of the student maintaining a home at a place other than that at which he resides during his course;

(e) intended to meet the cost of books and equipment or, if not so intended, an amount equal to [¹276];

(f) intended to meet travel expenses incurred as a result of his attendance on the course.

[¹(2A) Where in pursuance of an award a student is in receipt of a grant in respect of maintenance under regulation 17(b) of the Education (Mandatory Awards) Regulations 1991 (payments), there shall be excluded from his grant income a sum equal to the amount specified in paragraph 7(4) of Schedule 2 to those Regulations (disregard of travel costs), being the amount to be disregarded in respect of travel costs in the particular circumstances of his case.]

(3) A student's grant income, except any amount intended for the maintenance of dependants under Part 3 of Schedule 2 to the Education (Mandatory Awards) Regulations 1991 or intended for an older student under Part 4 of that Schedule, shall be apportioned—

(a) subject to paragraph (5), in a case where it is attributable to the period of study, equally between the weeks in that period;

(b) in any other case, equally between the weeks in the period in respect of which it is payable.

(4) Any amount intended for maintenance of dependants or for an older student under the provisions referred to in paragraph (3) shall be apportioned equally over a period of 52 weeks commencing with the week in which the period of study begins.

(5) In the case of a student on a sandwich course, any periods of experience within the period of study shall be excluded and the student's grant income shall be apportioned equally between the remaining weeks in that period.

AMENDMENTS

1. Income-related Benefits Schemes (Miscellaneous Amendments) (No. 2) Regulations 1994 (S.I. 1994 No. 1608), reg. 2 (September 6, 1994 or, where a student's period of study begins between August 1 and 31 1994, the first Tuesday of the period).

2. Income-related Benefits Schemes (Miscellaneous Amendments) (No. 3) Regulations 1992 (S.I. 1992 No. 2155), Sched., para. 13 (October 5, 1992).

DEFINITIONS

"grant income"—see reg. 41.
"payment"—see reg. 2(1).
"period of study"—see reg. 41.
"periods of experience"—*ibid.*
"sandwich course"—*ibid.*
"student"—*ibid.*
"week"—see reg. 2(1).

GENERAL NOTE

See the notes to reg. 38 of the Family Credit (General) Regulations.

Calculation of covenant income where a contribution is assessed

43.—(1) Where a student is in receipt of income by way of a grant during a period of study and a contribution has been assessed, the amount of his covenant income to be taken into account shall be the whole amount of his covenant income less, subject to paragraph (3), the amount of the contribution.

(2) The weekly amount of the student's covenant income shall be determined—

(a) by dividing the amount of income which falls to be taken into account under paragraph (1) by 52; and

(b) by disregarding from the resulting amount, £5.

(3) For the purposes of paragraph (1), the contribution shall be treated as increased by the amount, if any, by which the amount excluded under [¹regulation 42(2)(f) (calculation of grant income) falls short of the amount specified

in paragraph 7(4)(i) of Schedule 2 to the Education (Mandatory Awards) Regulations 1991 (travel expenditure)].

AMENDMENT

1. Income-related Benefits Schemes (Miscellaneous Amendments) (No. 3) Regulations 1992 (S.I. 1992 No. 2155), Sched., para. 14 (October 5, 1992).

DEFINITIONS

"contribution"—see reg. 41.
"covenant income"—*ibid.*
"grant"—*ibid.*
"standard maintenance grant"—*ibid.*
"student"—*ibid.*

GENERAL NOTE

See the notes to reg. 39 of the Family Credit (General) Regulations.

Covenant income where no grant income or no contribution is assessed

44.—(1) Where a student is not in receipt of income by way of a grant the amount of his covenant income shall be calculated as follows—
  (a) any sums intended for any expenditure specified in regulation 42(2)(a) to (d) (calculation of grant income), necessary as a result of his attendance on the course, shall be disregarded;
  (b) any covenant income, up to the amount of the standard maintenance grant, which is not so disregarded, shall be apportioned equally between the weeks of the period of study and there shall be disregarded from the covenant income to be so apportioned the amount which would have been disregarded [¹under regulation 42(2)(e) and (f) and (2A)] had the student been in receipt of the standard maintenance grant; and
  (c) the balance, if any, shall be divided by 52 and treated as weekly income of which shall be disregarded.
(2) Where a student is in receipt of income by way of a grant and no contribution has been assessed, the amount of his covenant income shall be calculated in accordance with sub-paragraphs (a) to (c) of paragraph (1), except that—
  (a) the value of the standard maintenance grant shall be abated by the amount of his grant income less an amount equal to the amount of any sums disregarded under regulation 42(2)(a) to (d); and
  (b) the amount to be disregarded under paragraph (1)(b) shall be abated by an amount equal to the amount of any sums disregarded [¹under regulation 42(2)(e) and (f) and (2A)].

AMENDMENT

1. Income-related Benefits Schemes (Miscellaneous Amendments) (No. 3) Regulations 1992 (S.I. 1992 No. 2155), Sched., para. 15 (October 5, 1992).

DEFINITIONS

"covenant income"—see reg. 41.
"grant"—*ibid.*
"grant income"—*ibid.*
"period of study"—*ibid.*
"standard maintenance grant"—*ibid.*
"student"—*ibid.*
"week"—see reg. 2(1).

GENERAL NOTE

See the notes to reg. 40 of the Family Credit (General) Regulations.

Relationship with amounts to be disregarded under Schedule 2

45. No part of a student's covenant income or grant income shall be disregarded under paragraph 12 of Schedule 3 and any other income to which sub-paragraph (1) of that paragraph applies shall be disregarded thereunder only to the extent that the amount disregarded under regulation 43(2)(b) (calculation of covenant income where a contribution is assessed) or, as the case may be, 44(1)(c) (covenant income where no grant income or no contribution is assessed) is less than £10.

DEFINITIONS

"covenant income"—see reg. 41.
"grant income"—*ibid.*
"student"—*ibid.*

GENERAL NOTE

See the notes to reg. 41 of the Family Credit (General) Regulations.

Other amounts to be disregarded

46. For the purposes of ascertaining income [¹other than grant income, covenant income and loans treated as income in accordance with regulation 47], any amounts intended for any expenditure specified in regulation 42(2) (calculation of grant income) necessary as a result of his attendance on the course shall be disregarded but only if, and to the extent that, the necessary expenditure exceeds or is likely to exceed the amount of the sums disregarded under regulation 42(2) [¹and (2A)], 43(3) and 44(1)(a) or (b) (calculation of grant income and covenant income) on like expenditure.

AMENDMENT

1. Income-related Benefits Schemes (Miscellaneous Amendents) Regulations 1994 (S.I. 1994 No. 527), reg. 27 (April 12, 1994).

DEFINITIONS

"covenant income"—see reg. 41.
"grant income"—*ibid.*

GENERAL NOTE

See the notes to reg. 42 of the Family Credit (General) Regulations.

Treatment of student loans

47.—(1) A loan which is made to a student pursuant to arrangements made under section 1 of the Education (Student Loans) Act 1990 or Article 3 of the Education (Student Loans) (Northern Ireland) Order 1990 shall be treated as income—

(2) In calculating the weekly amount of the loan to be taken into account as income—

(a) except where sub-paragraph (b) applies, the loan shall be apportioned equally between the weeks in the academic year in respect of which the loan is payable;

(b) in the case of a loan which is payable in respect of the final academic year of the course or if the course is only of one academic year's duration, in respect of that year the loan shall be apportioned equally between the weeks in the period beginning with the start of the final academic year or, as the case may be, the single academic year and ending with the last day of the course,

and from the weekly amount so apportioned there shall be disregarded £10.

(3) Any loan for which a student is eligible in respect of an academic year under the arrangements mentioned in paragraph (1) but which has not been acquired by him shall be treated as possessed by him and paragraphs (1) and (2) shall apply accordingly; and for the purposes of this paragraph the loan for which a student is eligible is the maximum amount payable to him under those arrangements.

GENERAL NOTE

See the notes to reg. 66(1) of the Income Support (General) Regulations.

Disregard of contribution

48. Where the claimant or his partner is a student and the income of one has been taken into account for the purpose of assessing a contribution to the student's grant, an amount equal to the amount of the contribution shall be disregarded for the purpose of calculating the income of the one liable to make that contribution.

DEFINITIONS

"claimant"—see reg. 2(1), reg. 12(1).
"contribution"—see reg. 41.
"grant"—*ibid.*
"partner"—see reg. 2(1).
"student"—see reg. 41.

GENERAL NOTE

See the notes to reg. 67 of the Income Support (General) Regulations. There is a trivial difference in drafting.

Disregard of tax refund

49. Any amount by way of a refund of tax deducted from a student's covenant income shall be disregarded in calculating the student's income or capital.

DEFINITIONS

"covenant income"—see reg. 41.
"student"—*ibid.*

GENERAL NOTE

See the notes to reg. 44 of the Family Credit (General) Regulations.

Disregard of changes occurring during summer vacation

50. In calculating a student's income there shall be disregarded any change

565

in the standard maintenance grant occurring in the recognised summer vacation appropriate to the student's course, if that vacation does not form part of his period of study[¹,] from the date on which the change occurred to the end of that vacation.

AMENDMENT

1. Income-related Benefits Schemes (Miscellaneous Amendments) (No. 3) Regulations 1992 (S.I. 1992 No. 2155), Sched., para. 16 (October 5, 1992).

DEFINITIONS

"period of study"—see reg. 41.
"standard maintenance grant"—*ibid.*
"student"—*ibid.*

GENERAL NOTE

See the notes to reg. 69 of the Income Support (General) Regulations. The differences in drafting do not seem to affect the substance.

PART VI

CALCULATION OF ENTITLEMENT

Determination of appropriate maximum disability working allowance

51.—(1) Subject to paragraphs (2) to (7), the appropriate maximum disability working allowance shall be the aggregate of the following allowances—
  (a) in respect of a single claimant, the allowance specified in column (2) of Schedule 5 at paragraph 1;
  (b) in respect of a claimant who is a member of a married or unmarried couple, or who is a lone parent who is treated as responsible for a child or young person by virtue of regulation 9 (circumstances in which a person is treated as responsible or not responsible for another), the allowance specified in column (2) of Schedule 5 at paragraph 2;
  (c) in respect of any child or young person for whom the claimant or his partner is treated as responsible by virtue of regulation 9 (circumstances in which a person is treated as responsible or not responsible for another), the allowance specified in column (2) of Schedule 5 at whichever description in paragraph 3 or 4 of column (1) fits the child or young person concerned.
[³(d) in respect of any child or young person to whom paragraph (1A) applies, the allowance specified in paragraph 5 of column (2) of Schedule 5.
  (1A) This paragraph applies to a child or young person for whom the claimant or his partner is responsible and who is a member of the claimant's household, and—
  (a) in respect of whom disability living allowance is payable, or has ceased to be payable solely because he is a patient; or
  (b) who is registered as blind in a register compiled by a local authority under section 29 of the National Assistance Act 1948 (welfare services) or, in Scotland, has been certified as blind and in consequence he is registered as blind in a register maintained by or on behalf of a regional or islands council; or
  (c) who ceased to be registered as blind in such a register within the 28 weeks immediately preceding the date of claim.

(1B) For the purposes of paragraph (1A)(a), "patient" has the same meaning it has in regulation 10.]

(2) Where a claimant or, as the case may be, the partner of a claimant is married polygamously to two or more members of the same household, the maximum amount shall include, in respect of every such member but the first, an additional allowance which equals—

(a) in the case of a person aged less than 18 years, the allowance specified in column (2) of Schedule 5 at paragraph 4(*a*) in column (1); or

(b) in any other case, the allowance specified in column (2) of Schedule 5 at paragraph 4(b) in column (1).

(3) For the purposes of paragraph (2), a person shall not be treated as a member of the same household as someone to whom he is married polygamously if he would not be so treated in the case of a monogamous marriage.

(4) Where the capital of a child or young person, if calculated in accordance with Part V (income and capital) in like manner as for the claimant, [²except as provided in regulation 30(1) (modifications in respect of children and young persons)], would exceed £3,000, the allowance in respect of that child or young person shall be nil.

(5) Where the weekly income of a child or young person, other than income consisting of payments of maintenance whether under a court order or not, calculated ['in accordance with Part V], exceeds the amount specified for that child or young person in Schedule 5, the allowance in respect of that child or young person shall be nil.

(6) Where a child or young person is, for the purposes of regulation 10(2)(*a*) (membership of the same household), a patient or in residential accommodation on account of physical or mental handicap or physical or mental illness and has been so accommodated for the 52 weeks immediately before the date of claim, the allowance in respect of that child or young person shall be nil.

(7) For the purposes of this regulation the amount of any disability working allowance and the age of any child or young person shall be determined by reference to the allowance specified in Schedule 5 and the age of the child or young person at the date on which the period under [⁴section 129(6) of the Contributions and Benefits Act] (period of award) begins.

AMENDMENTS

1. Income-related Benefits Schemes (Miscellaneous Amendments) (No. 3) Regulations 1992 (S.I. 1992 No. 2155), Sched., para. 17 (October 5, 1992).

2. Income-related Benefits Schemes (Miscellaneous Amendments) (No. 4) Regulations 1993 (S.I. 1993 No. 2119), reg. 44 (October 5, 1993).

3. Disability Working Allowance and Income Support (General) Amendment Regulations 1995 (S.I. 1995 No. 482), reg. 3 (April 11, 1995).

4. Income-related Benefits Schemes (Miscellaneous Amendments) Regulations 1995 (S.I. 1995 No. 516), reg. 7 (April 11, 1995).

DEFINITION

"child"—see 1986 Act, s.20(11) (SSCBA, s.137(1)).
"claimant"—see reg. 2(1).
"lone parent"—*ibid.*
"married couple"—see 1986 Act, s.84(1) (SSCBA, s.137(1)).
"partner"—see reg. 2(1).
"single claimant"—*ibid.*
"unmarried couple"—see 1986 Act, s.84(1) (SSCBA, s.137(1)).
"young person"—see reg. 2(1), reg. 8.

GENERAL NOTE

The determination of the maximum disability working allowance is the essential starting point in the calculation of benefit, just as it is for family credit. If the claimant's income is not more than the applicable amount specified in reg. 52, the maximum allowance is payable (Contributions and Benefits Act, s.129(5)(a); 1986 Act, s.21(3A)). If the income is above that amount, the maximum allowance is to be reduced at the rate specified in reg. 53 (Contributions and Benefits Act, s.129(5)(*b*); 1986 Act, s.21(3B)) The rate is 70 per cent., the same as for family credit.

Paragraph (1)
The structure for fixing the maximum disability working allowance is slightly different from family credit, because there is no requirement that the claimant should have a child in the household. Thus a maximum allowance for a single claimant has to be specified under sub-para. (a). Under sub-para. (b) there is the same maximum for a lone parent or a couple. To the allowance fixed under sub-para. (a) or (b) is added the appropriate amount for children and young persons for whom an adult is responsible under sub-para. (c) and, if applicable, sub-para. (d). Sub-para. (d) introduces a disabled child's allowance from April 11, 1995. The conditions for this are in para. (1A) and are similar to those for a disabled child premium in income support. See paras. (4) to (7) below for further rules for the allowances for children.
The amounts are specified in Sched. 5. The amount for a couple or lone parent is higher than the maximum family credit by the amount of the income support disability premium. It is not clear how the amount for a single claimant was calculated. The amounts for children under sub-para. (c) are the same as for family credit. The amount for a disabled child under sub-para. (d) is the same as the income support disabled child premium.
The effect of para. (7) is that the amount of the allowance is set according to the ages of children and the amounts specified as at the beginning of the award. See reg. 16(1A) and (1B) of the Claims and Payments Regulations.

Paragraphs (2) to (6)
See the notes to reg. 46 of the Family Credit (General) Regulations.

[¹Applicable amount of disability working allowance

52.—(1) The applicable amount] for the purposes of section 20(6A) of the Act [SSCBA, s.129(1)] (conditions of entitlement to disability working allowance) shall, in the case of a claimant who is—
    (a) single, be [²£54.75] per week;
    (b) a member of a married or unmarried couple, or a lone parent, be [²£73.00] per week.

(2) For the purposes of section 20(6D) of the Act [SSCBA, s.129(1)(c)] (date on which applicable amount is to be determined) the prescribed date is the date on which the period under section 20(6F) of the Act [SSCBA, s.129(6)] (period of the award) begins.

AMENDMENTS

1. Income-related Benefits Schemes (Miscellaneous Amendments) (No. 3) Regulations 1992 (S.I. 1992 No. 2155), Sched., para. 18 (October 5, 1992).
2. Social Security Benefits Up-rating Order 1995 (S.I. 1995 No. 559), art. 17(c) (April 11, 1995).

DEFINITIONS

    "the Act"—see reg. 2(1).
    "claimant"—*ibid.*
    "lone parent"—*ibid.*
    "married couple"—see 1986 Act, s.84(1) (SSCBA, s.137(1)).
    "single claimant"—see reg.2(1).
    "unmarried couple"—see 1986 Act, s.84(1) (SSCBA, s.137(1)).

GENERAL NOTE

See the note to reg. 51 for the calculation of benefit (and s.129(5) of the Contribution and Benefits Act; 1986 Act, s.21(3A) and (3B)). The applicable amount prescribed at the beginning of the period of award controls the calculation.

The applicable amount for couples and lone parents is the same as for family credit, the equivalent of the income support rate for couples both over 18. The applicable amount for single claimants has no equivalent in family credit. It is now above the income support figure for a single claimant aged 25 or over, having been increased as part of the changes associated with the introduction of incapacity benefit in April 1995.

Entitlement to disability working allowance where income exceeds the applicable amount

53. The prescribed percentage for the purpose of section 21 (3B) of the Act [SSCBA, s.129(5)(b)] (percentage of excess of income over applicable amount which is deducted from maximum disability working allowance) shall be 70 per cent.

DEFINITION

"the Act"—see reg. 2(1).

GENERAL NOTE

Where the income exceeds the applicable amount the maximum disability working allowance is reduced by 70 per cent. of the excess, just as for family credit.

PART VII

CHANGES OF CIRCUMSTANCES

Death of claimant

54.—(1) Except as provided in paragraph (2), an award of disability working allowance shall cease to have effect upon the death of the claimant.

(2) Where a claimant dies and is survived by a partner who was the claimant's partner at the date of claim, an award of disability working allowance made in the claimant's favour shall have effect for its unexpired period as if originally made in favour of the partner.

DEFINITIONS

"claimant"—see reg. 2(1).
"date of claim"—*ibid.*
"partner"—*ibid.*

GENERAL NOTE

See the notes to reg. 49 of the Family Credit (General) Regulations.

Prevention of duplication of awards of family credit, disability working allowance and income support

55. Where provision is made for the same child or young person in awards for overlapping periods, the first being an award of disability working allowance and the second an award of disability working allowance, family credit or income support, and at the start of the period of overlap that child or young person is no longer a member of the household of the claimant under the first award, the first award shall terminate with effect from the start of the period of overlap.

DEFINITIONS

"child"—see 1986 Act, s.20(11) (SSCBA, s.137(1)).
"claimant"—see reg. 2(1).
"young person"—*ibid.*, reg. 8.

[¹Overlapping awards

56.—(1) An award of disability working allowance (the new award) which is made in consequence of a claim in respect of a period beginning before the commencement of an existing award of disability working allowance (the existing award) and which overlaps with the period of the existing award, shall be treated as a relevant change of circumstances affecting the existing award and the existing award shall be reviewed and shall terminate with effect from the date on which the decision of the adjudication officer making the new award is notified to the claimant.

(2) An award of family credit which is made in consequence of a claim in respect of a period beginning before the commencement of an existing award of disability working allowance (the existing award) and which overlaps with the period of the existing award, shall be treated as a change of circumstances affecting the existing award and the existing award shall be reviewed and shall terminate with effect from the date on which the decision of the adjudication officer awarding family credit is notified to the claimant.]

AMENDMENT

1. Income-related Benefits Schemes (Miscellaneous Amendments) (No. 5) Regulations 1994 (S.I. 1994 No. 2139), reg. 8 (October 4, 1994).

DEFINITION

"claimant"—see reg. 2(1).

GENERAL NOTE

See the note to reg. 51 of the Family Credit Regulations.

[¹Reduced benefit direction

56A.—(1) The following occurrences shall be changes of circumstances which affect an award of disability working allowance and the rate at which it is payable—
   (a) a reduced benefit direction given by a child support officer under section 46(5) of the Child Support Act 1991;
   (b) the cessation or cancellation of a reduced benefit direction under Part IX of the maintenance regulations;
   (c) the suspension of a reduced benefit direction under regulation 48(1) of the maintenance regulations;
   (d) the removal of a suspension imposed under paragraph (1) of regulation 48 of the maintenance regulations in accordance with paragraph (3) of that regulation.
(2) In this regulation—
   (a) "child support officer" means a person appointed in accordance with section 13 of the Child Support Act 1991;
   (b) "the maintenance regulations" means the Child Support (Maintenance Assessment Procedure) Regulations 1992]

AMENDMENT

1. Income-related Benefits Schemes (Miscellaneous Amendments) Regulations 1993 (S.I. 1993 No. 315), reg. 20 (April 13, 1993).

GENERAL NOTE

See the note to reg. 51A of the Family Credit (General) Regulations. The application of reduced benefit directions under the Child Support Act 1991 to disability working allowance is required by reg. 34 of the Child Support (Maintenance Assessment Procedure) Regulations 1992.

PART VIII

ENTITLEMENT TO FAMILY CREDIT AND DISABILITY WORKING ALLOWANCE

Prescribed circumstances for entitlement to disability working allowance

57. For the purposes of section 20(6A)(d) of the Act [SSCBA, s.129(1)(d)] (prescribed circumstances) where a claimant or a member of his family is entitled to family credit, he is entitled to disability working allowance, if—
  (a) at the date of the claim for disability working allowance the award of family credit for him or a member of his family will expire within 28 days; and
  (b) the claimant is or would be otherwise entitled to disability working allowance by virtue of these Regulations; and
  (c) the claim for disability working allowance is made in respect of a period which commences immediately after the expiry of the award of family credit.

DEFINITIONS

"the Act"—see reg. 2(1).
"claimant"—*ibid.*
"date of claim"—*ibid.*
"family"—see 1986 Act, s.84(1) (SSCBA, s.137(1)).

SCHEDULES

SCHEDULE 1   **Regulation 3**

DISABILITY WHICH PUTS A PERSON AT A DISADVANTAGE IN GETTING A JOB

Part I

1. When standing he cannot keep his balance unless he continually holds onto something.
2. Using any crutches, walking frame, walking stick, prosthesis or similar walking aid which he habitually uses, he cannot walk a continuous distance of 100 metres along level ground without stopping or without suffering severe pain.
3. He can use neither of his hands behind his back as in the process of putting on a jacket or of tucking a shirt into trousers.
4. He can extend neither of his arms in front of him so as to shake hands with another person without difficulty.

5. He can put neither of his hands up to his head without difficulty so as to put on a hat.

6. Due to lack of manual dexterity he cannot pick up with each hand a coin which is not more than $2\frac{1}{2}$ centimetres in diameter.

7. He is not able to use his hands or arms to pick up a full jug of 1 litre capacity and pour from it into a cup, without difficulty.

8. He can turn neither of his hands sideways through 180°.

9. He is registered as blind or registered as partially sighted in a register compiled by a local authority under section 29(4)(g) of the National Assistance Act 1948 (welfare services) or, in Scotland, has been certified as blind or as partially sighted and in consequence registered as blind or partially sighted in a register maintained by or on behalf of a regional or island council.

10. He cannot see to read 16 point print at a distance greater than 20 centimetres, if appropriate, wearing the glasses he normally uses.

11. He cannot hear a telephone ring when he is in the same room as the telephone, if appropriate, using a hearing aid he normally uses.

12. In a quiet room he has difficulty in hearing what someone talking in a loud voice at a distance of 2 metres says, if appropriate, using a hearing aid he normally uses.

13. People who know him well have difficulty in understanding what he says.

14. When a person he knows well speaks to him, he has difficulty in understanding what that person says.

15. At least once a year during waking hours he is in a coma or has a fit in which he loses consciousness.

16. He has a mental illness for which he receives regular treatment under the supervision of a medically qualified person.

17. Due to mental disability he is often confused or forgetful.

18. He cannot do the simplest addition and subtraction.

19. Due to mental disability he strikes people or damages property or is unable to form normal social relationships.

20. He cannot normally sustain an 8 hour working day or a 5 day working week due to a medical condition or intermittent or continuous severe pain.

Part II

21. Subject to paragraph 24, there is payable to him—
(a) the highest or middle rate of the care component of disability living allowance.
(b) the higher rate of the mobility component of disability living allowance.
(c) an attendance allowance under section 35 of the Social Security Act [SSCBA, s.64],
(d) disablement benefit where the extent of the disablement is assessed at not less than 80 per cent. in accordance with section 57 of and Schedule 8 to the Social Security Act [SSCBA, s.103, Sched. 6],
(e) a war pension in respect of which the degree of disablement is certified at not less than 80 per cent.; and for the purposes of this sub-paragraph "war pension" means a war pension in accordance with section 25(4) of the Social Security Act 1989.
(f) mobility supplement, or
(g) a benefit corresponding to a benefit mentioned in sub-paragraphs (a)-(f), under any enactment having effect in Northern Ireland.

22. Subject to paragraph 24, for one or more of the 56 days immediately preceding the date when the initial claim for disability working allowance was made or treated as made, there was payable to him severe disablement allowance or a corresponding benefit under any enactment having effect in Northern Ireland.

23. Subject to paragraph 24, he has an invalid carriage or other vehicle provided by the Secretary of State under section 5(2)(a) of the National Health Service Act 1977 and Schedule 2 to that Act or under section 46 of the National Health Service (Scotland) Act

1978 or provided under Article 30(1) of the Health and Personal Social Services (Northern Ireland) Order 1972.

24. Paragraphs 21 to 23 are subject to the condition that no evidence is before the adjudication officer which gives him reasonable grounds for believing that in respect of an initial claim, none of the paragraphs in Part I or Part III of this Schedule apply to the claimant and in respect of a repeat claim, none of the paragraphs in Part I apply to the claimant.

Part III

25. As a result of an illness or accident he is undergoing a period of habilitation or rehabilitation.

DEFINITIONS

"claimant"—see reg. 2(1).
"the Social Security Act"—*ibid.*

GENERAL NOTE

See the notes to reg. 3 for the application of these tests to initial and repeat claims. For discussion of the substance of Sched.1, see Rowland, *Medical and Disability Appeal Tribunals: the Legislation.*

SCHEDULE 2   Regulations 19(2) and 21(2)

SUMS TO BE DISREGARDED IN THE CALCULATION OF EARNINGS

1. Any earnings derived from employment which are payable in a country outside the United Kingdom where there is a prohibition against the transfer to the United Kingdom of those earnings.

2. Any earnings of a child or young person.

3. Where a payment of earnings is made in a currency other than sterling, any banking charge or commission payable in converting that payment to sterling.

DEFINITIONS

"child"—see 1986 Act, s.20(11) (SSCBA, s.137(1)).
"earnings"—see reg. 2(1).
"young person"—*ibid.*, reg. 8.

GENERAL NOTE

The most important of these disregards is that in para. 2. Earnings of children and young persons are disregarded in all circumstances.

SCHEDULE 3   Regulation 27(2)

SUMS TO BE DISREGARDED IN THE CALCULATION OF INCOME OTHER THAN EARNINGS

1. Any amount paid by way of tax on income which is taken into account under regulation 27 (calculation of income other than earnings).

2. Any payment in respect of any expenses incurred by a claimant who is—
   (a) engaged by a charitable or [9voluntary organisation]; or

(b) a volunteer,

if he otherwise derives no remuneration or profit from the employment and is not to be treated as possessing any earnings under regulation 29(4) (notional income).

3. Any housing benefit or income support.

4. Any mobility allowance or disability living allowance.

5. Any concessionary payment made to compensate for the non-payment of—

(a) any payment specified in paragraph 4 or 7;

(b) income support.

6. Any mobility supplement or any payment intended to compensate for the non-payment of such a supplement.

7. Any attendance allowance.

8. Any payment to the claimant as holder of the Victoria Cross or of the George Cross or any analogous payment.

9. Any sum in respect of a course of study attended by a child or young person payable by virtue of regulations made under section 81 of the Education Act 1944 (assistance by means of scholarship or otherwise), or by virtue of section 2(1) of the Education Act 1962 (awards for courses of further education) or section 49 of the Education (Scotland) Act 1980 (power to assist persons to take advantage of educational facilities).

10. In the case of a student, any sums intended for any expenditure specified in paragraph (2) of regulation 42 (calculation of grant income) necessary as a result of his attendance on his course.

11. In the case of a claimant participating in arrangements for training made under section 2 of the Employment and Training Act 1973 or section 2 of the Enterprise and New Towns (Scotland) Act 1990 or attending a course at an employment rehabilitation centre established under section 2 of the 1973 Act—

(a) any travelling expenses reimbursed to the claimant;

(b) any living away from home allowance under section 2(2)(d) of the 1973 Act or section 2(4)(c) of the 1990 Act;

(c) any training premium, but this paragraph, except insofar as it relates to a payment under sub-paragraph (a), (b) or (c), does not apply to any part of any allowance under section 2(2)(d) of the 1973 Act or section 2(4)(c) of the 1990 Act.

12.—(1) Except where sub-paragraph (2) applies and subject to sub-paragraph (3) and paragraphs 29 and 33, £10 of any charitable payment or of any voluntary payment made or due to be made at regular intervals.

(2) Subject to sub-paragraph (3) and paragraph 33, any charitable payment or voluntary payment made or due to be made at regular intervals which is intended and used for an item other than food, ordinary clothing or footwear, household fuel, or housing costs of any member of the family, or is used for any personal community [²charge,] collective community charge contribution [² or council tax] for which any member of the family is liable.

(3) Sub-paragraphs (1) and (2) shall not apply to a payment which is made or due to be made by—

(a) a former partner of the claimant, or former parent of any member of the claimant's family; or

(b) the parent of a child or young person is a member of the claimant's family's.

(4) For the purposes of sub-paragraph (1) where a number of charitable or voluntary payments may fall to be taken into account they shall be treated as though they were one such payment.

(5) For the purposes of sub-paragraph (2) the expression "ordinary clothing or footwear" means clothing or footwear for normal daily use, but does not include school uniforms, or clothing or footwear used solely for sporting activities.

13.—(1) Where the claimant or his partner is treated as responsible for a child or young person by virtue of regulation 9 (circumstances in which a person is to be treated as responsible or not responsible for another), £15 of any payment of maintenance, whether under a court order or not, which is made or due to be made by—

(a) the claimant's former partner, or the claimant's partner's former partner; or

(b) the parent of a child or young person where that child or young person is a member of the claimant's family except where that parent is the claimant or the claimant's partner.

(2) For the purposes of sub-paragraph (1) where more than one maintenance payment falls to be taken into account in any week, all such payments shall be aggregated and treated as if they were a single payment.

14. Subject to paragraph 29, £10 of any of the following, namely—

(a) a war disablement pension or war widow's pension or a payment made to compensate for the non-payment of such a pension [⁶,except in so far as such a pension or payment falls to be disregarded under paragraphs 6 or 7];

(b) a pension paid by the Government of a country outside Great Britain which is either—
  (i) analogous to a war disablement pension; or
  (ii) analogous to a war widow's pension;

(c) a pension paid under any special provision made by the law of the Federal Republic of Germany or any part of it, or of the Republic of Austria, to victims of National Socialist persecution.

15. Any child benefit under Part I of the Child Benefit Act 1975 [SSCBA, Part IX].

16.—(1) Any income derived from capital to which the claimant is, or is treated under regulation 39 (capital jointly held) as, beneficially entitled but, but subject to sub-paragraph (2), not income derived from capital disregarded under paragraph 1, 2, 4, 13 or 26 to 30 of Schedule 4.

(2) Income derived from capital disregarded under paragraph 2, 4 or 26 to 30 of Schedule 4 but [³only to the extent of—

(a) any mortgage repayments made in respect of the dwelling or premises in the period during which that income accrued; or

(b) any council tax or water charges which the claimant is liable to pay in respect of the dwelling or premises and which are paid in the period during which that income accrued.]

17. Where a person receives income under an annuity purchased with a loan which satisfies the following conditions—

(a) that the loan was made as part of a scheme under which not less than 90 per cent. of the proceeds of the loan were applied to the purchase by the person to whom it was made of an annuity ending with his life or with the life of the survivor of two or more persons (in this paragraph referred to as "the annuitants") who include the person to whom the loan was made;

(b) that the interest on the loan is payable by the person to whom it was made or by one of the annuitants;

(c) that at the time the loan was made the person to whom it was made or each of the annuitants had attained the age of 65;

(d) that the loan was secured on a dwelling in Great Britain and the person to whom the loan was made or one of the annuitants owns an estate or interest in that dwelling; and

(e) that the person to whom the loan was made or one of the annuitants occupies the dwelling on which it was secured as his home at the time the interest is paid,

the amount, calculated on a weekly basis equal to—

  [⁸(i) where, or insofar as, section 369 of the Income and Corporation Taxes Act 1988 (mortgage interest payable under deduction of tax) applies to the payments of interest on the loan, the interest which is payable after deduction of a sum equal to income tax on such payments at the applicable percentage of income tax within the meaning of section 369(1A) of that Act;]

  (ii) in any other case the interest which is payable on the loan without deduction of such a sum.

[⁹18. Any payment made to the claimant by a person who normally resides with the claimant, which is a contribution towards that person's living and accommodation costs, except where that person is residing with the claimant in circumstances to which paragraph 19 or 38 or regulation 24(2) (earnings of self-employed earners) refers.]

[⁷19. Where the claimant occupies a dwelling as his home and the dwelling is also occupied by [⁹ another person], and there is a contractual liability to make payments to the claimant in respect of the occupation of the dwelling by that person or a member of his family—

    (a) £4 of the aggregate of any payments made in respect of any one week in respect of the occupation of the dwelling by that person or a member of his family, or by that person and a member of his family; and

    (b) a further [¹⁰£9.20], where the aggregate of any such payments is inclusive of an amount for heating.]

20. Any income in kind.

21. Any income which is payable in a country outside the United Kingdom where there is a prohibition against the transfer to the United Kingdom of that income.

22.—(1) Any payment made to the claimant in respect of a child or young person who is a member of his family—

    (a) in accordance with a scheme approved by the Secretary of State under section 57A of the Adoption Act 1976, or as the case may be, section 51 of the Adoption (Scotland) Act 1978 (schemes for payments of allowances to adopters);

    (b) which is a payment made by a local authority in pursuance of paragraph 15(1) of Schedule 1 to the Children Act 1989 (local authority contributions to a custodian to child's maintenance),

to the extent specified in sub-paragraph (2).

    (2) In the case of a child or young person—

    (a) to whom regulation 30 applies (capital in excess of £3,000), the whole payment;

    (b) to whom that regulation does not apply, so much of the weekly amount of the payment as exceeds the allowance in respect of that child or young person under Schedule 5.

23. Any payment made by a local authority to the claimant with whom a person is accommodated and maintained by virtue of arrangements made under section 23(2)(a) of the Children Act 1989 or, as the case may be, section 21 of the Social Work (Scotland) Act 1968 or by a voluntary organisation under section 59(1)(a) of the Children Act 1989 or by a care authority under regulation 9 of the Boarding Out and Fostering of Children (Scotland) Regulations 1985 (provision of accommodation and maintenance for children by local authorities and voluntary organisations).

24. Any payment made by a health authority, local authority or voluntary organisation to the claimant in respect of a person who is not normally a member of the claimant's household but is temporarily in his care.

25. Any payment made by a local authority under section 17 or 24 of the Children Act 1989 or, as the case may be, section 12, 24 or 26 of the Social Work (Scotland) Act 1968 (provision of services for children and their families and advice and assistance to certain children).

26. Any payment of income which under regulation 34 (income treated as capital) is to be treated as capital.

27. Any statutory maternity pay under Part V of the Act [SSCBA, Part XII] or maternity allowance under section 22 of the Social Security Act [SSCBA, s.35].

28. Any payment under paragraph 2 of Schedule 6 to the Act [SSCBA, s.148] (pensioners Christmas bonus).

29. The total of a claimant's income or, if he is a member of a family, the family's income and the income of any person which he is treated as possessing under regulation 12(2) (calculation of income and capital of members of claimant's family and of a polygamous marriage) to be disregarded under regulation 43(2)(b) (calculation of covenant income where a contribution is assessed), regulation 44(1)(c) (covenant income where no grant income or no contribution is assessed), regulation 47(2) (treatment of student loans) and paragraphs 12(1) and 14, shall in no case exceed £10 per week.

30. Where a payment of income is made in a currency other than sterling, any banking charge or commission payable in converting that payment into sterling.

31. Any statutory maternity pay under Part VI of the Social Security (Nothern Ireland) Order 1986 or maternity allowance under section 22 of the Social Security (Northern Ireland) Act 1975.

32. Any payment in respect of expenses to which regulation 21(2) (earnings of employed earners) applies.

33.—(1) Any payment made under the Macfarlane Trust, the Macfarlane (Special Payments) Trust, the Macfarlane (Special Payments) (No.2) Trust ("the Trusts"), ['the Fund][⁵, the Eileen Trust] or[⁴, the Independent Living Funds].

(2) Any payment by or on behalf of a person who suffered or is suffering from haemophilia ['or who is or was a qualifying person], or by or on behalf of his partner or former partner from whom he is not, or, where either that person or his former partner has died, was not, estranged or divorced, which derives from a payment under any of the Trusts to which sub-paragraph (1) refers and which is made to or for the benefit of—

(a) that person or that person's partner or former partner to whom this sub-paragraph refers;

(b) any child who is a member of that person's family or who was such a member and who is a member of the claimant's family; or

(c) any young person who is a member of that person's family or who was such a member and who is a member of the claimant's family.

(3) Any payment by a person who is suffering from haemophilia ['or who is a qualifying person], which derives from a payment under any of the Trusts to which sub-paragraph (1) refers, where—

(a) that person has no partner or former partner from whom he is not estranged or divorced, nor any child or young person who is or had been a member of that person's family; and

(b) the payment is made either—

(i) to that person's parent or step-parent, or

(ii) where that person at the date of the payment is a child, a young person or a student who has not completed his full-time education and has no parent or step-parent, to his guardian,

but only for a period from the date of the payment until the end of two years from that person's death.

(4) Any payment out of the estate of a person who suffered from haemophilia ['or who was a qualifying person], which derives from a payment under any of the Trusts to which sub-paragraph (1) refers, where—

(a) that person at the date of his death (the relevant date) had no partner or former partner from whom he was not estranged or divorced, nor any child or young person who was or had been a member of his family; and

(b) the payment is made either—

(i) to that person's parent or step-parent, or

(ii) where that person at the relevant date was a child, a young person or a student who had not completed his full education and had no parent or step-parent, to his guardian,

but only for a period of 2 years from the relevant date.

(5) In the case of a person to whom or for whose benefit a payment under sub-paragraph (1), (2), (3) or (4) is made, any income which derives from any payment of income or capital made under or deriving from any of the Trusts.

[¹(6) For the purposes of sub-paragraphs (2) to (5), any reference to the Trusts shall be construed as including a reference to the Fund [⁵ and the Eileen Trust].]

34. Any payment made by the Secretary of State to compensate for the loss (in whole or in part) of entitlement to housing benefit.

35. Any payment made by the Secretary of State to compensate a person who was entitled to supplementary benefit in respect of a period ending immediately before 11th

April 1988 but who did not become entitled to income support in respect of a period beginning with that day.

36. Any payment made by the Secretary of State to compensate for the loss of housing benefit supplement under regulation 19 of the Supplementary Benefit (Requirements) Regulations 1983.

37. Any payment made to a juror or witness in respect of attendance at court other than compensation for loss of earnings or for the loss of a benefit payable under the benefit Acts.

[⁷**38.** Where the claimant occupies a dwelling as his home and he provides in that dwelling board and lodging accommodation, an amount, in respect of each person for whom such accommodation is provided for the whole or any part of a week, equal to—

    (a) where the aggregate of any payments made in respect of any one week in respect of such accommodation provided to such person does not exceed £20.00, 100 per cent. of such payments; or

    (b) where the aggregate of any such payments exceeds £20.00, £20.00 and 50 per cent. of the excess over £20.00.]

39. Any community charge benefit.

40. Any payment in consequence of a reduction of a personal community charge pursuant to regulations under section 13A of the Local Government Finance Act 1988 or section 9A of the Abolition of Domestic Rates Etc. (Scotland) Act 1987 (reduction of liability for personal community charge) [²or reduction of council tax under section 13 or, as the case may be, section 80 of the Local Government Finance Act 1992 (reduction of liability for council tax).]

41. Any special war widows payment made under—

    (a) the Naval and Marine Pay and Pensions (Special War Widows Payment) Order 1990 made under section 3 of the Naval and Marine Pay and Pensions Act 1865;

    (b) the Royal Warrant dated 19th February 1990 amending the Schedule to the Army Pensions Warrant 1977;

    (c) the Queen's Order dated 26th February 1990 made under section 2 of the Air Force (Constitution) Act 1917;

    (d) the Home Guard War Widows Special Payments Regulations 1990 made under section 151 of the Reserve Forces Act 1980;

    (e) the Orders dated 19th February 1990 amending Orders made on 12th December 1980 concerning the Ulster Defence Regiment made in each case under section 140 of the Reserve Forces Act 1980;

and any analogous payment by the Secretary of State for Defence to any person who is not a person entitled under the provisions mentioned in sub-paragraphs (a) to (e) of this paragraph.

42.—(1) Any payment or repayment made—

    (a) as respects England and Wales, under regulation 3, 5 or 8 of the National Health Service (Travelling Expenses and Remission of Charges) Regulations 1988 (travelling expenses and health service supplies);

    (b) as respects Scotland, under regulation 3, 5 or 8 of the National Health Service (Travelling Expenses and Remission of Charges) (Scotland) Regulations 1988 (travelling expenses and health service supplies).

(2) Any payment or repayment made by the Secretary of State for Health, the Secretary of State for Scotland or the Secretary of State for Wales which is analogous to a payment or repayment mentioned in sub-paragraph (1).

43. Any payment made under regulation 9 to 11 or 13 of the Welfare Food Regulations 1988 (payments made in place of milk tokens or the supply of vitamins).

44. Any payment made either by the Secretary of State for the Home Department or by the Secretary of State for Scotland under a scheme established to assist relatives and other persons to visit persons in custody.

45. Any payment made, whether by the Secretary of State or any other person, under the Disabled Persons Employment Act 1944 or in accordance with arrangements made under section 2 of the Employment and Training Act 1973 to assist disabled persons to obtain or retain employment despite their disability.

46. Any family credit.

[³**47.** Any council tax benefit.

48. Any guardian's allowance.]

[⁷**49.** Where the claimant is in receipt of any benefit under Part II, III or V of the Contributions and Benefits Act, any increase in the rate of that benefit arising under Part IV (increases for dependants) or section 106(a) (unemployability supplement) of that Act where the dependant in respect of whom the increase is paid is not a member of the claimant's family.]

[⁸**50.** Any supplementary pension under article 29(1A) of the Naval, Military and Air Forces etc. (Disablement and Death) Service Pensions Order 1983 (pensions to widows).

51. In the case of a pension awarded at the supplementary rate under article 27(3) of the Personal Injuries (Civilians) Scheme 1983 (pensions to widows), the sum specified in paragraph 1(c) of Schedule 4 to that Scheme.

52.—(1) Any payment which is—
(a) made under any of the Dispensing Instruments to a widow of a person—
  (i) whose death was attributable to service in a capacity analogous to service as a member of the armed forces of the Crown; and
  (ii) whose service in such capacity terminated before 31st March 1973; and
(b) equal to the amount specified in article 29(1A) of the Naval, Military and Air Forces etc. (Disablement and Death) Service Pensions Order 1983 (pensions to widows).

(2) In this paragraph "the Dispensing Instruments" means the Order in Council of 19th December 1881, the Royal Warrant of 27th October 1884 and the Order by His Majesty of 14th January 1922 (exceptional grants of pay, non-effective pay and allowances).]

[⁹**53.** Any payment made by the Secretary of State to compensate for a reduction in a maintenance assessment made under the Child Support Act 1991.]

AMENDMENTS

1. Income-related Benefits Schemes and Social Security (Recoupment) Amendment Regulations 1992 (S.I. 1992 No. 1101), reg. 3(6) (May 7, 1992).

2. Income-related Benefits Schemes (Miscellaneous Amendments) Regulations 1993 (S.I. 1993 No. 315), Sched., para. 17 (April 1, 1993).

3. Income-related Benefits Schemes (Miscellaneous Amendments) Regulations 1993 (S.I. 1993 No. 315), reg. 21 (council tax and council tax benefit: April 1, 1993; otherwise: April 13, 1993).

4. Social Security Benefits (Miscellaneous Amendments) (No. 2) Regulations 1993 (S.I. 1993 No. 963), reg. 6(3) (April 22, 1993).

5. Income-related Benefits Schemes and Social Security (Recoupment) Amendment Regulations 1993 (S.I. 1993 No. 1249), reg. 5(4) (May 14, 1993).

6. Income-related Benefits Schemes (Miscellaneous Amendments) (No. 4) Regulations 1993 (S.I. 1993 No. 2119), reg. 45 (October 5, 1993).

7. Income-related Benefits Schemes (Miscellaneous Amendments) Regulations 1994 (S.I. 1994 No. 527), reg. 28 (April 12, 1994).

8. Income-related Benefits Schemes (Miscellaneous Amendments) (No. 5) Regulations 1994 (S.I. 1994 No. 2139), reg. 9 (October 4, 1994).

9. Income-related Benefits Schemes (Miscellaneous Amendments) Regulations 1995 (S.I. 1995 No. 516), reg. 8 (April 11, 1995).

10. Social Security Benefits Up-rating Order 1995 (S.I. 1995 No. 559), art. 17(d) (April 11, 1995).

DEFINITIONS

"the Act"—see reg. 2(1).
"attendance allowance"—*ibid.*
"child"—see 1986 Act, s.84(1) (SSCBA, s.137(1)).
"claimant"—see reg. 2(1).
"dwelling"—see 1986 Act, s.84(1) (SSCBA, s.137(1)).

"family"—see 1986 Act, s.20(11) (SSCBA, s.137(1)).
"local authority"—see 1986 Act, s.84(1).
"mobility allowance"—see reg. 2(1).
"mobility supplement"—*ibid.*
"payment"—*ibid.*
"qualifying person"—*ibid.*
"Social Security Act"—*ibid.*
"student"—*ibid.*,reg. 41.
"the Eileen Trust"—*ibid.*
"the Fund"—see reg. 2(1).
"the Independent Living Funds"—*ibid.*
"the Macfarlane (Special Payments) Trust"—*ibid.*
"the Macfarlane (Special Payments)(No.2) Trust"—*ibid.*
"the Macfarlane Trust"—*ibid.*
"voluntary organisation"—*ibid.*
"year of assessment"—see reg. 2(1).
"young person"—*ibid.*, reg. 8.

GENERAL NOTE

See the notes to Sched. 2 to the Family Credit (General) Regulations, with the necessary differences in cross-references. Para. 46 is an addition.

SCHEDULE 4   **Regulation 32(2)**

CAPITAL TO BE DISREGARDED

1. The dwelling, together with any garage, garden and outbuildings, normally occupied by the claimant as his home including any premises not so occupied which it is impracticable or unreasonable to sell separately, in particular, in Scotland, any croft land on which the dwelling is situated; but, notwithstanding regulation 12 (calculation of income and capital of members of claimant's family and of a polygamous marriage), only one dwelling shall be disregarded under this paragraph.

2. Any premises acquired for occupation by the claimant which he intends to occupy as his home within 26 weeks of the date of acquisition or such longer period as is reasonable in the circumstances to enable the claimant to obtain possession and commence occupation of the premises.

3. Any sum directly attributable to the proceeds of sale of any premises formerly occupied by the claimant as his home which is to be used for the purchase of other premises intended for such occupation within 26 weeks of the date of sale or such longer period as is reasonable in the circumstances to enable the claimant to complete the purchase.

4. Any premises occupied in whole or in part by a partner or relative (that is to say any close relative, grandparent, grandchild, uncle, aunt, nephew or niece) of any member of the family as his home, where that person is aged 60 or over or has been incapacitated for a continuous period of at least 13 weeks immediately preceding the date of the claim.

5. Any reversionary interest.

6.—(1) The assets of any business owned in whole or in part by the claimant and for the purposes of which he is engaged as a self-employed earner or, if he has ceased to be so engaged, for such period as may be reasonable in the circumstances to allow for disposal of any such asset.

(2) The assets of any business owned in whole or in part by the claimant where—

  (a) he has ceased to be engaged as a self-employed earner in that business by reason of some disease or bodily or mental disablement; and

  (b) he intends to become re-engaged as a self-employed earner in that business as soon as he recovers or is able to be re-engaged in that business,

for a period of 26 weeks from the date on which the claimant last ceased to be engaged in that business, or, if it is unreasonable to expect him to become re-engaged in that

580

business within that period, for such longer period as is reasonable in the circumstances to enable him to become so re-engaged.

7. Any sum attributable to the proceeds of sale of any asset of such a business which is re-invested or to be re-invested in the business within 13 weeks of the date of sale or such longer period as may be reasonable to allow for the re-investment.

8. Any arrears of, or any concessionary payment made to compensate for arrears due to non-payment of—

(a) any payment specified in paragraphs 4, 6, or 7 of Schedule 3;

(b) an income-related benefit or supplementary benefit under the Supplementary Benefits Act 1976, family income supplement under the Family Income Supplements Act 1970 or housing benefit under Part II of the Social Security and Housing Benefits Act 1982,

but only for a period of 52 weeks from the date of the receipt of the arrears or of the concessionary payment.

9. Any sum—

(a) paid to the claimant in consequence of damage to, or loss of, the home or any personal possession and intended for its repair or replacement; or

(b) acquired by the claimant (whether as a loan or otherwise) on the express condition that it is to be used for effecting essential repairs or improvements to the home,

which is to be used for the intended purpose, for a period of 26 weeks from the date on which it was so paid or acquired or such longer period as is reasonable in the circumstances to enable the claimant to effect the repairs, replacement or improvements.

10. Any sum—

(a) deposited with a housing association as defined in section 1(1) of the Housing Associations Act 1985 or section 338(1) of the Housing (Scotland) Act 1987 as a condition of occupying the home;

(b) which was so deposited and which is to be used for the purchase of another home,

for the period of 26 weeks or such longer period as may be reasonable in the circumstances to complete the purchase.

11. Any personal possessions except those which have been acquired by the claimant with the intention of reducing his capital in order to secure entitlement to disability working allowance or to increase the amount of that benefit.

12. The value of the right to receive any income under an annuity or the surrender value (if any) of such an annuity.

13. Where the funds of a trust are derived from a payment made in consequence of any personal injury to the claimant, the value of the trust fund and the value of the right to receive any payment under that trust.

14. The value of the right to receive any income under a life interest or from a liferent.

15. The value of the right to receive any income which is disregarded under paragraph 1 of Schedule 2 or 21 of Schedule 3.

16. The surrender value of any policy of life insurance.

17. Where any payment of capital falls to be made by instalments, the value of the right to receive any outstanding instalments.

18. Any payment made by a local authority under [²section 17 or 24] of the Children Act 1989 or, as the case may be, section 12, 24 or 26 of the Social Work (Scotland) Act 1968 (provision of services for children and their families and advice and assistance for certain children).

19. Any social fund payment under Part III of the Act [SSCBA, Part VIII].

20. Any refund of tax which falls to be deducted under section 26 of the Finance Act 1982 (deductions of tax from certain loan interest) on a payment of relevant loan interest for the purpose of acquiring an interest in the home or carrying out repairs or improvements to the home.

21. Any capital which by virtue of regulations 28 (capital treated as income)[⁶, 30(1) (modifications in respect of children and young persons)] or 47 (treatment of student loans) is to be treated as income.

22. Where a payment of capital is made in a currency other than sterling, any banking charge or commission payable in converting that payment to sterling.

23.—(1) Any payment made under the Macfarlane Trust, the Macfarlane (Special Payments) Trust, the Macfarlane (Special Payments) (No. 2) Trust ("the Trusts"), [¹the Fund][⁵, the Eileen Trust] or [³the Independent Living Funds].

(2) Any payment by or on behalf of a person who suffered or who is suffering from haemophilia [¹or who is or was a qualifying person], or by or on behalf of his partner or former partner from whom he is not or, where either that person or his former partner has died, was not estranged or divorced, which derives from a payment made under any of the Trusts to which sub-paragraph (1) refers and which is made to or for the benefit of—

(a) that person or that person's partner or former partner to whom this sub-paragraph refers;

(b) any child who is a member of that person's family or who was such a member and who is a member of the claimant's family; or

(c) any young person who is a member of that person's family or who was such a member and who is a member of the claimant's family.

(3) Any payment by a person who is suffering from haemophilia [¹or who is a qualifying person], which derives from a payment under any of the Trusts to which sub-paragraph (1) refers, where—

(a) that person has no partner or former partner from whom he is not estranged or divorced, nor any child or young person who is or had been a member of that person's family; and

(b) the payment is made either—

(i) to that person's parent or step-parent; or

(ii) where that person at the date of the payment is a child, a young person or a student who has not completed his full-time education and has no parent or step-parent, to his guardian,

but only for a period from the date of the payment until the end of two years from that person's death.

(4) Any payment out of the estate of a person who suffered from haemophilia [¹or who was a qualifying person], which derives from a payment under any of the Trusts to which sub-paragraph (1) refers, where—

(a) that person at the date of his death (the relevant date) had no partner or former partner from whom he was not estranged or divorced, nor any child or young person who was or had been a member of his family; and

(b) the payment is made either—

(i) to that person's parent or step-parent, or

(ii) where that person at the relevant date was a child, a young person or a student who had not completed his education and had no parent or step-parent, to his guardian,

but only for a period of 2 years from the relevant date.

(5) In the case of a person to whom or for whose benefit a payment under sub-paragraph (1), (2), (3) or (4) is made, any capital resource which derives from any payment of income or capital made under or deriving from any of the Trusts.

[¹(6) For the purposes of sub-paragraphs (2) to (5), any reference to the Trusts shall be construed as including a reference to the Fund [⁵and the Eileen Trust].]

24. The value of the right to receive an occupational or personal pension.

25. The value of the right to receive any rent.

26.—(1) Where a claimant has ceased to occupy what was formerly the dwelling occupied as the home following his estrangement or divorce from his former partner, that dwelling for a period of 26 weeks from the date on which he ceased to occupy that dwelling.

(2) In this paragraph "dwelling" includes any garage, garden and outbuildings which were formerly occupied by the claimant as his home and any premises not so occupied which it is impracticable or unreasonable to sell separately, in particular, in Scotland, any croft land on which the dwelling is situated.

27. Any premises where the claimant is taking reasonable steps to dispose of those premises, for a period of 26 weeks from the date on which he first took such steps, or such longer period as is reasonable in the circumstances to enable him to dispose of those premises.

28. Any premises which the claimant intends to occupy as his home, and in respect of which he is taking steps to obtain possession and has sought legal advice, or has commenced legal proceedings, with a view to obtaining possession, for a period of 26 weeks from the date on which he first sought such advice or first commenced such proceedings whichever is the earlier, or such longer period as is reasonable in the circumstances to enable him to obtain possession and commence occupation of those premises.

29. Any premises which the claimant intends to occupy as his home to which essential repairs or alterations are required in order to render them fit for such occupation, for a period of 26 weeks from the date on which the claimant first takes steps to effect those repairs or alterations, or such longer period as is reasonable in the circumstances to enable those repairs or alterations to be carried out and the claimant to commence occupation of the premises.

30. Any premises occupied in whole or in part by the former partner of a claimant as his home; but this provision shall not apply where the former partner is a person from whom the claimant is estranged or divorced.

31. Any payment in kind made by a charity or under the Macfarlane (Special Payments) Trust[¹, the Macfarlane (Special Payments) (No. 2) Trust[⁴, the Fund or the independent Living (1993) Fund]].

32. [⁶£200 of any payment, or, if the payment is less than £200, the whole of any payment] made under section 2 of the Employment and Training Act 1973 (functions of the Secretary of State) or section 2 of the Enterprise and New Towns (Scotland) Act 1990 as a training bonus to a person participating in arrangements for training made under either of those sections but only for a period of 52 weeks from the date of the receipt of that payment.

33. Any payment made by the Secretary of State to compensate for the loss (in the whole or in part) of entitlement to housing benefit.

34. Any payment made by the Secretary of State to compensate a person who was entitled to supplementary benefit in respect of a period ending immediately before 11th April 1988 but who did not become entitled to income support in respect of a period beginning with that day.

35. Any payment made by the Secretary of State to compensate for the loss of housing benefit supplement under regulation 19 of the Supplementary Benefit (Requirements) Regulations 1983.

36. Any payment made to a juror or witness in respect of attendance at court other than compensation for loss of earnings or for the loss of a benefit payable under the benefit Acts.

37. Any payment in consequence of a reduction of a personal community charge pursuant to regulations under section 13A of the Local Government Finance Act 1988 or section 9A of the Abolition of Domestic Rates Etc (Scotland) Act 1987 (reduction of liability for personal community charge) [²or reduction of council tax under section 13 or, as the case may be, section 80 of the Local Government Finance Act 1992 (reduction of liability for council tax),] but only for a period of 52 weeks from the date of receipt of the payment.

38. Any grant made to the claimant in accordance with a scheme made under section 129 of the Housing Act 1988 or section 66 of the Housing (Scotland) Act 1988 (schemes for payments to assist local housing authority and local authority tenants to obtain other accommodation) which is to be used—

    (a) to purchase premises intended for occupation as his home; or

    (b) to carry out repairs or alterations which are required to render premises fit for occupation as his home,

for a period of 26 weeks from the date on which he received such a grant or such longer period as is reasonable in the circumstances to enable the purchase, repairs or alterations to be completed and the claimant to commence occupation of those premises as his home.

39.—Any payment or repayment made—

    (a) as respects England and Wales, under regulation 3, 5 or 8 of the National Health Service (Travelling Expenses and Remission of Charges) Regulations 1988 (travelling expenses and health service supplies);

    (b) as respects Scotland, under regulation 3, 5 or 8 of the National Health Service (Travelling Expenses and Remission of Charges) (Scotland) 1988 (travelling expenses and health service supplies);

but only for a period of 52 weeks from the date of receipt of the payment or repayment.

(2) Any payment or repayment made by the Secretary of State for Health, the Secretary of State for Scotland or the Secretary of State for Wales which is analogous to a payment or repayment mentioned in sub-paragraph (1); but only for a period of 52 weeks from the date of receipt of the payment or repayment.

40. Any payment made under regulations 9 to 11 or 13 of the Welfare Food Regulations 1988 (payments made in place of milk tokens or the supply of vitamins), but only for a period of 52 weeks from the date of receipt of the payment.

41. Any payment made either by the Secretary of State for the Home Department or by the Secretary of State for Scotland under a scheme established to assist relatives and other persons to visit persons in custody, but only for a period of 52 weeks from the date of receipt of the payment.

42. Any arrears of special war widows payment which is disregarded under paragraph 41 of Schedule 3 (sums to be disregarded in the calculation of income other than earnings) [⁷ or of any amount which is disregarded under paragraph 50, 51 or 52 of that Schedule], but only for a period of 52 weeks from the date of receipt of the arrears.

43. Any payment made, whether by the Secretary of State or any other person, under the Disabled Persons Employment Act 1944 or in accordance with arrangements made under section 2 of the Employment and Training Act 1973 to assist disabled persons to obtain or retain employment despite their disability.

44. Any payment made by a local authority under section 3 of the Disabled (Employment) Act 1958 to homeworkers assisted under the Blind Homeworkers' Scheme.

[⁷**45.** Any sum of capital administered on behalf of a person under the age of 18 by the High Court under the provisions of Order 80 of the Rules of the Supreme Court, the County Court under Order 10 of the County Court Rules 1981, or the Court of Protection, where such sum derives from—

    (a) an award of damages for a personal injury to that person; or

    (b) compensation for the death of one or both parents.

46. Any sum of capital administered on behalf of a person under the age of 18 in accordance with an order made under Rule 43.15 of the Act of Sederunt (Rules of the Court of Session 1994) 1994, or under Rule 131 of the Act of Sederunt (Rules of the Court, consolidation and amendment) 1965, or under Rule 36.14 of the Ordinary Cause Rules 1993, or under Rule 128 of the Ordinary Cause Rules, where such sum derives from—

    (a) an award of damages for a personal injury to that person; or

    (b) compensation for the death of one or both parents.]

[⁸**47.** Any payment made by the Secretary of State to compensate for a reduction in a maintenance assessment made under the Child Support Act 1991, but only for a period of 52 weeks from the date of receipt of that payment.]

AMENDMENTS

    1. Income-related Benefits Schemes and Social Security (Recoupment) Amendment Regulations 1992 (S.I. 1992 No. 1101), reg. 3(7) (May 7, 1992).

    2. Income-related Benefits Schemes (Miscellaneous Amendments) Regulations 1993 (S.I. 1993 No. 315), Sched., para. 18 (April 1, 1993).

    3. Social Security Benefits (Miscellaneous Amendments) (No. 2) Regulations 1993 (S.I. 1993 No. 963), reg. 6(3) (April 22, 1993).

    4. Social Security Benefits (Miscellaneous Amendments) (No. 2) Regulations 1993 (S.I. 1993 No. 963), reg. 6(5) (April 22, 1993).

5. Income-related Benefits Schemes and Social Security (Recoupment) Amendment Regulations 1993 (S.I. 1993 No. 1249), reg. 5(5) (May 14, 1993).

6. Income-related Benefits Schemes (Miscellaneous Amendments) (No. 4) Regulations 1993 (S.I. 1993 No. 2119), reg. 46 (October 5, 1993).

7. Income-related Benefits Schemes (Miscellaneous Amendments) (No. 5) Regulations 1994 (S.I. 1994 No. 2139), reg. 10 (October 4, 1994).

8. Income-related Benefits Schemes (Miscellaneous Amendments) Regulations 1995 (S.I. 1995 No. 516), reg. 9 (April 11, 1995).

DEFINITIONS

"the Act"—see reg. 2(1).
"claimant"—see reg. 2(1), reg. 12(1).
"close relative"—see reg. 2(1).
"date of claim"—*ibid.*
"dwelling"—see 1986 Act, s.84(1) (SSCBA, s.137(1)).
"family"—see 1986 Act, s.20(11) (SSCBA, s.137(1)).
"income-related benefit"—see 1986 Act, s.84(1).
"occupational pension"—see reg. 2(1).
"partner"—*ibid.*
"policy of life insurance"—*ibid.*
"qualifying person"—*ibid.*
"self-employed earner"—*ibid.*
"the Eileen Trust"—*ibid.*
"the Fund"—*ibid.*
"the Independent Living Funds"—*ibid.*
"the Independent Living (1993) Fund"—*ibid.*
"the Macfarlane (Special Payments) Trust"—*ibid.*
"the Macfarlane (Special Payments) (No. 2) Trust"—*ibid.*
"the Macfarlane Trust"—*ibid.*

GENERAL NOTE

See the notes to Sched. 3 to the Family Credit (General) Regulations, with the necessary changes in cross-references. There are some simplifications in the form of these provisions, *e.g.* paras. 27 and 33.

SCHEDULE 5   **Regulations 51**

DETERMINATION OF APPROPRIATE MAXIMUM DISABILITY WORKING ALLOWANCE

Column (1)	Column (2)
Claimant, child, young person	*Amount of allowance*
1. Single claimant.	[¹£46.85];
2. Claimant who is a member of a married or unmarried couple, or is a lone parent.	[¹£73.40];
3. Child— (a) aged less than 11 years; (b) aged not less than 11 but less than 16 years.	(a) [¹£11.40]; (b) [¹£18.90];
4. Young persons— (a) aged not less than 16 but less than 18 years; (b) aged not less than 18 but less than 19 years.	(a) [¹£23.45]; (b) [¹£32.80];
[²**5.** Child or young person to whom regulation 51(1A) applies (disabled child or young person).	£19.80].

AMENDMENTS

1. Social Security Benefits Up-rating Order 1995 (S.I 1995 No. 559), art. 17(e) and Sched. 3 (April 11, 1995).
2. Disability Working Allowance and Income Support (General) Amendment Regulations 1995 (S.I. 1995 No. 482), reg. 4 (April 11, 1995).

DEFINITIONS

"child"—see 1986 Act, s.20(11) (SSCBA, s.137(1)).
"claimant"—see reg. 2(1).
"lone parent"—*ibid.*
"married couple"—see 1986 Act, s.20(11) (SSCBA, s.137(1)).
"single claimant"—see reg. 2(1).
"unmarried couple"—see 1986 Act, s.20(11) (SSCBA, s.137(1)).
"young person"—see reg. 2(1), reg. 8.

GENERAL NOTE

See notes to reg. 51.

Disability Working Allowance and Income Support (General) Amendment Regulations 1995

(S.I. 1995 No. 482)

Made by the Secretary of State under ss. 124(1)(d)(i) and (3), 129(2B)(b) and (c) and (8), 135(1), 137(1) and 175(1), (3) and (4) of the Social Security Contributions and Benefits Act 1992 and s. 12(1) of the Social Security (Incapacity for Work) Act 1994

[In force April 13, 1995]

Transitional provisions with respect to the Disability Working Allowance Regulations

18.—(1) Where invalidity pension was payable to the claimant for one or more of the 56 days immediately preceding the date on which the claim for disability working allowance was made or was treated as made, the payments shall be treated for the purposes of section 129(2)(a)(i) of the Contributions and Benefits Act as payments of long-term incapacity benefit.

(2) Any day on which a claimant was entitled to invalidity pension under sections 33, 40 or 41 of the Contributions and Benefits Act as in force on 12th April 1995 shall be treated for the purposes of section 129(2A)(b) of the Contributions and Benefits Act as a day on which he was entitled to long-term incapacity benefit.

GENERAL NOTE

See the notes to s. 129(2) and (2A) of the Contributions and Benefits Act.

PART V

THE SOCIAL FUND

Social Fund Cold Weather Payments (General) Regulations 1988

(S.I. 1988 No. 1724)

Made by the Secretary of State under ss.32(2A) and 84(1) of the Social Security Act 1986 and s.166(1) to (3A) of the Social Security Act 1975.

<small>GENERAL NOTE</small>

The cold weather payments scheme has been in operation since April 1988, but has undergone several changes in that time. The most significant has been that taking effect in November 1991. It stemmed from a general review announced in February 1991, when the temperature conditions were deemed to be triggered for the whole country for two weeks and the weekly amount of the payment was increased from £5 to £6.

Since s.138(2) of the Contributions and Benefits Act (1986 Act. s.32(2A)) provides the merest framework, the changes have been made by amendment of these Regulations. There are three main changes from November 1991. First, no separate claim needs to be, or can be, made for a cold weather payment. Entitlement simply depends on a person being in the right category of income support recipient and on the temperature conditions being triggered for the area in which he lives. Second, the temperature conditions can be triggered by a forecast, rather than waiting for a week of cold weather to have happened. Thus payments can potentially be made at the time that expenditure is needed, not after the event.

Third, the system of attaching areas to weather stations has been revised. It is now based on postcode areas, rather than DSS Local Office areas (which no longer exist under the Benefits Agency) or local government areas. The system can be more discriminating, but some weather stations still cover areas a long way away, and there have been complaints about bizarre differences in treatment within towns and cities.

It appears that a decision to make a payment will be made by an AO, but since no claim is possible there will be no notification to a person that a payment will not be made. If a person does not receive a payment to which he thinks he is entitled, it appears that he will have to request a negative AO's decision before there is something to appeal against.

Citation, commencement and interpretation

1.—(1) These regulations may be cited as the Social Fund Cold Weather Payments (General) Regulations 1988 and shall come into force on 7th November 1988.

(2) [³Schedule 2 to these Regulations (meaning of references to Post Office postcode areas and sectors) shall have effect and] in these Regulations, unless the context otherwise requires—

"the Act" means the Social Security Act 1986;

"the General Regulations" means the Income Support (General) Regulations 1987;

"child" has the meaning assigned to it by section 20(11) of the Act [SSCBA, s.137(1)];

[²"claimant" means a person who is claiming or has claimed income support;]

"family" has the meaning assigned to it by section 20(11) of the Act [SSCBA, s.137(1)] and for the purposes of these Regulations includes persons who are members of a polygamous marriage;

[²"forecast" means a weather forecast produced by the Meteorological Office of the Ministry of Defence and supplied to the Department of Social Security on a daily basis which provides the expected average mean daily temperature for a period of 7 consecutive days;

"forecasted period of cold weather" means a period of 7 consecutive days, during which the average of the mean daily temperature for that period is forecasted to be equal to or below 0 degrees celsius; and for the purposes of this definition where a day forms part of a forecasted period of cold weather it shall not form part of any other such forecasted period;]

"home" means the dwelling, together with any garage, garden and outbuildings normally occupied by the claimant as his home, including any premises not so occupied which it is impracticable or unreasonable to sell separately in particular, in Scotland, any croft land on which the dwelling is situated;

"income support" means income support under Part II of the Act [SSCBA, Part VII] and includes transitional addition, personal expenses addition and special transitional addition as defined in the Income Support (Transitional) Regulations 1987;

"married couple" means a man and a woman who are married to each other and are members of the same household;]

"mean daily temperature" means, in respect of a day, the average of the maximum temperature and minimum temperature recorded at a station for that day;

[²"overlap period" means any period of a day or days, where a day forms part of a recorded period of cold weather and also forms part of a forecasted period of cold weather;]

[¹"partner" means one of a married or unmarried couple or a member of a polygamous relationship;] [². . .]

"polygamous marriage" means any marriage during the subsistence of which a party to it is married to more than one person and the ceremony of marriage took place under the law of a country which permits polygamy;

[³"postcode", except in the definition below of "sector", includes a part of a postcode;]

"recorded period of cold weather" means a period of 7 consecutive days, during which the average of the mean daily temperature recorded for that period was equal to or below 0 degrees celsius; and for the purposes of this definition where a day forms part of a recorded period of cold weather it shall not form part of any other such recorded period;

"sector" means the area identified by the number which commences the second part of a Post Office postcode;]

"station" means a National Climatological Message Station.

[¹"unmarried couple" means a man and a woman who are not married to each other but are living together as husband and wife.]

[¹(2A) For the purposes of these Regulations, a person shall be treated as a member of a polygamous relationship where, but for the fact that the relationship includes more than two persons, he would be one of a married or unmarried couple.]

(3) In these Regulations, unless the context otherwise requires, a reference to a numbered regulation is to the regulation in these Regulations bearing that number and a reference in a regulation to a numbered paragraph or sub-paragraph is to the paragraph or sub-paragraph in that regulation bearing that number.

AMENDMENTS

1. Social Fund (Miscellaneous Amendments) Regulations 1990 (S.I. 1990 No. 580), reg. 3 (April 9, 1990).

2. Social Fund Cold Weather Payments (General) Amendment No. 2 Regulations 1991 (S.I. 1991 No. 2238), reg. 2 (November 1, 1991).

3. Social Fund Cold Weather Payments (General) Amendment (No. 2) Regulations 1992 (S.I. 1992 No. 2448), reg. 2 (November 1, 1992).

"*home.*" See notes to reg. 2(1) of the Income Support (General) Regulations under "dwelling occupied as the home".

"*forecasted period of cold weather.*" The original definition of a "period of cold weather" required it to run from a Monday to a Sunday. Since the test of the average of the mean daily temperature (*i.e.* the average of maximum and minimum temperature for each day) for the seven days being below 0 degrees celsius is a tough one, to have required also that the weather conformed to calendar weeks would have made the operation of the regulation excessively arbitrary. Thus, any consecutive seven days over which the average temperature test is met will do.

The departure in November 1991 is to include a period where the temperature is forecasted to meet the test. See reg. 2 for the interrelationship with periods where the temperature test is actually met. If a day falls into a forecasted period of cold weather it cannot count in any other forecasted period, but it can be part of a recorded period of cold weather (see the definition of "overlap period").

In the cold weather payments scheme under the Supplementary Benefit (Single Payments) Regulations the crucial average temperature was 1.5 degrees celsius, rather than 0 degrees celsius.

"*recorded period of cold weather.*" See the notes on a forecasted period and the definition of "overlap period."

"*unmarried couple.*" *and* "*married couple*" See notes to s.137(1) of the Contributions and Benefits Act (1986 Act, s.20(11)).

[¹Prescribed description of persons

1A. The description of persons prescribed as persons to whom a payment may be made out of the Social Fund to meet expenses for heating under section 32(2A) of the Act [SSCBA, s.138(2)] is claimants who have been awarded income support in respect of at least one day during the recorded or the forecasted period of cold weather specified in regulation 2(1)(a) and either—

   (i) whose applicable amount includes one or more of the premiums specified in paragraphs 9 to 14 of Part III of Schedule 2 to the General Regulations [², but does not include the allowance specified in paragraph 2A of that Schedule (residential allowances)]; or

  (ii) whose family includes a member aged less than 5.]

AMENDMENTS

1. Social Fund Cold Weather Payments (General) Amendment No. 3 Regulations 1991 (S.I. 1991 No. 2448), reg. 2 (November 1, 1991).

2. Social Fund Cold Weather Payments (General) Amendment Regulations 1993 (S.I. 1993 No. 2450), reg. 2 (November 1, 1993).

DEFINITIONS

    "the Act"—see reg 1(2).
    "the General Regulations"—*ibid.*
    "claimant"—*ibid.*
    "family"—*ibid.*
    "forecasted period of cold weather"—*ibid.*
    "income support"—*ibid.*
    "recorded period of cold weather"—*ibid.*

GENERAL NOTE

Only claimants who have been awarded income support for at least one day in a period of cold weather (forecasted or recorded) can qualify for a payment. Merely having underlying entitlement to income support will not do. However, only certain claimants meet the conditions prescribed by reg. 1A. The claimant's income support must include one of the pensioner or disability premiums (but from November 1, 1993, claimants who live in a residential care or nursing home and do not have a preserved right do not qualify), or there must be a child under five in the household. Since no claim for a cold weather payment is possible, the income support AO will identify qualifying claimants and make a payment automatically.

[¹Prescribed circumstances

2.—(1) The prescribed circumstances in which a payment may be made out of the social fund to meet expenses for heating under section 32(2A) of the Act [SSCBA, s.138(2)] are—

(a) subject to paragraphs (3), (4) and (5)—

    (i) there is a recorded period of cold weather at a station [³identified] in column (1) of Schedule 1 to these Regulations or, if that station is unable to provide temperature information for the period in question, the nearest such station to that station able to provide temperature information for that period; or

    (ii) there is a forecasted period of cold weather at a station [³identified] in column (1) of Schedule 1 to these Regulations; and

(b) the home of the claimant is, or by virtue of paragraph (2)(*b*) is treated as, situated in a Post Office postcode area [³or part of such an area] in respect of which the first mentioned station in sub-paragraph (a)(i) or the station mentioned in sub-paragraph (a)(ii) of this paragraph, as the case may be, is the designated station; [².. .]

(c) [².. .]

(2) For the purposes of this regulation—

(a) the station [³identified] in column (1) of Schedule 1 to these Regulations is the designated station for the Post Office postcode areas [³or parts thereof identified] in the corresponding paragraph in column (2) of that Schedule;

(b) where the home of the claimant is not situated within a Post Office postcode area [³or part of such an area identified] in column (2) of that Schedule, it shall be treated as situated within the Post Office postcode area [³or part of such an area] nearest to it [³identified] in that column.

(3) Subject to paragraphs (4) and (5) where a recorded period of cold weather is joined by an overlap period to a forecasted period of cold weather a payment under paragraph (1) may only be made in respect of the forecasted period of cold weather.

(4) Where—

(a) there is a continuous period of forecasted periods of cold weather, each of which is linked by an overlap period; and

(b) the total number of recorded periods of cold weather during that continuous period is greater than the total number of forecasted periods of cold weather,

a payment in respect of the last recorded period of cold weather may also be made under paragraph (1).

(5) Where—

(a) a claimant [²falls within the description of persons prescribed in Regulation 1A and] satisfies the prescribed circumstances for a payment under paragraph (1) above in respect of a recorded period of cold weather; and

(b) a payment in respect of the recorded period of cold weather does not fall to be made by virtue of paragraph (4); and

(c) the claimant does not [²fall within the description of persons prescribed in Regulation 1A] above in respect of the forecasted period of cold weather which is linked to the recorded period of cold weather by an overlap period,

a payment in respect of that recorded period of cold weather may also be made under paragraph (1).

AMENDMENTS

1. Social Fund Cold Weather Payments (General) Amendments No. 2 Regulations 1991 (S.I. 1991 No. 2238) reg. 3 (November 1, 1991).
2. Social Fund Cold Weather Payments (General) Amendment No. 3 Regulations 1991 (S.I. 1991 No. 2448), reg. 3 (November 1, 1991).
3. Social Fund Cold Weather Payments (General) Amendment (No. 2) Regulations 1992 (S.I. 1992 No. 2448), reg. 3 (November 1, 1992).

DEFINITIONS

"the Act"—see reg. 1(2).
"the General Regulations"—*ibid.*
"claimant"—*ibid.*
"family"—*ibid.*
"forecasted period of cold weather"—*ibid.*
"home"—*ibid.*
"income support"—*ibid.*
"overlap period"—*ibid.*
"Post Office postcode area"—*ibid.*, Sched. 2.
"recorded period of cold weather"—see reg. 1(2).
"station"—*ibid.*

GENERAL NOTE

Section 138(2) of the Contributions and Benefits Act (1986 Act, s.32(2A)) allows any circumstances to be prescribed. Reg. 1A prescribes the categories of income support recipients who can qualify.

The qualifications under reg. 2 have become rather more complex in November 1991. Under para. (1)(a) and (b), a period of cold weather (i.e. seven consecutive days) must be either recorded or forecast at the weather station relevant to the claimant's home. If a period of cold weather is forecast, but the forecast turns out to be wrong and there are not seven consecutive days of the necessary temperature actually recorded, the situation is simple. Only the forecast period is relevant. Things become more complicated where there is a recorded period of cold weather which coincides wholly or partly with the forecasted period. While an individual day can only count as part of one recorded period of cold weather or one forecasted period of cold weather (see the definitions in reg. 1(2)), it can be part of both a recorded and a forecasted period. There is then an overlap period, again defined in reg. 1(2). Since the aim is, if possible, to make the payment before the extra heating is required, the general rule, under para. (3), is that payment is to be made only for the forecasted period. However, that rule would lead to unfairness if, for instance, recorded periods of cold weather come at the beginning and end of a continuous series, with forecasted periods only starting towards the end of the first recorded period and finishing towards the start of the last recorded period. In such circumstances, payments can be made for an extra recorded period over the number of forecasted periods (para. (4)). Also, if the claimant does not qualify under reg. 1A for any day of the forecasted period, but does qualify for a day of the recorded period, then a payment can be made for the recorded period (para. (5)).

Prescribed amount

3. [¹. . .] The amount of the payment in respect of each period of cold weather shall be [²£7].

AMENDMENTS

1. Social Fund Cold Weather Payments (General) Amendment No. 2 Regulations 1991 (S.I. 1991 No. 2238), reg. 4 (November 1, 1991).
2. Social Fund Cold Weather Payments (General) Amendment Regulations 1994 (S.I. 1994 No. 2593) reg. 2 (November 1, 1994).

GENERAL NOTE

The fixed payment is £7 for each week which counts under regs. 1A and 2. The amount had been fixed at £5 from 1988, until it was increased to £6 in February 1991, at the same time as the temperature condition was deemed to have been triggered for the whole country for two weeks. It was increased to £7 in November 1994. The Government has announced that it will go up to £8.50 in November 1995.

Effect and calculation of capital

4. [¹. . .]

<small>AMENDMENT</small>

1. Social Fund Cold Weather Payments (General) Amendment No. 2 Regulations 1991 (S.I. 1991 No. 2238), reg. 5 (November 1, 1991).

<small>GENERAL NOTE</small>

There is now no capital limit for cold weather payments.

SCHEDULES

[¹SCHEDULE 1

Regulation 2

Column (1)	Column (2)
National Climatological Message Station	*[²Identification of Post Office postcode areas or parts thereof]*
1. ABERDEEN AIRPORT	AB1–3, AB20, AB22, AB23, AB30, AB32, AB41–43, AB51–54. DD8–11. PH11.
[³2. ABERPORTH	SA35–48, SA61–73. SY23–25.]
3. AUGHTON	CH5–8. FY1–8. L1–49, L60–66. LA1. that part of LA2 which consists of sectors: LA2 6 LA2 9, LA2 0, LA3, LA4. LL15–19, LL22. PR1–9. WA9–12.
[⁴4. AVIEMORE	AB31, AB33, AB34, AB36, AB37. IV4, IV6, IV13. PH18–26.]
[⁴. . .] 6. BIRMINGHAM AIRPORT	[⁴. . .] B1–21, B23–38, B40, B42–50, B60–76, B80, B90–98. CV1–8, CV10–12, CV21–23, CV31–37. DY1–13. WR1–15. WS1–6, WS8–10. WV1–4, WV9–14.
7. BOSCOMBE DOWN	BA12. SO20. SN9. SP1–5, SP7–11.
[³8. BOULMER	NE22, NE24, NE61–71. TD12, TD15.]

Column (1)	Column (2)
National Climatological Message Station	*[²Identification of Post Office postcode areas or parts thereof]*
9. BOURNEMOUTH AIRPORT	BH1–25, BH31.
	DT1–8, DT10, DT11.
	SP6.
[⁴9A. BRAEMAR	AB 35.]
[³. . .]	[³. . .]
[²11. BRIZE NORTON	GL1–8, GL10, GL11, GL14–20, GL50–56.
	HP17–22, HP27.
	OX1–18, OX20, OX33, OX44
	SN7.]
[⁴12. CARLISLE	CA1–11, CA15–17.
	DG16.
	LA6—10, LA22, LA23.]
13. CHIVENOR	EX1–12, EX15–23, EX31–39.
	PL16.
	TQ1–6, TQ9–14.
[³14. CILFYNYDD	CF8, CF37–48.
	LD3.
	NP2–5, NP7, NP8, NP44.
	That part of NP1 which consists of sectors: NP1 4, NP1 5, NP1 6, NP1 7 and NP1 8.]
15. COLTISHALL	IP18, IP24.
	NR1–18, NR24–35.
[³. . .]	[³. . .]
17. CULDROSE	TR12, TR13, TR17–27.
[³. . .]	[³. . .]
19. DUMFRIES (DRUNGANS)	DG1, DG2, DG5–7, DG11, DG12.
20. DUNKESWELL	EX13, EX14.
21. EASTHAMSTEAD	GU11, GU12, GU14, GU17, GU26, GU30.
	GU34, GU35.
	RG1–17, RG21–28.
[³22. EDINBURGH AIRPORT	EH1–37, EH39–42, EH47–49, EH51–55.
	FK1–21.
	KY3, KY4, KY11, KY12.
	TD5, TD11, TD13, TD14.]
[³23. ESKDALEMUIR	DG3, DG4, DG10, DG13, DG14.
	EH38, EH43–46.
	ML12.
	TD1–4, TD6–10.]
24. ESKMEALS	CA12–14, CA18–28.
	LA5, LA11–21.
[²25. FINNINGLEY	DN1–14.
	S1–14, S17, S19,
	That part of S30 which consists of sectors: S30 3, S30 4,
	S31, S60–66, S70–75.]
26. GATWICK AIRPORT	CR3, CR5, CR6.
	GU5–10, GU27–29, GU31.
	KT20.
	RH1–19.
	SM7.
	TN1–4, TN8–18.
[³27. GLASGOW AIRPORT	G1–5, G11–15, G20–23, G31–34, G40–46, G51–53, G60–69, G71–78, G81–84.
	KA1–26, KA28–30.
	ML1–11.
	PA1–27, PA32, PA36.]

Column (1)	Column (2)
National Climatological Message Station	*[²Identification of Post Office postcode areas or parts thereof]*
28. HEATHROW AIRPORT	AL1–5, AL9, AL10. BR1–4, BR6, BR7. CR0, CR2, CR4, CR7, CR8. E1–18. EC1–4. EN1–11. GU1–4, GU12, GU15, GU16, GU18–25. HA0–9. HP1–16, HP23. IG1–11. KT1–19, KT21–24. N1–22. NW1–11. SE1–28. SL0–9. SM1–6. SW1–20. TW1–20. UB1–10. W1–14. WC1, WC2. WD1–7.
29. HERSTMONCIEUX	BN1–18, BN20–27, BN41–45. RH20. TN5–7, TN19–22, TN31–40.
[⁴. . .] [³31. KINLOSS	[⁴. . .] AB38, AB44, AB45, AB55, AB56. IV1–3, IV5, IV7–12, IV14–20, IV30–32, IV36.]
32. KIRKWALL	KW15–17.

[²33. LEEDS WEATHER CENTRE	That part of HD8 which consists of sectors:
	    HD8-8,
	    HD8-9.
	HKG1–5.
	LS1–28.
	WF1–17.
	YO1–5, YO8.]

[³34. LEEMING	DH1–3, DH6–9. DL1–17. NE1–13, NE15–21, NE28, NE39–49. TS1–9, TS14–23 and that part of TS12 which consists of sector: TS12 3. YO6, YO7, YO17, YO18 and that part of YO21 which consists of sector: YO21 2.]
35. LERWICK	ZE1–3.
36. LEUCHARS	DD1–7. KY1–2, KY5–10, KY13–16. PH1–10, PH12–17.
37. LYNEHAM	BA13–15. SN1–6, SN8, SN10–16.
[³38. MACHRIHANISH	KA 27. PA28–31, PA41–49, PA60, PA61.]
[⁴39. MANCHESTER	BB1–3, BB5–7. BL0–9. CH1–4. CW1–12. That part of LA2 which consists of sectors:

Column (1)	Column (2)
National Climatological Message Station	*[²Identification of Post Office postcode areas or parts thereof]*
	LA2 7, LA2 8.
	M1–35, M38, M40, M41, M43–46.
	OL1, OL2, OL4–12, OL16.
	SK1–11, SK15, SK16.
	SY14.
	WA1–8, WA13–16.
	WN1–8.]
40. MANSTON	BR5, BR8.
	CT1–21.
	DA1–18.
	ME1–20.
	TN23–30.
41. MARHAM	IP25, IP26.
	NR19–23.
	PE13, PE14, PE30–38.
42. MOUNT BATTEN	PL1–12, PL14, P17–21.
	TQ7, TQ8.
43. MUMBLES	SA1–20, SA31–34.
[³. . .]	[³. . .]
[³45. RHOOSE	BA1–3, BA11.
	BS1–27.
	CF1–5, CF7, CF31–36, CF61–64.
	GL9,
	GL12,
	GL13.
	That part of NP1 which consists of sectors:
	NP10,
	NP19,
	NP6,
	NP9.]
46. ST. MAWGAN	PL13, PL15, PL22–35.
	TR1–11, TR14–16.
47. SHAWBURY	B77–79.
	DY14.
	HR1–9.
	LD1, LD2, LD4–8.
	LL11–14, LL20, LL21.
	ST1–13, ST15–21.
	SY1, SY15-19, SY21, SY22.
	TF1–13.
	WS7, WS11–15.
	WV5–8, WV15, WV16.
[⁴48. SOUTHAMPTON WEATHER CENTRE	GU32, GU33.
	PO1–22, PO30–41.
	SO1–5, SO14–19, SO21–24, SO30–32. SO40–43, SO45, SO50–SO53.]
49. STANSTED	AL6–8.
	CB10, CB11.
	CM0–24.
	CO8, CO9.
	RM1–18.
	SG1–14.
	SS0–9, SS11–17.
50. STORNOWAY	PA80–88.
51. TIREE	IV21–23, IV26, IV40–49, IV51–56.
	PA34, PA37, PA62–78.
	PH36, PH38–44.

Column (1)	Column (2)
National Climatological Message Station	*[²Identification of Post Office postcode areas or parts thereof]*
52. TRAWSFYNDD	LL23, LL35–39, LL51, LL52. SY20.
[³52A. TULLOCH BRIDGE	PA33, PA35, PA38–40. PH30–35, PH37.]
[²53. TYNEMOUTH	DH4, DH5. NE23, NE25–27, NE29–38. SR1–8. TS27–29.]
54. VALLEY	LL24–34, LL53–78.
[³55. WADDINGTON	DN15–21, DN31–40, HU1–20. LN1–13. NG23, NG24, NG31–34. PE9–12, PE20–25.]
[²56. WATNALL	CV9, CV13. DE1–7, DE11–15, DE21–24, DE45, DE55, DE56, DE65, DE72–75. DN22. LE1–18, LE65, LE67. NG1–22, NG25. S18, S40–45, S80, S81. ST14.]
[⁴57. WATTISHAM	CB8, CB9. CO1–7, CO10–16. IP1–17, IP19–23, IP27–33.]
[³58. WHITBY COASTGUARD	TS10, TS11, TS13, TS24–26 and that part of TS12 which consists of sectors: TS12 1, TS12 2, YO11–16, YO22, YO25 and that part of YO21 which consists of sectors: YO21 1, YO21 3.]
59. WHITHORN	DG8, DG9.
60. WICK	IV24, IV25, IV27, IV28. KW1–3, KW5–14.
[³61. WILSDEN	BB4, BB8–12. BD1–24. HD1–7, and that part of HD8 which consists of sector: HD80. HX1–7. LS29. OL3, OL13–15. That part of S30 which consists of sectors: S30 1, S30 2, S30 5, S30 6. SK12–14, SK17.]
[⁴62. WYTON	CB1–7. LU1–7 MK1–19, MK40–46. NN1–18, NN29. PE1–8, PE15–19. SG15–19.]
63. YEOVILTON	BA4–10, BA16, BA20–22. BS28. DT9. TA1–24.]

AMENDMENTS

1. Social Fund Cold Weather Payments (General) Amendment No. 2 Regulations 1991 (S.I. 1991 No. 2238), reg. 6 (November 1, 1991).
2. Social Fund Cold Weather Payments (General) Amendment (No. 2) Regulations 1992 (S.I. 1992 No. 2448), reg. 4 and Sched. 1 (November 1, 1992).
3. Social Fund Cold Weather Payments (General) Amendment Regulations 1993 (S.I. 1993 No. 2450), reg. 3 and Sched. 1 (November 1, 1993).
4. Social Fund Cold Weather Payments (General) Amendment Regulations 1994 (S.I. 1994 No. 2593), reg. 3 and Sched. 1 (November 1, 1994).

DEFINITION

"postcode"—see reg. 1(2).

[¹SCHEDULE 2   **Regulation 1(2)**

POST OFFICE POSTCODE AREAS AND SECTORS

1.—(1) In these Regulations a reference to an identified Post Office postcode area is a reference to that part of Great Britain which is identified by the postcode in question in the Postcode Atlas of Great Britain and Northern Ireland published by John Bartholomew & Son Ltd. in 1989 except that, in the case of a Post Office postcode area identified by a postcode specified in column (1) of Table 1 below, such a reference is a reference to that part of Great Britain which is so identified in the postcode map published by Datamaps Ltd. which is described opposite thereto in columns (2), (3) and (4) of the said Table.

TABLE 1

Column (1)	Column (2)	Column (3)	Column (4)
Postcodes	*Map No.*	*Map Area*	*Year of Publication*
AB2, AB4, AB5, AB20, AB22, AB23, AB41–45, AB51–56	56	Buchan & Gordon	1991
AB3, AB30–38	52 & 56	Aberdeen & Deeside Buchan & Gordon	1991
BH21, BH31	5	New Forest & Isle of Wight	1991
[²CF61–64	12	Cardiff & Glamorgan	1993]
CR2–8	9	London & Surrey	1991
DE4, DE45	29	The Peak & South Yorkshire	1992
DE2, DE3, DE5–7, DE21–24, DE56, DE65, DE72–75, LE6, LE65, LE67	24	Derby & Nottingham	1992
HP17, HP27, OX5, OX8, OX9, OX18, OX20, OX33, OX44	14	Oxford	1992
[²LE8, LE18 NN1–18	19 & 20	Birmingham & Northampton	1993]
[³M38, M40, M41, M43–46.	G14	Greater Manchester, Merseyside and Cheshire	1994
SO14–19, SO30–32, SO40, SO45, SO50, SO53	G3	Hampshire and the Isle of Wight	1994]

2. In these Regulations a reference to an identified sector of a Post Office postcode area identified by a postcode specified in column (1) of Table 2 below is a reference to that part of that area which is identified by the sector's postcode in the postcode map published by John Bartholomew & Son Ltd. which is described in columns (2) to (5) of the said Table opposite that area's postcode.

TABLE 2

Column (1)	Column (2)	Column (3)	Column (4)	Column (5)
Post-codes	*Map No.*	*Map Area*	*ISBN No.*	*Year of Publication*
CF8	12	Cardiff & Glamorgan	07028 0512 28.99	1988
HD8	29	The Peak and South Yorkshire	07028 05297	1989
LA2	31	Lancashire	07028 0531 98.99	1987
LN4	25 & 30	Fenland	07028 0525 48.99	1987
		Lincoln	07028 0530 08.99	1987
NP1	13	Hereford & Gloucester	07028 0513 08.99	1987
S30	20	The Peak and South Yorkshire	07028 05297	1989]

AMENDMENTS

1. Social Fund Cold Weather Payments (General) Amendment (No. 2) Regulations 1992 (S.I. 1992 No. 2448), reg. 5 and Sched. 2 (November 1, 1992).
2. Social Fund Cold Weather Payments (General) Amendment Regulations 1993 (S.I. 1993 No. 2450), reg. 4 and Sched. 2 (November 1, 1993).
3. Social Fund Cold Weather Payments (General) Amendment Regulations 1994 (S.I. 1994 No. 2593), reg. 4 and Sched. 2 (November 1, 1994).

GENERAL NOTE

The ISBN of the Postcode Atlas of Great Britain and Northern Ireland is 0702809187.

Social Fund Maternity and Funeral Expenses (General) Regulations 1987

(S.I. 1987 No. 481)

Made by the Secretary of State under the Social Security Act 1986, ss. 32(2)(a), 84(1) and 89(1), and the Supplementary Benefits Act 1976, ss. 3, 4 and 34.

ARRANGEMENT OF REGULATIONS

PART I

GENERAL

1. Citation and commencement
2. Revocation
3. Interpretation
4. Provision against double payment

PART II

PAYMENTS FOR MATERNITY EXPENSES

5. Entitlement to a maternity payment

6. Persons affected by a trade dispute

PART I

GENERAL

Citation and commencement

1. These regulations may be cited as the Social Fund Maternity and Funeral Expenses (General) Regulations 1987 and shall come into force on 6th April 1987.

Revocation

2. The Social Fund Maternity and Funeral Expenses (General) Regulations 1986 are hereby revoked.

Interpretation

3.—(1) In these regulations unless the context otherwise requires—
[¹"the Act" means the Social Security Act 1986;]
"child" means a person under the age of 16 [³or a young person within the meaning of regulation 14 of the Income Support (General) Regulations 1987;]

"claimant" means a person claiming a social fund payment in respect of maternity or funeral expenses;

[⁵"close relative" means a parent, parent-in-law, son, son-in-law, daughter, daughter-in-law, step-parent, step-son, step-daughter, brother, sister or partner of any of the preceding persons;]

"confinement" means labour resulting in the issue of a living child, or labour after [⁴24 weeks] of pregnancy resulting in the issue of a child whether alive or dead;

"family" means—

    (a) a married or unmarried couple and any children who are members of the same household and for whom one of the couple is or both are responsible;

    (b) a person who is not a member of a married or unmarried couple and any children who are members of the same household and for whom that person is responsible;

    (c) persons who are members of the same household and between whom there is a polygamous relationship and any children who are members of the same household and for whom a member of the polygamous relationship is responsible;

[¹. . .]

"funeral" means a burial or a cremation;

"funeral payment" is to be construed in accordance with regulation 7;

[¹. . .]

"married couple" means a man and a woman who are married to each other and are members of the same household;

"maternity payment" is to be construed in accordance with regulation 5;

"partner" means one of a married or unmarried couple or a member of a polygamous relationship;

"occupational pension scheme" has the same meaning as in the Social Security Pensions Act 1975;

[¹"person affected by a trade dispute" means a person—

    (a) to whom section 23 of the Act [SSCBA, s.126] applies; or

    (b) to whom that section would apply if a claim to income support were made by or in respect of him;]

[⁵"responsible person" is to be construed in accordance with regulation 7(1)(b);]

[¹. . .]

[⁴"still-born child" has the same meaning as in section 12 of the Births and Deaths Registration Act 1926 and section 56(1) of the Registrations of Births, Deaths and Marriages (Scotland) Act 1965 as they are amended by section 1 of the Still-birth (Definition) Act 1992;]

"unmarried couple" means a man and a woman who are not married to each other but are living together as husband and wife.

[¹(2) For the purposes of these Regulations, two persons are to be treated as not being members of the same household in the circumstances set out in regulation 16(2) and (3) of the Income Support (General) Regulations 1987.]

(3) For the purposes of these Regulations, a person shall be treated as a member of a polygamous relationship where, but for the fact that the relationship includes more than two persons, he would be one of a married or unmarried couple.

(4) In these Regulations, unless the context otherwise requires, any reference to a numbered regulation is a reference to the regulation bearing that number in these regulations and any reference in a regulation to a numbered paragraph is a reference to the paragraph of that regulation bearing that number.

1. Social Fund Maternity and Funeral Expenses (General) Amendment Regulations 1988 (S.I. 1988 No. 36), reg. 2 (April 11, 1988).
2. Social Fund Maternity and Funeral Expenses (General) Amendment Regulations 1989 (S.I. 1989 No. 379), reg. 2 (April 1, 1989).
3. Social Fund (Miscellaneous Amendments) Regulations 1990 (S.I. 1990 No. 580), reg. 5 (April 9, 1990).
4. Social Fund Maternity and Funeral Expenses (General) Amendment Regulations 1992 (S.I. 1992 No. 2149), reg. 2 (October 1, 1992).
5. Social Fund Maternity and Funeral Expenses (General) Amendment Regulations 1994 (S.I. 1994 No. 506), reg. 2 (April 1, 1994).

GENERAL NOTE

Paragraph (1)
"confinement." Note that a payment can be made for a stillbirth only if it occurs after the 24th week of the pregnancy (reduced from 28 weeks in October 1992).

"family." Note that the definition differs slightly from that in s.137(1) of the Contributions and Benefits Act (1986 Act, s.20(11)), which applies for the purposes of income support, family credit and disability working allowance. So far as married and unmarried couples go, the approach is the same (see the notes to s.137(1)). Para. (2) goes further than the income support rules by deeming members of a couple not to be members of the same household in these circumstances. The new form of para. (2) does not cover the circumstances in which people are treated as members of the same household, so that presumably the general law on when membership of a household endures through a temporary absence will apply (see *England v. Secretary of State for Social Services* [1982] 3 F.L.R. 222; *Taylor v. Supplemntary Benefit Officer (R(FIS) 5/85)*; *Santos v. Santos* [1972] 2 All E.R. 247).

Until the amendment in April 1990 the definition of "child" meant that beyond the age of 15 a child could not be part of the family although continuing in secondary education and not entitled to income support in her own right. Thus some 16–18-year-old mothers were excluded from maternity payments. The new reference to young persons, as defined in reg. 14 of the Income Support (General) Regulations, remedies this.

"funeral." The old form of the Single Payments Regulations on funerals left it unclear whether "funeral" meant the ceremonies or religious services which accompany burial or cremation, or simply "burial." *R(SB)23/86* held that, in that context, it meant the latter. The present definition does make it clear it is the burial or cremation which is covered, rather than any accompanying or religious services.

"still-born child." The definition referred to is "a child which has issued forth from its mother after the twenty-fourth week of pregnancy and which did not at any time after being completely expelled from its mother draw breath or show any other signs of life."

Provision against double payment

4.—(1) Subject to paragraph (2), no maternity payment shall be made under these Regulations if such a payment has already been made in respect of the child in question.

(2) Notwithstanding that a maternity payment has been made to the natural mother of a child or to one of her family, a second such payment may, subject to the following provisions of these Regulations, be made to the adoptive parents of the child in question.

(3) No funeral payment shall be made under these Regulations if such a payment has already been made in respect of the funeral expenses in question.

DEFINITIONS

"child"—see reg. 3(1).
"family"—*ibid.*
"funeral payment"—*ibid.*
"maternity payment"—*ibid.*

GENERAL NOTE

Paras. (1) and (3) contain a straightforward rule preventing double payments. Only a lawful payment bars another payment (*CG 30/1990*). So where the first payment was made to the partner of the maternity grant claimant (who was the income support claimant) and not to her, this did not prevent her receiving a payment.

Regs. 12(3) and 13(3) prevented social fund payments being made where a single payment had been made in respect of the same confinement, adoption or funeral. Paragraph (2) provides an exception as it allows the adoptive parents of a child to receive a payment although a payment has already been made for the natural mother. So a single payment made for the natural mother did not exclude a later social fund payment to the adoptive parents (reg. 12(3)).

PART II

PAYMENTS FOR MATERNITY EXPENSES

Entitlement

5.—(1) Subject to regulation 6 and Parts IV and V of these Regulations, a payment to meet maternity expenses (referred to in these regulations as a "maternity payment") shall be made only where—
[¹(a) the claimant or the claimant's partner has, in respect of the date of the claim for a maternity payment, been awarded either income support [², family credit or disability working allowance]; and]
  (b) either—
    (i) the claimant or, if the claimant is a member of a family, one of the family is pregnant or has given birth to a child [³or still-born child]; or
    (ii) the claimant or the claimant's partner or both of them have adopted a child not exceeding the age of twelve months at the date of the claim; and
  (c) the claim is made within the period specified for such a claim [¹in regulation 19 of, and Schedule 4 to, the Social Security (Claims and Payments Regulations 1987.]
[³(2) Subject to Part IV of these Regulations, the amount of a maternity payment shall be—
  (a) where the claim is made before confinement, £100 in respect of each expected child;
  (b) where the claim is made after confinement, £100 in respect of each child, including any still-born child;
  (c) where the claim is made after a child has already been adopted, £100 in respect of that child.]

AMENDMENTS

1. Social Fund Maternity and Funeral Expenses (General) Amendment Regulations 1988 (S.I. 1988 No. 36), reg. 3 (April 11, 1988).
2. Disability Living Allowance and Disability Working Allowance (Consequential Provisions) Regulations 1991 (S.I. 1991 No. 2742), reg. 10 (April 6, 1992).
3. Social Fund Maternity and Funeral Expenses (General) Amendment Regulations 1992 (S.I. 1992 No. 2149), reg. 3 (October 1, 1992).

DEFINITIONS

"child"—see reg. 3(1).
"claimant"—*ibid.*

"confinement"—*ibid.*
"family"—*ibid.*
"partner"—*ibid.*
"still-born child"—*ibid.*

GENERAL NOTE

Paragraph (1)
The three conditions specified must all be satisfied for a payment to be made but no needs have to be proved beyond them. Under sub-para. (a) either the person claiming the maternity payment or that person's partner must have been awarded income support, family credit or disability working allowance. The original form of this regulation referred to the claimant being "in receipt" of benefit, which probably meant "entitled to receive benefit" (*R(SB)12/87*). Now the crucial matter is an award, rather than the actual payment of benefit. Although para. (a) talks of the claimant having been awarded benefit, an award which is made after the date of the claim for a maternity payment (*e.g.* following an appeal or a review) will presumably do, provided that it covers the date of claim. The original form of reg. 5 also left unclear the exact date on which this condition had to be satisfied. This is now fixed as the date of claim.

Under sub-para. (b), the issues will normally be simple ones of fact. The October 1992 amendments to reg. 3 and this regulation mean that a payment can be made when a child is still-born after a confinement of at least 24 weeks. Note that while a payment can be made in advance of the actual birth of a child to a member of the family, in the case of an adoption one can only be made after the event. See the definition of "family" in reg. 3(1) and the notes to s.137(1) of the Contributions and Benefits Act (1986 Act, s.20(11)).

Under sub-para. (c), the period within which the claim has to be made begins 11 weeks before the first day of the expected week of confinement and ends three months after the actual date of confinement (or the date of the adoption order, in the case of an adopted baby) (Claims and Payments Regulations, Sched. 4, para. 8). The period may be extended for good cause (Claims and Payments Regulations, reg. 19(2)). See para. 1066 of the Social Fund Maternity and Funeral Payments Guide for suggestions of acceptable evidence of what is the expected week of confinement.

The other major rule of eligibility is imposed by Part IV of the Regulations, which applies a £500 or £1,000 capital rule (like that for single payments). Part V contains transitional provisions.

Paragraph (2)
The amount of the payment is (from April 1990) £100 per child, having been at £85 for two years, which will not go very far. Note the effect of the £500 and £1,000 capital rule (reg. 9). Although para. (2) is not expressly made subject to Part V, reg. 12(4) secured that any maternity grant awarded (before its abolition on April 6, 1987) in respect of the same confinement was to be deducted from what would otherwise have been awarded.

Persons affected by a trade dispute

6. Where the claimant or the claimant's partner is a person affected by a trade dispute, a maternity payment shall be made only if—
   (a) in the case where the claimant or the claimant's partner is in receipt of [¹income support], the trade dispute has, at the date of the claim for that payment, continued for not less than six weeks; or
   (b) in the case where the claimant or the claimant's partner is in receipt of [¹family credit], the claim in respect of which [¹family credit] was awarded was made before the beginning of the trade dispute[²; or
   (c) in the case where the claimant or the claimant's partner is in receipt of disability working allowance, the claim in respect of which disability working allowance was awarded was made before the beginning of the trade dispute.]

AMENDMENTS

1. Social Fund Maternity and Funeral Expenses (General) Amendment Regulations 1988 (S.I. 1988 No. 36) reg. 4 (April 11, 1988).
2. Disability Living Allowance and Disability Working Allowance (Consequential Provisions) Regulations 1991 (S.I. 1991 No. 2742), reg. 10 (April 6, 1992).

DEFINITIONS

"claimant"—see reg. 3(1).
"maternity payment"—*ibid.*
"partner"—*ibid.*
"person affected by a trade dispute"—*ibid.*

GENERAL NOTE

Para. (a) took over a similar rule which used to be in the Supplementary Benefit (Trade Disputes and Recovery from Earnings) Regulations, but the excluding period is reduced from 11 weeks to six weeks. The crucial date is that of the claim for the maternity payment. It may sometimes be difficult to tell when a trade dispute started, since the dispute is to be distinguished from the stoppage of work due to it. See reg. 3(1) for "person affected by a trade dispute."

Paras. (b) and (c) only exclude payments where the claim for family credit or disability working allowance was made after the beginning of the trade dispute.

PART III

PAYMENTS FOR FUNERAL EXPENSES

Entitlement

7.—(1) Subject to regulation 8 and Parts IV and V of these Regulations, a social fund payment to meet funeral expenses (referred to in these regulations as a "funeral payment") shall be made only where—
[²(a) the claimant or the claimant's partner in respect of the date of the claim for a funeral payment—
   (i) has been awarded income support, family credit, disability working allowance, housing benefit or council tax benefit where, in the case of council tax benefit, that benefit is awarded by virtue only of the claimant or his partner having fulfilled the conditions of entitlement specified in section 131(3) to (5) of the Social Security Contributions and Benefits Act 1992 (entitlement to the appropriate maximum council tax benefit); or
   (ii) is a person to whom, by virtue of sub-section (7) of section 131 of that Act, sub-section (6) of that section applies where, on a claim for council tax benefit, the conditions of entitlement specified in section 131(3) and (6) for an award of the alternative maximum council tax benefit are fulfilled; and]
[³(b) the claimant (in this Part of these Regulations referred to as "the responsible person") accepts responsibility for the costs of a funeral and—
   (i) the responsible person was the partner of the deceased; or
   (ii) where the responsible person or that person's partner was a close relative of the deceased, it is reasonable for the responsible person to accept responsibility for those costs and there is no other person who was equally or more closely related to the deceased whom, on comparing that other person's income and capital with that of the responsible person and taking account of the nature and extent of that other person's contact with the deceased, it is reasonable to expect to meet those costs; or
   (iii) where neither head (i) nor (ii) applies, it is reasonable in view of the extent of the responsible person's or partner's acquaintanceship with the deceased for that person to accept responsibility for those costs; and]
  (c) the funeral takes place in the United Kingdom; and

(d) the claim is made within the period specified for such a claim [¹in regulation 19 of, and Schedule 4 to, the Social Security (Claims and Payments) Regulations 1987.]

(2) Subject to regulation 8 and Part IV of these Regulations the amount of a funeral payment shall be an amount sufficient to meet any of the following essential expenses which fall to be met by the [³responsible person]:—

(a) the cost of any necessary documentation;

(b) the cost of an ordinary coffin [²and, in the case of cremation, the cost of an ordinary urn];

(c) the cost of transport for the coffin and bearers and one additional car;

(d) the reasonable cost of flowers from the [³responsible person];

(e) undertaker's fees and gratuities, chaplain's, organist's and cemetery or crematorium fees for a simple funeral;

(f) the cost of any additional expenses arising from a requirement of the religious faith of the deceased, not in excess of £75;

(g) where the death occurred away from the deceased's home, the costs of transporting the body within the United Kingdom to that home or to the undertaker's premises or to a chapel of rest; and

(h) the reasonable travelling costs of one return journey within the United Kingdom by the [³responsible person] in connection with either the arrangement of or attendance at the funeral.

[¹(3) In this regulation any reference to housing benefit includes a reference, in Scotland, to housing benefit in the form of a community charge rebate.]

AMENDMENTS

1. Social Fund Maternity and Funeral Expenses (General) Amendment Regulations 1989 (S.I. 1989 No. 379), reg. 3 (April 1, 1989).
2. Social Fund Maternity and Funeral Expenses (General) Amendment Regulations 1993 (S.I. 1993 No. 479), reg. 2 (April 1, 1993).
3. Social Fund Maternity and Funeral Expenses (General) Amendment Regulations 1994 (S.I. 1994 No. 506), reg. 3 (April 1, 1994).

DEFINITIONS

"claimant"—see reg. 3(1).
"close relative"—*ibid.*
"family"—*ibid.*
"funeral"—*ibid.*
"partner"—*ibid.*

GENERAL NOTE

This provision replaces both the contributory death grant, which had stood at £30 for many years, and reg. 8 of the Supplementary Benefit (Single Payments) Regulations. It provides effectively the same level of payment as under the Single Payments Regulations, but under wider conditions. The definition of funeral in reg. 3(1) avoids the problems of interpretation revealed in *R(SB) 23/86*. It is the cost of a burial or a cremation which is covered, rather than the accompanying ceremonies. Para. (1) deals with entitlement; para. (2) defines the amount of the payment.

The Government intends to impose a ceiling on the amount that can be awarded for a funeral payment, introduce a new priority order for deciding who is treated as "the responsible person", and tighten up the financial test that is applied where the deceased has more than one surviving close relative. It is understood that these new rules will come into force in June 1995. See the 1995 Supplement for the new regulations.

Paragraph (1)
All four conditions specified must be satisfied.
Sub-para. (a). An award of housing benefit or the maximum council tax benefit to either the claimant or his partner will do, as well as an award of income support, family credit or disability

working allowance, which widens entitlement quite considerably. The award must be in respect of the date of claim for the funeral payment (see notes to reg. 5(1)).

On head (ii), para. 2005 of the *Social Fund Maternity and Funeral Payments Guide* now states that if alternative maximum council tax benefit (usually known as second adult rebate) is the qualifying benefit, it is the person in respect of whom the second adult rebate has been awarded (*i.e.* the non-householder) who can qualify for a funeral payment, not the householder who receives the council tax benefit. Although this is logical, since it is the circumstances of the non-householder, not the householder, that warrant the rebate, it is not entirely clear that this is achieved by the wording of head (ii), which arguably may cover both people.

Sub-para. (b). This condition has been tightened up since April 1, 1994. It is now necessary for the claimant to have accepted responsibility for the costs of the funeral and to come within one of the categories in sub-para. (b). Head (i) is straightforward. Under (ii) the claimant or his partner has to be a close relative (see reg. 3(1)) of the deceased and it must be reasonable for the claimant to accept responsibility where there are no other equally close or closer relatives who can reasonably be expected to do so, taking into account their income, capital and contact with the person who has died. If neither (i) nor (ii) apply, a funeral payment can be made if it is reasonable for the claimant to accept responsibility, given his or his partner's acquaintance with the deceased. This is wide enough to cover, for example, friends, and relatives other than close relatives, subject to the AO or SSAT accepting that it is reasonable for the claimant to pay for the funeral. The decision in *CSB 488/1982*, that the fact that someone else makes the arrangements does not mean that the claimant has not taken responsibility for the costs, is applicable. The *Social Fund Maternity and Funeral Payments Guide* has now been amended (see paras. 2109–2113) so that it no longer implies that the test is who is responsible for arranging the funeral. It may be that if the person making the arrangements enters into a direct contractual relationship with an undertaker (rather than as agent for the claimant) that person has taken responsibility for the costs. In *CIS 85/1991* (which was to have been reported as *R(IS) 9/93* but has been withdrawn from reporting) the Commissioner follows *CSB 423/1989* in holding that if another person has initially made a contract with the undertakers the claimant may assume liability for the funeral costs by a novation of the contract under which the claimant assumes the other person's liability and the undertakers release the other person from his liability. The novation requires the consent of all three parties, but no consideration or further payment is necessary. Providing that the claimant comes within one of the heads in sub-para. (b) and has assumed responsibility for the costs before the AO's decision is made (or possibly before the claim is made) the condition is satisfied. Often, arrangements will be made without thinking about the legal niceties, and a commonsense view should be taken.

Sub-para (c). The funeral, *i.e.* the burial or cremation, must take place in the United Kingdom, *i.e.* Great Britain and Northern Ireland (Interpretation Act 1978, Sched. 1). *CIS 51/1990*, to be reported as *R(IS)7/94*, decided that this provision does not discriminate against Irish nationals and so does not contravene EC Directive 1612/68 on social and tax advantages, but the decision was set aside by the Court of Appeal in *O'Flynn v. Chief Adjudication Officer* (July 29, 1992). The Court of Appeal considered that the Commissioner had made a basic mistake in discrimination law in assuming that, because an Irish national could have arranged affairs so as to qualify for a payment, there was no discrimination. It is not clear that the Commissioner did make that assumption, but at any rate it is clear that it needs to be asked whether there is a disproportionate impact on nationals from other Member States in the practical difficulties of qualifying for a funeral payment. The Commissioner rehearing the *O'Flynn* case has referred it to the ECJ for a preliminary ruling on the test to be applied for establishing discrimination in these circumstances. At the time of writing the result of the reference is not yet known.

The argument that sub-para. (c) is unlawful under the Race Relations Act 1976 was rejected in *R v. Secretary of State for Social Security ex parte Nessa, The Times*, November 15, 1994. Section 75 of the 1976 Act states that the Act applies to acts done by, *inter alia*, Ministers, as it applies to acts done by a private person. But Auld J. holds that acts of a governmental nature, such as the making of regulations, were not subject to the control of the 1976 Act as they were not acts of a kind that could be done by a private person.

Sub-para (d). The time-limit is specified in para. 9 of Sched. 4 to the Claims and Payments Regulations as three months from the date of the funeral (not, as before, the date of death).

Entitlement is subject to the £500 or £1,000 capital rule in Part IV, and to the transitional provisions in reg. 12.

Paragraph (2)

The basic elements of the payment, set out in sub-paras. (a) to (g), are taken from the Single Payments Regulations.

All of the listed expenses are to be treated as essential. Since some categories contain an express limitation to reasonable costs and some do not, the Commissioner's view in *R(IS) 14/92* that the word "reasonable" should be read in even where it is not expressed is hard to support.

On the facts of *R(IS) 14/92* the funeral was conducted by the Burial Society of the United Synagogue, which was unable to break down the cost of £1325 into the cost of individual items. The SSAT allowed the amount of an average funeral (£800) plus an additional £75 for the requirements of a religious faith. The Commissioner holds that this approach was not permissible. Instead the SSAT had to consider whether the items paid for by the cost of the funeral were allowable under para. (2). If they were, then the cost was to be allowed. The provision in para. (2)(e) refers to expenses over and above those set out in the other sub-paragraphs, rather than the enhanced cost of a Jewish funeral over a Christian or secular funeral.

There are some helpful decisions on the provisions in the Single Payments Regulations, which are relevant to identical or similar provisions here. A plain coffin has become an ordinary coffin, but the meaning seems the same (*R(SB) 46/84*). "Necessary documentation" has been held not to include the cost of obituary notices in newspapers (*R(SB) 46/84, CSB 552/1984*). *The Social Fund Maternity and Funeral Payments Guide* (para. 2302) suggests that the phrase would include the death certificate, or additional certificates required for a cremation. The fees for a "simple funeral" are to be met. The same phrase was used in the Single Payments Regulations, where it was held to cover the costs of an ordinary grave in a local authority cemetery (*R(SB) 46/84*). In *CSB 28/1988* it was held that neither a double private grave (at £143) nor a common law grave, which might be opened for up to six people and where no headstone was allowed (at £69) came within this test. A simple funeral generally is an unpretentious one. The deceased's "home" under sub-para. (g) is the accommodation where he normally lived prior to his death (*R(IS) 11/91*). The provision in sub-para. (h) is taken from reg. 22 of the Single Payments Regulations, but the restriction to one return journey is new. The natural reading is probably that the responsible member can have one journey either for arranging the funeral or attending it. However, it is bound to be argued that the responsible member can have one journey for each purpose. Others who are relatives of the deceased may be eligible for a community care grant for the cost of travel to and from a funeral in the United Kingdom (see direction 4(b)(ii), below). The applicant must be a member of a family containing a claimant in receipt of income support.

From the amount calculated under para. (2) must be deducted the amounts listed in reg. 8. These do not include the value of the deceased's estate, but by virtue of s.78(4) of the Administration Act (1986 Act, s.32(4)) any funeral payment from the social fund is a first charge on the estate.

Finally, the £500 or £1,000 capital rule must be applied (reg. 9). However, since there is no requirement of need, it is no bar to payment that a claimant has already met the funeral costs by the date of claim. The normal time-limit for claiming is three months from the date of the death. Reg. 9(2)(e) secures that if the amount of capital as at the date of claim has been reduced by a payment towards the expenses of the funeral in question, the amount of the payment is to be added back. If the funeral costs have not been paid at the date of claim any funeral payment is to be made direct to the creditor (Claims and Payments Regulations, reg. 35(2)).

Paragraph (3)
This definition is now unnecessary.

Deductions from an award of a funeral payment

8. There shall be deducted from the amount of any award which would, but for this regulation, be made under regulation 7 the following amounts:—

    (a) the amount of any assets of the deceased which are available to the ['responsible person] (on application or otherwise) or any other member of his family without probate or letters of administration having been granted;

    (b) the amount of any lump sum due to the ['responsible person] or any other member of his family on the death of the deceased by virtue of any insurance policy, occupational pension scheme, or burial club or any analogous arrangement;

    (c) the amount of any contribution which has been received by the ['responsible person] or any other member of his family from a charity or a relative of his or of the deceased, but only to the extent that that amount or, if more than one contribution has been received, the aggregate of such amounts exceeds the cost of any funeral expenses other than those specified in regulation 7(2);

(d) the amount of any funeral grant, made out of public funds, in respect of the death of a person who was entitled to a war disablement pension.

AMENDMENT

1. Social Fund Maternity and Funeral Expenses (General) Amendment Regulations 1994 (S.I. 1994 No. 506), reg. 4 (April 1, 1994).

DEFINITIONS

"family"—see reg. 3(1).
"occupational pension scheme"—see 1986 Act, s.84(1) (PSA, s.1).
"responsible person"—see reg. 3(1).

GENERAL NOTE

The amounts specified are to be deducted from the amount calculated under reg. 7, it would appear before the £500 or £1000 capital rule is applied.

Sub-para. (a). Under the Administration of Estates (Small Payments) Act 1965 certain sums can be distributed from the estate to beneficiaries without a grant of probate or letters of administration. The current limit is £5,000. In addition many statutes regulating Post Office and building society accounts, savings certificates, etc., (but not, after privatisation, Trustee Savings Bank accounts) allow payment to be made after the owner's death. There is a similar power for most social security benefits. For details, see Parry & Clark, *The Law of Succession* (8th ed.), pp. 165–7, and *Halsbury's Laws of England* (4th ed.), Vol. 17, para. 970. One problem is that these provisions are generally merely permissive, so that payment cannot be demanded as of right. In *R(IS) 14/91* the Commissioner indicates that in straightforward cases it may be concluded that such an amount is available on application. However, the circumstances (*e.g.* some dispute between next of kin of equal status) may point to the opposite conclusion. *R(IS) 14/91* also decides that evidence of availability of assets from the date of death up to the date of the AO's decision is relevant. Thus where the claim was made on the date of death, a sum of £1300 in the deceased's building society account was available, although the claimant did not obtain the money until a week later. Nor was that conclusion defeated by the fact that before the AO's decision the claimant had distributed or spent most of the money. Funeral expenses are a first charge on the estate (*R(SB) 18/84*). If there are liquid assets in the estate, these may be immediately available for funeral expenses regardless of other debts. In *R(IS) 12/93* arrears of attendance allowance for the deceased were paid to the claimant as next-of-kin. The Commissioner holds that the arrears were available. Since they exceeded the cost of the funeral, no award was made.

Sub-para. (b). For this paragraph to apply the amount must be due to the claimant or a member of his family. Due must mean legally due. Sometimes such a member will have a clear legal entitlement under an insurance policy or a pension scheme. Sometimes trustees may have a discretion as to who should be paid a lump sum. In these circumstances no amount can be legally due until the trustees have exercised that discretion.

Sub-para. (c). This paragraph only applies to sums which have actually been received, presumably at the date of claim, since that is the date specified in reg. 7(1), although *R(IS) 14/91* casts doubt on this. Only payments from charities or from relatives of the deceased or the claimant's family count. Payments from anyone else do not count, except to the extent that they may increase the claimant's capital. Any relevant payments received are first to be set against funeral expenses not covered by reg. 7(2), *e.g.* unreasonable flowers or extra cars or the provision of a headstone. Then only the excess is to be deducted from the funeral payment. Note that only expenses of the burial or cremation can be brought into this calculation. It cannot be used to cover other kinds of expenses, of which obituary notices might be an example. However, if a contribution is expressed to be for expenses which are not funeral expenses it would be fair to exclude it from para. (c).

Sub-para. (d). This paragraph is straightforward.

PART IV

EFFECT OF CAPITAL

Effect of capital

9.—[²(1) Where—
(a) a claimant or a claimant's partner is aged 60 or over and the claimant has capital which is in excess of £1,000; or
(b) the claimant is or, if he has a partner, both he and his partner are aged under 60 and the claimant has capital which is in excess of £500,
a maternity payment or funeral payment which, but for this regulation, would be payable shall be payable only if, and to the extent that, the amount of the payment is more than the excess.]
[¹(2) For the purposes of paragraph (1)—
(a) any capital possessed by any person whose capital is for the purposes— of entitlement to income support, treated as that of the claimant by virtue of section 22(5) of the Social Security Act 1986 [SSCBA, s.136(1)] or the provisions of regulation 23(3) of the Income Support (General) Regulations 1987 (calculation of income and capital) shall be treated as that of the claimant;
(b) subject to paragraph (3), the claimant's capital shall be calculated in the same manner as his capital is calculated under the Income Support (General) Regulations 1987 for the purposes of determining his entitlement to income support.
(3) For the purposes of paragraph (1)—
(a) any sum acquired by the claimant (whether as a loan or otherwise) on the express condition that it is to be used to meet the funeral expenses in respect of which the claim is made shall be disregarded;
(b) in the case of a claim for a maternity payment or a funeral payment which is made within 12 months of the death of the husband of the claimant, any lump sum payable to that claimant as a widow by virtue of section 24 of the Social Security Act 1975 [SSCBA, s.36] shall be disregarded;
(c) the amount of any payment out of capital, other than capital disregarded under sub-paragraphs (a) and (b) above or under regulation 47 of, and Schedule 10 to, the Income Support (General) Regulations 1987 (capital disregards), which has already been made towards the funeral expenses (whether or not the expenses are within the scope of regulation 7(2), shall be added back to that capital as if the payment had not been made.]

AMENDMENTS

1. Social Fund Maternity and Funeral Expenses (General) Amendment Regulations 1989 (S.I. 1989 No. 379), reg. 4 (April 1, 1989).
2. Social Fund (Miscellaneous Amendments) Regulations 1990 (S.I. 1990 No. 580), reg. 7 (April 9, 1990).

DEFINITIONS

"the Act"—see reg. 3(1).
"claimant"—*ibid.*
"funeral payment"—*ibid.*
"maternity payment"—*ibid.*

Paragraph (1)

Any excess of the claimant's capital over £500, or £1,000 if either the claimant or his partner is aged over 59, is to be set against the amount of a payment calculated under Part II or III. This may wipe out the entitlement, or if the initial amount of the payment is higher than the excess the difference is paid.

Reg. 9 does not specify the date at which capital is to be calculated. It was clear under the Single Payments Regulations that the date of claim was the crucial date. It is possible that for social fund purposes changes in capital up to the date of decision are relevant, and this seems to be in line with the approach in *R(IS) 14/91* (see note to reg. 8(a)). The Commissioner there did point out that reg. 8 is not concerned with entitlement, but with deductions from an award. Thus it can still be argued that the capital test should be applied at the date fixed in reg. 5(1)(a) and 7(1)(a), *i.e.* the date of claim. But not all the elements of entitlement can necessarily be identified at that date (see reg. 7(1)(c)), so that the question remains open.

Paragraph (2)

Because a social fund payment is not income support, the income support capital rules have to be specifically incorporated.

Sub-para. (a). Section 136(1) of the Contributions and Benefits Act (1986 Act, s.22(5)) provides that the capital of all members of the claimant's family (as defined in s.137(1); 1986 Act, s.20(11)) counts as the claimant's. But see the immediate effect of sub-para. (b) below. Reg. 23(3) of the Income Support (General) Regulations deals with polygamous marriages (but not other polygamous relationships).

Sub-para. (b). The new form of this sub-paragraph makes clear that capital is to be calculated in the same way as for income support, subject to the special rules set out in para. (3). There may be some difficulties in directly applying those rules. For instance, if a claimant gives away money so as to get below the £500 or £1000 capital rule, he would not seem to be fixed with notional capital of the amount given away under reg. 51(1) of the Income Support (General) Regulations. That regulation only applies where the person's purpose is to secure or increase entitlement to income support. A social fund payment is not income support. Equally, if a claimant spends capital on personal possessions so as to get below the limit, the disregard of the value of personal possessions in para. 10 of Sched. 10 to the Income Support (General) Regulations (incorporated by reg. 9(2)(b) above) still applies.

Note that there is no general requirement under the income support rules that capital should be available before it is taken into account. Availability may sometimes be a factor in assessing market value.

Paragraph (3)

These are special rules for social fund payments, where the income support rules do not necessarily apply.

Sub-para. (a). Sums acquired by the claimant in these circumstances would probably not be part of the claimant's capital anyway (see *Barclays Bank Ltd. v. Quistclose Investments Ltd.* [1970] A.C. 567; *R(SB) 53/83; R(SB) 1/85; R(SB) 12/86*).

Sub-para. (b). A payment under s.36 of the Contributions and Benefits Act (1975 Act, s.24) is known as a widow's payment. It is a contributory benefit of £1,000 paid to widows, intended to help with immediate "bereavement associated" expenses. It is to be disregarded for a year from the date of the husband's death, in the case of both funeral and maternity payments.

Sub-para. (c). This provision applies only to funeral payments. If (presumably before the date of claim) capital which is not disregarded under sub-paras. (a) or (b) or Sched. 10 to the Income Support (General) Regulations has been used for funeral expenses, then the amount used is to be added back into the claimant's capital. A payment for funeral expenses which fall outside reg. 7(2) is caught by this provision, but not a payment for expenses which are not truly funeral expenses (*e.g.* obituary notices).

Assessment of capital

10. [¹. . .]

AMENDMENT

1. Social Fund Maternity and Funeral Expenses (General) Amendment Regulations 1989 (S.I. 1989 No. 379), reg. 5 (April 15, 1989).

PART V

TRANSITIONAL PROVISIONS

Interpretation of Parts V and VI

11. In this Part and Part VI of these Regulations—
"the Single Payments Regulations" means the Supplementary Benefit (Single
Payments) Regulations 1981;
"the Trade Dispute Regulations" means the Supplementary Benefit (Trade
Disputes and Recovery from Earnings) Regulations 1980;
"the Urgent Cases Regulations" means the Supplementary Benefit (Urgent
Cases) Regulations 1981.

Transitional arrangements—maternity payments

12.—(1) Subject to paragraph (2), no maternity payment shall be made in the
case where the confinement or adoption occurred before 6th April 1987.

(2) Subject to paragraph (3), a maternity payment may be made, so long as
the claimant satisfies the conditions of Part II of these Regulations, in respect
of a confinement or adoption which occurred on or after 9th March 1987 but
only if the claimant or his partner was or would have been, had a claim been
made, entitled to supplementary benefit for any period including 9th March 1987
or beginning after that date which falls before the coming into operation of these
Regulations.

(3) No maternity payment shall be made in a case where, in respect of the
same confinement or adoption, the claimant or his partner has received or is
entitled to a single payment of supplementary benefit by virtue of regulation 7
of the Single Payments Regulations or an additional requirement was applicable
by virtue of regulation 7 of the Trade Disputes Regulations.

(4) The amount of a maternity payment shall be reduced by the amount of an
award, in respect of the same confinement, of a maternity grant under section
21 of the Social Security Act 1975.

DEFINITIONS

   "claimant"—see reg. 3(1).
   "confinement"—*ibid.*
   "maternity payment"—*ibid.*
   "partner"—*ibid.*
   "Single Payments Regulations"—see reg. 11.
   "Trade Disputes Regulations"—*ibid.*

GENERAL NOTE

The general rule, under para. (1), is that maternity payments can only be made for births or
adoptions after April 5, 1987. Up to that date reg. 7 of the Single Payments Regulations was still
in operation. However, the crucial date under those regulations is the date of claim, so that if a
claim was not made before April 6, 1987, no payment for maternity expenses under reg. 7 can be
paid. Therefore, if no single payment has been made (para. (3)) a social fund payment can be made
for births or adoptions occurring after March 8, 1987 (para. (2)). The ordinary conditions of regs. 4
and 5 must be met, and in addition the claimant or his partner must have satisfied the conditions
for entitlement to weekly supplementary benefit for some time between March 9 and April 5, 1987,
inclusive. Reg. 19 of the Claims and Payments Regulations on good cause for late claims may be
relevant.

Note that para. (3) provides a general exclusion when there has already been a single payment or
trade dispute payment for the same birth or adoption. Similarly, under para. (4) if there has been an
award of maternity grant the £25 is to be deducted from any social fund payment.

Transitional payments—funeral payments

13.—(1) Subject to paragraph (2) no funeral payment shall be made where the deceased died before 6th April 1987.

(2) Subject to paragraph (3) a funeral payment may be made, so long as the claimant satisfies the conditions of regulation 6, where the deceased died on or after 9th March 1987 but only if the claimant or his partner was or would have been, had a claim been made, entitled to supplementary benefit for any period including 9th March 1987 or beginning after that date which falls before the coming into operation of these Regulations.

(3) No funeral payment shall be made in the case where, in respect of the same funeral, the claimant or his partner has received or is entitled to a single payment of supplementary benefit by virtue of regulation 8 of the Single Payments Regulations or an additional requirement was applicable by virtue of regulation 7A of the Trade Disputes Regulations.

(4) The amount of a funeral payment shall be reduced by the amount of an award, in respect of the same funeral, of a death grant under section 32 of the Social Security Act 1975 unless that grant has been spent on any item in respect of which a funeral payment would otherwise have been made.

DEFINITIONS

"claimant"—see reg. 3(1).
"funeral"—*ibid.*
"funeral payment"—*ibid.*
"partner"—*ibid.*
"Single Payments Regulations"—see reg. 11.
"Trade Disputes Regulations"—*ibid.*

GENERAL NOTE

The general rule, under para. (1), is that funeral payments can only be made for deaths occurring after April 5, 1987. Up to that date, reg. 8 of the Single Payments Regulations was still in operation. But the crucial thing under those regulations is the date of claim and if no claim had been made before April 6, 1987, no single payment could be awarded. Therefore, providing that no single payment or trade dispute payment has been made (para. (3)) a social fund payment can be made for deaths after March 8, 1987. The ordinary conditions of reg. 6 must be met, and in addition the claimant or his partner must for some period between March 9 and April 5, 1987, inclusive, have satisfied the conditions for entitlement to weekly supplementary benefit. Reg. 19 of the Claims and Payments Regulations on good cause for late claims may be relevant.

Para. (3) provides a general exception from entitlement. Under para. (4) the amount of a social fund payment is to be reduced by the amount of any death grant awarded, unless the grant has been spent on an item covered by reg. 6(2). Presumably in this case, a social fund payment will not be made for that item because the person will not have taken responsibility for that item.

PART VI

CONSEQUENTIAL AMENDMENTS

14., 15., and **16.** [*Omitted*]

Social Fund (Application for Review) Regulations 1988

(S.I. 1988 No. 34)

Made by the Secretary of State under the Social Security Act 1986, ss.34(1) and (3) and 84(1).

These regulations prescribe the procedure for applying for a review in cases in which decisions on the social fund are taken by social fund officers rather than AOs. Thus they apply to budgeting loans, crisis loans and community care grants, but not to maternity or funeral payments or payments for exceptionally cold weather.

Citation, commencement and interpretation

1.—(1) These Regulations may be cited as the Social Fund (Application for review) Regulations 1988 and shall come into force on 11th April 1988.

(2) Any reference in regulation 2 of these Regulations to a numbered paragraph is a reference to the paragraph in that regulation bearing that number.

Manner of making application for review or further review and time limits

2.—(1) Any application for—
   (a) a review of any determination made by a social fund officer;
   (b) a further review by a social fund inspector of a determination of a social fund officer which has been reviewed,
shall be in writing and shall be made within the time specified in paragraph (2) by sending or delivering it to an office of the Department of Social Security.

(2) The time specified for the purposes of paragraph (1) is—
   (a) in the case of an application to which paragraph (1)(a) applies, 28 days from the date on which the determination to which that application relates was issued;
   (b) in the case of an application to which paragraph (1)(b) applies, 28 days from the date on which the determination on review was issued.

(3) The time specified in paragraph (2) may be extended for special reasons, even though the time so specified may already have expired, by the social fund officer or, as the case may be, the social fund inspector.

(4) The application for review or, as the case may be, further review shall contain particulars of the specific grounds on which it is made and shall be signed by the person making the application.

(5) Where it appears to the social fund officer or, as the case may be, the social fund inspector that a person has submitted an application which is incomplete in that it contains insufficient particulars to enable any material question to be determined, he may request that person to furnish within a specified time such further particulars as may be reasonably required to complete the application; and if the person does so the application shall be treated as having been made within the time specified in paragraph (2) or, as the case may be, extended under paragraph (3).

[[1](6) Where an application is to be made on behalf of a person to whom the determination relates, that person shall signify in writing his consent to the application being made on his behalf unless the person making the application is a person appointed by the Secretary of State under regulation 33(1) of the Social Security (Claims and Payments) Regulations 1987 to act on behalf of the person to whom the determination relates.]

(7) For the purposes of paragraph (2) the date on which a determination or a determination on review is issued is the date on which notice of that determination was given or sent to the applicant for review or further review, and, if sent by post to the applicant's last known or notified address, that notice shall be treated for the purposes of this regulation as having been sent on the day that it was posted.

AMENDMENT

1. Social Fund (Miscellaneous Amendments) Regulations 1990 (S.I. 1990 No. 580), reg. 2 (April 9, 1990).

Social Fund (Applications) Regulations 1988

(S.I. 1988 No. 524)

Citation, commencement and interpretation

1.—(1) These Regulations may be cited as the Social Fund (Applications) Regulations 1988 and shall come into force on 11th April 1988.

(2) In these Regulations, unless the context otherwise requires—

"the Act" means the Social Security Act 1986;

"appropriate office" means an office of the Department of Social Security.

Form and manner in which an application is to be made

2.—(1) Every application for a payment out of the social fund under section 32(2)(b) of the Act [SSCBA, s.138(1)(b)] payment to meet needs other than in prescribed circumstances) shall be made in writing, on a form approved by the Secretary of State and completed in accordance with the instructions on that form, or in such other manner, being in writing, as the Secretary of State may accept as sufficient in the circumstances of any particular case.

(2) Forms of application shall be supplied, without charge, by such persons as the Secretary of State may appoint or authorise for that purpose.

(3) Every application shall be delivered or sent to an appropriate office.

(4) Where an application is to be made on behalf of a person, that person shall signify in writing his consent to the application being made on his behalf unless the person making the application is a person appointed by the Secretary of State under regulation 33(1) of the Social Security (Claims and Payments) Regulations 1987 to act on the beneficiary's behalf. (5) Where it appears to the Secretary of State that an application which has been submitted is incomplete in that—

(a) the form approved has been used but it has not been completed in accordance with the instructions given on that form, the Secretary of State may return the form to the person making the application for proper completion by him; or

(b) it contains insufficient particulars to enable any material question to be determined, the Secretary of State may request that person to furnish in writing or by attendance at the appropriate office such further particulars as may reasonably be required to complete the application.

[¹Time at which an application is to be treated as made

3. The time at which an application to which regulation 2 above applies is to be treated as made shall be—

(a) in the case of an application which meets the requirements of regulation 2(1), the date on which it is received in an appropriate office;

(b) in the case of an application which does not meet the requirements of regulation 2(1), but where the person complies with the requirements of the Secretary of State pursuant to regulation 2(5), the date on which the application was received in an appropriate office in the first instance.]

AMENDMENT

1. Social Fund (Miscellaneous Provisions) Regulations 1990 (S.I. 1990 No. 1788), reg. 4 (September 24, 1990).

Social Fund (Miscellaneous Provisions) Regulations 1990

(S.I. 1990 No. 1788)

Citation, commencement and interpretation

1.—(1) These Regulations may be cited as the Social Fund (Micellaneous Provisions) Regulations 1990 and shall come into force on 24th September 1990.

(2) In these Regulations, "the Act" means the Social Security Act 1986.

Condition to be satisfied before payment of a social fund award

2.—(1) Before a payment of an award out of the social fund under section 32(2)(b) of the Act [SSCBA, s. 138(1)(b)] (payment to meet needs other than in prescribed circumstances) is made for a category of need which is specified in directions given by the Secretary of State to be repayable, the person by or on behalf of whom the application was made shall notify the Secretary of State in writing of his agreement to the terms and conditions of which he has been notified by the Secretary of State in accordance with subsection (4A) of section 33 of the Act [SSCBA, s. 139(4)] within 14 days of the date on which that notification was issued to that person.

(2) The time specified in paragraph (1) above may be extended by the Secretary of State for special reasons, even though the time so specified may already have expired.

Circumstances in which an award is to be extinguished

3. An award of a payment out of the social fund under section 32(2)(b) of the Act [SSCBA, s.138(1)(b)] shall be extinguished where—

(a) the person by or on behalf of whom the application was made fails to satisfy the condition in regulation 2(1) above, within the time there specified or as extended under regulation 2(2), as the case may be; or

(b) the payment has been made to the person by or on behalf of whom the application was made or to a third party but the person or the third party, as the case may be, has failed to present for payment the instrument of payment within 12 months of its issue.

Social Fund (Recovery by Deductions from Benefits) Regulations 1988

(S.I. 1988 No. 35)

Made by the Secretary of State under the Social Security Act 1986, ss. 33(6) and 84(1).

Citation and commencement

1. These Regulations may be cited as the Social Fund (Recovery by Deductions from Benefits) Regulations 1988 and shall come into force on 11th April 1988.

Interpretation

2. In these Regulations "the principal Act" means the Social Security Act 1975.

Benefits from which an award from the social fund may be recovered

3. The following benefits are prescribed for the purposes of section 33(6) of the Social Security Act 1986 [SSAA, s.78(2)] as benefits from which an award from the social fund may be recovered by deduction—

 (a) income support;
 (b) family credit;
 (c) unemployment benefit under section 14(1)(a) of the principal Act [SSCBA, s.25];
[²(d) incapacity benefit under section 86A of the Social Security Contributions and Benefits Act 1992;]
 (e) [².. .];
 (f) [².. .];
 (g) maternity allowance under section 22(1) of the principal Act [SSCBA, s.34];
 (h) widowed mother's allowance under section 25(1) and (2) of the principal Act [SSCBA, s.37];
 (i) widow's pension under section 26(1) of the principal Act [SSCBA, s.38];
 (j) retirement pension (Categories A and B) under sections 28(1) and 29(1) of the principal Act [SSCBA, ss.44 and 49];
 (k) severe disablement allowance under section 36 of the principal Act [SSCBA, s.68];
 (l) invalid care allowance under section 37 of the principal Act [SSCBA, s.70];
 (m) retirement pension (Categories C and D) under section 39(1) of the principal Act [SSCBA, s.78];
 (n) age addition under section 40(1) and (2) of the principal Act [SSCBA, s.79];
 (o) increases to unemployment benefit, [²incapacity benefit] and Category A, B and C retirement pension under section 41(1) of the principal Act [SSCBA, s.80];
 (p) increases to unemployment benefit, [²short-term incapacity benefit] and maternity allowance under section 44(1) and (2) of the principal Act [SSCBA, s.82];
 (q) increases to Category A and Category C retirement pension or to [²long-term incapacity benefit] under section 45(2) of the principal Act [SSCBA, s.83];
 (r) increases to Category A retirement pension under section 45A(1) of the principal Act [SSCBA, s.84];
 (s) increases to Category A and Category C retirement pension and [²long-term incapacity benefit] under section 46(2) of the principal Act [SSCBA, s.85];
 (t) increase to [²long-term incapacity benefit] under section 47(1) of the principal Act [SSCBA, s.86];
 (u) increases to severe disablement allowance and invalid care allowance payable under section 49(a) and (b) of the principal Act [SSCBA, s.90];
 (v) disablement benefit under section 57(1) of the principal Act [SSCBA, s.103];
 (w) reduced earnings allowance under section 59A(1) of the principal Act [SSCBA, s.106];
 (x) industrial death benefit under section 67 to 70 to the principal Act [SSCBA, s. 106];
 (y) additions to Category A and Category B retirement pension under sections 6 to 10 of, and Schedule 1 to, the Social Security Pensions Act 1975;
 (z) additional pension payable as widows benefit under sections 6 and 13 of the Social Security Pensions Act 1975;
 (aa) [².. .];
 (bb) [².. .];
 (cc) graduated retirement benefit under sections 36 and 37 of the National Insurance Act 1965;

[¹(dd) disability working allowance under section 20 of the Social Security Act 1986 [SSCBA, s.129].]

AMENDMENT

1. Disability Living Allowance and Disability Working Allowance (Consequential Provisions) Regulations 1991 (S.I. 1991 No. 2742), reg. 14 (April 6, 1992).
2. Social Security (Incapacity Benefit) (Consequential and Transitional Amendments and Savings) Regulations 1995 (S.I. 1995 No. 829), reg. 20 (April 13, 1995).

GENERAL NOTE

See the notes to s. 78(2) of the Administration Act.

Social Fund Directions

Directions issued by the Secretary of State for Social Security under sections 138(1)(b), 140(2), 140(3) and 140(4) of the Social Security contributions and Benefits Act 1992 and sections 66(7), 66(8)(a) and (b) and 168(5) of the Social Security Administration Act 1992.

ARRANGEMENT OF DIRECTIONS

GENERAL

BUDGETING LOANS

CRISIS LOANS

COMMUNITY CARE GRANTS

REVIEWS

THE BUDGET

GENERAL

Needs which may be met by social fund payments

1. The needs which may be met by social fund payments awarded under section s.138(1)(b) of the Social Security Contributions and Benefits Act 1992 are those set out in directions 2, 3 and 4 below.

2. Subject to direction 8, a social fund payment may be awarded to assist an applicant to meet important intermittent expenses (except those excluded by these directions) for which it may be difficult to budget.

3. Subject to directions 14, 16 and 17, a social fund payment may be awarded to assist an applicant to meet expenses (except those excluded by these directions)—

  (a) in an emergency, or as a consequence of a disaster, provided that the provision of such assistance is the only means by which serious damage or serious risk to the health or safety of that person, or to a member of his family, may be prevented; or

  (b) where the expenses are rent in advance payable to a landlord who is not a local authority and a social fund payment is being awarded under Direction 4(a)(i).

3A. *[Deleted with effect from November 27, 1991]*

4. Subject to directions 25 and 26, a social fund payment may be awarded to promote community care—

  (a) by assisting an applicant with expenses, including expenses of travel within the United Kingdom (except those excluded by these directions) where such assistance will—

    (i) help the applicant, a member of his family or other person for whom the applicant (or a member of his family) will be providing care, to re-establish himself in the community following a stay in institutional or residential care; or

    (ii) help the applicant, a member of his family or other person for whom the applicant (or a member of his family) will be providing care, to remain in the community rather than enter institutional or residential care; or

    (iii) ease exceptional pressures on the applicant and his family; or

    (iv) allow the applicant or his partner to care for a prisoner or young offender on release on temporary licence under rule 6 of the Prison Rules 1964 or, in Scotland, on temporary release under Part XIV of the Prisons and Young Offenders Institutions (Scotland) Rules 1994; or

  (b) by assisting an applicant and one or more members of his family, or any of those persons, with expenses of travel including any reasonable charges for overnight accommodation within the United Kingdom in order to—

    (i) visit someone who is ill; or

    (ii) attend a relative's funeral; or

    (iii) ease a domestic crisis; or

    (iv) visit a child who is with the other parent pending a court decision; or

    (v) move to suitable accommodation.

4A. *[Deleted with effect from November 27, 1991]*

Grants and loans

5. Any award within direction 2 or 3 shall include a determination that it is repayable; an award within direction 2 is referred to in these directions as a budgeting loan and an award within direction 3 is referred to as a crisis loan.

6. Any award within direction 4 shall not include a determination that it is repayable; an award within direction 4 is referred to in these directions as a community care grant.

6A. *[Deleted with effect from November 27, 1991]*

Repeat applications

7. A social fund officer shall not determine an application for any payment from the social fund made within 26 weeks of a previous application for a loan or grant for the same item or service for which a payment has already been awarded or refused unless;

    (a) there has been a relevant change in the applicant's circumstances; or

    (b) the application is for a budgeting loan and at the time of the previous application for a loan or grant he would have been ineligible for a budgeting loan because he did not satisfy the provisions of direction 8(1)(c).

BUDGETING LOANS

Eligibility

8. (1) A social fund payment under direction 2 shall only be awarded to an applicant if at the date of the determination of the application—

    (a) he is in receipt of income support; and

    (b) neither he nor his partner is disqualified under section 27 of the Social Security Contributions and Benefits Act 1992 (trade disputes) from receiving unemployment benefit, nor would they be so disqualified if otherwise entitled to that benefit; and

    (c) for each week of the 26 weeks immediately preceding the date of determination of the application he has been in receipt of income support, or the partner of someone in receipt of income support.

(2) For the purpose of paragraph (1)(c), where the applicant or, as the case may be, the partner, has been in receipt of income support for two separate periods, the second of which includes the date of the determination of the application, and those periods are separated by an interval of not more than 14 days, those periods, or the later of those periods and that interval, may be treated as a continuous period of receipt of income support.

Effect of capital

9. (1) Where—

    (a) the applicant, or his partner, is aged 60 or over and the total capital resources of the applicant and his partner exceed £1000; or

    (b) the applicant is, or if he has a partner, both are aged under 60 and the total capital resources of the applicant and his partner exceed £500,

any budgeting loan which would but for this direction be awarded shall be awarded only if, and to the extent that, the amount of the award is more than the excess.

(2) In this direction "total capital resources" shall be calculated in accordance with Chapter VI of and Schedule 10 to the Income Support (General) Regulations 1987 (capital), except that any payments made from the Family Fund to the applicant or to his partner or children are to be disregarded.

Maximum and minimum amounts

10. The minimum that may be awarded as a budgeting loan is £30, and the maximum is the difference between any sum already repayable to the social fund by the applicant and his partner and £1000.

11. No budgeting loan may be awarded in excess of the amount which the applicant is likely to be able to repay.

Exclusions

12. A budgeting loan may not be awarded in respect of any of the following items of expense—

    (a) any need which occurs outside the United Kingdom;

(b) an educational or training need including clothing and tools;
(c) distinctive school uniform or sports clothes or equipment;
(d) travelling expenses to or from school;
(e) school meals and meals taken during school holidays by children who are entitled to free school meals;
(f) expenses in connection with court (legal) proceedings (including a community service order) such as legal fees, court fees, fines, costs, damages, subsistence or travelling expenses (other than a crisis loan for emergency travelling expenses where an applicant is stranded away from home);
(g) removal charges where an applicant is permanently rehoused following the imposition of a compulsory purchase order, or a redevelopment or closing order, or a compulsory exchange of tenancies, or pursuant to a housing authority's statutory duty to the homeless under the Housing Act 1985 or Part II of the Housing (Scotland) Act 1987;
(h) domestic assistance and respite care;
(i) any repair to property of any body mentioned in section 80(1) of the Housing Act 1985 or section 61(2)(a) of the Housing (Scotland) Act 1987 and, in the case of Scotland, any repair to property of any housing trust in existence on 13 November 1953;
(j) a medical, surgical, optical, aural or dental item or service;
(k) work related expenses;
(l) debts to government departments;
(m) investments;
(n) the cost of mains fuel consumption and associated standing charges;
(o) housing costs, including repairs and improvements to which the Income Support (General) Regulations 1987 Schedule 3 paragraph 8(3) refers and including deposits to secure accommodation, mortgage payments, water rates, sewerage rates, service charges, rent, residential charges for hostels, and all other charges for accommodation, whether or not such charges include payment for meals and/or services, other than:
  (i) payments for intermittent housing costs not met by housing benefit or income support or for which direct payments cannot be implemented such as the cost of emptying cess pits or septic tanks; or
  (ii) rent in advance where the landlord is not a local authority; or
  (iii) where such charges are payable in advance to secure board and lodging accommodation, or residential accommodation in hostels, but not any part of such charges not relating to accommodation, for example meals, services, or deposits; or
  (iv) minor repairs and improvements;
(p) council tax, council water charges, arrears of community charge, collective community charge contributions or community water charges.

13. [*Direction 13 has been deleted. It required applications to be made in writing on the approved form (unless the Secretary of State allowed otherwise). This is now provided for in the Social Fund (Applications) Regulations 1988 (S.I. 1988 No. 524).*]

CRISIS LOANS

Eligibility

14. A social fund payment under direction 3 shall only be awarded to an applicant if at the date when the application is determined;
  (a) he is aged 16 or over; and
  (b) he is without sufficient resources to meet the immediate short-term needs of himself or his family, or both himself and his family.

15. A crisis loan may not be awarded in respect of a person who is—

(a) a resident in accommodation to which Part III of the National Assistance Act 1948 or Part IV of the Social Work (Scotland) Act 1968 applies, or in a nursing home or residential care home or a hospital in-patient, unless it is planned that the person will be discharged within the following two weeks; or

(b) a prisoner or person who is lawfully detained or is on release on temporary licence under rule 6 of the Prison Rules 1964 or, in Scotland, on temporary release under Part XIV of the Prisons and Young Offenders Institutions (Scotland) Rules 1994; or

(c) a person who is a member of and fully maintained by a religious order; or

(d) a person who is (or would be) treated as a person in full time relevant education for the purpose of income support and, as a result, falls into a category whereby he is not (or would not be) entitled to income support.

16. Where the applicant is:

(a) a full time student except where he is in receipt of income support; or

(b) a person who is (or would be) treated as a person from abroad for the purposes of income support and, as a result, falls into a category whereby he is not (or would not be) entitled to income support

a social fund payment under direction 3 shall only be awarded in order to alleviate the consequences of a disaster.

17. Where the applicant or his partner is disqualified under section 27 of the Social Security Contributions and Benefits Act 1992 (trade disputes) from receiving unemployment benefit or would be so disqualified if otherwise entitled to that benefit, the expenses for which a crisis loan might otherwise be awarded are limited to—

(a) expenses which are a consequence of a disaster; and

(b) expenses, outside (a), in respect of items required for the purpose only of cooking or space heating (including fireguards).

Maximum awards

18. The maximum amount that may be awarded as a crisis loan in respect of living expenses for applicants, other than people whose applicable amount is reduced on the basis of voluntary unemployment is the aggregate of—

(a) an amount equal to 75% of the appropriate income support personal allowance for the applicant and any partner; and

(b) an amount equal to the income support personal allowance at the rate applicable to children under 11, for each child

but must not in any case exceed the difference between any sum already repayable to the Social Fund by the applicant and his partner and £1000.

19. [*Direction 19 has been deleted*]

20. The maximum amount that may be awarded as a crisis loan in respect of living expenses for applicants whose applicable amount is reduced on the basis of voluntary unemployment is—

(a) the aggregate of—

(i) an amount equal to 75% of the appropriate income support personal allowance for the applicant and any partner; and

(ii) an amount equal to the income support personal allowance at the rate applicable to children under 11, for each child; or

(b) the income support applicable amount payable in such circumstances

whichever is the lower, but must not in any case exceed the difference between any sum already repayable to the Social Fund by the applicant and his partner and £1000.

21. The maximum amount which may be awarded in respect of any item or service which is within direction 3 (crisis loans) is the lesser of—

  (a) in the case of an existing item, the cost of repair; or

  (b) the reasonable costs of replacing an existing item, or purchasing a new item or service (including delivery and installation)

but the amount must not in any case exceed the difference between any sum already repayable to the Social Fund by the applicant and his partner and £1000.

22. No crisis loan may be awarded in excess of the amount which the applicant is likely to be able to repay.

Exclusions

23. (1) A crisis loan may not be awarded in respect of any expenses which are excluded:

  (a) in the case of any budgeting loan by direction 12(a)–(m); or

  (b) by direction 17.

(2) In addition to the expenses excluded by paragraph (1), a crisis loan may not be awarded for any expenses in respect of any of the following items—

  (a) installation, rental and call charges for a telephone;

  (b) mobility needs;

  (c) holidays;

  (d) a television or radio, or licence, aerial or rental charges for a television or radio;

  (e) garaging, parking, purchase, and running costs of any motor vehicle except where payment is being considered for emergency travelling expenses;

  (f) housing costs, including repairs and improvements to which the Income Support (General) Regulations 1987 Schedule 3 paragraph 8(3) refers and including deposits to secure accommodation, mortgage payments, water rates, sewerage rates, service charges, rent and analogous charges for accommodation, other than:

    (i) payments for intermittent housing costs not met by housing benefit or income support or for which direct payments cannot be implemented such as the cost of emptying cess pits or septic tanks; or

    (ii) rent in advance where the landlord is not a local authority; or

    (iii) charges for board and lodging accommodation and residential charges for hostels, but not deposits, whether included in the total charge or not; or

    (iv) minor repairs and improvements;

  (g) council tax, council water charges, arrears of community charge, collective community charge contributions or community water charges.

24. [*Direction 24 has been deleted*]

COMMUNITY CARE GRANTS

Eligibility

25. A social fund payment under direction 4 shall only be awarded to an applicant if:

  (a) subject to paragraph (b) of this direction, he is in receipt of income support at the date the application is treated as made; or

  (b) in a case where the conditions set out in direction 4(a)(i) are satisfied, at the date the application is treated as made, it is planned that the applicant will be discharged within six weeks, is likely to receive income support upon discharge.

26. Where the applicant, or his partner, is disqualified under section 27 of the Social Security Contributions and Benefits Act 1992 (trade disputes) from receiving unemployment benefit, or would be so disqualified if otherwise entitled to that benefit, a community care grant may not be made except in respect of travelling expenses within the United Kingdom in the following situations—

(a) if the visit is made by a partner or dependant who is not affected by the trade dispute, an award may be made in respect of travelling expenses for
  (i) a visit to a patient who is a close relative or who was prior to his admission to hospital or similar institution a member of the same household; or
  (ii) a visit to a person who is a close relative or who was prior to his illness a member of the same household as the visitor and is critically ill but not in hospital or similar institution;

(b) if the visit is made by a person who is affected by the trade dispute, an award may be made in respect of travelling expenses for
  (i) a visit to a partner in hospital or similar institution; or
  (ii) a visit to a dependant in hospital or similar institution, if the person affected by the trade dispute has no partner living with him who would be eligible for an award within paragraph (*a*) of this direction, or the partner is also in hospital or similar institution; or
  (iii) a visit to a critically ill close relative or member of the household of the person affected by the trade dispute, whether or not he is in hospital or similar institution.

Effect of capital

27. (1) Where—
  (a) the applicant, or his partner, is aged 60 or over and the total capital resources of the applicant and his partner exceed £1000; or
  (b) the applicant is, or if he has a partner both are aged under 60 and the total capital resources of the applicant and his partner exceed £500
any community care grant which would but for this direction be awarded shall be awarded only if, and to the extent that, the amount of the award is more than the excess.

(2) In this direction "total capital resources" shall be calculated in accordance with Chapter VI of and Schedule 10 to the Income Support (General) Regulations 1987 (capital), except that any payments made from the Family Fund to the applicant or to his partner or children are to be disregarded.

Minimum awards

28. (a) Subject to paragraph (b) below, the minimum amount that may be awarded under direction 4(a) (community care grants other than for travelling expenses) is £30.

(b) The minimum amount of £30 shall not apply in respect of awards made towards the living expenses of a prisoner or young offender for a period of home leave.

Exclusions

29. A community care grant may not be awarded in respect of any expenses which are excluded in the case of budgeting loans by direction 12(a)–(m) nor in respect of—
  (a) installation, rental and call charges for a telephone;
  (b) any expenses which the local authority has a statutory duty to meet;
  (c) costs of fuel consumption and any associated standing charges;
  (d) housing costs, including repairs and improvements to which the Income

Support (General) Regulations 1987 Schedule 3 paragraph 8(3) refers and including deposits to secure accommodation, mortgage payments, water rates, sewerage rates, service charges, rent, and all other charges for accommodation, whether or not such charges include payment for meals and/or services other than:

    (i) minor repairs and improvements; or

    (ii) charges for accommodation applied for under direction 4(b);

(e) council tax, council water charges, arrears of community charge, collect-ive community charge contributions or community water charges.

(f) any daily living expenses such as food and groceries, except:

    (i) where such expenses are incurred in caring for a prisoner or young offender on release on temporary licence under rule 6 of the Prison Rules 1964, or, in Scotland, on temporary release under Part XIV of the Prisons and Young Offenders Institutions (Scotland) Rules 1994; or

    (ii) where a crisis loan cannot be awarded for such expenses because the maximum amount referred to in direction 18 has already been reached.

29A. [*Direction 29A has been deleted with effect from November 27, 1991*]
29B. [*Direction 29B has been deleted with effect from November 27, 1991*]
29C. [*Direction 29C has been deleted with effect from November 27, 1991*]
30. [*Direction 30 has been deleted*]

REVIEWS

Circumstances in which a determination is to be reviewed

31. A social fund officer must review a determination made by himself or some other social fund officer, including a determination made by a social fund officer on a previous review, where it appears to him that the decision:

(a) was based on a mistake as to the law or the directions;

(b) was given in ignorance of, or was based on a mistake as to, some material fact; or

(c) there has been any relevant change of circumstances since the decision was given.

Manner in which a review is to be conducted

32. Having reviewed a determination initially under direction 39, a social fund officer in thereafter reviewing the determination must have full regard to:

(a) all the circumstances which existed at the time the original determination was made;

(b) any new evidence which has since been produced; and

(c) any relevant change of circumstances.

33. If a social fund officer decides not to revise a determination wholly in the applicant's favour the applicant must be given the opportunity to attend an interview, accompanied by a friend or representative if he wishes, with the social fund officer before a determination is made.

34. If an applicant attends an interview with the social fund officer he must be given:

(a) an explanation of the reasons for the determination complained of;

(b) an opportunity to make any representations, including the provision of additional evidence, in relation to his application.

35. The social fund officer must make a written record of any representations made at the interview by the applicant in relation to his case, and this must be agreed with the applicant.

36.—(1) Where an applicant has attended an interview offered in accordance with Direction 33, or declines or fails to attend an interview, and the social fund officer decides to revise a determination and:

(a) makes an award where one was previously refused; or

(b) increases an existing award; or

(c) leaves the amount of an existing award unchanged but reduces the amount of the award to be repaid,

he shall inform the applicant of his determination in writing and also inform him that if he does not agree the revised determination, it will be reviewed by a social fund review officer.

(2) Where the applicant does not accept the revised determination made under paragraph (1) or the social fund officer determines not to revise the previous determination, the social fund officer must pass all the papers relevent to the application to a social fund review officer, who will freshly determine the review application (making a written record of his decision) and that determination will supersede that of the social fund officer.

37. If an applicant indicates in writing that he does not wish to proceed with his application the social fund officer or social fund review officer should take no further action unless satisfied that he should conduct a review in accordance with Direction 31 (circumstances in which a determination is to be reviewed).

38. The social fund review officer shall consider carefully any cases referred by the social fund inspector for redetermination. He should take into account any reasons given by the social fund inspector in reaching his decision to refer the matter to him, remedy any defects drawn attention to by the social fund inspector and note that he has done so when determining the case afresh.

39. In reviewing a determination a social fund officer must have full regard initially to:

(a) whether the SFO applied the law correctly in arriving at his decision. In particular:

— that the decision is sustainable on the evidence;

— that the SFO took all relevant considerations into account and did not take irrelevant considerations into account;

— that the SFO interpreted the law including Secretary of State directions—correctly;

(b) whether the SFO acted fairly and exercised his discretion to arrive at a conclusion that was reasonable in the circumstances — *i.e.* a decision that a reasonable SFO could have reached;

(c) whether the required procedural steps have been followed; that the applicant had sufficient opportunity to put his case; and there has been no bias.

THE BUDGET

40. Social fund officers shall control and manage the amounts allocated to them so as to give priority to high priority needs throughout the period of the allocation.

41. The Area social fund officer shall:

(a) make a plan of the level of expenditure for the relevant social fund officers throughout the period of the allocation; and

(b) issue guidance which specifies the high, medium and low priority needs which are specified for grants which may be awarded under direction 4 and loans which may be awarded under directions 2 and 3 and the levels of priority which may be met from the allocation; and

(c) on at least one occasion during every month monitor and review the plan made under paragraph (a) and the guidance under paragraph (b); and

(d) revise the plan and guidance as is necessary to ensure the planned level of expenditure is not exceeded for the period of the allocation.

42. A social fund officer or group of social fund officers shall not in the period of the allocation make an award—

(a) in accordance with direction 2 (budgeting loan) or direction 3 (crisis loan) which in the aggregate with other awards in accordance with those directions in that period exceeds the allocation to that social fund officer or group of social fund officers in that period; or

(b) in accordance with direction 4 (community care grants) which in the aggregate with other awards in accordance with that direction in the period exceeds the allocation to that social fund officer or group of social fund officers in that period.

GENERAL NOTE

These directions relate to social fund payments under s.138(1)(b) of the Contributions and Benefits Act (1986 Act, s.32(2)(b)), where decisions are made by social fund officers (SFOs), not AOs, and there is therefore no right of appeal to a SSAT. Section 140(2) of the Contributions and Benefits Act (1986 Act, s.33(10)) requires a SFO to determine questions in accordance with general directions issued by the Secretary of State. A SFO must also take account of general guidance issued by the Secretary of State. Both guidance and directions are contained in the *Social Fund Guide*, compiled by the Benefits Agency. The directions are reproduced as set out in Volume 2 and dated April 1, 1995. Apart from the two volumes containing the Sectretary of State's directions and guidance, there is also a *Decision and Review Guide*, a *Customer and Application Details Guide*, a *Money Advice Guide* and a *Social Fund Review Officers' Guide*. In addition, there is a separate volume dealing with maternity and funeral payments.

Several aspects of these directions have come under challenge in a series of judicial review cases. The most general challenge was raised in *R. v. Social Fund Officer and Secretary of State for Social Services, ex p. Stitt*, where it was argued that the 1986 Act did not give the Secretary of State power to make directions restricting the categories of need which could be considered for payments out of the Fund. This would have resulted in the striking down of directions 12, 17, 23 and 29. An associated case which would have directly raised the issue of whether the Secretary of State had power to make directions restricting the categories of persons eligible for payments was discontinued following the death of the applicant. However, the Divisional Court (*The Times*, February 23, 1990; *The Independent*, February 23, 1990) held that there was power to make directions which can reasonably be regarded as necessary for the proper control and management of the Social Fund.

The Court of Appeal (*The Times*, July 4, 1990) agreed that there was power to make the directions, but suggested that the power was free of the control and management restriction. Leave to appeal to the House of Lords was refused. In *R. v. Secretary of State for Social Security, ex parte Healey* and the associated actions *Ellison and Stitt II* (*The Times*, December 31, 1991) the Court of Appeal re-affirms this approach. See the notes to s.138(1)(b) of the Contributions and Benefits Act (1986 Act, s.32(2)(b)).

R. v. Social Fund Inspector, ex parte Sherwin, The Times, February 23, 1990; *The Independent*, February 23, 1990, raised a question on the interpretation of direction 4(a)(i) on community care grants. The application was for a grant to set up home in a local authority tenancy granted to someone in a homeless persons' hostel. The application was refused because the applicant had not been in the hostel for the three months laid down in the guidance in what was then the *Social Fund Manual*. The Divisional Court held that the direction should be interpreted in a common sense way and not with a technicality which would conflict with the obvious policy of the direction. Thus, looking at direction 4(a)(i) along with direction 4(a)(ii), the word "re-establish" should not be interpreted strictly and not too much weight given to the three month period.

In the *Healey* case (see above) the same common sense approach, to give effect to the obvious intent of the directions, was commended. But the Court of Appeal in fact construes direction 4 rather strictly. Mr. Healey was single. He moved from a psychiatric hospital to residential care, sharing a house which had permanent staff. It was unlikely that he would be able to live more independently. He claimed a community care grant of £150 for new clothes. The refusal of the grant was upheld on the ground that he did not come under either direction 4(a)(i) or (iii). In order to re-establish himself in the community the person must be actually or imminently in the community following a stay in care. A move in that direction is not enough. The Court of Appeal did not need to deal with the conclusion of the Divisional Court below that a grant could not ease exceptional pressures on Mr. Healey and his family, because he did not have a family.

The question of re-establishment in the community was also an issue in *R. v. Social Fund Inspector, ex parte Ahmed Mohammed* (*The Times*, November 25, 1992). The applicant was a single woman who had been living in a refugee camp in Somalia before coming to the U.K. and applying for asylum. She was initially placed in temporary accommodation and then allocated a flat. She applied for a community care grant of £500 to furnish the flat. The refusal of the application was confirmed by the SFI on the ground that she could not re-establish herself in the community in the U.K. because she had not previously lived in that community. Brooke J. upholds that decision, considering the ordinary meaning of "re-establish" and the normal territorial application of a U.K. statute.

In another case heard at the same time, *R. v. Social Fund Inspector, ex parte Ali*, Brooke J. considered the circumstances in which the provision of an item would ease exceptional pressures on a family (direction 4(a)(iii)). The applicant lived with his wife and five children in a damp flat. All the children were in poor health (one with a heart condition). Three were under five. The application was for a community care grant for a replacement refrigerator. The SFI accepted that the family was under exceptional stress, but considered that provision of a refrigerator would not ease the particular pressure. She accepted that shopping for food every day would be more inconvenient than being able to store food and medicine but not more expensive. Brooke J. decides that that approach was flawed in that the SFI should have looked at the totality of the family's needs and considered the possibility that an adult would not be able to shop every day (for instance if children were ill). On the evidence the only reasonable conclusion was that it would make managing the large family easier if it was not necessary to shop every day, so that direction 4(a)(iii) was satisfied. But the authorities would then have to consider priorities and the budget.

In *R. v. Secretary of State for Social Security, ex parte Smith, The Times*, April 22, 1991, the exclusion of housing costs in direction 29(d) was in issue. The claim was for a grant to buy a caravan. The Divisional Court holds that housing costs are the costs of a person's accommodation and that there should be no distinction between movable and immovable accommodation.

R. v. Social Fund Inspector and Secretary of State for Social Security, ex parte Roberts, The Times, February 23, 1990; *The Independent*, February 23, 1990, raised the nature of the review process, and the role of the budget, which was not then covered in the directions. The existing guidance to SFOs was struck down as it was expressed not in the language of guidance, but of direction. The result was that SFOs were obliged to do no more than have regard to the budget under s.33(9) (Contributions and Benefits Act, s.140(1)). In September 1990, the Secretary of State issued directions 40 to 42, requiring SFOs to keep to local budgets. The *Roberts* case was directed particularly to review by the Social Fund Inspector, on which see below, but may have implications for reviews by the SFO. See also *R. v. Social Fund Inspector, ex parte Ledicott* in the notes to the Directions to Social Fund Inspectors.

R v. Social Fund Inspector, ex parte Connick (June 8, 1993, unreported) concerned an application for a community care grant to buy incontinence pads. Hidden J. decides that the exclusion of a medical item in directions 12(j) and 29 does not cover items in ordinary use. He holds that directions 12(j) and 29 in directing that a community care grant "may not be awarded" for a medical, etc., item or service were mandatory and permitted no discretion. However, the SFI had applied the wrong test in deciding that since the pads would not be needed unless there was a medical problem they were a medical item. Items are not medical items just because the need for them arose from a medical condition. That conclusion is in line with Commissioners' decisions *R(SB) 23/87* and *CSB 1482/85* on the slightly different provision in reg. 6(2)(n) of the Supplementary Benefits (Single Payments) Regulations, to which Hidden J. referred. It is also in accord with the guidance in the Social Fund Guide (para. 4212).

In *R v. Social Fund Inspector ex parte Ibrahim* (November 9, 1993, unreported) Turner J. holds that in interpreting direction 4(a)(i) the question to be asked was whether the accommodation (in that case a hostel for single women) was set up to provide institutional or residential care, rather than did the applicant receive such care. Para. 3202 of the guidance has since been amended to put more emphasis on examining in each case the actual care a particular applicant is receiving.

On repayment of social fund loans by deductions from benefits, see the notes to s. 78(2) of the Administration Act.

The Directions issued by the Secretary of State for Social Security under sections 138(1)(b), 140(2) and 140(3) of the Social Security Contributions and Benefits Act 1992 and sections 66(7) and 66(8)(a) and (b) of the Social Security Administration Act 1992 to the Social Fund Inspectors.

Role of Social Fund Inspectors

1. In reviewing a determination a social fund inspector must have full regard initially to:
- (a) whether the SFO applied the law correctly in arriving at his decision on review. In particular:
  - — that the decision is sustainable on the evidence;
  - — that the SFO took all relevant considerations into account and did not take irrelevant considerations into account;
  - — that the SFO interpreted the law including Secretary of State directions correctly;
- (b) whether the SFO acted fairly and exercised his discretion to arrive at a conclusion that was reasonable in the circumstances—i.e. a decision that a reasonable SFO could have reached;
- (c) whether the required procedural steps have been followed; that the applicant had sufficient opportunity to put his case; and there has been no bias.

Social Fund Inspectors reviews

2. If in reviewing a determination initially, a social fund inspector is satisfied that the decision was reached correctly, having regard to the factors in direction 1, the social fund inspector in reviewing the determination thereafter must have full regard to
- (a) all the circumstances, including the state of the budget and local priorities, that existed at the time the original decision was made;
- (b) any new evidence which has since been produced; and
- (c) any relevant changes of circumstances.

GENERAL NOTE

In the *Roberts* and *Ellison* cases (see above), it was held first that the Secretary of State had power under s.34 of the 1986 Act, now s.66 of the Administration Act, to make directions limiting the scope of review and second that the directions actually made required a two-stage process. The first stage involved an investigation similar to that carried out on judicial review. The second stage goes beyond that in requiring the examination of new evidence and changes of circumstances, but does not involve a complete rehearing. In *R. v. Social Fund Inspector, ex parte Ledicott, The Times,* May 24, 1995, Sedley J. holds that a SFI conducting a review should apply the law as in force at the date of her decision, not the law as it stood at the date of the SFO's decision that is the subject of the review. In his view, Direction 2 which permitted the SFI, *inter alia*, to take account of any relevant change of circumstances (which would include a change in the law) was within the terms of s. 66(4) of the Administration Act. Sedley J. did not consider that this interpretation involved any retrospectivity, but if it did, the wording of s. 66(4) was wide enough to provide a statutory licence for any retrospectivity that existed.

PART VI

ADJUDICATION AND ADMINISTRATION

Social Security Administration Act 1992

(1992 c. 5)

PART I

CLAIMS FOR AND PAYMENTS AND GENERAL ADMINISTRATION OF BENEFIT

Necessity of Claim

Entitlement to benefit dependent on claim

1.—(1) Except in such cases as may be prescribed, and subject to the following provisions of this section and to section 3 below, no person shall be entitled to any benefit unless, in addition to any other conditions relating to that benefit being satisfied—

    (a) he makes a claim for it in the manner, and within the time, prescribed in relation to that benefit by regulations under this Part of this Act; or

    (b) he is treated by virtue of such regulations as making a claim for it.

(2) Where under subsection (1) above a person is required to make a claim or to be treated as making a claim for a benefit in order to be entitled to it—

    (a) if the benefit is a widow's payment, she shall not be entitled to it in respect of a death occurring more than 12 months before the date on which the claim is made or treated as made; and

    (b) if the benefit is any other benefit except disablement benefit or reduced earnings allowance, the person shall not be entitled to it in respect of any period more than 12 months before that date,

except as provided by section 3 below.

(3) [*Omitted as applying only to attendance allowance and disability living allowance*]

(4) In this section and in section 2 below "benefit" means—

    (a) benefit as defined in section 122 of the Contributions and Benefits Act; and

    (b) any income-related benefit.

(5) This section (which corresponds to section 165A of the 1975 Act, as it had effect immediately before this Act came into force) applies to claims made on or after 1st October 1990 or treated by virtue of regulations under that section or this section as having been made on or after that date.

(6) Schedule 1 to this Act shall have effect in relation to other claims.

DERIVATION

Social Security Act 1975, s.165A.

DEFINITIONS

    "the 1975 Act"—see s.191.
    "claim"—*ibid.*
    "disablement benefit"—*ibid.*
    "the Contributions and Benefits Act"—*ibid.*
    "income-related benefit"—*ibid.*
    "prescribe"—*ibid.*

GENERAL NOTE

Subsection 1

The general rule is that there cannot be entitlement to benefit unless a claim is made for it. Section 1 applies to income-related benefits, *i.e.* including income support, family credit and disability working allowance, but excluding supplementary benefit or FIS or payments from the social fund (subs. (4)). "Benefit" as defined in s.122 of the Contributions and Benefits Act does not include income-related benefits. Section 1 applies to claims made on or after October 1, 1990. Sched. 1 deals with earlier claims.

The introduction of the predecessor of s.1 was precipitated by the decision of the House of Lords in *Insurance Officer v. McCaffrey* [1984] 1 W. L. R. 1353 that (subject to an express provision to the contrary) a person was entitled to benefit if he met the conditions of entitlement even though he had not made a claim for that benefit. Claiming went to payability, not entitlement. This was contrary to the long-standing assumption of the DSS and was corrected with effect from September 2, 1985.

Section 3, which is excluded from the operation of s.1, deals with late claims for widow's benefits where the death of the spouse is difficult to establish.

Subsection 2

This provision imposes an overall limit of 12 months to the entitlement to benefit before the date of claim. Not all benefits are caught by subs.(1) and there is a further exclusion in para. (b). Reg.

19 of and Sched. 4 to the Claims and Payments Regulations impose the ordinary time-limits for claiming and allow many of those limits to be extended where the claimant proves good cause for the delay. In the case of income support, family credit, disability working allowance and social fund maternity and funeral payments, where there is such an extension the claim is then treated as made on the first day of the period for which the claim is allowed to relate (reg. 6(3)). Although the drafting is not at all clear, the reference in subs.(2) to the 12-month limit from the date on which the claim is made or is treated as made seems to make the limit start from the date fixed by reg. 6(3). However, reg. 19(4) prevents an extension for good cause in the benefits covered by reg. 6(3) leading to entitlement earlier than 12 months before the actual date of claim. But the restriction seems to stem from that regulation and not from s.1(2), or the earlier forms set out in Sched. 1.

Retrospective effect of provisions making entitlement to benefit dependent on claim

2.—(1) This section applies where a claim for benefit is made or treated as made at any time on or after 2nd September 1985 (the date on which section 165A of the 1975 Act (general provision as to necessity of claim for entitlement to benefit), as originally enacted, came into force) in respect of a period the whole or any part of which falls on or after that date.

(2) Where this section applies, any question arising as to—

    (a) whether the claimant is or was at any time (whether before, on or after 2nd September 1985) entitled to the benefit in question, or to any other benefit on which his entitlement to that benefit depends; or

    (b) in a case where the claimant's entitlement to the benefit depends on the entitlement of another person to a benefit, whether that other person is or was so entitled,

shall be determined as if the relevant claim enactment and any regulations made under or referred to in that enactment had also been in force, with any necessary modifications, at all times relevant for the purpose of determining the entitlement of the claimant, and, where applicable, of the other person, to the benefit or benefits in question (including the entitlement of any person to any benefit on which that entitlement depends, and so on).

(3) In this section "the relevant claim enactment" means section 1 above as it has effect in relation to the claim referred to in subsection (1) above.

(4) In any case where—

    (a) a claim for benefit was made or treated as made (whether before, on or after 2nd September 1985, and whether by the same claimant as the claim referred to in subsection (1) above or not), and benefit was awarded on that claim, in respect of a period falling wholly or partly before that date; but

    (b) that award would not have been made had the current requirements applied in relation to claims for benefit, whenever made, in respect of periods before that date; and

    (c) entitlement to the benefit claimed as mentioned in subsection (1) above depends on whether the claimant or some other person was previously entitled or treated as entitled to that or some other benefit,

then, in determining whether the conditions of entitlement to the benefit so claimed are satisfied, the person to whom benefit was awarded as mentioned in paragraphs (a) and (b) above shall be taken to have been entitled to the benefit so awarded, notwithstanding anything in subsection (2) above.

(5) In subsection (4) above "the current requirements" means—

    (a) the relevant claim enactment, and any regulations made or treated as made under that enactment, or referred to in it, as in force at the time of the claim referred to in subsection (1) above, with any necessary modifications; and

    (b) subsection (1) (with the omission of the words following "at any time") and subsections (2) and (3) above.

DERIVATION

Social Security Act 1975, s.165B.

DEFINITIONS

"the 1975 Act"—s.191.
"benefit"—see s.1(1).
"claim"—see s.191.
"claimant"—*ibid.*

GENERAL NOTE

There are a number of benefits where entitlement can depend on whether a person was entitled to a benefit at some earlier date (*e.g.* on reaching pensionable age). While the predecessor of s.1 clearly governed such questions from September 2, 1985, onwards, it was arguable that in relation to earlier dates the *McCaffrey* principle (see note to s.1(1) above) had to be applied. *R(S) 2/91* decided that that argument was correct. The predecessor of s.2 was inserted by the Social Security Act 1990 to reverse the effect of that decision and to do so retrospectively back to September 2, 1985.

The form of s.2 is complex and the retrospective effects are difficult to work out. It only applies to claims made or treated as made on or after September 2, 1985 (subs.(1)). Thus very late appeals or very long good causes for late claim might not be affected. Then on any such claim if a question of entitlement at any other date arises (including dates before September 2, 1985) that question is to be decided according to the principle of s.1 as it was in force at the relevant time (subs.(2)). The only exception to this is that if for any period benefit has been awarded following a claim, that beneficiary is to be treated as entitled to that benefit even though under the current requirements he would not be (subs.(4)).

Claims and payments regulations

Regulations about claims for and payments of benefit

5.—(1) Regulations may provide—
(a) for requiring a claim for a benefit to which this section applies to be made by such person, in such manner and within such time as may be prescribed;
(b) for treating such a claim made in such circumstances as may be prescribed as having been made at such date earlier or later than that at which it is made as may be prescribed;
(c) for permitting such a claim to be made, or treated as if made, for a period wholly or partly after the date on which it is made;
(d) for permitting an award on such a claim to be made for such a period subject to the condition that the claimant satisfies the requirements for entitlement when benefit becomes payable under the award;
(e) for a review of any such award if those requirements are found not to have been satisfied;
(f) for the disallowance on any ground of a person's claim for a benefit to which this section applies to be treated as a disallowance of any further claim by that person for that benefit until the grounds of the original disallowance have ceased to exist;
(g) for enabling one person to act for another in relation to a claim for a benefit to which this section applies and for enabling such a claim to be made and proceeded with in the name of a person who has died;
(h) for requiring any information or evidence needed for the determination of such a claim or of any question arising in connection with such a claim to be furnished by such person as may be prescribed in accordance with the regulations;
(i) for the person to whom, time when and manner in which a benefit to

which this section applies is to be paid and for the information and evidence to be furnished in connection with the payment of such a benefit;

(j) for notice to be given of any change of circumstances affecting the continuance of entitlement to such a benefit or payment of such a benefit;

(k) for the day on which entitlement to such a benefit is to begin or end;

(l) for calculating the amounts of such a benefit according to a prescribed scale or otherwise adjusting them so as to avoid fractional amounts or facilitate computation;

(m) for extinguishing the right to payment of such a benefit if payment is not obtained within such period, not being less than 12 months, as may be prescribed from the date on which the right is treated under the regulations as having arisen;

(n) for suspending payment, in whole or in part, where it appears to the Secretary of State that a question arises whether—
   (i) the conditions for entitlement are or were fulfilled;
   (ii) an award ought to be revised;
   (iii) an appeal ought to be brought against an award;

(o) for withholding payments of a benefit to which this section applies in prescribed circumstances and for subsequently making withheld payments in prescribed circumstances;

(p) for the circumstances and manner in which payments of such a benefit may be made to another person on behalf of the beneficiary for any purpose, which may be to discharge, in whole or in part, an obligation of the beneficiary or any other person;

(q) for the payment or distribution of such a benefit to or among persons claiming to be entitled on the death of any person and for dispensing with strict proof of their title;

(r) for the making of a payment on account of such a benefit—
   (i) where no claim has been made and it is impracticable for one to be made immediately;
   (ii) where a claim has been made and it is impracticable for the claim or an appeal, reference, review or application relating to it to be immediately determined;
   (iii) where an award has been made but it is impracticable to pay the whole immediately.

(2) This section applies to the following benefits—
(a) benefits as defined in section 122 of the Contributions and Benefits Act;
(b) income support;
(c) family credit;
(d) disability working allowance;
(e) housing benefit;
(f) any social fund payments such as are mentioned in section 138(1)(a) a or 2) of the Contributions and Benefits Act;
(g) child benefit; and
(h) Christmas bonus.

(3), (4) & (5) [*Omitted as not applying to income-related benefits, except housing benefit.*]

DERIVATION

Subss. (1) and (2): Social Security Act 1986, s.51(1) and (2).

DEFINITIONS

"the Contributions and Benefits Act"—see s.191.
"prescribed"—*ibid.*

Community charge benefits, etc.

Relationship between community charge benefits and other benefits

7.—(1) Regulations may provide for a claim for one relevant benefit to be treated, either in the alternative or in addition, as a claim for any other relevant benefit that may be prescribed.

(2) Regulations may provide for treating a payment made or right conferred by virtue of regulations—

(a) under section 5(1)(r) above; or

(b) under section 6(1)(r) to (t) above,

as made or conferred on account of any relevant benefit that is subsequently awarded or paid.

(3) For the purposes of subsections (1) and (2) above relevant benefits are—

(a) any benefit to which section 5 above applies; and

(b) [¹council tax benefit].

DERIVATION

Social Security Act 1986, s.51B.

AMENDMENT

1. Local Government Finance Act 1992, Sched. 9, para. 13 (April 1, 1993).

DEFINITIONS

"claim"—see s.191.
"prescribed"—*ibid.*

GENERAL NOTE

Subsection (1)
See Claims and Payments Regulations, Sched. 1.

Subsection (2)
See the Social Security (Payments on account, Overpayments and Recovery) Regulations, regs. 5 to 8.

Disability working allowance

Initial claims and repeat claims

11.—(1) In this section—

"initial claim" means a claim for a disability working allowance made by a person—

(a) to whom it has not previously been payable; or

(b) to whom it has not been payable during the period of 2 years immediately preceding the date on which the claim is made or is treated as made; and

"repeat claim" means any other claim for a disability working allowance.

(2) On an initial claim a declaration by a claimant that he has a physical or mental disability which puts him at a disadvantage in getting a job is conclusive, except in such circumstances as may be prescribed, that for the purposes of section 129(1)(b) of the Contributions and Benefits Act he has such a disability (in accordance with regulations under section 129(3) of that Act).

(3) If—

(a) a repeat claim is made or treated as made not later than the end of the period of 8 weeks commencing with the last day of the claimant's previous award; and

  (b) on the claim which resulted in that award he qualified under section 129(2) of the Contributions and Benefits Act by virtue—
    (i) of paragraph (a) of that subsection; or
    (ii) of there being payable to him a benefit under an enactment having effect in Northern Ireland and corresponding to a benefit mentioned in that paragraph,

he shall be treated on the repeat claim as if he still so qualified.

DERIVATION

Social Security Act 1986, s.27B(1) to (3).

DEFINITION

"the Contributions and Benefits Act"—see s.191.

GENERAL NOTE

Section 11 supplies some special rules under which some parts of the qualifications for disability working allowance are deemed to be satisfied.

Subsection (1)
An initial claim is one made by a person who has never been entitled to disability working allowance or whose last week of entitlement was more than two years before the date of claim. Any other claim is a repeat claim.

Subsection (2)
On an initial claim a claimant's declaration, on the elaborate self-assessment claim form, that he has a disability which puts him at a disadvantage in getting a job is conclusive. This general rule does not apply if the claim itself contains indications to the contrary or the AO has before him evidence pointing to the contrary (Disability Working Allowance (General) Regulations, reg. 4).

Subsection (3)
This provision applies to claimants who have been awarded disability working allowance on the basis that they were entitled to higher rate short-term incapacity benefit, long-term incapacity benefit (or invalidity benefit: reg. 18(1) of the Disability Working Allowance and Income Support (General) Amendment Regulations 1995, p. 586), severe disablement allowance or income support, housing benefit or council tax benefit with the disability premium or pensioner premium for disability or any Northern Ireland equivalent (see Contributions and Benefits Act, s.129(2)(a) and (4) and Disability Working Allowance Regulations, reg. 7). When such an award expires and the repeat claim is made within eight weeks, the claimant is deemed to satisfy the requirement. Thus if a claimant initially qualifies on this ground and continues to satisfy the other conditions of entitlement, awards may continue indefinitely.

The social fund

Necessity of application for certain payments

  12.—(1) A social fund payment such as is mentioned in section 138(1)(b) of the Contributions and Benefits Act may be awarded to a person only if an application for such a payment has been made by him or on his behalf in such form and manner as may be prescribed.
  (2) The Secretary of State may by regulations—
  (a) make provision with respect to the time at which an application for such a social fund payment is to be treated as made;
  (b) prescribe conditions that must be satisfied before any determination in connection with such an application may be made or any award of such a payment may be paid;
  (c) prescribe circumstances in which such an award becomes extinguished.

DERIVATION

Social Security Act 1986, s.33(1) and (13).

DEFINITIONS

"the Contributions and Benefits Act"—see s.191.
"prescribed"—*ibid.*

GENERAL NOTE

Subsection (1)
This provision applies to the "ordinary" social fund, not to funeral or maternity payments or cold weather payments. See the Social Fund (Applications) Regulations.

Subsection (2)
See the Social Fund (Miscellaneous Provisions) Regulations.

[¹*Payments in respect of mortgage interest etc.*

Payment out of benefit of sums in respect of mortgage interest etc.

15A.—(1) This section applies in relation to cases where—
(a) mortgage interest is payable to a qualifying lender by a person ("the borrower") who is entitled, or whose partner, former partner or qualifying associate is entitled, to income support; and
(b) a sum in respect of that mortgage interest is or was brought into account in determining the applicable amount for the purposes of income support in the case of the borrower or the partner, former partner or qualifying associate;
and any reference in this section to "the relevant beneficiary" is a reference to the person whose applicable amount for the purposes of income support is or was determined as mentioned in paragraph (b) above.

(2) Without prejudice to paragraphs (i) and (p) of section 5(1) above, regulations may, in relation to cases where this section applies, make provision—
(a) requiring that, in prescribed circumstances, a prescribed part of any relevant benefits to which the relevant beneficiary is entitled shall be paid by the Secretary of State directly to the qualifying lender and applied by that lender towards the discharge of the liability in respect of the mortgage interest;
(b) for the expenses of the Secretary of State in administering the making of payments under the regulations to be defrayed, in whole or in part, at the expense of qualifying lenders, whether by requiring them to pay prescribed fees or by deducting and retaining a prescribed part of the payments that would otherwise be made to them under the regulations or by such other method as may be prescribed;
(c) for requiring a qualifying lender, in a case where by virtue of paragraph (b) above the amount of the payment made to him under the regulations is less than it would otherwise have been, to credit against the liability in respect of the mortgage interest (in addition to the payment actually made) an amount equal to the difference between—
  (i) the payment that would have been so made, apart from paragraph (b) above; and
  (ii) the payment actually made;
and, in any such case, for treating the amount so credited as properly paid on account of benefit due to the relevant beneficiary;
(d) for enabling a body which, or person who, would otherwise be a qualify-

ing lender to elect not to be regarded as such for the purposes of this section, other than this paragraph;

   (e) for the recovery from any body or person—

      (i) of any sums paid to that body or person by way of payment under the regulations that ought not to have been so paid; or

      (ii) of any fees or other sums due from that body or person by virtue of paragraph (b) above;

   (f) for cases where the same person is the borrower in relation to mortgage interest payable in respect of two or more different loans; and

   (g) for any person of a prescribed class or description who would otherwise be regarded for the purposes of this section as the borrower in relation to any mortgage interest not to be so regarded, except for the purposes of this paragraph;

but the Secretary of State shall not make any regulations under paragraph (b) above unless he has consulted with such organisations representing qualifying lenders likely to be affected by the regulations as he considers appropriate.

(3) The bodies and persons who are "qualifying lenders" for the purposes of this section are—

   (a) any authorised institution, within the meaning of the Banking Act 1987, to which section 67 of that Act applies (companies and partnerships which may describe themselves as banks etc),

   (b) any building society incorporated under the Building Societies Act 1986,

   (c) any body or person carrying on insurance business, within the meaning of the Insurance Companies Act 1982,

   (d) any county council, district council, islands council or London Borough Council,

   (e) the common Council of the City of London,

   (f) the Council of the Isles of Scilly,

   (g) any new town corporation,

and such bodies or persons not falling within the above paragraphs as may be prescribed.

(4) In this section—

"mortgage interest" means interest on a loan which is secured by a mortgage of or charge over land, or (in Scotland) by a heritable security, and which has been taken out to defray money applied for any of the following purposes, that is to say—

   (a) acquiring any residential land which was intended, at the time of the acquisition, for occupation by the borrower as his home;

   (b) carrying out repairs or improvements to any residential land which was intended, at the time of taking out the loan, for occupation by the borrower as his home;

   (c) paying off another loan; or

   (d) any prescribed purpose not falling within paragraphs (a) to (c) above;

but interest shall be regarded as mortgage interest by virtue of paragraph (c) above only to the extent that interest on that other loan would have been regarded as mortgage interest for the purposes of this section had the loan not been paid off;

"partner" means—

   (a) any person to whom the borrower is married and who is a member of the same household as the borrower; or

   (b) any person to whom the borrower is not married but who lives together with the borrower as husband and wife, otherwise than in prescribed circumstances;

and "former partner" means a person who has at some time been, but no longer is, the borrower's partner;

"qualifying associate", in relation to the borrower, means a person who, for the purposes of income support, falls to be treated by regulations under Part VII of the Contributions and Benefits Act as responsible for so much of the expenditure which relates to housing costs (within the meaning of those regulations) as consists of any of the mortgage interest payable by the borrower, and who falls to be so treated because—

   (a) the borrower is not meeting those costs, so that the person has to meet them if he is to continue to live in the dwelling occupied as his home; and

   (b) the person is one whom it is reasonable, in the circumstances, to treat as liable to meet those costs;

"relevant benefits" means such of the following benefits as may be prescribed, namely—

   (a) benefits, as defined in section 122 of the Contributions and Benefits Act;

   (b) income support;

"residential land" means any land which consists of or includes a dwelling.

(5) For the purposes of this section, regulations may make provision—

   (a) as to circumstances in which residential land is or is not to be treated as intended for occupation by the borrower as his home; or

   (b) as to circumstances in which persons are to be treated as being or not being members of the same household.]

AMENDMENT

1. Social Security (Mortgage Interest Payments) Act 1992, s.1(12) and Sched., para. 1 (July 1, 1992; the equivalent amendment to the Social Security Act 1986 came into force on March 16, 1992).

DEFINITION

"Contributions and Benefits Act"—see s.191.

GENERAL NOTE

Section 15A authorises the regulations which set out the meat of the scheme for direct payment to lenders of the element of housing costs in income support to cover mortgage interest and supplies some basic definitions. The main provisions are in Sched. 9A to the Claims and Payments Regulations.

Emergency payments

Emergency payments by local authorities and other bodies

   16.—(1) The Secretary of State may make arrangements—

   (a) with a local authority to which this section applies; or

   (b) with any other body,

for the making on his behalf by members of the staff of any such authority or body of payments on account of benefits to which section 5 above applies in circumstances corresponding to those in which the Secretary of State himself has the power to make such payments under subsection (1)(r) of that section; and a local authority to which this section applies shall have power to enter into any such arrangements.

   (2) A payment under any such arrangements shall be treated for the purposes of any Act of Parliament or instrument made under an Act of Parliament as if it had been made by the Secretary of State.

   (3) The Secretary of State shall repay a local authority or other body such amount as he determines to be the reasonable administrative expenses incurred

by the authority or body in making payments in accordance with arrangements under this subsection.

(4) The local authorities to which this section applies are—

(a) a local authority as defined in section 270(1) of the Local Government Act 1972, other than a parish or community council;

(b) the Common Council of the City of London; and

(c) a local authority as defined in section 235(1) of the Local Government (Scotland) Act 1973.

DERIVATION

Social Security Act 1988, s.8.

PART II

ADJUDICATION

Adjudication by adjudication officers

Claims and questions to be submitted to adjudication officer

20.—(1) Subject to section 54 below, there shall be submitted forthwith to an adjudication officer for determination in accordance with this Part of this Act—

(a) any claim for a benefit to which this section applies;

(b) subject to subsection (2) below, any question arising in connection with a claim for, or award of, such a benefit; and

[¹(c) any question whether, if he otherwise had a right to it, a person would be disqualified under or by virtue of any provision of the Contributions and Benefits Act for receiving a benefit to which this section applies.]

(2) Subsection (1) above does not apply to any question which falls to be determined otherwise than by an adjudication officer.

(3) [*Omitted as not applying to income-related benefits*]

(4) If—

(a) a person submits a question relating to the age, marriage or death of any person; and

(b) it appears to the adjudication officer that the question may arise if the person who has submitted it to him submits a claim to a benefit to which this section applies,

the adjudication officer may determine the question.

(5) Different aspects of the same claim or question may be submitted to different adjudication officers; and for that purpose this section and the other provisions of this Part of this Act with respect to the determination of claims and questions shall apply with any necessary modifications.

(6) This section applies to the following benefits—

(a) benefits as defined in section 122 of the Contributions and Benefits Act;

(b) income support;

(c) family credit;

(d) disability working allowance;

(e) any social fund payment such as is mentioned in section 138(1)(a) or (2) of the Contributions and Benefits Act;

(f) child benefit;

(g) statutory sick pay; and

(h) statutory maternity pay.

Derivation

Social Security Act 1975, s.98.

Amendment

1. Social Security (Incapacity for Work) Act 1994, Sched. 1, para. 46 (April 13, 1995).

Definition

"the Contributions and Benefits Act"—see s.191.

General Note

Subsection (1)
See subs.(6) for the benefits to which this section applies.

In *R. v. Secretary of State for Social Services, ex parte CPAG and others* [1990] 2 Q.B. 540, the Court of Appeal decided that the duty to submit a claim "forthwith" did not arise until the DSS was in possession of the basic information necessary to determine the claim. The obligation on the claimant under reg. 7(1) of the Claims and Payments Regulations to supply such evidence etc. as the Secretary of State requires is relevant to this stage of the claim (*R(IS) 4/93*). However, once the basic information is there, the CPAG case holds that any need for verification does not justify delay in submitting the claim to the AO. It would then be for the AO to make enquiries, if he considered that verification was necessary.

In *R(SB) 29/84* the Tribunal of Commissioners (by a majority) held that the question whether payment had actually been made following an award (*i.e.* what should happen following an allegedly lost giro) was not a "question relating to supplementary benefit" (Supplementary Benefits Act 1976, s.2(1)), and therefore was not a matter for an AO or SSAT. Any remedy was to be pursued through the courts. *R(IS) 7/91* holds, after an exhaustive review of the legislation, that the result is the same under the predecessor of subs.(1)(b). The question whether the Secretary of State has implemented an award of benefit is not a question in connection with an award of benefit.

Subsection (6)
Under para. (e) s.20 applies to funeral and maternity payments and cold weather payments from the social fund.

Decision of adjudication officer

21.—(1) An adjudication officer to whom a claim or question is submitted under section 20 above (other than a claim which under section 30(12) or (13) or 35(7) below falls to be treated as an application for a review) shall take it into consideration and, so far as practicable, dispose of it, in accordance with this section, and with procedure regulations under section 59 below, within 14 days of its submission to him.

(2) Subject to subsection (3) and section 37 below, the adjudication officer may decide a claim or question himself or refer it to a social security appeal tribunal.

(3) The adjudication officer must decide a claim for or a question relating to attendance allowance, a disability living allowance or a disability working allowance himself.

(4) Where an adjudication officer refers a question as to, or in connection with, entitlement to statutory sick pay or statutory maternity pay to a social security appeal tribunal, the employee and employer shall each be given notice in writing of the reference.

(5) In any other case notice in writing of the reference shall be given to the claimant.

(6) Where—
(a) a case has been referred to a social security appeal tribunal ("the tribunal"); and

    (b) the claimant makes a further claim which raises the same or similar questions; and

    (c) that further claim is referred to the tribunal by the adjudication officer,

then the tribunal may proceed to determine the further claim whether or not notice of its reference has been given to the claimant under subsection (4) or (5) above.

DERIVATION

Social Security Act 1975, s.99.

GENERAL NOTE

Subsection (1)

The general rule is that the AO should make a decision within 14 days, once the claim or question is submitted to him under s.20. In *R. v. Secretary of State for Social Services, ex parte CPAG and others* [1990] 2 Q. B. 540, the Court of Appeal upheld Schiemann J.'s decision that there was no breach of the predecessor of subs.(1) if a heavy work load prevented an AO from disposing of the claim or question within the 14 days. It was clear that the Act intended that claims should be dealt with expeditiously, but this was merely one factor which the Secretary of State had to consider in exercising his discretion as to the number of AOs to appoint. He was under no duty to appoint enough AOs to deal with all claims within 14 days.

It also appears that the need to obtain verification of information may make it not practicable to reach a decision within 14 days. *R(SB) 29/83* mentions the obligation of a claimant under the equivalent of reg. 7 of the Claims and Payments Regulations to provide such evidence, information, etc., as required by the Secretary of State as being relevant to practicability. But the supplementary benefit provision on adjudication made the AO's duty expressly subject to the equivalent of reg. 7. Section 21(1) is significantly different, as pointed out in *R(IS) 4/93*. Once a claim or question has been referred to the AO. the question of whether reg. 7 is satisfied is irrelevant to the issue of entitlement. The principle stated in *R(SB) 29/83*, that after a reasonable length of time, even if further information is not forthcoming, the AO must make a decision on the evidence available to him, still holds. Then, if the decision is adverse, the claimant has something to appeal against and the adequacy of the information before the AO can be dealt with by the SSAT applying the appropriate burden of proof *(R(IS) 4/93)*.

Note that there is no longer a power for the Secretary of State to deem a claim to have been withdrawn if the information required under reg. 7 is not produced.

It has been held that an AO does not "discharge responsibilities of a judicial nature" (Glidewell L.J. in *Jones v. Department of Employment* [1988] 1 All E. R. 725, 733), but clearly the AO's administrative decisions must be reached in a judicial manner. The investigatory functions most recently emphasised in the *CPAG* case, do not extend to a duty to investigate the claimant's entire financial situation on a review *(Duggan v. Chief Adjudication Officer, The Times*, December 19, 1988; *R(SB) 13/89)*.

The Court of Appeal in *Chief Adjudication Officer v. Foster* [1992] Q.B. 31, [1991] 3 All E.R. 846 decided that the AO (as well as social security appeal tribunals and Commissioners) must reach decisions on the basis that all regulations are validly made, on the ground that only the High Court or the Court of Appeal has the jurisdiction to declare regulations *ultra vires*. The House of Lords *(Foster v. Chief Adjudication Officer* [1993] A. C. 754, [1993] 1 All E.R. 705) disagreed and held that Social Security Commissioners have undoubted jurisdiction, in the course of deciding issues within their statutory powers, to determine whether regulations have been validly made or not. See the notes to s.23 for more details. Lord Bridge accepts that "if the Commissioner can base his decision in any case on the invalidity of some provision in regulations made under the Act, it must follow that appeal tribunals and adjudication officers can do likewise." He rejects the arguments which persuaded the Court of Appeal to the contrary. These were that it cannot have been intended that officials of the level and qualifications of AOs should have the power to question the validity of regulations made by the Secretary of State particularly when the Secretary of State cannot be a party to proceedings before an appeal tribunal. Lord Bridge suggests that in any case where there was a challenge to the vires of a regulation an AO would use the power in subs. (2) to refer the claim to a SSAT, where the views of the Secretary of State could in practice be put through the AO.

An AO cannot be bound by any assurance given by an employee of the DSS about a claimant's entitlement, but must come to a proper decision on the law applicable to the case. Even if a claimant had relied on a statement from or on behalf of an AO, this requirement to carry out the statutory duty prevents an estoppel arising *(R(SB) 14/88, R(SB) 14/89* and Woolf L.J. refusing leave to appeal in *R(SB) 4/91).*

The claims excluded from the operation of subs. (1) by the words in brackets are certain claims for disability living allowance or disability working allowance. Under ss.30(12) and 35(7), if an award of either of those benefits has been made for a period, a further claim made within that period is treated as an application to review the existing award. Under s.30(13), where an AO's decision is not to award one of those benefits or attendance allowance, any further claim made during the period prescribed for applying for a review of that decision on any ground (*i.e.* three months: Adjudication Regulations, reg. 26A) is treated as an application for review.

Subsection (2)

The AO no longer has express power to decide questions in any particular way. The power to make references to the SSAT in supplementary benefit and FIS cases was new in 1984. The procedure is used sparingly in income support and family credit cases, but is sometimes invoked where there is a conflict of evidence which the AO feels unable to resolve. According to Lord Bridge in *Foster v. Chief Adjudication Officer* [1993] A.C. 754, [1993] 1 All E.R. 705 it should be used if the validity of any regulations is challenged before the AO. The effect of subs. (3) is that such references cannot be made in disability working allowance cases. Section 37 is concerned with the reference of special questions.

Subsection (3)

In these cases the AO must determine the claim or question himself, and so cannot refer a matter to a SSAT. This is no doubt because the process of appeal for these benefits must start with a review by another AO before there can be an appeal to the SSAT.

Subsection (5)

Subs. (5) does not prescribe any particular period in advance of the hearing for the written notice of a reference to be given. The Tribunal of Commissioners in *R(S) 5/86* decides that whatever is a reasonable time in the circumstances is the test. The same decision holds that the requirement that the reference is to be in writing cannot be waived by the claimant. Note the exception introduced by subs. (6) which has been in operation since April 1990.

Subsection (6)

Once a case has been properly referred to a SSAT under subs. (2) a further claim raising similar questions may be referred to the SSAT for decision without notice in writing being given to the claimant. It is obviously desirable that notice that the SSAT is to be asked to deal with the further claim should be given to the claimant if possible.

Appeals from adjudication officers—general

Appeal to social security appeal tribunal

22.—(1) Subject to subsection (3) below, where the adjudication officer has decided a claim or question other than a claim or question relating to an attendance allowance, a disability living allowance or a disability working allowance—

    (a) if it relates to statutory sick pay or statutory maternity pay, the employee and employer concerned shall each have a right to appeal to a social security appeal tribunal; and

    (b) in any other case the claimant shall have a right to do so.

(2) A person with a right of appeal under this section shall be given such notice of a decision falling within subsection (1) above and of that right as may be prescribed.

(3) No appeal lies under this section where—

    (a) in connection with the decision of the adjudication officer there has arisen any question which under or by virtue of this Act falls to be determined otherwise than by an adjudication officer; and

    (b) the question has been determined; and

(c) the adjudication officer certifies that the decision on that question is the sole ground of his decision.

(4) Regulations may make provision as to the manner in which, and the time within which, appeals are to be brought.

(5) Where an adjudication officer has determined that any amount, other than an amount—

(a) of an attendance allowance;

(b) of a disability living allowance;

(c) of a disability working allowance;

(d) of statutory sick pay; or

(e) of statutory maternity pay,

is recoverable under or by virtue of section 71 or 74 below, any person from whom he has determined that it is recoverable shall have the same right of appeal to a social security appeal tribunal as a claimant.

(6) [*Omitted as only applying to industrial injuries benefits*]

(7) Subsection (2) above shall apply to a person with a right of appeal under subsection (5) or (6) above as it applies to a claimant.

DERIVATION

Social Security Act 1975, s.100.

GENERAL NOTE

Subsection (1)

There is a general right of appeal for a claimant against any decision of an AO on any claim or question. Note that under subs. (5) a person from whom an overpayment of most benefits has been determined to be recoverable has the same right of appeal as a claimant. Subsection (1) does not cover disability working allowance. See ss. 30 to 33.

Subsection (2)

See the Adjudication Regulations, particularly regs. 20 and 63.

Subsection (3)

This procedure is unlikely to affect appeals on income-related benefits.

Subsection (4)

See reg. 3 and Sched. 2 to the Adjudication Regulations.

Subsection (5)

A person from whom it is determined that an overpayment of most benefits is recoverable has a right to appeal against the AO's decision to that effect. This applies to overpayments under s.71 (misrepresentation or failure to disclose) and s.74 (duplication of income support and other payments). A person falling within subs. (5) must be given notice of the decision and the right of appeal (subss. (7) and (2)).

The benefits listed in paras. (a) to (e) are excluded from the operation of subs. (5). See s.32(9) for rights of appeal against decisions on the recoverability of disability working allowance.

Appeal from social security appeal tribunal to Commissioner

23.—(1) Subject to the provisions of this section, an appeal lies to a Commissioner from any decision of a social security appeal tribunal under section 22 above on the ground that the decision of the tribunal was erroneous in point of law.

(2) [*Omitted as only applying to statutory sick pay and statutory maternity pay*]

(3) In any other case an appeal lies under this section at the instance of any of the following—

(a) an adjudication officer;

    (b) the claimant;

    (c) in any of the cases mentioned in subsection (5) below, a trade union; and

    (d) a person from whom it is determined that any amount is recoverable under section 71(1) or 74 below.

    (4) [*Omitted as only applying to industrial injuries benefits*]

    (5) The following are the cases in which an appeal lies at the instance of a trade union—

    (a) where the claimant is a member of the union at the time of the appeal and was so immediately before the question at issue arose;

    (b) where that question in any way relates to a deceased person who was a member of the union at the time of his death;

    (c) [*Omitted as only applying to industrial injuries benefits*]

    (6) Subsections (2), (3) and (5) above, as they apply to a trade union, apply also to any other association which exists to promote the interests and welfare of its members.

    (7) Where the Commissioner holds that the decision was erroneous in point of law, he shall set it aside and—

    (a) he shall have the power—

        (i) to give the decision which he considers the tribunal should have given, if he can do so without making fresh or further findings of fact; or

        (ii) if he considers it expedient, to make such findings and to give such decision as he considers appropriate in the light of them; and

    (b) in any other case he shall refer the case to a tribunal with directions for its determination.

    (8) Subject to any direction of the Commissioner, the tribunal on a reference under subsection (7)(*b*) above shall consist of persons who were not members of the tribunal which gave the erroneous decision.

    (9) No appeal lies under this section without the leave—

    (a) of the person who was the chairman of the tribunal when the decision was given or, in a prescribed case, the leave of some other chairman; or

    (b) subject to and in accordance with regulations, of a Commissioner.

    (10) Regulations may make provision as to the manner in which, and the time within which, appeals are to be brought and applications made for leave to appeal.

DERIVATION

Social Security Act 1975, s.101.

DEFINITIONS

    "Commissioner"—see s.191.
    "prescribed"—*ibid.*

GENERAL NOTE

Subsection (1)

There may only be an appeal from a decision under s.22 to the Commissioner on the ground that the SSAT made an error of law. See s.34 for disability working allowance cases. Note also the requirement under subs. (10) for leave to appeal to be given by the SSAT chairman (or a substitute) or a Commissioner.

There are conflicting Commissioners' decisions about whether there is an appealable decision where a SSAT adjourns the hearing of an appeal. In *CSIS 118/1990* the SSAT had determined that a recoverable overpayment had been made, but adjourned the question of the amount of the overpayment. The Commissioner holds that an appeal was possible in relation to the issues which the SSAT had decided, declining to follow the decision of the Tribunal of Commissioners in *CA 126/1989* because that decision did not mention *R v. Medical Appeal Tribunal (Midland Region), ex parte*

Carrarini [1966] 1 W.L.R. 883 or *CSU 14/64*. However, in *CSB 83/1991* the Commissioner followed *CA 126/1989*, holding that the *Carrarini* case was not in point because there the tribunal's decision was to refuse to adjourn. He held that there is only a right of appeal from a final decision of a SSAT, which finally disposes of the issues before it. In *CIS 628/1992* where the SSAT had failed to deal with all the issues arising on an appeal, it is held that there was no decision within the meaning of s.23 against which an appeal could be made. The Commissioner declines to follow *CSIS 118/1990*, holding that s.20(5) does not authorise the division of a claim or question into parts so that a decision dealing with some parts and adjourning others may be appealed to the Commissioner. See the notes to reg. 25 of the Adjudication Regulations for the guidance given in *CIS 628/ 1992* as to how to proceed in such a case. It is suggested that in the current state of the authorities, SSAT chairmen should follow *CSB 83/1991*, *CA 126/1989*, and *CIS 628/1992*. These are followed in *CIS 260/1993*. See also *CIS 451/1992* in the notes to reg. 25.

But where a SSAT decides that there has been a recoverable overpayment and remits the calculation of the amount to the AO, subject to reference back in case of disagreement, that is a sufficiently complete decision for the purposes of s. 23 (*R(SB) 15/87*, *CSB 83/1991*, *Riches v. Social Security Commissioner* (Court of Session, May 4, 1993 and *CIS 628/1992*). In this situation the only matter remaining is that of quantification, the tribunal having determined the issues of legal principle. *CIS 501/1993* holds that a SSAT's decision to refer a question to the ECJ for a preliminary ruling is a final decision and so appealable to the Commissioner.

CIS 749/1991 and *CS 159/1991* deal with a similar point but in relation to a Commissioner's decision. In *CIS 749/1991* the Commissioner who initially heard the appeal held that the claimant was entitled to housing costs in respect of a loan for a loft conversion; he went on to state that in the event of disagreement as to the arrears due or the implementation of the decision the matter was to be referred to him for determination. There was a dispute as what parts of the loan were allowable, but unfortunately the Commissioner died before the matter could be determined. The Commissioner who then dealt with the case held that "referred to me" meant "referred to me in my office as a duly appointed Social Security Commissioner", with the result that he could deal with the outstanding question in the case. Further, the decision that had been given by the first Commissioner was a final decision, in the sense that an appeal could have been brought against it; what had happened was that a further decision was necessary because the outstanding matter could not be resolved by agreement. This was different from the situation where an appeal had been adjourned part-heard, in which case a different Commissioner would have had to hold a complete rehearing. But he was bound by the first Commissioner's decision, as that Commissioner would have been if he had been able to deal with the outstanding issue. To the extent that *CIS 442/1992* suggested that there had to be an entire rehearing before a different Commissioner he declined to follow it.

In *CS 159/1991* the Commissioner had allowed the claimant's appeal against refusal of invalidity benefit and directed that if there was a dispute as to the sum owing after the offsetting of the unemployment benefit that the claimant had received against the arrears of invalidity benefit due, the matter was to be referred to him for determination. The claimant did not agree the calculation, but sadly the Commissioner (the same Commissioner) died before the hearing could be restored. The Commissioner to whom this case was referred (who was the Commissioner in *CIS 442/1992*) holds that if the decision had been incomplete he would have had to decide the whole appeal afresh. However, the first Commissioner's decision was not incomplete as he had determined the entire subject matter of the appeal. The correct calculation of the benefit due was not before the first Commissioner and he did not have jurisdiction on this question. This was not a case where the subject matter of the appeal involved the actual calculation. The second Commissioner in *CS 159/ 1991* disagrees with the approach taken in *CIS 749/1991*. In his view, the question of the meaning of "referred to *me*" only arose if the first Commissioner's decision was incomplete because decisions could not be split into parts. The approach of *CIS 749/1991* is certainly less cumbersome in practice, since if the disputed items of the claimant's housing costs had not been dealt with in this way, presumably it would have been necessary either for the AO to issue a formal determination, with a fresh right of appeal, or for the first Commissioner's decision to be set aside.

CDWA/1/1992 holds that a Commissioner does have power, even after he has given his decision, to inquire into a complaint that the decision has not been properly implemented. The Commissioner can give a supplemental decision. The supplemental decision cannot subtract from, or vary, the original decision; it can only supplement it. In fact, the Commissioner in *CDWA/1/1992* decides that his decision had been fully implemented by the award of disability working allowance for 26 weeks and that the question of any subsequent award was not within his jurisdiction.

There are a number of other parts of the Commissioners' jurisdiction where appeal is on a point of law only and the well established tests have been taken over here. In *R(SB) 6/81* the most accurate and concise summary is said to be that set out in *R(A) 1/72*. This holds that a decision would be wrong in law if:

(i) it contained a false proposition of law on its face;

(ii) it was supported by no evidence; or

(iii) the facts found were such that no person acting judicially and properly instructed as to the relevant law could have come to the determination in question.

CSB 29/81 refers *to R(I) 14/75*, which sets out the three heads quoted above and adds:

(iv) breach of the requirements of natural justice; and

(v) failure to state adequate reasons.

The formula of five headings is adopted in *R(SB) 11/83* (although by reference to decisions of the courts rather than the Commissioners) and is now clearly accepted. A retrospective change in the law can render a decision, which was correct at the time it was made, erroneous in law so that it may be appealed, or reviewed under s.25(2) if made by an AO (*CF 22/1992*, to be reported as *R(F) 1/95*). (Such a change can also amount to a change of circumstances: see *Chief Adjudication Officer v. McKiernon*, Court of Appeal, July 8, 1993, in the notes to s.25.)

The result of the House of Lord's decision in *Foster v. Chief Adjudication Officer* [1993] A.C. 754, [1993] 1 All E.R. 705 is that it is an error of law under head (i) for a SSAT to rely on a regulation which has not been validly made, even though it has not been declared to be *ultra vires* in judicial review proceedings. This result was found to be desirable because it avoids the duplication of proceedings that would have been caused by forcing parties into separate judicial review actions to test validity and because the courts will have the benefit of the Commissioners' expert views on the question of validity if an appeal is taken beyond the Commissioners.

Having disposed of the objections to AOs and SSATs having the power to determine the validity of regulations (see the notes to s.21(1)), Lord Bridge was left with three objections to giving the words "erroneous in point of law" their ordinary meaning in the context of the Commissioners' jurisdiction. The first was that the same words were used in the part of the legislation dealing with adjudication by the Secretary of State and it could not have been intended to give the Secretary of State power to decide whether he had acted *ultra vires* or not. Lord Bridge shows that in fact such a power is necessary. The second objection was that the Commissioners have no power to declare regulations *ultra vires*. Lord Bridge holds that the absence of that power does not throw any light on the Commissioners' power to determine incidentally to a decision on an appeal that a regulation is *ultra vires*. The third objection was more constitutional, that if the Commissioners have jurisdiction to question the *vires* of a regulation then that jurisdiction must embrace challenges on the basis of irrationality or unreasonableness as well as illegality. Lord Bridge avoided the issue by saying that the challenge in *Foster* was solely on the basis of illegality—that the regulations were not within the scope of the enabling power—and that there was no doubt of the Commissioners' jurisdiction on illegality.

This approach leaves two uncertainties: first what is the power of the ordinary courts to strike down regulations which have been approved by Parliament on the ground of irrationality; and second whether there is any difference between the courts' powers and those of the Commissioners. On the first question, Lord Bridge suggests that while Lord Jauncey in *City of Edinburgh District Council v. Secretary of State for Scotland* (1985) S.L.T. 551 held that a statutory instrument considered by Parliament could only be held to be *ultra vires* if it was patently defective, *i.e.* where it was not authorised by the enabling statute or the required procedure was not followed, the House of Lords in *R v. Secretary of State for the Environment, ex parte Nottinghamshire County Council* [1986] A.C. 240 left open possible exceptions from the rule that the courts may not strike down statutory instruments on the ground of irrationality. He says that the *Foster* case did not provide the occasion to decide whether those exceptions should exist. However, Lord Scarman's speech in the *Nottinghamshire* case appears to limit the exceptions where there has been Parliamentary approval of the instrument or decision under challenge, to situations where there has been bad faith or misconduct by the Minister concerned, in the form of misleading Parliament. That is a very limited exception. It is unfortunate that the House of Lords has left doubt about its existence or scope. It certainly made no reference to it in deciding that the October 1989 amendment to the definition of non-dependant in reg. 3 was not open to challenge for irrationality.

The second uncertainty is raised by what Lord Bridge says after referring to the possible exceptions to Lord Jauncey's approach in the *City of Edinburgh* case:

"But I have no doubt that the Social Security Commissioners have good pragmatic reasons not to take it on themselves to identify any such exceptional case, but to leave that to the higher courts, who, as Lord Jauncey pointed out, have never yet done so in any reported case."

This seems to suggest that the Commissioners should refuse to consider any challenges to regulations on the ground of irrationality (which are bound to be made given the uncertainties left by *Foster*). However, that approach would deprive the higher courts of the benefits of the Commissioners' expert views on the issue. Lord Bridge's reference to "pragmatic reasons" also suggests that the Commissioners' legal jurisdiction is co-extensive with that of the ordinary courts (whatever that is).

In *CIS 391/1992* a Tribunal of Commissioners had to decide how to exercise that jurisdiction. The Tribunal holds that *Foster* clearly states that the Commissioners do have jurisdiction to consider whether a regulation is invalid on the ground of irrationality. It was submitted by the *amicus curiae* in the case that Lord Bridge's approach could be taken to mean that Commissioners should not be astute to find secondary legislation irrational. The Tribunal appear to have taken this on board in stating that this jurisdiction should only be exercised where a determination whether or not a regulation is valid is necessary to the determination of the issue which arises and if a serious issue of irrationality arises. Oddly, however, the Commissioners deal with possible irrationality in *CIS 391/ 1992* in terms of whether the Secretary of State had taken leave of his senses, when it appears from the endorsement of the *Nottinghamshire* case in *Foster* that it is necessary to find bad faith or misconduct by the Secretary of State, in the form of a misleading of Parliament. If Commissioners have this jurisdiction so must SSATs and AOs.

In determining whether there is an error of law under head (ii) it is necessary to look at all the evidence presented to the tribunal, not only that recorded in the findings of fact or the chairman's notes of evidence. It is only if a decision cannot be supported looking at the totality of the evidence presented that an error of law is committed (*CSB 15/82, R(SB) 16/82, R(S) 1/88*). If an item of evidence was not before the SSAT, it cannot in itself be an error of law not to have considered it. The Commissioners have held that they are not restricted to looking at the formal SSAT documents but may consider any reliable account of what evidence was presented (*CSB 34/81, R(SB) 10/82, R(SB) 18/83*). However, the approach to such accounts is somewhat cautious. The Commissioner in *R(SB) 10/82* suggested an over-elaborate procedure for producing an account agreed between the parties to be referred to the SSAT chairman. That view is rejected in *R(M) 1/89*. The Tribunal of Commissioners there holds that it is a matter for the Commissioner's discretion what evidence about the proceedings to admit.

Subsections (2) to (6)

These provisions define the parties who may make an appeal from a SSAT and deal with trade unions and other organisations.

Subsection (7)

This important provision on the powers of the Commissioner seems oddly placed in the middle of s.23. His powers in supplementary benefit and FIS cases were until April 6, 1987 contained in reg. 27 of the 1984 Adjudication Regulations. Under those provisions if the Commissioner found an error of law he had to send the appeal back to a SSAT unless it was expedient for him to give the decision which the SSAT should have given. If sufficient facts had not been found by the SSAT (a common situation when the SSAT has gone wrong in law) the Commissioner could not give the decision which the SSAT should have given. There was some criticism of this procedure, which could be ponderous and time-consuming.

Para. (a)(i) confirms the power of the Commissioner to give the decision the SSAT should have given where no further findings of fact are necessary. Para. (a)(ii) gives the power (new in 1987) for the Commissioner, when he considers it expedient, to make fresh or further findings of fact and then to give a decision in the light of those findings. The power has been used by Commissioners in a large number of appeals, including *R(SB) 11/88* and *CSB 176/1987*. In the first decision, the Commissioner held that the power existed from April 6, 1987, and that it did not matter that the SSAT decision was before that date. In the second, the Commissioner called for quite a lot of new evidence, although there was no real dispute over the facts. A Commissioner is more likely to send factual disputes back to a SSAT, although practice varies. The power is most often used where the SSAT has failed to make express findings on matters which are not in dispute or on which the result of the existing evidence is clear. There may be some difficulty if a Commissioner is making a decision partly on his own assessment of evidence and partly on the SSAT's assessment of evidence which the Commissioner has not seen.

If para. (a) does not apply, then under para. (b) the case must be referred to a SSAT with directions. These have normally included a direction that no members of the original SSAT should be on the new one, as is now expressly required by subs. (8) unless the Commissioner directs otherwise. See *CIS 749/1991* and *CS 159/1991* above.

Subsection (9)

A party who wishes to appeal from a SSAT decision must get leave either from the chairman of the SSAT (or a substitute under reg. 26(4) of the Adjudication Regulations) or a Commissioner. Reg. 26 deals with the procedure for applying for leave to the chairman, and the time limit is three months (Adjudication Regulations, Sched. 2, para. 7). If the chairman refuses leave, a party has 42 days to apply to a Commissioner for leave (Social Security Commissioners Procedure Regulations

1987, reg. 3). A Commissioner may deal with late applications if, for special reasons, he thinks fit (regs. 3(2) and (5)).

A mere assertion of a mistake of law is not enough for leave to be granted. There must be some material in the case indicating that there is a sensible argument in support *(R(SB) 1/81)*. There is, in the nature of things, not much further guidance given to chairmen about whether to give leave or not. The most helpful statement is in para. 30 of *R(S) 4/82*. The Commissioners stress that the chairman's discretion is unfettered providing that it is exercised in a judicial manner, but say that chairmen should bear in mind that the object of requiring leave to be given is to restrict appeals to those which are neither hopeless nor frivolous and raise a serious issue. If the conduct of the tribunal's proceedings is seriously in question, leave should be given, but if the allegations are general, with no supporting detail, leave should be refused. The party always has another chance by applying to the Commissioner for leave.

It is suggested that if the grounds put forward by the claimant or the AO do not contain any allegations of error of law (either expressly or by obvious implication) then the SSAT chairman should refuse leave to appeal. In particular, if the complaint is that the SSAT should have made a different decision on the facts, or that there is some new or different evidence which was not put to the SSAT *(R(S) 1/88)*, that is not good enough. It is suggested that normally the chairman should not give leave simply because, on looking beyond the application, he considers that there might be some error of law in the SSAT's decision, such as inadequate findings of fact or reasons. That is something which is better dealt with by a Commissioner if the claimant or the AO makes a further application for leave to appeal.

If the Commissioner refuses leave to appeal that is not a decision within the meaning of s.24 below (Social Security Act 1980, s.14) and so cannot be appealed to the Court of Appeal (*Bland v. CSBO* [1983] 1 All E. R. 537, *R(SB) 12/83, Kuganathan v. Chief Adjudication Officer, The Times*, March 1, 1995). There is no right of appeal from a refusal of leave by a chairman. The only right of appeal is from a decision of a SSAT.

Subsection (10)

See the Adjudication Regulations, regs. 3 and 26 and Sched. 2, and the Social Security Commissioners Procedure Regulations 1987 (S.I. 1987 No. 214). On late appeals see the notes to reg. 3(3) of the Adjudication Regulations. *CIS 550/1993* holds that service by courier is not service by post within reg. 30(3) of the Social Security Commissioners Procedure Regulations.

An appeal to the Court of Appeal in *CIS 39/1993 (Fiore)* that is currently in progress raises a point on the construction of regs. 15(2) and 29(1)(b) of the Commissioners Procedure Regulations. The claimant's request for an oral hearing of his appeal to the Commissioner had been refused by a Nominated Officer. It is contended that only the power to *grant* an oral hearing may be delegated to a Nominated Officer, whereas the power to *refuse* an oral hearing has to be exercised by a Commissioner. This is certainly arguable on the wording of reg. 29(1)(b) itself.

Appeal from Commissioners on point of law

24.—(1) Subject to subsections (2) and (3) below, an appeal on a question of law shall lie to the appropriate court from any decision of a Commissioner [[1]or given in consequence of a reference under section 112(4) of the 1975 Act (which enabled a medical appeal tribunal to refer a question of law to a Commissioner)].

(2) No appeal under this section shall lie from a decision except—

  (a) with the leave of the Commissioner who gave the decision or, in a prescribed case, with the leave of a Commissioner selected in accordance with regulations; or

  (b) if he refuses leave, with the leave of the appropriate court.

(3) An application for leave under this section in respect of a Commissioner's decision may only be made by—

  (a) a person who, before the proceedings before the Commissioner were begun, was entitled to appeal to the Commissioner from the decision to which the Commissioner's decision relates;

  (b) any other person who was a party to the proceedings in which the first decision mentioned in paragraph (a) was given;

  (c) the Secretary of State, in a case where he is not entitled to apply for leave by virtue of paragraph (a) or (b) above;

  (d) any other person who is authorised by regulations to apply for leave;

and regulations may make provision with respect to the manner in which and the time within which applications must be made to a Commissioner for leave under this section and with respect to the procedure for dealing with such applications.

(4) On an application to a Commissioner for leave under this section it shall be the duty of the Commissioner to specify as the appropriate court—

    (a) the Court of Appeal if it appears to him that the relevant place is in England or Wales;

    (b) the Court of Session if it appears to him that the relevant place is in Scotland; and

    (c) the Court of Appeal in Northern Ireland if it appears to him that the relevant place is in Northern Ireland,

except that if it appears to him, having regard to the circumstances of the case and in particular to the convenience of the persons who may be parties to the proposed appeal, that he should specify a different court mentioned in paragraphs (a) to (c) above as the appropriate court, it shall be his duty to specify that court as the appropriate court.

(5) In this section—

    "the appropriate court", except in subsection (4) above, means the court specified in pursuance of that subsection;

    "the relevant place", in relation to an application for leave to appeal from a decision of a Commissioner, means the premises where the authority whose decision was the subject of the Commissioner's decision usually exercises its functions.

[¹(5A) In relation to a decision of a Commissioner which was given in consequence of a reference under section 112(4) of the 1975 Act subsections (3) and (5) of this section shall have effect with such modifications as may be prescribed by regulations.]

(6) The powers to make regulations conferred by this section shall be exercisable by the Lord Chancellor.

DERIVATION

Social Security Act 1980, s.14.

AMENDMENT

1. Social Security (Consequential Provisions) Act 1992, Sched. 4, paras. 1 and 12 (until the repeal of s.14(7) of the Social Security Act 1980 in Sched. 9 to the Social Security Act 1989 comes into force).

DEFINITIONS

"the Commissioner"—see s.191.
"prescribed"—*ibid.*

GENERAL NOTE

This section provides for an appeal on a point of law to the Court of Appeal, Court of Session or Court of Appeal in Northern Ireland, as appropriate, from a decision of a Commissioner, with the leave of a Commissioner or the court. See the Social Security Commissioners Procedure Regulations 1987 (S.I. 1987 No. 214).

For the procedure applicable in Scotland, see Books of Sederunt, Rules of Court, rules 290 and 293B (inserted by S.I. 1980 No. 1745 (s.151)).

A decision of a Commissioner to grant or refuse leave to appeal to the Commissioner is not a "decision" from which an appeal may lie under this section (*Bland v. Chief Supplementary Benefit Officer* [1983] 1 All E.R. 537, *Kuganathan v. Chief Adjudication Officer, The Times,* March 1, 1995).

See also the notes to s. 23(1) on the question of when there is a final decision.

Reviews—general

Review of decisions

25.—(1) Subject to the following provisions of this section, any decision under this Act of an adjudication officer, a social security appeal tribunal or a Commissioner (other than a decision relating to an attendance allowance, a disability living allowance or a disability working allowance) may be reviewed at any time by an adjudication officer or, on a reference by an adjudication officer, by a social security appeal tribunal, if—

(a) the officer or tribunal is satisfied that the decision was given in ignorance of, or was based on a mistake as to, some material fact; or

(b) there has been any relevant change of circumstances since the decision was given; or

(c) it is anticipated that a relevant change of circumstances will so occur; or

(d) the decision was based on a decision of a question which under or by virtue of this Act falls to be determined otherwise than by an adjudication officer, and the decision of that question is revised; or

(e) the decision falls to be reviewed under section [¹25A(4) or (5)] of the Contributions and Benefits Act.

(2) Any decision of an adjudication officer (other than a decision relating to an attendance allowance, a disability living allowance or a disability working allowance) may be reviewed, upon the ground that it was erroneous in point of law, by an adjudication officer or, on a reference from an adjudication officer, by a social security appeal tribunal.

(3) Regulations may provide that a decision may not be reviewed on the ground mentioned in subsection (1)(a) above unless the officer or tribunal is satisfied as mentioned in that paragraph by fresh evidence.

(4) In their application to family credit, subsection (1)(b) and (c) above shall have effect subject to section 128(3) of the Contributions and Benefits Act (change of circumstances not to affect award or rate during specified period).

(5) Where a decision is reviewed on the ground mentioned in subsection (1)(c) above, the decision given on the review—

(a) shall take effect on the day prescribed for that purpose by reference to the date on which the relevant change of circumstances is expected to occur; and

(b) shall be reviewed again if the relevant change of circumstances either does not occur or occurs otherwise than on that date.

DERIVATION

Subs. (1): Social Security Act 1975, s.104(1).
Subs. (2): 1975 Act, s.104(1A).
Subs. (3): 1975 Act, s.104(1).
Subs. (4): Social Security Act 1986, s.52(8).
Subs. (5): 1975 Act, s.104(1ZA).

AMENDMENT

1. Social Security (Incapacity for Work) Act 1994, Sched. 1, para. 47 (April 13, 1995).

DEFINITIONS

"Commissioner"—see s.191.
"the Contributions and Benefits Act"—*ibid.*
"prescribed"—*ibid.*

Social Security Administration Act 1992

Section 25 does not apply to disability working allowance. See ss.30 to 35 for reviews and appeals in that benefit.

Subsection (1)

Any decision to which s.25 applies may be reviewed by an AO on one of the five grounds set out in paras. (a) to (e). Where, as is normally the case for income support, an award is for an indefinite period (Claims and Payments Regulations, reg. 17(1)), any alteration to that award must be by way of review and revision. The principle flows from the fundamental rule in s.60 of the Administration Act (1975 Act, s.117(1)) that a decision on a claim, for whatever period covered by the decision, is final, subject to the processes of appeal or review under s.25 (see *CSSB 544/ 1989* and the Common Appendix to the group of decisions including *CSSB 281/1989*). Even if the award is for a definite period, any alteration of that award within that period is subject to the same limitation.

There are a number of potential exceptions to this general principle. The first is under reg. 17(4) of the Claims and Payments Regulations, which is being used as the basis for submissions that awards made for days after the date of claim may be terminated whenever the claimant ceases to satisfy the conditions of entitlement. But see the notes to reg. 17(4) for the limitations of this provision. The second is that ss.159 and 160 below provide for most alterations in rates of income support and some prescribed figures to take effect automatically without the need for a decision by an AO. Where some kind of transitional addition is in payment, review by an AO under reg. 69(3A) of the Adjudication Regulations is necessary. Some powers of review in income support cases are given directly by reg. 69(4) and reg. 69(2) sets out circumstances in which review under s.25(1) is not to take place (but note that para. 7(8) of Sched. 3 to the Income Support Regulations was revoked on April 11, 1994). However, outside these circumstances s.25(1) provides the general rule.

The significance of this is that it is clearly established (see, *e.g. CSB 376/1983* applying *R(I) 1/ 71* and *CI 11/77*) that the onus lies on the person wanting the review to establish both facts justifying the review and the correctness of the subsequent revised decision. That will be the normal situation but if the other party wishes the decision to be revised in some other way, the onus will be on that party (*CIS 247/1991*). Thus if, as in *CSB 376/1983*, the AO withdraws benefit on a change of circumstances when there is insufficient information to work out benefit, he has to justify the decision on the balance of probabilities. He cannot simply rely on the claimant not having proved his right to benefit. The same approach is taken in *CIS 1/1988*. If it is the claimant requesting the review (*e.g.* by raising the question whether a previous decision denying benefit should be revised: *R(SB) 9/84*), then the onus is on him. Although s.26(1) mentions an application in writing to the AO, a request for review may be oral or even implied (*CSB 336/1987*). *CIS 30/1993* confirms that a failure to identify a ground for review will be an error of law, even if there clearly was a relevant change of circumstances which could provide grounds for review. The SSAT (and the AO) had to be clear about the nature of the decision being made, because of the importance of the correct placing of the burden of proof.

A number of recent Commissioners have illuminated the general area of review through a detailed examination of review in supplementary benefit cases. The individual decisions are noted in the 1991 Supplement. The most general point is that in principle it is for the party seeking a review to identify the decision which he wishes to have reviewed (*CSSB 540/1989* and *CIS 77/1992*). Only once that is done can any potential grounds for review be properly identified. However, if, as was often the case, the claimant was not properly notified of the exact terms of an AO's decision (see Adjudication Regulations, reg. 63), due allowances must be made (*CSSB 470/1989*). If what is being put forward is a change of circumstances after the date of the decision, it will not be so important to establish the grounds of the original decision.

Secondly, doubt is cast on the proposition in *R(A) 2/90* that once one ground of review of a determination is established the whole determination is open to reconsideration (*CSSB 238/1989*). Even if this were right about an attendance allowance decision, the Commissioner holds that it does not apply to supplementary benefit decisions. Supplementary benefit awards (and, it would seem by analogy, income support awards) are made up of a continuing award of benefit co-existing with a series of review adjustments to particular elements of the award (*CSSB 238/1989* and the Common Appendix to the group of decisions including *CSSB 281/1989*). Thus where there are grounds for review of one element this does not in itself allow review of any other elements. And if one element is revised on review, that does not affect the existence of the underlying continuing award or the other elements of it, unless a separate ground of review exists in relation to those other elements. That approach is applied to income support in *CIS 77/1992* and *CIS 303/1992* (to be reported as *R(IS) 15/93*). In *CIS 303/1992*, in distinction to *CIS 77/1992*, a separate ground of review was put forward before the SSAT and should have been dealt with under s.36. Previous decisions appearing to suggest that a decision on review completely supersedes the decision reviewed are shown to be limited to decisions which are different in nature to supplementary benefit decisions and are indivisible, such as decisions that an overpayment is recoverable (*CSB 64/1986* and *R(SB) 15/87*) or attendance allowance cases where the review is in effect the first stage of an appeal (*R(A) 5/89*). See also *R(SB) 1/82* and *R(P) 1/82*. And see *CAO v. Eggleton and Others* (the appeal from *CIS 566/1991* and *CIS 788/1991*) below.

Perhaps the most controversial and difficult part of these decisions is the proposition that a request for review must be directed at the last operative decision dealing with the element of which review is sought (Common Appendix to group of decisions including *CSSB 281/1989*, as explained and expanded in *CSSB 238/1989* and *CSSB 544/1989*). If there has been a series of review decisions on that element, the chain must be traced backwards, at each decision asking whether grounds for review of the immediately preceding decision exist. However, the basis for this proposition has not yet been clearly established, and its application could cause considerable problems for claimants and for the DSS. For instance, if an old award is discovered to have been based on a misrepresentation of a material fact, must the AO trace a chain of review back to the relevant decision in order to carry out the review and revision which is a necessary basis of a decision on recoverability of the overpayment? *R(IS) 11/93* holds, without discussing any of the decisions cited above, that any supplementary benefit decision is open to review. *CIS 566/1991* dealt with the effect on the original decision of an AO's refusal to revise on review and *CIS 788/1991* with the effect where there had been a partial revision on review. In both cases the claimants had applied for a review of their income support so as to include a severe disability premium (following *CIS 180/1989*) and then obtained leave to bring a late appeal against the original decision awarding income support in April 1988. In *CIS 566/1991* the claimant's application for review was not made until August 1990, and the AO refused to revise the original decision because of s.104(7) and (8) of the Social Security Act 1975, now s.69 of the Administration Act. The AO argued that a late appeal could not be admitted because the original decision awarding benefit in April 1988 had been replaced by the review decision. This was rejected by the Commissioner who held that a decision refusing to revise did not alter the previous decision (applying para. 13 of *CSSB 540/1989*). In *CIS 788/1991* the AO had revised the original decision but limited payment of arrears to 12 months before the request for review under reg. 69 of the Ajudication Regulations. The Commissioner held that where a decision had only been partially revised the original decision was not superseded (see *CSSB 238/1989* and *R(P) 1/82*).

Both decisions were appealed. In *Chief Adjudication Officer v. Eggleton and Others* (March 17, 1995) the Court of Appeal dismissed the appeals. The Court holds that in *Eggleton* (and all the other cases except *James* (*CIS 788/1991*)) there had in fact been no review. Such evidence as there was (for example, specimen letters to the claimants following the request for a review) demonstrated a refusal to review (because of s. 69) rather than a review. But where there had been a review, as in *James*, the question of whether an original decision lapsed or was superseded when it was reviewed depended on the nature and the extent of the review. If the whole of the original decision was revised from the date on which it was made, there was nothing left of it and it therefore could not be appealed. But if it was only varied in part, or from a particular date, for example because revision was precluded after a certain date, the original decision subsisted, save as affected by the review, and was thus susceptible to appeal (or late appeal: see the notes to reg. 3(3) of the Adjudication Regulations on late appeals). Similarly, where the power to revise was limited by s. 69, the original decision remained operative for the period prior to review. The Court disagreed with the opposite conclusion reached by the Court of Appeal in Northern Ireland in *Thompson v. DHSS* (September 8, 1993, unreported). The Court rejected the CAO's submission that the implication of s. 29 (review following appeal) was that decisions are superseded upon review. Moreover, it was noteworthy that there was no equivalent in the adjudication scheme for income support to s. 32(1). If it had been intended that an award on review replaced the award the subject of the review in the case of income support, a similar express provision to s. 32(1) would have been expected. The Court referred to *R(A) 5/89*, among other decisions, but pointed out that there were important differences between the adjudication schemes for income support and the benefits covered by ss. 30–35. The Court did not consider that there was any inconsistency between the reasoning in *R(A) 5/89* and its own conclusion.

The lack of distinction in the Court's judgment, at least in places, between review and revision on review is not very helpful. But the tenor of the judgment is clear. Where a review does not lead to revision, the effect is that the original decision remains in existence. But see below for discussion of the effect of reg. 69 of the Adjudication Regulations.

Paragraphs (a) to (c)

These paragraphs cover the grounds of ignorance of or mistake as to a material fact and relevant change of circumstances. Mistake or ignorance presupposes that the material fact existed at the date of the decision which someone wishes to review *(CIS 650/1991)*. Relevant change of circumstances requires that a material fact has changed since the date of that decision. For both purposes it is necessary to identify what is a material fact.

The Commissioners have drawn a distinction between material facts and conclusions of fact (*e.g.* that a person is incapable of work, or is cohabiting). In *R(I) 3/75* (applied in *R(S) 4/86*) it is held that review is not allowed if the AO is simply satisfied that a mistaken inference was drawn from the evidence. He must go further and prove "that the inference might not have been drawn, or that a different inference might have been drawn, if the determining authority had not been ignorant of some specific fact of which it could have been aware, or had not been mistaken as to some specific fact which it took into consideration." This principle was also applied in *R(A) 2/81*. The Court of Appeal in *Saker v. Secretary of State for Social Services (R(I) 2/88)* has expressly decided that for a fact to be material it is not necessary that knowledge of it would have altered the decision. It is enough that the fact is one that would have called for serious consideration by the authority which made the decision and might well have affected its decision.

In *R(A) 2/90*, the Commissioner applied this approach to the question of when a change of circumstances is relevant. This throws doubt on decisions such as *R(I) 56/54* and *R(A) 4/81*, where it is said that the change of circumstances must make the original decision cease to be correct. This test may be too stringent, given the authority of *Saker*, but a reported decision would clarify this important area. It is accepted that merely obtaining a different medical opinion is not a change of circumstances, although it may be evidence of an underlying change (*R(S) 6/78, R(S) 4/86*). A change in the law may amount to a change of circumstances (*R(A) 4/81* and *R(SB) 4/92*), even if it operates retrospectively (*R(G) 3/58* and *Chief Adjudication Officer v. McKiernon*, C.A., July 8, 1993), from the date of the change. The *McKiernon* case means that a retrospective change of law constitutes grounds for reviewing a decision of an AO, SSAT or Commissioner, even though the decision was correct given the law at the time it was made. However, the Court of Appeal in *McKiernon* considered that a court judgment declaring the law to be different from what had previously been supposed was probably not a relevant change of circumstances.

It is not clear quite how subs. (2) allowing review where a decision was erroneous in law affects the principles noted above. If a wrong inference is drawn from correct primary facts because the wrong legal test is applied, that is clearly an error of law. If no person properly directing himself as to the law could have drawn that inference from those primary facts, then that will be an error of law (cf. *R(A) 1/72, R(I) 14/75*). But if the AO simply changes his mind about an "inference of fact" there has been no error of law. A retrospective change in the law will enable review under subs.(2) (*CF 22/1992*, to be reported as *R(F) 1/95*).

Paragraph (d)

This paragraph applies where the income support etc. decision was based on a decision made by someone other than the AO, typically the Secretary of State. If that other decision is revised, the income support, etc., decision is to be reviewed and revised in line with it.

Paragraph (e)

These provisions of the Contributions and Benefits Act deal with availability and actively seeking work in unemployment benefit.

Regs. 69 to 71 of the Adjudication Regulations prevent any revision on review from making benefit payable or increasing the amount of benefit payable more than 52 weeks before the request for review. These provisions were originally introduced in response to the confirmation in *R(SB) 9/84* that the existing regulations did not impose any time limit on the review of decisions denying benefit or single payments. However, they are now subject to reg. 64A, which has from August 31, 1991, replaced the controversial reg. 72, allowing the 12 month limit to be lifted in deserving cases. A SSAT should consider whether there are grounds for review of an identified decision and, if so, whether that decision should be revised, and from what date, before considering regs. 69 to 71 and reg. 72 or 64A (*CSSB 470/1989* and *R(SB) 4/92*), particularly if the SSAT's decision is to alter past entitlement in some way. It may be that in exceptional cases, where it is plain that there can be no practical advantage to the claimant from a review and revision if the conditions of reg. 72 or 64A are not satisfied, for a SSAT to deal only with that point if it is adverse to the claimant (*CSB 56/1992*). But as explained in *CIS 714/1991*, in the great majority of cases it is necessary first to identify any grounds for review and revision and it is desirable in all cases for SSATs to follow the logical chain of the regulations. It should be remembered that reg. 69 only prevents revision so as to make more benefit payable. It is possible that a claimant may derive a practical advantage from a revision of a decision to the effect that he is entitled to benefit or increased benefit, even if that benefit or increased benefit is not payable (*e.g.* a decision that a claimant was entitled to more supplementary benefit could affect his income support by means of a higher transitional addition). The Court of Appeal in *CAO v. Eggleton and Others* (see above) considered that where revision was precluded the original decision remained in existence (*i.e.* that any review was of no effect). But the Court did not expressly deal with the point that reg. 69 only prevents revision so as to make more benefit payable.

Subsection (2)

Note that only AO decisions may be reviewed on the ground of error of law, not decisions of SSATs or the Commissioners. Otherwise the provisions on appeals would be undermined. See the notes to s.23 for "error of law". Review on this ground is subject to the restrictions of reg. 69 of the Adjudication Regulations, with the exemptions in reg. 64A, and s.69. See notes to s.69 and in particular *Bate v. Chief Adjudication Officer and Secretary of State for Social Security, The Times*, December 12, 1994, discussed at the end of the notes.

This provision was first extended to "national insurance" benefits on April 23, 1984. *R(P) 1/85* decides that a decision relating to one of those benefits made before that date may subsequently be reviewed, but may not be revised. That was a case where the revision would have removed a claimant's entitlement, so that the principle probably does not apply where the revision would lead to entitlement or increased entitlement to benefit. However, a power to review supplementary benefit decisions for error of law existed from the beginning of the scheme (and appears also to have existed for national assistance). The principle of *R(P) 1/85* is therefore not a bar to review and revision of supplementary benefit and national assistance decisions for error of law. But see the notes to reg. 49 of the Claims and Payments Regulations.

Subsection (3)

No regulations have yet been made prescribing circumstances in which fresh evidence is required to trigger review.

Subsection (4)

Awards of family credit, which are normally made for a fixed period of 26 weeks, may not generally be reviewed on the ground of an actual or anticipated change of circumstances (see s.128(3) of the Contributions and Benefits Act).

Subsection (5)

There are special rules where there is review in advance of an anticipated change of circumstances under subs. (1)(c). The decision on review takes effect on the date identified by para. 7 of Sched. 7 to the Claims and Payments Regulations. There must be a further review if the change does not happen at all, or on a different date.

Procedure for reviews

26.—(1) A question may be raised with a view to a review under section 25 above by means of an application in writing to an adjudication officer, stating the grounds of the application.

(2) On receipt of any such application, the adjudication officer shall proceed to deal with or refer any question arising on it in accordance with sections 21 to 23 above.

(3) Regulations may provide for enabling, or requiring, in prescribed circumstances, a review under section 25 above notwithstanding that no application for a review has been made under subsection (1) above.

DERIVATION

Social Security Act 1975, s.104(2) to (3A).

GENERAL NOTE

Subsection (1)

Although this provides a useful procedure, it is not compulsory (*CSB 336/1987*). On general principle review should occur at any time if the AO is satisfied that the conditions are met, wherever the evidence comes from. But doubt was cast on this conclusion by the introduction of the predecessor of subs. (3) in 1987, after the time relevant to *CSB 336/1987*. In the Common Appendix to the group of decisions including *CSSB 281/1989*, the Commissioner suggests that the duty is on the

Secretary of State to submit in writing to the AO any requests for review received, in whatever form, from claimants.

Subsection (3)
This power is only doubtfully necessary (see notes to subs. (1)). No regulations have yet been made.

Reviews under s.25—supplementary

27.—(1) Regulations—
  (a) may prescribe what are, or are not, relevant changes of circumstances for the purposes of section 25 above; and
  (b) may make provision restricting the payment of any benefit, or any increase of benefit, to which a person would, but for this subsection, be entitled by reason of review in respect of any period before or after the review (whether that period falls wholly or partly before or after the making of the regulations).
  (2) [*Omitted as not applying to income-related benefits*]

DEFINITION

Social Security Act 1975, s.104(5).

DEFINITION

"prescribe"—see s.191.

GENERAL NOTE

On para. (*a*), see regs. 51 and 51A of the Family Credit (General) Regulations and regs. 56 and 56A of the Disability Working Allowance (General) Regulations. On para. (*b*) see regs. 69 to 71 of the Adjudication Regulations.

Appeals following reviews or refusals to review

28. A decision given on a review under section 25 above, and a refusal to review a decision under that section, shall be subject to appeal in like manner as an original decision, and sections 21 to 23 above shall, with the necessary modifications, apply in relation to a decision given on such a review as they apply to the original decision of a question.

DERIVATION

Social Security Act 1975, s.104(4).

GENERAL NOTE

The ordinary rights to appeal arise from a revised decision given on review or a refusal to review. This can be a useful way of getting round the time limits on appealing from an AO's decision. A request to review the decision will, if it does not produce all that the claimant wants, generate a fresh right of appeal.
In *CIS 354/1994* the claimant's housing costs had been restricted under para. 10(4) of Sched. 3 to the Income Support Regulations. He appealed against an AO's decision on review amending the calculation of his housing costs. It is held that the AO's review decision implied a continuance of the restriction and so opened up all the questions involved in the calculation of the claimant's housing costs, including whether the restriction had been properly imposed initially.

Review after claimant appeals

29. Where a claimant has appealed against a decision of an adjudication officer and the decision is reviewed by an adjudication officer under section 25 above—

(a) if the adjudication officer considers that the decision which he has made on the review is the same as the decision that would have been made on the appeal had every ground of the claimant's appeal succeeded, then the appeal shall lapse; but

(b) in any other case, the review shall be of no effect and the appeal shall proceed accordingly.

DERIVATION

Social Security Act 1975, s.104(3B).

GENERAL NOTE

The predecessor of this provision made an important change in the relationship between review and appeals. Previously, it was established, at least in relation to some types of decision, that if a decision was reviewed it ceased to exist, being replaced by the decision made on review *(R(SB) 1/ 82, R(SB) 15/87)*. The effect was that any appeal already lodged against the original decision would "lapse," because there was nothing left for the appeal to bite on *(R(A) 5/89*, which contains an authoritative review of all the earlier decisions). It is now clear from *CSSB 238/1989* that this only applies to decisions which are in their nature indivisible, like decisions that an overpayment is recoverable *(R(SB) 15/87)* or attendance allowance decisions reviewed in what is effectively the first stage of the appeal process *(R(A) 5/89)*. In other cases, a review of one element of a decision leaves the rest of it intact *(R(P) 5/89)*. Commissioners had in any event been able to get round the inconvenient effects of this principle in some circumstances, by treating the appeal as against the revised decision although no notice of appeal had been given *(R(SB) 15/87)*. The suggestion in *R(SB) 1/82*, that if an appeal had been lodged a decision should not be reviewed unless the revised decision gave the claimant everything that could have been obtained in the appeal, was only patchily applied.

Now, for reviews after April 5, 1990, if there is an appeal pending from an AO decision, a review is only of effect if the AO considers that the revised decision is the same as would have been made if every ground of the claimant's appeal had succeeded. In this case, but no other, the appeal lapses. This effect turns on the AO's opinion, but, as a matter of general principle, if the claimant disputes that the revised decision is the same as if every ground of the appeal had succeeded, the issue ought to go to the SSAT in the original appeal, although the amendment to reg. 24(1) of the Adjudication Regulations suggests otherwise. Note that the grounds set out in the claimant's appeal are the crucial elements, not further arguments which might be raised against the AO's decision (see reg. 3(5) of the Adjudication Regulations).

Note also that s.29 only applies to reviews of AO decisions, not to reviews of SSAT or Commissioners' decisions.

Attendance allowance, disability living allowance and disability working allowance

Reviews of decisions of adjudication officers

30.—(1) On an application under this section made within the prescribed period, a decision of an adjudication officer under section 21 above which relates to an attendance allowance, a disability living allowance or a disability working allowance may be reviewed on any ground subject, in the case of disability working allowance, to section 129(6) of the Contributions and Benefits Act.

(2) to (4) [*Omitted as not applying to disability working allowance*]

(5) On an application under this section made after the end of the prescribed period, a decision of an adjudication officer under section 21 above which relates to a disability working allowance may be reviewed if—

(a) the adjudication officer is satisfied that the decision was given in ignorance of, or was based on a mistake as to, some material fact; or

(b) subject to section 129(6) of the Contributions and Benefits Act, there has been any prescribed change of circumstances since the decision was given; or

(c) the decision was erroneous in point of law; or

(d) the decision was to make an award for a period wholly or partly after the date on which the claim was made or treated as made but subject to a condition being fulfilled and that condition has not been fulfilled,

but regulations may provide that a decision may not be reviewed on the ground mentioned in paragraph (a) above unless the officer is satisfied as mentioned in that paragraph by fresh evidence.

(6) The claimant shall be given such notification as may be prescribed of a decision which may be reviewed under this section and of his right to a review under subsection (1) above.

(7) A question may be raised with a view to a review under this section by means of an application made in writing to an adjudication officer stating the grounds of the application and supplying such information and evidence as may be prescribed.

(8) Regulations—

(a) may provide for enabling, or requiring, in prescribed circumstances, a review under this section notwithstanding that no application under subsection (7) above has been made; and

(b) if they do so provide, shall specify under which provision of this section a review carried out by virtue of any such regulations falls.

(9) Reviews under this section shall be carried out by adjudication officers.

(10) Different aspects of any question which arises on such a review may be dealt with by different adjudication officers; and for this purpose this section and the other provisions of this Part of this Act which relate to reviews under this section shall apply with any necessary modifications.

(11) If a review is under subsection (1) above, the officer who took the decision under review shall not deal with any question which arises on the review.

(12) [*Omitted as not applying to disability working allowance*]

(13) Where—

(a) a claim for an attendance allowance, a disability living allowance or a disability working allowance in respect of a person has been refused; and

(b) a further claim for the same allowance is made in respect of him within the period prescribed under subsection (1) above,

the further claim shall be treated as an application for a review under that subsection.

DERIVATION

Subs. (1): Social Security Act 1975, s.100A(1).
Subs. (5): 1975 Act, s.100A(2) and (3).
Subss. (6) to (13): 1975 Act, s.100A(5) to (12).

DEFINITIONS

"the Contributions and Benefits Act"—see s.191.
"prescribed"—*ibid.*

GENERAL NOTE

Section 30 deals with two types of review in disability working allowance cases. The first, under subs. (1), is review as the first stage of appeal against the initial AO's decision. The second, under subs. (5), is the "ordinary" review, but on slightly more restricted grounds than provided in s.25(1).

Subsection (1)

There is no provision in the legislation for an appeal from the initial decision of an AO under s.21 on a disability working allowance claim. Therefore, a claimant dissatisfied with the initial decision must apply for a review under this provision. The application must be made within the prescribed period. *i.e.* three months from the date on which notice of the AO's decision was given (Adjudication Regulations, reg. 26A). It seems that because review can only be considered "on an application under this section," the claimant must make an application and it must, under subs. (7), be made in writing to an AO. Although the words of subs. (7) are merely permissive, the words of subs. (1) seem to produce a different result to those of s.26(1). This is unfortunate, because review on specified grounds under subs. (5) is not available until after the end of the prescribed period unless there has already been a review under subs. (1). If, for instance, an AO notices just after an initial decision has been issued to the claimant that there has been an error of law, it appears that the decision cannot be reviewed unless the AO invites the claimant to apply for a review. Possibly an application could be made to the AO by a person acting on behalf of the Secretary of State.

Once an application has been made, review may be on any ground. This obviously covers mistake or ignorance of material facts as at the date of the decision or an error of law. But it can also cover a difference of opinion as to what conclusion to draw from the material facts, and changes of circumstances after the date of the decision. However, there are a number of limitations. First, if the AO has made an award of disability working allowance, there can be no review on the basis of a change of circumstances (Contributions and Benefits Act. s,129(6)). Second, if the AO's initial decision was not to make an award, any revised decision on review under subs. (1) can only take effect from the date of the application for review (Adjudication Regulations, reg. 70B(1)). This rule seems completely wrong if review is the first stage of the appeal process and it reveals that the decision has been mistaken from the outset, but is clearly set out in the regulations. See the notes to reg. 70B for more details.

If, after a decision refusing an award, a claimant makes a new claim during the prescribed period it is to be treated as an application for review under subs. (1) (subs. (13)).

The review is to be carried out by a different AO to the AO who made the initial decision (subss. (9) and (11)). The claimant has a right of appeal to a tribunal under s.33(1).

Subsection (5)

See the notes to subs. (1) for the argument that the opening words of this subsection mean that an application in writing to the AO is necessary before review can be considered. The argument that an application can be made on behalf of the Secretary of State is much stronger here, otherwise there would be no way of reviewing an award wrongly made to a claimant.

Normally an application under subs. (5) has to be made after the end of the prescribed period of three months from the date on which notice of the AO's initial decision was given (Adjudication Regulations, reg. 26A(1)). But if there has been a decision on review under subs. (1), whether favourable or unfavourable to the claimant, then an application under subs. (5) can be made at any time to review that decision (s.31(1)).

See the notes to s.25(1)(a) and (b) and (2) for review under paras. (a), (b), and (c). Section 129(6) of the Contributions and Benefits Act prevents review of an award of disability working allowance, or of the level of benefit, on the ground of change of circumstances, except where regulations prescribe otherwise. No regulations have been made requiring fresh evidence to be produced for para. (a), but see reg. 70B(2) of the Adjudication Regulations.

Para. (d) is roughly equivalent to reg. 17(4) of the Claims and Payments Regulations, which appears to apply a condition to awards of benefit including disability working allowance.

If a person is dissatisfied with a refusal to review or a decision on review, then there must be an application for a further review under the conditions of subs. (1) before there can be an appeal to a tribunal (s.31(2)).

Subsection (6)

Separate provision needs to be made for requiring notice of initial disability working allowance decisions and the right to apply for review under subs. (1) because of the exclusion in s.22(1).

Subsection (7)

This subsection only says that review "may" be started by an application in writing to an AO, but the wording of subss. (1) and (5) seems to require there to be such an application. In the ordinary case the application will be made by the claimant, but if circumstances showing that a ground for review has arisen come to the DSS's attention a person acting on behalf of the Secretary of State should make an application to the AO. Otherwise, there is no way of reviewing a decision based on a misrepresentation or failure to disclose material facts by the claimant. The principle should hold where the review would be in favour of the claimant.

No regulations have been made specifying any particular information or evidence to be supplied with the application.

Subsection (8)

No regulations have been made under subs. (8).

Subsections (9) to (11)

Applications for review must be decided initially by an AO. There is no power for the AO to refer a question to a tribunal (*cf.* s.21(3)).

Where the review is under subs. (1) the AO who carries out the review must be a different person from the AO who made the initial decision.

Subsection (13)

If an AO's decision is to refuse the claim and another claim is made within the prescribed period (three months from the date of notice of the AO's decision: Adjudication Regulations, reg. 26A(1)), the claim is to be treated as an application for review under subs. (1). The first claim is then to be treated as having been made on the date of the second claim (Claims and Payments Regulations, reg. 6(11)). In any case any award made on the review could only take effect from that date (Adjudication Regulations, reg. 70B(1)).

Further reviews

31.—(1) Subsections (2), (4) and (5) of section 30 above shall apply to a decision on a review under subsection (1) of that section as they apply to a decision of an adjudication officer under section 21 above but as if the words "made after the end of the prescribed period" were omitted from each subsection.

(2) Subsections (1), (2), (4) and (5) of section 30 above shall apply—

(a) to a decision on a review under subsection (2), (4) or (5) of that section; and

(b) to a refusal to review a decision under subsection (2), (4) or (5) of that section,

as they apply to a decision of an adjudication officer under section 21 above.

(3) The claimant shall be given such notification as may be prescribed—

(a) of a decision on a review under section 30 above;

(b) if the review was under section 30(1), of his right of appeal under section 33 below; and

(c) if it was under section 30(2), (4) or (5), of his right to a further review under section 30(1).

DERIVATION

Social Security Act 1975, s.100B.

DEFINITION

"prescribed"—see s.191.

GENERAL NOTE

Subsection (1)

A decision on a review under s.30(1) may be reviewed as if it was an initial decision by an AO, but with no need to wait the prescribed three months.

Subsection (2)

If a person wishes to challenge a refusal to review under s.30(5) (s.30(2) and (4) only apply to disability living allowance and attendance allowance), there must first be an application for further review under s.30(1) before there can be an appeal to a tribunal.

Subsection (3)

Notice must be given to the claimant of all decisions on review under s.30 (which must include a refusal to review under s.30(5)) and of the appropriate rights of appeal or further review

(Adjudication Regulations, reg. 20(1)). Separate provision is necessary because of the exclusion in s.22(1).

Reviews of decisions as to attendance allowance, disability living allowance or disability working allowance—supplementary

32.—(1) An award of an attendance allowance, a disability living allowance or a disability working allowance on a review under section 30 above replaces any award which was the subject of the review.

(2)–(6) [*Omitted as not applying to disability working allowance*]

(7) Where a claimant has appealed against a decision of an adjudication officer under section 33 below and the decision is reviewed again under section 30(2), (4) or (5) above by an adjudication officer, then—

(a) if the adjudication officer considers that the decision which he has made on the review is the same as the decision that would have been made on the appeal had every ground of the appeal succeeded, then the appeal shall lapse; but

(b) in any other case, the review shall be of no effect and the appeal shall proceed accordingly.

(8) Regulations may make provision restricting the payment of any benefit, or any increase of benefit, to which a person would, but for this subsection, be entitled by reason of a review in respect of any period before or after the review (whether that period falls wholly or partly before or after the making of the regulations).

(9) Where an adjudication officer has determined that any amount paid by way of an attendance allowance, a disability living allowance or a disability working allowance is recoverable under or by virtue of section 71 below, any person from whom he has determined that it is recoverable shall have the same right of review under section 30 above as a claimant.

(10) This Act and the Contributions and Benefits Act shall have effect in relation to a review by virtue of subsection (9) above as if any reference to the claimant were a reference to a person from whom the adjudication officer has determined that the amount in question is recoverable.

DERIVATION

Subs. (1): Social Security Act 1975, s.100C(1).
Subss. (6) to (10): 1975 Act, s.100C(6) to (10).

DEFINITIONS

"the Contributions and Benefits Act"—see s.191.
"prescribed"—*ibid.*

GENERAL NOTE

Subsection (1)
See reg. 70B(1) of the Adjudication Regulations for the date from which a replacement award of disability working allowance on review can take effect.

Subsection (7)
See notes to s.29.

Subsection (8)
See reg. 70B(2) of the Adjudication Regulations.

Subsections (9) and (10)
Where an AO has decided that an overpayment of disability working allowance has been made and is recoverable under s.71, the review and appeal process is the same as for an initial claim.

Appeals following reviews

33.—(1) Where an adjudication officer has given a decision on a review under section 30(1) above, the claimant or such other person as may be prescribed may appeal—

(a) in prescribed cases, to a disability appeal tribunal; and

(b) in any other case, to a social security appeal tribunal.

(2) Regulations may make provision as to the manner in which, and the time within which, appeals are to be brought.

(3) An award on an appeal under this section replaces any award which was the subject of the appeal.

(4)–(6) [*Omitted as not applying to disability working allowance*]

DERIVATION

Social Security Act 1975, s.100D.

DEFINITION

"prescribed"—see s.191.

GENERAL NOTE

Subsection (1)

Where there has been a review under s.30(1) following an initial decision on disability working allowance by an AO the claimant may appeal to a tribunal. The effect of paras. (a) and (b) seems to be that if appeal to a disability appeal tribunal (DAT) is possible, that is where the appeal must go. It is only where appeal to the DAT is not possible that the appeal goes to the SSAT. Reg. 26C(1) of the Adjudication Regulations prescribes that the claimant may appeal to the DAT where either a disability question or both a disability question and any other question relating to disability working allowance arises. A disability question for this purpose is whether a person has a physical or mental disability which puts him at a disadvantage in getting a job (Contributions and Benefits Act, s.129(1)(b) and Sched. 1 to the Disability Working Allowance (General) Regulations). Thus a SSAT may never consider a disability question, since if such a question first arises in the course of an appeal properly made to a SSAT, the SSAT cannot deal with it (s.36(2)). But a DAT has to consider all the conditions of entitlement to disability working allowance if a disability question arises along with other matters.

Subsection (2)

See Sched. 2 to the Adjudication Regulations.

Appeal from social security appeal tribunals or disability appeal tribunals to Commissioners and appeals from Commissioners

34.—(1) Subject to the provisions of this section, an appeal lies to a Commissioner from any decision of a social security appeal tribunal or disability appeal tribunal under section 33 above on the ground that the decision of the tribunal was erroneous in point of law.

(2) An appeal lies under this section at the instance of any of the following—

(a) an adjudication officer;

(b) the claimant;

(c) a trade union—

(i) where the claimant is a member of the union at the time of the appeal and was so immediately before the question at issue arose;

(ii) where that question in any way relates to a deceased person who was a member of the union at the time of his death; and

(d) a person from whom it is determined that any amount is recoverable under section 71(1) below.

(3) Subsection (2) above, as it applies to a trade union, applies also to any other association which exists to promote the interests and welfare of its members.

(4) Subsections (7) to (10) of section 23 above have effect for the purposes of this section as they have effect for the purposes of that section.

(5) Section 24 above applies to a decision of a Commissioner under this section as it applies to a decision of a Commissioner under section 23 above.

DERIVATION

Subss. (1) to (3): Social Security Act 1975, s.101(1) to (4).

DEFINITION

"Commissioner"—see s.191.

GENERAL NOTE

Subsection (1)
See notes to s.23(1).

Subsections (2) and (3)
See notes to s.23(3), (5) and (6).

Subsection (4)
See notes to s.23(7) to (10).

Subsection (5)
See notes to s.24. Subs. (5) is probably redundant as s.24 was finally drafted.

Reviews of decisions on appeal

35.—(1) & (2) [*Omitted as not relating to disability working allowance*]
(3) Any decision under this Act of a social security appeal tribunal, a disability appeal tribunal or a Commissioner which relates to a disability working allowance may be reviewed at any time by an adjudication officer if—
   (a) he is satisfied that the decision was given in ignorance of, or was based on a mistake as to, some material fact; or
   (b) subject to section 129(7) of the Contributions and Benefits Act, there has been any prescribed change of circumstances since the decision was given; or
   (c) the decision was to make an award for a period wholly or partly after the date on which the claim was made or treated as made but subject to a condition being fulfilled and that condition has not been fulfilled,
but regulations may provide that a decision may not be reviewed on the ground mentioned in paragraph (a) above unless the officer is satisfied as mentioned in that paragraph by fresh evidence.

(4) A question may be raised with a view to a review under this section by means of an application made in writing to an adjudication officer stating the grounds of the application and supplying such information and evidence as may be prescribed.

(5) Regulations may provide for enabling or requiring, in prescribed circumstances, a review under this section notwithstanding that no application for a review has been made under subsection (4) above.

(6) Reviews under this section shall be carried out by adjudication officers.

(7) [*Omitted as not applying to disability working allowance*]

(8) Subsections (1), (2), (4) and (5) of section 30 above shall apply—
   (a) to a decision on a review under this section; and

(b) to a refusal to review a decision such as is mentioned in subsection (1) above,

as they apply to a decision of an adjudication officer under section 21 above.

(9) The person whose claim was the subject of the appeal the decision on which has been reviewed under this section shall be given such notification as may be prescribed—

(a) of the decision on the review; and

(b) of his right to a further review under section 30(1) above.

(10) Regulations may make provision restricting the payment of any benefit, or any increase of benefit, to which a person would, but for this subsection, be entitled by reason of a review in respect of any period before or after the review (whether that period falls wholly or partly before or after the making of the regulations).

(11) [*Omitted as not applying to disability working allowance*]

(12) Section 30(10) above and section 32(1) to (5) above shall apply in relation to a review under this section as they apply to a review under section 30 above.

DERIVATION

Subss. (3) and (4): Social Security Act 1975, s.104A(1) to (3).
Subs. (5): 1975 Act, s.104(3A).
Subs. (6): 1975 Act, s.104A(4).
Subss. (8) and (9): 1975 Act, s.104A(6) and (7).
Subs. (10): 1975 Act, s.104(5)(b).
Subs. (11): 1975 Act, s.104(1ZA).
Subs. (12): 1975 Act, s.104A(8).

DEFINITIONS

"Commissioner"—see s.191.
"the Contributions and Benefits Act"—*ibid*.
"prescribed"—*ibid*.

GENERAL NOTE

Subsection (3)

See the notes to s.30(5). A decision of a SSAT, a DAT or a Commissioner cannot be reviewed as being erroneous in point of law, otherwise the appeal process would be subverted. To make sense, the reference in para. (b) should be to s.129(6) of the Contributions and Benefits Act. See regs. 56 and 56A of the Disability Working Allowance (General) Regulations.

Note that review under subs.(3) does not have to be "on an application made under this section." Therefore it seems that an application under subs.(4) is just one way of raising the question of review and that an AO can carry out a review without an application having been made.

Subsections (4) and (5)

See notes to s.26(1) and (3). No regulations have been made under this subsection prescribing any information to be provided.

Subsection (8)

If the claimant is dissatisfied with the decision on a review under this section he must apply for a further review under s.30(1) before he can appeal to a tribunal.

Questions first arising on appeal

Questions first arising on appeal

36.—(1) Where a question which but for this section would fall to be determined by an adjudication officer first arises in the course of an appeal to a social security appeal tribunal, a disability appeal tribunal or a Commissioner, the tribunal, subject to subsection (2) below, or the Commissioner may, if they or he think fit, proceed to determine the question notwithstanding that it has not been considered by an adjudication officer.

(2) A social security appeal tribunal may not determine a question by virtue of subsection (1) above if an appeal in relation to such a question would have lain to a disability appeal tribunal.

DERIVATION

Social Security Act 1975, s.102.

DEFINITION

"Commissioner"—see s.191.

GENERAL NOTE

Subsection (1)

A provision in similar terms to this has existed for some time for benefits falling directly under the 1975 Act. The extension to social fund, supplementary benefit and FIS cases raised problems. Before April 6, 1987, the SSAT's powers in supplementary benefit and FIS cases were defined in reg. 71 of the 1984 Adjudication Regulations. In a number of decisions (see the notes to reg. 71(2) in the 1986 edition of this book for details) the Commissioners held that the SSAT could only deal with matters "within the purview of the original claim" *(R(SB) 9/81)*. While there was only one claim for the whole of weekly supplementary benefit, there were separate claims for each item for which a single payment was claimed *(R(SB) 42/83)*. Thus, on an appeal from a refusal of a single payment the SSAT could not make a decision about the rate of weekly benefit, unless exceptionally the original claim could be said to cover both a single payment claim and a request to review weekly benefit. Several decisions commented that there was nothing in the supplementary benefit legislation corresponding to s.102 of the 1975 Act *(R(SB) 1/82, R(SB) 14/82, R(SB) 42/83)*.

Now s.36 replaces s.102 of the 1975 Act and does apply in income support, family credit and disability working allowance cases. What is its effect? It might at first sight appear to allow a SSAT or Commissioner to go outside the purview of the original claim, although there is little scope for this under the new regulations. However, s.36 only applies to questions which arise in the course of an appeal. This does not mean in the course of the hearing of the appeal *(CS 101/1986)*. The question must be connected with whatever question is properly before the SSAT in the appeal. In *CIS 807/1992* the claimant asked for a review of her supplementary benefit entitlement. The AO never made a decision on this application but the matter reached a SSAT as the claimant had appealed against another decision in connection with her income support. The SSAT assumed jurisdiction in reliance on s.102(1) of the Social Security Act 1975 (now s.36(1)). The Commissioner holds that the question of the claimant's entitlement to additional supplementary benefit had not first arisen "in the course of an appeal" but in connection with a request for a review. There was no appeal in the course of which it could first arise as there had been no initial adjudication. The SSAT's decision was made without authority and was of no effect. The Commissioner also states that "considered" in subs. (1) means "fully considered". As the AO had not reached a decision on the claimant's request for a review of her supplementary benefit he had not "considered" it within subs. (1). *CS 104/1987* confirms that s.36 can only be invoked where the question *first* arises in the course of an appeal. Thus if an AO has decided a question, from which decision no appeal has been made, the SSAT cannot deal with that question under s.36 as it does not first arise in the course of the appeal. The suggestion in *CS 101/1986* that the section could be used where a question might have been referred to the SSAT, but was not, might then be restricted to cases where the AO has not made a decision on that question. But there is growing support for giving a wider scope to s.36. In two recent decisions Commissioners have held that SSATs, should consider issues of review beyond the scope of the original application. In *R(IS) 11/93* review was sought from 1979. Before the SSAT the period from 1973 was raised and dealt with. That was held to be proper. In *CIS 303/1992* (to be reported as *R(IS) 15/93*) a review of housing costs for mortgage interest by the AO was in issue. Before the SSAT the claimant argued that her housing costs should no longer be restricted. It was held that the SSAT was wrong to refuse to consider that point. See also *CSB 1272/1989* (notes to s.71(5)).

In addition, there are two controls. First, the SSAT has a discretion to decide the new question. It may consider the argument that when the only appeal from the SSAT is on the ground of error of law, the claimant may be deprived of a stage in the appeal process if the SSAT, rather than the AO, makes an initial decision. But in *CIS 21/1993* the Commissioner says that where the new question is clearly tied to the matter in front of the tribunal, it should determine it under subs. (1), or ensure that the AO will consider it. The Commissioner states: "this is an inquisitorial jurisdiction and it is full of procedural pitfalls. Claimants cannot be expected to take the right points and s.36 exists to introduce some flexibility in the interests of justice". Second, the principles of natural justice would require that a SSAT should not make a decision on a new point if all parties have not had a fair opportunity of dealing with it (*R(F) 1/72*).

The power under s.36 applies to Commissioners as well as SSATs.

Subsection (2)

If a SSAT is hearing a disability working allowance appeal and a question arises for the first time about whether the claimant satisfies the condition in s.129(1)(b) of the Contributions and Benefits Act (physical or mental disability which puts the claimant at a disadvantage in getting a job), then the SSAT cannot deal with that question. If there is such a disability question (with or without some other point in dispute) when an appeal is made, the whole appeal goes to the DAT (s.33(1) and Adjudication Regulations, reg. 26C). But it appears that if an appeal has properly gone to the SSAT before the disability question first arises, then the SSAT should continue to deal with the questions raised in the original appeal. By definition, the disability question must have been decided by the AO under s.30(1) in the claimant's favour, otherwise the appeal would already be before the DAT. If something comes to light in the SSAT appeal which casts doubt on that, but the SSAT determines all the other questions in the claimant's favour, there is a difficult question on the SSAT's proper course of action. Should it make an award of disability working allowance, and leave the AO to review that award under s.35(3), or simply determine the questions before it and leave the AO to review the disability question? On balance, the first alternative seems more in line with the scheme of the legislation.

Reference of special questions

Reference of special questions

37.—(1) Subject to subsection (2) below—

(a) if on consideration of any claim or question an adjudication officer is of opinion that there arises any question which under or by virtue of this Act falls to be determined otherwise than by an adjudication officer, he shall refer the question for such determination; and

(b) if on consideration of any claim or question a social security appeal tribunal or Commissioner is of opinion that any such question arises, the tribunal or Commissioner shall direct it to be referred by an adjudication officer for such determination.

(2) The person or tribunal making or directing the reference shall then deal with any other question as if the referred question had not arisen.

(3) The adjudication officer, tribunal or Commissioner may—

(a) postpone the reference of, or dealing with, any question until other questions have been determined;

(b) in cases where the determination of any question disposes of a claim or any part of it, make an award or decide that an award cannot be made, as to the claim or that part of it, without referring or dealing with, or before the determination of, any other question.

DERIVATION

Social Security Act 1975, s.103.

Adjudication officers and the Chief Adjudication Officer

Adjudication officers

38.—(1) Adjudication officers shall be appointed by the Secretary of State, subject to the consent of the Treasury as to number, and may include—

(a) officers of the Department of Employment appointed with the concurrence of the Secretary of State in charge of that Department; or

(b) officers of the Northern Ireland Department appointed with the concurrence of that Department.

(2) An adjudication officer may be appointed to perform all the functions of adjudication officers under any enactment or such functions of such officers as may be specified in his instrument of appointment.

DERIVATION

Social Security Act 1975, s.97(1) and (1A).

DEFINITION

"the Northern Ireland Department"—see s.191.

GENERAL NOTE

Subsection (1)
The Secretary of State is not obliged to appoint enough AOs to dispose of all claims submitted to them within 14 days under s.21(1) (*R. v. Secretary of State for Social Services, ex parte CPAG* [1990] 2 Q.B. 540).

Subsection (2)
The current instrument of appointment was signed by the Secretary of State on February 28, 1992, and is reproduced as Appendix 1 to Part 01 of the *Adjudication Officers' Guide*. It directs that all persons appointed shall carry out all the functions of AOs, unless specifically designated to exercise only specified functions. In practice, most AOs will deal with only a limited number of benefits, but will formally have the power to carry out any AO function.

See reg. 64 of the Adjudication Regulations for the consequences of the limited practical range of expertise of individual AOs.

The Chief Adjudication Officer

39.—(1) The Secretary of State shall appoint a Chief Adjudication Officer.

(2) It shall be the duty of the Chief Adjudication Officer to advice adjudication officers on the performance of their functions under this or any other Act.

(3) The Chief Adjudication Officer shall keep under review the operation of the system of adjudication by adjudication officers and matters connected with the operation of that system.

(4) The Chief Adjudication Officer shall report annually in writing to the Secretary of State on the standards of adjudication and the Secretary of State shall publish his report.

DERIVATION

Social Security Act 1975, s.97(IB) to (IE).

GENERAL NOTE

The Chief Adjudication Officer combines the functions of the former Chief Insurance Officer and the Chief Supplementary Benefit Officer. But his advisory duties were given statutory expression for the first time in 1984. The duty to report publicly on standards of adjudication was also new. The CAO's first report was published in 1986. This and the subsequent annual reports contain much interesting and critical material. The more recent reports contain fascinating material on the relationship of the adjudication system with the Benefits Agency.

Social security appeal tribunals

Panels for appointment to social security appeal tribunals

40.—(1) The President shall constitute for the whole of Great Britain, to act for such areas as he thinks fit and be composed of such persons as he thinks fit to appoint, panels of persons to act as members of social security appeal tribunals.

(2) The panel for an area shall be composed of persons appearing to the President to have knowledge or experience of conditions in the area and to be representative of persons living or working in the area.

(3) Before appointing members of a panel, the President shall take into consideration any recommendations from such organisations or persons as he considers appropriate.

(4) The members of the panels shall hold office for such period as the President may direct, but the President may at any time terminate the appointment of any member of a panel.

DERIVATION

Social Security Act 1975, Sched. 10, para. 1(1) to (6).

DEFINITION

"President"—see s.191.

GENERAL NOTE

The President of Social Security Appeal Tribunals etc. is to appoint members to a national panel and assign them to particular areas.

There is now one panel of members. The temporary survival after April 1984 of the two panels left over from the old supplementary benefit appeal tribunals and national insurance local tribunals, conceded in order to get the Health and Social Services and Social Security Adjudications Act 1983 through Parliament before the 1983 General Election, came to an end on September 26, 1984. This was in fulfilment of the Government's original intention.

The test for appointment under subs.(2) is a dual one. The member must have knowledge or experience of conditions in the area to which the appointment applies and be representative of persons living or working in the area. The first part seems to be a watered down version of the old SBAT test for "Secretary of State's" members, omitting the requirement of knowledge or experience of the problems of people living on low incomes. This requirement was presumably thought inappropriate to the wider jurisdiction of the SSAT, but it is a pity that it should be lost altogether. It is far from clear what the "representative" test requires. The intention apparently is that the range of organisations consulted about membership under subs.(3) should be widened out from Trade Councils, Chambers of Commerce, etc., to include groups representing ethnic minorities, the disabled, one-parent families, etc. This is laudable in an attempt to secure a balanced panel, although of course it does not secure any specific balance on an individual tribunal. However, the member does not have to be nominated by an organisation. The test is not of a representative in that sense. The test is whether a person is representative of the local population. Individuals who do not belong to groups or organisations are also eligible, and may have much to offer.

Constitution of social security appeal tribunals

41.—(1) A social security appeal tribunal shall consist of a chairman and two other persons.

(2) The members of a social security appeal tribunal other than the chairman shall be drawn from the appropriate panel constituted under section 40 above.

(3) The President shall nominate the chairman.

(4) The President may nominate as chairman—

  (a) himself;

  (b) one of the full-time chairmen appointed under section 51(1) below; or

  (c) a person drawn from the panel appointed by the Lord Chancellor or, as the case may be, the Lord President of the Court of Session under ['section 6 of the Tribunals and Inquiries Act 1992].

(5) No person shall be appointed chairman of a tribunal under subsection (4)(c) above unless he has a 5 year general qualification or he is an advocate or solicitor in Scotland of at least 5 years' standing.

(6) If practicable, at least one of the members of the appeal tribunal hearing a case shall be of the same sex as the claimant.

(7) Schedule 2 to this Act shall have effect for supplementing this section.

DERIVATION

Subss. (1) to (5): Social Security Act 1975, s.97(2) to (2E).
Subs. (6): 1975 Act, Sched. 10, para. 1(6).
Subs. (7): 1975 Act, s.97(4).

AMENDMENT

1. Tribunals and Inquiries Act 1992, Sched. 3, para. 36 (October 1, 1992).

DEFINITIONS

"5 year general qualification"—see s.191.
"President"—*ibid.*

GENERAL NOTE

Subsection (1)
For the appointment of chairmen, see subss. (3) to (5). For the appointment of the other members, see subs.(2). For an overriding condition on the composition of each particular tribunal hearing an appeal, see subs.(6).

Subsection (2)
There is now one panel for each area from which members of a particular tribunal are chosen. The old division between the Trades Council members and the Secretary of State's members on supplementary benefit appeal tribunals and between employers' and employees' representatives on national insurance local tribunals has gone. There is no longer any guarantee of having a member from any particular background on any individual tribunal. Members need no longer be summoned in turn to sit on tribunals. See s.40 for appointment to the panel of members.

Subsection (4)
The panel referred to in para. (c) is of the ordinary part-time chairmen of SSATs, appointed by the Lord Chancellor (or the Lord President in Scotland). The President assigns chairmen to act in particular areas.
See s.51 for regional and other full-time chairmen.

Subsection (5)
Since 1984 part-time chairmen have had to have professional legal qualifications. This was a controversial provision, which required the discarding of some highly experienced and knowledge-able supplementary benefit appeal tribunal chairmen. However, it was probably inevitable in view of the excessive legalisation of the supplementary benefit system detailed in past editions of this book. What remains controversial is the requirement of professional legal qualifications (which, to put it kindly, do not guarantee any knowledge of, or interest in, social security law), rather than some other evidence of legal skills (*e.g.* a law degree).
From January 1, 1991, the nature of the required professional legal qualification in England and Wales has changed, following the reforms embodied in the Courts and Legal Services Act 1990. A person has a general qualification under s.71 of that Act if he has a right of audience, granted by an authorised body, in relation to any class of proceedings in the Supreme Court or all proceedings in county courts or magistrates' courts. To meet tests of having had a qualification for a particular length of time a person must currently hold the qualification and have held it for the required number of years, not necessarily consecutive (s.71(5)). There are transitional provisions under which solicitors and barristers admitted or called before 1991 are deemed to have been granted the appropriate right of audience.

Subsection (6)
This provision causes difficulty while only about 25 per cent. of members are women. The President's policy on appointments is to attempt to redress this imbalance.

The Commissioner in *R(SB) 2/88* holds that practicability imposes quite a strict requirement. The provision is mandatory, and if the SSAT does not have a member of the same sex as the claimant it must be shown that it was not practicable to do otherwise. This cannot be presumed. The chairman should ask the clerk about the circumstances, and endorse the record of decision (AT3) accordingly. If non-practicability cannot be proved the SSAT's decision will be in error of law even though the claimant consents to the hearing continuing. However, the Commissioner in *CS 99/1993* holds that a claimant may consent to a tribunal proceeding. He points out that even where a procedural rule is expressed in mandatory terms it can be waived by the party for whose benefit it exists (unless it is a matter where there is a wider public interest in compliance with the rule). In *CSB 36/1992* the Commissioner set aside the SSAT's decision as it appeared as though subs. (6) had just been overlooked. If it is not practicable to have a member of the same sex as the claimant it might be appropriate to offer the claimant an adjournment.

The President and full-time chairmen of tribunals

The President of social security appeal tribunals, medical appeal tribunals and disability appeal tribunals and regional chairmen and other full-time chairmen.

51.—(1) The Lord Chancellor may, after consultation with the Lord Advocate, appoint—
    (a) a President of social security appeal tribunals, medical appeal tribunals and disability appeal tribunals; and
    (b) regional and other full-time chairmen of such tribunals.

(2) A person is qualified to be appointed President if he has a 10 year general qualification or he is an advocate or solicitor in Scotland of at least 10 years' standing.

(3) A person is qualified to be appointed a full-time chairman if he has a 5 year general qualification or he is an advocate or solicitor in Scotland of at least 5 years' standing.

(4) Schedule 2 to this Act shall have effect for supplementing this section.

DERIVATION

Social Security Act 1975, Sched. 10, para. 1A(1) to (3).

DEFINITIONS

    "5 year general qualification"—see s.191.
    "10 year general qualification"—*ibid*.

GENERAL NOTE

One of the major innovations in the reform of tribunals in 1984 was the appointment of a President who took over the appointment of SSAT members and clerks as well as the training of chairmen and members. In effect, the administration of SSATs has been removed from the DSS into the hands of an entirely independent agency. The reality of this independence has largely been secured, but still depends on the resources allowed to the President by the Treasury. The President has now added DATs and CSATs (see para. 1 of Sched. 3 to the Child Support Act 1991) to his remit.

The first incumbent, Judge H. J. Byrt, took up his post towards the end of 1983 and completed his initial term of office in 1988. He was replaced by Judge Derek Holden in February 1990, who served until August 1992. The current President is Judge Keith Bassingthwaighte.

Section 51 also provides for the appointment of regional chairmen and full-time chairmen. Regional chairmen have been appointed for each of the seven (now reduced to six) DSS regions in Britain. This innovation can be seen as a reflection of the success of the four senior chairmen who had previously been responsible for SBATs and did a great deal to improve the standards of independence and expertise in those tribunals. The regional chairmen have smaller geographical areas to cope with, but must deal also with former NILTs, medical appeal tribunals, DATs and now CSATs (see para. 4 of Sched. 3 to the Child Support Act 1991). The regional chairmen carry out many of the statutory functions of the President, *e.g.* training, arranging meetings and appointing members, within the overall framework set by the President.

Power is also given to appoint other full-time chairmen. Initially seven were appointed, but following the recent extensions in the tribunals' jurisdiction, several additional appointments have been made in each region. In the past, they seem to have acted mainly as "troubleshooters," a resource to be called in to help clear backlogs of appeals in particular places or maybe to take particularly difficult cases. They have also had a large role in training, and with the number of tribunals expanding beyond what an individual regional chairman can handle, are increasingly taking on an administrative role.

Some dislike the development of full-time chairmen as much as the requirement of professional legal qualifications for part-time chairmen, as eroding the connections of chairmen with the local community. With the further expansion of the range of tribunals under the President's supervision, it is likely that even more full-time chairmen will be appointed; the trend certainly seems to be in this direction. It is certainly becoming increasingly unrealistic to expect part-time chairmen to keep on top of the entire range of the SSAT's jurisdiction, as well as possibly DATs, medical appeal tribunals and CSATs, and maintain the expertise to exercise a true independence of judgment.

Social Security Commissioners

Appointment of Commissioners

52.—(1) Her Majesty may from time to time appoint, from among persons who have a 10 year general qualification or advocates or solicitors in Scotland of at least 10 years' standing—

(a) a Chief Social Security Commissioner; and

(b) such number of other Social Security Commissioners, as Her Majesty thinks fit.

(2) If the Lord Chancellor considers that, in order to facilitate the disposal of the business of Social Security Commissioners, he should make an appointment in pursuance of this subsection, he may appoint—

(a) a person who has a 10 year general qualification; or

(b) an advocate or solicitor in Scotland of at least 10 years' standing; or

(c) a member of the bar of Northern Ireland or solicitor of the Supreme Court of Northern Ireland of at least 10 years' standing,

to be a Social Security Commissioner (but to be known as a deputy Commissioner) for such period or on such occasions as the Lord Chancellor thinks fit.

(3) When the Lord Chancellor proposes to exercise the power conferred on him by subsection (2) above, it shall be his duty to consult the Lord Advocate with respect to the proposal.

(4) Schedule 2 to this Act shall have effect for supplementing this section.

DERIVATION

Subs. (1): Social Security Act 1975, s.97(3).
Subss. (2) and (3): Social Security Act 1980, s.13(5) and (6).

DEFINITION

"10 year general qualification"—see s.191.

References by authorities

Power of adjudicating authorities to refer matters to experts

53.—(1) An authority to which this section applies may refer any question of special difficulty arising for decision by the authority to one or more experts for examination and report.

(2) The authorities to which this section applies are—

(a) an adjudication officer;

(b) an adjudicating medical practitioner, or two or more such practitioners acting together;

(c) a specially qualified adjudicating medical practitioner appointed by virtue of section 62 below, or two or more such practitioners acting together;

(d) a social security appeal tribunal;

(e) a disability appeal tribunal;

(f) a medical appeal tribunal;

(g) a Commissioner;

(h) the Secretary of State.

(3) Regulations may prescribe cases in which a Commissioner shall not exercise the power conferred by subsection (1) above.

(4) In this section "expert" means a person appearing to the authority to have knowledge or experience which would be relevant in determining the question of special difficulty.

DERIVATION

Social Security Act 1975, s.115A.

DEFINITIONS

"Commissioner"—see s.191.
"prescribed"—*ibid.*

GENERAL NOTE

This general power may be useful to SSATs in exceptional circumstances, perhaps being more relevants to AOs or MATs and DATs. The question must be of special difficulty and needs to be carefully specified. The power should not be used to get the SSAT off the hook of coming to a decision on conflicting evidence.

Claims relating to attendance allowance, disability living allowance and disability working allowance

54.—(1) Before a claim for an attendance allowance, a disability living allowance or a disability working allowance or any question relating to such an allowance is submitted to an adjudication officer under section 20 above the Secretary of State may refer the person in respect of whom the claim is made or the question is raised to a medical practitioner for such examination and report as appears to him to be necessary—

(a) for the purpose of providing the adjudication officer with information for use in determining the claim or question; or

(b) for the purpose of general monitoring of claims for attendance allowances, disability living allowances and disability working allowances.

(2) An adjudication officer may refer—

(a) a person in respect of whom such a claim is made or such a question is raised;

(b) a person who has applied or is treated as having applied for a review under section 30 or 35 above,

to a medical practitioner for such examination and report as appears to the adjudication officer to be needed to enable him to reach a decision on the claim or question or the matter under review.

(3) [*Omitted as not applying to disability working allowance*]

(4) An adjudication officer may refer for advice any case relating to disability working allowance to such a medical practitioner.

(5) & (6) [*Omitted as not applying to disability working allowance*]

(7) A medical practitioner who is an officer of the Secretary of State and to whom a question relating to disability working allowance is referred under section 53 above may obtain information about it from another medical practitioner.

(8) Where—

(a) the Secretary of State has exercised the power conferred on him by sub-section (1) above or an adjudication officer has exercised the power conferred on him by subsection (2) above; and

(b) the medical practitioner requests the person referred to him to attend for or submit himself to medical examination; but

(c) he fails without good cause to do so,

the adjudication officer shall decide the claim or question or matter under review against him.

DERIVATION

Social Security Act 1975, s.115C.

GENERAL NOTE

The powers contained in this section will in disability working allowance cases mainly be used in relation to the disability question under s.129(1)(*b*) of the Contributions and Benefits Act, which is not a concern of the SSAT.

Determination of questions of special difficulty

Assessors

56.—(1) Where it appears to an authority to which this section applies that a matter before the authority involves a question of fact of special difficulty, then, unless regulations otherwise provide, the authority may direct that in dealing with that matter they shall have the assistance of one or more assessors.

(2) The authorities to which this section applies are—

(a) two or more adjudicating medical practitioners acting together;

(b) two or more specially qualified adjudicating medical practitioners, appointed by virtue of section 62 below, acting together;

(c) a social security appeal tribunal;

(d) a disability appeal tribunal;

(e) a medical appeal tribunal;

(f) a Commissioner;

(g) the Secretary of State.

DERIVATION

Social Security Act 1975, s.115B.

GENERAL NOTE

Presumably the principles laid down in *R(I) 14/51* in relation to earlier legislation will continue to apply. The assessor's role is to assist the authority to understand the factual issues and to evaluate the evidence. He does not himself give evidence and so cannot be questioned by the parties to the proceedings. His advice should be summarised and the parties given the opportunity to comment on it. *CS 175/ 1992* holds that a medically qualified member of a SSAT was not performing an analogous role to that of a medical assessor when putting her expert interpretation on the evidence presented to the tribunal. An assessor is not entitled to be present while the decision is being made (regs. 2(2) and 4(6) of the Adjudication Regulations) whereas clearly a member is, and indeed, must be.

Tribunal of 3 Commissioners

57.—(1) If it appears to the Chief Social Security Commissioner (or, in the case of his inability to act, to such other of the Commissioners as he may have nominated to act for the purpose) that an appeal falling to be heard by one of the Commissioners involves a question of law of special difficulty, he may direct that the appeal be dealt with, not by that Commissioner alone, but by a Tribunal consisting of any 3 of the Commissioners.

(2) If the decision of the Tribunal is not unanimous, the decision of the majority shall be the decision of the Tribunal.

DERIVATION

Social Security Act 1975, s.116.

GENERAL NOTE

Under the legislation in force before April 1984 there was no express power for the Chief Commissioner to convene a Tribunal of Commissioners in supplementary benefit or FIS cases. The power was found by implication (*R(FIS) 1/82*). It is often invoked where individual Commissioners have reached conflicting decisions. Individual Commissioners are bound to follow a decision of a Tribunal of Commissioners, unless there are compelling reasons to the contrary (*R(I) 12/75* and *CM 44/1991*, to be reported as *R(M)2/94*). A Tribunal of Commissioners may depart from a previous Tribunal decision if satisfied that it was wrong (*R(U) 4/88*).

With the expansion in the number of Commissioners it can no longer be guaranteed that the approach adopted by the three Commissioners on a Tribunal will be accepted by the Commissioners as a whole. In recent years, a number of Tribunal decisions have been left unreported. This may be because of lack of support by the Commissioners as a whole, but it is impossible from the outside to tell. A SSAT must follow a Tribunal's decision, whether reported or unreported, in preference to a decision of an individual Commissioner. Possibly, if the individual Commissioner finds compelling reasons for departing from an unreported Tribunal decision, a SSAT would be entitled to follow the individual Commissioner.

Regulations

Regulations as to the determination of questions and matters arising out of, or pending, reviews and appeals

58.—(1) Subject to the provisions of this Act, provision may be made by regulations for the determination—

(a) by the Secretary of State; or

(b) by a person or tribunal appointed in accordance with the regulations, of any question arising under or in connection with the Contributions and Benefits Act or the former legislation, including a claim for benefit.

(2) In this section "the former legislation" means the National Insurance Acts 1965 to 1974 and the National Insurance (Industrial Injuries) Acts 1965 to 1974 and the 1975 Act and Part II of the 1986 Act.

(3) Regulations under subsection (1) above may modify, add to or exclude any provisions of this Part of this Act, so far as relating to any questions to which the regulations relate.

(4)–(8) [*Omitted as not applying to SSATs*]

DERIVATION

Social Security Act 1975, s.114(1) and (2).

DEFINITIONS

"the 1975 Act"—see s.191.
"the 1986 Act"—*ibid.*
"the Contributions and Benefits Act"—*ibid.*

Procedure

59.—(1) Regulations (in this section referred to as "procedure regulations") may make any such provision as is specified in Schedule 3 to this Act.

(2) Procedure regulations may deal differently with claims and questions relating to—

(a) benefit under Parts II to IV of the Contributions and Benefits Act;

(b) industrial injuries benefit;

(c) each of the other benefits to which section 20 above applies.

(3)–(5) [*Omitted as not applying to SSATs*]

(6) It is hereby declared—

(a) that the power to prescribe procedure includes power to make provision as to the representation of one person, at any hearing of a case, by another person whether having professional qualifications or not; and

(b) that the power to provide for the manner in which questions arising for determination by the Secretary of State are to be raised includes power to make provision with respect to the formulation of any such questions, whether, arising on a reference under section 117 below or otherwise.

(7) Except so far as it may be applied in relation to England and Wales by procedure regulations, the Arbitration Act 1950 shall not apply to any proceedings under this Part of this Act.

DERIVATION

Social Security Act 1975, ss.115(1) to (3), and (6) to (7).

DEFINITIONS

"the Contributions and Benefits Act"—see s.191.
"industrial injuries benefit"—*ibid*.

GENERAL NOTE

See Sched. 3 and the Adjudication Regulations.

Finality of decisions

60.—(1) Subject to the provisions of this Part of this Act, the decision of any claim or question in accordance with the foregoing provisions of this Part of this Act shall be final; and subject to the provisions of any regulations under section 58 above, the decision of any claim or question in accordance with those regulations shall be final.

(2) Subsection (1) above shall not make any finding of fact or other determination embodied in or necessary to a decision, or on which it is based, conclusive for the purpose of any further decision.

(3)–(5) [*Omitted as not applying to income-related benefits*]

DERIVATION

Social Security Act 1975, s.117(1) and (2).

GENERAL NOTE

Jones v. Department of Employment [1988] 1 All E.R. 725 decides that an AO cannot be sued for negligently making a decision, partly because of the effect of the predecessor of s.60. The principle of finality is fundamental to the system of social security adjudication. It means that once a decision is made on a claim or question, it can only be altered within the period covered by the decision when a power to do so is expressly granted by the legislation, as on appeal or review. See reg. 17 of the Claims and Payments Regulation for the period covered by a claim and an award. Disallowance of a claim for an open-ended period operates down to the date of the decision (*R(S) 14/81*).

Although decisions are final, under subs. (2) findings of fact or other determinations are not conclusive for further decision. It used to be the case that decisions of the insurance officer on certain questions were conclusive for supplementary benefit purposes. This issue is now covered by reg. 64 of the Adjudication Regulations. The issue is only really a live one before a tribunal, and here it is clear from reg. 64 that, although an AO must first make a decision on a relevant question, the SSAT can deal with both income support and the national insurance or child benefit question together.

Subs. (2) also confirms that on a fresh claim, issues of fact and law are for decision afresh. For instance, if an income support claim is rejected on the ground that a claimant has notional capital under the deprivation rule, a claim a month or a week later cannot be rejected simply by reference to the earlier decision.

Regulations about supplementary matters relating to determinations

61.—(1) Regulations may make provision as respects matters arising—
  (a) pending the determination under this Act (whether in the first instance or on an appeal or reference, and whether originally or on review)—
    (i) of any claim for benefit to which this section applies; or
    (ii) of any question affecting any person's right to such benefit or its receipt; or
    (iii) of any person's liability for contributionss under Part I of the Contributions and Benefits Act; or
  (b) out of the revision on appeal or review of any decision under this Act on any such claim or question.

(2) Without prejudice to the generality of subsection (1) above, regulations thereunder may include provision as to the date from which any decision on a review is to have effect or to be deemed to have had effect.

(3) [*Omitted as not applying to income-related benefits*]

(4) This section applies—
  (a) to benefit as defined in section 122 of the Contributions and Benefits Act;
  (b) to child benefit;
  (c) to statutory sick pay;
  (d) to statutory maternity pay;
  (e) to income support;
  (f) to family credit;
  (g) to disability working allowance; and
  (h) to any social fund payments such as are mentioned in section 138(1)(a) or (2) of the Contributions and Benefits Act.

DERIVATION

Social Security Act 1975, s.119(3) and (4)(a).

DEFINITION

"the Contributions and Benefits Act"—see s.191.

GENERAL NOTE

See the Adjudication Regulations and the Claims and Payments Regulations.

[*Incapacity for work*

Adjudication: incapacity for work

61A.—(1) The following provisions apply in relation to the determination, for any purpose for which the provisions of Part XIIA of the Contributions and Benefits Act apply, whether a person—
  (a) is, or is to be treated as, capable or incapable of work, or

   (b) falls to be disqualified for any period in accordance with regulations under section 171E of that Act,

and to the determination for any such purpose of such other related questions as may be prescribed.

(2) Provision may be made by regulations for a determination made for one such purpose to be treated as conclusive for another such purpose.

Regulations may in particular provide that a determination that a person is disqualified for any period in accordance with regulations under section 171E of the Contributions and Benefits Act shall have effect for such purposes as may be prescribed as a determination that he is to be treated as capable of work for that period, and *vice versa*.

(3) Provision may be made by regulations for questions of such descriptions as may be prescribed to be determined by an adjudication officer, notwithstanding that other questions fall to be determined by another authority.

(4) Provision may be made by regulations—

   (a) requiring a social security appeal tribunal to sit with one or more medical assessors in such classes of case as may be prescribed, and

   (b) as to the constitution of panels of medical practitioners to act as medical assessors in such cases;

and regulations under this subsection may confer on the President, or such other person as may be prescribed, such functions as may be prescribed.]

AMENDMENT

1. Social Security (Incapacity for Work) Act 1994, s. 6(2) (April 13, 1995).

DEFINITION

"the Contributions and Benefits Act"—see s. 191.

GENERAL NOTE

For the details of the new rules for deciding incapacity for work see *Bonner, Non-Means Tested Benefits: the Legislation*, (1995 ed.). See also the notes to para. 5 of Sched. 1 to the Income Support Regulations for a brief summary. The framework is in Part XIIA of the Contributions and Benefits Act (s.171A-G) and this section; the main detail of the new rules is mostly in the Social Security (Incapacity for Work) (General) Regulations 1995 (S.I. 1995 No. 311).

Subsection (2)

See reg. 19 of the Incapacity for Work (General) Regulations on the first part, and reg. 18 on the second.

Subsection (3)

See reg. 20 of the Incapacity for Work (General) Regulations.

Subsection (4)

Reg. 21 of the Incapacity for Work (General) Regulations provides that a SSAT must sit with a medical assessor in any case that involves consideration of whether the claimant satisfies the "all work test". For details of this test and when it applies, see *Bonner, Non-Means Tested Benefits: the Legislation*, (1965 ed.). Whether an assessor is required will be a matter for the chairman under reg. 2(1)(a) of the Adjudication Regulations; if one is required, but not present, the hearing will have to be postponed and relisted with an assessor present. See reg. 5(1A) of the Adjudication Regulations which from May 1994 gives a chairman power to postpone a hearing without any application being made.

Presumably the case law on s. 56 (power to appoint assessors in cases of special difficulty) will apply; see the notes to s. 56. An assessor is not a member of the tribunal and should enter and leave the room with the parties. An assessor should not participate in any appeal in which he has knowledge of the appellant. The role of the assessor is to give impartial advice to the tribunal; the parties must be given the opportunity to comment on anything he says, but cannot cross-examine him. He should not ask questions himself except through the chairman, and may not physically examine the claimant (*R(I) 14/51*).

It is understand that future amendments to the Adjudication Regulations will provide that the medical assessor may not comment on the claimant's capacity for work, or whether any particular "descriptor" applies (see the Schedule to the Social Security (Incapacity for Work) (General) Regulations 1995 (S.I. 1995 No 311) for the "descriptors" involved in the new "all work test"). But an assessor will be provided with a copy of the tribunal papers and shown any documents presented during the hearing. So it seems that the assessor's role in an incapacity for work appeal will be to assist the tribunal to understand and evaluate the evidence, by, for example, explaining medical terms, or the significance of, or side-effects of, any medication, or the likely consequences of any condition. He may also suggest that further medical evidence needs to be obtained. But the decision as to whether the particular claimant is or is not incapable of work remains that of the tribunal alone.

Social fund officers and inspectors and the social fund Commissioner

Social fund officers

64.—(1) The Secretary of State shall appoint officers, to be known as "social fund officers", for the purpose of performing functions in relation to payments out of the social fund such as are mentioned in section 138(1)(b) of the Contributions and Benefits Act.

(2) A social fund officer may be appointed to perform all the functions of social fund officers or such functions of such officers as may be specified in his instrument of appointment.

(3) The Secretary of State may nominate for an area a social fund officer who shall issue general guidance to the other social fund officers in the area about such matters relating to the social fund as the Secretary of State may specify.

DERIVATION

Social Security Act 1986, s.32(8) to (10).

DEFINITION

"the Contributions and Benefits Act"—see s.191.

GENERAL NOTE

Subsection (3)
See s.140(5) of the Contributions and Benefits Act and s.66(9) below for the status of guidance issued by area social fund officers.

The social fund Commissioner and inspectors

65.—(1) There shall continue to be an officer, to be known as "the social fund Commissioner" (in this section referred to as "the Commissioner").

(2) The Commissioner shall be appointed by the Secretary of State.

(3) The Commissioner—
  (a) shall appoint such social fund inspectors; and
  (b) may appoint such officers and staff for himself and for social fund inspectors,
as he thinks fit, but with the consent of the Secretary of State and the Treasury as to numbers.

(4) Appointments under subsection (3) above shall be made from persons made available to the Commissioner by the Secretary of State.

(5) It shall be the duty of the Commissioner—
  (a) to monitor the quality of decisions of social fund inspectors and give

them such advice and assistance as he thinks fit to improve the standard of their decisions;

(b) to arrange such training of social fund inspectors as he considers appropriate; and

(c) to carry out such other functions in connection with the work of social fund inspectors as the Secretary of State may direct.

(6) The Commissioner shall report annually in writing to the Secretary of State on the standards of reviews by social fund inspectors and the Secretary of State shall publish his report.

DERIVATION

Social Security Act 1986, s.35.

GENERAL NOTE

The Annual Reports of the Social Fund Commissioner contain much interesting material. Inspectors have been recruited from outside and inside the DSS and have established an independence of operation.

Reviews

66.—(1) A social fund officer—

(a) shall review a determination made under the Contributions and Benefits Act by himself or some other social fund officer, if an application for review is made within such time and in such form and manner as may be prescribed by or on behalf of the person who applied for the payment to which the determination relates; and

(b) may review such a determination in such other circumstances as he thinks fit;

and may exercise on a review any power exercisable by an officer under Part VIII of the Contributions and Benefits Act.

(2) The power to review a determination conferred on a social fund officer by subsection (1) above includes power to review a determination made by a social fund officer on a previous review.

(3) On an application made by or on behalf of the person to whom a determination relates within such time and in such form and manner as may be prescribed a determination of a social fund officer which has been reviewed shall be further reviewed by a social fund inspector.

(4) On a review a social fund inspector shall have the following powers—

(a) power to confirm the determination made by the social fund officer;

(b) power to make any determination which a social fund officer could have made;

(c) power to refer the matter to a social fund officer for determination.

(5) A social fund inspector may review a determination under subsection (3) above made by himself or by some other social fund inspector.

(6) In determining a question on a review a social fund officer or social fund inspector shall have regard, subject to subsection (7) below, to all the circumstances of the case and, in particular, to the matters specified in section 140(1)(a) to (e) of the Contributions and Benefits Act.

(7) An officer or inspector shall determine any question on a review in accordance with any general directions issued by the Secretary of State under section 140(2) of the Contributions and Benefits Act and any general directions issued by him with regard to reviews and in determining any such question shall take account of any general guidance issued by him under that subsection or with regard to reviews.

(8) Directions under this section may specify—

(a) the circumstances in which a determination is to be reviewed; and

(b) the manner in which a review is to be conducted.

(9) In reviewing a question under this section a social fund officer shall take account (subject to any directions or guidance issued by the Secretary of State under this section) of any guidance issued by the social fund officer nominated for his area under section 64(3) above.

(10) A social fund inspector reviewing a determination shall be under the same duties in relation to such guidance as the social fund officer or inspector who made the determination.

DERIVATION

Subss.(1) to (8): Social Security Act 1986, s.34.
Subss.(9) and (10): 1986 Act, s.32(11) and (12).

DEFINITION

"the Contributions and Benefits Act"—see s.191.

GENERAL NOTE

Subsections (1) and (3)
See the Social Fund (Application for Review) Regulations 1988.

Subsections (7) and (8)
See directions 31 to 42 of the Secretary of State's directions to SFOs and the directions to SFIs, together with the notes to those directions.

Restrictions on entitlement to benefit following erroneous decision

Restrictions on entitlement to benefit in certain cases of error

68.—(1) This section applies where—

(a) on the determination, whenever made of a Commissioner or the court (the "relevant determination"), a decision made by an adjudicating authority is or was found to have been erroneous in point of law; and

(b) after both—

(i) 13th July 1990 (the date of the coming into force of section 165D of the 1975 Act, the provision of that Act corresponding to this section); and

(ii) the date of the relevant determination,

a claim which falls, or which would apart from this section fall, to be decided in accordance with the relevant determination is made or treated under section 7(1) above as made by any person for any benefit.

(2) Where this section applies, any question which arises on, or on the review of a decision which is referable to, the claim mentioned in subsection (1)(b) above and which relates to the entitlement of the claimant or any other person to any benefit—

(a) in respect of a period before the relevant date; or

(b) in the case of a widow's payment, in respect of a death occurring before that date,

shall be determined as if the decision referred to in subsection (1)(a) above had been found by the Commissioner or court in question not to have been erroneous in point of law.

(3) In determining whether a person is entitled to benefit in a case where—

(a) his entitlement depends on his having been entitled to the same or some other benefit before attaining a particular age; and

(b) he attained that age—

    (i) before both the date of the relevant determination and the date of the claim referred to in subsection (1)(b) above, but

    (ii) not before the earliest day in respect of which benefit could, apart from this section, have been awarded on that claim,

subsection (2) above shall be disregarded for the purpose only of determining the question whether he was entitled as mentioned in paragraph (a) above.

(4) In this section—

"adjudicating authority" means—

    (a) an adjudication officer or, where the original decision was given on a reference under section 21(2) or 25(1) above, a social security appeal tribunal, a disability appeal tribunal or a medical appeal tribunal;

    (b) any of the following former bodies or officers, that is to say, the National Assistance Board, the Supplementary Benefits Commission, the Attendance Allowance Board, a benefit officer, an insurance officer or a supplement officer; or

    (c) any of the officers who, or tribunals or other bodies which, in Northern Ireland correspond to those mentioned in paragraph (a) or (b) above;

"benefit" means—

    (a) benefit as defined in section 122 of the Contributions and Benefits Act; and

    (b) any income-related benefit;

"the court" means the High Court, the Court of Appeal, the Court of Session, the High Court or Court of Appeal in Northern Ireland, the House of Lords or the Court of Justice of the European Community;

"the relevant date" means whichever is the latest of—

    (a) the date of the relevant determination;

    (b) the date which falls 12 months before the date on which the claim referred to in subsection (1)(b) above is made or treated under section 7(1) above as made; and

    (c) the earliest date in respect of which the claimant would, apart from this section, be entitled on that claim to the benefit in question.

(5) For the purpose of this section—

  (a) any reference in this section to entitlement to benefit includes a reference to entitlement—

    (i) to any increase in the rate of a benefit; or

    (ii) to a benefit, or increase of benefit, at a particular rate; and

  (b) any reference to a decision which is "referable to" a claim is a reference to—

    (i) a decision on the claim,

    (ii) a decision on a review of the decision on the claim, or

    (iii) a decision on a subsequent review of the decision on the review, and so on.

(6) The date of the relevant determination shall, in prescribed cases, be determined for the purposes of this section in accordance with any regulations made for that purpose.

<small>DERIVATION</small>

Social Security Act 1975, s.165D.

<small>DEFINITIONS</small>

"the 1975 Act"—see s.191.
"Commissioner"—*ibid.*
"the Contributions and Benefits Act"—*ibid.*
"income-related benefit"—*ibid.*

See the notes to s.69 below for the general background and effect of ss. 68 and 69, and for discussion of the definitions in s.68(4).

Section 68 can only apply when a claim is actually made after the date of some Commissioner's or court decision which finds the DSS view of the law to be wrong. Then, in so far as the claim can be treated as for a period before the date of claim and the claimant would otherwise be entitled to benefit, entitlement for any period before the "relevant date" is to be determined as if the decision had gone the other way (subs. (2)). The "relevant date" is either the date of the decision or 12 months before the actual date of claim, if later (subs. (4), paras.(a) and (b) of the definition). Para. (c) of the definition merely seems to confirm what would be the case anyway.

There is a small exception in subs. (3) where payment of benefit is not in issue, but merely establishing an entitlement to a benefit at a particular age.

Determination of questions on review following erroneous decisions

69.—(1) Subsection (2) below applies in any case where—

(a) on the determination, whenever made, of a Commissioner or the court (the "relevant determination"), a decision made by an adjudicating authority is or was found to have been erroneous in point of law; and

(b) in consequence of that determination, any other decision—

    (i) which was made before the date of that determination; and

    (ii) which is referable to a claim made or treated as made by any person for any benefit,

falls (or would, apart from subsection (2) below, fall) to be revised on a review carried out under section 25(2) above on or after 13th July 1990 (the date of the passing of the Social Security Act 1990, which added to the 1975 Act sections 104(7) to (10), corresponding to this section) or on a review under section 30 above on the ground that the decision under review was erroneous in point of law.

(2) Where this subsection applies, any question arising on the review referred to in subsection (1)(b) above, or on any subsequent review of a decision which is referable to the same claim, as to any person's entitlement to, or right to payment of, any benefit—

(a) in respect of any period before the date of the relevant determination; or

(b) in the case of widow's payment, in respect of a death occurring before the date,

shall be determined as if the decision referred to in subsection (1)(a) above had been found by the Commissioner or court in question not to have been erroneous in point of law.

(3) In determining whether a person is entitled to benefit in a case where his entitlement depends on his having been entitled to the same or some other benefit before attaining a particular age, subsection (2) above shall be disregarded for the purpose only of determining the question whether he was so entitled before attaining that age.

(4) For the purposes of this section—

(a) "adjudicating authority" and "the court" have the same meaning as they have in section 68 above;

(b) any reference to—

    (i) a person's entitlement to benefit; or

    (ii) a decision which is referable to a claim, shall be constructed in accordance with subsection (5) of that section; and

(c) the date of the relevant determination shall, in prescribed cases, be determined in accordance with any regulations made under subsection (6) of that section.

Social Security Act 1975, s.104(7) to (10).

DEFINITIONS

"the 1975 Act"—see s.191.
"Commissioner"—*ibid.*

GENERAL NOTE

The predecessor of s.69 formed a package with the predecessor of s.68 on claims when they were introduced in 1990. The aim is that where an established interpretation of the law is overturned by a decision of a Social Security Commissioner or a higher court, effect can only be given to the new interpretation for other claimants on review or a fresh claim with effect from the date of that decision (the decision is referred to below as the J decision and the date as the J Day).

Background

The general rule on claims for benefit is that there can be no entitlement for a period more than 12 months before the actual date of claim, however good the cause for delay in claiming (s.1(2); 1975 Act, s.165A(2)). None of the exceptions to the general rule applies to income-related benefits. Thus if a possible entitlement is revealed by the J decision and the person has not previously claimed, that limit applies.

If the person has already had a decision on a claim and applies for a review of that decision based on the new interpretation, again there is a general limit of 12 months before the date of the request for review (Adjudication Regulations, regs. 65 and 69 to 71). However, there was until August 31, 1991, an exemption from this limit under reg. 72(1) of the Adjudication Regulations where, among other things, the decision to be reviewed was erroneous by reason of a mistake made by an adjudication officer (AO). Acting on a mistaken view of the law could obviously come within reg. 72(1) (*R(SB) 10/91* and *CIS 11/1991*), so that a revision on review triggered by the J decision could go back to the date of the original decision. Alarm about this effect led to the insertion of reg. 72(2) from September 1, 1987, which provided that reg. 72 should not apply where review was on the ground that the original decision was erroneous in law by reason of the J decision. The result was that in such cases the normal 12 month limit applied. The argument that the original decision was not erroneous by reason of the J decision, but was simply revealed to have been erroneous all along was rejected in *R(SB)11/89*.

In an investigation by the Parliamentary Commissioner for Administration (the Ombudsman) into the decision of the Secretary of State about how extensively to trawl back for past entitlements following a Commissioner's decision on the offsetting of payments of occupational pension against dependency additions to invalidity benefit, the Ombudsman raised the effect of reg. 72(2) of the Adjudication Regulations (Case No. C191/88, Fourth Report of the PCA for 1989–90). He was concerned that the longer the delay in identifying a claimant's case as requiring review the more benefit was lost, because of the absolute time limit recently reintroduced. He was not convinced that this effect was brought to Ministers' attention. In the course of responding to that point the DSS said that it would introduce a common start date for entitlement on review in such cases, but gave no indication of what sort of date would be chosen. The new provisions introduced by the Social Security Act 1990 were said to be in fulfilment of this undertaking. See H.L. Hansard, May 21, 1990, Vol. 519, cols. 684–6 (Lord Henley).

Reg. 72 of the Adjudication Regulations has been replaced with effect from August 31, 1991 by reg. 64A, which also allows the 12 month limit on review to be lifted, but uses a more restricted approach to errors of law. See the notes to that regulation.

The new provisions

The new provisions came into force on July 13, 1990. Because, as discussed below, there has been a significant change in the legislation in the Administration Act, in force from July 1, 1992, it is necessary carefully to separate the legal position before July 1, 1992, from the position after that date.

First, note that the new provisions apply where a claim is made or a review is requested after J Day. If the effect of the J decision is an issue in adjudicating on a claim or request for review made before that date, then ss.68 and 69 do not apply at all.

There are a number of important definitions. The first is of a J decision, or in the statutory words "a relevant determination." It is "a determination, whenever made, of a Commissioner or the court ... [whereby] a decision made by an adjudicating authority is or was found to have been erroneous in point of law" (s.68(1)(a) and s.69(1)(a)).

An "adjudicating authority" was originally defined to cover an AO or any of his legislative predecessors, a SSAT, a MAT, the Attendance Allowance Board, the Supplementary Benefits Commission or the National Assistance Board. The DAT was added in April 1991. However, the form of words in the 1992 Act (s.68(4)) has introduced a significant change. Tribunals are only included where the original decision was given on a reference by the AO to a SSAT under s.21(2) or 25(1). There was no condition of this kind in the pre-July 1992 legislation. The change is not covered by a Law Commission recommendation (see the Report on the consolidation of certain enactments relating to Social Security: Law Com. No. 203). Therefore, it must have been considered to come within the corrections and minor improvements which can properly be authorised by s.2 of the Consolidation of Enactments (Procedure) Act 1949. The Joint Committee on Consolidation Bills (HL Paper 23–I, HC Paper 141–I, Session 1991–2) gave their opinion that this was so (although they also considered that the Administration Act and the Contributions and Benefits Act represented "pure consolidation" of the existing law), so that presumably the new form has to be accepted. See below for some of the resulting problems.

"The court" includes everything above the Commissioner (s.68(4)). Then if any decision made before J Day falls to be revised on review carried out on or after July 13, 1990, "in consequence of that determination" (s.69(1)(b)), entitlement before J Day is to be determined as if the adjudicating authority's decision had been found not to be erroneous in point of law (s.69(2)). In addition, reg. 64B of the Adjudication Regulations requires the revised decision on review to take effect only from J Day. This important change is operative from March 9, 1992. Alternatively, if a new claim is made after J Day, entitlement before that date is to be decided on the same assumption (s.68(2)). These provisions do not seem to achieve the intended aim, and give rise to a number of problems.

The problems

The aim of the provisions is clear—a common start date for revising other claimants' entitlements when an appeal overturns the previously accepted DSS interpretation of the law. The main political argument against their introduction was that the start date was placed unacceptably and unfairly late at J Day. While reg. 72(2) of the Adjudication Regulations still existed there was only a common start date when the review took place within 12 months of J Day. For reviews which take place after reg. 64A has taken over, the 12-month limit will only be lifted if the J Decision shows that the previous interpretation involved errors of law of particular kinds (see reg. 64A(3)). But the form of the new provisions both before and after July 1, 1992, raises more fundamental problems.

The provisions have now been considered by the Court of Appeal in *Bate v. Chief Adjudication Officer and Secretary of State for Social Security, The Times,* December 12, 1994 (the appeal from *CIS 787/1991*). Before dealing with that decision some of the problems with the provisions are described. The argument on the pre-July 1992 form of the provisions is as follows. For the new rules to apply a Commissioner or higher court must have found an adjudicating authority's decision to be erroneous in point of law. Thus, if a SSAT adopts the AO's view of the law and the Commissioner holds the SSAT to have made an error of law, the new rules apply. But if a SSAT differs from the AO and the Commissioner holds that the SSAT has not made an error of law, the condition in the predecessor of s.68(1)(a) and s.69(1)(a) is not met. The Commissioner's jurisdiction is only to determine whether the SSAT has made an error of law. Although the reasons for his determination may include an indication that the AO's decision was erroneous in point of law, this is not something which is "found" "on the determination". The words "erroneous in point of law" are precisely those used in describing the Commissioner's powers on an appeal from a SSAT (see s.23(7)). A similar point can be made if the AO's view is accepted by the SSAT and the Commissioner, but the Court of Appeal finds the Commissioner to have been in error of law. The Commissioner is not within the definition of "adjudicating authority." The Court of Appeal will not have "found" an adjudicating authority's decision to be erroneous in point of law and the new rules do not apply.

On this view, there might seem to be no point in the inclusion of the AO in the definition of "adjudicating authority," for there is no way in which a Commissioner or court within the normal appeal structure can "find" an AO's decision to be erroneous in point of law. However, even after the House of Lords' decision in *Foster v. Chief Adjudication Officer* [1993] A.C. 754, [1993] 1 All E.R. 705, an AO's decision may be taken directly to a court in an application for judicial review. It is therefore arguable that if the Divisional Court or some other court decides that a regulation relied on by an AO is *ultra vires*, this involves finding that the AO's decision was erroneous in point of law.

If this general argument is correct, the pre-July 1992 rules applied capriciously, depending on the precise history of the appeal before the J decision. This view was not shared by the DSS. The contrary view is that "found" does not have any technical meaning, so that if a Commissioner or a court takes a different view of the law to that taken by an AO, this amounts to finding the decision made by the AO to be erroneous in point of law. However, there remains considerable scope for argument that the new rules do not apply in the circumstances identified above. It may be that the change in the legislation from July 1, 1992, was an attempt to "clarify" the law, but it can be argued that since a consolidating Act can only make corrections and minor improvements the "clarification" cannot affect the proper interpretation of the legislation as it stood before July 1, 1992.

The form of the definition of "adjudicating authority" in force with effect from July 1, 1992 (s.68(4), applied in s.69(4)(a)) adds even further difficulties. It appears to exclude SSATs, DATs and MATs except where the original decision was given on a reference under s.21(2) or s.25(2). Under these provisions, an AO need not make a decision on a claim or an application for review, but may refer the claim or application to a SSAT for decision. The SSAT then makes the original decision on the claim or review. Thus a SSAT deciding an appeal is not an adjudicating authority. In the case of DATs or MATs the original decision cannot have been given on a reference under either of those provisions, which only apply to SSATs. Since the condition seems to govern SSATs, DATs and MATs, this has the effect of excluding DATs and MATs from the definition entirely. If tribunals are excluded from the definition except in the case where the SSAT makes an original decision on a reference, the argument put forward above about the pre-July 1992 law would mean that no Commissioner or court decision which put forward a different interpretation of the law from that adopted by an AO in an original decision could "find" a decision of an adjudicating authority erroneous in point of law, whether it upheld the view of a SSAT or not. This would give ss.68 and 69 such a very narrow application, that it must bolster the contrary argument mentioned above, on the basis that otherwise there would be little point in having ss.68 and 69. If the change does have this effect, and the argument made above about the pre-July 1992 law is right, the change seems to go well beyond a correction or minor improvement. However, in the context of a restriction on claimants' entitlements in a highly technical area, the argument for giving the actual words of the legislation their strictly logical meaning or that they have no effective meaning is a strong one.

There are also difficulties on some other issues. If the new rules apply, the decision of the relevant adjudicating authority is to be assumed not to have been erroneous in point of law. What if the AO decides according to the accepted DSS interpretation, the SSAT reaches the same result but for peculiar and different reasons and the Commissioner decides that a third approach is correct? It appears, pre-July 1, 1992, to be the SSAT decision which must be assumed not to be erroneous in law, thus incorporating its reasons rather than the DSS interpretation. Similarly, if the SSAT decision is erroneous in several respects, only one of which is the matter which would trigger the review, it appears that all the errors must be assumed not to be errors. On the basis of the Commissioner's decision in *CIS 787/1991* (see below), it is the AO's decision which is assumed to be correct. However, reg. 64B of the Adjudication Regulations may have rendered these arguments academic from March 9, 1992.

There is a link to the problem of identifying which of a series of decisions ought to count as the J decision. The question is which decision is it in consequence of which decisions on other claimants' claims fall to be revised on review as erroneous in point of law. AOs commonly do not carry out such reviews if a single Commissioner's decision goes against the DSS view, especially if an appeal is being taken to the Court of Appeal. If the Court of Appeal then confirms the Commissioner's decision, the J Day ought to be the date of the Commissioner's decision. But if there are a series of equally authoritative decisions which one establishes the J Day? It ought to be the earliest one. If the decision which therefore is to be reviewed and revised as erroneous in point of law was made after this J Day, the review based on the effect of the J decision is free of the new rules. The condition in subs. (1)(b)(i) is not met.

Finally, the new provisions may well be ineffective in relation to rulings on the effect of European Community law by the European Court of Justice (see the definition of "court" in s.68(4)) and by British courts. For the British legislature to remove a person's entitlement based on such a ruling would be a breach of the obligation in EC law to provide an adequate remedy. See *Von Colson* [1984] E.C.R. 1891. In *Johnson v. Chief Adjudication Officer* (ECJ C-410/92, judgment delivered on December 6, 1994), the ECJ held that the 12 month limit on arrears of benefit (now in s.1(2); reg. 19(4) Claims and Payments Regulations) could be applied even where a claim was based on the direct effect of EC Directive 79/7 (equal treatment for men and women in matters of social security) and the Directive had not been properly transposed into United Kingdom law within the prescribed period. However, it is difficult to reconcile this judgment with that of the ECJ in *Emmott v. Minister for Social Welfare* [1991] E.C.R. 1-4569, where the ECJ had disapplied a national rule on the limitation period for instituting judicial review proceedings. Although the ECJ drew a distinction between time limits on bringing proceedings at all and time limits on payments of arrears, what was at stake in *Emmott* and *Johnson* was in fact the same – payment of benefit for a past period. It is suggested that s.69 would seem to fall on the *Emmott* side of the line rather than the *Johnson* side, since the efect of s.69 may be the denial of any benefit (or virtually any benefit), particularly if amending regulations are speedily introduced.

The "Bate" case

The Commissioner in the *"Bate"* case (*CIS 787/1991*) recognised many of the problems described in the first five paragraphs above. But the conclusion he drew from the otherwise restricted scope of the provisions was that "found" was used in a very broad sense to include a case where a Commissioner or a court took a different view of the law from the AO. He reached this conclusion without considering the changes in the Administration Act, but noted that his approach would mean that the pre and post July 1992 positions were consistent. It would also prevent many, although not all, inconsistencies in the application of the provisions.

The Court of Appeal in *Bate v. Chief Adjudication Officer and the Secretary of State for Social Security, The Times*, December 12, 1994, does not deal with the arguments based on the significance of the word "found", but bases its judgment on a different point. The Court decides that s.69(1) and (2) is directed solely to the AO, or, on a reference under s.21(2) or s.25(1), the SSAT, conducting the review. The assumption required by subs. (2) does not have to be made by the Commissioner or the appellate courts because before them the question does not "arise on the review" but on an appeal from a refusal to entertain a review. Millett L.J. points out that subs. (2) does not say that the question arising on the review has to be determined as if the decision of the AO in the earlier case had been correct in law, which would give that decision statutory force, but only that it is to be determined as if the Commissioner had found it to be correct in law, which gives it the status of a decision of a Commissioner but no more. Subs. (2) did not "purport to change the law, but rather to rewrite history". What decision the Commissioner actually made did not affect the Court of Appeal, or strictly speaking, the Commissioner who was not obliged to follow his own decisions. Further, the definition of "the court" in s.68(4) (applied to s.69 by subs.(4)(a)) did not include the Commissioner. If subs. (2) was directed to the Commissioner and the Court of Appeal, this would mean that the outcome of the claimant's appeal depended on the Commissioner's decision in the earlier case not being appealed to and upheld by the Court of Appeal, since if it had been, the Court would be bound by a previous decision of its own which it would be required to assume had been to the opposite effect.

The result of the Court's judgment is that, although an AO has to apply the assumption in subs. (2), a Commissioner or a court hearing an appeal from its application is free, and thus obliged, to reconsider the substantive issue. For the position of SSATs see below.

This remarkable decision emasculates the anti-test case rule since, as Millett L.J. acknowledges, it means that the only effect of the rule is to delay payment of benefit arrears until an appellate level is reached. Once an application for review reaches an appellate level, reg. 64A(3) of the Adjudication Regulations would seem to disapply the normal 12 month limit on arrears in reg. 69 in this situation (see the notes to reg. 64A(3)). Unsurprisingly the CAO and the Secretary of State have been granted leave to appeal to the House of Lords, but this appeal will not be heard for some months. In the meantime the position of SSATs is not entirely clear. The Court of Appeal's judgment only specifically refers to SSATs in the context of their making the original decision on the claim when a reference has been made by an AO; it does not deal with the position when SSATs are performing their more normal function of hearing appeals against AOs' decisions. Much of the Court of Appeal's reasoning suggests that SSATs are not bound by the assumption in subs. (2) either, because they hear appeals from the AO's application of the rule. On the other hand, Millett L.J.'s reference to applications for review under s.25(2) "[beginning], in effect, at an appellate level for which leave is required", could indicate otherwise.

Another issue is whether the effect of s.69(1) and (2) in relation to the period before the J day is that there is to be no review, or a review but no revision, of decisions on other claimants' entitlement. The Court of Appeal in *Bate* seems (at least in places) to take the former view, although the point is not dealt with explicitly. In *Chief Adjudication Officer v. Eggleton and Others*, (March 17, 1995) the Court of Appeal found on the evidence that no reviews had been carried out where s.69 had been applied to the period at issue. Stuart-Smith L.J. did not consider that an AO "has to go through the farcical process of actually conducting a review and then deciding that he cannot revise the decision because of s.104(7) and (8) [s.69(1) and (2)]. He may equally well refuse to review the decision at all". That case also decides that the extent of the revision on review determines how much of the original decision remains in existence. See the notes to s.25. Note also the effect of reg. 64B of the Adjudication Regulations.

Correction of errors

Regulations as to correction of errors and setting aside of decisions

70.—(1) Regulations may make provision with respect to—

(a) the correction of accidental errors in any decision or record of a decision given with respect to a claim or question arising under or in connection with any relevant enactment by a body or person authorised to decide the claim or question; and

(b) the setting aside of any such decision in a case where it appears just to set the decision aside on the ground that—

   (i) a document relating to the proceedings in which the decision was given was not sent to, or was not received at an appropriate time by, a party to the proceedings or a party's representative or was not received at an appropriate time by the body or person who gave the decision; or

   (ii) a party to the proceedings or a party's representative was not present at a hearing related to the proceedings.

(2) Nothing in subsection (1) above shall be construed as derogating from any power to correct errors or set aside decisions which is exercisable apart from regulations made by virtue of that subsection.

(3) In this section "relevant enactment" means any enactment contained in—

(a) the National Insurance Acts 1965 to 1974;

(b) the National Insurance (Industrial Injuries) Acts 1965 to 1974;

(c) the Industrial Injuries and Diseases (Old Cases) Acts 1967 to 1974;

(d) the Social Security Act 1973;

(e) the Social Security Acts 1975 to 1991;

(f) the Old Cases Act;

(g) the Child Benefit Act 1975;

(h) the Family Income Supplements Act 1970;

(i) the Supplementary Benefits Act 1976; or

(j) the Contributions and Benefits Act.

DERIVATION

National Insurance Act 1974, s.6(1) and (3).

DEFINITIONS

"the Contributions and Benefits Act"—see s.191.
"the Old Cases Act"—*ibid.*

GENERAL NOTE

See regs. 10 to 12 of the Adjudication Regulations. The form of subs. (1)(b), which reproduces the earlier legislation, only authorises reg. 11(a) and (b). Reg. 11(c) is made under para. 2 of Sched. 3 (*R(U) 3/89*).

PART III

OVERPAYMENTS AND ADJUSTMENTS OF BENEFIT

Misrepresentation, etc.

Overpayments—general

71.—(1) Where it is determined that, whether fraudulently or otherwise, any person has misrepresented, or failed to disclose, any material fact and in consequence of the misrepresentation or failure—

(a) a payment has been made in respect of a benefit to which this section applies; or

(b) any sum recoverable by or on behalf of the Secretary of State in connection with any such payment has not been recovered,

the Secretary of State shall be entitled to recover the amount of any payment which he would not have made or any sum which he would have received but for the misrepresentation or failure to disclose.

(2) Where any such determination as is referred to in subsection (1) above is made on an appeal or review, there shall also be determined in the course of the appeal or review the question whether any, and if so what, amount is recoverable under that subsection by the Secretary of State.

(3) An amount recoverable under subsection (1) above is in all cases recoverable from the person who misrepresented the fact or failed to disclose it.

(4) In relation to cases where payments of a benefit to which this section applies have been credited to a bank account or other account under arrangements made with the agreement of the beneficiary or a person acting for him, circumstances may be prescribed in which the Secretary of State is to be entitled to recover any amount paid in excess of entitlement; but any such regulations shall not apply in relation to any payment unless before he agreed to the arrangements such notice of the effect of the regulations as may be prescribed was given in such manner as may be prescribed to the beneficiary or to a person acting for him.

(5) Except where regulations otherwise prescribe, an amount shall not be recoverable under subsection (1) above or regulations under subsection (4) above unless—

(a) the determination in pursuance of which it was paid has been reversed or varied on an appeal or revised on a review; and

(b) it has been determined on the appeal or review that the amount is so recoverable.

(6) Regulations may provide—

(a) that amounts recoverable under subsection (1) above or regulations under subsection (4) above shall be calculated or estimated in such manner or on such basis as may be prescribed;

(b) for treating any amount paid to any person under an award which is subsequently determined was not payable—

(i) as properly paid; or

(ii) as paid on account of a payment which it is determined should be or should have been made, and for reducing or withholding any arrears payable by virtue of the subsequent determination;

(c) for treating any amount paid to one person in respect of another as properly paid for any period for which it is not payable in cases where in consequence of a subsequent determination—

(i) the other person is himself entitled to a payment for that period; or

(ii) a third person is entitled in priority to the payee to a payment for that period in respect of the other person,

and for reducing or withholding any arrears payable for that period by virtue of the subsequent determination.

(7) Circumstances may be prescribed in which a payment on account made by virtue of section 5(1)(r) above may be recovered to the extent that it exceeds entitlement.

(8) Where any amount paid is recoverable under—

(a) subsection (1) above;

(b) regulations under subsection (4) or (7) above; or

(c) section 74 below.

it may, without prejudice to any other method of recovery, be recovered by deduction from prescribed benefits.

(9) Where any amount paid in respect of a married or unmarried couple is recoverable as mentioned in subsection (8) above, it may, without prejudice to

any other method of recovery, be recovered, in such circumstances as may be prescribed, by deduction from prescribed benefits payable to either of them.

(10) Any amount recoverable under the provisions mentioned in subsection (8) above—

(a) if the person from whom it is recoverable resides in England and Wales and the county court so orders, shall be recoverable by execution issued from the county court or otherwise as if it were payable under an order of that court; and

(b) if he resides in Scotland, shall be enforced in like manner as an extract registered decree arbitral bearing a warrant for execution issued by the sheriff court of any sheriffdom in Scotland.

(11) This section applies to the following benefits—

(a) benefits as defined in section 122 of the Contributions and Benefits Act;

(b) subject to section 72 below, income support;

(c) family credit:

(d) disability working allowance;

(e) any social fund payments such as are mentioned in section 138(1)(a) or (2) of the Contributions and Benefits Act; and

(f) child benefit.

DERIVATION

Social Security Act 1986, s.53.

DEFINITIONS

"the Contributions and Benefits Act"—see s.191.
"married couple"—see Contributions and Benefits Act, s.137.
"prescribed"—see s.191.
"unmarried couple"—see Contributions and Benefits Act, s.137.

GENERAL NOTE

The predecessor of s.71 (s.53 of the 1986 Act) was intended to produce a common rule on overpayments across all social security benefits. Since the new rule was based on the old supplementary benefit rule (Supplementary Benefits Act 1976, s.20), many of the existing principles developed in Commissioners' decisions will continue to be relevant.

In *Plewa v. Chief Adjudication Officer* [1995] A.C. 249, [1994] 3 All E.R. 323, the question was whether s. 53 had retrospective effect, so as to apply to all determinations of overpayments as part of reviews carried out on or after April 6, 1987 (when the section came into force), regardless of when the overpayment occurred. The Court of Appeal in *Secretary of State for Social Security v. Tunnicliffe* [1991] 2 All E.R. 712 had held that it did (see the 1994 edition for details of this decision). Section 53 replaced s. 119 of the Social Security Act 1975 (which applied to overpayments of non-means tested benefits) and s. 20 of the 1976 Act. Although the requirements of s. 53 and s. 20 were very similar, there were substantial differences from s. 119. It was pointed out to the House of Lords in *Plewa* that under s. 53 third parties who misrepresented or failed to disclose a material fact (however innocently) could be required to make a repayment, even though they personally never received any benefit, whereas this was not possible in the case of s. 119 (although it was under s. 20). This point had not been put to the Court of Appeal in *Tunnicliffe*. Lord Woolf, who delivered the main judgment in *Plewa*, considered that it might have materially affected the Court's decision if it had. He accepted that s. 53 was therefore "creating an entirely new obligation" to which the common law presumption against statutes having retrospective effect (see Lord Brightman in *Yew Bon Tew v. Kenderaan Bas Mara* [1983] 1 A.C. 553 at p. 558) applied "with full effect". In addition, Lord Woolf would have given more weight than the Court of Appeal did in *Tunnicliffe* to the possible unfairness to claimants if s. 53 had retrospective effect, because of the removal of the defence of due care and diligence. He also held that although there was no transitional provision, this did not mean that some overpayments would be irrecoverable. The effect of s. 16 of the Interpretation Act 1978 was to enable the Secretary of State still to recover under s. 119 or s. 20 if prior to April 6, 1987 a claimant would have been liable to repay under those sections.

This judgment will obviously have most impact on the recovery of overpayments of non-means tested benefits made before April 6, 1987 because of the differences between the test in s. 119 and

s. 53. The test in s. 20 was very similar to that in s. 53 (although there was no equivalent of what is now s. 71(5)). However, a SSAT dealing with any overpayment of supplementary benefit which occurred before April 6, 1987 must apply s. 20 to that payment. In addition, it must apply s. 20 to any part of the overpayment occurring after April 5, 1987 that was a consequence of a misrepresentation or failure to disclose a material fact made before that date (see Lord Woolf's summary of the effect of the judgment in *Plewa* at [1995] A.C. 260.) Section 53 (now s. 71) only applies where both the overpayment occurred, and the misrepresentation or failure to disclose was made, on or after April 6, 1987 (*CIS 332/1993*).

It does not matter how far back the overpayments occurred. The time limits of the Limitation Act 1980 have no application to proceedings before the adjudicating authorities and do not start to run until there has been a determination under s.71 or one of its predecessors giving the Secretary of State the right of recovery (*R(SB) 5/91, R(A) 2/86* and *CIS 26/1994*).

The question of recovery itself lies solely within the jurisdiction of the Secretary of State (*R(SB) 5/91*). A SSAT cannot stipulate in its decision that recovery is not to be carried out, although if it finds there are mitigating circumstances, it could request the Secretary of State to consider not pursuing recovery. However in *CSIS 37/1994*, by the time the claimant's appeal reached the Commissioner, the Compensation Recovery Unit had already effected recovery from his damages award of any benefit that might have been overpaid to the claimant. In view of the law's general prohibition against double recovery, the Commissioner directs the new SSAT to indicate, if they did find that there had been a recoverable overpayment, that the Secretary of State had no further right of recovery against the claimant.

Subsection (1)

This expresses the general rule on recovery of overpayments. There is no provision for the recovery of administrative costs, and if payments are made which go beyond what has been awarded by an AO recovery is a matter for the civil law (see *CSB 830/1985* on the old s.20).

Before considering the main elements of the rule, note the important condition imposed by subss. (2) and (5) that an overpayment determination can only be made in the course of a review of the decision awarding benefit (or an appeal from that decision). A SSAT must be satisfied that a valid review and revision has taken place before considering the rest of s.71. This can be overlooked, which causes great difficulties. See the notes to subs. (5) for further details.

For the right of recovery to exist, a person must have misrepresented or failed to disclose a material fact. Then it must be shown that a payment of benefit, or non-recovery, was a consequence of the misrepresentation or failure to disclose. Finally the amount recoverable must be determined. *R(SB) 2/92* decides that the words "whether fraudulently or otherwise" do not impose any further condition of there having been some kind of dishonesty. This decision was upheld by the Court of Appeal in *Page v. Chief Adjudication Officer* (*The Times*, July 4, 1991, and appendix to *R(SB) 2/92*). The Court of Appeal holds that the plain meaning of the words is "whether fraudulently or not."

It was clearly established under the old s.20 that the burden of proof of all issues lay on the AO (*R(SB) 34/83*). The same will apply to s.71. It was also established that if an initial decision is based on a failure to disclose (or misrepresentation), it is open to a SSAT to base its decision on misrepresentation (or failure to disclose), provided that the claimant has had a fair opportunity of dealing with that new point (*R(SB) 40/84*).

AOs' submissions to SSATS in overpayment cases frequently quote the six tests propounded in *R(SB) 54/83* for recovery on the ground of failure to disclose: (i) failure to disclose (ii) where disclosure could reasonably be expected (iii) of a material fact (iv) by a person who knew that fact (v) as a consequence of which expenditure was incurred (vi) by the Secretary of State who seeks to recover it. In *CSIS 51/1994* the Commissioner states that it is not necessary for a tribunal to expressly deal with all 6 tests in every case. Where there was, for example, no doubt as to the claimant's knowledge of the material fact (the claimant's contention was that *he* had informed the DSS of the changes in his mortgage interest rate), the tribunal's failure to make an express finding on that point did not vitiate their decision. The six tests were of great assistance in identifying the salient points that arose in any case, but they should be applied intelligently by AOs and SSATS.

Material fact

Section 71 only applies where there has been a misrepresentation of or a failure to disclose a material fact. There is often a concentration on the circumstances of a failure to disclose or a misrepresentation and the significance of whether something is a material fact or not is forgotten. There are three main limitations imposed.

First, matters of law are not covered. It is established for purposes of review that a mistake of law is not a mistake of material fact (*R(G) 18/52*). Entitlement to benefit is a conclusion of law based on findings of fact. This has now been expressly stated by Evans L.J. in *Jones and Sharples v. Chief Adjudication Officer* [1994] 1 All E.R. 225. He holds that the representation "I am entitled to the above sum" at the end of the standard order book declaration is one of law, not fact, and so cannot ground recovery under s.53 (now s.71). The other two judges (Stuart-Smith L.J. and Dillon L.J.) did not have to deal with this question in view of their interpretation of the second part of this declaration (see below). Thus Evans L.J.'s conclusion that a representation of entitlement to benefit is one of law is the most authoritative statement so far on the point, and SSATs should draw a distinction between matters of material fact and law. *CS 102/1993* has now expressly decided that "I am entitled to the above sum" in this context is a representation of law.

Secondly, in the context of the powers to review contained in s.25(1), the Commissioners have drawn a distinction between material facts and conclusions of fact, or inferences from primary fact (*R(I) 3/75, R(A) 2/81* and *R(S) 4/86*, discussed in the note to s.25). The same principle should apply here, so that only misrepresentations or failures to disclose primary facts can found recovery under s.71. So a representation that the claimant was incapable of work would not be enough in itself, unless it contained by necessary implication a representation that the claimant's underlying condition had not changed.

The third requirement is that the fact in issue is a *material* fact. In the context of review, the Court of Appeal in *Saker v. Secretary of State for Social Services (R(I) 2/88)* has decided that for a fact to be material it is not necessary that knowledge of it would have altered the decision. It is enough that the fact is one which would have called for serious consideration by the authority which made the decision and which might well have affected the decision. No doubt the same interpretation should be given to "material fact" here, as was effectively done in *CSB 1006/1985*, but since it is only benefit which would not have been paid but for the misrepresentation or failure to disclose which can be recovered under s.71, it is necessary that knowledge of the material fact would have altered the decision awarding benefit. In *R(SB) 2/91* a student was alleged to have failed to disclose that his course was full-time. The Commissioner held that since a student's own opinion of whether the course was full-time was irrelevant (the objective classification of the course being the issue) disclosure was not reasonably to be expected. Although the Commissioner does not expressly say that the student's opinion was not a material fact, the points he makes about the relevant information having to be gathered from the institution at which the claimant was studying lead inevitably to that conclusion.

There is, however, an extra complication in s.71 cases. When considering review, only facts material to the question of entitlement are relevant. Under s.71 it may be that facts relevant to the payment of benefit are also relevant. So if a claimant wrongly declares that he has correctly reported any fact which could affect the amount of his payment, this does not seem to be a misrepresentation of a material fact in the review sense. But following the Court of Appeal's decision in *Jones and Sharples v. Chief Adjudication Officer* [1994] 1 All E.R. 225 there will have been a misrepresentation of a material fact for the purposes of s.71. See below under *Misrepresentation*.

Misrepresentation

The meaning of misrepresentation is fairly clear. It requires an actual statement to have been made which is untrue (*CSB 1006/1985*). The statement of material fact may be oral or written, or in some circumstances may arise from conduct, *e.g.* cashing a giro-cheque. But in this last case there must be some positive conduct from which a statement can be implied, rather than a failure to act. An example where this principle worked in the claimant's favour is *R(SB) 18/85*. The claimant had signed a statement of his resources which omitted his Army pension, but he had produced his pension book to the officer who had filled in the form. The Commissioner holds that the circumstances surrounding the completion of a form must be looked at in deciding what has been represented. If the claimant had qualified the written form by saying that the Army pension should be taken into account, the writing could only be taken into account subject to that qualification. The same result would follow if he had indicated by his actions (*e.g.* producing the pension book) that the pension should be taken into account.

In *CS 102/1993* notification of an AO's review decision that he was no longer entitled to invalidity benefit was sent to the claimant on March 13, 1992 and he was asked to return his order book. The claimant cashed the order for 11 to 17 March on March 17 and the DSS received the order book on March 18. The AO decided that the claimant had been overpaid £72.12p, which was recoverable on the grounds of misrepresentation. The Commissioner holds that the representation "I am entitled to the above sum" at the end of the standard order book declaration is one of law. However, by his conduct in signing the order book, a claimant could make a representation of fact that he believed that there was a current award in his favour (see *CSB 249/89*). Following *Jones* (see below) there would be a misrepresentation of fact if he did not believe this. The Commissioner also holds that even though the payment was made after the award had been reviewed it was still a payment "in

697

respect of a benefit'' for the purposes of s. 53(1)(a) (now s. 71(1)(a)). Further, although it had not been determined on the review that the amount was recoverable (because at the time the invalidity benefit was reviewed there had been no overpayment) and so s. 53(4)(b) (now s. 71(5)(b)) had not been complied with, the Commissioner finds that this was a case where reg. 12 of the Payments Regulations could apply. The circumstances of the overpayment did not provide a basis for a further review and revision of the invalidity benefit award and so reg. 12 applied.

Even where there is a straightforward written statement its precise terms must be considered. In *CSB 1006/1985* the declaration on the B1 form (since changed) signed by the claimant was ''as far as I know the information on this form is true and complete.'' Although a capital resource was omitted from the form, there was no misrepresentation because the claimant honestly believed that the resource was not available to him. The same declaration had been signed by Mr Sharples in *Jones and Sharples v. Chief Adjudication Officer* [1994] 1 All E.R. 225. On his claim form for supplementary benefit Mr Sharples had ticked the ''No'' box in answer to the question about whether any member of the assessment unit had any life insurance or endowment policies. Unknown to him his partner had inherited a number of policies, of sufficient value that there was no entitlement to supplementary benefit. The Court of Appeal unanimously holds that the signed declaration qualified the answers on the rest of the B1 form and there had been no misrepresentation. This decision will apply to other forms where there is a general declaration at the end. But everything will depend on the drafting of the particular form and the wording of the particular declaration.

The declaration at issue in Mr Jones's case was that signed by him when cashing his income support order book. It was the standard order book declaration which reads ''I declare that I have read and understand all the instructions in this order book, that I have correctly reported any facts which could affect the amount of my payment and that I am entitled to the above sum''. An overpayment had occurred because, due to the proper procedure not being followed, Mr Jones's income support had not taken account of his receipt of unemployment benefit. Mr Jones had stated when claiming income support that he had applied for unemployment benefit, but he did not report its subsequent award. Recovery was sought on the ground of misrepresentation. Evans L.J., dissenting, accepts the submission made on behalf of Mr Jones that the declaration in the order book contained no representation as to any material fact. A material fact for the purposes of s.53 (now s.71) is one relevant to the calculation of benefit. Whether or not Mr Jones had *reported* material facts was not itself a material fact. His declaration did not make any statement or misrepresentation as to the material facts themselves. The representation ''I am entitled to the above sum'' was one of law, not fact. Mr Jones's appeal was, however, dismissed by the majority of the Court of Appeal. Stuart-Smith L.J. holds that the statement that ''I have correctly reported any facts which could affect the amount of my benefit'' was a statement of a material fact because unless the statement was true Mr Jones was not entitled to the amount of benefit received. Therefore there was a misrepresentation of a material fact within s.53 (now s.71). Dillon L.J. simply holds that since the declaration was incorrect, the overpayment was recoverable. But the reasoning of the majority is deficient and does not answer Evans L.J.'s cogent analysis. What leads to non-entitlement is the existence of the facts which affect the amount of benefit, not whether those facts have been disclosed or not. Nevertheless, the majority's approach has to be applied by SSATs and Commissioners.

It must be noted, however, that Stuart-Smith L.J. and Dillon L.J. qualified the declaration by implying the words ''known to me'' after ''correctly reported any facts''. Dillon L.J. stated that the ''representation must be limited, as a matter both of common sense and law, to a representation that [the claimant] has disclosed or reported all material facts known to him, since he cannot sensibly be expected to represent that he has disclosed all material facts that are not known to him''. Dillon L.J. concluded reluctantly that it could not be further limited to disclosure of facts that could reasonably be expected. (*CSB 790/1988*, which decided to the contrary, should therefore not be followed.) The claimant does not have to know that the fact is material (*CIS 695/1992*). Thus, signing the standard order book declaration will only amount to a misrepresentation if all the material facts known to the claimant have not been disclosed. Therefore, the AO will have to show that the claimant did know the fact, that it was a material fact, and not, for example, an inference from primary facts (see under *Material Fact* above) and that it has not been disclosed.

In *CP 34/1993*, however, the Commissioner holds that the claimant's knowledge of the material fact when signing the standard order book declaration is irrelevant. In his view the statements of Stuart-Smith L.J. and Dillon L.J. in *Jones* were *obiter* (*i.e.* not necessary to the decision) and ran contrary to authority that knowledge is not material as far as innocent misrepresentation is concerned (see, for example, *Page v. CAO* above). He therefore declined to follow them. But, as is stated in *CIS 695/1992*, the Court of Appeal's approach in *Jones* is not in conflict with *Page*. What the Court of Appeal was referring to in *Jones* was not the nature of misrepresentation, but the nature of the declaration at issue. The majority's statements in *Jones* were concerned with what exactly the alleged misrepresentation consisted of, rather than whether, once a misrepresentation had been established, the claimant's innocence was of any relevance. Moreover, although technically *obiter*, the majority's statements in *Jones* do seem central to their decision.

There have been other cases where the unqualified nature of a declaration has worked against the claimant, for example, *R(SB) 9/86*. There the claimant regularly signed declarations that his circumstances had not changed although (unknown to him) his wife's earnings had gone up. The Commissioner says that the claimant should have added something like "not to my knowledge" to his declaration. This may not be necessary to avoid recovery in the future if words such as those implied by the Court of Appeal in *Jones* were also held to qualify other similar declarations. However, it will all depend on the wording of the declaration. In *Jones* the Court of Appeal accepted that a claimant could only report the facts known to him. This may not be applicable in relation to other declarations, for example, if the claimant signs a declaration that the answers on the form are correct and complete. It is not known what would happen if a claimant tried adding to, or crossing out some of, a declaration on an order book or form.

R(SB) 9/85 illustrates that a wholly innocent misrepresentation may trigger recovery. The section applies whether the person acts "fraudulently or otherwise" (see *Page v. Chief Adjudication Officer*, above). In *R(SB) 9/85* the rule that the absence of knowledge of the facts which make the statement untrue is irrelevant is justified on the ground that misrepresentation is based on positive and deliberate action. Similarly, the reasonableness of any belief that a fact was not material is irrelevant *(R(SB) 18/85)*. In *R(SB) 3/90* it is suggested that a future case might have to determine whether mental incapacity could prevent there being a misrepresentation at all. On the facts, where the claimant was at the crucial time recovering from a nervous breakdown and treatment including ECT and drugs, there was a misrepresentation, but it was wholly innocent. Subsequent cases have accepted that mental incapacity could prevent there being a misrepresentation. In *CSB 1093/1989* the Commissioner applied the common law principles relating to *non est factum*, a defence that a document signed by a person was not his deed, and suggests that the necessary degree of understanding required to say that the person's mind went with his pen varies according to the nature of the transaction involved. In the social security context, if a claimant has signed a benefit order, the question would be whether he appreciates that the document was a benefit order which was to be cashed. This confines the effect of mental incapacity within quite narrow limits. Expert medical evidence of the claimant's mental capacity at the time would be particularly relevant. In *CIS 545/ 1992* the Commissioner's approach was broader. He rejected the argument that the doctrine of *non est factum* was relevant, since it could only apply in a contractual context and a claim for benefit was not a contract. However, he held that as the claimant lacked the power of reasoning necessary for her to be negligent in the legal sense she was mentally incapable of making a misrepresentation. The Commissioner went on to state that in the case of a claimant who was subject to an order of the Court of Protection there should be a presumption that he or she was personally incapable of making any valid representation with regard to entitlement to benefit, and that a heavy onus would rest upon anyone seeking to rebut that presumption. The decision contains a useful discussion of the effect of Court of Protection orders. The Commissioner points out that the Court has extensive and exclusive powers over all aspects of a person's property and affairs, which, until a receiver is appointed, are exercised by the Court. Thus, until he was appointed receiver the claimant's son had no legal responsibilities *vis-á-vis* his mother, and indeed, no right to take any action on her behalf. After his appointment the son had disclosed the claimant's capital when he became aware of the need to do so and therefore no liability attached to him. The CAO appealed against this decision to the Court of Appeal, which in *Chief Adjudication Officer v. Sherriff, The Times*, May 10, 1995, allowed the appeal. The Court rejected the argument that the claimant had to know that a representation was being made, since if she had the capacity to make a claim, she had the capacity to make a representation. Although the nursing home had filled in the claim form on the claimant's behalf, she had signed the form herself. She had thus made any representations it contained her own. If the claimant was mentally incapable of understanding that she was making a representation, she also lacked the necessary mental capacity to make a claim. If that had been the case, since it was a necessary condition of entitlement to benefit that a valid claim had been made, the income support that had been paid would be recoverable not under s. 53(1) (now subs. (1)) but on the ordinary principles of restitution. In *Sherriff* the Court of Appeal viewed the claim and the misrepresentation as indivisible and considered that the question of whether the claimant was capable of making a representation was answered by whether she had the capacity to make a claim. But what if the representation is not made on the claim form but elsewhere?

See also *CSB 218/1991* where the Commissioner holds that a claimant who was senile and did not understand her actions, but for whom no representative had been appointed for benefit purposes could not escape the consequences of the misrepresentation that she had made on the claim form.

Note also *CIS 222/1991* under *"Causation"* below.

Failure to disclose

A failure to disclose is a much more troublesome concept, and there is a good deal of confusing case-law. An essential background is that reg. 32 of the Claims and Payments Regulations imposes a duty on claimants entitled to benefit to notify the Secretary of State in writing of any change of circumstance specified in the notice of determination or order book or any other change which the person might reasonably be expected to know might affect the right to benefit. However, there is not a straightforward link with s.71. For example, recovery may be pursued against any person who fails to disclose or misrepresents a material fact (see, *e.g. R(SB) 21/82* (spouse) and *R(SB) 28/83* (receiver of a mentally infirm person's estate)). Such persons may not be covered by reg. 32. Secondly, the right of recovery only arises under the conditions of s.71. If an order book required a claimant to notify the Secretary of State of a fact which was not material, a failure to do so would not trigger s.71. See above for what amounts to a material fact. Although reg. 32 requires notification in writing it has long been settled that an oral disclosure is as effective as one in writing for the purposes of s.71 (*CSB 688/1982* and *R(SB) 40/84*).

What does disclosure mean? In *R(SB) 15/87* a Tribunal of Commissioners holds, adopting an opinion in an Australian case, that it is a statement of a fact so as to reveal that which so far as the discloser knows was previously unknown to the person to whom the statement is made. This is in line with the ordinary everyday meaning of "disclose." Once disclosure has been made to a particular person there can be no question of there being an obligation to repeat that disclosure to the same person. The question of to whom disclosure is to be made is considered below.

The Act uses the words "fails to disclose," not "does not disclose." Therefore it is necessary to consider what amounts to such a failure. In *CSB 53/1981* (a decision of a Tribunal of Commissioners, but not reported) the statement of Diplock J. in *R.* v. *Medical Appeal Tribunal (North Midland Region), ex p. Hubble* [1958] 2 Q. B. 228, 242, was applied to the old section 20. "'Non-disclosure' in the context of the subsection, where it is coupled with misrepresentation, means a failure to disclose a fact known to the person who does not disclose it ... It is innocent if the person failing to disclose the fact does not appreciate its materiality, fraudulent if he does." In *CSB 53/1981*, the claimant had either overlooked or failed to appreciate the relevance of £1000 of premium bonds, so was innocent, but had still failed to disclose. This approach gives the impression that if a fact is material and is known to the person, no other factors are relevant. It is certainly the case that knowledge of the fact is an essential requirement. Where the person is the owner of an asset and has once known of its existence, he will normally be fixed with that knowledge even if he later forgets about it (*R(SB) 21/82*, para. 20(4)). However, in some cases a person may not be mentally capable of knowing that he continues to possess the asset. This was so in *R(SB) 28/83*, where the Commissioner says that it must be shown that the person either knew or with reasonable diligence ought to have known that he possessed the assets. In *R(SB) 40/84* there was a possibility that, in view of her advanced age, the claimant had never known that her superannuation had been increased. Similar arguments can be applied, for instance, to the addition of interest to Building Society accounts. Knowledge of this process can normally be assumed if a person knows of the account, but depending on the medical evidence, may not exist in some circumstances. *CA 303/1992* holds that mental capacity is only relevant to the question whether or not the claimant knew the material fact. It is not relevant to the claimant's ability to understand the materiality of the fact. If the person from whom recovery is sought is not the owner of the asset, it seems that there is less room for assumptions and that knowledge of its existence must be proved (*R(SB) 21/82*, para. 20(4)). This is expanded in *CIS 734/1992* where the Commissioner distinguishes between the standard of the duty to disclose of a receiver and an appointee. In the case of a receiver appointed by the Court of Protection, since he has precise information as to the assets, constructive knowledge (*i.e.* what a person ought to know) is enough. However, as far as an appointee is concerned, it is necessary to show that he actually had sufficient knowledge of the material fact.

Once it is proved that the person has sufficient knowledge of a material fact, there must still be something which amounts to a "failure." In para. 4(2) of *R(SB) 21/82* the Commissioner says that this "necessarily imports the concept of some breach of obligation, moral or legal—*i.e.* the non-disclosure must have occurred in circumstances in which, at lowest, disclosure by the person in question was reasonably to be expected." This statement has been accepted in many decisions, including *R(SB) 28/83*, *R(SB) 54/83* and *R(SB) 15/87*, but does not provide a simple solution to problems when it is also clear that an innocent failure to disclose can trigger the right to recover. In *CSB 1006/1985* it is suggested that the statement does not apply at all where non-disclosure by the claimant himself of an asset of his own is being considered. This is probably going too far, but it is necessary to attempt to spell out some limitations. First, the test is an objective one (*CF 26/1990*). It must depend on what a reasonable person in the position of the person from whom recovery is sought, with that person's knowledge, would have done. Thus, in general the fact that, as in *CSB 1006/1985*, the claimant did not consider that an asset was relevant, would be irrelevant. A reasonable person would not take that view. (See also *CA 303/1992* above.) But if, say, a DSS official had expressly assured the claimant that an undoubtedly material fact did not need to be disclosed, this surely would create a situation in which disclosure was not reasonably to be expected. This would be in line with the result of *R(SB) 3/81* where a course of conduct which had evolved over several years between the DSS and the claimant concerning the handing over of P60s was held to have affected the claimant's obligation.

A slight extension is shown in *CSB 727/1987*, where it is held that the terms of a DSS form and the answers given by the claimant are relevant to whether a later disclosure is reasonably to be expected. The claim for supplementary benefit was made soon after the birth of the claimant's child. On the claim form she said that she was owed family allowance and had applied for child benefit and one parent benefit. Supplementary benefit was awarded without any deduction for child benefit or one parent benefit. The claimant's child benefit and one parent benefit order book was sent to her on December 17, 1984. She did not notify the local supplementary benefit office until February 24, 1986, and in the meantime supplementary benefit was paid without taking account of the income from child benefit and one parent benefit. Most SSATs would have regarded this as an open and shut case of failure to disclose, but the Commissioner holds that in these circumstances disclosure was not reasonably to be expected. The claimant had given detailed answers about her claims and made it clear that she regarded child benefit and one parent benefit as due to her. She might then expect not to have to report their actual receipt. Although her supplementary benefit did not go down, she might well have thought that such benefits did not affect the amount of supplementary benefit. The questions on the claim form could easily have led her to think that her answers were all the information the DSS required unless they expressly asked for more. Nor did the instructions in the supplementary benefit order book alter the situation, since they concerned reporting income or benefit not already reported to the Issuing Office. The claimant could justifiably think that she had already reported the benefits. The decision must depend on its particular facts, and some of the Commissioner's assumptions might not have held up under close examination of the claimant's actual knowledge, but it does indicate the necessity to consider what is reasonably to be expected in a broad context.

The general principle has been applied in a number of unreported decisions. In *CSB 677/1986* a supplementary benefit claimant was also in receipt of sickness benefit, both being administered in the same local office. He received a notification from the local office that he had progressed from sickness benefit to invalidity benefit (paid at a higher rate). The claimant did not inform the supplementary benefit section, but the Commissioner held that he could not reasonably be expected to inform the office which had informed him, especially if the notes in his order book turned out to refer simply to the "issuing office." In *CSB 1246/1986* it was held that there was no obligation to disclose the annual up-rating of unemployment benefit, since this was public knowledge. *CSB 790/1988* takes the same line as *CSB 677/1986* on whether, when an order book instructs a claimant to report changes to "the issuing office," a claimant would reasonably expect to have to report to one part of an integrated local office receipt of benefit from another part. Precise proof of what instructions were included in the order book actually issued to the claimant was crucial in *CP 20/1990*. An increase of benefit for the claimant's wife was improperly awarded, then excluded from payment by an administrative procedure, but allegedly actually paid to the claimant. The Commissioner says that in an ordinary case where proper awards are made, a photocopy of the Departmental record of the award and the issue of order books, together with a specimen of the order books current at the time will suffice to show the instructions given in the book about disclosure. But here it could not be assumed that the appropriate order book with the appropriate instructions had been issued.

CSB 510/1987 decided that advice from the claimant's solicitor and barrister that she did not need to tell the Department about an increase in her children's maintenance payments could make disclosure not reasonably expected.

In *CS 130/1992* the Commissioner suggests that disclosure of an intention to start work, if the intention was sufficiently settled so that an AO could reasonably review an award on the basis of it, may suffice, even if the actual start of work is not disclosed.

In *R(SB) 2/91* the Commissioner held that a claimant could not reasonably be expected to disclose a matter which was irrelevant to the question on which entitlement depended. However, it is expecting too much for a claimant to assess whether a matter is relevant or not, and this case would have been better dealt with on the basis that what was not disclosed was not a material fact (see above).

If one is concerned with disclosure by the claimant of someone else's asset (*e.g.* in *R(SB) 54/83*, the fact that the claimant's wife was working), the *R(SB) 21/82* test may be useful in marginal cases. Its most direct application will be, as in *R(SB) 21/82* itself, in deciding whether some person other than the claimant is under an obligation to disclose. *R(SB) 28/83* is a further example. Since the receiver of the mentally infirm claimant knew of his assets and knew or ought to have known that he was receiving supplementary benefit, he came under an obligation to disclose.

The next issue is to whom must disclosure be made. The leading decision is now *R(SB) 15/87*. Since the concern under the old s.20 was with breaches of the obligation to disclose which had the consequence that the Secretary of State incurred expenditure, it was held that the obligation was to disclose to a member or members of staff of an office of the Department handling the transaction giving rise to the expenditure. Although the wording of s.71 is somewhat different, it is thought that the obligation would be similar, relating to the office handling the claim giving rise to the payment of benefit alleged to have been overpaid. The Tribunal rejects the argument that disclosure to any member of the staff of the Department or to anyone in the "integrated office" in which the claimant was claiming would do. It is accepted that the claimant cannot be expected to identify the precise person dealing with his claim, but the Tribunal is then rather vague about how the obligation is to be fulfilled. They say it is best fulfilled by disclosure to the local office either on a claim form or making sufficient reference to the claim for the information to be referred to the proper person. If this is done, then there can be no further duty to disclose that matter. In the case of a claimant who is required to be available for work and thus has to deliver his claim form to the unemployment benefit office (UBO), disclosure on a claim form delivered there fulfils the duty. The Tribunal also accepts the decision in *R(SB) 54/83* that if an officer in another office accepts information in circumstances which make it reasonable for the claimant to think that the information will be passed on to the proper local office the duty is fulfilled. It holds that it is only in this kind of situation that there is a continuing duty of disclosure, as suggested in para. 18 of *R(SB) 54/83*. If the claimant should subsequently have realised that the information had not reached the proper person then a further obligation to disclose to the proper person would arise. The Tribunal expressly leaves open the question whether the claimant must actually know that the information has not got through.

Although the decision in *R(SB) 15/87* clears up a number of points, it does still leave some uncertainties. The major one is in what circumstances disclosure to the UBO might fulfil the claimant's obligation. It was suggested in *R(SB) 54/83* that in the case of a claimant who is required to declare his availability for work at, and is paid through, the UBO, the UBO is the agent of the supplementary benefit office, so that notice to the UBO would be imputed to the supplementary benefit office (and now the office dealing with income support). The Commissioner did not have to decide the point, but the issue was exhaustively discussed by a Tribunal of Commissioners in *R(SB) 36/84* and *CSB 397/1983*. There is an identical appendix in both decisions setting out in detail the arrangements between the DHSS and the Department of Employment (DE), who administer UBOs. The preliminary conclusion is that having regard to the past 40 years' arrangements, in particular those under which payment to claimants required to register or be available for work is made on the instructions of the UBO, there is an agency relationship. The decisions were not directly to do with recovery of overpayments, but the result in this context would be as suggested in *R(SB) 54/83*, regardless of the fact that the two Departments are otherwise independent. Some earlier decisions like *CSB 14/1982* must now be rejected as being based on mistaken assumptions about the independence of Departments (although it is clear that the principle can only apply in the special case of claimants paid through the UBO). However, the point has been treated as one of fact for each SSAT, rather than a matter on which a definite legal answer has been given (*R(SB) 10/85*).

The Tribunal of Commissioners in *R(SB) 15/87* certainly does not expressly reject the agency argument. Some doubt is raised because the Tribunal mention several ways of fulfilling the duty of disclosure, including delivering a claim form to the UBO, without mentioning the general agency argument. There is an obscure passage (para. 30) on causation (see below) which refers to para. 6549 of the *S Manual*. This does not seem to be relevant, but para. 6548 said that claimants who were required to be available were required to declare their earnings at the UBO. This reinforces the agency argument, but the context in the Tribunal's decision is of a situation where the claimant is said to have failed to disclose. In *R(SB) 2/91* it was accepted by the representative of the Chief Adjudication Officer that the DE were the agents of the DHSS for the purposes of the payment of supplementary benefit, so that information given to the UBO constituted information given to the supplementary benefit section of the DHSS. This view was approved by the Commissioner. The weight of the decisions is clearly that the DE now acts as the agent of the DSS in cases in which income support is paid through the UBO, so that in those cases disclosure to the UBO is disclosure to the office dealing with the claim, and there can be no question of a continuing duty to disclose.

In *CSB 699/1986* the Commissioner considers the circumstances in which, once disclosure has been made, there is no further obligation to disclose "the same matter." He suggests that the "same matter" is not restricted to one-off events, but could extend to a continuing state of affairs, such as the receipt of another benefit. But a transition from sickness to invalidity benefit would be a different matter. Similarly, disclosure on the claim form on a previous claim for the same benefit does not lift the duty to disclose on a fresh claim (*R(SB) 3/90*).

R(SB) 15/87 also deals with the question of by whom disclosure can be made in order to fulfil the claimant's obligation. One daughter, for whom the claimant had received benefit as a dependant, had made a claim in her own right for supplementary benefit at the same office. In respect of another child who started a YTS course, the child benefit book had been surrendered to the contributory benefits section of the same office by the claimant's wife. The Tribunal holds that neither of these actions was sufficient disclosure in relation to the claimant's entitlement to benefit for the children. Disclosure can be made by a third party on behalf of the claimant. but if this is done in the course of a separate transaction, the information must be given to the relevant benefit office and the claimant must know that it has been done and reasonably believe that it is unnecessary for him to take any action himself. In *Riches v. Social Security Commissioner* (Court of Session, May 4, 1993), it was accepted that it was reasonable for the claimant to assume that his wife had disclosed that he was getting invalidity benefit for her when she herself claimed sickness benefit, as she had done this in past claims. However, there was a continuing duty to disclose in these circumstances, and the claimant should have taken further steps when there was no follow-up action by the DSS.

CSB 347/1983 (approved in *R(SB) 10/85*) holds that while an AO might discharge his initial burden of proof by showing that there is no official record of a change of circumstances, thus leaving it for the claimant to prove on a balance of probabilities that he had made a disclosure, this only applies if a proper foundation is laid by evidence (not mere assertion) as to the instructions for recording information and how these are in practice carried out. The distinction between evidence and assertion is strongly supported in *CSB 1195/1984*. The claimant said that she had told two visiting officers that she was receiving unemployment benefit, but there was no official record of such a statement. The Commissioner stresses that what the claimant says about her own acts is evidence, while what a presenting officer says is not evidence unless backed up by personal knowledge of the facts. He says that the new SSAT should call the two visiting officers to give evidence. If they failed to appear without adequate excuse, the weight of the assertions alleged to have been made by them would be reduced to little or nothing. In *CSB 615/1985* it is stressed that there is no rule that only documentary evidence is admissible or that oral evidence requires corroboration.

Causation

It must be shown by the AO that any overpayment resulted from the misrepresentation or failure to disclose. In *R(SB) 3/81* the SBAT simply failed to look at the issue. In *R(SB) 21/82* the Commissioner holds that the right to recovery arises "only on a clearly stipulated causal basis." In that case the claimant's wife had made declarations in 1969 and 1971, but made no more until after the claimant's death in 1979. It was not clear how far any overpayment of benefit was in consequence of those earlier declarations when there were many intervening declarations by the claimant. It is clear that if a claimant has disclosed a material fact to the relevant office in relation to the relevant claim there can be no recovery of subsequent benefit based on a failure to disclose that fact. This was decided in *CSB 688/1982* and *CSB 347/1983*, and confirmed in *R(SB) 15/87*. On principle, it would seem that proper disclosure would rob a subsequent misrepresentation of any causative effect. This appeared to be the result in *CSB 688/1982*, where the claimant orally disclosed to an officer that he had a mine-worker's pension. The officer omitted this from the statement which the claimant then signed as a true and complete statement of his circumstances. The Commissioner holds that the disclosure was fatal to the right of recovery. Although this had been put only on the ground of failure to disclose, the Commissioner felt able to make the decision that the overpayment was not recoverable. Since there had obviously been a misrepresentation, it looked as though the Commissioner must have considered that it could have no legal effect. However, in the very similar case of *R(SB) 18/85* the same Commissioner concentrates on the misrepresentation (see above) and makes no mention of the causation issue. It may be that since the appeal had to be sent back to the SBAT for proper findings of fact, the decision should be regarded as neutral on the causation issue. Whether disclosure does rob a subsequent misrepresentation of causative effect would seem to depend to some extent on the circumstances. In *R(SB) 3/90* the basic principle that if a misrepresentation induces a person to act it is irrelevant that the person had a means of verifying the information was applied. But the disclosure relied on in that case was in an earlier claim. During the currency of one claim the principle of *R(SB) 15/87* would undermine that approach where the means of verification stems from the claimant's disclosure. In *CSB 108/1992* the claimant argued that the fact that he had been advised in 1965/66 that he did not have to disclose his war pension absolved him from any charge of misrepresentation despite the fact that between then and 1985 when the DSS found out about the pension he had made at least 43 written misrepresentations. The Commissioner holds that that advice meant that there had been no contemporaneous misrepresentation, but that it did not assist the claimant in relation to subsequent statements. Clearly the length of time involved in this case (was it reasonable for the claimant to assume that something he was told in 1965 remained valid in 1985?) was a relevant factor. However, in *CS 130/1992* the Commissioner takes the view that contemporaneity may not be essential in all circumstances. A claimant can rely on prior qualification of a misrepresentation if the earlier disclosure was in sufficiently clear terms that the claimant could reasonably believe that it had not been overlooked.

The most controversial issue here is the effect of the breakdown of procedures within the DSS for notifying the income support office that a person has been awarded some other benefit (see, *e.g., Income Support Guide*, Other Benefits Vol. 2, paras. 4010–4049 for the child benefit procedure). The argument is that even though a claimant may have failed to disclose receipt of the other benefit the operative cause of the overpayment is the failure of the administrative procedure to get notice of entitlement to the other benefit from the other section concerned to the income support office. This argument has been rejected in a number of Commissioner's decisions, most recently in *CSB 64/1986* and *R(SB) 3/90*. The question asked there is, would the Secretary of State have avoided the relevant expenditure if the claimant had not failed to disclose the relevant material fact? If the answer is "yes," then the failure is the cause of the expenditure. The DSS procedure is in that sense a back-up one. The validity of this approach is confirmed by the Court of Appeal in *Duggan v. Chief Adjudication Officer (R(SB) 13/89)*. The claimant had failed to disclose his wife's unemployment benefit, but argued that on a review the AO should have investigated the full financial situation. It is held that if one cause of the overpayment was the failure to disclose, the overpayment is recoverable. The new wording in s.71, describing the amount recoverable as any payment which the Secretary of State would not have made but for the misrepresentation or failure to disclose, reinforces this conclusion.

However, it is vital to note that the principles just set out only apply when the other section of the DSS fails to inform the income support section. It is different if the information is received, but the income support section fails to act on it. The Tribunal of Commissioners in *R(SB) 15/87* recognise that if the DSS procedure works it may break the causal link between the claimant's failure and the overpayment. This is now explicitly dealt with in *CIS 159/1990*, where the Child Benefit Centre informed the local office dealing with the income support claim of the issue of an order book with an increased amount of child benefit, plus some arrears. The claimant did not report the arrival of the order book. The Commissioner holds that the overpayment was not in consequence of the failure to disclose, because the local office already knew of the material fact.

Note that if income support is paid while a claimant is waiting for a decision on entitlement for another benefit and arrears of the other benefit are paid for this period, any excess income support cannot be recovered under this section, since it does not result from a failure to disclose. But s.74 and the Payments Regulations will operate to allow the excess to be deducted from the arrears of the other benefit or recovered from the recipient.

CIS/222/1991 and *CIS 395/1992* should also be mentioned. In *CIS 222/1991* the Commissioner holds that if the claimant's answers on the claim form are plainly inconsistent and ambiguous this puts the AO on notice to investigate the position. If this is not done, any overpayment is not recoverable as it is due to error on the part of the Department rather than a misrepresentation by the claimant. In *CIS 395/1992* the claimant, who had been living in a women's aid refuge, returned to live with her husband. She gave him her income support order book to send back to the local office as she thought he was now claiming for the family. Her order book was subsequently cashed. The Commissioner holds that if the husband had cashed the orders without her knowledge, the payments made were not in consequence of her failure to disclose that she had left the refuge. The effective cause of the over-payment was the husband's theft of the order book, not the claimant's failure to disclose.

Amount of overpayment

The calculation of the amount to be recovered has given considerable problems in the past. Subs. (6)(a) below allows regulations to be made on this issue. Regs. 13 and 14 of the Payments Regulations are relevant.

The starting point is the amount of benefit which would not have been paid but for the misrepresentation or failure to disclose. This is in line with the approach set out in *R(SB) 20/84* and *R(SB) 10/85* of looking at what the revised decision would be when the full facts are known. Normally there is no difficulty in determining the amount of benefit which was actually paid, but there may be exceptional cases, like *CP 20/1990*, where evidence of the amounts of payment, rather than a second-hand description, is required.

A controversial question under the pre-April 1987 law was how far it was possible to take account of underpayments of benefit against the overpayment. Reg. 13(b) of the Payments Regulations provides that from the gross amount of the overpayment is to be deducted any additional amount of benefit which should have been awarded on the basis of the claim as originally presented or with the addition of the facts misrepresented or not disclosed. This allows a somewhat more extensive set-off than under the old law (for which, see *R(SB) 20/84, R(SB) 10/85* and *R(SB) 11/86*). *R(IS)*

5/92 confirms that the reg. 13(b) deduction is not limited to the period after the beginning of the overpayment, but can go back to the date of claim. But the examination of the additional amount which would have been payable must be based on the claim as originally presented, or with the addition of the material facts misrepresented or not disclosed. Thus, if, for instance, evidence suggesting that a premium should have been allowed is produced for the first time once an overpayment has been determined by an AO, the amount of that premium is not to be offset against the gross amount of the overpayment (confirming the result of *CSB 615/1985*). In that case, any arrears must be obtained through the ordinary process of review under s.25, and subject to the 12 month limit imposed by reg. 69 of the Adjudication Regulations. If the award of benefit has been reviewed, *e.g.* to include a premium, but the arrears have not yet been paid when the overpayment is determined, there can be an offset under regs. 5(2), Case 1, and 13(a). Any other offset under reg. 5 is to be deducted, but no other deduction for underpayments is to be made. In *R(IS) 5/92* the Commissioner construes "claim as presented" in reg. 13(b)(i) as including facts that would be discovered by "any reasonable enquiry . . . prompted by the claim form". This is applied in *CIS 137/1992* to require the AO to consider reg. 8(3) of the Income Support Regulations (income support on hardship grounds) where it has been decided that neither para. 5 nor 6 of Sched. 1 apply to the claimant but she does not make herself available for work. The Commissioner states that there is always the possibility of hardship where a person is left on an income below the level of reduced income support; the fact that her claim form did not reveal that she would suffer hardship if no benefit was paid was thus not material. *CIS 137/1992* further points out that reg. 13 is concerned with deductions from an overpayment and so only comes into play after the overpayment has been calculated. The review which results in a decision as to the amount of benefit that ought to have been paid is therefore to be carried out without any fetter being imposed by reg. 13.

Another problem now dealt with by regulations arises when the misrepresentation or failure to disclose is of capital resources. If it emerged that a claimant who had been in receipt of income support or family credit for a few years throughout had capital of £1 over the limit, it would be most unfair to require repayment of the whole amount of benefit. If the capital had been properly taken into account, so that benefit was not initially awarded, the capital would have immediately been reduced below the limit in order to provide for living expenses. So the Commissioners applied the "diminishing capital" principle (*CSB 53/1981, CSBO v. Leary*, appendix to *R(SB) 6/85, R(SB) 15/85*). The position is now governed by reg. 14 of the Payments Regulations. This provides for the reduction of the figure of capital resources at quarterly intervals from the beginning of the overpayment period by the amount overpaid in income support or family credit in the previous quarter. No other reduction of the actual amount of capital resources is allowed (reg. 14(2)). Under the Commissioners' approach the notional reduction had to be made week by week. It will be considerably easier to make the calculation at 13 week intervals, but the tendency will be for smaller reductions of the overpayment to be produced.

It is for the AO to prove the existence and amount of capital taken into account in calculating an overpayment (*R(SB) 21/82*). Here, sums had suddenly appeared in Building Society accounts and there was no evidence where they had come from. The Commissioner commends the adoption of a lower figure of overpayment rather than a higher one based on the assumption that the capital assets had not been possessed before any evidence existed about them. The Commissioner in *R(SB) 34/83* agrees strongly on the burden of proof, but points out that if the person concerned was alive and failed to give any proper explanation of the origin of such sums, adverse inferences could be drawn against him, enabling the AO to discharge his burden of proof. He goes on to hold that the estate of a deceased person should be in the same position. Therefore, a heavy responsibility devolved on the executor to make every reasonable enquiry as to the origin of the money. But if after such efforts there was no evidence where the money came from the burden of proof on the AO would not have been discharged.

It is essential that on an appeal a SSAT should clearly state the amount which is recoverable, and state how that amount is calculated (*R(SB) 9/85*). If there is no dispute about the amount of the overpayment a SSAT may not need to describe the calculation (*CSB 218/1991*). If the SSAT cannot make the calculation at the time of their initial decision they can refer the matter back to the AO for recalculation on the basis determined by the SSAT, but only if the decision expressly allows the matter to be referred back to the SSAT if agreement cannot be reached on the recalculation (*R(SB) 11/86, R(SB) 15/87*). The suggestion in *CSB 83/1991* that this valuable practice is invalidated by subs. (2) is rightly rejected in *CIS 442/1992*. That decision also suggests that if there is a reference back to the SSAT, and the members of the new tribunal are not the same as those who sat on the tribunal which made the main decision, the whole matter, including the question of liability, must be reconsidered. The basis for this suggestion seems dubious. Such a decision is a final decision of the SSAT, and there seems to be no doubt that there can be an appeal to the Commissioner under s.23(1) from such a decision (see the notes to s.23(1) for further discussion).

One reason why SSATs must be careful to specify the amount recoverable is that often differing amounts are calculated by the AO after his initial decision. If this is done there was before April 1990 no bar to this operating as a review and revision of the initial decision. The initial decision, being on a single indivisible question, would thus be replaced and any appeal lodged against it would lapse. However, appeals in these circumstances were commonly continued as though they had not lapsed. In *CSB 64/1986*, where the claimant's representative insisted that the appeal was against the initial decision, the Commissioner held that the SSAT's decision was given without authority as the appeal had lapsed. In *R(SB) 15/87*, the appeal was treated as against the revised decision, although no notice of appeal against that decision had been given. The Tribunal of Commissioners holds that in this case the failure to comply with the procedural requirements, did not make the SSAT's proceedings a nullity. There had been substantial compliance with the requirements, there was no public interest in strict compliance and the claimant would be prejudiced if the procedural failure was not ignored, since the time for appealing against the revised decision had expired. The predecessor of s.29 of the Administration Act provided from April 1990 that once an appeal has been lodged, a review is to be of no effect unless it gives the claimant everything that the claimant could possibly obtain in the appeal, so that if there is merely a revision of the amount of an overpayment the appeal against the original decision continues in being.

Subsection (2)
See notes to subs. (5).

Subsection (3)
This provision confirms that amounts are recoverable from the person who made the misrepresentation or failed to make disclosure. Presumably the principle that after the person's death the overpayment is recoverable from his estate (*Secretary of State for Social Services v. Solly* [1974] 3 All E.R. 922, *R(SB) 21/82, R(SB) 28/83*) is not affected. Note that the time limit of the Limitation Act 1980 does not begin to run until there is a determination of an overpayment by an AO which gives the Secretary of State the right of recovery (*R(SB) 5/91, R(A) 2/86*). See also *CIS 26/1994* at the beginning of this note.

CIS 332/1992 decides that if an appointee signs a misrepresentation in the capacity of appointee, there can only be recovery from the claimant and not from her personally. Any misrepresentation or failure to disclose by the appointee acting in that capacity was attributable to the claimant and so any resulting overpayment was recoverable from the claimant (*R(SB) 28/83*). Thus, if in this situation it was as if the claimant had personally misrepresented or failed to disclose the material fact, it could not at the same time be said that the appointee had personally misrepresented or failed to disclose the fact. When a person was acting in the capacity of an appointee she was not a third party in the sense that had been considered by the House of Lords in *Plewa*, but her acts and omissions were those of the claimant's. The situation would of course be different if the appointee had been acting in a personal capacity. The Commissioner declined to follow *CIS 734/1992* which held that where the appointment was made because of the claimant's mental incapacity, any failure to disclose by the appointee could not be imputed to the claimant and so the overpayment was recoverable from the appointee personally.

Subsection (4)
This provision applies where benefit is directly credited to an account. See reg. 21 of the Claims and Payments Regulations and reg. 11 of the Payments Regulations.

Subsection (5)
The general rule here is taken over from that for contributory benefits, that recovery of an overpayment should follow a revision on review of the decision awarding benefit or its variation on appeal. The result is that if the conditions for review are not met, then even though the initial decision was incorrect, no overpayment can be recovered. However, regulations may provide otherwise and have done so. Reg. 12 of the Payments Regulations provides that subs. (5) shall not apply where the fact and circumstances of the misrepresentation or non-disclosure do not provide a basis for reviewing and revising the initial decision. This formulation is rather obscure, but it seems to mean that if the conditions for review and revision do not exist there can still be a determination that an overpayment is recoverable. See *CS 102/1993* in the note to misrepresentation above for an example of where reg. 12 applied. But if the conditions for review and revision do exist then the determination of the recoverable overpayment must be made as part of the review decision or not at all (see also subs. (2)). *R(SB) 7/91* has now decided that this is so.

A number of decisions have held that (outside the exception in reg. 12 of the Payments Regulations) it is an essential pre-condition of an overpayment determination that there should be proof of a valid revision of entitlement on review. See *CSSB 105/1989*, followed in *CIS 179/1990* and *CIS 360/1990*. The principle is accepted in *CSSB 316/1989*, where the Commissioner also deals with the requirement of subs. (5) that the overpayment determination must be made "on the appeal or review." He says "[the] earliest possible correction of a continuing award which has been found to be incorrect is obviously desirable and I accept that an effective decision for the purposes of section 53(1), (1A) and (4) can be made notwithstanding that grounds of review and revisal of the award for the past and the future, which must of course be appropriate, are established at a date prior to the making of the decision establishing the detail of the overpayment." In *CSIS 64/1992* the Commissioner regards it as essential that the review decision be produced in any recovery case in order to show, not just that subs. (5) has been complied with, but also that the review itself has been properly carried out under s.25 (including taking account of any awards that should have been made in the claimant's favour), and that reg. 20 of the Adjudication Regulations has been complied with. In *CSIS 78/1993* the same Commissioner reiterates the necessity for proof of a proper prior review, at least in any case where this is challenged. This was not established by production of largely unintelligible computer print outs, which did not show the actual terms of the review, nor that this had been communicated to the claimant. If no evidence of a review is put before a tribunal, it is obliged to enquire into this. If it does not do so, the fact that a review decision could have been produced will not vitiate this error *(CSIS 62/1991)*.

There remains some uncertainty about what a SSAT should do if faced with an overpayment decision when there has not been a valid revision of entitlement on review. In *CSSB 105/1989*, *CSSB 316/1989* and *CSSB 540/1989*, the Commissioner suggests that the SSAT should simply determine that no valid AO's decision on the overpayment has been made. In *R(SB) 7/91* the Commissioner holds that the SSAT should determine that the AO's decision is of no force or effect. However, this seems to leave the possibility of an AO's reviewing the defective AO's decision for error of law under s.25(2) of the Administration Act (suggested in *CSSB 105/1989*) or of the AO starting the overpayment procedure all over again by a valid revision of entitlement on review. A SSAT's decision in this form does not decide that an overpayment can never be recovered. It secures that the proper process must be applied. But the final result may be the same and the claimant has to appeal yet again to challenge it. It may therefore be asked why the SSAT should not follow the general principle put forward in *CSSB 540/1989* that on appeal a SSAT can correct a defective review decision. In *CSSB 1272/1989* the Commissioner, in an effort to avoid the expense and delay of starting the whole process again, suggests that where in overpayments cases the AO has omitted to carry out a review, the SSAT should make good the omission using its power under s.36 of the Administration Act (1975 Act, s.102) to determine questions first arising in the course of the appeal. This approach seems rather dubious, since the review question seems to be part and parcel of the overpayment question already before the AO and the SSAT, and not one which first arises in the course of the appeal. In addition, none of the decisions mentioned earlier are cited in *CSB 1272/1989*. For these reasons the Commissioner in *CSIS 64/1992* and *CSIS 78/1993* did not consider that in overpayment cases a tribunal could itself conduct the review. The position thus remains somewhat unresolved until some authoritative decision emerges from the Commissioners. But at the moment the weight of authority would seem to be in favour of a SSAT determining that no valid overpayment decision has been made. There is in any case a difficulty in "correcting" an AO's decision where no review decision at all has been made. There may however be exceptional circumstances, for instance where a SSAT is clear that an overpayment would not be recoverable under s.71, where a SSAT should deal with the review issue *(cf. CSB 274/1990)*.

If there is no doubt that the AO has carried out a proper review and revision, it is not an error of law for the SSAT not to mention the issue, although it is better if it does *(CSIS 62/1991)*.

Subsection (6)
The Payments Regulations have been made under these powers.

Subsection (7)
See Part II of the Payments Regulations.

Subsection (8)
The benefits from which deductions may be made are prescribed by reg. 15 of the Payments Regulations. They include most social security benefits. Limits to the weekly amounts which may be deducted from income support and family credit are set by reg. 16. Reg. 20(2) of the 1987 Payments Regulations provides that subs. (8) also applies to amounts recoverable under any enactment repealed by the 1986 Act or regulation revoked by the 1987 Regulations. The Divisional Court in *R. v. Secretary of State for Social Services, ex parte Britnell, The Times*, January 27, 1989, decided that reg. 20(2) did not offend the rule of construction against retrospection. Its effect was

merely to provide an additional method of recovery where there was no dispute that a liability to repay existed. In the Court of Appeal (*The Times*, February 16, 1990) and the House of Lords ([1991]1 W.L.R. 198, [1991] 2 All E.R. 726), the point on retrospection was not argued and reg. 20(2) was found to have been validly made under s.89(1) of the 1986 Act.

Subsection (9)
See reg. 17 of the Payments Regulations.

Special provision as to recovery of income support

72.—(1) Where—
  (a) a direction under section 125(1) of the Contributions and Benefits Act is revoked; and
  (b) it is determined by an adjudication officer that, whether fraudulently or otherwise, any person has misrepresented, or failed to disclose, any material fact and in consequence of the misrepresentation or failure a payment of income support has been made during the relevant period to the person to whom the direction related,
an adjudication officer may determine that the Secretary of State shall be entitled to recover the amount of the payment.

  (2) In subsection (1) above "the relevant period" means—
  (a) if the revocation is under subsection (3) of section 125 of the Contributions and Benefits Act, the period beginning with the date of the change of circumstances and ending with the date of the revocation; and
  (b) if the revocation is under subsection (4) of that section, the period during which the direction was in force.

  (3) Where a direction under section 125(1) of the Contributions and Benefits Act is revoked, the Secretary of State may certify whether there has been misrepresentation of a material fact or failure to disclose a material fact.

  (4) If he certifies that there has been such misrepresentation or failure to disclose, he may also certify—
  (a) who made the misrepresentation or failed to make the disclosure; and
  (b) whether or not a payment of income support has been made in consequence of the misrepresentation or failure.

  (5) If he certifies that a payment has been made, he may certify the period during which income support would not have been paid but for the misrepresentation or failure to disclose.

  (6) A certificate under this section shall be conclusive for the purposes of this section as to any matter certified.

  (7) Section 71(3) and (6) to (11) above apply to income support recoverable under subsection (1) above as they apply to income support recoverable under section 71(1) above.

  (8) The other provisions of section 71 above do not apply to income support recoverable under subsection (1) above.

DERIVATION

Subs. (1): Social Security Act 1986, s.20(4E).
Subs. (2): 1986 Act, s.20(4H).
Subss. (3) to (6): 1986 Act, s.20(4J) to (4M).
Subss. (7) and (8): 1986 Act, s.20(4F) and (4G).

DEFINITION

"the Contributions and Benefits Act"—see s.191.

Section 125(1) of the Contributions and Benefits Act enables the Secretary of State to direct that a person under the age of 18 is to qualify for income support in order to avoid severe hardship. The direction may be revoked under s.125(3) on the ground of change of circumstances or under s.125(4) on the ground that a mistake or ignorance of material fact led to the determination that severe hardship would result if income support were not to be paid. A special provision is needed for recovery in cases of misrepresentation or failure to disclose because the revocation of the direction is not a review which can found action under s.71. Although the determination is made by the AO under subs. (1), the Secretary of State's certificate is conclusive on almost every issue (subss. (3) to (6)). The provisions of s.71 about the mechanics of recovery apply.

Adjustments of benefits

Income support and other payments

74.—(1) Where—
   (a) a payment by way of prescribed income is made after the date which is the prescribed date in relation to the payment; and
   (b) it is determined that an amount which has been paid by way of income support would not have been paid if the payment had been made on the prescribed date,
the Secretary of State shall be entitled to recover that amount from the person to whom it was paid.

(2) Where—
   (a) a prescribed payment which apart from this subsection falls to be made from public funds in the United Kingdom or under the law of any other member State is not made on or before the date which is the prescribed date in relation to the payment; and
   (b) it is determined that an amount ("the relevant amount") has been paid by way of income support that would not have been paid if the payment mentioned in paragraph (a) above had been made on the prescribed date,
then—
   (i) in the case of a payment from public funds in the United Kingdom, the authority responsible for making it may abate it by the relevant amount; and
   (ii) in the case of any other payment, the Secretary of State shall be entitled to receive the relevant amount out of the payment.

(3) Where—
   (a) a person (in this subsection referred to as A) is entitled to any prescribed benefit for any period in respect of another person (in this subsection referred to as B); and
   (b) either—
      (i) B has received income support for that period; or
      (ii) B was, during that period, a member of the same family as some person other than A who received income support for that period; and
   (c) the amount of the income support has been determined on the basis that A has not made payments for the maintenance of B at a rate equal to or exceeding the amount of the prescribed benefit,
the amount of the prescribed benefit may, at the discretion of the authority administering it, be abated by the amount by which the amounts paid by way of income support exceed what it is determined that they would have been had A, at the time the amount of the income support was determined, been making payments for the maintenance of B at a rate equal to the amount of the prescribed benefit.

(4) Where an amount could have been recovered by abatement by virtue of subsection (2) or (3) above but has not been so recovered, the Secretary of State may recover it otherwise than by way of abatement—

(a) in the case of an amount which could have been recovered by virtue of subsection (2) above, from the person to whom it was paid; and

(b) in the case of an amount which could have been recovered by virtue of subsection (3) above, from the person to whom the prescribed benefit in question was paid.

(5) Where a payment is made in a currency other than sterling, its value in sterling shall be determined for the purposes of this section in accordance with regulations.

DERIVATION

Social Security Act 1986, s.27.

DEFINITION

"prescribed"—see s.191.

GENERAL NOTE

Most of this section was originally, in substance, s.12 of the Supplementary Benefits Act 1976. There are changes in form from the old s.12, but the overall aim is the same, to prevent a claimant from getting a double payment when other sources of income are not paid on time. This is an important provision, which is often overlooked.

Subsection (1)

Prescribed income is defined in reg. 7(1) of the Social Security (Payments on account, Overpayments and Recovery) Regulations 1988 ("the Payments Regulations") as any income which is to be taken into account under Part V of the Income Support (General) Regulations. The prescribed date under reg. 7(2) is, in general, the first day of the period to which that income relates. If as a result of that income being paid after the prescribed date, more income support is paid than would have been paid if the income had been paid on the prescribed date, the excess may be recovered. Note that the right to recover is absolute and does not depend on lack of care on the claimant's part, or on the effect of this section having been pointed out. That approach is confirmed in *CIS 625/1991*, where the Commissioner rejected the argument that there had to be an investigation of what an AO would in practice have done if the income had been paid on time. An example would be where a claimant has not been paid part-time earnings when they were due and as a result has been paid income support on the basis of having no earnings. Once the arrears of wages are received, the excess benefit would be recoverable. Late payment of most social security benefits is covered in subss. (2) and (4), but can also come within subs. (1). For instance, if a claim is made for child benefit and while a decision is awaited income support is paid without any deduction for the amount of the expected child benefit, then if arrears of child benefit are eventually paid in full (*i.e.* the abatement procedure of subs. (2) does not work) the "excess" income support for the period covered by the arrears is recoverable under subs. (1) or (4).

It is essential that the dates on which prescribed income was due to be paid and on what dates due payments would have affected income support entitlement should be determined *(R(SB) 28/85* and *CIS 625/1991)*.

Subsection (2)

Prescribed payments are listed in reg. 8(1) of the Payments Regulations and include most social security benefits, training allowances and social security benefits from other EC countries. As under subs. (1), a claimant is not to keep excess income support resulting from late payment of one of the prescribed payments. However, the primary mechanism here where the payment is due from public funds in the U.K. is for the arrears due to be abated (*i.e.* reduced) by the amount of the excess income support (subs. (2)(a) and (i)). Note that the abatement may be applied to benefits due to another member of the claimant's family (*e.g.* retirement pension due to the wife of the income support claimant in *CSB 383/1988*). If this mechanism breaks down and the arrears are paid in full, then under subs. (1) or (4) the Secretary of State can recover the excess from the income support recipient.

In *R (IS) 14/94* the claimant's income support included a severe disability premium (SDP). Her daughter was later awarded invalid care allowance (ICA) for caring for the claimant and arrears for March 1989 to July 1990 were paid. The AO reviewed the decision awarding the claimant an SDP from March 1989 to July 1990 on the ground that it was made in ignorance of a material fact, and decided that the resulting overpayment was recoverable from the claimant under s.27 of the Social Security Act 1986 (now s.74). The Commissioner held that the arrears of ICA could have been abated under s.27(2) (now s.74(2)), despite the fact that the daughter was not a member of the claimant's family for the purposes of income support. An SDP would not have been paid if the award of ICA had been known. The Commissioner also rejected the argument that ICA was not "in payment" until July 1990 and so the condition in para. 13(2)(a)(iii) of Sched. 2 to the Income Support Regulations was satisfied. "In payment" did not mean timeously in payment. Since the power of abatement had not been exercised, the overpaid income support could be recovered under s.27(4) (now s.74(4)) from the claimant as the person to whom it had been paid. The claimant was granted leave to appeal against the Commissioner's decision by the Court of Appeal. However, the appeal was not proceeded with as the Secretary of State issued internal guidance stating that where a carer receives arrears of ICA and an SDP has been in payment to the person cared for, no recovery should be sought of the consequent overpayment of income support. The Commissioner's interpretation was therefore not tested before the Court of Appeal. However, if through the operation of s.74 a person who is entitled to benefit can be deprived of it because an overpayment of income support has been made to some other independent person, this seems arbitrary and unfair. The position has now been remedied in relation to SDP and arrears of ICA by the introduction of para. 13(3ZA) of Sched. 2 to the Income Support Regulations. See the notes to para. 13. This should avoid any question of an overpayment of an SDP by reason of a backdated award of ICA. One other point should be made. The Commissioner in *R(IS) 14/94* accepted that the claimant's income support was properly reviewed on the ground of ignorance of a material fact. But the correct ground would seem to have been change of circumstances. It is difficult to see how an AO can be said to have been ignorant of a fact which did not exist at the date of the decision (see *CIS 650/1991*).

In the case of other payments (which will normally be benefits due from other EC countries) recovery is the primary mechanism (subs. (2)(ii)). If the payment is routed through the DSS, as was the case for the arrears of a German invalidity pension in *R(SB) 3/91* (see also *R(SB) 1/91* and *CIS 501/1993*), a deduction can be made before the arrears are paid over to the claimant. Although reg. 8(1)(g) of the Payments Regulations makes a reference to EC Regulation 1408/71, the s.74 procedure is not limited to benefits obtained by virtue of the Regulation.

Once again, the operation of the provision is automatic. Any undertaking by the claimant to repay seems superfluous. However, the Secretary of State might choose not to enforce his right to recovery.

Under s.71(8)(c), amounts may be recovered by deduction from most benefits.

Subsection (3)

Prescribed benefits are listed in reg. 9 of the Payments Regulations. They are benefits, like child benefit, which can be claimed if a person (A) is contributing to the support of another person (B) at at least the rate of the benefit. If income support has been paid for B on the basis that this contribution was not paid, the prescribed benefit may be abated by the amount of the excess income support. If the abatement mechanism breaks down, the Secretary of State may recover the excess under subs. (4). Under s.71(8))(c), amounts may be recovered by deduction from most benefits.

Subsection (4)

See notes to subss. (2) & (3).

Subsection (5)

R(SB) 28/85 had revealed problems in valuing a payment of arrears in a foreign currency which might cover quite a long period during which exchange rates varied. This provision authorises regulations to be made to deal with the conversion. See reg. 10 of the Payments Regulations, which appears to require the actual net amount received to be taken into account, reversing the effect of *R(SB) 28/85*.

Social fund awards

Recovery of social fund awards

78.—(1) A social fund award which is repayable shall be recoverable by the Secretary of State.

(2) Without prejudice to any other method of recovery, the Secretary of State may recover an award by deduction from prescribed benefits.

(3) The Secretary of State may recover an award—

(a) from the person to or for the benefit of whom it was made;

(b) where that person is a member of a married or unmarried couple, from the other member of the couple;

(c) from a person who is liable to maintain the person by or on behalf of whom the application for the award was made or any person in relation to whose needs the award was made.

(4) Payments to meet funeral expenses may in all cases be recovered, as if they were funeral expenses, out of the estate of the deceased, and (subject to section 71 above) by no other means.

(5) In this section—

"married couple" means a man and woman who are married to each other and are members of the same household;

"unmarried couple" means a man and a woman who are not married to each other but are living together as husband and wife otherwise than in circumstances prescribed under section 132 of the Contributions and Benefits Act.

(6) For the purposes of this section—

(a) a man shall be liable to maintain his wife and any children of whom he is the father; and

(b) a woman shall be liable to maintain her husband and any children of whom she is the mother;

(c) a person shall be liable to maintain another person throughout any period in respect of which the first-mentioned person has, on or after 23rd May 1980 (the date of the passing of the Social Security Act 1980) and either alone or jointly with a further person, given an undertaking in writing in pursuance of immigration rules within the meaning of the Immigration Act 1971 to be responsible for the maintenance and accommodation of the other person; and

(d) "child" includes a person who has attained the age of 16 but not the age of 19 and in respect of whom either parent, or some person acting in place of either parent, is receiving income support.

(7) Any reference in subsection (6) above to children of whom the man or the woman is the father or mother shall be construed in accordance with section 1 of the Family Law Reform Act 1987.

(8) Subsection (7) above does not apply in Scotland, and in the application of subsection (6) above to Scotland any reference to children of whom the man or the woman is the father or the mother shall be construed as a reference to any such children whether or not their parents have ever been married to one another.

(9) A document bearing a certificate which—

(a) is signed by a person authorised in that behalf by the Secretary of State; and

(b) states that the document apart from the certificate is, or is a copy of, such an undertaking as is mentioned in subsection (6)(c) above,

shall be conclusive of the undertaking in question for the purposes of this section; and a certificate purporting to be so signed shall be deemed to be so signed until the contrary is proved.

DERIVATION

Subss. (1) to (3): Social Security Act 1986, s.33(5) to (7).
Subs. (4): 1986 Act, s.32(4).
Subs. (5): 1986 Act, s.33(12).
Subss. (6) to (9): 1986 Act, ss.26(3) to (6) and 33(8).

"prescribed"—see s.191.

GENERAL NOTE

Subsections (1) to (3)

These provisions give the framework for recovery of social fund loans. See the Social Fund (Recovery by Deductions from Benefits) Regulations 1988.

Income support is a prescribed benefit for the purposes of subs. (2) (reg. 3(a) of the Social Fund (Recovery by Deductions from Benefits) Regulations). *Mulvey v. Secretary of State for Social Security* (Outer House of the Court of Session, November 18, 1994) [1995] SCLR 102, challenged the Secretary of State's right to make deductions under subs. (2) from the claimant's income support after she had been sequestrated (the Scottish equivalent of being made bankrupt). Under the Bankruptcy (Scotland) Act 1985 post-sequestration income vests in the debtor (except in certain circumstances). In addition, it is not possible to set off post-sequestration income against a pre-sequestration debt, which has to be the subject of a claim in the sequestration. Lord Abernethy holds that subs. (2) had to be read together with the 1985 Act. He did not consider that when Parliament enacted the predecessor of subs. (2) (s. 33(6) of the 1986 Act), it intended to repeal the provisions of the 1985 Act in so far as they related to the recovery of social fund loans, but rather that s. 33(6) should be read with the existing bankruptcy law. If this was not the case, one creditor (the Secretary of State) would in effect obtain an unfair advantage at the expense of the other creditors. Lord Abernethy also did not consider that s. 187(1) of the Administration Act had any bearing on the issue. The result was that the Secretary of State was not entitled to recover Ms Mulvey's pre-sequestration social fund loans by deduction from her post-sequestration income support. It is understood that the Secretary of State has appealed to the Inner House of the Court of Session, which appeal is due to be heard in October 1995.

English bankruptcy law is not the same as Scottish sequestration law. However, it is arguable that s. 285 of the Insolvency Act 1986 produces the same effect in England and Wales, and that the decision in *Mulvey* means that post-bankruptcy deductions for social fund loans should not be made.

Subsection (4)

Subs. (4) contains an important provision for the recovery of any payment for funeral expenses out of the estate of the deceased. Reg. 8 of the Social Fund Maternity and Funeral Expenses (General) Regulations lists sums to be deducted in calculating the amount of a funeral payment. These include assets of the deceased which are available before probate or letters of administration have been granted. The old reg. 8(3)(a) of the Single Payments Regulations required the deduction of the value of the deceased's estate, but since it might take some time for the estate to become available, the provision in subs. (4) is preferable.

The funeral payment is to be recovered as if it was funeral expenses. Funeral expenses are a first charge on the estate, in priority to anything else (see *R(SB) 18/84*, paras. 8 and 10, for the law in England and Scotland). *CIS 616/1990* decides that the right to recover is given to the Secretary of State. The AO (and the SSAT) has no role in subs. (4).

The only other method of recovery is under s.71, which applies generally where there has been misrepresentation or a failure to disclose and does depend on a review of entitlement by an AO, followed by a determination of an overpayment.

Subsections (6) to (9)

See the notes to s.105.

Northern Ireland payments

Recovery of Northern Ireland payments

79. Without prejudice to any other method of recovery—

(a) amounts recoverable under any enactment or instrument having effect in Northern Ireland and corresponding to an enactment or instrument mentioned in section 71(8) above shall be recoverable by deduction from benefits prescribed under that subsection;

(b) amounts recoverable under any enactment having effect in Northern Ireland and corresponding to section 75 above shall be recoverable by deduction from benefits prescribed under subsection (4) of that section; and

(c) awards recoverable under Part III of the Northern Ireland Administration Act shall be recoverable by deduction from benefits prescribed under subsection (2) of section 78 above and subsection (3) of that section shall have effect in relation to such awards as it has effect in relation to such awards out of the social fund under this Act.

DERIVATION

Para. (a): Social Security Act 1986, s.53(7A).
Para. (b): 1986 Act, s.29(8).
Para. (c): 1986 Act, s.33(8A).

DEFINITIONS

"the Northern Ireland Administration Act"—see s.191.
"prescribed"—*ibid.*

PART V

INCOME SUPPORT AND THE DUTY TO MAINTAIN

Failure to maintain—general

105.—(1) If—

(a) any person persistently refuses or neglects to maintain himself or any person whom he is liable to maintain; and

(b) in consequence of his refusal or neglect income support is paid to or in respect of him or such a person,

he shall be guilty of an offence and liable on summary conviction to imprisonment for a term not exceeding 3 months or to a fine of an amount not exceeding level 4 on the standard scale or to both.

(2) For the purposes of subsection (1) above a person shall not be taken to refuse or neglect to maintain himself or any other person by reason only of anything done or omitted in furtherance of a trade dispute.

(3) Subsections (6) to (9) of section 78 above shall have effect for the purposes of this Part of this Act as they have effect for the purposes of that section.

DERIVATION

Social Security Act 1986, s.26.

GENERAL NOTE

Subsection (1)

The criminal offence created by subs. (1) of refusing or neglecting to maintain oneself is at first sight rather extraordinary, but it is only committed if as a consequence income support is paid. Prosecution is very much a last resort after the ordinary sanctions against voluntary unemployment have been used. In 1984/5 there were none (NACRO, *Enforcement of the Law Relating to Social Security*, para. 8.6). Prosecution of those who refuse or neglect to maintain others is more common.

Liability to maintain

Under subs. (3), liability to maintain another person for the purposes of Part V is tested according to s.78(6) to (9). Both men and women are liable to maintain their spouses and children. This liability remains in force despite the enactment of the Child Support Act 1991, with the result that the DSS retains its power to enforce that liability under ss.106 to 108. But although this power remains, in practice the DSS does not enforce the liability to maintain children now that the Child Support Agency has acquired this role. Note also that since April 5, 1993, the courts have not had power to make new orders for maintenance for children (s. 8(3) Child Support Act 1991).

The definition of child goes beyond the usual meaning in s.137 of the Contributions and Benefits Act of a person under 16 to include those under 19 who count as a dependant in someone else's income support entitlement (s.78(6)(d)). The effect of the reference in s.78(4) to s.1 of the Family Law Reform Act 1987 is that in determining whether a person is the father or mother of a child it is irrelevant whether the person was married to the other parent at the time of the birth or not. If a married couple divorce, their liability to maintain each other ceases for the purposes of Part V, but the obligation to maintain their children remains. This then is the remnant of the old family means-test that used to extend much wider until the Poor Law was finally "abolished" by the National Assistance Act 1948. For the enforcement of this liability, see ss.106 to 108, and for a criminal offence, subs. (1).

Section 78(6)(c) was new in 1980. In *R. v. W. London SBAT, ex p. Clarke* [1975] 1 W.L.R. 1396, SB7, the court had held that the sponsor of an immigrant was under no obligation to maintain the immigrant for supplementary benefit purposes. This position is now reversed, and s.78(9) provides for conclusive certificates of an undertaking to maintain to be produced. The liability to maintain is enforced under s.106. The SBC policy struck down in *Clarke*'s case had deemed the immigrant to be receiving the support from his sponsor even where it was not forthcoming. This is not now the case. It is only a resource when actually received.

Recovery of expenditure on benefit from person liable for maintenance

106.—(1) Subject to the following provisions of this section, if income support is claimed by or in respect of a person whom another person is liable to maintain or paid to or in respect of such a person, the Secretary of State may make a complaint against the liable person to a magistrates' court for an order under this section.

(2) On the hearing of a complaint under this section the court shall have regard to all the circumstances and, in particular, to the income of the liable person, and may order him to pay such sum, weekly or otherwise, as it may consider appropriate, except that in a case falling within section 78(6)(c) above that sum shall not include any amount which is not attributable to income support (whether paid before or after the making of the order).

(3) In determining whether to order any payments to be made in respect of income support for any period before the complaint was made, or the amount of any such payments, the court shall disregard any amount by which the liable person's income exceeds the income which was his during that period.

(4) Any payments ordered to be made under this section shall be made—
(a) to the Secretary of State in so far as they are attributable to any income support (whether paid before or after the making of the order);
(b) to the person claiming income support or (if different) the dependant; or
(c) to such other person as appears to the court expedient in the interests of the dependant.

(5) An order under this section shall be enforceable as a magistrates' court maintenance order within the meaning of section 150(1) of the Magistrates' Court Act 1980.

(6) In the application of this section to Scotland, subsection (5) above shall be omitted and for the references to a complaint and to a magistrates' court there shall be substituted respectively references to an application and to the sheriff.

(7) On an application under subsection (1) above a court in Scotland may make a finding as to the parentage of a child for the purpose of establishing whether a person is, for the purposes of section 105 above and this section, liable to maintain him.

Social Security Administration Act 1992

DERIVATION

Social Security Act 1986, s.24.

DEFINITION

"child"—see ss.105(3) and 78(b).

GENERAL NOTE

This section gives the DSS an independent right to enforce the liability to maintain in s.78(6), which now covers both spouses and children, by an order in the magistrates' court, providing that income support has been claimed or paid for the person sought to be maintained.

Children

From April 1993 the Child Support Act 1991 has introduced an entirely new system of determining and enforcing the liability of parents to maintain children, through the Child Support Agency. This book does not deal with that system, for which, see Jacobs and Douglas, *Child Support Legislation*. But the DSS's rights under s.106 remain in force not only between spouses, but also as between parents and children. It is not clear in what circumstances action against a parent may be taken under s.106 rather than through the Child Support Agency. The DSS have said that they do not intend to use the s. 106 power in relation to children, and this seems to be implicit in the Income Support Special Circumstances Guide, paras. 6000–6014. The Child Support Agency is in the process of phasing in applications for child support maintenance for income support claimants. It was originally intended that all income support claimants would have been required to apply under s. 6 of the Child Support Act 1991 by April 1996; however, there have been some delays in taking on cases. Despite the delays, claimants receiving maintenance under a court order or an arrangement with liable relative officers were given priority by the Child Support Agency and so there should no longer be any cases where maintenance for dependent children is still being dealt with by the Benefits Agency. Benefit may only be reduced for failure to comply with obligations under s. 6, not for failure to co-operate in relation to the liability to maintain in s. 78(6). Note also that since April 5, 1993, the courts have not had the power to make new orders for maintenance for children (s. 8(3) Child Support Act 1991).

Spouses

The usual procedure was last described in detail in Chapter 13 of the *Supplementary Benefits Handbook* (1984 ed.) and will presumably continue to apply, since it was repeated in essence in the DSS *Guide to Income Support*, although there were some administrative changes. The current Income Support Guide does not contain the liable relative procedure. This apparently is now in an internal guide called "Residual Liable Relatives and Proceedings Guide". The most common situation is where a breakdown of marriage leads to separation or divorce and the woman claims income support. The same procedures can apply if it is the man who claims benefit. If there has already been a divorce then there is no liability to maintain between the ex-spouses. If there has merely been a separation then the wife is entitled to benefit as a single person, but there will be an investigation of the circumstances to ensure that the separation is genuine. If the husband is already paying maintenance under a court order or the wife has taken proceedings herself which are reasonably advanced, no approach to the husband will be made by the DSS. Otherwise, the wife will be asked for information about the whereabouts of the liable relative (although producing the information cannot be made a condition of receiving benefit) and he will be contacted as soon as possible. The husband is asked to pay as much as he can, if possible enough to remove the need for income support to be paid to the wife and any children.

In deciding what level of payment is acceptable on a voluntary basis, it is understood that the following formula is used as a starting point. The income support personal allowances and premiums for the man are taken, plus rent, or mortgage payments, council tax and 15 per cent of his net wage. If the man has a new partner, two calculations are done—one as if the man was single and the other using joint incomes. The lower figure is then taken. The excess over this amount is regarded as available to be used as maintenance. But this is only a basis for discussion and payment of a lesser sum may be agreed, particularly if there are other essential expenses. Clearly there is scope for negotiation here. Thus if the man himself is receiving income support he would not be expected to pay anything.

If the husband is unwilling to make a payment voluntarily, although the DSS believe that he has sufficient income, then legal proceedings may be considered. The first step will be to see if the wife will take action. The official policy is that the wife will merely be advised on the advantages of taking proceedings herself (that she may get enough maintenance to lift her off benefit and that an order for maintenance will continue if she ceases to be entitled to income support, as by working full-time). The first advantage is likely to be real in only a small minority of cases and the force of the second has been reduced by the introduction of the procedure in s.107(3) to (14). The choice should be left entirely to the woman. A wife may of course take proceedings herself even though the DSS have accepted voluntary payments from the husband.

The courts have refused to adopt the "liable relative formula" in private proceedings by wives or ex-wives (*Shallow* v. *Shallow* [1979] Fam. 1) and will only have regard to the man's subsistence level. By this they mean the ordinary scale rates of benefit plus housing costs. A more realistic approach may have been presaged by *Allen* v. *Allen* [1986] 2 F.L.R. 265, where the Court of Appeal used the long-term scale rate (now disappeared) as a yardstick. In *Delaney* v. *Delaney* [1990] 2 F.L.R. 457, the Court of Appeal accepted the principle that where the man had insufficient resources after taking account of his reasonable commitments to a new family to maintain his former wife and family properly, a maintenance order should not financially cripple him where the wife is entitled to social security benefits. But no calculation of the man's income support level was made.

If the wife does not take proceedings, then the DSS may. The court is to have regard to all the circumstances, in particular the husband's resources, and may order him to pay whatever sum is appropriate (subs. (2)). Presumably, the same principles will govern the amount of an order as in a private application. There were some new provisions in s.107(1) in cases where the order included amounts for children, but it is not at all clear how these interacted with the general test of appropriateness under subs. (2). Note that since April 5, 1993 the courts have not had the power to make new orders for maintenance for children (s. 8(3) Child Support Act 1991). The wife's adultery or desertion or other conduct is only a factor to be taken into account, not a bar to any order. Nor is the existence of a separation agreement under which the wife agrees not to claim maintenance a bar (*National Assistance Board v. Parkes* [1955] 2 Q.B. 506). Although *Hulley v. Thompson* [1981] 1 W.L.R. 159 concerned only the liability to maintain children, because there had been a divorce, it showed that not even a consent order under which the man transferred the matrimonial home to his ex-wife and she agreed to receive no maintenance for herself or the children, barred the statutory liability to maintain the children. However, it seems that the existence of the order could be taken into account in deciding what amount it is appropriate for the man to pay.

Proceedings by the DSS are relatively rare. In 1979 there were only 431 (SBC Annual Report for 1979 (Cmnd. 8033), para. 8.30).

Recovery of expenditure on income support: additional amounts and transfer of orders

107.—(1) In any case where—

(a) the claim for income support referred to in section 106(1) above is or was made by the parent of one or more children in respect of both himself and those children; and

(b) the other parent is liable to maintain those children but, by virtue of not being the claimant's husband or wife, is not liable to maintain the claimant,

the sum which the court may order that other parent to pay under subsection (2) of that section may include an amount, determined in accordance with regulations, in respect of any income support paid to or for the claimant by virtue of such provisions as may be prescribed.

(2) Where the sum which a court orders a person to pay under section 106 above includes by virtue of subsection (1) above an amount (in this section referred to as a "personal allowance element") in respect of income support by virtue of paragraph 1(2) of Schedule 2 to the Income Support (General) Regulations 1987 (personal allowance for lone parent) the order shall separately identify the amount of the personal allowance element.

(3) In any case where—

(a) there is in force an order under subsection (2) of section 106 above made against a person ("the liable parent") who is the parent of one or more children, in respect of the other parent or the children; and

717

(b) payments under the order fall to be made to the Secretary of State by virtue of subsection (4)(a) of that section; and

(c) that other parent (''the dependent parent'') ceases to claim income support,

the Secretary of State may, by giving notice in writing to the court which made the order and to the liable parent and the dependent parent, transfer to the dependent parent the right to receive the payments under the order, exclusive of any personal allowance element, and to exercise the relevant rights in relation to the order, except so far as relating to that element.

(4) Notice under subsection (3) above shall not be given (and if purportedly given, shall be of no effect) at a time when there is in force a maintenance order made against the liable parent—

(a) in favour of the dependent parent or one or more of the children; or

(b) in favour of some other person for the benefit of the dependent parent or one or more of the children;

and if such a maintenance order is made at any time after notice under that subsection has been given, the order under section 106(2) above shall cease to have effect.

(5) In any case where—

(a) notice is given to a magistrates' court under subsection (3) above,

(b) payments under the order are required to be made by any method of payment falling within section 59(6) of the Magistrates' Courts Act 1980 (standing order, etc.), and

(c) the clerk to the justices for the petty sessions area for which the court is acting decides that payment by that method is no longer possible,

the clerk shall amend the order to provide that payments under the order shall be made by the liable parent to the clerk.

(6) Except as provided by subsections (8) and (12) below, where the Secretary of State gives notice under subsection (3) above, he shall cease to be entitled—

(a) to receive any payment under the order in respect of any personal allowance element; or

(b) to exercise the relevant rights, so far as relating to any such element,

notwithstanding that the dependent parent does not become entitled to receive any payment in respect of that element or to exercise the relevant rights so far as so relating.

(7) If, in a case where the Secretary of State gives notice under subsection (3) above, a payment under the order is or has been made to him wholly or partly in respect of the whole or any part of the period beginning with the day on which the transfer takes effect and ending with the day on which the notice under subsection (3) above is given to the liable parent, the Secretary of State shall—

(a) repay to or for the liable parent so much of the payment as is referable to any personal allowance element in respect of that period or, as the case may be, the part of it in question; and

(b) pay to or for the dependent parent so much of any remaining balance of the payment as is referable to that period or part;

and a payment under paragraph (b) above shall be taken to discharge, to that extent, the liability of the liable parent to the dependent parent under the order in respect of that period or part.

(8) If, in a case where the Secretary of State has given notice under subsection (3) above, the dependent parent makes a further claim for income support, then—

(a) the Secretary of State may, by giving a further notice in writing to the court which made the order and to the liable parent and the dependent parent, transfer back from the dependent parent to himself the right to receive the payments and to exercise the relevant rights; and

(b) that transfer shall revive the Secretary of State's right to receive payment under the order in respect of any personal allowance element and to exercise the relevant rights so far as relating to any such element.

(9) Subject to subsections (10) and (11) below, in any case where—

(a) notice is given to a magistrates' court under subsection (8) above, and

(b) the method of payment under the order which subsists immediately before the day on which the transfer under subsection (8) above takes effect differs from the method of payment which subsisted immediately before the day on which the transfer under subsection (3) above (or, as the case may be, the last such transfer) took effect,

the clerk to the justices for the petty sessions area for which the court is acting shall amend the order by reinstating the method of payment under the order which subsisted immediately before the day on which the transfer under subsection (3) above (or, as the case may be, the last such transfer) took effect.

(10) The clerk shall not amend the order under subsection (9) above if the Secretary of State gives notice in writing to the clerk, on or before the day on which notice under subsection (8) above is given, that the method of payment under the order which subsists immediately before the day on which the transfer under subsection (8) above takes effect is to continue.

(11) In any case where—

(a) notice is given to a magistrates' court under subsection (8) above,

(b) the method of payment under the order which subsisted immediately before the day on which the transfer under subsection (3) above (or, if there has been more than one such transfer, the last such transfer) took effect was any method of payment falling within section 59(6) of the Magistrates' Courts Act 1980 (standing order, etc.), and

(c) the clerk decides that payment by that method is no longer possible, the clerk shall amend the order to provide that payments under the order shall be made by the liable parent to the clerk.

(12) A transfer under subsection (3) or (8) above does not transfer or otherwise affect the right of any person—

(a) to receive a payment which fell due to him at a time before the transfer took effect; or

(b) to exercise the relevant rights in relation to any such payment;

and, where notice is given under subsection (3), subsection (6) above does not deprive the Secretary of State of his right to receive such a payment in respect of any personal allowance element or to exercise the relevant rights in relation to such a payment.

(13) For the purposes of this section—

(a) a transfer under subsection (3) above takes effect on the day on which the dependent parent ceases to be in receipt of income support in consequence of the cessation referred to in paragraph (c) of that subsection, and

(b) a transfer under subsection (8) above takes effect on—

(i) the first day in respect of which the dependent parent receives income support after the transfer under subsection (3) above took effect, or

(ii) such later day as may be specified for the purpose in the notice under subsection (8).

irrespective of the day on which notice under the subsection in question is given.

(14) Any notice required to be given to the liable parent under subsection (3) or (8) above shall be taken to have been given if it has been sent to his last known address.

(15) In this section—

"child" means a person under the age of 16, notwithstanding section 78(6)(d) above;

"court" shall be construed in accordance with section 106 above;

"maintenance order"—

    (a) in England and Wales, means—

        (i) any order for the making of periodical payments or for the payment of a lump sum which is, or has at any time been, a maintenance order within the meaning of the Attachment of Earnings Act 1971;

        (ii) any order under Part III of the Matrimonial and Family Proceedings Act 1984 (overseas divorce) for the making of periodical payments or for the payment of a lump sum;

    (b) in Scotland, has the meaning given by section 106 of the Debtors (Scotland) Act 1987, but disgarding paragraph (h) (alimentary bond or agreement);

"the relevant rights", in relation to an order under section 106(2) above, means the right to bring any proceedings, take any steps or do any other thing under or in relation to the order which the Secretary of State could have brought, taken or done apart from any transfer under this section.

DERIVATION

Social Security Act 1986, s.24A, as amended by the Maintenance Enforcement Act 1991, s.9, with effect from April 1, 1992 (Maintenance Enforcement Act 1991 Commencement No. 2 Order 1992 (S.I. 1992 No. 455)).

GENERAL NOTE

The predecessors of this section and s.108 formed one of the central strategic objectives of the Social Security Act 1990 (H. C. Hansard, April 3, 1990, Vol. 170, col. 1137 (Tony Newton); H. L. Hansard, April 20, 1990, Vol. 518, col. 234 (Lord Henley)), but were only introduced at the Report stage in the Commons. They therefore received relatively little Parliamentary discussion due to the operation of the guillotine. The Government has carried out a general review of the maintenance system, based on a survey of work in U.K. courts and DSS offices and study of overseas systems, and has produced radical proposals in *Children Come First* (Cm. 1264), now embodied in the Child Support Act 1991 from April 1993. Action had already been taken to tighten up the assessment of an absent parent's ability to pay maintenance for his family on income support. The new provisions were regarded as desirable in the short term to improve the effectiveness of the present system, pending the more radical reform (H. C. Hansard, March 28, Vol. 170, col. 566). However, ss.107 and 108 remain in force despite the implementation of the Child Support Act.

Section 107 contains two elements. The first relates to the situation where a lone parent is receiving income support, but the absent parent of the child(ren) is not liable to maintain the parent under s.78(6) because the parents are not or are no longer married. Where the DSS seeks its own order against the absent parent, courts are empowered to take into account income support relating to the lone parent in calculating the amount to be paid for the child(ren) and the DSS may of course take this into account in negotiating voluntary agreements. The second is to allow a DSS order to be transferred to the lone parent when that person comes off income support, rather than the lone parent having to obtain a separate private maintenance order. Note that since April 5, 1993, the courts have not had the power to make new orders for maintenance for children (s. 8(3) Child Support Act 1991).

Subsections (1) and (2)

These provisions comprise the first element identified above. They apply when both of conditions (a) and (b) in subs. (1) are satisfied. Under para. (a), s.106 gives the DSS power to obtain an order against a person who is liable to maintain a claimant of income support or a person included in the family for claiming purposes. Section 78(6) defines liability to maintain for this purpose. There is a liability to maintain a spouse and any children. Under s.78(6)(d) "child" includes a person aged 16 to 18 (inclusive) who is still a member of the claimant's family for income support purposes (*e.g.* because still in full-time education). However, s.107(15) provides that for the purposes of s.107 "child" is restricted to a person under the age of 16. Thus, lone parent claimants whose children are all over 15 will fall outside this provision. Under para. (b), the absent parent must not be married to the lone parent, so that the obligation to maintain under s.78(6) is only in respect of the child(ren). If both these conditions are met, a court may include whatever amount the regulations determine in respect of the income support paid for the lone parent. The Income Support (Liable Relatives) Regulations specify in general the children's personal allowances, family premium, lone parent premium. disabled child premium and the carer premium in respect of care for a child.

The intention was said to be that the regulation-making power "will be used to specify that once having looked at the allowances and premiums that are paid because there are children, the court should also have regard to the income support personal allowance paid for the mother" (H. C. Hansard, March 28, 1990, Vol. 170, col. 567). The Liable Relatives Regulations provide that if the liable parent has the means to pay in addition to the amounts already specified, a court order may include some or all of the dependent parent's personal allowance.

It is said that in a private maintenance order for children the court can take account of the parent's care costs and that social security law is thus being brought into line with family law. However, there is nothing as specific as s.107 in family law. The existing power of the court on orders sought by the DSS is already wide and it is not clear how much real difference the new powers will make. Under s.106(2) the court may order payment of such sum as it may consider appropriate. The assumption seems to be that not only could the personal allowance for a child under 16 be considered under this provision, but also the family premium (paid to all claimants with a child or young person (16–18) in the family) and the additional lone parent premium. If such amounts can be considered under the existing law (and they might be considered to reflect the care costs of the lone parent) there seems no reason why the court could not also consider some part of the parent's personal allowance if that was considered "appropriate." However, s. 107(1) and the Liable Relatives Regulations make the position clear, which should be an advantage.

It is notable that the court retains a discretion as to what amounts to consider and that the overriding factor under s.106(2) is what is appropriate. Under para. 1 of Sched. 2 to the Income Support (General) Regulations 1987 the personal allowance for a lone parent aged under 18 or over 24 is the same as for a single person with no dependants. There is only a difference (currently £9.70 p.w.) for those aged 18 to 24.

Subs. (2) provides that if the lone parent's personal allowance under Sched. 2 is covered by the order, this element must be separately identified. This has no bearing on subs. (1), but is relevant to the procedure set up by subss. (3) to (14).

Subsections (3) to (15)

These provisions contain the important procedure allowing the transfer of a DSS order to the lone parent on coming off income support. The conditions for transfer under subs. (3) are that in such a case (remembering that "child" is defined to cover only those under 16 (subs. (15)) the Secretary of State gives notice to the court which made the order and to both the parents. Then the right to enforce or apply for variation of the order (apart from any personal allowance element identified under subs. (2)) is transferred to the lone parent (known as "the dependent parent"). Thus, the personal allowance element, which is of no net benefit to the lone parent while she is on income support, is removed at the point when its value would actually be felt by the lone parent. The DSS can no longer enforce the personal allowance element of the order (subs. (6)). Under subs. (13)(a) the transfer takes effect on the day on which the dependent parent ceases to receive income support in consequence of ceasing to claim. This is a peculiar way of putting things. If the dependent parent's circumstances change (*e.g.* her capital goes over the cut-off limit or she starts full-time work) her entitlement to income support may be terminated on review by the AO under s.25. She may well then choose not to claim income support again, as it would be a useless exercise. The dependent parent could with some strain be said to cease to claim income support and so to satisfy subs. (3)(c), but the cessation of receipt of income support is not in consequence of the cessation of claiming but of the review and revision by the AO.

Subs. (3) is not to apply if a private maintenance order (see subs. (15) for definition) is in existence, and if the dependent parent obtains one after a transfer the right to enforce the DSS order disappears (subs. (4)).

If, after a transfer, the dependent parent makes another claim for income support (presumably only while still having children under 16), the Secretary of State may by giving notice to all parties re-transfer to the DSS the right to enforce the order and revive the personal allowance element on the dependent parent becoming entitled to income support (subss. (8) and (13)(b)). Presumably, the revival of the personal allowance element depends on the conditions of subss. (1) and (2) being met at the date of revival.

Reduction of expenditure on income support: certain maintenance orders to be enforceable by the Secretary of State

108.—(1) This section applies where—

(a) a person ("the claimant") who is the parent of one or more children is in receipt of income support either in respect of those children or in respect of both himself and those children; and

(b) there is in force a maintenance order made against the other parent ("the liable person")—

(i) in favour of the claimant or one or more of the children, or

(ii) in favour of some other person for the benefit of the claimant or one or more of the children,

and in this section "the primary recipient" means the person in whose favour that maintenance order was made.

(2) If, in a case where this section applies, the liable person fails to comply with any of the terms of the maintenance order—

(a) the Secretary of State may bring any proceedings or take any other steps to enforce the order that could have been brought or taken by or on behalf of the primary recipient; and

(b) any court before which proceedings are brought by the Secretary of State by virtue of paragraph (a) above shall have the same powers in connection with those proceedings as it would have had if they had been brought by the primary recipient.

(3) The Secretary of State's powers under this section are exercisable at his discretion and whether or not the primary recipient or any other person consents to their exercise; but any sums recovered by virtue of this section shall be payable to or for the primary recipient, as if the proceedings or steps in question had been brought or taken by him or on his behalf.

(4) The powers conferred on the Secretary of State by subsection (2)(a) above include power—

(a) to apply for the registration of the maintenance order under—

(i) section 17 of the Maintenance Orders Act 1950;

(ii) section 2 of the Maintenance Orders Act 1958; or

(iii) the Civil Jurisdiction and Judgments Act 1982; and

(b) to make an application under section 2 of the Maintenance Orders (Reciprocal Enforcement) Act 1972 (application for enforcement in reciprocating country).

(5) Where this section applies, the prescribed person shall in prescribed circumstances give the Secretary of State notice of any application—

(a) to alter, vary, suspend, discharge, revoke, revive, or enforce the maintenance order in question; or

(b) to remit arrears under that maintenance order;

and the Secretary of State shall be entitled to appear and be heard on the application.

(6) Where, by virtue of this section, the Secretary of State commences any proceedings to enforce a maintenance order, he shall, in relation to those proceedings, be treated for the purposes of any enactment or instrument relating to maintenance orders as if he were a person entitled to payment under the maintenance order in question (but shall not thereby become entitled to any such payment).

(7) Where, in any proceedings under this section in England and Wales, the court makes an order for the whole or any part of the arrears due under the maintenance order in question to be paid as a lump sum, the Secretary of State

shall inform the Legal Aid Board of the amount of that lump sum if he knows—

  (a) that the primary recipient either—

      (i) received legal aid under the Legal Aid Act 1974 in connection with the proceedings in which the maintenance order was made, or

      (ii) was an assisted party, within the meaning of the Legal Aid Act 1988, in those proceedings; and

  (b) that a sum remains unpaid on account of the contribution required of the primary recipient—

      (i) under section 9 of the Legal Aid Act 1974 in respect of those proceedings, or

      (ii) under section 16 of the Legal Aid Act 1988 in respect of the costs of his being represented under Part IV of that Act in those proceedings,

as the case may be.

(8) In this section "maintenance order" has the same meaning as it has in section 107 above but does not include any such order for the payment of a lump sum.

DERIVATION

Social Security Act 1986, s.24B.

GENERAL NOTE

Section 108 enables the DSS to enforce certain private maintenance orders in favour of lone parent claimants of income support. Only lone parents are covered by subs. (1)(a), and not mere separated or divorced spouses, but the maintenance order may be in favour either of the parent or the child(ren) or both. The Secretary of State may at his discretion and without the consent of the lone parent take steps (including those specified in subs. (5)) to enforce the order as if he were the person entitled to payment under the order (subss. (2), (3) and (6)). But any sums recovered are payable to the primary recipient under the order (subss. (3) and (6)). Under subs. (5) regulations may specify who has to inform the DSS of applications to vary, suspend etc the private order or to remit arrears. Reg. 3 of the Income Support (Liable Relatives) Regulations specifies various court officials. The Secretary of State is given the right to be heard on any such application, but has no power to make such an application, e.g. to increase the amount of an order. This is because subs. (2) only operates when there is a failure to comply with the terms (*i.e.* the existing terms) of the order.

Subs. (7) requires the Secretary of State to inform the Legal Aid Board when a lump sum of arrears is to be paid when the Board might be able to recover a contribution out of the lump sum.

Overall s.108 is a powerful weapon for the DSS to enforce the payment of maintenance orders. If the lone parent has her own order, which is not being paid, income support will make up the shortfall. There is thus no great incentive for the lone parent to go through all the hassle of enforcement, and there may be other circumstances making her reluctant to take action. The DSS will have no such inhibitions.

The Secretary of State predicted that the amount of maintenance recovered by the DSS in respect of lone parents on income support would rise to about £260 million in 1990–91, having gone up from £155 million in 1988–89 to £180 million in 1989–90 (H.C. Hansard, March 28, 1990, Vol. 170, col. 571). The predicted increase was partly based on the provisions now contained in ss.107 and 108 and partly on giving greater priority and resources to such work, with changes in the administrative guidance. These changes are to point up the need to stress to lone parents on benefits the advantages of reflecting the absent parent's proper responsibilities in the maintenance arrangements from the outset and also to indicate that the "normal expectation" should be that a lone parent will co-operate in establishing where responsibility lies. It is, however, recognised that there may be circumstances in which lone parents will not wish to name the father of a child. The White paper, *Children Come First*, proposed reductions in the lone parent's benefit if she declines without good cause to take maintenance proceedings. The Child Support Act 1991 imposes such an obligation only in relation to applications under the Act.

Diversion of arrested earnings to Secretary of State—Scotland

109.—(1) Where in Scotland a creditor who is enforcing a maintenance order or alimentary bond or agreement by a current maintenance arrestment or a con-joined arrestment order is in receipt of income support, the creditor may in writing authorise the Secretary of State to receive any sums payable under the arrestment or order until the creditor ceases to be in receipt of income support or in writing withdraws the authorisation, whichever occurs first.

(2) On the intimation by the Secretary of State—

(a) to the employer operating the current maintenance arrestment; or

(b) to the sheriff clerk operating the conjoined arrestment order;

of an authorisation under subsection (1) above, the employer or sheriff clerk shall, until notified by the Secretary of State that the authorisation has ceased to have effect, pay to the Secretary of State any sums which would otherwise be payable under the arrestment or order to the creditor.

DERIVATION

Social Security Act 1986, s.25A.

PART VII

PROVISION OF INFORMATION

The Registration Service

Provisions relating to age, death and marriage

124.—(1) Regulations made by the Registrar General under section 20 of the Registration Service Act 1953 or section 54 of the Registration of Births, Deaths and Marriages (Scotland) Act 1965 may provide for the furnishing by superin-tendent registrars and registrars, subject to the payment of such fee as may be prescribed by the regulations, of such information for the purposes—

(a) of the provisions of the Contributions and Benefits Act to which this section applies; and

(b) the provisions of this Act so far as they have effect in relation to matters arising under those provisions,

including copies or extracts from the registers in their custody, as may be so prescribed.

(2) This section applies to the following provisions of the Contributions and Benefits Act—

(a) Parts I to VI except section 108;

(b) Part VII, so far as it relates to income support and family credit;

(c) Part VIII, so far as it relates to any social fund payment such as is men-tioned in section 138(1)(a) or (2);

(d) Part IX;

(e) Part XI; and

(f) Part XII.

(3) Where the age, marriage or death of a person is required to be ascertained or proved for the purposes mentioned in subsection (1) above, any person—

(a) on presenting to the custodian of the register under the enactments relat-ing to the registration of births, marriages and deaths, in which particulars of the birth, marriage or death (as the case may be) of the first-mentioned person are entered, a duly completed requisition in writing in that behalf; and

(b) on payment of a fee of £1.50 in England and Wales and £4 in Scotland,

shall be entitled to obtain a copy, certified under the hand of the custodian, of the entry of those particulars.

(4) Requisitions for the purposes of subsection (3) above shall be in such form and contain such particulars as may from time to time be specified by the Registrar General, and suitable forms of requisition shall, on request, be supplied without charge by superintendent registrars and registrars.

(5) In this section—

(a) as it applies to England and Wales—

"Registrar General" means the Registrar General for England and Wales; and

"superintendent registrar" and "registrar" mean a superintendent registrar or, as the case may be, registrar for the purposes of the enactments relating to the registration of births, deaths and marriages; and

(b) as it applies to Scotland—

"Registrar General" means the Registrar General of Births, Deaths and Marriages for Scotland;

"registrar" means a district registrar, senior registrar or assistant registrar for the purposes of the enactment relating to the registration of births, deaths and marriages in Scotland.

DERIVATION

Social Security Act 1975, s.160.

DEFINITIONS

"the Contributions and Benefits Act"—see s.191.
"prescribed"—*ibid.*

Regulations as to notification of deaths

125.—(1) Regulations may provide that it shall be the duty of any of the following persons—

(a) the Registrar General for England and Wales;

(b) the Registrar General of Births, Deaths and Marriages for Scotland;

(c) each registrar of births and deaths,

to furnish the Secretary of State, for the purpose of his functions under the Contributions and Benefits Act and this Act and the functions of the Northern Ireland Department under any Northern Ireland legislation corresponding to either of them, with the prescribed particulars of such deaths as may be prescribed.

(2) The regulations may make provision as to the manner in which and the times at which the particulars are to be furnished.

DERIVATION

Social Security Act 1986, s.60.

DEFINITIONS

"the Contributions and Benefits Act"—see s.191.
"the Northern Ireland Department"—*ibid.*
"prescribed"—*ibid.*

Personal representatives—income support and supplementary benefit

Personal representatives to give information about the estate of a deceased person who was in receipt of income support or supplementary benefit

126.—(1) The personal representatives of a person who was in receipt of income support or supplementary benefit at any time before his death shall provide the Secretary of State with such information as he may require relating to the assets and liabilities of that person's estate.

(2) If the personal representatives fail to supply any information within 28 days of being required to do so under subsection (1) above, then—

 (a) the appropriate court may, on the application of the Secretary of State, make an order directing them to supply that information within such time as may be specified in the order; and

 (b) any such order may provide that all costs (or, in Scotland, expenses) of and incidental to the application shall be borne personally by any of the personal representatives.

(3) In this section "the appropriate court" means—

 (a) in England and Wales, a county court;

 (b) in Scotland, the sheriff;

and any application to the sheriff under this section shall be made by summary application.

<small>DERIVATION</small>

Social Security Act 1986, s.27A.

<small>GENERAL NOTE</small>

Under s.71(3) an overpayment which would have been recoverable from a person is recoverable from that person's estate (*Secretary of State for Social Services v. Solly* [1974] 3 All E.R. 922). Section 126 provides a specific obligation for the estate to provide information about the assets in it. However, s.126 only applies to the estates of income support or supplementary benefit claimants. It does not apply to family credit, FIS, disability working allowance, housing benefit or council tax benefit claimants, all of whom can be overpaid by concealing capital. Nor does it apply to anyone other than a recipient of income support or supplementary benefit. Sometimes a person other than a recipient may become liable to recovery by making a misrepresentation or failing to disclose a material fact *(R(SB) 21/82* and *R(SB) 28/83)*.

Maintenance proceedings

Furnishing of addresses for maintenance proceedings, etc.

133. The Secretary of State may incur expenses for the purpose of furnishing the address at which a man or woman is recorded by him as residing, where the address is required for the purpose of taking or carrying on legal proceedings to obtain or enforce an order for the making by the man or woman of payments—

 (a) for the maintenance of the man's wife or former wife, or the woman's husband or former husband; or

 (b) for the maintenance or education of any person as being the son or daughter of the man or his wife or former wife, or of the woman or her husband or former husband.

<small>DERIVATION</small>

Social Security Act 1975, s.161(1).

PART XI

COMPUTATION OF BENEFITS

Effect of alteration in the component rates of income support

159.—(1) Subject to such exceptions and conditions as may be prescribed, where—

(a) an award of income support is in force in favour of any person ("the recipient"); and

(b) there is an alteration in any of the relevant amounts, that is to say—
    (i) any of the component rates of income support;
    (ii) any of the other sums specified in regulations under Part VII of the Contributions and Benefits Act; or
    (iii) the recipient's benefit income; and

(c) the alteration affects the computation of the amount of income support to which the recipient is entitled,

then subsection (2) or (3) below (as the case may be) shall have effect.

(2) Where, in consequence of the alteration in question, the recipient becomes entitled to an increased or reduced amount of income support ("the new amount"), then, as from the commencing date, the amount of income support payable to or for the recipient under the award shall be the new amount, without any further decision of an adjudication officer, and the award shall have effect accordingly.

(3) Where, notwithstanding the alteration in question, the recipient continues on and after the commencing date to be entitled to the same amount of income support as before, the award shall continue in force accordingly.

(4) In any case where—

(a) there is an alteration in any of the relevant amounts; and

(b) before the commencing date (but after that date is fixed) an award of income support is made in favour of a person,

the award either may provide for income support to be paid as from the commencing date, in which case the amount shall be determined by reference to the relevant amounts which will be in force on that date, or may provide for an amount determined by reference to the amounts in force at the date of the award.

(5) In this section—

"alteration" means—
    (a) in relation to—
        (i) the component rates of income support; or
        (ii) any other sums specified in regulations under Part VII of the Contributions and Benefits Act,
    their alteration by or under any enactment whether or not contained in that Part; and
    (b) in relation to a person's benefit income, the alteration of any of the sums referred to in section 150 above—
        (i) by any enactment; or
        (ii) by an order under section 150 or 152 above,
    to the extent that any such alteration affects the amount of his benefit income;

"benefit income", in relation to any person, means so much of his income as consists of—
    (a) benefit under the Contributions and Benefits Act, other than income support; or
    (b) a war disablement pension or war widow's pension;

"the commencing date" in relation to an alteration, means the date on which the alteration comes into force in the case of the person in question;

"component rate", in relation to income support, means the amount of—
    (a) the sum referred to in section 126(5)(b)(i) and (ii) of the Contributions and Benefits Act; or
    (b) any of the sums specified in regulations under section 135(1) of that Act; and

"relevant amounts" has the meaning given by subsection (1)(b) above.

DERIVATION

Social Security Act 1986, s.64A.

DEFINITIONS

"the Contributions and Benefits Act"—see s.191.
"war disablement pension"—*ibid.*
"war widow's pension"—*ibid.*

GENERAL NOTE

The general rule under s.159 is that if there is an alteration in the prescribed figures for personal allowances, premiums, the relevant sum (*i.e.* assumed "strike pay" in trade dispute cases), or any social security benefits which count as income for income support purposes (subss.(1) and (5)), then any consequent change in the amount of income support which is payable takes effect automatically without the need for a decision by an AO (subs. (2)). Thus no right of appeal arises against the change in the amount, although the claimant can always request a review of the decision awarding benefit, as altered under s.159. The former power to review an award of income support in such circumstances has been removed by the amendment to reg. 69(3) of the Adjudication Regulations, except where some kind of transitional addition is in payment. In this latter case, there must be a review under reg. 69(3A) to give effect to the change.

Implementation of increases in income support due to attainment of particular ages

160.—(1) This section applies where—
  (a) an award of income support is in force in favour of a person ("the recipient"); and
  (b) there is a component which becomes applicable, or applicable at a particular rate, in his case if he or some other person attains a particular age.
(2) If, in a case where this section applies, the recipient or other person attains the particular age referred to in paragraph (b) of subsection (1) above and, in consequence—
  (a) the component in question becomes applicable, or applicable at a particular rate, in the recipient's case (whether or not some other component ceases, for the same reason, to be applicable, or applicable at a particular rate, in his case; and
  (b) after taking account of any such cessation, the recipient becomes entitled to an increased amount of income support,
then, except as provided by subsection (3) below, as from the day on which he becomes so entitled, the amount of income support payable to or for him under the award shall be that increased amount, without any further decision of an adjudication officer, and the award shall have effect accordingly.
(3) Subsection (2) above does not apply in any case where, in consequence of the recipient or other person attaining the age in question, some question arises in relation to the recipient's entitlement to any benefit under the Contributions and Benefits Act, other than—
  (a) the question whether the component concerned, or any other component, becomes or ceases to be applicable, or applicable at a particular rate, in his case; and
  (b) the question whether, in consequence, the amount of his income support falls to be varied.
(4) In this section "component", in relation to a person and his income support, means any of the sums specified in regulations under section 135(1) of the Contributions and Benefits Act.

DERIVATION

Social Security Act 1986, s.64B.

DEFINITION

"the Contributions and Benefits Act"—see s.191.

GENERAL NOTE

Section 160 extends the process begun by s.159 of taking routine adjustments in the amount of income support out of the ordinary mechanism of review by an AO under s.25.

PART XII

FINANCE

The social fund

167.—(1) The fund known as the social fund shall continue in being by that name.

(2) The social fund shall continue to be maintained under the control and management of the Secretary of State and payments out of it shall be made by him.

(3) The Secretary of State shall make payments into the social fund of such amounts, at such times and in such manner as he may with the approval of the Treasury determine.

(4) Accounts of the social fund shall be prepared in such form, and in such manner and at such times, as the Treasury may direct, and the Comptroller and Auditor General shall examine and certify every such account and shall lay copies of it, together with his report, before Parliament.

(5) The Secretary of State shall prepare an annual report on the social fund.

(6) A copy of every such report shall be laid before each House of Parliament.

DERIVATION

Subs.(1): Social Security Act 1986, s.32(1).
Subss. (2) to (6): 1986 Act, s.32(5) to (7B).

Allocations from social fund

168.—(1) The Secretary of State shall allocate amounts for payments from the social fund such as are mentioned in section 138(1)(b) of the Contributions and Benefits Act in a financial year.

(2) The Secretary of State may specify the amounts either as sums of money or by reference to money falling into the social fund on repayment or partial repayment of loans, or partly in the former and partly in the latter manner.

(3) Allocations—

(a) may be for payments by a particular social fund officer or group of social fund officers;

(b) may be for different amounts for different purposes;

(c) may be made at such time or times as the Secretary of State considers appropriate; and

(d) may be in addition to any other allocation to the same officer or group of officers or for the same purpose.

(4) The Secretary of State may at any time re-allocate amounts previously allocated, and subsections (2) and (3) above shall have effect in relation to a re-allocation as they have effect in relation to an allocation.

(5) The Secretary of State may give general directions to social fund officers or groups of social fund officers, or to any class of social fund officers, with respect to the control and management by social fund officers or groups of social fund officers of the amounts allocated to them under this section.

DERIVATION

Social Security Act 1986, s.32(8A) to (8E).

DEFINITION

"the Contributions and Benefits Act"—see s.191.

GENERAL NOTE

See the notes to the social fund directions.

Adjustments between social fund and other sources of finance

169.—(1) There shall be made—
(a) out of the social fund into the Consolidated Fund or the National Insurance Fund;
(b) into the social fund out of money provided by Parliament or the National Insurance Fund,
such payments by way of adjustment as the Secretary of State determines (in accordance with any directions of the Treasury) to be appropriate in consequence of any enactment or regulations relating to the repayment or offsetting of a benefit or other payment under the Contributions and Benefits Act.

(2) Where in any other circumstances payments fall to be made by way of adjustment—
(a) out of the social fund into the Consolidated Fund or the National Insurance Fund; or
(b) into the social fund out of money provided by Parliament or the National Insurance Fund,
then, in such cases or classes of cases as may be specified by the Secretary of State by order, the amount of the payments to be made shall be taken to be such, and payments on account of it shall be be made at such times and in such manner, as may be determined by the Secretary of State in accordance with any direction given by the Treasury.

DERIVATION

Social Security Act 1986, s.85(11) and (12).

DEFINITION

"the Contributions and Benefits Act"—see s.191.

PART XV

MISCELLANEOUS

Supplementary benefit etc.

Applications of provisions of Act to supplementary benefit etc.

186. Schedule 10 to this Act shall have effect for the purposes of making provision in relation to the benefits there mentioned.

Miscellaneous

Certain benefit to be inalienable

187.—(1) Subject to the provisions of this Act, every assignment of or charge on—
  (a) benefit as defined in section 122 of the Contributions and Benefits Act;
  (b) any income-related benefit; or
  (c) child benefit,
and every agreement to assign or charge such benefit shall be void; and, on the bankruptcy of a beneficiary, such benefit shall not pass to any trustee or other person acting on behalf of his creditors.
  (2) In the application of subsection (1) above to Scotland—
  (a) the reference to assignment of benefit shall be read as a reference to assignation, "assign" being construed accordingly;
  (b) the reference to a beneficiary's bankruptcy shall be read as a reference to the sequestration of his estate or the appointment on his estate of a judicial factor under section 41 of the Solicitors (Scotland) Act 1980.
  (3) In calculating for the purposes of section 5 of the Debtors Act 1869 or section 4 of the Civil Imprisonment (Scotland) Act 1882 the means of any beneficiary, no account shall be taken of any increase of disablement benefit in respect of a child or of industrial death benefit.

DERIVATION

  Social Security Act 1975, s.87.

DEFINITIONS

  "the Contributions and Benefits Act"—see s.191.
  "income-related benefit"—*ibid.*

PART XVI

GENERAL

Supplementary

Interpretation—general

191. In this Act, unless the context otherwise requires—
"the 1975 Act" means the Social Security Act 1975;
"the 1986 Act" means the Social Security Act 1986;
"benefit" means benefit under the Contributions and Benefits Act;
[*Omitted definitions not applying to the benefits in this book*]
"Commissioner" means the Chief Social Security Commissioner or any other Social Security Commissioner and includes a tribunal of 3 Commissioners constituted under section 57 above;
[*Omitted definition not applying to the benefits in this book*]

"the Consequential Provisions Act" means the Social Security (Consequential Provisions) Act 1992;

[*Omitted definition not applying to the benefits in this book*]

"the Contributions and Benefits Act" means the Social Security Contributions and Benefits Act 1992;

"disablement benefit" is to be construed in accordance with section 94(2)(*a*) of the Contributions and Benefits Act;

"the disablement questions" is to be construed in accordance with section 45 above;

"dwelling" means any residential accommodation, whether or not consisting of the whole or part of a building, and whether or not comprising separate and self-contained premises;

"5 year general qualification" is to be construed in accordance with section 71 of the Courts and Legal Services Act 1991;

[*Omitted definitions not applying to the benefits in this book*]

"income-related benefit" means—
  (a) income support;
  (b) family credit;
  (c) disability working allowance;
  (d) housing benefit; and
  [¹(e) council tax benefit];

"industrial injuries benefits" means benefit under Part V of the Contributions and Benefits Act, other than under Schedule 8;

[*Omitted definitions not applying benefits in this book*]

"local authority" means—
  (a) in relation to England and Wales, the council of a district or London borough, the Common Council of the City of London or the Council of the Isles of Scilly; and
  (b) in relation to Scotland, an islands or district council;

[*Omitted definitions not applying to the benefits in this book*]

"the Northern Ireland Department" means the Department of Health and Social Services for Northern Ireland;

"the Northern Ireland Administration Act" means the Social Security (Northern Ireland) Administration Act 1992;

"occupational pension scheme" has the same meaning as in section 66(1) of the Social Security Pensions Act 1975;

"the Old Cases Act" means the Industrial Injuries and Diseases (Old Cases) Act 1975;

[*Omitted definition not applying to the benefits in this book*]

"the Pensions Act" means the Social Security Pensions Act 1975;

"personal pension scheme" has the meaning assigned to it by section 84(1) of the 1986 Act;

"prescribe" means prescribe by regulations;

"President" means the President of social security appeal tribunals, disability appeal tribunals and medical appeal tribunals;

[*Omitted definitions not applying to the benefits in this book*]

"10 year general qualification" is to be construed in accordance with section 71 of the Courts and Legal Services Act 1991.

[*Omitted definition not applying to the benefits in this book*]

DERIVATION

Social Security Act 1975, Sched. 20 and Social Security Act 1986, s.84(1).

AMENDMENT

1. Local Government Finance Act 1992, Sched. 9, para. 25 (April 1, 1993).

Short title, commencement and extent

192.—(1) This Act may be cited as the Social Security Administration Act 1992.

(2) This Act is to be read, where appropriate, with the Contributions and Benefits Act and the Consequential Provisions Act.

(3) The enactments consolidated by this Act are repealed, in consequence of the consolidation, by the Consequential Provisions Act.

(4) Except as provided in Schedule 4 to the Consequential Provisions Act, this Act shall come into force on 1st July 1992.

(5) The following provisions extend to Northern Ireland—

section 24;

section 101;

section 170 (with Schedule 5);

section 177 (with Schedule 8); and

this section.

(6) Except as provided by this section, this Act does not extend to Northern Ireland.

DEFINITIONS

"the Consequential Provisions Act"—see s.191.
"the Contributions and Benefits Act"—*ibid.*

SCHEDULES

SCHEDULE 1   Section 1(6)

CLAIMS FOR BENEFIT MADE OR TREATED AS MADE BEFORE 1ST OCTOBER 1990

Claims made or treated as made on or after 2nd September 1985 and before 1st October 1986

1. Section 1 above shall have effect in relation to a claim made or treated as made on or after 2nd September 1985 and before 1st October 1986 as if the following subsections were substituted for subsections (1) to (3)—

"(1) Except in such cases as may be prescribed, no person shall be entitled to any benefit unless, in addition to any other conditions relating to that benefit being satisfied—

(a) he makes a claim for it—

　　(i) in the prescribed manner; and

　　(ii) subject to subsection (2) below, within the prescribed time; or

(b) by virtue of a provision of Chapter VI of Part II of the 1975 Act or of regulations made under such a provision he would have been treated as making a claim for it.

(2) Regulations shall provide for extending, subject to any prescribed conditions, the time within which a claim may be made in cases where it is not made within the prescribed time but good cause is shown for the delay.

(3) Notwithstanding any regulations made under this section, no person shall be entitled to any benefit (except disablement benefit or industrial death benefit) in respect of any period more than 12 months before the date on which the claim is made."

Claims made or treated as made on or after 1st October 1986 and before 6th April 1987

2. Section 1 above shall have effect in relation to a claim made or treated as made on or after 1st October 1986 and before 6th April 1987 as if the subsections set out in paragraph

1 above were substituted for subsections (1) to (3) but with the insertion in subsection (3) of the words ", reduced earnings allowance" after the words "disablement benefit".

Claims made or treated as made on or after 6th April 1987 and before 21st July 1989

3. Section 1 above shall have effect in relation to a claim made or treated as made on or after 6th April 1987 and before 21st July 1989, as if—

(a) the following subsection were substituted for subsection (1)—

"(1) Except in such cases as may be prescribed, no person shall be entitled to any benefit unless, in addition to any other conditions relating to that benefit being satisfied—

(a) he makes a claim for it in the prescribed manner and within the prescribed time; or

(b) by virtue of regulations made under section 51 of the 1986 Act he would have been treated as making a claim for it."; and

(b) there were omitted—

(i) from subsection (2), the words "except as provided by section 3 below"; and

(ii) subsection (3).

Claims made or treated as made on or after 21st July 1989 and before 13th July 1990

4. Section 1 above shall have effect in relation to a claim made or treated as made on or after 21st July 1989 and before 13th July 1990 as if there were omitted—

(a) from subsection (1), the words "and subject to the following provisions of this section and to section 3 below";

(b) from subsection (2), the words "except as provided by section 3 below"; and

(c) subsection (3).

Claims made or treated as made on or after 13th July 1990 and before 1st October 1990

5. Section 1 above shall have effect in relation to a claim made or treated as made on or after 13th July 1990 and before 1st October 1990 as if there were omitted—

(a) from subsection (1), the words "the following provisions of this section and to"; and

(b) subsection (3).

DEFINITIONS

"disablement benefit"—see s.191.
"prescribe"—*ibid.*

SCHEDULE 2   Sections 41, 43 and 50 to 52

COMMISSIONERS, TRIBUNALS ETC.—SUPPLEMENTARY PROVISIONS

Tenure of offices

1.—(1) Subject to the following provisions of this paragraph, the President and the regional and other full-time chairmen of social security appeal tribunals, medical appeal tribunals and disability appeal tribunals shall hold and vacate office in accordance with the terms of their appointment.

(2) Commissioners, the President and the full-time chairmen shall vacate their offices at the end of the completed year of service in which they attain the age of 72.

(3) Where the Lord Chancellor considers it desirable in the public interest to retain a Commissioner, the President or a full-time chairman in office after the time at which he would be required by sub-paragraph (2) above to vacate it, the Lord Chancellor may from time to time authorise his continuance in office until any date not later than that on which he attains the age of 75.

(4) A Commissioner, the President and a full-time chairman may be removed from office by the Lord Chancellor on the ground of incapacity or misbehaviour.

(5) Where the Lord Chancellor proposes to exercise a power conferred on him by sub-paragraph (3) or (4) above, it shall be his duty to consult the Lord Advocate with respect to the proposal.

(6) Nothing in sub-paragraph (2) or (3) above or in section 13 or 32 of the Judicial Pensions Act 1981 (which relate to pensions for Commissioners) shall apply to a person by virtue of his appointment in pursuance of section 52(2) above.

(7) Nothing in sub-paragraph (2) or (4) above applies to a Commissioner appointed before 23rd May 1980.

Remuneration etc. for President and Chairmen

2. The Secretary of State may pay, or make such payments towards the provision of, such remuneration, pensions, allowances or gratuities to or in respect of the President and full-time chairmen as, with the consent of the Treasury, he may determine.

Officers and staff

3. The President may appoint such officers and staff as he thinks fit—
(a) for himself;
(b) for the regional and other full-time chairmen;
(c) for social security appeal tribunals;
(d) for disability appeal tribunals; and
(e) for medical appeal tribunals,
with the consent of the Secretary of State and the Treasury as to numbers and as to remuneration and other terms and conditions of service.

Clerks to social security appeal tribunals and disability appeal tribunals

4.—(1) The President shall assign clerks to service the social security appeal tribunal for each area and the disability appeal tribunal for each area.

(2) The duty of summoning members of a panel to serve on such a tribunal shall be performed by the clerk to the tribunal.

Miscellaneous administrative duties of President

5. It shall be the duty of the President—
(a) to arrange—
   (i) such meetings of chairmen and members of social security appeal tribunals, chairmen and members of disability appeal tribunals and chairmen and members of medical appeal tribunals;
   (ii) such training for such chairmen and members, as he considers appropriate; and
(b) to secure that such works of reference relating to social security law as he considers appropriate are available for the use of chairmen and members of social security appeal tribunals, disability appeal tribunals and medical appeal tribunals.

Remuneration etc.

6. The Lord Chancellor shall pay to a Commissioner such salary or other remuneration, and such expenses incurred in connection with the work of a Commissioner or any tribunal presided over by a Commissioner, as may be determined by the Treasury.

7.—(1) The Secretary of State may pay—

(a) to any person specified in sub-paragraph (2) below, such remuneration and such travelling and other allowances;

(b) to any person specified in sub-paragraph (3) below, such travelling and other allowances; and

(c) subject to sub-paragraph (4) below, such other expenses in connection with the work of any person, tribunal or inquiry appointed or constituted under any provision of this Act,

as the Secretary of State with the consent of the Treasury may determine.

(2) The persons mentioned in sub-paragraph (1)(a) above are—

(a) any person (other than a Commissioner) appointed under this Act to determine questions or as a member of, or assessor to, a social security appeal tribunal, a disability appeal tribunal or a medical appeal tribunal; and

[¹(aa) a person appointed as medical assessor to a social security appeal tribunal under regulations under section 61A(4) above; and]

(b) a medical officer appointed under regulations under section 62 above.

(3) The persons mentioned in sub-paragraph (1)(b) above are—

(a) any person required to attend at any proceedings or inquiry under this Act; and

(b) any person required under this Act (whether for the purposes of this Act or otherwise) to attend for or to submit themselves to medical or other examination or treatment.

(4) Expenses are not payable under sub-paragraph (1)(c) above in connection with the work—

(a) of a tribunal presided over by a Commissioner; or

(b) of a social fund officer, a social fund inspector or the social fund Commissioner.

(5) In this paragraph references to travelling and other allowances include references to compensation for loss of remunerative time but such compensation shall not be paid to any person in respect of any time during which he is in receipt of remuneration under this paragraph.

Certificates of decisions

8. A document bearing a certificate which—

(a) is signed by a person authorised in that behalf by the Secretary of State; and

(b) states that the document, apart from the certificate, is a record of a decision—

    (i) of a Commissioner;

    (ii) of a social security appeal tribunal;

    (iii) of a disability appeal tribunal; or

    (iv) of an adjudication officer,

shall be conclusive evidence of the decision; and a certificate purporting to be so signed shall be deemed to be so signed unless the contrary is proved.

DERIVATION

Para. 1: Social Security Act 1975, Sched. 10, para. 1A and Social Security Act 1980, s.13.
Paras. 2 and 3: 1975 Act, Sched. 10, para. 1A(10) and (11).
Paras. 4 and 5: 1975 Act, Sched. 10, paras. 1B to 1D and Sched. 10A, para. 11.
Para. 6: 1975 Act, Sched. 10, para. 4.
Para. 7: 1975 Act, Sched. 10, para. 3 and Sched. 10A, para. 11.
Para. 8: Social Security Act 1980, s.17.

AMENDMENT

1. Social Security (Incapacity for Work) Act 1994, Sched. 1, para. 53 (April 13, 1995).

DEFINITIONS

"Commissioner"—see s.191.
"President"—*ibid.*

Paragraph 4

Of the President's detailed powers and duties, the duty to assign the clerk to SSATs and DATs (but, oddly, not to MATs) under para. 4 is particularly important. The fact that SBAT clerks were in the past DHSS employees had long been a source of criticism, although their role had become less prominent as SBATs themselves became stronger. The President's own regional offices have now been established for some years. Clerks work from these offices as part of the President's own staff and the independence of this system is now clearly established. The President also appoints clerks for CSATs (see para. 6 of Sched. 3 to the Child Support Act 1991).

Paragraph 5

The President's powers to arrange training and to provide materials are unlimited, but he is constrained by the budget allowed to him for these purposes.

SCHEDULE 3   Section 59

REGULATIONS AS TO PROCEDURE

Interpretation

1. In this Schedule "competent tribunal" means—

(a) a Commissioner;

(b) a social security appeal tribunal;

(c) a disability appeal tribunal;

(d) a medical appeal tribunal;

(e) an adjudicating medical practitioner.

Provision which may be made

2. Provision prescribing the procedure to be followed in connection with the consideration and determination of claims and questions by the Secretary of State, an adjudication officer and a competent tribunal, or in connection with the withdrawal of a claim.

3. Provision as to the striking out of proceedings for want of prosecution.

4. Provision as to the form which is to be used for any document, the evidence which is to be required and the circumstances in which any official record or certificate is to be sufficient or conclusive evidence.

5. Provision as to the time to be allowed—

(a) for producing any evidence; or

(b) for making an appeal.

6. Provision as to the manner in which, and the time within which, a question may be raised with a view to its decision by the Secretary of State under Part II of this Act or with a view to the review of a decision under that Part.

7. Provision for summoning persons to attend and give evidence or produce documents and for authorising the administration of oaths to witnesses.

8. Provision for authorising a competent tribunal consisting of two or more members to proceed with any case, with the consent of the claimant, in the absence of any member.

9. Provision for giving the chairman or acting chairman of a competent tribunal consisting of two or more members a second or casting vote where the number of members present is an even number.

10. Provision empowering the chairman of a social security appeal tribunal, a disability appeal tribunal or a medical tribunal to give directions for the disposal of any purported appeal which he is satisfied that the tribunal does not have jurisdiction to entertain.

11. Provision for the non-disclosure to a person of the particulars of any medical advice or medical evidence given or submitted for the purposes of a determination.

12. Provision for requiring or authorising the Secretary of State to hold, or to appoint a person to hold, an inquiry in connection with the consideration of any question by the Secretary of State.

DERIVATION

Social Security Act 1975, Sched. 13.

SCHEDULE 10   **Section 186**

SUPPLEMENTARY BENEFIT ETC.

Interpretation

1. In this Schedule—
"the former National Insurance Acts" means the National Insurance Act 1946 and the National Insurance Act 1965; and
"the former Industrial Injuries Acts" means the National Insurance (Industrial Injuries) Act 1946 and the National Insurance (Industrial Injuries) Act 1965.

Claims and payments

2.—(1) Section 5 above shall have effect in relation to the benefits specified in sub-paragraph (2) below as it has effect in relation to the benefits to which it applies by virtue of subsection (2).

(2) The benefits mentioned in sub-paragraph (1) above are benefits under—
(a) the former National Insurance Acts;
(b) the former Industrial Injuries Acts;
(c) the National Assistance Act 1948;
(d) the Supplementary Benefit Act 1966;
(e) the Supplementary Benefits Act 1976;
(f) the Family Income Supplements Act 1970.

Adjudication

3.—(1) Sections 20 to 29, 36 to 43, 51 to 61 and section 124 above shall have effect for the purposes of the benefits specified in paragraph 2(2) above as they have effect for the purposes of benefit within the meaning of section 122 of the Contributions and Benefits Act other than attendance allowance, disability living allowance and disability working allowance.

(2) Procedure regulations made under section 59 above by virtue of sub-paragraph (1) may make different provision in relation to each of the benefits specified in paragraph 2(2) above.

Overpayments etc.

4.—(1) Section 71 above shall have effect for the purposes of the benefits specified in paragraph 2(2) above as it has effect in relation to the benefits to which it applies by virtue of subsection (11).

(2) Section 74 above shall have effect in relation to supplementary benefit as it has effect in relation to income support.

(3) The reference to housing benefit in section 75 above includes a reference to housing benefits under Part II of the Social Security and Housing Benefits Act 1982.

Inspection

5. Section 110 above shall have effect as if it also applied to—
(a) the Supplementary Benefits Act 1976,

(b) the Family Income Supplements Act 1970.

Legal proceedings

6. Section 116 above shall have effect as if any reference to that Act in that section included—
(a) the National Assistance Act 1948;
(b) the Supplementary Benefit Act 1966;
(c) the Supplementary Benefits Act 1976;
(d) the Family Income Supplements Act 1970.

DERIVATION

Social Security Act 1986, Sched. 7.

DEFINITION

"the Contributions and Benefits Act"—see s.191.

Social Security (Consequential Provisions) Act 1992

(1992 c. 6)

ARRANGEMENT OF SECTIONS

SCHEDULES

Meaning of "the consolidating Acts"

1. In this Act—
"the consolidating Acts" means the Social Security Contributions and Benefits Act 1992 ("the Contributions and Benefits Act"), the Social Security Administration Act 1992 ("the Administration Act") and, so far as it reproduces the effect of the repealed enactments, this Act; and
"the repealed enactments" means the enactments repealed by this Act.

Continuity of the law

2.—(1) The substitution of the consolidating Acts for the repealed enactments does not affect the continuity of the law.

(2) Anything done or having effect as if done under or for the purposes of a provision of the repealed enactments has effect, if it could have been done under or for the purposes of the corresponding provision of the consolidating Acts, as if done under or for the purposes of that provision.

(3) Any reference, whether express or implied, in the consolidating Acts or any other enactment, instrument or document to a provision of the consolidating

Acts shall, so far as the context permits, be construed as including, in relation to the times, circumstances and purposes in relation to which the corresponding provision of the repealed enactments has effect, a reference to that corresponding provision.

(4) Any reference, whether express or implied, in any enactment, instrument or document to a provision of the repealed enactments shall be construed, so far as is required for continuing its effect, as including a reference to the corresponding provision of the consolidating Acts.

DEFINITIONS

"the consolidating Acts"—see s.1.
"the repealed enactments"—*ibid.*

GENERAL NOTE

These provisions spell out what would anyway be the effect under the Interpretation Act 1978. For the practical purposes of this book, the most important provision is subs. (4). Any reference in a regulation to a section of the repealed legislation is to be construed as including a reference to the corresponding section of the Administration Act or the Contributions and Benefits Act. These updated references are included in square brackets in the appropriate places in the regulations.

Repeals

3.—(1) The enactments mentioned in Schedule 1 to this Act are repealed to the extent specified in the third column of that Schedule.

(2) Those repeals include, in addition to repeals consequential on the consolidation of provisions in the consolidating Acts, repeals in accordance with the Recommendations of the Law Commission and the Scottish Law Commission, of section 30(6)(*b*) of the Social Security Act 1975, paragraphs 2 to 8 of Schedule 9 to that Act, paragraph 2(1) of Schedule 10 to that Act and section 10 of the Social Security Act 1988.

(3) The repeals have effect subject to any relevant savings in Schedule 3 to this Act.

DEFINITION

"the consolidating Acts"—see s.1.

Consequential amendments

4. The enactments mentioned in Schedule 2 to this Act shall have effect with the amendments there specified (being amendments consequential on the consolidating Acts).

DEFINITION

"the consolidating Acts"—see s.1.

Transitional provisions and savings

5.—(1) The transitional provisions and savings in Schedule 3 to this Act shall have effect.

(2) Nothing in that Schedule affects the general operation of section 16 of the Interpretation Act 1978 (general savings implied on repeal) or of the previous provisions of this Act.

The effect of s.16 of the Interpretation Act 1978 is that regulations validly made under the repealed legislation continue to be treated as validly made after the consolidating legislation has taken over. (*Cottingham v. Chief Adjudication Officer* and *Geary v. Chief Adjudication Officer*, C.A., December 2, 1992).

Transitory modifications

6. The transitory modifications in Schedule 4 to this Act shall have effect.

Short title, commencement and extent

7.—(1) This Act may be cited as the Social Security (Consequential Provisions) Act 1992.

(2) This Act shall come into force on 1st July 1992.

(3) Section 2 above and this section extend to Northern Ireland.

(4) Subject to subsection (5) below, where any enactment repealed or amended by this Act extends to any part of the United Kingdom, the repeal or enactment extends to that part.

(5) The repeals—

(a) of provisions of sections 10, 13 and 14 of the Social Security Act 1980 and Part II of Schedule 3 to that Act;

(b) of enactments amending those provisions;

(c) of paragraph 2 of Schedule 1 to the Capital Allowances Act 1990; and

(d) of section 17(8) and (9) of the Social Security Act 1990,

do not extend to Northern Ireland.

(6) Section 6 above and Schedule 4 to this Act extend to Northern Ireland in so far as they give effect to transitory modifications of provisions of the consolidating Acts which so extend.

(7) Except as provided by this section, this Act does not extend to Northern Ireland.

(8) Section 4 above extends to the Isle of Man so far as it relates to paragraphs 52 and 3 of Schedule 2 to this Act.

"the consolidating Acts"—see s.1.

SCHEDULE

SCHEDULE 3

Section 5

TRANSITIONAL PROVISIONS AND SAVINGS (INCLUDING SOME TRANSITIONAL PROVISIONS RETAINED FROM PREVIOUS ACTS)

Part I

General and Miscellaneous

Questions relating to contributions and benefits

1.—(1) A question other than a question arising under any of sections 1 to 3 of the Administration Act—

(a) whether a person is entitled to benefit in respect of a time before 1st July 1992;

(b) whether a person is liable to pay contributions in respect of such a time,

and any other question not arising under any of those sections with respect to benefit or contributions in respect of such a time is to be determined, subject to section 68 of the Administration Act, in accordance with provisions in force or deemed to be in force at that time.

(2) Subject to sub-paragraph (1) above, the consolidating Acts apply to matters arising before their commencement as to matters arising after it.

General saving for old savings

2. The repeal by this Act of an enactment previously repealed subject to savings (whether or not in the repealing enactment) does not affect the continued operation of those savings.

Documents referring to repealed enactments

3. Any document made, served or issued after this Act comes into force which contains a reference to any of the repealed enactments shall be construed, except so far as a contrary intention appears, as referring or, as the context may require, including a reference to the corresponding provision of the consolidating Acts.

Provisions relating to the coming into force of other provisions

4. The repeal by this Act of a provision providing for or relating to the coming into force of a provision reproduced in the consolidating Acts does not affect the operation of the first provision, in so far as it remains capable of having effect, in relation to the enactment reproducing the second provision.

Continuing powers to make transitional etc. regulations

5. Where immediately before 1st July 1992 the Secretary of State has power under any provision of the Social Security Acts 1975 to 1991 not reproduced in the consolidating Acts by regulations to make provision or savings in preparation for or in connection with the coming into force of a provision repealed by this Act but reproduced in the consolidating Acts, the power shall be construed as having effect in relation to the provision reproducing the repealed provision.

6. The repeal by this Act of a power by regulations to make provision or savings in preparation for or in connection with the coming into force of a provision reproduced in the consolidating Acts does not affect the power, in so far as it remains capable of having effect, in relation to the enactment reproducing the second provision.

Provisions contained in enactments by virtue of orders or regulations

7.—(1) Without prejudice to any express provision in the consolidating Acts, where this Act repeals any provision contained in any enactment by virtue of any order or regulations and the provision is reproduced in the consolidating Acts, the Secretary of State shall have the like power to make orders or regulations repealing or amending the provision of the consolidating Acts which reproduces the effect of the repealed provision as he had in relation to that provision.

(2) Sub-paragraph (1) above applies to a repealed provision which was amended by Schedule 7 to the Social Security Act 1989 as it applies to a provision not so amended.

Amending orders made after passing of Act

8. An order which is made under any of the repealed enactments after the passing of this Act and which amends any of the repealed enactments shall have the effect also of making a corresponding amendment of the consolidating Acts.

"the Administration Act"—see s.1.
"the consolidating Acts"—*ibid.*
"the repealed enactments"—*ibid.*

Social Security (Adjudication) Regulations 1986

(S.I. 1986 No. 2218)

Made by the Secretary of State under the Social Security Act 1986, ss.52(4), 89(1) and Sched. 7, the Health and Social Services and Social Security Adjudications Act 1983, Sched. 8, and various other provisions set out in Sched. 1.

ARRANGEMENT OF REGULATIONS

PART I

GENERAL

PART II

COMMON PROVISIONS

PART III

ADJUDICATING AUTHORITIES

SECTION B—ADJUDICATION OFFICERS

SECTION C—APPEAL TRIBUNALS

SECTION CA—DISABILITY ADJUDICATION

GENERAL NOTE

These regulations replaced the 1984 regulations as part of the move to produce common provisions for adjudication by AOs and SSATs across many different benefits. Several issues which were formerly in the 1984 regulations are now covered by sections of the Administration Act. These regulations no longer cover proceedings before the Social Security Commissioners, which are now subject to the Social Security Commissioners Procedure Regulations 1987 (S.I. 1987 No. 214).

PART I

GENERAL

Citation, commencement and interpretation

1.—(1) These regulations may be cited as the Social Security (Adjudication) Regulations 1986 and shall come into operation on 6th April 1987.
(2) In these regulations, unless the context otherwise requires:—
"the Acts" means [¹. . .] the Social Security Acts 1975 to 1986, the Industrial Injuries and Diseases (Old Cases) Act 1975, the Child Benefit Act 1975 [¹. . .];
"the 1975 Act" means the Social Security Act 1975;
"the 1982 Act" means the Social Security and Housing Benefits Act 1982;

"the 1983 Act" means the Health and Social Services and Social Security Adjudications Act 1983;

"the 1986 Act" means the Social Security Act 1986;

[³"the 1991 Act" means the Disability Living Allowance and Disability Working Allowance Act 1991;]

[⁵"the Administration Act" means the Social Security Administration Act 1992;]

"adjudicating authority" means, as the case may be, an adjudicating medical practitioner, the Chief or any other adjudication officer, an appeal tribunal, [⁴. . .], a medical appeal tribunal, [³a disability appeal tribunal,] a medical board or a special medical board;

"adjudicating medical authority" has the meaning assigned to it by regulation 27;

"adjudicating medical practitioner" means a medical practitioner appointed in accordance with paragraph 1 of Schedule 12 to the 1975 Act [SSAA, s.49];

"adjudication officer" means an officer appointed in accordance with section 97(1) of the 1975 Act [SSAA, s.38(1)];

"appeal tribunal" means a social security appeal tribunal constituted in accordance with section 97(2) to (2E) of the 1975 Act [SSAA, s.41];

[⁴. . .]

"Chief Adjudication Officer" means the Chief Adjudication Officer appointed under section 97(1B) of the 1975 Act [SSAA, s.39(1)];

"Chief Commissioner" means the Chief Social Security Commissioner appointed under section 97(3) of the 1975 Act [SSAA, s.52(1)];

"claimant" means a person who has claimed benefit under the Acts (including, in relation to an award or decision, a beneficiary under the award or [¹a person] affected by the decision) or from whom benefit is alleged to be recoverable, and in relation to statutory sick pay and statutory maternity pay includes both the employee alleged to be entitled to and the employer alleged to be liable to pay such pay;

"Commissioner" means the Chief or any other Social Security Commissioner appointed in accordance with section 97(3) of the 1975 Act [SSAA, s.52(1)] and includes a Tribunal of three such Commissioners constituted in accordance with section 11 of that Act [SSAA, s.57];

[³"disability appeal tribunal" means a tribunal constituted in accordance with Schedule 10A to the 1975 Act [SSAA, s.43];

"disability question" has the meaning assigned by regulation 26C(2);]

"full-time chairman" means a regional or other full-time chairman of appeal tribunals [³, disability appeal tribunals] and medical appeals tribunals appointed under paragraph 1A of Schedule 10 to the 1975 Act [SSAA, s.51];

[¹"income support" means income support under Part II of the 1986 Act [SSAA, Part VII] and includes personal expenses addition, special transitional addition and transitional addition as defined in the Income Support (Transitional) Regulations 1987;]

"inquiry" means an inquiry held pursuant to section 93(3) of the 1975 Act [SSAA, s.17(4)];

[²"local office" means an office of the Department of Social Security, an office of the Department of Employment or the office of the Chief Adjudication Officer;]

"medical appeal tribunal" means a tribunal constituted in accordance with Schedule 12 to the 1975 Act [SSAA, s.50];

"medical board" and "special medical board" have the meanings assigned to them by regulation 27;

"party to the proceedings" means—
- (a) the claimant [¹ . . .];
- (b) in proceedings before an appeal tribunal [³or a disability appeal tribunal], the adjudication officer;
- (c) in proceedings relating to the determination of a question included in section 93(1) of the 1975 Act [SSAA, s.17(1)], any person interested within the meaning of regulation 13;
- [¹(d) in any other proceedings, the adjudication officer and the Secretary of State except in proceedings in which the adjudication officer or the Secretary of State is the adjudicating authority;]
- (e) any other person appearing to the Secretary of State, the adjudicating authority or, in the case of a tribunal or board, its chairman or in relation to an inquiry, the person appointed to hold the inquiry, to be interested in the proceedings;

"the Prescribed Diseases Regulations" means the Social Security (Industrial Injuries) (Prescribed Diseases) Regulations 1985;

"President" means the President of social security appeal tribunals [³, disability appeal tribunals] and medical appeal tribunals appointed under paragraph 1A of Schedule 10 to the 1975 Act [SSAA, s.51];

"proceedings" means proceedings on a claim, application, appeal or reference to which these regulations apply;

[⁵"specially qualified adjudicating medical practitioner" means a specially qualified adjudicating medical practitioner appointed by virtue of section 62 of the Administration Act;] and

"the Supplementary Benefits Act" means the Supplementary Benefits Act 1976.

[¹(3) Where, by any provision of the Acts or of these Regulations—
- (a) any notice or other document is required to be given or sent to any office, that notice or document shall be treated as having been so given or sent on the day that it is received in that office; and
- (b) any notice or other document is required to be given or sent to any person, that notice or document shall, if sent by post to that person's last known or notified address, be treated as having been [²given or] sent on the day that it was posted.]

(4) [⁴. . .]

(5) Unless the context otherwise requires, any reference in these regulations to a numbered or lettered Part, Section, regulation or Schedule is a reference to the Part, Section, regulation or Schedule bearing that number or letter in these regulations and any reference in a regulation to a numbered paragraph is a reference to the paragraph of that regulation bearing that number.

[⁶(6) Unless otherwise provided, where by these Regulations any power is conferred on a chairman of an appeal tribunal, a medical appeal tribunal or a disability appeal tribunal then—
- (a) if the power is to be exercised at the hearing of an appeal or application, it shall be exercised by the chairman of the tribunal hearing the appeal or application; and
- (b) otherwise, it shall be exercised by a person who is eligible to be nominated to act as a chairman of an appeal tribunal under section 41 of the Administration Act.]

AMENDMENTS

1. Social Security (Adjudication) Amendment (No. 2) Regulations 1987 (S.I. 1987 No. 1970), reg. 2 (November 23, 1987 (income support), January 1, 1988 (family credit) and otherwise April 11, 1988).

2. Social Security (Adjudication) Amendment Regulations 1990 (S.I. 1990 No. 603), reg. 2 (April 6, 1990).

3. Social Security (Adjudication) Amendment (No. 3) Regulations 1991 (S.I. 1991 No. 2889), reg. 2 (February 3, 1992).

4. Social Security (Adjudication) Amendment (No. 3) Regulations 1991 (S.I. 1991 No. 2889), reg. 2 (April 6, 1992).

5. Social Security (Industrial Injuries and Adjudication) Regulations 1993 (S.I. 1993 No. 861), reg. 3 (April 19, 1993).

6. Social Security (Adjudication) Amendment Regulations 1994 (S.I. 1994 No. 1082), reg. 2 (May 11, 1994).

GENERAL NOTE

Paragraph (2)
The only one of the definitions which requires a note is that of "party to the proceedings." This phrase is used in many places and had formerly not been defined. The new definition makes the regulations a lot tidier. Note, under head (*b*), that the reference is to *the* AO. This probably refers to the AO who made the decision under appeal, although it might possibly extend to any AO currently concerned with the case. Such an AO would presumably fall within head (e) anyway. But the AO who made the original decision must remain a party to the proceedings.

Paragraph (3)
There had been doubt about the meaning of what was then reg. 1(5) of the 1984 Adjudication Regulations. The 1986 form of para. (3) makes the position clear. Where a notice is to be sent to an office, typically a DSS local office, it is deemed to have been sent on the day that it is received at that office. There will normally be a date of receipt stamped on such a document. Particularly cogent evidence, such as direct evidence of delivery by hand on an earlier date, would be required to displace the effect of such a stamp.

Where notice is to be given to a person and it is sent by post, then it is deemed to have been given on the day of posting. Service by courier is not service by post (*CIS 550/1993*). Again, there will normally be an official record of the date of posting, although perhaps claimants should be advised to keep all envelopes from the DSS for the postmark! The wording of sub-para. (b) has been brought into line with that of sub-para. (a), removing speculation about the possible difference in effect (see p. 337 of 1989 edition). Posting to the person's last notified (presumably notified to the body giving the notice) address will do. *R(SB) 55/83* held on a similar form of words to that in sub-para. (b) that proof that a notice had not arrived did not defeat the operation of the deeming. Nor was it a breach of natural justice for the tribunal to have heard the appeal in the absence of the claimant when it later transpired that he had had no notice of the hearing. His remedy was to apply for the tribunal decision to be set aside (see now reg. 11). Whenever a claimant complains of not having been notified of a hearing the matter should be referred forthwith to a SSAT under this procedure (*R(SB) 19/83*).

PART II

COMMON PROVISIONS

Procedure in connection with determinations; and right to representation

2.—(1) Subject to the provisions of the Acts and of these regulations—
  (a) the procedure in connection with the consideration and determination of any claim or question to which these regulations relate shall be such as the Secretary of State, the adjudicating authority or the person holding the inquiry, as the case may be, shall determine; so however that in the case of a tribunal or board, the procedure shall be such as the chairman shall determine;
  (b) any person who by virtue of the provisions of these regulations has the right to be heard at a hearing or an inquiry may be accompanied and may be represented by another person whether having professional qualifications or not and, for the purposes of the proceedings at any such hearing or inquiry, any such representative shall have all the rights and

powers to which the person whom he represents is entitled under the Acts and these regulations.

(2) For the purpose of arriving at their decision an appeal tribunal, a medical board, a special medical board[¹, a medical appeal tribunal or a disability appeal tribunal], as the case may be, shall, and for the purpose of discussing any question of procedure may, notwithstanding anything contained in these regulations, order all persons not being members of the tribunal or board, other than the person acting as clerk to the tribunal or board, to withdraw from the sitting of the tribunal or board, except that,

    (a) a member of the Council on Tribunals or of the Scottish Committee of the Council and the President and any full-time chairman; and

    (b) with the leave of the chairman of the tribunal or board, and if no person having the right to be heard objects, any person mentioned in regulation 4(6)(b) and (d) (except a person undergoing training as an adjudication officer or as an adjudicating medical practitioner),

may remain present at any such sitting.

(3) Nothing in these regulations shall prevent a member of the Council on Tribunals or of the Scottish Committee of the Council from being present at a hearing before an appeal tribunal[¹, a medical appeal tribunal or a disability appeal tribunal] or at any inquiry, in his capacity as such, notwithstanding that the hearing or inquiry is not in public.

AMENDMENT

1. Social Security (Adjudication) Amendment (No. 3) Regulations 1991 (S.I. 1991 No. 2889), reg. 3 (February 3, 1992).

DEFINITIONS

    "the Acts"—see reg. 1(2).
    "adjudicating authority"—*ibid.*
    "appeal tribunal"—*ibid.*
    "disability appeal tribunal"—*ibid.*
    "full-time chairman"—*ibid.*
    "inquiry"—*ibid.*
    "medical appeal tribunal"—*ibid.*
    "medical board"—see reg. 27.
    "President"—see reg. 1(2).
    "proceedings"—*ibid.*
    "special medical board"—see reg. 27.

GENERAL NOTE

Paragraph (1)(a)

Although the adjudicating authority is given discretion to decide matters of procedure, the rules laid down in the rest of these regulations must be followed (see in particular regs. 4 to 6). In the case of a SSAT a distinction has to be drawn between matters of substance, which are for the tribunal as a whole to decide, and matters of procedure, which are for the chairman.

Natural justice

In addition, the principles of natural justice must be followed. These principles can be summed up rather crudely by saying that both parties to an appeal must be given a fair hearing by an unbiased tribunal.

Bias

So far as bias goes, the *Guide to procedure* (2nd ed.), para. 50, probably sets out the position accurately (see *R v. Gough* [1993] 2 All E.R. 724, H.L.). If any member of the SSAT finds that he is personally acquainted with the appellant or has some other contact with him which might give the appearance of bias, he should not take part in the hearing. *CIS 6/1989* holds that the fact that the chairman had heard a previous appeal by the claimant does not constitute a breach of the rules of natural justice. If it is the chairman who is affected, then the appeal must be heard by a different tribunal. If it is a member who is affected, it is possible for the hearing to proceed in his absence under reg. 24(2). Where there is this strong connection the member should not take part even though the appellant and the presenting officer wish the hearing to proceed. They might think differently after knowing the outcome. If there is a remoter connection (and it is in the chairman's discretion where to draw the line) it would be enough for that to be declared at the beginning of the hearing and for the member to take part in the absence of any objection. Acquaintance with a representative is assumed not to give rise to any natural justice problems. Nonetheless, the tribunal should avoid giving any impression of partiality towards one side or the other. In particular, the arrangement of the furniture in the tribunal room should put the presenting officer in the same position as the appellant and/or any representative (*Guide to procedure* (2nd ed.), para. 48). This usually means facing the tribunal at the other side of a table. The presenting officer should not creep round the corner leaving the appellant alone facing the tribunal. The presence in the appeal papers of decisions by previous tribunals is not a breach of natural justice (*CS 176/1990*).

A rather peculiar situation was dealt with in *CSB 226/1981*. The appellant arrived late at the SBAT after her appeal had been determined in her absence. The SBAT re-heard the case fully and comprehensively, but determined against the appellant, as they had the first time. The Commissioner held this to be a breach of natural justice in that there may have been an appearance of injustice. The appellant could easily have thought that the members of the SBAT had already made up their minds against her. An impression strengthened by the fact that the decision form LT 235 appeared to be the one completed first time round, simply altered to record the appellant as present rather than not present. She should have been offered a rehearing by a differently constituted tribunal. But the Commissioner does point out that the situation would have been different if the claimant had consented to a rehearing by the same tribunal. She should have been offered the option of having her appeal reheard by a differently constituted tribunal, or asked whether she was willing to have a rehearing by the same tribunal. (Since the first "decision" had not yet been promulgated, it could be revoked or varied informally (see *R(I) 14/74*, para. 14).) Clearly if the claimant does consent to a fresh hearing by the same tribunal the appeal must be completely re-heard and a separate AT3 completed.

Another example of when a rehearing by a differently constituted tribunal may need to be offered is if in the course of a hearing a tribunal member says something which might indicate that his mind is already made up (although the indication of a preliminary view may be an acceptable way of saving time).

Inquisitorial jurisdiction

It is clear that the SSAT, like other social security tribunals, is inquisitorial (*R(SB) 2/83, R(IS) 12/91* and *Page v. Chief Adjudication Officer*, appendix to *R(SB) 2/92*). Its object is to reach the correct entitlement for the appellant, which should also be the object of the AO. The SSAT is not refereeing a game between two sides in the traditional manner of the courts. As it has most recently been put in *R(IS) 5/93*, with copious supporting authority, the SSAT's "investigatory function has as its object the ascertainment of the truth and is not restricted as in ordinary litigation where there are proceedings between parties, to accepting or rejecting the respective contentions of the claimant on the one hand and of the adjudication officer on the other."

This means that it is the duty of the SSAT to consider any point which could be made in favour of the claimant (*R(SB) 2/83*, para. 10; *R(SB) 30/84*). It is not clear how far the Commissioners extend this principle to matters of fact. In *R(SB) 2/83* they say that the SSAT is not expected to question the facts presented, especially if agreed by the appellant. On the other hand a factual point may be so obvious that it ought to be considered even though it was not put forward by the appellant. But since the primary duty is on the appellant to make out his case a decision will only be struck down for failure to identify such a factual point in the most clear-cut circumstances. This appears to leave it open to a SSAT (although not obligatory) to explore factual issues, to go behind general statements and to investigate matters that a non-expert might not realise were relevant. Such an approach would not amount to bias and a breach of the principles of natural justice. However, by the same token an appellant must expect his assertions to be tested by questioning from the SSAT and this does not amount to bias against him (see *R(S) 4/82*). The tribunal should also consider any points not put forward by the AO but it may be that the investigation need not be as elaborate, for the presenting officer can be expected to understand the point and to indicate whether the AO relies on it or not. However, if the AO makes a concession on a point of fact or law, that does not, in consequence of the inquisitorial nature of the jurisdiction, prevent the AO from relying on the point later (*R(IS) 14/93*.)

Fair hearing

The second element of natural justice is that each party must be given a fair opportunity to state his case. This is largely covered by the specific provisions of reg. 4(2) and (5), but some other points can be covered here. It is not necessarily a breach of the rules of natural justice to proceed in the absence of the claimant, but may be in some circumstances (see notes to reg. 4(3) and *R(SB) 23/82*). It is an important principle that each party should know what is the evidence against him and have a fair opportunity of countering it. So in *R(SB) 18/83* the presenting officer had put in evidence only one of a number of letters written by the claimant's accountants to the DSS. Since these letters were about the matter in dispute this was inconsistent with the objectivity expected of presenting officers and meant that the SBAT's decision was in breach of the rules of natural justice (*R. v. Leyland Justices, ex p. Hawthorne* [1979] Q.B. 283). If a new piece of evidence is produced for the first time before the SSAT, or an entirely new point of substance, it may be necessary for the hearing to be adjourned, to give the other party a fair opportunity of dealing with it (*Guide to procedure* (2nd ed.), paras. 61 and 65). The same would apply if a concession on some point was withdrawn, or questioned by a SSAT. Presenting officers are instructed to ask for an adjournment if an unreported Commissioner's decision is relied on for the first time at the hearing, often arguing that the AO who made the decision will not have had the opportunity to see the decision. Here, matters are not so clear-cut and, though an adjournment may be appropriate, the question should be whether the presenting officer has a fair opportunity to deal with the point rather than whether the original AO can consider it. Similarly, although SSAT members may use their own knowledge of the locality, etc., any information should be disclosed to both parties during the hearing (*Guide to procedure* (2nd ed.), para. 62). There is a thin line between using local knowledge and experience in the evaluation of evidence (perfectly proper) and relying on information which the parties should have the opportunity of commenting on. This approach is affirmed by the Commissioner in *CS 142/ 1991*, to be reported as *R(S) 1/94*, where a SSAT's decision was struck down because it was based on a member's experience of the kind of work done in Remploy workshops, which had not been mentioned during the hearing. But *CS 175/1992*, where one of the members was a doctor, fell on the other side of the line. The Commissioner holds that the member was merely putting her expert interpretation on the evidence given to the tribunal. There was no need for a member's opinion to be communicated in advance of the decision unless, for example, it raised a new issue. It would have been preferable if the member's medical qualifications had been mentioned at the beginning of the hearing (or when she was asking questions), but a failure to do so was not a breach of the rules of natural justice. The Commissioner also rejects the argument that she was performing a role analogous to that of an assessor (see the notes to s.56 of the Administration Act). If a SSAT is presented with new written evidence the proceedings should stop while this is read, since the tribunal must be seen to be giving the case its undivided attention (see *R. v. Marylebone Magistrates Court ex parte Joseph, The Independent*, April 30, 1993).

The Commissioners have taken into account the practicalities of tribunal arrangements and premises. In *CSB 453/1983* one of the claimant's complaints was that when he and his solicitor entered the tribunal room they found the presenting officer already there. The Commissioner says that decisions have been set aside on this ground alone. The presenting officer should leave the room even if on the previous appeal the claimant was not there. If this is not done for some reason, only an immediate explanation could ensure that justice was seen to be done. The mere fact that a presenting officer has been in the tribunal room on an earlier appeal with no appellant present appears to require no explanation (*CIS 6/1989*). In *CSB 483/1982* the presenting officer entered the tribunal room before the hearing to leave his hat and bag and to pass the time of day. The Commissioner stresses that the claimant must not feel that his case is being discussed behind his back, but the nature of the accommodation may make it necessary for the presenting officer to go into the room. Here, since the door was left open there was no breach of natural justice. If it had been closed there would have been! More recently *R(IS)15/94* has reinforced the importance of one party to an appeal, *e.g.* the presenting officer, not being in the presence of the tribunal before the other, even in a case where the presenting officer has been engaged in earlier cases. The correct course must be for the presenting officer to leave the tribunal room at the end of each hearing and not to enter it again until the next case is called.

Even if the presenting officer is not seen to enter the tribunal room, there may be a problem, as in *CIS 50/1990*. The claimant's father was representing her. The appeal was scheduled for 10 a.m., but the father was not brought by the clerk from the waiting room to the tribunal room until after 10.10 a.m. When they arrived, the door to the tribunal room was wide open and the presenting officer was waiting just outside. The Commissioner holds that these circumstances could cause a reasonable person to fear that justice might not fully have been done. The father might have thought that the presenting officer could have talked to the tribunal or overheard their preliminary discussions. The Commissioner rightly stresses that the door to the tribunal room should be kept closed until the appeal begins and that the claimant and/or representative and the presenting officer should be brought in together. Tribunals must be sensitive to appearances when many claimants and representatives are unfamiliar with the tribunal's custom and practice.

Paragraph (1)(b)

The issue of representation has a long and intricate history. Immediately before the November 1980 reforms the position was that an interested person had the right to be accompanied and represented by not more than two persons. The present provision has no limit of numbers. Thus, since under the Interpretation Act 1978, s.6(c), the singular includes the plural unless the context otherwise requires, it seems clear that there is no limit under this paragraph to the number of representatives or companions. The limit comes from the power of the chairman to control procedure under para. (1)(a). He can clearly determine what is an improper number of extra people at the hearing (compare the approach of the Divisional Court to "McKenzie friends" in *R. v. Leicester City Justices, ex p. Barrow* [1991] 2 All E.R. 437). There is no direct right of appeal from his decision (*CSB 103/ 1984*). The *Guide to procedure* (2nd ed.), para. 38(1) now makes it clear that the number of representatives permitted is a matter for the chairman.

The presenting officer's powers appear to stem from this provision as a representative of the AO who made the decision under appeal.

See the ITS President's Practice Direction No. 1 and the notes to this (p. 877).

Paragraph (2)

Here the main powers and duties are given to the tribunal, etc., not to the chairman. The effect is that a member of the Council on Tribunals, the President or a full-time chairman (not acting as chairman of the particular tribunal) is entitled to remain with the tribunal when they are discussing their decision. Trainee chairmen, members or clerks (reg. 4(6)(b)) may remain, but not trainee AOs (reg. 2(2)(b)) or a person supervising training of clerks or AOs (reg. 4(6)(c)). Anyone else may stay only if no party to the proceedings (regs. 4(5) and 1(2)), or their representative (reg. 2(1)(b)) objects. For a person to be in this category, the positive consent of all parties to the proceedings who are present is required (reg. 4(6)(d)). In practice this will mean the claimant and/or representative and the presenting officer representing the AO. But the chairman (no longer the tribunal) has to give leave, and it should be made clear that the person plays no part in making the decision. Although a party to the proceedings may not object to the clerk remaining in the room, it is open to the tribunal to require him to leave. This might conceivably be necessary to ensure natural justice, *e.g.* if the clerk has taken an over-active part in the hearing.

Paragraph (3)

This allows a member of the Council on Tribunals to remain during an oral hearing, even though it is in private. It should logically go in reg. 4(6).

Manner of making applications, appeals or references; and time limits

3.—(1) Any application, appeal or reference mentioned in column (1) of Schedule 2 shall be in writing and shall be made or given by sending or delivering it to the appropriate office within the specified time.

(2) In this regulation—

    (a) "the appropriate office" means the office specified in column (2) of Schedule 2 opposite the description of the relevant application, appeal or reference listed in column (1); and

    (b) "the specified time" means the time specified in column (3) of that Schedule opposite the description of the relevant application, appeal or reference so listed.

(3) The time specified by this regulation and Schedule 2 for the making of any application, appeal or reference (except an application to the chairman of an appeal tribunal[², a medical appeal tribunal or a disability appeal tribunal] for leave to appeal to a Commissioner) may be extended for special reasons, even though the time so limited may already have expired, and any application for an extension of time under this paragraph shall be made to and determined by the person or body to whom the application, appeal or reference is sought to be made or, in the case of a tribunal or board, its chairman.

(4) Any application under paragraph (3) for an extension of time which has been refused may not be renewed.

(5) Any application, appeal or reference under these regulations shall contain particulars of the grounds on which it is made or given [¹and, in the case of an appeal, it shall include sufficient particulars of the decision under appeal to enable that decision to be identified].

(6) Where it appears to the Secretary of State, an adjudication officer or the chairman of a tribunal or board that an application, appeal or reference which is made to him or to the tribunal or board gives insufficient particulars to enable the question at issue to be determined, he may require the person making the application, appeal or reference to furnish such further particulars as may reasonably be required.

[¹(7) A chairman of an appeal tribunal[², a medical appeal tribunal or a disability appeal tribunal] may give directions for the disposal of any purported appeal where he is satisfied that the tribunal does not have jurisdiction to entertain the appeal.]

AMENDMENTS

1. Social Security (Adjudication) Amendment Regulations 1990 (S.I. 1990 No. 603), reg. 3 (April 6, 1990).
2. Social Security (Adjudication) Amendment (No. 3) Regulations 1991 (S.I. 1991 No. 2889), reg. 4 (February 3, 1992).

DEFINITIONS

"the Acts"—see reg. 1(2).
"adjudication officer"—*ibid.*
"appeal tribunal"—*ibid.*
"Commissioner"—*ibid.*
"disability appeal tribunal"—*ibid.*
"medical appeal tribunal"—*ibid.*

GENERAL NOTE

Paragraphs (1) and (2)
These provisions apply the various time limits set out in Schedule 2.

Paragraph (3)
Allows time limits to be extended for "special reasons." In *CU 12/1994* (which concerned a similar provision in reg. 7(2) of the Social Security Commissioners Procedure Regulations 1987 (S.I. 1987 No. 214)) the Commissioner states that "special reasons" meant that something more than mere non-prejudice to the other party or the fact that the period of delay was only short had to be shown. There has to be something unusual in the history or facts of the case (*CSB 15/1994* and *CSB 123/1993*). But the words are wide and allow almost anything to be brought forward for consideration (*R v. Social Security Appeal Tribunal ex parte O'Hara*, Divisional Court, July 13, 1994). The special reasons need not relate to the delay as such, but can be found in the surrounding circumstances, such as the applicant's health and personal circumstances (*R(I) 5/91*, following *R(U) 8/68* and *R(M) 1/87*, and *ex parte O'Hara*). The merits of the case can be considered (*R(M) 1/87*, following *R v. Secretary of State for the Home Department, ex p. Mehta* [1975] 2 All E.R. 1084 and *CU 12/1994*). The fact that the decision under appeal is clearly wrong can be a factor. However, in *R(S) 8/85* the Commissioner held that an "alteration" in the law by a subsequent decision of a superior court was not *of itself* a ground for a substantial extension of time for a late appeal. This is somewhat difficult to reconcile with the clearly established breadth of "special reasons", and in particular with the fact that the merits of the case should be considered. It obviously cannot be relied upon to undermine the general principle that the discretion to extend the time limit has to be exercised individually in each case. Moreover, the Commissioner in *R(S) 8/85* was not saying that where a court decision overrules the previously accepted view of the law there cannot be "special reasons", but only that such a ruling was not a special reason *by itself*. Clearly all the circumstances have to be considered. In *ex parte O'Hara* the Divisional Court expressed surprise that in view of the claimant's disability her application to bring a late appeal (based on *CIS 180/89*: see notes to reg. 3(2B)–(2C) of the Income Support Regulations) had been refused, although

the Court did not find that it was perverse or unreasonable in the *Wednesbury* ([1948] 1 K.B. 223) sense and so did not grant her application for judicial review.

As has been pointed out (see "Late social security appeals" by Nick Warren in Legal Action, February 1994), there is clearly a "certain tension in the system" between the provisions restricting payment of arrears of benefit following reviews (see reg. 69 and s. 69 of the Administration Act) and the late appeal procedure. In *Chief Adjudication Officer v. Eggleton and Others* (Court of Appeal, March 17, 1995) Stuart-Smith L.J. observed (*obiter*) that "It seems to be plain that the intention of Parliamant is clearly to be derived from the effect of regulation 69 (in relation to income support) and s. 69 (in relation to reviews based on errors of law as a result of subsequent inconsistent decision). To give leave to appeal, long out of time, which has the intended effect of circumventing these provisions, seems to me to be wrong." But it is suggested that the existence of this "tension" should not be used to justify importing restrictions into the test of "special reasons" which the words themselves do not require. Parliament has not chosen to impose any time limitation on the admittance of late appeals. Indeed, the existence of the late appeals procedure has been referred to as a safeguard which justified the introduction of restrictions on arrears contained in ss. 68 and 69 of the Administration Act. Furthermore, review may not always be an available option (*e.g.* where a claimant seeks a late appeal against a SSAT's decision), since it is only an AO's decision that can be reviewed on the grounds of error of law (s. 25(2)).

If the case involves European law (for example, the claimant is alleging that the U.K. Government is in breach of its obligations under EC Directive 79/7 on equal treatment for men and women in matters of social security) time limits for bringing proceedings cannot be used to defeat the claim (*Emmott v. Minister for Social Welfare* [1991] E.C.R. 1–4569). The proper approach would normally be for the chairman to extend the time limit in these cases. The ECJ's reasoning in *Emmott* was based on whether the law was certain. The ECJ concluded that, so long as a directive had not been properly translated into national law, individuals were unable to ascertain the full extent of their rights. Only when that had happened could there be said to be the legal certainty which had to exist if individuals were to assert their rights. A similar argument would seem to be relevant in domestic law. If, for example, as in the *Bate* case (see the notes to s. 69), the Court of Appeal overturns an established interpretation of a particular regulation (to which there have even been several amendments based on that meaning), how can it be said that an individual could previously have asserted their rights, when before the Court of Appeal's judgment there had been no suggestion of the possibility of the regulation being construed in this way?

Chief Adjudication Officer v. Eggleton and Others (see the notes to s. 25 of the Administration Act) confirms that where a decision has been reviewed, the original decision remains in existence except as affected by the revision on review. Thus a late appeal against the original decision may still be admitted.

There is no obligation on the chairman to give reasons for extending the time limit, or not, and almost all applications are decided on the papers only. Exceptionally a chairman may decide to hold an oral hearing (but there is no right to this (*ex parte O'Hara*)).

CSB 15/1994 holds that if no valid leave to appeal has been granted, jurisdiction cannot be conferred on the tribunal by agreement of the parties. In *CSB 15/1994* the Commissioner also considered that para. (5) meant that an application for a late appeal was invalid unless it identified the date of the AO's decision against which it was sought to appeal. But this would seem to go beyond the requirements of para. (5), which are only that sufficient particulars are given to enable the decision under appeal to be identified. It places too heavy a burden on claimants, particularly as letters from the Benefits Agency usually only communicate the import of an AO's decision, not its actual terms or its date.

However, the three months for applying to a tribunal chairman for leave to appeal to a Commissioner cannot be extended. This is because if a party misses the limit the Commissioner has power to deal with a late application (Social Security Commissioners Procedure Regulations 1987, reg. 3(2)) although special reasons have to be shown.

In *CIS 68/1991*, to be reported as *R(IS) 5/94*, the claimant's appeal was withdrawn at the hearing with the leave of the chairman. He subsequently obtained leave to bring a late appeal. The SSAT declined to hear the apppeal on the ground of lack of jurisdiction. The Commissioner holds that the principle of *res judicata* (that once a matter has been adjudicated on by a competent authority another authority of the same level cannot readjudicate on the matter) did not apply. Where an appeal is withdrawn with the leave of the chairman or the AO's agreement there has been no decision by a tribunal and there is nothing to prevent a new appeal being made. It would be different if the first appeal had been dismissed by a SSAT.

Paragraph (4)

This paragraph prevents a party from having more than one bite at the cherry in requesting an extension of time. Since there is no appeal from a decision not to extend a time limit, this is a serious matter, although sometimes another application or appeal can be made. *CIS 93/1992* holds that the decision of a chairman is subject to reconsideration by the same chairman, particularly if new matters are brought to his attention. The only other method of challenge would be by way of judicial review.

Paragraphs (5) and (6)

These were new requirements in 1984, but their inter-relationship is still obscure. The intention of para. (5) seems to be that if, *e.g.* an appeal states no grounds it is not a valid appeal. It is not clear how much detail is required before one can say that "particulars of grounds" have been given. It is possible that "grounds" has a narrower meaning than "reasons" (see *R. v. Secretary of State for Social Services, ex p. Loveday, The Times*, February 18, 1983, and appendix to *R(M) 5/86*). A claimant is surely not expected to frame an appeal in terms of the regulations. At this stage the claimant may simply know what the AO's decision is, or he may have a statement of reasons under reg. 63(7). He is scarcely in a position to say that the AO has got the facts wrong or has misinterpreted reg. 51 of the Income Support (General) Regulations. It should suffice if the appeal can be connected to the right decision and it is now required that the appeal should sufficiently identify the decision appealed against.

This then simplifies the relationship with para. (6). Once a valid appeal has started to be processed, a chairman may require further particulars to be furnished.

The test is quite unrealistic. Very few appeals will give sufficient particulars to enable the question at issue to be determined. If they did there would be no need for the oral hearing which is compulsory for SSATs. Maybe the power is more relevant to AOs dealing with applications for review (see Administration Act, ss. 26 and 30; 1975 Act, s.104(2)), where there will never be an oral hearing. There seems to be no reason why tribunal chairmen or other adjudicating authorities could not have issued similar directions acting under their general powers, as the Social Security Commissioners have. The sanction against the failure to provide the information requested would be that there would be an evidential gap from which adverse inferences could be drawn (*cf. R(SB) 34/83*). But it is probably useful for them to have this express power, which may save delay arising from questions first being raised at the hearing. A problem under para. (6) is what is the consequence if the claimant, etc., fails to provide the particulars required? It appears that the appeal etc. remains in being, but will have to proceed with the evidential gap. It is possible that the power given to tribunal chairmen by reg. 7 to strike out proceedings for want of prosecution could be exercised where a person fails to respond to a requirement under para. (6). But, as pointed out in the notes to reg. 7, the exercise of that power could only be based solely on such a failure where the requirement under para. (6) is precise, gives a definite time limit and, preferably a warning of the consequences of failure to respond.

A further crucial question is, who makes these decisions? Since appeals to SSATs are still to be made to local offices of the DSS (Sched. 2) it is vital to the independence of the system that appeals should not be screened out by the DSS. The instructions given to AOs are that if some reasons, however poorly expressed, are given for an appeal it should be accepted. If no such grounds are stated, the claimant will be asked by the AO to provide a written statement of them. If the claimant does not provide such a statement or says that he will do so only at the hearing, the AO is to send the appeal and subsequent correspondence to the SSAT clerk to be put before a chairman. The chairman, it appears, is then to decide whether to admit the appeal. The chairman may well at this point be rather in the dark about the AO decision appealed against.

It should be said that it is often to the claimant's advantage to set out the reasons for his appeal in some detail. On receipt of an appeal, the AO will reconsider the original decision. If he thinks (maybe in the light of new information) that the decision is wrong, he will review and revise it. The first appeal may then lapse, in which case the claimant has a fresh right of appeal against the new decision. This can be a valuable procedure, and round about 30 per cent. of appeals lodged lapse in this way. Section 29 of the Administration Act (1975 Act, s.104(3B)) has, from April 6, 1990, provided that an appeal will lapse in such circumstances only if the AO considers that the revised decision is the same as that which would be given on the appeal if every ground succeeded. Otherwise, the review is of no effect. This new rule supplies another argument for ensuring that the notice of appeal includes all the grounds that could be put forward.

Paragraph (7)

Before April 1990 if an appeal was expressed to be made to the SSAT, a rejection of the appeal on the ground that it was outside the SSAT's jurisdiction could only properly be made by the whole tribunal. This was a cumbersome procedure, which was often ignored in practice, for instance in relation to decisions by social fund officers where the applicant purported to appeal to the SSAT. Para. (7) carries out the power to make regulations given by para. 7A of Sched. 13 to the 1975

Act (now para. 10 of Sched. 3 to the Administration Act). Although the wording of para. (7) could be more explicit, presumably the power to give directions for the "disposal" of an appeal covers the appeal's rejection or termination. The power may be exercised by any chairman of a SSAT, including a regional or full-time chairman. Note that there is no power for a chairman to give directions for the disposal of a reference to the SSAT, rather than an appeal (*R(I) 3/92*).

Since there is no appeal from such a ruling by a chairman, the scope of para. (7) has not been directly considered by the Commissioners. However, in *CI 78/1990* the issue was whether a Medical Appeal Tribunal (MAT 3) had jurisdiction to hear an appeal where a decision by MAT 1 had been set aside by MAT 2 acting beyond its powers. The Commissioner says that it would be "wholly inappropriate for a tribunal chairman to exercise that power (which is obviously suitable for misconceived or misdirected appeals) in a case where the lack of jurisdiction was considered to arise in the circumstances under consideration in this reference. It would be manifestly unsatisfactory for a tribunal chairman in effect to hold a setting aside determination invalid in a ruling made at his own hand, which would not be subject to appeal and which could be challenged only by judicial review." Similarly, in *CSB 1182/1989* the Commissioner expresses some doubt about what para. (7) empowers chairmen to do.

Oral hearings and inquiries

4.—(1) This regulation applies to any oral hearing of an application, appeal or reference and to any inquiry.

(2) Reasonable notice (being not less than 10 days beginning with the day on which the notice is given and ending on the day before the hearing of the case or, as the case may be, the inquiry is to take place) of the time and place of any oral hearing before an adjudicating authority or of an inquiry shall be given to every party to the proceedings, and if such notice has not been given to a person to whom it should have been given under the provisions of this paragraph the hearing or inquiry may proceed only with the consent of that person.

(3) If a party to the proceedings to whom notice has been given under paragraph (2) shall fail to appear at the hearing or inquiry the adjudicating authority or the person holding the inquiry may, having regard to all the circumstances including any explanation offered for the absence, proceed with the case or the inquiry notwithstanding his absence, or give such directions with a view to the determination of the case or conduct of the inquiry as it or he may think proper.

(4) Any oral hearing before an adjudicating authority shall be in public except where (in the case of an oral hearing) the claimant requests a private hearing or (in any case) the chairman or the person holding the inquiry is satisfied that intimate personal or financial circumstances may have to be disclosed or that considerations of public security are involved, in which case the hearing or inquiry shall be in private.

(5) At any oral hearing or inquiry any party to the proceedings shall be entitled to be present and be heard.

(6) The following persons shall also be entitled to be present at an oral hearing (whether or not it is otherwise in private) but shall take no part in the proceedings:—

(a) the President and any full-time chairman;

(b) any person undergoing training as a chairman or other member of an appeal tribunal[1, a medical appeal tribunal or a disability appeal tribunal, or as a clerk to any such tribunal], or as an adjudication officer or an adjudicating medical practitioner;

(c) any person acting on behalf of the President, the Chief Adjudication Officer or the Secretary of State in the training or supervision of clerks to appeal tribunals[1, medical appeal tribunals or disability appeal tribunals] or of adjudication officers or officers of the Secretary of State or in the monitoring of standards of adjudication by adjudication officers; and

(d) with the leave of the chairman of the tribunal or board, as the case may be, and the consent of every party to the proceedings actually present, any other person.

(7) At any inquiry (whether or not it is otherwise in private) the following persons shall be entitled to be present but shall take no part in the proceedings—

  (a) any person undergoing training as an officer of the Secretary of State; and

  (b) any person acting on behalf of the Secretary of State in the training or supervision of officers of the Secretary of State; and

  (c) with the leave of the person holding the inquiry and the consent of all parties to the proceedings actually present, any other person.

(8) Nothing in paragraph (6) affects the rights of any person mentioned in sub-paragraphs (a) and (b) at any hearing where he is sitting as a member of the tribunal, or acting as its clerk, and nothing in this regulation prevents the presence at an oral hearing or an inquiry of any witness.

(9) Any person entitled to be heard at an oral hearing or inquiry may address the adjudicating authority or person holding the inquiry and may give evidence, may call witnesses and may put questions directly to any other person called as a witness.

AMENDMENT

1. Social Security (Adjudication) Amendment (No. 3) Regulations 1991 (S.I. 1991 No. 2889), reg. 5 (February 3, 1992).

DEFINITIONS

"adjudicating authority"—see reg. 1(2).
"adjudicating medical practitioner"—*ibid.*
"adjudication officer"—*ibid.*
"appeal tribunal"—*ibid.*
"Chief Adjudication Officer"—*ibid.*
"disability appeal tribunal"—*ibid.*
"full-time chairman"—*ibid.*
"inquiry"—*ibid.*
"medical appeal tribunal"—*ibid.*
"party to the proceedings"—*ibid.*
"President"—*ibid.*
"proceedings"—*ibid.*

GENERAL NOTE

The arrangement of paragraphs is as follows
(1) General
(2) Notice of hearings
(3) Powers if party fails to appear
(4) Public or private hearing
(5) Parties entitled to be present
(6) Persons entitled to attend private hearing
(7) Persons entitled to attend private inquiry
(8) Presence of members, clerk or witness
(9) Rights of parties at hearing

Paragraph (2)

Reg. 1(3) deems the date on which notice has been given to be the date of posting. Under the 1984 Regulations the date was that on which the notice would have arrived in the ordinary course of the post. The limit is still 10 days ending on the day before the hearing. Thus, for a hearing on the 12th of a month, the notice must have been posted on or before the 1st of the month. It may be that in a complicated SSAT case more than 10 days notice would be reasonable.

The notice must be given to all parties to the proceedings. This phrase is now defined in reg. 1(2) and covers, as well as the claimant, any person appearing to be interested in the proceedings. See the notes to reg. 1(2). It is not the general practice to inform anyone other than the AO and the claimant (and any representative). There is likely only to be a problem if it is said that a decision should be set aside under reg. 11 on the ground that a document was not sent to an interested person. Reg. 4(2) no longer requires copies of the documents provided for a tribunal to be sent to the claimant, but the principle of natural justice that a person should know the case he has to meet certainly does require it.

If a person who has not received the required notice positively consents to the hearing going on nevertheless, then it may do so. If the claimant or his representative is present, there is little problem. If neither is present, *R(SB) 19/83* decides that the tribunal must ask the clerk if the claimant has been properly notified. The date of the return of the form (AT 6) formerly sent with the appeal papers may settle the matter. If not, the Commissioner holds that the hearing should be adjourned if due notification cannot be shown, preferably by evidence of the date of posting and a copy of the AT 6.

A national procedure for the listing of appeals was introduced for appeals lodged from September 1, 1992. As soon as notification of the appeal is received by the Independent Tribunal Service (ITS), a leaflet will be sent to the claimant giving details of the appeal process and advice about getting help from a representative. The AT2 submission will be sent to the claimant and any representative as soon as it is received from the AO. With it will be a newly designed form AT6 (AT6(Rev)) with a tear-off page on which the claimant is to indicate whether he intends to attend the hearing of the appeal or not and whether there are any dates on which attendance is impossible. A paragraph headed "The importance of answering promptly" says that if the tear-off is not returned, or the claimant does not contact the clerk, within 14 days of the date of the AT6 it will be assumed that the claimant does not wish to continue with the appeal and that consideration will be given to striking out the appeal for failure to proceed. A reply envelope is included.

If the tear-off is returned within the 14 days, the appeal will be listed (it is hoped for hearing within four weeks). The notice of the date of the hearing will say that the hearing is expected to go ahead on that date, but that a postponement is possible in unexpected circumstances. Apparently, no form or pre-paid envelope goes out with the notice by which the claimant can reply that he is unable to attend. SSAT chairmen and members have been advised, in some regions at least, that when a claimant has said that he will attend the hearing but does not do so, the hearing should normally proceed in his absence (but see the note to para. (3) below). See also para. 42 of the *Guide to procedure* (2nd ed.).

If the tear-off is not returned within the 14 days, consideration will be given to implementing the striking out procedure under reg. 7. This now starts with a letter (with a reply envelope) enclosing a chairman's direction under reg. 2(1)(a) requiring the claimant to state whether or not he wishes to attend the appeal hearing, or if he wishes to withdraw his appeal; the direction states that failure to reply within 21 days will lead to the instigation of the striking out procedure. If no reply is received, another letter (with a reply envelope) is sent by the clerk saying that it is now proposed to seek a striking out order and giving a further two weeks for the claimant to state why an order should not be made. If there is no response, a chairman is then asked to consider whether an order striking out the appeal should be made. If an order is made, a copy of it is sent to the claimant together with a letter informing him that he may apply to a tribunal chairman to have the appeal reinstated (now within 12 months: see May 1994 amendment to reg. 7(3)).

In previous editions it was argued that following the Court of Appeal's decision in *Executor of Evans v. Metropolitan Police Authority* [1992] I.R.L.R. 570 the use of the striking out procedure where claimants did not reply to say whether they would attend a SSAT hearing or not was misguided. The May 1994 amendments to reg. 7(1) and the revised striking out procedure outlined above are clearly designed (and would appear) to satisfy the requirement of an "intentional and contumelious disobedience of a peremptory order" as laid down in *Birkett v. James* (see the notes to reg. 7).

The listing procedure was also criticised in the 1992 Supplement, independently of its legal basis, as being inconsistent with the philosophy which has recently informed the development of SSATs and the ITS. A claimant has a right to appeal to a SSAT. The emphasis in the past has been on enabling a claimant to present his case as fully as possible. The statement of a presumption that the claimant does not wish to proceed with the appeal unless he returns the tear-off could give the impression that the claimant is imposing a burden on the appeal process which he must justify. While recognising that the non-attendance of claimants at hearings is a considerable problem, the new procedure was seen as an inappropriate response. This criticism remains.

See ITS President's Practice Direction No. 5 on domiciliary hearings (p. 880).

Paragraph (3)

This provision clearly gives the SSAT discretion to hear an appeal although the appellant does not attend and is not represented. If he has replied on the AT 6 tear-off that he wishes the appeal to be heard in his absence there is no problem. If he expressly asks for an adjournment for some good reason or gives a reason for not being able to attend on a particular date, then it may well be a breach of the rules of natural justice to proceed in the appellant's absence. Of course, an appellant is not entitled to string out the process indefinitely (especially if recovery of an overpayment is being sought by the DSS).

If the appellant had failed to reply on the AT 6 tear-off at all (and the appeal has not been struck out: see notes to para. (2)) or replies on the tear-off that he is going to attend but does not turn up, the SSAT's discretion is more open. In the first case, given that the appellant will have also been given notice of the date of the hearing, a decision by a SSAT to proceed in the appellant's absence would be hard to challenge. In the second case, the official guidance to SSATs is noted in the description of the September 1992 listing procedure in the note to para. (2). However, under that procedure no form or reply-paid envelope is sent to the appellant with the notice of the date of the hearing on which the appellant can say that he is unable to attend on the particular date. He must make a positive effort to contact ITS. In the necessary consideration of all relevant circumstances before deciding whether to proceed in the appellant's absence it is suggested that little weight should be given to the official guidance. Since a SSAT is an inquisitorial body, the central issue must be a balance of the ability of the SSAT to make the necessary findings of fact without evidence from the appellant against the principle that the appellant need only be given a fair opportunity to attend.

In *R(SB) 23/83* the Commissioner holds that SSATs should always enquire if the appellant has stated that he wishes to be present and would have set aside a decision if there was evidence that the SSAT acted in ignorance of such a statement. See para. 42 of the *Guide to procedure* (2nd ed.).

CSB 582/1987, followed in *CSB 383/1988*, holds that para. (3) does not give a SSAT an automatic authority to proceed if the AO or the presenting officer is not present. The AO is not just a party to the proceedings, but is in the position of *amicus curiae*, with a duty to present the facts and law objectively. If the AO is not present or represented there is a danger that the SSAT will not be properly informed about the facts and the law. If, as in *CSB 582/1987*, there is an implied request from the claimant for an adjournment so that questions can be put to the presenting officer, it is a breach of natural justice for the SSAT not to grant the adjournment.

A party to the proceedings may apply to have a SSAT decision set aside on the ground that he or his representative was not present at a hearing (reg. 11). If the proceedings have been struck out under reg. 7 they can be reinstated within 12 months under reg. 7(3).

Paragraph (4)

Before April 1984 all SBAT hearings were in private. NILT hearings were open to the public. The effect of this new rule is that a claimant (or his representative: reg. 2(1)(b)) can insist on a private hearing. Secondly, if intimate personal or financial circumstances may have to be disclosed, the hearing is to be private. This would cover many income support appeals to a SSAT, although this could hardly have been the intention. But see para. (6)(d). The third category, public security, will rarely arise.

Paragraph (5)

This provision does little more than spell out what is implicit in the notion of an oral hearing. Note that in the definition of "party to the proceedings" the reference is to "the adjudication officer." This appears to mean the AO who made the decision or reference. If the presenting officer is a different person he has the rights of a representative under reg. 2(1)(b).

Paragraph (6)

The rights of a person entitled to be heard are set out in para. (9).

These people may be present during a private hearing. For the deliberations of the tribunal, see reg. 2(2). The only DSS employees entitled to remain are those listed in sub-para. (c). Under sub-para. (d) anyone may be admitted with the leave of the chairman, although any party to the proceedings (or a representative: reg. 2(1)(b)) who is actually present has a veto.

Paragraph (7)

Deals with inquiries.

Paragraph (8)

Confirms that these people are entitled to take part in the proceedings despite para. (6). The new provision about witnesses is presumably also directed at para. (4). Because it only provides that reg. 4 is not to prevent the presence of a witness, it does not inhibit the chairman's power under reg. 2(1) to exclude witnesses from the hearing except when giving evidence.

Paragraph (9)

The rights set out here would probably be secured anyway by the rules of natural justice. But these elements are not in the chairman's discretion; they must be followed. So, for instance, a party has the right to put questions directly to any witness, not merely to put them through the chairman. However, the chairman has a discretion as to the limits of these rights. Thus he can determine that a party has had a sufficient opportunity of addressing the tribunal, or that evidence is irrelevant (see below). If he gets it wrong in a way which prejudices a full and fair hearing, this will be an error of law *(R(SB) 1/81, R(SB) 6/82)*.

Either party may call witnesses to give evidence. It is for the chairman to decide if they should be allowed in to the tribunal room from the start of the hearing, or only admitted at the point at which they are to give evidence *(Guide to procedure* (2nd ed.), para. 60). Usually the informality of the proceedings is such that a representative or person accompanying the claimant in practice gives evidence as a witness without any clear demarcation line, but there may be circumstances in which the importance of evidence being independent means that the witness should not hear what goes on before he gives evidence. A SSAT is not bound by the rules of evidence applied in courts, so that hearsay evidence (*i.e.* the witness is not giving evidence of his direct knowledge, but of someone else's knowledge) can be admitted. However, before admitting it the SSAT must "carefully weigh up its probative value, bearing in mind that the original maker of the statement is not present at the hearing to be questioned on what he actually saw" *(R(SB) 5/82,* and see *Guide to procedure* (2nd ed.), para. 57). But any evidence which has any probative value must be listened to before it is given its appropriate weight, regardless of whether it is hearsay or not *(R(IS) 5/93,* drawing on *R v. Deputy Industrial Injuries Commissioner, ex p Moore* [1965] 1 Q.B. 456 and *Miller v. Minister of Housing and Local Government* [1968] 1 W.L.R. 992). Often the evidence presented by the AO to a SSAT will be hearsay, such as written reports from supplementary benefit visiting officers or copies of records made by unidentified officers. If hearsay evidence is directly challenged it may sometimes be necessary to adjourn to enable a person who can give direct evidence to attend a hearing.

Although the rules say nothing about the admission of documents and written evidence, clearly these are valuable. Indeed, the Commissioners have insisted that since the presenting officer is not a witness, a mere statement by him is not evidence unless supported by some elementary statement from the source of the fact it is desired to submit *(CSB 13/82* [1982] J.S.W.L. 383, *CSB 420/1981* [1983] J.S.W.L. 375, *CSB 728/1984).* In *CSB 517/1982,* the Commissioner expressed disquiet at the refutation of the claimant's expert medical evidence by the statement in the papers that medical advice to the SBO was to the contrary. He held that the claimant was entitled to "chapter and verse" of any evidence relied on. This general approach to statements from presenting officers is confirmed by the Tribunal of Commissioners in *R(SB) 8/84.* There has more recently been a particularly strong statement in *R(SB) 10/86.* See also *CU 47/1993* where the SSAT erred in not asking to see the notes that the claimant stated he had made of his conversations with the UBO.

A representative has all the rights of an interested person, but someone merely accompanying the claimant does not (reg. 2(1)(b)). If a tribunal is aware of a fundamental misconception on the part of a representative it should disabuse him of his erroneous view (see *Dennis v. United Kingdom Central Council for Nursing, Midwifery, and Health Visiting, The Times,* April 2, 1993).

Postponement and adjournment

5.—(1) Where a person to whom notice of an oral hearing by an adjudicating authority or an inquiry has been given wishes to apply for that hearing or inquiry to be postponed he shall do so in writing to the chairman or, as the case may be, the person appointed to hold the inquiry stating his reasons for the application, and the chairman or person appointed may grant or refuse the application as he thinks fit.

[[1](1A) A chairman may of his own motion at any time before the beginning of the hearing postpone the hearing.]

(2) An oral hearing or an inquiry may be adjourned by the adjudicating authority or, as the case may be, the person appointed to hold the inquiry at any time on the application of any party to the proceedings or of its or his own motion.

AMENDMENT

1. Social Security (Adjudication) Amendment Regulations 1994 (S.I. 1994 No. 1082), reg. 3 (May 11, 1994).

Social Security (Adjudication) Regulations 1986

DEFINITIONS

"adjudicating authority"—see reg. 1(2).
"inquiry"—*ibid.*
"party to the proceedings"—*ibid.*

GENERAL NOTE

Paragraph (1) and (1A)
Para. (1) provides that where in advance a party wishes a hearing whose date has been fixed to be postponed, he is to apply in writing with reasons to the tribunal chairman. Then the decision is for the chairman, not the whole tribunal. From May 1994, para. (1A) will, in particular, allow postponements to be granted in response to telephone requests. If paras. (1) or (1A) have not been applied, there remains the general power for an adjudicating authority (which would mean a whole SSAT, not just the chairman) to adjourn under para. (2).

Paragraph (2)
If there has not been a postponement by the chairman, under paras. (1) or (1A), any adjournment (except maybe short adjournments which may be part of the chairman's power to control procedure) must be agreed by the tribunal as a whole. There are many occasions when an adjournment is appropriate. Apart from cases where the claimant fails to appear (see reg. 4(3)), another situation is where a new point of substance, either of law or fact, is raised in the course of the hearing. Here, the test must be whether both parties or their representatives have had a fair opportunity of dealing with the point. If a tribunal considers that further evidence, or the presence of a particular witness, is necessary in order to reach a proper decision then an adjournment should be considered. One factor to be weighed up is the likelihood that the evidence can be produced. Another is whether one party could have been expected to have produced the evidence earlier. In *R(SB) 10/86*, where the presenting officer asserted that beds were available at a particular shop at a particular price, but could produce no supporting evidence, the Commissioner said that if "the adjudication officer comes to the hearing unprepared to support his statement by evidence they [the SSAT] must either decide the appeal on the basis that the facts are unproved or adjourn to give the officer an opportunity of proving them. And where the claimant has been kept waiting they should hesitate to permit a further long wait." The undesirability of subjecting the claimant to delay and possibly a new hearing by a completely differently constituted tribunal is mentioned in the helpful discussion in paras. 65 and 66 of the *Guide to procedure* (2nd ed.).
Under the new listing procedure introduced in September 1992, if a claimant replies on the AT6 tear-off that he will attend a hearing, or if it is decided not to start the striking out procedure, notice of the date of the hearing will be given. The AT6 says that once the date of the hearing has been fixed a request to postpone the hearing will be granted only in exceptional circumstances. Advice has been given, in some regions at least, that if a claimant who has said that he will attend does not do so on the date fixed, the hearing should normally proceed in his absence. It is suggested that a decision to proceed in the claimant's absence can only properly be made after considering all the relevant circumstances and how far it is possible to determine the issues in the appeal without the claimant's evidence. Simply to follow advice from a regional or full-time chairman is a failure to act in a judicial manner. There is no form or pre-paid envelope sent with the notice of the date of the hearing on which a claimant can reply that he cannot attend on that date. The claimant must therefore take the initiative to bring any difficulties to the tribunal's notice.
Note that ITS President's Practice Direction No. 3 on adjournment pending a decision of a higher court or tribunal (see the 1994 edition) has been withdrawn.
In *R(SB) 2/88* the Commissioner suggests that if the SSAT does not contain a member of the same sex as the claimant, as required if practicable by s.41(6) of the Administration Act, an adjournment should be offered to the claimant. See the notes to s.41(6).

Withdrawal of applications, appeals and references

6.—(1) A person who has made an application to the chairman of the tribunal for leave to appeal to a Commissioner against a decision of an appeal tribunal[², a medical appeal tribunal or a disability appeal tribunal] may withdraw his application at any time before it is determined by giving written notice of intention to withdraw to the chairman.
(2) Any appeal to an adjudicating authority made under the Acts or these regulations may be withdrawn by the person who made the appeal—

(a) before the hearing begins by giving written notice of intention to withdraw to the adjudicating authority to whom the appeal was made and
with the consent in writing of—
  (i) in a case which originated in a decision of an adjudication officer,
  [¹an adjudication officer], or
  (ii) in any other case, the Secretary of State, and, in any case, of any
  other party to the proceedings; or
(b) after the hearing has begun, with the leave of the adjudicating authority
or, in the case of a tribunal or board, its chairman, at any time before the
determination is made.

(3) A reference by an adjudication officer to an appeal tribunal under section
99(2) of the 1975 Act [SSAA, s.21(2)] or to a medical board under regulation
42(3) or 57(2) or to a medical appeal tribunal under section 109(3) of the 1975
Act [SSAA, s.46(3)] may be withdrawn by him at any time before the reference
is determined by giving written notice of intention to withdraw to the adjudicating authority to whom the reference was made, but in the case of a reference
under section 109(3) of the 1975 Act [SSAA, s.46(3)] made at the instance of
the Secretary of State only with his consent.

(4) An application under regulation 14 for a decision of the Secretary of State
on any question may, with his leave, be withdrawn at any time before the
decision is given.

AMENDMENTS

1. Social Security (Adjudication) Amendment Regulations 1990 (S.I. 1990 No. 603), reg. 6 (April
6, 1990).
2. Social Security (Adjudication) Amendment (No. 3) Regulations 1991 (S.I. 1991 No. 2889),
reg. 6 (February 3, 1992).

DEFINITIONS

"the Acts"—see reg. 1(2).
"the 1975 Act"—*ibid.*
"adjudicating authority"—*ibid.*
"appeal tribunal"—*ibid.*
"adjudication officer"—*ibid.*
"Commissioner"—*ibid.*
"disability appeal tribunal"—*ibid.*
"medical appeal tribunal"—*ibid.*
"medical board"—see reg. 30.
"party to the proceedings"—see reg. 1(2).

GENERAL NOTE

Paragraph (1)
An application for leave to appeal may be withdrawn at any time before a determination is given.

Paragraph (2)
It might be questioned why a claimant's withdrawal of an appeal should not be automatically
effective, as is a withdrawal of a claim before it is determined. The answer is that there is a public
interest in ensuring that the correct entitlement is applied to the claimant, whether that leaves him
worse or better off than under the original decision. So a claimant should not automatically be
allowed to withdraw an appeal.
Sub-para. (a) applies before a hearing begins. It is not clear exactly when a hearing begins, but
the crucial point appears to be when the tribunal as a body begins its formal consideration of the
appeal. This would mean that para. (2) was in line with the pre-April 1984 NILT practice, rather
than that in the SBAT. It is also assumed that if there has been an adjourned hearing, then any
subsequent withdrawal must be dealt with under sub-para. (b), but even this is not certain (see reg.
24(3)). Note that under sub-para. (a) the appellant's written notice must be given to the adjudicating
authority. There is no particular form in which a withdrawal needs to be expressed. The form AT

6 sent out with the appeal papers has a box asking whether the claimant wishes to withdraw the appeal which can be ticked, and is probably the most common form of withdrawal. The consent must be obtained of all parties to the proceedings. Where the appeal is from an AO's decision, any AO may consent under para. (2)(a)(i), not just the AO who made the decision, as was the case before the April 1990 amendment. The consent of the AO who made the decision appears also to be necessary, since he is a party to the proceedings (see note to reg. 1(2)). However, it may be that this is overridden by para. (2)(a)(i).

Under sub-para. (b), when the hearing has begun, the matter is for the chairman, bearing in mind the public interest noted above, and the probable lack of expertise of the claimant. There is no requirement that the claimant's wish to withdraw should be in writing, and the consent or otherwise of any other parties is irrelevant, although a chairman may wish to ascertain the presenting officer's opinion.

Reg. 6 is silent about whether a withdrawn appeal can be "reinstated", in contrast to reg. 20(3) of the Social Security Commissioners Procedure Regulations (which leaves the question to the discretion of a Commissioner). *CIS 68/1991*, to be reported as *R(IS) 5/94*, decides that providing that any necessary leave to appeal out of time has been granted, a fresh appeal may be brought against an AO's decision, even though an earlier appeal against the same decision has been withdrawn under reg. 6. Where the chairman or an AO has agreed a withdrawal under para. (2) there has been no decision by a tribunal and so the principle of *res judicata* (that once a matter has been adjudicated on by a competent authority another authority of the same level cannot readjudicate on the matter) does not apply. It would be different if the first appeal had been dismissed by a SSAT.

Striking-out of proceedings for want of prosecution

7.—(1) The chairman of an appeal tribunal [¹, a medical appeal tribunal or a disability appeal tribunal] may, subject to paragraph (2), on the application of any party to the proceedings or of his own motion, strike out any application, appeal or reference for want of prosecution. [² including the failure of the appellant to comply with a direction given by the chairman under regulation 2(1)(a)].

(2) [² The chairman shall not make an order under paragraph (1) before a notice has been sent] to the person against whom it is proposed that any such order should be made giving him a reasonable opportunity to show cause why such an order should not be made.

(3) The chairman of an appeal tribunal [¹, a medical appeal tribunal or a disability appeal tribunal] may, on application by the party concerned, [² made not later than 12 months beginning with the date of the order made under paragraph (1),] give leave to reinstate any application, appeal or reference which has been struck out in accordance with paragraph (1).

AMENDMENT

1. Social Security (Adjudication) Amendment (No. 3) Regulations 1991 (S.I. 1991 No. 2889), reg. 7 (February 3, 1992).

2. Social Security (Adjudication) Amendment Regulations 1994 (S.I. 1994 No. 1082), reg. 4 (May 11, 1994).

DEFINITIONS

"appeal tribunal"—see reg. 1(2).
"disability appeal tribunal"—*ibid.*
"medical appeal tribunal"—*ibid.*
"party to the proceedings"—*ibid.*

GENERAL NOTE

This power to strike out applications, appeals and references for want of prosecution, *i.e.* failure to proceed at an acceptable rate, was introduced in April 1987. There is some doubt whether reg. 7 was validly made. The Adjudication Regulations 1986 were made by the Secretary of State on December 16, 1986. At that date Sched. 13 to the Social Security Act 1975 had not been amended to include para. 1A (now para. 3 of Sched. 3 to the Administration Act) giving the power to make regulations providing for the striking out of proceedings for want of prosecution. The amending provision in the Social Security Act 1986 (Sched. 5, para. 19) was not brought into force until April 6, 1987. Thus at the date of the making of the Adjudication Regulations there was no power in force to make reg. 7. It may be that the operation of s.13(b) of the Interpretation Act 1978 allowed the power contained in para. 1A to be exercised before the amendment to the 1975 Act came into force, although the situation is not that primarily envisaged under s.13. The argument has not yet been tested and is probably unlikely to be, so is not set out in full here.

Reg. 7 appears to give the chairman of a SSAT an unfettered discretion to strike out an application, appeal or reference whenever the circumstances appear appropriate. However, the Court of Appeal in *Executors of Evans v. Metropolitan Police Authority* [1992] I.R.L.R. 570 has held that it was inconceivable that a provision in similar terms in the Industrial Tribunal (Rules of Procedure) Regulations 1980 and 1985 gave an unfettered power. Rather, the principles laid down by the House of Lords in *Birkett v. James* [1978] A.C. 297 in relation to ordinary civil actions were applied, subject only to such adaptation as was required by the differences between industrial tribunal proceedings and actions in the ordinary courts. Although there are differences between industrial tribunal proceedings and SSAT proceedings, it seems clear that the *Birkett v. James* principles apply with the necessary adaptations. The industrial tribunal procedure does not contain the possibility of reinstating a struck-out appeal, as in reg. 7(3), but does have a right of appeal against the striking-out order, which does not exist when a SSAT chairman makes an order. The powers are more or less equally draconian.

In *Birkett v. James* Lord Diplock held that the power to strike out for want of prosecution should be exercised only where the court is satisfied:

"either (1) that the default has been intentional and contumelious, *e.g.* disobedience to a peremptory order of the court of conduct amounting to an abuse of the process of the court; or (2) (a) that there has been inordinate and inexcusable delay on the part of the plaintiff or his lawyers, and (b) that such delay will give rise to a substantial risk that it is not possible to have a fair trial of the issues in the action or is such as is likely to cause or to have caused serious prejudice to the defendants either as between themselves and the plaintiff or between each other or between them and a third party."

Under head (i), a peremptory order is one expressly requiring specified action by the plaintiff by a specified date. In the SSAT context an order made under statutory powers by a SSAT or a chairman (*e.g.* under reg. 3(6)) could be made in a peremptory form. It is doubtful if requirements imposed by SSAT clerks as part of the administrative process could be said to be equivalent to orders of the court. Under head (2), the degree of delay that might be unjustifiable in the SSAT context is debateable, but there must also be either some substantial risk to the ability of the SSAT to deal with the appeal fairly or some degree of prejudice to the DSS from the delay.

Presumably a chairman's direction under reg. 2(1)(a) can be made in a peremptory form. Clearly the purpose of the May 1994 amendment to para. (1), which specifically refers to a failure to comply with such a direction, is to provide a mechanism for the making of an order within the *Birkett v. James* principles and so facilitate the striking out of appeals where the claimant fails to reply to correspondence about his appeal. See also the notes to reg. 4(2) on the revised striking out procedure. These changes seem to work. For discussion of the position prior to this amendment and the revised procedure, see the 1994 edition.

However, in other cases SSAT chairmen should think carefully before exercising the power under reg. 7, especially if there has been no application for striking out from any party to the proceedings. If, for example, a requirement under reg. 3(6) is in sufficiently clear terms, with a clear time limit (and maybe a warning of the consequences of failing to comply), a failure to provide further particulars might amount to intentional and contumelious default. If a claimant repeatedly fails to turn up at hearings or continually asserts that he is not ready for a hearing, the power could be used, although it is not always easy to identify the difficulty in conducting a fair hearing. It will often be preferable for the tribunal to make a substantive decision on the appeal.

There is also an uncertainty as to the identity of the person "against whom" an order is made (who must under para. (2) be given an opportunity to show cause why an order should not be made). An appeal to a tribunal can only be made by a claimant, who will be the relevant person in such cases. But a reference can only be made by an AO (Administration Act, s.21(2): 1975 Act, s.99(2)). Presumably the person against whom an order would be made is the AO, but the claimant might be prejudiced by the failure of the tribunal to make a decision. Applications, *e.g.* for leave to appeal, may be made by any party.

Under para. (3) the party concerned, who can apply within 12 months to have the matter reinstated, must be the person identified under para. (2).

Medical references

8. [¹. . .].

AMENDMENT

1. Social Security (Adjudication) Amendment Regulations 1990 (S.I. 1990 No. 603), reg. 5 (April 6, 1990).

GENERAL NOTE

See s.53 of the Administration Act (1975 Act, s.115A).

Non-disclosure of medical evidence

9.—(1) Where, in connection with the consideration and determination of any claim or question, there is before an adjudicating authority medical advice or medical evidence relating to a person which has not been disclosed to him and in the opinion of the adjudicating authority or, in the case of a tribunal or board, its chairman, the disclosure to that person of that advice or evidence would be harmful to his health, such advice or evidence shall not be required to be disclosed to that person.

(2) Evidence such as is mentioned in paragraph (1) shall not be disclosed to any person acting for or representing the person to whom it relates or, in a case where a claim for benefit is made by reference to the disability of a person other than the claimant and the evidence relates to that other person, shall not be disclosed to the claimant or any person acting for or representing him, unless the adjudicating authority, or in the case of a tribunal or board its chairman, is satisfied that it is in the interests of the person to whom the evidence relates to do so.

(3) An adjudicating authority shall not be precluded from taking into account for the purposes of the determination evidence which has not been disclosed to a person under the provisions of paragraphs (1) or (2).

(4) In this regulation "adjudicating authority" includes the Secretary of State in a case involving a question which is for determination by him.

DEFINITION

"adjudicating authority"—see reg. 1(2).

GENERAL NOTE

This provision is fairly self-explanatory. Presumably, if non-disclosure is appropriate, a SSAT is absolved from including its findings relating to that medical evidence in the record of its decision under reg. 25(2).

Correction of accidental errors in decisions

10.—(1) Subject to regulation 12 (provisions common to regulations 10 and 11), accidental errors in any decision or record of a decision may at any time be corrected by the adjudicating authority who gave the decision or by an authority of like status.

(2) A correction made to, or to the record of, a decision shall be deemed to be part of the decision or of that record and written notice of it shall be given as soon as practicable to every party to the proceedings.

DEFINITIONS

"adjudicating authority"—see regs. 1(2) and 12(1).
"party to the proceedings"—see reg. 1(2).

GENERAL NOTE

Only accidental errors, such as slips of the pen or arithmetical errors or such like, can be corrected through this procedure (*CM 209/1987, CM 264/1993* and *CSI 57/1993*). It cannot be used for afterthoughts or corrections of failures to deal with particular points. Also, although it is the duty of the chairman of a SSAT to record the tribunal's decision (reg. 25(2)), it is the whole tribunal which has to correct any errors. It used to be the case that another SSAT could correct errors only if it was impracticable or would cause undue delay to reconvene the original tribunal. From April 1987 an authority of like status may make the correction in any case. It remains preferable that the original people, who will know best what they intended, should carry out the procedure.

It was held in *CSB 226/1981* that a "decision" does not exist until a copy of the written record is sent to the interested parties. Therefore up to that point the chairman of a SSAT may make corrections and additions (providing that these represent the reasoning of the tribunal as a whole) without invoking the procedure of reg. 10 (and see reg. 12(4)). This view is supported by the decision of the Tribunal of Commissioners in *CI 141/1987*. This indicates that an oral decision announced at the end of a hearing can be withdrawn or amended before it is promulgated in writing, within the limits of a judicial discretion. However, in *Gutzmore v. Wardly, The Times*, March 4, 1993, the Court of Appeal decides that inconsistency between the oral and written decision of an industrial tribunal required there to be a rehearing in the circumstances of that case. There seems to be less room for the application of these decisions in view of the new interim notice of award procedure. See the notes to reg. 25(3).

There can be no appeal from the determination to make a correction (reg. 12(3)) but time for appealing or applying for leave to appeal does not start to run until notice of the correction is given (regs. 12(2) and 1(3)). See *CSI 57/1993* in the notes to reg. 12(1) for the position where a tribunal has exceeded the power of correction under reg. 10.

Setting aside of decisions on certain grounds

11.—(1) Subject to regulation 12 (provisions common to regulations 10 and 11), on an application made by a party to the proceedings, a decision may be set aside by the adjudicating authority who gave the decision or by an authority of like status in a case where it appears just to set the decision aside on the ground that—

(a) a document relating to the proceedings in which the decision was given was not sent to, or was not received at an appropriate time by, a party to the proceedings or the party's representative or was not received at an appropriate time by the adjudicating authority who gave the decision; or

(b) a party to the proceedings in which the decision was given or the party's representative was not present at a hearing or inquiry relating to the proceedings; or

(c) the interests of justice so require.

(2) An application under this regulation shall be made in accordance with regulation 3 and Schedule 2.

(3) Where an application to set aside a decision is entertained under paragraph (1), every party to the proceedings shall be sent a copy of the application and shall be afforded a reasonable opportunity of making representations on it before the application is determined.

(4) Notice in writing of a determination on an application to set aside a decision shall be given to every party to the proceedings as soon as may be practicable and the notice shall contain a statement giving the reasons for the determination.

(5) For the purposes of determining under these regulations an application to set aside a decision there shall be disregarded regulation 1(3)(b) and any provision in any enactment or instrument to the effect that any notice or other document required or authorised to be given or sent to any person shall be deemed to have been given or sent if it was sent by post to that person's last known or notified address.

Definitions

"adjudicating authority"—see regs. 1(2) and 12(1).
"party to the proceedings"—see reg. 1(2).

GENERAL NOTE

Paragraph (1)

An application to have a decision set aside may be made by any party to the proceedings (see notes to reg. 1(2)). Under reg. 3(5) the application must specify the grounds on which it is made, and so presumably must refer in some way to at least one of conditions (a), (b) or (c). Particularly since the addition of (c) in April 1987, these are quite wide. The validity of para. (c) is accepted in *R(U) 3/89*. Under (a) the deeming provisions of reg. 1(3) and the Interpretation Act 1978 do not apply (para. (5)), so the question is whether documents did actually arrive at the right time. The standard case is where notice of a hearing was never received by the claimant or a representative, but the non-receipt of a letter or document from the claimant to the tribunal would equally satisfy (a). Under (b) absence from a hearing for whatever reason will do. *R(S) 12/81* decides that when a claimant has not attended the hearing it is irrelevant what evidence he might have given or whether it would have been likely to affect the decision. The question is whether the circumstances of his absence make it just to set the decision aside. For the overriding question in all cases is that of justice.

The addition of condition (c) cannot take away from any rights given by (a) and (b), but allows any deserving case to be considered. However, it can only apply to procedural matters, otherwise the right of appeal to the Commissioner and the finality of SSAT decisions, subject to appeal or review, would be undermined (but see *CM 278/1993*). In *R(S) 3/89* it is said (in relation to the equivalent provision in the Social Security Commissioners Procedure Regulations) that the provision is confined to cases where there have been obvious mistakes or procedural mishaps. In *R(U) 3/89* the Commissioner confines its scope to procedural irregularities, not least because the legislation authorising the making of this regulation deals only with procedure. In *R(SB) 4/90* the Commissioner who decided *R(S) 3/89* holds that he was wrong to mention obvious mistakes, and that the more limited approach of *R(U) 3/89* is right. In *R(SB) 4/90* a crucial regulation was not mentioned in an AO's submission to the "original" SSAT and was ignored in their decision. The AO applied for the decision to be set aside and another SSAT did so under reg. 11(1)(c). A subsequent SSAT heard the appeal and correctly decided against the claimant. On appeal, the Commissioner held that the subsequent SSAT's decision was a nullity because it was purporting to decide a question which had already been decided by the original SSAT, whose decision had not been validly set aside. The setting aside SSAT had no power to act as they did and therefore its determination was declared to be a nullity. Although there is no direct appeal from a determination to set aside (reg. 12(3)) this does not prevent the Commissioner from considering whether the subsequent SSAT had jurisdiction. *R(SB) 1/92* confirms that a failure by a party to produce sufficient evidence to satisfy a SSAT is not a procedural irregularity. SSAT 1 decided that an alleged overpayment was not recoverable, despite written statements from two witnesses that the claimant's wife was known to them as working under another name. The AO applied to have the decision set aside "in the interests of natural justice" (!) to enable the two witnesses to give oral evidence to a new SSAT. SSAT 2 did set aside the first decision and SSAT 3 decided the appeal against the claimant. The Commissioner holds that SSAT 3 had no jurisdiction to hear the appeal since SSAT 1's decision had not validly been set aside.

In *R(SB) 4/90* and *R(SB) 1/92*, the determination of the invalidity of the setting aside determination was made by a Commissioner. *R(G) 2/93* holds that in similar circumstances SSAT 3 would have jurisdiction even though SSAT 2 had no power to set aside the decision of SSAT 1. This was because the Commissioner, as confirmed by the House of Lords in *Foster v. Chief Adjudication Officer* [1993] A.C. 754; [1993] 1 All E.R. 705, has no judicial review powers to make declarations of invalidity. It is true that in *R(SB) 4/90* the Commissioner did purport to declare the decision of SSAT 2 (which was not under appeal to him) a nullity, but that may not have been necessary to his decision. The Commissioner in *R(G) 2/93* does not deal with *R(SB) 1/92* or *CI 78/1990* (see below), where the point is made that in order to determine whether SSAT 3 has jurisdiction it may be necessary incidentally to determine that SSAT 2 did not have jurisdiction. This can be done without purporting to declare as a general matter that the decision of SSAT 2 was a nullity. However, the existence of so many conflicting decisions meant that the central question could not be regarded as finally resolved. But now see *CI 79/1990* below.

If it is concluded that a Commissioner may set aside a decision by SSAT 3 in these circumstances, the question arises of what a tribunal in the position of SSAT 3 should do. *CI 78/1990* decides that if a setting aside determination is plainly invalid on its face, a subsequent tribunal may determine that it has no jurisdiction to hear the appeal. *R(SB) 1/92* accepts this principle. In general, an intervening setting aside determination should be accepted at face value by SSAT 3 and any detailed investigation should be left to the Commissioner. A SSAT requires a very clear case to impugn a determination of a body of equal status. However, there remains some difference of opinion about what amounts to plain invalidity on the face of a setting aside determination. On the facts of *R(SB) 1/92*, the Commissioner considered that SSAT 2's determination was not plainly invalid on its face, so

766

that SSAT 3 was right to hear the appeal. He gives as examples of plain invalidity, SSAT 2 not being properly constituted or notice of the application to set aside not having been given to all parties. In *CI 78/1990* the defect in the SSAT's proceedings was of a similar kind to that in *R(SB) 1/92*, but the Commissioner did not specifically say that the invalidity was not plain. It is clearly not satisfactory if SSAT 3 has to hear an appeal after a plainly defective setting aside by SSAT 2 and leave the claimant to the long delays and inconvenience of a further appeal to the Commissioner. Nor can SSAT 3 avoid impugning a determination of a body of equivalent status. If it accepts a plainly defective setting aside by SSAT 2, it has impugned a perfectly valid decision by SSAT 1.

The issue of the extent of the power of SSATs and Commissioners to examine the validity of intervening decisions and determinations has now been comprehensively examined by a Tribunal of Commissioners in *CI 79/1990*. The facts were that the claimant's appeal was dismissed by SSAT 1. He applied for the decision to be set aside, but SSAT 2 refused that application. He then applied for leave to appeal. In the light of information in that application, the chairman (who had chaired both SSAT 1 and 2) decided that the application to set aside should be reconsidered. SSAT 3 (with an entirely different membership) then set aside the decision of SSAT 1 and SSAT 4 allowed the claimant's appeal. The AO appealed, contending that SSAT 4 was not entitled to hear the appeal, since SSAT 2 had refused the application to set aside and there was no provision for this to be reversed.

The central question was whether the Tribunal of Commissioners had to accept that as a result of SSAT 3's determination SSAT 1's decision had ceased to exist, or could they in the course of establishing whether SSAT 4 had jurisdiction, examine whether SSAT 3's determination was effective to set aside SSAT 1's decision?

The Tribunal agreed with *R(G) 2/93* to the extent that it was clear (see *Foster*) that Commissioners do not have power to make declarations as to the validity of decisions or determinations not under appeal to them. Thus para. 17 of *R(SB) 4/90* was too wide. However, that did not mean that SSATs and Commissioners, in the course of determining whether an appeal tribunal had jurisdiction to hear an appeal, could not determine whether an intervening appeal tribunal's setting aside determination had been effective or not. To that extent the Tribunal agreed with *R(SB) 4/90*, *CI 78/1990* and *R(SB) 1/92*. But Commissioners and appeal tribunals could only consider whether the earlier appeal tribunal had jurisdiction in the narrow sense (see Lord Reid in *Anisminic v. Foreign Compensation Commission* [1967] 2 A.C. 147 at p. 171) of being able to enter into consideration of the matter before it. If the intervening appeal tribunal had made an error *within* jurisdiction, *e.g.* set aside a decision on grounds outside para. (1), that did not allow the validity of its decision or determination to be examined. Thus *R(SB) 4/90*, *CI 78/1990* and *R(SB) 1/92* were wrong in adopting a wider approach.

The essential elements to establish jurisdiction in a setting aside case were: a valid application by a prescribed person which had not already been determined (the Tribunal did not decide the question of whether it was possible to reconsider an application to set aside) and a properly constituted appeal tribunal which made the determination. (*Note*: reg. 24(2) does not apply to setting aside determinations). Failure to send a copy of the application to set aside to other parties to the proceedings (as required by para. (3)) did not deprive the appeal tribunal of jurisdiction (although this was a mandatory requirement, see the note to para. (3)).

Applying this to the circumstances in this case, the result was that SSAT 1's decision and SSAT 2's determination were made within jurisdiction; SSAT 3's determination was made without jurisdiction because the claimant's application to set aside had already been determined by SSAT 2 acting within jurisdiction. (The claimant's application for leave to appeal was not a request for reconsideration of his setting aside application, and the chairman had no authority to treat it as such or reconsider the determination of SSAT 2 himself.) Therefore SSAT 4 had no jurisdiction. SSAT 4 should have investigated whether it had jurisdiction. Although SSAT 4's decision was invalid it had sufficient legal existence to be susceptible to appeal (*Calvin v. Carr* [1980] A.C. 574, applied in para. 6 of *R(S) 13/81*). The consequence was that the claimant's application for leave to appeal against the decision of SSAT 1 remained outstanding and should be dealt with as quickly as possible.

CI 79/1990 is followed in *CIS 373/1994*. See also *CSI 57/1993* which applies *CI 79/1990* to a correction outside a tribunal's powers under reg. 10.

CI 78/1990 also decides that only "decisions" can be set aside under reg. 11. Since a setting aside ruling, although made by the whole tribunal, is a "determination," reg. 11 cannot be used to set aside a setting aside determination. There is a clear distinction in the language within reg. 11, which does not necessarily hold in other contexts. It may be possible for a tribunal to reconsider a refusal to set aside (by analogy with *CIS 93/1992*, see the notes to reg. 3(4)) if further information is provided. This question was referred to, but not decided by, the Tribunal of Commissioners in *CI 79/1990*.

The setting aside is to be done by the adjudicating authority which gave the original decision, or one of like status. So in the case of a SSAT, this requires all three members of the tribunal, not just the chairman (*R(G) 1/81*). There is now no restriction on the circumstances in which another, rather than the original, authority may set aside the decision. Since an "adjudicating authority" includes an AO, this procedure may, in exceptional circumstances, provide a useful alternative to a review of the AO's decision. But the limitation to procedural irregularities must be carefully observed.

In some cases, an oral hearing of the application may be made necessary by the principles of natural justice (*CU 270/1986*), but there is no general right to such a hearing (*CSB 172/1990*).

An AO may apply to have a SSAT decision set aside although the claimant objects (*R(SB) 31/ 85*).

Paragraph (2)

Under para. 8 of Sched. 2 an application to have a decision set aside must be made within three months beginning with the date on which notice of the decision was given to the applicant. See reg. 1(3) for calculating the limit. The time limit may be extended for special reasons under reg. 3(3). The application must state grounds (reg. 3(4)) and further particulars can be required (reg. 3(5)).

Paragraph (3)

Every person interested in the decision must be sent a copy of the application. This particularly includes AOs in the case of a SSAT decision. The importance of their representations was stressed in *R(S) 12/81*. The former practice of IOs in disclaiming their opportunity to make representations was disapproved of. It also appears from *R(S) 12/81* that although the word "representations" suggests something written, an oral hearing may be appropriate. The Commissioners there disapproved of the method of informal postal circulation used.

In *CS 453/1993* the Commissioner decides that the equivalent provision in the Social Security Commissioners Procedure Regulations 1987 (reg. 25(3)) did not require him to obtain the Secretary of State's representation on an application to set aside a refusal of leave to appeal. In that case the Secretary of State had had no previous involvement and the application to set aside was without merit. But the Tribunal of Commissioners in *CI 79/1990* holds that para. (3) is mandatory and that it would be an error of law for an appeal tribunal to determine a setting aside application without being satisfied that a copy of the application had been sent to all parties. Moreover, although it was not a statutory requirement, the Tribunal considered that the principles of natural justice required that where another party did make representations a copy had to be sent to the applicant who had to be given an opportunity to reply.

Paragraph (4)

Notice of the determination (*n.b.* it is not a "decision") with reasons is to be given. There is no appeal from the determination (reg. 11(3)), but a party could apply for judicial review (*Bland v. CSBO* [1983] 1 All E. R. 537, *R(SB) 12/83*) and the validity (but not the merits) of the determination can be raised in a subsequent SSAT hearing (see *R(SB) 4/90, R(SB) 1/92, CI 78/1990* and *CI 79/ 1990*, discussed in the note to para. (1)).

Paragraph (5)

Excludes the operation of reg. 1(3) and s.7 of the Interpretation Act 1978.

Provisions common to regulations 10 and 11

12.—(1) In regulations 10 and 11 "adjudicating authority" includes the Secretary of State.

(2) In calculating any period specified in Schedule 2 there shall be disregarded any day falling before the day on which notice was given of a correction of a decision or the record thereof pursuant to regulation 10 or on which notice is given of a determination that a decision shall not be set aside following an application made under regulation 11, as the case may be.

(3) There shall be no appeal against a correction made under regulation 10 or a refusal to make such a correction or against a determination given under regulation 11.

(4) Nothing in this Part shall be construed as derogating from any power to correct errors or set aside decisions which is exercisable apart from these regulations.

GENERAL NOTE

Most of these provisions are mentioned at the appropriate point in the notes to regs. 10 and 11. The time for appealing or applying for leave to appeal runs from the date of notice of a correction or that a decision is not to be set aside (para. (2)).

PART III

ADJUDICATING AUTHORITIES

SECTION B—ADJUDICATION OFFICERS

Notification of decisions

20.—(1) Subject to paragraph (2) and regulation 63 the decision of an adjudication officer on any claim or question and the reasons for it shall be notified in writing to the claimant who shall at the same time be informed—
[²(a) in the case of a decision of an adjudication officer—
    (i) under section 99 of the 1975 Act [SSAA, s.21] relating to attendance allowance, disability living allowance or disability working allowance, or
    (ii) on a review under section 100A(2) or (4) or section 104A of the 1975 Act [SSAA, ss. 30(2) and (4) and 35].
of his right to a review under section 100A(1) of that Act [SSAA, s.30(1)]:
  (b) in the case of a decision of an adjudication officer under section 100A(1) of that Act [SSAA, s.30(1)], of his right of appeal—
    (i) to a disability appeal tribunal where the appeal relates to the determination of a disability question, and
    (ii) to an appeal tribunal in any other case;
  (c) in all other cases, of his right of appeal to an appeal tribunal under section 100 of that Act [SSAA, s.22].]
(2) Paragraph (1) does not apply in relation to a decision (other than a decision given on review) awarding benefit for a period which begins immediately after a period in respect of which the claimant had been awarded benefit of the same kind and at the same rate as that awarded by the first-mentioned decision.
    (3) [¹. . .]

AMENDMENTS

1. Social Security (Adjudication) Amendment (No. 2) Regulations 1987 (S.I. 1987 No. 1970), reg. 4 (November 23, 1987 (income support); January 1, 1988 (family credit) and otherwise April 11, 1988).
2. Social Security (Adjudication) Amendment (No. 3) Regulations 1991 (S.I. 1991 No. 2889), reg. 8 (February 3, 1992).

DEFINITIONS

"the 1975 Act"—see reg. 1(2).
"adjudication officer"—*ibid.*
"appeal tribunal"—*ibid.*
"disability appeal tribunal"—*ibid.*
"disability question"—*ibid.*
"claimant"—*ibid.*

For the purposes of this book, reg. 20 applies to decisions on family credit, disability working allowance and social fund maternity, funeral and cold weather payments. Income support decisions are dealt with by reg. 63.

For all cases, there is an obligation under para. (1) on the AO to notify the claimant of the precise terms of any decision and the reasons for it. Then for family credit and social fund cases, the right of appeal direct to a SSAT must be mentioned under para. (1)(c). Since for disability working allowance a claimant must first apply for a review of the AO's initial decision, before having the right of appeal to a SSAT or DAT against the AO's decision given on review, the provisions of para. (1)(a) and (b) are more complex. If a disability question arises, whether alone or along with other issues, the appeal must be to a DAT (Administration Act, s.33(1) (1975 Act, s.100D(1)) and reg. 26C). Only if no disability question arises does the appeal go to a SSAT.

SECTION C—APPEAL TRIBUNALS

Oral hearing of appeals and references

24.—(1) An appeal tribunal shall [¹except where section 104(3B)(a) of the 1975 Act [SSAA, s.29] applies] hold an oral hearing of every appeal or reference made to them.

(2) Any case may with the consent of the claimant, but not otherwise, be proceeded with in the absence of any one member other than the chairman.

(3) Where an oral hearing is adjourned and at the hearing after the adjournment the tribunal is differently constituted, otherwise than through the operation on that occasion of paragraph (2), the proceedings at that hearing shall be by way of a complete rehearing of the case.

(4) [¹. . .].

(5) [¹. . .].

(6) Paragraphs (3) and (4) of regulation 23 apply to an appeal tribunal as they apply to an adjudication officer, except that a tribunal shall, instead of referring a question in accordance with paragraph (3)(a) of that regulation, direct it to be so referred by an adjudication officer.

AMENDMENT

1. Social Security (Adjudication) Amendment Regulations 1990 (S.I. 1990 No. 603), reg. 7 (April 6, 1990).

DEFINITIONS

"adjudication officer"—see reg. 1(2).
"appeal tribunal"—*ibid.*
"claimant"—*ibid.*

GENERAL NOTE

Paragraph (1)
The old provision for SBATs that a hearing was to be held as soon as may be reasonably practicable has gone. At the moment a hearing date is not fixed until the DSS have completed their review process, prepared their submissions and sent the papers to the SSAT clerk. It may be that under the independent Presidential system more direct control of listings may be exercised by the SSATs or by regional chairmen.

The exception from April 1990 is to take account of the operation of s.104(3B) of the 1975 Act (now Administration Act, s.29) on reviews and appeals. If an appeal lapses under that provision, because the AO considers that his revised decision on review is the same as would have been given on appeal if the claimant succeeded on every ground, no hearing of the appeal is to take place. However, since this procedure rests on the opinion of the AO, it is arguable that if the claimant disputes that he has got on review all that he could have received if all his grounds of appeal were successful, the appeal should proceed to the SSAT. But it must be admitted that the new wording of para. (1) suggests otherwise, so that the claimant would be left with his right of appeal against the revised decision.

If the claimant dies after lodging an appeal, a SSAT cannot hear the appeal unless there is a personal representative appointed under a grant of probate or letters of administration or an appointee appointed by the Secretary of State under reg. 30 of the Claims and Payments Regulations *(R(SB) 8/88)*. Once such an appointment is made, it has retrospective effect and the appeal can continue *(R(SB) 5/90, R(A) 1/92* and *CIS 379/1992)*. The same applies if the claimant dies before an AO makes a decision on the claim *(CIS 379/1992)*.

Paragraph (2)

A hearing may proceed in the absence of one member of the SSAT, other than the chairman, only with the consent of the claimant. Other parties, including the AO, now have no say in the matter. But the claimant's representative is given express power to consent on his behalf (reg. 2(1)(b)). Mere absence of objection will not do. If the claimant or a representative attends the hearing there will be no problem. If the claimant has returned the form AT 6, there is a question on it asking "Are you willing to have your appeal heard if the tribunal is incomplete?" If the claimant does not send the AT 6 back having answered "Yes" to this question and he does not have an authorised representative at the hearing the SSAT hearing cannot proceed.

Where a member is missing, the chairman has a casting vote (reg. 25(1)). The suggestion that unless this was explained to a claimant before his consent was given, a hearing might be in breach of natural justice was rejected in *CSB 389/1982*. But the Commissioner says that it is desirable that this explanation should be given before the final consent is obtained. The new SSAT decision forms (AT 3) now include in the box which a claimant can sign to give his consent the statement "I understand the Chairman will have a casting vote if required."

Paragraph (3)

The effect of this provision is that on an adjournment a SSAT cannot bind in any way the second tribunal, if its members are not exactly the same. The Tribunal of Commissioners in *R(U) 3/88* has settled some controversy on what a "complete rehearing" requires. The new SSAT is wholly unfettered by what happened at the previous hearing, so that the hearing starts afresh. Everything that requires to be established must be established, even if established before. But it is not compulsory that all oral evidence given at the previous hearing be repeated. The written record or part of it (*e.g.* a witness's statement) may be treated by the parties as an agreed statement of facts. If either party wishes a witness to be further examined, every effort should be made to secure the witness's attendance. Equally, it is open to either party to develop new points or produce new evidence. The excessively strict view of *CS 427/1984* is rejected. *CIS 740/1993* endorses the point in *R2/88 (IVB)* (a decision of a Northern Ireland Commissioner) that it should be recorded in the notes of evidence that a complete rehearing took place.

The difficulties involved in such a rehearing lead the Tribunal in *R(U) 3/88* to make a number of further suggestions. The first is that every effort should be made to avoid a change in the composition of the SSAT. In practice this will require a SSAT, on adjourning, to direct that the next hearing be before an identically constituted tribunal. In this case there need not be a complete rehearing. The second suggestion is that if the SSAT is not identically constituted then no member of the previous SSAT should sit on the new one. Otherwise there is a danger that one member has knowledge of evidence not shared by the other members. This suggestion seems not to have been adopted in practice. The danger is lessened if the nature of a rehearing is kept clearly in mind.

Paragraph (6)

Reg. 23 is about the reference of special questions in child benefit cases to the Secretary of State.

Decisions of appeal tribunals

25.—(1) The decision of the majority of the appeal tribunal shall be the decision of the tribunal but, where the tribunal consists of an even number, the chairman shall have a second or casting vote.

(2) The chairman of an appeal tribunal shall—

(a) record in writing all their decisions (whether on an appeal or on a reference from an adjudication officer); and

(b) include in the record of every decision a statement of the reasons for such decision and of their findings on questions of fact material thereto; and

    (c) if a decision is not unanimous, record a statement that one of the members dissented and the reasons given by him for so dissenting.

(3) As soon as may be practicable after a case has been decided by an appeal tribunal, a copy of the record of their decision made in accordance with this regulation shall be sent to every party to the proceedings who shall also be informed of the conditions governing appeals to a Commissioner.

DEFINITIONS

"adjudication officer"—see reg. 1(2).
"appeal tribunal"—*ibid.*
"Commissioner"—*ibid.*
"party to the proceedings"—*ibid.*

GENERAL NOTE

Paragraph (1)

Normally a simple majority will suffice. The chairman's vote has no extra value unless a member is missing. The reasons for any dissent must be recorded (para. (2)(c)). The references to "the tribunal" emphasise that no other person should take any part in the decision or the deliberations leading up to it. The Commissioner in *R(SB) 13/83* stresses that the tribunal and the clerk should not do anything that would suggest to the claimant that the clerk was participating in the decision-making.

The SSAT seems not to have any express powers in income support and family credit cases. On general principle, and by analogy with the previous practice in non-means tested benefit cases, the SSAT must reach and express a decision on the matter under appeal, as the AO does initially. This will be particularly important where it differs from the AO's decision (*R(SB) 20/82*). It cannot simply say "appeal allowed" or something similar. But the decision does not need to be quantified in pounds and pence. This can be left to the AO, particularly in cases where complicated calculations etc., might be necessary, providing that it is made clear that in the event of any dispute the appeal can be restored to the tribunal for final determination (*R(SB) 16/83*). See the notes to para. (2) below and the decisions referred to in the notes to s.23(1) of the Administration Act on the meaning of "decision". Although the SSAT no longer has the express power simply to confirm the AO's decision, and so ought to set out the decision in full, a decision in the old form might be acceptable providing that it was absolutely clear what decision was being confirmed (see *R(SB) 9/85*, especially on the situation where the AO's decision has been revised). *CS 99/1993* suggests that where a SSAT does not allow an appeal and the AO's decision is quite long, it is better for the tribunal to say simply "the appeal is dismissed", or "the AO's decision is confirmed", thereby preserving the terms of the original decision, rather than record an incomplete decision. In that case, although the SSAT's reasons made it clear that it recognised that it was dealing with a review decision, the decision recorded in box 3 on form AT3 did not do so.

Paragraph (2)

The obligation to complete the record of the SSAT's decision is on the chairman, rather than the tribunal as a whole. This would seem to allow a chairman to complete the record after the decisions have been made, in the absence of the other members. However, it must remain the chairman's duty to ensure that the record represents the corporate view of all three members (*CSSB 1/1982*, approved in *R(SB) 13/83*). It would be at least polite for a chairman to ask the other members' permission to complete the record in their absence.

The Commissioners have consistently held that it is only permissible for the record to be made by the clerk at the chairman's specific direction (*CSSB 1/1982*, approved in *R(SB) 13/83*; *CSB 226/1981*). While there is nothing in the regulations to prevent a chairman from asking a clerk for drafting suggestions, it is clear that such a practice would be frowned on and is now virtually unknown. The AT3 form for the record of SSAT proceedings provides no more space than the old LT 235 did. The practice is for the form to be completed by hand (although dictating machines are also used). From this a typed copy is prepared by the President's staff to be sent to the parties (see para. (3)). The original record will often be scrappy and hard to read. The case-load of most tribunals means that there is not time for meticulous care if the record is to be completed immediately after the decision is reached. There is an obvious tension between the desirability of making the record immediately with the assistance of members and the necessity to meet the standards of legal precision and comprehensiveness required by the Commissioners and legitimately expected by the parties.

Although the regulations do not say anything about the recording of the evidence presented, there is a large box (although still only half a page) provided for this purpose on form AT3 and the Commissioners have held that it is obligatory for the chairman to make a note of evidence, either on form AT3 or on a document which will accompany it (see most recently *CSSB 212/1987*, confirming that failure to record a note of evidence, if there is any dispute, is an error of law). See para. 59 of the *Guide to procedure* (2nd ed.). If the clerk takes notes or lists documents produced and these are used by the tribunal, they should be available to the parties. It is wrong for the clerk's notes to be put forward as the chairman's, but it is proper for him to endorse them as in accordance with his recollection (*R(SB) 13/83*).

Sub-para. (a). Every decision must be recorded. *CSB 635/1982* confirms that if a specific request is made for an adjournment the tribunal is bound to record its decision on that request. It is implied here that the tribunal must make a decision on every matter in issue in the appeal or reference. In *R(SB) 6/81* the tribunal failed to record any conclusion at all on the claimant's appeal for clothes for himself, as opposed to his wife, and so breached this rule. *CIS 628/1992* decides that where the SSAT has failed to deal with all the issues arising on an appeal there is no decision within the meaning of s.23(1) of the Administration Act. The SSAT had purported to refer to an AO substantive matters going beyond questions of calculation or quantification. The Commissioner gives the following guidance to AOs and SSATs in this situation. The AO should not determine the outstanding issues, even with the consent of the claimant, but the appeal should be placed before the tribunal again. If it is not practicable to re-constitute the same tribunal, none of its members should sit on the tribunal for the resumed hearing. If the tribunal is not identically constituted, there must be a complete rehearing (within the guidelines given in para.7 of *R(U) 3/88*). If it is the same tribunal, evidence given at the earlier hearing need not be given again, but the tribunal will not be bound by any finding of fact or any conclusion reached at the previous hearing. If the SSAT is minded to differ from any finding of fact or conclusion it previously reached, it must ensure that the parties have a fair opportunity to deal with this. In *CIS 451/1992* the SSAT chose to deal with a preliminary point only and gave leave to appeal on that issue. The Commissioner refers to the House of Lords' criticism in *Tilling v. Whiteman* [1990] A.C. 1 of such a practice, and their Lordships' suggestion that it should be confined to cases where the facts are complicated and the legal issues short, or to exceptional cases.

In *CSIS 28/1992* and *CSIS 40/1992* (to be reported as *R(IS) 17/94*) a Tribunal of Commissioners holds that a SSAT should deal with the position from the date of claim down to the date of its decision, preferring the approach of another Tribunal of Commissioners in *CIS 391/1992* and *CIS 417/1992* to that of *CIS 649/1992*, where the Commissioner decided that an adjudicating authority should only consider the position as at the date from which benefit is sought. *CIS 649/1992* is also inconsistent with, for example, *CIS 654/1991* (to be reported as *R(IS) 3/93*), *CIS 181/1993*, *CIS 30/1993*, *CIS 267/1993* and *CIS 563/1991*. (The "down to the date of the decision" approach was not applied in *CSB 123/1993* but the Commissioner emphasises that this was due to the "abnormal" situation in that case.) Thus the clear weight of the authorities is that the period before a tribunal will extend down to the date of its decision, unless the running of the claim has been terminated at some earlier date. A new claim submitted while the original claim is under appeal does not automatically end the running of the original claim, although this will be the case if an undisputed award is made on the new claim (para. 11 of *R(S) 1/83*). See also *CIS 701/1993*. Clearly an express termination or withdrawal by the claimant would terminate the running of a claim, for example, if the claimant "signs off" on starting work (*CIS 240/1992*). But a failure to sign on does not indicate that the original claim has terminated (*CIS 563/1991*).

This "down to the date of the decision" principle applies whether the decision under appeal is an initial decision on a claim or a review decision (*CIS 30/1993*). It means that a conclusion that the claimant is not entitled to income support in one week does not prevent an adjudicating authority from finding that there is entitlement in a later week (*CIS 267/1993*). In *CIS 30/1993* the Commissioner states that "parity of treatment and elementary fairness requires that, if a decision confirming the termination of entitlement on review is to be given an effect beyond the operative date of the review, the decision should be able to award benefit for any weeks within the period of entitlement in which the conditions of entitlement were met". The Commissioner draws support for this conclusion from *CIS 391/1992*. But in *CS 879/1995* the Commissioner dissents from this, holding that when an award has been terminated on review, subsequent entitlement can only be established by a fresh claim. In his view the Tribunal of Commissioners in *CIS 391/1992* were only saying that the new appeal tribunal should identify whether at any time during the period down to the date of its decision entitlement had ceased. It was not authority for the proposition put forward in *CIS 30/1993*. He considered that once an earlier claim had been finally disposed of, no further award could be made without a new claim. But is this not the point? A claim will not be finally disposed of until any appeal relating to it has been fully resolved. Thus if the claimant maintains that he is still entitled to (or has become re-entitled to) benefit despite a review decision terminating his entitlement, surely there *is* a continuing claim on which the tribunal has a duty to adjudicate.

Sub-para. (b). In *R(SB) 6/81* and *R(SB) 11/82* the general test of the adequacy of reasons set out in *R(A) 1/72* was adopted. There is a requirement "to do more than only state the conclusion, and for the determining authority to state that on the evidence the authority is not satisfied that the statutory conditions are met, does no more than this ... the minimum requirement must at least be that the claimant, looking at the decision should be able to discern on the face of it reasons why the evidence failed to satisfy the authority." This test was expressly adopted in, *e.g. R(SB) 6/81* and *R(SB) 11/82*, and implicitly adopted in many more decisions. Most of the specific instances of failure to state adequate reasons mentioned below are merely elaborations of the basic principle that both parties should be able to see why the decision was made.

It is now clear that a failure to state adequate reasons is in itself an error of law. Some decisions adopted the formulation in *Crake v. SBC, Butterworth v. SBC* [1982] 1 All E.R. 498 that there was an error of law only when the reasons were so inadequate as to indicate that the tribunal had failed to direct their minds to the proper questions or evidence. However, the Commissioners have later (particularly in *R(SB) 11/82* and *R(SB) 11/83*) distinguished *Crake* as resting on the pre-November 1980 law and held that any failure to give proper reasons is a denial of justice and thus an error of law. The Tribunal of Commissioners in *R(SB) 26/83* confirmed that a failure either to find material facts or to state adequate reasons is in itself an error of law.

Findings of fact

There are a great many Commissioners' decisions holding that tribunals have failed to make adequate findings of fact. For if the tribunal gets its legal approach wrong or does not get to grips with the legal complexities this is almost bound to be reflected in a failure to make findings on the right issues. A good example is *R(SB) 5/82*. But although there is agreement about the general test (see above) there is some difference of approach in applying that test. On the one side are decisions like *R(SB) 5/81*, indicating that a record of reasons or findings in the detail or style of a reasoned court judgment is not expected and that so long as findings of fact are clear, there need not be a detailed enumeration, and *CSB 568/1981*, where a statement that the statutory conditions were not met was in the circumstances enough to make it clear that the presenting officer's argument on the facts was accepted. On the other hand are decisions like *R(SB) 23/82* indicating that findings of primary facts must be made, not simply secondary findings reflecting the terms of regulations and *R(SB) 18/83* indicating that findings have to be made on all submissions put to the tribunal. So far as there is any trend it is probably towards requiring more detailed findings of fact, but perhaps the key is in this statement in *R(SB) 5/81*. "It is not possible to lay down a general rule for recording findings and reasons since that depends on the nature of the evidence and of the case before them [the tribunal]."

What is clear is that conclusions of fact must be recorded, not merely what was said about the issue *(R(SB) 42/84)*. The SSAT must state whether evidence recorded is accepted or rejected *(R(SB) 8/84*, para. 25). It seems to be accepted that this can be done by reference to other documents, providing the result is unambiguous and clear (see *Guide to procedure* (2nd ed.), para. 75). The Commissioners have frequently warned that a mere adoption of the facts as set out in box 5 of form AT2 (the AO's written submission to the SSAT) is unlikely to be sufficient. In *R(IS) 4/93* it is said that it is acceptable for a SSAT to make findings of fact solely by reference to the summary of facts on form AT2 only where what are incorporated are conclusions of fact, rather than mere contentions or statements of evidence, and where findings on all relevant matters are made. To record in box 2 of the form AT3 (findings of fact) "As Box 1" *(CIS 685/1992)*, or "The basic facts are set out in the first paragraph of Box 1" *(R(IS) 9/94)*, did not constitute findings of fact as it was not possible to tell what parts of the claimant's evidence and the presenting officer's submissions were accepted.

There is no rule that the claimant's evidence always has to be corroborated, *e.g.* by medical evidence *(R(S) 2/51*, applied in the instructive decision in *R(SB) 33/85)*. *CSB 615/1985* reminds tribunals that oral evidence is as admissible as documentary evidence and does not necessarily require corroboration.

Reasons for decisions

There is a rather similar difference of approach to the level of detail required in the giving of reasons. Many cases clearly fail the test by merely stating a conclusion. A good example is *R(SB) 31/83:* "The tribunal faced with conflicting evidence decided that the benefit officer had correctly applied Resources Regulation 4(1)." But in more complex cases, there is on the one hand the approach of *R(SB) 5/81* and *CSB 568/1981* that detailed reference to all regulations concerned is not necessary so long as it appears that the tribunal have not misinterpreted them. On the other hand is the approach of *CSB 26/1981* indicating that particularly in single payments cases regulations relied on should be identified down to paragraphs and sub-paragraphs, and *CSB 32/1981* indicating that a complicated inter-relationship between two sets of regulations had to be dealt with. Once again the key is probably that it all depends on the circumstances and that the test is whether the losing party is left in the dark as to why he lost. A tribunal is not required to deal with every regulation which does not assist the claimant if those regulations were never in contention *(CSB 1291/1985)*.

Sub-para. (c). A failure to record the reasons given by the dissenting member is an error of law in itself *(CSB 389/1982)*.

Paragraph (3)

It was argued in *CSB 830/1985* that the sending of an unsigned transcript to the claimant did not satisfy para. (3). But the Commissioner points out that the obligation is to send "a copy of the record" of the decision, not the decision itself. A typed copy is a copy. Only the original should actually be signed by the chairman. The suggestion that a typed copy should be verified with the chairman before being sent out (supported particularly where the chairman dictates the record onto tape by *CP 30/1986*) is not followed in practice.

See ITS President's Practice Direction No. 2 on the delivery of tribunal decisions on the day of the hearing (p. 878), and No. 7 on signing interim award notices (p. 881). The interim notice of award procedure for locally administered DSS benefits started on September 1, 1993 and has since been extended to unemployment benefit and centrally administered benefits. If the SSAT decides the appeal in the claimant's favour so that a payment is due to the claimant, the chairman will complete a form AT3(A) in the same words that will appear in Box 3 of the AT3. When the parties are called back into the room to inform them of the tribunal's decision, they will also be handed a copy of the AT3(A). The chairman should explain that the full decision will be sent later but that the purpose of the procedure is to enable the AO to authorise payment without waiting for the full decision. The chairman should also explain about the parties' rights of appeal and that if the AO decides to appeal, payment of the award may be suspended. It remains to be seen whether the procedure will speed up the payment of awards to appellants.

CSB 342/1986 decided that the AT3(A) form that was in use in 1988 (see p. 316 of the 1988 edition) was not a final decision of the SSAT. By mistake the AT3(A) had stated that the appeal had been allowed, whereas the true decision, as recorded on the AT3, was that it had been disallowed. The Commissioner held that the final decision of the SSAT was only promulgated when the full record of it was sent. However, he also held that if an error of this kind occurred justice could only be done by a further hearing. If the error is discovered before the AT3 is promulgated the parties should be given the opportunity to appear before the SSAT (which presumably should be identically constituted) to make representations. If it is not discovered until after the AT3 is promulgated the Commissioner suggests that the decision could be set aside; reg.11(1)(c) would seem to apply.

The date of the decision continues to be the date of issue of the AT3. See para. 6 of Practice Direction No. 7.

Application for leave to appeal to a Commissioner from an appeal tribunal

26.—(1) Subject to the following provisions of this regulation and to regulation 74(4), an application to the chairman of an appeal tribunal for leave to appeal to a Commissioner from a decision of an appeal tribunal shall be made—

(a) orally at the hearing after the decision is announced by the tribunal; or

(b) as provided by regulation 3 and Schedule 2.

(2) Where an application in writing for leave to appeal is made by an adjudication officer the clerk to the tribunal shall, as soon as may be practicable, send a copy of the application to every other party to the proceedings.

(3) The decision of the chairman on an application for leave to appeal made under paragraph (1)(a) shall be recorded in the record of the proceedings of the tribunal, and on an application under paragraph (1)(a) shall be recorded in writing and a copy shall be sent to each party to the proceedings.

(4) Where in any case it is impracticable, or it would be likely to cause undue delay for an application for leave to appeal against a decision of an appeal

tribunal to be determined by the person who was the chairman of that tribunal, that application shall be determined by any other person qualified under section 97(2D) of the 1975 Act [SSAA, s.41(4)] to act as a chairman of appeal tribunals.

DEFINITIONS

"1975 Act"—see reg. 1(2).
"adjudication officer"—*ibid.*
"appeal tribunal"—*ibid.*
"Commissioner"—*ibid.*
"party to the proceedings"—*ibid.*

GENERAL NOTE

Paragraph (1)

Under s.23(9) of the Administration Act (1975 Act, s.101(5A)) an appeal lies from SSATs only with the leave of the chairman or a Commissioner, regardless of the nature of the decision. The application can be made orally at the SSAT hearing after the decision is announced. This of course requires the decision to have been given at the hearing, which was not the general SBAT practice, but is now the norm. But the full reasons will not be available and the application for leave must give grounds even though not in writing (reg. 3(5)). Thus the alternative of an application under para. 5 of Sched. 2 is likely to be more common. The application must be delivered to the office of the clerk to the SSAT within three months from the date when the notice of the SSAT decision was given. There is no appeal from a chairman's refusal of leave to appeal (*Bland v. CSBO* [1993] 1 All E.R. 537, *R(SB) 12/83*), but in this case the disappointed party may apply to the Commissioner for leave to appeal under s.23(9)(b) of the Administration Act (1975 Act, s.101(5A)(b)). This is to be done within 42 days (Social Security Commissioners Procedure Regulations 1987, reg. 3(3)). *CIS 550/1993* holds that in computing the 42 day period, the day of notification of the refusal of leave is not to be counted. The same principle applies to reg. 7(1) of the Social Security Commissioners Procedure Regulations, which requires notice of appeal to be served within 42 days of the notification of grant of leave. If the time limit for applying to the chairman is missed a party may still go straight to a Commissioner with his application, which may be accepted for special reasons.

In *R(S) 4/82* a Tribunal of Commissioners holds that the chairman's discretion whether or not to grant leave is unfettered, providing that he exercises it in a judicial manner. But they draw attention to the object of the legislation (in NILT cases then only requiring leave if the tribunal had been unanimous) to restrict appeals to those which are neither hopeless nor frivolous and raise a serious issue. If the conduct of the tribunal proceedings is seriously in question, leave should be given. But if the complaint is in general terms only, leave should be refused. There is always another bite of the cherry before the Commissioner. See further the notes to s.23(9) of the Administration Act.

Usually, the application goes to the person who chaired the SSAT, but there is provision under para. (4) for other chairmen to deal with it.

Paragraph (4)

Where it is impracticable or would cause undue delay to go to the original chairman, the application can go to any legally qualified chairman.

[¹SECTION CA—DISABILITY ADJUDICATION

Prescribed period

26A.—(1) Subject to paragraph (2), the prescribed period for the purposes of section 100A(1), (2) and (4) of the 1975 Act [SSAA, s.30(1), (2), (4) and (5)] shall be three months beginning with the date on which notice in writing of the decision of the adjudication officer under section 99 of the 1975 Act [SSAA, s.21] was given to the claimant.

(2) Where a claimant submits an application for review under section 100A(1) of the 1975 Act [SSAA, s.30(1)] by post which would have arrived in a local office in the ordinary course of the post within the period prescribed by paragraph (1) but is delayed by postal disruption caused by industrial action whether

within the postal service or elsewhere, that period shall expire on the day the application is received in the local office if that day does not fall within the period prescribed by paragraph (1).]

AMENDMENT

1. Social Security (Adjudication) Amendment (No. 3) Regulations 1991 (S.I. 1991 No. 2889), reg. 9 (February 3, 1992).

DEFINITIONS

"the 1975 Act"—see reg. 1(2).
"adjudication officer"—*ibid.*
"claimant"—*ibid.*
"local office"—*ibid.*

GENERAL NOTE

The three-month period prescibed in reg. 26A provides the limit within which the application for review on any ground of an AO's initial decision (in effect, the first stage of appeal) must be made, and beyond which review on the usual grounds is available.

See reg. 1(3) for the general rule about the dates when notices are to be treated as given to claimants and applications etc are to be treated as made. Para. (2) allows an extension to the three months where an application is delayed by industrial action. There is no other provision for extending the three months for special reasons or good cause. Therefore, it is particularly important for claimants and advisers to keep the time-limit in mind. Under reg. 26B, applications must be made to local offices.

See the notes to s.30 of the Administration Act for the question of when an application for review is necessary.

[¹Manner of making applications for review under section 100A(1) of the 1975 Act [SSAA, s. 30(1)]

26B. An application for a review of a decision of an adjudication officer under section 100A(1), (2) and (4) of the 1975 Act [SSAA, s.30(1), (2), (4) and (5)] shall be made to a local office.]

AMENDMENT

1. Social Security (Adjudication) Amendment (No. 3) Regulations 1991 (S.I. 1991 No. 2889), reg. 9 (February 3, 1992).

DEFINITIONS

"the 1975 Act"—see reg. 1(2).
"adjudication officer"—*ibid.*
"local office"—*ibid.*

[¹Appeal to a disability appeal tribunal

26C.—(1) The claimant may appeal to a disability appeal tribunal from a decision of an adjudication officer under section 100A(1) of the 1975 Act [SSAA, s.30(1)] in any case in which there arises—
  (a) a disability question; or
  (b) both a disability question and any other question relating to attendance allowance, disability living allowance or disability working allowance.
  (2) In this regulation "disability question" means a question as to—
  (a) whether the claimant satisfies the conditions for entitlement to—
  (i)–(iii) [*Omitted as not applying to disability working allowance*]

777

(iv) a disability working allowance specified in section 20(6A)(b) of the Social Security Act 1986 [SSCBA, s.129(1)(b)];

(b)–(d) [*Omitted as not applying to disability working allowance*]

<small>AMENDMENT</small>

1. Social Security (Adjudication) Amendment (No. 3) Regulations 1991 (S.I. 1991 No. 2889), reg. 9 (February 3, 1992).

<small>DEFINITIONS</small>

"the 1975 Act"—see reg. 1(2).
"adjudication officer"—*ibid.*
"attendance allowance"—*ibid.*
"claimant"—*ibid.*
"disability appeal tribunal"—*ibid.*
"disability question"—*ibid.*

<small>GENERAL NOTE</small>

This provision is made under s.33(1) of the Administration Act (1975 Act, s.100D(1)). Although it uses the word "may," in fact it does not give the claimant any choice about what kind of tribunal to appeal to. Under s.33(1)(a), the claimant may appeal to a DAT in prescribed cases. It is only in another case that there can be an appeal to a SSAT. Thus, if the regulations allow an appeal to a DAT, appeal to a SSAT is excluded.

The "disability question" under para. (2)(a)(iv) is whether the claimant has a physical or mental disability which puts him at a disadvantage in getting a job. If this is the only ground for not awarding the claimant disability working allowance, then the appeal must be to a DAT, which is particularly qualified to decide that question. In these circumstances, the AO may not have made a calculation of the claimant's weekly income to determine the level of the potential entitlement. If the DAT decides the disability question in the claimant's favour, it would seem that it ought to go on and determine all the questions necessary to decide whether the claimant is entitled to disability working allowance and, if so, of what amount. If a DAT refers any calculation back to the AO it should be on the basis that the appeal is to be returned to the DAT for final decision if there is not agreement about the result.

Although it appears odd that a DAT, rather than a SSAT, should determine the non-disability questions, this is expressly required by para. (1)(b) where an appeal raises both a disability question and some other question. The appeal on all questions must go to a DAT.

If in the course of an appeal before a SSAT a disability question arises for the first time, the SSAT may not determine that question under the powers of s.36 of the Administration Act (1975 Act, s.102). It is rather hard to envisage how this could happen, because by definition the disability question must originally have been determined in the claimant's favour for the appeal to have gone to the SSAT. See the notes to s.36 for more discussion.

[¹Persons who may appeal to disability appeal tribunals and appeal tribunals

26D. A person purporting to act on behalf of a person who is terminally ill as defined in section 35(2C) of the 1975 Act [SSAA, s.66(2)], whether or not that other person is acting with his knowledge or authority, may appeal to a disability appeal tribunal or an appeal tribunal, as appropriate, in accordance with section 100D(1) of that Act [SSAA, s.33(1)] in any case where the ground of appeal is that that person is or was at any time terminally ill.]

<small>AMENDMENT</small>

1. Social Security (Adjudication) Amendment (No. 3) Regulations 1991 (S.I. 1991 No. 2889), reg. 9 (February 3, 1992).

<small>DEFINITIONS</small>

"the 1975 Act"—see reg. 1(2).

"appeal tribunal"—*ibid.*
"disability appeal tribunal"—*ibid.*

GENERAL NOTE

Under s.33(1) of the Administration Act appeals to tribunals must be made by the claimant or other prescribed persons. This provision is the only prescription. It cannot apply to disability working allowance, because being terminally ill is not a relevant ground of appeal. Therefore, for disability working allowance the appeal must be made by the claimant (or an official appointee) personally and not by some other person or group, unless expressly authorised by the claimant.

PART IV

PROVISIONS RELATING TO PARTICULAR BENEFITS OR PROCEDURES

[¹SECTION C—INCOME SUPPORT

Notification of decisions in income support cases

63.—(1) Subject to paragraphs (2), (3) and (4) the decision of an adjudication officer on any claim or question relating to income support shall be notified in writing to the claimant who shall at the same time be notified of his right to request a statement of the reasons for that decision and of his right of appeal to an appeal tribunal.

(2) Where, under arrangements made by the Secretary of State either throughout or in any part of Great Britain, income support is payable together with a benefit under the 1975 Act, notice of the aggregate amount so payable shall be notice for the purpose of paragraph (1).

(3) Written notice shall not be required of any determination awarding benefit which is implemented by a cash payment if in all the circumstances it would be impracticable to give such a notice.

(4) Written notice shall not be required of a determination terminating entitlement to income support if the reason for the termination is already known to the claimant or it is otherwise reasonable in the circumstances not to give such notice.

(5) So far as may be practicable, and subject to paragraph (6), where a claimant is notified of a decision under paragraph (1) or (2) the Secretary of State shall also give or send him a written notice of assessment showing—

  (a) the total amounts of the personal allowances, family premium, other premiums and housing costs determined under Part IV of the Income Support (General) Regulations 1987 as are appropriate in his case; and
  (b) the income taken into account; and
  (c) any personal expenses addition, special transitional addition and transitional addition payable under the Income Support (Transitional) Regulations 1987.

(6) Paragraph (5) shall not apply to any determination—

  (a) that income support is not payable for any reason other than that the claimant's income exceeds the applicable amount;
  (b) made on review under regulation 69, either under paragraph (3) of that regulation or where in other cases under that regulation the Secretary of State considers a written notice of assessment unnecessary;
  (c) in respect of a claimant to whom [²section 23A] of the 1986 Act [SSCBA, s.127] (return to work after trade dispute) applies.

(7) If, within the time limited by regulation 3 and Schedule 2 for the bringing of an appeal against an adjudication officer's decision the claimant requests a

779

statement of the reasons for that decision he shall be given such a statement in writing and shall again be informed of his right of appeal.]

AMENDMENTS

1. Social Security (Adjudication) Amendment (No. 2) Regulations 1987 (S.I. 1987 No. 1970), reg. 8 (November 23, 1987).
2. Social Security (Common Provisions) Miscellaneous Amendments Regulations 1988 (S.I. 1988 No. 1725), reg. 2(5) (November 7, 1988).

DEFINITIONS

"the 1975 Act"—see reg. 1(2).
"adjudication officer"—*ibid.*
"appeal tribunal"—*ibid.*
"claimant"—*ibid.*
"income support"—*ibid.*

GENERAL NOTE

Paragraph (1)
Paras. (2), (3) and (4) supply exceptions to the general obligation to provide a written decision. The right to a statement of reasons is under para. (7). A notice of assessment, showing how benefit is worked out (normally on a form A14) is dealt with in paras. (5) and (6).

The obligation under para. (1) is to provide the actual and complete terms of the decision in writing to the claimant (Common Appendix to *CSSB 281/1989* and associated decisions and *CSSB 540/1989*). The implication of this requirement is that the AO has to record all decisions in writing. The Commissioner in the Common Appendix shows graphically how this requirement has not been met in the past, particularly in supplementary benefit cases, where decisions often have to be "reconstructed" from ticks on forms and such-like evidence of what was done. This is particularly troublesome in review cases, where the terms of and reasons for the decision review of which is sought are vital. See *CSIS 78/1993* in the notes to s. 71(5) of the Administration Act.

The obligation applies to review decisions as well as initial decisions on a claim (subject to the exception in para. (4)). It is not uncommon for an AO to terminate or alter an award without referring to any grounds for review. If such a decision comes before a SSAT, it may normally correct the deficiency by dealing with the grounds of review itself (*CSSB 540/1989*).

Paragraph (2)
Presumably a statement of the aggregate amount must still be accompanied by notification of the right to request reasons and the right of appeal.

Paragraphs (3) and (4)
The circumstances in which, under para. (4), it is reasonable not to give written notice of the termination of entitlement must be severely limited. It looks as though the obligation to notify the claimant of his right to receive reasons and the right of appeal disappears along with the obligation to give written notice (to which it is attached in para. (1)), although it is to be hoped that in practice the information is given.

Paragraph (5)
The general rule is that if a written notice has to be given under paras. (1) and (2) a notice showing the assessment of requirements and resources (A14) must be given. The exceptions are listed in para. (6).

Paragraph (6)
However, the overall obligation is subject to the condition of practicability. It is not clear whether shortage of staff would be relevant to this issue.

A notice of assessment need not be given in the following circumstances:
(a) where entitlement is denied on any ground except that income exceeds the applicable amount;
(b) where there is a review of a continuing entitlement and the Secretary of State considers a notice unnecessary (it would be a nuisance to have to produce a new notice every time the amount of benefit went up or down); and
(c) where the claimant is entitled for the first 15 days of return to work after a trade dispute.

Paragraph (7)

This is important provision. It is often said that a proportion of appeals are really about getting a proper explanation of the decision and that once this is provided in the appeal papers the claimant is satisfied. It is to be hoped that this provision will enable that process to take place without the time and expense involved in starting the appeal process. It will only achieve this if the statements of reasons are both full and understandable.

The procedure may also be another way of getting a decision looked at again, without invoking the appeal process. The search for reasons may reveal mistakes in the original decision, which the AO should then correct by review.

Under para. 4 of Sched. 2, a claimant has three months from the date on which notice of the AO's decision was given to appeal. The request for reasons must be made within this period, which can be extended (reg. 3(3)). Until April 1987, the time for appealing ran from the date on which a statement of reasons was given. But now that the normal period has been extended from 28 days to three months, this concession is considered unnecessary. But a long delay in producing a statement of reasons might well influence a chairman to extend the period for appealing.

[¹Income support and social fund questions not immediately determinable

64.—[³(1) Where on consideration of a claim or question relating to income support or to payment of maternity expenses from the Social Fund under Part VIII of the Social Security Contributions and Benefits Act 1992 it appears to an adjudication officer that the claimant's entitlement to, or the rate or amount of, such benefit depends on the determination of—

(a) the question as to what housing costs are to be included in the claimant's applicable amount by virtue of regulation 17(1)(e) or 18(1)(f) of, and Schedule 3 to, the Income Support (General) Regulations 1987 (applicable amounts) and the adjudication officer is satisfied that not all of those housing costs can be immediately determined, he shall proceed to determine the claim or question on the assumption that the housing costs to be included in the claimant's applicable amount are those that can be immediately determined;

(b) any of the questions mentioned in paragraph (3), and he is satisfied that the question cannot be immediately determined, he shall proceed to determine the claim or question on the assumption that the determination of the question so mentioned will be adverse to the claimant.

(2) Without prejudice to the power of an adjudication officer to refer any claim or question to an appeal tribunal under section 21(2) of the Administration Act and notwithstanding the provisions of section 22 of that Act, on an appeal to an appeal tribunal in any case where the adjudication officer has applied the provisions of paragraph (1) in relation to any of the questions mentioned or referred to in that paragraph, the tribunal shall not determine any such question until it has been determined by an adjudication officer.]

(3) The questions referred to in paragraphs (1) and (2) are—

(a) whether in relation to any person the applicable amount falls to be reduced or disregarded to any extent by virtue of section 23(3) of the 1986 Act [SSCBA, s.126(3)] (persons affected by trade disputes);

(b) whether regulation 22 of the Income Support (General) Regulations 1987 (reductions in applicable amounts in certain cases of actual or notional unemployment benefit disqualification) applies to a person by virtue of paragraph (4)(c)(iii) of that regulation and, if so, the period of its application by virtue of paragraph (6)(c) of that regulation;

(c) whether by virtue of regulation 9(1) of the Income Support (General) Regulations 1987 (persons treated as available for employment) a person is to be treated as available for employment and whether by virtue of regulation 10(1)(b), (d) or (g) of those Regulations he is not to be so treated;

(d) whether for the purposes of regulation 12 of the Income Support

(General) Regulations 1987 (relevant education) a person is by virtue of
that regulation to be treated as receiving relevant education;

(e) [². . .];

(f) whether for the purposes of regulation 10(1)(a) of the Income Support
(General) Regulations 1987 (circumstances in which claimants are not
to be treated as available for work) after a situation in any [². . .] employment has been properly notified to a claimant as vacant or about to
become vacant he has without good cause refused or failed to apply for
that situation or refused to accept that situation when offered to him.]

[²(g) whether regulation 10A of the Income Support (General) Regulations
1987 (circumstances in which a claimant is not required to seek employment actively or is treated as seeking employment actively) by the virtue
of paragraphs (3) or (4) of that regulation.]

[³(h) whether in relation to any claimant the applicable amount includes severe
disability premium by virtue of regulation 17(1)(d) or 18(1)(e) of, and
paragraph 13 of Schedule 2 to, the Income Support (General) Regulations
1987 (applicable amounts).]

AMENDMENTS

1. Social Security (Adjudication) Amendment (No. 2) Regulations 1987 (S.I. 1987 No. 1970),
reg. 8 (November 23, 1987).
2. Social Security (Adjudication) Amendment Regulations 1989 (S.I. 1989 No. 1689), reg. 4
(October 9, 1989).
3. Social Security (Adjudication) Amendment (No. 2) Regulations 1994 (S.I. 1994 No. 2686),
reg. 2 (November 14, 1994).

DEFINITIONS

"the 1975 Act"—see reg. 1(2).
"the 1986 Act"—*ibid.*
"adjudication officer"—*ibid.*
"appeal tribunal"—*ibid.*
"claimant"—*ibid.*
"income support"—*ibid.*

GENERAL NOTE

The substance of this important provision has been in place since 1984.
The procedure has the effect that all decisions are made by an AO exercising a social fund or
income support jurisdiction. The AO merely has the power to defer making a final decision. The
result is that on an appeal to a SSAT, which must be against the social fund or income support
decision, once all the questions are determined, all the issues are before the SSAT, including the
correctness of the answers to all of the questions (*R(SB) 22/85*, para. 21(2)).

Paragraph (1)
Where one of the questions listed in para. (3) arises before the AO on a social fund or income
support claim he has a choice of courses. He may decide that he can determine the question himself
immediately. He may consider that the answer is clear, there may be an existing decision on, *e.g.*,
child benefit or unemployment benefit which he decides to adopt, or he may informally consult
another AO specialising in child benefit or unemployment benefit. Whatever the reason, if the question is decided immediately, reg. 64 does not apply. There has been an ordinary adjudication with
the ordinary rights of appeal. Note also that reg. 64 does not apply at all in some circumstances
where the income support decision depends on the decision on another benefit. The main example
is the reduction in benefit under reg. 22(4)(c)(i) and (ii) of the Income Support (General) Regulations.
If the AO decides that he cannot immediately determine a question listed in para. (3), then paras.
(1)(b) and (2) do come into play. Under para. (1)(b) the claimant's entitlement must be determined
on the assumption that the question will be answered adversely to him. This means adversely from
the income support point of view (*R(SB) 22/82*). Para. (2) deals with the effect on appeals. Once
again, even if the question is passed on to another AO for decision, that AO, even if purporting to

decide the question as part of his child benefit or unemployment benefit jurisdiction, will do so under the income support or social fund jurisdiction. The proper procedure, no doubt, is for the income support AO to make the determination after a delay for consulting the other AO. If the eventual determination of the question is adverse to the claimant, the interim treatment of his entitlement is confirmed, although he has a right of appeal. If the eventual determination is favourable to the claimant, the initial decision on entitlement must be reviewed under reg. 69(4)(b).

Para. (1)(a), which concerns cases where the claimant's full housing costs cannot be immediately determined, is new from November 1994.

If the AO is proceeding under reg. 64 the claimant should be told this expressly, at the latest at the time of any appeal *(R(IS) 6/91)*. The claimant is entitled to know what rights of appeal he has.

Paragraph (2)
Where an AO has made his decision on an assumption under para. (1), a SSAT is not to decide any such question until that question has been decided by an AO. In practice it seems that when an AO makes such an initial decision and there is an appeal on the question whose decision is delayed, the AO will not prepare his submissions and send the papers on to the SSAT clerk until both decisions have been made. Then the SSAT has jurisdiction to deal with both decisions together and the reasons for both will be given on the tribunal papers *(R(SB) 22/85)*.

This leaves the situation where the AO makes some mistake, or perhaps bases his decision on a ground which is rejected by the SSAT on appeal, and one of these questions arises for the first time before the SSAT. The SSAT is not prevented from dealing with the question by para. (2) because there will not have been a decision under para. (1). There is nothing in the regulations to give the SSAT power to refer the question to an AO. Thus the SSAT has jurisdiction to decide the question which is relevant to income support or social fund entitlement. This conclusion is reinforced by the fact that s.36 of the Administration Act (1975 Act, s.102) allowing a SSAT to determine questions first arising in the course of an appeal, applies to income support and social fund cases. The control must come from the principles of natural justice. If a new issue, particularly one turning on legislation with which the presenting officer is not familiar, is raised at a hearing, then the presenting officer may legitimately request an adjournment in order to be able to deal with the issue. The same would apply if the claimant or his representative were to be unexpectedly asked to deal with a new issue.

Paragraph (3)
The precision of the references to other regulations in para. (3) must be carefully noted. See the notes to those regulations. Sub-para. (g) is new from November 1994.

SECTION D—REVIEW OF DECISIONS

[¹Date from which revised decision has effect on a review

64A.—(1) In the case of a review to which either paragraph (2) or paragraph (3) applies, the decision given shall have effect from the date from which the decision being reviewed had effect or from such earlier date as the authority giving the decision being reviewed could have awarded benefit had that authority taken account of the evidence mentioned in paragraph (2) or not overlooked or misconstrued some provision or determination as mentioned in paragraph (3).

(2) This paragraph applies to a review under [²sections 100A(2)(a) and (4), 104(1)(a) and 104A(1)(a) of the 1975 Act] [SSAA, ss.30(2)(a), (4) and (5)(a), 25(1)(a) and 35(1)(a)] (review for error of fact) of any decision, whether that decision was made before or after the coming into force of this regulation, where the reviewing authority, that is to say the adjudication officer or, as the case may be, the appeal tribunal, is satisfied that—

(a) the evidence upon which it is relying to revise the decision under review is specific evidence which the authority which was then determining the claim or question had before it at the time of making the decision under review and which was directly relevant to the determination of that claim or question but which that authority failed to take into account; or

(b) the evidence upon which it is relying to revise the decision under review is a document or other record containing such evidence which at the time of making the submission to the authority which was then to determine the claim or question, the officer of the Department of Social Security, the Department of Employment or the former Department of Health and Social Security who made the submission had in his possession but failed to submit; or

(c) the evidence upon which it is relying to revise the decision under review did not exist and could not have been obtained at that time, but was produced to an officer of one of those departments or to the authority which made that decision as soon as reasonably practicable after it became available to the claimant.

(3) This paragraph applies to a review under [²sections 100A(2)(d) and 104(1A) of the 1975 Act] [SSAA, ss.30(2)(d) and (5)(c) and 25(2)] (review for error of law) of any decision, whether that decision was made before or after the coming into force of this regulation, where the adjudication officer or, as the case may be, the appeal tribunal, is satisfied that the adjudication officer, in giving the decision under review, overlooked or misconstrued either—

(a) some provision in an Act of Parliament or in any Order or Regulations; or
(b) a determination of the Commissioner or the court,

which, had he taken it properly into account, would have resulted in a higher award of benefit or, where no award was made, an award of benefit.

(4) The following provisions of this section, including regulation 69 as continued in force by regulation 13 of the Social Security (Adjudication) Amendment (No. 2) Regulations 1987 and as amended by regulation 10 of those Regulations, are subject to the provisions of this regulation.

(5) In this regulation "court" has the same meaning as it has in section 165D of the Act [SSAA, s.68].]

AMENDMENTS

1. Social Security (Adjudication) Amendment (No. 2) Regulations 1991 (S.I. 1991 No. 1950), reg. 2 (August 31, 1991).
2. Social Security (Adjudication) Amendment (No. 3) Regulations 1991 (S.I. 1991 No. 2889), reg. 12 (April 6, 1992).

GENERAL NOTE

This new provision replaces reg. 72, with the same effect of lifting the normal 12-month limit to backdating on a review, from August 31, 1991. On general principle, the new conditions would apply to reviews requested or, if not requested, carried out from that date, while the old rules would apply to reviews before that date (*R(SB) 26/83, R(SB) 48/83* and *CIS 11/1991*). However, this is expressly confirmed by reg. 3 of the 1991 amending Regulations, which provides that the new rules do not apply to reviews pursuant to applications for review made before August 31, 1991.

The date of the coming into force of the amendment is itself a matter of some controversy. The first amending Regulations were made on August 19, 1991, and were due to come into force on September 11, 1991. The Government became concerned at the prospect of mass applications for review being submitted before September 11. On August 30, without notice, the No. 2 amending Regulations were made, coming into force the next day and thus cutting off the possibility of new applications being made to which reg. 72 would apply.

There had been difficulties in the interpretation of reg. 72. The Government was concerned that it was being exploited by applications for review of every decision made on a claim from a person's 16th birthday. The DSS proposed an amendment which would have simply prevented arrears of supplementary benefit or national assistance being awarded in a review decision. This provoked considerable opposition and the Social Security Advisory Committee rejected it in principle (see Cm. 1607 for their report, which also describes the background). The SSAC's suggestion was that if it was thought that reg. 72 was being used in wider circumstances than those originally intended, the solution was to define the conditions which merited the payment of arrears more closely. This, as set out in the Secretary of State's statement in Cm. 1607, is what has been done in the new reg. 64A.

If either para. (2) or para. (3) applies, the 12-month limit on payment of benefit following review in regs. 69 and 71 (as well as reg. 65 on most social security benefits) does not apply. See the amendments to those regulations. The decision (which must mean the revised decision on review) then has effect either from the date on which the decision under review took effect or from an earlier date from which benefit could have been awarded in that decision. There may be some difficulties if the decision being reviewed is itself a refusal to review or a revised decision given on review. The powers on review which existed at that time would then seem to control how far back entitlement could have gone from that decision. The interaction with the principles set out in the Common Appendix to *CSSB 281/1989*, etc., *CSSB 238/1989* and *CSSB 544/1989* will require careful working out. See also *Chief Adjudication Officer v. Eggleton and Others*, Court of Appeal, March 17, 1995 (effect on decision of no, or only partial, revision on review) in the notes to s. 25 of the Administration Act.

Paras. (2) and (3) helpfully provide expressly that they apply whether the decision under review was made before or after August 31, 1991.

Paragraph (2)

This provision covers cases where review is on the ground that the decision was made in ignorance of or under a mistake as to some material fact. Note that it does not cover reviews on the ground of change of circumstances. The 12-month limit is lifted if one of the three alternative conditions is satisfied. These are carefully drawn, although there are still several areas of uncertainty.

Under sub-para. (a) the authority making the decision under review (*i.e.* the AO, a SSAT or a Commissioner giving the decision the SSAT should have given) must have failed to take into account specific evidence which was before it at the time. It is not clear what "specific" evidence is. The underlying intention is no doubt that a claimant should point to some particular piece of evidence which was ignored, rather than make generalised assertions that circumstances could not have been taken into account, but the degree of specification needed is obscure. There are also difficulties in talking about evidence, not about the material fact of which it is evidence. The structure might make sense where there is a clear distinction between the AO making a decision on the basis of evidence submitted and officers acting for the Secretary of State in gathering evidence. However, the practice in supplementary benefit and national assistance was for such a distinction often to be blurred. A visiting officer who went to see the claimant's home circumstances might also be the AO who made the decision. Is what the AO saw with his own eyes specific evidence which was before him? The specific evidence must also be "directly relevant" to the decision under review. The test of whether a fact is material is whether it would have called for serious consideration, not that it would necessarily have led to a different decision if it had been known (*Saker v. Secretary of State for Social Services, R(I) 2/88*). Does the "directly relevant" test require that the evidence would definitely have led to a different decision? The precise words suggest not, so that the reviewing authority, once the conditions for review are met, can draw different inferences and conclusions from the same primary facts.

Under sub-para. (b) the evidence on which review is based must have been in the possession of an officer of the DSS/DHSS or the Department of Employment, but not been submitted to the AO, SSAT or Commissioner. The same difficulty as noted in relation to sub-para. (a), the blurring of roles in the administration of supplementary benefit and national assistance, will appear here. The evidence of the material fact must also be embodied in some document or record which an officer failed to submit. It is hard to see how the evidence can be a document containing such evidence, but the above seems to be the most sensible construction.

Finally, under sub-para. (c) the evidence of the material fact must have not existed at the time of the decision under review. The material fact must have existed at the time for there to be ignorance or a mistake as to it. There is a second condition that evidence of that fact could not have been obtained at the time. This is a particularly tough test: it is not a question of reasonableness or practicality but of possibility. If these two hurdles are crossed, it must be shown that the evidence was produced to the DSS, Department of Employment or the AO as soon as reasonably practicable after it became available to the claimant. The test is not when it comes to the claimant's knowledge, but when it becomes available to him. If the evidence is in the hands of an adviser or representative, is it available to the claimant?

It is understood that the DSS has apparently accepted that sub-para. (c) can apply where an income support decision is reviewed (to award, for example, a severe disability premium) following an award of attendance allowance or disability living allowance that is backdated for more than 12 months. The basis of this is that the AO made a mistake as to fact (the AO believed that the claimant was not entitled to this benefit when in fact he was) when he made the income support decision. In this situation the DSS say that full arrears, not limited to 52 weeks, can be paid.

These alternative tests certainly define clearly deserving cases, but only time will tell whether the lines have been drawn too strictly.

If review is sought going back a long way, it is quite likely that documents relating to the original decision will have been destroyed under the DSS's arrangements for clearing storage space. In those circumstances, no presumptions can be drawn about the contents of the destroyed documents (*R(IS) 11/92*). A claimant may then well be unable to show that the conditions of paras. (a) or (b) have been satisfied. *R(IS) 11/92* shows that *The Ophelia* [1916] 2 A.C. 206 merely applied the established rules of evidence to the effect that if a person destroys documents with the intention of destroying evidence, then in any litigation concerning that person the contents of the destroyed documents are presumed to have gone against that person's case. Para. 7 of *CSB 1288/1985* gave a mistaken view of the effect of *The Ophelia*.

Paragraph (3)

This provision covers cases of review for error of law. Only AO's decisions may be reviewed under this power, not decisions of a SSAT or Commissioner. The error of law must be of one of the two kinds specified.

The first (sub-para. (a)) is overlooking or misconstruing some provision in an Act of Parliament, Order or Regulations. By definition, the provision must be in force at the relevant time (or there would not be an error of law) and in existence at the date of the decision (so that retrospective legislation does not count). However, it does not matter for these purposes (where the hurdle of s.69 of the Administration Act must already have been overcome) that the misconstruction is revealed as such by a decision of the courts or the Commissioner which comes after the date of the decision under review. Note that European Community legislation, even though directly effective in English law, is not included. But if a decision was reviewed as given in error of European Community law which was part of English law that same law would require an adequate remedy to be provided.

The second kind of error of law (sub-para. (b)) is overlooking or misconstruing a determination of the Commissioner or the court. The court means the High Court, the Court of Appeal, the Scottish and Northern Irish equivalents, the House of Lords and the European Court of Justice (para. (5) and Administration Act, s.68(4); 1975 Act, s.165D(4)). By definition, the determination which is overlooked or misconstrued must have been made before the date of the decision under review. Since under the Interpretation Act the singular includes the plural unless the context requires otherwise, misconstruing the combined effect of a number of decisions would seem to fall within para. (3). As under para. (2), it does not matter that it is a Commissioner's or court decision after the decision under review which reveals that some earlier Commissioner's or court decision has been misconstrued or overlooked. It must nevertheless be shown that if the effect of the decision or decisions had been properly taken into account the decision under review would have been more favourable to the claimant.

[¹Review of decisions to which section 104(7) of the 1975 Act [SSAA, s.69(1)] applies

64B. In any case to which subsection (7) of section 104 of the 1975 Act [SSAA, s.69(1)] applies, the decision given on review shall have effect from the date of the relevant determination within the meaning of that subsection whether the decision which is being reviewed was made before, on or after 9th March 1992.]

AMENDMENT

1. Social Security (Miscellaneous Provisions) Amendment Regulations 1992 (S.I. 1992 No. 247), reg. 7 (March 9, 1992).

DEFINITION

"the 1975 Act"—see reg. 1(2).

GENERAL NOTE

Section 69(1) of the Administration Act (1975 Act, s.104(7)) deals with the effect of "test cases" on reviews of entitlements in the cases of other claimants, and lays down the legal basis on which entitlement before the date of the test case (*i.e.* the "relevant determination") must be decided. The effect of reg. 64B seems to make that result academic, by only allowing a review to have effect from the date of the test case. This makes it all the more important to establish exactly what cases s.69(1) applies to. Note *Chief Adjudication Officer v. Eggleton and Others* (Court of Appeal, March 17, 1995) on the effect on decisions where there is no, or only partial, revision on review (see the notes to s. 25 of the Administration Act). As to when s. 69(1) applies, see *Bate v. Chief Adjudication Officer and the Secretary of State for Social Security, The Times,* December 12, 1994, in the notes to s. 69 and the extensive discussion in those notes.

[¹Review in income support cases

69.—(1) [³Except in a case to which regulation 64A(2) or (3) [⁵or regulation 64B] applies], a determination on a claim or question relating to income support shall not be revised on review under section 104 of the 1975 Act [SSAA, s.25] so as to make income support payable or to increase the amount of income support payable in respect of—

(a) any period which falls more than 12 months before the date on which the review was requested or, where no request is made, the date of review; or

(b) any past period which falls within the period of 12 months mentioned in sub-paragraph (a) and has been followed by termination or interruption of entitlement to income support and—

  (i) the total amount of the increase would be £5 or less, or

  (ii) the grounds for review are a material fact or relevant change of circumstances of which the claimant was aware but of which he previously failed to furnish information to the Secretary of State.

(2) A change mentioned in paragraph 7(8) of Schedule 3 to the Income Support (General) Regulations 1987 (fall in interest rates or reduction of outstanding loan capital) shall be deemed not to be a change of circumstances if the amount of the instalments payable to the lender remains constant but, in such a case, where a determination is subsequently reviewed under section 104(1)(b) of the 1975 Act [SSAA, s.25(1)(b)], that review shall also take account of any such change.

[²(3) Section 64A of the 1986 Act [SSAA, s.159], (which relates to the effect of alterations in the component rates of income support) shall not apply to any award of income support in force in favour of a person where there is applicable to that person—

(a) any amount determined in accordance with regulation 17(2) to (7) of the Income Support (General) Regulations 1987; or

(b) any protected sum determined in accordance with Schedule 3A or 3B of those Regulations; or

(c) any transitional addition, personal expenses addition or special transitional addition applicable under Part II of the Income Support (Transitional) Regulations 1987 (transitional protection).

(3A) Where section 64A of the 1986 Act [SSAA, s.159] does not apply to an award of income support by virtue of paragraph (3), that award may be reviewed by an adjudication officer, or on a reference by him, by an appeal tribunal for the sole purpose of giving effect to any change made by an order under section 63 of the 1986 Act [SSAA, s.150].]

(4) A determination relating to income support made by an adjudicating authority or a Commissioner shall be reviewed by an adjudication officer or, on a reference by him, by an appeal tribunal where this is necessary to give effect to—

(a) regulation 22 of the Income Support (General) Regulations 1987 (reductions in applicable amounts in certain cases of actual or notional unemployment benefit disqualification); or

(b) a determination given on a question to which regulation 64 applies; or

(c) a change of circumstances to which regulation 14 (reduction and termination of transitional and personal expenses addition) and regulation 15 (special transitional addition) of the Income Support (Transitional) Regulations 1987 applies [²....].

[⁴(5) Where a claimant in receipt of income support, other than a claimant to whom Part II of Schedule 4 to the Income Support (General) Regulations 1987 applies, lives in a nursing home or residential care home and he is absent from the home for a period of less than one week, that absence shall not be treated as a relevant change of circumstances for the purposes of section 104(1)(b) and (bb) of the 1975 Act [SSAA, ss.25(1)(b) and (c)].

(6) In paragraph (5), "nursing home" and "residential care home" have the same meanings as they have in regulation 19 of the Income Support (General) Regulations 1987.]

AMENDMENTS

1. Social Security (Adjudication) Amendment (No. 2) Regulations 1987 (S.I. 1987 No. 1970), reg. 10 (November 23, 1987).
2. Social Security (Adjudication) Amendment Regulations 1989 (S.I. 1989 No. 1689), reg. 5 (October 9, 1989).
3. Social Security (Adjudication) Amendment (No. 2) Regulations 1991 (S.I. 1991 No. 1950), reg. 2 (August 31, 1991).
4. Social Security (Miscellaneous Provisions) Amendment Regulations 1991 (S.I. 1991 No. 2284), reg. 2 (November 1, 1991).
5. Social Security (Miscellaneous Provisions) Amendment Regulations 1992 (S.I. 1992 No. 247), reg. 7 (March 9, 1992).

DEFINITIONS

"the 1975 Act"—see reg. 1(2).
"the 1986 Act"—*ibid.*
"adjudicating authority"—*ibid.*
"adjudication officer"—*ibid.*
"appeal tribunal"—*ibid.*
"Commissioner"—*ibid.*
"income support"—*ibid.*

GENERAL NOTE

Note that the pre-April 1988 form of reg. 69 is preserved in force (and has been amended) for supplementary benefit purposes.

Paras. (1) and (2) impose limits or qualifications on the power to review decisions under s.25 of the Administration Act (1975 Act, s.104). But the power granted by reg. 72 and then reg. 64A to award benefit free of these limitations in cases of official error or newly discovered evidence must be carefully noted. Paras. (3) and (3A) concern the effect of s.159 of the Administration Act (1986 Act, s.64A). Para. (3A) and para. (4) allow review to take place outside s.25 (1975 Act. s.104) in some circumstances.

Paragraph (1)
Sub-paras. (a) and (b) make it crystal clear that in ordinary cases (*i.e.* outside those covered by reg. 72 or now reg. 64A) a revision on review under s.25 of the Administration Act (1975 Act, s.104) (but not the rest of reg. 69) cannot make weekly benefit payable, or increase the amount of benefit, more than 12 months before the date review was requested, or the date of review if no request was made.

Logically, reg. 69 should only be considered once it has been determined that there are grounds for review of an identified decision which would, apart from reg. 69, lead to review (*CSSB 470/1989* and *R(SB) 4/92*). Then reg. 69 prevents the revision having effect on the payability of benefit for any period prior to the 12-month limit. A revision of entitlement, without payment, may still be of advantage to the claimant. For instance, if supplementary benefit entitlement immediately before April 11, 1988, is revised on review, that may have an effect on the claimant's income support transitional addition. That is because reg. 9 of the Income Support (Transitional) Regulations 1987 defines a person's total benefit income in their last week of supplementary benefit in terms of entitlement, not payment or payability. That is one reason why the Commissioner's view expressed in *CSB 56/1992*, that a SSAT need not consider the issues of review and revision if it is plain that because of regs. 69 and 72 or 64A the claimant can gain no practical advantage from the review, must be treated with caution (see *CIS 714/1991*). It also promotes clarity of thought for a SSAT to follow the logical chain of the regulations. Clearly, if a decision is to make benefit payable on review within the 12-month limit the issues of review and revision must be fully dealt with. Note that *CIS 788/1991* held that where a decision has only been partially revised on review because of the 12 months limit in reg. 69, the review is restricted to the period covered by the revisal. Thus a late appeal can be admitted against the original decision that remains in existence for any prior period. This decision has been confirmed by the Court of Appeal in *Chief Adjudication Officer v. Eggleton and Others* (March 17, 1995). See the notes to s.25 of the Administration Act.

Presumably the question of what in sub-para. (b) is meant by "failing" to furnish information will be decided on the same basis as the meaning of "failure to disclose" in s.71 of the Administration Act (1986 Act, s.53) (see extensive notes to that section).

If reg. 69 limits the amount of benefit payable on review, it must then be considered whether reg. 64A (for reviews requested, or if not requested carried out, from August 31, 1991) or reg. 72 (for reviews requested etc. before August 31, 1991, but after April 5, 1987) applies to lift the limit.

A revision on review may remove or decrease entitlement for any past period, without time limit, providing it seems that the ground of review relied on existed in relation to the benefit in question at the time that it was paid (*R(P) 1/85*). Then the question of the Secretary of State's right to recover an overpayment under s.71 is raised.

The limitations of the old rule (contained in reg. 4 of the Determination of Questions Regulations) were exposed in *R(SB) 9/84*. The wording of sub-para. (b) has also been clarified to meet the points made in *R(SB) 48/83*. That decision also makes it clear that the AO's power to review decisions is fixed by the statutory provisions in force at the date review is requested. Similar limitations to those imposed by reg. 69 have applied since April 23, 1984.

Paragraph (2)

Para. 7(8) of Sched. 3 to the Income Support Regulations was revoked on April 11, 1994. See the notes to para. 7(8) for the probable alternative effect of para. 7(4C) of Sched. 3 where the interest actually charged by the lender does not alter until the annual review date.

An increase in the amount of interest paid leads to an immediate revision on review.

Paragraphs (3) and (3A)

The normal rule under s.159 of the Administration Act (1986 Act, s.64A) is that alterations in the prescribed rates of benefit take effect automatically without any decision being given by an AO. The new form of para. (3) preserves the review process where a transitional addition of some kind under the 1987 Transitional Regulations or the General Regulations is in payment. The right to review where s.159 does not apply is created independently by para. (3A). Since the decision is to be made by an AO, there ought to be a right of appeal to a SSAT (possibly under s.22(1) of the Administration Act (1975 Act, s.100(1)). But there is not the express provision which is made in ordinary cases of review by s.28 of the Administration Act (1975 Act, s.104(4)), so that the position is not entirely clear.

Paragraph (4)

Sub-paras. (a) and (b) confirm that where an AO has made an income-support decision on the assumption that a decision on another question will be adverse to the claimant but that decision turns out to be favourable, then the income support decision is to be reviewed.

Paragraphs (5) and (6)

Claimants entitled to the special rates of income support for residents in residential care or nursing homes cannot have benefit reviewed for a change of circumstances on an absence of less than a week.

[¹Repayment of student loan not a change of circumstances

69A. The repayment of a loan to which regulation 66A of the Income Support (General) Regulations 1987 (treatment of student loans) applies shall not be treated as a relevant change of circumstances for the purposes of section 104(1)(b) and (bb) of the 1975 Act [SSAA, s.25(1)(b) and (c)].]

AMENDMENT

1. Social Security (Miscellaneous Provisions) Amendment Regulations 1991 (S.I. 1991 No. 2284), reg. 3 (November 1, 1991).

DEFINITION

"the 1975 Act"—see reg. 1(2).

[¹Review in family credit cases

70. Where a review under section 104(1)(a) of the 1975 Act [SSAA s.25(1)(a)] of a decision relating to family credit arises from a disclosure of a material fact of which the person who claimed family credit was, or could reasonably have been expected to be, aware but of which he previously failed to furnish information to the Secretary of State, then if that review would result in either a new award of family credit or an increase in the amount of family credit payable, such new award or increase shall not be payable in respect of any period earlier than 12 months before the date on which that person first furnished that information.]

AMENDMENT

1. Social Security (Adjudication) Amendment (No. 2) Regulations 1987 (S.I. 1987 No. 1970), reg. 11 (January 1, 1988).

DEFINITIONS

"the 1975 Act"—see reg. 1(2).
"adjudicating authority"—*ibid.*

GENERAL NOTE

Reg. 70 is not made subject to reg. 64A, it seems because the limits it imposes on review in family credit cases are within what would be allowed by reg. 64A.

A review on the ground of ignorance of or mistake as to some material fact is normally without limit. But if it results from the disclosure of a fact which the claimant knew or could reasonably have been expected to know, but had not been disclosed to the DSS, no extra benefit can be paid for a period earlier than 12 months before the date of disclosure.

[¹Repayment of student loan not a change of circumstances

[70A. The repayment of a loan to which regulation 42A of the Family Credit (General) Regulations 1987 (treatment of student loans) applies shall not be treated as a relevant change of circumstances for the purposes of section 104(1)(b) and (bb) of the 1975 Act [SSAA, s.25(1)(b) and (c)].]

AMENDMENT

1. Social Security (Miscellaneous Provisions) Amendment Regulations 1991 (S.I. 1991 No. 2284), reg. 4 (November 1, 1991).

DEFINITION

"the 1975 Act"—see reg. 1(2).

[¹Review in disability working allowance cases

70B.—(1) Where a claim for disability working allowance has been refused and either—

(a) an application for review of the decision is made under section 100A(1) of the 1975 Act [SSAA, s.30(1)]; or

(b) a further claim for disability working allowance is made within the period prescribed under section 100A(1) [s.30(1)] and is accordingly treated as an application for review in accordance with section 100A(12) of the 1975 Act [SSAA, s.30(13)]

then, if that review results in an award of disability working allowance, the decision on review shall have effect from the date on which the application for review is made or the further claim is made whichever is appropriate.

(2) Where a review under section 100A(1) or (2)(a) or 104A(1)(a) of the 1975 Act [SSAA, ss.30(1), (5)(a) and 35(1)(a)] of a decision relating to disability working allowance arises from a disclosure of a material fact of which the person who claimed disability working allowance was, or could reasonably have been expected to be, aware but of which he previously failed to furnish information to the Secretary of State, then if that review would result in either a new award of disability working allowance or an increase in the amount of diasability working allowance payable, the decision on review shall not have effect in respect of any period earlier than 12 months before the date on which the person first furnished that information.]

AMENDMENT

1. Social Security (Adjudication) Amendment (No. 3) Regulations 1991 (S.I. 1991 No. 2889), reg. 14 (February 3, 1992).

DEFINITION

"the 1975 Act"—see reg. 1(2).

GENERAL NOTE

Paragraph (1)
This provision establishes a special rule for the review which is the first stage of appeal in disability working allowance. Under s.30(1) of the Administration Act (1975 Act, s.100A(1)) an application for review on any ground may be made within three months of notification of the initial AO's decision under s.21 (1975 Act, s.99). If that initial decision was to refuse to make an award of disability working allowance, any further claim within the three months is treated as an application for review (Administration Act, s.30(13); 1975 Act, s.100A(12)). Where there is an actual or deemed application for review following a refusal of an award, any award following the review can only take effect from the date of that application, not the date of the original claim. This rule seems most unfair, especially if the initial AO makes a clear mistake, but there is no other provision to lift the effect of reg. 70B. Reg. 64A does not apply to a review under s.30(1) of the Administration Act (1975 Act, s.100A(1)).
If the initial AO's decision is to make an award of disability working allowance, so that the application for review is about the amount or duration of the award, para. (1) does not apply. The general principle that the review should operate from the beginning of the award will operate.

Paragraph (2)
This is the equivalent of reg. 70 on family credit. It will rarely apply to review under s.30(1) of the Administration Act (1975 Act, s.100A(1)). An application for such a review has to be made within three months of notification of the initial AO's decision, so that the 12 month limit of para. (2) can only be of relevance if information is produced long after the application is made.

Review in social fund maternity and funeral expenses cases

71. [²Except in a case to which regulation 64A(2) or (3) applies] a determination on a claim or question relating to maternity or funeral expenses [¹or expenses for heating which appear to the Secretary of State to have been or to be likely to be incurred in cold weather] out of the social fund under Part III of the 1986 Act [SSCBA, Part VIII] shall not be revised on review under section 104 of the 1975 Act [SSAA, s.25] so as to make such expenses payable or to increase the amount of such expenses payable in respect of a determination of a claim for such expenses made more than 12 months before the date on which the review was requested or, where no request is made, the date of review.

AMENDMENTS

1. Social Security (Common Provisions) Miscellaneous Amendment Regulations 1988 (S.I. 1988 No. 1725), reg. 2(6) (November 7, 1988).
2. Social Security (Adjudication) Amendment (No. 2) Regulations 1991 (S.I. 1991 No. 1950), reg. 2 (August 31, 1991).

DEFINITIONS

"the 1975 Act"—see reg. 1(2).
"the 1986 Act"—*ibid.*

GENERAL NOTE

The normal limit on review leading to an extra payment is 12 months before the date on which review is requested. If entitlement to social fund payments is to be determined as at the date of claim. then review on the ground of change of circumstances will not be possible, but this point remains to be settled. Note the exemptions from the 12 month limit in cases of official error or newly discovered evidence (reg. 64A, replacing reg. 72).

[Reg. 72 below is revoked with effect from August 31, 1991: see General Note]

Exemption from limitations on payments of arrears of benefit

72.—[[1](1) Subject to paragraph (2),] nothing in this section shall operate so as to limit the amount of benefit or additional benefit that may be awarded on a review of a decision if the adjudicating authority making the review is satisfied either—

(a) that the decision under review was erroneous by reason only of a mistake made, or something done or omitted to be done by an officer of the [[2]Department of Social Security] or of the Department of Employment acting as such, or by an adjudicating authority or the clerk or other officer of such an authority, and that the claimant and anyone acting for him neither caused nor materially contributed to that mistake, act or omission; or

(b) that where the grounds for review are that the decision was given in ignorance of or was based on a mistake as to a material fact, those grounds are established by evidence which was not before the adjudicating authority which gave the decision; that the claimant and anyone acting for him could not reasonably have produced that evidence to the authority at or before the time the decision was given, and that it has been produced as soon as reasonably practicable.

[[1](2) This regulation shall not apply to a review of a decision by an adjudication officer or, on a reference by an adjudication officer, by an appeal tribunal, where the ground for review is that the decision was erroneous in point of law by virtue of a determination by a Commissioner, the High Court, the Court of Appeal, the Court of Session, the House of Lords or the Court of Justice of the European Communities given subsequent to the decision.]

AMENDMENTS

1. Social Security (Adjudication) Amendment Regulations 1987 (S.I. 1987 No. 1424), reg. 2 (September 1, 1987).

2. Transfer of Functions (Health and Social Security) Order 1988 (S.I. 1988 No. 1843), art. 3(4) (November 28, 1988).

Revocation: Social Security (Adjudication) Amendment (No. 2) Regulations 1991 (S.I. 1991 No. 1950), reg. 2(5) (August 31, 1991).

DEFINITIONS

"adjudicating authority"—see reg. 1(2).
"adjudication officer"—*ibid.*
"appeal tribunal"—*ibid.*
"claimant"—*ibid.*
"Commissioner"—*ibid.*

GENERAL NOTE

Although reg. 72 has been revoked, the text and the notes are being retained because it will still govern outstanding applications and appeals. Reg. 3 of the Social Security (Adjudication) Amendment (No. 2) Regulations 1991 confirms that reg. 72 continues to apply to applications for review made before August 31, 1991.

Paragraph (1)
The provision gave a very welcome power from April 6, 1987 to allow arrears of benefit to be paid free of the limits otherwise imposed in Section D of Part IV of these regulations in cases where the claimant was clearly not to blame for the mistaken decision. Formerly, there had been quite a bit of criticism of the imbalance between the power of the Secretary of State to recover past overpayments of benefit without limit of time and the power to pay arrears representing past underpayments. It is particularly significant that the power to make awards is given to the adjudicating authority making the review, not to the Secretary of State. Presumably if an AO refuses to review a decision and on appeal a SSAT does review and revise the decision the same power under reg. 72 is available to the SSAT.

In *CSB 1153/1989*, the Commissioner, disagreeing with *CSB 271/1990* and *CSB 433/1989*, held that reg. 72 lifts the limits on entitlements to arrears of benefit in reviews requested or, if not requested, carried out from April 6, 1987, onwards. It did not matter that any mistake by an AO leading to an erroneous decision was made before the regulation came into force. The Commissioner held that this does not offend the presumption against retrospectivity because it does not adversely affect any rights of the claimant. And to take the opposite view would mean that reg. 72 would have had no practical effect until 12 months after it came into force. *CSB 1153/1989* is in accord with the general principle described in *R(SB) 48/83*, that the powers available on a review are those given by the review legislation at the date of the review, and has settled the issue. It is true that in *R(P) 1/85* it was held that while s.104(1A) of the 1975 Act (now s.25(2) of the Administration Act) on review for error of law could be used to review AOs' decisions made before it came into force in relation to "national insurance" benefits (April 23, 1984) it did not allow the revision of entitlement before that date. However, that was a case where the revision would have been to remove entitlement under an award of benefit. The Commissioner held that s.104(1A) should not operate retrospectively to remove an accrued entitlement. That objection does not exist where the effect of revision on review would be to create a new entitlement or to increase the amount of benefit. Although there would be a retrospective effect on the liabilities of the DSS, it is arguable that it is not an unfair one when, by definition, the original decision was made under an error of law.

CSB 112/1993 decides that reg. 72 could apply to an application for review made in 1991 even though the review application concerned the same issue (higher rate heating addition) which had been the subject of a review in 1985. At that time backdating on review was limited to 52 weeks under reg. 87 of the Social Security (Adjudication) Regulation 1984. The claimant had appealed to a tribunal in 1985 which had upheld the AO's decision on backdating. The Commissioner holds that the principle of *res judicata* (that once a matter has been adjudicated on by a competent authority another authority of the same level cannot readjudicate on the matter) did not apply in relation to the matters before the 1992 tribunal. The 1985 tribunal had had no opportunity to consider the factual issues raised by reg. 72, since, of course, the regulation was not in force at that time. Thus the claimant was entitled to have these questions considered. Nor did s. 60 of the Administration Act mean that the 1985 tribunal's decision was final in relation to the issues raised by the claimant's 1991 application.

Reg. 72 only needs to be considered once it has been determined that reg. 69 or 71 limits the payment of benefit following a revision of a decision on review. It is desirable that in all cases a

SSAT follows through this logical sequence (*CIS 714/1991*). A SSAT must certainly deal with all the issues if its decision is to make some benefit payable on the review (*CSSB 470/1989*). It may be that if it is plain that the claimant cannot satisfy the conditions of reg. 72 and cannot then derive any practical benefit from the review (on which see the notes to reg. 69), a SSAT need only deal with reg. 72 (*CSB 56/1992*). But even then it must be determined what grounds of review have been established in order to tell whether reg. 72(1)(b) might apply or not.

The lifting of the time limit on payment of benefit for past periods occurs only when either sub-para. (a) or (b) is satisfied. The conditions are quite complex and must all be met.

Under both sub-paragraphs the claimant will need to establish the circumstances of the decision under review in order to meet the conditions. If the DSS has destroyed the documents relating to that decision in the course of its normal "weeding" procedure, the claimant may be left with a gap in the evidence. Arguments have been made that the principle of *The Ophelia* [1916] 2 A.C. 206, as explained in *CSB 1288/1985*, was that the contents of the destroyed documents should be presumed to go against the interests of the DSS and in favour of the claimant. *R(IS) 11/92* decides that that strong presumption does not arise in such circumstances. It only arises when documents are destroyed with the intention to destroy evidence.

Sub-para. (a). Under this head the decision must be wrong solely because of official error or omission, either of a DSS or DE employee or of an adjudicating authority or clerk. In *R(SB) 10/91*, the Commissioner says that the regulation applies only to "clear mistakes of fact or law in relation to an actual issue in a given case at a time when the officer of the relevant Department, etc., was actively required by his duties under the social security legislation to arrive at a decision or take some administrative act. It certainly does not impose a general duty on the officers etc. of the Department of their own accord constantly to keep all cases under review in order to see whether or not any particular exempting regulation might apply." *R(SB) 2/93* holds that visiting officers should not be taken to be under a duty to interrogate claimants as to every conceivable circumstance which might affect supplementary benefit. "Mistakes" are limited to clear and obvious mistakes on the facts disclosed or which the office had reason to believe were relevant. So where the claimant had said that he hoped to obtain work in the near future, it was not an error or omission for the visiting officer not to enquire about his health. *CIS 11/1991* confirms that an error of law can amount to a mistake under sub-para. (a).

R(P) 1/92 holds that a failure to take account of a future contingency, in that case the likelihood of the claimant being divorced, and to advise the claimant on the effect which this would have on her benefit situation cannot render the AO's decision erroneous. The error must lie in the decision itself.

Any erroneous decision could not be solely due to an official mistake if the claimant had caused or materially contributed to the mistake, so that the end of the paragraph is really spelling out the implication of the first part. Here the claimant's obligation under reg. 32 of the Claims and Payments Regulations to notify the Secretary of State of changes of circumstances which he might reasonably be expected to know might affect his right to benefit must be relevant. See the discussion of causation in the notes to s.71 of the Administration Act.

Sub-para. (b). Here evidence must have come to light which was not before the adjudicating authority when the original decision was made. Secondly, neither the claimant nor anyone acting on his behalf must have been able reasonably to have produced that evidence before that original decision was made. The question of what factors can be taken into account in deciding the issue of reasonableness here will be a difficult one. The test seems to be related to the particular claimant concerned, rather than some hypothetical reasonable claimant. Thirdly, the evidence must have been produced (who to?) as soon as reasonably practicable. Thus any unnecessary delay may prejudice the right to arrears although the mistake in the original decision was not the claimant's fault.

Paragraph (2)

The intention of this addition to the original form of reg. 72 seems to have been to contain the knock-on effect of test cases which are decided against the DSS. If it applies, it means that the ordinary 12 month rule of reg. 69 defines the extent of arrears payable on review (although extra-statutory payments may be considered). It was argued in the 1988 edition that the scope of para. (2) is limited in the following way. If a decision of a Commissioner or a court shows that an accepted interpretation of a regulation is wrong, that decision merely reveals what the law has been all along. Decisions made on the mistaken interpretation are not erroneous in law by virtue of the appeal decision. They are erroneous because they got the law wrong. Where para. (2) will apply is in the situation where decisions are made according to one appeal decision, which is then overruled by a more authoritative decision. However, in *R(SB) 11/89* a Tribunal of Commissioners has rejected such limitations. Decisions had been made based on regulations later declared *ultra vires* by the Court of Appeal in the *Cotton* case. The Tribunal would have applied para. (2) in these circumstances. Although it was not necessary for them actually to do so, this is an authoritative expression of view within the social security system, despite its constitutional weakness. The Commissioner in *CIS 11/1991* holds that the ruling in *R(SB) 11/89* only applies when the request for review is made after the decision of the Commissioner or court which reveals the AO's error of law. Since the powers on review are determined as at the date of the request for review, and that is the start of the 12 month limit in reg. 69, the claimant should not be prejudiced by the chance that a Commissioner or court decision confirming his, rather than the AO's, view of the law emerges after his request. This analysis of reg. 72(2) seems cogent. *R(IS) 10/92* confirms that the application of reg. 72(2) is not confined to the situation where a claimant has asked for a review because he knew of a relevant Commissioner's decision. The grounds for review are not limited to those put forward by the claimant; the determining factor is what in fact are the grounds for review.

It has been argued that para. (2) does not cover a SSAT hearing an appeal from an AO's revised decision on review or refusal to review. The words of para. (2) only mention a SSAT dealing with a reference by an AO, where the AO has not made a decision, but the argument is misconceived. The legislation does not define the powers of SSATs. Section 104(1) and (1A) of the 1975 Act (Administration Act, s.25(1) and (2)) equally only refers to a SSAT dealing with a reference, yet a right of appeal to a SSAT from an AO is expressly provided in s.104(4). The SSAT on such an appeal must have the power to make a decision. On principle, that power must be to do what an AO could do in the circumstances. The SSAT must equally be subject to the restrictions of reg. 72(2).

Part V

Transitional Provisions Savings and Revocations

Transitional provisions

73.—(1) These regulations shall apply—

(a) to any claim or question under the National Insurance Acts 1965 to 1974 or the National Insurance (Industrial Injuries) Acts 1965 to 1974 as they apply to a corresponding claim or question under the 1975 Act, and for this purpose questions relating to graduated contributions and payments in lieu of contributions shall be treated as questions relating to contributions; and

(b) to any claim or question under the National Assistance Act 1948 or the Supplementary Benefits Act 1966 as they apply to a corresponding claim or question under the Supplementary Benefits Act.

(2) Subject to paragraph (7), anything done or begun pursuant to any provision of Part III (including Schedules 10 to 13) of the 1975 Act which was amended by section 52 of and Schedule 5 to, or repealed by section 86 of and Schedule 11 to the 1986 Act or pursuant to any regulations made under those provisions or revoked by these regulations, shall be deemed to have been done or, as the case may be, continued pursuant to those provisions as amended or the provisions of these regulations.

(3) So much of any document as refers expressly or by implication to any regulation made under the enactments mentioned in paragraph (2) or revoked by these regulations shall, if and so far as the context permits, for the purposes of these regulations be treated as referring to the corresponding provision of these regulations.

(4) Nothing in paragraphs (2) and (3) shall be taken as affecting the general application of the rules for the construction of Acts of Parliament contained in sections 15 to 17 of the Interpretation Act 1978 (repealing enactments) with regard to the effect of revocations.

(5) Notwithstanding their repeal, sections 64, 65, 66 and 97 of the National Insurance Act 1965 and section 80 of that Act, in so far as it relates to payments in respect of any matter arising out of Part III of the 1975 Act, shall continue

in force for the purpose of disposing of any question, appeal or other matter to which they relate (whether arising by virtue of regulations made under the Social Security (Consequential Provisions) Act 1975 or otherwise).

(6) Without prejudice to the powers conferred on the Lord Chancellor or the Lord President of the Court of Session by section 7 of the Tribunals and Inquiries Act 1971 or on the Secretary of State or the President by Part III of and Schedules 10 and 12 to the 1975 Act, any person who, immediately before the coming into force of section 25 of and Schedule 8 to the 1983 Act, held a subsisting appointment as—

(a) a member of any panel of persons constituted under the said section from which were selected chairmen of National Insurance Local Tribunals (constituted under section 97(2) of the 1975 Act) or, as the case may be, of Supplementary Benefit Appeal Tribunals (constituted under Schedule 4 to the Supplementary Benefits Act) shall be deemed to have been appointed to the panel from which chairmen of appeal tribunals are selected for a period corresponding to that of his subsisting appointment;

(b) a member of either of the tribunal membership panels mentioned in section 97(2)(a) of the 1975 Act and paragraph 1(a) of Schedule 4 to the Supplementary Benefits Act (representing employers and earners other than employed earners) shall be deemed to have been appointed to the panel constituted by the President under paragraph 1(4) of Schedule 10 to the 1975 Act for a period corresponding to that of his subsisting appointment;

(c) a member of either of the tribunal membership panels mentioned in section 97(2)(b) of the 1975 Act and paragraph 1(b) of Schedule 4 to the Supplementary Benefits Act (representing employed earners) shall be deemed to have been appointed to the panel constituted by the President under paragraph 1(3) of Schedule 10 to the 1975 Act for a period corresponding to that of his subsisting appointment;

(d) a clerk to any National Insurance Local Tribunal or Supplementary Benefit Appeal Tribunal shall be deemed to have been assigned by the President as a clerk to the appeal tribunal for the area in question;

(e) a member of a pneumoconiosis medical panel (under regulation 49 of the Prescribed Diseases Regulations) shall be deemed to have been appointed as a specially qualified adjudicating medical practitioner.

(7) Except in relation to proceedings before a Commissioner but notwithstanding paragraph (2) where, before the coming into operation of these regulations, the time limited by any enactment, rule or regulation mentioned in that paragraph for the making of any application, appeal or reference has begun to run, that time limit shall continue to apply, and the application, appeal or reference shall be made to the same person or body and in the same manner, as if the relevant enactment, rule or regulation had continued in force without amendment.

DEFINITIONS

"the 1975 Act"—see reg. 1(2).
"the 1986 Act"—*ibid.*
"appeal tribunal"—*ibid.*
"Commissioner"—*ibid.*
"the Prescribed Diseases Regulations"—*ibid.*
"President"—*ibid.*
"specially qualified adjudicating medical practitioner"—*ibid.*
"the Supplementary Benefits Act"—*ibid.*

Saving for existing chairmen of tribunals

74.—(1) Notwithstanding any enactment any person who, immediately before the coming into force of section 25 of and Schedule 8 to the 1983 Act was a member of either of the panels referred to in regulation 73(6)(*a*) shall, though not a barrister, advocate or solicitor, or not of 5 years standing as such, be eligible for appointment or reappointment to the panel from which chairmen of appeal tribunals are selected for any period or periods before 23rd April 1989.

(2) Any person mentioned in paragraph (1) who, before 23rd April 1989, becomes a barrister, advocate or solicitor shall remain eligible for appointment or reappointment for any period or periods during the 5 years from the date of his call or admission.

(3) An appeal tribunal the chairman of which is eligible for appointment as such by virtue only of paragraph (1) shall not determine any appeal or reference other than an appeal or reference relating to a claim or question arising under the Supplementary Benefits Act or the Family Income Supplements Act 1970.

(4) An application for leave to appeal to a Commissioner against a decision of an appeal tribunal presided over by a chairman who is eligible for appointment as such by virtue only of paragraph (1) shall not be determined by that chairman but shall instead be referred to and determined by the President or a full-time chairman.

DEFINITIONS

"the 1983 Act"—see reg. 1(2).
"appeal tribunal"—*ibid.*
"Commissioner"—*ibid.*
"full-time chairman"—*ibid.*
"President"—*ibid.*
"the Supplementary Benefits Act"—*ibid.*

GENERAL NOTE

Paragraph (1)
This allowed non-legally qualified chairmen to continue for up to five years from the start of the new system. Their powers are subject to paras. (3) and (4). The intention, as announced by the President of SSATs, was that in general such chairmen would serve out the remaining period of their existing appointments and would only be offered a re-appointment if there was some difficulty or delay in finding legally qualified chairmen for their area.

Paragraph (2)
Any non-legally qualified chairman who became a solicitor or barrister before April 23, 1989, counts immediately as qualified under s.97(2E) of the Social Security Act 1975 (now s.41(4) of the Administration Act) without having to wait the normal five years from the date of admission or call.

Paragraph (3)
Non-legally qualified chairmen continuing under para. (1) could only hear supplementary benefit and FIS appeals. Can this apply to income support, social fund and family credit cases?

Paragraph (4)
A non-legally qualified chairman continuing under para. (1) could not deal with an application for leave to appeal to a Commissioner. Any application had to be referred to a regional or other full-time chairman or the President.

Revocations

75. Except in so far as they apply to proceedings before a Commissioner, the regulations set out in column (1) of Schedule 4 are revoked to the extent mentioned in column (3) of that Schedule.

DEFINITIONS

"Commissioner"—see reg. 1(2).
"proceedings"—*ibid.*

GENERAL NOTE

Schedule 4 is not set out below. The major revocation is of the 1984 Adjudication Regulations.

SCHEDULES

SCHEDULE 2

TIME LIMITS FOR MAKING APPLICATIONS, APPEALS OR REFERENCES

Column (1)	Column (2)	Column (3)
Application, appeal or reference	*Appropriate office*	*Specified time*
4. Appeal to an appeal tribunal from a decision of an adjudication officer (section 100(1) of the 1975 Act, [SSAA, s.22(1)]).	A local office.	3 months beginning with the date when notice of the decision was given to the appellant.
[²4A. Appeal to a disability appeal tribunal from a decision on review of an adjudication officer under section 100A(1) of the 1975 Act [SSAA, s.30(1)].	A local office.	3 months beginning with the date when notice in writing of the decision was given to the appellant.
4B. Appeal to an appeal tribunal from a decision on a review of an adjudication officer under section 100A(1) of the 1975 Act [SSAA, s.30(1)].	A local office.	3 months beginning with the date when notice in writing of the decision was given to the appellant.]
5. Application to the chairman for leave to appeal to a Commissioner from the decision of an appeal tribunal (regulation 26(1)).	The office of the clerk to the appeal tribunal.	3 months beginning with the date when a copy of the record of the decision was given to the applicant.
8. Application to an adjudicating authority to set aside its decision (regulation 11(2)).	A local office of the Department of [¹. . .] Social Security or, in the case of unemployment benefit, either at such an office or at a local office of the Department of Employment or, in any case, at the office of the authority who gave the decision.	3 months beginning with the date when notice in writing of the decision was given to the applicant.

AMENDMENTS

1. Social Security (Adjudication) Amendment Regulations 1990 (S.I. 1990 No. 603), reg. 11 (April 6, 1990).
2. Social Security (Adjudication) Amendment (No. 3) Regulations 1991 (S.I. 1991 No. 2889), reg. 15 (February 3, 1992).

DEFINITIONS

"the 1975 Act"—see reg. 1(2).
"adjudicating authority"—*ibid.*
"adjudication officer"—*ibid.*
"appeal tribunal"—*ibid.*
"Commissioner"—*ibid.*
"local office"—*ibid.*

GENERAL NOTE

See notes to reg. 1(3) for the dates on which notices, etc., are deemed to have been given. See the notes to the regulations referred to for further information on rights of appeal. The time-limits for making the applications and appeals mentioned in Sched. 2 end on or before the last day of the period (*Trow v. Ind Coope (West Midlands) Ltd.* [1967] 2 Q.B. 899 referred to in *CIS 550/1993*). The time-limits can be extended for special reasons by leave granted under reg. 3(3).

Social Security (Claims and Payments) Regulations 1987

(S.I. 1987 No. 1968)

Made by the secretary of state under ss.165a and 166(2) of the social Security Act 1975, s.6(1) of the Child Benefit Act 1975 and ss.21(7), 51(1)(a) to (s), 54(1) and 84(1) of the Social Security Act 1986.

REGULATIONS REPRODUCED

PART I

GENERAL

PART II

CLAIMS

PART III

PAYMENTS

PART I

GENERAL

Citation and commencement

1. These Regulations may be cited as the Social Security (Claims and Payments) Regulations 1987 and shall come into operation on 11th April 1988.

Interpretation

2.—(1) In these Regulations, unless the context otherwise requires—
"adjudicating authority" means any person or body with responsibility under the Social Security Acts 1975 to 1986 [SSAA], and regulations made

thereunder, for the determination of claims for benefit and questions arising in connection with a claim for, or award of, or disqualification for
receiving benefits;

"appropriate office" means an office of the [²Department of Social Security]
or the Department of Employment;

"claim for benefit" includes—

    (a) an application for a declaration that an accident was an industrial
accident;

    (b) [³. . .]

    (c) an application for the review of an award or a decision for the pur-
pose of obtaining any increase of benefit [⁶in respect of a child or
adult dependant under the Social Security Act 1975 or an increase in
disablement benefit under section 60 (special hardship), 61 (constant
attendance), 62 (hospital treatment allowance) or 63 (exceptionally
severe disablement) of the Social Security Act 1975], but does not
include any other application for the review of an award or a
decision;

[⁸"instrument for benefit payment" means an instrument issued by the Secretary of State under regulation 20A on the presentation of which benefit
due to a beneficiary shall be paid in accordance with the arrangements
set out in that regulation;]

"long-term benefits" means any retirement pension, a widowed mother's
allowance, a widow's pension, attendance allowance, [⁵disability living
allowance], invalid care allowance, guardian's allowance, any pension
or allowance for industrial injury or disease and any increase in any such
benefit;

"married couple" means a man and a woman who are married to each other
and are members of the same household;

"partner" means one of a married or unmarried couple; [⁴. . .]

"unmarried couple" means a man and a woman who are not married to
each other but are living together as husband and wife otherwise than in
prescribed circumstances; and

"week" means a period of 7 days beginning with midnight between Saturday
and Sunday.

(2) Unless the context otherwise requires, any reference in these Regulations
to—

    (a) a numbered regulation, Part or Schedule is a reference to the regulation,
Part or Schedule bearing that number in these Regulations and any reference in a regulation to a numbered paragraph is a reference to the paragraph of that regulation having that number;

    (b) a benefit includes any benefit under the Social Security Act 1975
[SSCBA], child benefit under Part I of the Child Benefit Act 1975,
income support[⁷, family credit and disability working allowance under
the Social Security Act 1986 [SSCBA] and any social fund payments
such as are mentioned in section 32(2)(a) [¹and section 32(2A)] of that
Act [SSCBA, s.138(1)(a) and (2)].

(3) For the purposes of the provisions of these Regulations relating to the
making of claims every increase of benefit under the Social Security Act 1975
[SSCBA] shall be treated as a separate benefit and so shall an increase in the
weekly amount of benefit under regulation 2(2) of the Child Benefit and Social
Security (Fixing and Adjustment of Rates) Regulations 1976.

AMENDMENTS

1. Social Security (Common Provisions) Miscellaneous Amendment Regulations 1988 (S.I. 1988
No. 1725), reg. 3 (November 7, 1988).

2. Transfer of Functions (Health and Social Security) Order 1988 (S.I. 1988 No. 1843), art. 3(4) (November 28, 1988).

3. Social Security (Medical Evidence, Claims and Payments) Amendment Regulations 1989 (S.I. 1989 No. 1686), reg. 3 (October 9, 1989).

4. Social Security (Miscellaneous Provisions) Amendment Regulations 1991 (S.I. 1991 No. 2284), reg. 5 (November 1, 1991).

5. Social Security (Claims and Payments) Amendment Regulations 1991 (S.I. 1991 No. 2741), reg. 2(a) (February 3, 1992).

6. Social Security (Miscellaneous Provisions) Amendment Regulations 1992 (S.I. 1992 No. 247), reg. 9 (March 9, 1992).

7. Social Security (Claims and Payments) Amendment Regulations 1991 (S.I. 1991 No. 2741), reg. 2(b) (March 10, 1992).

8. Social Security (Claims and Payments) Amendment (No. 4) Regulations 1994 (S.I. 1994 No. 3196), reg. 2 (January 10, 1995).

GENERAL NOTE

"claim for benefit." Under sub-para. (c) a claim includes, for the purposes of these Regulations, an application for review for the purpose of securing any increase of benefit. The March 1992 amendment restricts the scope of this provision to applications for review to obtain increases for spouses or dependants or the listed industrial injury "benefits" which are (or were, since special hardship allowance and hospital treatment allowance have ceased to exist) technically not separate benefits, but increases of disablement benefit. In *CIS 515/1990,* the Commissioner took the view that the pre-amendment form of the definition applied to any application for review which requested an increase in the amount of any benefit. The subsequent amendment cannot affect the authority of this decision before the date of the amendment, but para. (3) makes it dubious.

See the notes to s.137(1) of the Contributions and Benefits Act for "married couple" and "unmarried couple."

PART II

CLAIMS

Making a claim for benefit

4.—(1) Every claim for benefit shall be made in writing on a form approved by the Secretary of State [³for the purpose of the benefit for which the claim is made], or in such other manner, being in writing, as the Secretary of State may accept as sufficient in the circumstances of any particular case.

(2) In the case of a claim for family credit, where a married or unmarried couple is included in the family, the claim shall be made by the woman, unless the Secretary of State is satisfied that it would be reasonable to accept a claim by the man.

(3) In the case of a married or unmarried couple, a claim for income support shall be made by whichever partner they agree should so claim or, in default of agreement, by such one of them as the Secretary of State shall in his discretion determine.

[²(3A) In the case of a married or unmarried couple where both partners satisfy the conditions set out in Section 20(6A) of the Social Security Act 1986 [SSCBA, s.129(1)], a claim for disability working allowance shall be made by whichever partner they agree should so claim, or in default of agreement, by such one of them as the Secretary of State shall determine.]

(4) Where one of a married or unmarried couple is entitled to income support under an award and, with his agreement, his partner claims income support that entitlement shall terminate on the day before that claim is made or treated as made.

(5) Forms of claim shall be supplied without charge by such persons as the Secretary of State may appoint or authorise for that purpose.

(6) Every claim shall be delivered or sent to an appropriate office, which, in the case of unemployment benefit, shall be such office, [¹or to such other place], as the Secretary of State may specify.

(7) If a claim is defective at the date when it is received or has been made in writing but not on the form approved for the time being, the Secretary of State may refer the claim to the person making it or, as the case may be, supply him with the approved form, and if the form is received properly completed within one month, or such longer period as the Secretary of State may consider reasonable, from the date on which it is so referred or supplied, the Secretary of State shall treat the claim as if it has been duly made in the first instance.

(8) A claim which is made on the form approved for the time being is, for the purposes of paragraph (7), properly completed if completed in accordance with the instructions on the form and defective if not so completed.

AMENDMENTS

1. Social Security (Miscellaneous Provisions) Amendment Regulations 1990 (S.I. 1990 No. 2208), reg. 8 (December 5, 1990).
2. Social Security (Claims and Payments) Amendment Regulations 1991 (S.I. 1991 No. 2741), reg. 3 (February 3, 1992).
3. Social Security (Miscellaneous Provisions) Amendment Regulations 1992 (S.I. 1992 No. 247), reg. 10 (March 9, 1992).

DEFINITIONS

"appropriate office"—see reg. 2(1).
"benefit"—see reg. 2(2).
"claim for benefit"—see reg. 2(1).
"married couple"—*ibid.*
"partner"—*ibid.*
"unmarried couple"—*ibid.*

GENERAL NOTE

Paragraph (1)
Claims for benefit must be made in writing, normally on an official form, although the Secretary of State may accept some other kind of written claim. In such a case, under para. (7), the Secretary of State may require the claimant to fill in the proper form. If this is done in the proper time the claim is treated as duly made in the first instance. It no longer seems possible for an oral claim to be accepted, or for the old procedure when claimants were given B1 forms to fill in, to be followed (see *CSB 900/1985* and *CSB 841/1986*). The request for a B1 at the UBO was treated as an oral claim. If the form was returned properly completed within the 21 days then mentioned on the form, the Secretary of State would exercise his discretion to treat the claim as made on the date of the oral claim. That precise discretion no longer exists. Now there are two administrative possibilities. One is that some form of written claim is made, when under para. (7) there is a month to provide a properly completed form. The second is that the Secretary of State, under reg. 19(3), extends the time for claiming up to a month and this seems to be the accepted procedure. B1 forms contain a warning that benefit may be lost if they are not returned within a month. In this second case the claim, if properly made within the month, is treated under reg. 6(3) as made at the beginning of the period specified by the Secretary of State under reg. 19(3)(a) (which presumably will be equal to the time taken to return the claim form).

Paragraph (2)
In family credit cases, if a couple is involved, the claim must normally be made by the woman. The Secretary of State has discretion to accept a claim from the man.

Paragraph (3)
In income support cases, where a couple is involved, either partner can be the claimant. The exceptionally complex rules of reg. 1A of the Supplementary Benefit (Aggregation) Regulations,

incorporating the "nominated breadwinner" scheme, are abandoned. There is now free choice. If the couple cannot jointly agree who should claim, the Secretary of State is to break the tie. There are still some differences in entitlement according to which partner is the claimant, particularly since only the claimant is required to be available for work. In addition, head (b) of para. 12(1) of Sched. 2 to the Income Support Regulations (disability and higher pensioner premium) can only be satisfied by the claimant. But there is now no long-term rate and the full-time employment of either partner excludes entitlement to income support. See reg. 7(2). Under the Income Support (Transitional) Regulations transitional protection is lost if the claimant for the couple changes. *CIS 8/1990* and *CIS 375/1990* challenged this rule on the grounds that it was indirectly discriminatory against women (since in 98 per cent. of couples (at that time) the man was the claimant). Following the ECJ's decision in the *Cresswell* case that income support is not covered by EC Directive 79/7 on equal treatment for men and women in social security (see the notes to reg. 36 of the Income Support Regulations), the claimants could not rely on European law. The Commissioner also rejects a submission that the Sex Discrimination Act 1975 prevented the discriminatory effect of regs. 2 and 10 of the Transitional Regulations. Para. (4) below deals with changes of partner.

Paragraph (3A)

Normally a claim for disability working allowance must be made by the person who is disabled and in remunerative work. Under para. (3A), if both partners in a couple satisfy the conditions of entitlement, they may choose which one of them is to claim. If they cannot choose, the Secretary of State makes the decision.

Paragraph (4)

If there is a change of claimant within a couple in the middle of a continuing income support claim, the claims are not to overlap. The change is a matter of a new claim for benefit, not review as it was for supplementary benefit (*R(SB) 1/93*). In *CSIS 66/1992* the Commissioner rejects the argument that para. (4) combined with s.20(9) of the Social Security Act 1986 (SSCBA s.134(2)) meant that a change of claimant could not be backdated. If the claimant could show good cause for her delay in claiming, regs. 19(2) and 6(3) enabled her claim to be backdated to the date from which she had good cause (subject to the 12 month limit in reg. 19(4)). Duplication of payment could be avoided by the AO reviewing the claimant's husband's entitlement for any past period in respect of which the claimant was held to be entitled to benefit and applying reg. 5(1) and (2), Case 1, of the Payments Regulations. By becoming the claimant the wife qualified for a disability premium. There is a specific provision in para. 19 of Sched. 7 to the Income Support Regulations for arrears of a disability premium in these circumstances.

Paragraph (6)

The claim must be delivered or sent to the appropriate office. In *CS 175/1988* the claimant took a claim form to the local office. The counter-clerk told him to get his employer to correct a mistake and he took it away. The Commissioner holds that a claim was not made on that date, because it was not lodged, but merely shown to the clerk for advice. This distinction is unrealistic.

In *CSIS 48/1992* the Commissioner considered the effect of para. (6) in the light of s.7 and s.23 of the Interpretation Act 1978. He concludes that the effect of these provisions is that a claim for a social security benefit is a document authorised by an Act to be served by post, which is presumed to have been delivered in the ordinary course of post unless this is proved not to have been the case. The SSAT should therefore have considered whether it accepted that the claim had been posted, and, if so, whether the presumption of delivery had been rebutted by the AO. *CSIS 48/1992* has been followed in *CIS 759/1992*.

Paragraph (7)

This provision deals with written claims not made on the proper form (for which, see para. (1)), and situations where the proper form is not completed according to the instructions (see para. 8)). The Secretary of State may simply treat this as an ineffective attempt to claim, but also has power to refer the form back to the claimant. Then there is one month (extendable by the Secretary of State) to complete the form properly, in which case the claim is treated as made on the date of the original attempt to claim (see reg. 6(1)(b)).

Amendment and withdrawal of claim

5.—(1) A person who has made a claim may amend it at any time by notice in writing received in an appropriate office before a determination has been made on the claim, and any claim so amended may be treated as if it had been so amended in the first instance.

(2) A person who has made a claim may withdraw it at any time before a determination has been made on it, by notice to an appropriate office, and any such notice of withdrawal shall have effect when it is received.

DEFINITION

"appropriate office"—see reg. 2(1).

Date of claim

6.—(1) [³Subject to the following provisions of this regulation] the date on which a claim is made shall be—
  (a) in the case of a claim which meets the requirements of regulation 4(1), the date on which it is received in an appropriate office;
  (b) in the case of a claim which does not meet the requirements of regulation 4(1) but which is treated, under regulation 4(7) as having been duly made, the date on which the claim was received in an appropriate office in the first instance.

(2) [¹. . .]

[¹(3) In the case of a claim for income support, family credit[⁷, disability working allowance] or a social fund payment for maternity or funeral expenses [⁵. . .], where the time for claiming is extended under regulation 19 the claim shall be treated as made on the first day of the period in respect of which the claim is, by reason of the operation of that regulation, timeously made.

(4) Paragraph (3) shall not apply when the time for claiming income support[⁷, family credit or disability working allowance] has been extended under regulation 19 and the failure to claim within the prescribed time for the purposes of that regulation is for the reason only that the claim has been sent by post.]

[²(5) Where a person submits a claim for attendance allowance [⁶or disability living allowance or a request under paragraph (8)] by post and the arrival of that [⁶claim or request] at an appropriate office is delayed by postal disruption caused by industrial action, whether within the postal service or elsewhere, the [⁶claim or request] shall be treated as received on the day on which it would have been received if it had been delivered in the ordinary course of post.]

[³(6) Where—
  (a) on or after 9th April 1990 a person satisfies the capital condition in section 22(6) of the Social Security Act 1986 [SSCBA, s.134(1)] for income support and he would not have satisfied that condition had the amount prescribed under regulation 45 of the Income Support (General) Regulation 1987 been £6,000; and
  (b) a claim for that benefit is received from him in an appropriate office not later than 27th May 1990;
the claim shall be treated as made on the date [⁴not later than 5th December 1990] determined in accordance with paragraph (7).

(7) For the purpose of paragraph (6), where—
  (a) the claimant satisfies the other conditions of entitlement to income support on the date on which he satisfies the capital condition, the date shall be the date on which he satisfies that condition;
  (b) the claimant does not satisfy the other conditions of entitlement to income support on the date on which he satisfies the capital condition, the date shall be the date on which he satisfies the conditions of entitlement to that benefit.]

[⁶(8) [⁸Subject to paragraph (8A),] where—
  (a) a request is received in an appropriate office for a claim form for disability living allowance or attendance allowance; and

(b) in response to the request a claim form for disability living allowance or attendance is issued from an appropriate office; and

(c) within the time specified the claim form properly completed is received in an appropriate office,

the date on which the claim is made shall be the date which the request was received in the appropriate office.

[⁸(8A) Where, in a case which would otherwise fall within paragraph (8), it is not possible to determine the date when the request for a claim form was received in an appropriate office because of a failure to record that date, the claim shall be treated as having been made on the date 6 weeks before the date on which the properly completed claim form is received in an appropriate office.]

(9) [⁹In paragraph (8) and (8A)]—

"a claim form" means a form approved by the Secretary of State under regulation 4(1); "properly completed" has the meaning assigned by regulation 4(8);

"the time specified" means 6 weeks from the date on which the request was received or such longer period as the Secretary of State may consider reasonable.]

[⁷(10) Where a person starts a job on a Monday or Tuesday in any week and he makes a claim for disability working allowance in that week the claim shall be treated as made on the Tuesday of that week.

(11) Where a claim for disability working allowance in respect of a person has been refused and a further claim for the same allowance is made in respect of him within the period prescribed under section 100A(1) of the Social Security Act 1975 [SSAA, s.30(1)] and that further claim has been treated as an application for review in accordance with section 100A(12) of that Act [SSAA, s.30(13)] then the original claim shall be treated as made on the date on which the further claim is made or treated as made.]

AMENDMENTS

1. Social Security (Claims and Payments) Amendment Regulations 1988 (S.I. 1988 No. 522), reg. 2 (April 11, 1988).

2. Social Security (Medical Evidence, Claims and Payments) Amendment Regulations 1989 (S.I. 1989 No. 1686), reg. 4 (October 9, 1989).

3. Social Security (Claims and Payments) Amendment Regulations 1990 (S.I. 1990 No. 725), reg. 2 (April 9, 1990).

4. Social Security (Miscellaneous Provisions) Amendment Regulations (S.I. 1990 No. 2208), reg. 9 (December 5, 1990).

5. Social Security (Miscellaneous Provisions) Amendment Regulations 1991 (S.I. 1991 No. 2284), reg. 6 (November 1, 1991).

6. Social Security (Claims and Payments) Amendment Regulations 1991 (S.I. 1991 No. 2741), reg. 4 (February 3, 1992).

7. Social Security (Claims and Payments) Amendment Regulations 1991 (S.I. 1991 No. 2741), reg. 4 (March 10, 1992).

8. Social Security (Claims and Payments) Amendment (No. 3) Regulations 1993 (S.I. 1993 No. 2113), reg. 3 (September 27, 1993).

9. Social Security (Claims and Payments) Amendment Regulations 1994 (S.I. 1994 No. 2319), reg. 2 (October 3, 1994).

DEFINITIONS

"appropriate office"—see reg. 2(1).
"claim for benefit"—*ibid.*
"week"—*ibid.*

GENERAL NOTE

Paragraph (1)

A properly completed claim on the proper form is made on the date that it is received in a DSS office or UBO. See *CS 175/1988*, discussed in the notes to reg. 4(6). If a claim is treated as properly made under reg. 4(7), it is made on the date when the original attempt to claim was received.

R(SB) 8/89 holds that if the DSS puts it out of its power to receive a claim, as by closing its office and arranging with the Post Office not to deliver mail, *e.g.* on a Saturday, then if that day is the day on which the claim would have been delivered, it is the date of claim. It can be said that by making the arrangement with the Post Office the DSS constitute the Post Office bailees of the mail (see *Hodgson v. Armstrong* [1967] Q.B. 299 and *Lang v. Devon General Limited* [1987] I.C.R. 4). The Commissioner does not deal expressly with the situation where the office is closed, but there is no arrangement about the mail, *e.g.* if an office is closed on a Saturday and the Saturday and Monday mail is all stamped with the Monday date in the office. Here, principle would suggest that if it can be shown that in the normal course of the post delivery would have been on the Saturday, then the Saturday is the date of receipt and the date of claim. If a claimant proves a delivery by hand when the office is closed, the date of delivery is the date of receipt.

See *CSIS 48/1992* in the notes to reg. 4(6) on the presumption of delivery for claims sent by post.

Paragraph (3)

In cases where good cause for a late claim is shown, the claim is treated as made at the beginning of the period of good cause plus any prescribed time for claiming. Initial claims for family credit and disability working allowance and claims for income support have to be made on the first day of the period claimed for (Sched. 4, paras. 6, 7 and 11). Claims for social fund payments for maternity and funeral expenses can be made after the event (Sched. 4, paras. 8 and 9A).

Paragraph (4)

The interaction of this provision with others is far from clear (at least to me). It does not look as though it can apply directly in a case where the Secretary of State has extended the time for claiming by up to a month under reg. 19(3). If the claim is not actually made (*i.e.* received: para. (1)) within the extended period, the claim is not timeously made and para. (3) above does not apply anyway. Para. (4) seems to apply when the last link in a chain of good cause under reg. 19(2) is a delay in the post, so that the date of claim in such a case is the date of receipt.

Paragraphs (6) and (7)

These provisions create a special rule on the increase of the capital limit for income support to £8,000. Where, from April 9, 1990, a claimant has capital of more than £6,000 but not more than £8,000, a claim made before May 28, 1990, can be back-dated to the date on which all the conditions of entitlement are satisfied.

Paragraph (10)

Where a claimant starts work on a Monday or Tuesday and makes a claim for disability working allowance at any time in that week (*i.e.* Sunday to Saturday), the claim is treated as made on the Tuesday. Disability working allowance benefit weeks begin on Tuesdays (reg. 16(3)(b)).

Paragraph (11)

In these circumstances, where a further claim for disability working allowance is treated as an application for review under s.30(1) of the Administration Act (1975 Act, s.100A(1)), any award on that review can only have effect from the date of the further claim (Adjudication Regulations, reg. 70B(1)). Treating the original claim as having been made at the same date seems to require that all the conditions of entitlement in s.129(1) of the Contributions and Benefits Act (1986 Act, s.20(6A)) must be satisfied at that date. Even if the original AO's decision was clearly wrong it seems that benefit cannot be awarded for the intervening dates.

Evidence and information

7.—(1) Every person who makes a claim for benefit shall furnish such certificates, documents, information and evidence in connection with the claim, or any question arising out of it, as may be required by the Secretary of State and shall do so within one month of being required to do so or such longer period as the Secretary of State may consider reasonable.

(2) Where a benefit may be claimed by either of two partners or where entitlement to or the amount of any benefit is or may be affected by the circumstances of a partner, the Secretary of State may require the partner other than the claimant to certify in writing whether he agrees to the claimant making the claim or, as the case may be, that he confirms the information given about his circumstances.

(3) In the case of a claim for family credit [¹or disability working allowance], the employer of the claimant or, as the case may be, of the partner shall furnish such certificates, documents, information and evidence in connection with the claim or any question arising out of it as may be required by the Secretary of State.

AMENDMENT

1. Social Security (Claims and Payments) Amendment Regulations 1991 (S.I. 1991 No. 2741), reg. 5 (March 10, 1992).

DEFINITIONS

"benefit"—see reg. 2(2).
"claim for benefit"—see reg. 2(1).
"partner"—*ibid.*

GENERAL NOTE

This obligation does not arise until a valid claim has been made (*CSB 841/1986*). A failure to produce the information required may mean that a claim does not have to be submitted "forthwith" to the AO (Administration Act, s.20; 1975 Act, s.98). There is no direct sanction for a failure to comply with the requirement. The old supplementary benefit rule allowing a claim to be deemed to have been withdrawn has not been translated into the present Claims and Payments Regulations. After a lapse of a reasonable time, the Secretary of State should refer the claim to the AO to make a decision on the evidence available (*R(SB) 29/83*). If there is a significant gap in the evidence the claimant is likely not to have proved his entitlement on the balance of probabilities. Reg. 7 is only relevant to s.20 of the Administration Act. Once the claim has been referred to the AO the question of whether reg. 7 is satisfied or not is not directly relevant (*R(IS) 4/93*).

See reg. 32 for the continuing obligations of beneficiaries.

Attendance in person

8.—(1) Subject to any directions given by the Secretary of State in any particular case [¹or class of case], a person who is claiming unemployment benefit or who is claiming income support and is required by section 20(3)(d)(i) of the Social Security Act 1986 [SSCBA, s.124(1)(d)(i)] to be available for employment, shall attend in person at such unemployment benefit office as the Secretary of State may direct.

(2) Every person who makes a claim for benefit shall attend at such office or place and on such days and at such times as the Secretary of State may direct, for the purpose of furnishing certificates, documents, information and evidence under regulation 7, if reasonably so required by the Secretary of State.

AMENDMENT

1. Social Security (Miscellaneous Provisions) Amendment Regulations 1992 (S.I. 1992 No. 247), reg. 11 (March 9, 1992).

DEFINITIONS

"benefit"—see reg. 2(2).

"claim for benefit"—see reg. 2(1).

GENERAL NOTE

Note that the attendance at the UBO is not to make claims for income support every fortnight or whatever, but to make declarations of availability for and active seeking of work.

See reg. 37AA(3) for the withholding of benefit where a person fails to attend at the UBO and reg. 37AB for payment of benefit which has been withheld.

Interchange with claims for other benefits

9.—(1) Where it appears that a person who has made a claim for benefit specified in column (1) of Part I of Schedule 1 may be entitled to the benefit specified opposite it in column (2) of that Part, any such claim may be treated by the Secretary of State as a claim alternatively, or in addition, to the benefit specified opposite to it in that column.

(2)–(7) [*Omitted as not applying to income-related benefits*]

DEFINITIONS

"benefit"—see reg. 2(2).
"claim for benefit"—see reg. 2(1).

GENERAL NOTE

See Sched. 1.

Advance claims and awards

13.—(1) Where, although a person does not satisfy the requirements for entitlement to benefit on the date on which a claim is made, the adjudicating authority is of the opinion that unless there is a change of circumstances he will satisfy those requirements for a period beginning on a day ("the relevant day") not more than 3 months after the date on which the claim is made, then that authority may—

    (a) treat the claim as if made for a period beginning with the relevant day; and

    (b) award benefit accordingly, subject to the condition that the person satisfies the requirements for entitlement when benefit becomes payable under the award.

(2) An award under paragraph (1)(b) shall be reviewed by the adjudicating authority if the requirements for entitlement are found not to have been satisfied on the relevant day.

(3) [⁵Subject to paragraph (4), paragraphs (1) and (2) do not] apply to any claim for maternity allowance, attendance allowance, [²disability living allowance], retirement pension or increase, family credit [⁴disability working allowance], or any claim within regulation 11(1)(a) or (b).

[¹(4) Paragraphs (1) and (2) of this regulation shall apply to a claim for family credit made—

    (a) on or after 10th March 1992 and before 7th April 1992;

    (b) in respect of a period beginning on or after 7th April 1992; and

    (c) by a person who, if he is a member of a married or unmarried couple, he or the other member of the couple, is engaged and normally engaged in remunerative work for not less than 16 but less than 24 hours a week on the date the claim is made.

(5) In paragraph (4)(c) "remunerative work" and "engaged and normally engaged in remunerative work" shall be construed in accordance with regulations 4 and 5 respectively of the Family Credit (General) Regulations 1987

[³save that in their application to paragraph 4(c) those regulations shall be read as though for the words "not less than 24 hours" there were substituted the words "not less than 16 hours but less than 24 hours"].]

[⁵(6) Where a person claims family credit or disability working allowance but does not satisfy the requirements for entitlement to that benefit on the date on which the claim is made, and the adjudicating authority is of the opinion that he will satisfy those requirements for a period beginning on a day not more than 3 days after the date on which the claim is made, the adjudicating authority may treat the claim as if made for a period beginning with that day, and award benefit accordingly.]

AMENDMENTS

1. Social Security (Miscellaneous Provisions) Amendment Regulations 1991 (S.I. 1991 No. 2284), reg. 7 (November 1, 1991).
2. Social Security (Claims and Payments) Amendment Regulations 1991 (S.I. 1991 No. 2741), reg. 6(a) (February 3, 1992).
3. Social Security (Miscellaneous Provisions) Amendment Regulations 1992 (S.I. 1992 No. 247), reg. 13 (March 9, 1992).
4. Social Security (Claims and Payments) Amendment Regulations 1991 (S.I. 1991 No. 2741), reg. 6(b) (March 10, 1992).
5. Social Security (Claims and Payments) Amendment Regulations 1994 (S.I. 1994 No. 2319), reg. 3 (October 3, 1994).

DEFINITIONS

"adjudicating authority"—see reg. 2(1).
"benefit"—see reg. 2(2).
"married couple"—see reg. 2(1).
"unmarried couple"—*ibid.*

GENERAL NOTE

Paras. (1) and (2) contain a useful power in income support and social fund maternity and funeral expenses cases, to make awards in advance, subject to review if circumstances change.

The general rule in para. (3) is that the power in paras. (1) and (2) does not apply to family credit, but para. (4) allows advance claims immediately in advance of the change in the number of qualifying hours from 24 to 16 in April 1992. See also para. (6).

The power in paras. (1) and (2) does not apply to disability working allowance (para. (3)), but see reg. 13B for claims in advance of the start of the scheme, and para. (6).

From October 1994, para. (6) allows family credit and disability working allowance claims to be made up to three days in advance.

[¹Advance claim for and award of disability working allowance

13B.—(1) Where a person makes a claim for disability working allowance on or after 10th March 1992 and before 7th April 1992 the adjudicating authority may—

(a) treat the claim as if it were made for a period beginning on 7th April 1992; and

(b) An award benefit accordingly, subject to the condition that the person satisfies the requirements for entitlement on 7th April 1992.

(2) An award under paragraph (1)(b) shall be reviewed by the adjudicating authority if the requirements for entitlement are found not to have been satisfied on 7th April 1992.]

AMENDMENT

1. Social Security (Claims and Payments) Amendment Regulations 1991 (S.I. 1991 No. 2741), reg. 7(2) (March 10, 1992).

DEFINITION

"adjudicating authority"—see reg. 2(1).

GENERAL NOTE

This allows an advance claim in the few weeks immediately before the start of the scheme on April 7, 1992.

Cold weather payments

15A. [¹ . . .]

AMENDMENT

1. Social Security (Miscellaneous Provisions) Amendment Regulations 1991 (S.I. 1991 No. 2284), reg. 8 (November 1, 1991).

GENERAL NOTE

Claims for cold weather payments are no longer necessary or possible.

Date of entitlement under an award for the purpose of payability of benefit and effective date of change of rate

16.—(1) For the purpose only of determining the day from which benefit is to become payable, where a benefit other than one of those specified in paragraph (4) is awarded for a period of a week, or weeks, and the earliest date on which entitlement would otherwise commence is not the first day of a benefit week, entitlement shall begin on the first day of the benefit week next following.

[¹(1A) Where a claim for family credit is made in accordance with paragraph 7(a) [²or (aa)] of Schedule 4 for a period following the expiration of an existing award of family credit [²or disability working allowance], entitlement shall begin on the day after the expiration of that award.

(1B) Where a claim for family credit [²or disability working allowance] is made on or after the date when an up-rating order is made under section 63(2) of the Social Security Act 1986 [SSAA, s.150], but before the date when that order comes into force, and—

(a) an award cannot be made on that claim as at the date it is made but could have been made if that order were then in force, and

(b) the period beginning with the date of claim and ending immediately before the date when the order came into force does not exceed 28 days,

entitlement shall begin from the date the up-rating order comes into force.]

[²(1C) Where a claim for disability working allowance is made in accordance with paragraph 11(a) or (b) of Schedule 4 for a period following the expiration of an existing award of disability working allowance or family credit, entitlement shall begin on the day after the expiration of that award.]

(2) Where there is a change in the rate of any benefit to which paragraph (1) applies the change, if it would otherwise take effect on a day which is not the appropriate pay day for that benefit, shall take effect from the appropriate pay day next following.

[¹(3) For the purposes of this regulation the first day of the benefit week—

(a) in the case of child benefit is Monday,

(b) in the case of family credit [²or disability working allowance] is Tuesday, and

(c) in any other case is the day of the week on which the benefit is payable in accordance with regulation 22 (long-term benefits).]

(4) The benefits specified for exclusion from the scope of paragraph (1) are unemployment benefit, [³incapacity benefit], maternity allowance, [¹. . .], severe disablement allowance, income support [¹. . .] and any increase of those benefits.

AMENDMENTS

1. Social Security (Claims and Payments) Amendment Regulations 1988 (S.I. 1988 No. 522), reg. 3 (April 11, 1988).
2. Social Security (Claims and Payments) Amendment Regulations 1991 (S.I. 1991 No. 2741), reg. 9 (March 10, 1992).
3. Social Security (Claims and Payments) Amendment (No. 2) Regulations 1994 (S.I. 1994 No. 2943), reg. 6 (April 13, 1995).

DEFINITIONS

"benefit"—see reg. 2(2).
"week"—see reg. 2(1).

GENERAL NOTE

Reg. 16 does not apply to income support (para. (4)). See Sched. 7 for the income support rules. Reg. 16 is inappropriate for social fund payments. It does apply to family credit and disability working allowance. Para. (1) supplies the normal rule for the beginning of entitlement, *i.e.* the first day of the benefit week beginning on the date of claim or in the following six days. Note that under para. (3) and reg. 27 the family credit and disability working allowance pay-day is a Tuesday, and it is paid in arrears. Paras.(1A) to (1C) provide for awards of family credit or disability working allowance which follow on from an award of family credit or disability working allowance to begin on the day after the end of the previous award.

Duration of awards

17.—(1) Subject to the provisions of this regulation and of section [²37ZA(3) of the Social Security Act 1975 (disability living allowance) and section] 20(6) [³and (6F)] of the Social Security Act 1986 (family credit [³and disability working allowance]) [SSCBA, ss. 71(3), 128(3) and 129(6)] a claim for benefit shall be treated as made for an indefinite period and any award of benefit on that claim shall be made for an indefinite period.

[¹(1A) Where an award of income support is made in respect of a married or unmarried couple (as defined in section 20(11) of the Social Security Act 1986 [SSCBA, s.137(1)]) and one member of the couple is, at the date of claim, a person to whom section 23 of that Act [SSCBA, s.126] applies, the award of benefit shall cease when the person to whom section 23 [SSCBA, s.126] applies returns to work with the same employer.]

(2) [*Omitted as relating only to unemployment benefit*]

(3) If, in any case outside paragraph (2), it would be inappropriate to treat a claim as made and to make an award for an indefinite period (for example where a relevant change of circumstances is reasonably to be expected in the near future) the claim shall be treated as made and the award shall be for a definite period which is appropriate in the circumstances.

(4) In any case where benefit is awarded in respect of days subsequent to the date of claim the award shall be subject to the condition that the claimant satisfies the requirements for entitlement; and where those requirements are not satisfied the award shall be reviewed.

(5) [*Omitted as relating only to unemployment benefit*]

AMENDMENTS

1. Social Security (Claims and Payments) Amendment Regulations 1988 (S.I. 1988 No. 522), reg. 4 (April 11, 1988).
2. Social Security (Claims and Payments) Amendment Regulations 1991 (S.I. 1991 No. 2741), reg. 10 (February 3, 1992).

3. Social Security (Claims and Payments) Amendment Regulations 1991 (S.I. 1991 No. 2741), reg. 10 (March 10, 1992).

DEFINITIONS

"benefit"—see reg. 2(2).
"claim for benefit"—see reg. 2(1).

GENERAL NOTE

Paragraph (1)

A claim for income support is generally to be treated as for an indefinite period, and an award is for an indefinite period. The presumption in para. (1) is a strong one (*CIS 267/1993*, discussed in the note to para. (3)). Any subsequent change in or removal of entitlement must be by way of review under s.25 of the Administration Act (1975 Act, s.104) or under para. (4). See *CIS 620/1990*. An exception is provided in para. (3). Family credit and disability working allowance is payable for a period of 26 weeks and is not affected by change of circumstances (Contributions and Benefits Act, ss.128(3) and 129(6); 1986 Act, ss.20(6) and (6A)). The running of a claim is not automatically terminated by the submission of a new claim, although this will be the case if an undisputed award is made on the new claim (para. 11 of *R(S) 1/83*, applied in *CIS 181/1993* and *CIS 82/1993*). See also *CIS 701/1993*. An express withdrawal or termination will end a claim, for example, if the claimant "signs off" on starting work (*CIS 240/1992*). But a failure to sign on does not indicate that the claim has terminated (*CIS 563/1991*).

Note *CSIS 28/1992* and *CSIS 40/1992* (to be reported as *R(IS) 17/94*) in which a Tribunal of Commissioners holds that a SSAT should deal with the position from the date of claim down to the date of its decision, preferring the approach of another Tribunal of Commissioners in *CIS 391/1992* and *CIS 417/1992* to that of *CIS 649/1992*, where the Commissioner decided that an adjudicating authority should only consider the position as at the date from which benefit is sought. *CIS 649/1992* is also inconsistent with, for example, *CIS 654/1991* (to be reported as *R(IS) 3/93*), *CIS 30/1993*, *CIS 181/1993*, *CIS 267/1993* and *CIS 563/1991*. See the notes to reg. 25(2) of the Adjudication Regulations for further discussion of this important point, and in particular whether the effect of the "down to the date of the decision" principle is that a decision confirming termination of entitlement on review can award benefit for weeks within the period covered by the decision in which the conditions of entitlement *are* met.

Paragraph (1A)

An award of income support for a couple, where at the date of claim one partner was caught by the trade dispute rule (Contributions and Benefits Act, s.126; 1986 Act, s.23), ends when that partner returns to work with the same employer. It appears that a fresh claim has to be made under s.127 of the Contributions and Benefits Act (1986 Act, s.23A) for the first 15 days back at work.

Paragraph (3)

If an award of income support for an indefinite period is inappropriate then an award can be made for a definite period. The discretion to determine what is or is not appropriate should be exercised in an informed, reasonable and practical manner (*CIS 83/1990*). In *CIS 267/1993* the Commissioner states that what is appropriate or inappropriate has to be determined in the light of all the circumstances and the relevant legislative provisions. The claimant normally worked a 37 hour week but went onto a period of short time, working one week on and one week off. There was a possibility that he might be called in on non-working weeks. The claimant therefore argued that his claim should be considered on a week by week basis and that he was entitled to income support in the weeks off. The Commissioner, however, holds that in deciding whether the claimant was engaged in remunerative work under reg. 5 of the Income Support (General) Regulations, the question whether his hours of work fluctuated had to be looked at over a period which was longer than a week because the aim was to decide the hours worked in a week. This indicated that the claim was to be treated as made for an indefinite period, rather than a definite period, or series of definite periods. Although a claim may be limited to certain weeks that did not prevent an adjudicating authority from treating it as made for an indefinite period. However, the fact that an adjudicating authority could deal with a claim down to the date of its decision must mean that it could make an award limited to only some of the weeks in that period. As regards weeks after the date of the adjudicating authority's decision, clearly an award for an indefinite period could be made under reg. 17(1). However, the Commissioner considered that an award for a definite period, or periods, in the future could only be made for periods defined by particular dates.

813

Para. (3) refers as an example of when a definite award might be appropriate to a case where a change of circumstances is reasonably expected in the near future. Examples might be that a person is about to start a job or become a student. However. there may be other situations in which an award for an indefinite period is inappropriate, as illustrated by *R(S) 1/92*. In that case the Commissioner holds that the fact that the time was approaching when the claimant's incapacity to work would have to be tested against a wider field of employment could justify the making of an award for a definite period, although no change in the claimant's medical condition was anticipated.

An award is to be presumed to be for an indefinite period unless it is expressly made for a definite period. Even if the award is expressly made for a definite period, on appeal the SSAT may investigate whether the AO has shown that an indefinite award was inappropriate (see *CIS 267/1993* above).

Para. (3) can obviously apply to an initial claim, when entitlement begins on the date of claim (Sched. 7, para. 6(2A)) and continues for the appropriate period. It was held in relation to the corresponding supplementary benefit provision that an indefinite award could be reviewed and replaced by a definite award when the end of entitlement was foreseeable (*CSB 1053/1986*). However, it appears that such a procedure is not now possible under para. (3) where the initial claim and award were made for an indefinite period. If at some later date the end of entitlement becomes foreseeable, that is no ground for treating the claim as having been made for a definite period, which is the first stage of making an award for a definite period. It seems that the proper procedure in these circumstances is either to wait until the event occurs and then review the award on a change of circumstances (Administration Act, s.25(1)(b); 1975 Act, s.104(1)(b)) or review the award in advance on an anticipated change of circumstances (s.25(1)(c); s.104(1)).

See Sched. 7, para. 7 for the date from which a revised decision on a change of circumstances is to take effect.

Paragraph (4)

This provision will apply to virtually every income support, family credit and disability working allowance award, for it covers all cases where benefit is awarded for days subsequent to the date of claim. Initial claims for income support, family credit and disability working allowance have to be made on the first day of the period claimed for (Sched. 4, paras. 6 and 7). The predecessor of para. (4) applied to sickness and invalidity benefits and para. (4) has been used most commonly in that context. However, its use in income support cases has been approved in *R(IS) 20/93* and *CIS 620/1990*.

Para. (4) apparently requires an award to be reviewed whenever the claimant does not satisfy the requirements for entitlement. In *R(S) 5/89* a Tribunal of Commissioners held that a similar, but not identical, power in relation to sickness and invalidity benefit in reg. 11 of the 1979 Claims and Payments Regulations was independent of s.104 of the 1975 Act (now s.25 of the Administration Act). They put the burden of showing that the claimant had ceased to satisfy the requirements for entitlement on the AO. *R(S) 3/90* expressly holds that the burden of proving the conditions for a review under para. (4) is on the AO. This is a matter that is often overlooked by AOs and SSATs. As the Commissioner stresses in *CIS 620/1990*, this is a matter of substance and not a technicality.

R(S) 1/92 confirms that all that the AO needs to show is that the claimant ceased to satisfy the requirements for entitlement. He does not have to show any change in the primary facts, and rules such as that a different medical opinion does not in itself justify a review (*R(S) 4/86*) are not appropriate. The scope of para. (4) is very sweeping because the ground for review has wrapped up in it the conclusion that the award of benefit be revised so as to terminate entitlement. The AO needs no warrant to consider whether para. (4) applies to terminate entitlement other than his own opinion that the claimant does not satisfy the conditions for entitlement (*R(S) 3/94*).

However, *CIS 627/1992* (now renumbered as *CIS 627A/1992*) holds that if a claimant is still entitled to income support, albeit on different conditions, the "requirements for entitlement" have not ceased to be satisfied. Thus, where the AO has decided that a claimant has ceased to be incapable of work but the claimant signs on as available for work, or satisfies reg. 8(2) or (3) of the Income Support Regulations, or indeed any other para. of Sched. 1 to those Regulations, any review should be carried out under s.25 of the Administration Act, not para. (4). This means that the AO will have to establish grounds for review under s.25 (see the notes to s.25). A different medical opinion is not a change of circumstances, although it may be evidence of an underlying change if there is other evidence of this, *e.g.*, if a person has resumed work or has completely recovered (*R(S) 6/78, R(S) 4/86*). In *CIS 251/1993* the only question, following the AO's decision that the claimant was not incapable of work, was whether she had ceased to satisfy the condition for a disability premium. The claimant continued to qualify for the basic rate of income support as para. 13 of Sched. 1 applied to her. The Commissioner applies *CIS 627A/1992*, holding that the review of her entitlement to the disability premium had to be carried out under s.25, not reg. 17(4), and that the AO should have identified the relevant change of circumstances. He suggests that if the time had come when it was appropriate to consider the claimant's capacity for work in relation to a wider field of employment than her regular employment, that might be regarded as a relevant change of circumstances. If this is right, this could only provide possible grounds for a s. 25 review the first time that a claimant is found fit for alternative work by the Benefits Agency's Medical Services. But in *CSIS 92/1994* the Commissioner considered that para. (4) could be used if the only question was entitlement to the disability premium. In his view, review under para. (4) was not restricted to cases where the whole income support award would be terminated but could be used to revise a component of it. But the clear import of *CIS 627A/1992*, and *CIS 45/1994* which follows it, is that review under para. (4) is not available where a claimant remains entitled to income support to some extent, even though the amount of benefit has reduced or the conditions for entitlement are different. It is suggested that in the current state of the authorities *CIS 627A/1992*, CIS 251/1993 and *CIS 45/1994* should be followed in preference to *CSIS 92/1994*. It should be noted that the guidance that was issued to AOs after *CIS 627A/1992* had been decided was incorrect. It suggested that s. 25 grounds for review only had to be shown if the claimant remained entitled to income support (*e.g.*, as a lone parent), but that para. (4) could be used if the claimant was not still entitled to income support because he was required to be available for employment. This plainly misinterpreted *CIS 627A/ 1992*, which held that the "requirements of entitlement" had not ceased to be satisfied if the claimant was still entitled to income support albeit on *different conditions* (emphasis added) and at a lower rate. But it was also at variance with the usual AO's decision in these cases which normally only deals with the question of entitlement on the ground of incapacity. If, following the AO's review, a claimant is required to be available for employment, entitlement to income support *will* continue, albeit on different conditions (as long as the claimant is available for employment, or reg. 8(2) or (3) of the Income Support Regulations applies).

CIS 45/1994 concerned the form of para. 5 of Sched. 1 to the Income Support Regulations that was in force up to March 31, 1994 (see the 1993 edition). This did not require a claimant to prove that he was incapable of work; he simply had to submit medical evidence, provided that an AO had not determined that he was not incapable of work. The Commissioner holds that it was therefore probable that an AO would not have made a decision on the claimant's capacity for work (he did not qualify for sickness or invalidity benefit) until this question was considered after the claimant had been found "fit within limits" following a medical examination. When the AO made his decision that the claimant was not incapable of work it was not a review decision because there was no existing decision on capacity for work. It was a free-standing decision given under para. 5 of Sched. 1. (However, because of the form of para. 5, the burden of proof that the claimant was not incapable of work was on the AO.) The making of this decision was a relevant change of circumstances that provided a ground for review under s. 25. The Commissioner had already decided, following *CIS 627A/1992*, that review under para. (4) was not possible. The form of para. 5 of Sched. 1 has changed twice since this decision and the reasoning does not apply to either of the latest two forms. AOs will therefore have to show some other s. 25 ground for review after March 30, 1994. But the Commissioner's clearly expressed view that review under para. (4) is not available if the claimant remains entitled to income support to any extent should be noted.

In income support cases para. (4) has been most commonly used in the past where an AO has decided that a claimant is no longer entitled to income support on the ground of incapacity for work. But, for the reasons explained above, if the claimant is entitled to income support on other grounds this is not possible. The AO will have to establish grounds for review under s. 25. What if the AO originally carried out the review under para. (4), but is able to show s. 25 grounds for review at the appeal hearing? Can the SSAT correct the position, or does the AO have to go back to square one? Decisions such as *CSSB 540/1989* (see para. 13) would seem to suggest that the AO's decision will not be completely vitiated and can be corrected by a tribunal on appeal.

Note *CIS 413/1992* where the Commissioner holds that when an award of benefit was terminated retrospectively, this could not be done under reg. 17(4), but only on a review under s.104 of the Social Security Act 1975 (SSAA s.25). See also *CSIS 92/1994* on this point.

However, there is considerable doubt whether para. (4) can validly have application to all income support, family credit and disability working allowance awards. The authority for making the provision appears to be in s.51(1)(d) and (e) of the 1986 Act (now Administration Act, s.5(1)(d) and (e). Section 51(1)(d) allows regulations permitting an award for days after the date of claim to be made subject to the condition that the claimant satisfies the requirements for entitlement when benefit becomes payable. It is only such awards which may be reviewed if the requirements are found not to have been satisfied (s.51(1)(e)). These provisions probably allow regulations to impose the condition on awards automatically, as para. (4) seems to do.

More importantly, s.51(1)(d) may permit the test of satisfying the requirements for entitlement to be imposed only at the outset of the award. The use of the phrase "when benefit becomes payable under the award" certainly suggests a test only at that point (although *R(S) 3/94* is to the contrary). The terms of s.79(3)(c) of the 1975 Act, which gave power for the making of the regulation with which *R(S) 5/89* was concerned, were significantly different. They allowed review where the requirements were found "not to have been satisfied at some time during the period of the award." If this argument is right, para. (4) cannot validly apply to a failure to meet the condition during the course of an indefinite award. The traditional protection of s.25 of the Administration Act (1975 Act, s.104) would then apply.

Following the decision of the House of Lords in *Foster v. Chief Adjudication Officer* [1993] A.C. 754, [1993] 1 All E.R. 705 the validity of para. (4) may be challenged in an appeal to a SSAT or a Commissioner. Until that question is authoritatively decided it may still be possible to argue about what para. (4) actually means. *R(S) 5/89* dealt with a significantly differently worded regulation. *R(S) 3/90* and *R(S) 1/92* assume that para. (4) applies to a failure to satisfy the requirements for entitlement during the period of an award, but no argument to the contrary was put forward. They did not settle the question whether the words of para. (4), taking into account the statutory power under which they were enacted, only allow review where a claimant does not satisfy the requirements at the outset of the award. However, the argument was specifically put and categorically rejected in *R(S) 3/94*, where the Commissioner made plain his view that para. (4) allows review at any point during the course of an award. Therefore it seems that unless para. (4) is determined to be ultra vires, it must in the current state of the authorities be given its full apparent effect. But note *CIS 627/1992, CIS 251/1993, CIS 45/1994* and *CIS 413/1992* above.

Time for claiming benefit

19.—(1) Subject to the provisions of Schedule 5 the prescribed time for claiming any benefit specified in column (1) of Schedule 4 shall be the appropriate time specified opposite that benefit in column (2) of that Schedule.

(2) Where the claimant proves that there was good cause, throughout the period from the expiry of the prescribed time for making the claim for the failure to claim a benefit specified in column (1) of Schedule 4 before the date on which the claim was made the prescribed time shall, subject to section 165A of the Social Security Act 1975 [SSAA, s.1] (12 months limit on entitlement before the date of claim) and [¹paragraph (4)], be extended to the date on which the claim is made.

[⁴(2A) In the case of a claim for income support[⁶, family credit or disability working allowance], where the claimant does not prove that there was good cause for the failure to claim throughout the period specified in paragraph (2) but does prove that there was good cause throughout the period from a date subsequent to the expiry of the prescribed time to the date on which the claim was made, the claim shall be treated as made on—

    (a) that subsequent date if it is not more than 12 months before the date on which the claim was made; or

    (b) in any other case the date 12 months before the date on which the claim was made.]

(3) Where a claim is made for any benefit specified in column (1) of Schedule 4 and the Secretary of State certifies that to do so would be consistent with the proper administration of the Social Security Acts, [²the prescribed time shall be extended—

    (a) except in a case to which sub-paragraph (b) applies [⁷and if the time prescribed in relation to that benefit in column (2) of that Schedule is less than one month, by such period as may be specified in the certificate, but not so as to extend the prescribed time for claiming to more than one month;] and

    (b) where the benefit claimed is family credit [⁵or disability working allowance] and there has been a previous award of that benefit, to one month from the day following the 14th day after the last day of that award.]

(4) The prescribed time for claiming income support, family credit [⁵, disability working allowance] or a social fund payment for maternity or funeral expenses [³...] shall not be extended under paragraph (2) so as to give entitlement to benefit in respect of any period or, as the case may be, any birth, adoption or funeral occurring, more than 12 months before the date of claim.

(5) [¹. . .]
(6) & (7) [*Omitted as not relating to income-related benefits*]

AMENDMENTS

1. Social Security (Claims and Payments) Amendment Regulations 1988 (S.I. 1988 No. 522), reg. 5 (April 11, 1988).
2. Social Security (Medical Evidence, Claims and Payments) Amendment Regulations 1989 (S.I. 1989 No. 1686), reg. 5 (October 9, 1989).
3. Social Security (Miscellaneous Provisions) Amendment Regulations 1991 (S.I. 1991 No. 2284), reg. 9 (November 1, 1991).
4. Social Security (Miscellaneous Provisions) Amendment Regulations 1992 (S.I. 1992 No. 247), reg. 14 (March 9, 1992).
5. Social Security (Claims and Payments) Amendment Regulations 1991 (S.I. 1991 No. 2741), reg. 11 (March 10, 1992).
6. Social Security (Miscellaneous Provisions) Amendment (No. 2) Regulations 1992 (S.I. 1992 No. 2595), reg. 3 (November 16, 1992).
7. Social Security (Claims and Payments) Amendment (No. 3) Regulations 1993 (S.I. 1993 No. 2113), reg. 3 (September 27, 1993).

GENERAL NOTE

Paragraph (1)
See Sched. 4. Sched. 5 does not apply to income support, family credit, disability working allowance or social fund payments.

Paragraph (2)
Where the claimant proves continuous good cause for the delay in claiming back from the actual date of claim to the end of the prescribed time for claiming, the time for claiming is to be extended to the date of the actual claim. The technique is different from the supplementary benefit provision, which directly treated the claim as made on the first day of the period for which good cause could be shown. The change is the result of the new form of s.165A of the Social Security Act 1975 substituted from April 1987 (now contained in s.1 of the Administration Act). If the prescribed time is extended to include the date of claim, a claim for one of the benefits covered by this book is treated as made on the first day of the period the subject of the claim (reg. 6(3)).

The prescribed time for claiming each benefit in Sched. 4 must be looked at carefully. For para. (2) to operate, the good cause must exist continuously from the end of the prescribed time to the actual date of claim. Absence of good cause before the end of the prescribed time is irrelevant. For income support, the prescribed time is the first day of the period for which a claim is made. In the past, it was therefore crucial for the claimant to choose the right date to claim back to. If the claim was back to a date earlier than the date back to which good cause could be proved, para. (2) could not operate at all (*CIS 529/1990*). Para. (2A) now allows a claim to go back to the beginning of the period of good cause in such circumstances. The prescribed time for initial claims for family credit and disability working allowance is the same, but with more extended periods for repeat claims. The prescribed time for social fund maternity and funeral payments is quite long.

The meaning of "good cause" was summarised in *R(SB) 6/83*, where the national insurance interpretation was adopted. No doubt the same principles will apply under the 1987 Regulations. The fundamental meaning of good cause is "some fact which, having regard to all the circumstances (including the claimant's state of health and the information which he had received and that which he might have obtained) would probably have caused a reasonable person of his age and experience to act (or fail to act) as the claimant did" (*R(S) 2/63*). The elaboration of this test in *R(SB) 6/83* in considering when ignorance of a person's rights might be reasonable should be noted, along with much more detail in the notes to this regulation in Bonner, *Non-Means Tested Benefits*. See also Partington, *Claim in Time: time limits in social security law* (3rd ed., 1994). In *CIS 663/1992* the claimant delayed sending in the B1 claim form because he was trying to obtain information relating to his mortgage. The declaration at the end of the B1 states, "I understand that if I give information which is incorrect or incomplete, action may be taken against me. I declare that the information I have given on this form is correct and complete". The Commissioner holds that this could cause a claimant to believe he ought to obtain precise information before returning the form. The claimant had shown good cause for the delay. Note also *CIS 643/1993* and *CIS 21/1993*. The latter case concerned the implications for the claimant's income support claim of a reallocation of unemployment benefit under reg. 9(5) of the Social Security (General Benefit) Regulations 1982 (S.I. 1982 No. 1408) and will be of great assistance to any tribunal dealing with such a case.

The exception for the operation of s.1 of the Administration Act (1975 Act, s.165A) and para. (4) is important. Section 1(2)(b) provides that where a person is required to make a claim in order to be entitled to a benefit (as is the case for income support, family credit, disability working allowance and social fund maternity and funeral expenses payments) there is to be no entitlement earlier than 12 months before the date on which the claim was made or was treated as made. This would at first sight appear to allow entitlement to go back for 12 months from the date on which the claim is treated as made under reg. 6(3), although this conclusion is put forward very tentatively. Para. (4) appears to be more restrictive (see below).

Paragraph (2A)

This provision is necessary because of the way Sched. 4 defines the time limit for claiming income support, *i.e.* the first day of the period in respect of which the claim is made. If on June 1, 1992, a person claims income support from January 1, 1992, the time for claiming can only be extended to June 1 under para. (2) if the claimant proves that he had good cause for the delay in claiming throughout the period from January 1 to June 1. The claim is then treated as having been made on January 1 (reg. 6(3)). If he proves that he had good cause from March 1 to June 1 (for instance because of misleading official advice), but not before March 1, the claim cannot under para. (2) be treated as validly made from March 1. This appears unfair, and is different from the position for some other benefits where the prescribed time for claiming is put differently. Para. (2A) reverses the position for income support and family credit, but only for claims made from March 9, 1992 onwards. It was extended to disability working allowance from November 16, 1992.

Paragraph (3)

Here the extension of up to a month depends on a certificate from the Secretary of State. Otherwise all decisions under reg. 19 are for the AO. In *CSIS 61/1992* it was emphasised by the Commissioner that where a claim is made outside the time limit specified in Sched. 4, the Secretary of State must consider whether an extension of the period under reg. 19(3) is appropriate before the AO considers the claim. In his view the anonymous endorsement commonly made on claim forms to indicate the decision under reg. 19(3) is unsatisfactory. It leaves it open for doubt to arise whether the AO has usurped the functions of the Secretary of State by making the decision under reg. 19(3). The new (from September 1993) form of para. (3)(a) provides that where the prescribed time for claiming is less than one month, this can be extended for *up to* one month (the previous wording was "to one month"). For the benefits covered by this book this means income support and initial claims for family credit and disability working allowance. Normally, if a claimant attends an office to make a claim and is given a claim form to take away, complete and post in, this power is exercised to give up to a month for the return of the form. If the claim is made within the month it is treated as made at the beginning of the period to which it relates (reg. 6(3)). See also regs. 4(1) and (7) and reg. 6(1). Note the special provision for family credit and disability working allowance renewal claims.

Paragraph (4)

This provision prevents the good cause provision of para. (2) from operating so as to give entitlement in income support, family credit, disability working allowance or social fund cases more than 12 months before the date of claim. An immediate question is whether "the date of claim" means the date of the actual claim or the date on which the claim is treated as made under reg. 6(3). See *CIS 385/1992*. Since the reference is simply to the "date of claim," and not, as in s.1(2) of the Administration Act (1975 Act, s.165A(2)), to the date on which the claim is treated as made, the first interpretation appears correct. This is reinforced by the fact that para. (4) prevents the extension of the time for claiming under para. (2), which is a pre-condition for the operation of reg. 6(3).

Thus entitlement cannot be taken back beyond 12 months however good the cause.

PART III

PAYMENTS

Time and manner of payment: general provision

20. Subject to the provisions of [¹regulations 20A to 27], benefit shall be paid in accordance with an award as soon as is reasonably practicable after the award has been made, by means of an instrument of payment or by such other means as appears to the Secretary of State to be appropriate in the circumstances of any particular case.

AMENDMENT

1. Social Security (Claims and Payments) Amendment (No. 4) Regulations 1994 (S.I. 1994 No. 3196), reg. 3 (January 10, 1995).

DEFINITION

"benefit"—see reg. 2(2).

[¹ Payment on presentation of an instrument for benefit payment

20A.—(1) Where it appears to the Secretary of State to be appropriate in any class of case, benefit due to a beneficiary falling within such a class shall be paid on presentation of an instrument for benefit payment in accordance with the arrangements set out in this regulation.

(2) Where a beneficiary falls within a class mentioned in paragraph (1), the Secretary of State shall issue an instrument for benefit payment to—
  (a) that beneficiary;
  (b) the person authorised by that beneficiary to act on his behalf;
  (c) the person appointed by the Secretary of State under regulation 33 to act on behalf of that beneficiary; or
  (d) the person to whom benefit is to be paid on that beneficiary's behalf further to a direction by the Secretary of State under regulation 34.

(3) Instruments for benefit payment shall be in such form as the Secretary of State may from time to time approve.

(4) Benefit shall not be paid under this regulation other than to—
  (a) a person to whom an instrument for benefit payment has been issued in accordance with paragraph (2); or
  (b) a person not falling within sub-paragraph (a) who has been authorised by a beneficiary to whom an instrument for benefit payment has been issued to act on his behalf.

(5) The Secretary of State shall provide the paying agent with information as to the amount of benefit, if any, due to the beneficiary where the paying agent uses the instrument for benefit payment to request that information.

(6) Where a paying agent pays benefit in accordance with this regulation, the person receiving it shall sign a receipt in a form approved by the Secretary of State and such signature shall be sufficient discharge to the Secretary of State for any sum so paid.

(7) In this regulation, "paying agent" means a person authorised by the Secretary of State to make payments of benefit in accordance with the arrangements for payment set out in this regulation.]

AMENDMENT

1. Social Security (Claims and Payments) Amendment (No. 4) Regulations 1994 (S.I. 1994 No. 3196), reg. 4 (January 10, 1995).

DEFINITIONS

"instrument for benefit payment"—see reg. 2(1).
"benefit"—see reg. 2(2).

GENERAL NOTE

This regulation and the amendments to regs. 27 and 47 have been introduced as a consequence of the Government's plans to eventually replace benefit order books by social security payment cards.

Direct credit transfer

21.—(1) Subject to the provisions of this regulation, [¹benefit to which this regulation applies] may, on the application of the person claiming, or entitled to it, and with the consent of the Secretary of State, be paid by way of automated [¹. . .] credit transfer into a bank or other account—

   (a) in the name of the person entitled to benefit, or his spouse [³or partner], or a person acting on his behalf, or

   (b) in the joint names of the person entitled to benefit and his spouse [³or partner], or the person entitled to benefit and a person acting on his behalf.

   (2) An application for benefit to be paid in accordance with paragraph (1)—

   (a) shall be in writing on a form approved for the purpose by the Secretary of State or in such other manner, being in writing, as he may accept as sufficient in the circumstances, and

   (b) shall contain a statement or be accompanied by a written statement made by the applicant declaring that he has read and understood the conditions applicable to payment of benefit in accordance with this regulation

   (3) [²Subject to paragraph (3A)] benefit shall be paid in accordance with paragraph (1) within seven days of the last day of each successive period of entitlement as may be provided in the application.

   [²(3A) Income Support shall be paid in accordance with paragraph (1) within 7 days of the time determined for the payment of income support in accordance with Schedule 7.]

   (4) In respect of benefit which is the subject of an arrangement for payment under this regulation, the Secretary of State may make a particular payment by credit transfer otherwise than is provided by paragraph (3) [²or (3A)] if it appears to him appropriate to do so for the purpose of—

   (a) paying any arrears of benefit, or

   (b) making a payment in respect of a terminal period of an award or for any similar purpose.

   (5) The arrangement for benefit to be payable in accordance with this regulation may be terminated—

   (a) by the person entitled to benefit or a person acting on his behalf by notice in writing delivered or sent to an appropriate office or

   (b) by the Secretary of State if the arrangement seems to him to be no longer appropriate to the circumstances of the particular case.

   [¹(6) This regulation applies to the payment of retirement pension, widow's pension, widowed mother's allowance, child benefit, attendance allowance, disability living allowance, disability working allowance, mobility allowance, family credit [²unemployment benefit, income support, [⁴incapacity benefit], severe disablement allowance] and any increase of those benefits payable in respect of a child or adult dependant.]

AMENDMENTS

1. Social Security (Miscellaneous Provisions) Amendment Regulations 1992 (S.I. 1992 No. 247), reg. 15 (March 9, 1992).
   2. Social Security (Claims and Payments) Amendment (No. 2) Regulations 1993 (S.I. 1993 No. 1113), reg. 2 (May 12, 1993).
   3. Social Security (Claims and Payments) Amendment Regulations 1994 (S.I. 1994 No. 2319), reg. 4 (October 3, 1994).

4. Social Security (Claims and Payments) Amendment (No. 2) Regulations 1994 (S.I. 1994 No. 2943), reg. 8 (April 13, 1995).

DEFINITION

"appropriate office"—see reg. 2(1).
"partner"—*ibid.*.

GENERAL NOTE

Until May 12, 1993, it was not possible for income support to be paid by direct credit transfer.

Income support

26.—(1) [³Subject to regulation 21 (direct credit transfer), Schedule 7] shall have effect for determining the manner in and time at which income support is to be paid, the day when any change of circumstances affecting entitlement is to have effect and the day when entitlement to income support is to begin.

(2) Where income support paid by means of a book of serial orders is increased [²or reduced] on review by an amount which, with any previous such increase [²or reduction], is less than 50 pence per week, the Secretary of State may defer payment of that increase [²or disregard the reduction] until not later than either—

(a) the termination of entitlement; or

(b) the expiration of the period of one week from the date specified for payment in the last order in that book of serial orders,

whichever is the earlier.

[²(3) Where income support is payable to a beneficiary by means of a book of serial orders and a payment to a third party under Schedule 9 is increased on review so that the amount of income support payable to the beneficiary is reduced by an amount which with any previous reduction is less than 50 pence per week, the Secretary of State may make the payment to the third party and disregard the reduction in respect of the beneficiary for the period to which the book relates.]

(4) Where the entitlement to income support is less than 10 pence or, in the case of a beneficiary to whom [¹section 23(a)] of the Social Security Act 1986 [SSCBA, s.126] applies, £5, that amount shall not be payable unless the claimant is also entitled to payment of any other benefit with which income support [²may be paid] under arrangements made by the Secretary of State.

AMENDMENTS

1. Social Security (Claims and Payments) Amendment Regulations 1988 (S.I. 1988 No. 522), reg. 6 (April 11, 1988).

2. Social Security (Claims and Payments and Payments on account, Overpayments and Recovery) Amendment Regulations 1989 (S.I. 1989 No. 136), reg. 2 (February 27, 1989).

3. Social Security (Claims and Payments) Amendment (No. 2) Regulations 1993 (S.I. 1993) (No. 1113), reg. 3 (May 12, 1993).

[¹Family credit and disability working allowance

27.—(1) Subject to regulation 21 [²and paragraph (1A)], family credit and disability working allowance shall be payable in respect of any benefit week on the Tuesday next following the end of that week by means of a book of serial orders [³or on presentation of an instrument for benefit payment] unless in any case the Secretary of State arranges otherwise.

[²(1A) Subject to paragraph (2), where an amount of family credit or disability working allowance becomes payable which is at a weekly rate of not more than

£4.00, that amount shall, if the Secretary of State so directs, be payable as soon as practicable by means of a single payment; except that if that amount represents an increase in the amount of either of those benefits which has previously been paid in respect of the same period, this paragraph shall apply only if that previous payment was made by means of a single payment.]

(2) Where the entitlement to family credit or disability working allowance is less than 50 pence a week that amount shall not be payable.

AMENDMENTS

1. Social Security (Claims and Payments) Amendment Regulations 1991 (S.I. 1991 No. 2741), reg. 14 (April 6, 1992).
2. Social Security (Claims and Payments) Amendment (No. 3) Regulations 1993 (S.I. 1993 No. 2113), reg. 3 (October 25, 1993).
3. Social Security (Claims and Payments) Amendment (No. 4) Regulations 1994 (S.I. 1994 No. 3196), reg. 7 (January 10, 1995).

GENERAL NOTE

From October 25, 1993, family credit and disability working allowance of £4 or less a week can be paid in a lump sum at the beginning of an award. If the award of £4 or less is an increase of a previous award for the same period, it will only be paid in a lump sum if the previous award was so paid. The stated purpose of this provision is to recognise the costs (including childcare costs) of starting work.

Fractional amounts of benefit

28. Where the amount of any benefit payable would, but for this regulation, include a fraction of a penny, that fraction shall be disregarded if it is less than half a penny and shall otherwise be treated as a penny.

DEFINITION

"benefit"—see reg. 2(2).

Payment to a person under age 18

29. Where a person who is awarded benefit is under the age of 18, his signature on any instrument of payment shall be a sufficient discharge to the Secretary of State for any sum paid under such instrument.

DEFINITION

"benefit"—see reg. 2(2).

Payments on death

30.—(1) On the death of a person who has made a claim for benefit, the Secretary of State may appoint such person as he may think fit to proceed with the claim.

(2) Subject to paragraph (4), any sum payable by way of benefit which is payable under an award on a claim proceeded with under paragraph (1) may be paid or distributed by the Secretary of State to or amongst persons over the age of 16 claiming as personal representatives, legatees, next of kin, or creditors of the deceased (or, where the deceased was illegitimate, to or amongst other persons over the age of 16), and the provisions of regulation 38 (extinguishment of right) shall apply to any such payment or distribution; and—

(a) the receipt of any such person shall be a good discharge to the Secretary of State for any sum so paid; and

(b) where the Secretary of State is satisfied that any such sum or part thereof is needed for the benefit of any person under the age of 16, he may obtain a good discharge therefor by paying the sum or part thereof to a person over that age who satisfies the Secretary of State that he will apply the sum so paid for the benefit of the person under the age of 16.

(3) Subject to paragraph (2), any sum payable by way of benefit to the deceased, payment of which he had not obtained at the date of his death, may, unless the right thereto was already extinguished at that date, be paid or distributed to or amongst such persons as are mentioned in paragraph (2), and regulation 38 shall apply to any such payment or distribution, except that, for the purpose of that regulation, the period of 12 months shall be calculated from the date on which the right to payment of any sum is treated as having arisen in relation to any such person and not from the date on which that right is treated as having arisen in relation to the deceased.

(4) Paragraphs (2) and (3) shall not apply in any case unless written application for the payment of any such sum is made to the Secretary of State within 12 months from the date of the deceased's death or within such longer period as the Secretary of State may allow in any particular case.

(5), (6), (6A), (6B) & (7) [*Omitted as not relating to income-related benefits*]

(8) The Secretary of State may dispense with strict proof of the title of any person claiming in accordance with the provisions of this regulation.

(9) In paragraph (2) "next of kin" means—

(a) in England and Wales, the persons who would take beneficially on an intestacy; and

(b) in Scotland, the persons entitled to the moveable estate of the deceased on intestacy.

DEFINITION

"benefit"—see reg. 2(2).

Information to be given when obtaining payment of benefit

32.—(1) Every beneficiary and every person by whom or on whose behalf sums payable by way of benefit are receivable shall furnish in such manner and at such times as the Secretary of State may determine such certificates and other documents and such information or facts affecting the right to benefit or to its receipt as the Secretary of State may require (either as a condition on which any sum or sums shall be receivable or otherwise), and in particular shall notify the Secretary of State of any change of circumstances which he might reasonably be expected to know might affect the right to benefit, or to its receipt, as soon as reasonably practicable after its occurrence, by giving notice in writing [¹(unless the Secretary of State determines in any particular case to accept notice given otherwise than in writing)] of any such change to the appropriate office.

(2) Where any sum is receivable on account of an increase of benefit in respect of an adult dependant, the Secretary of State may require the beneficiary to furnish a declaration signed by such dependant confirming the particulars respecting him, which have been given by the claimant.

AMENDMENT

1. Social Security (Miscellaneous Provisions) Amendment (No. 2) Regulations 1992 (S.I. 1992 No. 2595), reg. 4 (November 16, 1992).

DEFINITIONS

"benefit"—see reg. 2(2).

"appropriate office"—see reg. 2(1).
"beneficiary"—see Social Security Act 1975, Sched. 20.

GENERAL NOTE

Notes in order books and on notices of determination require claimants to inform the DSS of various changes of circumstances, and there is also a general duty to report changes of circumstances which the claimant might reasonably be expected to know might affect entitlement. This obligation can be relevant to the recoverability of an overpayment under s.71 of the Administration Act (Social Security Act 1986, s.53). Although reg. 32 requires notice generally to be given in writing, the Secretary of State can now accept notification otherwise than in writing. Oral disclosures have always counted as disclosure under s.71 (*R(SB) 40/84*).

See reg. 37AA(1) for the withholding of benefit if para. (1) is not complied with and reg. 37AB for payment of benefit that has been withheld.

PART IV

THIRD PARTIES

Persons unable to act

33.—(1) Where—
(a) a person is, or is alleged to be, entitled to benefit, whether or not a claim for benefit has been made by him or on his behalf; and
(b) that person is unable for the time being to act; and either
(c) no receiver has been appointed by the Court of Protection with power to claim, or as the case may be, receive benefit on his behalf; or
(d) in Scotland, his estate is not being administered by any tutor, curator or other guardian acting or appointed in terms of law,
the Secretary of State may, upon written application made to him by a person who, if a natural person, is over the age of 18, appoint that person to exercise, on behalf of the person who is unable to act, any right to which that person may be entitled and to receive and deal on his behalf with any sums payable to him.

(2) Where the Secretary of State has made an appointment under paragraph (1)—
(a) he may at any time revoke it;
(b) the person appointed may resign his office after having given one month's notice in writing to the Secretary of State of his intention to do so;
(c) any such appointment shall terminate when the Secretary of State is notified that a receiver or other person to whom paragraph (1)(c) or (d) applies has been appointed.

(3) Anything required by these regulations to be done by or to any person who is for the time being unable to act may be done by or to the receiver, tutor, curator or other guardian, if any, or by or to the person appointed under this regulation or regulation 43 [¹(disability living allowance for a child)] and the receipt of any person so appointed shall be a good discharge to the Secretary of State for any sum paid.

AMENDMENT

1. Social Security (Claims and Payments) Amendment Regulations 1991 (S.I. 1991 No. 2741), reg. 16 (February 3, 1992).

DEFINITIONS

"benefit"—see reg. 2(2).
"claim for benefit"—see reg. 2(1).

GENERAL NOTE

Even if no appointment has been made, a claim made by a person unable to act, or by an "unauthorised person" on their behalf, is still valid (*CIS 812/1992*, applying para. 8 of *R(SB) 9/84* where a Tribunal of Commissioners holds that in the absence of any challenge at the time the Secretary of State must be deemed to have accepted that the claim was made in sufficient manner). In *Walsh v. CAO* (Consent Order, January 19, 1995) the Court of Appeal also applied *R(SB) 9/84* when setting aside *CIS 638/1991* in which the Commissioner had held that a claim made on behalf of a person unable to act by a person who had not been formally appointed was a nullity.

Note that any subsequent appointment has retrospective effect (*R(SB) 5/90*).

CIS 812/1992 also confirms that if there has been no appointment it is only necessary to decide whether the claimant has good cause for a late claim; it is not necessary to consider the reasonableness of the failure to claim of a person who has been acting informally on his behalf. The Commissioner declines to follow paras. 12 and 13 of *R(IS) 5/91* since this could not be reconciled with paras. 9 and 10 of *R(SB) 9/84* (which was a Tribunal of Commissioners' decision).

Payment to another person on the beneficiary's behalf

34. The Secretary of State may direct that benefit shall be paid, wholly or in part, to [¹another natural person] on the beneficiary's behalf if such a direction as to payment appears to the Secretary of State to be necessary for protecting the interests of the beneficiary, or any child or dependant in respect of whom benefit is payable.

AMENDMENT

1. Social Security (Miscellaneous Provisions) Amendment (No. 2) Regulations 1992 (S.I. 1992 No. 2595), reg. 5 (January 4, 1993).

DEFINITIONS

"beneficiary"—see Social Security Act 1975, Sched. 20.
"benefit"—see reg. 2(2).
"child"—see 1986 Act, s 20(11).

[¹Deductions of mortgage interest which shall be made from benefit and paid to qualifying lenders

34A.—(1) In relation to cases to which section 51C(1) of the Social Security Act 1986 [SSAA, s.15A(1)] (payment out of benefit of sums in respect of mortgage interest etc.) applies and in the circumstances specified in Schedule 9A, such part of any relevant benefits to which a relevant beneficiary is entitled as may be specified in that Schedule shall be paid by the Secretary of State directly to the qualifying lender and shall be applied by that lender towards the discharge of the liability in respect of that mortgage interest.

(2) The provisions of Schedule 9A shall have effect in relation to mortgage interest payments.]

AMENDMENT

1. Social Security (Claims and Payments) Amendment Regulations 1992 (S.I. 1992 No. 1026), reg. 3 (May 25, 1992).

DEFINITIONS

"qualifying lender"—see Administration Act, s.15A(3).

"relevant beneficiary"—see Administration Act, s.15A(1).
"relevant benefits"—see Administration Act, s.15A(4).

[¹[³Deductions which may be made from benefit and paid to third parties

35.—(1) Except as provided for in regulation 34A and Schedule 9A, deductions] may be made from benefit and direct payments may be made to third parties on behalf of a beneficiary in accordance with the provisions of Schedule 9.

(2) Where a social fund payment for maternity or funeral expenses [²or expenses for heating which appear to the Secretary of State to have been or to be likely to be incurred in cold weather] is made, wholly or in part, in respect of a debt which is, or will be, due to a third person, the instrument of payment may be, and in the case of funeral expenses shall be, made payable to that person and it may, in any case, be delivered or sent to that person as a direct payment.]

AMENDMENTS

1. Social Security (Claims and Payments) Amendment Regulations 1988 (S.I. 1988 No. 522, reg. 7 (April 11, 1988).

2. Social Security (Common Provisions) Miscellaneous Amendment Regulations 1988 (S.I. 1988 No. 1725), reg. 3, (November 7, 1988).

3. Social Security (Claims and Payments) Amendment Regulations 1992 (S.I. 1992 No. 1026), reg. 4 (May 25, 1992).

DEFINITIONS

"beneficiary"—see Social Security Act 1975, Sched. 20.
"benefit"—see reg. 2(2).

[¹Transitional provisions for persons in hostels or certain residential accommodation

35A.—(1) In this regulation—
"benefit week" has the same meaning as it has in Schedule 7, paragraph 4;
"specified benefit" has the same meaning as it has in Schedule 9, paragraph 1; and
"Schedule 3B" means Schedule 3B to the Income Support (General) Regulations 1987.

(2) Expressions used in this regulation and in Schedule 3B have, unless the context otherwise requires, the same meanings in this regulation as they have in that Schedule.

(3) Where—
(a) immediately before the coming into force of Schedule 3B a beneficiary was in, or temporarily absent from, a hostel and a payment in respect of his accommodation charges was, or would but for that absence have been, made for the first week to a third party under—
   (i) Schedule 9, paragraph 4 (miscellaneous accommodation costs), or
   (ii) regulation 34 (payment to another person on the beneficiary's behalf); and
(b) the beneficiary is entitled to eligible housing benefit for the period mentioned in sub-paragraph (b) of the expression "eligible housing benefit"; and
(c) the beneficiary continues to reside in the same hostel,
the adjudicating authority shall in a case to which paragraph (6) applies determine that an amount of specified benefit shall, subject to paragraphs (8) and (9), be paid to that third party.

(4) Where a beneficiary is in, or is temporarily absent from, accommodation which—

(a) was a hostel before the March benefit week; and

(b) in the second week is residential accommodation within the meaning of regulation 21 of the Income Support (General) Regulations 1987,

paragraph (3) shall apply as if sub-paragraph (b) was omitted and as if the reference to paragraph (6) was a reference to paragraph (7).

(5) An amount of specified benefit shall not be paid to a third party under paragraph (3), as applied by paragraph (4), where the beneficiary—

(a) is in residential accommodation in the benefit week which commences in the period of 7 consecutive days beginning on 9th October 1989, but

(b) is a person to whom a protected sum is not applicable in accordance with paragraph 3(3) of Schedule 3B.

(6) This paragraph applies in a case where—

(a) the amount of the eligible housing benefit referred to in paragraph (3)(b) is less than

(b) the amount of the direct payment or the payment under regulation 34 in respect of the first week or the amount which would have been payable but for the temporary absence of the beneficiary in the first week;

and where this paragraph applies the amount of the specified benefit determined in accordance with paragraph (3) shall be the difference between the amounts specified in sub-paragraphs (a) and (b).

(7) This paragraph applies where the applicable amount which was appropriate to the beneficiary by way of personal expenses in the first week is less than the total applicable amount appropriate to the beneficiary in the second week; and where this paragraph applies the amount of the specified benefit determined in accordance with paragraph (3) as applied by paragraph (4) shall be the difference between those two amounts.

(8) Where immediately before the coming into force of Schedule 3B a beneficiary was temporarily absent from a hostel and the charge levied on him during that period of absence was less than the full charge for the accommodation, an amount of specified benefit shall not be paid to the third party in respect of the period for which less than the full charge was levied but shall be paid when the full charge is levied.

(9) Specified benefit shall not be paid to a third party in accordance with this regulation unless the amount of the beneficiary's award of the specified benefit is not less than the total of the amount otherwise authorised to be so paid under this regulation plus 10 pence.

(10) For the purposes of paragraph (3)(c) residence shall be regarded as continuous where the only absences occurred during the permitted period and for this purpose "permitted period" has the same meaning as it has in regulation 3A of the Income Support (General) Regulations 1987.

(11) This regulation shall cease to apply, where a beneficiary's benefit week in the week commencing 2nd April 1990—

(i) begins on that day, on the day immediately following 8th April 1990;

(ii) begins on a day other than that day, on the day immediately following the last day in his benefit week.]

AMENDMENT

1. Social Security (Medical Evidence, Claims and Payments) Amendment Regulations 1989 (S.I. 1989 No. 1686), reg. 6 (October 9, 1989).

DEFINITIONS

"adjudicating authority"—see reg. 2(1).

"beneficiary"—see Social Security Act 1975, Sched. 20.
"eligible housing benefit"—see Income Support (General) Regulations, Sched. 3B, para. 1(1).
"first week"—*ibid.*
"hostel"—*ibid.*
"March benefit week"—*ibid.*
"second week"—*ibid.*

Payment to a partner as an alternative payee

36. Where one of a married or unmarried couple residing together is entitled to child benefit or family credit the Secretary of State may make arrangements whereby that benefit, as well as being payable to the person entitled to it, may, in the alternative, be paid to that person's partner on behalf of the person entitled.

DEFINITIONS

"married couple"—see reg. 2(1).
"partner"—*ibid.*
"unmarried couple"—*ibid.*

PART V

SUSPENSION AND EXTINGUISHMENT

[¹ Suspension in individual cases

37.—(1) Where it appears to the Secretary of State that a question arises whether—
(a) the conditions for entitlement are or were fulfilled;
(b) an award ought to be revised; or
(c) subject to paragraph (2), an appeal ought to be brought against an award, the Secretary of State may direct that payment of benefit under an award be suspended, in whole or in part, pending the determination of that question on review, appeal or reference.
(2) Where it appears to the Secretary of State that a question arises under paragraph (1)(c), he may only give directions that payment of benefit under the award be suspended [²within the relevant period]
(3) A suspension of benefit under paragraph (1)(c) shall cease unless, [²within the relevant period], the claimant is given notice in writing that either an appeal or an application or petition for leave to appeal, whichever is appropriate, has been made against that decision.
(4) Where the claimant has been given notice [²within the relevant period] that either an appeal or an application or petition for leave to appeal has been made, the suspension may continue until the appeal or the application or the petition and any subsequent appeal have been determined.
[²(5) For the purposes of this regulation—
(a) "relevant period" means—
(i) where the appeal in question would fall to be determined by a Social Security Commissioner, the period of one month; and
(ii) in any other case, the period of 3 months,
beginning with the date on which notice in writing of the decision in question and of the reasons for it is received by the adjudication officer; and
(b) a claimant is to be treated as having been given the notice required by

paragraph (3) on the date that it is posted to him at his last known address.]]

AMENDMENTS

1. Social Security (Miscellaneous Provisions) Amendment Regulations 1992 (S.I. 1992 No. 247), reg. 16 (March 9, 1992).
2. Social Security (Claims and Payments) Amendment (No. 3) Regulations 1993 (SI 1993 No. 2113), reg. 3(6) (September 27, 1993).

DEFINITION

"benefit"—see reg. 2(2).

GENERAL NOTE

This regulation and regs. 37A and 37B represent a recasting and an intended clarification of the previous reg. 37. Unfortunately, they do not fully succeed in this second aim (although the latest form (from September 27, 1993) of reg. 37A certainly makes more sense) mainly because of the need to keep to the powers conferred by s.51(1)(p) of the Social Security Act 1986 (now s.5(1)(n) of the Administration Act). The new reg. 37 deals with broadly two situations. The first, under para. (1)(a) and (b), is where there is a question whether the conditions of entitlement for a claimant are satisfied or whether an award ought to be revised. The second, under para. (1)(c), concerns awards made on appeal. In both cases, all matters are for the Secretary of State to determine, so that no appeal lies to a SSAT or a Commissioner against any determination. Challenge through judicial review would be possible.

Paragraphs (1)(a) and (b)
By definition an award of benefit has been made, by an AO, by a SSAT or by a Commissioner or a court giving the decision which a SSAT should have given. Therefore, the award may be altered only by review or appeal. If the Secretary of State considers that there is a question whether the conditions of entitlement are satisfied at any date from the beginning of the award or whether the award should be revised, he may direct that payment under the award is to be suspended. Presumably, a question whether a ground for review exists involves the question whether the award ought to be revised. The direction may then continue until a review is carried out. If the outcome of the review is not to revise the award of benefit, arrears will be paid. If the outcome is to revise the award, no overpayment will have been incurred.
Note that a decision of a SSAT or a Commissioner may be reviewed by an AO on the grounds of mistake or ignorance of a material fact or a relevant change of circumstances (Administration Act, s.25(1); 1975 Act, s.104(1)).
There is some doubt whether para. (1)(a) can apply when the question over the fulfilment of the conditions of entitlement arises in the context of whether to appeal against a decision, since that is specifically dealt with in para. (1)(c). However, because of the uncertainties surrounding para. (1)(c), para (1)(a) may have to be considered.
See reg. 37B for questions about whether overpayments of benefit are recoverable.

Paragraph (1)(c)
Since an AO cannot appeal against an AO's decision, this provision applies to awards made by decisions of a SSAT or a Commissioner exercising the power in s.23(7)(a) of the Administration Act (1975 Act s.101(5)(a)). On appeal from the Commissioner, the Court of Appeal or the Court of Session has all the authority of the Commissioner (Supreme Court Act 1981, s.15(2)). Therefore, the courts can make an award in the same circumstances in which the Commissioner can, but a confirmation by the Court of Appeal of an award made by the Commissioner would not seem itself to be an award. In that latter situation, para (1)(c) does not apply directly to a question whether to appeal to the House of Lords against a decision of the Court of Appeal or the Court of Session. If the Secretary of State considers that an appeal ought to be made against a decision making an award, then providing he gives the direction within the period specified in para. (5)(a), he may suspend payment of the award (para. (2)). The period in para. (5)(a) is one month beginning with the date of receipt of the full decision by the AO in the case of an appeal to a Social Security Commissioner, and three months in any other case. Within this period, the claimant must be given written notice that the appeal process has been started, otherwise the suspension ends (para. (3)). But para. (3) does not invalidate an appeal if the notice is not given within a month (*CSB 72/1992*).

However, the question of how long the suspension can last is left very obscure. Para. (1) on its own makes little sense. The question in sub-para. (c) is "whether . . . an appeal ought to be brought against an award." Para. (1) gives power to suspend payment of benefit "pending the determination of that question." The question whether an appeal ought to be brought is determined by an appeal being started, but this is not a determination "on review, appeal or reference." Para. (1) either does not make sense or would terminate the suspension when the appeal is started, which is clearly not the intention of the rest of the regulation. Therefore, one has to look to para. (4), which provides that if the notice referred to in para. (3) has been given, the suspension may continue until the appeal or the application or petition for leave to appeal and any subsequent appeal have been determined. The order of these phrases follows the order in which the various ways of starting an appeal are set out. This starts with a direct appeal, which is not usually possible. Usually, leave to appeal is necessary. So the next in order are applications or petitions for leave to appeal. If leave is granted, then an appeal can be made and determined. The really obscure point is whether "any subsequent appeal" refers only to the appeal for which leave was given or whether it can refer to further appeals.

Take an example of a SSAT decision awarding benefit, contrary to the AO's view of the law. The AO applies for leave to appeal and the Secretary of State decides to suspend payment of the SSAT's award under para. (1)(c). Leave to appeal is granted. On the appeal the Commissioner upholds the SSAT's decision. The AO applies for and is granted leave to appeal to the Court of Appeal. Under para. (4), the suspension of payment can clearly continue up to the date of the Commissioner's decision. But is that the determination of any subsequent appeal following the application for leave, or can the initial suspension continue until the determination of the appeal to the Court of Appeal, or even a further appeal to the House of Lords? There is certainly a good argument that the words of the regulation are not clear enough to produce this adverse effect on the claimant. Then it would appear that para. (1)(c) cannot be applied afresh to the Commissioner's decision (or to the upholding of that decision by the Court of Appeal) because that decision was not an award of benefit. On the other hand, it can be argued that the plain words simply refer to appeals which follow after the award.

If the restrictive argument put above is correct then the Secretary of State might have to rely on the general power of suspension under para. (1)(a).

It is certainly unfortunate that the considerable efforts to achieve clarity seem to have missed their mark. Nor is there likely to be any authoritative clarification because the issues never get before the Commissioners, being entirely matters for the Secretary of State.

Paragraph (5)

This provision makes the start of the one or three months period relevant under paras. (2) to (4) the date of actual receipt of written notice of the decision by the AO. This means the full record of the decision with reasons, not any preliminary indication of the decision, nor the interim notice of award (AT3(A)). The reference to the AO presumably means the AO who made the decision under appeal, or it may extend to any AO currently concerned with the appeal. But the claimant is deemed to have received the notice under para. (3) on the day it is posted to him (para. (5)(b)).

[¹Suspension in identical cases

[²**37A.**—(1) Where it appears to the Secretary of State that—
- (a) an appeal has been brought or a question arises whether an appeal ought to be brought against a decision of a Social Security Commissioner or of the appropriate court in relation to a case ("the primary case"); and
- (b) if such an appeal were to be allowed a question would arise in relation to another case ("the secondary case") whether the award of benefit (whether the same benefit as in the primary case or not) in that case ought to be revised.

he may direct that payment of benefit under the award in the secondary case be suspended, in whole or in part—
- (i) until the time limit for making an application or lodging a petition for leave to appeal in the primary case has expired; or
- (ii) if such an application is made or petition lodged, until that application or petition and any consequent appeal has been determined.
  whichever is the later.

(2) In this regulation "appeal" includes an appeal in relation to an application for judicial review in accordance with Order 53 of the Rules of the Supreme

Court 1965 or, in Scotland, an appeal in relation to such an application under the supervisory jurisdiction of the Court of Session, and, in relation to such an application "the appropriate court" includes the High Court or, as the case may be, the Court of Session.]]

AMENDMENTS

1. Social Security (Miscellaneous Provisions) Amendment Regulations 1992 (S.I. 1992 No. 247), reg. 16 (March 9, 1992).
2. Social Security (Claims and Payments) Amendment (No. 3) Regulations 1993 (S.I. 1993 No 2113), reg. 3(7) (September 27, 1993).

DEFINITION

"benefit"—see reg. 2(2).

GENERAL NOTE

The intended aim of reg. 37A is to authorise suspension of payment of other claimants' benefit while an appeal in the "primary case" is brought. A new form of reg. 37A was introduced on September 27, 1993. This applies where an appeal against a decision of a Social Security Commissioner or court has been made or the Secretary of State considers that such an appeal ought to be instituted. If a successful appeal would raise the question as to whether the award of benefit to another claimant ought to be revised, payment of that other claimant's benefit may be suspended until the time limit for applying for leave to appeal in the primary case has expired, or, if a leave application is made, until the question under appeal is determined. The benefits involved do not have to be the same, but presumably the same legal issue must be in question. It does not matter that the time limits and conditions of reg. 37 are not met in the case of the claimant involved in the appeal.

The previous form of reg. 37A was limited to situations in which there was a question whether an appeal ought to be brought against an *award* in the primary case. The new form also applies where the decision in the primary case is not an award, *e.g.* a decision by a Social Security Commissioner upholding an award by a SSAT, or an appeal in respect of an application for judicial review (para. (2)). See the discussion in the notes to reg. 37 as to the scope of the powers to make regs. 37 and 37A conferred by what is now s.5(1)(n) of the Administration Act. However, under the new form of reg. 37A the question that has to arise includes whether the award in the secondary case ought to be revised (para. (1)(b)). The power relied upon, therefore, is presumably that contained in s.5(1)(n)(ii). But it is arguable that there has to be something that raises a question in the Secretary of State's mind about the secondary case itself at the time the decision to suspend in that case is taken. If the question as to whether the award in the secondary case ought to be revised would only arise when and if the appeal in the primary case is allowed, as para. (1)(b) seems to envisage, it may be that this is not within the scope of the powers contained in s.5(1)(n).

[¹Withholding of benefit in prescribed circumstances

37AA.—(1) Where a person who is in receipt of benefit fails to comply with the provisions of regulation 32(1), in so far as they relate to documents, information or facts required by the Secretary of State, that benefit may be withheld, in whole or in part, from a date not earlier than 28 days after the date on which the requirement is imposed.

(2) Where the Secretary of State is satisfied that the last known address of a person who is in receipt of benefit is not the address at which that person is residing or that a serious doubt exists as to whether that person is residing at that address, that benefit may be withheld from the date on which the Secretary of State is so satisfied or such later date as he may determine.

(3) Where it appears to the Secretary of State that a person who is claiming income support is, under the provisions of regulation 8, required to attend an unemployment benefit office in person, but that person has failed to do so, benefit may be withheld from a date not earlier than the date following that on which that person last attended an unemployment benefit office under the provisions of regulation 8.

(4) Where a person—
   (a) claims any benefit, and entitlement to that benefit depends on his being incapable of work during the period to which his claim relates; or
   (b) claims income support, but is not required to be available for employment by virtue of paragraph 5 of Schedule 1 to the Income Support (General) Regulations 1987

and that person fails to provide evidence of incapacity in accordance with regulation 2 of the Social Security (Medical Evidence) Regulations 1976 (evidence of incapacity for work), that benefit may be withheld from the date from which he has ceased to comply with the requirements of that regulation, or as soon as practicable thereafter.]

AMENDMENT

1. Social Security (Claims and Payments) Amendment Regulations 1994 (S.I. 1994 No. 2319), reg. 6 (October 3, 1994).

DEFINITION

"benefit"—see reg. 2(2).

[¹Payment of withheld benefit

37AB.—(1) Subject to paragraph (2), where the circumstances in which any benefit that has been withheld under the provisions of regulation 37AA no longer exist, and—
   (a) the Secretary of State is satisfied that no question arises in connection with the award of that benefit, payments of that benefit shall be made;
   (b) a question arises in connection with the award of that benefit and that question has been determined, payments of benefit that the beneficiary is entitled to in accordance with that determination shall be made.
(2) Subject to paragraph (3)—
   (a) a payment of any sum by way of benefit shall not be made under paragraph (1) after the expiration of a period of 12 months from the date the right to that payment arose;
   (b) where a person from whom benefit has been withheld satisfies the adjudicating authority that there was good cause for his failure to act from a day within the period specified in sub-paragraph (a) and continuing after the expiration of that period, the period specified in that sub-paragraph shall be extended to the date on which the adjudicating authority is so satisfied, or the date on which good cause ceases, whichever is the earlier.
(3) For the purposes of paragraph (2), the following periods shall be disregarded—
   (a) any period during which the Secretary of State possesses information which is sufficient—
      (i) to enable him to be satisfied that no question arises in connection with the award of that benefit, or
      (ii) to enable him to decide that a question does arise in connection with the award of that benefit;
   (b) in a case where a question in connection with the award of the benefit arises, the period commencing on the date the question is submitted to an adjudication officer and ending on the date that question is finally determined.]

AMENDMENT

1. Social Security (Claims and Payments) Amendment Regulations 1994 (S.I. 1994 No. 2319), reg. 6 (October 3, 1994).

"benefit"—see reg. 2(2).

[¹Witholding payment of arrears of benefit

37B. Where it appears to the Secretary of State that a question has arisen whether any amount paid or payable to a person by way of, or in connection with a claim for, benefit is recoverable under section 27 or 53 of the Social Security Act 1986 [SSAA, ss.74 and 71], or regulations made under either section, he may direct that any payment of arrears of benefit to that person shall be suspended, in whole or in part, pending determination of that question.]

AMENDMENT

1. Social Security (Miscellaneous Provisions) Amendment Regulations 1992 (S.I. 1992 No. 247), reg. 16 (March 9, 1992).

DEFINITION

"benefit"—see reg. 2(2).

GENERAL NOTE

It does not seem to be necessary that the arrears of benefit withheld under this regulation relate to the same period, or even the same benefit, as that to which the potential overpayment relates.

Extinguishment of right to payment of sums by way of benefit where payment is not obtained within the prescribed period

38.—(1) [¹Subject to paragraph (2A), the right to payment of any sum by way of benefit shall be extinguished] where payment of that sum is not obtained within the period of 12 months from the date on which the right is to be treated as having arisen; and for the purposes of this regulation the right shall be treated as having arisen—
  (a) in relation to any such sum contained in an instrument of payment which has been given or sent to the person to whom it is payable, or to a place approved by the Secretary of State for collection by him (whether or not received or collected as the case may be)—
    (i) on the date of the said instrument of payment, or
    (ii) if a further instrument of payment has been so given or sent as a replacement, on the date of the last such instrument of payment;
  (b) in relation to any such sum to which sub-paragraph (a) does not apply, where notice is given (whether orally or in writing) or is sent that the sum contained in the notice is ready for collection on the date of the notice or, if more than one such notice is given or sent, the date of the first such notice;
  (c) in relation to any such sum to which neither (a) nor (b) applies, on such date as the Secretary of State determines.
  (2) The giving or sending of an instrument of payment under paragraph 1(a), or of a notice under paragraph (1)(b), shall be effective for the purposes of that paragraph, even where the sum contained in that instrument, or notice, is more or less than the sum which the person concerned has the right to receive.
  [¹(2A) Where a question arises whether the right to payment of any sum by way of benefit has been extinguished by the operation of this regulation and the adjudicating authority is satisfied that—
    (a) the Secretary of State has first received written notice requesting payment of that sum after the expiration of 12 months; and

(b) from a day within that period of 12 months and continuing until the day the written notice was given, there was good cause for not giving the notice; and

[²(c) the Secretary of State has certified either—

    (i) that no instrument of payment has been given or sent to the person to whom it is payable and that no payment has been made under the provisions of regulation 21 (automated credit transfer); or

    (ii) that such instrument has been produced to him and that no further instrument has been issued as a replacement,]

the period of 12 months shall be extended to the date on which the adjudicating authority decides that question, and this regulation shall accordingly apply as though the right to payment had arisen on that date.]

(3) For the purposes of paragraph (1) the date of an instrument of payment is the date of issue of that instrument or, if the instrument specifies a date which is the earliest date on which payment can be obtained on the instrument and which is later than the date of issue, that date.

(4) This regulation shall apply to a person authorised or appointed to act on behalf of a beneficiary as it applies to a beneficiary.

(5) [*Omitted as not applying to income-related benefits*]

AMENDMENTS

1. Social Security (Medical Evidence, Claims and Payments) Amendment Regulations 1989 (S.I. 1989 No. 1686), reg. 7 (October 9, 1989).
2. Social Security (Claims and Payments) Amendment (No. 3) Regulations 1993 (S.I. 1993 No. 2113), reg. 3(8) (September 27, 1993).

DEFINITIONS

"beneficiary"—see Social Security Act 1975, Sched. 20.
"benefit"—see reg. 2(2).

GENERAL NOTE

See *R(A) 2/93* on the pre-October 1989 form of reg. 38.

The new form applies to decisions extinguishing the right from October 9, 1989, onwards *(R/ (P) 3/93)*. The claimant only has to produce the instrument of payment under para. (2A)(c) if one was issued to him.

PART VII

MISCELLANEOUS

[¹**Instruments of payment, etc and instruments for benefit payment**

47.—(1) Instruments of payment, books of serial orders and instruments for benefit payment issued by the Secretary of State shall remain his property.

(2) Any person having an instrument of payment or book of serial orders shall, on ceasing to be entitled to the benefit to which such instrument or book relates, or when so required by the Secretary of State, deliver it to the Secretary of State or such other person as he may direct.

(3) Any person having an instrument for benefit payment shall, when so required by the Secretary of State, deliver it to the Secretary of State or such other person as he may direct.]

AMENDMENT

1. Social Security (Claims and Payments) Amendment (No. 4) Regulations 1994 (S.I. 1994 No. 3196), reg. 8 (January 10, 1995).

DEFINITIONS

"instrument for benefit payment"—see reg. 2(1).
"benefit"—see reg. 2(2).

Revocations

48. The regulations specified in column (1) of Schedule 10 to these regulations are hereby revoked to the extent mentioned in column (2) of that Schedule, in exercise of the powers specified in column (3).

Savings

49. [¹. . .]

AMENDMENT

1. Social Security (Miscellaneous Provisions) Amendment (No. 2) Regulations 1992 (S.I. 1992 No. 2595), reg. 6 (November 16, 1992).

GENERAL NOTE

Reg. 49 maintained in force regulations about claims and reviews relating to supplementary benefit and family income support. See *CIS 465/1991*. Because its terms led to the mistaken impression that the substantive terms of the schemes survived the repeal of the Supplementary Benefits Act 1976 and the Family Income Supplements Act 1970 by the Social Security Act 1986, reg. 49 has been revoked from November 16, 1992. See *R(SB) 1/94*. It is not immediately apparent that reg. 49 was necessary in order to allow claims to be made for supplementary benefit for periods prior to April 11, 1988, and reviews of entitlement for such periods to be carried out. Therefore its revocation may have no effect on such matters. See Sched. 10 to the Administration Act.

SCHEDULES

SCHEDULE 1   **Regulation 9(1)**

PART I

BENEFIT CLAIMED AND OTHER BENEFIT WHICH MAY BE TREATED AS IF CLAIMED IN ADDITION OR IN THE ALTERNATIVE

Column (1)	Column (2)
Benefit Claimed	*Alternative Benefit*
Income support	Supplementary benefit, or an invalid care allowance.
[¹Disability working allowance	Family credit.
Family credit	Disability working allowance.]

AMENDMENT

1. Social Security (Claims and Payments) Amendment Regulations 1991 (S.I. 1991 No. 2741), reg. 25 (March 10, 1992).

SCHEDULE 4   **Regulation 19(1)**

Part I

Prescribed Times for Claiming Benefit

Column (1)	Column (2)
Description of benefit	*Prescribed time for claiming benefit*
6. Income support.	The first day of the period in respect of which the claim is made.
7. Family credit.	(a) Where family credit has previously been claimed and awarded the period beginning 28 days before and ending 14 days after the last day of that award; [³(aa) where disability working allowance has previously been claimed and awarded the period beginning 42 days before and ending 14 days after the last day of that award of disability working allowance;] (b) subject to [³(a) and (aa)], the first day of the period in respect of which the claim is made. [¹(c) where a claim for family credit is treated as if made for a period beginning with the relevant day by virtue of regulation 13 of these Regulations, the period beginning on 10th March 1992 and ending on 6th April 1992.]
8. Social fund payment in respect of maternity expenses.	The period beginning 11 weeks before the first day of the expected week of confinement and ending 3 months after the actual date of confinement or, in the case of an adopted baby, the date of the adoption order.
9. Social fund payment in respect of funeral expenses.	3 months from the date of the funeral.
9A. [²...]	
[³**11.** Disability working allowance.	(a) Where disability working allowance has previously been claimed and awarded the period beginning 42 days before and ending 14 days after the last day of that award; (b) where family credit has previously been claimed and awarded the period beginning 28 days before and ending 14 days after the last day of that award of family credit; (c) subject to (c) and (b), the first day of the period in respect of which the claim is made; (d) where a claim for disability working allowance is made by virtue of regulation 13B(1), the period beginning on 10th March 1992 and ending on 6th April 1992.]

For the purposes of this Schedule—

"actual date of confinement" means the date of the issue of the child or, if the woman is confined of twins or a greater number of children, the date of the issue of the last of them; and

"confinement" means labour resulting in the issue of a living child, or labour after 28 weeks of pregnancy resulting in the issue of a child whether alive or dead.

AMENDMENTS

1. Social Security (Miscellaneous Provisions) Amendment Regulations 1991 (S.I. 1991 No. 2284), reg. 10 (November 1, 1991).
2. Social Security (Miscellaneous Provisions) Amendment Regulations 1991 (S.I. 1991 No. 2284), reg. 11 (November 1, 1991).
3. Social Security (Claims and Payments) Amendment Regulations 1991 (S.I. 1991 No. 2741), reg. 26 (March 10, 1992).

SCHEDULE 7

Regulation 26

MANNER AND TIME OF PAYMENT, EFFECTIVE DATE OF CHANGE OF CIRCUMSTANCES AND COMMENCEMENT OF ENTITLEMENT IN INCOME SUPPORT CASES

Manner of payment

1. Except as otherwise provided in these Regulations income support shall be paid in arrears in accordance with the award by means of an instrument of payment.

Time of payment

2. Income support shall be paid in advance where the claimant is—
(a) in receipt of retirement pension; or
(b) over pensionable age and not in receipt of unemployment benefit, ['incapacity benefit or severe disablement allowance and is not a person to whom section 126 of the Social Security Contributions and Benefits Act 1992 (trade disputes) applies] unless he was in receipt of income support immediately before the trade dispute began; or
(c) in receipt of widow's benefit and is not registering or required to register as available for work or providing or required to provide medical evidence of incapacity for work; or
(d) a person to whom ['section 23(a)] of the Social Security Act 1986 [SSCBA, s.127] applies, but only for the period of 15 days mentioned in that subsection.

[²2A.—(1) For the purposes of this paragraph—
(a) "public holiday" means, as the case may be, Christmas Day, Good Friday or a Bank Holiday under the Banking and Financial Dealings Act 1971 or in Scotland local holidays, and
(b) "office closure" means a period during which an office of the Department of Social Security or associated office is closed in connection with a public holiday.

(2) Where income support is normally paid in arrears and the day on which the benefit is payable by reason of paragraph 3 is affected by office closure it may for that benefit week be paid wholly in advance or partly in advance and partly in arrears and on such a day as the Secretary of State may direct.

(3) Where under this paragraph income support is paid either in advance or partly in advance and partly in arrears it shall for any other purposes be treated as if it was paid in arrears.]

[³3.—(1) Subject to [⁷sub-paragraph (1A) and to] any direction given by the Secretary of State in accordance with sub-paragraph (2), income support in respect of any benefit week shall, if the beneficiary is entitled to a relevant social security benefit or would be so entitled but for failure to satisfy the contribution conditions or had not exhausted his entitlement, be paid on the day and at the intervals appropriate to payment of that benefit.

[⁷(1A) Subject to sub-paragraph (2), where income support is paid to a person on the grounds of incapacity for work, that entitlement commenced on or after 13th April 1995, and no relevant social security benefit is paid to that person, the income support shall be paid fortnightly in arrears.]

(2) The Secretary of State may direct that income support in respect of any benefit week shall be paid at such intervals and on such days as he may in any particular case or class of case determine.

3A.—(1) Income support for any part-week shall be paid in accordance with an award on such day as the Secretary of State may in any particular case direct.

(2) In this paragraph, "part-week" has the same meaning as it has in Part VII of the Income Support (General) Regulations 1987.]

4. [¹In this Schedule]—

"benefit week" means, if the beneficiary is entitled to a relevant social security benefit or would be so entitled but for failure to satisfy the contribution conditions or had not exhausted his entitlement, the week corresponding to the week in respect of which that benefit is paid, and in any other case a period of 7 days beginning or ending with such day as the Secretary of State may direct;

[¹"Income Support Regulations" means the Income Support (General) Regulations 1987;] and

"relevant social security benefit" means unemployment benefit, [⁷incapacity benefit], severe disablement allowance, retirement pension or widow's benefit.

Payment of small amounts of income support

5. Where the amount of income support is less than .00 a week the Secretary of State may direct that it shall be paid at such intervals as may be specified not exceeding 13 weeks.

Commencement of entitlement to income support

6.—(1) Subject to sub-paragraphs (3) and (4), in a case where income support is payable in arrears entitlement shall commence on the date of claim.

(2) [¹Subject to sub-paragraphs (2A) and (3)], in a case where, under paragraph 2, income support is payable in advance entitlement shall commence on the date of claim if that day is a day for payment of income support as determined under paragraph 3 but otherwise on the first such day after the date of claim.

[¹(2A) Where income support is awarded under regulation 17(3) for a definite period which is not a benefit week or a multiple of such a week entitlement shall commence on the date of claim.

(3) In a case where regulation 13 applies, entitlement shall commence on the day which is the relevant day for the purposes of that regulation [⁵except where income support is paid in advance, when entitlement shall commence on the relevant day, if that day is a day for payment as determined under paragraph 3 but otherwise on the first day for payment after the relevant day].]

(4) [¹. . .]

[¹(5) If a claim is made by a claimant within 3 days of the date on which he became resident at a resettlement unit or at a place provided by a voluntary organisation for purposes similar to the purposes for which resettlement units are provided by the Secretary of State or at a centre providing facilities for the rehabilitation of alcoholics or drug addicts and is so resident for the purposes of that rehabilitation, then it shall be treated as having been made on the day he became so resident.

(5A) In the preceding paragraph "resettlement unit" means accommodation provided under section 30 of and paragraph 2 of Schedule 5 to the Supplementary Benefits Act 1976.]

(6) Where, in consequence of a further claim for income support such as is mentioned in sub-paragraph 4(7) of Schedule 3 to the Income Support (General) Regulations 1987, a claimant is treated as occupying a dwelling as his home for a period before moving in, that further claim shall be treated as having been made on the date from which he is treated as so occupying the dwelling or the date of the claim made before he moved in to the dwelling and referred to in that subparagraph, whichever is the later.

[⁴Date when change of circumstances is to take effect

7.—(1) Subject to the following sub-paragraphs, where the amount of income support payable under an award is changed because of a change of circumstances that change shall have effect—

    (i) where income support is paid in arrears, from the first day of the benefit week in which the change occurs or is expected to occur; or

    (ii) where income support is paid in advance, from the date of the relevant change of circumstances, or the day on which the relevant change of circumstances is expected to occur, if either of those days is the first day of the benefit week and otherwise from the next following such day, and

for the purposes of this paragraph any period of residence in temporary accommodation pursuant to arrangements for training under section 2 of the Employment and Training Act 1973 [⁵or section 2 of the Enterprise and New Towns (Scotland) Act 1990] for a period which is expected to last for seven days or less shall not be regarded as a change of circumstances.]

(2) In the cases set out in sub-paragraph (3) the decision given on review shall have effect on the day on which the relevant change of circumstances occurs or is expected to occur.

(3) The cases referred in sub-paragraph (2) are where—

    (a) income support is paid in arrears and entitlement ends, or is expected to end, for a reason other than that the claimant no longer satisfies the provisions of section 20(3)(b) of the Social Security Act 1986 [SSCBA, s.124(1)(b)];

    (b) a child or young person referred to in regulation 16(6) of the Income Support Regulations (child in care of a local authority or detained in custody) lives, or is expected to live, with the claimant for part only of the benefit week;

    (c) a claimant or his partner (as defined in regulation 2(1) of the Income Support Regulations) enters, or is expected to enter, a nursing home or a residential care home (as defined in regulation 19(3) of those Regulations) or residential accommodation (as defined in regulation 21(3)(a) to (d) of those Regulations) for a period of not more than 8 weeks;

    (d) a person referred to in paragraphs 1, 2, 3 or 18 of Schedule 7 to the Income Support Regulations either—

        (i) ceases, or is expected to cease, to be a patient, or

        (ii) a member of his family ceases, or is expected to cease, to be a patient, in either case for a period of less than a week;

[⁶(dd) a person referred to in paragraph 8 of Schedule 7 to the Income Support Regulations either—

        (i) ceases to be a prisoner, or.

        (ii) becomes a prisoner;]

    (e) a person to whom section 23 of the Social Security Act 1986 [SSCBA, s.126] (trade disputes) applies either—

        (i) becomes incapable of work by reason of disease or bodily or mental disablement, or

        (ii) enters the maternity period (as defined in section 23(2) of that Act) or the day is known on which that person is expected to enter the maternity period;

    (f) during the currency of a claim the claimant makes a claim for a relevant social security benefit—

        (i) the result of which is that his benefit week changes; or

        (ii) under regulation 13 and an award of that benefit on the relevant day for the purposes of that regulation means that his benefit week is expected to change.

    (4) Where income is treated as paid on a particular day under regulation 31(1)(b) or (2) of the Income Support Regulations (date on which income is treated as paid) any relevant change of circumstances which occurs, or is expected to occur, resulting from that payment shall have effect on the day on which it was treated as paid.

    (5) Where the relevant change of circumstances requires, or is expected to require, a reduction in the amount of income support then, if the Secretary of State certifies that it will be impracticable to give effect to that reduction from the day prescribed in the preceding sub-paragraphs, except where (3)(f) or (4) apply, the change shall have effect either from the first day of the following benefit week or, where the relevant change of circumstances is expected to occur, from the first day of the benefit week following that in which that change of circumstances is expected to occur.

    (6) Where in the cases set out in sub-paragraphs (b), (c), (d), (e) and (f) of paragraph (3) the review has been carried out under section 104(1)(b) of the Social Security Act 1975 and the circumstances which have caused the award to be revised cease to apply and the award is reviewed and revised again that second change of circumstances shall take effect from the date of the second change.

AMENDMENTS

    1. Social Security (Claims and Payments) Amendment Regulations 1988 (S.I. 1988 No. 522), reg. 10 (April 11, 1988).

    2. Social Security (Claims and Payments and Payments on account, Overpayments and Recovery) Amendment Regulations 1989 (S.I. 1989 No. 136), reg. 2(b) (February 27, 1989).

    3. Social Security (Medical Evidence, Claims and Payments) Amendment Regulations 1989 (S.I. 1989 No. 1686), reg. 8 (October 9, 1989).

    4. Social Security (Miscellaneous Provisions) Amendment Regulations 1990 (S.I. 1990 No. 2208), reg. 15 (December 5, 1990).

    5. Enterprise (Scotland) Consequential Amendments Order 1991 (S.I. 1991 No. 387), art. 2 and Sched. (April 1, 1991).

    6. Social Security (Miscellaneous Provisions) Amendment Regulations 1992 (S.I. 1992 No. 247), reg. 17 (March 9, 1992).

    7. Social Security (Claims and Payments) Amendment (No. 2) Regulations 1994 (S.I. 1994 No. 2943), reg. 14 (April 13, 1995).

GENERAL NOTE

Paragraph 1

    One of the most significant changes from supplementary benefit is encapsulated in this provision. The general rule is that income support is paid in arrears, rather than in advance. This is perhaps a further step in the integration of means-tested benefits (where the approach in the past has been to make the benefit available at the time of need) with other kinds of benefit. Exceptions to the general rule are in paras. 2 and 2A. The day of payment is dealt with in paras. 3 to 4.

    If a claimant is without resources until the first payment of income support at the end of the first benefit week then there may be eligibility for a crisis loan under the social fund (*Social Fund Guide*, para. 5422). Any resources actually available or which could be obtained in time to meet the need must be considered. A crisis loan may be made for living expenses (see Social Fund Directions 18–20).

    On the changeover to income support from April 11, 1988, a special transitional payment of income support was to be paid after that date to bridge the gap from supplementary benefit paid in advance to income support paid in arrears (Income Support (Transitional) Regulations, reg. 7).

Paragraph 2

    These categories of claimant are paid income support in advance. Apart from pensioners and most widows, those returning to work after a trade dispute are covered.

Paragraphs 3 and 4

Where a claimant meets the conditions of entitlement for one of the benefits listed as a "relevant social security benefit," the income support benefit week, pay-day and interval of payment is the same as for that benefit. Thus, the unemployed are paid fortnightly in arrears (reg. 24(1)), although under reg. 24 the Secretary of State can arrange payment at other intervals (*e.g.* weekly). Otherwise the benefit week is to be defined by the Secretary of State. Income support paid for a definite period under reg. 17(3) need not be in terms of benefit weeks. Para. 3A provides that payments for part-weeks may be made as the Secretary of State directs.

Paragraph 6

The general rule for income support paid in arrears is that entitlement begins on the date of claim. The first payment on the pay day at the end of the first benefit week (or the second benefit week in the case of the unemployed) can thus be precisely calculated to include the right number of days. Payments can then continue on a weekly basis.

If income support is paid in advance, then, as for supplementary benefit, entitlement begins on the next pay day following the claim or coinciding with the date of claim.

Where the award is for a definite period under reg. 17(3) entitlement begins with the date of claim (sub-para. (2A)). Sub-para. (3) deals with the special case of advance awards. Sub-paras. (5) and (6) cover other special cases.

Paragraph 7

This provision deals with the date on which a review on the ground of a change of circumstances (Administration Act, s.25(1)(b); 1975 Act, s.104(1)(b) and reg. 17(4)) or an anticipated change of circumstances (Administration Act, s.25(1)(c); 1975 Act, s.104(1)(bb)) takes effect. The review legislation does not specify the date on which a revised decision on review is to take effect.

Although sub-paras. (1) refers to the amount of income support payable being changed, it is apparent from the rest of para. 7 that changes which result in entitlement to income support being entirely removed are equally covered. Sub-para. (1) establishes two general rules, which are subject to exceptions in sub-paras. (2) to (6).

The general rule where benefit is paid in arrears is that the change of circumstances is to take effect from the first day of the benefit week (defined in para. 4) in which it occurs, or is expected to occur (sub-para. (1)(i)). Where benefit is paid in advance the change takes effect from the first day of the benefit week which starts on the date of the change or in the next six days (sub-para. (1)(ii)). Sub-para. (3) lists cases in which the change of circumstances takes effect on the date of the change. The most important is (a), which covers the ending of entitlement (other than on capital grounds) where benefit is being paid in arrears. Sub-para. (4) deals with changes in most payments of income. Sub-para. (5) provides a general exception allowing the effect of a change to be deferred to the next benefit week following the normal day, if the Secretary of State certifies that it would be impracticable to follow the normal rule.

SCHEDULE 9   **Regulation 35**

DEDUCTIONS FROM BENEFIT AND DIRECT PAYMENT TO THIRD PARTIES

Interpretation

1. In this Schedule—

[¹¹"the Community Charges Regulations" means the Community Charges (Deductions from Income Support (No. 2) Regulations 1990;

"the Community Charges (Scotland) Regulations" means the Community Charges (Deductions from Income Support) (Scotland) Regulations 1989;]

"family" in the case of a claimant who is not a member of a family means that claimant;

[¹¹"the Fines Regulations" means the Fines (Deductions from Income Support) Regulations 1992;]

[⁶"5 per cent. of the personal allowance for the single claimant aged not less than 25" means where the percentage is not a multiple of 5 pence the sum obtained by rounding that 5 per cent. to the next higher such multiple;

"hostel" means a building other than a residential care home or nursing home within the meaning of regulation 19(3) of the Income Support Regulations or residential accommodation within the meaning of regulation 21(3) of those Regulations—

    (a) in which there is provided for persons generally, or for a class of persons. accommodation, otherwise than in separate and self-contained premises, and either board or facilities of a kind set out in paragraph 4A(1)(d) below adequate to the needs of those persons and—

    (b) which is—

        (i) managed by or owned by a housing association registered with the Housing Corporation established by the Housing Act 1964; or

        (ii) managed or owned by a housing association registered with Scottish Homes established by the Housing (Scotland) Act 1988; or

        (iii) operated other than on a commercial basis and in respect of which funds are provided wholly or in part by a government department or a local authority; or

        (iv) managed by a voluntary organisation or charity and provides care, support or supervision with a view to assisting those persons to be rehabilitated or resettled within the community.

    (c) In sub-paragraph (iv) above, "voluntary organisation" shall mean a body the activities of which are carried out otherwise than for profit, but shall not include any public or local authority;

"housing authority" means a local authority, a new town corporation, Scottish Homes or the Rural Development Board for Rural Wales;]

"The Housing Benefit Regulations" means the Housing Benefit (General) Regulations 1987;

"housing costs" means those costs specified in [⁶paragraph 1(a), (aa),] (b), (c) (but in the case of ground rent or feu duty only when paid with service charges), (d), (e) and (f) of Schedule 3 to the Income Support Regulations [⁶and payments analogous to those specified in this definition];

[²"income support" means income support under Part II of the Social Security Act 1986 [SSCBA, Part VII] and includes transitional addition, personal expenses addition and special transitional addition as defined in the Income Support (Transitional) Regulations 1987;]

"the Income Support Regulations" means the Income Support (General) Regulations 1987;

"miscellaneous accommodation costs" has the meaning assigned by paragraph 4(1);

"mortgage payment" means a payment attributable to [⁶interest on a loan whether or not secured by way of a mortgage or under a heritable security] which falls to be met under paragraph 7 of Schedule 3 to the Income Support Regulations (interest on loans to acquire an interest in the home); and for the purposes of this Schedule includes interest payable on loans which falls to be met under paragraph 8 of that Schedule (interest on loans for repairs and improvements to the home) [¹²,minus any amount which is not allowed under paragraph 10 of that Schedule or deducted under paragraph 11 of that Schedule];

"specified benefit" means income support either alone or together with any unemployment, [¹⁴incapacity benefit], retirement pension or severe disablement allowance which is paid by means of the same instrument of payment;

"personal allowance for a single claimant aged not less than 25 years" means the amount specified in [⁶paragraph 1(1)(e)] of column 2 of Schedule 2 to the Income Support Regulations;

[². . .]

"rent" has the meaning assigned to it in the Housing Benefit Regulations and, for the purposes of this Schedule

    (a) includes any water charges which are paid with or as part of the rent;

    (b) where in any particular case a claimant's rent includes elements which would

not otherwise fall to be treated as rent, references to rent shall include those
elements; and

(c) references to "rent" include references to part only of the rent; and

[⁸"water charges" means charges for water or sewerage under Chapter I of Part V of
the Water Industry Act 1991;]

[⁶"water undertaker" means a company which has been appointed under section 11(1)
of the Water Act 1989 to be the water or sewerage undertaker for any area in
England and Wales.]

General

2.—(1) The specified benefit may be paid direct to a third party in accordance with
the following provisions of this Schedule in discharge of a liability of the beneficiary or
his partner to that third party in respect of—

(a) housing costs;

(b) miscellaneous accommodation costs;

[⁶(bb) hostel payments;]

(c) service charges for fuel, and rent not falling within head (a) above;

(d) fuel costs; [¹⁰. . .]

(e) water charges [¹⁰and

(f) payments in place of payments of child support maintenance under section 43(1)
of the Child Support Act 1991 and regulation 28 of the Child Support
(Maintenance Assessments and Special Cases) Regulations 1992.]

(2) No payment to a third party may be made under this Schedule under the amount
of the beneficiary's award of the specified benefit is not less than the total of the amount
otherwise authorised to be so paid under this Schedule plus 10 pence.

(3) A payment to be made to a third party under this Schedule shall be made, at such
intervals as the Secretary of State may direct, on behalf of and in discharge (in whole or
in part) of the obligation of the beneficiary or, as the case may be, of his partner, in
respect of which the payment is made.

Housing costs

3.—(1) Subject to [⁷sub-paragraphs (4) to (6)] and paragraph 8, where a beneficiary
who has been awarded the specified benefit or his partner is in debt for any item of
housing costs which continues to be applicable to the beneficiary in the determination of
his applicable amount, the adjudicating authority may, if in its opinion it would be in the
interests of the family to do so, determine that the amount of the award of the specified
benefit ("the amount deductible") calculated in accordance with the following sub-
paragraphs shall be paid in accordance with sub-paragraph 2(3).

(2) [⁷Subject to sub-paragraphs (2A) and (3)], the amount deductible shall be such
weekly aggregate of the following as is appropriate:—

(a) in respect of any debt to which sub-paragraph (1) applies, or where the debt owed
is in respect of an amount which includes more than one item of housing costs, a
weekly amount equal to 5 per cent. of the personal allowance for a single claimant
aged not less than 25 [¹. . .] for such period as it is necessary to discharge the
debt, so however that in aggregate the weekly amount calculated under this sub-
paragraph shall not exceed 3 times that 5 per cent.;

(b) for each such debt—

(i) in respect of mortgage payments, the weekly amount of the mortgage payment in that case; and

(ii) for any other housing item, the actual weekly cost necessary in respect of
continuing needs for the relevant items,

and the adjudicating authority may direct that, when the debt is discharged, the amount
determined under sub-paragraph (b) shall be the amount deductible.

[⁷(2A) Where a payment falls to be made to a third party in accordance with this Schedule, and—
(a) more than one item of housing costs falls to be taken into account in determining the beneficiary's applicable amount; and
(b) in accordance with paragraph 10 or paragraph 11 of Schedule 3 to the Income Support Regulations an amount is not allowed or a deduction falls to be made from the amount to be met by way of housing costs,

then in calculating the amount deductible, the weekly aggregate amount ascertained in accordance with sub-paragraph (2) shall be reduced by an amount determined by applying the formula—

$$C \times \frac{B}{A}$$

where—
A = housing costs;
B = the item of housing costs which falls to be paid to a third party under this Schedule;
C = the sum which is not allowed or falls to be deducted in accordance with paragraph 10 or, as the case may be, paragraph 11 of Schedule 3 to the Income Support Regulations.]

(3) Where the aggregate amount calculated under sub-paragraph (2) is such that paragraph 2(2) would operate to prevent any payment under this paragraph being made that aggregate amount shall be adjusted so that 10 pence of the award is payable to the beneficiary.

(4) Sub-paragraph (1) shall not apply to any debt which is either—
(a) in respect of mortgage payments and the beneficiary or his partner has in the preceding 12 weeks paid sums equal to [⁸or greater than] 8 week's mortgage payments due in that period; or
(b) for any other item of housing costs and is less than half the annual amount due to be paid by the beneficiary or his partner in respect of that item,

unless, in either case, in the opinion of the adjudicating authority it is in the overriding interests of the family that paragraph (1) should apply.

[⁷(5) No amount shall be paid pursuant to this paragraph in respect of mortgage interest in any case where a specified part of relevant benefits—
(a) is required to be paid directly to a qualifying lender under regulation 34A and Schedule 9A; or
(b) would have been required to be paid to a body which, or a person who, would otherwise have been a qualifying lender but for an election given under paragraph 9 of Schedule 9A not to be regarded as such.

(6) In sub-paragraph (5), "specified part" and "relevant benefits" have the meanings given to them in paragraph 1 of Schedule 9A.]

Miscellaneous accommodation costs

[⁹4.—(1) Where an award of income support—
(a) is made to a person in a residential care home or nursing home as defined in regulation 19(3) of the Income Support Regulations, or
(b) includes an amount under Schedule 4 (persons in residential care and nursing homes) or paragraph 13 (residential accommodation) or 13A (Polish resettlement) of Schedule 7 to the Income Support Regulations,

(hereafter in this paragraph referred to as "miscellaneous accommodation costs")] the adjudicating authority may determine that an amount of the specified benefit shall be paid direct to the person or body to whom the charges in respect of that accommodation are payable, but, except in a case to which paragraph [⁶13A] [⁴. . .] of Schedule 7 to the Income Support Regulations apply or where the accommodation is [²run by a voluntary organisation either for purposes similar to the purposes for which resettlement units are provided] or which provides facilities for alcoholics or drug addicts, only if the adjudicating authority is satisfied that the beneficiary has failed to budget for the charges and that it is in the interests of the family.

(2) [²Subject to sub-paragraph (3), in relation to miscellaneous accommodation costs the amount] of any payment of income support to a third party determined [²under sub-paragraph (1)] shall be—

(a) the amount of the award under paragraph 1(1)(a) of Schedule 4 to the Income Support Regulations excluding any increase under paragraph 2(2) of that Schedule; or

[⁹(aa) an amount equal to the amount of any payment the beneficiary is liable to make to the local authority under section 22 of the National Assistance Act 1948;]

[¹²(ab) in a case where the beneficiary does not have a preserved right within the meaning of regulation 19 of the Income Support Regulations and is not liable to make a payment to a local authority under section 22 of the National Assistance Act 1948 an amount equal to the amount of the award of income support payable to the claimant but excluding an amount, if any, which when added to any other income of the beneficiary (as determined in accordance with regulation 28 of the Income Support Regulations) will equal the aggregate of the amounts—

　　(i) prescribed by paragraph 13 of Schedule 4 to the Income Support Regulations; and

　　(ii) where the charge for the accommodation does not include the provision of all meals, an amount calculated under paragraph 2(2)(b) of that Schedule.]

(b) [⁴. . .]

(c) the amount of the award [²under paragraph 13(1)(a), (b), (c), or (e)], [⁴or, as the case may be, 14] of Schedule 7 to those Regulations excluding the amount allowed by those paragraphs in respect of personal expenses.

as the case may be.

[²(3) In relation to miscellaneous accommodation costs, where an award of income support is calculated in accordance with Part VII of the Income Support Regulations, (calculation of income support for part-weeks) the amount of any payment of income support to a third party determined under sub-paragraph (1) shall be—

(a) where the amount is calculated under regulation 73(1) of the Income Support Regulations an amount calculated in accordance with sub-paragraph (2)(a), (b), or as the case may be (c), [⁶divided by 7 and multiplied by the number of days in the part-week]; or

(b) where an amount is calculated under regulation 73(2) of those regulations an amount calculated in accordance with regulation 73(4)(a)(i) or (b)(i) as the case may be;

and no payment shall be made to a third party under this sub-paragraph where the Secretary of State certifies it would be impracticable to do so in that particular case.

(4) Where the amount calculated under sub-paragraph (2) or (3) is such that paragraph 2(2) would operate to prevent any payment under this paragraph being made the amount shall be adjusted so that 10 pence of the award is payable to the beneficiary.]

[⁶Hostel payments

4A.—(1) This paragraph applies to a beneficiary if—

(a) he has been awarded specified benefit; and

(b) he or his partner has claimed housing benefit in the form of a rent rebate or rent allowance; and

(c) he or his partner is resident in a hostel; and

(d) the charge for that hostel includes a payment, whether direct or indirect, for one or more of the following services—

　　(i) water;

　　(ii) a service charge for fuel;

　　(iii) meals;

　　(iv) laundry;

    (v) cleaning (other than communal areas).

    (2) Subject to sub-paragraph (3) below, where a beneficiary [⁸. . .] has been awarded specified benefit the adjudicating authority may determine that an amount of specified benefit shall be paid to the person or body to whom the charges referred to in sub-paragraph (1)(d) above are or would be payable.

    (3) The amount of any payment to a third party under this paragraph shall be either—
    (a) the aggregate of the amounts determined by a housing authority in accordance with the provisions specified in sub-paragraph (4); or
    (b) if no amount has been determined under paragraph (a) of this sub-paragraph, an amount which the adjudicating authority estimates to be the amount which is likely to be so determined.

    (4) The provisions referred to in sub-paragraph (3)(a) above are regulation 10(6) of, and paragraphs 1(a)(ii) and (iv), [⁸1A, 2, 3 and either 5(1)(b) or 5(2) or 5(2A)] of Schedule 1 to, the Housing Benefit Regulations.

    (5) Sub-paragraph (2) above shall not apply to a deduction in respect of a service charge for fuel if that charge is one such as is mentioned in paragraph 5(5) of Schedule 1 to the Housing Benefit Regulations (variable service charges for fuel) unless the adjudicating authority is satisfied on the evidence available at the date of the determination that the amount of the charge does not normally alter more than twice in any one year.

    (6) Where an award of income support is calculated in accordance with regulation 73(1) of the Income Support Regulations (calculation of income support for part-weeks) the amount of any payment of income support to a third party determined under sub-paragraph (2) above shall be an amount calculated in accordance with sub-paragraph (3)(a) or (b) above divided by 7 and multiplied by the number of days in the part-week and no payment shall be made under this sub-paragraph where the Secretary of State certifies that it would be impracticable to do so in that particular case.]

Service charges for fuel, and rent not falling within paragraph 2(1)(a)

    5.—(1) Subject to paragraph 8, this paragraph applies to a beneficiary if—
    (a) he has been awarded the specified benefit; and
    (b) he or his partner is entitled to housing benefit in the form of a rent rebate or rent allowance; and
    (c) he or his partner has arrears of rent which equal or exceed four times the full weekly rent payable and—
        (i) there are arrears of rent in respect of at least 8 weeks and the landlord has requested the Secretary of State to make payments in accordance with this paragraph; or
        (ii) there are arrears of rent in respect of less than 8 weeks and in the opinion of the adjudicating authority it is in the overriding interests of the family that payments shall be made in accordance with this paragraph.

    (2) For the purposes of sub-paragraph (1) arrears of rent do not include—
    (a) the 20 per cent. of eligible rates excluded from a rent allowance under regulation 61 of the Housing Benefit Regulations (maximum housing benefit); or
    (b) any amount falls to be deducted when assessing a person's rent rebate or rent allowance under regulation 63 of those Regulations (non-dependants).

    (3) Subject to sub-paragraph (4), the adjudicating authority shall determine that a weekly amount of the specified benefit awarded to the beneficiary shall be paid to his or his partner's landlord if—
    (a) he or his partner is entitled to housing benefit and in calculating that benefit a deduction is made under regulation 10(3) of the Housing Benefit Regulations in respect of either or both of water charges or service charges for fuel; and
    (b) the amount of the beneficiary's award is not less than the amount of the deduction, and the amount to be paid shall be equal to the amount of the deduction.

    (4) Sub-paragraph (3) shall not apply to a deduction in respect of a service charge for fuel if that charge is one such as is mentioned in paragraph 5(5) of Schedule 1 to the

Housing Benefit Regulations (variable service charges for fuel) unless the adjudicating authority is satisfied on the evidence available at the date of the determination that the amount of the charge does not normally alter more than twice in any one year.

(5) Where the aggregate amount calculated in accordance with sub-paragraphs 5(3) and (6) exceeds a sum equal to 25 per cent. of the applicable amount for the family as is awarded under heads (a) to (d) of regulation 17 (applicable amounts) or [¹heads (a) to (e)] of regulation 18(1) (polygamous marriages) of the Income Support Regulations a determination under this paragraph shall be made only with the consent of the beneficiary.

(6) In a case to which sub-paragraph (1) applies the adjudicating authority may determine that a weekly amount of the specified benefit awarded to that beneficiary equal to 5 per cent. of the personal allowance for a single claimant aged not less than 25 [⁶. . .] shall be paid to his landlord until the debt is discharged.

[⁸(7) Immediately after the discharge of any arrears of rent to which sub-paragraph (1) applies and in respect of which a determination has been made under sub-paragraph (6) the adjudicating authority may, if satisfied that it would be in the interests of the family to do so, direct that an amount, equal to the amount by which the eligible rent is to be reduced by virtue of regulation 10(3) of the Housing Benefit Regulations in respect of charges for water or service charges for fuel or both, shall be deductible.]

Fuel costs

6.—(1) Subject to sub-paragraph (6) and paragraph 8, where a beneficiary who has been awarded the specified benefit or his partner is in debt for any item of mains gas or mains electricity [¹³including any charges for the reconnection of gas or disconnection or reconnection of electricity] ("fuel item") to an amount not less than the rate of personal allowance for a single claimant aged not less than 25 and continues to require that fuel, the adjudicating authority, if in its opinion it would be in the interests of the family to do so, may determine that the amount of the award of the specified benefit ("the amount deductible") calculated in accordance with the following paragraphs shall be paid to the person or body to whom payment is due in accordance with paragraph 2(3).

(2) The amount deductible shall, in respect of any fuel item, be such weekly aggregate of the following as is appropriate:—

[⁶(a) in respect of each debt to which sub-paragraph (1) applies ("the original debt"), a weekly amount equal to 5 per cent. of the personal allowance for a person aged not less than 25 for such period as is necessary to discharge the original debt, but the aggregate of the amounts, calculated under this paragraph shall not exceed twice 5 per cent. of the personal allowance for a single claimant aged not less than 25;]

(b) except where current consumption is paid for by other means (for example pre-payment meter), an amount equal to the estimated average weekly cost necessary to meet the continuing needs for that fuel item, varied, where appropriate, in accordance with sub-paragraph (4)(a).

(3) [⁶. . .]

(4) Where an amount is being paid direct to a person or body on behalf of the beneficiary or his partner in accordance with a determination under sub-paragraph (1) and that determination falls to be reviewed—

(a) where since the date of that determination the average weekly cost estimated for the purpose of sub-paragraph (2)(b) has either exceeded or proved insufficient to meet the actual cost of continuing consumption so that in respect of the continuing needs for that fuel item the beneficiary or his partner is in credit or, as the case may be, a further debt has accrued, the adjudicating authority may determine that the weekly amount calculated under that paragraph shall, for a period of 26 weeks [⁸or such longer period as may be reasonable in the circumstances of the case], be adjusted so as to take account of that credit or further debt;

(b) where an original debt in respect of any fuel item has been discharged the adjudicating authority may determine that the amount deductible in respect of that fuel item shall be the amount determined under sub-paragraph (2)(b).

(5) [⁶. . .]

(6) Subject to paragraph 8 where [⁶. . .] the aggregate amount calculated in accordance with sub-paragraph (2) exceeds a sum equal to 25 per cent. of the applicable amount for the family as is awarded under heads (a) to (d) of regulation 17 or [¹heads (a) to (e)] of regulation 18(1) of the Income Support Regulations, a determination under this paragraph shall be made only with the consent of the beneficiary.

(7) [⁶. . .]

[⁶Water charges

7.—(1) This paragraph does not apply where water charges are paid with rent; and in this paragraph "original debt" means the debt to which sub-paragraph (2) applies, [¹³including any disconnection or reconnection charges and any other costs (including legal costs) arising out of that debt].

(2) Where a beneficiary or his partner is liable, whether directly or indirectly, for water charges and is in debt for those charges, the adjudicating authority may determine, subject to paragraph 8, that a weekly amount of the specified benefit shall be paid either to a water undertaker to whom that debt is owed, or to the person or body authorised to collect water charges for that undertaker, [⁸but only if the authority is satisfied that the beneficiary or his partner has failed to budget for those charges, and that it would be in the interests of the family to make the determination.]

(3) Where water charges are determined by means of a water meter, the weekly amount to be paid under sub-paragraph (2) shall be the aggregate of—

(a) in respect of the original debt, an amount equal to 5 per cent. of the personal allowance for a single claimant aged not less than 25 years; and

(b) the amount which the adjudicating authority estimates to be the average weekly cost necessary to meet the continuing need for water consumption.

(4) Where the sum estimated in accordance with sub-paragraph (3)(b) proves to be greater or less than the average weekly cost necessary to meet continuing need for water consumption so that a beneficiary or his partner accrues a credit, or as the case may be a further debt, the adjudicating authority may determine that the sum so estimated shall be adjusted for a period of 26 weeks [⁸or such longer period as may be reasonable in the circumstances of the case] to take account of that credit or further debt.

(5) Where water charges are determined other than by means of a water meter the weekly amount to be paid under sub-paragraph (2) shall be the aggregate of—

(a) the amount referred to in sub-paragraph (3)(a); and

(b) an amount equal to the weekly cost necessary to meet the continuing need for water consumption.

(6) Where the original debt in respect of water charges is discharged, the adjudicating authority may direct that the amount deductible shall be—

(a) where water charges are determined by means of a water meter, the amount determined under sub-paragraph (3)(b) taking into account any adjustment that may have been made in accordance with sub-paragraph (4); and

(b) in any other case, the amount determined under sub-paragraph (5)(b).

(7) Where the beneficiary or his partner is in debt to two water undertakers—

(a) only one weekly amount under sub-paragraph (3)(a) or (5)(a) shall be deducted; and

(b) a deduction in respect of an original debt for sewerage shall only be made after the whole debt in respect of an original debt for water has been paid; and

(c) deductions in respect of continuing charges for both water and for sewerage may be made at the same time.

(8) Subject to paragraph 8 (maximum amounts of payments to third parties), where the aggregate amount calculated in accordance with sub-paragraphs (3), (4), (5) and (6) exceeds a sum equal to 25 per cent. of the applicable amount for the family as is awarded

under heads (a) to (d) of regulation 17(1) or heads (a) to (e) of regulation 18(1) of the Income Support Regulations, a determination under this paragraph shall be made only with the consent of the beneficiary.

[¹⁰Payments in place of payments of child support maintenance

7A.—[¹²(1)Subject to paragraph (2), where a child support officer (within the meaning of section 13 of the Child Support Act 1991) has determined that section 43 of that Act and regulation 28 of the Child Support (Maintenance Assessments and Special Cases) Regulations 1992 (contribution to maintenance by deduction from benefit) apply in relation to a beneficiary or his partner, the adjudicating authority shall (subject to paragraph 8), if it is satisfied that there is sufficient specified benefit in payment, determine that a weekly amount of that benefit shall be deducted by the Secretary of State for transmission to the person or persons entitled to it.]

(2) Not more than one deduction shall be made under [¹²sub-paragraph (1)] in any one benefit week as defined in paragraph 4 of Schedule 7.

(3) The amount of specified benefit to be paid under this paragraph shall be the amount prescribed by regulation 28(2) of the Child Support (Maintenance Assessments and Special Cases) Regulations 1992 for the purposes of section 43(2)(a) of the Child Support Act 1991 (that is to say 5 per cent. of the personal allowance for a single claimant aged not less than 25).]

Maximum amount of payments to third parties

8.—(1) The maximum aggregate amount payable under sub-paragraphs 3(2)(a), 5(6), 6(2)(a)[⁶, 7(3)(a)[¹¹, 7(5)(a) and 7A]] [⁷and sub-paragraph 3(5) of Schedule 9A][¹¹, and [¹³regulation 7 of the Council Tax Regulations] and regulation 6 of the Fines Regulations] shall not exceed an amount equal to 3 times 5 per cent. of the personal allowance for a single claimant aged not less than 25 years.

(2) The maximum [⁵aggregate] amount payable under [⁶paragraphs 3(2)(a), 5, 6 and 7] shall not without the consent of the beneficiary, exceed a sum equal to 25 per cent. of so much of the applicable amount for the family as is awarded under heads (a) to (d) [⁶of regulation 17(1)] or [¹heads (a) to (e)] of regulation 18(1) of the Income Support Regulations.

[⁷(3) Where the aggregate of the amounts payable under the provisions mentioned in sub-paragraph (2) does not exceed the sum there mentioned ("the specified sum") but does exceed that sum where the aggregate includes in addition any amount required to be paid in accordance with paragraph 3(5) of Schedule 9A, then in relation to the amounts payable under the provisions mentioned in sub-paragraph (2) the consent of the beneficiary is required to the payment of so much of the specified sum as represents the amount by which that sum is so exceeded.]

Priority as between certain debts

[¹¹**9.**—(1)(A) Where in any one week—
(a) more than one of the paragraphs 3 to 7A are applicable to the beneficiary; or
(b) one or more of those paragraphs are applicable to the beneficiary and one or more of the following provisions, namely, Schedule 9A, regulation 2 of the Community Charges Regulations, regulation 2 of the Community Charges (Scotland) Regulations, regulation 6 of the Fines Regulations and regulation 7 of the Council Tax Regulations also applies; and
(c) the amount of the specified benefit which may be made to third parties is insufficient to meet the whole of the liabilities for which provision is made;
the order of priorities specified in sub-paragraph (1)(B) shall apply.

(1)(B) The order of priorities which shall apply in sub-paragraph (1)(A) is—
(za) any liability mentioned in Schedule 9A;

(a) any liability mentioned in paragraph 3 (housing costs);
(b) any liability mentioned in paragraph 5 (service charges for fuel and rent not falling within paragraph 2(1)(a));
(c) any liability mentioned in paragraph 6 (fuel costs);
(d) any liability mentioned in paragraph 7 (water charges);
(e) any liability mentioned in regulation 2 of the Community Charges Regulations (deductions from income support), regulation 2 of the Community Charges (Scotland) Regulations (deductions from income support) or any liability mentioned in regulation 7 of the Council Tax Regulations (deductions from debtor's income support);
(f) any liability mentioned in regulation 6 of the Fines Regulations (deductions from offenders income support);
(g) any liability mentioned in paragraph 7A (payments in place of payments of child support maintenance).]

(2) As between liability for items of housing costs liabilities in respect of mortgage payments shall have priority over all other items.

(3) As between liabilities for items of gas or electricity the adjudicating authority shall give priority to whichever liability it considers it would, having regard to the circumstances and to any requests of the beneficiary, be appropriate to discharge.

(4) [⁶. . .]

AMENDMENTS

1. Social Security (Claims and Payments) Amendment Regulations 1988 (S.I. 1988 No. 522), reg. 11 (April 11, 1988).
2. Social Security (Claims and Payments and Payments on account, Overpayments and Recovery) Amendment Regulations 1989 (S.I. 1989 No. 136), reg. 2(7) (February 27, 1989).
3. Social Security (Claims and Payments and Payments on account, Overpayments and Recovery) Amendment Regulations 1989 (S.I. 1989 No. 136), reg. 2(7) (April 10, 1989).
4. Social Security (Medical Evidence, Claims and Payments) Amendment Regulations 1989 (S.I. No. 1686), reg. 9 (October 9, 1989).
5. Social Security (Miscellaneous Provisions) Amendment Regulations 1990 (S.I. 1990 No. 2208), reg. 16 (December 5, 1990).
6. Social Security (Miscellaneous Provisions) Amendment Regulations 1991 (S.I. 1991 No. 2284), regs. 12 to 20 (November 1, 1991).
7. Social Security (Claims and Payments) Amendment Regulations 1992 (S.I. 1992 No. 1026), reg. 5 (May 25, 1992).
8. Social Security (Miscellaneous Provisions) Amendment (No. 2) Regulations 1992 (S.I. 1992 No. 2595), reg. 8 (November 16, 1992).
9. Social Security Benefits (Amendments Consequential Upon the Introduction of Community Care) Regulations 1992 (S.I. 1992 No. 3147), Sched. 1, para. 8 (April 1, 1993).
10. Social Security (Claims and Payments) Amendment Regulations 1993 (S.I. 1993 No. 478), reg. 2 (April 1, 1993).
11. Deductions from Income Support (Miscellaneous Amendment) Regulations 1993 (S.I. 1993 No. 495), reg. 2 (April 1, 1993).
12. Social Security (Claims and Payments) Amendment (No. 3) Regulations 1993 (S.I. 1993 No. 2113), reg. 3 (September 27, 1993).
13. Social Security (Claims and Payments) Amendment Regulations 1994 (S.I. 1994 No. 2319), reg. 7 (October 3, 1994).
14. Social Security (Claims and Payments) Amendment (No. 2) Regulations 1994 (S.I. 1994 No. 2943), reg. 15 (April 13, 1995).

DEFINITIONS

"adjudicating authority"—see reg. 2(1).
"beneficiary"—see Social Security Act 1975, Sched. 20.
"family"—see 1986 Act, s.20(11) (SSCBA, s.137(1)).
"partner"—see reg. 2(1).
"qualifying lender"—see Administration Act, s.15A(3).

Note that these references are only to phrases defined outside Sched. 9 itself. See para. 1 for definitions special to Sched. 9.

GENERAL NOTE

The provisions for part of weekly benefit to be diverted direct to a third party are of great importance in determining the actual weekly incomes of claimants. There have been changes in the provisions on fuel and water charges and Sched. 9A now deals specifically with payments of mortgage interest.

On deductions in respect of rent arrears under para. 5(6), *CIS 220/1994* holds that the arrears must be proved, at least where these are disputed. In addition, the existence of an arguable counterclaim in possession proceedings is a matter that an adjudicating authority might properly take into account in deciding whether to exercise the discretionary power to make deductions under para. 5(6).

[¹SCHEDULE 9A

DEDUCTIONS OF MORTGAGE INTEREST FROM BENEFIT AND PAYMENT TO QUALIFYING LENDERS

Interpretation

1. In this Schedule—
"5 per cent. of the personal allowance for the single claimant aged not less than 25" means where the percentage is not a multiple of 5 pence, the sum obtained by rounding that 5 per cent. to the next higher such multiple;
"personal allowance for a single aged not less than 25 years" means the amount specified in paragraph 1(1)(e) of column 2 of Schedule 2 to the Income Support Regulations;
"Income Support Regulations" means the Income Support (General) Regulations 1987;
"relevant benefits" means the benefits prescribed in paragraph 5;
"specified part" shall be construed in accordance with paragraph 3.

Specified circumstances

2.—(1) The circumstances referred to in regulation 34A are that—
(a) the amount to be met under paragraph 7 or as the case may be paragraph 8 of Schedule 3 to the Income Support Regulations in determining the relevant beneficiary's applicable amount is 100 per cent. of the eligible interest in his case; and
(b) the relevant benefits to which a relevant beneficiary is entitled are payable in respect of a period of 7 days or a multiple of such a period.

(2) For the purposes of determining whether 100 per cent. of the eligible interest referred to in sub-paragraph (1)(a) is met in determining a relevant beneficiary's applicable amount, no account shall be taken of any amounts not allowed under paragraph 10 (restrictions on payment of housing costs) or deducted under paragraph 11 (non-dependant deductions) of Schedule 3 to the Income Support Regulations.

(3) In this paragraph, the expression "eligible interest" has the meaning it bears in paragraph 7 of Schedule 3 to the Income Support Regulations by virtue of sub-paragraph (3) of that paragraph.

Specified part of relevant benefit

3.—(1) Subject to the following provisions of this paragraph, the part of any relevant benefits which, [²as determined by the adjudicating authority] in accordance with regulation 34A, shall be paid by the Secretary of State directly to a qualifying lender ("the

851

specified part'') is a sum equal to the amount of the mortgage interest to be met under paragraphs 7 and 8 of Schedule 3 to the Income Support Regulations.

(2) Where, in determining a relevant beneficiary's applicable amount for the purposes of income support, an amount is not allowed or a deduction falls to be made in accordance with paragraph 10 or paragraph 11 of Schedule 3 to the Income Support Regulations (excessive housing costs and non-dependant deductions) then the specified part referred to in sub-paragraph (1) of this paragraph is the mortgage interest to be met under paragraphs 7 and 8 of Schedule 3 to the Income Support Regulations minus the amount not allowed or, as the case may be, the deduction made.

(3) Where, in determining a relevant beneficiary's applicable amount for the purposes of income support—

    (a) a sum in respect of housing costs is brought into account in addition to a sum in respect of mortgage interest; and

    (b) in accordance with paragraph 10 or paragraph 11 of Schedule 3 to the Income Support Regulations an amount is not allowed or a deduction falls to be made from the amount to be met under that Schedule,

then the specified part referred to in sub-paragraph (1) of this paragraph is the mortgage interest minus a sum calculated by applying the formula—

$$C \times \frac{B}{A}$$

where—

    A = the eligible housing costs within the meaning of paragraph 1 of Schedule 3 to the Income Support Regulations;

    B = the mortgage interest to be met under paragraphs 7 and 8 of Schedule 3 to the Income Support Regulations which is payable to a qualifying lender by the borrower;

    C = the sum which is not allowed or falls to be deducted in accordance with paragraph 10 or paragraph 11 of Schedule 3 to the Income Support Regulations.

(4) Where a payment is being made under a policy of insurance taken out by a beneficiary to insure against the risk of his being unable to maintain repayments of mortgage interest to a qualifying lender, then the amount of any relevant benefits payable to that lender shall be reduced by a sum equivalent to so much of the amount payable under the policy of insurance as represents payments in respect of mortgage interest.

(5) Subject to sub-paragraphs (6), (7) and (8), where the borrower is in arrears with the payment of mortgage interest on a loan which he is liable to make to a qualifying lender, then the specified part shall include a sum equal to 5 per cent. of the personal allowance for a single claimant aged not less than 25 years (''an additional sum'').

(6) Where the borrower is in arrears with the payment of mortgage interest in respect of more than one loan, the sum included in the specified part under sub-paragraph (5) shall not exceed 3 times a sum equal to 5 per cent. of the personal allowance for a single claimant aged not less than 25 years.

(7) Except in relation to an award of income support made before 25th May 1992, where as a result of the operation of paragraph 7(1)(b)(ii) of Schedule 3 to the Income Support Regulations (only 50 per cent. of eligible interest payable during the first 16 weeks of payment of income support) a borrower is in arrears with the payment of mortgage interest in respect of a loan which he is liable to make to a qualifying lender no additional sum shall be included in the specified part by reference to those arrears.

(8) Where the amount of any relevant benefits to which a relevant beneficiary is entitled is less than the sum which would, but for this sub-paragraph, have been the specified part, then the specified part shall be the amount of any relevant benefits to which the relevant beneficiary is entitled less 10p.

Direct payment: more than one loan

4.—(1) This paragraph applies where the borrower is liable to pay mortgage interest in respect of two or more different loans.

(2) Subject to the following provisions of this paragraph, the Secretary of State shall pay to the qualifying lender or, if there is more than one qualifying lender, to each qualifying lender—

(a) a sum equal to the mortgage interest to be met under paragraphs 7 and 8 of Schedule 3 to the Income Support Regulations in respect of each loan made by that lender, plus

(b) any additional amount attributable to a particular loan which may, under paragraph 3(5), have been taken into account in calculating the specified part.

(3) If, by virtue of deductions made under either paragraph 3(2) or 3(3), the specified part is less than the amount payable by the borrower in respect of mortgage interest, then the sum payable under sub-paragraph (2)(a) shall be minus such proportion of the sum subtracted under those sub-paragraphs as is attributable to the particular loan.

(4) Paragraph 3(4) shall apply to reduce the amount payable to a qualifying lender mentioned in sub-paragraph (2) above as it applies to reduce the amount of any relevant benefits payable to a qualifying lender under paragraph 3.

(5) Where the specified part is the part referred to in paragraph 3(8), the Secretary of State shall pay the specified part directly to the qualifying lenders to whom mortgage interest is payable by the borrower in order of the priority of mortgages or (in Scotland) in accordance with the preference in ranking of heritable securities.

Relevant benefits

5.—(1) Subject to sub-paragraph (2), the following benefits shall be relevant benefits in addition to income support, namely, unemployment benefit, [⁴incapacity benefit], retirement pension and severe disablement allowance.

(2) The benefits referred to in sub-paragraph (1) are only relevant benefits when paid together with income support by means of the same instrument of payment.

Time and manner of payments

6. Payments to qualifying lenders under regulation 34A and this Schedule shall be made in arrears at intervals of 4 weeks.

Fees payable by qualifying lenders

7. For the purposes of defraying the expenses of the Secretary of State in administering the making of payments under regulation 34A and this Schedule a qualifying lender shall pay to the Secretary of State a fee of [³£0.80] in respect of each payment made under regulation 34A and this Schedule.

Qualifying lenders

8. The following bodies and persons shall be qualifying lenders—

(a) the Housing Corporation;

(b) Housing for Wales;

(c) Scottish Homes;

(d) the Development Board for Rural Wales; and

(e) any body incorporated under the Companies Act 1985 whose main objects include the making of loans secured by a mortgage of or a charge over land or (in Scotland) by a heritable security.

Election not to be regarded as a qualifying lender

9.—(1) A body which, or a person who, would otherwise be a qualifying lender may elect not to be regarded as such for the purposes of these Regulations by giving notice of election under this paragraph to the Secretary of State in accordance with sub-paragraphs (2) and (3).

(2) Subject to sub-paragraph (3), notice of election shall be given in writing—

(a) in the case of the financial year 1992 to 1993, before 23rd May 1992 and shall take effect on that date; and

(b) in the case of any other financial year, before 1st February in the preceding year and shall take effect on 1st April following the giving of the notice.

(3) A body which, or a person who, becomes a qualifying lender during a financial year and who wishes to elect not to be regarded as such for the purposes of these Regulations shall give notice of election in writing within a period of six weeks from the date on which the person or body becomes a qualifying lender.

(4) Regulation 34A shall not apply to a body which, or a person who, becomes a qualifying lender during a financial year for a period of six weeks from the date on which the person or body became a qualifying lender unless, either before the start of that period or at any time during that period, the person or body notifies the Secretary of State in writing that this sub-paragraph should not apply.

(5) A body which, or a person who, has made an election under this paragraph may revoke that election by giving notice in writing to the Secretary of State before 1st February in any financial year and the revocation shall take effect on the 1st April following the giving of the notice.

(6) Where a notice under this paragraph is sent by post it shall be treated as having been given on the day it was posted.

Provision of information

10.—(1) A qualifying lender shall provide the Secretary of State with information relating to—

(a) the mortgage interest payable by a borrower;

(b) the amount of the loan;

(c) the purpose for which the loan is made;

(d) the amount outstanding on the loan on which the mortgage interest is payable;

(e) any change in the amount of interest payable by the borrower;

at the times specified in sub-paragraphs (2) and (3).

(2) The information referred to in heads (a), (b), (c) and (d) of sub-paragraph (1) shall be provided at the request of the Secretary of State when a claim for income support is made and a sum in respect of mortgage interest is to be brought into account in determining the applicable amount.

(3) The information referred to in heads (d) and (e) of sub-paragraph (1) shall be provided at the request of the Secretary of State—

(a) when a claim for income support ceases to be paid to a relevant beneficiary; and

(b) once every 12 months notwithstanding that, in relation to head (d), the information may already have been provided during the period of 12 months preceding the date of the Secretary of State's request.

Recovery of sums wrongly paid

11.—(1) Where sums have been paid to a qualifying lender under regulation 34A which ought not to have been paid for one or both of the reasons mentioned in sub-paragraph (2) of this paragraph, the qualifying lender shall, at the request of the Secretary of State, repay the sum overpaid.

(2) The reasons referred to in sub-paragraph (1) of this paragraph are—

(a) that—

(i) the rate at which the borrower pays mortgage interest has been reduced or the amount outstanding on the loan has been reduced, and

(ii) as a result of this reduction the applicable amount of the relevant beneficiary has also been reduced, but

(iii) no corresponding reduction was made to the specified part; or

(b) subject to paragraph (3), that the relevant beneficiary has ceased to be entitled to any relevant benefits.

(3) A qualifying lender shall only repay sums which ought not to have been paid for the reason mentioned in sub-paragraph (2)(b) of this paragraph if the Secretary of State has requested that lender to repay the sums within a period of 4 weeks starting with the last day on which the relevant beneficiary was entitled to any relevant benefits.]

AMENDMENTS

1. Social Security (Claims and Payments) Amendment Regulations 1992 (S.I. 1992 No. 1026), reg. 6 and Sched. (May 25, 1992).
2. Social Security (Claims and Payments) Amendment (No. 3) Regulations 1993 (S.I. 1993 No. 2113), reg. 3 (September 27, 1993).
3. Social Security (Claims and Payments) Amendment (No. 3) Regulations 1994 (S.I. 1994 No. 2944), reg. 2 (April 1, 1995).
4. Social Security (Claims and Payments) Amendment (No. 2) Regulations 1994 (S.I. 1994 No. 2943), reg. 16 (April 13, 1995).

DEFINITIONS

"mortgage interest"—see Administration Act, s.15A(4).
"qualifying lender"—see Administration Act, s.15A(3).
"relevant beneficiary"—see Administration Act, s.15A(1).

GENERAL NOTE

Para. 11 only authorises recovery of overpaid interest in the circumstances specified in sub-paras. (2) and (3). What is not clear is who decides that the interest has been overpaid. The Benefits Agency's standard letter indicates that this is decided by the Secretary of State, but it is certainly arguable that this is the type of decision that should be made by an AO.

Social Security (Payments on account, Overpayments and Recovery) Regulations 1987

(S.I. 1987 No. 491)

Made by the Secretary of State under the Social Security Act 1986, ss.27, 51(1)(t), 84(1) and 89.

Transitional provisions

20.—(1) [*Revoked by the 1988 Regulations*].

(2) Section 53(7) and (9) [SSAA, s.71(8) and (10)] (recovery by deductions from benefit and recovery through the county court or sheriff court) and Part VII of these regulations (the process of recovery) shall apply to any amount recoverable or repayable under any enactment repealed by the Act or any regulations revoked by these regulations as if it were an amount recoverable under section 53(1) [SSAA, s.71(1)].

(3) Section 53(9) [SSAA, s.71(10)] shall apply to any amount which was, or would have been, recoverable through the county court or sheriff court under enactments repealed by the Act as if it was an amount recoverable under section 53(1) [SSAA, s.71(1)].

GENERAL NOTE

These provisions are specifically continued in force (along with reg. 19 and the Schedule thereto— not reproduced) beyond the general revocation of the 1987 Regulations on April 6, 1988, by reg. 31(1) of the 1988 Regulations. "The Act" is the 1986 Act.

Social Security (Payments on account, Overpayments and Recovery) Regulations 1988

(S.I. 1988 No. 664)

Made by the Secretary of State under the Social Security Act 1986, ss.23(8), 27, 51(1)(t), (u), 53, 83(1), 84(1) and 89.

ARRANGEMENT OF REGULATIONS

PART I

GENERAL

PART II

INTERIM PAYMENTS

PART III

OFFSETTING

PART IV

PREVENTION OF DUPLICATION OF PAYMENTS

PART V

DIRECT CREDIT TRANSFER OVERPAYMENTS

PART VI

REVISION OF DETERMINATION AND CALCULATION OF AMOUNT RECOVERABLE

PART VII

THE PROCESS OF RECOVERY

PART I

GENERAL

Citation, commencement and interpretation

1.—(1) These regulations may be cited as the Social Security (Payments on account, Overpayments and Recovery) Regulations 1988 and shall come into force on 6th April 1988.

(2) In these Regulations, unless the context otherwise requires—

"the Act" means the Social Security Act 1986;

"adjudicating authority" means, as the case may be, the Chief or any other adjudication officer, a social security appeal tribunal, [²a disability appeal tribunal] the Chief or any other Social Security Commissioner or a Tribunal of Commissioners;

"benefit" means any benefit under the Social Security Act 1975 [SSCBA, Parts II to V], child benefit, family credit, income support and [¹any social fund payment under sections 32(2)(a) and 32(2A) of the Act [SSCBA, s.138(1)(a) and (2)] [³and any incapacity benefit under sections 30A(1) and (5) of the Contributions and Benefits Act]];

"child benefit" means benefit under Part I of the Child Benefit Act 1975 [SSCBA, Part IX];

"the Claims and Payments Regulations" means the Social Security (Claims and Payments) Regulations 1987;

[³"the Contributions and Benefits Act" means the Social Security Contributions and Benefits Act 1992;]

[²"disability living allowance" means a disability living allowance under section 37ZA of the Social Security Act 1975 [SSCBA, s.71];

"disability working allowance" means a disability working allowance under section 20 of the Act [SSCBA, s.129];]

"family credit" means family credit under Part II of the Act [SSCBA, Part VII];

"guardian's allowance" means an allowance under section 38 of the Social
    Security Act 1975 [SSCBA, s.77];
"income support" means income support under Part II of the Act [SSCBA,
    Part VII] and includes personal expenses addition, special transitional
    addition and transitional addition as defined in the Income Support
    (Transitional) Regulations 1987;
"Income Support Regulations" means the Income Support (General) Regula-
    tions 1987;
"severe disablement allowance" means an allowance under section 36 of the
    Social Security Act 1975 [SSCBA, s.68].

(3) Unless the context otherwise requires, any reference in these regulations
to a numbered Part or regulation is a reference to the Part or regulation bearing
that number in these Regulations and any reference in a regulation to a numbered
paragraph is a reference to the paragraph of that regulation bearing that number.

AMENDMENTS

1. Social Security (Claims and Payments and Payments on account, Overpayments and Recovery)
Amendment Regulations 1989 (S.I. 1989 No. 136), reg. 3 (February 27, 1989).
2. Disability Living Allowance and Disability Working Allowance (Consequential Provisions)
Regulations 1991 (S.I. 1991 No. 2742), reg. 15 (April 6, 1992).
3. Social Security (Incapacity Benefit) (Consequential and Transitional Amendments and Savings)
Regulations 1995 (S.I. 1995 No. 829), reg. 21(2) (April 13, 1995).

PART II

INTERIM PAYMENTS

Making of interim payments

2.—(1) The Secretary of State may, in his discretion, make an interim payment, that is to say a payment on account of any benefit to which it appears to
him that a person is or may be entitled, in the following circumstances—
  (a) a claim for that benefit has not been made in accordance with the Claims
      and Payments Regulations and it is impracticable for such a claim to be
      made immediately; or
  (b) a claim for that benefit has been so made, but it is impracticable for it or
      a reference, review, application or appeal which relates to it to be deter-
      mined immediately; or
  (c) an award of that benefit has been made but it is impracticable for the
      beneficiary to be paid immediately, except by means of an interim
      payment.
(2) [¹Subject to paragraph (3)] on or before the making of an interim payment
the recipient shall be given notice in writing of his liability under this Part to
have it brought into account and to repay any overpayment.
(3) [*Omitted as only applying to disability living allowance*]
[²(4) Where an interim payment of income support is made because a payment
to which the recipient is entitled by way of child support maintenance under
the Child Support Act 1991, or periodical payments under a maintenance agreement within the meaning of section 9(1) of that Act or under a maintenance
order within the meaning of section 107(15) of the Social Security Administration Act 1992, has not been made, the requirement in paragraph (2) of this
regulation to give notice shall be omitted.]

AMENDMENTS

1. Disability Living Allowance and Disability Working Allowance (Consequential Provisions) Regulations 1991 (S.I. 1991 No. 2742), reg. 15 (April 6, 1992).
2. Social Security (Payments on account, Overpayments and Recovery) Amendment Regulations 1993 (S.I. 1993 No. 650), reg. 2 (April 5, 1993).

GENERAL NOTE

Interim payments are made at the discretion of the Secretary of State. Thus there is no right of appeal and any refusal can only be challenged (other than by making further representations) by judicial review. The test is not whether it is "clear" that the person will qualify for a particular benefit, but whether it appears to the Secretary of State that he "is or may be entitled" to that benefit (*R v. Secretary of State for Social Security, ex parte Sarwar, Getachew and Urbanek*, High Court, April 11, 1995). Thus the Secretary of State can decide to make interim payments even where entitlement to, for example, income support is not certain. Interim payments are recoverable if the person is subsequently found not to be entitled to the benefit claimed (see reg. 4).

The introduction of an habitual residence rule for income support from August 1, 1994 (see the additional definition of "person from abroad" in reg. 21(3) of the Income Support Regulations) has focussed fresh attention on this regulation. Most claimants who fail the test will not be eligible for urgent cases payments under reg. 70(3) of the Income Support Regulations and so face a delay of what can be several months until their appeal is heard without any benefit. Although they can apply for their appeal to be expedited, it is understood that in some areas at least, habitual residence appeals are only being expedited as a class, not individually. This has led to many claimants asking for interim payments pending the hearing of their appeals, and some judicial review applications of refusals to make interim payments. This in turn has precipitated the issue of new guidance on interim payments (see the Income Support Payments Guide paras. 6000–6019).

Clearly, as the new guidance emphasises, each case should be treated on its own merits. Factors such as the strength of the case and the hardship that will be suffered, particularly in view of the length of time it will take for a claim to be determined or an appeal to be heard, are obviously relevant. The guidance suggests that an interim payment will not normally be made if, for example, a basic condition of entitlement is in doubt. But this seems to ignore the fact that the basic test for an interim payment is whether the claimant "is or *may* be entitled" to any benefit. In cases such as habitual residence which currently involves the application of an imprecise and subjective test and where there are many complex unresolved legal issues, it would seem very difficult for the Secretary of State to predict with certainty that a person is not entitled to income support. As the SSAC commented in para. 34 of its report on the proposal to introduce the habitual residence rule (Cm 2609): "The basic difficulty of an habitual residence test [is that] . . . it allows for the construction of a case for or against the claimant in almost every circumstance".

Bringing interim payments into account

[¹3. Where it is practicable to do so and, where notice is required to be given under regulation 2(2), such notice has been given—

(a) any interim payment, other than an interim payment made in the circumstances mentioned in regulation 2(4),—

    (i) which was made in anticipation of an award of benefit shall be offset by the adjudicating authority in reduction of the benefit to be awarded; and

    (ii) whether or not made in anticipation of an award, which is not offset under sub-paragraph (i) shall be deducted by the Secretary of State from—

        (a) the sum payable under the award of benefit on account of which the interim payment was made; or

        (b) any sum payable under any subsequent award of the same benefit to the same person; and

(b) any interim payment made in the circumstances mentioned in regulation 2(4) shall be offset by the Secretary of State against any sum received by him in respect of arrears of child support maintenance payable to the person to whom the interim payment was made.]

AMENDMENT

1. Social Security (Payments on account, Overpayments and Recovery) Amendment Regulations 1993 (S.I. 1993 No. 650), reg. 2 (April 5, 1993).

Recovery of overpaid interim payments

4.—(1) Where the adjudicating authority has determined that an interim payment has been overpaid in circumstances which fall within paragraph (3) and ['where notice is required to be given under regulation 2(2), such notice has been given], that authority shall determine the amount of the overpayment.

(2) The amount of the overpayment shall be recoverable by the Secretary of State, by the same procedures and subject to the same conditions as if it were recoverable under section 53(1) of the Act [SSAA, s.71(1)].

(3) The circumstances in which an interim payment may be determined to have been overpaid are as follows:—

    (a) an interim payment has been made under regulation 2(1)(a) or (b) but—

        (i) the recipient has failed to make a claim in accordance with the Claims and Payments Regulations as soon as practicable, or has made a claim which is either defective or is not made on the form approved for the time being by the Secretary of State and the Secretary of State has not treated the claim as duly made under regulation 4(7) of the Claims and Payments Regulations; or

        (ii) it has been determined that there is no entitlement on the claim, or that the entitlement is less than the amount of the interim payment or that benefit is not payable; or

        (iii) the claim has been withdrawn under regulation 5(2) of the Claims and Payments Regulations; or

    (b) an interim payment has been made under regulation 2(1)(c) which exceeds the entitlement under the award of benefit on account of which the interim payment was made['; or

    (c) an interim payment of income support has been made under regulation 2(1)(b) in the circumstances mentioned in regulation 2(4).]

(4) For the purposes of this regulation a claim is defective if it is made on the form approved for the time being by the Secretary of State but is not completed in accordance with the instructions on the form.

AMENDMENT

1. Social Security (Payments on account, Overpayments and Recovery) Amendment Regulations 1993 (S.I. 1993 No. 650), reg. 2 (April 5, 1993).

PART III

OFFSETTING

Offsetting prior payment against subsequent award

5.—(1) Subject to regulation 6 (exception from offset of recoverable overpayment), any sum paid in respect of a period covered by a subsequent determination in any of the cases set out in paragraph (2) shall be offset against arrears of entitlement under the subsequent determination and, except to the extent that the sum exceeds the arrears, shall be treated as properly paid on account of them.

(2) Paragraph (1) applies in the following cases—

Case 1: Payment under an award which is revised, reversed or varied
Where a person has been paid a sum by way of benefit under an award which is subsequently varied on appeal or revised on a review.

Case 2: Award or payment of benefit in lieu
Where a person has been paid a sum by way of benefit under the original award and it is subsequently determined, on review or appeal, that another benefit should be awarded or is payable in lieu of the first.

Case 3: Child benefit and severe disablement allowance
Where either—

(a) a person has been awarded and paid child benefit for a period in respect of which severe disablement allowance is subsequently determined to be payable to the child concerned; or

(b) severe disablement allowance is awarded and paid for a period in respect of which child benefit is subsequently awarded to someone else, the child concerned in the subsequent determination being the beneficiary of the original award.

Case 4: Increase of benefit for dependant
Where a person has been paid a sum by way of an increase in respect of a dependent person under the original award and it is subsequently determined that that other person is entitled to benefit for that period, or that a third person is entitled to the increase for that period in priority to the beneficiary of the original award.

Case 5: Increase of benefit for partner
Where a person has been paid a sum by way of an increase in respect of a partner (as defined in regulation 2 of the Income Support Regulations) and it is subsequently determined that that other person is entitled to benefit for that period.

(3) Where an amount has been deducted under regulation 13(*b*) (sums to be deducted in calculating recoverable amounts) an equivalent sum shall be offset against any arrears of entitlement of that person under a subsequent award of income support for the period to which the deducted amount relates.

(4) Where child benefit which has been paid under an award in favour of a person (the original beneficiary) is subsequently awarded to someone else for any week, the benefit shall nevertheless be treated as properly paid if it was received by someone other than the original beneficiary, who—

(a) either had the child living with him or was contributing towards the cost of providing for the child at a weekly rate which was not less than the weekly rate under the original award, and

(b) could have been entitled to child benefit in respect of that child for that week had a claim been made in time.

(5) Any amount which is treated, under paragraph (4), as properly paid shall be deducted from the amount payable to the beneficiary under the subsequent award.

Exception from offset of recoverable overpayment

6. No amount may be offset under regulation 5(1) which has been determined to be a recoverable overpayment for the purposes of section 53(1) of the Act [SSAA, s.71(1)].

PART IV

PREVENTION OF DUPLICATION OF PAYMENTS

Duplication and prescribed income

7.—[¹(1) For the purposes of section 74(1) of the Social Security Administra-

tion Act 1992 (income support and other payments), a person's prescribed income is—
- (a) income required to be taken into account in accordance with Part V of the Income Support Regulations, except for the income specified in sub-paragraph (b); and]
- [²(b) income which, if it were actually paid, would be required to be taken into account in accordance with Chapter VIIA of Part V of the Income Support Regulations (child support maintenance); but only in so far as it relates to the period beginning with the effective date of the maintenance assessment under which it is payable, as determined in accordance with regulation 30 of the Child Support (Maintenance Assessment Procedure) Regulations 1992, and ending with the first day which is a day specified by the Secretary of State under regulation 4(1) of the Child Support (Collection and Enforcement) Regulations 1992 as being a day on which payment of child support maintenance under that maintenance assessment is due.]

(2) The prescribed date in relation to any payment of income prescribed by [¹paragraph (1)(a)] is—
- (a) where it is made in respect of a specific day or period, that day or the first day of the period;
- (b) where it is not so made, the day or the first day of the period to which it is fairly attributable.

[²(3) Subject to paragraph (4), the prescribed date in relation to any payment of income prescribed by paragraph (1)(b) is the last day of the maintenance period, determined in accordance with regulation 33 of the Child Support (Maintenance Assessment Procedure) Regulations 1992, to which it relates.

(4) Where the period referred to in paragraph (1)(b) does not consist of a number of complete maintenance periods the prescribed date in relation to income prescribed by that sub-paragraph which relates to any part of that period which is not a complete maintenance period is the last day of that period.]

AMENDMENTS

1. Social Security (Payments on account, Overpayments and Recovery) Amendment Regulations 1993 (S.I. 1993 No. 650), reg. 2, as amended by reg. 4 of the Social Security (Miscellaneous Provisions) Amendment Regulations 1993 (S.I. 1993 No. 846) (April 5, 1993).
2. Social Security (Payments on account, Overpayments and Recovery) Amendment Regulations 1993 (S.I. 1993 No. 650), reg. 2, as amended by reg. 4 of the Social Security (Miscellaneous Provisions) Amendment Regulations 1993 (S.I. 1993 No. 846) (April 19, 1993).

GENERAL NOTE

See the notes to s.74(1) of the Administration Act.

Under s.54 of the Child Support Act 1991 "maintenance assessment" means an assessment of maintenance made under that Act, including, except where regulations prescribe otherwise, an interim assessment. Under reg. 30 of the Child Support (Maintenance Assessment Procedure) Regulations 1992, the effective date of a new assessment is usually, when the application was made by the person with care of the child, the date on which a maintenance enquiry form was sent to the absent parent or, where the application was made by the absent parent, the date on which an effective maintenance form was received by the Secretary of State. Arrears will inevitably accrue while the assessment is being made. In the meantime income support can be paid in full to the parent with care. When the arrears are paid, the amount of "overpaid" income support is recoverable under s.74(1) of the Administration Act.

See the notes to reg. 60C of the Income Support (General) Regulations for the interaction with payments of other arrears of child support maintenance, which are excluded from the operation of s.74(1).

Duplication and prescribed payments

8.—(1) For the purposes of section 27(2) of the Act [SSAA, s.74(2)] (recovery

of amount of benefit awarded because prescribed payment not made on prescribed date), the payment of any of the following is a prescribed payment:—

(a) any benefit under the Social Security Act 1975 [SSCBA, Parts II to V]
other than any grant or gratuity or a widow's payment;

(b) any child benefit;

(c) any family credit;

(d) any war disablement pension or war widow's pension which is not in the
form of a gratuity and any payment which the Secretary of State accepts
as analogous to any such pension;

(e) any allowance paid under the Job Release Act 1977;

(f) any allowance payable by or on behalf of [²Scottish Enterprise Highlands
and Islands Enterprise or] [¹the Secretary of State] to or in respect of a
person for his maintenance for any period during which he is following
a course of training or instruction provided or approved by [²Scottish
Enterprise Highlands and Islands Enterprise or] [¹the Secretary of State]

(g) any payment of benefit under the legislation of any member State other
than the United Kingdom concerning the branches of social security mentioned in Article 4(1) of Regulation (EEC) No. 1408/71 on the application of social security schemes to employed persons, to self-employed
persons and to members of their families moving within the Community,
whether or not the benefit has been acquired by virtue of the provisions
of that Regulation. [³(h) any disability working allowance.]

(2) The prescribed date, in relation to any payment prescribed by paragraph
(1) is the date by which receipt of or entitlement to that benefit would have to
be notified to the Secretary of State if it were to be taken into account in determining, whether on review or otherwise, the amount of or entitlement to income
support.

AMENDMENTS

1. Employment Act 1989, Sched. 5, paras. 1 and 4 (November 16, 1989).
2. Enterprise (Scotland) Consequential Amendments Order 1991 (S.I. 1991 No. 387), art. 14
(April 1, 1991).
3. Disability Living Allowance and Disability Working Allowance (Consequential Provisions)
Regulations 1991 (S.I. 1991 No. 2742), reg. 15 (April 6, 1992).

GENERAL NOTE

See the notes to s.74(2) of the Administration Act.

Duplication and maintenance payments

9. For the purposes of section 27(3) of the Act [SSAA, s.74(3)] (recovery of
amount of benefit awarded because maintenance payments not made), the following benefits are prescribed:—

(a) child benefit;

(b) increase for dependants of any benefit under the Social Security Act 1975
[SSCBA, Parts II to V];

(c) child's special allowance under section 31 of the Social Security Act
1975 [SSCBA, s.56]; and

(d) guardian's allowance.

GENERAL NOTE

See the notes to s.74(3) of the Administration Act.

Conversion of payments made in a foreign currency

10. Where a payment of income prescribed by regulation 7(1), or a payment prescribed by regulation 8(1), is made in a currency other than sterling, its value in sterling, for the purposes of section 27 of the Act [SSAA, s.74] and this Part, shall be determined, after conversion by the Bank of England, or by [¹any institution which is authorised under the Banking Act 1987], as the net sterling sum into which it is converted, after any banking charge or commission on the transaction has been deducted.

AMENDMENT

1. Social Security (Payments on account, Overpayments and Recovery) Amendment Regulations 1988 (S.I. 1988 No. 688), reg. 2(2) (April 11, 1988).

PART V

DIRECT CREDIT TRANSFER OVERPAYMENTS

Recovery of overpayments by automated or other direct credit transfer

11.—(1) Where it is determined by the adjudicating authority that a payment in excess of entitlement has been credited to a bank or other account under an arrangement for automated or other direct credit transfer made in accordance with regulation 21 of the Claims and Payments Regulations and that the conditions prescribed by paragraph (2) are satisfied, the excess, or the specified part of it to which the Secretary of State's certificate relates, shall be recoverable under this regulation.

(2) The prescribed conditions for recoverability under paragraph (1) are as follows—

    (a) the Secretary of State has certified that the payment in excess of entitlement, or a specified part of it, is materially due to the arrangements for payments to be made by automated or other direct credit transfer; and

    (b) notice of the effect which this regulation would have, in the event of an overpayment, was given in writing to the beneficiary, or to a person acting for him, before he agreed to the arrangement.

(3) Where the arrangement was agreed to before April 6, 1987 the condition prescribed by paragraph (2)(b) need not be satisfied in any case where the application for benefit to be paid by automated or other direct credit transfer contained a statement, or was accompanied by a written statement made by the applicant, which complied with the provisions of regulation 16A(3)(b) and (8) of the Social Security (Claims and Payments) Regulations 1979 or, as the case may be, regulation 7(2)(b) and (6) of the Child Benefit (Claims and Payments) Regulations 1984.

PART VI

REVISION OF DETERMINATION AND CALCULATION OF AMOUNT RECOVERABLE

Circumstances in which determination need not be revised

12. Section 53(4) of the Act [SSAA, s.71(5)] (recoverability dependent on reversal, variation or revision of determination) shall not apply where the fact and circumstances of the misrepresentation or non-disclosure do not provide a basis for reviewing and revising the determination under which payment was made.

GENERAL NOTE

See the notes to s.71(5) of the Administration Act.

Sums to be deducted in calculating recoverable amounts

13. In calculating the amounts recoverable under section 53(1) of the Act [SSAA, s.71(1)] or regulation 11, where there has been an overpayment of benefit, the adjudicating authority shall deduct—
    (a) any amount which has been offset under Part III;
    (b) any additional amount of income support which was not payable under the original, or any other, determination, but which should have been determined to be payable—
        (i) on the basis of the claim as presented to the adjudicating authority, or
        (ii) on the basis of the claim as it would have appeared had the misrepresentation or non-disclosure been remedied before the determination;
but no other deduction shall be made in respect of any other entitlement to benefit which may be, or might have been, determined to exist.

GENERAL NOTE

See the notes to s.71(1) of the Administration Act, under the heading *Amount of overpayment*.

Quarterly diminution of capital resources

14.—(1) For the purposes of section 53(1) of the Act [SSAA, s.71(1)], where income support[1, family credit or disability working allowance] has been overpaid in consequence of a misrepresentation as to the capital a claimant possesses or a failure to disclose its existence, the adjudicating authority shall treat that capital as having been reduced at the end of each quarter from the start of the overpayment period by the amount overpaid by way of income support[1, family credit or disability working allowance] within that quarter.

(2) Capital shall not be treated as reduced over any period other than a quarter or in circumstances other than those for which paragraph (1) provides.

(3) In this regulation—
"a quarter" means a period of 13 weeks starting with the first day on which the overpayment period began and ending on the 90th consecutive day thereafter.

"overpayment period" is a period during which income support [1, family credit or disability working allowance] is overpaid in consequence of a misrepresentation as to capital or a failure to disclose its existence.

AMENDMENT

1. Disability Living Allowance and Disability Working Allowance (Consequential Provisions) Regulations 1991 (S.I. 1991 No. 2742), reg. 15 (April 6, 1992).

GENERAL NOTE

See the notes to s.71(1) of the Administration Act, under the heading *Amount of overpayment*.

PART VII

THE PROCESS OF RECOVERY

Recovery by deduction from benefits

15.—(1) Subject to regulation 16, where any amount is recoverable under sections 27 or 53(1) of the Act [SSAA, ss.74 or 71(1)], or under these Regulations, that amount shall be recoverable by the Secretary of State from any of the benefits prescribed by the next paragraph, to which the person from whom [¹the amount is determined] to be recoverable is entitled.

(2) The following benefits are prescribed for the purposes of this regulation—
- (a) subject to paragraphs (1) and (2) of regulation 16, any benefit under the Social Security Act 1975 [SSCBA, Parts II to V];
- (b) subject to paragraphs (1) and (2) of regulation 16, any child benefit;
- (c) any family credit;
- (d) subject to regulation 16, any income support.
- [²(e) any disability working allowance.]
- [³(f) any incapacity benefit.]

AMENDMENTS

1. Social Security (Payments on account, Overpayments and Recovery) Amendment Regulations 1988 (S.I. 1988 No. 688), reg. 2(3) (April 11, 1988).
2. Disability Living Allowance and Disability Working Allowance (Consequential Provisions) Regulations 1991 (S.I. 1991 No. 2742), reg. 15 (April 6, 1992).
3. Social Security (Incapacity Benefit) (Consequential and Transitional Amendments and Savings) Regulations 1995 (S.I. 1995 No. 829), reg. 21(3) (April 13, 1995).

Limitations on deductions from prescribed benefits

16.—(1) Deductions may not be made from entitlement to the benefits prescribed by paragraph (2) except as a means of recovering an overpayment of the benefit from which the deduction is to be made.

(2) The benefits [¹prescribed] for the purposes of paragraph (1) are guardian's allowance, [². . .] and child benefit.

(3) Regulation 15 shall apply without limitation to any payment of arrears of benefit other than any arrears caused by the operation of regulation 37(1) of the Claims and Payments Regulations (suspension of payments).

(4) Regulation 15 shall apply to the amount of income support to which a person is presently entitled only to the extent that there may, subject to paragraphs 8 and 9 of Schedule 9 to the Claims and Payments Regulations, be recovered in respect of any one benefit week—
- (a) in a case to which paragraph (5) applies, not more than the amount there specified; and
- (b) in any other case, 3 times 5 per cent. of the personal allowance for a single claimant aged not less than 25, that 5 per cent. being, where it is not a multiple of 5 pence, rounded to the next higher such multiple.

(5) Where the person responsible for the misrepresentation of or failure to disclose a material fact has, by reason thereof, been found guilty of an offence under section 55 of the Act [SSAA, s.112] or under any other enactment, or has made a written statement after caution in admission of deception or fraud for the purpose of obtaining benefit, the amount mentioned in paragraph (4)(a) shall be 4 times 5 per cent. of the personal allowance for a single claimant aged not less than 25, that 5 per cent. being, where it is not a multiple of 10 pence, rounded to the nearest such multiple or, if it is a multiple of 5 pence but not of 10 pence, the next higher multiple of 10 pence.

(6) Where, in the calculation of the income of a person to whom the income support is payable, the amount of earnings or other income falling to be taken into account is reduced by paragraphs 4 to 9 of Schedule 8 to the Income Support Regulations (sums to be disregarded in the calculation of earnings) or paragraphs 15 and 16 of Schedule 9 to those Regulations (sums to be disregarded in the calculation of income other than earnings) the weekly amount applicable under paragraph (4) may be increased by not more than half the amount of the

reduction, and any increase under this paragraph has priority over any increase which would, but for this paragraph, be made under paragraph 6(5) of Schedule 9 to the Claims and Payments Regulations.

(7) Regulation 15 shall not be applied to a specified benefit so as to reduce the benefit in any one benefit week to less than 10 pence.

(8) In this regulation—

"benefit week" means the week corresponding to the week in respect of which the benefit is paid;

"personal allowance for a single claimant aged not less than 25" means the amount specified in paragraph 1(1)(c) of column 2 of Schedule 2 to the Income Support Regulations;

"specified benefit" means income support either alone or together with any unemployment, [³ incapacity benefit], retirement pension or severe disablement allowance which is paid by means of the same instrument of payment;

"written statement after caution" means—

(i) in England and Wales, a written statement made in accordance with the Police and Criminal Evidence Act 1984 (Codes of Practice) (No. 1) Order 1985, or, before that Order came into operation, the Judges Rules;

(ii) in Scotland, a written statement duly witnessed by two persons.

AMENDMENTS

1. Social Security (Payments on account, Overpayments and Recovery) Amendment Regulations 1988 (S.I. 1988 No. 688), reg. 2(4) (April 11, 1988).
2. Disability Living Allowance and Disability Working Allowance (Consequential Provisions) Regulations 1991 (S.I. 1991 No. 2742), reg. 15 (April 6, 1992).
3. Social Security (Incapacity Benefit) (Consequential and Transitional Amendments and Savings) Regulations 1995 (S.I. 1995 No. 829), reg. 21(4) (April 13, 1995).

Recovery from couples

17. In the case of an overpayment of income support[¹, family credit or disability working allowance] to one of a married or unmarried couple, the amount recoverable by deduction, in accordance with regulation 15, may be recovered by deduction from income support[¹, family credit or disability working allowance] payable to either of them, provided that the two of them are a married or unmarried couple at the date of the deduction.

AMENDMENT

1. Disability Living Allowance and Disability Working Allowance (Consequential Provisions) Regulations 1991 (S.I. 1991 No. 2742), reg. 15 (April 6, 1992).

PART VIII

RECOVERY BY DEDUCTIONS FROM EARNINGS FOLLOWING TRADE DISPUTE

Recovery by deductions from earnings

18.—(1) Any sum paid to a person on an award of income support made to him by virtue of section 23(8) of the Act [SSCBA, s.127] (effect of return to work after a trade dispute) shall be recoverable from him in accordance with this Part of these Regulations.

867

(2) In this Part, unless the context otherwise requires—

"available earnings" means the earnings, including any remuneration paid by or on behalf of an employer to an employee who is for the time being unable to work owing to sickness, which remain payable to a claimant on any pay-day after deduction by his employer of all amounts lawfully deductible by the employer otherwise than by virtue of a deduction notice;

"claimant" means a person to whom an award is made by virtue of section 23(8) of the Act [SSCBA, s.127];

"deduction notice" means a notice under regulation 20 or 25; "employment" means employment (including employment which has been suspended but not terminated) in remunerative work, and related expressions shall be construed accordingly;

"pay-day" means an occasion on which earnings are paid to a claimant;

"protected earnings" means protected earnings as determined by an adjudicating authority, in accordance with regulation 19(2), under regulation 19(1)(a) or 24;

"recoverable amount" means the amount (determined in accordance with regulation 20(3) or (5) or regulation 25(2)(a)) by reference to which deductions are to be made by an employer from a claimant's earnings by virtue of a deduction notice;

"repaid by the claimant" means paid by the claimant directly to the Secretary of State by way of repayment of income support otherwise recoverable under this Part of these Regulations.

(3) Any notice or other document required or authorised to be given or sent to any person under the provisions of this Part shall be deemed to have been given or sent if it was sent by post to that person in accordance with paragraph (6) of regulation 27 where that regulation applies and, in any other case, at his ordinary or last known address or in the case of an employer at the last place of business where the claimant to which it relates is employed, and if so sent to have been given or sent on the day on which it was posted.

Award and protected earnings

19.—(1) Where an adjudicating authority determines that a person claiming income support is entitled by virtue of section 23(8) of the Act [SSCBA, s.127] (effect of return to work after a trade dispute) and makes an award to him accordingly he shall determine the claimant's protected earnings (that is to say the amount below which his actual earnings must not be reduced by any deduction made under this Part).

(2) The adjudicating authority shall include in his decision—

(a) the amount of income support awarded together with a statement that the claimant is a person entitled by virtue of section 23(8) of the Act [SSCBA, s.127] and that accordingly any sum paid to him on that award will be recoverable from him as provided in this Part;

(b) the amount of the claimant's protected earnings, and

(c) a statement of the claimant's duty under regulation 28 (duty to give notice of cessation or resumption of employment).

[¹(3) The protected earnings of the claimant shall be the sum determined by—

(a) taking the sum specified in paragraph (4),

(b) adding the sum specified in paragraph (5), and

(c) subtracting from the result any child benefit which falls to be taken into account in calculating his income for the purposes of Part V of the Income Support Regulations.]

(4) The sum referred to in paragraph (3)(a) shall be the aggregate of the

amounts calculated under regulation 17(a) to (d), 18(a) to (e), 20 or 21, as the case may be, of the Income Support Regulations.

(5) The sum referred to in paragraph (3)(b) shall be £27 except where the sum referred to in paragraph (3)(a) includes an amount calculated under regulation 20 in which case the sum shall be £8.00.

AMENDMENT

1. Social Security (Payments on account, Overpayments and Recovery) Amendment Regulations 1988 (S.I. 1988 No. 688), reg. 2(5) (April 11, 1988).

Service and contents of deduction notices

20.—(1) Where the amount of income support has not already been repaid by the claimant, the Secretary of State shall serve a deduction notice on the employer of the claimant.

(2) A deduction notice shall contain the following particulars—

(a) particulars enabling the employer to identify the claimant;

(b) the recoverable amount;

(c) the claimant's protected earnings as specified in the notification of award.

(3) Subject to paragraph (5) the recoverable amount shall be—

(a) the amount specified in the decision as having been awarded to the claimant by way of income support; reduced by

(b) the amount (if any) which has been repaid by the claimant before the date of the deduction notice.

(4) If a further award relating to the claimant is made the Secretary of State shall cancel the deduction notice (giving written notice of the cancellation to the employer and the claimant) and serve on the employer a further deduction notice.

(5) The recoverable amount to be specified in the further deduction notice shall be the sum of—

(a) the amount determined by applying paragraph (3) to the further award; and

(b) the recoverable amount specified in the cancelled deduction notice less any part of that amount which before the date of the further notice has already been deducted by virtue of the cancelled notice or repaid by the claimant.

Period for which deduction notice has effect

21.—(1) A deduction notice shall come into force when it is served on the employer of the claimant to whom it relates and shall cease to have effect as soon as any of the following conditions is fulfilled—

(a) the notice is cancelled by virtue of regulation 20(4) or paragraph (2) of this regulation;

(b) the claimant ceases to be in the employment of the person on whom the notice was served;

(c) the aggregate of—

(i) any part of the recoverable amount repaid by the claimant on or after the date of the deduction notice, and

(ii) the total amount deducted by virtue of the notice,

reaches the recoverable amount;

(d) there has elapsed a period of 26 weeks beginning with the date of the notice.

(2) The Secretary of State may at any time give a direction in writing cancelling a deduction notice and—

(a) he shall cause a copy of the direction to be served on the employer concerned and on the claimant;

(b) the direction shall take effect when a copy of it is served on the employer concerned.

Effect of deduction notice

22.—(1) Where a deduction notice is in force the following provisions of this regulation shall apply as regards any relevant pay-day.

(2) Where a claimant's earnings include any bonus, commission or other similar payment which is paid other than on a day on which the remainder of his earnings is paid, then in order to calculate his available earnings for the purposes of this regulation any such bonus, commission or other similar payment shall be treated as being paid to him on the next day of payment of the remainder of his earnings instead of on the day of actual payment.

(3) If on a relevant pay-day a claimant's available earnings—

(a) do not exceed his protected earnings by at least £1, no deduction shall be made;

(b) do exceed his protected earnings by at least £1, his employer shall deduct from the claimant's available earnings one half of the excess over his protected earnings,

so however that where earnings are paid other than weekly the amount of the protected earnings and the figure of £1 shall be adjusted accordingly, in particular—

(c) where earnings are paid monthly, they shall for this purpose be treated as paid every five weeks (and the protected earnings and the figure of £1 accordingly multiplied by five);

(d) where earnings are paid daily, the protected earnings and the figure of £1 shall be divided by five,

and if, in any case to which sub-paragraph (c) or (d) does not apply, there is doubt as to the adjustment to be made this shall be determined by the Secretary of State on the application of the employer or the claimant.

(4) Where on a relevant pay-day earnings are payable to the claimant in respect of more than one pay-day the amount of the protected earnings and the figure of £1 referred to in the preceding paragraph, adjusted where appropriate in accordance with the provisions of that paragraph, shall be multiplied by the number of pay-days to which the earnings relate.

(5) Notwithstanding anything in paragraph (3)—

(a) the employer shall not make a deduction on a relevant pay-day if the claimant satisfies him that up to that day he has not obtained payment of the income support to which the deduction notice relates;

(b) the employer shall not on any relevant pay-day deduct from the claimant's earnings by virtue of the deduction notice an amount greater than the excess of the recoverable amount over the aggregate of all such amounts as, in relation to that notice, are mentioned in regulation 21(1)(c)(i) and (ii); and

(c) where the amount of any deduction which by this regulation the employer is required to make would otherwise include a fraction of 1p, that amount shall be reduced by that fraction.

(6) For the purpose of this regulation ''relevant pay-day'' means any pay-day beginning with—

(a) the first pay-day falling after the expiration of the period of one month from the date on which the deduction notice comes into force; or

(b) if the employer so chooses, any earlier pay-day after the notice has come into force.

Increase of amount of award on appeal or review

23. If the amount of the award is increased, whether on appeal or on review by an adjudicating authority, this Part shall have effect as if on the date on which the amount of the award was increased—

(a) the amount of the increase was the recoverable amount; and

(b) the claimant's protected earnings were the earnings subsequently reviewed under regulation 24.

Review of determination of protected earnings

24.—(1) A determination of a claimant's protected earnings, whether made under ['regulation 19(1)] or under this regulation, may be reviewed by an adjudicating authority if he is satisfied that it was based on a mistake as to the law or was made in ignorance of, or was based on a mistake as to, some material fact.

(2) Where the claimant's protected earnings are reviewed under paragraph (1) the Secretary of State shall give the employer written notice varying the deduction notice by substituting for the amount of the protected earnings as there specified (or as previously reviewed under this regulation) the amount of the protected earnings determined on review.

(3) Variation of a deduction notice under paragraph (2) shall take effect either from the end of the period of 10 working days beginning with the day on which notice of the variation is given to the employer or, if the employer so chooses, at any earlier time after notice is given.

AMENDMENT

1. Social Security (Payments on account, Overpayments and Recovery) Amendment Regulations 1988 (S.I. 1988 No. 688), reg. 2(6) (April 11, 1988).

Power to serve further deduction notice on resumption of employment

25.—(1) Where a deduction notice has ceased to have effect by reason of the claimant ceasing to be in the employment of the person on whom the notice was served, the Secretary of State may, if he thinks fit, serve a further deduction notice on any person by whom the claimant is for the time being employed.

(2) Notwithstanding anything in the foregoing provisions of these Regulations, in any such deduction notice—

(a) the recoverable amount shall be equal to the recoverable amount as specified in the previous deduction notice less the aggregate of—

(i) the total of any amounts required to be deducted by virtue of that notice, and

(ii) any additional part of that recoverable amount repaid by the claimant on or after the date of that notice,

or, where this regulation applies in respect of more than one such previous notice, the aggregate of the amounts as so calculated in respect of each such notice;

(b) the amount specified as the claimant's protected earnings shall be the same as that so specified in the last deduction notice relating to him which was previously in force or as subsequently reviewed under regulation 24.

Right of Secretary of State to recover direct from claimant

26. Where the Secretary of State has received a notification of award and it is at any time not practicable for him, by means of a deduction notice, to effect recovery of the recoverable amount or of so much of that amount as remains to be recovered from the claimant, the amount which remains to be recovered shall, by virtue of this regulation, be recoverable from the claimant by the Secretary of State.

Duties and liabilities of employers

27.—(1) An employer shall keep a record of the available earnings of each claimant who is an employee in respect of whom a deduction notice is in force and of the payments which he makes in pursuance of the notice.

(2) A record of every deduction made by an employer under a deduction notice on any pay-day shall be given or sent by him to the Secretary of State, together with payment of the amount deduced, by not later than the 19th day of the following month.

(3) Where by reason only of the circumstances mentioned in regulation 22(5)(a) the employer makes no deduction from a claimant's weekly earnings on any pay-day he shall within 10 working days after that pay-day give notice of that fact to the Secretary of State.

(4) Where a deduction notice is cancelled by virtue of regulation 20(4) or 21(2) or ceases to have effect by virtue of regulation 21(1) the employer shall within 10 working days after the date on which the notice is cancelled or, as the case may be, ceases to have effect—

    (a) return the notice to the Secretary of State and, where regulation 21(1) applies, give notice of the reason for its return;

    (b) give notice, in relation to each relevant pay-day (as defined in regulation 22(6)), of the available earnings of the claimant and of any deduction made from those earnings.

(5) If on any pay-day to which regulation 22(3)(b) applies the employer makes no deduction from a claimant's available earnings, or makes a smaller deduction than he was thereby required to make, and in consequence any amount is not deducted while the deduction notice, or any further notice which under regulation 20(4) cancels that notice, has effect—

    (a) the amount which is not deducted shall, without prejudice to any other method of recovery from the claimant or otherwise, be recoverable from the employer by the Secretary of State; and

    (b) any amount so recovered shall, for the purposes of these Regulations, be deemed to have been repaid by the claimant.

(6) All records and notices to which this regulation applies shall given or sent to the Secretary of State, on a form approved by him, at such office of the ['Department of Social Security] as he may direct.

Amendment

1. Transfer of Functions (Health and Social Security) Order 1988 (S.I. 1988 No. 1843), art. 3(4) (November 28, 1988).

Claimants to give notice of cessation or resumption of employment

28.—(1) Where a claimant ceases to be in the employment of a person on whom a deduction notice relating to him has been duly served knowing that the full amount of the recoverable amount has not been deducted from his earnings or otherwise recovered by the Secretary of State, he shall give notice within 10 working days to the Secretary of State of his address and of the date of such cessation of employment.

(2) Where on or after such cessation the claimant resumes employment (whether with the same or some other employer) he shall within 10 working days give notice to the Secretary of State of the name of the employer and of the address of his place of employment.

Failure to notify

29. If a person fails to comply with any requirement under regulation 27 or 28 to give notice of any matter to the Secretary of State he shall be guilty of an offence and liable on summary conviction to a fine not exceeding—
  (a) for any one offence, level 3 on the standard scale; or
  (b) for an offence of continuing any such contravention, £40 for each day on which it is so continued.

PART IX

REVOCATION, TRANSITIONAL PROVISIONS AND SAVINGS

Revocation

30. Subject to regulation 31(3), the Social Security (Payments on account, Overpayments and Recovery) Regulations 1987 are hereby revoked except for regulations 19 and the Schedule thereto and 20(2) and (3) which shall continue in force.

Transitional provisions

31.—(1) These Regulations shall apply to any question relating to the repayment or recoverability of family income supplement and supplementary benefit as though the definition of "benefit" in regulation 1(2) included references to both those benefits and as though any reference in Part VIII to income support was a reference to income support and supplementary benefit.

(2) Anything done or begun under the Social Security (Payments on account, Overpayments and Recovery) Regulations 1987 or Part IV of the Supplementary Benefit (Trade Disputes and Recovery from Earnings) Regulations 1980 shall be deemed to have been done or, as the case may be, continued under the corresponding provisions of these Regulations.

(3) Where this regulation applies—
  (a) regulation 3(b)(ii) shall have effect as though for the words "the same benefit" there were substituted the words "income support" if the interim payment was of supplementary benefit and "family credit" if the interim payment was of family income supplement;
  (b) regulation 13(b) shall have effect as though for the words "income support" there were substituted the words "supplementary benefit".

(4) In this Part—

"family income supplement" means benefit under the Family Income Supplements Act 1970;

"supplementary benefit" means benefit under Part I of the Supplementary Benefits Act 1976.

PART VII

ITS PRESIDENT'S PRACTICE DIRECTIONS

No. 1

Practice directions: general

1. This and subsequent Practice Directions are issued by me pursuant to my appointment as President of Social Security Appeal Tribunals, Medical Appeal Tribunals, Disability Appeal Tribunals and Child Support Appeal Tribunals under section 51 of the Social Security Administration Act 1992 and Schedule 3 paragraph 1(1) of the Child Support Act 1991, and in part fulfilment of my duties under Schedule 2 paragraph 5 of the Social Security Administration Act 1992 and Schedule 3 paragraph 1(2) of the Child Support Act 1991.

2. It is my intention to issue Practice Directions from time to time to guide Tribunals and their Chairmen in the exercise of their statutory functions. Such Directions will be numbered in sequence [^{1}. . .] and may be published.

3. Unless the contrary is indicated, all Practice Directions will apply to all Social Security Appeal Tribunals, Medical Appeal Tribunals, Disability Appeal Tribunals and Child Support Appeal Tribunals.

4. Subject to any provision of legislation or regulations, and to any binding decision of the courts or the Social Security or Child Support Commissioners, Practice Directions should be followed by Tribunals and Chairmen in the absence of compelling reasons to the contrary.

5. Each Practice Direction will remain in force unless and until it is revoked by a subsequent Practice Direction.

6. This Practice Direction will be referred to as ITS President's Practice Direction No. 1 of 1993 and comes into force on 1 July 1993.

AMENDMENT

1. ITS President's Practice Direction No. 6 (January 31, 1994).

GENERAL NOTE

The issue of Practice Directions to tribunals by the President of ITS is a very interesting development. It is perhaps a reflection of the widening scope of ITS's responsibilities and the need for increased guidance at national level. However, there are several unanswered questions about the basis of the Practice Directions which have been issued. These questions stem from the fact that the word "practice" can cover a variety of matters.

None of the legislative provisions cited in para. 1 of Practice Direction No. 1 give the President specific authority to issue such directions. Section 51 of the Administration Act and para. 1(1) of Sched. 3 to the Child Support Act simply provide for the appointment of a President. Para. 5 of Sched. 2 to the Administration Act (partly mirrored in para. 1(2) of Sched. 3 to the Child Support Act) requires the President, as he considers appropriate, to arrange meetings and training for chairmen and members and to make works of reference relating to social security law available. Arguably, the Practice Directions are part of the training function or constitute works of reference on social security law, but para. 5 does not appear to authorise the President to create rules which are binding on tribunal chairmen or members. No doubt, on matters which properly fall within the area of the administration of tribunals (or practice in a narrow sense) the President can direct what should be done. Practice Direction No. 4 on No Smoking Policy and Tribunals is a prime example of such a direction. The ability to give such directions can be said to be inherent in the appointment of a President, with the power to appoint staff to run the tribunal system. But since the office of President is a creation of statute, there would seem to be no inherent power to give binding directions outside

877

that area, on matters of practice in a wider sense of how the tribunal or a chairman comes to a decision on an issue raised in the case before the tribunal. There can be no objection to recommendations of best practice being put forward. Indeed, such recommendations can be of great value. Nor can there be any objection in principle to the President's indicating that he will take into account in considering the re-appointment of chairmen and members a failure to implement such recommendations (although some of the warnings in the first set of Practice Directions are rather heavy-handed).

The difficulty is in para. 4 of Practice Direction No. 1. Although this only says that Practice Directions *should* be followed, rather than *shall* be followed, the tenor of para. 4 (from the references to contrary provisions) is that chairmen and members should regard themselves as bound by Practice Directions. In my view, Practice Directions can only have that effect in matters of administration or practice in the narrow sense, and in other matters relating to practice in the wider sense tribunals' primary obligation is to carry out their judicial functions in accordance with the principles of natural justice and with the relevant legislation and case law. Tribunals may properly have regard to the President's Practice Directions outside the area of administration as an indication of good practice, but there is a danger that they may be held to have committed an error of law if they simply apply a provision in a Practice Direction without considering all the relevant circumstances.

Particular applications of this general approach are noted briefly after the end of each Practice Direction.

See Practice Direction No. 6 as to the amended numbering of these Practice Directions.

No. 2

Delivery of tribunal decisions on the day of the hearing

1. This Practice Direction is made in accordance with ITS President's Practice Direction No. 1 of 1993.

2. A Tribunal Chairman must in person and orally tell the parties to a hearing the result of the hearing at the conclusion of the hearing in the absence of compelling reason to the contrary.

3. Paragraph 2 applies whether the decision is to adjourn, postpone, allow, allow in part, refuse, or any other decision.

4. The Chairman should normally use non-technical general language to indicate the decision and its effect and explain that a full written decision will follow.

5. This Practice Direction applies whether or not a short-form written decision (AT3A) is given.

6. Paragraph 2 does not apply where the only party present is an Adjudication or Child Support Officer.

7. For the purposes of paragraph 2 the following are compelling reasons to the contrary where the Chairman is of the opinion that one or more applies:

    (a) A party does not or cannot wait to hear the decision.

    (b) Because of disability a party cannot hear or understand the decision.

    (c) There is reason to believe that if told the decision the party will become distressed or distraught.

    (d) There is reason to believe that a party will become violent to himself or another, or to property, if told the decision at the conclusion of the hearing.

    (e) The decision is too complex to explain to a party without causing undue confusion or anxiety.

    (f) There is some other compelling reason.

8. Failure to comply with this Practice Direction will be taken into account when considering the re-appointment of a Part-time Chairman.

9. Inconsistency between the decision delivered orally, that on the AT3A, and the full decision on the AT3 will normally constitute grounds for the decision to be set aside pursuant to Social Security (Adjudication) Regulations 1986 reg. 11(1)(c) or Child Support Appeal Tribunals (Procedure) Regulations 1992 reg. 15(1)(c).

10. This Practice Direction will be referred to as ITS President's Practice Direction No. 2 of 1993 and comes into force on 1 Sep 93.

The question of giving an oral decision to the parties following the hearing may fall within the area of administration, in which it is suggested above that the President may give binding directions. The exceptions in para. 7 to the general rule are comprehensive enough that no chairman should have difficulty in following the direction. A general objection by members to the practice of giving the decision orally would not in itself be a sufficient reason for not following the practice.

The short-form written decision (AT3(A)) referred to in para. 5 is a form which is to be used where appeals relate to the benefits listed in para. 3 of Practice Direction No. 7 and the tribunal's decision will result in the payment of extra benefit to the claimant. When the AT3(A) was introduced in September 1993, it only covered benefits that were locally administered by the DSS, but it now also applies to unemployment benefit and disability living allowance and disability working allowance appeals. From July 1995 it is to be extended to family credit and child benefit. The chairman records the decision on the AT3(A), exactly as it is to be recorded in Box 3 of form AT3. Copies are handed or sent to the claimant and to the presenting officer. The procedure to be followed in connection with the form AT3(A) is now set out in Practice Direction No. 7. The DSS and the Employment Service have agreed to make payments on the strength of receipt of the AT3(A), but it is not known how much quicker in practice this results in benefit due as a result of a tribunal's hearing being paid.

Para. 9 cannot be taken as prescribing the course to be followed on an application to set aside a decision in the circumstances described, but see *Gutzmore v. Wardly, The Times*, March 4, 1993 in the notes to regs. 10. See also the notes to reg. 25(3) of the Adjudication Regulations.

No. 3

Adjournment pending a decision of a higher court or other tribunal

[Withdrawn with effect from June 1, 1995]

This Practice Direction (see the 1994 edition) has been withdrawn from June 1, 1995. The question of whether an adjournment or postponement should be granted pending the result of a "test case" should continue to be decided in accordance with general principles. See the notes to reg. 5 of the Adjudication Regulations.

No. 4

No smoking policy and tribunals

1. This Practice Direction is made in accordance with ITS President's Practice Direction No. 1 of 1993.

2. It is the responsibility of the Chairman to ensure that there is no smoking in the Tribunal hearing room, whether or not a hearing is in progress and irrespective of whether the person wishing to smoke is a member of the Tribunal, a member of the ITS staff, a party or witness at the hearing, an observer or is present in any other capacity.

3. The Chairman and members have a personal responsibility to comply with the rule that they may not smoke at any time in the hearing room and observance of this rule is a condition of continued appointment to the Tribunals operated by the Independent Tribunal Service.

4. Administrative arrangements already ensure that appropriate notices are posted to discourage smoking in all parts of Tribunal suites.

5. This Practice Direction will be referred to as ITS President's Practice Direction No. 4 of 1993 and comes into force on 16 Jul 93 and remains in force unless and until revoked by a subsequent Practice Direction.

GENERAL NOTE

The regulation of smoking on ITS premises is clearly within the President's authority. The rules are welcome, but there are many worse failings of chairmen and members than the smoking of an illicit cigarette.

No. 5

Tribunals and domiciliary hearings

1. This Practice Direction is made in accordance with ITS President's Practice Direction No. 1 of 1993.

2. Tribunals do have power to hold domiciliary hearings in appropriate cases but a Tribunal is never under a legal obligation to hold such a hearing.

3. A domiciliary hearing must not be ordered or arranged before the Tribunal has sat to hear the case except by the President or a Regional or Full Time Chairman, who shall not do so except in a case where it is obvious that there is no other reasonable means of ensuring that a just decision is made by the Tribunal, taking into account the principles set out below for Tribunals.

4. A Tribunal, having sat to hear a case, may order that the hearing be adjourned for a domiciliary hearing to take place but shall not do so unless it is satisfied that:

(a) There is insufficient evidence before it on which to allow an appeal in full and that

(b) Sufficient evidence to reach a just decision cannot reasonably be obtained in some other way including those indicated in paragraph 5 below and that

(c) There is no other reasonable way to obtain the attendance of the parties, including those indicated in paragraph 6 below.

5. For the purposes of paragraph 4 above, other ways of obtaining evidence include:

(a) requesting the attendance of a family member, a carer, or some other witness who could give the evidence that could be given by the parties;

(b) requesting written or recorded evidence from the parties, a carer or some other witness;

(c) referring a question of special difficulty to an expert (including a General Practitioner) for report under section 53 of the Social Security Administration Act 1992;

(d) the exercise of the power of the Chairman to require further particulars under Regulation 3(6) of the Social Security (Adjudication) Regulations 1986.

6. For the purposes of paragraph 4 above, other ways of obtaining the attendance of the parties include:

(a) Providing a taxi or a private hire car to bring the parties all the way from home to the Tribunal hearing at the usual venue and to return them to home;

(b) Arranging for the parties to be brought all the way from home to the usual venue by St John's Ambulance or similar suitable vehicle and to return them to home.

7. In determining the appropriate course of action the Tribunal shall take into account the following considerations:

(a) that members of the Tribunal may have disabilities which would cause difficulties in arranging a domiciliary hearing;

(b) it is preferable to adjourn for another hearing at the usual venue, rather than to arrange an unnecessary domiciliary hearing.

8. This Practice Direction will be referred to as ITS President's Practice Direction No. 5 of 1993 and comes into force on 1 Sep 93.

GENERAL NOTE

The question of whether a domiciliary hearing should be arranged seems to be on the borderline between practice in the narrow and wider senses as I have defined them. It is probably just on the administration side. The approach suggested is full of common sense and allows considerable flexibility to take account of the need to ensure that claimants have a real opportunity to state their case to the tribunal.

No. 6

Practice Directions: General [Amendment]

1. With effect from the issue of this Practice Direction paragraph 2 of ITS President's Practice Direction No. 1 of 1993 is amended by deleting the words "within each calendar year" so that all such Directions will be numbered in one sequence without reference to the calendar year in which they were issued.

2. This Practice Direction will be referred to as ITS President's Practice Direction No 6 and comes into force on 31 Jan 94 and remains in force unless and until revoked by a subsequent Practice Direction.

No. 7

Signing Interim Notices

1. This Practice Direction is made in accordance with ITS President's Practice Direction No 1 of 1993 and applies only to Social Security Appeal Tribunals and Disability Appeal Tribunals.

2. In this Practice Direction the Interim Notice is referred to as the AT3(A), [DAT28[A] for Disability Appeals], and the Decision Form is referred to as the AT3, [DAT28 for Disability Appeals].

3. The AT3[A] or the DAT28[A] and three copies should be completed and signed by the Chairman immediately an appeal or reference has been decided which has the consequence that further payment may be due to the claimant of one or more of the following benefits:

(a) Income Support;

(b) Incapacity Benefit, Sickness Benefit or Invalidity Benefit;

(c) Maternity Benefit;

(d) Unemployment Benefit;

(e) Disability Living Allowance;

(f) Disability Working Allowance.

4. The wording of the AT3[A] [DAT28[A] must be the same as the wording in Box 3 of the AT3 [DAT28]. Copies must be handed to such of the parties as are present. The Chairman should retain a copy of the AT3[A] [DAT28[A]] until the AT3 [DAT28] has been fully completed.

5. The Chairman should explain to any appellant and appellant's representative who is present that a full decision will be sent by post subsequently, that the AT3[A] [DAT28[A]] will enable the Department to make payment without waiting for the full decision, but that payment may be suspended if there is an appeal by the Adjudication Officer against the Tribunal's decision. [Please refer to suggested advice to Chairmen re [UB] Appeals].

6. The issue of the AT3[A] or the DAT28[A] does not affect rights of appeal against the Tribunal's decision. Leave to appeal may still be given at the hearing. The date of the decision will still be the date of issue of the AT3 or the DAT28.

7. This Practice Direction will be referred to as ITS President's Practice Direction No 7 and comes into force on 13 April 1995; it replaces Practice Direction No 7 issued on 1 December 1994.

GENERAL NOTE

This Practice Direction would seem to fall within the realm of administration. See Practice Direction No. 2 and the notes to that Direction and the notes to reg. 25(3) of the Adjudication Regulations.

The new form of this Practice Direction is similar to the previous form. It has been expanded to include unemployment benefit, disability living allowance, disability working allowance and incapacity benefit appeals.

The suggested advice to chairmen in the case of unemployment benefit appeals, referred to in para. 5, is that, in view of factors (such as the claimant's contribution record and recovery of benefit already paid) that could affect whether a payment of unemployment benefit will be made following the tribunal's decision, they should emphasise that whether any benefit is payable as a result of the tribunal's decision will be decided by the Employment Service.

INDEX